D1104056

The Professional Counselor's Desk Reference

Dr. Irmo Marini is Professor in the Department of Rehabilitation in the College of Health Sciences and Human Services at the University of Texas Pan-American in Edinburg, Texas. He received his PhD in Rehabilitation at Auburn University and a master's degree in Clinical Psychology from Lakehead University, in Thunder Bay, Canada, where he also was Director of Lakehead University's Counseling and Career Center. He has national certifications as a Certified Rehabilitation Counselor (CRC) and a Certified Life Care Planner (CLCP). Dr. Marini is on the editorial boards of several rehabilitation counseling journals and has more than 65 journal and book chapter publications. He also writes a quarterly column for the *Psychosocial Process,* the official journal of the American Association of Spinal Cord Injury Psychologists and Social Workers. He is the recipient of four outstanding faculty awards in scholarship and two in teaching. Dr. Marini is former Chair of the Commission on Rehabilitation Counselor Certification, the national certifying body of more than 16,000 rehabilitation counselors in the United States and Canada, and is past President of the American Rehabilitation Counseling Association. Dr. Marini owns and operates Marini & Associates, forensic rehabilitation consultants specializing in vocational assessments and life-care planning in legal cases involving personal injuries.

Dr. Mark A. Stebnicki is Professor and Director of the Graduate Program in Rehabilitation Counseling at East Carolina University, in Greenville, North Carolina. He holds a doctoral degree in rehabilitation counseling (PhD), is a Licensed Professional Counselor (LPC) in North Carolina, and has national certifications as a Certified Rehabilitation Counselor (CRC) and a Certified Case Manager (CCM). He is also certified by the Washington DC–based crisis response team National Organization for Victim Assistance (NOVA). He has more than 18 years' experience working with the psychosocial aspects of adolescents and adults with mental health conditions and chronic illnesses and disabilities. Dr. Stebnicki is an active teacher, researcher, and practitioner. He is the author of *Empathy Fatigue: Healing the Mind, Body, and Spirit of Professional Counselors* (Springer Publishing, 2008) as well as two other books on adolescent mental health and youth at risk. He has written more than 24 articles in peer-reviewed journals and presented regionally, statewide, and nationally at well over 60 seminars, workshops, and conferences on topics that range from empathy fatigue, youth violence, and traumatic stress to the psychosocial aspects of adults with chronic illnesses and disabilities. Dr. Stebnicki served on the crisis response team for the Westside Middle School shootings in Jonesboro, AR (March 24, 1998), and has done many stress debriefings with private companies, schools, and government employees after incidents of workplace violence, hurricanes, tornadoes, and floods. His youth violence program, the Identification, Early Intervention, Prevention, and Preparation (IEPP) Program, has been awarded national recognition by the American Counseling Association (ACA) Foundation for its vision and excellence in the area of youth violence prevention. Other accolades include consulting with former President Bill Clinton's staff on addressing the students of Columbine High School after their critical incident (April 20, 1999).

The Professional Counselor's Desk Reference

Edited by Irmo Marini, PhD, CRC, CLCP
Mark A. Stebnicki, PhD, LPC, CRC, CCM

SPRINGER PUBLISHING COMPANY
New York

Springer Publishing Company, Inc.
11 West 42nd Street
New York, NY 10036
www.springerpub.com

Acquisitions Editor: Philip Laughlin
Production Editor: Julia Rosen
Cover design: Steven Pisano
Composition: Apex CoVantage, LLC

08 09 10 11/ 5 4 3 2 1

Library of Congress Cataloging-in-Publication Data

Marini, Irmo.
  The professional counselor's desk reference / Irmo Marini, Mark A. Stebnicki.
      p. cm.
    Includes bibliographical references and index.
    ISBN 978–0–8261–1547–8 (alk. paper)
    1. Counseling—Handbooks, manuals, etc.   I. Stebnicki, Mark A.   II. Title.
    BF636.6.M37 2008
    158'.3—dc22   2008024569

Printed in the United States of America by Hamilton Printing.

The author and the publisher of this Work have made every effort to use sources believed to be reliable to provide information that is accurate and compatible with the standards generally accepted at the time of publication. The author and publisher shall not be liable for any special, consequential, or exemplary damages resulting, in whole or in part, from the readers' use of, or reliance on, the information contained in this book.

The publisher has no responsibility for the persistence or accuracy of URLs for external or third-party Internet Web sites referred to in this publication and does not guarantee that any content on such Web sites is, or will remain, accurate or appropriate.

Dedication

Contents

SECTION I

Contributors

Jennifer R. Adams, PhD, NCC
Assistant Professor
School Counseling Program
    Coordinator
West Virginia University
Morgantown, WV

Paul P. Alston, PhD, CRC
Professor, Chair of Department
    of Rehabilitation Studies
East Carolina University
Greenville, NC

Leticia Arellano-Morales, PhD
Associate Professor, Department
    of Psychology
Director of Research, Mosaic
    Cultural Institute
University of La Verne
La Verne, CA

Dawn C. Brislin, MS
Doctoral Student
The Pennsylvania State
    University
University Park, PA

Philip Brownell, MDiv, PsyD
Registered Clinical Psychologist,
    Organizational Consultant,
    and Coach—Bermuda
Licensed Clinical Psychologist,
    Oregon and North
    Carolina—USA
Director, The Gestalt Training
    Institute of Bermuda

Susanne M. Bruyère, PhD, CRC
Director of the Employment and
    Disability Institute
Cornell University
Ithaca, NY

David Burnhill, MA
Counselor Education Doctoral
    Student
University of Maryland
College Park, MD

Jon Carlson, PsyD, EdD, ABPP
Distinguished Professor,
    Psychology and Counseling
Governors State University
University Park, IL

JoLynn V. Carney, PhD, LPCC-S
Associate Professor of Counselor
  Education and Supervision
The Pennsylvania State
  University
University Park, PA

Mary Louise Cashel, PhD
Associate Professor
Department of Psychology
Southern Illinois University at
  Carbondale
Carbondale, IL

Fong Chan, PhD, CRC
Professor and Director of Clinical
  Training
Department of Rehabilitation
  Psychology and Special
  Education
University of Wisconsin–Madison
Madison, WI

**Martha H. Chapin, PhD, LPC,
  CRC, CDMS**
Associate Professor and Director,
  Undergraduate Rehabilitation
  Services Program
East Carolina University
Greenville, NC

Chih Chin Chou, PhD
Assistant Professor
Special Education, Rehabilitation,
  and School Psychology
University of Arizona
Tucson, AZ

John C. Christopher, PhD
Professor of Counseling
Health and Human Development
Montana State University
Bozeman, MT

Julie Chronister, PhD, CRC
Assistant Professor
Department of Counseling
College of Health and Human
  Services
San Francisco State University
San Francisco, CA

Grant Corbett
Principal of Behavior Change
  Solutions Inc.
St. Catherine's, Ontario, Canada

William Crimando, PhD, CRC
Professor, Program Coordinator
  of Rehabilitation
  Administration and Services
Rehabilitation Institute
Southern Illinois University at
  Carbondale
Carbondale, IL

**Norman C. Dasenbrook, MS,
  LCPC**
Private Practice Consultant
Walsh & Dasenbrook Consulting
Rockford, IL

**Dibya Devika Choudhuri, PhD,
  LPC, ACS**
Associate Professor, Graduate
  Coordinator of Advertising
Eastern Michigan University
Ypsilanti, MI

Shengli Dong, MS, Ed
Counselor Education Doctoral
  Student
University of Maryland
College Park, MD

Suzanne M. Dugger, EdD
Professor and School Counseling
  Program Coordinator
Eastern Michigan University
Ypsilanti, MI

Glacia Ethridge, MA, CRC
Counselor Education Doctoral
    Student
University of Maryland
College Park, MD

Ellen S. Fabian, PhD, CRC
Associate Professor and Director
Rehabilitation Program
University of Maryland
College Park, MD

Angela D. Ferguson, PhD
Director, Counseling Psychology
    Program
Human Development and
    Psychoeducational Studies
Howard University
Washington, DC

Perry C. Francis, EdD, LPC, NCC
Associate Professor of
    Counseling and Coordinator
    for Counseling Services
College of Education, Clinical
    Suite, Counseling Clinic
Eastern Michigan University
Ypsilanti, MI

**Arthur Freeman, EdD, ABPP,
    HSPP**
Graduate Coordinator in
    Psychology and Counseling
Governors State University
University Park, IL

**Gregory G. Garske, PhD, LPCC,
    CRC**
Professor and Graduate
    Coordinator
Mental Health and School
    Counseling Program
Bowling Green State University
Bowling Green, OH

**Samuel T. Gladding, PhD, NCC,
    CCMHC, LPC, LPA**
Department of Counseling
Wake Forest University
Winston-Salem, NC

Jeannie A. Golden, PhD
Assistant Professor
Department of Psychology
East Carolina University
Greenville, NC

**Lloyd R. Goodwin, Jr.,
    PhD, LPC, LCAS, CRC,
    MAC, CCS, ACS**
Professor, Director of Graduate
    Program in Substance
    Abuse and Clinical
    Counseling
East Carolina University
Greenville, NC

Noreen M. Graf, RhD, CRC
Professor
Department of Rehabilitation
University of Texas
    Pan-American
Edinburg, TX

Joan S. Grant, DSN, RN, CS
Professor
School of Nursing
University of Alabama at
    Birmingham
Birmingham, AL

**Debra A. Harley, PhD, LPC,
    CRC, CCFC**
Professor, Chair of Department
    of Special Education and
    Rehabilitation Counseling
University of Kentucky
Lexington, KY

Michael T. Hartley, PhD, CRC
Assistant Professor
Department of Rehabilitation
    Studies
East Carolina University
Greenville, NC

James T. Herbert, PhD, CRC, LPC
Professor-in-Charge,
    Rehabilitation Service
    Program
The Pennsylvania State
    University
University Park, PA

David B. Hershenson, PhD
Adjunct Faculty Department
    of Counseling and School
    Psychology
University of
    Massachusetts–Boston
Boston, MA

Euchay N. Horsman, MS, CRC, LPCI
Doctoral Student
Rehabilitation Counseling
    Program
Southern Illinois University
Carbondale, IL

Brian Hutchison, MEd
Doctoral Candidate
Department of Counselor
    Education
The Pennsylvania State
    University
University Park, PA

Ed Jacobs, PhD, LPC, NCC
Associate Professor and
    Coordinator of
    Counseling
Department of Counseling,
    Rehabilitation Counseling,
    and Counseling
    Psychology
West Virginia University
Morgantown, WV

Jean Johnson, PhD
Assistant Professor
Division of Psychology and
    Counseling
Governors State University
University Park, IL

Sara P. Johnston
Doctoral Student
Division of Counseling,
    Rehabilitation, and Student
    Development
University of Iowa
Iowa City, IA

Charlene M. Kampfe, PhD, CRC
Professor
Department of Special Education,
    Rehabilitation, and School
    Counseling
University of Arizona
Tucson, AR

David Kaplan, PhD, NCC
Chief Professional Officer
American Counseling Association
Alexandria, VA

Nikolaos Kazantzis, PhD
Professor
Massey University
Auckland, New Zealand

Norman L. Keltner, EdD, RN
Professor
School of Nursing
University of Alabama at
  Birmingham
Birmingham, AL

Kriss A. Kevorkian, MSW, PhD
Assistant Professor
Department of Social Work
University of Wisconsin at
  Eau Claire
Eau Claire, WI

Jessica E. Lambert, MS
Doctoral Student
Department of Counseling and
  Psychology
State University of New York
  at Albany
Albany, NY

**Simone F. Lambert, PhD, LPC,
  NCC**
Assistant Professor, Counselor
  Education
Virginia Tech
Falls Church, VA

**Michael J. Leahy, PhD, LPC,
  CRC**
Professor and Director
Office of Rehabilitation and
  Disability Studies
Michigan State University
East Lansing, MI

**Kim L. MacDonald-Wilson,
  ScD, CRC, CPRP**
Assistant Professor
Rehabilitation Counseling
  and Counselor Education
  Programs
University of Maryland
College Park, MD

Irmo Marini, PhD, CRC, CLCP
Professor
Department of Rehabilitation
University of Texas
  Pan-American
Edinburg, TX

**Jennifer Todd McDonough, MS,
  CRC**
Associate Director,
  Training
Rehabilitation Research and
  Training Center on Workplace
  Supports
Virginia Commonwealth
  University
Richmond, VA

Nancy McWilliams, PhD
Visiting Professor
Graduate School of
  Applied and Professional
  Psychology
Rutgers, The State University of
  New Jersey
Piscataway, NJ

**Gail Mears, PsyD, NCC,
  LCMHC**
Associate Professor and Chair
  of Counselor Education and
  School Psychology
Plymouth State University
Plymouth, NH

Eva Miller, PhD, CRC
Associate Professor, Licensed
  Psychologist
Department of Rehabilitation
University of Texas
  Pan-American
Edinburg, TX

Nathalie D. Mizelle, PhD, CRC, LPC
Assistant Professor
Department of Rehabilitation
    Studies
East Carolina University
Greenville, NC

Sharon E. Morgillo Freeman, PhD, MSN, CARN-AP, APRN-BC
CEO Center for Brief Therapy,
    PC and The Freeman Institute
    Corporation
Associate Professor, Continuing
    Education
Indiana/Purdue Universities
Fort Wayne, IN

Nancy Newport, LPC, LMFT
Psychotherapist, Private Practice,
    Specializing in Trauma
    and Couples and Family
    Counseling
Adjunct Professor
George Mason University
Fairfax, VA

Spencer G. Niles, DEd, LPC, NCC
Incoming Editor, *Journal of
    Counseling & Development*
Professor and Department Head
Counselor Education,
    Counseling Psychology, and
    Rehabilitation Services
The Pennsylvania State
    University
University Park, PA

Rhoda Olkin, PhD
Distinguished Professor
Executive Director, Institute on
    Disability
California School of Professional
    Psychology
Alliant International University
San Francisco, CA

Nancy A. Pachana, PhD
Professor
University of Queensland
Brisbane, Australia

Nansook Park, PhD, NCSP
Associate Professor
Department of Psychology
University of Rhode Island
Kingston, RI

Nando Pelusi, PhD
Private Practice
Contributing Editor, *Psychology
    Today*
Brooklyn, NY

Christopher Peterson, PhD
Professor
Department of Psychology
University of Michigan
Ann Arbor, MI

David B. Peterson, PhD, CRC, NCC
Licensed Psychologist
Associate Professor, Coordinator
    of Program in Rehabilitation
    Services
California State University
Los Angeles, CA

Eniko Rak
Doctoral Student
Rehabilitation Counselor
    Education Program
Michigan State University
East Lansing, MI

Chuck Reid, PhD, CRC
Associate Professor
Department of Rehabilitation
University of Texas Pan-American
Edinburg, TX

Ted F. Riggar, EdD
Professor, Rehabilitation Services
    and Administrative Program
Rehabilitation Institute

Southern Illinois University at
  Carbondale
Carbondale, IL

Blanca Robles, MS, CRC
Student Counselor
University of Texas Pan-American
Edinburg, TX

Valerie J. Rodriguez, MS, CRC
Rehabilitation Counselor
Division of Assistive and
  Rehabilitative Services
San Antonio, TX

Maria G. Romero, MS, CRC
Doctoral Student
Department of Rehabilitation
  Psychology
University of Wisconsin–Madison
Madison, WI

Joshua Rosenthal, PsyD
President
Therapy Match, Inc.
Cliffside Park, NJ

**Shawn P. Saladin, PhD, CRC,
  CPM**
Assistant Professor, Coordinator
  of Deaf Rehabilitation Program
University of Texas Pan-American
Edinburg, TX

**Marcia J. Scherer, PhD, MPH,
  CRC**
President
Institute for Matching Person
  and Technology
Professor of Orthopedics and
  Rehabilitation
University of Rochester Medical
  Center
Webster, NY

**Chris J. Schimmel, EdS, LPC,
  NCC**
Instructor, Counseling
  Program
Marshall University Graduate
  Program
Huntington, WV

Kirk J. Schneider, PhD
Psychologist
Saybrook Graduate School
San Francisco, CA

Sandra T. Sigmon, PhD
Professor
Department of Psychology
University of Maine
Orono, ME

Winona F. Simms, PhD
Associate Dean and Director of
  American Indian and Alaska
  Native Program
Stanford University
Palo Alto, CA

David J. Simourd, PhD
Psychologist, Algonquin
  Correctional Evaluation
  Services
Kingston, Ontario, Canada

Wendy F. Sims, MA
Doctoral Student
Counseling and Counseling
  Psychology Program
Oklahoma State University
Tulsa, OK

Steven R. Sligar, EdD
Assistant Professor
Director of Graduate Program in
  Vocational Evaluation
East Carolina University
Greenville, NC

Julie Smart, PhD, CRC, LPC, NCC, ABDA, CCFC
Professor
Department of Special Education and Rehabilitation
Utah State University
Logan, UT

Adina J. Smith, PhD
Associate Professor
Department of Health and Human Development
Montana State University
Bozeman, MT

Mark A. Stebnicki, PhD, LPC, CRC, CCM
Professor, Director of Graduate Program in Rehabilitation Counseling
East Carolina University
Greenville, NC

Vilia M. Tarvydas, PhD, LMHC, CRC
Professor and Program Coordinator, Graduate Programs in Rehabilitation
Division of Counseling, Rehabilitation, and Student Development
University of Iowa
Iowa City, IA

Stephen W. Thomas, EdD, CRC, CVE
Professor and Dean
College of Allied Health Sciences
East Carolina University
Greenville, NC

Jill Thorngren, PhD, LCPC
Associate Professor, Marriage and Family Counseling
Montana State University
Bozeman, MT

Geoffrey L. Thorpe, PhD, ABPP
Professor
Psychology Department
University of Maine
Orono, ME

John S. Wadsworth, PhD
Associate Professor
Department of Counseling, Rehabilitation, and Student Development
College of Education
University of Iowa
Iowa City, IA

Robert J. Walsh, MA, LCPC, NCC
Private Practice Consultant
Walsh & Dasenbrook Consulting
Rockford, IL

Paul H. Wehman, PhD
Professor, Department of Physical Medicine and Rehabilitation
Chairman, Division of Rehabilitation Research
Director, Rehabilitation Research and Training Center on Workplace Supports
Virginia Commonwealth University
Richmond, VA

Robert A. Williams, PhD
Associate Professor
Department of Counseling
San Francisco State University
San Francisco, CA

Carrie Wintero
wd, PhD
Associate Professor
Counseling and Counseling
    Psychology Program
Oklahoma State University
Tulsa, OK

Noel Ysasi, MS
Rehabilitation Consultant
Marini & Associates
McAllen, TX

Stephen A. Zanskas, PhD, CRC
Assistant Professor and Program
    Coordinator
Rehabilitation Counseling
    Program
The University of Memphis
Memphis, TN

Foreword

Students and seasoned counseling professionals often need to review different books to find what they are looking for to address their concerns. Many would treasure a book that contains a wealth of practical information. This unique handbook contains this wealth of information on a variety of topics that will be of interest to counseling students, counselor educators, and practitioners in the mental health field. Each section of this reference work is structured within the framework of the CACREP and CORE accreditation standards. Readers who want to answer the following questions will find 81 chapters that offer up-to-date information:

- What are the roles and functions of professional counselors?
- What are some issues in the practice of clinical supervision?
- What are some new areas in ethics in the counseling profession?
- What are some practical guidelines in reducing ethical and legal risks?
- How can homework be integrated into the practice of counseling?
- How can counselors effectively address multicultural issues in their practices?
- What are some unique issues facing mental health counselors who work in rural settings?
- What are some of the key concepts of contemporary counseling theories?

- How can career counseling address challenges across the lifespan?
- What do counselors need to know about assessment and diagnosis?
- How can the DSM-IV-TR be used?
- What are some key issues facing counselors who work with couples, families, and groups?
- What are some emerging areas in counseling specific populations?
- How are empathy fatigue, burnout, and self-care of vital importance to every counselor?
- What is the place of religion and spirituality in counseling?

This book will be a useful reference tool that practitioners can turn to when they want specific information on any of the topics listed above. Most of the chapters contain current references and places the readers can contact for further information. The PCDR can be used as a supplementary text in various courses in counseling programs. Those who are studying for the professional counselor's licensing examination will find the various categories of the core counseling standards to be a useful review for preparing for an examination.

I found the chapters to be well-written, organized in a clear manner, and presented in a balanced way. Current literature was used to support the discussion of the variety of topics covered in this single volume. Experts in the content areas did a high-quality job of presenting their ideas in a direct way that makes for easy comprehension. This is a reference work that people will want to keep.

This will also be a valuable resource for continuing education programs. Community mental health agencies may want to order copies of this handbook for those who work in the agency. It would be most useful as a discussion tool and also for in-service education and training.

Gerald Corey, EdD in Counseling Psychology, ABPP
Professor Emeritus of Human Services and Counseling
California State University, Fullerton

Preface

There are multiple indicators to suggest there is an identity shift in the foundational principles and practices of the counseling profession. This is due to state-mediated professional counselor licensure laws, the increase in required coursework (to 60 semester hours) within many accredited counselor education programs, the recognition of specialty certifications as well as other credentials that demonstrate counselor competence, and equivalent opportunities to collect third-party reimbursement for the provision of counseling-related services. Indeed, we are in a state of transition to differentiate professional counselors (i.e., state-licensed LPCs [licensed professional counselors]) from other counseling professions such as in psychology and social work. Overall, the profession looks and feels much different now than when it was first conceived by our lineage of creative practitioners, consumer advocates, highly productive counselor educators, and visionaries from the 1950s–1970s.

As Leahy, Rak, and Zanskus as well as Tarvydas and Hartley point out in the first section (professional identity) of the *Professional Counselor's Desk Reference* (*PCDR*), we have evolved as a group of specialty areas (e.g., vocational, school, mental health, marriage and family, and rehabilitation counseling) that practice a common core of competencies and possess similar foundational concepts and skills. Accordingly, counselors are now differentiated by their employment setting, the types of clients served, and the counseling services provided. Interestingly, early professional counselors appeared to lack a professional identity despite practicing within their own specialty areas. This was due in part to (1) a lack of research defining best practices in counseling, (2) limited preprofessional counselor training programs, (3) a lack of regulations that included counselor certification and licensure, and (4) a poorly-defined code of ethics. This is not the case today. We have much to be proud of because our profession has widely recognized leaders in state and national professional counseling associations, counselor credentialing entities, as well as congressional representatives who advocate for inclusion of services provided by qualified LPCs. Our professional identity now has a brief history that is marked by a wellspring of therapeutic outcome as well as role and function studies, state laws mandating that LPCs have access to insurance panels, as well as national standards and guidelines for providing competent and ethical practice in the counseling profession.

The *Professional Counselor's Desk Reference* is a reflection of our identity as professional counselors for the start of the 21st century. A review of the table of contents demonstrates an impressive body of research and practice guidelines offered by many well-known practitioners, counselor educators, and researchers. Accordingly, we have reached a pivotal point in our professional identity as LPCs continue to expand into other counseling specialty settings that have been traditionally marked by psychologists and social workers.

Regardless of scope of practice and counseling specialty, we have been challenged with counseling a more diverse group of individuals than in the early days of the profession. We are hopeful that the *Professional Counselor's Desk Reference* can be used as a resource offering a framework for understanding this change from providing traditional counseling services to the interrelationships between counseling individuals, groups, and families, and the importance of maintaining a professional identity through professional counseling associations.

At the core of working from this perspective, it is essential to understand that we have much to gain by (1) working with other accrediting and credentialing bodies in an interdisciplinary environment; (2) increasing our capacity for partnering, collaborating, organizing, and uniting state and national professional counseling associations with one voice for the profession; and (3) cultivating the spirit to thrive as a profession where state counselor licensure is reciprocal with all states. Thus, the interconnectedness between different systems makes up the whole of our structure and professional counseling identity.

Indeed, a profession that is licensable has the capability to negotiate third-party contracts with Medicare, Medicaid, and private insurance; can function independently (not under the supervision or referral of a psychologist or medical professional); and can enjoy the benefits and opportunities afforded to other counseling professions. Advancing the practice of professional counseling requires an increased recognition of and sensitivity to the diversity of specialty areas in counseling and expanding opportunities in this dynamic sociopolitical environment so that we may communicate with one voice.

Introduction

The field of counseling is a continually expanding and challenging profession that has a prolific history of facilitating person-centered, couples, family, and group therapeutic services for children, adolescents, and adults. Many consumers of counseling services report chronic and persistent mental health conditions such as substance abuse or addictions, depression and anxiety, acute stress, and a multitude of other life-adjustment issues. As we have found in our own clinical practice, rarely do we treat individuals with just a mental health condition. Oftentimes, there appears to be a coexisting medical and/or situational circumstance that hinders the individual's functional capacity to achieve optimal levels of mental and physical well-being.

The *Professional Counselor's Desk Reference* (*PCDR*) is the first of its kind that serves as an authoritative resource written for both preprofessionals working toward counselor licensure and certification as well as seasoned counselors, counselor educators, clinical supervisors, psychologists, and social workers. Our intent in writing and editing the *Professional Counselor's Desk Reference* is to provide professionals with a quick desk reference guide based on the 10 core content and knowledge areas as described in both the Council for Accreditation of Counseling and Related Education Programs (CACREP) and Council on Rehabilitation Education (CORE) accreditation standards. It also offers an excellent resource for graduate-level coursework that relates to an orientation to the counseling profession. To advance this mission, we asked each of our chapter contributors to submit four multiple-choice questions based on the material in his or her chapter. Although the

300-plus multiple-choice questions do not cover all the possible curricula required by the CACREP and CORE accreditation standards, they serve as an original guide to good counseling practices written by more than 100 professionals who understand the roles and functions of professional counselors and the knowledge, awareness, and skills that lead to competent and ethical counseling practices.

The *Professional Counselor's Desk Reference* includes 81 chapters and collaborative works from more than 100 different contributing authors, each with extensive expertise in his or her own specialty area as outlined in the table of contents. Most of our chapter contributors have well over 25 years of clinical practice, teaching, and research experience within their specialty area. Many of these authors have written several books and/or have numerous articles published in peer-reviewed journals within their discipline. The *Professional Counselor's Desk Reference* is didactic in its coverage, containing numerous how-to chapters with examples such as starting your own private practice, professional disclosure statements, conducting intake interviews, developing treatment plans, negotiating third-party contracts with insurance companies, ensuring clients return after the first session, and strategies for motivating and providing homework assignments for clients. Additionally, there are chapters that relate to counseling strategies and techniques for counseling persons with psychiatric disabilities, providing services in rural settings, and working therapeutically with children, older adults, adult offenders, persons with substance abuse or addiction problems, college student adjustment concerns, end-of-life issues, and counseling persons with various other types of mental and physical disabilities. The *Professional Counselor's Desk Reference* is contemporary in its focus as well, addressing spirituality-religiosity issues, the increasing interest in providing disaster mental-health counseling, positive psychology and wellness, dealing with counselor impairment and fatigue syndromes such as empathy fatigue, and counseling the increasing elderly population and their family members.

Perhaps the most significant contribution of the *Professional Counselor's Desk Reference* is its interdisciplinary approach that is inclusive across all counseling disciplines. The content offered appears to more accurately reflect the realities that we see in everyday practice with our clients. The intent of the *Professional Counselor's Desk Reference* is to provide both insight and practical strategies for working with the complexity of real-life issues clients may present with in counseling. Although the *Professional Counselor's Desk Reference* is not designed as an end-all guide that offers all the necessary counseling skills for working in all situations, the majority of chapters provide a comprehensive list of references and resources for further reading on the topic. Each counselor of course must still determine when appropriate referrals need to be made. The full value of such a desk reference, however, is that various counseling specialties can learn from each other's practice strategies to become more knowledgeable in dealing with numerous client issues.

The *Professional Counselor's Desk Reference* provides professionals with chapters organized into the combined 10 CACREP and CORE content areas that address the awareness, knowledge, and skills to work with children, adolescents, individuals, groups, couples, families, and persons from diverse cultural backgrounds. The content areas include:

- Professional counseling identity
- Ethical and practice management issues
- Case management and consultation issues
- Multicultural counseling awareness
- Counseling theories and techniques
- Career counseling and human growth
- Assessment and diagnosis
- Counseling couples, families, and groups
- Counseling specific populations
- Contemporary issues in counseling

Special features of the *Professional Counselor's Desk Reference* include:

- Tools and information to begin establishing a private practice
- Bulleted how-to strategies and counseling techniques in working with specific populations under various environmental and complex circumstances
- A comprehensive list of references and Internet sites for further reading
- A comprehensive 300-plus-item multiple-choice test reflecting each chapter's content
- Easy-to-read tables, graphics, and figures to capture a holistic picture of the client's situational circumstances
- Usable common counseling formatted documents, including a professional disclosure statement, intake interview, treatment plan, checklists, mental and physical functional capacity evaluations, and summary guidelines
- A comprehensive index and author listing at the end of the book
- Concise informational tools and resource introductions, such as ethical practice guidelines, HIPAA regulations, using the *Diagnostic and Statistical Manual of Mental Disorders (DSM–IV–TR)* and the International Classification of Functioning (ICF)
- Quick reference information that can be integrated into PowerPoint presentations

Overall, the *Professional Counselor's Desk Reference* has something valuable for preprofessional counselors and students enrolled in a graduate-level counselor education program, clinical supervisors, counselor educators, and seasoned counselors. Although we have attempted to cover a comprehensive list of counseling issues, there are many other content areas that will be added to future editions of the *Professional Counselor's Desk Reference*. As such, we welcome your feedback regarding other important counseling topics that would benefit our colleagues.

Finally, we would like to thank our more than 100 contributing authors who made the *Professional Counselor's Desk Reference* possible. We were extremely fortunate to have many "first-round draft choices" say yes to contributing one or more chapters to the *Professional Counselor's Desk Reference*. We solicited contributions from many of the American Counseling Association (ACA) subdivisions, fellow colleagues, well-known practitioners who work within their specialty area, distinguished counselor educators, and some highly productive master's- and doctoral-level students to join in developing these works. Together, they made coediting the *Professional Counselor's Desk Reference* a much easier task. In most instances, many of our chapter contributors who have written numerous books and journal articles on their topic did not have to struggle with which appropriate material to include in their chapter, but rather the major decision was what content they should leave out. As such, each chapter is applied in nature and represents decades of combined experiences in psychology and counseling research, teaching, and practice. It is our hope that you will find the *Professional Counselor's Desk Reference* a valuable resource that offers the combined wisdom of many authors to assist you in providing the optimal level of awareness, knowledge, and skills to work with a diversity of clients in an increasingly complex world.

Irmo and Mark

Section A

The Identity of Professional Counselors

1

A Brief History of Counseling and Specialty Areas of Practice

MICHAEL J. LEAHY, ENIKO RAK, AND STEPHEN A. ZANSKAS

HISTORICAL ROOTS OF THE COUNSELING PROFESSION

THE HISTORY OF counseling is a fascinating evolutionary process, particularly in relation to how the profession developed, and how quickly it has evolved through the professionalization process during the past half century. Counseling principally evolved as a profession from the development and maturation of specialty areas of counseling practice (e.g., school counseling, rehabilitation counseling, mental health counseling) that shared a common core of professional competencies and foundational concepts (Hosie, 1995; Myers, 1995; Sweeney, 1995). Historical, philosophical, and societal trends and public policy have all contributed to the development of the various counseling specialties.

Rather than the profession of counseling evolving first, followed by a logical sequence of specialization of practice (as evident in the medical

and legal professions), the specialty areas actually emerged first in response to a variety of human needs and were only later conceptualized
as belonging to the common professional home of counseling. This
unusual sequence of professional emergence has had a direct impact
on the institutions, regulatory bodies, and professional associations
that represent the profession and the specialty areas of practice. Myers
(1995) indicated that specializations in the counseling profession have
been based on unique employment settings, clients served, techniques
employed, or a blend of required knowledge and client populations.
Herr (1999) has suggested that the

> content of counseling, with whom the counselor works, and the degree
> to which counseling is seen as a vital and important sociopolitical in-
> stitution derive from major social, economic, and political themes that
> affect the individual and group psychology. Thus images, beliefs, narra-
> tives, and realities that compose the national macrosystems also have a
> ripple effect through the subsystems—community, school, workplace,
> and family—in which people interact with institutions and with other
> individuals to negotiate their identity, their sense of purpose, and their
> meaning. (p. x)

For the most part, the counseling specialty areas emerged to address
specific client needs, within the system and environmental context
that Herr (1999) describes above, and early practitioners in these special
practice areas had limited preservice education and supervision, did
not have well-defined codes of ethics, were not regulated (certification
and licensure), may not have been aware of the values and needs of
diverse populations, and did not have access to research that could help
define best practices for counselors (Capuzzi & Stauffer, 2008).

Although the term *counseling* appeared for the first time in print in
1931, the practice of this helping relationship started well before that
date. For example, psychological healing was used in ancient Greece and
Rome thousands of years ago (Jackson, 1999). Considered an adjacent
process of guidance at the beginning of the 20th century, counseling is
now considered a profession. It was in the *Workbook in Vocations,* added
as a supplement to Proctor's publication *Educational and Vocational
Guidance,* where the word *counseling* was first introduced (Aubrey, 1982).
Today, counseling is a vibrant professional discipline that is taught at
the preservice graduate level in accredited university programs throughout this country. It is practiced under state and federal licensure and
certification standards and has its own professional organizations,
philosophy and principles, professional standards, and ethical codes
of conduct. Professional counselors provide services through different
specialties in diverse settings (Sweeney, 2001). A series of significant
political, social, and cultural events led to these accomplishments.

The purpose of this chapter is to briefly review and highlight the major events that led to development of professional counseling, including the numerous professional specialty groups that make up the family of professional disciplines in counseling that provide services to a wide-ranging population of clients in highly diverse practice settings. For interested readers who may want a more detailed history of counseling than is possible in this brief chapter, there are a number of excellent resources available in print (e.g., Gibson & Mitchell, 1990; Gladding, 2004; Locke, Myers, & Herr, 2001; Petterson & Nisenholz, 1991), as well as more detailed descriptions of the specialty areas (e.g., Capuzzi & Stauffer, 2008; Riggar & Maki, 2004).

THE EARLY YEARS

THE ORIGINS OF the counseling profession in the United States have generally been attributed to Frank Parsons, "the father of the guidance movement," who established the first formal career counseling center in Boston in 1909 (Hartung & Blustein, 2002). This center offered assistance to young people in vocational selection and other work-related issues. The first decades of the 20th century included major events that launched the guidance movement in this country. Industrialization, mass migration to large cities, compulsory education, immigration, the women's movement, and the emergence of psychometrics led to changes that increased needs for assessment and guidance. Migrant workers and war veterans needed expert guidance to help find suitable occupations in various industries (Aubrey, 1982). At the beginning of the century, "visiting teachers" performed social welfare functions to students who showed adjustment problems (Sedlak, 1997). Parson's book, *Choosing a Vocation,* published in 1909, was a capstone event in the emerging guidance movement and its corollary process: counseling. Counseling was seen as a helpful tool to accomplish the goals of guidance.

Another early influential reformer was Jesse Davis, who as a high school principal introduced vocational guidance into public education. He believed in the idea of *call to a vocation,* creating the opportunity for students to explore possible vocations. Parsons also inspired Boston school superintendent Stratton Brooks to introduce guidance practices in local schools, although Jesse Davis is generally credited with the naturalization of educational guidance. During these formative years, guidance was delivered in regular classrooms just like any other subject of the curriculum (Aubrey, 1982). Formal training of teachers in guidance began in 1911 at Harvard College (Nugent, 1990). A third pioneer, frequently mentioned in the literature, was Clifford Beers, an early advocate for reform in mental health facilities. His book, *A Mind That Found Itself,* published in 1908, described the regrettable conditions he witnessed firsthand as a patient (Gladding, 2004).

These reforms introduced guidance into schools, a practice that soon became mandated by the passage of the Smith-Hughes Act in 1917 (Aubrey, 1977). This legislation made funding available to provide vocational education in public schools. Educational guidance increased in the 1920s because of emerging issues in school settings that included the expanded curriculum and an increase in the number of students due to compulsory education laws. Another series of important events for counseling in this era was the establishment of the first marriage and family counseling center in New York City by Abraham and Hannah Stone in 1929 (Nugent, 1990); the passage of the Soldiers Rehabilitation Act in 1918; the Smith Fess Act of 1920, which mandated counseling and guidance services for individuals with service-related disabilities (pre–Veterans Administration program legislation); and civilians with disabilities who had the capacity to enter or reenter employment as an outcome of services.

During the 1920s and 1930s, guidance and counseling began a significant shift from a predominantly selection-focused test-and-tell approach to a conceptualization of guidance that was focused primarily on personal adjustment and human developmental issues (Aubrey, 1982). There is no question that in the early stages of the 20th century, the field of counseling was heavily influenced by the vocational guidance movement, the mental health movement, and the study of individual differences, particularly in relation to psychometry (Petterson & Nisenholz, 1991). Furthermore, as Petterson and Nisenholz (1991) succinctly point out, "in large part, counseling developed from a non-medical, non-psychoanalytic point of view" (p. 100).

THE MIDDLE YEARS—THE PROFESSIONALIZATION OF COUNSELING PRACTICE

COUNSELING GAINED CONSIDERABLE autonomy and visibility by the middle of the century. The debut of Carl Rogers, the great pioneer of humanistic approaches and founder of client-centered counseling, prompted this process of individualization. Rogers's (1942) book, *Counseling and Psychotherapy,* revolutionized the counseling profession. The trait-and-factor approach was gradually replaced or at least supplemented by a nondirective, humanistic approach to counseling. Rogers brought the client-centered orientation into the fields of psychotherapy and counseling. The client-centered approach (now termed *person-centered*), founded on humanistic principles, became known as the third force in psychology and counseling, next to psychoanalysis and behaviorism. In the 1950s other orientations emerged to offer a basis of theoretical and methodological grounding in counseling practice. There were also a number of critical developments achieved through legislation and public policy that initiated a process of professionalization in the counseling specialty areas. For example, the Vocational Rehabilitation Act Amendments of 1954 provided funding to university programs and students to train rehabilitation counselors at the graduate level to work with individuals with disabilities (Leahy, 2004). The National Defense Education Act of 1958 (Aubrey, 1982) provided funding for schools to select students with potential for scientific and academic work (Sweeney, 2001). Another major contribution of this law was to provide funds to train counselors (Bradley & Cox, 2001). The Community Mental Health Centers Act of 1963 was another significant legislative piece that launched counseling in community and health institutions. This law started a trend that made counseling available and accessible to diverse groups in highly diverse practice settings.

Professions have been defined as full-time occupations that are characterized by specific education or training requirements, professional associations, established codes of ethics, and public recognition (Rothman, 1998). The transition from an occupation to a profession occurs through a dynamic and continuous process (Rothman, 1998). For most of the counseling specialty areas, the period of time from the early 1950s through the 1970s represents a 30-year period in which significant strides were made in relation to professionalization of practice. Specialty areas of counseling practice that made significant progress during this period included school counseling, rehabilitation counseling, mental health counseling, marriage and family counseling, addictions counseling, and career counseling. According to Myers (1995), the American Counseling Association (ACA) has created specialty divisions consulting with the four following groups to determine a counseling specialty: the Council for Accreditation of Counseling and Related Educational Programs (CACREP), the Council on Rehabilitation Education (CORE), the National Board for Certified Counselors (NBCC), and the Commission on Rehabilitation Counselor Certification (CRCC).

CONTEMPORARY PRACTICE—PROFESSIONAL IDENTITY AND RECOGNITION

ONE OF THE critical issues that continues to challenge the counseling profession and related specialty areas is professional identity and professional unification (Remley, 1993; Sweeney, 2001). Because the profession of counseling evolved initially as specialty areas, this unusual sequence of professional development has directly impacted on its identity. Contemporary practice also is characterized as both unified and fragmented. However, the family of professional disciplines in counseling provides services to a wide range of clients in highly diverse practice settings. In fact, some of the specialty areas developed their own codes of ethics, and in the case of rehabilitation counseling, established independent regulatory bodies (i.e., certification and accreditation) prior to the development of these mechanisms within the general counseling field.

In the early 1990s there was a specific initiative to address the unity and professional identity issues within the counseling specialty areas (Remley, 1993). These efforts continue today, although one of the lessons learned during these earlier initiatives was the critical significance of the specialty areas to the individual practitioner's professional identity. Practitioners typically identify first with their specialty area of practice, and secondarily with the profession of counseling. In the sections that follow we will highlight developments in professional associations, education and training, and practitioner credentials that demonstrate the significant progress that has been made in the professionalization arena over the past 30 years. While these areas, along with codes of professional ethics for counselors, will be covered more extensively elsewhere in this text, they are significant milestones in the history of counseling and related specializations and deserve attention here.

PROFESSIONAL ASSOCIATIONS

ANY DISCUSSION OF the history of counseling needs to address the professional associations that represent its vital interests (Goodyear, 1984). The first professional association to comprehensively represent counselors was the American Personal and Guidance Association (APGA) founded in 1952. Over time the name was changed to the American Association for Counseling and Development (AACD) in 1983, and again in 1992 when the organization became the ACA. This organization is by far the largest association of counselors in the world, with more than 40,000 members and 19 divisions representing its diverse community of counselors, who share that the goal of counseling is to facilitate individual adjustment and development across the life span.

The 19 unique divisions within the ACA represent areas of specialized practice (e.g., school counseling, rehabilitation counseling, mental health counseling, marriage and family counseling, addictions counseling, and career counseling) and special interest areas (e.g., assessment in counseling; adult development and aging; counselor education and supervision; spiritual, ethical, and religious values; and social justice) that relate to a broad constituency of counselors regardless of their specialty area of practice. There are also a number of other professional associations outside of the ACA that provide additional opportunities for counselors from distinct specialty areas, including organizations at the state level.

EDUCATION AND TRAINING

THE MAJORITY OF master's-level counselor education programs consist of 48 or 60 semester hours of credits. Counselor education programs are accredited by two primary institutional accreditation organizations: CORE and CACREP. The similarity between the two organizations' goals and objectives and an interest in the promotion of a unified counselor identity has led to proposals to merge the two organizations in recent years. However, these organizations have not been merged at this point in time.

The accreditation organization for rehabilitation counselor education is CORE (Leahy & Szymanski, 1995). Incorporated in 1972, CORE's stated purpose is "to promote the effective delivery of rehabilitation services to individuals with disabilities by promoting and fostering continuing review and improvement of master's degree level RCE [rehabilitation counselor education] programs" (CORE, 2001, p. 2). Currently, there are 102 master's degree programs accredited by CORE (CORE Master's Programs in Rehabilitation Counselor Education, 2006–2007 Academic Year).

CACREP was incorporated in 1981, nearly 9 years after the development of CORE. In 1993, CACREP (2006) articulated its mission "to promote the professional competence of counseling and related practitioners through the development of preparation standards, encouragement of excellence in program development, and accreditation of professional preparation programs" (*About CACREP*, section 3). CACREP currently accredits 210 programs and 10 entry-level master's degree program categories, which include addiction counseling; community counseling; college counseling; career counseling; gerontological counseling; marital, couple, and family counseling; clinical mental health counseling; student affairs and college counseling; student affairs practice in higher education—college counseling emphasis; student affairs practice in higher education—professional practice emphasis; and school counseling. The council also recognizes 50 doctoral programs in counselor education and supervision (CACREP, 2008, Directory of Accredited Programs).

PRACTITIONER CREDENTIALS

COUNSELOR CERTIFICATION BEGAN with the movement to certify teachers and school counselors in the 1940s and 1950s (Forrest & Stone, 1991). The primary impetus for counselor certification remained with school counselors until 1973 when the CRCC was the first organization to establish a credentialing process for counseling and rehabilitation professionals (Leahy & Szymanski, 1995). Examination and certification standards for the Certified Rehabilitation Counselor (CRC) credential have been established through empirical research throughout the CRCC's history (Leahy & Szymanski, 1995).

Engels, Minor, Sampson, and Splete (1995) indicated that the NBCC represents a common foundation for all of the counseling specialties. The NBCC was incorporated in 1982, some 9 years after the CRCC, to establish and monitor a national counselor certification system. The NBCC certification program has established standards for counselors' training, experience, and performance on the National Counselor Examination for Licensure and Certification (NCE). The National Certified Counselor (NCC) is the primary credential offered by NBCC. The NCC is a prerequisite for the NBCC specialty certifications in school counseling, clinical mental health counseling, and addictions counseling (NBCC, 2007).

Licensing of professional counselors has contributed to the public's recognition of counseling as a profession (Remley, 1995). The counselor licensure movement began in the early 1970s (Bradley, 1995). Although the primary purpose of licensure is public protection, the counseling profession's interest in licensure was also a reaction to prevent restriction by other professions (Hosie, 1995). Virginia became the first state to license professional counselors in 1975 (Bradley, 1995). By 1994, 41 states and the District of Columbia regulated the counseling profession (Bradley, 1995), and in 2007, Nevada became the 49th state to license counselors (American Counseling Association, 2007). While there has been some fragmentation in relation to certification and accreditation efforts within the counseling specialty areas, there has been a much more unified voice in relation to counselor licensure.

CURRENT AND FUTURE CHALLENGES

THE FUNDAMENTAL PURPOSE of counseling is to address human needs emerging in response to the ongoing changes that define dynamic societies (Herr, 1999). There is no question that the counseling specialty areas, and the profession as a whole, have made remarkable strides and accomplishments over the past 100 years or so in responding to these human needs. According to the U.S. Department of Labor, Bureau of Labor Statistics' *Occupational Outlook Handbook* (2008), there were 636,000 jobs held by counselors in this country in 2006, with an occupational outlook expected to grow faster than average over the years to come. The distribution of these jobs include educational, vocational, and school counselors (260,000); rehabilitation counselors (141,000); mental health counselors (100,000); substance abuse and behavioral disorder counselors (83,000); marriage and family therapists (25,000); and all other counselors (27,000).

American society always has been diverse. Projections indicate further diversification along various dimensions, such as age, racial and ethnic affiliation, sexual orientation, family patterns, and disability, that will continue to challenge the counseling profession to respond. Major demographic shifts are predicted that will have profound implications for counseling, raising the need for enhanced competencies to serve an increasingly diverse group of individuals.

Other issues that will impact the practice of counseling in the years to come include the aging of American society (Himes, 2001), the anticipated increase in disability (partially related to aging and advanced medical practices), significant changes in the world of work, and advancements in technology. The next chapter in the history of counseling and related specializations is currently in progress, and to some degree its success will depend on how well these issues are understood and addressed in practice by professional counselors from all the specialty areas.

REFERENCES

American Counseling Association (ACA). (2007). *Nevada is 49th state to license professional counselors.* Retrieved July 7, 2008, from http://www.counseling.org/PressRoom/PressReleases.aspx?AGuid=cd2c9dad-427f-4135-af98-3801251526bf

Aubrey, R. F. (1977). Historical development of guidance and counseling and implications for the future. *Personnel and Guidance Journal, 55,* 288–295.

Aubrey, R. F. (1982). A house divided: Guidance and counseling in twentieth-century America. *Personnel and Guidance Journal, 60,* 198–204.

Bradley, L. (1995). Certification and licensure issues. *Journal of Counseling and Development, 74*(2), 185–186.

Bradley, R. W., & Cox, J. A. (2001). Counseling: Evolution of the profession. In D. Locke, J. Myers, & E. Herr (Eds.), *The handbook of counseling* (pp. 27–41). Thousand Oaks, CA: Sage.

Capuzzi, D., & Stauffer, M. D. (2008). *Foundations of addictions counseling.* Boston: Pearson Education.

Council for Accreditation of Counseling and Related Educational Programs. (2008). *About CACREP*. Retrieved August 12, 2007, from http://www.cacrep.org/AboutCACREP.html

Council on Rehabilitation Education. (2001). *Mission and objectives*. Retrieved August 12, 2007, from http://www.core-rehab.org/manual/manual.html#mission

Council on Rehabilitation Education. (2006). *2005–2006 CORE profile*. Retrieved August 12, 2007, from http://www.core-rehab.org/

Engels, D., Minor, C., Sampson, J., & Splete, H. (1995). Career counseling specialty: History, development, and prospect. *Journal of Counseling and Development, 74*(2), 134–138.

Forrest, D., & Stone, L. (1991). Counselor certification. In F. O. Bradley (Ed.), *Credentialing in counseling* (pp. 13–23). Alexandria, VA: American Association for Counseling and Development.

Gibson, R. L., & Mitchell, M. H. (1990). *Introduction to counseling and guidance* (3rd ed.). New York: Macmillan.

Gladding, S. T. (2004). *Counseling: A comprehensive profession* (5th ed.). Englewood Cliffs, NJ: Merrill/Prentice-Hall.

Goodyear, R. K. (1984). On our journal's evolution: Historical developments, transitions, and future directions. *Journal of Counseling and Development, 63*, 3–9.

Hartung, P., & Blustein, D. (2002). Reason, intuition, and social justice: Elaborating on Parson's career decision-making model. *Journal of Counseling and Development, 80*(1), 41–47.

Herr, E. L. (1999). *Counseling in a dynamic society: Context and practices for the 21st century* (2nd ed.). Alexandria, VA: American Counseling Association.

Himes, C. L. (2001). Elderly Americans. *Population Bulletin, 4*, 27–28.

Hosie, T. (1995). Counseling specialties: A case of basic preparation rather than advanced specialization. *Journal of Counseling and Development, 74*(2), 177–180.

Jackson, S. W. (1999). Care of the psyche: A history of psychological healing. New Haven, CT: Yale University Press.

Leahy, M. J. (2004). Qualified providers of rehabilitation counseling services. In T. F. Riggar & D. R. Maki (Eds.), *The handbook of rehabilitation counseling* (pp. 142–158). New York: Springer Publishing.

Leahy, M., & Szymanski, E. (1995). Rehabilitation counseling: Evolution and current status. *Journal of Counseling and Development, 74*(2), 163–166.

Locke, D., Myers, J., & Herr, E. (Eds.). (2001). *The handbook of counseling*. Thousand Oaks, CA: Sage.

Myers, J. (1995). Specialties in counseling: Rich heritage or force for fragmentation? *Journal of Counseling and Development, 74*(2), 115–116.

National Board for Certified Counselors. (2007). *History of NBCC*. Retrieved August 12, 2007, from http://www.nbcc.org/about

Nugent, F. A. (1990). *An introduction to the profession of counseling*. Columbus, OH: Merrill.

Petterson, J. V., & Nisenholz, B. (1991). *Orientation to counseling* (2nd ed.). Boston: Allyn and Bacon.

Remley, T. P. (1993). Rehabilitation counseling: A scholarly model for the generic profession of counseling. *Rehabilitation Counseling Bulletin, 37*(2), 182–186.

Remley, T. (1995). A proposed alternative to the licensing of specialties in counseling. *Journal of Counseling and Development, 74*(2), 126–129.

Riggar, T. F., & Maki, D. R. (Eds.). (2004). *The handbook of rehabilitation counseling.* New York: Springer Publishing.

Rogers, C. R. (1942). *Counseling and psychotherapy: Newer concepts in practice.* Boston/New York: Houghton Mifflin.

Rothman, R. A. (1998). *Working: Sociological perspectives* (2nd ed.). Upper Saddle River, NJ: Prentice-Hall.

Sedlak, M. W. (1997). The uneasy alliance of mental health services and schools: An historical perspective. *American Journal of Orthopsychiatry, 67,* 349–362.

Sweeney, T. (1995). Accreditation, credentialing, professionalization: The role of specialties. *Journal of Counseling and Development, 74*(2), 117–125.

Sweeney, T. J. (2001). Counseling: Historical origins and philosophical roots. In D. Locke, J. Myers, & E. Herr (Eds.), *The handbook of counseling* (pp. 3–26). Thousand Oaks, CA: Sage.

U.S. Department of Labor, Bureau of Labor Statistics. (2008). *Occupational outlook handbook [OOH].* Retrieved July 7, 2008, from http://www.bls.gov/oco/ocos067.htm

2

The Roles and Functions of Professional Counselors

JULIE CHRONISTER, CHIH CHIN CHOU,
AND FONG CHAN

COUNSELING INVOLVES A voluntary and confidential process that occurs within the context of a professional relationship, in which individuals, groups, or families work toward gaining an understanding of self and others that will allow them to successfully solve problems and resolve conflicts in their daily lives (Altekruse, Harris, & Brandt, 2001). Although counseling is a function of many helping disciplines (e.g., counseling, social work, and psychology), the field of counseling is a distinct profession that has an accrediting body, an ethical code, recommended curriculum, professional organizations, credentials, and licensure in most states (Gale & Austin, 2003). In fact, professional counselors occupy more than 600,000 jobs in the United States and the employment rate is expected to grow faster than average by 2014 (U.S. Department of Labor, Bureau of Labor Statistics, 2007). Given the professionalization of counseling and the anticipated job growth, the purpose of this chapter is to provide readers with an overview of the roles, functions, and knowledge base of counselors and address the professional issues that influence the identity and practice of counselors today.

COUNSELOR ROLES

THE PRIMARY ROLE of a counselor is to assist clients in reaching their optimal level of psychosocial functioning through resolving negative patterns, prevention, rehabilitation, and improving quality of life (Hershenson & Power, 1987). In doing this, counselors apply "mental health, psychological, or human development principles, through cognitive, affective, behavioral or systemic intervention strategies, that address wellness, personal growth, or career development, as well as pathology" (American Counseling Association [ACA], 2007). A counselor's role can be differentiated from other helping professions by its focus on viewing problems as naturally occurring developmental events that are a manifestation of the person, system, and culture. As such, counselors consider the individual's life stage, developmental history, context and broader sociocultural issues in assessment and treatment. Less emphasis is placed on making diagnostic decisions and remediation; most often, counselors focus their treatment on developmental growth and prevention, competencies, strengths, coping, resources, negotiating life transitions, and managing stressors (Van Hesteren & Ivey, 1990).

COUNSELOR FUNCTIONS

THE NATIONAL BOARD for Certified Counselors (NBCC) conducted a job analysis to identify the essential job functions of professional counselors (National Board for Certified Counselors [NBCC], 1995). Their study identified five major work behavior dimensions: (1) fundamental counseling practices (e.g., obtain informed consent, conduct interview, listen actively, help set counseling goals, and counsel clients concerning personal changes); (2) counseling for career development (e.g., use interest inventories, help client develop decision-making skills, and use occupational information in counseling); (3) counseling groups (e.g., inform clients of group counseling guidelines and goals, observe group members' behaviors, use structured activities during group counseling, and use group counseling leadership techniques); (4) counseling families (e.g., clarify family counseling goals, counsel concerning family member interaction and family change, develop family conflict resolution strategies); and (5) professional practices (e.g., participate in case conferences, conduct community outreach, and serve as a liaison with other agencies). Similarly, the Commission on Rehabilitation Counselor Certification (CRCC, n.d.) identified the following counselor functions: (1) counseling (individual, group, marriage, family) and psychotherapy, (2) guidance and consultation, (3) appraisal, (4) diagnostic and treatment planning for persons with psychological disorders or disabilities, (5) functional assessments and career counseling for persons adjusting to a disability, (6) referrals, and (7) research. Additional functions may include advocacy, case management, crisis management, and outreach.

Counseling and *psychotherapy* involve the development of a counseling relationship in which the counselor interacts with one or more clients who are seeking support in making life changes associated with intra- and interpersonal related to family or other social ties, educational adjustment, employment, rehabilitation, aging, mental health, and empowerment (ACA, 2007; Thomas, Berven, & Chan, 2004). The process involves assisting clients in exploring their present functioning and formulating new ways of behaving, feeling, and thinking to achieve personal goals. Thus, counseling entails both choice and change and progresses through distinct stages such as exploration, goal setting, and action (ACA, 2007). Effective delivery of counseling and psychotherapy requires

> establishing a therapeutic working relationship with individuals served; communicating with individuals in facilitative, helpful ways; obtaining information from individuals in a comprehensive and thorough manner, helping them to tell their stories and explain their problems and needs; understanding and conceptualizing behavior and problems in ways that will facilitate treatment and service planning; and facilitating follow-through on commitments and compliance with treatment and service plans that individuals have decided to pursue. (Thomas et al., 2004, p. 4)

In the past, counseling and psychotherapy were considered two distinct functions. Specifically, psychotherapy was considered to be longer in duration, have greater depth and intensity, require more training, and address personality reorganization as opposed to more reality-based problems. Psychotherapy has also been considered the treatment for individuals with severe psychopathology, while counseling is applied to more "normal" problems of living, decision making, and personal growth (Thomas et al., 2004). Today, however, most scholars concede that counseling and psychotherapy are synonymous (Corsini, 1989).

Guidance and *consultation* are also important functions of professional counselors. These two functions focus less on the process of psychological change and more on making life choices and decisions or solving immediate problems related to others. Guidance activities involve assisting people in making important choices and identifying values; consultation involves providing assistance with resolving problems related to a third party (ACA, 2007). *Appraisal* refers to selecting, administering, scoring, and interpreting instruments designed to assess an individual's attitudes, abilities, achievements, interests, and personal characteristics. *Referral* involves making a referral to another specialist based on the needs of a client. *Research* involves systematic efforts to collect, evaluate, interpret, and apply procedures related to improving the understanding and delivery of counseling services to clients (ACA, 2007).

Because professional counseling is practiced in different settings (i.e., community or state agency, mental health clinic, school, college, career center) with different clients (individual, group, family), a number of counseling specialties have evolved over the years (i.e., rehabilitation, mental health, school, career, college, marriage and family, community, and gerontological). Thus, counseling functions vary according to the context and the clientele. For example, *rehabilitation counselors* work with clients with disabilities and/or chronic illnesses in settings such as state vocational rehabilitation agencies, hospitals, community-based programs, school-to-work programs, private rehabilitation agencies, and businesses. They focus on understanding existing problems, barriers, and potentials in order to facilitate the client's effective use of personal and environmental resources for career, personal, social, and community adjustment following disability (Parker & Szymanski, 1998). The profession of rehabilitation counseling has taken the lead in empirically identifying job functions unique to rehabilitation counselors (e.g., Leahy, Chan, & Saunders, 2003). In fact, rehabilitation scholars have been conducting studies to determine the roles and functions of rehabilitation counselors for the past 45 years. In a recent study, Leahy et al. (2003) identified vocational counseling and consultation, counseling interventions, community-based rehabilitation service activities, case management, applied research, assessment, and professional advocacy as the major job functions of rehabilitation counselors. They reported that on a daily basis, the most frequently performed functions include case management, professional advocacy, and counseling, followed by vocational consultation, assessment, utilization of community-based services, and applied research (Leahy et al., 2003).

Mental health counselors also have a long history of establishing their professional identity. Mental health counselors practice in a variety of settings including, but not limited to, independent practice, community agencies, managed behavioral health care organizations, integrated delivery systems, hospitals, employee assistance programs, and substance abuse treatment centers. They work with individuals, couples, families, adolescents, and children and provide assessment and diagnosis, counseling and psychotherapy, treatment planning and utilization review, brief solution-focused therapy, alcohol and substance abuse treatment, psychoeducational and prevention programs, and crisis management (American Mental Health Counselors Association [AMHCA], 2007). Mental health counseling focuses on the promotion and maintenance of mental health, the prevention and treatment of mental illness, the identification and modification of etiologic, diagnostic, and systems correlates of mental health, mental illness and related dysfunction, and the improvement of the mental health service delivery system (Spruill & Fong, 1990).

Marriage and family and community counselors have similar roles and functions as mental health counselors but are considered separate and distinct entities, with the distinguishing characteristics of these specialties depending heavily on the training curriculum and the state in which the specialty is practiced. In general, mental health, community, marriage, and family counseling can be differentiated from other specialties by their focus on addressing psychological issues such as depression, substance abuse, suicide, stress management, family, parenting, and marital or other relationship problems. Marriage and family counseling in particular has long been defined as an intervention aimed at ameliorating not only relationship problems but also mental and emotional disorders within the context of family and larger social systems (American Association for Marriage and Family Therapy [AAMFT], 2007). These counselors work in various settings such as outpatient clinics, hospitals, community-based health agencies, mental health centers, family support services, child protective services, domestic violence centers, substance abuse centers, pastoral counseling, corrections, and business and industry.

School counselors work primarily in K–12 settings and perform counseling-related functions to promote student achievement, including curriculum activities, student planning, individual or group counseling, standardized test administration and interpretation, consultation with parents and teachers, and system support (Altekruse et al., 2001; American School Counseling Association [ASCA], 2007). Similarly, *college counselors* also promote student achievement but work with traditional and nontraditional students at the college level in either community or four-year institutions. College counselors provide both counseling and student services (i.e., academic advising, educational planning, transfer issues, financial aid and scholarship needs, and academic probation) and often assist students in managing the balance of school, family, and work.

Career counselors work in settings such as high schools, colleges, career centers, advising offices, private industry, governmental agencies, and private practice offices. They assist people in making decisions related to career and life directions and focus on providing vocational guidance, work adjustment, career education, job placement, and occupational information. Additional functions may include academic advising, employee assistance, retirement planning, job stressors, and organizational consultation across the life cycle.

Gerontological counselors work with older persons in settings such as senior centers, family service agencies, residential and long-term care facilities, adult day care, and recreational and wellness programs. This specialty is differentiated by its focus on helping older individuals cope with changes associated with aging. Gerontological counselors often function as advocates and focus on short-term goals that emphasize the present life situation of the client.

KNOWLEDGE AREAS

A CORE SET OF knowledge areas has been identified by accreditation and certification bodies related to the counseling profession. Specifically, the Council on Rehabilitation Education (CORE), the Council for Accreditation of Counseling and Related Educational Programs (CACREP), as well as national certification bodies (e.g., Commission on Rehabilitation Counselor Certification [CRCC], National Board for Certified Counselors [NBCC]) have all identified core knowledge areas necessary for counselor training. Common to all of these entities are the following eight core knowledge areas: Professional Identity, Social and Cultural Diversity, Human Growth and Development, Career Development, Helping Relationships, Group Work, Assessment, and Research and Program Evaluation (Council for Accreditation of Counseling and Related Educational Programs [CACREP], 2001). In addition, there are supplementary knowledge areas identified for training in specific counseling specialties. For example, CACREP requires students to have knowledge specific to their specialization (e.g., career, college, school) in Foundations, the Contextual Dimen-sion, and the Knowledge and Skills for Practice.

The core knowledge areas for rehabilitation counseling vary slightly because the profession has its own accreditation body, CORE, separate from CACREP. The knowledge areas for rehabilitation counseling include the eight areas listed above plus knowledge in Medical, Functional and Environmental Aspects of Disability, and Rehabilitation Services and Resources. In addition, Leahy et al. (2003) identified six knowledge and skills domains important for contemporary rehabilitation counseling, including (1) career counseling, assessment, and consultation; (2) counseling theories, techniques, and applications;

(3) rehabilitation services and resources; (4) case and caseload management; (5) health care and disability systems; and (6) medical, functional, and environmental implications of disability.

Importantly, not all counseling specialties are accredited by CORE or CACREP (i.e., addiction counseling, pastoral counseling), and therefore the knowledge areas may vary. Further, many training programs offer electives for students interested in a more focused emphasis in a certain specialty. For example, within rehabilitation counseling, knowledge in psychiatric rehabilitation or substance abuse may be important for those counselors planning to work in these areas. Finally, students may have dual specializations allowing them to broaden their knowledge and skill repertoire and ensure eligibility for national certifications and state licensure.

PROFESSIONAL ISSUES

ALTHOUGH SCHOLARS HAVE identified key ingredients in the counseling profession, a unique identity that serves to conceptually unify counselors continues to be elusive. As a result, the title *professional counselor* "lacks sufficient specificity to secure its role in the eyes of other mental health professionals and the general public" (Gale & Austin, 2003, p. 3). A number of historical and contemporary factors have contributed to this challenge. For example, the profession evolved from, and continues to rely on, the contributions from multiple disciplines (e.g., education, social work, and psychology), regardless of the profession's distinct roots in education (Ivey & Van Hesteren, 1990). According to Weinrach (1987), "its identity has always been confusing, even to those who have worked in the field for several decades. Counseling falls somewhere between education and psychology; its literature, theories, and role models come from these two disciplines" (p. 397).

Various counseling scholars have, over the years, attempted to delineate the defining aspects of the profession of counseling. The most common distinguishing characteristic identified is the counseling profession's preventive, developmental focus, wherein counselors work with a person's so-called normal developmental conflicts, whereas other helping professionals focus on diagnosis and remediation with persons with dysfunctional behavior or severe mental illness (ACA, 2007; Nugent, 1994). Research shows, however, that diagnosis and remediation are primary duties of some counselors (Altekruse & Sexton, 1995). Indeed, the helping professions share much in common and the interdisciplinary nature of these professions has produced a rich consortium of information. Nonetheless, the roles and functions shared across these disciplines have made delineating the profession of counseling difficult.

The lack of a specific counseling identity may also reflect the internal diversity within the counseling field. The counseling profession has a historical tradition of specialties and divisions (Myers, 1995). For example, the American Personnel and Guidance Association (APGA) was initially formed through the alliance of four specialty groups: career, student development, counselor education and supervision, and teacher education. Today, there are numerous counseling specialties (i.e., rehabilitation, mental health, school, college, career, gerontological, community, marriage and family) that vary in terms of setting, population, training, professional affiliation, certification, and accreditation. Some specialties are based on work settings (i.e., school and college) and some are based on specific client populations (i.e., rehabilitation and gerontology). In addition, there are a number of professional affiliations that are based on a specialty (e.g., American Rehabilitation Counseling Association [ARCA], American School Counselor Association [ASCA]), a technique (e.g., specialists in group work), or a combination of knowledge competencies and client populations (e.g., multicultural counseling and development; Myers, 1995). And, some counseling specialties, such as rehabilitation counseling, have a number of professional organizations attached to the specialty, such as the National Rehabilitation Association (NRA), ARCA, the National Rehabilitation Counseling Association (NRCA), and the Rehabilitation Counselors and Educators Association (RCEA).

Another challenge that may detract from a unified profession is the fact that accreditation, certification, and licensure for professional counselors vary depending on the specialty and state requirements. For example, there are two primary accreditation bodies for counselor training programs: CACREP and CORE—with the majority of specialties falling under CACREP and rehabilitation counseling under CORE. The merging of these two accreditation bodies has received widespread attention and is under consideration.

Among those specialties accredited by CACREP there is diversity in training standards. For example, the community counseling specialty emphasizes a preventive-developmental model and requires 48 semester units and 700 hours of clinical experience. Conversely, the mental health specialty emphasizes diagnosis and treatment and requires 12 additional units and 300 more hours of clinical experience. Importantly, not all counselor training programs follow national accreditation guidelines in determining their core curricula. In fact, some counseling specialties are not eligible for CACREP or CORE accreditation (i.e., substance abuse counseling).

In regard to national certification, counselors may elect to be certified through the CRCC or the NBCC depending on their training. The NBCC grants the general practice credential National Certified Counselor but also offers specialty certifications in school, mental health, addiction counseling, and gerontological counseling, which supplement the national certified counselor designation. The CRCC grants the practice credential Certified Rehabilitation Counselor. In addition to national certifications, many states have certifications requirements. For example, school counselors are typically certified by each state's department of education. Indeed, these forces may muddle the perceptions of school counselors' role and function in schools: Are they teachers, counselors, or teachers plus counselors?

Notably, accreditation and certification bodies accredit or certify specialties rather than counselor training programs, or general counselors; therefore, there is diversity and redundancy in the process. For example, CACREP accredits training programs in School, Career, College, Community, Gerontological, Mental Health, Student Affairs, and Marriage, Couple and Family Therapy/Counseling—but not a general counseling program. Therefore, if a program also includes a rehabilitation counseling track, the program will need both CORE and CACREP at this point. Further, the specialties accredited by CACREP do not necessarily coincide with certifications available through NBCC (Myers, 1995). For example, marriage and family, community, and rehabilitation counselors are not qualified to sit for the NBCC exam. Most often, counselors take additional coursework in another specialization that qualifies for certification in order to take the NBCC or CRCC exams.

In regard to state licensure, at present, 49 states have licensure laws for professional counselors. However, there is diversity in the state licensure titles and practice domains. Most states have agreed on a general "licensed professional counselor" title, yet some have licensure in designated specialties (e.g., marriage and family counseling, mental health), leaving those students specializing in other counseling areas unable to easily apply for licensure. Even though social workers and psychologists have specialties, they have only one license, which likely contributes to the identity confusion of professional counselors (Altekruse et al., 2001). Finally, state portability for counselor licensure is unavailable, preventing counselors from easily transferring their training to a new state.

In conclusion, the shared practice and knowledge domains of counselors and other helping professions coupled with the diversity within the counseling profession has, on the one hand, produced a rich, comprehensive, and inclusive field; yet, on the other hand, it has contributed to a disjointed identity that lacks clear roles and functions. In fact, regardless of training, affiliations, and credentials, social workers, psychologists, and counselors often share the same clientele, apply a common theoretical framework, and compete for the same jobs, in which they are hired to perform the same tasks and hold the same responsibilities. To remain competitive, counselors need to be perceived as different from other helping professionals and equally, if not more, effective in carrying out counseling services. To do this, it has been suggested that there be a core training model based on the remedial model (diagnosis and treatment), with an added emphasis on the preventive-developmental model (Altekruse et al., 2001). In addition, scholars propose that professional counselors need to have the knowledge and skills to work with clients in their respective developmental stages and learn strategies and approaches that help to prevent mental illness. Finally, competent counselors need to be aware of research, use approaches based on positive outcomes, maintain active status in professional affiliations, have the appropriate license or certification, and adhere to appropriate ethical codes (Altekruse et al., 2001).

REFERENCES

Altekruse, M. K., Harris, H. L., & Brandt, M. A. (2001). The role of the professional counselor in the 21st century. *Counseling and Human Development, 34*, 1–10.

Altekruse, M. K., & Sexton, T. L. (Eds.). (1995). *Mental health counseling in the 90s: A research report for training and practice*. Tampa, FL: National Commission for Mental Health Counseling.

American Association for Marriage and Family Therapy. (2007). *About the American association for marriage and family therapy*. Retrieved July 27, 2007, from http://www.aamft.org/about/Aboutaamft.asp

American Counseling Association. (1995). *Policies and procedures manual of the American Counseling Association*. Alexandria, VA: Author.

American Counseling Association. (2007). *Definition of counseling*. Retrieved July 27, 2007, from http://www.counseling.org/Resources/Consumers Media.aspx

American Mental Health Counselors Association. (2007). *About AMHCA*. Retrieved June 28, 2007, from http://www.amhca.org/about/

American School Counseling Association. (2007). *Careers/roles*. Retrieved June 29, 2007, from http://www.schoolcounselor.org/content

Commission on Rehabilitation Counselor Certification. (n.d.). *Scope of practice for rehabilitation counseling*. Rolling Meadows, IL: Author.

Corsini, R. J. (1989). Introduction. In R. J. Corsini and D. Wedding (Eds.), *Current Psychotherapies* (4th ed., pp. 1–16). Itasca, IL: Peacock.

Council for Accreditation of Counseling and Related Educational Programs. (2001). *CACREP accreditation manual*. Alexandria, VA: Author.

Gale, A. U., & Austin, B. D. (2003). Professionalism's challenges to professional counselors' collective identity. *Journal of Counseling and Development, 81*, 3–10.

Hershenson, D. B., & Power, P. W. (1987). *Mental health counseling: Theory and practice*. New York: Pergamon Press.

Ivey, A. E., & Van Hesteren, F. (1990). Counseling and development: "No one can do it all but it all needs to be done." *Journal of Counseling and Development, 68*, 534–536.

Leahy, M. J., Chan, F., & Saunders, J. (2003). Job functions and knowledge requirements of certified rehabilitation counselors in the 21st century. *Rehabilitation Counseling Bulletin, 46*, 66–81.

Myers, J. (1995). Specialties in counseling: Rich heritage or force for fragmentation? *Journal of Counseling and Development, 74*, 115–116.

National Board for Certified Counselors. (1995). *National counselor examination for licensure and certification. Preliminary technical manual*. Greensboro, NC: Author.

Nugent, F. A. (1994). *An introduction to the profession of counseling* (2nd ed.). Upper Saddle River, NJ: Merrill/Prentice Hall.

Parker, R. M., & Szymanski, E. M. (1998). *Rehabilitation counseling: Basics and beyond* (3rd ed.). Austin, TX: Pro-Ed.

Spruill, D. A., & Fong, M. L. (1990). Defining the domain of mental health counseling: From identity confusion to consensus. *Journal of Mental Health Counseling, 12*, 12–14.

Thomas, K. R., Berven, N. L., & Chan, F. (2004). An introduction to counseling for rehabilitation health professionals. In F. Chan, N. L. Berven, & K. R. Thomas (Eds.), *Counseling theories and techniques for rehabilitation health professionals* (pp. 3–16). New York: Springer Publishing.

U.S. Department of Labor, Bureau of Labor Statistics. (2007). *Occupational outlook handbook*. Retrieved July 29, 2007, from http://www.bls.gov/oco/ocos067.htm

Van Hesteren, F., & Ivey, A. E. (1990). Counseling and development: Toward a new identity for a profession in transition. *Journal of Counseling and Development, 68*, 524–528.

Weinrach, S. G. (1987). Some serious and some not so serious reactions to AACD and its journals. *Journal of Counseling and Development, 65*, 395–399.

3

What Practitioners Need to Know About Professional Credentialing

Vilia M. Tarvydas and Michael T. Hartley

TTAINING LICENSURE IS a critical event in the career of many counselors. Nonetheless, licensure and credentialing are often either misunderstood or seen as mysterious processes. Even the terms used to describe the various forms of credentials can be confusing. The American Counseling Association (American Counseling Association [ACA], 2008) notes that credentialing serves to regulate the counseling profession and to protect the public safety by establishing the minimum standards of knowledge and skill for professional counselors.

Licensure, certification, and accreditation are distinct forms of credentialing (ACA, 2007). *Licensure* is a governmentally sanctioned credential that regulates which professionals can be reimbursed legally by third-party and private payers for general counseling services (ACA, 2007). *Certification* is a more specific marker of professional expertise, typically created by professional groups to convey which counselors can provide specialty types of counseling services (e.g., Master Addiction Counselor; ACA, 2007). *Accreditation* is a voluntary process that educational programs undergo in order to identify themselves as programs that meet the minimum educational standards necessary for graduates of the profession and may lead to eligibility for licensure and certification (ACA, 2007). The primary accreditation bodies for graduate-level training in the field of counseling are the Council for Accreditation of Counseling and Related Educational Programs (CACREP) and the Council on Rehabilitation Education (CORE; ACA, 2008). Often graduates of CORE-accredited and other counseling programs gain licensure through curriculum equivalency provisions in licensure standards that accept courses conforming to required core counselor education curricular areas. A regional accreditation body also often is written into the licensure law, such as the National Council of Accreditation for Teacher Education (NCATE; ACA, 2008). This chapter addresses what counselors need to know about licensure and certification, including trends and considerations that counselors may need to monitor. The chapter concludes with basic tips for counselors interested in licensure and certification.

LICENSURE

Each state in the United States is responsible for issuing counseling licenses and enforcing disciplinary actions in its own jurisdiction (ACA, 2008). Licensure is based on the legal precedent that states can pass laws that "protect the health, safety and welfare of its citizens" (ACA, 2007, p. 1). Once a licensure law is passed by a specific state, individuals who are not licensed in that state are prohibited from engaging in professional activities that include counseling if both the title of counseling and its practice are regulated (ACA, 2007). Throughout this section of the chapter, the practice of counseling is defined as it is written into an individual state licensure law in a scope of practice statement, its related definitions, and professional disclosure statements if required by the state. One benefit of counselor licensure is that it is often associated with the legal ability to receive reimbursement from third-party (e.g., insurance companies) and private payers for the provision of counseling services. The major benefit to consumers of counseling services is that it ensures licensed counselors have attained minimum standards of education and supervised experience and have passed a basic examination of knowledge. More important, unethical or incompetent practitioners may be disciplined and/or removed by licensure boards to protect consumers.

Licensure is also a form of professional recognition. In disaster relief, for example, the American Red Cross sends Licensed Professional Counselors (LPCs) to provide crisis mental health services (American Red Cross, 2008). Currently, 49 states, not including California, have adopted counselor licensure laws. If licensure legislation passes in California by the end of 2008, there will be counselor licensure laws in all 50 states (ACA, 2008). This achievement is remarkable considering that the first counselor licensure bill was passed in Virginia as recently as 1976 (ACA, 2008).

In the U.S. legal system, there are two types of licensure laws: (1) title-only, and (2) practice legislation (ACA, 2008). *Title-only legislation* prohibits individuals from calling themselves counselors unless they meet the educational and clinical standards outlined in the law (Leahy, 2004). Title-only legislation does not prohibit nonqualified individuals from engaging in the practice of counseling (ACA, 2008) if they do not utilize the specific legally prohibited title. *Practice legislation,* in contrast, prohibits the practice of professional counseling unless the individual is licensed in that state (ACA, 2008). The ACA recommends the passage of title and practice legislation, as opposed to title-only legislation (Glosoff, Benshoff, Hosie, & Maki, 1995). Practice acts are considered to be more protective of the public safety (ACA, 2008). The majority of states have some form of practice legislation; only seven states have title-only acts (ACA, 2008).

From state to state, there are differences in counselor licensure laws that can be confusing for both counselors and consumers of counseling. It is not possible to summarize all of the differences in this chapter. However, the differences counselors need to be aware of will be highlighted for the purpose of understanding how their state licensure law fits with the other states. The most common licensure title is LPC, with 34 states offering a LPC credential. Some states offer more than one title or type of license, so the total number of professional titles is greater than 49. See Table 3.1 for a glimpse into the complexity of professional titles offered in the United States.

According to the ACA publication *Licensure Requirements for Professional Counselors* (2008), a general trend of a majority of state licensure laws requires 60 credit hours of graduate course work, 48 credit hours of which need to be a master's degree in counseling or a related master's degree. Furthermore, in most states, applicants are required to obtain 3,000 hours or more of supervised clinical experience (ACA, 2008). This is a requirement of the "supervised experience" standard. Finally, all states require that applicants have passed a comprehensive examination, such as the National Counseling Examination (NCE; ACA, 2008). There are 13 states that will also accept the Certified Rehabilitation Counselor (CRC) exam (Commission on Rehabilitation Counselor Certification [CRCC], 2007). Increasingly, individual state licensure boards are adopting the ACA Code of Ethics. The most recent count has 19 states adopting the ACA code (ACA, 2008). This movement

TABLE 3.1 Licensure Titles Across the United States

Professional Title	States
Licensed Professional Counselor (LPC)	34 states
Licensed Mental Health Counselor (LMHC)	7 states
Licensed Clinical Professional Counselor (LCPC)	7 states
Licensed Professional Clinical Counselor (LPCC)	5 states
Licensed Professional Counselor of Mental Health (LPCMH)	2 states
Licensed Clinical Mental Health Counselor (LCMHC)	3 states
Registered Counselor (RC)	2 states
Licensed Professional Counselor–Mental Health Service Provider (LPC-MHSP)	1 state
Licensed Mental Health Practitioner (LMHP)	1 state
Certified Professional Counselor (CPC)	1 state
Licensed Independent Mental Health Practitioner (LIMHP/LPC)	1 state

is a positive trend for counselors because counselors are required to adhere to both the state statute and its specific disciplinary rules or rules of conduct, as well as the ACA professional code of ethics.

Arguably the most critical component in counselor licensure legislation is the professional *scope of practice* statement. The professional scope of practice statement is a broad statement of the counselor's background in terms of the education, credentials, professional experiences, counseling approaches and strategies, and other services that the licensed counselor is ethically and competently able to provide to clients and consumers of counseling services (ACA, 2008). Scope of practice statements are grounded in the knowledge and skills of a profession (ACA, 2008); however, there are individual differences that exist from state to state. Some states have adopted a general scope of practice while other states have adopted a scope of practice that is more connected to mental health services. In general, states that have adopted a broad scope of practice across populations and settings often use the professional occupational title LPC. Those states that have a more narrow scope of practice focused on counseling persons with emotional and cognitive problems often use the professional title Licensed Mental Health Counselor (LMHC). Despite that some state licensure laws prohibit individuals who are not licensed to practice counseling, some work settings are exempt from such restrictions. Many of these work settings are highly regulated or supervised environments (e.g., prisons, state-vocational rehabilitation, college career centers, and pastoral counselors) in contrast to independent, private practices. Licensure laws that regulate private practice work settings are typically less structured.

One highly debated scope of practice issue has been the ability of counselors to provide assessment services. For example, since 1997 professional counselors in the state of Indiana have rallied against a licensure law that gave psychologists exclusive rights to all forms of testing, including vocational assessments (Fair Access Coalition on Testing [FACT], 2007). The Fair Access Coalition on Testing (FACT) became a critical component in advocating against this type of restriction in Indiana and other states. For instance, the Indiana governor removed the psychology board's authority to create a Restricted Test List (RTL) because it encroached on the counseling profession's scope of practice (FACT, 2007). There is a range of professional groups represented in FACT, including marriage and family therapists, creative arts therapists, school psychologists, certified case managers, rehabilitation counselors, school counselors, and mental health counselors (FACT, 2007).

Due to the diversity in scope of practice statements, counselors need to examine the professional activities as written into their licensure law statute. Further, counselors need to differentiate their individual scope of practice from the professional scope of practice statement (Cottone & Tarvydas, 2007). Ethically, the individual counselor's scope of practice that governs his or her own professional practice must be based on his or her own set of knowledge, abilities, and skills even though it must be drawn from the profession's overall scope of practice as defined in the statute (Cottone & Tarvydas, 2007). Regardless of the professional scope of practice statement, counselors are ethically bound to practice within these individual boundaries. If counselors are moving across states, they should examine the scope of practice to make sure it fits with their individual scope of practice.

CERTIFICATION

T HE PURPOSE OF certification is to protect the public safety by helping clients find professionals who have appropriate training. Professional counselors who also possess certifications are recognized for their training, expertise, and competence within a specialty area of counseling (ACA, 2007). Some examples of credentialing bodies that issue specialty certifications include the National Board of Certified Counselors (NBCC; National Board of Certified Counselors [NBCC], 2007), which certifies counselors for general practice as National Certified Counselors (NCCs) or for some specialty practices, such as the Master of Addictions Counselor (MAC) and National Certified School

Counselors (NCSC); the Commission on Rehabilitation Counselor Certification (CRCC; CRCC, 2007), which certifies CRCs; the National Career Development Association (NCDA), which certifies Master Career Counselors (MCCs) and Master Career Development Professionals (MCDPs) (Pope, 2006).

Certifications are much like the medical professions where medical doctors are licensed by their state to practice general medicine, yet voluntarily apply for board certifications to inform consumers of their expertise in a specialty field (i.e., allergist, cardiologist, endocrinologist). Thus, certification is critical to the hiring and selection of personnel in a variety of work settings.

The first certification body in professional counseling was the CRCC, which was established in 1974. The CRCC has been a leader in establishing role and function studies for the profession of rehabilitation counseling. There are currently 16,122 professionals who hold an active CRC certification. CRCC certifies rehabilitation counselors working in a variety of settings for people with mental and physical disabilities (CRCC, 2007).

Following the establishment of CRCC, the NBCC (2007) was created in 1982 by the ACA. Although the NBCC and the ACA have strong historical ties and work together to further the profession of counseling, the two organizations are separate entities with different goals (NBCC, 2007). There are currently 41,015 professionals with an active NCC certification. Several NBCC certifications cross over with other certification bodies. As an example, the NCDA, the primary organization that represents career counselors, and one of the 19 divisions within the ACA, now regulates a credential in career development, the MCC, which is similar to the National Certified Career Counselor (NCCC) (Pope & Tarvydas, 2007). The NBCC had offered the NCCC, and although NBCC does not offer a new NCCC certification, it still has 577 active NCCC certifications.

It appears that 19 counseling specialty divisions within the ACA are developing specific professionalization agendas that may influence the counselor certification process. Recently, specialty groups within the counseling profession, specifically the American Mental Health Counseling Association (AMHCA), the American Rehabilitation Counseling Association (ARCA), and the American School Counseling Association (ASCA), were allowed to establish their own administration separate from the ACA (Cottone & Tarvydas, 2007). In the future, as counseling grows, certification may become even more of a political and economic process as the trend toward credentialing rather than professionalism gains influence. Practitioners should be aware of which organizations provide the certification and why.

TRENDS AND CONSIDERATIONS

C REDENTIALING IS RAPIDLY evolving. As this chapter was being written, the states of Nevada and California are in the process of passing a counselor licensure law. With such rapid progress in professional credentialing, professional counselors need to look ahead for opportunities and challenges in licensure laws and national certification standards. The following four examples of practice and credentialing trends may be of interest to practitioners for the purpose of maximizing their knowledge and awareness of professional developments and expanding employment opportunities.

PROFESSIONAL COUNSELING FUND

AS THE HEALTH care system continues to be politically influenced, it is necessary for counselors to have a voice on Capitol Hill. Recently, a group of leaders in the counseling profession formed a political action committee to promote the counseling profession and the welfare of clients through participation in the national political process (Professional Counseling Fund, 2007). The Professional Counseling Fund was created to influence the U.S. political system through "political contributions to candidates and incumbents of political office at the federal level who support the political goals of the Counseling Profession" (p. 1). One of the goals is to ensure that counselors have access to the professional opportunities that are associated with licensure and certification and access to third-party reimbursement for counseling services. As legislators on Capitol Hill debate health care issues, the Professional Counseling Fund may be one mechanism for the counseling profession to advocate for counselors and their clients to be included in health care reforms. For more information, go to http://counselingfund.org

GLOBALIZATION AND CREDENTIALS

GLOBALIZATION IS HERE to stay, whether we like it or not. An evolution of the popular Career Development Facilitator (CDF) credential is the Global Career Development Facilitator (GCDF), an international credential. The GCDF project was developed in 1997 to recognize the training and background of those working internationally in career development fields and to establish minimum competency areas (Center for Credentialing and Education, 2008). Today, the GCDF is used by individuals who work in a variety of career development settings in the following countries: Bulgaria, Canada, China, Germany, Korea, Japan, New Zealand, Romania, Turkey, and the United States

(Center for Credentialing and Education, 2008). Benefits of the GCDF certification include professional recognition, a national/portable and marketable credential, and clarification of a scope of practice (Center for Credentialing and Education, 2008). Ironically, establishing uniform credentialing standards will likely be more easily done internationally than here in the United States since credentials are being established at the national level rather than on a state-by-state basis. This movement may accelerate the trend toward international credentialing, especially for third world countries where paraprofessional credentialing is in high demand. In third world countries it is difficult to train master's level counselors and there is a demand for mental health facilitators who are trained in basic counseling and case management skills to address disaster relief.

Web-Based Counseling

THE ADVENT OF Internet technology is connected to globalization and has created access to counseling across the Web and around the world. For the last decade, leaders in the counseling field have been unsure about how to shape and regulate the growing practice of cyber-counseling. In 1999, the ACA developed standards for counselors providing counseling services over the Internet (ACA, 1999). However, this professional organization had no way to effectively enforce the standards. In 2005, the NBCC created a document, *The Practice of Internet Counseling* (NBCC, 2005). These standards were a step forward, but one that did not have an effective way to regulate Web-based counseling across certain legal jurisdictions either. Recently, in a pioneering effort to regulate the provision of Web-based counseling, Arkansas decided to include Web-based counseling in its licensure law (State of Arkansas, 2006). The licensure law states that counselors who provide Web-based counseling in the state of Arkansas need to be licensed and to follow the NBCC best practices document. The Arkansas licensure board has taken a step forward in the ability to regulate Web-based counseling. In the future, the use of Internet technology and benefits from the growth of telehealth legal practice standards in medicine and other professions will assist the counseling field to adopt standards that will provide more realistic and effective regulation.

National Credentials Registry and Counselor Mobility

THE VARIETY OF counselor licensure laws nationally presents a serious problem for professional counselors in their ability to move from state to state without disruption and the ability to practice counseling.

The American Association of State Counseling Boards (AASCB) is the national organization that provides a forum and technical information for state licensure boards. The AASCB does not want to lose skilled practitioners as they move across states and apply for reciprocity, and seeks to decrease the time-consuming and frustrating difficulties for both licensees and regulators alike in the reciprocity process. Therefore AASCB created the National Credentials Registry (NCR) to create a credentials portfolio for counselors who are reviewed and certified as conforming to two levels of standards qualifications (American Association of State Counseling Boards [AASCB], 2007). The goal of the NCR is to establish fluidity across states through streamlining the transfer of an individual's educational and clinical background (AASCB, 2007). Once a counselor has practiced for 5 years as a licensed counselor without a disciplinary action, he or she may have his or her name placed in the NCR, which ensures the ability to move across states when his or her individual credentials are presented, reviewed, and certified. The goal of the NCR is to create a system of portability to help counselors move across state lines without a disruption in their ability to practice. For more information, go to National Credentials Registry on the AASCB Web site, http://www.aascb.org

TIPS

T HIS CHAPTER CONCLUDES with tips for counselors who wish to maximize their successful experiences with credentialing.

- If you are planning to become a licensed professional counselor, research the requirements by contacting the counselor licensure board directly. Do not rely on secondhand information or old handouts. Licensure laws, rules, and regulations may change at any time, so go right to the source. These boards have administrators who will be helpful, and they maintain Web sites that will provide the necessary information. Once you have this information, fill out a spare application form as a trial run. Use this to talk to board staff about the specialty area you plan to practice.
- If you are making career decisions, research the requirements of any state in which you plan to practice. This may assist you in making practical decisions about any additional coursework that you need to take to be licensed in a particular state.
- If you are not successful in meeting state counselor licensure requirements, state boards have an appeals and/or waiver procedure. Be reasonable in your attempts to appeal your case. Staff will be able to help you most effectively if you remain calm and

professional and listen to their advice on how to proceed. If you are not successful, try to be flexible and open. For example, you may have to take another course to meet state licensure requirements. Additional coursework and/or continuing educational credits may be applied toward a certification that you already possess. So tell yourself that new learning can be fun and not a tragedy if you plan ahead. Many applicants make the mistake of overreacting and waste time pursuing their appeals or complaints to board staff.

* If licensed in the last 5 years, send credentials to the AASCB credentials bank. If you have not received a disciplinary action, you can establish your portfolio and have your name listed in the NCR. This process protects you from such unforeseen problems as the death of a counseling supervisor or loss of educational records in a disaster. For more information go to http://www.aascb.org

* Start keeping track of credentials early. Maintain specific, detailed, and contemporaneous records of training and professional experiences early on, specifically, course descriptions, transcripts and course catalog, practicum and internship responsibilities, and supervisor credentials (including all license types and numbers) and contact information, job descriptions, old jobs, verification of supervision, and client contact hours.

* Write a professional disclosure or individual scope of practice statement. Compare this statement with the scope of practice written into the licensure law. If a counselor is interested in broadening his or her scope of practice, the ACA Code of Ethics provides guidelines for creating an intentional plan that addresses how to reduce risks to clients and ensures that the counselor is receiving competent training and supervision.

* Maintain professional practice insurance for both malpractice (civil tort) and state licensure board disciplinary actions. You may need an attorney to defend yourself in actions before either state licensure boards or in the courts.

CONCLUSION

IN CONCLUSION, CREDENTIALING protects the consumer of counseling services and public safety by establishing the minimum standards of professional knowledge and skill. Credentialing is likely to evolve rapidly as the U.S. health care system becomes more politicized. However, individual counselors who attain licensure and certification, and who serve their clients ethically and competently, demonstrate the value and importance of counselors to our entire society. Beyond that, they enjoy a meaningful and valued career of which they may be proud.

REFERENCES

American Association of State Counseling Boards. (2007). Retrieved July 7, 2008, from www.aascb.org/

American Counseling Association. (1999). *Ethical standards for Internet on-line counseling.* Retrieved July 7, 2008, from www.counseling.org

American Counseling Association. (2007). *Licensure and certification.* Retrieved July 7, 2008, from www.counseling.org

American Counseling Association. (2008). *Licensure requirements for professional counselors.* Alexandria, VA: Author.

American Red Cross. (2008). Retrieved July 7, 2008, from www.redcross.org

Center for Credentialing and Education. (2008). *Global career development facilitator.* Retrieved July 7, 2008, from www.cce-global.org

Commission on Rehabilitation Counselor Certification. (2007). Retrieved July 7, 2008, from www.crccertification.com

Cottone, R. R., & Tarvydas, V. M. (2007). *Counseling ethics and decision making* (3rd ed.). Upper Saddle River, NJ: Pearson.

Fair Access Coalition on Testing. (2007). Retrieved July 7, 2008, from www .fairaccess.org

Glosoff, H., Benshoff, J., Hosie, T., & Maki, D. (1995). The 1994 model legislation for licensed professional counselors. *Journal of Counseling and Development, 74,* 209–220.

Leahy, M. J. (2004). Qualified providers. In T. F. Riggar & D. R. Maki (Eds.), *Handbook of rehabilitation counseling* (pp. 142–158). New York: Springer Publishing.

National Board for Certified Counselors. (2005). *The practice of Internet counseling.* Retrieved July 7, 2008, from www.nbcc.org

National Board for Certified Counselors. (2007). Retrieved July 7, 2008, from www.nbcc.org

Pope, M. (2006). You've just got to have standards: On licensing, ethics, certification, and accreditation. In M. Pope (Ed.), *Professional counseling 101: Building a strong professional identity* (pp. 65–70). Alexandria, VA: American Counseling Association.

Pope, M., & Tarvydas, V. M. (2007). Career counseling. In R. R. Cottone & V. M. Tarvydas (Eds.), *Counseling ethics and decision making* (3rd ed., pp. 283–300). Upper Saddle River, NJ: Pearson.

Professional Counseling Fund. (2007). Retrieved July 7, 2008, from counseling fund.org

State of Arkansas. (2006). *Arkansas Code Annotated 17–27–101 et seq.*

4

Clinical Supervision for Developing Counselors

Dawn C. Brislin and James T. Herbert

As part of professional counselor licensure requirements, most states mandate between 2,000 and 3,000 hours of post-graduate, supervised clinical experience (Lum, 2007). In order to make an informed choice about seeking clinical supervision, persons interested in becoming licensed professional counselors should be aware of effective and ethical supervision aspects prior to arranging supervision. Further, counselors new to the profession should develop an awareness of supervisory models, theories, and practices when selecting an appropriate clinical supervisor. This chapter will help developing counselors, particularly those persons seeking professional licensure, to better understand relevant issues as applied to clinical supervision.

Supervision has been described as a means of transmitting skills and knowledge to all levels of counselors (Maki & Delworth, 1995) by providing a continuous cycle of feedback, practice, and additional feedback via consistent assessment of strengths and areas for counselor improvement (Borders, 1991). Within professional counseling practice, supervision comprises both administrative and clinical aspects. Whereas administrative supervision typically addresses client case management and related facility or agency service delivery documentation, clinical supervision focuses on the counselor's professional development within the client–counselor relationship (Herbert & Trusty, 2006). Although researchers have presented various definitions regarding clinical supervision (Bernard & Goodyear, 2004; Herbert, 2004a; Maki & Delworth, 1995), the most commonly used, and the one referred to in this chapter, is provided by Bernard and Goodyear (2004):

> Supervision is an intervention provided by a more senior member of a profession to a more junior member or members of that same profession. The relationship is evaluative, extends over time, and has the simultaneous purposes of enhancing the professional functioning of the more junior person(s), monitoring the quality of professional services offered to the clients that she, he, or they see, and serving as a gatekeeper for those who are to enter the particular profession. (p. 8)

In keeping with this definition, Maki and Delworth (1995) assert that supervision allows for enhancement of professional growth by providing education and consultation to developing professionals. It is also essential to note that, although professional growth is an important component to the supervisory relationship, client welfare and protection are of paramount value (Bernard & Goodyear, 2004; Pearson, 2000).

QUALITIES OF EFFECTIVE SUPERVISION

SUPERVISION ENCOMPASSES VARYING formats depending on supervisee and supervisor availability, needs, and preferences. These formats, discussed by Herbert (2004b), include self-supervision, individual or one-to-one supervision, group supervision, and team supervision. With the exception of self-supervision where there is no external feedback provided to the counselor, beginning counselors should consider benefits and preferences when receiving supervision from one supervisor who either works in the same as (internal supervisor) or outside of (external supervisor) the counselor's work setting (i.e., one-to-one supervision).

In certain situations, supervision is provided to several counselors simultaneously by one or several supervisors. As a group, this format benefits individual members about issues that other counselors are confronting. This social-learning aspect may assist each counselor to expand in areas that could be potentially problematic in the future. The disadvantage of this format is that it may not provide sufficient time and intensity that one-to-one supervision provides. Team supervision, which is a variation of group supervision, refers to supervision that usually occurs within the same work setting provided by a group of supervisors from various disciplines (e.g., within a hospital setting).

Deciding on which clinical supervision format is appropriate for each counselor depends on individual supervisee needs, employment setting resources, and availability of supervision. In addition, supervisor role and process may vary depending on the type of counseling services provided.

School counselors, mental health counselors, and rehabilitation counselors have distinct needs for supervision within their respective professional roles and counseling settings (Thielsen & Leahy, 2001). Supervision in school counseling, for example, may focus more on administrative supervision or on program development supervision as opposed to clinical supervision (Roberts & Borders, 1994) and may be more likely to occur as peer supervision (Page, 1994). Supervision within mental health delineations of counseling, however, will likely focus on clinical aspects of counseling (Magnuson, Norem, & Wilcoxon, 2000). Conversely, supervision practices within rehabilitation counseling practice may vary widely depending on employment setting (i.e., public sector vocational rehabilitation, private for-profit proprietary rehabilitation) and may, as in school counseling settings, take a greater administrative or program evaluation focus (Herbert, 2004a).

Given various foci of clinical supervision within the professional disciplines, it is recommended that counselors seek supervision within their specific scope of practice. Counselors must also consult state regulatory boards to ensure that supervision is provided according to designated jurisdiction because some states require that supervisors be board approved prior to beginning supervision (Lum, 2007).

EFFECTIVE SUPERVISION PRACTICE

SIMILAR TO THE variety of counseling theories used in professional practice, there are parallel and unique theories and models as applied to clinical supervision, and as several writers suggest (e.g., Bernard & Goodyear, 2004; Herbert, 2004b; Pearson, 2006), effective supervisors rely on these models to inform practice. Integration of a conceptual model provides the supervisor with an informed rationale for what supervision practices are used, supervisory issues addressed, and techniques used to promote professional growth for each counselor being supervised (Pearson, 2001). Supervisors may draw from three distinct types of supervision models and/or combine components to form their own theoretical orientation. Within clinical supervision practice, the primary supervision models include theory orientation models, which involve providing supervision consistent with assumptions and interventions consistent with a specific counseling theoretical approach (e.g., cognitive behavioral, person-centered, or existential); developmental models, which require supervision interventions as a function of unique counselor skill and professional identity development; and social role models, which promote supervisee skill development in relationship to supervisor roles (e.g., counselor, consultant, and teacher; Bernard & Goodyear, 2004).

Of the three supervisory models, developmental models are the most widely researched within the counseling supervision literature. These models include focusing on cyclical (e.g., Loganbil, Hardy, & Delworth, 1982, as cited in Bernard & Goodyear, 2004) and continuous (e.g., Renstad & Skovholt, 2003, as cited in Bernard & Goodyear, 2004) patterns of professional development as well as integrated developmental approaches (e.g., Stoltenberg, 1981, as cited in Bernard & Goodyear, 2004) that examine how people at different cognitive levels think, reason, and understand their environment. Use of developmental models within supervision allows the supervisor to identify basic developmental needs of the counselor (supervisee) and how the supervisor can best assist in the counselor's continued professional development.

Social Role Models are used within the context of various counseling theories. The most widely used Social Role Models include the Discrimination Model (Bernard, 1997, as cited in Bernard & Goodyear, 2004), which allows the supervisor to fill three roles (i.e., counselor, consultant, and teacher) while focusing on the supervisee's intervention skills, conceptualization skills, and personalization skills; the Hawkins and Shohet Model (Hawkins & Shohet, 1989, as cited in Bernard & Goodyear, 2004), in which the supervisor is expected to use different roles or styles depending on supervisee need and focus of supervision; and the Holloway Systems Model (Holloway, 1995, as cited in Bernard & Goodyear, 2004), which considers the supervisory relationship and unique characteristics relevant to the supervisor, work setting, client, and supervisee. In addition, a review of clinical supervision approaches indicates that effective clinical supervisors consistently exhibit certain basic qualities. Specifically, clinical supervisors perceived by their supervisees as creative, sincere, genuine, positive, and respectful of individual differences generally are evaluated as more effective at implementing supervisory practices and creating a safe atmosphere for beginning counselors to accept responsibility for their actions and consequences (Herbert, 1997).

SUPERVISION METHODS

BECAUSE OF THE evaluative nature of clinical supervision, documentation of client–counselor interactions often represents the central focus, and as such, it requires supervisors to have an understanding of these interactions. Often, these interactions are audiotaped or videotaped so that counselors and supervisors may review taped sessions together or independently. The benefit of this review method is that it provides a direct account of what actually happened. The disadvantage is that the counselor–client session has already occurred, and should the supervisor wish to intervene, it can only be done after the fact. This direct delayed supervision approach is perhaps the most common approach used in clinical supervision within the helping professions such as rehabilitation counseling (Herbert 2004a). Other delayed but more indirect methods that involve the counselor providing a verbal case summary or written account of the session (e.g., using client–counselor process notes) can complement the use of audio or video client–counselor sessions. In certain instances, supervisors may want to interact more directly through live observation of client–counselor sessions and provide simultaneous supervision. Although this method has the benefit of being immediately responsive to counselor needs, it has the potential of disrupting the client–counselor process. All of these methods as well as those using role play, modeling, microskills training, and interpersonal process recall offer supervisors options in providing effective clinical supervision (Bernard & Goodyear, 2004; Borders & Brown, 2005).

The manner in which any of the aforementioned methods are delivered can be further enhanced with available technology and, by doing so, provide supervisors with greater flexibility. For example, one approach to providing live supervision involves using a two-way mirror in which the supervisor is able to observe counselor–client interactions while, at the same time, the supervisor is not seen by either party. Because of additional costs in construction and additional room space needed for a designated supervision room, most counseling settings do not provide counseling rooms with two-way mirrors. As a technological adaptation to providing live supervision without the use of two-way mirrors, supervisors may use recording equipment within the counseling session and watch the session from a separate viewing area. They can also provide visual feedback by using a television monitor with computer interface to type supervisor comments that may or may not be visible to the client. In addition, supervisors can use a hearing device placed in one of the counselor's ears and provide immediate feedback to the supervisee. Beyond these adaptations, a more practical and increasingly more common approach is to observe counseling sessions using built-in cameras found in many personal laptop computers.

Perhaps more than any of these technological advances, the use of online supervision offers greater opportunities for counselors to receive clinical supervision. In some instances such as counselors who work in isolated settings or communities, availability of qualified supervisors may be limited. E-supervision, which can be used as a complement to traditional face-to-face supervision or used as an independent supervisory approach, provides continuous access to the supervisor, as well as the ability for timely and convenient feedback (Stebnicki & Glover, 2001). Used with a group of counselors who are separated by geographic distances, e-supervision or cyber-supervision can not only establish a supportive learning community but also provides increased opportunities for equal participation (Borders & Brown, 2005; Stebnicki & Glover, 2001).

As an additional tool to e-supervision, recent advances in digitizing taped counseling sessions allow supervisors to focus on specific aspects of the counseling process. Once the counseling session is reviewed, the supervisor develops a schema using computer software that contains aspects relevant to supervision. For example, the supervisor may want to focus on occurrences where the counselor demonstrated advanced empathy, used positive confrontation effectively, or implemented a counseling intervention consistent with the counselor's theoretical orientation. These types of technological advances, whether through software programs or other audiovisuals, aid the supervisory process by providing visual cues for interpersonal process recall (Borders & Brown, 2005).

PROFESSIONAL DISCLOSURE STATEMENTS

COUNSELORS SEEKING SUPERVISION should be aware of appropriate documents and contracts that will aid them in understanding supervisor expectations, roles, and procedures. Generally, a supervisor should provide counselor-supervisees with a professional disclosure statement that gives them an outline of the supervisor's educational background, credentials, and specialized training in supervision. This statement should also incorporate the supervisor's areas of professional competence as well as a brief overview of supervisory models and counseling theories that inform his or her practice (Magnuson et al., 2000).

At the onset of arranging supervision, a written supervisory contract should address number and frequency of supervision sessions, identify when and how contact will be established (e.g., e-mail, phone, mail), as well as give instructions on how both supervisor and supervisee should prepare for each session (Borders & Brown, 2005). This preparation can include completing case notes, reviewing audio- or videotapes that demonstrate effective and less effective counseling skills, or other activities such as providing process notes of each session that describe counseling content, client–counselor process (transference and countertransference) issues, and internal dialogue experienced by the counselor throughout the session. The supervisory contract should also address how many clients will be seen during supervision, which supervisory formats (i.e., individual, team, group) and methods (e.g., audiotape or videotape, role play, interpersonal recall) will be used, what evaluation methods will be used to document progress, how many supervision sessions will be provided, and, if relevant, supervision fees and when payment is due, what procedures will be used to maintain client and counselor confidentiality, and how emergency situations will be handled (Borders & Brown, 2005).

SUPERVISEE PERSONAL GROWTH

GIVEN THAT CLINICAL supervision often includes personal and professional issues that impact the client–counselor relationship, examination of counselor thoughts and feelings during clinical supervision often occurs. During these instances, the counselor-supervisee may elicit countertransference, transference, anxiety, and resistance that may be uncomfortable (Pearson, 2000, 2001). For this reason, supervisees must understand that clinical supervision can be emotionally challenging. Therefore, counselors participating in clinical supervision should consider what skills and knowledge they wish to gain from the supervisory relationship (Students & Pearson, 2004). Once these initial considerations are agreed upon, supervisees will likely complete a second contract that details individual learning goals and objectives (Borders & Brown, 2005).

ETHICS IN SUPERVISION

SINCE ONE OF the primary foci of supervision is to protect each client's welfare, it is essential that both supervisor and supervisee understand ethical issues that commonly arise during supervision. Much like the counseling relationship, supervisees should be aware that supervisors are both ethically and legally responsible for services and actions of their supervisees (Blackwell, Strohmer, Belcas, & Burton, 2002). Beyond this responsibility, there are several ethical concerns that can arise within the supervisory relationship in and of itself. Of these, the most commonly identified issues focus on dual relationships, competence, consultation, informed consent, due process, evaluation, and vicarious liability (Bernard & Goodyear, 2004; Blackwell et al., 2002; Borders & Brown, 2005; Magnuson et al., 2000). Unique to the supervisory relationship is the recognized power differential that the clinical supervisor holds because this person is accountable not only for client treatment and services provided by his or her supervisees but also for the ongoing professional development of each counselor-supervisee (Magnuson et al., 2000). Since the supervisor can be held liable for all evaluative material and any negligent act on behalf of the counselor-supervisee, it is important that each supervisor carry professional liability insurance and keep detailed records of supervision sessions (Borders & Brown, 2005; Pearson, 2000). Failure to provide consistent and ongoing feedback creates an ethical concern for both supervisee and supervisor (Blackwell et al., 2002).

In accordance with these responsibilities, counseling supervisors must adhere to *The Ethical Guidelines for Counseling Supervisors* (Association for Counselor Education and Supervision, 1993). Supervisors may also hold membership within various professional organizations depending on their specialty and therefore should follow these ethical guidelines as well. Conflict codes may present an ethical dilemma for the supervisor relationship and should be considered when choosing an appropriate supervisor (Saunders & Peck, 2001).

CONCLUSION

COUNSELORS SEEKING SUPERVISION should be aware of basic issues that surround the supervisory process, including the importance of integrating supervision models and counseling theories into supervision, basic responsibilities of each supervisor and supervisee as outlined in an agreed written contract, and ethical concerns within supervision practice. Consultation with state jurisdictions on requirements for licensure should be considered when choosing an appropriate supervisor. Supervision should provide less experienced counselors with additional opportunities to build upon basic skills, provide better services to the clients they serve, and help them continue to develop professionally within their individual scope of practice.

REFERENCES

Association for Counselor Education and Supervision. (1993). *Ethical guidelines for counseling supervisors*. Retrieved December 18, 2007, from http://www.acesonline.net/ethical_guidelines.asp

Bernard, J. M., & Goodyear, R. K. (2004). *Fundamentals of clinical supervision* (3rd ed.). Boston: Pearson Education.

Blackwell, T. L., Strohmer, D. C., Belcas, E. M., & Burton, K. A. (2002). Ethics in rehabilitation counselor supervision. *Rehabilitation Counseling Bulletin, 45,* 240–247.

Borders, L. D. (1991). Supervision does not equal evaluation. *School Counselor, 38*(4), 253–255.

Borders, L. D., & Brown, L. L. (2005). *The new handbook of counseling supervision.* Mahwah, NJ: Erlbaum.

Herbert, J. (1997). Quality assurance: Administration and supervision. In D. R. Maki & T. F. Riggar (Eds.), *Rehabilitation counseling: Profession and practice* (pp. 247–258). New York: Springer Publishing.

Herbert, J. (2004a). Clinical supervision in rehabilitation settings. In F. Chan, N. L. Berven, & K. R. Thomas (Eds.), *Counseling theories and techniques for rehabilitation health professionals* (pp. 405–422). New York: Springer Publishing.

Herbert, J. (2004b). Clinical supervision. In T. F. Riggar & D. R. Maki (Eds.), *Handbook of rehabilitation counseling* (pp. 289–304). New York: Springer Publishing.

Herbert, J. T., & Trusty, J. (2006). Clinical supervision practices and satisfaction within the public vocational rehabilitation program. *Rehabilitation Counseling Bulletin, 49,* 66–80.

Lum, C. (2007). *Licensure requirements for professional counselors: A state-by-state report.* Alexandria, VA: American Counseling Association.

Magnuson, S., Norem, K., & Wilcoxon, A. (2000). Clinical supervision of prelicensed counselors: Recommendations for consideration and practice. *Journal of Mental Health Counseling, 22*(2), 176–188.

Maki, D. R., & Delworth, U. (1995). Clinical supervision: A definition and model for the rehabilitation counseling profession. *Rehabilitation Counseling Bulletin, 38,* 282–294.

Page, B. J. (1994). Post-degree clinical supervision of school counselors. *School Counselor, 42,* 32–40.

Pearson, Q. M. (2000). Opportunities and challenges in the supervisory relationship: Implications for counselor supervision. *Journal of Mental Health Counseling, 22,* 283–294.

Pearson, Q. M. (2001). A case in clinical supervision: A framework for putting theory into practice. *Journal of Mental Health Counseling, 23,* 174–183.

Pearson, Q. M. (2006). Psychotherapy-driven supervision: Integrating counseling theories into role-based supervision. *Journal of Mental Health Counseling, 28,* 241–252.

Roberts, E. B., & Borders, L. D. (1994). Supervision of school counselors: Administrative, program and counseling. *School Counselor, 41,* 149–157.

Saunders, J. L., & Peck, S. L. (2001). The code of professional ethics for rehabilitation counselors: The administrator and supervisor perspective. *Journal of Applied Rehabilitation Counseling, 32*(4), 20–26.

Stebnicki, M. A., & Glover, N. M. (2001). E-supervision as a complementary approach to traditional face-to-face clinical supervision in rehabilitation counseling: Problems and solutions. *Rehabilitation Education, 15,* 283–293.

Students, C., & Pearson, Q. M. (2004). Getting the most out of clinical supervision: Strategies for mental health. *Journal of Mental Health Counseling, 26,* 361–373.

Thielsen, V. A., & Leahy, M. J. (2001). Essential knowledge and skills for effective clinical supervision in rehabilitation counseling. *Rehabilitation Counseling Bulletin, 44,* 196–208.

Section B

Professional, Ethical, and Practice Management Issues in Counseling

5

Tools and Strategies for Developing Your Own Counseling Private Practice

NORMAN C. DASENBROOK
AND ROBERT J. WALSH

PRIVATE PRACTICE FOR most counselors has been an elusive goal. Now with licensure in most states and the ability to bill third-party payers, the goal has become more realistic. Being a well-trained and ethical counselor is the foundation for starting a private practice, but while being competent is essential, the challenge is to think outside of traditional training. The authors' experience as private practice counselors and practice consultants for more than three decades has found the following tools and strategies to be what breeds success in private practice.

Successful counselors in private practice challenge themselves to be businesspersons. As a counselor in private practice, one needs to see oneself as the CEO of a corporation, not only needing to make good clinical decisions, but also needing to make good business decisions. Good business decisions inherently involve some risk, and risk taking has a tendency to make counselors uncomfortable. However, private practice aspirations will require feeling uncomfortable, managing that anxiety, and using it as motivation. Discomfort may come from competing with other counselors, fearing failure, ensuring fees are collected, justifying medically necessary services to a managed care company, speaking in public, or self-promotion. Being uncomfortable, managing it, and using it motivationally—will make you a better businessperson.

As a counselor in private practice, one needs to see oneself as an *entrepreneur*. An entrepreneur as defined by Webster's dictionary is someone who "organizes, manages, and assumes the risks of a business or enterprise." In the 1990s many counselors resisted managed health care and the need to cooperate with insurance companies. However, entrepreneurial counselors that took the opportunity to understand and work with these systems and institutions found it could be both professionally and financially rewarding. Rather than being discouraged by obstacles and threats to starting a practice, one must look for ways to practice better, smarter, or more efficiently, with an eye on the bottom line.

A counselor in private practice also needs to see himself or herself as a *consultant*. Counselors are experts in human behavior and relationships. These skills apply not only to clients and their families but also to business, industry, organizations, and institutions. Anywhere people want to improve relationships or need to interact with each other, there is a potential need for services of a counselor. Counselors have the skill set necessary to be organizational development consultants.

A private practice counselor additionally needs to see himself or herself as a *marketing* person. Networking with others is always a good opportunity to promote a practice. Practice promotion can occur by attending a school staffing on a client, making appointments with potential referral sources, or offering to give a speech to a gathering. Promotional opportunities can also arise when bidding on consulting or therapeutic contracts, getting involved with professional organizations, or engaging in political activity (reminiscent of the 1960s). A marketing person seizes every opportunity to promote the practice. If not, another counselor will.

Lastly, as a counselor in private practice, one needs to see oneself and the practice in terms of *multiple income streams*. It is rare these days to make a satisfying living from a traditional office practice. Generally, it takes many income streams to thrive in private practice, whether that is by taking part-time employment at an agency, school, or employee assistance program (EAP), teaching, writing, lecturing, consulting, mediating, litigation contracting, supervising, and performing related work. Do not attempt to put all of the private practice eggs in one basket. Just as the approach to private practice needs to be diverse, so does the vision of the counselor. The counselor in private practice can be a good businessperson and still be a compassionate counselor. The two are not mutually exclusive.

Once the business paradigm is firmly in place and potential income streams have been identified, consultation with an attorney and tax advisor is necessary to determine what type of business entity would be appropriate. The most common types of business entities for counselors in private practice are sole proprietor, professional limited liability company (PLLC), and professional service corporation. Laws that affect business entities vary from state to state, so legal and tax consultation is essential.

In our seminars, we challenge counselors to see themselves as providing a unique and valuable service that is cost-effective, enriches people's lives, and promotes growth and development. Moreover, that service has a tremendous value in the marketplace. However, determining fees and fee collection can be difficult for most counselors.

In order to set fees, compare what other mental health professionals with like credentials in your location charge to help determine a fee range. In setting fees, resist the temptation to undercharge. Undercharging will not attract new clients. Set fees in the mid to upper range of what other professionals in the area are charging. Moreover, resist the temptation to offer a sliding fee schedule. Sliding fee schedules are difficult to administer and a potential source of conflict. Rather than reducing fees, consider taking on a few clients pro bono (at no charge).

Developing an ongoing marketing plan is essential to any business, and counseling is no different. Not only does a practice need to be launched, but it also needs to be self-sustaining. Codes of ethics help give some guidance in this area. Additionally, Robert Walsh's 8-Step Method in *The Complete Guide to Private Practice for Licensed Mental Health Professionals* (Walsh & Dasenbrook, 2007) is an excellent example of a marketing plan, emphasizing public speaking as the main component to marketing counseling services.

While public speaking is one of the most productive marketing strategies, a great marketing plan includes numerous other components. Common sense and a professional approach will help to market a practice directly to potential clients and referral sources.

Before embarking on a marketing plan, development of professional marketing material is essential. Key marketing pieces are letterhead and logo, business card, brochure, and Web site. These marketing pieces need to look clean and sharp. Less is more! Most marketing consultants will advise that blank space is a good thing. Resist the temptation to give too much information, thus confusing the client or referral source. Be cautious not to overpower the marketing piece with too much color, logo, or symbols that could be confusing. While this sounds painfully obvious, we have seen some awful marketing material.

Business cards should contain just enough information to identify the counselor and credentials, one or two specialties, basic contact information, and Web site address. Brochures can be more informative, but again resist the temptation to give too much information, rendering the brochure overwhelming or confusing. A picture (head shot by a professional photographer) can help the potential client or referral source make a connection. Keep the biographical information brief. As with the business card, the Web site should be included.

The business card and brochure direct the client and referral source to your Web site. The Web site can give greater detail and all the information necessary to inform clients and referral sources of the counselors, credentials, specialties, training, policies, treatment approaches and information. Links to other resources add value to the Web site.

A good marketing plan will directly target clients and those individuals and services (potential referral sources) that come in contact with potential clients. Marketing consultants will advise that repetition is important. Do not market the practice with only one or two big projects; think smaller and more often.

In marketing directly to potential clients, public speaking is a good plan. Giving talks or speeches is an excellent way to promote the practice. Church groups, civic organizations, support groups, schools, parent-teacher organizations (PTOs), associations, professional societies, and women's and men's groups are always looking for speakers for their meetings. Disseminating marketing pieces or a one-page handout with the practice contact information is recommended. Most of these groups will promote the speech, especially if it is free or low cost.

To prospect potential referral sources, make a list of individuals, agencies, businesses, and organizations that may have contact with the types of clients appropriate for the practice. For example, if the practice niche is adolescents, it would be appropriate to market to pediatricians and family physicians, middle and high schools, principals, counselors, employee assistance programs, probation departments, police departments, United Way agencies, churches and synagogues, community mental health centers, community centers, parent support groups, substance abuse treatment centers, and other counselors who only treat children or adults. Send these potential referral sources the practice marketing pieces and direct them to the practice Web site for more information. After a few weeks, follow up with a phone call, requesting a meeting. Remember, think repetition.

Successful counselors in private practice are very connected and involved with business and other helping professionals. This can be accomplished by joining local, state, and national organizations. Consider joining the local chamber of commerce, Kiwanis, toastmasters/toastmistresses, and so forth. Volunteer to work on a political campaign, for a cause, or to serve on the board of directors of a United Way agency, and other organizations. Join the state counseling organization and its appropriate division or professional society, and get involved. On a national level, join the American Counseling Association and other national professional organizations that are related to the practice. Contribute to political action committees like the Professional Counseling Fund (counselingfund .org), and meet and support local politicians who are favorable to the practice and client population.

Once the practice is beginning to attract clients, each client then becomes a potential referral source. Every client offers a potential opportunity to expand the practice. The obvious way is for a satisfied client to recommend the practice to others. Another way to expand the practice is through what is referred to as *cross-pollination*. Just as it is beneficial for plants to share pollen, it is beneficial for counselors and other professionals to share information. This can be initiated while adhering to all release of information requirements. Within the informed consent document should be a coordination of treatment clause that allows the counselor to contact others who are involved in the care of the client. Whenever a coordination of treatment contact is made, it is a marketing opportunity. These contacts are a professional and ethical responsibility, and at the same time, they provide conduits to help market the practice.

For example, when a client referral is from a physician, sending a thank you letter with a brochure or business card, along with basic clinical information for the patient's chart, is appropriate. A follow-up call to discuss the client is good for coordination of treatment and a way for marketing more directly to the physician. Take opportunities to drop off fruit or lunch to the physician's staff. This will be on their minds whenever one of the patients needs a referral to a counselor.

If the client is a student and has an educational issue, it is an excellent idea to call the counselor, social worker, or special education coordinator at the school to ask for input in treatment planning. Consider asking the student's family for an invitation to the student's individual education plan (IEP) or annual review. At these meetings, act as an observer, giving input only when asked. Leaving a brochure or card is usually welcome. Schools look for competent counselors when they wish to refer outside the district. Most schools have a list of good counselors.

Marketing the practice to the schools may earn an invitation as a speaker at teacher institutes, PTO meetings, or district parent education fairs. The authors have even been asked to keynote the beginning-of-the-year teacher gatherings and have had teachers from these districts contact them for personal and marital counseling. If the school refers a student with medical issues, and the family has signed the coordination of treatment document, it is wise to contact the physician with a letter or call. This is a courtesy contact (and it may be required by state law or a managed-care contractual agreement) to let the physician know of the treatment of his or her patient with ADD, anxiety, or other mental health issues. If the practices niche is working with adults, obtain client permission to contact the internist, gynecologist, or other specialist. The fear of irritating the physician is usually unfounded. Because physicians spend an average of 7 minutes with patients, most MDs welcome a counselor ally. Once again, when another of the physician's patients needs a counselor, the marketing efforts may pay off. Visiting clients who have been hospitalized by a psychiatrist is a thoughtful and professional gesture. Most psychiatrists will write orders in the patient's chart that allow the outside counselor to visit. When signing in at the front desk, drop off the practice card or brochure. The authors have had many clients referred upon discharge from the hospital for outpatient treatment because the personnel at the hospital saw that they were competent and professional.

When accepting a referral from a friend of a client, a managed care company, EAP, or other referral source, use cross-pollination. Make sure to coordinate with physicians, schools, and even lawyers if it is appropriate, but keep in mind that ethics require a release of information. A small, limited practice can grow fairly rapidly using the cross-pollination method. One of the most encouraging comments ever received was when a new client said, "I was given your name by our school and the next day our pediatrician gave us your card, and with those two referrals we feel pretty good about coming to see you."

Looking ahead, the prospect of private practice for counselors continues to be a viable career path. However, more work needs to be done. In the past 30 years counselors have passed licensure laws, lobbied to have counseling services recognized by the insurance and managed-care industry, increased parity with the other helping professions, and advocated for the rights of clients. In the future, counselors will need licensure in all 50 states, license portability, the right to practice in all private and governmental programs, and the ability to continue to advocate for clients. These past accomplishments and future needs speak to another tool or strategy for success in private practice: the ability of all counselors, regardless of specialty, to speak with one voice for the good of the profession and the clients served.

RESOURCES

Covey, S. R. (1989). *The seven habits of highly effective people*. New York: Fireside Books.

Dasenbrook, N. C., & Mastroianni, M. D. (2003). *Harnessing the power of conflict: Leading, living, learning*. Rockford, IL: Crysand Press.
Rosenthal, J. R. (2007). *Ask the expert*. Retrieved April 15, 2007, from http://therapymatch.com/new/?p=resorces&c=84
Walsh, R. J., & Dasenbrook, N. C. (2007). *Frequently asked questions*. Retrieved April 6, 2007, from http://www.counseling-privatepractice.com/faq.php

REFERENCE

Walsh, R. J., & Dasenbrook, N. C. (2007). *The complete guide to private practice for licensed mental health professionals* (3rd ed.). Rockford, IL: Crysand Press.

6

New Concepts in Counseling Ethics

David Kaplan

T H E **A C A C O D E** *of Ethics* (American Counseling Association, 2005; available at www.counseling.org) is revised every 10 years, and a new edition was published in late 2005. Many significant and substantial changes in the areas of counseling ethics occurred over the decade from 1995–2005, and the revised code of ethics therefore contains major updates and important new concepts. This chapter provides an overview of new concepts in counseling ethics in 10 areas: confidentiality, dual relationships, romantic and sexual interactions, end-of-life care for terminally ill clients, cultural sensitivity, diagnosis, interventions, practice termination, technology, and deceased clients. Readers may want to note that additional resources focusing on the revised *ACA Code of Ethics* are available on the American Counseling Association (ACA) Web site at www.counseling.org/ethics

THE END OF CLEAR AND IMMINENT DANGER

I MAGINE THE FOLLOWING scenario: A client is extremely distraught over being fired just 2 hours ago. He states that he is immediately going to go to the interstate highway at a very specific location, climb over the fence, and jump into traffic. The client then informs you that he doesn't want you to tell anyone or to make any effort to interfere.

I don't think it would take very long for most of us to decide that we would not agree to the client's request. In doing so, what criteria would you use to justify your decision to break confidentiality? If you are like me, you can still hear the words that have been drummed into all professional counselors in graduate school; we would break confidentiality because there was clear and imminent danger.

Not anymore. The term *clear and imminent danger* can no longer be found in the *ACA Code of Ethics*. It has been replaced by *serious and foreseeable harm* (see section B.2.a). Why was this change made? A major reason was to bring the language for determining the need to break confidentiality into line with the most famous legal trial in counseling: *Tarasoff v. Regents of the University of California*. In the Tarasoff case, the judge ruled that confidentiality must be broken if there is serious and foreseeable harm.

What is the difference between the now-outdated clear and imminent danger and its replacement, serious and foreseeable harm? The honest answer is that at this point, we really don't know. The ACA Ethics Committee is going to need some test cases in order to make rulings that flesh out the difference between the two. In the meantime, the committee has recommended the following: Treat serious and foreseeable harm exactly the same as you would clear and imminent danger. If you have a situation with a client in which you would break confidentiality under clear and imminent danger, then go ahead and break confidentiality. If you have a situation in which under clear and imminent danger you would not have broken confidentiality, then do not break confidentiality. This recommendation will change over time as the aforementioned ethics test cases occur, so keep up with the literature in this area.

ALLOWING DUAL RELATIONSHIPS

A SECOND NEW concept in counseling ethics focuses on a major change in the revised *ACA Code of Ethics*: the end of the notion that you always need to avoid dual relationships. In fact, you will not see the term *dual relationships* anywhere in the entire 22-page revised ethics code. This can come as somewhat of a shock to those who have been around awhile and were taught from their first class in graduate school that professional counselors never engage in a dual relationship with a client.

The 2005 *ACA Code of Ethics* has replaced dual relationships with the concept of *beneficial versus harmful relationships* (see section A.5.d). A counselor and client can now evaluate whether a nonprofessional interaction would be beneficial for the client. If the interaction is beneficial, the counselor can go ahead and engage in the interaction. As an example, if a client invites you to her child's wedding you now have the opportunity to have a thorough discussion with the client as to the benefits and the concerns about attending the wedding ceremony—what could go right and what could go wrong. If after this discussion both you and the client feel that it would clearly be beneficial for you to attend the client's child's wedding, you may certainly do so. Section A.5.d provides additional examples of nonprofessional interactions that a counselor may engage in with a client when appropriate: a commitment ceremony, a graduation ceremony, hospital visits to an ill family member, and mutual membership in a professional association, organization, or community.

ROMANTIC AND SEXUAL RELATIONSHIPS

THE 2005 ACA *Code of Ethics* continues to prohibit romantic and sexual interactions between counselor and client. It should be noted, however, that the timeframe prohibiting sexual or romantic contacts with former clients has now increased from 2 to 5 years.

A new concept in the revised ethics code has to do with romantic or sexual relationships with family members of clients. Section A.5.b states that counselors are now explicitly prohibited from having sex or a romantic relationship with the partners or family members of clients for a 5-year period. This new mandate was developed due to the realization that some counselors were conducting child counseling and subsequently asking the parent out on a date, or they were providing family counseling and pursuing a romantic relationship with a family member who attended one or more sessions.

END-OF-LIFE CARE FOR TERMINALLY ILL CLIENTS

THE PREVIOUS SECTION spoke to ethical mandates about love. This section speaks to ethical concepts for counselors about death. There is a new section (A.9) of the revised *ACA Code of Ethics* that covers end-of-life care for terminally ill clients. Section A.9 does two things: It gives counselors permission to work with terminally ill clients who wish to explore their end-of-life options, and it gives permission to keep discussions with terminally ill clients who are considering hastening their death confidential.

Section A.9 grew out of the Oregon assisted-suicide law, which gives physicians permission to assist terminally ill patients who wish to hasten their death. Of course, counselors would never be involved in the practice of medicine and would never get involved in the actual administration of any drugs that would end a terminally ill patient's life. However, with Oregon's new assisted-suicide law, the question arises as to whether counseling a terminally ill client with a presenting issue of deciding whether to hasten death is violating the edict to do no harm. If so, does that mean that a counselor then has to break confidentiality if a terminally ill patient tells him or her that he is contemplating hastening his death? Section A.9 of the revised *ACA Code of Ethics* makes it clear that in and of itself, a terminally ill client who wishes to explore his or her end-of-life options is not in serious and foreseeable harm, and a counselor does not need to break confidentiality simply because a terminally ill client brought up these issues.

A NEW FOCUS ON CULTURAL SENSITIVITY

O**VER THE PAST** decade, the counseling profession has made great strides in addressing the needs of a culturally diverse society. In order to keep pace with this progress, one of the mandates given to the ACA Ethics Revision Task Force was to infuse multiculturalism and diversity throughout the 2005 *ACA Code of Ethics*.

Section B.1.a of the revised ethics code is titled "Multicultural Diversity Considerations" and states the following: "Counselors maintain awareness and sensitivity regarding cultural meanings of confidentiality and privacy. Counselors respect different views toward disclosure of information. Counselors hold ongoing discussions with clients as to how, when, and with whom information is to be shared."

In discussing the implications of section B.1.a, Courtland Lee, a member of the ACA Ethics Revision Task Force, has noted that the essence of multiculturalism is reflected in the difference between individualistic societies—those that value the individual—and collectivist societies—those that focus on and value the group (Kaplan et al., in press). An example of the cultural meaning of confidentiality in a collectivist society is provided by Tammy Bringaze, another member of the Ethics Revision Task Force (Kaplan et al., in press). Dr. Bringaze works with women from Afghanistan, and many of her clients have recently emigrated from the Middle East. During a session with an Afghani woman, the door opened and one of the client's close Afghani friends walked in and joined in the conversation. Fortunately, Dr. Bringaze knew that the Afghani collectivist society views it as perfectly appropriate for close friends to be involved in a discussion of personal matters with a counselor. If Dr. Bringaze had taken a Western individualistic perspective and told the friend to leave the office immediately because of the confidential nature of the session, both women would have been greatly offended and Dr. Bringaze would likely have never seen her client again.

A second new concept reflecting on the ethical responsibility to be culturally sensitive is found within section A.2.c of the revised ethics code: "Counselors communicate information in ways that are both developmentally and culturally appropriate." In an interview provided in Kaplan et al. (in press), Courtland Lee gives an example of fulfilling this new mandate when working with African American youth:

> Another example of the importance of cultural sensitivity regarding confidentiality and the disclosure of information revolves around disciplining a child. When an African American kid tells you, "I got in trouble and I'm afraid to go home because my mom is going to give me a whipping!" it sounds really harsh, as if the kid is going to get the heck beat out of him with a whip. But in the African-American community the term "whipping" generally refers to a form of mild discipline. So understanding how words and meanings are different in different cultures is important.

PERMISSION TO REFRAIN FROM MAKING A DIAGNOSIS

W E N O W C O M E to a new concept that the counseling profession can be very proud of. With the implementation of the 2005 *ACA Code of Ethics*, professional counseling is now the only mental health profession that gives explicit permission to refrain from making a *Diagnostic and Statistical Manual of Mental Disorders (DSM)* diagnosis when it is in the best interest of the client to do so. The permission to refrain from making a diagnosis is not something you will find in the ethics code of psychology, social work, marriage and family therapy, or any other mental health–related profession.

As background, the ACA Ethics Revision Task Force was aware that diagnosis has been abused in the past. For example, there have been people of color who have been diagnosed as mentally ill when their symptoms were really a result of oppression, poverty, and racism. A second example revolves around the increasing diagnosis of Attention Deficit Disorder in children who have been exhibiting normal behaviors of childhood. In addition, ACA has received reports that many counselors have been forced into giving a *DSM* Axis I diagnosis when none exists due to the pressures of receiving reimbursement from health insurance companies.

The Ethics Revision Task Force approached these issues by creating sections E.5.c and E.5.d. Section E.5.c, titled "Historical and Social

Prejudices in the Diagnosis of Pathology," states the following: "Counselors recognize historical and social prejudices in the misdiagnosis and pathologizing of certain individuals and groups and the role of mental health professionals in perpetuating these prejudices through diagnosis and treatment." Section E.5.d, titled "Refraining From Diagnosis," states: "Counselors may refrain from making and/or reporting a diagnosis if they believe it would cause harm to the client or others." Section E.5.d is truly groundbreaking. For the first time, there is a specific statement in the *ACA Code of Ethics* that permits counselors to refrain from making a *DSM* diagnosis if it is in the best interest of the client not to have a diagnosis.

As an example, a college counselor may be working with a student who is depressed and will also be applying to the CIA for employment. The counselor may decide not to give an Axis I diagnosis, knowing that doing so would mean that the client is automatically ineligible for a position with the CIA. Another example focuses on clients with an Axis II personality disorder. There are some clients who become despondent over having a personality disorder, especially if they read texts and articles that state that a personality disorder is hard to treat or incurable. A counselor who has such a client may now ethically choose to refrain from reporting a diagnosis on Axis II.

NEW MANDATES FOR SELECTING INTERVENTIONS

THE 2005 REVISION of the *ACA Code of Ethics* has an important new mandate about selecting interventions. There were two factors involved in creating section C.6.e, "Scientific Bases for Treatment Modalities." The first was the need to advance the profession by setting the expectation that counselors utilize approaches, theories, and techniques that are grounded in theory or have an empirical or scientific foundation. The second factor was the need to provide a mechanism for the ACA Ethics Committee to review so-called fringe interventions for potential harm.

With the above as background, let us take a look at the section (C.6.e) in the revised *ACA Code of Ethics* (2005) that speaks to the new mandate for selecting interventions: "Counselors use techniques/procedures/modalities that are grounded in theory and/or have an empirical or scientific foundation. Counselors who do not must define the techniques/procedures as 'unproven' or 'developing' and explain the potential risks and ethical considerations of using such techniques and procedures and take steps to protect clients from possible harm."

It should be noted that section C.6.e does not prohibit counselors from utilizing techniques, procedures, or modalities that do not have an empirical or theoretical base. However, it does state that such approaches must be defined as unproven or developing and that the potential risks and ethical considerations of using the technique or procedure must be explained.

You may also want to note that the ACA Ethics Committee has reviewed its first fringe intervention—reparative-conversion therapy. Reparative-conversion therapy purports to change homosexuals into heterosexuals. The Ethics Committee has formally ruled that this intervention is not grounded in theory and does not have an empirical or scientific foundation. Therefore, any counselor either using reparative-conversion therapy or referring for reparative-conversion therapy must define it as unproven or developing, explain the potential risks and ethical considerations, and take any steps necessary to protect the client from possible harm.

NEW REQUIREMENTS TO HAVE A TRANSFER PLAN

AN INTERESTING NEW section in the revised *ACA Code of Ethics* (2005) requires counselors to now think about the end of their practice from the very beginning. Section C.2.h, "Counselor Incapacitation or Termination of Practice," states the following: "When counselors leave a practice, they follow a prepared plan for transfer of clients and files. Counselors prepare and disseminate to an identified colleague or records custodian a plan for the transfer of clients and files in case of their incapacitation, death, or termination of practice."

This new ethics mandate arose from awareness that harm was being done to clients when their counselor moved to another city, became disabled due to an illness or accident, or suddenly died. In many such cases, clients were unable to transfer records to their new counselor. Other clients who needed their records and past history were denied much-needed disability payments. Still other clients simply wanted the peace of mind of keeping track of their records after their counselor died or moved away.

Section C.2.h now makes it clear that from the very first day of starting a practice, every counselor needs a plan in place for the transfer of clients and files in the event that the counselor moves to another area, becomes incapacitated, or dies. For many counselors who work in schools and agencies, this will be fairly simple. It means identifying the school or agency as your record keeper and establishing a system within the institution to transfer records to a new counselor. Counselors in private practice should find another practitioner who will agree to be the records custodian. The counselor's informed-consent document can then be amended to include a statement informing clients where they can find their records in the event of a sudden ending to the practice. Counselors should also consider stating in their Last Will and Testament the name and contact information of the records custodian and instructions for transferring client records. This will help the counselor's loved ones to know how case notes and other records should be treated posthumously.

ETHICAL USE OF TECHNOLOGY IN COUNSELING

THE REVISED *ACA* *Code of Ethics* has a greatly expanded section devoted to technology (A.12): "Technology Applications." In the previous 1995 edition, technological applications received less than one half of one column. In the 2005 code, technology covers two and a half columns, making it the largest single section within the *ACA Code of Ethics*. This indicates that technology has become an integral part of counseling.

It is beyond the scope of this chapter to review all of the important new concepts about the use of technology contained in section A.12 of the revised *ACA Code of Ethics*. One new mandate that does deserves attention is the requirement that counselors conducting distance counseling through the Internet, telephone, or other technology establish a method for verifying client identification. The Ethics Revision Task Force recognized that a counselor providing distance counseling needs to be sure that the person on the other end of the phone or computer is the actual client. There are two important reasons for that. First, of course, is the issue of confidentiality. If a friend, sibling, parent, or partner signs on as the client, a counselor is likely to disclose information that would constitute a breach of confidentiality. Second, it is important to know the actual identity of the client in the event that a counselor determines that there is serious and foreseeable harm to self or others and needs to implement the duty to warn. The counselor will be unable to assist the authorities to locate the client if it turns out that the name was an alias and the contact information was fictitious.

OBLIGATIONS FOR PROTECTING THE CONFIDENTIALITY OF THE DECEASED

THE FINAL NEW concept in counseling ethics for review is contained in one sentence. However, this does not diminish its importance. The revised *ACA Code of Ethics* (2005) has a new requirement to protect the confidentiality of a client who has died. Section B.3.f,

"Deceased Clients," states the following: "Counselors protect the confidentiality of deceased clients consistent with the legal requirements and agency or setting policies."

The Ethics Revision Task Force felt that it was important to make this statement, in part, because of mental health professionals who had sold their stories to tabloids after famous clients had died. These mental health professionals felt that confidentiality could be broken once their clients were deceased and that information stated during counseling sessions was fair game to be sold to the highest bidder.

In response to the posthumous disclosures described above, the ACA Ethics Revision Task Force wanted to make it clear that confidentiality extends beyond death. Simply put, section B.3.f implies that all of the rules about confidentiality that applied when a client was alive continue to apply after a client dies. For further information regarding the most recently released ACA code of ethics, visit www.counseling.org

REFERENCES

American Counseling Association. (2005). *ACA code of ethics*. Alexandria, VA: Author.

Kaplan, D., Kocet, M. M., Cottone, R. R., Glosoff, H. L., Miranti, J. G., Moll, E. C., et al. (in press). New mandates and imperatives in the revised ACA code of ethics. *Journal of Counseling and Development*.

7

A Synopsis of the Health Insurance Portability and Accountability Act

BLANCA ROBLES

PASSAGE OF THE 1996 Health Insurance Portability and Accountability Act (HIPAA) was originally an effort by Congress to ensure portability of health insurance between jobs for American workers. An Administrative Simplification section was included to cut costs and regulate the manner in which electronic transactions were performed by the health care industry. Congress entrusted the Department of Health and Human Services (DHHS) to develop privacy and security requirements to ensure confidentiality on forms containing individually identifiable health information. This chapter provides a brief overview of HIPAA regarding mental health services, compliance issues for providers, filing and investigating complaints, violation penalties, glossary of terms, and resource links for more detailed information.

HIPAA's TWO TITLES

TITLE I PROTECTS health insurance coverage for workers and their families when they change or lose their jobs. In other words, it lowers the probability or risks of losing existing coverage and being unable to switch or buy coverage in the event that their employer's health plan is no longer available.

Title II requires the DHHS to establish national standards for electronic health care transactions and addresses the security and privacy of health information. Covered entities must provide a *privacy notice* stating their privacy practices and limiting the *use* and *disclosure* of information as required under the rule to all patients.

Patients must be informed of their rights and are required to sign the appropriate forms authorizing the health care provider to obtain and/or provide information to other health care providers as relevant. The provider of services would use this form when trying to obtain any records from other hospitals, doctors, labs, and so forth. If patients desire to obtain access to their own medical records from entities such as doctors, hospitals, or clinics, the DHHS stipulates that they would be entitled to receive their records within 30 days after services are rendered. It also states that these entities may, at their discretion, charge patients for copying and providing personal records to their patients. There are no restrictions as to how much entities may charge per page for copying records.

In addition, the DHHS makes clear that the new federal privacy standards do not affect or preempt state laws that provide additional privacy protections for patients. It is the responsibility of health care providers to remain abreast of the requirements particular or specific to the state where their services are rendered. Stronger state laws that may include more restrictive privacy provisions (e.g., those covering mental health, HIV infection, and AIDS information) continue to apply, providing patients additional protections.

WHO IS REQUIRED TO COMPLY?

AS PER THE DHHS, all *covered entities* are required to comply. The Centers for Disease Control and Prevention Web site indicates the following types of health care organizations are defined as "covered entities" by the Privacy Rule: (1) all who choose to transmit administrative and financial health information electronically, (2) all *health plans,* and (3) all *health care clearinghouses.* The HIPAA standards do not apply to individuals unless they are acting in some capacity on behalf of a covered entity, and not on behalf of themselves.

HOW DOES A COVERED ENTITY ENSURE COMPLIANCE?

THE OFFICE FOR Civil Rights (OCR) under HIPAA indicates compliance must be ensured by instituting the following:

- ❖ *Written privacy procedures.* The rule requires covered entities to have written privacy procedures, including a description of staff that has access to protected information, how it will be used, and when it may be disclosed. Covered entities generally must take steps to ensure that any business associates who have access to protected information agree to the same limitations on the use and disclosure of that information.
- ❖ *Employee training and a privacy officer.* Covered entities must train their employees in their privacy procedures and must designate an individual to be responsible for ensuring the procedures are followed. If covered entities learn an employee failed to follow these procedures, they must take appropriate disciplinary action.

The act places the final responsibility for compliance on the covered entity, not the individual worker. The HIPAA Compliance Rule Standards include definitions for three levels of security:

- ❖ *Administrative security*—assignment of security responsibility to an individual
- ❖ *Physical security*—required to protect electronic systems, equipment, and data
- ❖ *Technical security*—authentication and encryption used to control access to data

There are 10 standard transactions for Electronic Data Interchange (EDI) for the transmission of health care data that HIPAA has identified. Claims information, payment and remittance advice, and claims status and inquiry are examples of standard transactions. Current Procedural Terminology (CPT) codes, *International Classification of Diseases (ICD)*, and Healthcare Common Procedure Coding System (HCPCS) are examples of *code sets* for procedures and diagnoses.

Transactions are activities involving the transfer of health care information for specific purposes. Under HIPAA, if a health care provider engages in one of the identified transactions (see glossary of terms), the provider must comply with the standard for that transaction. Every provider who does business electronically must use the same health care transactions, code sets, and identifiers, per HIPAA requirements.

HIPAA APPLICATION TO MENTAL HEALTH AND SUBSTANCE ABUSE SERVICE PROVIDERS

REGARDING THE USE and Disclosure of Psychotherapy Notes under 45 CFR 164.508(a)(2), (a)(3), indicates authorization for psychotherapy notes other than the transaction provisions in §164.532, the covered entity must obtain an authorization for any use or disclosure of psychotherapy notes, except in these instances: (1) use by the originator of the psychotherapy notes for treatment; (2) use or disclosure by the covered entity for its own training programs in which students, trainees, or practitioners in mental health learn under supervision to practice or improve their skills in group, joint, family, or individual counseling; or (3) use or disclosure by the covered entity to defend itself in a legal action or other proceeding brought by the individual.

All psychotherapy notes recorded on any medium (paper, electronic) by a mental health professional such as a licensed counselor or psychologist must be kept by the author and filed separately from the rest of the patient's medical record to maintain a higher standard of protection. Psychotherapy notes are defined as "process notes," not "progress notes." In addition, psychotherapy notes do not include medication prescription and monitoring, counseling session start and stop times, the modalities and frequencies of treatment furnished, results of clinical tests, and any summary of diagnosis, functional status, the treatment plan, symptoms, prognosis, and progress to date.

The Authorization for Use and Disclosure of Health Information, Form IHS-810, must be dated, signed by the patient, legal guardian if the patient is a minor or incompetent, or the patient's personal representative, and the box for Psychotherapy Notes must be checked. The authorization should not be used in conjunction with other disclosures or uses.

WHO CAN FILE A COMPLAINT AND WHAT ARE THE REQUIREMENTS?

ACCORDING TO HIPAA Administrative Simplification Regulation Text published in March 2006, section 160.306(a), a person who believes a covered entity is not complying with the administrative simplification provisions may file a complaint with the secretary.

Under this section, complaints must (1) be filed in writing, either on paper or electronically; (2) name the person that is the subject of the complaint and describe the acts or omissions believed to be in violation of the applicable administrative simplification provision(s); (3) be filed within 180 days of when the complainant knew or should have known that the act or omission in question occurred, unless this time limit is waived by the secretary for good cause shown; and (4) note that the secretary may prescribe additional procedures for the filing of complaints as well as the place and manner of filing by notice in the Federal Register.

WHAT DOES AN INVESTIGATION ENTAIL?

T HE OCR UNDER HIPAA monitors and ensures compliance with the act. Enforcement is generally complaint driven. When appropriate, the OCR can impose civil monetary penalties for violations of the Privacy Rule provisions. Potential criminal violations of the law would be referred to the U.S. Department of Justice for further investigation and appropriate action.

The secretary may investigate complaints filed under this section that may include a review of the pertinent policies, procedures, or practices of the covered entity and of the circumstances regarding any alleged violation. At the time of initial written communication with the covered entity about the complaint, the secretary will describe the act(s) and/or omission(s) that are the basis of the complaint. The covered entity or health care provider's responsibilities for complying with the investigation include (1) providing records and compliance reports in a timely manner; (2) cooperating with complaint investigators and compliance reviews; and (3) permitting access to information by the secretary during normal business hours to its facilities, books, records, accounts, and other sources of information, including protected health information, that are pertinent to ascertaining compliance with the applicable administrative simplification provisions. If any information required of a covered entity is in the exclusive possession of any other agency, institution, or person and the other agency, institution, or person fails or refuses to furnish the information, the covered entity must so certify and set forth what efforts it has made to obtain the information.

Protected health information obtained by the secretary in connection with an investigation or compliance review will not be disclosed by the secretary except if necessary for ascertaining or enforcing compliance with the applicable administrative simplification provisions, or if otherwise required by law.

WHAT ARE VIOLATION PENALTIES?

C ONGRESS PROVIDED CIVIL and criminal penalties for covered entities that misuse personal health information. For civil violations of the standards, OCR may impose monetary penalties up to $100 per violation or $25,000 per year for each requirement or provision violated. Criminal penalties apply for certain actions such as knowingly obtaining protected health information in violation of the law. Criminal penalties can range up to $50,000 and 1 year in prison for certain offenses; up to $100,000 and up to 5 years in prison if the offense is committed under false pretenses; and up to $250,000 and up to 10 years in prison if the offense is committed with the intent to sell, transfer, or use protected health information for commercial advantage, personal gain, or malicious harm.

INFORMATION STORAGE AND REVIEWS

NEITHER THE DHHS nor the OCR endorse any software storage programs regarding the security of patient personal records. Covered entities should conduct risk analysis in relation to information being transmitted electronically, including the use of any portable devices such as laptops, PDAs, USB flash drives, and so forth. Wireless access points must be encrypted and assigned strong passwords. Annual reviews of the covered entity should be performed internally to assess all areas and improve compliance, which would show OCR good faith effort in complying with all standards in case a complaint was filed.

HIPAA ADMINISTRATIVE SIMPLIFICATION REGULATION TEXT TERMINOLOGY

AUTHORIZATION. AN INDIVIDUAL'S written permission to allow a covered entity to use or disclose specified protected health information (PHI) for a particular purpose. Except as otherwise permitted by the rule, a covered entity may not use or disclose PHI for research purposes without a valid authorization.

Code sets. The codes used to identify specific diagnoses and clinical procedures on claims and encounter forms.

Confidentiality. The protection of individually identifiable information as required by state and federal legal requirements and partners policies.

Covered entity. A health plan, a health care clearinghouse, or a health care provider that transmits health information in electronic form in connection with a transaction for which the DHHS has adopted a standard.

Disclosure. The release, transfer, access to, or divulging of information in any other manner outside the entity holding the information.

Health care. Care, services, or supplies related to the health of an individual, including (1) preventive, diagnostic, therapeutic, rehabilitative, maintenance, or palliative care, and counseling, service, assessment, or procedure with respect to the physical or mental condition, or functional status, of an individual that affects the structure or function of the body; and (2) sale or dispensing of a drug, device, equipment, or other item in accordance with a prescription.

Health care clearinghouse. A public or private entity, including a billing service, repricing company, community health management information system, or community health information system, and so-called value-added networks and switches that either process or facilitate the processing of health information received from another entity in a nonstandard format or containing nonstandard data content into standard data elements or a standard transaction, or receive a standard transaction from another entity and process or facilitate the processing of health information into a nonstandard format or nonstandard data content for the receiving entity.

Health care provider. A provider of services, as defined in section 1861(u) of the act, 42 U.S.C. 1395x(u); a provider of medical or health services, as defined in section 1861(s) of the act, 42 U.S.C. 1395x(s); and any other person or organization that furnishes, bills, or is paid for health care in the normal course of business.

Individually identifiable health information. Information that is a subset of health information, including demographic information collected from an individual, and (1) is created or received by a health care provider, health plan, employer, or health care clearinghouse; and (2) relates to the past, present, or future physical or mental health or condition of an individual; the provision of health care to an individual; or the past, present, or future payment for the provision of health care to an individual; and (1) that identifies the individual; or (2) with respect to which there is a reasonable basis to believe the information can be used to identify the individual.

Privacy notice. Institution-wide notice describing the practices of the covered entity regarding PHI. Health care providers and other covered entities must give the notice to patients and research subjects and should obtain signed acknowledgments of receipt. Internal and external uses of protected health information are explained. It is the responsibility of the researcher to provide a copy of the privacy notice to any subject who has not already received one. If the researcher does provide the notice, the researcher should also obtain the subject's written acknowledgment of receipt.

Small health plan. A health plan with annual receipts of $5 million or less.

Transaction. The transmission of information between two parties to carry out financial or administrative activities related to health care. It includes the following types of information transmissions:

1. Health care claims or equivalent encounter information
2. Health care payment and remittance advice

3. Coordination of benefits
4. Health care claim status
5. Enrollment and disenrollment in a health plan
6. Eligibility for a health plan
7. Health plan premium payments
8. Referral certification and authorization
9. First report of injury
10. Health claims attachments
11. Other transactions that the secretary may prescribe by regulation

Treatment. The provision of health care by one or more health care providers. Treatment includes any consultation, referral, or other exchanges of information to manage a patient's care. The privacy notice explains that the HIPAA privacy rule allows partners and their affiliates to use and disclose protected health information for treatment purposes without specific authorization.

Use. With respect to individually identifiable health information, the sharing, employment, application, utilization, examination, or analysis of such information within the entity or health care component (for hybrid entities) that maintains such information.

Waiver or alteration of authorization. The documentation that the covered entity obtains from a researcher or an Institutional Review Board (IRB) or a Privacy Board that states that the IRB or Privacy Board has waived or altered the Privacy Rule's requirement that an individual must authorize a covered entity to use or disclose the individual's PHI for research purposes.

[65 FR 82798, December 28, 2000, as amended at 67 FR 38019, May 31, 2002; 67 FR 53266, August 14, 2002; 68 FR 8374, February 20, 2003; 71 FR 8424, February 16, 2006]

RESOURCES

Department of Health and Human Services, http://www.hhs.gov/ocr/hipaa
http://www.hipaacompliance101.com/hipaa-rules.htm
http://www.hhs.gov/ocr/hipaa/assist.html
http://www.hhs.gov/ocr/AdminSimpRegText.pdf
http://www.hhs.gov/ohrp/documents/OHRPRegulations.pdf
http://healthcare.partners.org/phsirb/hipaaglos.htm#g23#g23
http://privacyruleandresearch.nih.gov/dictionary.asp
Centers for Disease Control, http://www.cdc.gov/privacyrule/Guidance/PRmmwrguidance.pdf

FEDERAL GOVERNMENT RESOURCES

DHHS Office for Civil Rights—HIPAA guidelines: http://www.hhs.gov/ocr/hipaa

Centers for Disease Control—Privacy Rule guidelines: http://www.cdc.gov/privacyrule

Centers for Medicare and Medicaid Services: http://www.cms.gov/hipaa

Health Resources and Services Administration: http://www.hrsa.gov/website.htm

National Center for Health Statistics: http://www.cdc.gov/nchs/otheract/phdsc/phdsc.htm

National Committee on Vital and Health Statistics: http://www.ncvhs.hhs.gov/

National Health Information Infrastructure: http://www.health.gov/ncvhs-nhii/

Indian Health Service: http://www.ihs.gov/AdminMngrResources/HIPAA/index.cfm

National Institutes of Health: http://privacyruleandresearch.nih.gov

Substance Abuse and Mental Health Services Administration: http://www.samhsa.gov/hipaa/

8

Contracting Strategies With Managed Care and Other Agencies

ROBERT J. WALSH AND
NORMAN C. DASENBROOK

MANAGED HEALTH CARE

MANY PRACTICE-BUILDING books and seminars suggest that a counselor can enjoy a thriving private practice without insurance and managed care reimbursements. The assertion is that becoming a provider is difficult, which is true, and that the bureaucracy and paperwork is brain numbing, also true. Despite the headaches, it's worth the trouble. Unless the clinician practices in a very affluent area (and if so, hundreds of other therapists will be there too), it is important to realize managed care is an important part of the private practice business.

Several years ago, when licensed mental health counselors were not included on any insurance panels or reimbursed by any insurance companies, a counselors' conference was held on managed care and insurance issues. A national expert on managed care was invited to help explain what counselors were up against as they tried to be recognized as providers on insurance plans. In one of the presentations the expert used the analogy of a train and indicated that the managed care train had left the station and for licensed counselors to get on that train would be a difficult task.

Well, counselors *are* on the train now, thanks to hard work by many state and national counseling organizations. Mental health counselors are accepted as third-party payees by more than 40 national and regional managed care and insurance companies. A comprehensive list of managed health care and insurance companies that accept counselors is available at the American Counseling Association's (ACA) Web site, www.counseling.org, and in the book *The Complete Guide to Private Practice for Licensed Mental Health Professionals* (Walsh & Dasenbrook, 2007). The number of insurance providers that accept counselors varies from state to state, but the trend is toward managed care companies, employee assistance plans (EAPs), and union benefit funds recognizing—and paying—counselors.

What does that mean for the experienced therapist who would like to start a private practice? What about the newly licensed graduate? The truth is, there are still seats on the train, and good, solid, effective therapists can have a seat.

TYPES OF MANAGED CARE

UNDERSTANDING THE LANGUAGE of managed health care plans can be confusing and overwhelming, even to people who think they know insurance. Managed health care plans negotiate lower prices with therapists so that employers can give their employees discounted services. There are three types of managed health care plans. The first is the HMO, or health maintenance organization. The HMO negotiates with medical providers to reduce the fees for their services and names specific providers that must be used for the employee to receive the health insurance benefits. A list of approved providers is often given to the employee or is accessible via the Internet. Often, with the HMO, specialists can only be seen through the recommendation of the primary physician. The HMO often requires less co-pay from the employee. If providing services to a client with an HMO, the clinician will need to work with the client's doctor to get preapproval for services.

Another type of managed health care plan is the PPO, or preferred provider organization. These plans also negotiate for reduced cost to the employee, yet with the PPO the employee can choose any provider. There are usually two lists of therapists with a PPO. There is the Member Provider, which generally provides services at the same cost as an HMO provider, and then there is the Non-Member Provider, whose cost to the employee may be a little more. Because of the acceptance of Non-Member Providers, often referred to as Out-of-Network Providers, PPOs offer employees more freedom to see specialists of their own choice. This is without the recommendation of the primary care physician. The clinician may still need to earn preapproval for the client with PPOs, however, and should plan to charge a client for his or her first visit until service coverage can be checked.

The third type of managed care plan is the POS, or point of service plan. This is similar to the HMO in that the employee chooses a specific doctor, who works as a gateway to a specialist. Anytime the employee needs treatment for something specific, the POS doctor has to be contacted first. The counselor will need to work more closely with a POS doctor when servicing clients with this type of insurance.

Some clients do not have managed care insurance, but carry indemnity insurance. With regular indemnity insurance, no referral by the primary doctor is necessary and the client can see any qualified provider. This insurance, while not especially common, offers the most freedom to employees, and the simplest billing for mental health providers.

BACK DOOR METHOD FOR GAINING ACCESS TO MANAGED CARE

IN MOST STATES, up to 80% of the top companies will pay mental health counselors third-party reimbursement. To be eligible for payment from these insurance companies, the clinician may need to apply to each company and earn provider status, which means inclusion on the insurance's approved mental health provider panel. But what if the counselor is not on the new client's panel? What if a panel is closed in that particular area? The authors have learned how to get in the back door of managed care companies. Using this method helps clinicians become ad hoc providers; that is, they are accepted for that one client. In many cases, once accepted in the insurance company's system, the counselor is given provider status and may even be referred new clients from the managed care company.

The back door system is predicated on a few factors. The first is the motivated client. When a new client calls, especially if the call is based on a doctor's, teacher's, or friend's strong recommendation, the client is highly motivated to make the insurance work. The counselor must ask the client to petition the employers in a clear, polite way, requesting that the managed care company consider paying the chosen mental health clinician. The letter should point out the credentials, license, and experience of this therapist and explain that the therapist meets the requirements of the state for a license as a professional. If the client was referred by a physician, that information is included as well. This letter goes to the benefits manager or whoever coordinates insurance for the company. A copy is sent to the insurance or managed care company's provider relations director. Contact information for managed care companies' provider relations departments is available at the ACA Web site, http://www.counseling.org/Counselors/PrivatePracticePointers.aspx

The second letter of the petition comes from the licensed mental health counselor. This letter is sent to the managed care or insurance company with a copy to the client's employer. The counselor must always obtain a release from the client to send these letters. In this letter, the counselor writes a request for consideration of payment for services, including professional qualifications, and information explaining why the counselor is a good fit for this client. The insurance company's provider relations department should respond to the request within 2 weeks. Phone call follow-ups will help expedite this process after the 2 weeks pass. In the meantime, it is recommended that a payment plan be set up with the new client charging what the insurance company would pay. An agreement is made that the money will be reimbursed once the insurance company responds with payment.

It was not long ago that the biggest insurance providers did not accept counselors as mental health providers at all. This has turned around, and now counselors are members of most major insurance panels. However, the clinician may come upon an insurance company that does not recognize counselors at all. If this is the case, a third letter is needed. This should come from the state's counseling association chapter. The state counseling association sends the insurance company or managed care company a letter on the counselor's behalf, stating the case for accepting licensed counselors into the managed care panel. Along with this letter, the state's counseling association should send a brochure explaining exactly what your state counseling licensure involves. State organizations should be happy to provide this service to members. If a letter has not been created yet, counselors in that state must form a committee to draft one.

Templates of all three letters are available through the ACA Web site, http://www.counseling.org/Counselors/PrivatePracticePointers.aspx, and in Walsh & Dasenbrook (2007).

NATIONAL PROVIDER IDENTIFIER AND THE COUNCIL FOR AFFORDABLE QUALITY HEALTH CARE

A LL LICENSED COUNSELORS who work with insurance and managed care plans must use the National Provider Identifier (NPI) number when filing an insurance claim. The Administrative Simplification provisions of the Health Insurance Portability and Accountability Act of 1996 (HIPAA) mandated the adoption of a standard unique identifier for each health care provider. Information can be obtained at its Web site, http://www.cms.hhs.gov/nationalprovident stand/, and an application can be downloaded at https://nppes.cms .hhs.gov/NPPES/Welcome.do

Another organization, the Council for Affordable Quality Healthcare (CAQH; www.caqh.org), can help streamline applications to managed care and insurance panels. Through this organization, formed by a consortium of insurance companies, a counselor can submit a credentialing application that can be accessed by more than 100 insurance and managed health care companies. The authors recommend going through Aetna Insurance's Credentialing Customer Service Department online. Aetna has a helpful link on its Web site that will facilitate this process at http://www.aetna.com/provider/ credentialing.html. Interested counselors should follow the directions to fill out the Aetna application request form in order to be added to the CAQH–Aetna Provider Application Roster. If help with this is needed, Netsource Billing (866-441-1591) will process the CAQH application for a fee. Additional information regarding these issues can be found on the ACA Web site http://www.counseling .org/Counselors/. Click on Private Practice Pointers (note: this is a members-only section).

REIMBURSEMENT ISSUES

T HE SPECTER OF managed care has occasionally caused anxiety and frustration for counselors, but many times the issues can be tackled with an old-fashioned problem-solving approach. For example, counselors sometimes hear that insurance companies are planning to reduce rates of reimbursement to mental health professionals. However, according to the provider relations departments of seven of the top managed care and insurance companies, there were no plans in the works to reduce fees. In fact, when asked if there was a way to get an *increase* in reimbursement, one offered a 12% increase; another made no promises but said it was reviewing a possible increase across the country in 2007. A major behavioral health company said it will consider a rate increase for counselors after it received a request in writing outlining the reasons, and the largest managed care company reviews its rates based on audits state by state.

One of the companies that refers many clients offered an increase from $65 to $70, and another of the bigger ones gave a raise from $60 to $67. Finally, one of the top five said it will give a $5 raise to $70 for EAPs and $75 on regular managed care. While these companies report that they will not deal with national professional organizations about payment issues, the authors have found that they will deal with individual providers. Overall, it has been found, and has been proven, that polite inquiry and persistence is most effective in dealing with managed care issues.

For advocacy purposes, the list of the largest managed care and insurance companies is available at the ACA Web site, www.counseling.org, in the Members Only section, and in Walsh and Dasenbrook (2007).

ELECTRONIC CLAIMS SUBMISSION

ELECTRONIC CLAIMS SUBMISSION is not only becoming the more efficient way of sending insurance claims, in some instances it is becoming a requirement. Some insurance carriers will delay paper claims processing up to 28 days while electronic claims submissions can take just 24–48 hours. That is money in the pocket faster! There are multiple options available for submitting claims electronically. All contracts with billing services maintain signed HIPAA agreements.

Medical billing software systems. A medical billing software system allows the counselor to keep patient information on the computer and send claims directly to a clearinghouse that will properly format and send the claim to the insurance carriers. Clearinghouses can send electronic claims to most insurance carriers. This option is one of the more expensive because of the up-front cost of the medical billing software and the additional monthly per-claim cost for sending each claim electronically.

Online billing for each insurance carrier. Some insurance carriers allow billing directly from their Web sites by setting up an account with them. Many times the clinician can also utilize eligibility information and claims tracking as well. There is no cost to this option. It is very easy to access the insurance carriers' Web sites. The counselor must be an in-network provider for this option and have access to each insurance carrier's Web page to enter claims.

Online Web sites for entering claims. Monthly agreements can be purchased to enter patient information and claims online through sites such as www.enshealth.com and www.carepaths.com. There is usually only a monthly fee, regardless of the number of claims sent. This does not require purchasing software. Instead, the counselor completes all patient information online for claims (i.e., name, address, date of birth, insurance information, etc.). This option does not offer direct patient billing or other services such as preauthorization or tracking.

Outsourcing to a medical billing service company. Third-party medical billing services can handle all billing tasks, including insurance and patient billing. The charge for this service is usually a set percentage of collections. There is no need to purchase software, upgrades, or worry about compliance issues. All claims are handled by the billing company, so the clinician needs to make sure the service chosen is reliable and thorough. One billing service that has a good reputation is NetSource Billing (www.netsourcebilling.com) and another one is NaviNet Claims (www.navinetclaims.com).

COST-EFFECTIVE STRATEGIES

SUPERBILL. A SUPERBILL is a term for a billing format for counselors who want to handle billing in a simplified manner. Using this strategy allows the client to submit the bill directly to the insurance company. This form is all the client needs to file with his or her own insurance; it takes the counselor out of the billing loop and saves money on computers, billing software, even postage. It is particularly good for the new counselor, starting on a shoestring. A superbill is usually one page. It has to contain the counselor's name, the practice name and address, phone number, date and place of service, tax ID, NPI number, state license number, checklist of Current Procedural Terminology (CPT) codes, a place to write *Diagnostic and Statistical Manual of Mental Disorders (DSM)* or *International Classification of Diseases (ICD)* diagnosis codes, the charge for service and the payment, balance due, and signature of the clinician. Any local printer can make three attached pages with NCR carbonless paper. One copy goes in the client file to keep a record of payment. Two copies are given to the client: one is a receipt for personal records, and the other can be sent to the insurance company so the client can be reimbursed by his or her insurance plan. With the superbill, the counselor can ask for payment at the time of the session and saves money by not purchasing billing software. An example of this type of form can be found in *The Complete Guide to Private Practice for Licensed Mental Health Professionals* (Walsh & Dasenbrook, 2007).

Billing software and the zip-zap office procedure. If a counselor wishes to bill the insurance company as an added service client, he or she can consider several good quality billing software programs. These all automatically print out the complete insurance billing form, called CMS-1500 or the Health Care Financing Administration (HCFA). Handwriting the HCFA (CMS-1500) billing form is no longer a viable option as one or two managed care companies no longer accept handwritten forms, and many strongly discourage this practice. From among the more popular billing software programs, the authors chose EZ Claims for personal office use. The program keeps track of bills outstanding. It also offers electronic filing for an extra cost. Others that are good are Shrinkrapt, Sum Time, and TheraManager. The consensus of counselors surveyed is that Therapist Helper is one of the best, but costly. EZ Claims, less expensive, allows the counselor to click on a date, press the Enter key, and the HCFA (CMS-1500) appears at the printer. This is done as the client writes the co-pay check and schedules the next appointment right in front of the desk. The counselor envelopes them at the end of the night and mails the bunch— zip, zap. The appointment book, the file cabinet with client folders, the billing receipts, the appointment reminder card, the computer with the HCFAs, and the printer are all within reach of the clinician's swivel chair. A handful of bills is mailed to the insurance companies at the end of the day, all labeled and printed by the software. Other billing software products not mentioned here may be also very good, and private practice billing software can easily be shopped on the Internet.

CONCLUSION

TWENTY YEARS AGO it felt like counselors were wandering in the desert, trying to find their way. There were few practice manuals to map the way. Being an entrepreneur was a foreign concept, and few counselors were trained in business.

Graduate programs were designed to teach clinical skills, not business skills. Counselors were trained primarily to work in schools or social service agencies, while psychologists, psychiatrists, and even social workers were working in private practice. At that time managed care had just entered the insurance industry and most states didn't even have licensure for counselors. The rules and regulations, ethics guidelines, and professional organizations for the professional counselor were just forming. Since then, counseling professionals have learned to deal with managed care through trial and error and have had success. All of these lessons have led to benefit and profit from managed care. By learning to use managed care, counselors are now able to help clients utilize their employee benefits to defray the cost of counseling and also make a good living in private practice. The professional mental health counselor is finally on the train.

RESOURCES

Aetna®. (2005). *We want you to know®*. Retrieved November 15, 2006, from http://www.aetna.com/provider/credentialing.html

Centers for Medicare and Medicaid Services. (2006). *National Provider Identifier Standards*. Retrieved November 15, 2006, from http://www.cms.hhs .gov/NationalProvIdentStand/

Council for Affordable Quality Healthcare. (2006). *Universal Credentialing Datasource®*. Retrieved November 15, 2006, from http://www.caqh.org/

Walsh, R. J., & Dasenbrook, N. C. (2007). *Frequently asked questions*. Retrieved April 6, 2007, from http://www.counseling-privatepractice.com/faq.php

Walsh, R. J., & Dasenbrook, N. C. (2007). *Private practice pointers*. Retrieved November 15, 2007, from http://www.counseling.org/Counselors/ PrivatePracticePointers.aspx

Zappia, D. (2007). *So you want to send claims electronically*. Retrieved April 16, 2007, from http://www.netsourcebilling.com

REFERENCE

Walsh, R. J., & Dasenbrook, N. C. (2007). *The complete guide to private practice for licensed mental health professionals* (3rd ed.). Rockford, IL: Crysand Press.

9

Computerized Practice Resource Tools

JOSHUA ROSENTHAL

THE IMPACT OF the Internet and computers on private practice is most obvious in the areas of billing and marketing. Electronic (versus paper) claim submission is a major money saver for insurance companies and the government (e.g., reducing processing fees from $6 to 50 cents per claim on average) and offers clinicians the best chance for reduced paperwork, increased cash flow, and reduced claim rejections. In terms of marketing, as patients have gravitated to the Internet for information gathering, so too have clinicians begun to market and advertise their practices online.

ELECTRONIC BILLING

THE KEY PLAYERS in electronic billing include commercial and government insurance carriers or payers, clearinghouses, and software vendors. As with paper claim submission, insurance carriers or payers (e.g., Oxford, Cigna, United Behavioral Health, Aetna, BCBS, Medicare, and Champus/Tricare) still retain the most control since they control the cash flow. In addition, payers also control the flow of patient information, such as eligibility (i.e., 270s), authorizations, electronic explanation of benefits (EOBs) or remittance advice (i.e., 835s), and claim status (i.e., 276s). Providers need this information for a host of reasons, but mostly to ensure prompt and correct payment. Since payers dictate both the flow of money and information, clearinghouses and software vendors compete for direct links into their data processing centers.

In exchange for millions in savings on administrative duties and postage, payers are slowly opening their patient data centers to allow in clearinghouses and software vendors. Whoever has the highest connectivity or direct connection with the payers will ultimately attract the most providers. Moreover, since payers don't charge for electronic billing, there is a strong demand by software vendors to bypass clearinghouses by creating direct connections between their customers (i.e., providers) and payers. One such vendor, Post-n-Track, boasts a free "secure web tunnel" with big payers such as Cigna, Oxford, and United Healthcare. However, you still need software to complete your Health Care Financing Administration (HCFA) 1500 claim forms. Naturally, clearinghouses make their money by middling providers and payers and are willing to pay top dollar for the highest payer connectivity. For example, Emdeon (formerly WebMD or Envoy) is the largest clearinghouse in the United States simply because of its connectivity and exclusive partnerships with the largest payers.

Two new features that are slowly making noise are electronic EOBs (i.e., 835s) and direct-connect claim submission (e.g., ANSI X12 837s). Instead of receiving paper EOBs by mail and then having to enter in the payment information manually, 835s can be autoposted into each patient's account. Direct-connect claim submission is a new way for providers to communicate with payers without paying to use a clearinghouse. The problem is that many clearinghouses and software vendors advertise 835s and direct connections, but very few payers actually support them. However, it is only a matter of time before the technology catches up.

Though you will rarely deal with the clearinghouses directly since their services are typically resold via software vendors, it is important to know what clearinghouses do and cost. Like automated, electronic post offices, the main functions of a clearinghouse are to format, check, and transmit your claims to and from many payers at a time. In addition, they encrypt and decrypt your claims to ensure patient information is protected according to the Health Insurance Portability and Accountability Act (HIPAA). Only two clearinghouses (OfficeAlley and ENS) allow you to submit claims online without billing software. OfficeAlley actually provides free claim submission to providers because it makes its money by charging payers (roughly 5 to 20 cents per claim). Although seemingly attractive, many payers elect not to use OfficeAlly because payers can generate more business and profit from other clearinghouses that charge software vendors and providers to submit claims electronically.

As for the rest of the big clearinghouses (e.g., Emdeon, Proxymed, THIN, GatewayEDI, Ettch, Iplexus, Claimsnet), they each offer different pricing structures and payer lists. The real worth of any clearinghouse, however, depends not only on the size of its payer list, but also on the connectivity it shares with your payers. Since electronic billing involves more than just submitting claims, one should consider not only pricing but also connectivity when choosing a clearinghouse; paying more per claim or monthly can be justified if the clearinghouse allows you to avoid countless hours on the phone verifying benefits, getting authorizations, checking claim statuses, and reviewing and in-putting EOBs.

Since mental health doesn't produce the same volume as medicine, there are fewer companies investing time and money developing soft-ware packages, and thus, fewer billing options to choose from. Besides allowing you to complete and submit a digital HCFA, billing packages often offer integrated claim tracking, note-taking, scheduling, and ac-counting features. Additional services might include autoposting of credit card payments and 835s, PDA data-syncing, remote access, and ANSI X12 direct submission.

There are generally two types of self-service billing solutions: Web-based and computer-based. Web-based programs operate through your Internet browser so there is no software to purchase or down-load. These are good if you work from more than one office or want to hire an administrative assistant to work remotely, since all your pa-tient information can be shared online via any computer with broad-band Internet access. And because the programs operate from a remote server, all patient files and claims are automatically backed up. Some programs (e.g., CarePaths and MyClientsPlus) charge a monthly fee, while others (e.g., PsyQuel) charge per claim.

Computer-based practice-management programs specific to mental health (e.g., Delphi/PBS, Helper, QuicDoc, ShrinkRapt, SumTime, The Therapist, and TheraManager) are typically sold as a base package start-ing at around $500 with different add-on modules (e.g., note-taking, scheduling, case management, electronic billing, etc.) for an extra charge. Stand-alone electronic billing programs (e.g., EZClaim) are another op-tion if you don't need a complete practice-management solution.

Whether your billing software is Web- or computer-based, make sure the support package matches your needs. Some offer free support and software upgrades, while other packages charge as much as $300 per year. Again, choose based on your needs; if you do better with a live person, paying less for only e-mail support might cost you more (i.e., in billable hours) in the end.

Now that you know the lingo, are familiar with the key players, and know how the system works, here are things to consider before purchasing a software package. First, start with the insurance companies by following links on their Web sites to provider billing resources. If they accept claims electronically, they should tell you which clearinghouses and software vendors already work with their systems, and the level of connectivity they offer. Though a good place to start, do not accept their recommendations without shopping around. Their Web sites are not always updated so newer and less expensive clearinghouses and software vendors may also work equally as well.

Second, identify those software features you need from those available. If you are completely new to third-party billing (including paper billing), choosing software may feel overwhelming. Consult with colleagues and ask about specific features and modules (e.g., note-taking, scheduler, etc.) included in the billing software, any existing relationship between the software vendor and your payers, the cost per claim for electronic versus paper claims, the number of claims you can submit per month, any setup or monthly fees, and the cost for customer or technical support or software upgrades.

Finally, make sure to test-drive the billing software demos. Nearly every software vendor will give you a free demo of its billing software to practice with. Don't pass on this opportunity or you might miss a needed feature or pay for unnecessary features.

EFFECTIVE WEB DESIGN AND INTERNET MARKETING

MORE AND MORE private practitioners are adding Web sites to their marketing programs to attract patients searching online for mental health information, which in turn can ultimately lead to new patient referrals. But just having a Web site is not enough; it must captivate visitors and have great visibility in Google and Yahoo.

When patients get a recommendation for therapy from their internist, insurance directory, family, or friends, their first instinct is to do online research to determine if it's a good match. Before initiating contact to set up the first appointment, prospective patients want to know if you provide the type of service they're looking for, if you can be trusted, if you take their insurance or how much you cost out of pocket, and if your location and availability fit with their schedule. A great Web site can answer all of these questions and much more.

Overall, effective practice Web sites include four key ingredients. First, they have a clean, captivating, and welcoming design, which includes a balance between the text and images and different pictures on each page. The text and background colors are easy to read, and there is no horizontal scrolling or blocks of highlighted text. Second, they have a simple and easy-to-use navigation system. Moving from page to page and within pages follows a predictable pattern toward making contact. Regardless of practice size, every practice Web site should strive for a simple navigation system, with commonly used pages such as Home, About Me/Us, Services, Therapy Investment, Resources, Getting Started, FAQs, and Contact. Third, effective practice Web sites include educational and informative content. Education-based marketing is the best way to increase credibility and repeat visitors with specific and relevant information, rather than outside links to associations and other Web sites. Also, short, concise paragraphs and bullets are easier to read than lengthy pages of text. Finally, effective practice Web sites have a clear call-to-action. That is, the purpose of the Web site is obvious to visitors. Do you want visitors to call you, e-mail you, or buy your book? Is your contact information and availability easily visible and current? Specificity creates desirability; consider adding specific times that visitors can call for phone consultations.

However, using your Web site as a comparison tool for outside referrals is only half the equation. Creating the most attractive, easy-to-use, and informative Web site is a waste of time and money if no one sees it, which is why understanding Internet marketing is so important. There are many direct and indirect ways to increase your Web site's visibility, including adding keyword-rich content, search engine optimization (SEO), pay-per-click (PPC) advertising, submitting online articles, and many others. The goal is to position your Web site where prospective patients and referral sources can find and use your services or products.

According to a 2002 Harris Poll survey, adults search mainly through portals or search engines rather than by going directly to particular sites (Taylor, 2002). This demonstrates the critical importance to practitioners of the need to be quickly and easily accessible through search engines and portals. According to a recent online report from Danny Sullivan (2006) of SearchEngineWatch.com, about 70% of Internet users at home and work prefer Google and Yahoo, followed by MSN (11%) and AOL (7%). This means that if you want to be noticed, you must be easily visible in Google and Yahoo Search.

During the Web site development process, it's a good idea to pay attention to search engine visibility as there are many things you can do to increase your chance for a higher ranking in the natural or manual listings (left column). Keep in mind, however, that none of these tactics alone will guarantee a top 10 ranking in Google; PPC is the only way to do that (more details below).

First, choose a domain name (or URL) that reflects your geography, services, and/or clientele, which will in turn mimic the keywords people use when searching. To minimize misspellings, try to keep the domain name at three words or less and avoid hyphens if possible. Although it is preferable, your domain name does not have to match your business name or entity. Second, title your Web site pages with relevant keywords. You'll notice these titles at the very top left of the Internet browser. Obviously, pick keywords that match what you offer on your Web site. Third, choose keywords and a description for your meta tags that accurately reflect what you offer. Keywords (20) are those that potential visitors are likely to use in searching for your services, while the description is a brief synopsis (20 words) of your Web site that will be used in your search engine listings. Fourth, try to use lots of keyword-rich text throughout your Web site, and especially in the first 30 words on each page. For instance, if you specialize in working with traumatic brain injury (TBI) patients, make sure to have *TBI* and *traumatic brain injury* as text, not images, throughout your Web site. Adding relevant articles to your Web site to increase its size is also helpful. Fifth, since Google and Yahoo prefer Web sites with lots of external links, you could list links to several Web sites in your Additional Information section, and/or offer to exchange links with colleagues and associations. However, this could lead prospective patients astray, so be conscientious about tracking visitor browsing habits with your Web site traffic reports. Finally, for those with Web design skills, Google Help provides additional tips to make your Web site more search robot friendly, which can boost your rankings.

Once your Web site is completed, the next step is to submit it to the search engines for listing approval. To get your Web site in their natural search results, you can either wait for their search robot to find your Web site, or you can submit it manually for free by using their Submit/Suggest a Site link. It's also a good idea to apply for a listing in their directories, since their directories feed their search results. Yahoo charges $299 to be listed in its directory, but Google's directory (dmoz .org) is free to join. For a small fee ($25–$75), most designers will submit your Web site for you using special software that speeds up your listing approval time and gets your Web site into more directories.

The only two direct ways to increase your Web site's visibility in Google and Yahoo are SEO and PPC. The first, SEO, refers to Web site programming tactics and strategies designed to trick the search engines into ranking your Web site higher than it would be naturally. Professionals who offer this type of service typically charge an initial fee to perform keyword research and several hundred dollars a month, with a 6-month so-called soft guarantee that your Web site will be listed on the first page of Google and Yahoo. The guarantee is not definitive because many of the factors and variables used in SEO change daily according to keyword demand and tactics used by competitors. Overall, SEO can be expensive initially but tends to produce better long-term results.

Unlike SEO, which can take many months to show results, PPC can get your Web site ranked number one (in the top and right column) in Google within hours. Google's program is called Google Adwords and Yahoo's version is called Local/Sponsored Search. Both PPC programs allow you to bid on particular keywords based on popularity and demand by competitors. Each time a visitor searches with your keyword and clicks thru to your Web site, you pay for the click. The best part about PPC is that you have complete control of your advertising budget and can easily track your return on investment (ROI), not to mention select keywords only for your particular location (e.g., child therapist New York). However, there is always the risk that you will pay for clicks that do not result in new business. If you don't want to spend the time doing keyword research or monitoring your account, consider hiring a professional.

Due to the high volume and rate that search engines pull information from directories and online news sources, one of the best ways to increase Web site traffic is to submit online articles. If your target is other mental health professionals, try submitting articles to mental health trade publications with online counterparts, such as *Counselor Magazine, Psychotherapy Networker*, and *National Psychologist*. Sometimes if they won't run your article in their print or online magazine, they will offer you a spot in their online newsletter or e-zine. If you want to market to the general public, try online health portals such as WebMD.com, PsychologyToday.com, Prevention.com, MedicalNewsToday.com, and NYTimes.com. Another way to submit your articles is to use an online PR service, such as Prweb.com, Ezinearticles.com, or Webwire.com. These services range in cost from $10–$619 per submission, but another PR service, Goarticles.com, is free. Knowing how to write the right article for the right news source at the right time is only half the battle; you also need to be persistent and skillful at building relationships with editors and journalists.

In addition to SEO, PPC, and submitting articles, there are several other ways to increase your Web site traffic and online exposure. First, purchase several domains and forward them to your main Web site using a 302 permanent forward and add the proper keywords and description in the domain setup. As with the initial domain selection during the design phase, choose additional domain names or URLs that include keywords relevant to your geography, services, and/or clientele. One domain for your name and one that describes your practice tends to work well. Second, try to use your hosted e-mail account (e.g., JRosenthal@TherapyMatch.com) as much as possible, especially when responding to Web site inquiries or posting to Listservs or on-line groups. Not only does it appear more professional and help with branding, it's a mini advertisement for your Web site. Third, add your Web site to your e-mail signature so that every e-mail you send has your contact information and Web site at the bottom. Also, add your Web site to all your print marketing materials (e.g., business card, brochure, etc.). Fourth, send an e-mail announcement about your Web site and practice to friends, family, and colleagues. You'd be surprised how often a friend of a friend in need of your services will eventually find his or her way to your Web site and initiate contact. Fifth, if you have the time and material, start your own blog (Web log) via Blogger.com. Not only is it free, but it's one of today's fastest-growing ways to spread your word (Walker, 2006) and build credibility as an expert in virtually any industry. Plus, blogs are heavily responsible for feeding search engines and great for redirecting visitors to your Web site. Sixth, develop an e-zine or online newsletter. This can be done for free via your hosting plan by adding a subscription box to your Web site and using the group e-mail program. E-zines are great for maintaining ongoing contact with Web site visitors. Seventh, add real simple syndication (RSS) feeds to your Web site as a way of attracting visitors and boosting search engine rankings. The RSS allows you to display information from other Web sites in real-time, such as the latest mental health news and research. However, as previously mentioned, adding outside links can work against your intended course of contact and inhibit visitors from calling. Eighth, join online patient referral directories, such as psychologytoday.com, which for a small fee will allow you to advertise your practice. Ninth, join online groups, message boards, and Listservs via state associations and local community groups. You can find them by searching in Yahoo and Google groups.

CONCLUSION

USING COMPUTERS AND the Internet in your practice can save tremendous amounts of time and money, especially in the areas of billing and marketing. If you plan to work with third-party payers, you will eventually need to familiarize yourself with electronic billing. Though it can seem daunting at first, the advantages dramatically outweigh the hassles of choosing a billing system. As with any solid marketing plan, diversification offers the best opportunity to increase your exposure and reach new clientele. While your Web site will increase exposure directly from the Internet, additional practice-building tactics (e.g., writing articles, presenting, networking, etc.) should also be included in your marketing plan. The fact that you are interested in Web sites and Internet marketing means that you are headed in the right direction. In the past, clinicians believed they could launch and grow their practice without marketing. However, due to increasing competition among disciplines and decreasing reimbursement rates from insurance companies, the Internet is becoming increasingly popular among mental health professionals as a viable and cost-effective practice-building resource.

REFERENCES

Sullivan, D. (2006, January 24). *Nielsen NetRatings search engine ratings.* Retrieved August 5, 2005, from http://searchenginewatch.com/reports/article.php/2156451http://searchenginewatch.com/reports/article.php/2156451

Taylor, H. (2002). Cyberchondriacs update. *Harris Interactive–The Harris Poll.* Retrieved June 28, 2005, from http://www.harrisinteractive.com/harris_poll/index.asp?PID=299

Walker, L. (2006, April 4). New trends in online traffic. *Washingtonpost.com.* Retrieved June 7, 2006, from http://www.washingtonpost.com/wp-dyn/content/article/2006/04/03/AR2006040301692.html

10

Managing Risk in Ethical and Legal Situations

Vilia M. Tarvydas and Sara P. Johnston

Marjorie Stevens (not her real name) works as a counselor for a mental health office in a small Midwestern city of approximately 35,000 people. Marjorie has been licensed in her state as a mental health counselor for 11 years. She is also a Certified Rehabilitation Counselor (CRC) and a National Certified Counselor (NCC). After a particularly tough day at work, she arrives home to find a letter in her mailbox from the state's Department of Professional Licensure. Her heart skips a beat as she begins to read. The letter informs her that the department is investigating an ethics complaint by one of her clients. The client reported that Marjorie gave the client advice on the treatment of a skin care condition (psoriasis) and sold the client skin care products during the time that the client also was receiving counseling services from Marjorie at the mental health office. The complaint goes on to state that Marjorie rented an apartment in a building she owns to the client's stepdaughter. The client's stepdaughter was behind on rent by several months, and the client reported that Marjorie asked the client during a counseling session about the stepdaughter's finances. The client stated that Marjorie requested that the client encourage her stepdaughter to bring her rent current. The complaint also states that Marjorie disclosed her professional relationship with the client to the client's stepdaughter. The stepdaughter was previously unaware that the client was seeking treatment for mental health issues from Marjorie. The complaint alleges that Marjorie has engaged in unprofessional conduct. Specifically, (1) Marjorie benefited financially from the counseling relationship with a client and a client's family member, contrary to accepted professional practices; (2) Marjorie disclosed client information to a person outside of the mental health agency without the client's written permission to disclose such information, contrary to accepted professional practices; and (3) Marjorie operated outside the scope of her practice by giving the client advice on a medical condition, contrary to accepted professional practices. The complaint states that Marjorie must contact the department to respond to the allegations, and bring with her all records pertaining to the client.

WHAT SHOULD MARJORIE do next? Understandably, a counselor who receives an ethics complaint from his or her state licensing board may feel a wide range of emotions, including fear, anger, confusion, betrayal, and sadness. However, it is important that the counselor refrain from acting on emotion or impulse. Rather, before responding to the complaint, the counselor should become as informed about the situation as possible, including learning what his or her rights and responsibilities are in such situations (Koocher & Keith-Spiegel, 1998a; Remley & Herlihy, 2007).

This chapter provides counselors with guidance on responding to ethics complaints. It begins with information on ethical complaints and the complaint process. Next, it provides guidance on how to respond to a complaint. The chapter ends with advice on how to minimize risk with the goal of avoiding the complaint process altogether.

ETHICAL COMPLAINTS

THE PRIMARY GOAL of state licensure boards, accreditation and certification agencies, as well as professional organizations is the protection of the public. This protection serves both counselors and clients. For example, state licensure boards ensure that persons holding themselves out as counselors have the appropriate experience and training to engage in counseling activities properly (professional title and practice protection for counselors); and that properly trained counselors provide services to clients in a safe and ethical manner, protecting clients from harm (American Counseling Association [ACA], 2008; Cottone & Tarvydas, 2007; Remley & Herlihy, 2007; Welfel, 2006). National certification agencies, such as the National Board for Certified Counselors (NBCC) and the Commission on Rehabilitation Counselor Certification (CRCC; Commission on Rehabilitation Counselor Certification [CRCC], 2001), and professional organizations, such as the American Counseling Association (ACA), have developed mandatory codes of ethics that outline the components of ethical practice. All organization members or certificants must follow the code of ethics or be subject to sanctions that range from formal investigation by the organization to referral to state licensure officials for disciplinary action (for current versions of professional codes of ethics, see the ACA, www.counseling.org; the NBCC, http://www.nbcc.org/; and the CRCC, http://www.crccertification.com/). For example, professional organizations that receive an ethical complaint involving sexual or other abuse of a client are mandated to report the complaint to the counselor's state licensing board. The licensing board then will refer the matter to the state department of justice for civil or criminal prosecution (National Board for Certified Counselors [NBCC], 2007; Remley & Herlihy, 2007).

Number and types of complaints. It is important for counselors to note that formal ethics complaints, such as the one received by Marjorie from her state licensing board, are a relatively uncommon experience in the field of counseling. For example, it is estimated than less than 1% of licensed counselors have ever been the subject of an ethics complaint to a state board (Neukrug, Milliken, & Walden, 2001). Similarly, professional organizations, such as the ACA, report that although it has upward of 60,000 members, the organization received just 12 complaints for the year 2002–2003 (Welfel, 2006), and 6 concerning members for the year 2006–2007 (Sanabria & Freeman, 2008).

Counselor misperceptions. Counselors tend to worry more about malpractice or civil tort lawsuits. In reality counselors more often are investigated by their state licensure boards or professional organizations than they are sued in civil or criminal court (Welfel, 2006). Another misconception involves the most common types of ethical complaints. When asked to name the most common ethical complaint, most counselors will answer sexual or other abuse. However, research shows that the most common ethical complaints against counselors involve boundary issues, such as personal or financial relationships with clients that are not therapeutic in nature. Another common ethical complaint involves poor or incomplete record keeping (Caudill, 1985a, 1985b).

Exposure to risk. Information about complaints filed suggests that practicing counselors do not need to worry unnecessarily about being the subject of an ethics complaint. However, it is important to note that many authorities suggest that the number of ethical violations is much higher than what is reported to state licensing boards and professional organizations (Welfel, 2006). This phenomenon may be because clients do not know their rights, do not know how to file a complaint, or, alternatively, choose not to file a complaint because they fear repercussions (Welfel, 2006). Also, counselors may engage in unethical behavior for a wide range of reasons, some of which can affect even the most well-intentioned practitioner, exposing them to ethicolegal risk. Reasons noted by Wheeler and Bertram (2008) include intentional disregard, unintentional disregard (e.g., being innocently unaware or lazy), and being in the wrong place at the wrong time.

THE COMPLAINT PROCESS

Is there any way that Marjorie could have seen the risk and pre-vented it? Alternatively, what if Marjorie saw the risk and chose to do nothing about it? Finally, how can Marjorie better manage professional risk in her practice so she can avoid being in this situation again?

Ware (1971) states that counselors should neither look to the law as a way to solve complex professional dilemmas nor should counselors develop an overly cautious or fearful approach to the law. Rather, counselors should seek a balance of knowledge of and respect for the law. Knowledge of the law may assist counselors in avoiding potential legal issues, increase their awareness of potential legal conflicts, and promote better understanding of the appropriate response to legal situations (Cottone & Tarvydas, 2007). "Although counselors are not expected to have advanced legal knowledge, they are obligated to have basic knowledge of their own state statutes and case law related to their profession" (Cottone & Tarvydas, 2007, p. 51). Indeed, it is a wise counselor who knows that a code of ethics is a minimum standard that governs his or her practice, and follows not only that code of ethics but also is familiar with the rules and statutes that govern counseling practice in the state and municipality in which he or she resides. The *ACA Code of Ethics* has been adopted in 19 states that license counselors (ACA, 2008), and it is widely considered to be the primary source of ethical standards for the counseling profession to be supplemented by other codes that relate to the specific practice in which the counselor is engaged.

Definitions. One way that counselors can improve their knowledge of the law and how it affects the counseling profession is to become familiar with the language of ethical complaints, including legal terminology or so-called legalese. The next section of the chapter will provide a brief overview of some of the more common ethical and legal terms counselors may encounter in ethical complaints.

Often one of the most confusing concepts for counselors is *credentialing*. A credential simply indicates that a counselor's education and experience has been reviewed by a professional or legal body, and he or she can legitimately hold himself or herself out as a professional possessing specific knowledge and skills that meet the minimum standards of the profession (Remley & Herlihy, 2007). There are many types of credentials. Some are *mandatory*, meaning a counselor must possess the credential in order to practice legally as a counselor; to practice in a specific setting, such as a school; or to work with a specific diagnosis, such as substance abuse. Other types of credentials are optional or *voluntary*, which means that a counselor is not required to possess the credential in order to practice legally as a counselor (Remley & Herlihy, 2007). Voluntary credentials include certification by certification bodies, such as the NBCC and the CRCC.

Marjorie holds several types of credentials. First, she is a graduate of an accredited master's degree program. *Accreditation* is a process whereby a master's program adheres to specific educational and training standards set by an accreditation board. The master's degree program Marjorie graduated from is accredited by both the Council for Accreditation of Counseling and Related Educational Programs (CACREP), which is an affiliate of the ACA, and the Council on Rehabilitation Education (CORE).

Second, she is a licensed mental health counselor in her state, which is a mandatory credential required by the state in which she lives and the setting in which she practices, a mental health center. Each state sets its own education, experience, and testing requirements for licensure as a counselor. Finally, Marjorie is also a Certified Rehabilitation Counselor (CRC) and a National Certified Counselor (NCC). The CRC and NCC credentials are both voluntary credentials. They were granted to Marjorie by the two national certification bodies (NBCC and CRCC) after a review of her education, experience, and her score on a required national credentialing exam (Remley & Herlihy, 2007). Unlike state licensure, which is valid only in the state in which the license was granted, voluntary national certification is valid across the entire nation. National certification agencies use the same education, experience, and testing requirements for all counselors regardless of the state in which they practice (Remley & Herlihy, 2007).

A helpful tool in understanding the relationships among the various credentialing bodies is the Governance Pyramid (see Figure 10.1).

The complaint Marjorie received was from her state licensure board, not from one of the national certification bodies. This means the outcome of the complaint process will impact her state licensure credential. This particular complaint may or may not impact her two national certification credentials depending on whether she is found to be guilty of a serious enough ethical violation to merit informing these bodies and/or the state board is empowered to notify these bodies of the sanctions after the adjudicatory process is complete.

Perhaps the most important term relevant to legal proceedings as applied to the counseling profession is the term *competence*. In order to ensure the safety and well-being of their clients, counselors must possess the necessary education, skills, and diligence needed to work effectively with clients in a therapeutic relationship (Cottone & Tarvydas, 2007; Welfel, 2006).

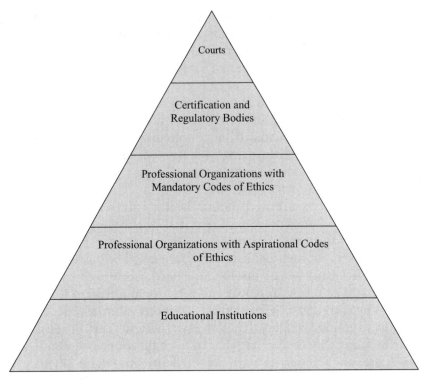

FIGURE 10.1 Ethicolegal governance system for counseling.
From "Ethics," by V. M. Tarvydas, 2004, in *Handbook of Rehabilitation Counseling,*
edited by T. F. Riggar and D. R. Maki, New York: Springer Publishing. Copyright 2004 by
V. M. Tarvydas. Reprinted with permission.

Working with clients within a specific knowledge and experience base is known as practicing within one's *scope of practice.* Counselors who practice within their scope of practice limit their exposure to legal complaints (Cottone & Tarvydas, 2007). In the case example at the beginning of the chapter, Marjorie has been charged with practicing outside her scope of practice by providing medical advice to a client. Professional organizations (ACA), licensing boards (individual states), and national certification bodies (CRCC, NBCC) and accreditation agencies (CACREP, CORE) define the scope of practice for counseling in general. The scope of practice is a written statement that outlines the knowledge and skills that define the counseling profession and the practice of counseling. The scope of a *specialty practice,* such as mental health and school counseling, is defined by state licensing and credentialing bodies, as well as professional organizations governing the particular specialty (Cottone & Tarvydas, 2007; Nystul, 2006; Remley & Herlihy, 2007).

Counselors should also be familiar with how their particular states define the scope of counseling practice within their own *jurisdictions,* or, in other words, their particular geographic locations (Garner, 2005). Counselors can find their state's laws governing counseling practice within their individual state's licensure laws. These laws are often adopted from national professional counseling organizations (ACA, 2008). Each state may add rules or statutes for its own purposes, for example, a rule to prohibit falsifying information on an application. The ACA has published a manual titled *Licensure Requirements for Professional Counselors* (2008), which provides contact information for each state's licensure board, as well as information on professional associations, scope of practice, and insurance reimbursement.

RESPONDING TO THE COMPLAINT

B ECAUSE OF THE risk of harm that incompetent practice poses to clients, counselors are held to high standards by the law. There are four legal entities that regulate the practice of counseling: (1) professional ethics committees; (2) state licensure boards; (3) criminal courts; and (4) civil courts (Pope & Vasquez, 1998). Professional ethics committees and state licensure boards have been discussed in the previous section. This section will explain the court system briefly as it applies to ethical complaints in counseling (for extended information see Wheeler & Bertram, 2008).

The laws that govern citizens of the United States can be divided into four types, or levels, of law. The first is U.S. constitutional law, which was codified into the Constitution by the country's founders and can be changed only by a U.S. Supreme Court decision and/or ratification by a majority of the 50 states. The second level of law is federal law, which governs national policies, such as Social Security. The third and fourth levels of law are state and local, and it is these levels that most affect the practice of counseling (Remley & Herlihy, 2007). As mentioned in the first section of the chapter, counselors are licensed to practice by their individual states, and there may be variations from state to state in the way counseling practice is defined. State statutes set forth the scope of practice for counseling within any given jurisdiction (Cottone & Tarvydas, 2007). At the local level, counselors need to be familiar with their individual city or county rules and regulations, as these typically govern agency funding and administrative decisions. Each of the four levels of law has a court system associated with it. The U.S. Supreme Court and the 89 federal district courts (http://www.uscourts.gov) are responsible for the Constitutional and federal levels of law. Counselors will not typically have dealings with these courts on an individual level; however, counselors must be familiar with relevant federal court decisions that may affect their counseling practice, such as *Tarasoff v. Regents of the University of California* (17 Cal. 3d 425, 551 P.2d 334, 131 Cal. Rptr. 14 [Cal. 1976]). Federal courts have defined the duty to protect individuals who may be in danger due to threats made by a client through the record *Tarasoff* and other related cases have established through subsequent case law (Cottone & Tarvydas, 2007). In general, it is the state and local courts that may become involved if a counselor receives an ethical complaint.

Counselors should also be familiar with the two types of laws: *criminal* and *civil*. Criminal law involves the relationship between citizens and the government. Criminal law encompasses the regulations citizens within a jurisdiction are expected to follow. For example, there are federal and state laws that prohibit citizens from speeding or robbing banks. An example pertaining to counseling practice is that counselors are prohibited by many states from engaging in sexual relationships with clients. In a criminal case, the governmental body (federal, state, or local) will bring a legal action against a citizen breaking the law (Cottone & Tarvydas, 2007), and penalties may include imprisonment.

Civil law, in contrast, encompasses the relationship between citizens of a particular jurisdiction (federal, state, or local). A civil case involves a legal dispute between citizens. A court may fix, or *remedy*, the dispute by awarding money, or other forms of *compensation*, to the citizen whom the court judges to have been wronged or harmed by the dispute. It is the responsibility of the person who did the harm to pay the compensation to the wronged person. For example, the so-called wrong can be a failure to do something, such as failure to pay rent, in the case of a landlord versus a tenant. In the case of a client versus a counselor, the wrong is termed *malpractice*. There are four parts or elements of a malpractice claim that must be proven before a counselor can be charged with malpractice (either civilly or criminally):

1. The counselor and the client have entered into a *professional relationship* with one another, and as a result, the counselor owes the client a duty of care.
2. The counselor *fails in this duty of care* either as the result of negligent or substandard care.
3. The client is either physically or materially *harmed* by this care.
4. The conduct of the counselor was the *proximate cause* of the harm or injury to the client (Cottone & Tarvydas, pp. 51–52).

The first two elements are known as *negligence*; in other words, engaging in behavior you should not have engaged in, or not behaving in a way you should have behaved. The second two elements require that the negligence be the proximate cause of the harm; in other words, the behavior of the counselor can be shown to have caused the harm to the client (Welfel, 2006).

Although counselors typically are very concerned about being found guilty of malpractice, in reality it can be quite difficult to prove all four elements of a malpractice case. In Marjorie's case, the complaint would most likely take the form of an ethics violation rather than a malpractice claim because it appears that all four of the elements would be difficult to prove.

The formal complaint process. Marjorie should read the complaint thoroughly in order to understand what it is charging her with and what is expected of her. Any complaint brings with it the Constitutional *right to due process.* This right simply means that Marjorie, or any other counselor charged with malpractice, has the right to be treated fairly by the court system, including the right to notice of the charge and the basis for the charge; the right to an attorney; the right to present evidence in his or her defense and to question witnesses for the opposing side; and the right to receive a written decision. In addition, Marjorie should thoroughly review the complaint and respond to the complaint in an appropriate manner (see Table 10.1).

Informal complaints and ethical dilemmas. Counselors may receive complaints that never rise to the formal level, yet must still be resolved. How does a counselor resolve a complaint informally, either within his or her employment setting or within the counselor–client relationship? There are many ethical dilemmas that arise in counseling practice that never rise to the formal or informal complaint level, yet must be resolved so that the counselor may continue to provide competent counseling services to clients (Cottone & Tarvydas, 2007; Welfel, 2005). Counselors can resolve informal complaints through the use of an ethical decision-making model.

Ethical decision-making models. There are many ethical decision-making models to which counselors can refer for help in resolving informal complaints and ethical dilemmas that arise in counseling practice (see, for example, Cottone & Tarvydas, 2007; Remley & Herlihy, 2007; Welfel, 2006). Counselors are encouraged to review the suggested references and choose a model that is a good fit for them individually and within their particular practice setting. All ethical decision-making models contain the following five components:

1. Determine whether there is an ethical issue that needs to be addressed.
2. Determine if there is a conflict between two ethical principles (e.g., autonomy and justice).

TABLE 10.1 Guidelines for Responding to an Ethical or Legal Complaint

A. What is the source of the complaint?

1. Who is the complaint from? A state licensing board or a professional organization?
2. Is it an inquiry or a charge?
3. How clear is the complaint (explanation of allegations)?
4. Have all documents related to the complaint or inquiry been provided?

B. How do I proceed in a professional manner?

1. Maintain a professional demeanor at all times; refrain from becoming emotional and upset.
2. Notify your employer immediately.
3. Notify your professional liability insurance carrier immediately.
4. Do not contact the complainant directly.
5. Obtain consultation from peers.
6. Determine whether an attorney should be contacted.
7. Know how to find an attorney. Contact the American Bar Association, http://www .abanet.org/. (Note: The professional liability insurance offered to ACA members will provide legal counsel to policyholders accused of an ethics or legal violation.)
8. If you decide to retain the services of an attorney, follow your attorney's advice.

C. How do I respond to the complaint?

1. Assess the credibility of the charge(s) (e.g., are they accurate?).
2. Review all notes and documentation that will assist you in responding to the charges.
3. Respond personally or through an attorney to the charge.
4. If you hire an attorney, do not respond until your attorney reviews your response.
5. Limit the scope of your response and respond only to the charges contained within the complaint.
6. Interpret the events; provide your account.
7. Provide documentation.
8. Provide mitigating circumstances.
9. If you don't dispute the charge, begin remediation activities.
10. Determine what discipline or sanctions may be appropriate.
11. Know your right of appeal.

D. How do I take care of myself and prevent this from happening again?

1. Seek emotional support from friends, colleagues, and family members, but do not discuss details of the case with them.
2. Seek professional counseling if you believe the legal dispute is negatively affecting your ability to work effectively with your clients.
3. If you are guilty of an ethics breach, seek help from professional counseling, continuing education programs, and/or additional supervision or consultation to prevent future ethics breaches.

Note. Adapted from Koocher & Keith-Spiegel, 1998b; *Ethical, Legal, and Professional Issues in Counseling* (2nd ed.), by T. P. Remley & B. Herlihy, 2007. Upper Saddle River, NJ: Pearson Education; *Ethics in Counseling and Psychotherapy: Standards, Research, and Emerging Issues* (3rd ed.), by E. R. Welfel, 2006. Belmont, CA: Thomson Brooks/Cole.

3. Address contextual issues (e.g., sources of potential bias).
4. Formulate a plan of action.
5. Implement the plan of action (Nystul, 2006).

PREVENTION AND MAINTENANCE

Is THERE ANY way Marjorie could have seen the risk and avoided it? What if Marjorie did see the risk but did nothing to prevent it? Ethicolegal risk anticipation, assessment, and management are prominent in more modern ethical standards (e.g., the *ACA Code of Ethics*) and practices.

It is important for counselors to practice good ethics hygiene to minimize the chances of being involved in an ethical or legal complaint. There several ways counselors can practice good ethics hygiene. First, counselors should obtain professional training, certification, and licensure; become members of professional organizations; and complete continuing education coursework to update and maintain their clinical practice skills (Welfel, 2006). Second, counselors must become familiar with the laws and codes of ethics that govern their practice. Counselors should review their codes of ethics, so that if they are charged with an ethics or legal violation, they are familiar with necessary documentation procedures. Working knowledge of an ethical decision-making model also ensures that counselors address ethical dilemmas promptly and in a consistent manner (Cottone & Tarvydas, 2007; Welfel, 2006). Third, counselors should apply for and keep current a professional liability insurance policy. Many professional organizations, including the ACA, offer professional liability insurance that will provide legal counsel to members accused of an ethics or legal violation (note: insurance will not cover complaints with a felony component, such as sexual or other abuse of a client; Remley & Herlihy, 2007). Fourth, counselors should consult with peers on ethical dilemmas (Welfel, 2006).

Finally, counselors must be vigilant for the signs of burnout or compassion fatigue and practice self-care to ensure that they are not practicing in an impaired state that may harm clients (Cottone & Tarvydas, 2007; Welfel, 2006). The warning signs of burnout include fatigue, lack of empathy, loss of enthusiasm, substance abuse, withdrawal, and isolation. In addition, many clinicians who work with clients who have experienced trauma or who are in crisis may face an additional risk for burnout. Further, counselors who are experiencing a high level of stress in their own lives may inadvertently place clients at risk for harm due to their inability to focus on the client's issues (Welfel, 2005). Welfel (2005) proposes a model to assist counselors in monitoring their well-being and taking responsibility for mistakes before they rise to the level of a formal ethics or legal violation. These steps include (1) acknowledgment of the violation of a professional standard; (2) recognizing that a mistake has been made and engaging in actions to mitigate the mistake; (3) engaging in a process of self-evaluation to ensure that the mistake does not happen again.

RESOURCES

American Counseling Association Code of Ethics: http://www.counseling.org/Resources/CodeOfEthics/TP/Home/CT2.aspx

Brazelon: http://www.bazelon.com

Center for the Study of Ethics in the Professions, Illinois Institute of Technology: http://www.iit.edu/libraries/csep/codes/

Council on Licensure, Enforcement, and Regulation (CLEAR): http://www.clearhq.com

Federation of Associations of Regulatory Bodies (FARB): http://www.farb.org/mc/page.doc

Findlaw: http://www.findlaw.com

Ken Pope, PhD (general ethics, licensing, and practice information): http://kspope.com/ethcodes/index.php

MegaLaw: http://www.megalaw.com

REFERENCES

American Counseling Association. (2008). *Licensure requirements for professional counselors.* Alexandria, VA: Author.

Caudill, B. (1985a). *Malpractice and licensing pitfalls for therapists: A defense attorney's list.* Retrieved March 12, 2006, from http://www.kspope.com/ethics/malpractice.php

Caudill, O. B. (1985b). Risk management for psychotherapists: Avoiding the pitfalls. In L. VandeCreek & T. L. Jackson (Eds.), *Innovations in clinical practice: A source book* (vol. 20, pp. 391–395). Sarasota, FL: Professional Resource Press.

Commission on Rehabilitation Counselor Certification. (2001). *Code of professional ethics.* Retrieved December 1, 2007, from http://www.crccertification.com/pages/30code.html

Cottone, R. R., & Tarvydas, V. M. (2007). *Counseling ethics and decision making* (3rd ed.). Upper Saddle River, NJ: Merrill/Prentice-Hall.

Garner, B. A. (2005). *Black's law dictionary* (8th ed.). St Paul, MN: West.

Koocher, G. P., & Keith-Spiegel, P. (1998a). Guide to dealing with licensing board and ethics complaints. In G. P. Koocher, J. C. Norcress, &

S. S. Hill, III (Eds.), *Psychologists' desk reference* (pp. 434–442). New York: Oxford University Press.

Koocher, G. P., & Keith-Spiegel, P. (1998b). *Ethics in psychology: Professional standards and cases* (2nd ed.). New York: Oxford University Press.

National Board for Certified Counselors. (2007). *NBCC ethics information.* Retrieved December 1, 2007, from http://www.nbcc.org/ethics2

Neukrug, E. S., Milliken, T., & Walden, S. (2001). Ethics complaints against credentialed counselors: An updated survey of state licensing boards. *Counselor Education and Supervision, 41,* 57–70.

Nystul, M. S. (2006). *Introduction to counseling: An art and science perspective* (3rd ed.). Boston: Allyn & Bacon.

Pope, K., & Vasquez, M. J. T. (1998). *Ethics in psychology and counseling* (2nd ed.). San Francisco: Jossey-Bass.

Remley, T. P., & Herlihy, B. (2007). *Ethical, legal, and professional issues in counseling* (2nd ed.). Upper Saddle River, NJ: Pearson Education.

Sanabria, S., & Freeman, L. (2008). Report of the ACA Ethics Committee: 2006–2007. *Journal of Counseling and Development, 86,* 249–252.

Tarvydas, V. M. (2004). Ethics. In T. F. Riggar & D. R. Maki (Eds.), *Handbook of rehabilitation counseling* (pp. 108–170). New York: Springer Publishing.

Ware, M. L. (1971). The law and counselor ethics. *Personnel and Guidance Journal, 50,* 305–310.

Welfel, E. R. (2005). Accepting fallibility: A model for personal responsibility for nonegregious ethics infractions. *Counseling and Values, 49,* 121–131.

Welfel, E. R. (2006). *Ethics in counseling and psychotherapy: Standards, research, and emerging issues* (3rd ed.). Belmont, CA: Thomson Brooks/Cole.

Wheeler, A. M., & Bertram, B. (2008). *The counselor and the law: A guide to legal and ethical practice* (5th ed.). Alexandria, VA: American Counseling Association.

11

Professional Disclosure in Counseling

Lloyd R. Goodwin, Jr.

> Informed consent involves the right of clients to be informed about their therapy and to make autonomous decisions pertaining to it. (Corey, Corey, & Callanan, 2007, p. 156)

THE AMERICAN COUNSELING Association's (ACA, 2005) *Code of Ethics,* section A.2.a on informed consent, states the following:

> Clients have the freedom to choose whether to enter into or remain in a counseling relationship and need adequate information about the counseling process and the counselor. Counselors have an obligation to review in writing and verbally with clients the rights and responsibilities of both the counselor and the client. Informed consent is an ongoing part of the counseling process, and counselors appropriately document discussions of informed consent throughout the counseling relationship. (p. 4)

Professional disclosure statements disclose to clients the nature and boundaries of the counseling relationship they are about to enter. The written statement indicating that the client has been fully informed about the counseling relationship is signed by both the client and the counselor. "Disclosure statements are also legal contracts" (Remley & Herlihy, 2005, p. 81).

The types of information that ethically need to be spelled out in the written disclosure statement to secure informed consent are listed in the *ACA Code of Ethics* (2005) in section A.2.b:

> They [counselors] inform clients about issues such as, but not limited to, the following: purposes, goals, techniques, procedures, limitations, potential risks, and benefits of services; the counselor's qualifications, credentials, and relevant experience; continuation of services upon the incapacitation or death of a counselor; and other pertinent information. Counselors take steps to ensure that clients understand the implications of diagnosis, the intended use of tests and reports, fees, and billing arrangements. Clients have the right to confidentiality and to be provided with an explanation of its limitations (including how supervisors and/or treatment team professionals are involved); to obtain clear information about their records; to participate in the ongoing counseling plans; and to refuse any services or modality change and to be advised of the consequences of such refusal. (p. 4)

All states' counselor licensure boards have their own requirements for topics to include in professional disclosure statements, and these may vary slightly from the standards in the *ACA Code of Ethics* (2005).

ADDITIONAL TOPICS

IN ADDITION TO the elements listed in the code, other topics may be addressed to more fully explain the nature of counseling and the counselor's approach to counseling, which and avoid misunderstandings that may prevent potential lawsuits. These topics include the counselor's qualifications and credentials, including relevant degrees, licenses and certifications, areas of specialization, and experiences; theoretical orientation and types of techniques used; whether the counselor is a practicum student or intern; length and frequency of sessions, fees for each type of service provided (e.g., assessments, individual, group, marital, family, court appearances, consultations), and methods of payment accepted; policies for cancelling appointments, fees for cancelled sessions and telephone counseling sessions, and changes in fees; information regarding the benefits and limitations of treatment and sharing of client information under his or her insurance or managed care; the nature of relationships with referral sources, especially mandated services from the criminal justice system; the nature of information shared with parents or legal guardians when working with minors; procedures for contacting the counselor or a mental health crisis service in between sessions; information about alternatives to counseling such as mutual-help groups (e.g., Alcoholics Anonymous); a statement about supervision and colleague consultation, including the supervisor's qualifications, taped client sessions, and the way client information will be handled; potential implications of a mental disorder diagnosis such as stigma and denial of security clearance at certain jobs; coverage for interruptions in counseling such as vacations and illness; termination procedures; and the way to contact a supervisor, the state counselor licensure board, or professional associations to register a complaint against the counselor.

Minor children and vulnerable adults. "Counselors who provide services to minors and to others who lack legal competency must pay attention to the legal rights of parents and guardians" (Remley & Herlihy, 2005, p. 193). Because of their legal status in our society, children are not able to enter into contracts and technically do not have the right to consent to counseling. Their parents or legal guardians have the right to consent for them. Some states have statutes allowing minor children to seek counseling for special issues related to birth control, venereal disease, pregnancy and abortion, outpatient mental health services, or substance abuse treatment without the consent of a parent or legal guardian (Cottone & Tarvydas, 2007; Remley & Herlihy, 2005). Except in these cases, parents or legal guardians may have the right to know what occurs in counseling, and they may request termination of counseling at any time. The minor should be informed that what is discussed in counseling can be shared with the parent or legal guardian. Some counselors attempt to get parents or legal guardians to agree that they will respect the minor's right to confidentiality even though this may not be upheld legally (Cottone & Tarvydas, 2007). "The privacy rights of minor clients legally belong to their parents or guardians" (Remley & Herlihy, 2005, p. 195). "Emancipated minors, who are under the age of 18 but live separately from their parents, manage their own finances, and have been adjudicated legally emancipated by a judge, can enter into a contract for counseling" (Remley & Herlihy, 2005, p. 195).

Counselors should realize that any time they decide to withhold information from a parent, they assume responsibility if that information later leads to injuries for the client (Remley & Herlihy, 2005). It is prudent for counselors to assure parents at the beginning of the counseling relationship with their child that the counselor is concerned about their children's safety and best interests and will inform them if the child is in danger. Examples of potentially injurious behavior include certain types and methods of using psychoactive substances, engaging in unsafe and unprotected sexual activity, engaging in criminal activity, and other risky behaviors. As Remley and Herlihy (2005) point out, "To avoid situations in which parents demand information and minor clients refuse to authorize you to provide it, it is wise to have a thorough understanding with all parties regarding the issue of confidentiality before the counseling relationship is initiated" (p. 198).

The following areas of informed consent could lead to legal problems for counselors if not handled properly: failing to include required Health Insurance Portability and Accountability Act (HIPAA) elements; guaranteeing an outcome as a result of counseling; guaranteeing privacy with no exceptions; changing agreed-to fee arrangements; touching without implied or actual permission; misrepresenting credentials; failing to communicate the nature of counseling; or neglecting to warn client about possible stigma (Remley & Herlihy, 2005).

Licensure boards typically require counselors to submit a current copy of their written professional disclosure statement to the licensure board and provide a copy to each client prior to the performance of any counseling services. The counselor must retain a copy of the disclosure statement signed by the client.

A major challenge in developing a written disclosure statement is balancing the need to include enough information to clearly communicate the nature and parameters of the counseling experience and the need to avoid providing so much information as to overwhelm and intimidate the client. The counselor can always supplement the information verbally in reviewing the key points of the disclosure with the client. A sample written counselor disclosure statement designed for a private counseling practice is provided in Table 11.1. Disclosure statements may vary depending on the work setting. For example, counselors employed in organized work settings such as mental health, rehabilitation, or addiction programs will provide different information in some areas, such as fees for services.

As Remley and Herlihy (2005) point out, "A complete signed disclosure statement will fulfill a counselor's legal obligation to obtain informed consent from a client" (p. 84). Disclosure statements must be in plain English, culturally sensitive, and understandable to clients, including minors and individuals with impaired intellectual or cognitive ability. Ensuring informed consent is not a one-time event but a recurring process that continues throughout the counseling relationship as issues and questions arise. Some counselors and treatment programs give clients a written statement of client rights and responsibilities. The National Board for Certified Counselors (NBCC, 2007) has developed such a statement that may be downloaded from its Web site, http://www.nbcc.org/clientrights. The informed consent process is a way of engaging the participation of the client and outlining the rights and responsibilities of the client in the therapeutic process (Corey, et al., 2007).

TABLE 11.1 Professional Disclosure Statement for Counseling

PROFESSIONAL DISCLOSURE STATEMENT

Lloyd R. Goodwin, Jr., Ph.D., LPC, CRC-MAC, LCAS, CCS, ACS

Address

Office telephone number Cell phone number

e-mail address

I am pleased that you have selected me as your counselor or consultant. This document is designed to inform you about my credentials and background and to ensure that you understand our professional relationship.

Credentials

I earned a PhD in Counseling, Health, and Rehabilitation with a major in rehabilitation counseling in 1974 from Florida State University. I have been a professional counselor and counselor educator for more than 40 years. I am a Licensed Professional Counselor (LPC #____), Licensed Clinical Addictions Specialist (LCAS #____), and Certified Clinical Supervisor (CCS# ____) in North Carolina, and a nationally certified Rehabilitation Counselor with a specialty certification in substance abuse counseling (CRC-MAC # ____) and Approved Clinical Supervisor (ACS #____) credential.

Counseling Process and Theoretical Orientation

People can make better decisions if they have enough information and an understanding of how counseling works. Here are some aspects of counseling and psychotherapy as I perceive and practice it: Therapeutic counseling requires your active involvement, including efforts to change any self-defeating thoughts, feelings, and behaviors. You will be asked to work both during and between counseling sessions. There are no instant, painless, or passive cures, no "magic pills." Instead, ongoing personal and spiritual growth will occur with your conscious effort, which may include homework assignments and other projects. Often, individuals need to improve stress management skills, cognitions (e.g., beliefs and thought processes), emotional health, relationships, and general lifestyle if counseling is to be successful. Sometimes change will be relatively easy, but more often personal change takes much effort, time, and persistence. It is not uncommon to discover some psychological and behavior patterns that have been reinforced for more than 20 to 30 years and will not change with insight alone. These entrenched thinking and behavior patterns usually require much focused time and effort. Although these are some typical self-improvement goals for many individuals, I will assist you in identifying and achieving your personal development goals.

I use an eclectic counseling approach. Theoretically, I rely heavily on Rogerian person-centered, cognitive behavioral therapy (e.g., Button Therapy), Gestalt therapy, and transactional analysis approaches. These are well established, researched, and respected therapies. If specifically requested by a client, I use less well researched and more intuitive energy work techniques (e.g., Reiki healing) focusing on the energy field for individuals with an interest in metaphysical and spiritual development.

Populations Served

I provide counseling services to adolescents and adults with general mental health concerns, substance use disorders, and marital and family relationship problems.

(continued)

TABLE 11.1 *(Continued)*

When appropriate, I refer individuals to other mental health professionals and mutual-help groups such as Alcoholics Anonymous and Narcotics Anonymous.

Potential Benefits and Risks of Counseling

Mental health counseling and therapy can involve both benefits and risks.

Potential benefits. Potential benefits include becoming free from self-defeating and sometimes self-destructive behavior (e.g., substance abuse); developing more satisfying relationships with other people; becoming happier and more loving; becoming more centered, peaceful, and spiritual; and living a healthier lifestyle.

Potential risks. Risks include experiencing uncomfortable feelings or difficulties with friends and family members during the counseling, therapeutic, or rehabilitation process. Personal and spiritual growth often involves changes in our usual ways of functioning and relating that may involve considerable stress. Major life changes such as divorce and changing jobs or careers, although extremely distressful in the short run, may help us actualize healthier long-term mental health or career potentials. For example, an individual may realize that a goal of keeping a dysfunctional marriage together at all costs may not be in his or her, or the rest of the family's, best interests. Sometimes it is in the best interests of both spouses, as well as other family members, to separate.

Stigma of a mental disorder diagnosis. Treatment for a diagnosed mental disorder can result in social stigma and discrimination in work settings, including denied security clearance for certain types of jobs. A diagnosis of a mental disorder is required if you seek reimbursement from a third-party payer such as a health insurance or managed care company. In the event you wish to seek reimbursement and a diagnosis is required, I will inform you beforehand of the diagnosis I plan to submit to your health insurance or managed care company.

Confidentiality

I regard the information you share with me with the greatest respect, so I want us to be as clear as possible about how it will be handled. Generally, I will tell no one what you tell me without your written permission. The privacy and confidentiality of our conversations, and my records, is your right and is protected by state law and my profession's ethical principles in all but a few circumstances. There are three primary circumstances in which I cannot guarantee confidentiality, legally or ethically: (1) when I believe you intend to harm yourself or another person; (2) when I believe a child or elderly person has been, or will be, abused or neglected; and (3) in rare circumstances, mental health professionals can be ordered by a judge to release information. Other aspects of the confidential nature of our counseling relationship are explained below.

Minors. Individuals under 18 years of age will need to have a parent or legal guardian give written permission for my counseling services. If you are a minor under 18 years of age I will decide on an individual basis whether to accept you for counseling, if North Carolina statutes permit treatment of your condition without parental permission.

Parents or legal guardians of minors. It is important that your child trust and feel comfortable talking with me about personal matters. I expect that parents will respect the privacy arrangement between their children and me. Do not expect me to divulge their "secrets" and personal issues without their permission, for this is a sure way to impair our therapeutic relationship. I tell my minor clients that I will keep confidential

TABLE 11.1 *(Continued)*

what we talk about in our counseling sessions unless they tell me something that concerns me deeply about their personal or interpersonal welfare, in which case I will notify their parents. My decisions on sharing information with parents will be based on what I consider to be in the best interests of the child, and I will notify the child before I share any information with parents.

Marital and family counseling. In general I do not believe that keeping secrets from other family members is healthy in counseling. Thus, the confidentiality of what one family member or spouse tells me in private may be waived if I believe that it is in the best interests of the individual and the family. For example, an adolescent may share something with me that alarms me and needs to be shared with a parent.

Group counseling. Confidentiality in group counseling is imperative, and every group member is bound by confidentiality. It has been my experience that group members take the confidentiality commitment very seriously and violations are rare. However, even though I make every attempt to safeguard confidentiality in group counseling, I cannot guarantee that no group member will violate confidentiality.

Supervision and consultation. Periodically, I may seek consultation from a professional colleague to better serve my clients. I keep my clients' identity anonymous and share information on a need-to-know basis.

Support staff and consultants. Support staff such as secretaries, mental health consultants, and third-party insurance carriers are bound by the same confidentiality rules as I am, and they are committed to maintaining the privacy of your information.

Referral sources. With your written permission, I generally thank referral sources for trusting me with the task of helping people with their personal issues and may inform them of progress. When counseling is mandated by the court or criminal justice system, I will provide required information (e.g., to your probation/parole officer), which is generally related to your attendance at sessions, results of drug tests, and progress in counseling.

Health insurance and managed care companies. Insurance and other third-party companies usually require that I diagnose your mental health condition and indicate that you have a mental disorder before they will agree to reimburse you for therapeutic counseling services. In the event that a psychological diagnosis is required, I will inform you of the diagnosis that I plan to render before I submit it to the health insurance company. Any diagnosis made will become a part of your permanent insurance records and your employer's personnel records.

Otherwise, I will not tell anyone anything about your treatment, diagnosis, history, or even that you are a client, without your full knowledge and written permission.

Explanations of Dual Relationships

Although our sessions may be very intimate psychologically, it is important for you to realize that we have a professional relationship rather than a social one. Our contact will be limited to sessions you will arrange with me. Please do not invite me to social gatherings, offer me gifts, or ask me to relate to you in any way other than in the professional context of our counseling sessions. You will be best served while I am seeing you for counseling if our relationship stays strictly professional and if our sessions concentrate exclusively on your concerns. You will learn a great deal about me as we work together during your counseling experience. However, it is important for you to remember that you are experiencing me in my professional role. If we encounter each other in a public setting (e.g., grocery store) I will not acknowledge you unless you initiate the interaction in order to maintain your privacy.

(continued)

TABLE 11.1 *(Continued)*

Length and Frequency of Sessions

I assure you that my services will be rendered in a professional manner consistent with accepted ethical standards. Individual sessions are approximately 50 minutes in duration. Group therapy is approximately 90 minutes in duration. Marital and family sessions are usually between 60 and 90 minutes in duration. The number of sessions you will need to resolve your issues cannot be predetermined ahead of time, but can be estimated after the first session. Therapeutic effects take time to accumulate, and individuals can expect to meet for at least five sessions. After five sessions we can evaluate your status and determine whether more sessions are needed. We can continue to meet for as many sessions as mutually agreed on to successfully resolve your issues. You have the right to decline or terminate any counseling intervention you feel uncomfortable with during a counseling session and to terminate your counseling relationship with me at any time.

Treatment Outcome

Please note that it is impossible to guarantee any specific results regarding your counseling goals. Often, counseling and treatment goals change with increased understanding. Your counseling or treatment goals are likely to be modified during the therapeutic counseling process. However, counseling, treatment, personal, and spiritual growth will always be your goals. Together we will work to achieve the best possible results for you.

Fees and Methods of Payment

In return for a fee of $\_\_\_$ per individual session, $\$\_\_\_$ per group counseling session, and $\$\_\_\_$ per marital and family session, I agree to provide therapeutic counseling services for you. I provide substance abuse assessments for $\$\_\_\_$. The fee for telephone counseling sessions between in-office sessions is the same as for an individual session. Fees for consultation, supervision, presentations, and training are determined as needed. Clients will be notified at least 1 month in advance of any increase in counseling fees. My policy is that you pay in cash or by check for each session at the beginning of each session.

Partial sessions or missed appointments. Clients are responsible for full payment of a session if they show up late for the session. If unable to keep an appointment, please call to cancel or reschedule at least 24 hours in advance. Clients are responsible for payment of missed sessions if not cancelled 24 hours ahead of time.

Billing and Insurance Reimbursement

If you wish to seek reimbursement for my services from your health insurance company, I will complete any forms related to your reimbursement provided by you or the insurance company. However, you will need to pay me the total fee directly after each session and then you can receive reimbursements from insurance companies, if available.

Most health insurance companies will reimburse clients for my counseling and psychotherapy services. Those that do reimburse usually require that a standard amount be paid by you before reimbursement is allowed (deductible), and then usually only a percentage of my fee is reimbursable (i.e., you will probably have a "co-payment"). You should contact a company representative, usually the personnel

TABLE 11.1 *(Continued)*

office or human resources department, at your place of employment to determine whether your insurance company will reimburse you and obtain reimbursement details. However, *please remember that you are responsible, not your insurance company, for paying the fees agreed upon.*

Clients' Rights to See Files

A client has the right to see his or her file. However, a client does not have the right to see psychological tests and inventories that are copyrighted. I will be happy to go over with you any material in your file, including any psychological test results.

Termination

The counseling relationship may be terminated for nonpayment of services or noncompliant client behavior, or if I believe there is insufficient therapeutic progress. The client will be notified of the intent to terminate the counseling relationship at least one session ahead of the last session. In addition, I ask clients to let me know at least one session before the last session in order to deal with potential termination issues.

Emergency Contact Information

I can be reached at one of the following phone numbers at all times: xxx-xxx-xxxx (office) or xxx-xxx-xxxx (cell). If I am not available and you need to contact someone in a mental health emergency, you can contact the REAL Crises center at xxx-xxx-xxxx for crises counseling and referral or 911 for police assistance to secure crises psychiatric services at our local hospital.

Counselor's Vacations, Retirement, Death, or Impairment

In the event of my retirement, you will be notified ahead of time so you can decide on another mental health professional and the disposition of your counseling files. In the event of my untimely death, or impairment from a disability, Dr. _____ (xxx-xxx-xxxx), a mental health professional in Greenville, NC, is authorized to secure my counseling files and notify clients of my demise. Dr. _____ has also agreed to see my clients, if needed, if I should become temporarily unavailable due to vacations or illness.

Alternatives to Counseling

There are alternatives to counseling, often free of charge, available to individuals interested in working on their personal and spiritual growth. Examples include pastoral counseling through various religious establishments and mutual-help groups such as Alcoholics Anonymous, Narcotics Anonymous, and Al-Anon. I will be glad to discuss these options with you.

Complaint Procedures

If you are dissatisfied with any aspect of our work, please inform me immediately. This will make our work together more efficient and effective. If you think that you have been treated unfairly or unethically, by me or any other counselor, and cannot resolve this problem with me, you can contact the North Carolina Board of Licensed Professional Counselors at P.O. Box 21005, Raleigh, NC 27619-1005, 919-787-1980, for clarification of clients' rights as I have explained them or to lodge a complaint.

(continued)

TABLE 11.1 *(Continued)*

If you have any questions, feel free to ask. Please sign and date both copies of this form. A copy for your records will be returned to you. I will retain a copy in my confidential records.

Counselor's Signature	Date	Client's Signature	Date

Client's Signature	Date	Client's Signature	Date

Parent or Legal Guardian if Client Is a Minor or Adult Lacking Legal Competency	Date

Remley and Herlihy (2005) note that research supports the wisdom of clarifying the nature and boundaries of the counseling relationship and securing informed consent. They cite studies showing that clients want information about their prospective counselors (Braaten, Otto, & Handelsman, 1993; Hendrick, 1988); they perceive counselors who provide informed consent information as being more expert and trustworthy (Sullivan, Martin, & Handelsman, 1993); clients who have received appropriate information are more alert to possible negative consequences (Handler, 1990); and some legal problems can be avoided (Remley & Herlihy, 2005).

REFERENCES

American Counseling Association. (2005). *ACA code of ethics*. Alexandria, VA: Author.

Braaten, E. E., Otto, S., & Handelsman, M. M. (1993). What do people want to know about psychotherapy? *Psychotherapy, 30,* 565–570.

Corey, G., Corey, M. S., & Callanan, P. (2007). *Issues and ethics in the helping professions* (7th ed.). Belmont, CA: Thomson-Brooks/Cole.

Cottone, R. R., & Tarvydas, V. M. (2007). *Counseling ethics and decision making* (3rd ed.). Upper Saddle River, NJ: Pearson-Merrill/Prentice-Hall.

Handler, J. F. (1990). *Law and the search for community*. Philadelphia: University of Pennsylvania Press.

Hendrick, S. S. (1988). Counselor self-disclosure. *Journal of Counseling and Development, 66,* 419–424.

National Board for Certified Counselors. (2007). *What to expect as a client.* Greensboro, NC: Author. Retrieved January 8, 2008, from http://www.nbcc.org/clientrights

Remley, T. P., & Herlihy, B. (2005). *Ethical, legal, and professional issues in counseling* (2nd ed.). Upper Saddle River, NJ: Pearson-Merrill/Prentice-Hall.

Sullivan, T., Martin, W. L., & Handelsman, M. M. (1993). Practical benefits of an informed consent procedure: An empirical investigation. *Professional Psychology: Research and Practice, 24,* 160–163.

Section C

Case Management and Consultation Issues

12

Conducting an Intake Interview

GAIL MEARS

NTAKE INTERVIEWS, AS part of the assessment phase of counseling, gather information about the client's reasons for seeking counseling, current and past functioning, social history and interpersonal style, and goals for counseling (Seligman, 2004; Sommers-Flanagan & Sommers-Flanagan, 2003). This information allows the counselor to develop a framework in which to understand the clinical issues presented (diagnosis) and to collaboratively plan the counseling experience with the client (treatment plan). Developing rapport with the client is a primary concern during an intake interview and attention to cultural considerations is essential. This chapter will review dimensions of effective intake interviewing, including preparation, skills, and cultural competency, informed consent, and format.

PREPARATION

PREPARATION IS IMPORTANT for the effectiveness of an intake interview (Drummond & Jones, 2006; Karg & Wiens, 2005). This includes attention to space in which the interview will be conducted, a review of available client information, and consideration of the purpose of the interview. Symptom inventories and client questionnaires are frequently used to reduce the amount of information gathered during the intake interview and to enhance the accuracy of the intake assessment. Counselors should familiarize themselves with the information provided by clients before the intake interview and incorporate this information in their intake interviews, thus avoiding redundancy in the information-gathering process. The purpose of the intake needs to be identified as the intake interview process will be influenced by whether it is a diagnostic consultation, the first session of ongoing counseling or psychotherapy, or part of a more formal evaluation process (Karg & Wiens, 2005).

SKILLFUL INTERVIEWING

AN INTAKE INTERVIEW relying primarily on questions may leave clients feeling disconnected from the counselor and discouraged about the potential benefits of the counseling process. Questions, in the absence of empathic engagement, can feel intrusive and may result in clients feeling exposed and/or violated by the counselor. Learning how to skillfully elicit information, while maintaining an empathic stance, is a critical counseling competency (Hackney & Cormier, 2005; Seligman, 2004; Sommers-Flanagan & Sommers-Flanagan, 2003). The intake interview will likely be more effective if the counselor uses more open- than closed-ended questions and balances questions with empathic reflective responses. A good rule of thumb is to reflect on the client's response before asking another question.

During an intake interview, the client will undoubtedly touch on issues that are troubling and emotionally charged. It is important to respond to the client's distress while keeping the assessment goals of the intake process in mind. This means developing the art of responding empathically while keeping the information-gathering process moving forward. A skillful intake interview can, in and of itself, be a potent therapeutic experience for clients.

CULTURAL CONSIDERATIONS

CULTURALLY COMPETENT INTERVIEWERS are sensitive to differences in verbal and nonverbal communication styles (Ivey & Ivey, 2003). Clients come with preferences regarding directness of communication, use of questions, silence, eye contact, and other nonverbal dimensions of communication. To the extent possible, counselors should modify their interviewing style to respect these preferences. Counselors need to be particularly attuned to issues of power in the intake process and be careful not to inadvertently set up a situation in which clients feel shamed, silenced, or disempowered. It is vital that counselors make sure that the client understands the questions being asked during the interview and that any checklist or questionnaires used are nondiscriminating and understandable to the client.

FORMAT

THE SPECIFIC FORMAT of an intake interview varies depending on setting, the client's level of distress, the counselor's theoretical orientation, and the purpose of the prospective intervention. However, regardless of setting, intake interviews should orient the client to the intake process, provide information so that the client can give informed consent, allow the client an open-ended way to talk about the concerns he or she brings to counseling, gather information relevant to determining treatment needs, elicit the client's counseling expectations, and promote a sense of hope of positive outcome when appropriate. These elements of an intake interview are addressed in the following discussion.

ORIENTATION AND INFORMED CONSENT

THE INTAKE INTERVIEW is typically more counselor-directed than later counseling sessions. A broad range of information is gathered *in a systematic way* and the counselor typically take notes. It is important that the nature of the intake interview and how it may be different from the counseling process is discussed with the client (Hackney & Cormier, 2005). Clients need to give informed consent before entering into the intake process. Informed consent is an ethical imperative (American Counseling Association [ACA], 2005) and includes discussion of confidentiality and limits to confidentiality; the types of services that are offered by the counselor; prospective treatment options, including prospective benefits and risks and information about the counselor's training and counseling style; and information about procedural issues such as office hours, fees, and emergency services.

PRESENTING CONCERNS

A SIMPLE OPEN-ENDED question, "What brings you here?" provides an opportunity for clients to tell their story in a nondirected way and articulate their most pressing concerns. Empathic responses such as reflection of feelings, paraphrasing, and summarizing demonstrate the counselor's level of understanding and promote a sense of empathic engagement. A transition into more specific information gathering can naturally follow an accurate summarizing of the client's presenting concerns.

It is often very instructive to ask clients why they chose to come to counseling at this time. Sometimes clients struggle with distress for a very long time and only come into counseling due to a recent motivating event. It is also often useful at this stage to ask clients what they hope to gain from the counseling experience with more formal goal setting to follow.

INTAKE KEY QUESTIONS AND INFORMATION GATHERING

THE STRUCTURE AND the breadth of the intake interview is determined by many factors, including where the counseling is taking place, accreditation and insurance requirements, and the intensity of clients' distress or level of functional impairment. Typically, higher levels of client distress or dysfunction and more intense treatment settings call for more comprehensive intake interviews.

The following discussion outlines the range of information typically addressed in intake interviews (Barlow & Durand, 2003; Drummond & Jones, 2006; Hack & Cook, 1995; Seligman, 2004; Sommers-Flanagan & Sommers-Flanagan, 2003). However, not all settings will require or lend themselves to this level of comprehensiveness. It is likely that counselors will not be able to solicit all of this information in the first interview. Minimally, counselors should get biographical information; presenting problem and history of this problem; history of psychological or psychiatric and relevant medical treatment; current functioning, including an assessment of suicidal, homicidal, or other self- or other-harming ideation or plans; significant background events as identified by clients; and clients' hopes and expectations for the counseling process. Clients might be asked to fill out intake questionnaires and symptom checklists to aid in the information-gathering process. Accuracy of diagnosis is enhanced when structured instruments, information from family members, and/or behavioral assessments are used in addition to the intake interview (Karg & Wiens, 2005).

TYPICAL INFORMATION GATHERED AT INTAKE

BIOGRAPHICAL DATA. THIS includes client's name, age, gender, ethnicity, relationship status and living situation, and referral source.

History of past counseling or other psychological service. Has the client previously been in any type of counseling or received psychiatric services or psychological testing? What precipitated these services? Who was the provider? Is the client aware of a prior or existing diagnosis? How does the client feel about his or her experience in counseling?

Family history. Who is in the client's family of origin? What were significant family events? What is the quality of the client's relationship with family members? What role does family play in the client's current life? What is the client's current family structure (counselors should be mindful of the diverse nature of family structures)?

Developmental history. What were the circumstances of the client's birth? Did the client reach developmental milestones at expected ages?

Medical/physical history. Are there current or past medical conditions? What types of treatment has he or she had for the above-noted conditions? What medications are currently being taken? Who is the client's primary care provider? When did the client last receive medical care? What are the client's dietary practices? What types of exercise does the client engage in?

It is important for the client to be prepared to collaborate actively with health providers. Counselors should insist that clients consult with a medical provider when there is an indication of neglected health services, when the condition of concern has significant medical implications, or when the client presents with physical as well as emotional symptoms.

Educational/vocational/military history. What is the highest level of education the client has achieved and what is or was the quality of his or her school experiences? Has the client been evaluated for any learning issues? What is the client's work history (types of jobs and level of success with jobs)? Has the client been in the military? If so, what was his or her tour of duty? Was the client involved in combat situations? How successful was or is the client's military experience?

Substance use history. Does the client use illegal substances? Does the client use legal drugs (alcohol, nicotine, caffeine)? Is there a history of substance abuse in the client's family? If so, what was or is the nature of this abuse?

When taking a substance use history it is important to get specific information on duration, frequency, and level of substance use. Subjective reports of levels of use (e.g., "I drink a little" or "I smoke marijuana occasionally") should be followed by questions asking clients to quantify their use.

Spiritual and recreational activities. Does the client have practices, beliefs, or communities that provide a sense of meaning and connection for the client? This may or may not be in the form of an organized religion. Does the client have recreational activities that he or she finds pleasurable and aid in a sense of rejuvenation?

Mental status. The mental status exam evaluates current functioning and looks at a broad range of affective, cognitive, and behavioral domains. The formality with which a mental status exam is administered depends on the treatment context and the symptom severity or functional impairment of the client. When a client presents with more significant symptoms or a history of more impaired functioning, or the intake interview is being administered in a more restrictive environment (such as an inpatient facility), the mental status exam is typically administered in a more structured way. The mental status exam need not be a totally distinct portion of the intake interview. Much of the information associated with the mental status exam can be incorporated in the broader intake interview. The following discussion outlines typical dimensions of a mental status exam.

Appearance/behavior/attitude. How is the client dressed and what is his or her level of grooming (care should be taken to use descriptive versus evaluative language)? Does the client look his or her stated age? Does the client evidence any unusual behavior such as tics, unusual movements, or repetitive motions? Is the client's level of activity within expected ranges? What is the client's attitude toward the counselor and the intake process?

Affect and mood. Affect refers to observable indications of the client's emotions in the session and is determined by the counselor. How would you describe the client's display of emotionality during the interview? Did the client demonstrate a wide range of intense feelings as demonstrated by crying, laughing, and irritability? Did the client appear sad as evidenced by facial expression and crying? Did the client appear emotionless (flat), lacking outward emotional response to provocative clinical material? Was affect congruent with the content being discussed?

Mood refers to the client's report of his or her subjective internal feeling states and can be assessed by asking, "Could you describe how you have been feeling in general lately?"

Speech and thought content and organization. What is the client's style of speech (loudness, speed, and amount)? What is the content and organization of the client's thinking? Is the client preoccupied with particular concerns (such as "I am a worthless human being")? Does the client report obsessions (negative mental images or ideas that the client fends off with ritualized behaviors (compulsions)? Is there evidence of delusions, hallucinations, or illusions or other perceptual disturbances? Hallucinations are the presence of sensory experiences not experienced by others (seeing, hearing, tasting, or touching experiences). The most common form of hallucinations is auditory. Hallucinations involving other senses are often associated with organic causes. Delusions are ideas that are firmly held, unrealistic, and not shared by others (ideas of being persecuted, ideas of self-grandeur, ideas of reference). Illusions are distortions of existing sensory stimuli.

Orientation and cognitive functioning. Does the client appear oriented (knows who he or she is, where the meeting is taking place, what the date is)? Does the client appear to be of average, below average, or above average intelligence? Without a structured cognitive assessment this is only an estimate and is based on the client's vocabulary, apparent memory, speech content, and demonstrated complexity of thought.

Suicide and risk assessment. Does the client evidence any current suicidal or homicidal ideation? If so, does the client have a plan? Is there any history of self- or other-harming behaviors? Is the client impulsive? Does the client suffer from a mood disorder? Does the client suffer from a medical condition? Is the client's affect discrepant from the situations he or she reports (such as a lack of affect when describing a very painful story)? Is there a history of suicide in the client's family or social network? Does the client have significant social relationships and supports? Does the client abuse drugs or alcohol? Counselors should be aware of the factors associated with suicidal and homicidal risk.

Insight/judgment/reliability. Does the client understand the nature of his or her symptoms or functional impairments (insight)? Does the client make adaptive decisions for himself or herself and others despite symptoms of functional impairments (judgment)? Is the client an accurate reporter of his or her experiences (reliability)?

GOAL SETTING

An intake interview should end with a discussion of what comes next. The last part of the session provides an opportunity to review what the client's expected outcomes are, develop counseling goals, and identify resources and roadblocks to accomplishing these goals. Counselors should be careful not to impose goals or expectations that are beyond the client's resources or motivation. After reaching mutual agreement on counseling goals, the counselor can prepare the client for counseling with a brief discussion of the types of counseling interventions that will likely be helpful and the expected course of treatment. Hope is an important factor in the recovery process (Frank & Frank, 1993; Sperry, Carlson, & Kjos, 2003) and counselors should promote clients' hope that they can achieve reasonable counseling goals.

CONCLUSION

Intake interviews are an integral part of the counseling process. They require counselors to marry informed consent, information gathering, and rapport building. It is important for counselors to carefully consider the purpose of the intake interview, agency or insurance requirements, and client's presenting concerns in planning for an intake interview. An effective interview allows the counselor to accurately understand clients' presenting concerns, collaboratively consider outcome goals, develop a supportive relationship, and promote hope about the benefits of the counseling process.

REFERENCES

American Counseling Association. (2005). *ACA code of ethics* (3rd ed.). Alexandria, VA: Author.

Barlow, D. H., & Durand, V. M. (2003). *Essentials of abnormal psychology* (3rd ed.). Pacific Grove, CA: Wadsworth-Thomson Learning.

Drummond, R., & Jones, K. D. (2006). *Assessment procedures for counseling and helping professionals* (6th ed.). Upper Saddle River, NJ: Prentice-Hall.

Frank, J. D., & Frank, J. B. (1993). *Persuasion and healing: A comparative study of psychotherapy* (3rd ed.). Baltimore: Johns Hopkins Press.

Hack, T. F., & Cook, A. J. (1995). Getting started: Intake and initial sessions. In D. G. Martin & A. D. Moore (Eds.), *Basics of clinical practice: A guidebook for trainees in the helping professions* (pp. 46–74). Prospect Heights, IL: Waveland Press.

Hackney, H., & Cormier, S. (2005). *The professional counselor* (5th ed.). Boston: Pearson Education.

Ivey, A. E., & Ivey, M. B. (2003). *Intentional interviewing and counseling.* Pacific Grove, CA: Brooks/Cole-Thomson Learning.

Karg, R. S., & Wiens, A. N. (2005). Improving diagnostic and clinical interviewing. In G. P. Koocher, J. C. Norcross, & S. S. Hill (Eds.), *Psychologists' desk reference* (2nd ed., pp. 13–15). New York: Oxford University Press.

Seligman, L. (2004). *Technical and conceptual skills for mental health professionals.* Upper Saddle River, NJ: Pearson-Merrill/Prentice-Hall.

Sommers-Flanagan, J., & Sommers-Flanagan, R. (2003). *Clinical interviewing* (3rd ed.). Hoboken, NJ: Wiley.

Sperry, L., Carlson, J., & Kjos, D. (2003). *Becoming an effective therapist.* Boston: Pearson Education.

13

Resource Brokering: Managing the Referral Process

WILLIAM CRIMANDO

THE PROFESSIONAL COUNSELOR often takes on the role of *resource broker*. A resource broker is a professional who helps the client to identify, access, and successfully use any vendor who can provide a service or material good necessary to operationalize the client's service plan, that is, meet the client's developmental needs or therapeutic goals (cf. Colbert & Kulikowich, 2006; Moxley, 1989; Small, 2006). The term *brokering* suggests a two-way relationship. This relationship is implied by Moxley as he rationalizes brokering because "human service delivery systems are complex" (p. 96) and clients' knowledge about available services may be incomplete or inaccurate. Further, vendors, who may not actively engage in case finding, may be unaware of people who require their goods or services. Thus, the broker serves as an intermediary or liaison between the client and vendor. Besides Moxley, other writers have recognized the professional counselor's role in resource brokering. For example, Colbert and Kulikowich implored school counselors to prepare themselves to participate in brokering services. Small discussed a set of propositions regarding the reasons for, and means by which, personnel at childcare centers could broker resources for persons from lower socioeconomic backgrounds or those who are socially isolated. Finally, Malloy, Cheney, and Cormier (1998) described Project RENEW, which operationalized resource brokering on a large scale in an effort "to improve transition services for students with emotional and behavioral disorders" (p. 96).

Success as a resource broker depends on the professional counselor having in-depth knowledge about community and professional resources. Moxley (1989) described these knowledge areas: (1) availability, appropriateness, acceptability, and accessibility of community resources; (2) whether eligibility requirements are need based, diagnosis based, or means tested; (3) quality of service, identified through past experience, evaluation studies, and accrediting bodies; (4) the competence of potential resources for working with a particular type of client; (5) the motivation of vendors to work with a specific client; and (6) whether potential resources offer a broad or narrow range of services (see also Crimando, 2005). Besides the personal experiences of the professional counselor, such knowledge can be gained through interviews with clients and other agency counselors, reviews of caseloads, reviews of existing interagency service agreements, use of the counselor's personal or professional network, or use of published and online resource guides developed jointly by chambers of commerce, service providers, government offices, community mental health associations, and state advocacy associations. Development of a thorough knowledge base is likely to take time, as is the development and cultivation of a professional network. Both are invaluable because the professional counselor as resource broker must know who to contact and how to work through the various layers of bureaucracy at her or his own agency as well as potential vendors. Further, such knowledge will help the client have a successful experience with the service provider.

THE PROFESSIONAL COUNSELOR AND RESOURCE BROKERING

COLBERT AND KULIKOWICH (2006), writing about school counselors, asserted that counselors have three responsibilities as resource brokers: identifying resources, gaining access to resources, and ensuring effective use of resources. The following is a brief description of the major activities constituting fulfillment of these responsibilities.

IDENTIFYING AND SELECTING SERVICE PROVIDERS AND VENDORS

CRIMANDO (2005) IDENTIFIED a list of general criteria that may be used when identifying and choosing service providers, such as these:

1. Service cost and pricing structure
2. Qualifications of staff
3. Linkages the vendor has with others to meet special needs
4. Staff:client ratio
5. Reputation of provider
6. Whether client or family input is considered in planning the program

More important, Crimando (2005) implied that for certain clients general criteria should be eschewed in favor of more individualized criteria. For example, clients seeking brain injury rehabilitation may require service providers that employ a neuropsychology staff or a program setting consistent with preinjury lifestyle.

GAINING ACCESS TO RESOURCES: LINKING CLIENTS TO SERVICE PROVIDERS AND VENDORS

USE OF A COMMUNITY resource often begins with an informal telephone contact with the vendor, followed by a formal referral letter. The referral letter, which is frequently used in lieu of a service contract, provides documentation that can be reviewed (paper trail) and that secures the commitment of all parties involved (accountability; Crimando, 2005).

Composing the Referral Letter

Referral letters should include, minimally, these elements (Crimando, 2005):

1. *Client introduction.* Background information relevant to the presenting problem is needed to effectively serve the client. Depending on the vendor and the client's presenting problem, this may include the client's presenting symptoms and medical and psychological history, employment experience and goals, family and housing information, and the counselor's clinical impressions and concerns. Needless to say, before releasing this information, the counselor should make sure that the agency's policy on privacy and release of information is observed.
2. *The specific services needed.* The services being purchased, such as assistive technology consultation, medical evaluation, legal aid, or physical therapy, should be specified. If the services to be rendered include an evaluation, rather than making a general request for evaluation and assessment results, the specific questions of interest should be detailed. For example, a rehabilitation counselor may query physicians about the severity and prognosis of disability, conditions that exacerbate symptoms, work limitations imposed by the medical condition, and specific treatments that

may help the client (Roessler & Rubin, 2006). They may also ask psychologists about the degree to which the client's level of psychosocial adjustment is likely to be a barrier to rehabilitation or employment; the client's general functioning level and suitability for employment in specific situations such as high stress, work in close proximity with others, or work requiring a high tolerance for ambiguity; and the client's response to authority or supervision. A school counselor may request a general screening for attention deficit hyperactivity disorder from a psychologist but would be better advised to ask under what environmental conditions the client is most distractible, what conditions are most conducive to learning, and so forth.

3. *The monitoring mechanism.* The means by which the referral will be managed should be addressed, possibly including clearly stated goals and objectives, terms for renegotiating service costs if necessary, and procedures for joint case planning and quality assurance.

4. *Time lines.* Significant milestones, such as dates for planning meetings, client appointments, when initial impressions may be available, final reports, and when services will either be terminated or renegotiated, may be identified.

5. *Special considerations.* Finally, stipulations for ancillary services like transportation from and to home and lodging that the client may need in order to participate in the service should be made in the referral letter.

Meeting the Needs of the "Other Client"

As broker, the professional counselor has a secondary client, the prospective service provider. Recall that brokering suggests that the needs of both the primary and secondary client will be met. The referral process must then include provisions for the service provider. These include transmitting information releases and following confidentiality procedures required by the vendor, providing enough information so that the service provider has a chance of meeting the client's needs, and working with the provider to resolve any problems that may present themselves while the client is being served by the outside service provider.

ENSURING EFFICIENT AND EFFECTIVE USE OF RESOURCES: MONITORING AND EVALUATING THE REFERRAL

TWO COMPONENTS ARE necessary for ensuring the efficient and effective use of resources: continual monitoring of ongoing referrals, and the periodic evaluation of the service provider. Monitoring ongoing referrals is important to (1) make sure that the services are being provided as planned; (2) intervene when problems arise; and (3) determine if a referral should be discontinued, when it has no chance of success. On the other hand, periodic evaluation of outside service providers is beneficial to caseload management, making the best financial decisions, and the overall integrity of the service delivery system.

Monitoring

Moxley (1989) stated that monitoring need not involve elaborate and complicated processes. A number of informal activities can be helpful:

1. Consistent, well-timed contact, either by phone or in person, with the client will give the counselor the opportunity to identify problems, motivate the client who is not meeting his or her responsibilities, or provide positive feedback to the client who is actively engaged in services. Such contact will also help reduce any residual apprehensions the client has about the referral.
2. Routine contact should be made with the service provider, either by phone or, with caution, e-mail. Moxley (1989) insisted that counselors approach such contact in the spirit of determining what can be done to facilitate the referral, rather than "checking up" on the service provider.
3. Periodic staffings or *linkage meetings* (Moxley, 1989) may be held to review client progress, especially in the case in which the duration of services is likely to be prolonged or delayed.
4. Periodic written reports from the service provider, while not sufficient for monitoring because of the potential for bias, may be useful.

As previously discussed, any of these monitoring mechanisms should be stipulated in the referral letter, especially when they require action by the service provider.

Periodic Evaluation of Service Providers

Crimando (2005) identified four areas that require periodic evaluation: outcome, responsiveness to clients' primary and special needs, responsiveness to the referring counselor's needs, and responsiveness to the organization's needs.

1. *Outcome.* The primary area concerns whether the goals and objectives of referrals are routinely met. If referrals involved the purchase of material goods, of course, the issue should be whether these

goods were delivered when promised, in the quality promised, and in the quantity promised. For referrals involving a service, satisfactory progress is critical.

2. *Responsiveness to clients' primary and special needs.* While vendors' performance in responding to goals and objectives spelled out in the referral is crucial, the secondary needs of clients should also be considered. Questions can include these: "Are clients (or their families) routinely satisfied with how they are treated by this vendor?" and "Do clients feel involved, understood, respected, or safe by the vendor?"

3. *Responsiveness to the referring counselor's needs.* The counselor may evaluate the degree to which vendors have provided opportunities for having input on planning; sent useful, accurate, and timely reports; and cooperated in cost-containment efforts.

4. *Responsiveness to the organization's needs.* The counselor's organization may have specific needs, and their fulfillment should be evaluated. These needs include timely billing; satisfying legal, funding, and accreditation requirements; and providing appropriate data for program evaluation.

By routinely evaluating vendors in these areas, and comparing their experiences with those of other counselors, the counselor may identify vendors that are extraordinarily strong or weak in one or more areas. This information may be passed on to vendors, and it may be used to make decisions about whether to continue to use specific vendors.

THE CLIENT AND RESOURCE BROKERING: CLIENT INVOLVEMENT IN REFERRALS

THE PREVIOUS DISCUSSION should not lead one to believe that the client should be a passive recipient of referred services. The importance of client empowerment has long been recognized by social workers and professional counselors. For example, in vocational rehabilitation as practiced in the state-federal system, client empowerment has been featured in the legislation authorizing services since the 1978 amendments to the 1973 Vocational Rehabilitation Act, which required active client involvement in the development of the Individualized Written Rehabilitation Plan. This move toward involvement and client choice continued, and most recently was manifested in the establishment of a system by which clients are given vouchers with which to purchase services of their own choosing.

Optimally, it is important to involve the client in selecting and linking them with service providers (Moxley, 1989). There are two primary reasons for client involvement in service planning, including referral management. First, clients may be more committed and motivated to complete a plan that they have had a role in developing. Second, Moxley insisted that the professional counselor should consider any anxiety, apprehensiveness, and misunderstandings the client may have about the referral process (e.g., "Won't you be my counselor anymore?" or "How long will I be gone?") or a specific service provider (e.g., "Will there be other people like me at that program?" or "Are they going to know about my sexuality?"). Involvement of the client in the referral process may alleviate the confusion and apprehensions.

Involvement may be implemented in a number of ways (cf. Moxley, 1989):

1. The client or advocate should be apprised of the need for referral, that is, what steps in the service plan cannot be completed except through outside sources.
2. The counselor can instruct the client in identifying potential resources. He or she may already have some choices in mind and these should be considered. Of course, the implications of these choices, as well as those recommended by the counselor, should be thoroughly discussed.
3. The match between the client's needs and services offered by potential providers may be jointly assessed by the counselor and client. Here the counselor's knowledge of community and professional resources, as described previously, will bear on the ease with which clients (i.e., who may lack the training or motivation) are able to participate in this process.
4. Clients should be thoroughly informed about what can and cannot be achieved through the referral. The client's role in making the referral successful, that is, his or her responsibilities, should be addressed.
5. Plans for remedying any problems that the client may have in accessing services (i.e., those regarding transportation, physical accessibility, and hours of operation) may be jointly formulated.
6. Certain clients may also be instructed in how to assert their rights with the service provider.

ETHICAL CONSIDERATIONS

Although the knowledge, skills, and activities necessary to be a successful resource broker may seem overwhelming and tedious at times, the counselor may have a professional and ethical responsibility to act as resource broker. The discussion presented herein is consistent with ethical metaprinciples such as beneficence, nonmaleficence, fidelity, and autonomy (see Forester-Miller & Davis, 1996, for a complete discussion of principles). Beneficence suggests that the counselor has a responsibility to contribute to the client's welfare, while nonmaleficence is the principle of causing no harm to others. By identifying and utilizing the best community resources available, the client's therapeutic and developmental goals have a better chance of being met. When a counselor refuses to refer out to meet the needs of the client, the counselor, it could be argued, may be causing harm to the client. This is especially true if the counselor is practicing beyond his or her scope of responsibility or capacity. Thus, it is essential for counselors to go through the steps necessary to ensure the effectiveness of the referral. Fidelity involves honoring commitments to the client (i.e., putting the client's welfare first). This suggests that the counselor should continually monitor referrals and periodically evaluate service providers, potentially ending professional relationships with providers who fail to meet the needs of clients. Finally, autonomy encourages the counselor to allow an individual freedom of choice and action. "It addresses the responsibility of the counselor to encourage clients, when appropriate, to make their own decisions and to act on their own values" (Forester-Miller & Davis, 1996, p. 1). By allowing clients to take an active role in identifying and choosing community resources and giving them the tools to use those resources, the counselor, it is clear, empowers clients to act autonomously.

CONCLUSION

A RESOURCE BROKER is a professional who helps the client to identify, access, and use any vendor who can provide resources necessary to operationalize the client's service plan (Colbert & Kulikowich, 2006; Moxley, 1989; Small, 2006). The role of resource broker is important in helping the client thrive in service delivery systems that are often complex and difficult to understand. Resource brokers act in a liaison role between the client, the organization serving the client, and outside organizations from whom it is necessary to secure resources. The professional counselor, with whom the client is in a developmental or therapeutic relationship, is the ideal person to serve as resource broker. He or she has already established trust and rapport with the client, which may serve to alleviate the anxiety that clients may have about having to seek help from multiple agencies. The experienced, professional counselor is likely to have connections with a strong professional network, and the extensive knowledge of community resources necessary to be successful as a resource broker.

REFERENCES

Colbert, R. D., & Kulikowich, J. M. (2006). School counselors as resource brokers: The case for including teacher efficacy in data-driven programs. *Professional School Counseling, 9*(3), 216–222.

Crimando, W. (2005). Case management implications. In W. Crimando & T. F. Riggar (Eds.), *Community resources: A guide for human service workers* (2nd ed., pp. 8–18). Long Grove, IL: Waveland Press.

Forester-Miller, H., & Davis, T. (1996). *A practitioner's guide to ethical decision making.* Alexandria, VA: American Counseling Association.

Malloy, J. M., Cheney, D., & Cormier, G. M. (1998). Interagency collaboration and the transition to adulthood for students with emotional or behavioral disabilities. *Education & Treatment of Children, 21,* 18. Retrieved January 17, 2007, from Academic Search Premier [database], http://web.ebscohost.com

Moxley, D. P. (1989). *The practice of case management.* Newbury Park, CA: Sage Publications.

Roessler, R. R., & Rubin, S. E. (2006). *Case management and rehabilitation counseling: Procedures and techniques* (4th ed.). Austin, TX: Pro-Ed.

Small, M. L. (2006). Neighborhood institutions as resource brokers: Childcare centers, inter-organizational ties, and resource access among the poor. *Social Problems, 53,* 274–292.

14

How to Develop Treatment Plans

GAIL MEARS

TREATMENT PLANNING IS an essential part of the counseling process. It provides a mutually agreed upon road map of
counseling goals, objectives, and strategies to reach these goals
(Johnson & Johnson, 2003; Jongsma & Peterson, 1999; Seligman, 2004;
Sommers-Flanagan & Sommers-Flanagan, 2003). An effective treatment
plan addresses clients' presenting concerns and takes into account
motivation, available resources, social context, preferred coping styles,
and impediments to treatment. The counselor's area of expertise and
the context in which treatment is taking place are also considered.
Treatment goals serve the purposes of motivating client change, educating clients about helpful outcomes, and providing a way of evaluating the effectiveness of counseling interventions (Hackney & Cormier,
2005). The process of developing clearly articulated goals and objectives benefits clients, the counselors, mental health organizations, and
the psychotherapy field at large (Jongsma, 2005). This chapter will discuss the nuts and bolts of treatment planning and related issues.

TREATMENT PLANS AND MANAGED CARE

TREATMENT PLANNING EMERGED as a necessary counseling
practice in behavioral health settings in the 1970s as a means of
satisfying accreditation and funding requirements, and by the 1980s

managed care prompted increased attention to the need for clearly articulated treatment plans (Jongsma & Peterson, 1999). While the format of required plans will vary among managed care companies, the need for counselors to concisely articulate what they hope will be accomplished during counseling and how they plan to achieve objectives remains constant. It is important that the treatment plan be tied to diagnostic concerns. If, for example, the diagnosis is major depression, the treatment plan needs to reflect interventions that the extant literature suggests are indicated in the treatment of depression. Otherwise, the treatment plan will likely be called into question. When a counselor agrees to become part of a managed care panel of providers, it is important that the counselor has an understanding of the treatment expectations and limitations implied in this partnership. It is also important for clients to be brought into the discussion of what their insurance resources are and how the insurance company's requirements will affect treatment.

MULTICULTURAL CONSIDERATIONS

CLIENTS' SOCIAL CONTEXT is an important consideration in treatment planning. Culturally competent counselors understand that symptoms of emotional distress and the meaning that clients make of these symptoms are culturally bound. Similarly, a client's culture influences what types of interventions are acceptable and seen to be useful. Frank and Frank (1993), in their seminal review of the elements of healing relationships, note that a shared belief in the benefits of the helping process is a central characteristic of healing relationships. Important cultural considerations include the client's preferred coping style, worldview regarding health and ways to achieve health, social resources as defined by the client, level of acculturation, language, and feelings about negative self-disclosure. Additionally, the relationship between the client's distress and oppression needs to be examined and accounted for. Culturally competent treatment planning may need to include consultation regarding legal issues and social resources from within the client's culture (Cormier & Nurius, 2002, cited in Hackney & Cormier, 2005; Sommers-Flanagan & Sommers-Flanagan, 2003).

MOTIVATION AND READINESS FOR CHANGE

EFFECTIVE TREATMENT PLANS reflect the client's level of motivation and contain goals that are consistent with the client's readiness for change. Prochaska and DiClemente's model of the stages of change outlines five stages of change readiness including precontemplation, contemplation, preparation for change, action, and maintenance (Prochaska, Norcross, & DiClemente, 2005).

Clients in the *precontemplation* stage are not actively considering change nor committed to the change process. An example of someone in the precontemplation stage is the client who comes to counseling because someone else wants the client to change. Counseling goals and objectives that identify change as the counseling outcome are not consistent with the client's level of motivation. Goals, objectives, and interventions that address validation of the client's feelings, including resistance to change, are more consistent with this client's level of motivation.

During the *contemplation* stage, clients are still ambivalent about change but are actively engaged in considering the benefits of change. Treatment plans too focused on making behavioral changes overreach the client's commitment to change. In this stage, the focus needs to be on consideration of the benefits and possible drawbacks to change and raising awareness of the impact of the client's behavior on self and others.

During the *preparation for change* stage, clients have made a commitment to change and are setting the stage to make change possible. Treatment plans that focus on helping clients identify resources and roadblocks, provide support for desired changes, help the client develop a personal sense of efficacy around the possibility of change, and encourage a supportive social network for the desired changes are consistent with this level of readiness for change.

During the *action* stage, clients are engaged in the desired changes. Here, treatment plans should focus on avenues of continued support both internal and external. The focus is not on whether change should happen but rather on how to support continuation of desired habits.

The *maintenance* stage of change readiness assumes that the client is actively engaged in the desired behaviors and wants to ensure long-term success. In this instance, the focus is on developing ongoing mechanisms of support as well as planning for relapse prevention and control.

The following case illustrates the need to construct treatment plans that are consistent with clients' motivation:

> Susan comes to counseling due to feelings of sadness and disinterest in her daily activities. She reports that since her best friend moved to another state 3 months ago she has been feeling lonely and disinterested in activities that she previously enjoyed. She reports coming home from work, watching television, drinking three to four glasses of wine at night and going to bed very late. She works as an administrative assistant for a

school superintendent, and she reports that she has begun making more mistakes at work. She denies any suicidal ideation but is finding life increasingly boring and beginning to wonder, "What's the point?" Susan has a history of several episodes of major depression in her 20s. These periods coincided with the death of her sister and her parent's relocation to Florida. Susan is not sleeping well, has little energy, and feels herself to be unattractive and useless. She has gained 10 pounds in the past 3 months and was recently diagnosed with high blood pressure. Susan is interested in finding meaningful activities and feeling physically better. While she recognizes the link between loss and depression currently and historically, she reports that she is not really interested in talking much about her friend's move, her sister's death, or her relationship with her parents. She notes that she does not see the point in crying over spilt milk.

While alleviating depression is a major concern, the pathways used need to reflect the client's level of motivation and preferred coping style. Insisting on insight-oriented approaches that require an affective engagement with painful events may risk client frustration and alienation from the counseling process. One could say that Susan is precontemplative regarding the benefits of exploring the relationships between losses and depression. This client is, however, quite motivated to engage in behavioral changes regarding exercise, socialization, and alcohol consumption. In this case an effective treatment plan would validate her reluctance to engage in insight-oriented interventions (ironically, a supportive exploration of why she does not wish to do this may in fact promote a future willingness to examine these issues) and focus on those changes she is ready to make.

THEORETICAL ORIENTATION AND TREATMENT PLANS

COUNSELORS' THEORETICAL ORIENTATION provides a framework for counseling and informs treatment goals, objectives, and interventions to achieve these objectives. A counselor operating within the context of a particular theory will conceptualize the client's presenting concerns and helpful interventions through the counselor's theoretical lens. For example, counselors operating from a behavioral lens will understand the client's problems in terms of maladaptive learning and will likely be drawn to interventions that rely on learning principles and behavioral rehearsal. Counselors operating from a person-centered lens will understand the client's problems from the perspective of conditional worth and the absence of authenticity and will rely on interventions that reflect a belief in the provision of empathy, unconditional positive regard, and congruency as the medium of change.

From an integrated theoretical lens, clients are viewed holistically and seen as biologically grounded, thinking, feeling, and behaving people embedded in particular social, cultural, and political contexts. Treatment plans will result from an evaluation of what types of interventions will be most effective in addressing the client's presenting concerns. As such, interventions will be drawn from multiple theoretical models. For example, when a client presents with feelings of sadness, the counselor and client will examine not only the subjective experience of sadness but will also consider the client's social networks, physical conditions, and ideas about self and others. A determination can then be made as to what interventions will be most beneficial to the client. Interventions that reflect behavior change may be drawn from behavioral models, interventions that target exploration of feeling and meaning in the client's life may be drawn from humanistic-existential and cognitive models, and interventions that target social networks might be drawn from systems models.

COMPREHENSIVE TREATMENT PLANNING

TREATMENT PLANNING STARTS with an accurate assessment of the client's presenting issues, diagnosis, and a clear understanding of what the client wants to see different in his or her life. It is important to take a holistic perspective and examine clients' issues from an emotional, cognitive, behavioral, social, and biological perspective. While treatment plans may not include all of these dimensions, they should be considered before developing a plan that focuses on some dimensions over others. Falvey, Bray, and Hebert (2005) found that more experienced therapists considered a broader scope of information than did novice therapists when developing treatment plans.

Seligman (2004) and Lazarus (Lazarus & Beutler, 1993; Lazarus & Lazarus, 2005) developed comprehensive models of assessment and treatment planning. These models take a holistic approach to understanding the client's presenting concerns and to the treatment process. Both of these models help counselors consider a broad range of client, counselor, and social considerations in treatment planning.

Seligman (2004) uses the acronym DO A CLIENT MAP as the outline for her model. The following are considered:

D What is the diagnosis?
O What are the outcome objectives?

A   What types of information need to be gathered to develop effective treatment?

C   What counselor characteristics will facilitate effective treatment?

L   Where should treatment be located (outpatient/inpatient, etc.)?

I   What types of interventions are indicated by the literature?

E   What should be the emphasis of treatment (present, past, future; insight-oriented, supportive, etc.)?

N   How many people should be involved in the treatment and who?

T   How frequent and how long should counseling sessions be?

M   Is a medication evaluation indicated?

A   Are there other adjunctive services that would support treatment (e.g., Alcoholics Anonymous)?

P   What is the prognosis? What outcomes can realistically be expected?

The BASIC ID model (Lazarus & Beutler, 1993; Lazarus & Lazurus, 2005) evaluates the following dimensions: behavior, affect, sensations, imagery, cognition, interpersonal relationships, and drugs and biology. Counselors evaluate problems that exist in each of these dimensions and base their treatment interventions on those areas that are problematic.

TREATMENT PLAN FORMATS

THE WAY THAT treatment plans are formatted depends on the requirements of the organization in which treatment takes place, and accreditation and insurance requirements. Jongsma and Peterson (1999) outline a six-step model that includes (1) problem selection, (2) problem definition, (3) goal development, (4) objective construction, (5) intervention creation, and (6) diagnosis determination. Sommers-Flanagan and Sommers-Flanagan (2003) note that appropriate treatment plans incorporate the outcome literature regarding the client's presenting concern; the counselor's skills, expertise, and counseling style; and the client's preferences regarding the counseling process.

Treatment goals are aspirational statements that are long-term in nature. An example of an aspirational goal is, "John Doe will effectively manage stress." Goals are broad-based positive outcomes and are related to the client's primary presenting concern and diagnostic considerations. Objectives, on the other hand, are shorter term, measurable outcomes. Interventions are the methods that counselors employ with clients to help clients meet their objectives.

If the goal is for the client to become an effective manager of stress, the objectives under this goal are short-term measurable outcomes that are in the service of ultimately achieving this goal. Exercising for

30 minutes three times per week is a short-term, observable, and measurable objective that will contribute to becoming an effective manager of stress. Participating in pleasurable social activity one time per week might be another objective supporting effective stress management. Clearly, the objectives are identified through a careful analysis of what contributes to the client's difficulties managing stress, what the client feels will be important steps in stress management, and what the client is actually motivated to do. Objectives should reflect treatments that the literature suggests are considered effective in addressing the client's diagnosis.

Interventions supporting the objective of exercising three times per week might include homework assignments that require the client to explore exercise options in his or her area; to identify impediments to exercise; and to identify people who can support the client's exercise program. Similarly, identifying social activities that the client has found pleasurable in the past; agreeing on gradually increasing levels of social interaction; identifying groups that the client might be willing to join; and examining self-statements that interfere with engaging in social activities are interventions that might be used to meet the objective of increased socialization.

Treatment plans target goals that are most important to clients. The number of goals should be limited, and each goal should be supported by realistic objectives. It can be overwhelming and confusing to clients and counselors alike when too many goals and objectives are identified as the focus of treatment.

Treatment plans, to be useful, are made explicit (preferably through a written agreement) and monitored on a regular basis. Counselors need to be flexible and willing to modify treatment goals when it becomes apparent that they are too ambitious or do not meet the client's evolving needs. A good treatment plan helps counselors answer the question, What are we trying to accomplish during our time together? When counselors find themselves unable to answer this question, it may be an indicator that the treatment plan has been waylaid or that the treatment plan needs to be reconsidered.

The following sample treatment plan refers back to the case of Susan illustrated earlier in this chapter. The treatment plan addresses her counseling interests and the symptoms with which she struggles.

Goal: Susan will enjoy positive mood.

Objective 1. Susan will increase her social network.

Intervention 1.a. Susan will identify at least one acquaintance with whom she would be willing to initiate some form of social contact.

Intervention 1.b. Through role plays, visualizations, and cognitive reframing, Susan will develop the confidence to initiate social contact with at least one identified person.

Intervention 1.c. Susan will explore social groups in her area and identify those which she would consider joining.

Intervention 1.d. Susan will examine negative self-messages that inhibit her from joining groups.

Objective 2. Susan will decrease her alcohol consumption.

Intervention 2.a. Susan will identify behaviors that contribute to increased alcohol consumption, including the identification of evening activities that do not allow for alcohol use.

Objective 3. Susan will exercise at least three times per week.

Intervention 3.a. Susan will identify physical activities she has enjoyed in the past.

Intervention 3.b. Susan will identify at least one person she feels would be interested in joining her in some form of physical activity.

Intervention 3.c. Through role plays, visualizations, and cognitive strategies, Susan will develop the confidence to ask at least one identified person to join her in some physical activity.

Intervention 3.d. Susan will consult with her primary care provider (PCP) regarding her overall health before beginning an exercise program.

Objective 4. Susan will learn to manage depressive symptoms.

Intervention 4.a. Susan will read psychoeducational material regarding depression and its management.

Intervention 4.b. Susan will consult with her physician regarding her identified symptoms of depression.

Intervention 4.c. Susan will explore the pros and cons of talking about her experiences of loss and their relationship to her depression.

CONCLUSION

TREATMENT PLANNING IS an essential part of the counseling process. It is no longer acceptable to have vague ideas regarding the course and expected outcome of treatment. Clients need to be actively engaged in the treatment planning process with treatment goals reflecting areas that are most important to clients. Treatment plans should address both client's desired changes and diagnostic concerns. Consideration should be given to the intensity of treatment needs, counselor's areas of skill, as well as other adjunctive services that might facilitate reaching target goals. A holistic lens ensures that treatment plans are based on an assessment of multiple dimensions of clients' lives with the areas implicated in the clients' distress as the targets of treatment.

REFERENCES

Falvey, J. E., Bray, T. E., & Hebert, D. J. (2005). Case conceptualization and treatment planning: Investigation of problem-solving and clinical judgment. *Journal of Mental Health Counseling, 27*(4), 348–372.

Frank, J., & Frank, J. (1993). *Persuasion and healing: A comparative study of psychotherapy* (3rd ed.). Baltimore: Johns Hopkins Press.

Hackney, H., & Cormier, S. (2005). *The professional counselor* (5th ed.). Boston: Pearson Education.

Johnson, D., & Johnson, S. (2003). *Real world treatment planning.* Pacific Grove, CA: Brooks/Cole-Thomson Learning.

Jongsma, A. E. (2005). Psychotherapy treatment plan writing. In G. P. Koocher, J. C. Norcross, & S. S. Hill (Eds.), *Psychologists' desk reference* (2nd ed., pp. 232–235). New York: Oxford University Press.

Jongsma, A. E., & Peterson, L. M. (1999). *The complete adult psychotherapy treatment planner* (2nd ed.). New York: Wiley.

Lazarus, A. A., & Beutler, L. E. (1993). On technical eclecticism. *Journal of Counseling and Development, 71*(4), 381–385.

Lazarus, A. L., & Lazarus, C. N. (2005). Clinical purposes of the multimodal life history inventory. In G. P. Koocher, J. C. Norcross, & S. S. Hill (Eds.), *Psychologists' desk reference* (2nd ed., pp. 232–235). New York: Oxford University Press.

Prochaska, J. O., Norcross, J. C., & DiClemente, C. C. (2005). Stages of change: Prescriptive guidelines. In G. P. Koocher, J. C. Norcross, & S. S. Hill (Eds.), *Psychologists' desk reference* (2nd ed., pp. 226–231). New York: Oxford University Press.

Seligman, L. (2004). *Technical and conceptual skills for mental health professionals.* Upper Saddle River, NJ: Pearson-Merrill/Prentice Hall.

Sommers-Flannagan, J., & Sommers-Flannagan, R. (2003). *Clinical interviewing* (3rd ed.). Hoboken, NJ: Wiley.

15

Enhancing Client Return After the First Session, and Alternatively Dealing With Early Termination

IRMO MARINI

T HIS CHAPTER EXPLORES two separate, but very common, occurrences in the counseling process: (1) clients who do not return after the first session, and (2) effectively dealing with early termination of counseling. Most practitioners are all too familiar with one or both of these phenomena in counseling and are often left wondering what happened during the process for it to end prematurely or to never begin. As such, this section addresses probable reasons why clients do not return following the first session and offers practical strategies regarding how to minimize this occurrence. Separately, potential reasons for early termination of counseling and strategies to minimize this occurrence are explored.

ENHANCING CLIENT RETURN FOLLOWING THE FIRST SESSION

THE STATISTICS ARE somewhat staggering regarding the rate of attrition in returning to counseling following the first session. Sue and Sue (2003) cite findings indicating that in counseling interactions between a White counselor and a person of minority, the percentage of clients that return for a second visit is less than 50%. In cases where White clients are involved, there is an attrition rate of approximately 30% for a second visit. Psychologically, it often takes a tremendous amount of thought, motivation, and courage for individuals to eventually decide to seek out counseling services to begin with, so what is it then between the counselor and client interaction dynamics that ultimately leads a client to not return?

In the case of White counselors and minority clients (see chapter 18 for a lengthier discussion), Sue and Sue (2003) suggest that part of the problem is counselor insensitivity regarding ethnic or racial cultural differences. Counselor bias or opposing belief systems may be directly or indirectly conveyed to the minority client, who ultimately decides the counselor is judgmental, unable to relate or empathize, or simply not perceived competent enough to appreciate the cultural differences. The past decade has seen numerous books on multicultural competency as well as its integration into the *American Counseling Association Code of Ethics* (Sue et al., 1998; www.counseling.org).

Aside from cultural differences, however, there are most likely other factors at work here as well, especially since White clients do not return for a second session about one-third of the time. In some instances, although clients may show up for the first session believing they are ready to make a perceived needed life change, they ultimately may decide otherwise during the session if the counselor appropriately conveys the work that may need to be done, and essentially that there is no quick-cure magic pill.

STAGES OF CHANGE

IN MOTIVATIONAL INTERVIEWING, Miller and Rollnick (2002) discuss Prochaska and DiClemente's six stages of change regarding the reluctant or unsure client who may be resistant to making changes. Counselors who are unaware of the different stages of change for resistant clients may otherwise believe that because the client has shown up at the counselor's door, he or she must be ready and motivated to take the necessary steps to change. Unfortunately, this is not always the case. Miller and Rollnick define the six sequential stages as (1) *precontemplation*—the individual is not yet considering the need for change or does not perceive having a problem. Most clients who voluntarily come to counseling on their own volition likely are not at this stage. Persons typically entering at this stage might be court-mandated persons with alcoholism who do not believe they have a drinking problem; (2) *contemplation*—a period of ambivalence in which clients realize they have some problems but are unsure whether they need to change their behavior. Many counselors likely see clients at this stage, who after the first session may decide it is too much work and convince themselves that their problems are not so bad after all. A skilled counselor may be able to motivate such a client to return. However, if the counselor begins to list counseling strategies and homework, he or she is likely to lose the client; (3) *determination*—this is the period in which clients realize their problem is a concern and decide to do something about it. They come to counseling looking for strategies to change. If the session does not go well, clients may slip back into contemplation. If a good rapport is not established with a counselor, the client will likely seek out another counselor. In any instance, the stage allows the window of opportunity for clients to begin working on making a change; (4) *action*—during this stage, clients are onboard and ready to actively engage in behavior, thought, and affect change. This may mean smoking or drinking cessation, assertiveness training, changing thought patterns, weight loss behaviors, and so forth; (5) *maintenance*—the stage at which clients are attempting to maintain their changed behavior. Monitoring a client's maintenance so that a relapse doesn't occur becomes particularly important; and (6) *relapse*—the potential for client relapse must be met with reassurance that the setback does not mean the client is a failure, but rather that relapse is to be expected. If this occurs, the client reenters the action stage and explores the reasons why relapse occurred. Prochaska, Norcross, and DiClemente (1994) indicate that only about 20% of the population is able to maintain their desired change on the first attempt.

Prochaska (as cited by Kelley, 2006) notes the importance of basic Carl Roger's client-centered interpersonal skills such as warmth, genuineness, and caring as among the most cited reasons as to how and why clients choose a counselor. A caring personal style as opposed to a formal or "I'm the expert" approach serves to not intimidate a new client. Counselor expertise is also found to be most important. As such, Kelley notes the importance of warmth and self-disclosure during the first session, in which the counselor discloses his or her education and training background. In actuality, most licensing and certifying bodies mandate that counselors provide a written professional disclosure statement to new clients during the initial session. The statement generally includes counselor name; degree, discipline, institution, and year; listing of all licenses and certifications; number of years of counseling service and populations served; description of services offered; length of sessions and fees charged as well as cancellation policy; methods of reimbursement; a statement regarding diagnosis and it becoming a part of a client's record; an explanation of confidentiality and duty to warn; information on where to file complaints; and finally, a place for both parties to sign. Professional disclosure provides clients with answers to many questions they might otherwise have about the process, policies, and procedures. Again, if the counselor overwhelms a potential new client and then inundates him or her with how long and hard a process counseling is going to be, clients may not return. As such, the skilled counselor will disclose the necessary information while at the same time not overwhelm a new client. Prochaska (as cited by Kelley, 2006) states that reversing deeply embedded behaviors takes an average of 6 months to change, and cites 14 counseling sessions on average to move from the action stage to the maintenance stage.

As noted above, establishing a good rapport with a new client is paramount during the first session. Prochaska (as cited by Kelley, 2006) cites lack of empathy as a second main reason why clients terminate therapy. Some counselors unfortunately are entrenched in a medical model–type paradigm in which they view themselves as the expert to be faithfully listened to, and the client as a submissive bystander in counseling. This cold and perceived uncaring approach may be a key factor as to why clients do not return. Indeed, Kelley states that counselor warmth and empathy, and a caring attitude, may not only be the single most important factor for clients returning but also with regard to client progress in therapy. This finding, of course, is what Carl Rogers (1989) has propounded for more than 30 years.

Regarding other specific strategies for ensuring clients' return for a second visit, counselors may want to view the situation as a job interview. Some strategies would include the following:

1. Introduce yourself in a caring way; give a firm handshake with a smile; offer a beverage. Some employer job interview studies suggest that employers make a decision to hire within the first 2 minutes. First impressions are likely just as important in meeting a new counselor.
2. Review the professional disclosure statement in a nonrushed, relaxed manner, allowing for questions and making sure not to overwhelm the client.
3. Kelley (2006) recommends preparing for the second session by giving clients three things: an appointment card that includes a no-show policy fee, a relevant homework assignment or some readings (not too burdensome), and an affirmation card or statement that clients can read each day to motivate them to return.

4. Kelley also advises follow-up welcome letters and perhaps a satisfaction survey with the letter following the first session. This makes it more difficult for clients not to show up when the counselor has taken the time to formally welcome them as well as ask for feedback regarding how the session went. She recommends that if clients do not show up for an appointment, the counselor should phone to see why. If no response, another satisfaction survey could be resent once again to obtain feedback.

Overall, counselor demeanor in conveying a warm, caring, and genuine attitude in all communications with clients typically is able to better establish a good rapport. Going over professional disclosure information as well as the counseling process without overwhelming the client is critical to ensuring client return. Practical strategies, such as an appointment and affirmation card, and a small relevant homework or reading assignment, work to motivate client commitment. Finally, sending follow-up welcome letters, calling clients if they miss an appointment, and mailing a satisfaction survey all convey a counselor who cares.

DEALING WITH EARLY TERMINATION

RESEARCH REGARDING EARLY termination of therapy has for the most part been speculative and theoretical, rather than empirically derived (Roe, Dekel, Harel, & Fennig, 2006). Central questions regarding early termination deal with Who decides when therapy ends? How should it be handled? When should it end? These are all questions that most counselors have little education or training on, and ones that practitioners are often uncertain about. On the surface, termination should revolve around whether treatment goals have been attained. Interestingly, the difference in perception between counselor and client as to whether and when explicit treatment goals have been met is often debatable, and subsequently, the result of an awkward or unplanned termination.

Treatment goals and length of treatment will vary depending on counselor theoretical orientation. Cognitive behavior therapy, for example, is usually short term, focusing primarily on symptom reduction through the development of client coping skills and self-efficacy, and less emphasis on the client–counselor relationship (Goldfried, 2002). Experiential therapy, on the other hand, focuses on change as a process and termination being more of a choice rather than an endpoint after accomplishing goals. The counselor weans away from providing his or her input slowly, thus gradually empowering clients to make their own decisions. Psychodynamic therapy may have as one of its goals to explore separation and loss emotion as therapy comes to an end.

From the available empirical literature, Kramer (1986) interviewed 20 private practice psychotherapists and found that they rarely discussed termination with clients, nor did they take the time to prepare clients for termination of therapy. When a client decided to end therapy, therapists tended to attribute the client's request as a form of acting out or avoiding highly emotionally laden topics. Related studies show similar findings in that therapists cite lack of motivation (Rosenbaum & Horowitz, 1983), client improvement (Pekarik & Finney-Owen, 1987), and client resistance (Lane, 1984) as common reasons for client early termination. Conversely, Hunsley, Aubry, Verstervelt, and Vito (1999) assessed client and counselor reasons for termination. Although having met goals was rated highest by the client and counselor (44% versus 39%, respectively), other reasons cited were vastly different. For example, 34% of clients rated dissatisfaction as the reason for termination, but virtually none of the counselors rated this item. Similar findings of mutually agreed-upon goal attainment, situational circumstances, or dissatisfaction with counseling have been found in other studies (Renk & Dinger, 2002; Todd, Deane, & Bragdon, 2003).

In Roe et al.'s (2006) study of 84 private practice clients who had been in counseling for 6–27 months, the authors found the most commonly cited reasons for client termination of therapy were circumstantial (financial 54%, external reasons 30%), achievement of treatment goals (45%), dissatisfaction with therapist (36%), dissatisfaction with therapy (i.e., became stuck 16%, not helpful to begin with 6%, psychotherapy became negative 8%, and disagreements about therapeutic technique 9%), need for independence (14%), and busy with a new relationship (12%). It appears from these findings that clients may perceive they have gotten better and met their goals, while counselors may not agree. In addition, situational circumstances such as finances, new relationship, or other reasons may lead to early termination. Finally, it appears that some therapy sessions go stagnant or turn negative after a time as perceived by clients, while counselors may not be remotely aware of the fact that their clients are no longer benefiting from counseling. In this instance, some clients feel stuck, decide the therapy wasn't helpful to begin with, feel a need to become more independent, or disagree with the techniques being used.

So what can be synthesized from available research into practical strategies for counselors regarding termination of therapy? First is the realization that clients may terminate counseling for circumstantial reasons, having nothing to do with the counselor or his or her practices.

161

*Enhancing Client
Return After the
First Session,
and Alternatively
Dealing With Earl*
Termination

Second, clients may early terminate because they perceive they have met their goals, have become more independent, and have obtained self-growth. Counselors may disagree and see termination as a defensive maneuver when this is not the case. Third, counselors must have the insight to know when sessions have become stagnant and there are no signs of improvement or further improvement. Finally, it appears in some cases that, although counseling may have started off well, some clients report the counselor and his or her techniques have taken a downward turn and become more negative. Practical strategies for counselors include the following:

1. After collaboratively establishing treatment goals at the beginning of counseling, periodically review and go over how the client perceives progress is being made. This occasional assessment can minimize client perceptions of feeling stuck or that counseling has in fact become negative. Reevaluating and modifying treatment goals would then be in order.
2. Counselors must be able to objectively evaluate whether a client's request for what appears to be early termination is a valid one. Some counselors may think the decision is premature; others may not want to lose the business. In cases where the counselor believes the client's work is not yet done, a frank discussion regarding whether the client is dissatisfied with some aspect of the process or whether the client has progressed enough to move forward without accomplishing all the goals should be assessed. If the client simply does not return, a follow-up phone call to determine why is appropriate.
3. Since the counseling process should be a collaborative one, counselors are advised to include their clients in determining and describing counseling techniques. As noted in previous studies, some clients terminate therapy because they did not like the techniques being used. This suggests that some counselors try techniques without disclosing them to the client beforehand.
4. Develop a satisfaction survey. In all cases, regardless of early termination or mutually agreed-upon treatment goals being met, counselors should seek ongoing feedback regarding their services. Ideally, surveys should be mailed out to clients with a self-addressed stamped envelope and the survey should be anonymous, so the client does not feel the pressure to respond in a socially desirable manner. When counselors begin receiving consistent negative responses regarding their style or technique, this is valuable information regarding improving services.

CONCLUSION

THE REAL-LIFE NUANCES of the counseling process often involve clients not returning for a second visit or, alternatively, clients terminating counseling without reason. Counselors are often left wondering if it was something they said or did. Most counseling programs do not adequately deal with this common occurrence because many educators and practitioners believe clients are ready and motivated to change when they come for counseling. As noted from theory on change and empirical research regarding early termination, some clients may be contemplating change but not ready to make it. Although counselors must cover a great deal of policy and procedure information regarding professional disclosure during the first session, they must be cautious not to overwhelm the client who is only contemplating a needed change. In addition, establishing a rapport by conveying caring, warmth, and genuineness during the first and subsequent sessions is most important in retaining clients. Counselor competence and expertise is equally important. Collaboratively establishing treatment goals, and then periodically reviewing the progress of these goals, helps to minimize differing perceptions between counselor and client as to whether goals are completed or near completion. This procedure should ultimately minimize the occurrence of early termination, provided there are no other circumstantial reasons. Finally, in all instances, counselors, no matter how seemingly successful, should solicit ongoing feedback from clients regarding satisfaction with counseling. By continuing to hone their skills, counselors can be assured they are offering quality services. Indeed, with excellent client feedback, counselors may be able to further market their services via former client endorsements.

REFERENCES

Goldfried, M. R. (2002). A cognitive-behavioral perspective on termination. *Journal of Psychotherapy Integration, 12*(3), 364–372.

Hunsley, J., Aubry, T. D., Verstervelt, C. M., & Vito, D. (1999). Comparing therapist and client perspectives on reasons for psychotherapy termination. *Psychotherapy, 36*(4), 380–388.

Kelley, L. (2006). Motivating clients to show up for their next scheduled visit. *Counseling Today*. Arlington, VA: American Counseling Association.

Kramer, S. A. (1986). The termination process in open-ended psychotherapy: Guidelines for clinical practice. *Psychotherapy, 23*(4), 526–531.

Lane, R. C. (1984). The difficult patient, resistance, and the negative therapeutic reaction: A review of the literature. *Current Issues in Psychoanalytic Practice, 1*(4), 83–106.

163

*Enhancing Client
Return After the
First Session,
and Alternatively
Dealing With Early
Termination*

Miller, W. R., & Rollnick, S. (2002). *Motivational interviewing: Preparing people for change* (2nd ed.). New York: Guilford Press.

Pekarik, G., & Finney-Owen, K. (1987). Out-patient clinic therapist attitudes and beliefs relevant to client dropout. *Community Mental Health Journal, 23,* 120–130.

Prochaska, J. O., Norcross, J., & DiClemente, C. (1994). *Changing for good: A revolutionary six stage program for overcoming bad habits and moving your life positively forward*. New York: Avon Books.

Renk, K., & Dinger, T. M. (2002). Reasons for therapy termination in a university psychology clinic. *Journal of Clinical Psychology, 58*(9), 1173–1181.

Roe, D., Dekel, R., Harel, G., & Fennig, S. (2006). Client's reasons for terminating psychotherapy: A quantitative and qualitative inquiry. *Psychology and Psychotherapy: Research and Practice, 79,* 529–538.

Rogers, C. (1989). *On becoming a person: A therapist's view of psychotherapy*. New York: Houghton Mifflin.

Rosenbaum, R., & Horowitz, M. J. (1983). Motivation for psychotherapy: A factorial and conceptual analysis. *Psychotherapy: Theory, & Practice, 20*(3), 346–354.

Sue, D. W., Carter, R. T., Cases, J. M., Fouad, N. A., Ivey, A. E., Jensen, M., et al. (1998). *Multicultural counseling competencies: Individual and organizational development*. Thousand Oaks, CA: Sage Publications.

Sue, D. W., & Sue, D. (2003). *Counseling the culturally diverse: Theory and practice* (3rd ed.). New York: Wiley.

Todd, D. M., Deane, F. P., & Bragdon, R. A. (2003). Client and therapist reasons for termination: A conceptualization and preliminary validation. *Journal of Clinical Psychology, 59,* 133–147.

16

Effective Use of Therapeutic Homework Assignments

NANCY A. PACHANA AND NIKOLAOS KAZANTZIS

HOMEWORK ASSIGNMENTS ARE meaningful and intentional therapeutic activities incorporated into counseling and psychotherapy to facilitate client adjustment and benefit. This chapter presents an overview of a guiding model for clinical practice for the use of homework with a broad spectrum of clients and presenting problems. As with many aspects of clinical practice, these guidelines will be most effective if tailored to meet the individual client's goals for therapy. Specific suggestions for increasing counselors' skills in incorporating homework assignments into the therapy process are provided. The foundation for this material is primarily based on the work of Aaron T. Beck's (1976) cognitive theory and system of psychotherapy.

Use of between-session time for augmenting psychological treatment dates from its suggested utility by early psychodynamic practitioners through to its contemporary elaboration and central focus in cognitive behavior therapy contexts. Within the practice of cognitive behavior and behavioral therapies, as well as other models of therapy (e.g., client-centered, emotion-focused experiential, and constructivist therapies; see Kazantzis, Lampropoulos, & Deane, 2005), homework is envisioned to serve clients' practice, maintenance, and generalization of therapeutic skills.

DEFINING HOMEWORK ASSIGNMENTS

HOMEWORK AS IT is implemented in both research and clinical practice is quite heterogeneous, and different therapeutic models operationalize homework differently. Any type of between-session therapeutic activity has the potential to qualify as homework. Certainly, behaviors and cognitions are commonly addressed by homework, but better accessing of emotions, or addressing interpersonal relationships, are examples of other directions that homework can take. The particular selection of specific homework tasks is ideally guided by the theoretical framework in which the therapist is working. For instance, a cognitive behavior therapist is primarily interested in helping clients to learn skills to relieve distress through evaluating their surface level cognitions, testing out their rules and assumptions, or gathering prospective evidence to strengthen positive core level beliefs about themselves, other people, the world, and the future that were not identified in childhood. In the client-centered approaches, client-initiated homework assignments are exclusively encouraged, rather than homework that is content or process directed by the therapist (Kazantzis & L'Abate, 2007). Whatever their nature, between session activities can assist in increasing the impact of gains made in therapy on clients' lives. Making appropriate suggestions about how clients might facilitate their own learning between sessions can help achieve this goal. Thus, the emphasis on homework as a process for facilitating learning is common to all psychotherapies. Therapeutic homework is different from schoolwork in that it is not graded, cannot be "passed" or "failed," and even noncompletion provides useful information (i.e., knowing what does not work for clients is helpful). For this reason, we do not recommend the use of the term *homework* with clients, as it may be problematic and viewed as reflecting the "assigned" and "compulsory" nature of the activity, which must be complied with and then "judged" by the therapist. Many clients may see such assignments as emphasizing a power differential in the therapeutic relationship, or it may exacerbate other issues within the therapeutic dynamic (e.g., age differences between therapist and client). If well presented in a collaborative fashion, however, such *self-help assignments* or *home practice activities* can assist clients not only to cement learning but to address other foci of therapy.

THEORETICAL AND EMPIRICAL SUPPORT

A THEORETICAL FRAMEWORK to explain the mechanisms be-hind how clients engage in homework assignments, and how such successful engagement can augment psychotherapy outcomes, is outlined in Kazantzis, Deane, Ronan, and L'Abate (2005). The behavioral literature suggests that key elements to the successful introduction of homework include therapist engagement and positive endorsement of this aspect of therapy, careful consideration of issues around generalizing newly learned positive responses in the clients' own contexts, and the need for regular practice of said responses. The literature emphasizes the role of client beliefs at the time when specific tasks are first suggested and practiced in session; when the specifics of when, where, how often, and how long are collaboratively discussed; and when clients reflect and synthesize their between-session experience in terms of their therapy goals. Thus, as outlined in the Kazantzis and colleagues practitioner volume, the interplay of classical and operant processes, with client attitudes threaded throughout the process, is integral to understanding client engagement with homework.

Empirical work on homework to date tends to concentrate on fairly basic associations between ratings of homework compliance and symptom reduction. The data support various assertions, namely, (1) psychotherapy involving homework produces better clinical outcomes when contrasted with a comparable psychotherapy without homework; (2) client engagement with homework is associated (and can be taken as an indicator) of positive outcome; (3) practitioners from various theoretical approaches and training backgrounds report the use of homework; and (4) in anonymous surveys, practitioners do not self-report the use of homework in a manner consistent with recommendations for practice appearing in the literature (Kazantzis & Deane, 1999).

There is also empirical support for the importance of client beliefs about between-session activities. One study found a surprisingly low 41% concordance rate between therapist and client perceptions of the assigned homework (Scheel, Hoggan, Willie, McDonald, & Tonin, 1998), underscoring the value of having clients review their understanding of the rationale and purpose of any homework activity. Another study (Conoley, Padula, Payton, & Daniels, 1994) identified three key predictors of client acceptability of homework activities: (1) the link between treatment goals and the content of the assignment, (2) the difficulty level of the assignment, and (3) the extent to which the homework was designed to build on client strengths. This chapter builds on this theoretical and empirical support and highlights key issues in using homework based on the Kazantzis, Deane et al. (2005) guiding model for clinical practice.

THE IMPORTANCE OF THE THERAPEUTIC ALLIANCE/RELATIONSHIP

THE NATURE OF the therapeutic relationship, as well as the therapist's assumptions and behaviors in using homework assignments in practice, can influence the success of any between-session activities recommended to the client. While a strong therapeutic relationship can be supposed to facilitate the effective utilization of homework by the client, the fact that homework is often assigned from the first session poses a significant challenge. This challenge underscores the necessity of a firm understanding of potential uses and limitations of a flexible range of homework options, as well as the need to present the idea of homework in a careful and considered manner.

A collaborative approach and active involvement of the client is required to facilitate the development of successful between-session activities (Trygon & Winograd, 2001). Barriers to such collaborative work from all parties must be addressed. Distrust, unrealistic expectations, and fear of failure on the part of either the therapist or the client can disrupt homework, and ultimately, the therapy process itself. The therapist's empathic, curious, and genuine style can steer the process of discussing homework far away from a therapy environment where a client is socialized as a passive recipient of interventions, or where the therapist is directive or punitive regarding nonengagement of tasks. Clear communication at all points, encouragement of voicing questions or concerns, and willingness to be flexible and revise strategies and directions, again on the parts of all parties to therapy, can help avoid disengagement with homework activities.

Consistency on the part of the therapist sends the message that homework is an important part of the therapy, at all phases of therapy. If homework is not reviewed or planned strategically, sensitively, and above all, consistently, then the client may arrive at a host of negative assumptions. For example, the client may believe that the therapist did not feel the homework was important, or did not believe that the client was capable of completing the activity. Such assumptions can have a negative impact on future between-session activities as well as in-session progress.

KEY ISSUES IN INCORPORATING HOMEWORK INTO PRACTICE

HOMEWORK ENGAGES A client in a significant portion of time outside of the therapy session. Thus, a substantial amount of time is required in session to successfully develop homework activities.

Generally speaking, the therapist can view the integration of home-work into therapy as a three-stage process comprising the selection (design), discussion of the specifics, and review of homework tasks.

SELECTING (DESIGNING) HOMEWORK TASKS

SELECTING HOMEWORK IS, of course, vital, and predicated on sev-eral factors. A therapist might wish to choose activities that derive closely from the model of therapy to be followed in sessions, as in Aaron T. Beck's (1976) system of psychotherapy. When therapy sessions follow such a model (e.g., graded exposure for phobia, social phobia, panic, and obsessive-compulsive disorders), there can be some broad predetermined schedule of assignments based on the theoretical model explaining the etiology and maintenance of the disorder treated. Additionally, published therapy resources also provide flexible lists of homework assignments for various problems and populations (e.g., Bevilacqua & Dattilio, 2001).

Homework should be relevant to the client's goals. Failure to link the content of between-session activities to treatment goals jointly shared by the therapist and client is likely to make such activities ir-relevant or unhelpful. Likewise, homework should be aligned with the client's existing coping strategies. Clients often present with strong evidence that at least a portion of their current coping strategies are effective in providing relief from their emotional distress. The educa-tion and conceptualization processes in psychotherapy are ways to as-sist clients to evaluate to what extent their strategies are either helpful or serving to maintain their presenting problems. With this in mind, efforts to include the client's input in all aspects of homework discus-sions are vital.

The design of future between-session activities can proceed, with any relevant information with obstacles to completion already in mind. A rationale for the proposed homework activity should be presented, one that is congruent with the client's treatment goals and ability lev-els. A collaborative approach should ensure that the task is well defined and feasible. In-session practice of the activity, if appropriate, will give the client immediate experience of the benefits of the task, thereby boosting motivation and the client's sense of mastery. Homework as-signments can also be practiced using hypothetical situations in im-agery or in role plays with the therapist.

Practitioners may also wish to use empirically supported activities where possible. However, while there is limited empirical support for specific assignments (see review in Kazantzis, Deane et al., 2005), per-haps the nature of between-session activities, collaboratively arrived at and tailored to best meet individual needs and contexts, argues against the feasibility of such empirical reassurances. Moreover, two clients carrying out similar activities may experience activities very differently, arriving at unique experiential outcomes. There will also optimally be a dynamic relationship between in-session content and between-session activities. This relationship mitigates against having acutely distinct homework content.

A prudent rule of thumb is for therapists to only assign homework that they would be prepared to carry out themselves. A useful activity for therapists to engage in, particularly novice therapists, is to complete homework activities themselves from time to time. This is useful in enabling the therapist to fully appreciate what is involved in a given assignment, as well as an opportunity to encounter any potential external barriers or internal qualms about the nature and completion of the tasks themselves.

SPECIFICS OF THE HOMEWORK TASK

THE DISCUSSION ON specifics of the homework task ideally includes both practical issues, such as how frequent the activity is, as well as issues regarding external pressures from the environment (i.e., lack of support or resistance to the activities from family members), fears of failure and other beliefs on the part of the client, or other individual issues raised by the particular activity. Such discussions can have a direct and facilitative impact on the nature of broader issues and directions of therapy for a client in general.

Realistic appraisals of what homework can be accomplished by the client are essential to ensuring a positive learning experience. Such appraisals can be facilitated by having the client generate willingness, readiness, and confidence ratings regarding his or her perceived ability to complete the between-session activity. It is best if the therapist and client discuss all practical aspects of the homework before the rating is given (i.e., when, where, how often, how long). Using a scale from 0 to 100, where 0 represents "not at all willing/ready/confident" and 100 represents "totally willing/ready/confident," the client can indicate his or her beliefs about the activities under discussion before leaving the session. As a guideline, when ratings are less than 70%, the therapist should renegotiate the homework activity, considering perceived difficulty, potential barriers, and the benefits to the completion of the activity. When such discussions have been productive, the final confidence rating serves as a verbal commitment that the client intends to engage with the activities as suggested.

The therapist should ask the client to summarize the rationale and his or her expectations regarding the homework designed. Perceived task difficulty should be discussed and a rating obtained as discussed above. Finally, a written note of the homework for the client should be made for future reference of both parties.

REVIEWING HOMEWORK ASSIGNMENTS

THERE IS THE need to review the between-session activity from the previous week. At the outset of the following session, the therapist should discuss both the quality and quantity of completed activity as well as noncompletion. Reinforcement in the form of genuine praise should be offered for homework completed, and an attempt made to conceptualize with the client any portions of homework that were not completed. Here, problem solving of barriers to completion can assist with the planning of future homework.

There is strong empirical support for the association between homework completion and treatment outcome in cognitive behavioral approaches, with data accumulating for other therapy models. Moreover, there is emerging evidence to suggest that the quality of the client's homework is a strong predictor of treatment outcome. Therapists can thus regard the degree of learning through the completion of homework (above and beyond mere compliance) as a key indicator of treatment outcome.

Homework noncompletion is a common occurrence and should be expected by practitioners. In the majority of cases, this will involve some proportion of homework left uncompleted by some proportion of clients at various times, rather than wholesale disengagement with homework per se. However, as was alluded to above, much may be learned from how and why a particular activity was not completed, knowledge that may advance therapy in other areas as well. While a discussion of homework noncompletion may reveal client beliefs about the assignment (e.g., misunderstanding the homework, or seeing it as irrelevant in situ), it may also reveal a broader issue of the therapy process itself being off track, prompting the therapist and client to reevaluate and adjust conceptualizations and treatment goals.

COMMON DIFFICULTIES

COMMON DIFFICULTIES WITH homework include not linking homework to the treatment goals and individual conceptualization and selection of an assignment that does not address the client's presenting problem (Beck, 2005). Therapists may underestimate the demands of the particular homework activity, fail to be specific in outlining and explaining the exact nature of the task, or expect clients to work on the activities at a rate that is unrealistic. Therapists may assume clients will understand how to proceed with an activity when in fact modeling or practice of the activity in session would have been invaluable. Such in-session practice may also highlight potential barriers to the successful completion of homework.

Practical problem solving around ways to handle potential obstacles to completing activities in the real world can greatly enhance a client's confidence in his or her ability not only to complete a specific homework activity but also in a broader sense to reach desired treatment goals. The working through of the details of how to handle larger than anticipated crowds at an outing, for example, can prevent the client from abandoning a task altogether. Practical obstacles should be carefully distinguished from client's beliefs about the activity or his or her ability to negotiate it. Presenting activities as "experiments" to be conducted and carefully recorded by the client can reinforce the notion that whatever happens, useful data can be generated and brought back to the therapy session for discussion. This can be a point to suggest the keeping of therapy notes on the part of the client. Notes on in-session and between-session activities can strengthen the collaboration, provide a helpful reminder of key points, and serve as a repository of successful strategies available to the client after the completion of therapy.

CONCLUSION

THIS CHAPTER PRESENTS an overview of a guiding model for clinical practice for the use of homework with a broad spectrum of clients with presenting problems. Individualized homework assignments are envisioned to serve clients' practice, maintenance, and generalization of therapeutic skills using a variety of counseling and psychotherapy approaches. Homework is an effective element of counseling, leading to improved outcomes when clients engage in tasks and experience learning or refinement of adaptive skills. Tailoring homework to meet individual client needs in the selection (design), discussion of specifics, and review of homework assignments is critical for maximizing the opportunity for homework exercises to be effective.

REFERENCES

Beck, A. T. (1976). *Cognitive therapy and the emotional disorders*. New York: International Universities Press.

Beck, J. S. (2005). *Cognitive therapy for challenging problems*. New York: Guilford Press.

Bevilacqua, L. J., & Dattilio, F. M. (2001). *Brief family therapy homework planner*. New York: Wiley.

Conoley, C. W., Padula, M. A., Payton, D. S., & Daniels, J. A. (1994). Predictors of client implementation of counselor recommendations: Match with problem, difficulty level, and building on client strengths. *Journal of Counseling Psychology, 41*, 3–7.

Kazantzis, N., & Deane, F. P. (1999). Psychologists' use of homework assignments in clinical practice. *Professional Psychology: Research and Practice, 30*, 581–585.

Kazantzis, N., Deane, F. P., Ronan, K. R., & L'Abate, L. (2005). *Using homework assignments in cognitive behavior therapy*. New York: Routledge.

Kazantzis, N., & L'Abate, L. (2007). *Handbook of homework assignments in psychotherapy: Research, practice, and prevention*. New York: Springer Publishing.

Kazantzis, N., Lampropoulos, G. L., & Deane, F. P. (2005). A national survey of practicing psychologists' use and attitudes towards homework in psychotherapy. *Journal of Consulting and Clinical Psychology, 73*, 742–748.

Scheel, M. J., Hoggan, K., Willie, D., McDonald, K., & Tonin, S. (1998, August). *Client understanding of homework determined through therapist delivery*. Poster session presented at the 106th Annual Convention of the American Psychological Association, San Francisco, CA.

Trygon, S. G., & Winograd, G. (2001). Goal consensus and collaboration. *Psychotherapy, 38*, 385–389.

17

Community Resources Used in Counseling

MARTHA H. CHAPIN

FOR COUNSELING TO be effective one needs to treat the whole person. Since counselors may not be able to meet all of their clients' needs, they may need to make a referral to another resource. This chapter will define community resources, referrals, and ways of locating and maintaining a community resource database. It will also provide some service providers that may be useful to counselors throughout the client's life span.

Community resources have been defined by Crimando (2005) as public or private agencies within a geographic area that provide a service for one's clients, oneselves, or one's organization and may or may not charge a fee. To be beneficial, one's clients must be eligible for the services provided. Clients can be referred to agencies providing a single, specialized service or multiple services within the same facility (Crimando, 2005).

Before making a referral to a community resource the counselor should thoroughly assess the client's needs, then determine the most appropriate resource to meet those needs (Chapin, 2005b; Crimando, 2005). Crimando provides a list of questions to consider before making a referral that includes obtaining general information about the agency (e.g., purpose and eligibility requirements), services provided, staff-to-client ratio, staff qualifications, referral procedures, agency capacity, program planning, cost, and reporting guidelines.

Today, the Internet expedites locating community resources and may provide more current information than printed resources such as telephone directories or specialized community resource directories (Chapin, 2005b; Crimando, 2005). The library may also have Internet resource guides available in areas such as nursing and health care (Chapin, 2005b). The Internet does not provide an all-inclusive list of resources and requires a more astute evaluation of the resource to verify legitimacy. Resources can also be obtained from colleagues, other clients' case files, referral sources, vendors, local hospitals, nursing homes, and rehabilitation centers. Physician referral services can help in locating medical specialists. Local and national disability organizations can provide information specific to a particular disability (Chapin, 2005b).

Once a client has had a positive, successful experience with a community resource, the counselor wants to develop a mechanism to track the resource. A notebook or a computer software database can be used to list the type of service provided, provider name, address, phone number, e-mail and Web address, information needed at the time of referral (Chapin, 2005b), and the counselor and client's experience with the resource.

MEDICAL, FUNCTIONAL, ENVIRONMENTAL, AND PSYCHOSOCIAL RESOURCES

To LOCATE A professional counselor with a particular area of expertise, one can contact either the state license or national certification board in the particular area of expertise. For example, the American Counseling Association (http://www.counseling.org/) provides a listing of all 50 state licensing boards. Certification boards such as the Commission on Rehabilitation Counselor Certification (http://www.crccertification.com/) and the National Board for Certified Counselors (http://www.nbcc.org/) can also be found online. Credentialing agencies also provide information on professional practice and ethical guidelines.

One place to locate a list of organizations certifying professionals is at the National Organization of Competence Assurance (NOCA) Web site (http://www.noca.org/). This site also provides a complete list of NOCA organizational members. The NOCA sets quality standards for organizations that credential various professionals (http://www.noca.org/NCCAAccreditation/Standards/tabid/93/Default.aspx), including the National Commission for Certifying Agencies (NCCA), the accrediting body for NOCA. The commission provides a list of accredited certification organizations and programs (http://www.noca

.org/NCCAAccreditation/AccreditedCertificationPrograms/tabid/120/ Default.aspx). Many professional counseling certification organizations can be found at the NCCA Web site, including the certification board for National Certified Counselors, Certified Rehabilitation Counselors, Addiction Specialist, and Forensic Counselors. There is also a Directory of Licensure Boards (http://www.aamft.org/resources/ Online_Directories/boardcontacts.asp) that may expedite one's search for licensed professionals.

The U.S. Department of Health and Human Services (USDHHS) (http://www.hhs.gov/) provides access to resources for health care facilities, health insurance, medical records, nursing homes, physicians and other health professionals, and information on research and clinical trials. The USDHHS Resource Locator (http://www.hhs.gov/resource/) provides a list of agencies serving the aged, children, blind, deaf and hard of hearing, developmental disabilities, minorities, persons requiring mental health and substance abuse services, information about education services, environmental issues, rural health, social services, and vocational rehabilitation services. Generally, a state agency related to one of these areas can be located by checking the individual state department of health and human services Web site.

Clients may need to be referred to a specialized physician or require the assistance of other allied health professionals. Professional association and certification Web sites for many of these occupations can be found in Table 17.1. As is true in counseling, some allied health professionals provide overlapping services. For example, depending on the type of assessment tool utilized, a functional capacity evaluation can be completed by an occupational therapist, physical therapist, rehabilitation counselor, or vocational evaluator.

For some resources such as personal care attendants, it is difficult to locate a central Internet site. The telephone directory can be used to locate personal care attendants under the category of home health services. Day care and long-term care facilities can also be located in the telephone directory under key phrases such as adult homes, day care centers for adults, nursing homes, homes and institutions, and rest homes.

The Commission on Accreditation of Rehabilitation Facilities (http://www.carf.org/) and its provider search site (http://www.carf .org/consumer.aspx?content=ConsumerSearch&id=7) can be used to locate resources on aging services; behavioral health; child and youth; durable medical equipment; prosthetics, orthotics, and supplies; employment and community services; medical rehabilitation; and opioid treatment programs.

Employment and career development are essential services to facilitate human growth and development. Table 17.2 provides a list of possible resources to address clients' employment and career development needs.

TABLE 17.1   Medical and Allied Health Professional References

Profession	Credentialing body	Home page
Marriage and family therapy	American Association of Marriage and Family Therapy *Locator:*	http://www.aamft.org/faqs/index_nm.asp http://www.therapistlocator.net/
Nursing	National Council of State Boards of Nursing *Locator:*	https://www.ncsbn.org/boards.htm https://www.ncsbn.org/515.htm
Occupational therapy	American Occupational Therapy Association *Locator:*	http://www.aota.org/ http://www.aota.org/#state
	National Board for Certification in Occupational Therapy, Inc.	http://www.nbcot.org/webarticles/anmviewer.asp?a=79&z=16
	Association for Driver Rehabilitation Specialists	http://www.driver-ed.org/i4a/pages/index.cfm?pageid=1
	Certified Driver Rehabilitation Specialists Directory	http://www.driver-ed.org/custom/directory-cdrs/?pageid=320&showTitle=1
Orthotics, prosthetics, and pedorthics	American Board for Certification in Orthotics, Prosthetics, and Pedorthics	http://www.nctrc.org/
Physical therapy	American Physical Therapy Association	http://www.apta.org//AM/
	❖ American Board of Physical Therapy Specialties	http://www.apta.org/AM/Template.cfm?Section=ABPTS1&Template=/TaggedPage/TaggedPageDisplay.cfm&TPLID=42&ContentID=14391
Physicians	American Medical Association	http://www.ama-assn.org
Psychologists	American Psychological Association *Locator:*	http://www.apa.org/ http://locator.apa.org
Sex counselors, educators, and therapists	American Association of Sexuality Educators, Counselors and Therapists *Locator:*	http://www.aasect.org/default.asp http://www.aasect.org/directory.asp
	Society for Sex Therapy and Research *Locator:*	http://www.sstarnet.org/ http://www.sstarnet.org/directory.cfm

(continued)

TABLE 17.1 *(Continued)*

Profession	Credentialing body	Home page
Speech and language pathologists and audiologists	American Speech-Language-Hearing Association *Locator:*	http://www.asha.org/default.htm http://www.asha.org/findpro/
Therapeutic recreation	National Council for Therapeutic Recreation Certification Recreational Therapist *Locator:*	http://www.nctrc.org/ https://www.nctrc.org/verifyform.cfm

TABLE 17.2 Employment and Career Development Needs and Issues in Human Growth and Development

Resources	Agency or organization	Web site
Advocacy and guardianship	North American Securities Administrators Association	http://www.nasaa.org
Aging	National Council on Aging	http://www.ncoa.org/
Crisis/disaster counseling	American Red Cross training	http://www.redcross.org/flash/course01_v01/
Disability organizations	Directory of Disability Related Organizations	http://www.ilru.org/html/publications/directory/other_organizations.htm
Domestic violence programs	U.S. Department of Justice Office of Violence Against Women	http://www.usdoj.gov/ovw/
	Help for victims hotline numbers	http://www.usdoj.gov/ovw/hotnum.htm
	National Coalition Against Domestic Violence	http://ncadv.org
	National Committee for the Prevention of Elder Abuse	http://www.preventelderabuse.org/elderabuse/domestic.html
Employment and career development	America's Career InfoNet	http://www.acinet.org
	Job Accommodation Network	http://janweb.icdi.wvu.edu/
	One Stop Career Centers America's Service Locator	http://www.servicelocator.org/
	O*NET—Occupational Information Network	http://www.doleta.gov/programs/onet/

(continued)

TABLE 17.2 *(Continued)*

Resources	Agency or organization	Web site
Home and hospice care, medical equipment supplies	National Association for Home Care and Hospice	http://www.nahc.org/
	❧ Comparison of home health care agencies that are Medicare certified	www.medicare.gov/ HHCompare/Home.asp
Independent living	ILRU Directory for Independent Living and Statewide Independent Living Councils	http://www.ilru.org/html/ publications/directory/ index.html
	❧ Directory of Disability Related Organizations	http://www.ilru.org/html/ publications/directory/ other_organizations.htm
Products and rehabilitation equipment resources	AbleData	http://www.abledata.com/
	ADA/IT Technical Assistance Centers Resource Center	http://www.abledata.com/ abledata.cfm?pageid=1135 73&top=161090&ksec tionid=19326
	Rehabilitation Engineering and Assistive Technology Society of North America	http://www.resna.org/ index.php
	❧ Directory of members	http://www.resna .org/ProfessOrg/Directory/ Directory.php
Medical information	Center for Disease Control and Prevention—Injury Center	http://www.cdc.gov/ncipc/
	National Institutes of Health	http://www.nih.gov
	WebMD	http://www.webmd.com

BENEFIT SYSTEMS

COUNSELORS WILL WANT to contact their clients' insurance benefit provider prior to providing services as benefits vary by state and policy. Questions regarding Social Security benefits can be obtained from the Social Security Administration Web site (www.ssa .gov) or a local office. Workers' Compensation benefits are legislated by the state and require a review of the state's Workers' Compensation Web site and possibly contact with the Workers' Compensation insurance carrier. Short- and long-term disability benefits also vary depending on the policy provider and whether the policy is an individual or group policy. Contact with the disability insurance provider can help counselors answer questions regarding benefits. Auto insurance companies need to be contacted directly to answer questions regarding coverage since auto insurance benefits vary by state and are dependent on the benefits selected by the policyholder (Chapin, 2005a).

The development of a community resource database is an ongoing process. The database changes as new client issues arise, agencies go out of business, or the quality of services provided by an agency change. The lists of resources in this chapter are not intended to be all-inclusive and do not endorse or guarantee the quality or competence of any of the human service professionals. Counselors and clients need to assess professional competence based on the services provided and through reference checks (Chapin, 2005b). The resources listed are for information purposes only.

REFERENCES

Chapin, M. H. (2005a). Case management in private sector rehabilitation. In F. Chan, M. J. Leahy, & J. L. Saunders (Eds.), *Case management for rehabilitation health professionals* (2nd ed., Vol. 1, pp. 304–329). Osage Beach, MO: Aspen Professional Services.

Chapin, M. H. (2005b). Community resources. In F. Chan, M. J. Leahy, & J. L. Saunders (Eds.), *Case management for rehabilitation health professionals* (2nd ed., Vol. 1, pp. 176–196). Osage Beach, MO: Aspen Professional Services.

Crimando, W. (2005). Case management implications. In W. Crimando & T. F. Riggar (Eds.), *Community resources: A guide for human service workers* (2nd ed., pp. 8–18). Long Grove, IL: Waveland Press.

Section D

Multicultural Counseling Issues

18

The Elephant in the Room: Cultural Distrust Directed at White Counselors

EUCHAY N. HORSMAN, VALERIE J. RODRIGUEZ, AND IRMO MARINI

THIS CHAPTER EXPLORES some of the possible underpinnings behind Sue and Sue's (1990) citation that in counseling situations with minorities, more than 50% of clients do not return for a second visit with a counselor. Obviously there is a disconnect at some point during that first session, whether it be gender preference, perceived counselor competence, age difference, appearance of the counselor, or some unknown variable as to why clients initially seek out help but then do not return. Alternatively, Sue and Sue allude to potential cultural insensitivity of a White counselor toward minority clients, and/or perhaps perceived bias as well. This potential elephant in the room may lie deep within the past history of cultural distrust that many persons have toward the White race in America such as stories that are passed down by their parents and grandparents (Terrell & Terrell, 1981). Here, we explore a brief definition of culture and define the major ethnic and racial groups and subgroups within. A brief history behind some of the transgressions by White Americans toward racial and ethnic minorities is discussed to provide counselors with some perspective on the possible reasoning behind each minority group's lack of trust. Those characteristics of culture that transcend time, acts of legislation, and cursory attempts at equality are explored.

DEFINITIONS OF MAJOR ETHNIC AND RACIAL GROUPS IN THE UNITED STATES

THERE ARE NUMEROUS definitions of culture. Barnes and Mercer's (2003) definition of culture as "a link with the past as well as a guide to the present [which] . . . includes the ties that bind as well as what divide human groups" (p. 89) is relevant within the context of this chapter. Another definition includes Samovar and Porter's (1997) definition in which culture is defined as "the deposit of knowledge, experience, beliefs, values, attitudes, meanings, hierarchies, religion, notions of time, roles, spatial relations, concepts of the universe, and material objects and possessions acquired by a group of people in the course of generations through individual and group striving" (pp. 12–13). These definitions perhaps provide some perspective regarding cultural distrust in the United States of America.

American Indian or Alaska Native. Persons having origins in any of the original peoples of North and South America (including Central America), and who maintain tribal affiliations or community attachment. A definition of American Indian includes people who either indicate their race as "American Indian," report being a member of a specific Indian tribe, or report such tribal affiliation as Canadian Indian, French American Indian, or Spanish American Indian. Most Alaska Natives identify themselves as Eskimo, Aleut, and Alaska Indian and/or Arctic Slope, Inupiat, Yupik, Alutiiq, Egegik, and Pribilovian. The major Alaska tribes include the Alaskan Athabaskan, Tlingit, and Haida.

Asian. Persons having origin in any of the original peoples of the Far East, Southeast Asia, or any of the Indian subcontinents. These include, for example, Cambodia, China, India, Japan, Korea, Malaysia, Pakistan, the Philippine Islands, Thailand, and Vietnam.

Black or African American. Persons having origins in any of the Black racial groups of Africa. Other recognized terms are *Haitian* or *Negro* in addition to Black or African American.

Hispanic, Chicano, or Latino. Persons of Cuban, Mexican, Puerto Rican, South or Central American, or other Spanish culture descent, regardless of race. The term *Spanish* can be used in addition to Hispanic or Latino.

White, Anglo, Caucasian, or European American. Persons originating from Europe, the Middle East, or North Africa. Terms such as White, Caucasian, Anglo, and European American are used interchangeably.

Although minority groups are discussed here in general terms, it should be noted that there are wide-ranging within-group differences, and experiences of minority groups may be totally different. Some of these differences are based on the level of acculturation and assimilation into American culture.

HISTORICAL OVERVIEW

THOUGH THE UNITED STATES is a diverse country with legal and social structures that proclaim equal rights (egalitarianism) and justice for all, fairness and justice have not always been modeled. The fact that the founders of this country were themselves freedom seekers who fled their native lands to escape harsh and inhumane treatment ironically did not stop them from treating one another, those indigenous groups they encountered on arrival, and the slaves they brought to help them build the nation with utmost cruelty (Prewitt, 2002; Sue & Sue, 2003). This scarred history of minority groups in the United States tends to make many other minority groups uneasy around, and untrusting of, the majority. Stark racism and systemic degradation and dehumanization of members of minority ethnic groups were accepted practices in the United States for more than 150 years. Even in more recent times, racist attitudes are manifest in everyday interactions and occasionally lead to protests and rioting in extreme cases (Asante, 2003; Johnson, 1995). Such incidents as the Rodney King beating, the Dorismond and Diallo police shootings, and the Louima case in which officers beat and then sodomized Louima with a plunger create fears and tensions among many minority groups (*Frontline*, n.d.).

Ethnic and racial minorities in the United States are still connected to yet vivid histories of segregation, oppression, marginalization, and discrimination. Prewitt (2002) gives a chronological overview of the origins of the demographic framework of the United States, starting from the first recorded census in 1790. Prewitt notes that the high percentage of the foreign-born population in the country today (approximately 10%) is not a new phenomenon. The demographic makeup of the foreign-born population in the country today is comparatively different from that of the 19th and 20th centuries.

Some of the transgressions of European American settlers during this period include (1) taking over North American Indian land by force, (2) the enslavement and treatment of African Americans as subhuman, (3) the Chinese Exclusion Act of 1882, and (4) the evacuation and internment of more than 100,000 Japanese Americans and immigrants during World War II in 1942. These major events highlight the grim beginnings of exclusionist and prejudicial sentiment of the majority culture that has largely resulted in the divisions, disharmony, and distrust still covertly prevalent (Leung, 1996; Prewitt, 2002; Sue & Sue, 2003) in the country. What follows is a discussion of the major ethnic and racial dynamics in the country and some of the key minority groups' experiences that may have led to much of the cultural distrust experienced today (Prewitt, 2002; U.S. Census Bureau, 2002).

EXPERIENCES OF AMERICAN INDIANS

ACCORDING TO THE 2000 census, American Indians and Alaska Natives accounted for 0.9% or 2,475,956 of the overall U.S. population. These ethnic groups at one time accounted for 1% of the population in 1790; however, the consequences of disease, war, and the loss of the American Indian ways of life ultimately decimated this population, resulting in a 90% decline since the group's initial contact with Europeans (Johnson, 1999; Sue & Sue, 2003). Wilson (1997) suggests that much of the American Indian histories are missing from history books. Many American Indians do not trust that White American historians have accurately written historical accounts of the American Indian history. Wilson further argues that who we know today as American Indians, and even the name *Indian,* is of European American ancestry, as a political designation.

Because of displacement, regrouping, and forced adaptation to a new lifestyle fashioned by White Americans, American Indians lost at least some of their own cultures and all of their ways of life (Johnson, 1999; Sue & Sue, 2003; Wilson, 1997). American Indians are groups of peoples that have experienced ongoing, unimaginable forms of discrimination and hatred that have been kept much less publicized than other ethnic groups' experiences. From 1785 to 1866, for example, American Indians experienced legal discrimination and deception by White Americans in that, of the more than 400 land treaties the two groups signed, none was kept. Every single treaty was deceptively broken by White Americans. Some of the events that stripped American Indians of their land, dignity, cultures, loved ones, and ways of life included the (1) Indian Removal Act of 1830, which imposed relocation of Indian Nations (including the Trail of Tears); (2) *Cherokee Nation v. Georgia* case of 1831, ruling tribes as dependencies and not foreign nations, thus permitting unequal treatment; (3) Massacre at Sand Creek of 1864, a heinous act of treachery as wagon train riders outside of Denver invited a tribe of more than 200 Indians for dinner, then murdered all tribe members and hung their bodies as symbols of victory; (4) Dawes General Allotment Act of 1887, which used a blood quantum test to steal more than 100 million acres of American Indian land, leaving countless landless; and (5) Massacre of 1890 at Wounded Knee, an incident in which the U.S. Cavalry shot and killed approximately 300 American Indians for taking part in the Ghost Dance, a ritual that signified American Indians' renouncing of tribal affiliation (Sonneborn, 2001).

Even today, it appears the American society still makes mockery of American Indian cultures and values when stereotyped images of American Indians are inconsiderately paraded in the media, including movies, television, and children's toys. Athletic teams adopt derogatory nicknames, thinking nothing of the meanings and reflections of those names on American Indian cultures.

In addition to these transgressions, American Indians have also had to continually face other issues, such as attempting to obtain voting rights and political representation. There has also been an absence of civil rights protection in cases of police brutality and other discriminatory acts within the criminal justice system. American Indians also are underrepresented in the workforce, have insufficient training and education, are at higher risk for poverty, lack technical assistance, and have inadequate funding for tribal court systems and law enforcement agencies, limited legal resources, and overall poorer outcomes within the health care system (Hayden, 2004). Older American Indians experience higher mortality rates with 6 to 11 years less life expectancy compared to White Americans. Common health concerns among American Indians include circulatory and respiratory system conditions, arthritis, low vision problems, diabetes, oral health, and high blood pressure (Dahlen, Eagleshield, Gragert, & Ide, 2006). Young and old alike also experience problems with alcohol and substance abuse, domestic violence, suicide, lower levels of education, financial support, and cultural identity conflicts, especially in the decision to move or stay on a reservation (Clark & Kelley, 1992; Sue & Sue, 2003). American Indians represent such a small percentage of the U.S. population that they are never represented as a cause for concern in any presidential election.

American Indians pass down the following cautionary advice to the younger generations in reference to dominant White society in general, and in particular, those in authority: "Don't ask them for anything; you won't get it anyways. Always agree with them. Humble yourself to them, they like it. Don't cross them, ever, or you or someone in your family will pay. Never speak up to defend yourself. Never call attention to yourself. Do these things and they might let you live in peace. At least you will live" (Locust, 1998, p. 55).

IMPLICATIONS FOR COUNSELING

ALTHOUGH A MORE detailed analysis of American Indians is provided in chapter 19, counseling implications with this population include knowledge pertaining to their beliefs, religion/spirituality, native healing practices, geographic/social isolation, language, and psychological/socioeconomic conditions. The issue of trust/distrust and the ability of the counselor to understand and be nonjudgmental of the American Indian client's ways can be the most crucial factor in establishing rapport and facilitating a successful counseling relationship (Braswell & Wong, 1994; D'Alonzo, Giordano, & Oyenque, 1996).

EXPERIENCES OF ASIAN AMERICANS

ASIAN AMERICANS COMPRISE a diverse group of persons from a variety of ethnic origins, despite obvious differences in Asian cultural beliefs and values, political orientation, and social experiences. There are more than 14 identified ethnic groups, including Asia Pacific Americans—Chinese, Filipino, Japanese, Asian Indian, Korean, Vietnamese, Hawaiian, Laotian, Cambodian, Thai, Hmong, Samoan, Guamanian, Tongan, and others (Fong & Shinagawa, 2000). It is only natural that these groups have different cultural attributes, including language and religion. Popular culture and mainstream attitudes present Asian Americans constituting one ethnic group; however, it is essential to understand that each of these groups has had its own history and unique experience in the United States.

Subgroups of Asians made initial entries into the country at different periods, making each group's history different from those of the others. For example, in a discussion of what he termed the "standard periodization," Okihiro (2001) describes the time between 1848 and 1882 as "the period of immigration, characterized by open immigration of Asians into the US" (p. 35). During this period, men from China in an effort to escape poverty in their home country came to the United States in sizeable numbers, most of them intending to work for a few years and return to China. At the same time as those immigrating to the U.S. mainland, large numbers of Chinese men also migrated to Hawaii where they supplied contract labor for Hawaiian sugar plantations (Boyd, 1971; Okihiro, 2001; Prewitt, 2002). This period ended with the enactment of the Chinese Exclusion Act of 1882, which barred Chinese laborers and their spouses and relatives from entering the United States. The act was later broadened to include all Chinese people and was not repealed until 1943 when China became an American ally at the beginning of World War II (Kim-Rupnow, 2001; Liu, 2001; Okihiro, 2001).

Boyd (1971) noted that though the Chinese were initially received with open arms as they supplied much-needed labor, wage and economic competition between the Chinese and White workers "and the distrust of the different cultural ways of the Chinese led to the Chinese Exclusion Act of 1882" (p. 48). While new immigrants were restricted from coming in, those already in the country were forbidden to intermarry. They faced special taxation, institutional racism, persistent humiliation, violence, loss of property and livelihood, and sometimes loss of life (Chan, 1998). These conditions negatively impacted the development of family life among early Chinese immigrants in the United States (Lee, 1996).

Transgressions against Japanese Americans largely began on February 19, 1942, when President Franklin Roosevelt authorized the internment (forced removal and detention of approximately 120,000 Japanese and Japanese Americans from the West Coast of the United States) with Executive Order 9066, which allowed local military commanders to designate "military areas" as exclusion zones during World War II. An astounding 62% of the imprisoned detainees were U.S. citizens. Men, women, and children were sent unwillingly to camps called War Relocation Centers in remote areas of the United States. Explanation for relocation was not given by the U.S. government, and some imprisoned Japanese Americans were found guilty of crimes that were perceived as a threat to national security. This large group of Japanese was forced to relocate and leave behind their homes, families, jobs, and perhaps more important, the safety of a life that should have never been taken away. Japanese who were imprisoned were held in these camps without plumbing or cooking facilities and in tarpaper-covered barracks without the right to a civil trial. By 1945, President Roosevelt rescinded the order, bringing an end to the internment camps. Clearly, White Americans used prejudice and discriminatory acts to put an end to the previous economic success Japanese American farmers and business owners had worked so hard to obtain (Fremon, 1996).

IMPLICATIONS FOR COUNSELING

ALTHOUGH CHOUDHURI IN chapter 21 offers a more detailed cultural perspective on Asian Americans and Pacific Islanders, counselors should be aware that Asian Americans may have collectivistic and hierarchical familial orientation. Mental health problems among Asian Americans are perceived as shameful. They often do not seek outside treatment for depression or other psychological problems. Mental health problems among Asian Americans are typically expressed via physical or somatic complaints such as headaches, tiredness, restlessness, and changes in sleep patterns or appetite (Sue & Sue, 2003). Counselors must be mindful of the Asian American focus on the concepts of yin and yang harmony of the body, religious beliefs, and the preference for a more directive, tangible type of counseling approach. Counselors should offer more concrete strategies as opposed to long-term psycho-therapeutic insight–based counseling strategies.

EXPERIENCES OF AFRICAN AMERICANS

AFRICAN AMERICANS ALONG with American Indians share the longest history of inhumane treatment in the United States at the hands of some White Americans. The forceful removal of African Americans from their homeland has created a cultural mistrust of many White European Americans over the centuries (Library of Congress, n.d.; Okihiro, 2001; Prewitt, 2002). Leaving the violent past behind has not been possible for many African Americans, as negative attitudes and stereotypes still exist with racial tensions erupting from time to time when incidents of inequity occur (Asante, 2003). Despite laws and constitutional amendments that aim to eradicate such practices, racism and discrimination and the consequent isolation, low educational attainment, and low socioeconomic status among African Americans are still pervasive issues this ethnic group must deal with.

The African American struggle for equality and identity as a unique cultural group is chronicled in a number of books, Web sites, and other media. Among these are the Library of Congress' *Time Line of African American History: 1852–1925,* Molefi Kete Asante's (2003) *Erasing Racism: The Survival of the American Nation,* and Carter Wilson's (1996) *Racism: From Slavery to Advanced Capitalism,* all of which indicate a lengthy history of slavery, racism, and inhumane treatment. The struggle apparently continues for many African Americans because people's attitudes cannot be mandated, and discriminatory practices periodically surface in many aspects of American life. When blatant and publicized discrimination or prejudice occurs, racial unrest generally follows.

The 1966 Hough Riots of Hough, Cleveland, prompted a 6-day standoff between the predominantly African American communities of Cleveland and Cleveland's local law enforcement. The incident occurred when two White restaurant owners denied an African American woman seeking donations access to the restaurant. Later, an African American male was denied a glass of ice after purchasing wine. Tension had previously built up in the community, reportedly rising from such practices as African American customers being overcharged for services. Also, African Americans predominantly lived in the Cleveland ghettos, prompting Commissioner Theodore Hesburgh of the U.S. Commission on Civil Rights to report the living conditions as the worst he had ever seen. The riots ended with one African American female fatality by police gunfire. There were also more than 275 arrests and more than 240 fires reported.

The Detroit Riot of 1967 began as a direct result of racial tensions between African Americans and Whites as they competed for wartime jobs and limited housing. The civil disturbance lasted 5 full days with violent rioting. At the conclusion of the riots, police and military troops sought to regain control of the city, leaving 43 people dead, 1,189 injured, and more than 7,000 people arrested (Toonari, n.d.).

The 1992 Rodney King riot is a further example of racial tension and perceived inequity, and also an evidence of continued racial tension in the country. Mr. King, an African American male, was unnecessarily kicked and beaten by four White Los Angeles police officers after a high-speed chase. The videotaped and highly publicized incident ignited 4 days of rioting predominantly by African Americans in Los Angeles and ultimately led to 55 deaths, 2,383 injuries, and more than $1 billion in property damages. After only one of the four police officers was indicted and given a 30-month jail sentence, angry protesters began rioting due to the almost all-White jury's decision (Linder, 1993).

Another Los Angeles incident was the 1994 O. J. Simpson murder trial. Although this trial did not spark riots, the 75% Black jury found Simpson not guilty despite alleged credible evidence to the contrary. Posttrial public polling showed that although the vast majority of White Americans believed Simpson was guilty of murder, the vast majority of African Americans believed him to be not guilty.

IMPLICATIONS FOR COUNSELING

ALTHOUGH A MORE extensive reading on the multicultural issues facing African Americans is found in this text (chapter 20), some implications for counseling are addressed here. African Americans' history of oppression and discrimination ultimately leads to the cultural mistrust and suspicion of some White counselors that presents major barriers to establishing a rapport or the likelihood of African American clients returning for a second visit. Alston and Bell (1996) cited suspicion, unwillingness to engage, fear of consequences, doubt and/or insecurity about the sequence of events, a sense of powerlessness, and cautious attitudes in counseling situations between African American clients and White counselors. African Americans also have low expectations of the counseling relationship with White counselors and possess negative attitudes toward seeking help from predominantly White-staffed clinics (Alston, 2004; Alston & Bell, 1996). Counselors must be able to understand and acknowledge that clients' perceived discrimination actually exists. This ultimately reflects on the restricted employment opportunities, housing applications, health care treatment, as well as many other areas. Overall, African Americans, like other minority groups, tend to prefer a direct counseling style with tangible strategies for problem solving, solution-focused approaches that may include advocacy and promotion of civil rights (Sue & Sue, 2003).

EXPERIENCES OF HISPANIC/ LATINO AMERICANS

THERE ARE NEARLY 20 recognized subcategories within the Hispanic American category, which, at 44.3 million in 2006, was estimated to be the largest minority population in the United States. It is projected that by the year 2050, Hispanics will constitute 24% of the overall U.S. population (Adam, 2007). This minority group has its indigenous roots from Cuba, Mexico, Puerto Rico, South and Central America, and other Spanish cultures. Terms such as *Latino/Latina, Spanish, Chicano/Chicana, Mexican, Puerto Rican, Tejano/Tejana* are additional ones that one might hear used in reference to Hispanic and Latino Americans.

Although purportedly not treated as harshly as American Indian and African American minority groups, the Hispanic population has also experienced oppression and discrimination in the United States. For example, the 1848 Treaty of Guadalupe Hidalgo ended the war between Mexico and the United States and allowed Mexicans to remain on American soil and to become legal citizens. Mexicans were also to receive land so they could establish residency and Spanish was to be recognized as a legitimate language. These terms of the treaty were never practiced, and approximately 500,000 Mexicans were forced to rent land from the U.S. government (Novas, 2003).

Over time, Mexican Americans began to constitute a larger segment of the American workforce during the 1800s with the boon of workers needed for mining operations and building the railroad. Mexican immigrants migrated by the tens of thousands all the way into the early 1900s, vying for these and agricultural jobs (*Chicano Immigration,* 2006). Many also escaped to the United States during the Mexican Revolution, because immigration remained unrestricted and open until the 1930s when it came under closer U.S. scrutiny. Operation Wetback of 1954, as well as the 1986 Immigration Reform and Control Act (IRCA), was established in efforts to close the door on Mexican immigration. Operation Wetback allowed the nation's Border Patrol to have powerful control over enforcement. The IRCA fined employers approximately $3,000 for every illegal alien they had working for them. It was estimated that 1 million Mexicans a year were sent back to Mexico under these programs, while an estimated 3 million continue to immigrate illegally on a yearly basis (Novas, 2003). The debate on authorized and unauthorized immigration from Mexico continues today.

Other forms of oppression and discrimination against Hispanics also began in the 1930s when the United States attempted to control the population of Puerto Rico because of perceived rapid and uncontrollable growth. Some in the United States perceived Puerto Rico as an underdeveloped third world country against which superior White civilization should be safeguarded. Thus, the United States influenced the Puerto Rican government to enforce female sterilization. Approximately one-third of young females coming to the United States to work were sterilized. A 1973 report titled "Opportunities of Employment, Education, & Training" outlined the Sterilization Plan that spanned the 1930s to 1970s, initiated due to the convenience of U.S. manufacturing companies who needed cheap labor free from childcare concerns. This incidence of sterilization within this ethnic group is the highest in the world with an estimated 35% of Puerto Rican females sterilized by 1968 (Aviles & Vargas, 1997).

IMPLICATIONS FOR COUNSELING

CHAPTER 22 DISCUSSES this population more in depth, noting that Hispanics generally believe that people are born with dignity and the right to respect. Clients may believe that the inner- self or spirit is more important than the physical body. This belief certainly is different from that of White, middle-class societal views of independence and accomplishment (Foster, 1982). The Hispanic English proficiency is an important factor to consider in the counseling process. Many Hispanics who speak conversational English might still use Spanish to depict emotions, as they might feel more comfortable or better able to articulate their feelings in Spanish. White counselors must recognize language and not mistake this for the client's hesitancy to engage in the counseling process. White counselors should also not misinterpret English proficiency as the client's flat affect or their lack of insight (Altarriba & Bauer, 1998).

Counselors should be familiar with the types of stressors typically associated with a client's acculturation status and help him or her determine to what degree stressors are present in his or her life. For low acculturated Hispanic American clients, stressors may include homesickness, vulnerability in the new culture, isolation, and grief over the loss of what is left behind. Environmental factors, such as poverty, low levels of education, poor or lacking health care, higher rates of disability, overrepresentation in physical labor jobs, and social injustice, may intensify these stressors (Ramos, 2005). Traditional Mexican American beliefs in *curanderos* or folk healers are often relied on for spiritual, psychological, and physical healing. Counselors need to know how to work with these beliefs and not dismiss them. Examples of common folk illnesses where curanderos may be consulted include *mal ojo* ("evil eye"), *susto* ("magical fright"), and *embrujo* ("hex"; Trevino, 1991).

CONCLUSION

IT MAY BE argued that the vast majority of inhumane treatment toward minority persons is largely a part of America's dark past. However, there continues to be periodic reports of discrimination, violence, and prejudice toward minority groups that dictate otherwise. Although many would agree we have come a long way at mending racial/ethnic relations, others believe we have a long way to go (Sue & Sue, 2003).

Good rapport building between client and clinician is imperative, and both parties must recognize their own biases, stereotypes, values, and belief systems before moving forward in guiding the counseling relationship. Projecting biases and stereotypical attitudes on clients can create conflict if one is not culturally competent or empathetic with the client's particular situation. It is crucial for clinicians to recognize the client's interpersonal styles and circumstances (e.g., acculturated, bicultural, culturally immersed, or traditional) and work with them accordingly.

REFERENCES

Adam, M. (2007). Our Hispanic heritage: Where did we come from and where are we going? *Hispanic Outlook, 10*, 10–16.

Alston, R. J. (2004). African Americans with disabilities and the Social Security Administration's return-to-work incentives. *Journal of Disability Policy Studies, 14*(4), 216–221.

Alston, R. J., & Bell, T. J. (1996). Cultural mistrust and the rehabilitation enigma for African Americans. *Journal of Rehabilitation, 62*(2), 16–20.

Altarriba, J., & Bauer, L. M. (1998). Counseling the Hispanic client: Cuban Americans, Mexican Americans, and Puerto Ricans. *Journal of Counseling and Development, 76*(4), 389–397.

Asante, M. K. (2003). *Erasing racism: The survival of the American nation.* Amherst, NY: Prometheus Books.

Aviles, L. A., & Vargas, Y. A. (1997). Aboration in Puerto Rico: The limits of colonial legality. *Reproductive Health Matters, 9*, 56–65.

Barnes, C., & Mercer, G. (2003). *Disability.* Malden, MA: Blackwell.

Boyd, M. (1971). Oriental immigration: The experience of the Chinese, Japanese, and Filipino populations in the US. *International Migration Review, 5*(1), 48–61.

Braswell, M. E., & Wong, H. D. (1994). Perceptions of rehabilitation counselors regarding Native American healing practices. *Journal of Rehabilitation, 60*(2), 33–37.

Chan, S. (1998). *Major problems in Asian American history*. Boston: Houghton Mifflin.

Chicano Immigration. (2006). Retrieved November 1, 2007, from http://www .thehispanicamerican.com/chicano-immigration/

Clark, S., & Kelley, S. D. M. (1992). Traditional Native American values: Conflict or concordance in rehabilitation? *Journal of Rehabilitation, 58*(2), 23–28.

Dahlen, B., Eagleshield, J., Gragert, M., & Ide, B. (2006). Needs assessment of Standing Rock elders. *Journal of Cultural Diversity, 13*, 186–189.

D'Alonzo, B. J., Giordano, G., & Oyenque, W. (1996). American Indian vocational rehabilitation services: A unique project. *American Rehabilitation, 22*(1), 20–26.

Fong, T. P., & Shinagawa, L. H. (Eds.). (2000). *Asian Americans: Experiences and perspectives*. Upper Saddle River, NJ: Prentice-Hall.

Foster, D. (Ed.). (1982). *Sourcebook of Hispanic culture in the US*. Chicago: American Library Association.

Fremon, D. (1996). *Japanese-American internment in American history*. Springfield, NJ: Enslow.

FRONTLINE. (2001). *Interview with Gregory Yates on February 6, 2001*. Retrieved June 26, 2007, from http://www.pbs.org/wgbh/pages/frontline/shows/ lapd/interviews/yates.html

Hayden, T. (2004). *A modern life: After decades of discrimination, poverty, and despair, American Indians can finally look toward a better future*. Retrieved November 1, 2007, from U.S. News and World Report Web site: www .usnews.com/usnews/culture/articles/041004/4native.htm

Johnson, O. (1995). Integrating the "underclass": Confronting America's enduring apartheid. *Stanford Law Review, 47*(4), 787–818.

Johnson, T. (1999). American historical images in file: The Native American experience. *Indians of North America*. Long Beach: California State University. Retrieved November 17, 2005, from http://www.csulb .edu/projects/ais/nae/

Kim-Rupnow, W. S. (2001). *An introduction to Korean culture for rehabilitation service providers*. University of Buffalo, State University of New York, Center for International Rehabilitation Research Information and Exchange. Retrieved June 2, 2005, from http://cirrie.buffalo.edu/korea.html

Lee, E. (1996). Chinese families. In M. McGoldrick, J. Geordano, & J. K. Pearce (Eds.), *Ethnicity and family therapy* (pp. 249–267). New York: Guilford Press.

Leung, P. (1996). Asian Americans and rehabilitation: Some important variables. *Journal of Applied Rehabilitation Counseling, 19*(4), 16–35.

Library of Congress. (n.d.). *Time line of African American history: 1852–1925*. Retrieved November 15, 2005, from http://memory.loc.gov/ammem/ aap/timeline.html

Linder, D. O. (1993). Los Angeles police officers' (Rodney King beating) trials. Retrieved November 1, 2007, from http://www.law.umkc.edu/faculty/projects/ftrials/lapd/lapd.html

Liu, G. Z. (2001). *Chinese culture and disability: Information for U.S. service providers.* New York: Center for International Rehabilitation Research Information and Exchange. Retrieved November 23, 2005, from http://cirrie.buffalo.edu/mseries.html

Locust, C. (1998). Counseling strategies with Native American clients. *Directions in Rehabilitation Counseling, 9*(5), 51–63.

Novas, H. (2003). *Everything you need to know about Latino history.* New York: Plume.

Okihiro, G. Y. (2001). *The Columbia guide to Asian American history.* New York: Columbia University Press.

Prewitt, K. (2002). Demography, diversity, and democracy: The 2000 census story. *The Brookings Review, 20*(1), 6–9. Retrieved November 2, 2005, from http://www.brookings.edu/press/review/winter2002/prewitt.htm

Ramos, B. M. (2005). Acculturation and depression among Puerto Ricans in the mainland. *Social Work Research, 29*(2), 95–105.

Samovar, L. A., & Porter, R. E. (Eds.). (1997). *Intercultural communication: A reader* (8th ed.). Florence, KY: Wadsworth.

Sonneborn, L. (2001). *Chronology of American Indian history: The trail of the wind.* New York: Facts on File.

Sue, D. W., & Sue, D. (1990). *Counseling the culturally diverse: Theory and practice* (2nd ed.). New York: Wiley.

Sue, D. W., & Sue, D. (2003). *Counseling the culturally diverse: Theory and practice* (3rd ed.). New York: Wiley.

Terrell, F., & Terrell, S. (1981). An inventory to measure cultural mistrust among Blacks. *The Western Journal of Black Studies, 5,* 180–185.

Toonari. (n.d.). *Detroit riot of 1967.* Retrieved November 1, 2007, from http://www.africanaonline.com/reports_detroit.htm

Trevino, B. (1991). Cultural characteristics of Mexican Americans: Issues in rehabilitation counseling and services. *Journal of Rehabilitation, 57,* 21–25.

U.S. Census Bureau. (2002). *Profiles of general demographic characteristics, 2000 Census of Population and Housing, U.S. 2000.* Retrieved November 22, 2005, from http://www.census.gov/prod/cen2000/dp1/2kh00.pdf

Wilson, A. C. (1997). Power of the spoken word: Native oral traditions in American Indian history. In Donald L. Fixico (Ed.), *Rethinking American Indian history* (pp. 101–116). Albuquerque: University of New Mexico Press.

Wilson, C. A. (1996). *Racism: From slavery to advanced capitalism.* Thousand Oaks, CA: Sage.

19

The Native American Indian Client

WINONA F. SIMMS

T HE UNIQUENESS OF Native American Indian (NAI) people in the United States is founded on rich and diverse cultures
that have enabled this population to survive severe political,
economic, and environmental hardship. Over time these indigenous
peoples have maintained language, cultural practices, and dynamic traditions that have provided them with a meaningful understanding of
the world and the events that affected their existence and well-being.
While it is true that the strengths exhibited in meeting the challenges
to survive have allowed Native people to avoid eradication, the impact
of past obstacles can be viewed as having damaging effects on the emotional well-being of individuals, tribal entities, and groups that have
carried into the present (Brave Heart, Maria Yellow Horse, & LeMyra,
1998). This fragile strength is just one of many dualities in the life of a
Native person and is an important aspect of being able to see the whole
person and to begin to interpret relevant mental health issues.

Counselors, psychologists, psychiatrists, and other mental health
providers and therapists have an obligation to bear in mind the cultural differences of all clients in their vulnerable states. "A clinician
who is unfamiliar with the nuances of an individual's cultural frame
of reference may incorrectly judge as psychopathology those normal variations in behavior, belief, or experience that are particular
to the individual's culture" (American Psychiatric Association, 1994,
p. xxiv). Adherence to this obligation is the foundation for developing

a therapeutic relationship with a Native American Indian that is truly therapeutic. Respect for cultural beliefs and ways of living and thinking, regardless of how alien they may seem to the caregiver, will encourage the Native client to develop trust and more fully participate in his or her own healing process (Simms, 1999, p. 29).

FACTORS THAT AFFECT NATIVE AMERICAN INDIANS

LANGUAGE AND NAMES

THERE MAY NOT exist an accurate term to use for the indigenous people of North America and Alaska. The misnomer *Indian* was used by Christopher Columbus based on his mistaken understanding of where he was in the world. Names used by individuals, as well as the words for tribes and groups of people, were sometimes changed due to the difficulty that Europeans had in hearing and/or learning the languages spoken in the Americas. Tribal names used today may also have gone through several changes. An example is given by Dr. Richard Grounds, who directs a language immersion project in Oklahoma that is designed to retain the Euchee (or Yuchi) language and develop fluent speakers. Dr. Grounds relates that the historical use of Euchee as a tribal name was the result of a misinterpretation of the word *Zo-ya-ha*, which meant "People of the Sun." As a confounding result, the people of this tribal nation today disagree on whether to spell their name *Yuchi* or *Euchee*. This depends on which translation of their name they rely on (personal communication, April 28, 2008).

Native American Indian is a term that attempts to reflect the various references that describe indigenous people of the North American continent. Although Alaska Natives are included under this term, it is recognized that this group as well as most of the hundreds of groups being referenced prefer to be called by their tribal affiliation. No judgment is made as to whether those Native people who live beyond the borders of the United States and/or who are native to the Hawaiian Islands should be included or excluded from this population. As such, Native American Indian and Native will be used interchangeably.

CULTURAL VALIDATION

IT IS IMPORTANT that therapists learn as much as they can about the Native American Indian client because of the importance their identity and beliefs have for them as people with proud histories. It's also important because these people are the original inhabitants of the lands where they are now minorities and they maintain strong connections to the land and the sacred sites that were home to their ancestors. If a therapist does not take these concerns into consideration there may be a sense of disconnect for the client and the chances of a client returning to therapy are reduced (Sue, Allen, & Conaway, 1981). Native people also may be leery of counseling due to an unsettling history with White culture. Lockart (1981) surmises, "In the counseling of Indian clients, the issue of trust takes on new dimensions. No longer is the issue of trust necessarily based in the present; it takes on a historic perspective that is even harder to deal with. It is essential that the conscientious counselor be aware of the existence of this distrust and its basis, and try to understand its magnitude in order that the counseling relationship is effective" (pp. 31–32).

NATIVE AMERICAN INDIAN DEMOGRAPHICS

ACCORDING TO THE U.S. Census Bureau, there are 562 federally recognized tribes in the United States, and the estimated population of American Indians, Alaska Natives, or Native Hawaiians is 4.5 million or 1.5% of the U.S. population. This figure is reflective of individuals from more than one race. The median age is 30.7 with about 1.3 million under the age of 18 and 336,000 aged 65 or older. More than 100,000 Natives live in just 12 states: California, Oklahoma, Arizona, New Mexico, Washington, Michigan, Florida, Texas, New York, North Carolina, Hawaii, and Alaska. Only 34% of these Natives live on what is referred to as a reservation or Indian lands (U.S. Census Bureau, 2005). "The number of American Indians who live on reservations and trust lands (areas with boundaries established by treaty, statute, and executive or court order) has decreased substantially in the past few decades" (U.S. Public Health Service, 2001, p. 81). Because reservation lands tend to be rural in nature, there are few employment opportunities, which, in turn, affects financial resources.

POVERTY

THE 2005 CENSUS found that Natives are twice as likely to live in poverty as Whites in the U.S. population, that is, 25.7% versus 12.4%. When clearly one-quarter of the total Native population lives in poverty, there are subsequent socioeconomic indicators that influence the lives of these people, such as the quality of education, employment opportunities, adequate health care, and ability to overcome these barriers. With unemployment rates for Natives reported as three times that of White unemployment statistics, the problem of poverty is exacerbated (U.S. Department of Education, 2005, p. xi).

EDUCATION

HIGH POVERTY LEVELS are frequently followed by lower rates of educational obtainment. In 2003 the Census Bureau reported that Natives between the ages of 18 and 24 were less likely to be enrolled in a college or university than their White, Asian, and Black peers (U.S. Census Bureau, 2003, p. 98). In *Status and Trends in the Education of American Indians and Alaska Natives* (U.S. Department of Education, 2005), it was reported that 58.3% of the total Native population have high school degrees or less. Only 11% have completed a bachelor's degree or an advanced degree as compared to 24% of the total population. In 2000 Natives with graduate degrees represented 2% as compared to Whites who had 6% and Asians who held 8% (U.S. Department of Education, 2005, p. 106). Sixty percent of Native college enrollees are female and 40% are male (U.S. Department of Education, 2005).

Clearly, Native students face more challenges in college than other groups because of a lower percentage that take advanced science classes in high school (U.S. Department of Education, 2005, p. 66). In part, this may be due to the fact that American Indian and Alaska Native students are 2.53 times more likely to be in special education courses for learning disability and 2.89 times more likely to receive services for delayed development than all other racial groups combined (U.S. Department of Education, 2005).

The National Indian Education Association (2007) in *Native Education: 101 Basic Facts About American Indian, Alaska Native, and Native Hawaiian Education* reports that Native youth attend various types of schools:

1. Public schools on tribal lands—funded by individual states and subject to state standards and assessments.
2. Bureau of Indian Affairs (BIA) schools—federal and tribally operated schools that serve American Indian students. As a result of treaty rights, statutes, court decisions, and other commitments, the Bureau of Indian Education (BIE), housed in the Department of the Interior, has the responsibility for 184 elementary and secondary schools and dormitories located on 63 reservations, in 23 states, and representing 238 different tribes.
3. Tribal contract or grant schools—elementary schools, secondary schools, or dormitories that receive operating funds under a contract or grant with BIE/BIA under the Indian Self Determination and Education Assistance Act [25 U.S.C. 450 et seq.] or under the Tribally Controlled School Act of 1988 [25 U.S.C. 2501 et seq.].

4. Tribally controlled community colleges—located on or near reservation communities to provide postsecondary learning opportunities for American Indian and Alaska Native students. There are currently 35 of these tribal schools.

SOVEREIGNTY AND CITIZENSHIP

NATIVE AMERICAN INDIANS have a unique relationship with the U.S. government that makes them unlike any other minority or ethnic group. Legal, political, and historical policies and decisions with regard to Natives make a thorough understanding of who is or isn't an *Indian* or tribal member complicated. Suffice it to say that the general premise is that Native groups prior to discovery had original sovereignty over their affairs and tribal matters as citizens of that nation (Canby, 1998). Decisions by Chief Justice Marshall in the mid 1800s have relevance to sovereignty issues in the present (Canby, 1998, pp. 13–18). Dictum in *Winton v. Amos* (255 U.S. 373 [1921]) and *United States v. Nice* (241 U.S. 591 [1916]) help explain other aspects of citizenship with their holding that "While the 1924 statute makes all native-born Indians United States citizens, it is the Fourteenth Amendment that makes them citizens of the states where they reside as well. The status of Indians as citizens of the United States and of the individual states does not interfere with the Indians' relationship to their tribes or with the trust relationship between the tribes and the federal government" (Canby, 1998, p. 324). The trust or fiduciary relationship and the government-to-government relationship between Native people and the United States is founded on historical occurrences that give deeper and more complex dimensions to the study of American Indian Natives, and thus, the difficulty in adequately referencing this unique minority group with a name that is all-inclusive.

VALUES

SUE (1981, TABLE 17.1), in a comparison of the values of Native Americans and Anglos, highlights important differences in cultural perspective. While Anglo or White culture emphasizes youthfulness, Native culture recognizes and respects their elders for their wisdom. One could also view the elders in the tribe or community as those who are the culture carriers of tradition and experience. The elders not only carry the stories of their culture but also the language and the knowledge of ceremonies that heal, bring vision, and restore and maintain harmony to individuals and the tribe. As long as the language and ceremonies are in the memory bank of the culture, there is reason to believe that the culture is still vital and strong and able to sustain itself. Sue further indicates that Native culture is centered on religion, as compared to Anglos who view religion as individualistic. Duran and Duran (1995) refer to the notion of religion as a movement to a cosmic reality through a harmonious existence. They state that

> Native Americans had a very well structured society in which everyone's role and place was well defined. Our family systems and self-governance supported these roles and functions, and everyone felt valued as a member of the community. . . . This holistic worldview allowed Native Americans to have a unified awareness or perception of the physical, psychological, and spiritual phenomena that make up the totality of human existence or consciousness. In the experience of such a unified awareness, there was also a close integration with cosmological realities as they were experienced or perceived. . . . Native American people were able to have a centered awareness that was fluid and nonstatic. The centered awareness allowed for a harmonious attitude toward the world, as exemplified by a tribal collective way of life versus an individualistic approach. The harmony idea is best illustrated by the acceptance and being part of the mystery of existence versus the ongoing struggle to understand the world through a logical positivistic approach, as exemplified by Western science. (pp. 44–45)

Other Native values reflect an emphasis on sharing and cooperation, the extended family and tribe, present-time centeredness, and an abiding respect for their elders. In contrast, majority or White culture emphasizes saving, domination, competition, individualism, a future time orientation, and the nuclear family (Herring, 1999; Sue & Sue, 1990). Additionally, ceremonies and family were integral parts of Native life and critical to the survival of the tribe. Ceremonies and rituals helped youth know who they were and when they were to become and behave as an adult. Older family members and grandparents guided their young people into these roles, and the community was always present to witness traditions that supported healings, vision quests, and honoring. Through these cultural differences it is easy to see how confusing it is for a Native person to live and think in one culture and, yet, be required to function in the majority culture with its expectations and demands. If harmony/balance or disharmony/lack of balance were seen as interchangeable with mental health or mental illness, counseling issues with Natives might be approachable from more than one cultural perspective.

NATIVE AMERICAN MENTAL HEALTH CONCERNS

ASSESSING THE PROBLEM

YURKOVICH AND HOPKINS-LATTERGRASS (2004) led a research team that interviewed and evaluated Native American Indians experiencing mental health dilemmas across four reservation areas in North Dakota, representative of some eight different tribal affiliations, including Dakota Sioux, Assinaboine Sioux, Lakota Sioux, Chippewa/Ojibwa, Arikara, Mandan, Hidatsa, and Navajo. The findings of their assessment indicated there were 12 mental health diagnoses: depression, chronic alcoholism, chemical abuse, post-traumatic stress disorder (PTSD) or traumatic life processes, anxiety (many types), panic disorder, schizophrenia (with/without psychosis, paranoia), bipolar disorder, anger out of control, dissociative identity disorder (DID; multiple personality disorder), dysthymia, and phobias. This project is noted because of the importance of gathering good research information on minority populations on sensitive topics in a respectful manner.

The analysis used also identified some critical Native perspectives on the definition of health. Health was perceived as being in balance or having a sense of harmony/equilibrium, and not being out of control with respect to the cognitive, emotional, physical, and spiritual quadrants. Health was also described as "being empowered through knowledge, hope, sense of control/well being, and purpose to manage their illness while using the formal and informal health care system as support resources" (Yurkovich & Hopkins-Lattergrass, 2004, p. 3).

As another phase of mental health service delivery, Yurkovich and Hopkins-Lattergrass (2004) listed what was found as workable services for clients on reservations. They include talk therapy, group therapy and support groups, emergency toll-free hotlines with immediate access to health care providers (not reservation bound), education about illness and its management for personal empowerment, mediation management, a secure environment to live and socialize in, and meaningful doing (e.g., residential setting, community center, or psychiatric social club). Opportunities to contribute to meaningful doing such as volunteering or sheltered work settings that provide altruistic experiences was also recommended as well as residential treatment for chemical addictions (Yurkovich & Hopkins-Lattergrass, 2004, p. 7).

PROMINENT MENTAL HEALTH ISSUES

COMPREHENSIVE STUDIES OF Native American health issues are lacking in the research, but Yurkovich and Hopkins-Lattergrass (2004) suggest that depression, chronic alcoholism, chemical abuse, and PTSD may not be unusual mental health diagnoses among rural/reservation Native adults. Tirado (2006) reported that on a northern Minnesota reservation, suicide and substance abuse were the leading risk factors for youth. Psychiatric disorders, depression, attention deficit hyperactivity disorder (ADHD), bipolar disorder, alcohol and drug abuse, and aggressive disruptive disorder were also found to be indicators that may lead to a suicide attempt.

In the article "The Darkest Hour" Tirado (2006) reports that on a Minnesota reservation in 2006 there had been 69 youth suicide attempts and that 81% of ninth-grade girls and 43% of ninth-grade boys had contemplated suicide. U.S. Department of Health and Human Services (DHHS) statistics were also cited, reporting that 12.8% of Native youth 12–17 years old are binge drinkers and 2.9% are heavy drinkers. A 2000 DHHS (DHHS, 2001) report further indicated that 12.6% of Native Americans are illicit drug users in contrast to 6.4% of Whites.

CONCLUSION: MENTAL HEALTH SERVICE AS A SOLUTION

MENTAL HEALTH PROVIDERS cannot afford to get bogged down with the heaviness of the challenge to provide good mental health services to Native populations. As a profession, counseling continues to research ways in which to better serve clients and/or help structure appropriate treatment (Simms, 1995). Recognizing the dualistic nature of clients from a Native background is a first step to recognizing within-group variances and level of acculturation (Herring, 1999). Herring (1999) further asserts that mental health professionals "may need to become systemic change agents, intervening in environments that impede the development of Native peoples. In particular, helping professionals will need to create a culturally affirmative environment in which to accomplish their helping goals" (p. 75).

In order to achieve the above objectives, Herring (1997) suggests that counselors "(1) address openly the issue of dissimilar ethnic relationships rather than pretending that no differences exist; (2) evaluate the degree of acculturation of the client; (3) be open to allowing other family members to participate in the counseling session; (4) allow time for trust to develop before focusing on deeper feelings; (5) use counseling strategies that elicit practical solutions to problems; (6) maintain eye contact as appropriate; (7) respect the uses of silence; (8) demonstrate honor and respect for the client's culture; and (9) maintain the highest level of confidentiality" (p. 75).

Simms (1999) recommends that once differences between cultures are recognized and respected, the client can decide whether to pursue counseling based on (1) the provision of information about the treatment process, (2) freedom to express comfort or discomfort with the treatment strategies, (3) having self-confidence nurtured as he or she begins to take control of his or her own "healing," (4) encouragement to explore his or her identity as a Native American Indian person in a non-Indian culture, and (5) the practitioner's openness to integrating Indian and traditional intervention strategies in the interest of the client's total well-being (p. 30).

The healing process for the client is facilitated by simple strategies regardless of the race or culture of the counselor. "Embracing the world view of the client, educating the client about the treatment process, mobilizing hope, and respecting the client's freedom to choose whether or not to pursue treatment" (Simms, 1999, p. 30) allows the client to invest in his or her therapy outcomes.

REFERENCES

American Psychiatric Association. (1994). *Diagnostic and statistical manual of mental disorders* (4th ed.). Washington, DC: Author.

Brave Heart, Maria Yellow Horse, & LeMyra, M. (1998). *American Indian and Alaska Native Mental Health Research, 8*(2), 60–82.

Canby, W. C. (1998). *American Indian law in a nutshell* (3rd ed.). St. Paul, MN: West Group.

Duran, E., & Duran, B. (1995). *Native American postcolonial psychology.* Albany: State University of New York Press.

Herring, R. D. (1997). Synergetic counseling and Native American Indian studies. *Journal of Counseling and Development, 74,* 542–547.

Herring, R. D. (1999). *Counseling with Native American Indians and Alaska Natives.* Los Angeles: Sage Publications.

Lockhart, B. (1981). Historic distrust and the counseling of American Indians and Alaska Natives. *White Cloud Journal, (2)*3, 31–34.

National Indian Education Association. (2007). *Native education: 101 basic facts about American Indian, Alaska Native, and Native Hawaiian education.* Washington, DC: Author in partnership with the National Education Association.

Simms, W. F. (1995). *Cultural identification and cultural mistrust: A study among Native American Indian college students.* Unpublished doctoral dissertation, Oklahoma State University, Stillwater, Oklahoma.

Simms, W. F. (1999). The Native American Indian client: A tale of two cultures. In Y. M. Jenkins (Ed.), *Diversity in college settings: Directives for helping professionals* (pp. 21–35). New York: Routledge.

Sue, D. W., & Sue, D. (1990). Culture-specific strategies in counseling: A conceptual framework. *Professional Psychology, 21,* 423–433.

Sue, S. (1981). *Counseling the culturally different: Theory and practice.* New York: Wiley.

Sue, S., Allen, D. B., & Conaway, L. (1981). The responsiveness and equality of mental health care to Chicanos and Native Americans. *American Journal of Community Psychology, 6,* 137–146.

Tirado, M. (2006, January). The darkest hour: Native American youth and suicide. *American Indian Report, 12*(1), 10–13.

U.S. Census Bureau. (2003). *Current population reports.* Washington, DC: U.S. Department of Commerce.

U.S. Census Bureau. (2005). *Current population reports.* Washington, DC: U.S. Department of Commerce.

U.S. Department of Education. (2005, August). *Status and trends in the education of American Indians and Alaska Natives.* Washington, DC: National Center for Education Statistics.

U.S. Public Health Service. (2001). *Mental health: Culture, race, and ethnicity: A supplement to mental health: A report of the Surgeon General* (pp. 79–104). Washington, DC: U.S. Department of Health and Human Services.

Yurkovich, E., & Hopkins-Lattergrass, I. (2004). *A needs assessment focused on defining health and health seeking behaviors of Native American Indians experiencing severe and persistent mental illness. Phase II: Preliminary findings.* Grand Forks, ND: University of North Dakota, College of Nursing.

20

Multicultural Issues in Counseling African Americans

CHUCK REID

AFRICAN AMERICANS REPRESENT approximately 13% of the American population, 35.8 million with a projected population of 61.3 million by 2050 (U.S. Census Bureau, 2004). They have been a part of American society since its inception, yet conditions for this population are dismal in many social areas. Statistically, African Americans have a shorter life expectancy with males living approximately 7 years less than any other racial group. They also experience more health issues: 40% of males die prematurely of cardiovascular disease compared to 21% of White males. African American males are also five times more likely to die of HIV/AIDS than are White males. African Americans also have poor, if any, health insurance compared to Whites. Although the numbers are decreasing, Black children have a 2.4% higher uninsured rate than White children. One in five Blacks lacked insurance coverage in 2003 while that number was one in 10 for Whites (Hargraves, 2004); while 47.8% of Latinos had employer health coverage, 53.9% of Blacks had employer health coverage, and 73.5% of Whites had health coverage.

In the area of employment, the unemployment rate for Blacks is more than twice as high (8.2% for Blacks versus 3.9% for Whites) as the White population, and the poverty rate is approximately three times as high (Anderson, 1995; Felton, Parson, Misener, & Oldaker, 1997).

Racism and poverty are manifested in African American incarceration rates. According to Freeburg (1995), approximately one-third of young African American men are in jail, on parole, or on probation. That is higher than the percentage of African American males who attend colleges or universities.

It is difficult to generalize about groups, as within-group differences can be as great as between-group differences. For example, in 2001 there were about 112,000 African American households with wealth of more than $1 million and approximately 333,000 African American households had wealth of about half a million. Although some progress has been made regarding income disparities between African Americans who are well-off and those who are not, the debate continues regarding the marginalization of this group in the United States, compared to the more positive outlook for African American groups outside the United States such as in Canada. There seems to be some positive direction toward economic parity with Whites; however, poverty still exists in many African American communities. The U.S. Census Bureau (2005) indicates that among African Americans the underclass is shrinking, the middle class is growing rapidly, and the ranks of the wealthy continue to grow. Unemployment for African Americans has dropped in recent years and the poverty rate is under 25% (U.S. Census Bureau, 2005).

In 2004, only Asian Americans had a higher median income than African American workers. African Americans had the highest level of male-female income parity of all ethnic groups in the United States. Among American minority groups, only Asian Americans were more likely to hold white-collar occupations (management, professional, and related fields), and African Americans were no more or less likely than Whites to work in the service industry. In 2001, more than half of African American households of married couples earned $50,000 or more, and African Americans collectively attain higher levels of education than immigrants to the United States (U.S. Census Bureau, 2005).

A BRIEF HISTORY

T HE TERM AFRICAN American as a descriptor includes many segments of the American population, including populations brought to America from West Africa during the slave trade. The term is the current statement of group identification, beginning with identification by oppressors onto oppressed to self-identification (Hutchinson, 1994).

The first Africans were brought to the New World by the Spanish, but the population who eventually became African Americans were introduced to the Americas by the British colonists. The Africans and the colonists originally coexisted with some Africans and colonists being indentured servants. As time passed, the number of White indentured servants decreased, and they were replaced by African slaves. By the 18th century, the enslavement of Africans had become an institution (Bennett, 1982). Despite slavery, Africans tried to develop a sense of community. This was difficult as there was no common language or culture. Africans were brought to America from many different regions of West Africa; they had different family structures and religions. Some were enemies in Africa, and it sometimes took generations for tribal animosities to subside. By the end of the 18th century, Africans as slaves and freemen had acculturated to American society. They fought on both sides during the Revolutionary War, but they did not benefit from America's freedom. It would take a civil war to bring about even a semblance of freedom (Bennett, 1982).

The American Civil War (1861–1865) and the 13th Amendment to the U.S. Constitution (1865) resulted in the abolishment of chattel slavery in the United States. During the Jim Crow era, African Americans were subject to de jure segregation and discrimination and were kept almost entirely out of political power. The American Civil Rights Movement scored a series of victories from the 1940s into the early 1970s that put an end to de jure segregation and discrimination, made inroads against de facto segregation and discrimination, increased opportunities for African Americans to enter the middle class, and brought African American voices into American politics. Although progress has been made, African Americans continue the struggle for equality in American society. African Americans are a diverse group. Now two main commonalities within this group are the legacy of slavery and the color of skin.

AFRICAN AMERICAN VALUES AND ISSUES

FAMILY VALUES

AFRICAN AMERICAN FAMILIES are becoming more matriarchal. The number of married couples has been steadily decreasing, from 68% in 1970, 56% in 1980 to 47% in the late 1990s (U.S. Census Bureau, 2005). Seventy percent of lower-class African American families are headed by women and almost 60% of births are by unwed Black females. Although this information may seem discouraging, there are some mitigating factors.

The middle class is strengthening and growing. The basis structure of African American families has some strengths also. An extended family network provides economic and emotional support. Childrearing is often shared by older children, friends, and other relatives. The families have role adaptability, kinship bonds are strong, there is a strong achievement and work ethic, and there is a strong religious orientation (McCollum, 1997). African American males and females value assertiveness, and although the home may be headed by women, men are often around providing support. Many African American children have self-respect and positive self-esteem despite the specter of racism and discrimination. Husbands are generally supportive and not threatened by their wife's desire to work.

EDUCATION

EDUCATION IS OFTEN thought of as a key to success in the African American community. Although the education of Whites and Blacks has not reached parity, African Americans have made great strides. African Americans have a high school completion rate of 84%, and 71% of African American parents believe that science education is important. Racial integration is important to 79% of African American parents, and 80% of African American parents want academic standards to be raised. The *Journal of Blacks in Higher Education* (2006) revealed that about 60% of African Americans between the ages of 3 and 34 were enrolled in school in 2003 and that there were in the same year 12,660 African American faculty with tenure in American higher education. Despite the progress that has been made educationally, statistics are grim for African American males.

Nationally, about 25% of African American males between the ages of 18 and 24 attended college in 2000. During the same time frame and within the same age group, 35% of African American females and 36% of the general population attended college. African American men have the lowest graduation rate of any group from NCAA Division I institutions; 35% for them, 59% for White males, 46% for Hispanic males, 41% for American Indian males, and 45% for African American women after 6 years. In 1999 there were 25% more African American males in prison than there were enrolled in college. Many colleges and universities have initiatives to address the situation of African American males in higher education (Maxwell, 2004).

RELIGION AND SPIRITUALITY

RELIGION AND SPIRITUALITY are an important part of American culture and this is no less so for the African American community. Religious participation provides opportunities for leadership, self-expression, and community involvement (Sue & Sue, 2003). As with other groups, African Americans practice a number of religions and forms of spirituality.

Most African Americans are Protestant Christians. Although during slavery African beliefs were suppressed, some of those practices survived and were integrated into the Black Christian Church. African rhythms, lively singing, and a message of equality and hope for the future were hallmarks of this form of Christianity. The Black Church became a link between Black and White communities during the Civil Rights Movement (Bennett, 1982). Today, Islam and traditional African religions are making headway in the African American community. People are turning to these religions in an effort to return to and connect with African origins.

ISSUES OF RACIAL IDENTITY, RACISM, AND DISCRIMINATION

SKIN COLOR AND the legacy of slavery are strong underpinnings of African American identity. They are what separate the African American experience in America from all other groups. These two experiences are the foundation of African American racial identity as well as racism and discrimination against African Americans. Skin color and the legacy of slavery have been instrumental in the formulation of the culture and worldviews of African Americans.

Many African Americans, as do other minorities, experience a sequential process of racial identity, developing from non-Afrocentric to Afrocentric. Cross (1991, 1995) described a number of changes: preencounter, encounter, immersion-emersion, internalization, and internalization-commitment. In the preencounter stage, the individual devalues Black culture and values White culture. In the encounter stage, the individual begins to question, due to crisis or challenge, his or her previous way of thinking and begins to reinterpret the world. In the immersion-emersion stage, the individual withdraws from the dominant culture and focuses on the African American culture. In the internalization stage, the person becomes more secure and resolves conflicts between the old and new identities. Finally, during the internalization-commitment stage, the individual develops and verbalizes his or her commitment to social justice, social change, and civil rights for all (see Atkinson, Morton, & Sue, 1979; Sue & Sue, 2003). Racism and discrimination have helped to create a range of defensive, coping, and survival responses by African Americans. These include organizations that mirror White organizations such as the National Bar Association because African Americans were not allowed into the American Bar Association and the National Medical Association because of exclusion from the American Medical Association. There often exists paranoia of the system by African Americans as the system was controlled by Whites who were seen as the oppressor. Black vernacular English developed as a way for African Americans to communicate among themselves and not be understood by the general population. It also created a dialect of English that did not exist before. Suspicion of the medical and mental health systems was also developed as coping and survival systems (Sue & Sue, 2003).

MENTAL HEALTH ISSUES

WHEN CONCEPTUALIZING MENTAL health issues of African Americans, it may be better to use nonlinear scientific approaches and ecological theory to examine the etiology and course of emotional health challenges of this population. An accurate assessment of African American issues should seek to describe conditions where so-called abnormal behaviors may be normal reactions to social and environmental conditions. That is to say that some behavioral pathology in this population may be the result of dynamic ecological systems instead of the result of intrapsychological deficits (Pedersen, Draguns, Lonner, & Trimble, 2008).

There are reports by the Epidemiological Catchment Area studies that African Americans have a higher rate of mental disorders than the general population; however, when socioeconomic issues are factored in, the difference is all but eliminated (Pedersen et al., 2008). African Americans have been overdiagnosed with schizophrenia and affective disorders and underdiagnosed with depression. Much of this inaccurate diagnosis was due to diagnostic biases and reaction to racism. This generalized reaction to racism can be perceived as a national adaptation to oppressive conditions. Das, Olson, McCurtis, and Weissman (2006) indicated that practitioners avoid cultural influences by exploring "somatic and neuro-vegetative systems rather than mood or cognitive symptoms" (p. 30). This way of approaching Black people undermines their psychological functioning and gives the implication that clinicians could ignore symptoms that they do not understand, rather than broadening their cultural perspectives.

Other mental health issues for African Americans include suicide and exposure to violence. For young African Americans between the ages of 10 to 14, the suicide rates have increased at almost twice the rate of Whites of a comparable age. When considering exposure to violence, murder is the top cause of death for young African Americans (Feldman, 2006). About 25% of Black youth who have experienced or witnessed violence meet the criteria for post-traumatic stress disorder (Fitzpatrick & Boldizar, 1993).

STRATEGIES AND GUIDELINES FOR COUNSELING AFRICAN AMERICANS

WHEN COUNSELING GROUPS who are different, counselors must be aware of their own values and biases as well as the values of others. Sue and Sue (2003) outlined some guidelines for working with people who are African American:

1. If the client is referred, determine his or her feelings about counseling and how it may be useful to the client. Explain your relationship with the referring agency and the limits of confidentiality.
2. Identify the expectations and worldviews of African American clients, find out what they think counseling is, and explore their feelings about counseling. Determine how they view the problem and possible solutions. For example, many African Americans may view problems as being caused by a racist, oppressive society rather than a problem of their own making.
3. Establish an egalitarian relationship with the client. In contrast to other ethnic groups, most African Americans tend to establish a personal commonality with the counselor. This relates to the concept of the counselor showing that he or she can relate to some of the issues of concern to African Americans. This may be accomplished by self-disclosure by the counselor. If the client appears hostile or aloof, discussing some noncounseling topics may be useful.
4. Determine how clients have responded to discrimination and racism in healthy and unhealthy ways. Examine issues around racial identity. If needed, elements of African American culture should be incorporated into counseling. For example, explore reasons why racism may not be the cause of the problem because exploring alternative reasons or causes of problems is healthier than being stuck on one track. Also, spirituality can be incorporated into counseling.
5. Assess clients' strengths (e.g., social support networks). Do not dismiss issues such as racism as "just an excuse"; instead, help the client identify alternative means of dealing with problems.
6. Determine if any external factors are contributing to the presenting problem.

CONCLUSION

AFRICAN AMERICANS CONSTITUTE approximately 13% of the American population. They have been an integral part of this society since its conception, yet they face a myriad of issues. These issues include health issues, employment issues, health insurance issues, racism, and discrimination. African Americans are incarcerated at higher rates than any other group and draconian drug laws have a detrimental effect on the population. The mental health community has had difficulty addressing the issues of African Americans, and there is a dearth of appropriate treatment models to address the particular needs of the population.

Many factors influence the African American client and the importance of each factor may overlap depending on the individual. An African American who is middle class living in a White neighborhood may have a different developmental pattern from an African American living in a poor Black neighborhood. The counselor should completely assess internal and external issues involving the African American client.

In spite of the above-mentioned issues, African Americans continue to make positive strides in society. There have been improvements in health care, education, and employment to name a few areas. The task is to continue improving the lot of the population in a culturally sensitive way.

REFERENCES

Anderson, N. B. (1995). Behavioural and sociocultural perspectives on ethnicity and health: An introduction to the special issue. *Health Psychology, 14,* 591–598.

Atkinson, D. R., Morton, G., & Sue, D. W. (1979). *Counseling American minorities: A cross cultural perspective.* Dubuque, IA: W. C. Brown.

Bennett, L., Jr. (1982). *Before the Mayflower: A history of Black America.* New York: Johnson.

Cross, W. E. (1991). *Shades of Black: Diversity in African American identity.* Philadelphia: Temple University Press.

Cross, W. E. (1995). The psychology of Nigrescence: Revising the Cross model. In J. G. Ponterotto, J. M. Casas, L. A. Suzuki, & C. M. Alexander (Eds.), *Handbook of multicultural counseling* (pp. 93–122). Thousand Oaks, CA: Sage Publications.

Das, A. K., Olson, M., McCurtis, H. L., & Weissman, M. M. (2006). Depression in African Americans: Breaking barriers to detection and treatment. *Journal of Family Practice, 55*(1), 30–39.

Feldman, R. S. (2006). *Development across the life span* (4th ed.). Upper Saddle River, NJ: Pearson/Prentice-Hall.

Felton, G. M., Parson, M. A., Misener, T. R., & Oldaker, S. (1997). Health promoting behaviour of black and white college women. *Western Journal of Nursing Research, 19,* 654–664.

Fitzpatrick, K. M., & Boldizar, J. P. (1993). The prevalence and consequences of exposure to violence among African American youth. *Journal of the American Academy of Child and Adolescent Psychiatry, 32,* 424–430.

Freeberg, L. (1995, October 5). One of three blacks in 20s has trouble with law. *Seattle Post Intelligence,* pp. A1, A8.

Hargraves, J. L. (2004, October). *Trends in health insurance coverage and access among Black, Latino and White Americans, 2001–2003* (Tracking Report No. 11). Washington, DC: Center for Studying Health Center Change.

Hutchinson, E. O. (1994). *The assassination of the Black male image.* Los Angeles: Middle Passage Press.

Journal of Blacks in Higher Education. (2005/2006, Winter). *Vital statistics.* Retrieved June 13, 2007, from http://www. jbhe.com/vital/50_index.html

Maxwell, B. (2004, January). On campus grim statistics for African American men. *St. Petersburg Times Columns Online.* Retrieved November 3, 2007, from http://www.sptimes.com/2004/01/04Columns/On_campus_grim_stati .shtml

McCollum, V. J. C. (1997). Evolution of the African American family personality. *Journal of Multicultural Counseling and Development, 25,* 219–229.

Pedersen, P. B., Draguns, J. G., Lonner, W. J., & Trimble, J. E. (Eds.). (2008). *Counseling across cultures* (6th ed.). Thousand Oaks, CA: Sage Publications.

Sue, D. W., & Sue, D. (2003). *Counseling the culturally diverse: Theory and practice* (3rd ed.). New York: Wiley.

U.S. Census Bureau. (2004). *Population profile of the United States.* Washington, DC: U.S. Government Printing Office.

U.S. Census Bureau. (2005). *Data highlights.* Retrieved November 3, 2007, from www.census.gov

21

Multicultural Issues in Counseling Asian Americans

Dibya D. Choudhuri

A SIAN AMERICAN AND Pacific Islanders (AAPIs) are the second-fastest-growing group, after Hispanics, among the four federally designated racial and ethnic minority groups in the United States. Currently at 10.6 million people (about 4% of the total U.S. population), AAPIs are projected to reach 8% or 41 million U.S. residents by the year 2050 (U.S. Census Bureau, 2004). Members of this group are very diverse, with various origins and distinct immigration histories, levels of acculturation, socioeconomic characteristics, and health profiles. While generalized statements that are applicable across the subgroups are difficult to make, AAPIs collectively exhibit a wide range of strengths such as family cohesion, educational achievements, and motivation for upward mobility as well as risk factors for mental illness such as preimmigration trauma from harsh social conditions, discrimination, and acculturative stress.

DEMOGRAPHICS

A SIAN AMERICAN AND Pacific Islanders have roots in at least 29 Asian countries and 20 Pacific Islander cultures (U.S. Census Bureau, 2004). Members of this group speak more than 100 languages and belong to numerous religions; most (95%) are of Asian origin, while the rest (5%) are Pacific Islanders. The 2000 census states that Chinese Americans and Filipino Americans remain the first and second largest subpopulations, followed by Asian Indian Americans and Korean Americans (Barnes & Bennett, 2002).

The Asian American population is increasing primarily through immigration, with more than 60% born overseas as of 2001 (U.S. Census Bureau, 2004). This is a larger percentage of immigrants than any other minority group and close to 40% is estimated to have limited English-language proficiency, which could significantly impact knowledge of, access to, and usage of counseling services. For many of these individuals, English will be a second language and many will experience difficulties in adjusting to their new lives in the United States. Furthermore, many of these individuals may not be familiar with conventional forms of counseling or may not know how and where to seek help for their concerns. The rapid growth of the Asian American population does mean that counselors will encounter clients from these groups more frequently. It is estimated that by the year 2050, almost 1 in 10 people in the United States will be of AAPI descent (U.S. Census Bureau, 2004).

It is important to note that most Pacific Islanders are not immigrants; their ancestors were original inhabitants of land taken over by the United States a century ago. Clients from these populations as well as Asian Americans who are fourth- or fifth-generation Americans will deal with a very different set of social realities and experiences than new immigrants, one of which is the constant assignment of foreignness when the person is generationally American (Kurasaki, Okazaki, & Sue, 2002).

While the per capita income of AAPIs is almost as high as that for Whites, there are great differences between and within subgroups. For example, in 1995, while the national poverty rate was 13.1%, several Southeast Asian AAPI subgroups had elevated poverty levels such as Cambodian Americans (42.6%), Vietnamese Americans (25.7%), Laotian Americans (34.7%), and Hmong Americans (63.6%; Rumbaut, 1995). While there are many successful Southeast Asian and Pacific Islander Americans, the 14% household poverty rate for AAPIs is higher than that for non-Hispanic Whites at 8% (U.S. Census Bureau, 2004). This has implications for access to services since more than 2 million AAPIs remain uninsured.

Large education differences also exist among various AAPI subpopulations. For example, 88% of Japanese Americans have a high school diploma compared with only 31% of Hmong Americans, and 58% of Asian Indian Americans have a college degree compared to only 6% of Cambodian Americans or Laotian Americans (U.S. Census Bureau, 2004).

This in turn impacts counseling services, since applying a stereotype of educational attainment for every AAPI client may miss the actual struggles many AAPIs continue to face.

HISTORY PERSPECTIVE

HISTORICALLY, THE PRESENCE of Asians in North America can be traced to Filipino sailors in the mid-1500s, who settled around what is now Louisiana (Chan, 1991). The first large wave of migration from Asia to the United States was the Chinese who arrived in response to the discovery of gold in California in the 1800s, which fueled a backlash of discrimination and racism (Chan, 1991). A number of subsequent discriminatory laws were passed against the Chinese, culminating in the 1882 Chinese Exclusion Act that forbade more Chinese laborers from entering the United States. In response, workers from other Asian countries, starting with the Japanese in 1868, Koreans in 1903, and Filipinos in 1906, were recruited as field workers by planters on the mainland and Hawaii (Takaki, 1989). Asian Indians began arriving in 1907 to work on the railroads and in the Californian agricultural fields.

Anti-Asian sentiments (Chan, 1991) leading to discriminatory legislation, legal verdicts, and national policy culminated with the forced detainment of more than 100,000 Japanese Americans during World War II. These policies were somewhat reversed for Asian Indians, Chinese, Filipinos, and Koreans with the passing of the 1965 Immigration Act that attempted to lift the most severe restrictions (Takaki, 1989). The United States' political and military involvement in Southeast Asia through the Korean and Vietnam wars created a different migration of Korean, Vietnamese, Laotian, Hmong, and Cambodian individuals who came to the United States as refugees and exiles, often with great cultural shock, difficulties in acculturation, as well as legacies of trauma. In their adopted country, Asian immigrants continue to encounter discrimination. Pacific Islanders continue to encounter much of the same devastating institutionalized discrimination encountered by Native Americans (National Asian Pacific American Legal Consortium, 2001).

CULTURAL ASPECTS, BELIEFS, AND WORLDVIEW

THE RELATIVELY HIGH rates of marriage and low rates of divorce, along with a greater tendency to live in extended family households, indicate a strong orientation toward family among Asian Americans, for whom it serves as an important source of strength and resiliency (Kim et al., 2003). Based on a review of the literature, Kim, Atkinson, and Umemoto (2001) presented a summary of core cultural values.

Collective identity, family success, and shame. Asian Americans' self-worth and self-identity are strongly tied to their collective identity as members of a family. Thus, all family members have the responsibility to achieve success and to avoid bringing shame to the family. Hard work and perseverance are ways for individuals to achieve educational and occupational success, bringing success to the family. The fear of losing face can be a powerful motivating force for an Asian American to conform to the family's expectations and often may be used to suppress deviation from family norms.

Filial piety and deference to authority. Characterized as faithfulness to parents, this value is very significant and is exemplified by children offering respect, honor, loyalty, dutifulness, and sacrifice to their parents. Being obedient to parents and elders as well as concerned with their needs and wishes is important. Parental love is implicitly understood rather than expressed. The importance of family is believed to extend well beyond death, so that even deceased family members continue to be interested in the family's well-being and provide guidance. Those Asian Americans who adhere strongly to Asian cultural values tend to defer to authority figures for decision making and problem resolution.

Interpersonal harmony and reciprocity. Asian Americans may be accommodating, appeasing, and amenable, refraining from openly confronting others in order to maintain interpersonal harmony. Blending in as a part of the group rather than standing out, and exhibiting interpersonal virtues of patience, gentleness, and cooperation, are esteemed. The concurrent value of reciprocity implies that individuals should consider the needs of others before considering their own and in turn repay any favors, service, or gifts from others.

Restricted expression of emotion and interpersonal communication. With a high regard for emotional privacy, traditional Asian cultures encourage the suppression of emotional conflicts and discourage the full expression of emotions. Thus, many Asian Americans are taught to control themselves and exercise restraint. Many Asian Americans may be reserved in their interpersonal communication style and are generally discouraged from appearing boastful by talking about their accomplishments or expressing their opinions. Self-effacement, self-control, modesty, discretion, and humility are highly valued (Tsai, Knutson, & Fung, 2006). However, given the high-context cultures of origin, Asian Americans may use nonverbal communication processes, including subtle body expressions, to convey feelings nonverbally during both conversation and silence.

MENTAL HEALTH SERVICES

ALTHOUGH SOME STUDIES suggest higher rates of mental illness, there is wide variance of reported illness across different groups of Asian Americans (Takeuchi, Uehara, & Maramba, 1999). Asian Americans are distinguished by extremely low levels at which outside treatment is sought for mental health problems (Leong & Lau, 2001). They are also less likely than Whites to be psychiatric inpatients (Snowden & Cheung, 1990). Kim and colleagues (2003) found that Asian Americans would see a counselor only as the last resort, with friends and family being the first sources of support. Studies of Asian Americans have identified the barriers of stigma, suspiciousness, and a lack of awareness about the availability of services (Uba, 1994). Concurrently, among those who use services, they typically delay seeking outside help until their condition has become severe. As a result, Asian Americans are statistically likely to be underdiagnosed and often perceived as being "problem-free" (Takeuchi et al., 1999). Underutilization of services may also be explained by structural barriers such as limited English proficiency among some Asian immigrants and the inability to find culturally competent services. These phenomena are more pronounced for recent immigrants (Sue, 1994).

Post-traumatic stress disorder. Within the Asian community, refugees are at risk for post-traumatic stress disorder as a result of the trauma and terror preceding their immigration. Refugee experiences of groups such as Vietnamese, Indochinese, and Cambodians include imprisonment, death of family members or friends, physical abuse, and assault, as well as new stresses upon arriving in the United States (Mollica, Henderson, & Tor, 2002). These effects lasted many years postresettlement and increase the severity of the acculturative stress (Santos, 2006).

Acculturative stress. This refers to the difficulties that arise in the process of navigating the new culture. Psychological symptoms of acculturative stress include confusion, anxiety, depression, feelings of marginality and alienation, heightened psychosomatic symptom level, and identity confusion (Berry & Annis, 1974). It can negatively affect decision making, impair occupational functioning, contribute to role entrapment, heighten emotional strain, as well as contribute to ineffective client-counselor relations (Smart & Smart, 1995). Moyerman and Forman (1992) found that acculturative stress is positively correlated with psychosocial and health problems. This concept is extremely salient among Asian Americans, particularly new immigrants (Kim, 2007).

Intergenerational conflict. According to Chung (2001), this may occur across three dimensions as parents and children struggle with the demands of collectivist traditional values while living in a society that values individuality. The family dimension may impact communication with parents, pressure to follow cultural traditions, pressure to learn one's own Asian language, gendered expectations and concomitant roles to be followed, and expectations based on birth order and placement in the family hierarchy. Education and career dimensions generate conflict in the areas of time spent on studying versus recreation, the importance of academic achievement, emphasis on materialism and success, which school to attend and which major to study, and which career to pursue. The relational dimension are areas of conflict in terms of the generations disagreeing about when to date, who is considered appropriate, and when and whom to marry.

ASSESSMENT

IN WORKING EFFECTIVELY with AAPI clients, it is important to first perform a thorough and responsive assessment on the client's cultural background. The degree to which clients adhere to the norms and values of traditional culture versus the dominant cultural framework of U.S. society is important and can be assessed along four dimensions of behavior, values, knowledge, and cultural identity (Kim & Abreu, 2001). These can be assessed through learning about choice of friends; preferences for television programs and recreational activities; degree of contact with indigenous culture; language use; food choice; ideas and psychological explanations about health, illness, and wellness; as well as gendered attitudes and roles. Racial and cultural identity statuses can be assessed using the Racial and Cultural Identity Development Model (Sue & Sue, 2003). Assessing the extent to which clients have been victimized by oppression and whether clients' presenting issues might be related to this oppression is particularly important for generational Asian Americans and Pacific Islanders who may perceive their discriminatory experience as minorities as far more salient than cultural differences (Liang, Li, & Kim, 2004).

As discussed earlier, AAPIs tend to have negative attitudes about counseling and may be skeptical about the benefits from it. If the client reports a low level of credibility and less than positive attitudes, it would be crucial to address these attitudes early on and attend to the feelings of shame and embarrassment.

Many AAPI clients, particularly those who are strongly enculturated, may somaticize their psychological distress (Nishio & Bilmes, 1987). Hence, when working with these clients, it is helpful to learn about the clients' beliefs about the effects of psychological problems on their physical health.

COUNSELING APPROACHES

GIVEN THE HOLISTIC nature and integration of mind and body as well as collectivistic identity among AAPI populations, only a highly acculturated client would benefit from a strictly individualistic counseling approach that focused on self-actualization and individual achievement. Culturally sensitive counseling interventions would acknowledge and focus on issues such as family, responsibility, and accountability (Gim, Atkinson, & Kim, 1991; Zhang & Dixon, 2001). One of the first steps in the Cultural Accommodation Model (Leong & Lee, 2006) is to identify cultural disparities that are often ignored and then accommodate them by using current culturally specific concepts. This can be as preliminary as greeting clients in a family in order of their family hierarchy and using honorifics in greeting elders rather than first names or nicknames. On the other hand, it can include focusing on family goals and history in exploring client motivations.

While no specific counseling approaches are prohibited, they must be utilized appropriately with reference to cultural identity, and after the working alliance is strongly established. For instance, it would be inadvisable to strongly encourage emotional expression as curative in and of itself, since the client may well perceive it as weakness, indicative of a loss of control. Psychodynamic approaches that require exploring unresolved issues with family members may seem threatening and disrespectful. A humanistic approach that asks the client to collaboratively treat the counselor as an equal flies in the face of traditional deference to authority and may lead the client to expect little guidance and therefore lose hope in the counseling process (Merta, Ponterotto, & Brown, 1992). Cognitive approaches may conceptualize self-effacement and other traditional values of modesty and humility as negative self-concept, and a prescribed intervention of confronting negative self-talk with descriptions of one's achievements may seem boastful and distasteful.

Cultural values can assist the counseling process if harnessed appropriately. The deference to authority can result in the counselor having credibility and be perceived more favorably (Atkinson, Whiteley, & Gim, 1990). The valuing of interpersonal harmony can result in the client striving to build a strong working alliance with the counselor. Studies with actual clients suggest that Asian Americans prefer directive counseling styles to nondirective styles (Li & Kim, 2004) and that counselors who self-disclosed about successful strategies they had used in similar situations were perceived as more helpful than counselors who disclosed other types of personal information (Kim et al., 2003).

With some clients who are highly enculturated, simply using a culturally sensitive approach may be insufficient. It may be useful to enhance the treatment by concurrent referral to practitioners of indigenous healing methods. Studies have found that many Asian clients find these methods to be beneficial (Meng, Luo, & Halbreich, 2002). One approach is to provide holistic care, as well as address the interconnected nature of psychosomatic understandings of wellness, by directing the client to culturally appropriate exercise such as *ta'i chi ch'uan* or *yoga* that can enhance overall psychological well-being and mood (Sandlund & Norlander, 2000). Another approach is concurrent treatment by indigenous practitioners in modalities such as homeopathy or acupuncture. Based on principles of Chinese medicine in which health and illness are viewed in terms of a balance between the *yin* and the *yang* forces, acupuncture treatments have been used to enhance effectiveness in treating depression, anxiety disorders, alcoholism, and substance abuse (Meng et al., 2002). Community sources of support are also very effective, and AAPI clients report being open to seeking and receiving such support (Kim et al., 2003). For instance, a traditional Christian Korean American client may well benefit from developing a connection with the pastor of a Korean church (Park, 1989). As such, counselors should develop a good working relationship with agencies and organizations serving AAPIs. Familiarity with these services and practitioners will also lead to the counselor developing greater cultural expertise and sensitivity as well as expanding resources with whom to consult when dealing with complex client issues.

CONCLUSION

IN WORKING WITH AAPI clients, it is important that the counselor employ an individualized and personalized approach to each client, while acknowledging the historical, cultural, and social contexts of the client's experience. Counselors need to understand both the group's cultural orientation, as well as the extent to which the individual client may differ in such identification. Due to the large number of Asian immigrants, counselors need to understand the impact of acculturative stressors, the gap between the immigrant family experience with that of mainstream families, as well as attending to the social experience of being ethnic minorities.

REFERENCES

Atkinson, D. R., Whiteley, S., & Gim, R. H. (1990). Asian-American acculturation preferences for help providers. *Journal of College Student Development, 31,* 155–161.

Barnes, J. S., & Bennett, C. E. (2002). *The Asian population: 2000. Census 2002 brief.* Washington, DC: U.S. Department of Commerce.

Berry, J. W., & Annis, R. C. (1974). Acculturative stress: The role of ecology, culture and differentiation. *Journal of Cross-Cultural Psychology, 5,* 382–406.

Chan, S. (1991). *Asian Americans: An interpretative history.* Boston: Twayne.

Chung, R. H. G. (2001). Gender, ethnicity, and acculturation in intergenerational conflict of Asian American college students. *Cultural Diversity and Ethnic Minority Psychology, 7,* 376–386.

Gim, R. H., Atkinson, D. R., & Kim, S. J. (1991). Asian-American acculturation, counselor ethnicity and cultural sensitivity, and ratings of counselors. *Journal of Counseling Psychology, 38,* 57–62.

Kim, B. S. K. (2007). Acculturation and enculturation. In F. T. L. Leong, A. G. Inman, A. Ebreo, L. H. Yang, L. Kinoshito, & M. Fu (Eds.), *Handbook of Asian American psychology* (2nd ed., pp. 141–158). Thousand Oaks, CA: Sage Publications.

Kim, B. S. K., & Abreu, J. M. (2001). Acculturation measurement: Theory, current instruments, and future directions. In J. G. Ponterotto, J. M. Casas, L. A. Suzuki, & C. M. Alexander (Eds.), *Handbook of multicultural counseling* (2nd ed., pp. 394–424). Thousand Oaks, CA: Sage Publications.

Kim, B. S. K., Atkinson, D. R., & Umemoto, D. (2001). Asian cultural values and the counseling process: Current knowledge and directions for future research. *The Counseling Psychologist, 29,* 570–603.

Kim, B. S. K., Hill, C. E., Gelso, C. J., Goates, M. K., Asay, P. A., & Harbin, J. M. (2003). Counselor self-disclosure, East Asian American client adherence to Asian cultural values, and counseling process. *Journal of Counseling Psychology, 50,* 324–332.

Kurasaki, K. S., Okazaki, S., & Sue, S. (2002). *Asian American mental health: Assessment, theories and methods.* New York: Springer Publishing.

Liang, C. T., Li, L. C., & Kim, B. S. (2004). The Asian American racism-related stress inventory: Development factor analysis, reliability, and validity. *Journal of Counseling Psychology, 51*(1), 103–114.

Leong, F. T. L., & Lau, A. S. L. (2001). Barriers to providing effective mental health services to Asian Americans. *Mental Health Services Research, 3*(4), 210–214.

Leong, F. T., & Lee, S. (2006). A cultural accommodation model for cross-cultural psychotherapy: Illustrated with the case of Asian Americans. *Psychotherapy: Theory, Research, Practice, Training Special Issue: Culture, Race, and Ethnicity in Psychotherapy, 43*(4), 410–423.

Li, L. C., & Kim, B. S. K. (2004). Effects of counseling style and client adherence to Asian cultural values on counseling process with Asian American college students. *Journal of Counseling Psychology, 51,* 158–167.

Meng, F., Luo, H., & Halbreich, U. (2002). Concepts, techniques, and clinical applications of acupuncture. *Psychiatric Annals, 32,* 45–49.

Merta, R. J., Ponterotto, J. G., & Brown, R. D. (1992). Comparing the effectiveness of two directive styles in the academic counseling of foreign students. *Journal of Counseling Psychology, 39*, 214–218.

Mollica, R. F., Henderson, D. C., & Tor, S. (2002). Psychiatric effects of traumatic brain injury events in Cambodian survivors of mass violence. *British Journal of Psychiatry, 181*(4), 339–347.

Moyerman, D. R., & Forman, B. D. (1992). Acculturation and adjustment: A meta-analytic study. *Hispanic Journal of Behavioral Sciences, 14*, 163–200.

National Asian Pacific American Legal Consortium. (2001). *Backlash: When America turned on its own.* Washington, DC: Author.

Nishio, K., & Bilmes, M. (1987). Psychotherapy with southeastern Asian American clients. *Professional Psychology: Research and Practice, 18*(4), 342–346.

Office of the Surgeon General. (2001). *Mental health: Culture, race, and ethnicity. A supplement to mental health: A report of the Surgeon General.* Washington, DC: Department of Health and Human Services. Retrieved December 21, 2006, from http://mentalhealth.samhsa.gov/cre/toc.asp

Park, K. (1989). "Born again": What does it mean to Korean-Americans in New York City? *Journal of Ritual Studies, 3*(2), 287–301.

Rumbaut, R. G. (1995). Vietnamese, Loatian, and Cambodian Americans. In Min Pyong Gap (Ed.), *Asian Americans: Contemporary trends and issues* (pp. 232–270). Thousand Oaks, CA: Sage.

Sandlund, E. S., & Norlander, T. (2000). The effects of tai chi chuan relaxation and exercise on stress responses and well-being: An overview of research. *International Journal of Stress Management, 17*, 139–149.

Santos, F. S. (2006). The relationship of stress and loss to the severity and duration of chronic depression in Southeast Asian refugees (Doctoral dissertation, Alliant International University, 2006). *Dissertation Abstracts International: Section B: The Sciences and Engineering, 67*(4-B), 2242.

Smart, J. F., & Smart, D. W. (1995). Acculturative stress: The experience of the Hispanic immigrant. *The Counseling Psychologist, 23*, 25–42.

Snowden, L. R., & Cheung, F. H. (1990). Use of inpatient mental health services by members of ethnic minority groups. *American Psychologist, 45*, 347–355.

Sue, D. W. (1994). Asian-American mental health and help-seeking behavior: Comment on Solberg et al. (1994), Tata and Leong (1994), and Lin (1994). *Journal of Counseling Psychology, 41*, 292–295.

Sue, D. W., & Sue, D. (2003). *Counseling the culturally diverse: Theory and practice* (4th ed.). New York: Wiley.

Takaki, R. T. (1989). *Strangers from a different shore: A history of Asian Americans.* Boston: Little, Brown.

Takeuchi, D. T., & Uehara, E., & Maramba, G. (1999). Cultural diversity and mental health treatment. In A. V. Horwitz & T. Scheid (Eds.), *A handbook for the study of mental health: Social contexts, theories, and systems* (pp. 550–565). New York: Cambridge University Press.

Tsai, J. L., Knutson, B., & Fung, H. H. (2006). Cultural variation in affect valuation. *Journal of Personality and Social Psychology, 90*(2), 288–307.

Uba, L. (1994). *Asian Americans: Personality patterns, identity, and mental health.* New York: Guilford Press.

U.S. Census Bureau. (2004). *U.S. interim projections by age, sex, race, and Hispanic origin.* Retrieved December 21, 2006, from http://www.census .gov/ipc/www/usinterimproj/

Zhang, N., & Dixon, D. N. (2001). Multiculturally responsive counseling: Effects on Asian students' ratings of counselors. *Journal of Multicultural Counseling and Development, 29,* 253–262.

22

Mental Health Counseling With Hispanics/Latinos: The Role of Culture in Practice

Maria G. Romero

ACCORDING TO THE U.S. Census Bureau (2004) Hispanic/ Latinos (H/Ls) constitute the largest and fastest-growing ethnic minority group; there are approximately 37.4 million persons of Hispanic background living in the country. This number is projected to increase to about 50 million by the year 2020 (Arredondo, 2004). Due to the growing prevalence of the Hispanic population in the United States, and in mental health offices, it has become essential to develop models and approaches that will adequately meet the increasing mental health needs of this group (Kanel, 2002). This trend is expected to continue as Hispanics tend to be young, have high rates of births (Comas-Díaz, 2006), and have continued immigration (Kanel, 2002).

The terms *Hispanic* and *Latino* encompass individuals living in the United States with ancestry from Mexico, Puerto Rico, Cuba, El Salvador, the Dominican Republic, and other Latin American countries

(Sue & Sue, 2003). Each Hispanic subgroup faces distinct dilemmas: Mexicans and Mexican Americans experience the pressures of legalities and legalism; Puerto Ricans confront the challenges of dual identities; Cubans face the joys and pains of economic assimilation; Dominicans are subjected to some forms of racism because of their predominantly African phenotype; and countless South Americans contend with the ambiguities of detachment and belonging (Comas-Díaz, 2006). The term *Hispanic* is not widely accepted by all groups; some individuals prefer to be referred to as Latinos or *Chicanos* or self-identify based on country of origin or ancestry such as those from Mexico, who identify as *Mexicanos, Mexican American,* or *Spanish American* (Arredondo, 2004; Sue & Sue, 2003). The term Hispanic is not seen without controversy; however, the term *Hispanic/Latino* (H/L) will be employed throughout the chapter in an attempt to provide a common ground among these groups manifested through the Spanish language and customs.

MAJOR CONCERNS, PREVALENCE, AND THE NEED FOR MENTAL HEALTH SERVICES

HISPANIC/LATINOS POPULATE EVERY single state including Alaska and Hawaii; however, they make up a large percentage of the population in areas such as Arizona (16%), New Mexico (36%), and Miami (64%). The majority of Mexican Americans live in California and Texas (Sue & Sue, 2003). What was once described by the research as an underutilization of mental health services is now conceptualized as disparities in service delivery. Consequently, much attention is now being devoted to improving services and including the appraisal of institutional and organizational factors that may affect the relevance and fit of services of H/Ls (Manoleas & Garcia, 2003).

PREVALENCE OF MENTAL HEALTH ISSUES

MANY H/LS HAVE a high need for mental health services. There is evidence to suggest that H/Ls are at much higher risk for some mental health illnesses, but not others (Manoleas & Garcia, 2003). Their emotional needs include issues around ethnic identity, immigration, acculturation, and discrimination (Comas-Díaz, 2006). They also contend with loss, mourning, and adaptation stress while struggling with social, ethnic, and cultural conflicts in this country. It has been suggested that H/Ls' risk for mental illnesses is closely associated with the duration of time in the United States (Manoleas & Garcia; Weisman, 2005), suggesting an inverse relationship to acculturation. Some studies indicate that depression increases and social interest decreases with increasing levels of acculturation (Cuéllar, Siles, & Bracamontes, 2004). Moreover, among Mexican American immigrants, social and cultural assimilation into the U.S. culture increases vulnerability to alcohol addiction (Weisman, 2005). Barón and Constantine (as cited in Valdez, 2000) reported that acculturation occurs at different rates within different areas, such as behaviors and cognitions, which usually results in emotional distress and conflict. Other research has reported that the prevalence of post-traumatic stress disorder (PTSD) is higher in H/Ls than in their Anglo and African American counterparts (Pole, Best, Metzler, & Marmar, 2005, as cited in Comas-Díaz, 2006).

Research suggests that compared to Anglo Americans, Hispanics have less access to and availability of mental health services, are less likely to receive needed mental health services, often receive a poorer quality of mental health care, and are underrepresented in mental health research (Gelman, López, & Foster, 2005). The literature describes several reasons for this disparity between the H/L population with mental illness and utilization: (1) when seeking psychological assistance, Hispanics often encounter Eurocentric-based services that are insensitive to their cultural and spiritual experiences; (2) the lack of cultural sensitivity leads to the use of techniques and goals of mainstream psychology used by the dominant culture; and (3) an English-only climate may prevent clinicians from appreciating bilingualism (Comas-Díaz, 2006). The psychotherapist's inability to communicate in Spanish can compromise the quality of services delivered to bilingual Hispanics by creating a barrier to cultural understanding and misinterpretation of the client's communication. Significant efforts in research and practice are needed in making mental health services more relevant to H/Ls to address issues such as underutilization, disparities in services, and excessively high dropout rates (Manoleas & Garcia, 2003).

HISPANIC/LATINO CULTURE: TERMS AND DEFINITIONS

TRADITIONAL HISPANIC VALUES, CHARACTERISTICS, AND BEHAVIOR PATTERNS

THERE IS A significant and long-standing body of research across disciplines finding that culture informs clients' perceptions of their illness, their symptom presentation, their help-seeking expectations and behaviors, and therefore, the types of interventions they find acceptable; thus Gelman and colleagues (2005) suggest that an "understanding of culture is central to the creation and provision of adequate services" (p. 3). The following is information about the H/L culture that current practitioners may deem useful; however, it is not to say that this is an all-inclusive source for information.

Stereotypes of Hispanics on individual expectations, goals, and behaviors. Stereotypes as societal, consensually held beliefs about the characteristics of H/Ls tend to prescribe behavior (Niemann, 2004). Stereotypes tell H/Ls "who they are supposed to be and how they are supposed to behave and allow them to pass judgment on themselves and others based on these prescriptions and expectations" (p. 61). Stereotypes among H/Ls have a significant influence and greatly affect family relations, family functioning, and family members' goals and expectations. Some of the most prevalent types of stereotypes among H/Ls today, including dichotomous images for both men and women that define gender roles, have been associated with having an impact on psychopathology and will be briefly discussed in the following sections.

Familism, personalismo, and respect. For the past decade, much attention has been given to the importance of the family, social interactions, and collectivism among H/Ls in the literature (Niemann, 2004; Sue & Sue, 2003; Weisman, 2005). Individuals in H/L cultures consider the family to be the single most important social unit for the individual. Thus, in terms of mental health, it seems reasonable that individuals with strongly familistic tendencies might be motivated to view odd or disruptive behavior of a loved one in a more benign way to preserve the solidarity of the family (Weisman, 2005). Familism defines men and women's roles within the family, where women are mothers and wives and must prioritize the needs of family members above their own (Niemann, 2004). Young H/L individuals are expected to engage in behaviors that will prepare them for their expected adult roles in the family.

H/Ls place high value on characteristics such as respect (*respeto*) when interacting with other individuals, especially professionals such as medical doctors, teachers, and psychologists. Manoleas and Garcia (2003) suggest that it would not be appropriate to ask highly intrusive questions of H/L clients until it is clear that a level of trust and safety has been reached. Similarly, respect would also mean that a clinician may want to ask the client how he or she prefers to be addressed or assume the formal tense (in Spanish—*usted*) until invited to do otherwise. Once the relationship between therapist and client has been established, some H/Ls may ask therapists personal questions to place them within a context (e.g., "Where are you from? Are you married?") and/or express affection by embracing and kissing on the cheek during greetings and farewells. Clients may also offer their therapists invitations to weddings, graduations, baptisms, or other family events. The culturally competent therapist should be able to manage these requests accordingly and use cultural sensitivity, keeping in mind that declining these invitations may mean avoiding missed opportunities (Comas-Díaz, 2006).

FOLK HEALING AND *CURANDERISMO*: CURRENT STATUS

CURANDERISMO, A MEXICAN American folk healing practice, is the most widely studied of all belief systems in the social science literature (see Harris, Velásquez, White, & Renteria, 2004, for a review). The *curandero,* or the person providing the folk-healing services, is typically a person from the community who shares his or her clients' experiences, geographic location, socioeconomic status, class, language, religion, and beliefs regarding the cause of pathology. Their line of treatment is reported to supersede the services that typically can be offered by a physician, psychiatrist, psychologist, pastor, priest, or other mental health care worker (Harris et al., 2004). Table 22.1 outlines the symptom profile for the common types of conditions treated by a curandero/a, and how these conditions/syndromes may appear to be psychopathology in the *Diagnostic and Statistical Manual of Mental Disorders.*

TABLE 22.1 Symptom Profiles for Common *Curandera/o* Syndromes

Condition	Syndrome
Mal de ojo (evil eye)	One may interpret the behavior of a look, glance, or stare of a stranger or enemy as an attempt to inoculate him or her with this illness. Headaches, crying, irritability, restlessness, and stomach ailments are common symptoms.
Envidia (extreme jealousy)	A desire or jealousy resulting from an intense anger toward, dislike of, or jealousy of another. Symptoms often mimic a number of anxiety syndromes and may resemble a severe cold or fever.
Susto (extreme fright or fear)	Due to a traumatic experience. Symptoms mimic posttraumatic stress disorder: feeling keyed up or on edge, bodily complaints, restlessness, fatigue, major change in appetite, anhedonia, and depression.
Mal puesto (hexing)	May be placed by someone who is familiar with witchcraft. Symptoms include somatic complaints, GI problems, paranoia, and anxiety.

From "Folk Healing and *Curanderismo* Within the Contemporary Chicana/o Community: Current Status," by M. Harris, R. J. Velásquez, J. White, and T. Renteria, 2004, in *The Handbook of Chicana/o Psychology and Mental Health* (p. 118), edited by R. J. Velásquez, L. M. Arellano, and B. W. McNeill. Mahwah, NJ: Lawrence Erlbaum. Copyright 2004 by M. Harris, R. J. Velásquez, J. White, and T. Renteria. Reprinted with permission.

COUNSELING/TREATMENT OR PRACTICE TECHNIQUES WITH HISPANICS

MUCH HAS BEEN written about the need to be culturally sensitive when providing mental health services to H/Ls and the need for specialized clinical training to develop culturally sensitive therapists (Gelman et al., 2005). Due to the continued growth of this population in the United States and prevalence of mental health issues, it has become essential to develop models and approaches that will adequately meet the needs of this group. Several authors have addressed this need by providing suggestions regarding how to conduct initial sessions with H/Ls (Padilla & DeSnyder, 1985; Paniagua, 1994; and Velásquez et al., 1997, as cited in Sue & Sue, 2003) and/or specific recommendations for treating H/L men and women (Arredondo, 2004; Velásquez & Burton, 2004). The following is a summary of what has been presented in the literature as therapeutic approaches among the Hispanic population.

PSYCHOTHERAPY WITH HISPANIC WOMEN

HISPANIC WOMEN'S DEVELOPMENT has a historical context and is largely shaped by forces of historical colonization, marginality, bicultural identities, religious prescriptions, and their ongoing feminist efforts toward self-empowerment (Arredondo, 2004). Similar to other cultures, Hispanic women are socialized to be in roles of secondary or marginal status in their communities and families. The expectation for them to serve is ever present through the female's role as a daughter, sister, mother, godmother, or aunt. Other ideologies that promote a Hispanic woman's secondary status include (1) virginity until marriage, (2) the role of wife and mother being first, and the dictate to always be a (3) caring and compassionate woman (Arredondo, 2004).

According to Gil and Vazquez (1996) there are 10 commandments that women are socialized to abide by, such as knowing one's place, not wishing for more than being a housewife, not forsaking tradition, and not being unhappy with your man no matter what he does to you.

For more contemporary women who seek to go beyond these traditional role expectations, cultural conflict will likely occur (Arredondo, 2004).

Although the match between Hispanic women and therapist may seem ideal, it is important to keep in mind that H/L women in psychotherapy mirror all women. They are family members foremost, educators, victims of domestic violence, legislators, farm workers, performers, housekeepers, small business owners, activists, students, teenage mothers, writers, artists, physicians, immigration officers, and any of the other roles held by other men and women in the United States. Clinician's expectations of H/L female clients must neither be high or low; rather they must be suspended. Hispanic females must be allowed to tell their stories and then clinicians may engage (Arredondo, 2004).

PSYCHOTHERAPY WITH HISPANIC MEN

THE TREATMENT OF H/L men in psychotherapy remains one of the most challenging of all endeavors for the psychologist or therapist. Unlike Hispanic women, H/L men are less likely to voluntarily seek out treatment on their own because of emotional or psychological problems (Velásquez & Burton, 2004) but may show up for therapy for external reasons, including (1) court mandates, (2) pressures or ultimatums from family members (e.g., spouses or girlfriends), and (3) need for a specific problem to be solved as soon as possible. Hispanic/Latino men may walk into therapy full of anger or rage; anxious, defensive, or guarded; or ready to explode because they have repressed their feelings for a long time. For H/L men the idea of entering psychotherapy can be very intimidating, scary, unusual, threatening, and emasculating. This is largely influenced by their perceptions of psychotherapy as being only for women and that it is "chatting" time that would best be done with a friend and not a stranger (Velásquez & Burton, 2004). Psychotherapy with an H/L male requires an understanding of the many psychological layers that have been shaped and reinforced through parental socialization and peer relationships and are salient to the culture. Hispanic/Latino men who do seek out psychotherapy are likely to drop out or stop attending because these concepts are not fully understood by the psychologist.

Recommendations for Treating H/Ls in Psychotherapy (Sue & Sue, 2003; Velásquez & Burton, 2004)

- Establish a therapeutic alliance as soon as possible. Some older women may want to engage in small talk with the clinician. Research suggests that this is a good way to build rapport as this is an indication of personalism.
- Engage the client in clarifying or defining his or her role in the family and the community. The importance of family and personal relationships must be appreciated.
- Always be formal with H/Ls, especially if older. These clients, in general, are very respectful of the psychologist; formality should guide initial communications until the client indicates that a more informal discussion is acceptable.

- Be clear with the client about what psychotherapy is and is not and assess what his or her impressions are about therapy. Once things are clarified, the client is more likely to participate, which reduces the risk of dropping out.
- Identify any internal dialogue that the client may have (e.g., "I must be very strong," "I must put my family first"). Cognitive therapy appears to be an effective approach in working with H/Ls, especially those who tend to overrationalize or intellectualize.

CURRENT RESEARCH AND APPROACHES IN MENTAL HEALTH

THE ATTENTION IN research on culturally appropriate practices and competencies among therapists toward H/L individuals has increased in the last decade, prompting new areas of inquiry and modifications of current modalities such as cognitive behavior therapies. For example, Organista and Muñoz (1996) suggested that psychoeducational and cognitive behavior treatments (CBT) for H/Ls can be beneficial both for cultural and economic reasons. Given many H/L clients' expectations of immediate symptom relief, guidance and advice, and problem-centered approaches, CBT may be well suited for H/L clients. This approach quickly orients patients to treatment through education about mental illness and how interventions will help them with their problems. Kanel (2002) surveyed 268 Hispanics in southern California about their perceived mental health needs. They preferred counseling approaches in which the counselor gives a lot of advice, asks many questions, and focuses on current problems, especially family issues. It was also found that they preferred a therapeutic relationship that was both personal and professional and preferred counseling over medications to deal with mental health issues.

Other research has shown that family interventions are efficacious in treating adults with psychiatric disorders. Family-focused treatments, which provide psychoeducation, enhance coping skills, and improve family adaptation, have shown positive results in the treatment of schizophrenia (Weisman, 2005) and bipolar disorder (Rea, Tompson, Miklowitz, & Goldstein, 2003 as cited in Weisman, 2005). Other additional suggestions by researchers in incorporating cultural factors into current therapy include the idea of *Latino ethnic psychology*, which is described as a cultural resilient practice that attempts to restore "connectedness, foster liberation, and facilitate ethnic identity reformulation" among clients (Comas-Díaz, 2006). Essentially, Latino ethnic psychology aims at achieving a spiritual and existential type of wisdom that facilitates self-improvement.

CONCLUSION

THERE IS A strong need for counseling psychotherapies for ethnic minorities such as H/Ls that are both empirically supported and culturally sensitive given the tremendous growth and established mental health needs among this population. It is essential that researchers construct theories of counseling and psychotherapy and evaluate treatments grounded in the realities and experiences of H/Ls (Weisman, 2005). Currently, there is an emerging trend to assess the role that acculturation plays in facilitating or hindering the counseling process among immigrants and bicultural individuals such as H/Ls born in the United States (Valdez, 2000). Counselors must be culturally sensitive when treating H/Ls, keeping in mind traditional family patterns and gender norms, as well as other stresses that influence or can present as a mental health concern.

REFERENCES

Arredondo, P. (2004). Psychotherapy with Chicanas. In R. J. Velásquez, L. M. Arellano, & B. W. McNeill (Eds.), *The handbook of Chicana/o psychology and mental health* (pp. 231–250). Mahwah, NJ: Lawrence Erlbaum.

Comas-Díaz, L. (2006). Latino healing: The integration of ethnic psychology into psychotherapy. *Psychotherapy: Theory, Research, Practice, Training, 43,* 436–453.

Cuéllar, I., Siles, R. I., & Bracamontes, E. (2004). Acculturation: A psychological construct of continuing relevance for Chicana/o psychology. In R. J. Velásquez, L. M. Arellano, & B. W. McNeill (Eds.), *The handbook of Chicana/o psychology and mental health* (pp. 23–42). Mahwah, NJ: Lawrence Erlbaum.

Gelman, C. R., López, M., & Foster, R. P. (2005). Evaluating the impact of a cognitive-behavioral intervention with depressed Latinas: A preliminary report. *Social Work in Mental Health, 4,* 1–16.

Gil, R. M., & Vazquez, C. N. (1996). *The Maria paradox.* New York: Perigee Books.

Harris, M., Velásquez, R. J., White, J., & Renteria, T. (2004). Folk healing and *Curanderismo* within the contemporary Chicana/o community: Current status. In R. J. Velásquez, L. M. Arellano, & B. W. McNeill (Eds.), *The handbook of Chicana/o psychology and mental health* (pp. 111–125). Mahwah, NJ: Lawrence Erlbaum.

Kanel, K. (2002). Mental health needs of Spanish-speaking Latinos in southern California. *Hispanic Journal of Behavioral Sciences, 24,* 74–91.

Manoleas, P., & Garcia, B. (2003). Clinical algorithms as a toll for psychotherapy with Latino clients. *American Journal of Orthopsychiatry, 73,* 154–166.

Niemann, Y. F. (2004). Stereotypes of Chicanas and Chicanos: Impact on family functioning, individual expectations, goals, and behaviors. In R. J. Velásquez, L. M. Arellano, & B. W. McNeill (Eds.), *The handbook of Chicana/o psychology and mental health* (pp. 61–82). Mahwah, NJ: Lawrence Erlbaum.

Organista, K. C., & Muñoz, R. F. (1996). Cognitive behavioral therapy with Latinos. *Cognitive and Behavioral Practice, 3,* 255–270.

Sue, D. W., & Sue, D. (2003). *Counseling the culturally diverse: Theory and practice* (4th ed.). New York: Wiley.

U.S. Census Bureau. (2004). *Current population reports.* Washington, DC: U.S. Department of Commerce.

Valdez, J. N. (2000). Psychotherapy with bicultural Hispanic clients. *Psychotherapy, 37,* 240–246.

Velásquez, R. J., & Burton, M. P. (2004). Psychotherapy of men. In R. J. Velásquez, L. M. Arellano, & B. W. McNeill (Eds.), *The handbook of Chicana/o psychology and mental health* (pp. 177–192). Mahwah, NJ: Lawrence Erlbaum.

Weisman, A. (2005). Integrating culturally based approaches with existing interventions for Hispanic/Latino families coping with schizophrenia. *Psychotherapy: Theory, Research, Practice, Training, 42,* 178–197.

23

Counseling Persons From Middle Eastern Backgrounds

NATHALIE D. MIZELLE

REPORTS OF PREJUDICE and discrimination against Arab Americans have increased since the events of September 11, 2001 (Moradi & Talal Hasan, 2004). Perceived prejudice events are recognized as stressors that are linked to lowered mental health for those who experience such events. Frequently misrepresented and even vilified in the press (e.g., depicted as terrorists, "fanatics," or "oil sheiks"), Middle Eastern Americans are routinely negatively portrayed in the media and entertainment and are often the victims of stereo-types (Erickson & Al-Timimi, 2001; Nassar-McMillian & Hakim-Larson, 2003). Stereotyping has led to hostile attitudes toward the Middle Eastern American community. Hate crimes have increased, including harassment, threats, offensive language, physical aggression, religious aggression, discrimination, vandalism, and other hostile acts against this community. In addition, the legacy of 9/11 has increased such nega-tive attitudes, leading some Middle Eastern Americans to deny their heritage out of fear of discrimination and for fear of their lives. These stereotypes not only present serious challenges to Middle Eastern Americans' development of positive ethnic associations (Erickson & Al-Timimi, 2001; Jackson, 1997) but they also lead to biases and mistaken assumptions among the mental health professionals who serve them.

DEMOGRAPHICS

MIDDLE EASTERN AMERICANS originate from a geographical region stretching from Syria in the north to Yemen in the south, and from Morocco on the Atlantic Ocean in the west to the Persian Gulf countries in the east. It should be noted that they have been given many social and political designations, such as Palestinians, Jordanians, Egyptians, Lebanese, Iraqis, Syrians, and Yemenis, terms that refer to their country of origin. Such designations as Maronites, Copts, Melkites, Chaldeans, Greek Orthodox, Antiochian Orthodox, Protestant, Sunni Muslims, and Shiite Muslims refer to the religious affiliations (Khoury, 2002). Arab Americans are descendents of the Semites who originated in a vast region of enormous historical and cultural complexity. Today the region is called the Middle East. It is rich in natural resources as well as in religions. Here in the United States, it is estimated that approximately 3 million Middle Eastern Americans currently reside (Moradi & Talal Hasan, 2004). Middle Eastern Americans came to the United States in two waves, which occurred before and after World War II. The first wave began during the last quarter of the 19th century. Khoury (2002) reports that most of the newcomers were from the lower social classes and with little education. They were mainly Christian (90%), single males, and 75% were between 15–45 years of age. Other religious groups such as Muslims and Druze constituted minorities. About 50% of the first wave settled in the South and the other 50% split into two groups, each half immigrating to the East Coast and Midwest, respectively. The second wave began after World War II and continues to the present time. This migration appears to have been predicated chiefly on a need to escape the political turmoil in the Middle East. This wave has tended to comprise highly educated professionals such as doctors, lawyers, and engineers. They are predominately Muslim (60%) and married, and 50% range from ages 20–49 years old; females constitute about 45% of the total (Erickson & Al-Timimi, 2001; Moradi & Talal Hasan, 2004; Nassar-McMillian & Hakim-Larson, 2003).

RELIGION AND SPIRITUALITY

RELIGION OFTEN DICTATES the way of life in the Middle East. Religion plays an integral role in the lives of many Middle Eastern Americans and may be a central component of their identity (Erickson & Al-Timimi, 2001; Abudabbeh, 1996). Based on differences, Middle Eastern immigrants tend to reside in the United States near people from their respective homeland and/or who share the same religion. The reason for such proximity is based on the preservation of cultural values, customs, and traditions. The religious affiliations of Middle

Eastern Americans are as diverse as their national origins. In general, the community is divided into two distinct religious groups: Christian and Muslim. The majority of Middle Eastern Americans are Christians, although Islam is the predominant religion practiced throughout the Middle Eastern world. Within the Christian faith, Middle Eastern Americans may belong to one of the following sects: Maronite, Melkite Catholics, Greek Orthodox, Antiochian Orthodox, Protestant, or Roman Catholic. Within the Islamic faith, Middle Eastern Americans belong to one of the two major sects: Sunni or Shiite Muslims (Baker, 2003; Erickson & Al-Timimi, 2001; Khoury, 2002).

Communication can be illustrated by both the spoken and written forms of language. Arabic (Semitic language) was the mother tongue of the ancestors of Middle Eastern Americans. Also, most Middle Eastern Americans are conversant in some additional languages such as English, French, Italian, or Spanish, to name a few. Nonverbal communication can be explained as "all those stimuli within a communication setting, both humanly and environmentally generated, with the exception of verbal stimuli, that have potential message value of the sender or receiver" (Samovar, Porter, & Jain, 1981, p. 156). The nonverbal communication may be illustrated by examples of physical touch, such as greeting the opposite sex, as well as examples of appearance. During greeting, the Americanized group may touch by kissing, hugging, or shaking hands with a person of the opposite sex, depending on their relationship. The traditionalists, meanwhile, cannot touch due to either religious values or restrictive customs and traditions; their greeting tends to remain strictly verbal (Nassar-McMillian & Hakim-Larson, 2003).

The family is the central structure of Middle Eastern culture and plays a critical role in Middle Eastern social origination and in collective identity. This means that the development of an individual identity separate from that of the family or the community is typically not valued or encouraged (Al-Deen, 1991; Erickson & Al-Timimi, 2001). Middle Eastern cultures consider the enhancement of family honor and status an important goal for each family member, and conformity and placing family interests over individual ones are expected (Erickson & Al-Timimi, 2001). Extended families are very important in Middle Eastern culture and often live near or with each other. Within some Middle Eastern cultures, parents or families sometimes arrange a couple's marriage or aid in the selection of a partner (Baker, 2003; Erickson & Al-Timimi, 2001).

COUNSELING ISSUES

Relocating to a foreign culture can be complicated, challenging, and stressful. Among the factors that may affect Middle Eastern Americans' acculturation experiences are country or origin, length of time in the United States, reasons for emigration, whether they have family still living abroad, their ability to return to or visit their home country, and their long-term plans to stay in the United States (Ahmed & Lemkau, 2000). Additionally, language factors such as ability to speak English or the presence of a discernible accent may affect individuals' acculturation experiences or be a source of stress in their lives. Another factor to consider in understanding Middle Eastern Americans' cultural adjustment is their family's educational and economic status in their home country and the degree to which these have changed since coming to the United States, because such differences can be dramatic and represent a significant source of stress for families. Another source of stress may stem from being constantly profiled since 9/11 in attempting to board planes or other means of transportation, going through security, and being questioned more frequently about their whereabouts.

Middle Eastern Americans may have a general skepticism of the authority of mental health professionals, in part due to the negative connotations of mental illness. The concept of *mental disturbance* may be difficult for them to accept as a diagnosis. Clients may have strong fears about being branded *majnun* (pronounced "muhj-noon") or crazy, a term that can carry considerable stigma (Baker, 2003; Erickson & Al-Timimi, 2001; Okasha, 1999). Another factor contributing to reluctance to seek mental health services is the lack of experience with or exposure to Western counseling approaches. Family members are sought out for guidance and most of the time men seek guidance from an older man and women from an older woman (Abudabbeh, 1996; Erickson & Al-Timimi, 2001; Okasha, 1999). Additionally, individuals have a tendency to display emotional pain in physical terms or through physical complaints. For example, anxiety or depression may be described as an aching body or gastrointestinal concerns (Erickson & Al-Timimi, 2001; Okasha, 1999). Middle Eastern Americans are inclined to maintain their family ties and may be reluctant to engage in self-disclosure; therefore any services rendered will involve a longer period of time in order to develop the trust necessary for effective treatment (Erickson & Al-Timimi, 2001; Nassar-McMillian & Hakim-Larson, 2003).

To provide effective services to Middle Eastern clients, mental health professionals need to have an awareness of history, culture, and experiences beyond what they are exposed to. Counselors working with Middle Eastern Americans benefit from an awareness of cultural beliefs and differences. For example, a competent counselor could never ignore the influence of the Islamic religion in the life of the Middle Eastern client. Furthermore, counselors must certainly be aware of the influence of family and the roles men and women are expected to play in society. Encouraging a female client to engage in feminist activities would be tantamount to ostracizing her from her community.

Aside from values previously mentioned, counselors also benefit from an awareness of certain cultural differences that may stand in the way of open communication. For instance, when Middle Eastern clients engage in conversations, they typically stand much closer together than individuals from other cultures. In addition, they tend to engage in fixed eye contact during conversation. Moreover, some Middle Eastern clients of the same sex may tend to touch each other or hold hands when conversing or gesturing (Moradi & Talal Hasan, 2004; Nassar-McMillian & Hakim-Larson, 2003). The counselor must be aware of the Middle Eastern culture and judgments that may occur.

Most counselors are on clock time and therefore must be aware of not misdiagnosing their clients since a lot of Middle Eastern Americans may not have fixed or rigid time frames. Additionally, some women counselors may face resistance with an opposite-sex client who may have been socialized to confide in only same-sex confidants (Nassar-McMillian & Hakim-Larson, 2003). Another obstacle standing in the way of counseling persons of Middle Eastern descent may be the deep-rooted cultural belief in divine will. This is a traditional belief that people are helpless to control events and God has direct and ultimate control of all things that happen (Erickson & Al-Timimi, 2001). To this end, it is important to view Middle Eastern Americans' receptiveness to counseling, which may encompass an array of factors, including, but not limited to, religious background, cultural background, country of origin, educational level, community involvement, language spoken at home, and acculturation level, from a holistic perspective.

Since there are many complexities of the Middle Eastern American identity, counselors must make few assumptions regarding the identity of the client or his or her family. In working with Middle Eastern Americans, counselors need to be aware of ethnic identity or other issues of ethnicity that might come into fruition. Consequently, counselors must consider the overall context or intergenerational experiences of these clients and examine immigration and discrimination concerns. These roles are vital because counselors need to be aware of gender issues, shifts in cultural identity, and perhaps their own bias or stereotypes.

RESOURCES

Abraham, N. (1995). Arab Americans. In R. J. Vecoli, J. Gadens, A. Sheets, & R. V. Young (Eds.), *Gale encyclopedia of multicultural America* (Vol. 1, pp. 84–98). New York: Gale Research.

Baker, K. (1999). Acculturation and reacculturation influence: Multilayer contexts in therapy. *Clinical Psychology Review, 19*(8), 951–967.

Erickson, C., & Al-Timimi, N. (2001). Providing mental health services to Arab Americans: Recommendations and considerations. *Cultural Diversity and Ethnic Minority Psychology, 7*(4), 308–327.

Khoury, R. (2002). *Refugee mental health manual: Culturally competent practice with Arab-Americans*. Retrieved July 25, 2008, from http://www.arabacc .org/Refugee_Manual/body_refugee_manual.html

Nafisi, A. (2004). *Reading Lolita in Tehran: A memoir in books*. New York: Random House.

REFERENCES

Abudabbeh, N. (1996). Arab families. In M. McGoldrick, J. Giodana, & J. K. Pearce (Eds.), *Ethnicity and family therapy* (2nd ed., pp. 333–346). New York: Guilford Press.

Ahmed, S., & Lemkau, J. (2000). Cultural issues in the primary care of South Asians. *Journal of Immigrant Health, 2*(2), 89–96.

Al-Deen, N. (1991). Understanding Arab Americans: A matter of diversities. In A. Gonzalez, M. Houston, & V. Chen (Eds.), *Our voices* (pp. 18–23). Los Angeles: Roxbury.

Baker, K. (2003). Marital problems among Arab families: Between cultural and family therapy interventions. *Arab Studies Quarterly, 25*, 471–477.

Erickson, C., & Al-Timimi, N. (2001). Providing mental health services to Arab Americans: Recommendations and considerations: Cultural diversity and ethnic minority. *Psychology, 7*(4), 308–327.

Jackson, M. (1997). Counseling Arab Americans. In C. Lee (Ed.), *Multicultural issues in counseling: New approaches in diversity* (2nd ed., pp. 333–349). Alexandria, VA: American Counseling Association.

Khoury, R. (2002). *Refugee mental health manual: Culturally competent practice with Arab Americans*. Retrieved July 25, 2008, from http://www .routledgementalhealth.com/multicultural-counseling/ch12.pdf

Moradi, B., & Talal Hasan, N. (2004). Arab American persons' reported experience of discrimination and mental health: Mediating role of personal control. *Journal of Counseling Psychology, 51*(4), 414–428.

Nassar-McMillian, S., & Hakim-Larson, J. (2003). Counseling considerations among Arab Americans. *Journal of Counseling and Development, 81*(2), 150–159.

Okasha, A. (1999). Mental health in the Middle East: An Egyptian perspective. *Clinical Psychology Review, 19*(8), 917–933.

Samovar, L. A., Porter, R. F., & Jain, N. C. (1981). *Understanding intercultural communication*. Belmont, CA: Wadsworth.

24

Counseling White Americans

NATHALIE D. MIZELLE

LTHOUGH THE TERM *White American* is meant here to include Americans whose ancestors immigrated to the United States from a country in Europe, many Caucasian Americans would not immediately identify themselves as being from Europe for their cultural background. Many clients are likely to use the expressions *White, American, Caucasian, European American,* or *Anglo American.* Some White Americans are either unaware of or do not identify with the European aspects of their culture. However, because Americans from Europe are the dominant cultural force in the United States today, it is hoped that a greater understanding of the counseling issues particular to this group of people will also illuminate the extent to which the counseling profession itself, as a Eurocentric process, has developed (Das, 1995).

According to the 2000 census, German (42.9 million), Irish (30.5 million), and English (24.5 million) ethnic groups from northern Europe and Italians (15.7 million) from southern Europe are the most populous European ethnic groups in the United States (U.S. Census Bureau, 2006). Another 20.6 million Americans list their ancestry as *American* or the *United States.* According to the U.S. Census Bureau's estimation for 2006, 45% of American children under the age of 5 are minorities. In 2006, the nation's minority population reached 100.7 million, up more than 2 million people from a year earlier. Hispanics accounted for almost half (1.4 million) of the national population growth of 2.9 million between July 1, 2005, and July 1, 2006. In 35 of the country's 50 largest cities, White people are or soon will be in the minority.

White Americans use the mental health system in different ways from most minority groups and hold different views about mental health problems and their treatment. These concepts and cultural differences are addressed below.

NORTHERN EUROPEAN AMERICANS

NORTHERN EUROPEAN AMERICANS may include people whose families immigrated from England, Scotland, Wales, Ireland, France, Germany, Sweden, Norway, Denmark, Finland, Belgium, and so forth. Although there are many differences between, among, and within ethnic groups that emigrated from northern Europe, some important similarities are worth noting, especially as they have shaped current American culture. Four of these characteristics seem frequent among northern European immigrants: the importance of work in self-identity, an emphasis on individuality, suppression of feelings, and distancing as a mode of coping with interpersonal conflict.

Work as a predominant value may have roots in British culture. Sixty-five percent of the top executives of the largest American corporations in 1950, and 78% of Supreme Court justices through 1957, were of British heritage (Axelson, 1993). It is worth considering that these accomplishments may be indicative of political as well as economic power. A strong work value is also consistent with German, French, and other northern European cultures (Langelier & Langelier, 2005; McGill & Pearce, 2005; Winawer & Wetzel, 2005). In general, the work ethic has evolved in the United States to an emphasis on individual achievement, such that there is a dominant cultural expectation of individual success (McGill & Pearce, 2005). This core value, which may have originated in Calvinist philosophy, is evidenced in negative attitudes toward anyone who is not obviously successful—for example, some people of color, disabled persons, and people on welfare. In counseling, this value may be reflected in high self-expectations and corresponding feelings of failure as well as in positive motivation to work on relationships and other problems.

The northern European American, especially British, emphasis on individuality may bring with it feelings of alienation, emotional isolation, and withdrawal (McGill & Pearce, 2005). Das (1995) noted that many successful middle-class Americans feel alienated and lack a sense of community after putting their emphasis on individual achievement and the self.

Another commonality in northern European countries that appears to have become characteristic of mainstream American culture is a reluctance to directly express feelings, which has been noted in British, French, German, and Irish cultures (Langelier & Langelier, 2005; McGill & Pearce, 2005; McGoldrick, 2005; Winawer & Wetzel, 2005). Perhaps as a consequence, the expression of feelings often becomes a goal of counseling with European Americans, and several counseling techniques seem to have developed to address this need. Some examples are psychodrama, Rogerian reflection of feeling, and Gestalt *empty chair* techniques.

Northern European Americans may cope with interpersonal conflicts by distancing or cutting off the relationship, as is common in British, German, and Irish cultures (McGill & Pearce, 2005; McGoldrick, 2005; Winawer & Wetzel, 2005). Current European American concerns with divorce and teenage runaways may be indicators of this problem-solving style. Counseling techniques that focus on communication training and family therapy may have developed as remedies for such problematic interpersonal coping strategies.

SOUTHERN AND EASTERN EUROPEAN AMERICANS

AFTER 1900, AND prior to the 1965 Immigration Act, most immigrants to the United States came from southern and eastern European countries, such as Italy, Greece, Poland, and Russia (Stave, Sutherland, & Salerno, 1994). In 1882, 87% of immigrants were from northern and western European countries, but by 1907 the focus of immigration had shifted, and 81% were from southern and eastern European countries instead. Immigrants from southern and eastern European countries are sometimes called *White ethnic Americans* (Axelson, 1993). This term, however, seems to ignore the ethnic roots of northern and western European Americans. As cultural groups, southern and eastern European immigrants have some general cultural differences from northern Europeans that bear discussion: the importance of the family over the individual, expression of feelings, and prescribed roles as a mode of coping with interpersonal conflict.

As is commonly the case in Latino, African, Asian, and Native American cultures, family is of great importance to many southern European Americans (Johnson, 1985; Giordano, McGoldrick, & Guarino Klages, 2005; Killian & Agathangelou, 2005), so much so that the needs of the individual may be considered secondary. This can make individuation from the family a difficult issue, especially in contrast to popular emphasis on American independence. In fact, it may be contrary to southern

European American cultural norms to label particular family issues as individuation–enmeshment issues. Moving out of the house, going away to college, or marrying outside the culture could each be viewed by the family as an act of betrayal and might become a presenting problem in counseling (Johnson, 1985; Killian & Agathangelou, 2005; Sleek, 1995). It is essential that counselors inquire about and identify cultural values related to these issues.

European/White Americans value rugged individualism (Frame, 2003). It is common to believe that life struggles are centered in the self and that most problems can be overcome if enough individual effort is put forth (Frame, 2003). Indeed, any type of failure may be ascribed to personal weakness, whereas independence is highly valued. Emotional expression is another common theme among southern European cultures (Frame, 2003; Rosen & Weltman, 2005). For example, among many families with Jewish cultural backgrounds, expression of feelings may not only be accepted but may also be a highly valued part of family interaction (Rosen & Weltman, 2005). In other southern and eastern European cultures—Polish and Greek American, for example—some emotions related to joy or sexuality may be easily expressed, whereas other emotions that might indicate anxiety or weakness may be censored (Killian & Agathangelou, 2005; Mondykowski, 1982).

Proscribed roles for men and women may contribute to a more formalized behavioral conformity in carrying out relationships, with men often viewed as the authority and provider, and women viewed as the nurturer within the family sphere (Giordano et al., 2005; Rosen & Weltman, 2005). The implication for counseling is that models for interpersonal negotiation and gender role flexibility may be lacking in some southern European American homes (Giordano et al., 2005). This array of backgrounds may be an indication of a lack of cultural awareness among majority White or European American researchers about the importance and uniqueness of their own ethnic backgrounds, even though research results have found White racial identity attitudes to be related to racism toward others (Pope-Davis & Ottavi, 1994).

Many treatments for European Americans are already part of traditional counseling practice. Because most counseling techniques taught today were developed by European Americans (Ivey, Ivey, & Simek-Morgan, 1993), it seems logical that they would be effective when applied to European Americans. The rational explanations of psychodynamic approaches to counseling may be especially suited to British Americans (McGill & Pearce, 2005) and Jewish Americans (Rosen & Weltman, 2005). Sigmund Freud, originator of psychoanalysis, was northern European and Jewish. Carl Rogers and Virginia Satir, both European Americans living in the Midwest, developed counseling approaches that may be especially compatible to Midwestern British Americans, whereas structural and strategic family therapy approaches may be less helpful with these European Americans (McGill & Pearce, 2005). In contrast, structured, paradoxical techniques or positive refraining have been noted as possibly being more helpful to Irish Americans than nonverbal or body techniques (McGoldrick, 2005). Behavioral or action-oriented approaches have been described as culturally consistent for French Americans (Langelier & Langelier, 2005) and Polish Americans (Mondykowski, 1982). Meanwhile, Milan-style family counseling was developed by northern Italians and may be suited for issues of family enmeshment when it becomes problematic (Giordano et al., 2005).

COUNSELING ISSUES

SOCIAL CLASS CONSIDERATIONS

EUROPEAN AMERICANS AS a group have enjoyed social, political, and economic privileges not afforded others. For example, as of 2004, European Americans had higher household incomes ($49,101) than Latinos ($34,299), American Indians/Alaska Natives ($33,132), or Blacks ($30,355) and were less likely to live in poverty than were Blacks, American Indians/Alaska Natives, Latinos, or Asians. European Americans, too, were more likely to have health insurance (89%) than were Asians (82%), Blacks (80.2%), American Indians/Alaska Natives (71%), or Latinos (67.4%) (Frame, 2003). This economic power may be the result, in part, of race-based privilege in that White Americans may receive economic benefits and advantages just on the basis of being White. These statistics over-look, however, large numbers of European Americans (oftentimes in Appalachia or in the Southwest) who live in poverty or are marginalized. Some European Americans see their successes solely to be the result of hard work and may ignore or deny the social benefits of White racial identity (McIntosh, 1988). Sometimes issues that arise in counseling a White American client may be related to a lack of understanding of the impact of privilege on the client and ignorance related to race. Some scholars have noted the lack of emphasis on encouraging White people to explore what it means to be White or have called for White people to explore their own cultural identities (Pope-Davis & Ottavi, 1994).

SPIRITUALITY

RELIGION AND SPIRITUALITY are highly valued among White Americans (Frame, 2003). Spiritual differences, only one facet of cul-ture, are often confused with ethnic differences. As such, differences between groups might be more related to differences between Catholics and Protestants than between ethnic groups. When counseling White Americans, the ethnic variety within one specific religion or denomination creates further diversity in religious and spiritual expression. For example, Southern Baptists tend to ascribe to biblical literalism, require strict observance of moral codes of conduct, and take more conservative positions on social issues than do American Baptists of the North and Midwest (Frame, 2003, p. 129).

It is important for the counselor to assess the client's individual views of spirituality and to not assume that membership in a particular ethnic group implies religious convictions common to that group. The counselor should explore the dynamics and religious practices of the client's family of origin and ask about the importance of these customs for the individual, partner, and/or family members. There are other counseling considerations related to religion. For example, it may be counterproductive for a Catholic client to view counseling as if it were confession, a place to tell one's sins and seek forgiveness. On the other hand, Frame (2003) found that Jews were more likely to seek outpatient treatment than were Protestants or Catholics. Talking, insight, and complex explanations are culturally consistent with Jewish culture, making psychodynamic approaches to counseling a treatment of choice (Frame, 2003). It is also important to note that some White Americans are not particularly influenced by or reject their ethnic heritage in their religion and spirituality. Some clients entering counseling may be unaware of their ethnicity and the cultural values contributing to their distress; therefore, bringing their ethnic and religious heritage into their awareness may result in greater counseling fulfillment.

Counselors need to educate themselves and be aware that there are within-group differences. There is a dearth of information about techniques and approaches and theories about White Americans and counseling; however, there may be a discrepancy of a lack of cultural awareness among a majority of White American researchers and counselors about the importance and uniqueness of their own ethnic backgrounds. Counselors working with White Americans should also be mindful of their own judgments and stereotypes that may manifest from past history, politics, and assumptions.

RESOURCES

PRINT MEDIA

Bartlett, J. (1992). *Familiar quotations* (16th ed.). Boston: Little, Brown.

Carter, R. T. (1990). The relationship between racism and racial identity among White Americans: An exploratory investigation. *Journal of Counseling and Development, 69*, 46–50.

Folwarski, J., & Smolinsk, J. (2005). Polish families. In M. McGoldrick, J. Giordano, & N. Garcia-Preto (Eds.), *Ethnicity and family therapy* (3rd ed., pp. 741–755). New York: Guilford Press.

Herz, F. M., & Rosen, E. J. (1982). Jewish families. In M. McGoldrick, J. Pearce, & J. Giordano (Eds.), *Ethnicity and family therapy* (pp. 364–392). New York: Guilford Press.

Katz, J. H. (1989). *White awareness* (6th ed.). Norman: University of Oklahoma Press.

McGill, D. W., & Pearce, J. K. (1982). British families. In M. McGoldrick, J. Pearce, & J. Giordano (Eds.), *Ethnicity and family therapy* (pp. 457–479). New York: Guilford Press.

Neville, H. A., Worthington, R. L., & Spanierman, L. B. (2001). Race, power, and multicultural counseling psychology: Understanding White privilege and color-blind racial attitudes. In J. G. Ponterotto, J. M. Casas, L. A. Suzuki, & C. M. Alexander (Eds.), *Handbook of multicultural counseling* (2nd ed., pp. 257–288). Thousand Oaks, CA: Sage Publications.

Rotunno, M., & McGoldrick, M. (1982). Italian families. In M. McGoldrick, J. Pearce, & J. Giordano (Eds.), *Ethnicity and family therapy* (pp. 340–363). New York: Guilford Press.

Wise, T. (2005). *White like me: Reflections on race from a privileged son*. Brooklyn, NY: Soft Skull Press. A European American's quasi-memoir, arguing that racial privilege hurts all people.

MULTIMEDIA

Chase, D. (Producer). (1999). *Sopranos* [Videorecording]. New York: Home Box Office (HBO).

Mangold, J. (Director). (1999). *Girl Interrupted* [Movie]. Hollywood: Columbia, Tristar.

ORGANIZATIONS

Center for the Study of White American Culture: A Multiracial Organization. http://www.euroamerican.org/

REFERENCES

Axelson, J. A. (1993). *Counseling and development in a multicultural society*. Pacific Grove, CA: Brooks Cole.

Das, A. K. (1995). Rethinking multicultural counseling: Implications for counselor education. *Journal of Counseling and Development, 74*, 45–52.

Frame, M. (2003). *Integrating religion and spirituality into counseling*. Pacific Grove, CA: Thomson/Brooks Cole.

Giordano, J., McGoldrick, M., & Guarino Klages, J. (2005). Italian families. In M. McGoldrick, J. Giordano, & N. Garcia-Preto (Eds.), *Ethnicity and family therapy* (3rd ed., pp. 616–628). New York: Guilford Press.

Ivey, A. E., Ivey, M. B., & Simek-Morgan, K. (1993). *Counseling and psychotherapy: A multicultural perspective*. Boston: Allyn & Bacon.

Johnson, C. L. (1985). Socialization to family attachments. In C. L. Johnson (Ed.), *Growing up and growing old in Italian American families* (pp. 183–199). Rutgers, NJ: Rutgers University Press.

Killian, K. D., & Agathangelou, A. M. (2005). Greek families. In M. McGoldrick, J. Giordano, & N. Garcia-Preto (Eds.), *Ethnicity and family therapy* (3rd ed., pp. 573–585). New York: Guilford Press.

Langelier, R., & Langelier, P. (2005). French Canadian families. In M. McGoldrick, J. Giordano, & N. Garcia-Preto (Eds.), *Ethnicity and family therapy* (3rd ed., pp. 545–554). New York: Guilford Press.

McGill, D. W., & Pearce, J. K. (2005). American families with English ancestors from the colonial era: Anglo Americans. In M. McGoldrick, J. Giordano, & N. Garcia-Preto (Eds.), *Ethnicity and family therapy* (3rd ed., pp. 520–533). New York: Guilford Press.

McGoldrick, M. (2005). Irish families. In M. McGoldrick, J. Giordano, & N. Garcia-Preto (Eds.), *Ethnicity and family therapy* (3rd ed., pp. 595–615). New York: Guilford Press.

McIntosh, P. (1988). White privilege: Unpacking the invisible knapsack (Paper 189). White privilege and male privilege: A personal account of coming to see correspondences through work in women's studies. Excerpt from McIntosh, 1988, Working Paper #189, published in *Peace and Freedom* (July/August 1989); reprinted in *Independent School* (Winter 1990).

Mondykowski, S. M. (1982). Polish families. In M. McGoldrick, J. Pearce, & J. Giordano (Eds.), *Ethnicity and family therapy* (pp. 393–411). New York: Guilford Press.

Pope-Davis, D. B., & Ottavi, T. M. (1994). The relationship between racism and racial identity among White Americans: A replication and extension. *Journal of Counseling and Development, 72*(3), 293–297.

Rosen, E. J., & Weltman, S. F. (2005). Jewish families: An overview. In M. McGoldrick, J. Giordano, & N. Garcia-Preto (Eds.), *Ethnicity and family therapy* (3rd ed., pp. 667–679). New York: Guilford Press.

Sleek, S. (1995, September). Religion can play hidden role in relationships. *APA Monitor, 41*, 1. Retrieved May 5, 2008, from http://www.apa.org/monitor/peacea.html

Stave, B. M., Sutherland, J. F., with Salerno, A. (1994). *From the Old Country*. New York: Twayne.

U.S. Census Bureau. (2006). *American FactFinder: Population finder: Fact sheet*. Washington, DC: Author. Retrieved June 6, 2006, from http://factfinder.census.gov

Winawer, H., & Wetzel, N. A. (2005). German families. In M. McGoldrick, J. Giordano, & N. Garcia-Preto (Eds.), *Ethnicity and family therapy* (3rd ed., pp. 555–572). New York: Guilford Press.

25

Cultural Issues in Counseling Lesbians, Gays, and Bisexuals

Angela D. Ferguson

MUCH OF TRADITIONAL, Western psychological literature and theories has been rooted in Euro/American philosophy, values, and customs. Implicitly and explicitly, Western
psychology has attempted to explain human behavior and development through a Euro/American social structure that is based on
dominant–subordinate group dynamics (Fukuyama & Ferguson, 2000)
and has developed a normative standard of behavior against which
all other cultural groups are and continue to be compared. Consequently, the normative standard in Western counseling and psychology
is, and remains, based on a White, heterosexual, male, Christian, able-
bodied, middle-high socioeconomic status (SES), educated, and English-
speaking worldview. The counseling and psychology literature is
replete with comparative studies using a so-called normative group
with a minority group. The normative group is often composed of
dominant-member cultural beliefs, customs, and values consistent
with a majority-group worldview, thus leading researchers and clinicians to conclude that one group is more deficient, subordinate, or
defective than another group. This perspective, by definition, perpetuates a deficiency model of behavior and ignores the role and importance

of cultural contexts in the ways that people think, behave, and define their experiences and cultural identities.

The United States comprises multiple cultural groups that coexist, overlap, and sometimes contradict each other (Fukuyama & Ferguson, 2000). The emergence of multiculturalism within the field of counseling and psychology has brought attention to and emphasized the importance and salience of sociocultural factors that affect the psychological well-being and development of the individual. This area of psychology has also developed specific guidelines for mental health professionals to work effectively with people of color and lesbian, gay, and bisexual (LGB) individuals (American Psychological Association [APA], 2003). However, although guidelines have been developed to assist mental health professionals acquire appropriate and ethical skills to work more effectively with these populations, very little research is available to work effectively with LGB individuals who are members of ethnic/cultural groups (Greene, 1997; Miville & Ferguson, 2006).

This chapter will briefly highlight existing literature and research concerning identity development formation and the coming-out process for LGB individuals. It will then focus more specifically on cultural issues that exist within the gay, lesbian, and bisexual community and more closely focus on counseling considerations that will assist mental health professionals to work more effectively with LGB clients of color.

SEXUAL IDENTITY FORMATION OF LESBIAN, GAY, AND BISEXUAL INDIVIDUALS

EARLY COUNSELING AND psychological literature primarily focused on examining LGB individuals from a deficiency or *illness* model. This perspective did not allow mental health professionals to counsel LGB individuals from an affirmative perspective but rather from a negative, pathological perspective. Since the late 1970s, several sexual identity development models (primarily White, male) have emerged in the psychological literature (Cass, 1979; Coleman, 1982; Troiden, 1989). Sexual identity development models were constructed to better understand the coming-out process for LGB individuals. They were developmental or stage-based models that described a sequential process toward healthy identity development for individuals in marginalized and oppressed social groups. Specifically, LGB identity models provided a conceptual framework to describe the psychological and sociocultural identification as a lesbian, gay, or bisexual group member. Using these models to study LGB individuals, researchers and theorists could focus more on the process by which people became aware of their nonheterosexual identity, negotiated internalized and external forms of heterosexism and homophobia, and valued who they were as a sexual minority.

Typically, each model was constructed as a progressive sequential process of individual awareness of sexual identity that included gradual exploration, disclosure of this identity to others, and eventual acceptance of being lesbian or gay. These models introduced an entirely new way of understanding LGB individuals in that their focus was to better understand how individuals developed a positive LGB identity, particularly within a society that holds negative beliefs and stigmas about individuals who do not adhere to a heterosexual lifestyle. Using this perspective to explore the coming-out process, researchers and theorists were better able to explore LGB individuals from their worldview and from their definitions of what it meant to be LGB in a heterosexist society. As more attention was given to exploring LGB individuals from more confirmatory perspectives, some researchers were also aware that very little attention was given to LGB people of color (Chan, 1989; Morales, 1989) and began expanding LGB research to include the effects of cultural factors on identity development formation for LGB people of color.

CULTURAL IDENTITY AND GAY, LESBIAN, AND BISEXUAL PEOPLE

DURING THE PAST 30 years, there has been a significant increase in the number of studies that have explored the role of race and ethnicity on the psychosocial development of people of color; similarly, there has also been an increase in the exploration of gay and lesbian sexual orientations from affirmative perspectives (Greene, 1997). Exploration of race, gender, and sexual orientation prompted the development of various cultural identity models. They have provided a conceptual framework that describes the psychological process in which individuals move from nonacceptance to acceptance of a particular cultural identity (e.g., race, gender, sexual orientation). This line of empirical research has provided a significant contribution to the understanding of cultural factors relative to the development of the self (e.g., personal identity, self-esteem, self-concept), as well as to the understanding of the individual's psychological affiliation and connection to a particular cultural group and to the majority culture. However, a prominent criticism of identity development models (including sexual identity development models) is that they focus on a single sociocultural identity such as gender or race. Intersections of cultural social identities have largely been ignored in identity development research and scholarly discourses. Consequently, single-identity models overlook important dynamics that may exist for LGB people of color who often identify with more than one cultural group, such as the (1) salience of any one cultural group membership in relationship to other group memberships; (2) visibility or invisibility of identity(ies); (3) importance of cultural contexts in relationship to sexuality, family, and traditional cultural values; and (4) experiences of multiple forms of oppression (Fukuyama & Ferguson, 2000).

The integration of multiple group memberships can result in unique psychological stressors related to negotiating affiliations with multiple cultural group memberships. For many LGB people of color, experiences of social oppression, discrimination, and marginalization are connected with one or more of their cultural social identities. Any one of these oppressive forces can result in internalized negative feelings about oneself, as well as toward those included within that respective cultural group. Identification with a social group that is viewed negatively by society is filled with cognitive and affective challenges that must be negotiated and integrated with the self. Feelings of shame, inferiority, and reconciling distorted images and stereotypes of themselves as racial, gendered, or sexual minorities are just a few of the psychological challenges that many LGB individuals of color must manage as they develop a positive self-perception and acceptance of their social identity(ies). Consequently, integrating inner and outer perceptions of oneself becomes a complex process, potentially involving positive perceptions of oneself on a personal level, but also having to negotiate negative perceptions of oneself as a member of one or more stigmatized social groups. Commitment and resolution toward an integrated self becomes more complex in the face of negotiating and resolving multiple forms of oppression.

Culture and cultural contexts influence the way(s) in which we interpret information, behave, and interact with members in respective sociocultural groups, as well as with those outside of that sociocultural group. Sexual orientation is often viewed through the lens of one's cultural contexts, which dictate in part, the way in which individuals have learned to view their gender role, themselves as LGB, as well as the way in which group members view gender and sexual orientation. Cultural contexts also influence feelings of visibility or invisibility in cultural communities (Fukuyama & Ferguson, 2000). For example, LGB people of color may be coping with feelings of invisibility in their respective ethnic/racial communities as an LGB person, while also feeling very visible as an ethnic/racial person in the mainstream LGB and heterosexual communities. Developing a congruent sense of self and identity is challenging with these conflicting feelings of visibility/invisibility.

The process of coming out is a complex process, particularly in societal systems that normalize and perpetuate heterosexuality as natural.

The experience of feeling different from what is accepted by society can produce intense feelings of despair, lowered self-esteem, depression, anger, and feelings of disconnection and separation from family, friends, and community. For these, and a number of other possible reasons, LGB people of color may seek counseling services. Some may enter therapy in hopes of (1) resolving coming-out issues; (2) finding ways to cope with negotiating multiple nondominant social and cultural identities; (3) discussing family issues related to being an LGB person; (4) developing a better understanding of forming romantic relationship issues; (5) coping with religious conflicts; (6) dealing with personal intrapsychic issues; or a combination of one or more of these issues. Mental health professionals need to be prepared to discuss, assess, and develop effective treatment interventions for the LGB person of color. The following section will identify common therapeutic issues and considerations that mental health professionals should be aware of in order to provide therapeutically effective ways of working with LGB people of color.

THERAPEUTIC CONSIDERATIONS

Lesbian, gay, and bisexual people of color share some commonalities with White LGB individuals with respect to the coming-out process and involvement in the LGB community. However, they also experience unique differences from their White counterparts. It is important to emphasize that the discussion regarding therapeutic considerations highlights general themes that may surface for LGB people of color. Caution should be taken to avoid overgeneralizations about specific cultural/ethnic social groups and to be aware that there is great variation among LGB people of color in terms of their coming-out process, experiences of oppression and discrimination, affiliation with their respective cultural group(s), and salience of any one of their cultural social identities.

LGB people of color are almost always coping with one or more forms of prejudice and discrimination from several places in their lives. For some LGB people of color, they may only be aware of one or two forms of oppression in their lives (e.g., racism, heterosexism); however, each form of oppression may have deleterious effects on all aspects of an individual's identity development (e.g., race, gender, sexual orientation). Inasmuch as LGB people of color experience similar developmental coming-out milestones as their White LGB counterparts, cultural/racial factors often influence the coming-out process of LGB people of color in different ways than many of the traditional sexual identity models have described. For example, many LGB people of color experience discrimination and marginalization not only from respective majority racial group cultures but sometimes also from members of their own ethnic/racial social group. This experience of concurrent inclusion and exclusion may make it difficult for LGB people of color to fully embrace or feel full membership in any one of their nondominant cultural social groups. An example of this psychosocial stressor may occur when a gay Latino feels validated and supported in the Latino community relative to his gender and ethnicity, but this may only occur if he hides his sexual orientation due to heterosexism. When he is immersed in the mainstream LGB community, he may feel supported and validated relative to his sexual orientation, but not necessarily validated as a person of color due to experiences of racism. He may also feel validated and supported in both communities relative to his gender.

Social supports relative to racial/ethnic identity may not be the same social supports relative to the LGB community. LGB people of color may often find themselves having different social supports depending on the particular social group they are immersed in at any given time. Professional counselors who are aware of these kinds of issues can effectively address psychological issues related to internalized homophobia; feelings of disconnection and separation from family, friends, and other community supports; and possible suicidal ideation.

Many of the traditional identity developmental models discuss the importance of recognizing, acknowledging, and disclosing sexual identity to self and eventually to others (e.g., family, friends, community members) as a sign of health in the process of developing a positive sexual identity. However, many LGB people of color may diminish or hide their sexual orientation from their racial/ethnic sociocultural group for fear that disclosing their sexual identity may mean immediate separation and isolation from family, as well as separation from their racial/ethnic community that may have served as a protective barrier against racism. The possibility of separating oneself from the protective barrier against racism may cause LGB people of color to be selective in when and with whom they reveal their sexual orientation. Mental health professionals need to carefully discuss the decision of when to come out and to whom to come out to with their clients (Fukuyama & Ferguson, 2000).

Spirituality is an area that often goes unaddressed when working with LGB people. For many people in the heterosexual mainstream society, LGB people are often viewed as immoral and thus without religious beliefs. For many LGB people, spirituality and religion are salient dimensions of their life. Moreover, for many communities of color, spirituality and faith has been a core aspect and visible demonstration of their racial/ethnic culture for them, their families, and within their respective communities. The majority of the world's religious leaders have often imposed homonegative tenets and traditions as part of traditional religious practices, and many LGB people have internalized a deep sense of isolation, exclusion, and religious absence in their lives. Counseling professionals may find that LGB people of color often struggle to reconcile their feelings of homonegative beliefs and their desire to practice their form of religion or spirituality. Mental health professionals must explore their comfort level in discussing issues of religion and spirituality with LGB people and make sure not to unintentionally avoid or diminish this aspect of their clients' lives altogether or denounce their clients' sexual orientation due to the professionals' religious beliefs concerning LGB individuals.

COUNSELING IMPLICATIONS

WHEN WORKING WITH LGB people of color, counselors should consider the following recommendations: (1) counselors should familiarize themselves with the ways in which prejudice, discrimination, and multiple forms of oppression may emerge in society and acknowledge their occurrence and exploration of their resulting impact on the lives of LGB people of color; (2) counselors are additionally encouraged to examine their own views regarding heterosexuality, racism, and sexism in order to understand and deal with any unconscious biases toward working with LGB people of color; (3) although traditional models of identity development (e.g., race, gender, sexual orientation) may be helpful as a beginning step in becoming familiar with the developmental processes of forming a positive identity, counselors need to consider the ways in which negative LGB and negative racial/ethnic experiences may also intersect and have become internalized for clients; and (4) counselors should inquire about all dimensions of their client's identities, rather than remain focused on only one dimension. Social identities converge and intersect in uneven ways and the LGB person of color may feel positively about one dimension of his or her identity (gender), but negatively about another dimension (sexual orientation). The confluence of these factors may significantly affect the development, expression, salience, and acceptance of one or more identities (Fukuyama & Ferguson, 2000).

Lesbian, gay, and bisexual people of color represent a collective group and often share common experiences relative to coming-out issues. However, they also vary in terms of race/ethnicity; experiences of oppression, marginalization, and discrimination related to one or more of their social identities; and ways that they have internalized multiple cultural values, beliefs, behaviors, and expectations. For example, mental health professionals need to be aware that a client's problem, such as depression or discord in a relationship, can be the result of internalized messages of inferiority due to race, gender, and/or sexual orientation or to discordant messages of positive racial identification and negative sexual identification. These messages may cause individuals to form cognitive distortions about themselves and group members in a respective social group. Counseling interventions and therapeutic strategies need to address the intersection of psychological problems in the context of sociocultural histories, experiences of oppression, and the worldview of clients. In this way, they are consistent with multiple fluid/dynamic cultural contexts that can provide individuals with sensitivity and empathy that is congruent with their cognitive, emotional, and psychological experience.

REFERENCES

American Psychological Association. (2003). Guidelines on multicultural education, training, research, practice, and organizational change for psychologists. *American Psychologist, 58*(5), 377–402.

Cass, V. C. (1979). Homosexual identity formation: A theoretical model. *Journal of Homosexuality, 4,* 219–236.

Chan, C. S. (1989). Issues of identity development among Asian-American lesbians and gay men. *Journal of Counseling and Development, 68,* 16–20.

Coleman, E. (1982). Developmental stages of the coming out process. *Journal of Homosexuality, 7,* 31–43.

Fukuyama, M. A., & Ferguson, A. D. (2000). Lesbian, gay, and bisexual people of color: Understanding cultural complexity and multiple oppressions. In R. M. Perez, K. A. DeBord, & K. J. Bieschke (Eds.), *Handbook of counseling and psychotherapy with lesbian, gay, and bisexual clients* (pp. 81–105). Washington, DC: American Psychological Association.

Greene, B. (1997). Ethnic minority lesbians and gay men: Mental health and treatment issues. In B. Greene (Ed.), *Ethnic and cultural diversity among lesbians and gay men* (pp. 216–239). Newbury Park, CA: Sage Publications.

Miville, M. L., & Ferguson, A. D. (2006). Intersections of sexism and heterosexism with racism: Therapeutic implications. In M. G. Constantine & D. W. Sue, (Eds.), *Racism as a barrier to cultural competence in mental health and educational settings.* New York: Wiley.

Morales, E. S. (1989). Ethnic minority families and minority gays and lesbians. *Journal of Homosexuality, 17,* 217–239.

Troiden, R. (1989). The formation of homosexual identities. *Journal of Homosexuality, 17*(1/2), 43–73.

26

Rural Mental Health Counseling

ADINA J. SMITH, JILL THORNGREN, AND JOHN C. CHRISTOPHER

R URAL AREAS ARE often characterized by low population density, limited and fragile economic bases, high level of poverty, and limited access to metropolitan areas (Sawyer, Gale, & Lambert, 2006). Residents of rural communities experience mental health problems (e.g., depression, suicide, substance abuse) at a rate greater than or equal to urban communities (Sawyer et al., 2006). However, these individuals receive less treatment of any type for mental health conditions and less specialized mental health services (Hauenstein et al., 2006). A number of factors contribute to a lack of services and a lack of treatment in rural communities. This chapter will discuss the challenges counselors typically encounter when working in rural communities as well as suggestions for maximizing the opportunities that rural practice provides.

RURAL COMMUNITIES AND MENTAL HEALTH

B ECAUSE OF STRESSORS characteristic of rural areas such as poverty, single parenting, less formal education, unemployment, lack of health insurance, stigma surrounding mental illness, and inaccessible or inconsistent community resources, few opportunities may exist for receiving mental health care (e.g., Merwin, Snyder, & Katz, 2006; Wagenfeld, 2003). Moreover, those living in rural areas often must travel long distances for services. Even when rural individuals are able to access mental health services, they may not be able to pay for existing services, may not get the help they require, or may receive services at a primary health care facility, such as a rural public hospital or clinic. Mental health care by public facilities has been found to be inconsistent and unreliable (Blank, Fox, Hargrove, & Turner, 1995). Because those with severe mental illness are less likely to receive services necessary to maintain healthy functioning, they may be more likely to end up in crisis situations that could have been avoided with consistent care (Harowski, Turner, LeVine, Schank, & Leichter, 2006). This places undue stress on hospitals and law enforcement agencies who then have a high level of involvement in mental health issues (i.e., dealing with suicidal persons, psychosis, etc.; Smith, 2004).

Stigma regarding mental illness is particularly pronounced in rural areas (e.g., Esters, Cooker, & Ittenbach, 1998; Gamm, Stone, & Pittman, 2003) and may be related to lack of education, insufficient resources, isolation, and the value of autonomy (e.g., Kelleher, Taylor, & Rickert, 1992; Thorngren, 2003). Sirey and colleagues (2001) found that stigma not only dissuades people from help seeking for mental health but may also impede progress once individuals are engaged in the treatment process. Roberts, Battaglia, and Epstein (1999) note the "fishbowl" effect of rural communities in that others easily observe comings and goings at the mental health clinic and may even hear comments by staff members about patients. Even if clients or potential clients do not hold their own stigmatized views regarding mental health issues, the lack of anonymity, and the possibility of being the subject of rumors, may thwart care seeking.

Several other factors exist in rural communities that likely impede care seeking. One is the lack of awareness or recognition that there is a mental health issue. According to the University of Maryland Department of Family Science (2007), "Often rural residents are unaware of their mental health status, availability of services, or their eligibility for services" (p. 1). Another factor is that in farming or ranching rural communities, where being able to work is a priority, there exists a strong sense of individualism, a pull-yourself-up-by-your-bootstraps mentality where people are self-sufficient, self-reliant, and solve their own problems (Human & Wasem, 1991). One example of the importance of work in relation to mental illness was depicted in a study by Thorngren (2003), who found focus group participants widely believed that lack of work contributes to depression, and therefore, engaging in work alleviates depression. These findings also point to differences that can exist in the folk psychology of rural residents and the professional and personal outlook of mental health providers. Rural residents and counselors may have different assumptions about the nature of illness and healing, and these can constitute genuine cultural differences that need to be sensitively broached (Christopher & Smith, 2006). Thus, rural individuals who could benefit from mental health treatment may not seek assistance due to not recognizing the problem, cultural values such as individualism and stoicism, or a folk psychology that provides alternate views of etiology and treatment.

MENTAL HEALTH COUNSELING IN RURAL COMMUNITIES

NUMEROUS UNIQUE PROFESSIONAL challenges exist for counselors practicing in rural settings. Obtaining effective training and skills, unique ethical considerations (e.g., boundaries, dual relationships), understanding of rural culture, being integrated in the community, maintaining continuing education, relocation and professional isolation, limited resources, lack of integration of services and consultation, and government regulations and restrictions are several of the obstacles experienced by rural mental health professionals (Copans, 2006; Sawyer et al., 2006). The lack of funding for state and federal mental health initiatives since the 1990s has reached a crisis that significantly exacerbates the already existing challenges of providing outpatient mental health services for rural Americans (Wagenfeld, Murray, Mohatt, & DeBruyn, 1994).

While health care providers in public hospitals and clinics, such as physicians and nurses, are often the most accessible regarding the provision of mental health care, they rarely specialize in mental health care and receive little training in the way of diagnosis and intervention of mental illness (DeLeon, 2000). Also, although mental health professionals are frequently well trained in general practice, few graduate programs specialize in rural mental health provision (Murray & Keller, 1991; Sawyer et al., 2006). Therefore, mental health professionals who move to a rural community may not have been trained to understand rural culture and may experience their own biases toward individuals embracing rural ways. They also may not expect the degree of personal and professional isolation that can come with a rural practice. Rural mental health providers have fewer training opportunities, fewer colleagues with whom to discuss professional issues, and a greater variety of demands on their time than mental health providers in urban settings (DeLeon, 2000). According to Jameson and Blank (2007), mental health professionals who plan to serve rural populations need to receive training in graduate school in order to provide appropriate services.

For those already practicing, continuing education and consultation opportunities are critical for mental health counselors in rural communities but, ironically, are often unavailable locally.

In terms of mental health service delivery, Human and Wasem (1991) suggest that availability, accessibility, and acceptability are important aspects to consider in rural communities. *Availability* is determined by whether mental health services exist, especially in rural areas. *Accessibility* refers to whether individuals can actually receive existing services, including whether they can get to and purchase the services (e.g., to travel long distance without the existence of public transportation). For many, not having health insurance is a barrier to health care, including mental health care. Rural residents, especially women and low-income part-time workers, have been found to have a lack of health insurance, thus decreasing their access to mental health services (University of Maryland Department of Family Science, 2007). Another contributor to inaccessibility is a lack of mental health outreach to isolated communities (Human & Wasem, 1991). *Acceptability* is characterized by services offered in a way that is consistent with the value system of the community. Barriers to acceptability include self-reliance in managing problems, beliefs about the etiology and appropriate treatment of a mental disorder that are at odds with prevailing academic and professional opinion, and stigma and lack of education about mental illness and the mental health profession.

ACCESSIBILITY

INTEGRATION

As noted previously, access to mental health services often is impeded in rural areas due to lack of providers and lengthy distances between clients and providers. This issue is exacerbated by lack of integration between mental health care providers and primary care givers (Jameson & Blank, 2007). Several authors emphasize the importance of interdisciplinary collaboration and cooperation by mental health practitioners (e.g., Beeson, 1998; Wagenfeld et al., 1994). Such collaboration is suggested for several reasons. Individuals frequently suffer from multiple problems aside from the presenting mental health issue, for example, physical health and/or substance abuse. Health care providers, however, are not always comfortable considering diagnoses outside their particular realm of specialty or may be susceptible to making diagnostic errors. For instance, Rost, Smith, Matthews, and Guise (1994) found that nearly half of physicians in primary care settings misdiagnose depression. Uncertainty about the diagnosis, potential problems with reimbursement, and fear of client's future insurability were given as reasons for misdiagnosing (Jameson & Blank, 2007). Collaboration in rural areas also frequently includes non–health care professionals such as clergy, teachers, judges, police officers, and paraprofessionals (Heyman & VandenBos, 1989; Reed 1992), and appropriate care often requires the combined efforts of several professionals, each with expertise in specific areas.

It is suggested that care providers engage in continuing education that broadens their scope of understanding regarding client issues outside their area of expertise. For example, counselors and psychologists could provide information and training regarding depression and other mental health issues. Medical professionals could provide information regarding the physiological effects of eating disorders, and so on. Collaborative continuing education could alleviate much of the fear and uncertainty around respective diagnoses and increase the likelihood of consultation. While it is not recommended that one diagnose or treat outside of one's area of practice, it is highly encouraged that health care and non–health care professionals become aware of what each has to offer clients. A mental health provider can treat anxiety through talk and relaxation therapy and have little benefit if the client is suffering from an undiagnosed thyroid disorder!

TELEHEALTH

THE USE OF communications technology in the educational, clinical, training, administrative, and technological aspects of health care is known as *telehealth* and may have an impact on the delivery of services to clients in rural areas (Jameson & Blank, 2007). Telehealth can vary from e-mail communication to videoconferencing to more advanced computerized therapy programs (Jameson & Blank, 2007). While there are structural issues to consider, such as the availability of advanced technology and high speed Internet in rural areas, when available, this method may provide outreach services to those who would otherwise receive none. The relative anonymity of telehealth is one solution to avoiding the stigma that often surrounds seeking mental health services in rural communities.

Telehealth methods may also be utilized to lessen the isolation of practitioners in rural communities. Supervision can occur through videoconferencing as can a wide variety of continuing education trainings.

ACCEPTABILITY

WHILE ACCESSIBILITY CREATES challenges for rural mental health clients, some are still reluctant to accept services even when available. The field of mental health is often permeated with a certain negative connotation in rural areas. Stereotypical perceptions of mental health patients as *crazy* still abound. Esters and colleagues (1998) argued that the effects of this stigma are magnified among rural Americans. They hypothesize that this may be due not only to the stigma attached to mental health services but to the stigma attached to help-seeking in general.

Recognizing the difficulties inherent in making mental health more acceptable in rural areas, Hovestadt, Fenell, and Canfield (2002) outlined characteristics of effective providers of marital and family therapy (MFT) in rural settings. The six characteristics, listed below, are easily applied to other mental health professionals.

1. *Effective skills [in MFT].* Encompassed in this characteristic are the components of clinical flexibility and the ability to use a wide variety of approaches.

2. *Rural community understanding, appreciation, and participation.* Understanding the unique culture of rural people is crucial to fitting into the community and being viewed without suspicion. As described by participants in Thorngren's (2003) study, some of the characteristics of rural persons include having a strong connection to the land, valuing interpersonal connections, and developing good problem-solving abilities. These characteristics can easily be utilized in therapy once they are understood and appreciated by therapists.

3. *Personal characteristics and flexibility.* This category includes items such as being willing to integrate holistic interventions, multidisciplinary service delivery systems, involving family networks, offering self-help groups, offering home-based therapy, and ability to work with limited resources.

4. *Generalist with a nonspecialization foundation.* Encompassed here are the abilities of working with a broad range of presenting issues; utilizing various formats, that is, individual and group work and various techniques; not rigidly adhering to any single theory; and even being willing to engage in public speaking, news article writing, advocacy, and handling legal issues. As noted by Smith (2004): "Although collaboration is essential, in rural settings where only one or a few therapists exist, working with clients or issues beyond their level of expertise may be more the norm than the exception. Therefore, therapists are faced with utilizing a generalist approach rather than the specialization in which they were trained" (p. 4).

5. *Education, training, and experience [in MFT].* While this may appear irrelevant to those credentialed outside of MFT, Hovestadt and colleagues. indicated that what was necessary included understanding and assessing the environment from a systems

perspective, crisis intervention skills, the desire and ability to reduce stigma associated with mental health treatment, and active participation in formal and informal continuing education and supervision.

6. *Utilizing formal and informal community resources.* This includes working well with a range of community stakeholders (e.g., schools, courts, churches, law enforcement, etc.), willingness to utilize community networks, ability to coordinate services with various agencies, ability to work with professionals and nonprofessionals alike, and willingness to include extended family in treatment services.

The work of Hovestadt and colleagues (2002) and others (e.g., Jameson & Blank, 2007; Nickel, 2004; Smith, 2004; Thorngren, 2003; Weigel & Baker, 2002) indicates the need for flexibility, creativity, and cultural sensitivity when working in rural areas. None of these skills are foreign to mental health practitioners, regardless of setting. What may be unique, however, are ethical issues created by virtue of the nature of rural practice.

ETHICS AND RURAL MENTAL HEALTH CARE

DUAL RELATIONSHIPS

ONE OF THE most salient ethical issues in providing therapy in rural areas is that of dual relationships. As described by Nickel (2004), there is an ongoing debate among mental health professionals regarding the definition of dual relationships as well as the potential harm and benefits of such relationships. While the harmful nature of sexual relationships is well documented (Barnett & Yutrzenka, 2002; Nickel, 2004; Reamer, 2003), there still remains question about the feasibility of avoiding all nonsexual relationships with clients. This is particularly noteworthy when working with rural clients. As pointed out by Nickel, refusing to treat anyone with whom a therapist has had a nonclinical relationship may eliminate the entire client base in rural areas. It is cautioned that therapists evaluate engaging in dual relationships with rural clients on a case-by-case basis.

The updated American Counseling Association (ACA) *Code of Ethics* (2005) states the following:

A.5.d. Potentially Beneficial Interactions

When a counselor–client nonprofessional interaction with a client or former client may be potentially beneficial to the client or former client, the counselor must document in case records, prior to the interaction (when feasible), the rationale for such an interaction, the potential benefit, and anticipated consequences for the client or former client and other individuals significantly involved with the client or former client. Such interactions should be initiated with appropriate client consent.

Thus, counselors are not prohibited from engaging in nonsexual dual relationships with clients but are cautioned to ensure the benefits to the client before doing so. It is important to discuss with the clients the potential ramifications of engaging in dual relationships such as clients and counselors having public encounters, role conflicts, and limits to confidentiality.

BARTERING

PRACTITIONERS IN RURAL settings may also find that clients are more likely to want to barter for services than clients in more urban settings. The ACA (2005) *Code of Ethics* section A.10.d states that counselors may barter if the nature of the exchange is not exploitative and has potential benefit for the client. Counselors are urged to make bartering a contractual agreement with terms clearly outlined in a written document.

CONCLUSION

DESPITE THE INHERENT challenges of working with rural populations, the work can be exciting and rewarding. As with any clinical work, consultation with peers and colleagues, even via distance, is crucial to prevent therapist stagnation and burnout. In addition, therapists are encouraged to tap into the strengths of their rural clients and allow themselves to be taught about the culture in which these people survive and thrive. Values such as community involvement, connections between people and people and land, and problem solving, which are typically characteristic of rural populations, are integral to mental well-being.

REFERENCES

American Counseling Association. (2005). *Code of ethics and standards of practice*. Retrieved February 8, 2008, from http://www.counseling.org/Resources/CodeOfEthics/TP/Home/CT2.aspx

Barnett, J. E., & Yutrzenka, B. A. (2002). Nonsexual dual relationships in professional practice with special applications to rural and military communities. In A. A. Lazarus & O. Zur (Eds.), *Dual relationships and psychotherapy* (pp. 273–285). New York: Springer Publishing.

Beeson, P. G. (1998). Apples and oranges: The successful rural mental health practitioner at the turn of the century. *Rural Community Mental Health, 24,* 38–40.

Blank, M. B., Fox, J. C., Hargrove, D. S., & Turner, J. T. (1995). Critical issues in reforming rural mental health service delivery. *Community Mental Health Journal, 31,* 511–524.

Christopher, J. C., & Smith, A. J. (2006). A hermeneutic approach to culture and psychotherapy. In R. Moody & S. Palmer (Eds.), *Race, culture and psychotherapy: Critical perspective in multicultural practice* (pp. 265–280). New York: Brunner/Routledge.

Copans, S. (2006). Practical aspects of rural mental health care. In T. A. Petti & C. Salguero (Eds.), *Community child and adolescent psychiatry: A manual of clinical practice and consultation* (pp. 43–54). New Haven, CT: American Psychiatric Publishing.

DeLeon, P. H. (2000). Rural America: Our diamond in the rough. *Monitor on Psychology, 31*(7), 5.

Esters, I. G., Cooker, P. G., & Ittenbach, R. F. (1998). Effects of a unit of instruction in mental health on rural adolescents' conceptions of mental illness and attitudes about seeking help. *Adolescence, 33,* 469–477.

Gamm, L., Stone, S., & Pittman, S. (2003). Mental health and mental disorders: A rural challenge. In L. Gamm, L. Hutchison, B. Dabney, & A. Dorsey (Eds.), *Rural healthy people 2010: A companion document to healthy people 2010* (pp. 165–170). College Station, TX: The Texas A&M University System Health Science Center, School of Rural Public Health, Southwest Rural Health Research Center.

Harowski, K., Turner, A. L., LeVine, E., Schank, J. A., & Leichter, J. (2006). From our community to yours: Rural best perspectives on psychology practice, training, and advocacy. *Professional Psychology: Research and Practice, 37*(2), 158–164.

Hauenstein, E., Petterson, S., Rovnyak, V., Merwin, E., Heise, B., & Wagner, D. (2006). Rurality and mental health treatment. *Administration and Policy in Mental Health and Mental Health Service Research 34,* 255–267.

Heyman, S. R., & VandenBos, G. R. (1989). Developing local resources to enrich the practice of rural community psychology. *Hospital and Community Psychiatry, 40,* 21–23.

Hovestadt, A. J., Fenell, D. L., & Canfield, B. S. (2002). Characteristics of effective providers of marital and family therapy in rural mental health settings. *Journal of Marital and Family Therapy, 28,* 225–231.

Human, J., & Wasem, C. (1991). Rural mental health in America. *American Psychologist, 46,* 232–239.

Jameson, J. P., & Blank, M. B. (2007). The role of clinical psychology in rural mental health services: Defining problems and developing solutions. *Clinical Psychology: Science and Practice, 14*(3), 283–298.

Kelleher, K. J., Taylor, J. L., & Rickert, V. I. (1992). Mental health services for rural children and adolescents. *Clinical Psychology Review, 12*(8), 841–852.

Merwin, E., Snyder, A., & Katz, E. (2006). Differential access to quality rural healthcare: Professional and policy challenges. *Family and Community Health, 29*(3), 186–194.

Murray, J. D., & Keller, P. A. (1991). Psychology and rural America: Current status and future directions. *American Psychologist, 46,* 220–231.

Nickel, M. B. (2004). Professional boundaries: The dilemma of dual and multiple relationships in rural clinical practice. *Counseling and Clinical Psychology Journal, 1,* 17–22.

Reamer, F. G. (2003, January). Boundary issues in social work: Managing dual relationships. *Social Work, 48*(1), 121–134.

Reed, D. A. (1992). Adaptation: The key to community psychiatric practice in the rural setting. *Community Mental Health Journal, 28,* 141–150.

Roberts, L. W., Battaglia, J., & Epstein, R. S. (1999). Frontier ethics: Mental health care needs and ethical dilemmas in rural communities. *Psychiatric Services, 50*(4), 497–503.

Rost, K., Smith, R., Matthews, D. B., & Guise, B. (1994). The deliberate misdiagnosis of major depression in primary care. *Archives of Family Medicine, 3,* 333–337.

Sawyer, D., Gale, J., & Lambert, D. (2006). *Rural and frontier mental and behavioral health care: Barriers, effective policy strategies, best practices.* Waite Park, MN: National Association of Rural Mental Health.

Sirey, J. A., Bruce, M. L., Alexopoulos, G. S., Perlick, D. A., Raue, P., Friedman, S. J., et al. (2001). Perceived stigma as a predictor of treatment discontinuation in young and older outpatients with depression. *American Journal of Psychiatry, 158,* 479–481.

Smith, A. J. (2004). Rural mental health counseling: One example of practicing what the research preaches [Electronic version]. *Journal of Rural Community Psychology, E7*(1–9). Retrieved February 25, 2005, from http://www.marshall.edu/JRCP/

Thorngren, J. M. (2003). Rural mental health: A qualitative inquiry. *Journal of Rural Community Psychology, E6*(2). Retrieved July 17, 2008, from http://www.marshall.edu/jrcp/JRCP_E6_2_Throngren.htm

University of Maryland Department of Family Science. (2007). *Barriers to mental health access for rural residents.* College Park: University of Maryland.

Wagenfeld, M. O. (2003). A snapshot of rural and frontier America. In B. H. Stamm (Ed.), *Rural behavioral health care* (pp. 33–40). Washington, DC: American Psychological Association.

Wagenfeld, M. O., Murray, J. D., Mohatt, D. F., & DeBruyn, J. C. (Eds.). (1994). *Mental health and rural America 1980–1993: An overview and annotated bibliography (rev. ed.)* (NIMH Publication No. 94–3500). Rockville, MD: Office of Rural Health Policy, Health Resources and Services Administration: Office of Rural Mental Health Research, NPVM, NIH: U.S. Department of Health and Human Services, Public Health Service.

Weigel, D. J., & Baker, B. G. (2002). Unique issues in rural couple and family counseling. *The Family Journal: Counseling and Therapy for Couples and Families, 10*(1), 61–69.

27

Counseling Persons Who Are Deaf or Hard of Hearing

SHAWN P. SALADIN

HUMAN HISTORY SUGGESTS that humans have coped with hearing loss and Deafness for centuries, because it was addressed in some of the world's most ancient texts, including the writings of Plato and Aristotle, the Torah, and the Talmud. Hearing loss is now the most common sensory disability, with one in every 1,000 people in the United States born with a severe hearing loss or Deafness (Luxon et al., 2003; Nance, 2003; Robertson & Morton, 1999). Hearing loss may occur at any life stage. A person who is Deaf or hard of hearing from birth or in the first days of life has a *congenital* hearing loss. *Prelingual* hearing loss occurs prior to the development of meaningful speech. If hearing problems develop later in childhood or adulthood, an individual has an *acquired postlingual* hearing loss. Postlingual hearing loss may be *prevocational,* or occurring when an individual is school-aged (Tye-Murray, 2004), while the term *late deafened* describes people whose hearing loss occurs later in adulthood (Rehabilitation Services Administration, 1995).

CAUSES OF HEARING LOSS

TWO BROAD CATEGORIES of hearing loss exist: genetic and acquired. Genetic hearing loss may be inherited or occur spontaneously (Nance, 2003; Robertson & Morton, 1999). Approximately

75% of individuals with a severe or profound congenital hearing loss have an inherited genetic pattern occurring when both parents carry a recessive gene for hearing loss. About one-fourth of genetic hearing loss occurs when one parent carries a dominant gene for hearing loss. Only 1% of genetic hearing loss is due to isolated mutations in DNA or an X-linked trait (Smith & Taggart, 2004). Some genetic differences such as Pendred, Branchio-Oto-Renal (BOR), and Usher syndromes can result in profound sensorineural Deafness and differences in kidney, eye, and thyroid structure and function (Nance, 2003).

An acquired hearing loss develops later in childhood (usually after 5 years of age) or in adulthood. Acquired hearing loss is also considered postlingual, because it has occurred after the development of speech. At times, postlingual hearing losses are also further labeled prevocational to indicate a hearing loss occurring when a person is school-aged (Tye-Murray, 2004). Chronic ear infections, penetrating ear injuries, and aging are common causes of acquired hearing loss and Deafness. Occupational, recreational, and accidental noise exposure can also seriously injure the inner ear, resulting in noise-induced hearing loss (Nelson, Nelson, Concha-Barrientos, & Fingerhut, 2005). Other causes may include head injuries, inner ear disorders, or exposure to toxins (Robertson & Morton, 1999).

TYPES OF HEARING LOSS

REGARDLESS OF ETIOLOGY, hearing loss may be described as *sensorineural, conductive,* or *mixed.* Hearing loss stemming from conditions of the inner ear or auditory nerve is considered sensorineural in type. Usually, sensorineural hearing loss is due to damage to the pathway from the inner ear hair cells to the auditory nerve and the brain (Katz & White, 2001; Schow & Nerbonne, 1996). Sensorineural loss typically involves a reduction in perception of higher frequency sounds combined with low speech discrimination scores (Katz & White, 2001). Conductive hearing loss usually originates in the outer and middle ear. Most conductive hearing problems result from an inability of sound waves to conduct from the outer ear to ear drum and inner ear structures (Schow & Nerbonne, 1996). Excessive ear wax, a punctured eardrum, an ear infection, or irregularities in outer or middle ear shape are commonly related to conductive loss (Katz & White, 2001; Tye-Murray, 2004). Mixed hearing loss results from a combination of both conductive and sensorineural causes (Roeser, Buckley, & Stickney, 2000).

CULTURAL DEAFNESS

PEOPLE WHO ARE Deaf often report negative experiences with the hearing world (Demorest & Erdman, 1989; Lane, 1992; Lane, Hoffmeister, & Bahan, 1996; Schein, 1989), and the general public has historically considered Deafness from a medical or pathological context (Filer & Filer, 2000). However, over the last two decades the Deaf Pride movement has advanced a sociocultural definition of Deafness that represents a life and worldview that is manifested by the beliefs, values, and traditions unique to Deaf people and expressed through the use of American Sign Language (ASL; Lane, 1992; Lane, Hoffmeister, & Bahan, 1996).

Deaf culture does not identify Deafness as a disability but as the basis of a distinct cultural group (Padden & Humphries, 2005). The distinction between medical hearing loss and membership in the cultural group is made by capitalizing the term *Deaf* when referencing individuals in the Deaf cultural community (Lane et al., 1996; Padden & Humphries, 2005). A person may self-identify as culturally Deaf, although he or she may have a mild or moderate hearing loss. The converse may also be true; a person may have an audiologically profound hearing loss but identify with Deaf culture (Padden & Humphries, 2005).

Cultural transmission is primarily a function of residential schools for the Deaf, and for this reason, the Deaf community strongly resists public school mainstreaming or inclusion (Lane et al., 1996; Porter, 1999). In fact, residential schooling and the use of ASL are often considered the most important components of the culture (Filer & Filer, 2000; Porter, 1999; Reagan, 2002). As in other cultures, Deaf people rely on other individuals within their culture for behavioral norms and patterns, standards, and information, and interdependence is highly valued (Porter, 1999). Deaf culture includes—among many others facets—a historical understanding of the Deaf community; common literary, theatrical, and artistic traditions; and Deaf social groups. Individuals who are part of the Deaf world also tend to intermarry and often share a highly tolerant and cooperative parenting style.

MYTHS AND MISCONCEPTIONS
ABOUT DEAF PEOPLE

A NUMBER OF MISCONCEPTIONS about people who are Deaf exist, and these misconceptions may have unintended negative consequences for service planning and delivery. For instance, the general public often believes Deaf people can't speak, that all Deaf people are good speech readers (erroneously called lip reading), and that Deaf people have other special or heightened senses (Goldberg & Richburg, 2004; Williams & Finnegan, 2003). People also mistakenly believe sign language is universal, but as with spoken languages, signed languages vary greatly from country to country and region to region (Lane et al., 1996). Myths also persist related to Deaf parents and Deaf children—many people believe Deaf parents always give birth to Deaf children (Williams & Finnegan, 2003), a belief that has led to tragic and inhumane eugenics practices, forced sterilization, and marriage prohibitions. In truth, about 90% of parents of Deaf or hard of hearing children are hearing and 79% of Deaf children do not have siblings who are Deaf (Gallaudet Research Institute, 2003).

WORKING WITH PEOPLE WHO ARE DEAF

RESEARCH SUGGESTS THAT the severity of a person's hearing loss does not correlate strongly with adaptation to the hearing loss, and individual needs and preferences are highly variable (Schein, Bottum, Lawler, Madory, & Wantuch, 2001). First, and foremost, establishing and maintaining good attention and eye contact is necessary. It is acceptable to wave, thump a nearby surface, or gently tap a person who is Deaf or hard of hearing in order to gain the person's attention, and people with hearing loss may use these approaches to gain the attention of a hearing person as well (Foster, 1998). It is also important to articulate clearly, although overarticulation distorts the shape of the speaker's mouth and hinders speech reading. Speaking too quickly or too slowly may hinder speech reading and distort conversational cues, and it is important to face a person who is Deaf or hard of hearing during communication while avoiding obstructing the mouth (Arlinger, 2003; Luey, Glass, & Elliott, 1995).

While modifications to the environment vary, some general guidelines exist for creating environments that promote clear communication. Although it may seem counterintuitive, noisy situations are often difficult for people who are Deaf or hard of hearing (Scherich, 1996). Quiet surroundings interfere less with usable hearing. Extraneous noise may also be effectively managed through sound-absorbing carpeting or upholstery. Well-lit and glare-free settings are also very beneficial, as are surroundings that are free of objects or barriers to visual sight lines, allowing for clearly visible manual communication or speech reading (Geyer & Schroedel, 1999). Telephones, doorbells, and fire alarms may be modified through linkage to visual alerting devices such as flashing lights. These devices help alert Deaf or hard of hearing individuals to the presence of others or to situations that need immediate attention (Geyer & Schroedel, 1999). Tactile alerting devices, such as vibrating pagers, may also be helpful.

WORKING WITH INTERPRETERS

SOME INDIVIDUALS WHO are Deaf or hard of hearing may use sign language exclusively while others may use spoken language or a combination of the two. People who communicate manually often have difficulty participating in situations where few or no other people use sign language, and a qualified sign language interpreter may be required to facilitate communication. The knowledge, skills, and abilities of the sign language interpreter are of critical importance to the use of sign language (Gierl, 2000; Loew, Cahalan-Laitusis, Cook, & Harris, 2005). However, live translations can vary from interpreter to interpreter due to differences in language skills, competencies, and familiarity with the topic and content, and preferred communication style of the individual. Also, variability within and between signed languages can alter expressive accuracy and receptive understanding (Blennerhassett, 2000; Johnson, Kimball, & Brown, 2001; Rogers, 2005). When using interpreter services, the hearing speaker should address the Deaf or hard of hearing person directly; conversation should not be directed to the interpreter (Luey et al., 1995).

COUNSELING STRATEGIES AND ASSISTIVE TECHNOLOGY

TREATMENT AND MANAGEMENT of hearing loss is very important and usually involves provision of assistive listening devices. Assistive listening devices have been shown to benefit the consumer in the areas of social, emotional, and communication functioning, and include hearing aids and cochlear implants. Aural rehabilitation is another key management strategy, encompassing a variety of communication-focused methodologies. Another strategy may be to improve one's own ability to use sign language, and sign language classes for employers and co-workers may be available as an accommodation (Geyer & Schroedel, 1999).

ASSISTIVE LISTENING DEVICES

CONVENTIONAL ANALOG HEARING aids generate signals similar to the sound energy they receive and then amplify those signals (Martin

& Clark, 2006; Weinstein, 1996). Analog aids generally amplify all environmental sounds similarly and may be appropriate for various types of hearing loss. Programmable analog hearing aids store several different settings so that the consumer can change the level of amplification needed in different listening environments. Analog devices are the least costly type of hearing aid, a critical advantage for many consumers.

Digital hearing aids use technology termed digitized sound processing to provide an undistorted signal and to filter background sounds (National Research Council, 2005). Digital devices are significantly more expensive than analog alternatives (Wood & Lutman, 2004). People who do not benefit from conventional assistive listening devices may be candidates for a cochlear implant, a prosthetic device implanted in the inner ear that stimulates the auditory nerve directly through electrical impulses (Flexer & Wray, 1998; National Research Council, 2005). The age at which an individual undergoes cochlear implantation, the length and severity of Deafness prior to implantation, and whether the person possesses useful speech-reading skills are all critical factors that influence cochlear implant outcomes.

AURAL REHABILITATION

AUDITORY REHABILITATION METHODS use residual hearing abilities, either with or without assistive devices, with special attention to development of listening skills. Oral methods combine assistive listening devices, speech reading, and kinesthesis to develop speaking abilities. Speech reading allows an individual to comprehend speech by observing lip and facial movements along with body gestures as visual cues to determine what is being spoken and in what context. Aural rehabilitation may also include training in manual communication. Manual communication training prepares the individual to communicate through nonverbal techniques such as finger spelling and signed languages, including ASL, Signed English, and others. Total communication is an inclusive option that involves selecting the most effective and appropriate strategies from all other methods to maximize expressive and receptive communication (Nicolosi, Harryman, & Kresheck, 1996).

ACCOMMODATIONS AND ASSISTIVE TECHNOLOGY

ACCOMMODATIONS ARE MODIFICATIONS, auxiliary aids, and services made or used to reduce barriers to inclusion and to ameliorate functional limitations. Without accommodations, people who are Deaf or hard of hearing may be excluded from many communicative interactions with the hearing world (King, 1999). However, assistive technology (AT) and environmental modifications are particularly useful accommodation options for individuals who are Deaf (Geyer & Schroedel, 1999). Technologies routinely used by hearing people such as Web-based chat, electronic mail, or text messaging are also useful for people who are Deaf or hard of hearing. Additional communication technologies have been developed especially for people who are Deaf or hard of hearing and include text-based telephone relay systems and video relay systems.

ISSUES IN ACCOMMODATIONS

RESEARCH SUGGESTS PEOPLE who are Deaf or hard of hearing face a number of accommodation challenges. For instance, employers exhibit greater willingness in providing job accommodations to workers in managerial or other white-collar positions than to workers in less prestigious positions (Geyer & Schroedel, 1999; National Research Council, 2005; Scherich, 1996). Differences in hearing status may also account for differences in accommodations; in general, individuals who are Deaf are more likely to request and receive accommodations than those who are hard of hearing (Geyer & Schroedel, 1999). Additionally, larger companies or organizations generally provide accommodations more readily (Scherich, 1996).

ENVIRONMENTAL-OCCUPATIONAL HEARING REQUIREMENTS

ACROSS HOME, WORK, and leisure settings, individuals who are Deaf or hard of hearing may encounter situations that require an awareness of and response to sounds in the environment. The ability to detect sounds such as warning bells, alarms, or door chimes; the ability to locate the source of sounds; and an ability to make distinctions between sounds may be critical hearing functions needed in some work settings (International Organization for Standardization, 2003; National Research Council, 2005). For example, the inability to hear or localize warning buzzers, alarms, or bells is a vocational limitation that could, if unnoticed, result in injury to the person with the hearing loss or others in the working environment (Arlinger, 2003). In some instances, individuals may be excluded from military service and professions such as law enforcement fields if they have hearing loss (National Research Council, 2005).

CONCLUSION

DEAF OR HARD of hearing people often face marked inability to participate in reciprocal conversations and social interactions due to functional differences in audition and communication (Gallaudet Research Institute, 2003; Villaume et al., 1997). The population of people with hearing loss and other auditory disorders is very diverse, not only in terms of severity, configuration, onset, progression, and classification, but also in etiology. Functional limitations related to Deafness and hearing loss are largely dependent on prelingual versus postlingual occurrence, the severity of the hearing loss, and the presence or absence of other complicating factors such as a secondary disability, along with situational factors (Arlinger, 2003; Foster, 1998; Tye-Murray, 2004).

Counselors can develop and maintain positive working relationships with people who are Deaf and hard of hearing by being cognizant of a few points. It is important to be aware of the individual's cultural identity and his or her mode of communication (Padden & Humphries, 2005) as well as any assistive technology the person may require for effective communication. In the event interpreters are needed, identifying where to locate and how to utilize them in advance will also help (Luey et al., 1995). There are simple positive changes to the environment that would be beneficial to all clients, regardless of hearing status, such as reducing glare and background noise and having one person speak at a time. This will help with effective communication (Scherich, 1996; Wood & Lutman, 2004). Following these guidelines may foster positive communication experiences for both the counselor and the consumer, thus allowing more focus to be placed on the counseling issues rather than communication issues.

REFERENCES

Arlinger, S. (2003). Negative consequences of uncorrected hearing loss—a review. *International Journal of Audiology, 42*(2), 2S17–2S20.

Blennerhassett, L. (2000). Psychological assessments. In N. Kitson & P. Hindley (Eds.), *Mental health and deafness* (pp. 185–205). London: Whurr.

Demorest, M. E., & Erdman, S. A. (1989). Factor structure of the communication profile for the hearing impaired. *Journal of Speech and Hearing Disorders, 54,* 541–549.

Filer, R. D., & Filer, P. A. (2000). Practical considerations for counselors working with hearing children of deaf parents. *Journal of Counseling and Development, 78*(1), 38–43.

Flexer, C., & Wray, D. (1998). The auditory-verbal approach: The voice of experience: Cochlear implants for children from auditory-verbal and speech-language pathology perspectives. In B. Tucker (Ed.), *Cochlear implants: A handbook* (pp. 93–146). Jefferson, NC: McFarland.

Foster, S. (1998). Communication as social engagement: Implications for interactions between deaf and hearing persons. *Scandinavian Audiology, 27*(Suppl. 49), 116–124.

Gallaudet Research Institute. (2003). *Regional and national summary report of data from the 2002–2003 annual survey of deaf and hard of hearing children and youth*. Washington, DC: Author.

Geyer, P. D., & Schroedel, J. G. (1999). Conditions influencing the availability of accommodations for workers who are deaf or hard-of-hearing. *Journal of Rehabilitation, 65*(2), 42–50.

Gierl, M. J. (2000). Construct equivalence on translated achievement test. *Canadian Journal of Education, 25*(4), 280–296.

Goldberg, L. R., & Richburg, C. M. (2004). Minimal hearing impairment: Major myths with more than minimal implications. *Communication Disorders Quarterly, 25*(3), 152–160.

International Organization for Standardization. (2003). *Ergonomics—Danger signals for public work areas—Auditory danger signals* (ISO 7731:2003). Geneva, Switzerland: Author.

Johnson, E., Kimball, K., & Brown, S. O. (2001). American Sign Language as an accommodation during standards-based assessments. *Assessment for Effective Intervention, 26*(2), 39–47.

Katz, J., & White, T. P. (2001). Introduction to the handicap of hearing impairment. In R. H. Hull (Ed.), *Aural rehabilitation: Serving children and adults* (4th ed., pp. 21–39). New York: Singular.

King, T. W. (1999). *Assistive technology: Essential human factors*. Boston: Allyn & Bacon.

Lane, H. (1992). *The mask of benevolence: Disabling the deaf community*. New York: Knopf.

Lane, H., Hoffmeister, R., & Bahan, B. (1996). *A journey into the deaf world*. San Diego, CA: Dawn Sign Press.

Loew, R., Cahalan-Laitusis, C., Cook, L., & Harris, R. (2005). Access considerations and the provision of appropriate accommodations: A research perspective from a testing organization. In J. L. Mounty & D. S. Martin (Eds.), *Assessing deaf adults: Critical issues in testing and evaluation* (pp. 37–53). Washington, DC: Gallaudet University Press.

Luey, H. S., Glass, L., & Elliott, H. (1995). Hard-of-hearing or deaf: Issues of ears, language, culture, and identity. *Social Work, 40*(2), 177–181.

Luxon, L. M., Cohen, M., Coffey, R. A., Phelps, P. D., Britton, K. E., Jan, H., et al. (2003). Neuro-otological findings in Pendred syndrome. *International Journal of Audiology, 42*(2), 82–88.

Martin, F. N., & Clark, J. G. (2006). *Introduction to audiology* (9th ed.). New York: Allyn & Bacon.

Nance, W. E. (2003). The genetics of deafness. *Mental Retardation and Developmental Disabilities Research Reviews, 9*, 109–119.

National Research Council. (2005). *Hearing loss: Determining eligibility for Social Security benefits*. Committee on Disability Determination for Individuals With Hearing Impairments. Robert A. Dobie & Susan B. Van Hemel (Eds.). *Board on Behavioral, Cognitive, and Sensory Sciences, Division of Behavioral and Social Sciences and Education*. Washington, DC: The National Academies Press.

Nelson, D. I., Nelson, R. Y., Concha-Barrientos, M., & Fingerhut, M. (2005). The global burden of occupational noise exposure. *American Journal of Industrial Medicine, 48*(6), 446–458.

Nicolosi, L., Harryman, E., & Kresheck, J. (1996). *Terminology of communication disorders: Speech-language-hearing* (4th ed.). Baltimore, MD: Williams & Wilkins.

Padden, C., & Humphries, T. (2005). *Inside deaf culture*. Cambridge, MA: Harvard University Press.

Porter, A. (1999). Sign-language interpretation in psychotherapy with deaf patients. *American Journal of Psychotherapy, 53*(2), 163–176.

Reagan, T. (2002). Toward an archeology of deafness: Etic and emic constructions of identity in conflict. *Journal of Language, Identity, and Education, 1*(1), 41–66.

Rehabilitation Services Administration. (1995). *Reporting manual for the program impact reporting system* (RSA-911) (Information Memorandum RSA-1250, May 1). Washington, DC: U.S. Department of Education, Office of Special Education and Rehabilitation Services.

Robertson, N. G., & Morton, C. C. (1999). Beginning of a molecular era in hearing and deafness. *Clinical Genetics, 55*, 149–159.

Roeser, R. J., Buckley, K. A., & Stickney, G. S. (2000). Pure tone test. In R. J. Roeser, M. Valente, & H. Hosford-Dunn (Eds.), *Audiology diagnosis* (pp. 227–251). New York: Thieme.

Rogers, P. (2005). Sign language interpretation in testing environments. In J. L. Mounty & D. S. Martin (Eds.), *Assessing deaf adults: Critical issues in testing and evaluation* (pp. 109–122). Washington, DC: Gallaudet University Press.

Schein, J. D. (1989). *At home among strangers*. Washington, DC: Gallaudet University Press.

Schein, S., Bottum, E. B., Lawler, J. T., Madory, R., & Wantuch, E. (2001). Psychological challenges encountered by hearing impaired adults and their families. *Rehabilitation Psychology, 46*(4), 322–323.

Scherich, D. L. (1996). Job accommodations in the workplace for persons who are deaf or hard of hearing: Current practices and recommendations. *Journal of Rehabilitation, 62*(2), 27–35.

Schow, R. L., & Nerbonne, M. A. (1996). *Introduction to audiologic rehabilitation* (3rd ed.). Boston: Allyn & Bacon.

Smith, S. D., & Taggart, R. T. (2004). Genetic hearing loss with no associated abnormalities. In H. V. Toriello, W. Reardon, & R. J. Gorlin (Eds.),

Hereditary hearing loss and its syndromes (2nd ed., pp. 37–82). New York: Oxford University Press.

Tye-Murray, N. (2004). *Foundations of aural rehabilitation: Children, adults, and their family members* (2nd ed.). Clifton Park, NY: Thomson Learning.

Villaume, W. A., Brown, M. H., Darling, R., Richardson, D., Hawk, R. M., Henry, D. M., et al. (1997). Presbycusis and conversation: Elderly interactants adjusting to multiple hearing losses. *Research on Language and Social Interaction, 30*(3), 235–262.

Weinstein, B. E. (1996). Treatment efficacy: Hearing aids in the management of hearing loss in adults. *Journal of Speech and Hearing Research, 39*(5), S37–S45.

Williams, C. B., & Finnegan, M. (2003). From myth to reality: Sound information for teachers about students who are deaf. *Teaching Exceptional Children, 35*(3), 40–45.

Wood, S. A., & Lutman, M. E. (2004). Relative benefits of linear analogue and advanced digital hearing aids. *International Journal of Audiology, 43*(3), 144–155.

Section E

Counseling Theories and Techniques

28

Psychoanalysis

Nancy McWilliams

PSYCHOANALYSIS AND THE psychoanalytic therapies originated in Sigmund Freud's work in the 1890s with people then diagnosed with severe hysterical disorders (psychogenic loss of body functions, altered states of consciousness, seizures, etc.). Inspired by the charismatic French psychiatrist Jean Charcot, Freud originally experimented with hypnosis to relieve hysterical symptoms and asked his patients to recline on his office couch to be hypnotized. Soon, however, impressed by the work of his colleague, Josef Breuer, with a gifted woman who preferred to report her stream of consciousness, he dispensed with hypnosis and began recommending what became known as *free association,* urging all his patients to say whatever came to mind, no matter how socially inappropriate, irrational, or embarrassing. Thus was born the talking cure.

In this chapter, the evolution of psychoanalysis and the psychodynamic therapies from Freud's time through the present are reviewed, emphasizing the implications of the major psychoanalytic theories for psychotherapy and counseling. Foundational theoretical and technical concepts in this tradition are italicized. Space limitations prevent my covering analytic ways of helping children, couples, families, groups, and organizations; instead, I concentrate on psychoanalytic approaches developed for individual adults.

EARLY FREUDIAN THEORY AND TECHNIQUE

WHAT FREUD HEARD in the increasingly intimate disclosures of his early patients were stories of molestation and incest. He concluded that hysterical disorders (most of which would today be diagnosed as posttraumatic or somatization disorders) were caused by memories of childhood seduction that had been kept out of awareness but were being expressed symbolically by the illness. He applied concepts from the physics of his day to these narratives, labeling as *repression* the process by which disturbing memories are made unconscious. The idea that there are automatic means of keeping upsetting experiences out of awareness was the germ of the larger concept of *defenses,* unconscious ways we protect ourselves from unbearable thoughts, feelings, and sensations. When Freud's patients would eventually recall painful memories—with their emotional intensity—their symptoms would diminish. Early psychoanalytic therapy thus emphasized both *remembering* and *abreaction* (emotional catharsis).

Soon, Freud ran into problems similar to those that therapists working with traumatized clients would encounter a century later (e.g., that some so-called memories are not accurate recollections but constructions, affected by complex unconscious motives such as trying to say what the doctor wants to hear). He revised his theory of symptom formation—never denying that many people with hysterical afflictions have been molested, but emphasizing the drives, conflicts, and fantasies that his patients also exposed during free association. Finding comparable drives, conflicts, and fantasies in himself, he concluded that they were universal (and that they would complicate any experience of sexual exploitation). He began using the idea of *unconscious conflict* to understand the other so-called neuroses, as they were then diagnosed: phobias, obsessive-compulsive disorders, and nonpsychotic depressions. Adopting the notion of dynamism from 19th-century physics, Freud began referring to the *dynamicunconscious,* the source of the term *psychodynamic.*

As his patients spoke increasingly freely and traced their problems to their early years, Freud began speculating that neuroses are rooted in normative childhood concerns with successive oral, anal, and body-integrity themes. He connected depression with the first, obsessions and compulsions with the second, and phobias with the third, positing that if one's temperament and childhood experiences make it hard to master a given developmental phase, an unconscious *fixation* with the issues of that phase results. He began framing hysteria as a fixation on the phase from about age 3 to about age 6, which he dubbed *oedipal* because the sexual and aggressive fantasies common in children in that age range suggest the Greek story of Oedipus. Freud's mature thinking came to be called *drive theory* or *drive-conflict theory* because it emphasized children's normal erotic and aggressive strivings and their inevitable conflicts with both realistic and moral limitation.

As he struggled to help his patients face their inner struggles, Freud became fascinated with how his relationships with them in the present became infused with issues from their pasts. Despite his efforts to be strictly professional, some patients would fall in love with him; others would compete or defer anxiously. Their associations revealed that they were experiencing him as if he were an important childhood figure. Initially viewing this *transference* from past to present as a distraction from the therapeutic work, Freud eventually came to believe that in this process lies considerable power to rework the more painful legacies of childhood. If one is given the emotional power of a parent and is cast in a central and recurring childhood drama, perhaps one can make that story come out differently.

Freud saw his patients four or five days a week, asking them to associate freely while reclining on his couch (a holdover from hypnosis; he also did not like being stared at all day). Listening to their dreams, memories, and current preoccupations, he became struck with their inadvertent *repetitions* of past experiences in the present. *Analyzing the transference* became a hallmark of psychoanalytic treatment. He considered this version of therapy, which we now refer to as *classical psychoanalysis,* to be applicable only to people with neuroses (as opposed to, say, psychoses or addictions), but he also hoped that what he had learned about unconscious motivation, repetition, conflict, and defense could be applied to develop ways of helping a wider range of people. Subsequent analysts extended psychoanalysis accordingly.

Although contemporary psychoanalytic therapies have diverged considerably from their Freudian base, the core ingredients of all psychodynamic approaches are present in Freud's early work. These factors include an appreciation of (1) unconscious processes, (2) a valence to all mental life, (3) a developmental viewpoint, (4) the inevitability of conflict and defense, and (5) the ubiquity of transferential processes (Pincus, 2006). How an analytic therapist applies these understandings to clinical or counseling challenges depends on the specific client(s) and the context of the work.

EGO PSYCHOLOGY: THEORY AND TECHNIQUE

FROM THE 1920S on, especially in the United States, where psychoanalysis was for many decades widely defined (against Freud's wishes) as a medical activity characterized by standard medical procedures, analysts refined an approach that became known as *ego psychology.* It drew from Freud's (1923) *structural model,* in which the mind is conceived as an arena of competing demands from the *id* (primitive impulse), *ego* (sense of *I*), and *superego* (self-consciousness and conscience). The ego was portrayed as mediating between id, superego, and external reality, using both conscious coping skills and unconscious *defenses* (repression, denial, projection, rationalization, and others). Psychopathology was equated with defenses that may have been adaptive in childhood but were currently primitive, inflexible, or maladaptive.

The analytic tradition thus did not posit a qualitative difference between *sick* and *healthy* people or adaptations; all problems were seen as on a continuum, as variant aspects and problems of the human condition. Although the term *patient* (from the Latin "one who suffers") is still common in the analytic community because of the origins of psychoanalysis in psychiatry, I use the term *client* in what follows because as psychotherapy broadened beyond the medical community, that term became more acceptable to counselors. (The term *analysand* has also been used in analytic writing, meaning "someone who is undergoing psychoanalysis.")

Ego psychology theorists construed therapy in terms of efforts to make clients aware of their defenses and to help them develop more adequate ways to cope. To do this, they tried to foster a solid *working alliance,* or *therapeutic relationship,* in which the client felt warmly collaborative in looking at problematic parts of the self. As in any situation that engenders anxiety, the person's defensive patterns would appear in the therapeutic relationship in the form of *resistances* (obstacles to free expression and emotional aliveness). The analyst would interpret the resistances in an effort to interfere with their automatic deployment so that the client could consider other means of handling anxiety and other painful emotions.

Instead of urging clients to remember, or teaching them about their putative unconscious conflicts, as Freud had, ego-psychological analysts noted defenses as they manifested themselves as resistances in the therapeutic hour. Rather than speculating, for example, about a person's unconscious hostility from childhood, the therapist might remark, "I notice that every time you get close to any angry feelings toward me, you abruptly change the subject. What comes to mind about that?"

In an effort to allow transference reactions to elaborate themselves freely and fully, analysts tried to take a position of *neutrality* (refraining from advising or actively influencing the client or disclosing personal feelings) and *abstinence* (not exploiting the client in any way). *Interpretation* was idealized, and *insight* was assumed to be the agent of change. (During the ego psychology era, not everyone agreed about this explanation of healing. Alexander and French [1946] argued that what happens in effective therapy constitutes a "corrective emotional experience," as opposed to the attainment of insight via interpretation, but their work inspired considerable controversy because of worries in the analytic community that self-conscious efforts to offer corrective experiences verged on manipulation of the client.)

This overall approach, often labeled *exploratory,* was considered appropriate for people with neurotic conflicts and personality disorders of the hysterical, obsessive-compulsive, phobic, and depressive types. *Supportive therapy* was offered to clients with "ego weakness," such as those with psychotic tendencies. Supportive therapy was not well defined until the recent work of analysts such as Rockland (1992) and Pinsker (1997), but it was understood to involve efforts to build *ego strength* (resilience and capacity to cope realistically) by active emotional support, educative interventions, and emphasis on probable outcomes of alternative courses of action.

The relative isolation of psychoanalytic training institutes from other educational settings has contributed to significant misunderstandings of the nature of analytic therapies, even among academics and mental health professionals. Most contemporary analysts have rejected more sterile versions of ego-psychological technique and have continually modified their procedures to address the needs of different eras, cultures, and individuals. Nevertheless, a surprising number of people mistakenly equate psychoanalysis with the strict methods that mid-20th-century ego psychologists tried to observe with those clients they considered healthy enough to respond positively to exploratory work.

OBJECT RELATIONS AND INTERPERSONAL PSYCHOANALYSIS: THEORY AND TECHNIQUE

B Y T H E 1 9 5 0 S , some analysts were developing an orientation to psychotherapy that emphasized the *internalization of relationships* and the emotional themes associated with them. In the United Kingdom, this movement had the (misleadingly cold-sounding) name of *object relations theory*—in homage to Freud's original formulation of drives as having a source, aim, and *object,* the object usually being a person. In the United States, a somewhat parallel movement called itself *interpersonal psychoanalysis* (see Mitchell & Black, 1995).

This shift reflected, among other influences, therapists' experiences with children, with psychotic clients, and with people whose mental lives were characterized by dynamics other than the neurotic ones for which Freud had developed his approach (e.g., paranoid, schizoid, psychopathic, and narcissistic clients). As the interpersonal and object relations communities developed, they drew also on advances in empirical observation and research. They were especially interested in investigations of attachment and separation (see Blatt & Levy, 2003).

To object-relational and interpersonal analysts, the Freudian focus on drive, conflict, and defense seemed less relevant to their clients' problems than basic relationship issues. They found themselves accounting for psychopathology by reference to individuals' childhood interpersonal contexts rather than by reference to developmental fixation. Stressing basic *security operations* and *sense of self* more than issues of gratification and frustration, they were more likely, for example, to explain obsessive perfectionism in terms of experience with a controlling parent than in terms of fixation at the anal stage. The two explanations are not mutually exclusive, but emphasis on one versus the other has different implications for what one says to clients. ("You want to make a mess, but you're afraid to let yourself go" is not the same message as "You're terrified of your mother's criticism if you're not perfectly neat.")

One group of clients that analysts found easier to comprehend from an object relations perspective were those who came to be called *borderline*. This term arose from a clinical consensus that some people seem to live psychologically on the border between the neuroses and psychoses. It originally referred to clients with "stable instability" (Grinker, Werble, & Drye, 1968), who lack a cohesive *identity* and use primitive defenses such as *splitting* (seeing things as all good or all bad), yet who nonetheless have adequate grounding in reality. Such individuals oscillate between feeling controlled and engulfed when with others, and feeling abandoned and desperate when alone.

In therapy, clients in the borderline range would have powerful transferences that they could not see *as* transferences ("It's my bad luck to get a therapist exactly like my mother!"). Therapy was consequently intense, and analysts reported having powerful *countertransferences* (emotional reactions) to such clients. Object relations theories helped them hang in with people who might treat them as an omnipotent rescuer on Tuesday and a malevolent persecutor on Thursday. Eventually, several specific psychoanalytic therapies were developed to address the needs of this group (e.g., Meares's psychodynamic/interpersonal therapy, Kernberg's transference-focused therapy, Fonagy's mentalization-based therapy), all of which drew on object-relations concepts (see Bateman & Fonagy, 2004). Although distinct, all involve setting clear boundaries, addressing self-destructive behaviors, working in the here-and-now, tolerating affect storms, and fostering the capacity for *mentalization* (appreciating the separate subjective states of other people).

SELF PSYCHOLOGY: THEORY AND TECHNIQUE

BY THE SECOND half of the 20th century, analysts were encountering more and more nonpsychotic clients who suffered from feelings of internal emptiness, low self-esteem (often coexisting with grandiose claims or ambitions), and confusion about who they were. Their inner experience seemed difficult to represent in terms of either conflict/defense or internalized love objects. What seemed broken or stunted was their basic sense of self. Unable to value themselves from the inside, they craved repeated validation from outside. They tended to relate to others with either idealization (presumably improving their self-esteem by identifying with superior beings) or devaluation (improving their self-esteem by feeling superior). Their histories suggested that caregivers had used them to support their own self-esteem. Not having been loved uncritically themselves, they seemed unable to love others as they are.

Such clients are difficult to help by traditional interpretive means; in fact, Freud (1914) considered them untreatable. They resist making a comfortable alliance; they seem not to have analyzable transferences; and they may experience interpretation as judgmental or irrelevant or both. There gradually arose a rich literature, both clinical and empirical, on *narcissism,* the psychoanalytic term for the deficient self-state, and compensatory attitudes, of those with seriously diminished self-esteem. Otto Kernberg (1975), blending ego-psychological and object relations ideas, advocated interpreting their defensive devaluation and underlying envy. Heinz Kohut (1971, 1978), in contrast, construing their responses to the therapist as *self-object transferences* that call for acceptance rather than interpretation, argued that they need a primary experience of *empathic attunement.*

Kohut's position inspired the movement that became known as *self psychology.* His technical recommendations are reminiscent of Carl Rogers's (1951) emphasis on nonjudgmental acceptance, empathy, and authenticity, with the significant addition of Kohut's expectation that, given the predictable repetition of childhood shame experiences in the analytic relationship, the therapist would inevitably cause the client narcissistic injury and would have to repair such ruptures nondefensively. Progress would occur gradually as the client developed a *transmuting internalization* of the therapist; that is, the counselor's empathic voice would be slowly taken in.

As clinicians became oriented toward issues of self and the development of realistic and reliable self-esteem, they began seeing the applicability of a self-psychological orientation to all clients. Kohut and subsequent self psychologists restored empathy to the forefront of psychoanalytic healing and ushered in an era in which analysts became more flexible as they chose interventions not on the basis of whether they conformed to a standard technique but on the basis of whether they were genuinely empathically attuned.

RELATIONAL PSYCHOANALYSIS: THEORY AND TECHNIQUE

ALL THE FOREGOING orientations within psychoanalysis assume an analyst who is a relatively objective observer of the client and the therapy. The recent relational movement has challenged this assumption. Its leading thinkers have argued that the analyst's subjectivity is constantly affecting, and being affected by, the unconscious dynamics of both parties in the therapy dyad (see Wachtel, 2007). In this view, transference is not something that the client projects on to a blank-screen therapist but instead reflects the analyst's and client's *intersubjectivity*. Influenced by infant research, postmodern philosophy, relationally astute psychoanalytic forebears, and personal frustrations with rigidly "neutral" analysts, relational thinkers have accomplished a significant paradigm shift, widely dubbed the "relational turn" in psychoanalysis.

The relational community has also been influenced by evolving research and clinical experience with traumatized clients (see Herman, 1992) and has tended to emphasize *dissociation* over repression as the process that keeps painful mental contents out of awareness. Most reject Freud's topographical images of the layering of psychological processes (defense covering anxiety, anxiety covering conflict overdrives) and prefer to imagine the simultaneous coexistence of conscious mental life and *dissociated self-states*.

Triebel (2007) recently characterized relational therapy as "a field that is undergoing a continuous dynamic process: a therapeutic couple co-work with each other (consciously as well as unconsciously), and in favorable circumstances try to produce experiences that are healthier than the old ones" (p. 228). This way of construing therapeutic process resembles the older notion of "corrective emotional experience," except that Alexander and French had assumed that analysts could deliberately provide this from a stance of professional expertise. Relational theory, in contrast, posits that healing experiences evolve organically as both parties explore the psychoanalytic encounter as honestly as possible.

The relational movement has brought a more egalitarian sensibility to psychoanalysis. Relational analysts emphasize *not knowing* and *courting surprise* (Stern, 1997) rather than interpretation. Skeptical of those who claim to speak with clinical or scientific detachment, they assume they will find themselves participating in *enactments* (behavioral repetitions of themes from the client's life that evoke responsive themes from their own). This is a notable departure from the ego psychological notion of the client's "acting out" childhood dramas in a neutral setting. Instead of "interpreting the transference" ("You're experiencing me as if I'm your critical father"), relational analysts may note mutual enactments ("You and I seem to be relating to each other like a critical father and a criticized child"). If they believe it will deepen the work, they may share their emotional reactions. Progress is conceived in terms of reducing the unconscious polarities of "doer and done-to" (Benjamin, 1995) that organize much psychological experience, and in terms of an evolving capacity in client and therapist to tolerate "standing in the spaces" (Bromberg, 1998) between different self-states.

SHORT-TERM AND FOCUSED PSYCHOANALYTIC THERAPIES

THE ARCHITECTS OF most psychoanalytic theories have tended to assume that the therapist is the employee of the client and can be retained for as long as both the client and analyst deem advisable. Although Freud saw most of his patients for weeks or months, rather than years, later analysts found that more time was necessary for most people to make lasting changes. There were many efforts to streamline psychotherapy, however, starting quite early (see Messer & Warren, 1995). As therapy slowly lost its stigma, and as increasing numbers of clients sought it, market forces and other limiting factors began exerting pressures on practitioners to create short-term treatments based on psychoanalytic ideas. Many such approaches have been developed.

At the same time, analytic therapists treating the problems of specific populations (e.g., infants, children, couples, people with substance use disorders, people with schizophrenia and other psychoses, trauma victims, individuals in sexual, ethnic, or religious minorities) fashioned specialized approaches for their particular clients. Such therapies are too numerous to review here, but I mention them to make the point that what makes a therapy psychoanalytic is not a specific technique. Rather, it is whether there is a focus on *unconscious processes, especially as they are manifested, and potentially influenced, in the here-and-now relationship with the therapist.* Analytic understanding has influenced a range of treatments, from exploratory to supportive, from open-ended to time-limited, with highly diverse clients and problems.

EVALUATION OF PSYCHOANALYTIC THERAPIES

PSYCHOANALYTIC THERAPIES TEND to be complex, open-ended, and individualized, making them hard to investigate scientifically. Spurred by recent demands for evidence of effectiveness, however, analytic communities are becoming much more attentive to research. There are three general areas that lend empirical validation to psychodynamic approaches.

First, several meta-analyses have found that *relationship variables* account for more variance in therapy outcome than any other factor, including type of treatment (see Wampold, 2001). From Freud's discovery of transference, through the ego psychology emphasis on the alliance, to the current relational movement, the analytic tradition has studied and emphasized interpersonal connection. Individual differences—in both client and therapist—also correlate strongly with outcome, suggesting that the research paradigm of trying to find specific treatments for discrete *DSM* disorders may be the wrong way to approach psychotherapy research (Blatt & Zuroff, 2005).

Investigations by Weiss and Sampson and their colleagues (e.g., 1986) have given empirical support for the individualized nature of psychoanalytic treatment. They learned that each client approaches therapy or counseling hoping to disconfirm his or her unique unconscious *pathogenic beliefs*. To the extent that the relationship with the therapist does so, the client gets better. Appreciation of the fact that similar-appearing problems may be experienced vastly differently and call for different therapy styles based on individual dynamics is a hallmark of the psychoanalytic tradition. Robust evidence now supports the core convictions of psychodynamic therapists that relationship and personality factors are critical to healing and growth.

Second, outcome research on psychoanalysis and psychoanalytic treatments attests to their helpfulness (see Doidge, 1997). Some studies, especially the oldest, have serious methodological flaws (see McWilliams & Weinberger, 2003), but the overall take-home message is that psychoanalytic therapy works. The majority of clinicians surveyed in the *Consumer Reports* study of psychotherapy effectiveness (Seligman, 1995), which found that patients did better the more intensively, and the longer, they were in therapy, were analytically influenced. Randomized controlled trials of specific analytic treatments (see Westen, Novotny, & Thompson-Brenner, 2004) are also appearing, with encouraging results.

Finally, there are extensive empirical literatures on attachment, defense, emotion, personality, and other areas relevant to psychoanalytic conceptualization and treatment that support the theoretical models and clinical experiences of analytic therapists. Contemporary neuroscientists are meanwhile learning that, as Freud hoped long ago, we can now describe in biological terms many of the unconscious processes for which he could only formulate hypothetical structures and metaphors.

PROFESSIONAL AND CULTURAL CONSEQUENCES OF THE PSYCHOANALYTIC MOVEMENT

ALTERNATIVE THERAPY PARADIGMS, including those that have reacted against psychoanalysis, have incorporated many concepts from the psychodynamic clinical tradition. References to "working through," "secondary gain," "projection," "denial," "insecurity," and "attachment problems" all have origins in analytic thinking, whether they are applied to analytic treatments or to humanistic, family systems, or cognitive behavior therapies. Popular assessment instruments, such as the Myers-Briggs Type Indicator, Minnesota Multiphasic Personality Inventory, and Rorschach test, are based on psychodynamic concepts. Psychoanalytic themes have infused the arts, social sciences, literature, biography, and other areas of intellectual life.

When it was the "latest thing" in Western thinking, psychoanalysis was overvalued. Now that it has been around for more than a century, it tends to be dismissed as passé. Both attitudes are distortions of a complex reality. In a post-Freudian world, much of what was once surprising in psychoanalysis has been slowly assimilated and has come to be considered common knowledge. A person reporting an "identity crisis" is unknowingly quoting Erik Erikson (1959); people who accuse others of "defensiveness" are referencing ego psychology (A. Freud, 1936); my carpenter, who referred to his fastidiousness as "anal," was invoking early drive theory (Freud, 1908), as are parents who reassure themselves that their child is "going through a phase." Psychoanalysis has permeated the culture, for better and for worse. I hope I have conveyed in this chapter its most relevant contributions to the art and science of helping others.

REFERENCES

Alexander, F., & French, T. M. (1946). *Psychoanalytic therapy: Principles and application*. New York: Ronald Press.

Bateman, A., & Fonagy, P. (2004). *Psychotherapy for borderline personality disorder: Mentalization-based treatment*. New York: Oxford University Press.

Benjamin, J. (1995). *Like subjects, love objects: Essays on recognition and sexual difference*. New Haven, CT: Yale University Press.

Blatt, S. J., & Levy, K. N. (2003). Attachment theory, psychoanalysis, personality development, and psychopathology. *Psychoanalytic Inquiry, 23,* 102–150.

Blatt, S. J., & Zuroff, D. C. (2005). Empirical evaluation of the assumptions in identifying evidence based treatments in mental health. *Clinical Psychology Review, 25,* 459–486.

Bromberg, P. M. (1998). *Standing in the spaces: Essays on clinical process, trauma, and dissociation*. Hillsdale, NJ: Analytic Press.

Doidge, N. (1997). Empirical evidence for the efficacy of psychoanalytic psychotherapies and psychoanalysis: An overview. *Psychoanalytic Inquiry, 1997 Supplement,* 102–150.

Erikson, E. H. (1959). *Identity and the life cycle*. New York: W. W. Norton.

Freud, A. (1936). *The ego and the mechanisms of defense*. New York: International Universities Press, 1966.

Freud, S. (1908). *Character and anal eroticism*. Standard Edition, 9 (pp. 169–175). London: Hogarth Press.

Freud, S. (1914). *On narcissism: An introduction*. Standard Edition, 14 (pp. 67–102). London: Hogarth Press.

Freud, S. (1923). *The ego and the id.* Standard Edition, 19 (pp. 13–59). London: Hogarth Press.

Grinker, R. R., Werble, B., & Drye, R. C. (1968). *The borderline syndrome: A behavioral study of ego functions.* New York: Basic Books.

Herman, J. L. (1992). *Trauma and recovery: The aftermath of violence—from domestic abuse to political terror.* New York: Basic Books.

Kernberg, O. F. (1975). *Borderline conditions and pathological narcissism.* New York: Jason Aronson.

Kohut, H. (1971). *The analysis of the self.* New York: International Universities Press.

Kohut, H. (1978). *The restoration of the self.* New York: International Universities Press.

McWilliams, N., & Weinberger, J. (2003). Psychodynamic psychotherapy. In G. Stricker & T. Widiger (Eds.), *Comprehensive handbook of psychology: Vol. 8. Clinical psychology* (pp. 253–277). New York: Wiley.

Messer, S. B., & Warren, C. S. (1995). *Models of brief psychodynamic therapy: A comparative approach.* New York: Guilford Press.

Mitchell, S. A., & Black, M. J. (1995). *Freud and beyond: A history of modern psychoanalytic thought.* New York: Basic Books.

Pincus, D. (2006). Who is Freud and what does the new century behold? *Psychoanalytic Psychology, 23,* 367–372.

Pinsker, H. (1997). *A primer of supportive psychotherapy.* Hillsdale, NJ: Analytic Press.

Rockland, L. H. (1992). *Supportive therapy: A psychodynamic approach.* New York: Basic Books.

Rogers, C. R. (1951). *Client-centered therapy: Its current practice, implications, and theory.* Boston: Houghton Mifflin.

Seligman, M. E. P. (1995). The effectiveness of psychotherapy: The *Consumer Reports* Study. *American Psychological Association, 50,* 965–974.

Stern, D. B. (1997). *Unformulated experience: From dissociation to negotiation in psychoanalysis.* Hillsdale, NJ: Analytic Press.

Triebel, A. (2007). "Transitional subjects": Therapeutic persons being curative. *International Forum of Psychoanalysis, 16,* 228–234.

Wachtel, P. L. (2007). *Relational theory and the practice of psychotherapy.* New York: Guilford Press.

Wampold, B. E. (2001). *The great psychotherapy debate: Models, methods, and findings.* Mahwah, NJ: Lawrence Erlbaum.

Weiss, J., Sampson, H., & the Mount Zion Psychotherapy Research Group. (1986). *The psychoanalytic process: Theory, clinical observations, and empirical research.* New York: Guilford Press.

Westen, D., Novotny, C. M., & Thompson-Brenner, H. (2004). The empirical status of empirically supported psychotherapies: Assumptions, findings, and reporting in controlled clinical trials. *Psychological Bulletin, 130,* 631–663.

29

Basics of Cognitive Behavior Therapy

Arthur Freeman and
Sharon E. Morgillo Freeman

OGNITIVE BEHAVIOR THERAPY (CBT) serves as an umbrella term that encompasses aspects of a number of specific approaches, including Beck's cognitive therapy (Beck, 1995; Beck, Rush, Shaw, & Emery, 1979); McMullin's cognitive restructuring (McMullin, 2000); Ellis's rational emotive behavior therapy (Ellis & Dryden, 2007; Ellis & Maclaren, 1998); Goldfried's systematic rational restructuring (Goldfried, 1995); Lazarus's multimodal assessment (Lazarus, 1981); Linehan's dialectical behavior therapy (Linehan, 1993; Linehan, Dimeff, & Koerner, 2007); Meichenbaum's self-instructional training (Meichenbaum, 1977) or stress innoculation training (Jaremko & Meichenbaum, 1983); Young's Schema—focused therapy (Young, Klosko, & Weishaar, 2003); Hayes's acceptance and commitment therapy (Hayes, Strosahl, & Wilson, 1999); Ryle's cognitive analytic therapy (Ryle, 1995); and others. Over the years CBT has been applied to a variety of client populations (crisis problems, couples, children, suicidal clients) in a range of treatment settings (inpatient or outpatient, hospital, university counseling centers) and to the range of clinical problems. It has continued to be at the forefront of empirically supported therapies, with a large number of controlled studies indicating CBT has proven to be highly effective in treating a number of problems, including depression, anxiety, eating disorders, substance abuse, anger management and personality disorders, and in facilitating relapse prevention (Freeman, Felgoise, Nezu, Nezu, & Reinecke, 2005).

CBT originally evolved out of two traditions, the behavior therapy tradition and the psychodynamic tradition. Alfred Adler, a member of the early psychoanalytic circle, was not only a proponent of short-term therapy but one of the earliest progenitors of CBT. Typically, Adler informed his clients at the beginning of therapy that the process would take 8 to 10 weeks. He recommended that with more difficult cases the client be told the following about the length of therapy: "I don't know. Let us begin. In a month I shall ask you whether we are on the right track. If not, we shall break it off" (Ansbacher & Ansbacher, 1964, p. 201). Behavior therapy was one of the first major departures from the more traditional, psychodynamically oriented approaches to therapy. The research of Pavlov, Skinner, Watson, Wolpe and others helped to shape the behavior therapy tradition that emerged in the early to mid-1900s and into the 1950s to become popular in the late 20th and early 21st centuries. Cognitive behavior therapy stands as a meeting point for therapists from many different models. Behavior therapy called for the use of concrete, planned interventions and monitored progress continuously and often quantitatively. It also moved away from the *disease* conceptualization of psychological problems due to early faulty personality development and focused instead on the target behavior as a learned response. Problem behaviors were no longer seen as symptoms of an underlying process such as an unconscious expression of a blocked desire but were deemed the actual problems.

A small group of clinicians such as Aaron T. Beck and Albert Ellis, both earlier trained as psychoanalysts, had already been suggesting in their writing and lectures that thinking played a large mediating role in behavioral and emotional reactions to the world. This concept of a mediational model began to take shape. This mediational model was the beginning of cognitive behavior therapy (Freeman et al., 2005).

Recent trends in the field have made the need for short-term models of therapy an increasing necessity. Multiple factors have driven this increased interest and necessity in short-term models. For example, the nature of client problems will often dictate a short-term model for treatment of specific disorders. Based on empirical studies, a number of disorders have been clearly demonstrated to be treated in several sessions. Too, clients now seek quick, directive, symptomatic relief. Their motivation for extended therapy based on the erroneous but oft-quoted adage that problems took a long time to form, so will now need a long time for amelioration is gone. The wish to quickly feel better, to rid oneself of long-standing thoughts, actions, or behaviors, is not the result of a pathological need for instant gratification but the need to quickly and reasonably address a specific symptom. Clients have been empowered to ask for what they want without being intimidated by interpretations.

Another factor that has increased the need for short-term models is institutional or administrative constraints. Both inpatient and out-patient programs have shortened lengths of available treatment or services so as to be able to provide services to a broader number of in-dividuals with static or shrinking funding. This phenomenon has also been seen in community mental health centers, where resources are often limited. With the proliferation of health maintenance organiza-tions (HMOs) and increased demand for accountability for health care reimbursement, mental health providers must show positive gains after fewer sessions.

BASIC CONCEPTUAL FRAMEWORK

COGNITIVE BEHAVIORAL THERAPY has several defining elements in that it is

Active. The client must be involved in the therapeutic process not merely as an observer or as an occasional visitor but as a core and key participant. If the client cannot (or will not) be part of the process, therapy goals must be limited and even foreshortened.

Motivational. The therapist needs to take responsibility for help-ing to motivate the client toward a change in behavior, affect, or thinking. The therapist must be able to set up the format, setting, and rationale for the client to consider the value of change.

Directive. The therapist must be able to develop a treatment plan and then to help the client to understand, contribute to, and to use the treatment plan as a template for change. In effect, the therapist must have an idea of what the "finished product" sub-sequent to therapy will look like, so as to use the optimal inter-ventions, time them well, and choreograph the therapy.

Structured. CBT is structured in two ways. First, the overall therapy follows a structure that approximates the treatment plan. The individual session is structured so that every session has an iden-tifiable beginning, middle, and end. This is especially useful for those clients who come to therapy because their lives are con-fused and disorganized.

Collaborative. Therapeutic collaboration cannot be 50/50. For the severely depressed client, the possibility to generate 50% of the therapeutic effort is an impossible dream. Initially, the collabo-ration may be 90/10, with the therapist doing 90% of the work. For each client, the therapist must evaluate the client's ability and motivation for the therapy and then supply the balance of collaboration needed. Any therapist who has worked with adolescents has learned that the expectation or demand that the adolescent provide at least 50% of the energy and motivation for therapy has most often been disappointed.

Psychoeducational. The therapist works as a change agent. Many of the problems that bring (or drive) people to therapy involve skill deficits. These skills might include self-soothing (anxiety), taking a forward rather than backward view of experience (depression), problem solving (substance abuse), anger management (partner abuse), or increased ability to tolerate frustration. The therapist may have to teach by direct instruction, modeling, role playing, guided practice, or in vivo experience.

Problem oriented. Cognitive behavior therapy focuses on discrete problems rather than vague and amorphous goals of "feeling good," "getting better," or increasing self-esteem. The issues that bring people to therapy are more often complaints (depression) rather than the problems that constitute the depression (difficulty sleeping, low libido, apathy, etc.).

Solution focused. The CBT therapist works with the client on generating solutions, not simply gaining insight into the problems. The CBT therapist uses the Socratic dialogue to move the client toward a more problem-solving focus.

Dynamic. The dynamic level of CBT is to help the client to identify, understand, and to then modify his or her schema. The *schema* are the basic templates for understanding one's world. Schema may be personal, religious, cultural, age related, gender related, or family based. These so-called rules, learned in one's family of origin, are then modified throughout life by the interaction with family, friends, or institutions. The schema would encompass what was termed *superego* by the analysts.

Time limited. Each therapy session should, ideally, stand alone. A time-limited focus is not a number of sessions but rather a way of looking at therapy. Ellis has, on many occasions, demonstrated that a single session can have a marked positive effect on an individual.

CBT is based on several principles:

- There is an interaction between cognitions, affect, and behavior.
- Certain experiences evoke cognitions, explanation, and attributions about that situation.
- Cognitions may be made conscious and can be monitored and altered.
- Desired emotional and behavioral change can be achieved through cognitive change, just as cognitive change can be altered by actions or emotions.

What does this really mean? Two people can be in the exact same situation but have very different reactions to it based on their idiosyncratic internal dialogue, that is, what they are telling themselves about the situation. In fact, the same person can be in similar situations and react differently to them at different times. This indicates that there is a so-called filter through which we process experiences and that determines how we react to them. These mediating or filtering factors are what are termed schema. Our schema, or beliefs, about the world, other people, ourselves, and the potential for the future greatly influence our behavioral and emotional reactions. These activating events or triggers can be actual events, experiences, thoughts, memories, and anything else that causes a reaction. For example, reviewing past hurts and perceived injustice will likely lead to depression. If the individual views the world as dangerous or threatening, anxiety would result. If there is some specific object or situation that is perceived as dangerous, the result would be a phobic response. When an individual maintains a negative view of the future, hopelessness and suicide are possible. If an individual has thoughts of having been cheated or humiliated, anger is the common reaction. Or, thoughts of being abandoned will often lead to dependent feelings, thoughts, and behavior.

CBT advocates for the careful evaluation of our cognitions, behaviors, and emotions so that we can determine what is helpful and useful to us and what is self-defeating. The therapeutic goal is to work to change what is necessary in order to live full and satisfying lives. In this respect, CBT can also be seen as promoting a healthy philosophy of living. It is educative in that one goal is to help clients operate as their own therapists so that they are able to work through problems ultimately without the aid of a professional.

The power of the mind is incredible, and people look for evidence to support what they believe. If the evidence is not readily apparent, they will sometimes make it up or skew existing information in support of what they believe, for better or for worse. These are some typical cognitive distortions (Beck, 1995; Burns, 1980; Freeman, Pretzer, Fleming, & Simon, 1990, 2004):

- *All-or-none thinking (polarized or dichotomous thinking).* One sees a situation in terms of two mutually exclusive categories instead of a continuum with a spectrum of possibilities.
  Example: "If I don't succeed at this, I am a total and complete failure."
- *Catastrophizing/awfulizing:* When thinking about situations, one assumes the worst will happen and that it will be intolerable.
  Example: "If this relationship doesn't work out, then I'll never find anyone and will be miserable and alone for the rest of my life."

   Emotional reasoning: One assumes that because he or she feels something it must be true without actually scrutinizing the validity of the thinking and evidence that caused the emotion in the first place.
Example: "I'm anxious about this situation therefore I know it will end in disaster."

   "Should," "must," "have to," and "ought to" statements: One makes and holds on to rigid demands about how oneself, the world, and others have to be, despite evidence to the contrary, making it sometimes difficult to cope with the reality of a situation.
Example: "He should never act that way."

   Personalization: One attributes others' perceived negative behavior to oneself without considering the possibility of alternative explanations for the behavior.
Example: "She was cold to me because she's upset by something I did."

   Mind reading: One believes he or she knows without being told what other people are thinking and what their motivations are for behaviors.
Example: "She thinks I'm a superficial flake."

   Overgeneralization: One jumps to broad negative conclusions based on one experience or a series of experiences.
Example: "I didn't get this job just like I never get anything that I want."

   Labeling: One globally puts labels on oneself as opposed to labeling and rating specific behaviors or experiences.
Example: "I'm a complete failure," instead of "I failed to accomplish this."

   Disqualifying/discounting the positive: Positive experiences or behaviors that don't support one's negative outlook on a situation are automatically discounted, ignored, or explained away.
Example: "I only did well on the test because it was easy."

   Selective abstraction: One pays close and generally irrational attention to one or a couple negative details in a situation or experience and virtually ignores all other data.
Example: "I received high grades in all of my classes but one, which means I'm a terrible student."

   Minimization: Positive experiences or characteristics are acknowledged but generally treated as unimportant or insignificant.
Example: "My professional life is going well but it doesn't matter because my personal life is a disaster."

Clients are asked to be as specific and concrete about their goals as possible based on the belief that people stand a better chance of getting where they want to go if they know what that looks like. While the goal of being happier is perfectly legitimate, it is important to break it down into what will increase and decrease behaviorally, emotionally, and cognitively that will indicate the person has made strides toward this goal. This also allows the therapist and client to monitor progress during therapy.

Once therapy goals are identified, agreed upon, and prioritized, the therapist sets about helping the client start to identify and evaluate his or her thinking, behaving, and feeling that may be helpful and unhelpful. Through the use of Socratic questioning, CBT involves an ongoing assessment of the person and the problems throughout the therapy experience and is very sensitive to the idiosyncratic nature of an individual's problems (Beck, 1995). Once cognitive, behavioral, and emotive patterns are identified for change, the CBT therapist begins to introduce a variety of focused techniques to facilitate this process. These techniques are discussed later in this chapter.

COGNITIVE INTERVENTIONS

COGNITIVE INTERVENTIONS REPRESENT one of the cornerstones of CBT. As we noted earlier, cognitions, behaviors, and emotions are interconnected, so an intervention focused on one component is bound to influence the others. Once the client's unhelpful and self-defeating thinking is identified, it usually becomes an important focus of therapy. Two of the main goals of CBT are to help clients examine and challenge or dispute the current beliefs and thinking that causes them to have self-identified undesirable reactions and then to aid them in developing new, more useful, and helpful ways of thinking so as to further their goals. Some specific strategies include the following:

Self-help forms. These are employed in the identification of dysfunctional thinking. Clients are asked to write down the activating situation, their emotional and behavioral responses, and what they were thinking. They are then asked to identify their irrational thinking and potential rational responses that would have allowed them to respond in the way they would like to respond to this type of situation.

Challenging beliefs. Once a dysfunctional belief has been identified, the therapist sets about helping the client challenge it. For example:

> *Functional.* How is it helping you to believe this? Does it further your goals? Are there any negative consequences to thinking this way?
>
> *Empirical.* Where is the evidence this is true?

Logical. How does it follow from one point to another?
Friend. What advice would you give a friend in this situation?
Philosophical. Despite this, can you still lead a satisfying life?
Alternative. Is there an alternative explanation or way of thinking about this that is equally viable?

Writing an alternative assumption. People are most likely to give up an irrational or dysfunctional belief when they can see that it is not helping them and they have an alternative that they see as more adaptive and functional. So after disputing or challenging a client's belief, it is crucial to help the client develop a self-statement that is preferably in his or her words. Writing it down is helpful in terms of remembering and practicing it.

Advantages and disadvantages. The purpose is to keep the client fully aware of the reasons he or she has chosen to attempt the change so that if he or she starts to relapse the list can be used to shore up his or her motivation.

Role reversal. For clients who have an especially challenging time disputing their own thinking, the therapist can ask them to trade roles. They act as the "therapist" and the therapist voices the verbalized client beliefs. It also gives both client and therapist an idea of how entrenched the thinking is for the individual.

Recording therapy sessions. Having a client listen to his or her own therapy session provides one degree of separation, which sometimes allows the client to develop more insight and understanding about himself or herself.

Reframing. Another strategy is to ask the client to identify what the opportunities may be in a situation rather than solely focusing on the inherent threats and problems.

Bibliotherapy. Often CBT therapists will assign books, tapes, workshops, lectures, or anything else that's relevant and will supplement the work being done in therapy.

BEHAVIORAL INTERVENTIONS

BEHAVIORAL INTERVENTIONS CAN be especially helpful in promoting change in individuals who have a harder time making elegant core belief changes through cognitive methods. Clients may be limited by their intelligence or developmental level, or there may be communication problems that get in the way of using cognitive interventions.

Role playing/behavioral rehearsal. Clients may often find it helpful to practice situations such as discussions with co-workers or family members in the therapy session. It allows the client to receive coaching from the therapist and also to think through what he or she wants to say in a potentially emotional conversation.

Skills training. Clients may lack some life skills either on interpersonal or practical levels that are blocking their ability to reach their goals. Supplementing therapy with training in social skills, assertiveness skills, anger management skills, relaxation skills, computer skills, or other related areas may be especially helpful to some clients.

Modeling. Ask clients if they can identify someone in their life who they believe has a better way of handling a specific situation that they've identified they want to work on. Once they've identified that person ask them why they think the other person is better able to handle these situations. Then ask them to act the way that person would in the situation and see what happens in their thinking and feeling.

In vivo desensitization. This generally involves creating a so-called hierarchy of pain to deal with an anxiety-provoking situation. Through repeated, systematic exposure to increasingly provocative situations the client is asked to stay with the discomfort toward the ultimate goal of becoming desensitized to the triggers.

Graded task assignments. This entails having clients break large, potentially overwhelming, tasks into smaller steps that feel more manageable, with each step helping the client move toward the ultimate big goal.

Activity scheduling. An actual form can be used to have clients schedule their daily activities on an hour-by-hour basis to aid them in using their time more productively and effectively and reaping the cognitive and behavioral benefits of doing so.

Behavioral experiment. This is used in an effort to help clients behaviorally test out the validity of beliefs they hold. Clients may be asked to do something out of the ordinary (for them) in order to evaluate the results and their ability to handle the potential disapproval of others.

Fixed role therapy. People often wait to feel motivated or hopeful or happy before engaging in behaviors that support those thoughts and feelings. With some clients it is possible to jump start those thoughts and feelings by having the client agree to engage in some of the behaviors that would indicate success in those areas whether or not he or she "feels" like it.

The use of homework. The use of homework or between-session assignments is essential to CBT. Because the main objective of the approach is to help clients make effective and lasting changes in their lives, it is crucial that whatever is being discovered in the sessions be applied in the client's real life. The homework becomes the thread that connects the different sessions. By specifically doing something between sessions, clients are being educated to become their own therapist. After all, when therapy ends, everything is homework.

CONCLUSION

T HE PURPOSE OF this chapter is to provide a general overview of the cognitive behavioral history, model, and techniques and their application to counseling practice. CBT employs a number of distinct and unique therapeutic strategies in its practice. It is a collaborative effort and process between therapist and client, relying on the client's goals for therapy and in his or her life. This dynamic and exciting approach to therapy can be tailored to every client. By building on past successful efforts and avoiding avenues that have proven ineffective, therapists stand a better chance of helping their clients and establishing credibility with them.

REFERENCES

Ansbacher, H., & Ansbacher, R. (1964). *The individual psychology of Alfred Adler*. New York: Basic Books.

Beck, J. S. (1995). *Cognitive therapy: Basics and beyond*. New York: Guilford Press.

Beck, J. S., Rush, A. J., Shaw, B. F., & Emery, G. (1979). *Cognitive therapy and depression*. New York: Guilford Press.

Burns, D. (1980). *Feeling good*. New York: William Morrow.

Ellis, A., & Dryden, W. (2007). *The practice of rational emotive behavior therapy* (2nd ed.). New York: Springer Publishing.

Ellis, A., & Maclaren, C. (1998). *REBT: A therapist's guide*. Atascodero, CA: Impact.

Freeman, A., Felgoise, S. H., Nezu, A. M., Nezu, K. M., & Reinecke, M. (2005). *Encyclopedia of cognitive behavior therapy*. New York: Springer Publishing.

Freeman, A., Pretzer, J., Fleming, B., & Simon, K. (1990). *Clinical applications of cognitive therapy*. New York: Plenum.

Freeman, A., Pretzer, J., Fleming, B., & Simon, K. (2004). *Clinical applications of cognitive therapy* (2nd ed.). New York: Kluwer.

Goldfried, M. R. (1995). *From cognitive behavior therapy to psychotherapy integration: An evolving view*. New York: Springer Publishing.

Hayes, S. T., Strosahl, K. D., & Wilson, K. G. (1999). *Acceptance and commitment therapy: An experiential approach to behavior change*. New York: Guilford Press.

Jaremko, M., & Meichenbaum, D. (1983). *Stress reduction and prevention*. New York: Plenum.

Lazarus, A. A. (1981). *The practice of multimodal therapy: Systematic, comprehensive, and effective psychotherapy*. Baltimore: Johns Hopkins University Press.

Linehan, M. M. (1993). *Cognitive-behavioral treatment of borderline personality disorder*. New York: Guilford Press.

Linehan, M. M., Dimeff, L. A., & Koerner, K. (2007). *Dialectical behavior therapy in clinical practice: Applications across disorders*. New York: Guilford Press.

McMullin, R. E. (2000). *The new handbook of cognitive therapy techniques.* New York: W. W. Norton.

Meichenbaum, D. (1977). *Cognitive behavior modification.* New York: Plenum.

Ryle, A. (1995). *Cognitive analytic therapy: Developments in theory and practice.* Chichester, England: John Wiley & Sons.

Young, J. E., Klosko, J. S., & Weishaar, M. E. (2003). *Schema therapy: A practical guide.* New York: Guilford Press.

30

Reality Therapy

PAUL P. ALSTON

WHAT IS REALITY THERAPY?

IN HIS BOOK *Reality Therapy,* first published in 1965, Dr. William Glasser relates a conversation he had with his friend and mentor, Dr. G. L. Harrington. Toward the end of his training in psychiatry, which included a focus in psychoanalysis, Dr. Glasser expressed doubts about some of the basic tenets of psychoanalysis. Dr. Harrington reached across the desk, shook his hand, and said, "Join the club" (Glasser, 1965, p. 1). Dr. Glasser was surprised that his friend shared many of his views and vowed to develop an approach that was an "effective psychiatric treatment different from that generally accepted today" (p. 3).

Glasser's initial approach, described in *Reality Therapy* (1965), was designed to help people meet two basic human needs: "the need to love and be loved and the need to feel that we are worthwhile to ourselves and to others" (p. 9). To meet these needs, he believed people must become realistic and responsible and they must understand right and wrong. That is to say, people must learn to meet their needs without depriving others of their ability to meet their needs.

The therapeutic approach described in *Reality Therapy* achieved remarkable success, and the principles and practices were adopted by numerous counselors, especially those working with "hard to reach populations" such as disaffected youth and prisoners. Dr. Glasser, however, continued to update and revise not only the theory, but also aspects of recommended counselor practice. Perhaps the greatest change was made by Dr. Glasser when he incorporated the theory and principles of control theory into reality therapy (Glasser, 1998). The newer theoretical basis for reality therapy is described in his books *Control*

Theory in the Practice of Reality Therapy (1989) and *Choice Theory: A New Psychology of Personal Freedom* (1998, 2000). With this new approach, people are viewed as having five basic needs that must be met in order to feel good about their lives:

1. Love and belonging (supportive relationships)
2. Power (achievement and feeling worthwhile)
3. Fun (pleasure and enjoyment)
4. Freedom (autonomy, independence)
5. Survival (food, shelter)

Except for survival, a need that is met at least in most cultures and societies today, people spend their time and energy trying to meet these needs. It is important to note that difficulty in meeting those needs usually involves problems in relationships. For example, while freedom or autonomy would not seem to involve or require relationships, difficulties in meeting this need usually involve conflict with others. This led Dr. Glasser (1998) to conclude that all client problems are, at some level, problems in relationships. The counselor's role is to perform the following:

1. Assist clients to meet their needs in ways that are consistent with the clients' view/perception of success
2. Do not "break the rules" of the culture or society

USING A REALITY THERAPY APPROACH WITH CLIENTS

REALITY THERAPY FALLS within the general category of cognitive behavioral approaches and provides a framework that gives focus and structure to the process of working with clients. Rapport is emphasized, and a trusting relationship with the client is considered critical to effectiveness. It is understood that this can take longer with some clients, but the relationship is necessary for the client to be willing to take a look at himself or herself.

Clients' willingness to share their preferences and wants and consider the effectiveness of their own behavior is a crucial component of this approach. The process and techniques used in reality therapy are designed to encourage this in clients. Reality therapy is based theoretically on choice theory, and on the belief that clients are trying to meet the needs listed above. If they are unsatisfied or experiencing difficulty, it is because they do not feel one or more of these needs are being satisfactorily met. The role of the therapist is to assist clients in exploring which of their needs are not being met and in developing more effective behaviors/approaches to meet their need(s). Dr. Robert Wubbolding (2000) has developed a set of procedures that provide structure to this process. Referred to as WDEP (wants, direction/doing, evaluation, plan), the process serves as a guide to exploration and planning with a client.

The *W* or *wants* asks clients to clarify what they want in a number of life areas, including themselves, the world, spouses, work/boss, friends, spirituality, and any other area that appears important. Clients are viewed as having a personal so-called quality world in which they have specific pictures or expectations of ways their needs could or should be met. This is explored in detail so that the client can develop a clear picture of what he or she wants from life, relationships, and the world.

The *D* then moves the focus of counseling to the *direction* in which the clients' current behavior is taking them and asks clients to assess whether this is where they wish to go. It should be emphasized that the client is asked to make those judgments, not the therapist. "These questions are global and are an attempt to help clients increase their awareness of what their choices look like from a distance" (Wubbolding, 2000, p. 105). The *D* also stands for *doing,* and the therapist asks clients what exactly they are doing. This encourages clients to become more specific in describing their behavior, especially in areas of concern. Reality therapy is primarily behavioral in its approach to solutions. Clients are asked what they are doing, and what specific actions they are taking to make their preferences more likely to be realized in real life.

The *E* stands for *evaluation*. This is self-evaluation by the client, not the therapist, and it is considered the core of reality therapy. Clients are asked to make judgments about their own behaviors, not just describe them. They are asked whether their lives are the way they want them to be, whether what they want is realistic and helpful, and whether their behaviors are effective in getting them what they want (Wubbolding, 2000). Wubbolding notes that many people repeat behaviors that are not helpful or are even harmful, and thus need to be encouraged to ask, "Is this really helping me?" (p. 111). If the answer is no, then the client must consider relinquishing that behavior and developing another approach that is more likely to achieve what the client wants.

Evaluation also includes an assessment of how realistic or attainable goals are. One of the realities of life is that we do not have the power to change other people, and realistic assessments must take this into account. This process is cognitive, because the client is asked to make a judgment about how realistic a goal or preference is. If the conclusion is that a particular goal (e.g., a closer relationship with another person, promotion at work) is unrealistic, then clients are asked to consider changing the "pictures" they have in their heads about how to meet certain needs.

For example, a client may be asked to consider replacing the picture of a currently desired person with another person, or to consider other ways to meet needs for supportive relationships. If a desired promotion is deemed unlikely, the client may be asked to consider other ways to meet the need for achievement, which could include changing jobs or careers, or perhaps changing the way the person views the current job. The process of changing pictures of success may be difficult, but it is an important part of the process. Goals and behaviors must be realistic to have a reasonable chance for success, and at times clients may have to adjust their goals. The success of this process requires that the counselor and client have a trusting relationship. Reality therapy maintains that the counselor–client relationship is crucial to success.

The fourth stage of this process, the *P*, stands for *plan*. Assuming that clients have not decided that their lives are fine in every respect, they are asked to "make plans to more effectively fulfill their wants and needs without infringing on the rights of others to do the same" (Wubbolding, 2000, p. 150). The therapist might ask questions such as, "What would you like to do differently?" or "What could you do that might get better results?" or other questions designed to encourage clients to look at changing behaviors in order to achieve more satisfactory results. Plans are typically simple behavioral plans that are within the ability of the client to carry out, not requiring the assistance or cooperation of others. Wubbolding states that good plans are "simple/understandable, attainable/realistic, measurable/exact, immediate/soon, assisted by helper as needed, controlled by client, committed to, and consistent/repetitive" (p. 150).

The client's commitment to the plan is considered crucial to success. Planning occurs in three stages: "Could you?" "Would you?" and "Will you?" (Wubbolding, 2000, p. 151). The client is asked to make a strong specific commitment to carrying out the plan, and reality therapy suggests that often a written plan signed by the client to emphasize this commitment is useful.

Subsequent sessions of reality therapy are used to evaluate the effectiveness of the plans/solutions being carried out. If the client, for whatever reason, fails to carry out the agreed-upon plan, the reality therapy therapist does not criticize or berate the client. The therapist asks the client to evaluate this behavior (Did this help?), and make additional plans for the next period. An effort is then made to again get a commitment to carry out the original (or another) plan. Typically, success is achieved when the client develops behaviors that are more effective in meeting his or her needs. On occasion, clients may need to adjust their picture of how to meet a need (e.g., no matter what they do, a desired person is not interested in them) by changing to a more realistic picture of success.

How Clients Resolve Problems or Issues

MANY CLIENT PROBLEMS are the result of not making functional or realistic choices regarding their lives and behaviors. This may be for a variety of reasons, but for many, the failure is related to a lack of control over their lives. Many people lack confidence in their ability to make meaningful changes (learned helplessness), and therefore they adopt a reactive rather than a proactive approach to life. Also, clients may make choices that do not have reasonable chances of achieving their goals because they have not systematically assessed how their behaviors match up with their goals. They behave this way because that is just "who they are," which is a way of saying that this is the way they habitually behave or respond. They have not systematically evaluated the effectiveness of their behaviors. This lack of attention may be acceptable if habitual behaviors are working reasonably well, but if a person is experiencing frustration because some of his or her needs are not being met, the behaviors in this area deserve attention.

Problem behaviors may persist for other reasons, including lack of attention to or even a denial of consequences. Also, there may be conflict between short- and long-term consequences of behavior. Short-term consequences may be positive while long-term consequences are negative, but the remote consequences are ignored. The classic example of this is substance abuse, where long-term consequences of the behaviors are either denied or ignored. Realistically, however, all consequences must be considered when evaluating the usefulness of behaviors.

Clients resolve problems by confronting them. The focus during the early part of reality therapy is on having clients confront the effectiveness of their current behaviors in meeting their needs/goals. Clients are asked to look initially at what their goals and values are and then asked to assess whether their current behaviors are getting them "where they want to go." While this appears quite straightforward and perhaps even simplistic, the personal assessment and goal setting are critical to constructive change.

Goal establishment is the critical first stage in helping clients begin to make progress. It is essential that clients assess where they are in terms of meeting their needs in the areas mentioned above. They are asked to look at each of these areas and assess their satisfaction with the results. If they are unhappy in an area, they are then asked what they would view as success; what pictures they have in their heads that represent what they "really want." Clients are encouraged to be clear and specific about what they want out of life in each area.

Clients are then asked to assess the effectiveness of their current behaviors. In some, perhaps most, areas they may feel good about the results they are getting. In areas where they are somewhat dissatisfied, they are asked to examine what they are doing to get what they want. Then they are asked to evaluate whether this is working: "Is this behavior getting you what you want?" If the answer is no, then other behaviors or approaches are examined.

Assisting clients to be specific in examining their values and goals (what they want) is helpful in itself, and it also provides the basis for confronting ineffective behaviors. The evaluation clients are consistently asked to make is whether current behaviors are working, and this judgment requires clients to have a clear picture of what they want. Clients then can adopt behaviors that are more likely to help them meet their needs, and this is the path to greater personal success.

How to Foster Client Motivation

Client motivation is fostered by several factors, one of which is the attitude and perspective of the reality therapy counselor. A positive, trusting relationship is crucial to success, and the reality therapy counselor maintains an attitude of interest in and respect for the client. The counselor considers that clients have the ability to evaluate their own behavior and make better choices. This positive, caring attitude and "never-give-up" approach fosters client willingness to look at personal goals and behaviors and evaluate how realistic and effective they are. The positive, respectful attitude also affects client attitudes toward themselves (Pygmalion effect) and encourages the belief that things could be different and better.

The reality therapy focus on specific *do plans* and on a commitment to make changes in behavior is also motivating. These plans specify a change in behavior targeted at a specific problem or issue, and the client is asked to make a commitment (often in writing) to carry out the plan. The client is aware that the success of the plan will be discussed at the next session. Two aspects of this are motivating. One, the personal commitment to carry out a plan is motivating, since clients typically feel a need to honor their commitments. Second, knowledge that there is accountability in the form of looking at the success of the plan at the next session encourages the client to actually make changes in behavior.

A third motivator is behavioral. As the client makes changes and achieves some success, the client begins to feel better. Success also provides proof that the client can make positive changes and become more successful. This success becomes its own reward and is motivating for additional efforts to improve.

The Uniqueness of Reality Therapy

One of the most notable differences between reality therapy and other counseling approaches is that it does not accept the traditional view of mental illness and does not believe that psychiatric diagnoses are particularly useful in treatment. The focus is on client behavior and whether it is effective in meeting the needs of the client. Also, unlike some other approaches, reality therapy does not focus on the past and does not focus on symptoms. The focus is on present behaviors and how they may affect the future.

Another somewhat unique aspect of reality therapy is its insistence that clients first clarify in specific terms their wants (mental pictures) and goals; then these are used as a basis for systematically evaluating the effectiveness of behaviors. The insistence that clients, not the therapist, evaluate the effectiveness of client behaviors is a focal point of the approach. The use of do plans that involve specific changes in behavior that clients are asked to commit to, while not original with reality therapy, is also a focus of this approach. The counselor skills and knowledge required to conduct reality therapy are not unique. However, the process and areas of focus are unique and provide a structure that allows clients to gain control of their lives and use these principles throughout their lives.

REFERENCES

Glasser, W. (1965). *Reality therapy: A new approach to psychiatry*. New York: Harper & Row.

Glasser, W. (1998). *Choice theory: A new psychology of personal freedom*. New York: HarperCollins.

Glasser, W. (2000). *Counseling with choice theory: The new reality therapy*. New York: HarperCollins.

Wubbolding, R. (2000). *Reality therapy for the 21st century*. Muncie, IN: Taylor & Francis.

31

Existential-Humanistic Psychotherapy

KIRK J. SCHNEIDER

EXISTENTIAL-HUMANISTIC (E-H) psychotherapy is a coalescence of American humanistic psychology, which emphasized optimism, potential, and relatively rapid transformation, with European existential philosophy and psychology, which underscored challenge, uncertainty, and relatively gradual transformation (Burston, 2003; Moss, 2001; Yalom, 1980). On the humanistic side, E-H therapy drew its inspiration from such luminaries as Abraham Maslow, Carl Rogers, and Frederick (Fritz) Perls, and on the existential side, from such notables as Soren Kierkegaard, Friedrich Nietzsche, Martin Heidegger, and Jean Paul Sartre, as well as the methodological brilliance of Edmund Husserl, Maurice Merleau-Ponty, and William James (see Moss, 2001; Schneider, 2003; and Schneider & May, 1995, for elaborations).

Taken together, contemporary E-H therapy reflects a dynamic middle ground between circumspection and optimism, struggle and possibility, and realism and capacity for change (Bugental, 1987; May, 1981; Mendelowitz & Schneider, 2008; Schneider, 2003, 2008; Yalom, 1980). E-H therapy acknowledges the difficulties of transformation, but also the power of relationship, experiential searching, and responsibility to effect such transformation. At its best, E-H therapy neither under- nor overestimates human liberation; life in its paradoxical fullness, and indeed intensity, is the E-H therapist's domain (May, 1981; Schneider, 1999, 2004).

The thrust of E-H therapy, as Rollo May (1981), its founding spokesperson, put it, is "to set clients free," physically, cognitively, and emotionally (p. 19). Freedom is understood as the cultivation of choice within the natural and self-imposed (e.g., cultural) limits of living. Choice is understood further as responsibility, the "ability to respond" to the myriad forces within and about one. Although many forces are recognized as restrictive of the human capacity for choice, for example, influences that May (1981) termed *destiny*—genes, biology, culture, circumstance—they are nevertheless highly mutative, according to E-H theorists, in light of—and through the tussle with—choice. For E-H therapists, choice is the key to an engaged and meaningful life.

The second major concern of E-H therapy is the cultivation not just of intellectual or calculative decision making but decision making that is felt, sensed, or in short, experienced. The stress on the experiential is one of the primary areas of distinction between existential and other (e.g., cognitive behavioral, psychoanalytical) modes of practice. The experiential mode is characterized by four basic dimensions: immediacy, affectivity, kinesthesia (or embodiment), and profundity (or significance of impact; Schneider, 2008). By immediacy, E-H therapists mean that experience is fresh, living, "here and now"; by affectivity, we mean experience is distinguished by feeling or passion; by kinesthesia, we mean experience that is embodied or intensively sensed; and by profundity, we mean experience that has depth, impact, and transcendent significance.

The third major emphasis of E-H therapy is responsibility to (or the ability to respond to) newfound experiential understandings (May, 1981; Schneider, 2008). Responsibility is distinguished by the ability to face and transform experiential awareness into full-fledged values, directions, and actions. Generally, responsibility begins with acknowledgment of painful affects, for example, guilt, resignation, vengefulness, and rage; then it graduates to a realization of the significance of those affects for one's life; and finally, it manifests in some identifiable actions in the world, for example, a project, an expanded relationship, or a new job. However, the assumption of responsibility often leads to something much greater, something that cannot simply be characterized by identifiable behaviors, but in a renewed *freedom to be*. This freedom to be maximizes one's experience of life—both in its heights and its depths—not just identifiable goals. I (Schneider, 2004, 2008) call this *global transformation* in E-H therapy, the rediscovery of one's capacity for awe—the capacity to both humble oneself before, and marvel at, inquire into, life.

E-H therapists have a variety of means by which to facilitate the capacities for freedom, experiential reflection, and responsibility.

Some, such as Irvin Yalom (1980, 1989), emphasize the support and challenges of the therapist-client relationship to facilitate liberation. Yalom stresses the building of rapport and repeated challenges to clients to take responsibility for their difficulties. Further, Yalom homes in on the immediate and affective elements of his therapeutic contacts but refers little to the kinesthetic or somatic components.

Following the philosopher Martin Buber, Maurice Friedman (1995) also homes in on the interpersonal relationship but stresses the dimension of authenticity or the *I-thou* encounter as the key therapeutic dimension. The I-thou encounter, according to Friedman, is the dialectical process of being both present to and confirming of oneself, while simultaneously being open to and confirming of the other. The result of such an encounter is a "healing through meeting," as Friedman (1995, p. 309) put it, which is a healing of trust, deep self-searching, and responsibility. Through the therapist's I-thou encounter, in other words, the client is inspired to trust, enhance self-awareness, and take charge of his or her own distinct plight.

James Bugental (1976, 1987), on the other hand, accents the *intra* personal dimensions of freedom, experiential reflection, and responsibility. For Bugental, choice and responsibility are facilitated, not merely or mainly through therapist and client encounter, but through concerted invitations (and sometimes challenges) to clients to attend to their subtlest internal processes—flashes of feeling, twinges of sensation, and glimpses of imagination. Via these means, according to Bugental, clients discover their deepest yearnings, their strongest desires, but also, and equally, their thorniest impediments to these impulses. Bugental uses the example of the space suit to illustrate both the survival value and imprisonment of clients' self-world constructions of their lives. By supporting clients to grapple with the rivaling sides of themselves, both the side that endeavors to liberate and break through, as well as the side that conspires to hold the person back and regress them to a safer or earlier stage of functioning, Bugental helps clients to elucidate their conflicts, vivify their meanings, and renegotiate them into a fuller and more empowered state of functioning.

Similarly, Rollo May (1969, 1981) stresses the cultivation of what he terms *intentionality* in the therapeutic relationship. By intentionality, May refers to the "whole bodied" direction, orientation, or purpose that can result from E-H therapy. In his case examples, May shows how intellectualized or behaviorally programmed interventions persistently fall short with respect to the cultivation of intentionality, whereas profound struggle, both between the therapist and client and within the client, can, if appropriately supported, lead to such a quality. For May (as with most E-H therapists), the struggle for identity is essential—enhancing clarity, agency, and ultimately, commitment or intentionality in the engagement of one's life (Bohart & Tallman, 1999).

Finally, I have synthesized the above approaches to E-H therapy with an overarching approach that I term *existential-integrative* (EI) therapy (Schneider, 1999, 2008). Although in its early stages of development, the EI approach is gaining a notable base of support (e.g., see Schneider, 2008; and Schneider & Krug, in press, for an elaboration). In its essence, the EI model is one way to understand and coordinate a variety of therapeutic modalities within an overarching existential or experiential context. Each modality, in other words, is viewed as a "liberation condition," that encompasses ever-widening capacities for choice (e.g., from the physiological [medical], to the environmental [behavioral], to the intellectual [cognitive], to the psychosexual and relational [psychoanalytic], to the intersituational [or experiential]). The client's desire and capacity for change, which is in part determined by the therapist–client field, is the chief criterion by which modes may be engaged and transcended. For example, once a client has gained a foothold using techniques of cognitive behavior therapy, he or she may be ready for and desirous of a deeper level of contact.

THERAPEUTIC STANCES

THE EI APPROACH, which broadens E-H therapy's application to a diagnostically and ethnically diverse client base, is characterized by four basic stances. These stances are relevant to each of the liberation conditions but become integral at the experiential level of contact. They are (1) the cultivation of therapeutic presence (presence as ground); (2) the activation of therapeutic presence through struggle (presence as goal); (3) the encounter with the resistance to therapeutic struggle; and (4) the coalescence of the meaning, intentionality, and awe that can result from the struggle (Schneider, 2003; Schneider & Krug, in press). Please note that the following synopses cover the barest details of the above liberation conditions. For fuller elaborations, see Schneider (2003, 2008) and Schneider and Krug (in press).

THE CULTIVATION OF THERAPEUTIC PRESENCE: PRESENCE AS GROUND

PRESENCE IS THE soup, the seedbed of substantive E-H work (Yalom, 1980). Put more formally, presence holds and illuminates that which is palpably relevant (or "charged") within the client and between the client and therapist (Schneider, 2008).

Presence, in other words, provides two basic functions: an illuminating and a safety function. The illuminating function vivifies the construction of clients' (and therapists') experiential worlds, both the possibilities of those worlds and the blocks to manifesting those possibilities. Presence also illuminates clients' desires and capacities for change. This illumination helps, in turn, to guide the direction of therapy.

Second, presence provides a safety function or what Erik Craig (1986) calls sanctuary. This sense of sanctuary—or sacred space—holds and supports clients in the process of their struggle.

THE ACTIVATION OF THERAPEUTIC PRESENCE THROUGH INNER STRUGGLE: PRESENCE AS GOAL

As SUGGESTED ABOVE, presence not only forms the ground for E-H encounter, it also culminates in its goal. To the extent that clients can attune, at the most embodied levels, to their severest conflicts, healing in the E-H framework is likely to ensue. This healing is a kind of reoccupation of oneself—an immersion in the parts of oneself that one has designed a lifetime to avoid; and it is an integration thereby of the potential or openings that become manifest through that reoccupation. The question for this particular phase of the therapeutic process is, What are the ways and means to activate presence in the client? Or, how can therapists help to mobilize clients' presence (Bugental, 1987)?

Questions such as "Can you say more?" or "How does it feel to make that statement?" or "What really matters about what you've conveyed?" can help clients to mobilize their presence to emergent or conflictive material. There are myriad other ways to catalyze clients' presence (e.g., see my formulation of "embodied meditation," which involves somatic explorations of emergent and conflictive states [Schneider, 2008]). However, the upshot of the mobilization or activation of presence is to help clients "dwell" in previously "condemned" parts of themselves, and thereby assume responsibility for a fuller and more deliberative existence.

THE ENCOUNTER WITH THE RESISTANCE TO THERAPEUTIC STRUGGLE

As CLIENTS IMMERSE in the parts of themselves that they formerly denied, and as they begin to realize the stakes in those immersions, they are often terrified by the implications. Although change is welcome at one level by most clients, it is abhorred at another, and so the delicate problem of resistance or *blocks* to the activation of presence must be addressed. Resistances or "protections" as they are now increasingly called, are often approached in two basic ways—through *alerting* clients to how they stop or divert themselves from a fuller experiential engagement, and very occasionally (and circumspectly!) by *alarming* clients about this stoppage or diversion (Schneider, 2008). Resistance work must be artfully engaged because the therapist cannot live the client's life, and it is the client who must in the end decide whether and when he or she is ready to assume fuller responsibility for his or her life.

THE COALESCENCE OF THE MEANING, INTENTIONALITY, AND AWE THAT RESULTS FROM THERAPEUTIC STRUGGLE

AS CLIENTS INTENSIFY their awareness of how they've cut themselves off from a fuller and more rewarding life, they begin not only to clarify new life meanings, they live them. Clients, in other words, develop intentionality or a whole-bodied orientation toward a new life direction or value. This is an orientation that comes, not chiefly from the introduction of outside agents, such as medicines, or systematic programs, or even rational restructuring, but from the depths of their encounter with what it means to be, here and now, in their own unique skins. This substantive transformation is what also leads, for some E-H therapy clients (and perhaps many at varying levels), to a renewed capacity to be moved by life, not just by a specific goal or life direction. I call this capacity a rediscovery of the sense of awe (humility and wonder) toward life. This sense of the bigger picture of life, and of the capacity to be deeply moved, is one of the most powerful dimensions of E-H facilitation—and distinguishes it as a premier depth and spiritual orientation (May, 1981; Schneider, 2008; Mendelowitz & Schneider, 2008).

CASE EXAMPLE

CLIENT X FELT sure that he was despicable, plaguelike, and demonic. His parents had convinced him so over a period of 18 years, and not through the usual route of abuse and punishment, but exactly the opposite, through indulgence. Client X was led to believe he was a king, a seer, and a god. He was given everything, and praised for virtually every routine move. The result: as soon as client X hit adulthood, the trials and pressures of college, dating, and vocation, his bubble burst. No longer could he live under his former illusions but now had to face his inadequacies, inabilities to compete, and far-from-developed will. The convergence of these factors sent client X into a tailspin. His view of himself completely reversed—such that he now (in his 30s) repudiated himself whereas he had earlier glorified himself, and where he once saw a titan for whom every whim was fulfilled, he now saw an outcast for whom every desire was unreachable.

The work with client X is highly illustrative of the trust dimension in the activation of—as well as resistance to—presence. Although his self-hatred was formidable, it was not irrevocable. We spent many sessions acknowledging his anguish, self-pity, and guilt. There were many times when he could go only so far with these feelings and had to warp back into the semblance of self and self-image that he had constructed as a defense. But there were times, increasingly productive times, when he could glimpse a counterpart. For example, in the midst of his self-devaluing, he might suddenly become frustrated and realize moments of self-affirmation; that is, times where he actually liked himself, and liked being alive, regardless of the strokes he would receive from doting associates. At first this realization was fleeting but eventually, as he stayed with it, it became the major counterpoint to his despairing self-reproach. Back and forth he would swing, between burning self-debasement and gleaming self-validation—including compassion, appreciation, and even exultation at being alive. This latter quality was also connected to his growing sense of outrage, not only at his outdated sense of self, but at his upbringing and his well-intentioned but clueless parents. He began to realize that his lowliness was far from an inherent defect but a product of environment, circumstance, and in part, choice. In sum, client X eventually was able to discover an expanded sense of himself. This sense was neither behaviorally engineered nor cognitively reprogrammed, but *embodied,* wrought from his mental, physical, and emotional depths.

CONCLUSION

EXISTENTIAL-HUMANISTIC THERAPY IS a coalescence of American humanistic psychology, which stresses optimism, potential, and relatively rapid transformation, with European existential philosophy and psychology, which emphasizes challenge, uncertainty, and relatively gradual transformation. E-H therapy is characterized by the cultivation of freedom, experiential reflection, and responsibility. EI therapy, or the apprehension of diverse practice modalities within an overarching existential context, is one of the latest trends within E-H practice. This therapy has the advantage of addressing a broad array of clients, diagnostic issues, and therapeutic settings. The aim of EI therapy is to facilitate client freedom (defined as the capacity for choice within the natural and self-imposed limits of living). E-I therapy proceeds on the basis of clients' desires and capacities for change, and the liberation conditions available to impact those desires and capacities. In conjunction with clients' readiness for and capability of experiential (immediate, affective, kinesthetic, and profound) change, EI and E-H therapists draw on (1) the cultivation of therapeutic presence (presence as ground); (2) the activation of therapeutic presence through struggle (presence as goal); (3) the encounter with the resistance to therapeutic struggle; and (4) the coalescence of the meaning, intentionality, and awe that can result from the struggle (and implied working through of resistance).

In short, the E-H therapeutic orientation provides a deep and broad alternative to mainstream emphases on physiological, behavioral, or cognitive change. The wide-ranging emphasis on an expanded sense of being in E-H therapy is complemented by a stark recognition of the limits and difficulties that temper, and indeed, accentuate that sense of being. The poignant challenge of this dilemma is to help people respond to, as opposed to react against, their rivaling natures. Such a response is cultivated by presence, and presence is the seedbed for choice (depth, freedom, awe). To the extent that clients can develop choice, they can lead fuller, more empowered lives (see Bugental, 1976; Schneider, 2008; Schneider & May, 1995; and Yalom, 1989 for a wide array of case reports that illustrate these postulates).

SUGGESTED READINGS/WEB RESOURCES

Becker, E. (1973). *Denial of death*. New York: Free Press.

Cooper, M. (2003). *Existential therapies*. London: Sage.

Laing, R. D. (1969). *The divided self: An existential study in sanity and madness*. Middlesex, UK: Penguin.

May, R., Angel, E., & Ellenberger, H. (Eds.). (1958). *Existence: A new dimension in psychiatry and psychology*. New York: Basic Books.

Bugental, J. F. T. (Speaker). *Existential-humanistic psychotherapy in action*. [DVD]. Psychotherapy. Available online at http://www.psychotherapy.net

Existential-Humanistic Institute (EHI): http://www.ehinstitute.org or http://www.pacificinstitute.org

Hoffman, L. *Why become an existential therapist?* Retrieved February 24, 2008, from http://www.depth-psychotherapy-network.com/Student_Section/Orientation_Overviews/Existential_Psychotherapy/Existential_Psychotherapy_Students.htm

May, R. (Speaker). (2007). *Rollo May on existential psychotherapy*. [DVD]. Psychotherapy. Available online at http://www.psychotherapy.net

Schneider, K. J. (Speaker). (2006). *Existential therapy*. [DVD and online article]. American Psychological Association Systems of Psychotherapy Series 1. Available online at htpp://www.apa.org/videos

Yalom, I. (Speaker). *Irvin Yalom: Live case consultation*. [DVD]. Psychotherapy. Available online at http://www.psychotherapy.net

REFERENCES

Bohart, A. C., & Tallman, K. (1999). *How clients make therapy work: The process of active self-healing*. Washington, DC: American Psychological Association.

Bugental, J. F. T. (1976). *The search for existential identity: Patient-therapist dialogues in humanistic psychotherapy*. San Francisco: Jossey-Bass.

Bugental, J. F. T. (1987). *The art of the psychotherapist*. New York: W. W. Norton.

Burston, D. (2003). Existentialism, humanism, and psychotherapy. *Existential Analysis, 14*, 309–319.

Craig, P. E. (1986). Sanctuary and presence: An existential view of the therapist's contribution. *The Humanistic Psychologist, 14*(1), 22–28.

Friedman, M. (1995). The case of Dawn. In K. J. Schneider & R. May (Eds.), *The psychology of existence: An integrative, clinical perspective* (pp. 308–315). New York: McGraw-Hill.

May, R. (1969). *Love and will*. New York: W. W. Norton.

May, R. (1981). *Freedom and destiny*. New York: W. W. Norton.

Mendelowitz, E., & Schneider, K. (2008). Existential psychotherapy. In R. Corsini & D. Wedding (Eds.), *Current psychotherapies* (8th ed., pp. 295–327). Belmont, CA: Thompson/Brooks/Cole.

Moss, D. (2001). The roots and genealogy of humanistic psychology. In K. J. Schneider, J. F. T. Bugental, & J. F. Pierson (Eds.), *The handbook of humanistic psychology: Leading edges in theory, practice, and research* (pp. 5–20). Thousand Oaks, CA: Sage.

Schneider, K. (1999). *The paradoxical self: Toward an understanding of our contradictory nature* (2nd ed.). Amityville, NY: Humanity Books (an imprint of Prometheus Books).

Schneider, K. (2003). Existential-humanistic psychotherapies. In A. Gurman & S. Messer (Eds.), *Essential psychotherapies* (pp. 149–181). New York: Guilford Press.

Schneider, K. (2004). *Rediscovery of awe: Splendor, mystery, and the fluid center of life*. St. Paul, MN: Paragon House.

Schneider, K. J. (2008). *Existential-integrative psychotherapy: Guideposts to the core of practice*. New York: Routledge.

Schneider, K. J., & Krug, O. T. (in press). *Existential-humanistic therapy*. Washington, DC: American Psychological Association Press.

Schneider, K. J., & May, R. (Eds.). (1995). *The psychology of existence: An integrative, clinical perspective*. New York: McGraw-Hill.

Yalom, I. (1980). *Existential psychotherapy*. New York: Basic Books.

Yalom, I. (1989). *Love's executioner*. New York: Basic Books.

32

Rational Emotive Behavior Therapy

NANDO PELUSI

RATIONAL EMOTIVE BEHAVIOR therapy (REBT), developed by Albert Ellis in the 1950s, is a founding cognitive behavioral approach to treating psychological problems and is the basis for most of the cognitive behavioral approaches as studied and practiced today. REBT is a modern interpretation and outgrowth of the Stoic and Rationalist schools of philosophy. Ellis also built on the work of Adler and Horney. Ellis augmented the famous expression by Stoic philosopher Epictetus, "We are not disturbed by things, but by the views we take of them." REBT is an extension of that quote by Epictetus.

The main tenet of REBT is that so-called irrational thinking, questionable beliefs and philosophies (mostly held semiconsciously), can negatively affect our functioning in chronic and systematic ways. Our ability to find fulfillment in life is also impacted when we needlessly create disturbances in emotions and behaviors.

REBT has given rise to various branches of cognitive therapy, but, far from being a footnote in the history of psychotherapy, REBT continues to evolve as it had since the early 1950s, when a young psychoanalyst, Albert Ellis, grew ever more displeased with the unscientific nature and inefficiency of his field (Ellis, 1994).

MAIN TENETS

RATIONAL EMOTIVE BEHAVIOR therapy holds the assumption that we want to survive and be happy, and it proposes no particular set of values other than those two. Thus, it has little to say about preferences, culture, common practices, and traditions. Practitioners (REBTers) believe that a person's preferences, whatever they are, are rarely in question. Instead, as long as the preferences break no law, they should not become a discussion in therapy. It is a humanistic psychotherapy in that it posits that we only have this one life, in all probability, and advocates a pursuit of enlightened self-interest (pursuing one's goals, while taking care not to trample on those of others). It holds as a premise that a person is largely responsible for his or her own disturbance, and that we are not disturbed by past or present adversities.

The REBT premises include assertions about our thoughts and our construal of the world, the future, and our place in it. First, REBTers find that individuals perceive events, and evaluate them, with underlying premises and assumptions. These premises and assumptions include what Ellis called "musts." The cornerstone of REBT is the goal of uprooting these musts, oughts, and shoulds. A general *demandingness* is at the root of most human disturbance according to REBT.

REBT is not a psychology of personality per se but a psychotherapy of personality change. Thus, Ellis believes that shyness, anxiety, guilt, anger, and depression can be largely overcome by awareness, practice, disputation, and risk taking. The REBTer distinguishes between appropriate negative emotions and inappropriate negative emotions. Thus, some emotions are quite negative but very functional and appropriate to the circumstance. For example, emotions such as sadness, annoyance, irritation, displeasure, and grief tend to be appropriately reflective of circumstances that thwart our goals and frustrate us. At the same time, we exaggerate and extend our negative emotions into dysfunctional ones, such as going from concern to anxiety, and sadness to helplessness. The mediating factor, that is, what we tell ourselves, what we believe, tends to be self-reinforcing. Thus, if I predict that I will fail at something because "I'm a failure," then, when I fail, I can use that experience as evidence in support of my belief. Ellis purports to parse beliefs that are specious, insidious, and irrational. It is these irrational beliefs, or iBs, that make up the B-C connection in REBT.

Ellis's elegant ABCDE method neatly encapsulates the ideal procedure in a therapeutic encounter; it is also a mnemonic summary of how humans create their own disturbances.

A. *The activating event or adversity.* Most of us assume, Ellis asserts, that adversity directly causes our pain and suffering. And often, as in the case of real frustration and physical obstacles, this is true. However, we might even imagine it to exist, predict it might commence, or it might have happened long ago.

B. *The belief system.* We don't just perceive events in the world, we also evaluate them, and it is these evaluations that could lead to disturbances such as perfectionism, absolutistic thinking, dichotomous thinking, and overgeneralizing.

C. *Consequences of beliefs.* Consequences can be both behavioral and emotional. Undesirable emotional consequences, such as anxiety or depression, are the result of beliefs. Undesirable behavioral consequences can be changed, according to REBT, when beliefs are changed.

D. *Disputation,* or questioning of the irrational beliefs. Disputation employs a logical and empirical test for some proposition. Persistent questioning of irrational beliefs, such as, "Why must I absolutely do well to accept myself?" can help uproot long-held convictions.

E. *Effective new philosophy.* An answer to the disputing question, such as, "No reason I must do well, and I can still accept myself."

The main REBT principle is that conditions in life and past experiences do not cause our disturbances directly, but what we think about them does. We create our dysfunction by blaming our upset on the environment, or on our parents and others. Ellis's main view is that we were born with a tendency to upset ourselves, but it is correctable.

The next is the principle of the musts. Of all the genera of human irrationality, we get into the most serious trouble by dogmatically making demands of others and ourselves and commanding the environment and universe to behave according to our desires. The REBT premise that we are born with a tendency to get whiny and needy and to rant and rave at ourselves and at the universe is at the core of most emotional disturbance.

THE THREE MAIN MUSTS

THE MAIN DEMANDS in REBT that constitute a wide variety of disturbances can be categorized as Three Main Musts, and their corollaries. All of these beliefs interact and affect each other in nuanced ways, and the experienced practitioner would explore how that occurs. Most of these salient beliefs contain demands, in the form of Musts:

1. Musts on self: "I must do well, I must be loved."

   First derivative: awfulness: "It's totally bad, with no possibility of improvement."
   Second derivative: "I can't stand it, it's completely intolerable."
   Third derivative: "I'm no good, I'm an inferior person."

2. Musts on others: "You must treat me well and fairly."
   Derivatives: "It's terrible, I can't stand you, and you are a no-good person."

3. Musts on the world, and conditions: "Life must be fair, the world must treat me well."
   Derivatives: "Life is too hard; it's awful, horrible, and terrible. I can't stand it, and the world is a horrible place."

These three categories of musts comprise the core irrational beliefs. They give rise to the derivatives and corollaries that typical CBT approaches focus on. Unlike CBT, REBT gives primacy to the demands that cause the cognitive distortions, such as overgeneralization and jumping to conclusions.

REBT posits that we consciously or unconsciously escalate desires and preferences, which are good and delicious, into absolute commands: oughts, shoulds, and musts. Notice that these are cognitive constructs, and therefore REBT asks, "What are you telling yourself to make yourself upset?" The implication of this question is that disturbances come not just from circumstances and adversity but from what we believe, tell ourselves, and demand.

SECONDARY DISTURBANCES

WATCHING YOUR EMOTIONS about your emotions, potentially creating a vicious cycle of being upset. It is important to establish that beliefs, and not circumstances, create disturbances, and this is known as the B-C connection. This can be simply accomplished by asking, "What are you telling yourself to make yourself upset?"

As an illustration, and in order to demonstrate the actual practice of REBT, I will attempt to demonstrate my own application of it to my own problems in writing this chapter. The first activating event in question was the very generous invitation to contribute this chapter. I hesitated and fumbled around for a couple of days before I decided to do it. During that time, I experienced mild dread, avoidance, and some shame. Now, as an experienced practitioner of REBT, I knew that those emotions were not helpful. Therefore, what did I do? Instead of quickly zapping the irrational beliefs, I turned those unhelpful emotions into a new activating event! That is, I felt dread about feeling dread! This is an important step in REBT; that is, identifying the secondary problem. Often, the secondary problem is where things really go awry.

Obviously, wanting to cure myself of this indecision, I decided to get down to work. I identified what kinds of things I was telling myself to create feelings of dread about the feelings of dread. In this manner I wanted to stop the spiraling secondary problem. I discovered that I was telling myself, "I can't stand feeling dread, and I must get over it immediately!" Now what do we do in classical REBT? We dispute! My first dispute was, "Although it's annoying, why must I get over this dread immediately?" And another question, "Why can't I stand what I don't like?" These questions are important components in REBT, because they constitute the method by which we change our philosophies and our beliefs.

But what about the answers? The answers to those pointed disputations constitute what has been called a new effective philosophy. Therefore, in this case, my new effective philosophy (at the second level) is "I definitely can stand this feeling of dread, even though I don't like it one bit!" Another answer is, "There is no reason why I must get over this dysfunctional feeling immediately!"

We just addressed my secondary problem, the dread about the dread, about whether to contribute this chapter. Regarding the decision itself, I ask myself, "What am I telling myself to create dread about writing this chapter?" In REBT we look for the demand, in this case, it was a demand on myself, that I must make the right decision, and it must be comfortable. In addition, it must be easy as well as excellent! You can see that with those beliefs, I was creating an inordinate amount of pressure on myself, and it wasn't helping me at all. And now—on to disputation.

I ask myself, "Why is it a must that I make the right decision?" Notice that I am not telling myself, "I probably will make a pretty good decision." REBT is not positive thinking per se. It is a philosophical questioning of underlying absolute premise. The answer to the disputation is that there is no reason I must make the right decision. In fact, there is no guarantee that there even is a right decision.

TYPES OF IRRATIONALITY

IN DISPUTATION, THE REBT premise is that we address the four common types of irrational beliefs. First is the must. Second is the idea that an event could be "awful." The third type of irrational thinking would involve discomfort and would be in the form of, "I can't stand it." The fourth type of irrationality includes ego, in the form of total self-rating: "This adversity is a measure of my worth as a person."

Examples of the four types of irrationality mentioned above are contained in my simple problem, "I must make the right decision or it would be terrible, I couldn't stand making an error, and it would make me a failure." This exaggerated belief can happen very quickly, subtly, and even subconsciously. The REBT therapist quickly zeros in on it and discusses it explicitly with the client.

Since I am my own client in this example, let's take them individually. First, "Why must I do well?" Answer: "There exists no reason why I absolutely must do well, and in fact, I might do poorly, but why would it be awful?" Answer: "It cannot be awful, it can only be a hassle." "Could I stand, could I tolerate, doing a poor job, and getting criticized or rejected for it?" Answer: "Although I would feel disappointment, I probably could tolerate doing a poor job, and perhaps even learn something from it in the long run." "But wouldn't that make me a failure to get rejected?" "Wouldn't it be shameful?" Answer: "It would definitely be a failure, but it could not define me as a total failure as a person, since I could succeed at some point in some other endeavor, as I have in the past."

Notice the strong preferential component; it would be vastly better to do well, and I would work toward doing well, but a lot of the anxiety-provoking demand would be dismantled, reducing unhelpful pressure, and allowing me to get on with the task at hand.

REBT has long used examples such as the one offered above to demonstrate the applicability and practical usage of its psychotherapeutic message. For many years, Albert Ellis would conduct public demonstrations with volunteers from the audience. Knowing nothing about the individual, except what was discussed in public, and using only the REBT principles, he would quickly offer what he thought were the client's irrational beliefs. The volunteer would either agree or disagree, but the process proved productive, because eventually several messages would get through: You are responsible for your irrational thinking; you have the power of overcoming emotional distress; you can change your experience of adversity; and you can do this without decades of analysis.

REFERENCE

Ellis, A. (1994). *Reason and emotion in psychotherapy*. New York: Citadel Press.

33

Behavior Therapy

GEOFFREY L. THORPE AND SANDRA T. SIGMON

A S A SYSTEMATIC approach to assessment and treatment in the mental health arena, behavior therapy arose in the 1950s when innovators in South Africa, the United Kingdom, and the United States derived new treatment procedures from the principles of conditioning and learning in the tradition of experimental psychology. Initially put forward as an alternative to psychodynamic theory and practice, behavior therapy has been characterized by its adherence to empiricism and to modern forms of behaviorism. The practice of behavior therapy has many features in common with that of other forms of psychotherapy, for example, the development of a collaborative working relationship between client and therapist. Behavior therapy is distinguished by its use of particular techniques to address specified problems, by its allegiance to psychological experimentation, and by its commitment to empirical validation.

In application to the treatment of anxiety and related disorders, behavior therapy drew inspiration from studies of classical conditioning and experimental neurosis. Joseph Wolpe's systematic desensitization, developed from learning theories popular in the 1950s and 1960s, was among the earliest techniques used with outpatients. Systematic programs of gradually confronting feared situations therapeutically, in the imagination or in real life, are familiar features of contemporary behavioral practice with anxious clients. Assertiveness training, another of Wolpe's contributions that has since been refined and developed by Arnold Lazarus and others, addresses specific social skills deficits through coaching, modeling, and role playing (Wolpe & Lazarus, 1966).

An early application of anxiety-reduction techniques based on conditioning and learning principles was described by Jones (1956), who used "graded re-education" methods to treat a professional dancer with fears of performing in public. First, she practiced dancing by herself in a private garden behind the clinic. Then she danced with an audience of one, the therapist. When she was comfortable with that, another spectator joined the therapist to observe the client's performance. After progressing through a series of steps in each of which her audience grew incrementally larger, the client could eventually dance again before a large group, without anxiety.

The principles of positive reinforcement as studied by B. F. Skinner and his associates have been essential to the theoretical foundation of behavior therapy. From the behavioral perspective, environmental contingencies that operate to encourage some behaviors and weaken others are seen all around us—in homes, schools, workplaces, and even psychiatric hospital wards. Understanding the power of behavioral contingencies to influence both normal and abnormal behavior has led to treatment advances for even the most impaired clients. Changing unhelpful environmental contingencies can help promote more fulfilling and less distressing patterns of thought, emotion, and activity.

A classic example from Schaefer and Martin (1969) illustrates the power of positive reinforcement. Several inpatients with mental retardation had started deliberately banging their heads against the wall, causing injury to themselves and concern among the staff members. The administrator was baffled, because the ward staff were caring and sympathetic individuals who always came running to offer sympathy, attention, and even candy bars whenever patients injured themselves in that way. The psychologists who were called in to consult on this remarkable behavior pattern recommended to the staff that they continue to act in sympathetic and caring ways, and to keep on giving candy to the patients on occasion—but to do so only when the patients were acting appropriately, and never immediately after they had hurt themselves by head banging!

Showing that our behavior can be affected more by our expectancies and thought processes than by actual experiences or events, Albert Bandura and others influenced behavior therapists to attend to cognitive processes as important predictors of human behavior. This movement has been termed the second wave of behavior therapy (Hayes, 2004). Treatment techniques involving self-control and self-management are viable because clients can alter the contingencies affecting their own behavior. In Bandura's social learning theory, the three key elements of behavior, personal factors, and the environment interact to determine our psychological functioning. While in this model the essential change processes are cognitive, the effective therapeutic procedures involve behavioral enactments. For example, beneficial changes in self-efficacy—one's confidence in having the capability of handling stressful situations successfully—are best achieved by such methods as participant modeling, in which a therapist guides a client by demonstrating helpful behavioral strategies. The cognitive restructuring interventions of Albert Ellis, Donald Meichenbaum, and Aaron T. Beck rest on the idea that philosophical changes can help clients to be their own therapists by choosing more realistic and constructive perspectives on their lives and situations.

Behavior therapy interventions often look very similar to psychology studies as carried out in research laboratories. Viewing a client as if, in some respects, he or she were a participant in a carefully controlled study has been a strong tradition in behavior therapy.

Rosemary Nelson-Gray and others advanced the practice of behavior therapy by focusing on the all-important matter of assessment—before, during, and after treatment. Behavioral assessment is designed to provide detailed information that focuses and directs behavioral treatment. It began with highly specific observations of particular client behaviors in narrowly delineated surroundings. For example, behavioral avoidance tests help to clarify exactly which difficulties a client is experiencing in problem-relevant situations. The field of behavioral assessment gradually expanded to include measures of cognitive schemas, automatic thoughts, and attributional styles. Based on the triple response model (e.g., Eifert & Wilson, 1991) therapists assess the behavioral domains of motor behavior, verbal behavior, and physiological responses. Behavior therapists quickly learned the importance of assessing behavior across domains. Current assessment methods include structured interviews and rating scales, self-report questionnaires, behavior samples in analogues of troublesome situations, self-monitoring, direct observation, and monitoring of psychophysiological reactivity.

The exposure principle has been central to behavior therapists' treatment of situational anxiety disorders like specific phobias and obsessive-compulsive disorder. Drawn from the principles of conditioning and extinction, these methods help clients overcome excessive and unwarranted anxiety by encouraging them to encounter feared situations systematically so as to allow extinction processes to operate, thus relieving anxiety and distress and reducing unnecessary avoidance behavior. More complex patterns, such as panic attacks and generalized anxiety disorder, have called for more inventive techniques, such as urging clients to recreate the signs and symptoms of panic deliberately so as to learn to cope with them. These interoceptive exposure exercises represent an integral component in the successful treatment of panic attacks (e.g., Gould, Otto, & Pollack, 1995). Behavior therapists David Barlow, Edna Foa, and Gail Steketee have advanced the field with innovative interventions to treat the various anxiety disorders.

In treating post-traumatic stress disorder behavior therapists have focused on exposure methods and anxiety management training.

Attributional styles, learned helplessness, and emotional processing have proven to be useful theoretical concepts guiding treatment development. Recurrent traumatic nightmares can be treated successfully by dream reorganization methods and other novel behavior therapy techniques. Based on extinction processes, exposure to avoided stimuli associated with the trauma results in decreased anxiety.

A 10-year-old boy who had been involved in two automobile accidents complained of terrifying nightmares and a reluctance to sleep alone at night. Some dream elements involved trauma-relevant stimuli such as squealing tires and cars crashing, and others were more surreal and involved mysterious bad people who were bent on harming him. The therapist used a combination of systematic desensitization and dream reorganization methods to address these problems. Client and therapist progressed through a hierarchy of imagined scenes related to the original accidents. In addition, during the therapy sessions the client practiced giving a significant twist to the bad dream elements. He imagined that a heavily armed superhero came to help him, so that together they confronted the malevolent dream figures and overcame them. After 16 treatment sessions the boy was able to sleep alone, and his nightmares had been eliminated. He was still doing well when reassessed 6 months later (Palace & Johnston, 1989).

Behavioral treatment of depression involves a spectrum of interventions that include behavioral activation and cognitive therapy methods. Arguing that the most prominent behavioral feature of depression is reduced activity, Peter Lewinsohn and others have sought to increase depressive clients' involvement in behaviors that were interesting, absorbing, and fulfilling prior to the onset of the depressive episode. Using the Pleasant Events Schedule as a pertinent assessment device, behavior therapists can help their depressive clients by identifying suitable activities and urging clients to engage in them—whether or not they would look forward to doing so. The typical observation is that clients gradually become more active and involved in life, and progressively less depressive in mood, when they make a project of deliberate engagement in potentially rewarding activities. Behavioral activation is now regarded as a stand-alone treatment for depression and has been proposed as the effective mechanism behind the success of cognitive therapy (e.g., Cuijpers, van Straten, & Warmerdam, 2007). Beck's cognitive therapy had its origins in the treatment of depression, and direct efforts to collaborate with clients in setting up mini experiments to test—and, often, dislodge—their pessimistic appraisals of self, world, and future have proved to be a significant advance in psychological care. Interventions to help clients dispute their fleeting negative automatic thoughts and their more ingrained depressive schemas have earned strong empirical support as a treatment of choice for depression.

The behavioral treatment of personality disorders proceeds by assessing the specifics of the client's areas of distress and impairment and then bringing into play appropriate techniques selected from the wide array of available interventions. Establishing an effective rapport and positive working relationship with personality-disordered clients may constitute a significant component of the initial treatment plan. Aaron Beck, Arthur Freeman, and others have described specific treatment protocols for addressing some of the personality disorders, and Marsha Linehan has developed and tested a specific multifaceted treatment for borderline personality disorder that has drawn from her years of experience in researching social skills development and emotion regulation. This dialectical behavior therapy represents an empirically supported intervention that targets emotional dysregulation by promoting a structured, predictable therapeutic environment. Problem-solving training and emotion regulation are other key elements.

Behavior therapists working with children have often found it necessary to intervene constructively with the parents also, because the implementation of contingency management programs requires the active involvement of concerned adults. Parent training methods, based on operant and classical conditioning processes, are quite successful in helping parents change environmental contingencies that maintain their children's problematic behaviors (e.g., Reyno & McGrath, 2006). In the process of helping parents deal with their children's challenging behavior, therapists are commonly enough asked to help the parents with their own issues. That was one of the factors that led to the development of behavioral couples therapy. Other influences on the development of this subfield have been social exchange theory and systems theory. Typical behavioral couples therapy interventions include behavior exchange, communication skills training, and problem-solving training, all of which have received empirical support from controlled studies.

From its inception, behavior therapy has been applied in inpatient and other residential settings to remotivate and rehabilitate institutionalized individuals with severe and persistent mental disorders. Behavior therapists have addressed the social breakdown syndrome and attempted to counteract the negative consequences of institutionalization by employing interventions drawn from operant learning principles. Specific target behaviors have included mutism, hoarding, bizarre behavior, and social withdrawal. The token economy, pioneered by Teodoro Ayllon and Nathan Azrin in the 1960s, has been shown to produce clinically significant gains in inpatient settings with patients who have grown dependent on the institution, yet for whom discharge to the community could still be a realistic option. Social skills and problem-solving training have been essential adjunctive treatments in that context.

Behavior therapy techniques have also been used extensively in the behavioral medicine area. More and more psychologists are working in medical settings and have much to offer individuals who are coping with disease, injury, trauma, and chronic illnesses. For example, relaxation techniques are commonly used to help individuals reduce anxiety before surgery or painful diagnostic tests (e.g., Manyande & Salmon, 1998). Guided imagery techniques have been used to help cancer patients cope with the aversive side effects of chemotherapy (e.g., Roffe, Schmidt, & Ernst, 2005). Activity scheduling and behavioral pacing have long been used with individuals who live with chronic pain (Patterson, 2005). Biofeedback techniques can be helpful in teaching clients how to reduce muscle tension, heart rate, and respiration rate (e.g., Schwartz & Andrasik, 2003). Cognitive restructuring is often used to help individuals challenge catastrophic or unrealistic cognitions about their medical condition (e.g., Edelman & Kidman, 2000). Stress reduction strategies are often used to prepare discharged hospital patients to cope more effectively with upcoming stressors in their lives (e.g., Antoni, Lehman, & Klibourn, 2001). Behavior therapy techniques have contributed greatly to the medical arena and have resulted in better medical and psychological outcomes.

Over the past decade, behavior therapy has experienced another shift in the focus of treatment. Mindfulness techniques, termed the third wave in behavior therapy (Hayes, 2004), have led to significant reductions in the experience of problematic behaviors. These techniques have connections to Eastern philosophies and involve having clients experience their thoughts, emotions, and physiological sensations without evaluation. Acceptance and commitment therapy (ACT) adds a values component that encourages individuals to act in accordance with their values. It has been used successfully in the treatment of anxiety disorders, substance abuse, delusions, depression, and in couples therapy (Hayes, Follette, & Linehan, 2004). Although these new techniques have demonstrated early success, more research needs to be conducted with regard to the identification of client characteristics that might best benefit from these approaches.

Its prominent coverage in current textbooks on psychotherapy, its enormous professional literature, and the documented empirical success of its applications in practically all aspects of psychopathology and its care and treatment all bear witness to the central role played by behavior therapy in the contemporary mental health scene. Thirty years ago, behavior therapists' emphasis on experimental psychology drew criticism from some professionals who viewed a concern for the empirical validation of mental health interventions as somehow antihumanistic. This unfortunate bias on the part of some critics was revealed dramatically by Woolfolk, Woolfolk, and Wilson (1977). Undergraduate and graduate students in education and related fields viewed a videotape of a teacher using behavioral interventions with children. All students saw the same videotape, but the prefatory material differed for different audiences, selected at random. Some viewers were told that the methods portrayed were based on reinforcement principles studied by B. F. Skinner. Others were told that the teacher was demonstrating humanistic educational methods. The students' ratings of the videotaped demonstration were significantly more positive when it was described as humanistic education!

Today, it is commonplace for the behavioral principles of reinforcement and extinction to be accepted as fundamental influences on human behavior in all settings in which people interact with their physical and social environments. This near-universal acceptance of the importance of conditioning and learning phenomena in educational and mental health settings is partly the result of the substantial achievements of behavior therapy in recent decades as the leading exemplar of evidence-based mental health practice.

REFERENCES

Antoni, M. H., Lehman, J. M., & Klibourn, K. M. (2001). Cognitive-behavioral stress management intervention decreases the prevalence of depression and enhances benefit finding among women under treatment for early-stage breast cancer. *Health Psychology, 20*(1), 20–32.

Cuijpers, P., van Straten, A., & Warmerdam, L. (2007). Behavioral activation treatment of depression: A meta-analysis. *Clinical Psychology Review, 127,* 318–326.

Edelman, S., & Kidman, A. D. (2000). Application of cognitive behaviour therapy to patients who have advanced cancer. *Behaviour Change, 17,* 103–110.

Eifert, G. H., & Wilson, P. H. (1991). The triple response approach to assessment: A conceptual and methodological appraisal. *Behaviour Research and Therapy, 29,* 283–292.

Gould, R. A., Otto, M. W., & Pollack, M. H. (1995). A meta-analysis of treatment outcome for panic disorder. *Clinical Psychology Review, 15,* 819–844.

Hayes, S. C. (2004). Acceptance and commitment therapy, relational frame theory, and the third wave of behavioral and cognitive therapies. *Behavior Therapy, 35,* 639–665.

Hayes, S. C., Follette, V., & Linehan, M. (2004). *Mindfulness and acceptance: Expanding the cognitive-behavioral tradition.* New York: Guilford Press.

Jones, H. G. (1956). Application of conditioning and learning techniques to the treatment of a psychiatric patient. *Journal of Abnormal and Social Psychology, 52,* 414–419.

Manyande, A., & Salmon, P. (1998). Effects of pre-operative relaxation on post-operative analgesia: Immediate increase and delayed reduction. *British Journal of Health Psychology, 3,* 215–224.

Palace, E. M., & Johnston, C. (1989). Treatment of recurrent nightmares by the dream reorganization approach. *Journal of Behavior Therapy and Experimental Psychiatry, 20,* 219–226.

Patterson, D. R. (2005). Behavioral methods for chronic pain and illness: A reconsideration and appreciation. *Rehabilitation Psychology, 50,* 312–315.

Reyno, S. M., & McGrath, P. J. (2006). Predictors of parent training efficacy for child externalizing behavior problem—a meta-analytic review. *Journal of Child Psychology and Psychiatry, 47,* 99–111.

Roffe, L., Schmidt, K., & Ernst, E. (2005). A systematic review of guided imagery as an adjuvant cancer therapy. *Psycho-Oncology, 14,* 607–617.

Schaefer, H. H., & Martin, P. L. (1969). *Behavioral therapy.* New York: McGraw-Hill.

Schwartz, M. S., & Andrasik, F. (2003). *Biofeedback: A practitioner's guide* (3rd ed.). New York: Guilford Press.

Wolpe, J., & Lazarus, A. A. (1966). *Behavior therapy techniques.* New York: Pergamon.

Woolfolk, A. E., Woolfolk, R. L., & Wilson, G. T. (1977). A rose by any other name . . . : Labeling bias and attitudes toward behavior modification. *Journal of Consulting and Clinical Psychology, 45,* 184–191.

34

The Use of Multiracial Feminism Within Counseling

LETICIA ARELLANO-MORALES

FEMINISM IS A social and political movement that focuses on improving the status of women and establishing equity among men and women (Lorber, 2001). Despite popular thought, there is not a universal feminist theory but a myriad of feminist theories (Enns, 2004; Lorber, 2001). The issue of feminism is quite controversial and its utility is often questioned. Therefore, the purpose of this chapter is to introduce the utility of multiracial feminism within clinical practice, particularly with women of color. However, brief overviews regarding feminist theory, critiques of feminist theory, and feminist therapy are provided. Lastly, while the term *women of color* is used within this chapter to reference ethnic minority women, it is used to recognize other social locations beyond race and gender, to include lesbian, poor, disabled, older, and non-American women.

BRIEF OVERVIEW OF FEMINIST THEORY

A CENTRAL TENET OF feminism is that the *personal is political*, meaning "personal problems are often connected to or influenced by the political social climate in which people live" (Enns, 2004, p. 11). While gender inequality is a cornerstone of feminist theories, feminist theories of the past half-century can be grouped into three broad categories: gender reform feminisms, gender resistance feminisms, and gender rebellion feminisms (Lorber, 2001). Briefly stated, *gender reform feminisms* (liberal, Marxist, socialist, and postcolonial) focus on women's work in the family and economy as the source of gender inequality. *Gender resistance feminisms* (radical, lesbian, psychoanalytic, and standpoint) examine oppression and exploitation of women. Lastly, *gender rebellion feminisms* (multicultural, men, social construction, postmodern, and queer theory) examine the interconnections among gender, racial category, ethnicity, religion, social class, and sexual orientation to demonstrate how individuals are both advantaged and disadvantaged in complex stratification systems (Lorber, 2001, pp. 9–13).

CRITIQUES OF FEMINIST THEORY AND PRACTICE

WOMEN OF COLOR share a rich legacy of feminist consciousness and political activism. However, many do not identify as feminists and tend to view feminism as a pursuit of "White women" (Espín, 1995). One cause of their lack of association with the feminist movement was due to the exclusionary practices of White feminists (Comas-Díaz, 1991; Espín, 1995). Feminist theory and practice was largely developed by White middle-class women (Brown, 1994; Espín, 1995) and largely focused on sexism and patriarchy. These practices negated the concerns of women of color (Bing & Reid, 1996; Brown, 1994; Espín, 1995). While women indeed experience gender oppression, their experience of gender oppression is also influenced by other factors. Therefore, the primacy of gender ignores the inseparability of gender, ethnicity, class, sexuality, and other identities in the lives of women of color (Comas-Díaz, 1991). In addition, the realities of older, ethnic, working-class (Bing & Reid, 1996), disabled, and non–North American women are often excluded within feminist theory and practice (Brown, 1994).

The area of cultural solidarity also differed among feminists. For instance, the political activism of women of color did not exclude their male counterparts, as they worked alongside their male counterparts and families. Unfortunately, they often faced conflicting loyalties. For instance, advocacy for gender equality and challenging sexism within their respective communities resulted in an array of negative responses by family or community members. In addition, when women of color participated in mainstream feminist organizations, their concerns as ethnic women were often overlooked. Regrettably, many encountered blatant racism and elitism (Bing & Reid, 1996; Espín, 1994, 1995). Furthermore, they challenged the unacknowledged racial privilege of White women. However, it is only within the past decade or so that White feminists have acknowledged these criticisms and worked toward developing antiracist practices (Brown, 1994).

FEMINIST THERAPY

F EMINIST THERAPY EMERGED approximately four decades ago to specifically address the various psychological needs of women and to correct the sexism and bias within clinical practice. Feminist therapy has evolved with respect to theory, practice, and application, as various feminist therapies and techniques exist (Enns, 2004; Evans, Kincade, Marbley, & Seem, 2005). Various counseling and personality theories can also be integrated within feminist approaches (Enns, 2004). In addition, contemporary feminist therapy includes men, both as clients and therapists (Evans et al., 2005).

Although the perspectives of women of color were often absent within the area of feminist psychology, they are valuable contributors to feminist understandings of therapy. They provide insight into the understanding of how both gender and racial biases exist in the treatment of women and in psychological theories. They also demonstrate how the understanding and awareness of oppressive factors and sociopolitical forces allows for culturally sensitive therapy with various women of color (Comas-Díaz, 1987; Espín, 1993, 1995; Vasquez, 1994). Although the literature on feminist therapy with women of color is scant, a small body of literature addresses feminist practice and culturally sensitive perspectives with women of color.

For instance, Comas-Díaz (1987) asserts that an ethnocultural perspective, coupled with feminist therapy, is applicable in working with mainland Puerto Rican women. In addition, the tenet of empowerment allows for Puerto Rican women to (1) acknowledge the deleterious effects of racism and sexism, (2) address feelings of anger and self-degradation imposed by their status as ethnic minorities, (3) perceive themselves as causal agents in achieving solutions to their problems, (4) understand the interplay between the external environment and their inner reality, and (5) perceive opportunities to change the responses from the wider society.

MULTIRACIAL FEMINISM AND CLINICAL PRACTICE

G IVEN THE EXCLUSIONARY practices of many White feminists, multiracial feminism was developed to build a coalition among feminists of color (Arellano & Ayala-Alcantar, 2004). The primary goal of the coalition was to bring to the forefront the idea of race as a power system that interacts with other oppressive social structures in the construction of gender. This idea is the cornerstone of multiracial feminism and differentiates this theory from feminist theories that fail to recognize race as a critical factor of power. Building on various intellectual perspectives, multiracial feminism, developed by Baca Zinn and Dill (2000), integrates several emergent viewpoints created by women of color. As an "evolving body of theory and practice," multiracial feminism is informed by six basic tenets (Baca Zinn & Dill, 2000, p. 26). In addition to discussing these tenets, the feminist principles identified by Comas-Díaz (1987) in her work with mainland Puerto Rican women are also integrated to illustrate how both multiracial feminism and the principle of empowerment can be applied in clinical settings with women of color.

INTERLOCKING INEQUALITIES

THE FIRST TENET of multiracial feminism proposes that gender is a social structure that is constructed by a range of interlocking inequalities. As such, gender is experienced simultaneously with other social structures, such as race, class, and sexuality. The experience of being a man or woman is interlocked with other social locations, leading to "multiple ways" that individuals experience themselves as gendered beings (Baca Zinn & Dill, 2000, p. 26). This tenet also maintains that the range of gendered experiences created by these interlocking social locations results in inequalities. That is, certain locations are more oppressive than others, as they are the consequence of multiple systems of domination. People of the same race often experience race differently depending on their social locations.

A distinctive form of feminist therapy is the analysis of social, political, and economic oppression that individually and collectively affect women (Espín, 1994). Culturally sensitive therapy includes the understanding and awareness of oppressive factors and sociopolitical forces in the lives of women of color. Caution must be taken to ensure that women of color are not pathologized or regarded as helpless victims during their assessment or treatment. Interestingly, rather than using the term *pathology*, many feminists prefer to use the phrase "problems in living or coping strategies," based on the feminist assumption that the concerns of clients are inextricably connected to the social, political, and economic factors that influence their personal choices (Enns, 2004, p. 11). Individuals are not pathologized because it is understood that their thoughts, emotions, and behaviors are congruent with living in an oppressive society. In addition, their symptoms are regarded as strategies for coping with an unhealthy environment (Brown, 1992; Enns, 2004; Worell & Remer, 2003).

Brown (1992) argues that the problems experienced by persons with limited power in society can be conceptualized as reactions to oppression. The constant exposure to oppressive forces impacts their well-being. Therefore, when working with women of color it is important for them to acknowledge the deleterious effects of racism, sexism, and classism. As part of the therapeutic process, it is important for women of color to understand the interplay between the external environment and their inner reality. Feminist therapy focuses on helping clients identify the influence of external factors, such as gender role socialization, social rules, sexism, and other types of oppression, to help them separate internal from external sources of their mental health concerns. More specifically, the focus is on changing the unhealthy external situation and the internalized effects of that external situation, rather than helping the client adapt to a dysfunctional environment (Worell & Remer, 2003).

INTERSECTIONAL NATURE OF HIERARCHIES

THE SECOND TENET of multiracial feminism proposes that all hierarchies of social life are intersectional. For example, class, race, gender, and sexuality are components of social structures and social interaction. Men and women are embedded differently in locations as a result of these intersectional hierarchies. Social locations lead to differential forms of power and subjugation. As a result, men and women experience different forms of privilege and subordination based on their race, class, gender, and sexuality. While these social structures create disadvantages for women of color, they provide unacknowledged benefits for individuals who are at the top of these hierarchies, namely Whites, the upper class, and males (Baca Zinn & Dill, 2000, p. 26). As previously stated, the presenting problems of women of color are often associated with their less powerful position in society. While they may experience powerlessness due to their gender status, the intersecting impact of racism, classism, heterosexualism, and so forth also contributes to their sense of powerlessness. A natural outcome of identifying external sources of oppression is anger. Because women of color are often in touch with their anger due to these factors, their expression of anger is regarded as the misplaced expression of an angry minority (Comas-Díaz & Greene, 1994). Consequently, it is important for women of color to address their feelings of anger and self-degradation imposed by their status as ethnic minorities. As noted by Espín (1994), the validation, facilitation, and management of that anger is a source of strength in oppressive social contexts. Examining their experience of anger as well as learning how to manage and articulate their anger in a productive manner is empowering and also aids in preventing depression.

RELATIONAL NATURE OF DOMINANCE AND SUBORDINATION

THE THIRD TENET of multiracial feminism highlights the relational nature of dominance and subordination, as power is the basis of the differences among women. Therefore, this tenet challenges the notion of a universal experience of womanhood. Differences among women due to their race are connected in systematic ways. Baca Zinn and Dill (2000) propose that dominance and subordination exist across women. More specifically, they argue that race is a decisive social structure that creates differences among women and assists in the subjugation of women of color by White women (pp. 26–27).

Counselors must be cognizant not to replicate inequity or oppression within the therapeutic relationship (Vasquez, 1994). Instead, they must create an egalitarian therapeutic relationship and share power (Enns, 2004). Great care should be given to avoid reproducing power differentials that are inherent in society, particularly among White women and women of color. It is critical for White female counselors to be cognizant of the racial privileges that they possess as White women. In addition to acknowledging their racial privilege (and certainly other privileges), counselors must clarify their values and understand their potential impact on their clients (Enns, 2004). Similarly, counselors must acknowledge their countertransference and other factors that may impact the therapeutic process.

RESILIENCE AND STRENGTHS

THE FOURTH TENET of multiracial feminism explores the interplay between social structures and women's agency. While many women of color encounter barriers due to oppressive social structures, they fight and "create viable lives for themselves, their families, and communities" (Baca Zinn & Dill, 2000, p. 27). They resist and defy powerful forces that control them, thus exemplifying their strength and resilience. Also noted are their contributions as nurturing beings. Women's focus on mutuality, interdependence, and connectedness should be regarded as signs of health, balance, and strength for their loved ones, and not as weakness of character, as described by psychological theories that devalue women and value men (Flores-Ortiz, 1998). Therefore, it is important to endorse the principle of self-determination, more specifically, the assumption that the client is the best expert on her own experience. Counselors should regard their clients as competent, strong, and capable. As such, the therapeutic process should focus on identifying their strengths and resources. Counselors should regard women of color as causal agents in achieving solutions to their problems, and not simply as helpless or passive victims. In addition, through empowerment and as agents of change, women of color will continue to perceive opportunities to change the responses from the wider society.

INCLUSION OF DIVERSE METHODOLOGIES AND THEORETICAL APPROACHES

THE FIFTH TENET of multiracial feminism suggests the use of an array of methodological and theoretical frameworks when attempting to understand the experience of gender. Feminist critiques of traditional psychological inquiry argue that it is biased due to the androcentric, ethnocentric, restrictive, hierarchical, and context-free nature of such research (Worell & Remer, 2003). Consequently, it is limited in scope and often harmful to marginalized groups. In addition to challenging the tenets of traditional scientific inquiry, feminist scholars propose that feminist research should introduce women from all social locations and their diverse concerns and social contexts. Revised research practices should also identify areas that disempower women and their effects of such disempowerment. Scientific findings should be directed to benefit women and promote societal change (Worell & Remer, 2003).

Feminist scholars propose the use of a wide range of research methods, including qualitative, ethnographic, and other types of research methods. For example, the use of qualitative research allows for the examination of the lived experiences and realities of women of color. With respect to clinical practice, feminist therapy distinguishes itself from traditional therapies based on a nonsexist frame of reference. As such, when working with women of color, counselors should incorporate appropriate therapeutic modalities and develop new techniques that are compatible with the philosophies of feminist therapy. Most important, these diverse modalities should complement the sociocultural perspectives of the client.

UNDERSTANDINGS OF DIVERSE WOMEN

THE FINAL TENET of multiracial feminism gathers understandings based on the lived experiences of diverse and changing groups of women. As noted by Comas-Díaz and Greene (1994), "women of color are culturally and emotionally distinct from mainstream White women" (p. 4) based on their lived experiences. Women of color may define themselves within the context of their family, ethnic group, sexual orientation, and so forth (Comas-Díaz & Greene, 1994). They are also multidimensional and comprise various cultural and ethnic groups. While they may share similarities based on their experiences, they comprise highly heterogeneous populations and possess multiple forms of identity. In addition, significant within-group differences also exist among women from the same ethnic group based on their social locations and lived experiences. In working with clients or conducting research, it is important that we are informed by their lived experiences to understand their social world. Unfortunately, portrayals and images of women of color are often inaccurate or racist based on stereotypes. As such, women of color are creating their own identities and integrating multiple roles and realities. They are actively engaged in the process of "testing, refining, and reshaping" their own identities and images (Baca Zinn & Dill, 2000, p. 27). A multicultural knowledge base of interdisciplinary scholarship is needed to inform our theory, practice, and research. The use of a wide range of intellectual traditions that highlight the multiple voices of women of color in their own unique modalities will further highlight the richness and plurality of their realities.

RECOMMENDED READINGS

Adleman, J., & Enguidanos, G. M. (Eds.). (1995). *Racism in the lives of women: Testimony, theory, and guides to antiracist practice*. Binghamton, NY: Harrington Park Press.

Espín, O. M., & Gawelek, M. A. (1992). Women's diversity: Ethnicity, race, class, and gender in theories of feminist psychology. In L. S. Brown & M. Ballou (Eds.), *Personality and psychopathology: Feminist reappraisals* (pp. 88–107). New York: Guilford Press.

Greene, B. (1994). African American women. In L. Comas-Díaz & B. Greene (Eds.), *Women of color: Integrating ethnic and gender identities in psychotherapy* (pp. 10–29). New York: Guilford Press.

Hamby, S. L. (2000). The importance of community in a feminist analysis of domestic violence among American Indians. *American Journal of Community Psychology, 28,* 649–669.

Hooks, B. (1991). *Ain't I a woman: Black women and feminism*. Boston: South End Press.

Kallivayalil, D. (2007). Feminist therapy: Its use and implications for south Asian immigrant survivors of domestic violence. *Women and Therapy, 30,* 109–127.

Landrine, H. (Ed.). (1995). *Bringing cultural diversity to feminist psychology; Theory, research and practice*. Washington, DC: American Psychological Association Press.

Moraga, C., & Anzaldúa, G. (Eds.). (1983). *This bridge called my back: Writings by radical women of color*. New York: Kitchen Table.

Trotman, F. K. (2000). Feminist and psychodynamic psychotherapy with African American women: Some differences. In L. Jackson & B. Greene (Eds.),

Psychotherapy with African American women: Innovations in psychodynamic perspectives and practice (pp. 251–274). New York: Guilford Press.

Vasquez, M. J. T. (2002). Latinas: Exercise and empowerment from a feminist psychodynamic perspective. *Women and Therapy, 25,* 23–38.

Walker, A. (1983). *In search of our mother's gardens: Womanist prose.* San Diego, CA: Harcourt Brace Jovanovich.

REFERENCES

Arellano, L. M., & Ayala-Alcantar, C. (2004). Multiracial feminism for Chicana/o psychology. In R. J. Velasquez, L. M. Arellano, & B. McNeill (Eds.), *Handbook of Chicana/o psychology and mental health* (pp. 215–230). Mahwah, NJ: Erlbaum.

Baca Zinn, M., & Dill, B. (2000). Theorizing difference from multiracial feminism. In M. Baca Zinn, P. Hondagneu-Sotelo, & M. A. Messner (Eds.), *Gender through the prism of difference* (pp. 23–29). Boston: Allyn & Bacon.

Bing, V. M., & Reid, P. T. (1996). Unknown women and unknowing research: Consequences of color and class in feminist psychology. In N. R. Goldberger, J. M. Tarule, B. M. Clinchy, & M. F. Belenky (Eds.), *Knowledge, difference, and power: Essays inspired by women's ways of knowing* (pp. 175–202). New York: Basic Books.

Brown, L. S. (1992). A feminist critique of the personality disorders. In L. S. Brown & M. Ballou (Eds.), *Personality and psychopathology: Feminist reappraisals* (pp. 206–228). New York: Guilford Press.

Brown, L. S. (1994). *Subversive dialogues: Theory in feminist therapy.* New York: Basic Books.

Comas-Díaz, L. (1987). Feminist therapy with mainland Puerto Rican women. *Psychology of Women Quarterly, 11,* 461–474.

Comas-Díaz, L. (1991). Feminism and diversity in psychology: The case of women of color. *Psychology of Women Quarterly, 15,* 597–609.

Comas-Díaz, L., & Greene, B. (Eds.). (1994). *Women of color: Integrating ethnic and gender identities in psychotherapy.* New York: Guilford Press.

Enns, C. Z. (2004). *Feminist theories and feminist psychotherapies: Origins, themes and diversity* (2nd ed.). New York: Haworth Press.

Espín, O. M. (1993). Feminist therapy: Not for or by White women only. *The Counseling Psychologist, 21,* 103–108.

Espín, O. M. (1994). Feminist approaches. In L. Comas-Díaz & B. Greene (Eds.), *Women of color: Integrating ethnic and gender identities in psychotherapy* (pp. 265–286). New York: Guilford Press.

Espín, O. M. (1995). On knowing you are the unknown: Women of color constructing psychology. In J. Adleman & G. M. Enguidanos (Eds.), *Racism in the lives of women: Testimony, theory, and guides to antiracist practice* (pp. 251–259). Binghamton, NY: Harrington Park Press.

Evans, K. M., Kincade, E. A., Marbley, A. F., & Seem, S. R. (2005). Feminism and feminist therapy: Lessons from the past and hopes for the future. *Journal of Counseling and Development, 83,* 269–277.

Flores-Ortiz, Y. G. (1998). Voices from the couch: The co-creation of a Chicana psychology. In C. Trujillo (Ed.), *Living Chicana theory* (pp. 102–122). Berkeley, CA: Third Woman Press.

Lorber, J. (2001). *Gender inequality: Feminist theories and politics* (2nd ed.). Los Angeles: Roxbury.

Vasquez, M. J. T. (1994). Latinas. In L. Comas-Díaz & B. Greene (Eds.), *Women of color: Integrating ethnic and gender identities in psychotherapy* (pp. 114–138). New York: Guilford Press.

Worell, J., & Remer, P. (2003). *Feminist perspectives in therapy: Empowering diverse women* (2nd ed.). Hoboken, NJ: Wiley.

35

Disability-Affirmative Therapy

RHODA OLKIN

T HE PURPOSE OF this chapter is to acquaint therapists with the major concepts of disability-affirmative therapy (D-AT), focusing on five key concepts. These include (1) special knowledge areas (developmental history as affected by a disability, models of disability, disability community and culture, and psychosocial issues); (2) using the models of disability clinically; (3) making treatment accessible; (4) case formulation; and (5) being culturally affirmative. A basic tenet of D-AT is that incorporating information about disability will inform the case formulation such that it neither overinflates nor underestimates the role of disability.

SPECIAL KNOWLEDGE AREAS FOR D-AT

T HERE ARE FOUR areas of special knowledge about disability for the therapist who wants to use D-AT. These are the effects of disability on developmental history, understanding models of disability, disability community and culture, and psychosocial issues.

DEVELOPMENTAL HISTORY

ALTHOUGH GENERALLY CHILDREN with disabilities are more like than unlike children without disabilities (Olkin, 1997), there are some aspects of developmental history that can be affected by disability. Following are six areas to explore.

What is/was the client's socioeconomic and family background? Economic disadvantage often accompanies disability. Children with disabilities are more likely than their nondisabled peers to be raised in a single-parent family, to live alone with a mother, and to live below the poverty line. Factors associated with a family member's disability can be an ongoing economic stressor, and divorce can exacerbate this stress. Siblings of a child with a disability may have been protective and/or rejecting. Disability can profoundly affect current employment status, income, and standard of living. Persons with disabilities are more likely to be unemployed and underemployed, and to live below the poverty line. They are more likely to have government support and less likely to have private insurance. Women with disabilities are especially more likely to be single, compared to women without disabilities and men with and without disabilities; men with disabilities are more likely to be single than men without disabilities. One study found that parents with disabilities had $15,000 per year less than parents without disabilities living in the same neighborhood and school district (Olkin, Abrams, Preston, & Kirshbaum, 2006). Out-of-pocket expenses can be considerable, especially when house modifications are needed (Zelman & Olkin, 2007).

How was the person taught to understand the disability, that is, what model of disability did the parents/family subscribe to? Many parents make the decision to raise their child with a disability as *normal*, that is, as much like a nondisabled child as possible. But if a child is told that he or she is just like other children when this is not the case, then disability becomes a negative attribute, one that may not be talked about. By making disability unspeakable, the child doesn't learn how to talk about disability, how to respond to others as they react to the disability, or how to think about the disability as a part of the self. If these things are not learned as a child or a teen with disability, then they must be learned as an adult with disability, sometimes in therapy.

Was the person taught advocacy skills and medical decision making? If, as discussed above, the disability was rarely overtly discussed, and the child was not taught about handling the disability, then he or she may not have the skills required for self-advocacy and medical decision making as a young adult. How does one teach one's child to make decisions about surgery, braces, or assistive technologies? What are the procedures for teaching a child to understand what reasonable accommodations are possible, and how to assertively ask for them? Parents are as much in the dark about these issues as are the children. Mental health professionals may need to fill this role of giving guidance to parents.

Did the client experience medical traumas? Many children with disabilities have histories of multiple doctor visits, invasive and/or painful procedures, hospitalizations, separation from parents, exercise regimens, restrictions in activities, overfatigue, and scary and unfamiliar environments. These medical experiences, more common for children with disabilities than for nondisabled children, are the scary experiences that can get confused with the disability, and can make the disability itself seem scary. The trauma, more than the disability per se, may be a key therapeutic issue.

What is the person's romantic and sexual history? At the risk of overgeneralization across many types of disabilities, it is probable that adolescents with disabilities have a harder time being seen as potential romantic or sexual partners. Adolescents with disabilities, particularly developmental or intellectual disabilities, may not be taught about sexuality. Information about sexual techniques that accommodate the disability is not readily available. For these and many reasons, the romantic and sexual development of teens and young adults with disabilities may be somewhat behind those of nondisabled peers. In trying to understand the client's romantic relationships, there are several questions clinicians can consider (see Table 35.1).

What is the person's abuse history? The rate of sexual and physical abuse of children with disabilities is about 2.1 times greater than for nondisabled children (Olkin, 1999), and some disabilities may be caused by or exacerbated by abuse (Cohen, 1998; Conley-Jung & Olkin, 2001; Olkin et al., 2006). This makes it imperative that clinicians ask all clients with disabilities specifically about physical and sexual abuse. The abuse may have been from a person who would not have been in the child's life if not for the disability (e.g., a caregiver, a teacher's aid, a paratransit driver) and can involve behaviors not usually thought of as abuse (e.g., taking the batteries out of a wheelchair, leaving someone in the bathtub for several hours). Furthermore, the abuse may have gone undetected for longer, and the child's creditability may be viewed as compromised. Treatment may still resemble that of nondisabled

TABLE 35.1 Questions the Clinician Can Ask About the Client's Romantic Partners

1.	Does the client feel that he or she chooses partners as much as they choose him or her, or does he or she wait to be chosen?
2.	Does he or she stay in relationships that don't work longer than he or she should for fear that no one will find him or her attractive?
3.	Is he or she indiscriminant in hooking up with partners to prove his or her appeal?
4.	Is acceptance of him or her as a person with a disability a salient feature of his or her partners?
5.	How does the disability play a role in his or her relationships?

clients, but the increased physical vulnerability and interdependence of clients with disabilities may impact the therapy.

MODELS OF DISABILITY

A SECOND AREA of consideration is how clients conceptualize disability. Three ways of understanding disability are the Moral, Medical, and Social models. In the *Moral Model* disability has symbolic meaning, often religious in nature, that emanates from character, deeds, or beliefs. Intervention is moral or religious, focused on internal aspects of the person or family, rather than on the physical self. In the *Medical Model* disability has been stripped of the moral symbolism, and now is seen as representing abnormality contained within a person's corporeal self. Such abnormality is the province of medicine, and intervention focuses on amelioration of the abnormality to the greatest extent possible. In the *Social Model* disability is a social construct, and handicap lies in the mismatch between abilities and environment. Intervention is aimed at social, economic, political, environmental, and physical arenas, rather than on personal abilities or inabilities. People with disabilities still seek medical advances, but the collective focus is on nonpathologizing of disability as a ubiquitous human condition, and solutions are sought at the systemic level (Olkin, in press).

Each model has its benefits and limitations (Olkin, 2002). The Moral Model promotes faith or connection with a greater purpose but can incur shame. The Medical Model has spurred medical and technological advances that improve the lives of people with disabilities but tends toward a paternalistic stance and a view of disability as inherently pathological. The Social Model exorcizes personal blame and promotes community but can underplay the real day-to-day realities of living with impairments. Each model is double-sided, and one goal of D-AT is to help clients realize the positive aspects of the model and decrease its negative impact.

DISABILITY CULTURE

A THIRD AREA of consideration is disability culture and community (DCC). Since disability occurs in a person who has a sex, age, race/ethnicity, and sexual orientation, disability culture is not the only cultural group to which the person belongs. DCC does not have an agreed-upon definition but can be seen as including sociopolitical, economic, legal, and educational experiences, as well as music, art, history, humor, media images, food, and social connection. It includes 10 elements that bring the DCC together, and one element that is imposed on it (see Table 35.2).

TABLE 35.2   Eleven Elements of Disability Culture and Community (DCC)

Elements of DCC	Explanation
Definition of the in-group	The group defines itself, what it is called, and who belongs. Insiders are people with disabilities, their families, and those close to them. There is a shared identity as people with disabilities who are outsiders in the able-bodied community. Insiders use language to identify themselves: *PWD*—persons with disabilities; *ABs*—able-bodied persons—or *TABs*—temporarily able bodied; *HI*—hearing impairment; *LD*—learning disabilities. Important distinctions are made: *Blind* means little to no usable sight versus *low vision;* lowercase *deaf* indicates hearing loss, uppercase *Deaf* indicates cultural affiliation with the Deaf community. In a *chair* or *chair user* refers to a wheelchair. Older terms tend to take on derogatory meanings: *mental retardation* became *developmental disabilities* (DD), then *intellectual impairments*. Some terms that are not endorsed: *Special needs* implies that the needs of PWD are outside the norm. Euphemisms generally are not used (otherwise abled, handicapable) because this implies that disability is a derogatory word. Some derogatory words are discouraged, despite their widespread use in the media: *suffering from, afflicted with, persistent vegetative state, the mentality of an eight-year-old, useless limb, the good leg and the bad leg, mentally unstable, deranged, abnormal.* One term, *crippled,* is now experienced as inflammatory, especially in its shortened version, *crip*. It is used by insiders only.
Pride and values	PWD are subject to prejudice, discrimination, and stigma. In DCC this oppression is reversed into a sense of pride, belonging, identity, advocacy, activism, struggles, and survival. Attributes or goals valued within the DCC include comfort with disability, and personal and societal advocacy skills. There is generally acknowledged to be a separate but overlapping Deaf community, and the Deaf community and DCC join together for sociopolitical, economic, and legal purposes.
Shared model of disability	The DCC is relatively unified in its adherence to the social model (versus Medical or Moral), in which disability is a social construct, and the problems related to disability are mostly from social, economic, political, and interpersonal barriers. Regrettably, the insistence on the Social Model has unintentionally alienated many communities of color, whose concepts of interdependence, extended family, and religion may make them more comfortable with other models.
Shared social and personal histories	PWD are a protected class, which defines them as a group. The category of PWD is specifically defined as a protected group in federal laws (e.g., IDEA, the Rehabilitation Act, the ADA). The DCC shares a legal and political history. Personal histories may contain experiences of hospitalization, medical traumas, rehabilitation and physical therapy, separation from parents, cruelty by other children, being taught to hide or overcome the disability. Shared memories can be one of the bonds within the DCC.

(continued)

TABLE 35.2 *(Continued)*

Elements of DCC	Explanation
Common concerns	The DCC unites on issues of improving physical access, changing attitudinal barriers to equity, achieving civil rights for persons with disabilities, addressing chronic unemployment and underemployment, and supports for community living. Hotly debated issues are stem-cell research, prenatal testing, and right-to-die legislation. The political stance upholds the dignity of the disability community.
Culture	DCC is emerging in the areas of art, music, literature, and humor. Some artists are little known outside the disability community, and others are very well known (e.g., Itzak Perlman). To be included in this group means that the disability is embraced in some way (e.g., Perlman's activism to make concert halls of the world accessible). Some artists have disabilities but this is mostly incidental to their careers, and thus they are not viewed as spokespeople for the disability community.
Disability norms	The DCC has ways of communicating nonverbally to signify who is in the group, such as use of particular words. There also are norms that are different for various disabilities, such as a chair missing at a table indicating a place for someone using a wheelchair, using teeth to hold things when using crutches or manual wheelchairs, or leaving doors open so Deaf persons can find the group without knocking. Gatherings have acceptable orders (e.g., wheelchairs in back, Deaf people and interpreters in front). Exclusion of certain types of disabilities (e.g., persons with psychiatric disorders) is discouraged.
Role models	Children with disabilities may grow up without ever having personal contact with any adult with the same type of disability. So the lack of public role models takes on added importance. Some public role models are very well known (e.g., FDR), and others are well known in the disability community but less well known outside it. The DCC prefers to pick its own role models, though sometimes they are picked by outsiders.
Expertise	PWD have been so devalued that they rarely are assumed to be experts on disability, and the field is dominated by ABs. This domination is rarely questioned. The presence of PWD is noticeable; the absence of PWD is unremarkable. Thus the slogan "Nothing about us without us," which reflects the relative absence of PWD in key decision-making roles in government, city planning, budget making, accessibility evaluation, community care development, medicine, and psychology. PWD are underrepresented in most fields, especially teaching.
Assistive technology and devices	Assistive technology (AT) is an integral part of the person, and hence of the culture. One aspect of AT is that it can be experienced as a part of the body of the person using it. For example, leaning on the back

(*continued*)

TABLE 35.2 *(Continued)*

Elements of DCC	Explanation
	of someone's wheelchair is like putting a hand on his or her shoulder. In DCC respect for the body boundaries of people with disabilities is important, and this respect extends to their assistive devices as part of their personal space. AT and devices are parts of the body, functioning as extensions of the person, performing tasks with the person (not for the person—one walks with crutches).
Enforced group definition	This feature of the DCC is enforced by outsiders and reinforced by the media. PWD are seen as a group—the disabled—despite tremendous inter- and intragroup differences. There is the presumption of shared attributes. The disability becomes the key feature of identity. Even the empirical literature often conflates disabilities, as well as disability, with illness, and results overgeneralized to all PWD. This repeated aggregation is bolstered by an us–them view: from a nondisabled perspective (i.e., us) people with disabilities are united in the feature of being not-abled (i.e., them).

There are at least four questions that can help the clinician assess the client's knowledge of and receptivity to the DCC (see Table 35.3).

PSYCHOSOCIAL ISSUES

PSYCHOSOCIAL ISSUES RELATED to disability include age of onset and visibility of the disability, managing symptoms of fatigue and pain, and emotional regulation. Generally people with disabilities endorse psychosocial issues as their biggest barriers in living with a disability, rather than physical barriers.

Later-onset disabilities. One obvious difference between early and later onset disabilities is the existence of pre- and postdisability memories and experiences for those with later onset disabilities. Although many studies seem to indicate that by 5 years after a later onset disability differences between early and later onset disabilities are negligible, this may be due to lack of sophistication in the studies in terms of research questions and theory. (Table 35.4 shows a few of the potential differences between early and late onset disabilities.) The key point here is that clinicians will need to explore the disability onset and be aware of some issues unique to earlier or to later onset disabilities but

TABLE 35.3 Four Questions to Ask Clients About Disability Culture and Community (DCC)

Questions	Comments
Does the client know there is a DCC?	Has the client been introduced to the DCC (e.g., in college, through the office of disability services)? Can the persons with disabilities (PWD) identify disability events, publications, and/or national groups?
Has the client been exposed to the DCC?	Does the client feel a kinship to the DCC? Does the client know about organizations such as Not Dead Yet (re physician-assisted suicide), ADAPT (re accessible public transportation), or the National Association of Persons With Disabilities? Does the client affiliate with any other PWD? Was the client isolated from other PWD as a child? Does the client feel alienated from PWD rather than affiliation?
Does the client desire affiliation with the DCC?	PWD often describe their initial integration into the DCC as coming home. Others may feel alienated and repulsed. There may be tremendous ambivalence about being visibly a part of a DCC that is stigmatized. Clients may fear being politically incorrect or ignorant in the DCC or come across as ignorant about disability. The client may not want to be someone who stands out in a crowd.
Does the client know how to access the DCC, and if not, can the therapist provide guidance into the DCC?	Clients with disabilities don't automatically know how to locate the DCC. Thus therapists need to be able to introduce clients to the DCC. One problem is that the DCC is not very visible; disability is the hidden minority. A few of the avenues to the DCC are (1) independent living centers; (2) technology expositions; (3) magazines; (4) disability-specific support groups; (5) disability cultural events; (6) conferences; (7) national organizations and their national and local events; (8) specialized service providers; and (9) veteran's centers. Other PWD are the greatest source of information, resource sharing, understanding, and support. At first approach to the DCC, the client may feel strange, overwhelmed, ambivalent, overstimulated, angry, or depressed, and the therapist should be prepared for these reactions. Also, not everyone will become a part of the DCC, but the choice should not be made out of fear.

should not assume that the disability onset itself is a critical feature in the therapy, especially as the onset gets more distal.

Hidden disabilities. Hidden disabilities can include intellectual disabilities, cognitive disabilities (e.g., traumatic brain injury), systemic disabilities (multiple sclerosis, diabetes), and defects in particular body systems (e.g., kidneys, heart, hearing). Some of these may have visible

TABLE 35.4 Differences in Early and Late Onset Disabilities

Early Onset Disability	Late Onset Disability
More likely to use assistive techonlogy (AT) (Olkin et al., 2006)	May have higher rates of PTSD
Disability may be traumatic if it involves separation from parents, pain, medical procedures	Disability onset may be related to trauma (e.g., car accident, gunshot wound, war casualty, stroke)
Certain early onset disabilities favor certain groups (e.g., males and autism)	Certain later onset disabilities favor certain groups (e.g., SCI in young males; MS in Whites and females)
More related to genetics and prenatal factors as well as health care in pregnancy.	More related to lifestyle, health care, nutrition, environmental factors
Less likely to get married than nondisabled peers	More likely to already be married and then become disabled
Disability affects developmental processes and early-life learning	Self-concept and self-esteem formed prior to disability
Increased risk for physical and sexual abuse in childhood	Increased risk of abuse after disability

manifestations (e.g., when someone who is deaf uses sign language), but many will not. People with hidden disabilities have to decide when and to whom to reveal the disability. The decision to reveal a hidden disability can be difficult and personal. Once the information is told to even one other person the owner loses ownership of the information, and disclosure can incur social stigma, discrimination, and prejudice. Others may be surprised or disbelieving about a disability that is not visible, or even accusatory that the disability is being used for personal gain. Although this does happen, particularly in certain settings (workers compensation, battle, educational failure), there aren't that many perks associated with disability that make it worth the deception, and the stigma and prejudice surrounding disability make deception the exception.

Managing symptoms of fatigue and pain. Many very different disabilities include fatigue as a major symptom. Fatigue due to disability can lead to a depletion of energy or failure of muscles, which require time to regenerate. People with disability-related fatigue often refer to the shape of their week, looking at the total expenditure of energy over a period of days; what one does early in the week affects that latter part of the week. Other people may misinterpret when the person with a disability declines social invitations and misascribe it to internal qualities (uninterested or unfriendly).

Many physical and systemic disabilities have pain as one of the symptoms. Pain associated with disability can be acute (e.g., from overuse) and/or chronic (e.g., joint or muscle pain). It can be nociceptive (i.e., muscle or joint pain) and/or neuropathic (i.e., nerve pain). It can range from manageable (like background white noise) to unmanageable (interferes with activities; Zelman et al., 2004); those with long-term pain have *a relationship with pain* (Zelman & Olkin, 2007). The assessment of pain is necessarily complex, and ultimately pain is a subjective experience. Clients should be asked about their experience of pain and their understanding of its role in their lives, as well as the effects of pain on activities and functional limitations; they may have accrued functional limitations over time that affect quality of life.

Emotions. Disability often is assumed to be a loss, leading to the expectation that people with disabilities mourn their losses. The stage model of response to loss (denial, depression, anger, acceptance) is then imposed on this putative loss. However, this is not borne out by research, and the assumption of loss and mourning does a great disservice to people with disabilities. Depression is not the modal response to disability onset; depression after disability is best predicted by previous depression. Defining depression as normative results in accepting a condition that should be treated as aggressively as one would for persons without disabilities. So strong is the presumption of mourning that persons with disabilities who are not depressed are often labeled as being in denial. Conversely, people with disabilities are relentlessly portrayed as brave, courageous, inspirational, plucky, miraculously able to get up each morning and function, ever with a smile, despite the disability. Thus there is the paradoxical prescription to be both in mourning over the loss yet eternally plucky. These affective prescriptions are combined with an affective prohibition against anger, because anger is interpreted as denoting maladjustment to the disability. In spite of the pervasive stigma, discrimination, and oppression of people with disabilities, anger is seen decontextualized from its social roots, and attributed to personal characteristics. This combination of prescriptions (mourn yet be plucky) and prohibitions (do not be angry) is a powerful force.

USING THE MODELS OF DISABILITY CLINICALLY IN DISABILITY-AFFIRMATIVE THERAPY

THERE ARE MULTIPLE perspectives to consider, including the model of disability of the therapist, the supervisor, the client, the client's family, and the client's immediate community. Further information to be learned is about the effects of the model on the client's experiences, the extent to which the client experiences the benefits and the drawbacks of the model, and how the client's perspective interacts with his or her social environment. D-AT presumes that the therapist adopts the social model of disability, but the therapist must not impose any model on the client. The therapist's language should reflect the client's model, because talking in a different model from the client results in a cultural mismatch that can result in early drop out. Instead the therapist should ask questions to assess the client's model (see Guber [2007] for the beginnings of a model assessment tool), the client's comfort with the model, and openness to other perspectives and models. This has to be done in a supportive way that is free of any investment in which model fits the client. The goal is to maximize the benefits of the client's own model, and minimize its deficits.

This advice to follow the client's model may seem counter to the previous description of the DCC and helping clients find the DCC. Regardless of the client's view of disability, the DCC is valuable for support and information, and virtually all families with disabilities need information. Support groups and clinics specializing in particular disorders are sources of information about local resources (schools, doctors, medical supplies, etc.). The therapist needs to become familiar with an array of resources, including those that are culturally located (e.g., in Chinatown) and accessible by public transportation.

MAKING TREATMENT ACCESSIBLE

IT IS IMPORTANT that therapy not be experienced by the client as duplicating the discrimination, limitations, and barriers experienced in the outside world. Treatment should be accessible; this refers to both physical barriers as well as attitudinal issues. Physical access incorporates issues of public transportation, handicapped parking, automatic door openers, and a bathroom with a large stall and grab bars. In the office itself the client should be able to reach the consultation area without impediment, and transfer into a chair if desired. The temperature will not be right for everyone, but people with disabilities may experience heat or cold more profoundly, so blankets and fans can be kept handy. But just as important as physical access are other less tangible ways in which therapy should be accessible. Time of day and length of the appointment can be affected (e.g., due to need for public transportation, or fatigue early or later in the day). Consent forms should be available in large print or electronically. Substance abuse treatment cannot rigidly insist on eschewing all medications, even those with mood-altering properties. These are more subtle types of making therapy not only accessible but welcoming.

In therapy there are no taboo topics, including disability. At first the therapist may be uncertain as to the degree of relevance of the disability. Knowing when to ask the relevance is a therapist skill; knowing how to ask is rather straightforward: *What is your disability? How do you think your disability might be involved in this issue? Can you tell me about how you cope with your pain/fatigue/tendency to fall/memory problems? Is there some way I can make the therapy situation more accessible to you?* Knowing what not to ask is just as important: *What is your partner's disability?* (i.e., assuming only a person with a disability would marry the client with a disability). *How do you do your grocery shopping? Do you ever wish you didn't have a disability? What do you think you'd be like if you didn't have a disability? Do you think you are depressed because you are disabled? Did you/ your parents mourn the loss of your perfect, able, self?* To test a question before asking, the therapist can try substituting another word for disability (e.g., gay, Catholic, male) to see if it still seems like a useful question.

CASE FORMULATION

THE COMMONALITY TO therapy with diverse groups is to understand how to incorporate the diversity into the case formulation in just the appropriate amount. This is hard to titrate in the abstract. *How much of what the client says is related to the disability? What does it mean to say that an issue is disability related? If a client raises experiences more common for people with disabilities, does this make it a disability issue? If the disability went away, would the clinical issue go away?* These are just some of the questions that can inform the case formulation, which should incorporate the disability into the definition of the person without becoming the thing that defines the person. Just as being, say, a female is a part of the case formulation of a woman client, it is not the sole or even the most salient or relevant feature. On the other hand, being an adolescent would play a large role in any case formulation. Sometimes disability may be figure, and sometimes ground; the trick is to figure out which for each client.

Case formulation is dependent on theory. D-AT does not presume any particular theoretical orientation. However, D-AT does blend more readily with some orientations (interpersonal therapy, family therapy, cognitive behavior therapy, feminist therapy) than with others (the psychodynamic spectrum of approaches). Regardless, all therapists can incorporate ideas of cultural responsivity within their own theory, and apply those ideas to D-AT.

CULTURALLY AFFIRMATIVE THERAPY

DISABILITY-AFFIRMATIVE THERAPY assumes that disability is not inherently pathological or deviant, and in fact has value and worth. This does not mean that disability is a blessing in disguise or a gift, rather that, in a rather Zen way, it is what it is and has value the same way sex, religion, age, sexual orientation, or ethnicity do. That value is realized in the appreciation of what has been learned from having a disability, and from incorporating that learning into one's selfhood. Even if the client is not a part of the DCC he or she can still feel a sense of community and belonging.

Although many clients, with or without disabilities, come to therapy for reduction of symptoms (e.g., depression, anxiety, stress), removal of symptoms often is not a sufficient end to therapy—reduction of depression doesn't automatically lead to ability to experience joy. A goal of therapy with clients with disabilities may need to be full inclusion and maximal functioning. Although there may be initial focus on symptom reduction, this might be followed with helping the client understand the role of the disability and take ownership of it, manage the negative reactions of some others without internalizing them, and feel a part of any peer group. Although I have asserted that people with disabilities are necessarily bicultural, straddling both disability and nondisabled worlds (Olkin, 1999), some people with disabilities are not truly in either world. Children with disabilities generally are not raised in families, neighborhoods, or classrooms with other children or adults with disabilities and thus may develop into young adults who feel left out of both disability and nondisability communities.

Therapy by a nondisabled therapist with a client who has a disability is *cross cultural therapy*. Since most therapists cannot become truly culturally competent in disability, they need to be culturally aware, informed, and receptive. If the therapist is to avoid being self-conscious and deskilled (Heller & Harris, 1987), then he or she will have to master certain tasks. These include how to talk openly about disability, how to locate information about specific disabilities, understanding what the concepts of *accessible* and *reasonable accommodation* mean in practice, becoming familiar with local resources, and how to access support groups. Since disability is a highly stigmatized condition, it is probable that the therapist has learned myriad negative messages about disability and will experience some initial discomfort. Thus one of the most important skills is understanding and managing one's countertransference. However, it is not necessary to know the latest disability terminology or slang, as long as the therapist doesn't use derogatory or value-laden language (e.g., *suffers from* cerebral palsy; *in spite of* the disability).

Disability-affirmative therapy considers the political, legal, economic, financial, social, educational, and familial, as well as the personal, impact of disability in a cultural and historical context. Therapy does not necessarily address all of these areas, but D-AT is not necessarily limited to only the personal impact of disability. Similar to feminist therapy, it might include analysis of power dynamics, openness to advocacy and activism, contextualizing of disability, awareness of life span development and of internalized ableism, understanding of oppression, a focus on strengths and empowerment, and a commitment to equity and social change.

CONCLUSION

THERAPISTS UNDERSTAND THAT they best serve clients when they are familiar with the world of the client, including the client's culture. But learning about disability culture is not easy. Disability culture, like disability itself, often is hidden from the mainstream. Disability is not a topic most people are comfortable talking about, and one in which few psychologists receive training (Olkin & Pledger, 2003). This chapter is only one perspective on conceptualizing cases in which the client has a disability. The principal goal is to help counselors take the areas outlined here and infuse them into their own knowledge and skill base.

Important counseling traits include the ability for empathy, genuineness, acceptance, and humor; D-AT presumes these basic skills but posits that they are not in themselves sufficient. Additionally, some knowledge of disability norms and culture is essential, especially in certain phases of therapy. The beginning of treatment, from the first phone call through the first session, can signal to a client that the counselor is comfortable, knowledgeable, and open about the client's culture. (For a training DVD specific to the first session, see Olkin, 2005.) For example, simply asking about pain and fatigue can demonstrate that the therapist is aware of which conditions might have these symptoms. The knowledge base would include that the stage model of response to disability has been discredited, depression is not a normal response to disability, disability is not inherently pathological, removing negatives is not enough (deficit model). In particular, clinical supervisors must be sufficiently comfortable with and knowledgeable about disability to help their supervisees conduct D-AT.

Another phase in which knowledge of disability is critical is in developing the case formulation, and the ability to appropriately incorporate disability into the case formulation without over- or underestimating its role is a key goal of D-AT. Counselors have to use their clinical skills to assess whether the formulation is accurate and, as in any therapy, be alert to negative signs such as early termination, problems in the relationship, material being left unsaid, difficulty talking openly about disability issues, and failure to progress. Sharing the case formulation with the client is one way to evaluate its fit. Although this kind of transparency is not typical of all theoretical approaches, it is recommended particularly for working with clients with disabilities, because they are used to being discussed and having decisions made about them without their input. D-AT is designed to help counselors incorporate disability knowledge and culture into the treatment, making for a powerful combination to achieve desired results.

REFERENCES

Cohen, L. J. (1998). *Mothers' perceptions of the influence of their physical disabilities on the developmental tasks of children.* Unpublished doctoral dissertation, California School of Professional Psychology, Alameda.

Conley-Jung, C., & Olkin, R. (2001). Mothers with visual impairments or blindness raising young children. *Journal of Visual Impairment and Blindness, 91*(1), 14–29.

Guber, G. (2007). *Development of the Models of Disability Assessment Questionnaire.* Unpublished doctoral dissertation, California School of Professional Psychology, San Francisco.

Heller, T., & Harris, R. I. (1987). Special considerations in the psychological assessment of hearing impaired persons. In B. W. Heller, L. M. Flohr, & L. S. Zegans (Eds.), *Psychosocial interventions with sensorially disabled persons* (pp. 53–77). Orlando, FL: Grune & Stratton.

Olkin, R. (1997). Human rights of children with disabilities. *Women and Therapy, 20*(2), 29–42.

Olkin, R. (1999). *What psychotherapists should know about disability.* New York: Guilford Press.

Olkin, R. (2002). Could you hold the door for me? Including disability in diversity. *Cultural Diversity and Ethnic Minority Psychology, 8*(2), 130–137.

Olkin, R. (2005). *Disability-affirmative therapy: A beginner's guide* (Video #460). Available online at www.Emicrotraining.com

Olkin, R. (in press). Disability-affirmative therapy and case formulation: A template for understanding disability in a clinical context. *Counseling and Human Development.*

Olkin, R., Abrams, K., Preston, P., & Kirshbaum, M. (2006). Comparison of parents with and without disabilities raising teens: Information from the NHIS and two national surveys. *Rehabilitation Psychology, 51*(1), 43–49.

Olkin, R., & Pledger, C. (2003). Can disability studies and psychology join hands? *American Psychologist, 58*(4), 296–304.

Zelman, D., & Olkin, R. (2007). Post-polio syndrome related pain: Model of a mixed neuropathic-nociceptive pain condition. *Journal of Pain, 8*(4), S22.

Zelman, D., Smith, M., Hoffman, D., Edwards, L., Reed, P., Levine, E., et al. (2004). Acceptable, manageable, and tolerable days: Patient daily goals for medication management of persistent pain. *Journal of Pain and Symptoms Management, 28*(5), 474–487.

36

Adlerian Therapy

JON CARLSON AND JEAN JOHNSON

T HE INDIVIDUAL PSYCHOLOGY of Alfred Adler is based on a holistic, phenomenological understanding of human behavior. Adler used the term *individual psychology* for his approach in order to emphasize the indivisible (undivided or whole) nature of our personalities and refers to essential unity of the individual. This approach stresses holism, noting that one cannot understand an individual in parts (reductionism), but all aspects of a person must be understood in relationship and in connection to social systems (Mosak, 2005). The phenomenological perspective suggests that each person views situations from a unique point of view. We live our lives and "act as if" our view of the world is correct. When our views are distorted, our thinking becomes faulty and our behavior becomes inappropriate. Adlerians believe that all behavior has a purpose and occurs in a social context, noting that one's cognitive orientation and *lifestyle* (literally one's style of dealing with life) is created in the first few years of life and molded within the initial social setting, the family constellation. The lifestyle is the characteristic way that we act, think, perceive, and the way we live. It is from the lifestyle that we select the methods for coping with life's challenges and tasks.

Adlerians believe that all behavior is goal directed. People continually strive to attain in the future what they believe is important or significant. Adler believed that for all people there are three basic life tasks: work, friendship, and love-intimacy. The work task is addressed when work is meaningful and satisfying. The friendship task is addressed through satisfying relationships with others. The love or intimacy task is addressed by learning to love oneself as well as another. Adlerians have outlined three additional tasks, suggesting a need to master the recreational and spiritual tasks of life (Mosak, 2005) and also the task of parenting and the family (Dinkmeyer, Dinkmeyer, & Sperry, 1987). Mentally healthy people look to master each of these tasks or challenges of life.

Adlerian theory purports that humans are all social beings and therefore all behavior is socially embedded and has social meaning (Carlson, Watts, & Maniacci, 2005). As one of the first models of psychotherapy, Adler's theory emphasized the importance of relationships, of being connected to others. A hallmark of Adlerian theory is the emphasis on social interest, which is a feeling of cooperation with people, a sense of belonging to and participating in the common good. Social interest can be equated with empathy for others, and Adlerians view social interest as a measure of mental health, noting that as social interest develops, feelings of inferiority decrease.

Adlerian psychotherapy is a psychoeducational, present/future-oriented, and time-limited (or brief) approach (Carlson et al., 2005; Watts, 2003). Adlerians espouse a growth model, noting that our fates are never fixed and that individuals are always in the process of "becoming." Adlerians believe that the person experiencing difficulties in living or so-called psychopathology is not sick, but rather discouraged (Mosak, 2005). Psychopathology is a result of mistaken notions and faulty assumptions, low social interest, discouragement, and ineffective lifestyle. The task of psychotherapy then becomes one of encouraging the client to develop more social interests and a more effective lifestyle to achieve success in the tasks of life.

The Adlerian approach is a contemporary therapy as it is cognitive behavioral, culture-sensitive/multicultural, and integrative. Adler is a chameleon in that he appears to change form depending on the background against which he stands. Practically every other theory now claims him as a grandparent (e.g., person-centered, reality therapy, constructivist, cognitive, rational emotive, cognitive behavior, integrative, or family).

Adler was not only ahead of his time but also limited by the historical era he was part of. In summarizing Adler's important contributions that have influenced current practice, one notes that many would now strike you as rather obvious because they have formed the basis of so many other theories. Adler was able to reach a different constituency by introducing the following ideas:

1. The importance of thinking processes on feelings (he was the first cognitive therapist).
2. The impact of early family experiences and birth order on present behavior (he was among the first family therapists).
3. The value of constructing specific plans of action (he was the first to emphasize action strategies to follow insights).

4. The construction of an egalitarian, collaborative counseling relationship (moving far afield from the psychoanalysts who stressed neutral authority figures). He was the first to have the client sit and face the therapist.
5. An assessment of lifestyle issues and social behavior as they affect personality development. He stressed the importance of understanding a person and his or her culture.
6. Importance of skill training and education. Rather than employing a predominately medical model for diagnosing and treating problems, he preferred a more educational model where the therapist's role was as much a teacher and consultant as a doctor.

BASIC CONCEPTS OF ADLERIAN THERAPY

THE FOLLOWING CONCEPTS provide the basic guidelines for how an Adlerian therapist works with clients. The guidelines provide a checklist of those areas that an Adlerian will view as most critical.

Holism. The assumption in Adlerian psychology is that people are different than the sum of their parts. This entails looking at people as individuals, and not as parts or part functions (e.g., id, ego, drives, emotions). The mind and the body are viewed as an interconnected process that cannot be understood when separated. The clinical implication is that a therapist should look at the whole person when doing a complete assessment. In Adlerian terms, this means exploring the client's world from a holistic perspective that takes into consideration biological and social facets as well as psychological factors.

Encouragement. The inverse of discouragement, this means to give another courage and hope. Courage occurs when clients become aware of their strengths, at the same time they feel less alienated and alone. Encouragement begins with faith in clients and moves toward helping them use all of their personal and external resources.

Subjective or private logic. Each person creates his or her own reality. This is uniquely a subjective and private process, rather than one that is objective and universally agreed upon.

Basic mistakes. These are the self-defeating aspects of an individual's lifestyle. They also represent the first examples of irrational thinking that can be disputed. Often they reflect avoidance or withdrawal from others, excessive self-interest, or the desire for power.

Basic tasks. Adler believed that the questions of life could be grouped into three major areas: (1) the problems of communal life, (2) the problems of work, and (3) the problems of love.

Lifestyle. This is the attitudinal set or personality of an individual. This includes the convictions, choices, and values people develop that influence their decisions and behaviors. Adlerians see the lifestyle as the characteristic way one moves toward life goals. Once we understand the lifestyle of individuals, we can begin to make sense of their experiences, or at the very least, to help them to develop this for themselves.

Social interest. Adlerians believe that every individual has a responsibility to the community, as well as to himself or herself. This sense of social interest is an inadequate translation of the German phrase *gemeinschaftsgefuhl*, which more resembles a kind of "community feeling." Roughly defined, this means the kind of empathic bonding people feel for each other and the responsible actions and attitudes they take toward one another. It takes into account that we all are members of the human community; we all have responsibility to create a better world.

Compensation for inferiority and superiority. All of us have inferiority feelings since there are situations in which we wish to improve. The good news, however, is that feelings of inferiority can actually serve as catalysts to help us to strive to reach our goals.

Goals and belonging. All behavior is goal directed. People are constantly striving to reach self-declared goals that they believe will lead to happiness and satisfaction. We are all trying to find our place in the social world. During this process, we may engage in behavior that is neither helpful to us and is often disruptive to others.

Family constellation and birth order. You most likely take it for granted that birth order affects the ways a person might develop, but Adler was among the first to observe that sibling position might be a critical variable to consider. Clearly, an eldest child does not grow up in the same family, nor have the same parents, as would younger brothers and sisters.

FOUR STAGES OF ADLERIAN THERAPY

THE FIRST THING you should know is that therapy proceeds along a series of progressive stages that will strike you as quite logical. The four stages of Adlerian therapy are as follows:

> *Stage I: The relationship.* The first step in any therapy encounter is to establish a collaborative relationship. This is an empathic, supportive relationship, one that is based on democratic principles and essential equality. The therapist uses all the regular skills favored by any other professional at this stage, using well-timed questions and reflections of feeling and content, in order to build a solid alliance. It is now considered standard operating procedure to use empathy and support to establish a sense of trust. If that doesn't happen first, subsequent therapeutic efforts are likely to be less than successful.

Stage II: Assessment. A thorough history is explored, including family background, belief systems, cultural heritage, personal goals, and other facets of being human. Early recollections are also collected.

Stage III: Insight and interpretation. A key approach to Adlerian therapy is to identify the thought disturbances and core fears that get in the way. Practitioners are inclined to explore with clients their self-defeating thinking patterns that contribute to distorted perceptions (Mosak & Maniacci, 1999). Adlerians refer to these as *basic mistakes* or faulty logic.

Stage IV: Reorientation. Once clients develop sufficient insight into their problems the therapy shifts to action. Insight can be a wonderful thing, but only if it leads to constructive movement toward desired goals.

Because the Adlerian approach is both insight- and action-oriented, the therapist would be more directive in helping clients to convert their self-declared goals into specific homework assignments or tasks that can be completed between sessions. Adlerian therapists will give specific assignments that involve responding in a different fashion.

SELECTIVE THERAPEUTIC STRATEGIES

REFRAMING. THIS IS a process of helping a client see the same thing from a different perspective. The intervention is based around helping people to understand that everything can really be something else. Clients are helped to look at their situations in more positive ways.

The question. This is used to determine whether a problem is primarily physiological or psychological. The therapist asks, "What would be different if your problem was gone?"

The push-button technique. Clients are asked to remember a pleasant experience and an unpleasant one. This technique shows people that they have power to change/choose their feelings. The therapist helps clients to realize that they act one way in one situation and a different way in another.

Acting "as if." This involves suggesting to clients that they act "as if" they didn't have the problem for a week or two. This pretend exercise allows the client to take actions that, previously, would have seemed outside the realm of possibility.

Encouragement. This means to build courage in your client. Courage occurs when people become aware of their strengths, feel they belong, and have hope.

Midas technique. This strategy involves exaggerating the client's neurotic demands. The exaggeration allows for the client to laugh at his or her own position. Just like King Midas got his wish, the therapist can allow the client to take this into other areas.

Pleasing someone. The therapist urges the client to do something nice for someone else, an act of grace, a mitzvah, or a loving gesture. This is based on the importance of creating social interest in clients, to reach out beyond their own suffering to help others.

Avoiding the tar baby. This is a strategy to avoid supporting the client's self-defeating behaviors. The goal is to act in ways that no longer support the client's negative self-perceptions.

MAJOR CONCERNS OF THE ADLERIAN APPROACH

IT IS NOT so much that Adler himself tried to make his theory into something for everyone as it is his followers who have found ways to do so. You can find within this theory a little bit of everything that you will recognize from other approaches. One reason for this, of course, is so many other therapists have borrowed and adapted Adler's ideas for their own purposes. Some of the trademark techniques of specific theories like "spitting in a client's soup" (Gestalt), the "miracle question" (solution-focused), "reframing" (strategic), and many others really are ideas that were originally generated by Adler.

Nevertheless, one might get the distinct impression from studying this model that it seems to wander all over the place, from attention to the past to a focus on the present, from a cognitive, to a behavioral, to an affective approach. This, however, is believed to be a good strategy because the Adlerian theory gives counselors an overall framework from which to use a host of other methods that might appeal to them.

Perhaps Adler's greatest contribution is that he developed a theory that recognized and stressed the effects of social class, racism, and sex on the behavior of individuals. His ideas, therefore, are well received by those living in today's global society.

Most of the criticisms of the Adlerian approach show a lack of understanding of how the approach has evolved. For example, contemporary Adlerians do not undertake a complete lifestyle assessment. Adlerian approaches are tailored to the client and will rely on verbal interventions, logic, and insight dependent on the client's level of understanding. Adlerians are not really interested in the past and history but rather how one views (today) the past and history. Adlerians do very effective brief therapy (Carlson & Sperry, 2000) and are able to code for a full range of psychopathology (Sperry & Carlson, 1996).

A valid criticism is that Adler was pragmatic and spent more time training and treating than theorizing; therefore, the theory is not especially well defined. In fact, his ideas are somewhat vague and general, which makes it hard to research the basic concepts.

CONCLUSION

Adler was clearly way ahead of his time. He stressed the importance of understanding people in a whole or indivisible fashion. He was a positive psychologist and stressed that we should help people by focusing on their strengths and assets. He believed in the subjective view of the client as the most important reality. He understood that when our thinking is distorted we make mistakes that prevent us from liking others, liking ourselves, and finding satisfying work. He believed that we live in a social world in which healthy people contribute to the greater good of all humankind, and each person does so in a unique manner.

REFERENCES

Carlson, J., & Sperry, L. (2000). *Brief therapy with individuals and couples.* Phoenix, AZ: Zeig & Tucker.

Carlson, J. D., Watts, R. E., & Maniacci, M. (2005). *Adlerian psychotherapy.* Washington, DC: American Psychological Association.

Dinkmeyer, D. C., Dinkmeyer, D. C., Jr., & Sperry, L. (1987). *Adlerian counseling and psychotherapy* (2nd ed.). Columbus, OH: Merrill.

Mosak, H. H. (2005). Adlerian psychotherapy. In R. J. Corsini & D. Wedding (Eds.), *Current psychotherapies* (7th ed., pp. 52–95). Belmont, CA: Brooks/Cole.

Mosak, H. H., & Maniacci, M. (1999). *A primer of Adlerian psychology: The analytic-behavioral-cognitive psychology of Alfred Adler.* Philadelphia: Accelerated Development/Taylor and Francis.

Sperry, L., & Carlson, J. (Eds.). (1996). *Psychopathology and psychotherapy: From DSM–IV diagnoses to treatment* (2nd ed.). Philadelphia: Accelerated Development/Taylor and Francis.

Watts, R. E. (2003). *Adlerian, cognitive, and constructivist therapies: An integrative dialogue.* New York: Springer Publishing.

37

Brief Psychotherapy

EVA MILLER AND IRMO MARINI

DURING THE FIRST half of the 20th century, traditional psychoanalytic and psychodynamic therapies favored frequent treatment sessions lasting for months and even years. Beginning in the 1940s, alternative approaches, such as behavioral, person-centered, and systemic methods, that were designedly short-term began to emerge as a reaction to the typical 850-session psychoanalysis that was never within reach of most individuals or mental health systems in any country (Shapiro et al., 2003). In the 1960s, the priorities of community mental health services exerted further pressures toward brief interventions that could reach more clients. Since the 1970s, many health care systems in the United States have been developing practices such as managed care to reduce the number of psychotherapy sessions. The purpose of this chapter is to (1) define brief psychotherapy, (2) provide an overview of the types of brief psychotherapy, and (3) outline some of the major theoretical concepts and techniques associated with each of these therapeutic approaches.

A HISTORICAL CONTEXT

SINCE THE ADVENT of brief psychotherapy, one of the most common questions has been, "How much therapy is enough?" (Shapiro et al., 2003, p. 212). In countries where psychotherapy is established, most clients receive brief therapy lasting no more than 25 sessions. Others have suggested that a range of 3–12 sessions is sufficient for treating most mental health traits (e.g., Rothwell, 2005; Wettersten,

Lichtenberg, & Mallinckrodt, 2005). Overall, it appears most therapists believe that 12 to 25 sessions are sufficient for stimulating positive, enduring change in clients with a wide range of mental illnesses (Shapiro et al., 2003).

It is important to note that the definition of *brief* varies depending on the theoretical orientation of the therapist (Cameron, 2006). Additionally, brief therapy is dependent on the type of mental health condition, onset of the disorder, degree of client motivation, and the therapist's ability to establish an effective therapeutic alliance and assist clients in attaining therapeutic goals (Mander, 2005). Malan (1979) is credited with being the first to establish suitable criteria for brief therapy, positing from a conservative view, that only acute illnesses among well-adjusted personalities are appropriate for facilitating brief therapy. From a radical perspective, Malan suggested that improved mental health can often be achieved in severe, chronic illnesses in which brief therapy may be more suitable than long-term approaches. Malan and other early pioneers based their criteria for brief therapy on a list of decreasing treatable conditions such as hysteria, conversion symptoms, compulsive neurosis, character disturbance, perversions, addictions, lack of impulse control, and psychosis. Others (e.g., Goldfried, 2004) have suggested that brief therapy is not appropriate for addressing long-standing Axis II conditions such as borderline personality disorders.

DETERMINING "WHY NOW"

A CENTRAL CONCEPT IN brief therapy is the discovery of immediate issues clients present with in session and the therapists' attempts at answering the question "Why has this client decided to seek counseling now?" Budman and Gurman (1988) explore this domain by viewing the situation from an interpersonal-developmental-existential (I-D-E) perspective. Specifically, clients present with an interpersonal conflict(s), developmental life stage problem(s), and/or existential concerns (e.g., meaning and value of life), which often occurs after some event or situation. Research indicates that many persons entering therapy typically do so within 3 weeks to 6 months after experiencing some major unpleasant event (Barrett, 1979; Brown, 1978). Clients often enter therapy due to interpersonal conflicts with family members such as their children, spouses, or partners, while others enter therapy to try and resolve issues with friends and coworkers. Developmentally, some clients may feel that they are *off time* or out of sync regarding where they expect themselves to be at this stage in life. Finally, from an existential perspective, clients may question their value, meaning, or role in life after the death of a friend or relative.

Budman and Gurman (1988) narrow down the question of *why clients come for counseling* at this point in time due to a loss, developmental dysynchronies, interpersonal conflicts, symptomatic presentations, and personality disorders. The I-D-E framework focuses on "current here-and-now or there-and-now issues" (p. 37). Specific questions to ask clients within this framework include (1) What is the client's reason for seeking therapy at this time? (2) What is the client's age and approximate developmental stage? (3) Are there any significant recent or upcoming anniversaries? (4) Has the client experienced any major social support changes recently? (5) Is the client drinking and/or using drugs at this time? (6) Is the client initiating treatment because of outside pressure? (7) Is the client addicted to psychotherapy and/or using treatment as a reason not to change? and (8) Does the client desire symptomatic change only? (p. 37). Responses to these central questions allow counselors to home in more quickly as to why the client has come for counseling now.

PHILOSOPHICAL APPROACH

THE VALUES OF brief therapists tend to be different from those of traditional, long-term therapists. According to Budman and Gurman (1988), brief therapists subscribe to a parsimonious approach that entails the least costly and least invasive treatment; they believe significant psychological change can occur in brief therapy as opposed to slowly "chipping away" at long-standing psychopathology; and they endorse a *health* rather than an *illness* orientation that often accompanies psychiatric diagnosis. Brief therapists also take the client's presenting problem seriously and believe that understanding why a problem has arisen is often secondary or irrelevant to producing client change. They also contend that many changes will occur after therapy or between sessions, and, most important, brief therapists are typically present- or future-oriented (Budman & Gurman, 1988).

Some of the most salient technical elements to follow in brief therapy include (1) setting and maintaining realistic goals and maintaining a clear and specific focus; (2) high-level therapist activity (e.g., offering suggestions, asking leading questions, and assigning homework); (3) maintaining awareness of the limited number of sessions; (4) involving relatives and significant others in treatment as many clients' problems relate to issues with important people in their lives; (5) making use of naturally occurring therapies in the environment such as Alcoholics Anonymous, social clubs, and support groups; and (6) planned follow-up of brief therapy 1 year after termination (Budman & Gurman, 1988).

SOLUTION-FOCUSED BRIEF THERAPY

SOLUTION-FOCUSED BRIEF therapy (SFBT), developed by the late Steve de Shazer and his wife Insoo Kim Berg at the Brief Therapy Center in Milwaukee in the late 1970s, is one of the most widely used brief therapies in the world (Tepper, Dolan, McCollum, & Nelson, 2006). SFBT differs from traditional therapies by circumventing the past in favor of both the present and future. This paradigm shift entails having therapists ask clients questions designed to help them to visualize desired outcomes and to identify their strengths and resources as well as times when the problem was not evident. A basic assumption of SFBT is that clients are healthy and competent and have the ability to construct solutions that can enhance their lives. According to Corey (2009), there are a number of specific techniques and procedures associated with this particular approach:

- Establishing a collaborative relationship
- Facilitating pretherapy change (e.g., asking clients during the first session what they have done since making the appointment that has made a difference in their problem)
- Asking exception questions that direct clients to think about times when the problem did not exist or when it was not as intense
- Asking clients, "If a miracle happened and your problem was solved overnight, how would you know it was solved and what would be different?"
- Using scaling questions (e.g., "On a scale of 0 to 10, with 0 being how you felt when you entered therapy and 10 representing now that we have completed therapy.")
- Assigning homework between the first and second sessions
- Providing feedback to clients at the end of each session
- Being mindful of terminating therapy from the onset

Although SFBT has been criticized for its emphasis on rapid application of techniques at the expense of developing a sound therapeutic relationship (Wettersten et al., 2005), it has been shown to be effective in up to 90% of clients with many different types of mental health problems, including substance abuse, domestic violence offenders, post-traumatic stress disorder, at-risk adolescents, obesity, sexual abuse, and schizophrenia (Corey, 2009; de Shazer et al., 2005; Tepper et al., 2006). It has also been shown to yield therapeutic results with individuals treated for depression, relationship problems, anxiety, and substance abuse (Macdonald, 2005). In addition, this approach can be used in couples, family, and group therapy.

BRIEF INTERPERSONAL PSYCHOTHERAPY

BRIEF INTERPERSONAL PSYCHOTHERAPISTS (IPT) consider a high-quality working alliance between the therapist and client essential for facilitating positive outcomes. This approach emphasizes creating a collaborative relationship, encouraging client insight, facilitating the expression of conflicted emotions, and using the therapeutic relationship to provide a corrective emotional experience that will facilitate change (Teyber, 2006). Therapists focus on helping clients modify interpersonal relationships or change expectations about themselves, particularly in the areas of grief, interpersonal disputes, role transition, and interpersonal sensitivity that entails a client's difficulty in establishing and maintaining interpersonal relationships. Clients are also assisted in improving their social support network so they can better manage their current interpersonal distress.

Interpersonal psychotherapy has been shown to be efficacious in a number of psychiatric disorders such as depression in adolescents, older persons, and individuals who are HIV positive; postpartum depression; dysthymic disorder; bipolar disorder; and eating disorders (Stuart, 2004). In contrast to approaches such as cognitive therapy, which emphasizes a client's thought processes, IPT focuses on the client's current interpersonal communication with others in his or her social network. This therapeutic approach is time limited and is used in the acute phase of treatment. For example, for the acute treatment of depression and other major psychiatric illnesses, a course of 12–20 sessions is tapered over time (e.g., 6–10 sessions followed by a gradual increase in time between sessions). Therapists avoid diagnosing a specific illness and instead maintain their focus on one or two interpersonal problems. Therapists are also encouraged to establish contracts with their clients to end acute treatment after a specified number of sessions.

BRIEF COGNITIVE THERAPY

COGNITIVE THERAPY HAS been empirically proven to be a valid form of brief psychotherapy in more than 350 outcome studies across a variety of psychiatric disorders, including depression, generalized anxiety disorder, panic disorders, social phobias, obsessive-compulsive disorder, post-traumatic stress disorders, bulimia, and substance abuse (Beck & Bieling, 2004). This approach has also been shown to be effective in a number of medical conditions such as chronic fatigue syndrome, hypertension, fibromyalgia, vascular depression, cancer, diabetes, chronic pain, and migraine headaches

(White & Freeman, 2000). The overall goal of this approach is to help clients achieve a remission of their disorders by problem solving and reducing symptoms through a collaborative, empirical approach that teaches clients to view reality more clearly through examination of their distorted cognitions.

Brief cognitive therapy is highly structured and typically begins with an objective assessment (e.g., Beck Depression Inventory-II, Beck, Steer, & Brown, 1996) of the client's current symptoms at the onset of each session. During this mood evaluation, the therapist also requests verbal feedback about how the client has been feeling over the past week and compares the responses to those provided in previous weeks. From there, the therapist and client collaboratively develop an agenda for the session, followed by an in-depth discussion of one or two of the major identified problems. During this discussion, the therapist collects data, conceptualizes problems, presents hypotheses, and elicits key cognitions, feelings, and behaviors (Beck & Bieling, 2004). The client and therapist also engage in problem solving and evaluate the client's pattern of dysfunctional thoughts and beliefs. Sessions end with a summarization of the session and possible homework assignments for clients such as identifying and responding to distressing thoughts, journal writing, and activity monitoring. Brief cognitive therapists also draw on a number of techniques typically used in traditional cognitive therapy, including relaxation training, graded exposure, modification of underlying beliefs, imagery work, and response prevention. For example, people with obsessive-compulsive disorder may be encouraged to actively work to reduce their compulsive behaviors. As with other brief therapies, brief cognitive therapy entails between 12–20 sessions.

EVALUATING COMPETENCY IN BRIEF PSYCHOTHERAPY

MANNING, BEITMAN, AND Dewan (2004) provide a number of useful suggestions for counselors and therapists to use when evaluating their effectiveness in using brief psychotherapy interventions. The following highlights some of these major competencies:

- Establishing and maintaining professional boundaries
- Establishing a strong therapeutic alliance with clients
- Maintaining focus in treatment
- Effectively using a broad array of verbal interventions designed to provide hope, reassurance, guidance, reflection, confrontation, and interpretation

- Encouraging and reinforcing change
- Assessing client readiness for termination of treatment

Client feedback is also vital in evaluating the effectiveness of therapy. This may be accomplished by having clients complete brief objective assessments and/or by discussing the achievement of specific goals established at the onset of therapy.

TERMINATING THERAPY

FOR NO REAL apparent empirical reason, but now likely due to insurance coverage, psychologists and counselors have maintained the traditional 50-minute sessions once per week for more than 50 years. Milton Erickson (1980) was, however, a maverick at setting his own rules regarding session length and termination. In some cases, he would see clients for only a few brief sessions or minutes; on other occasions, under other client circumstances, he might see a client every day for hours over several days. His success in treating individuals with various disorders encourages us to perhaps think in nontraditional ways regarding number and length of sessions based on what is best for the client.

Since brief therapy is by its nature brief, counselors more frequently have to deal with termination, which for many is an uncertain and uncomfortable task. Because of the anticipated anxiety over clients who may become emotional at termination, some counselors may wonder if the client is truly ready to terminate therapy. In addition, some therapists debate whether a client's last session is really the end of therapy. On one side of the debate is the unrealistic and rigid perception that once termination occurs, a client is totally cured, never to experience mental health problems again. Therefore, an invitation to recontact the counselor in the future may be contradictory to many clients, especially if their therapist certifies that they are functioning much better psychologically. The other side to this issue, and the more empirically confirmed viewpoint, is that many clients return to counseling months or years later. They often do so over the course of their lives because they need immediate assistance in dealing with the ever-changing I-D-E dynamic (Patterson, Levene, & Breger, 1977). It is essential that counselors recognize that life is not static. It continually involves changes in one's interpersonal, developmental, and existential experience. Thus, returning to therapy should not be viewed as a failure. Accordingly, it becomes important in that counselors who are able to acknowledge that clients may likely seek mental health counseling periodically due to life adjustment circumstances may feel more comfortable with terminating therapy, and that the last brief therapy session may not necessarily be the last therapeutic intervention in that individual's life (Hartlaub, Martin, & Rhine, 1986; Patterson et al., 1977).

CONCLUSION

BRIEF THERAPY ACCORDING to meta-analysis traditionally runs anywhere between 12–25 sessions, depending on client circumstances. Counselors utilizing brief therapy are actively involved from the onset, establishing a collaborative rapport, being mindful of termination, summarizing each session, and giving homework following the first session. Homing in on the major client concern(s) by asking specific questions within the I-D-E framework quickly facilitates the direction therapy will take. The use of traditional therapies such as solution-focused, brief cognitive therapy, and brief interpersonal methods has been shown to be effective with a variety of client presenting problems. Finally, since termination of therapy is a frequent occurrence with counselors using brief therapy, counselors should become comfortable with the notion that clients may return in the future to deal with different life events, and saying goodbye really could perhaps be substituted for "Maybe we'll see you again." . . . and that's okay.

REFERENCES

Barrett, J. E. (1979). The relationship of life events to the onset of neurotic disorders. In J. E. Barrett (Ed.), *Stress and mental disorder* (pp. 87–109). New York: Raven Press.

Beck, A. T., Steer, R. A., & Brown, G. K. (1996). *Beck Depression Inventory—Second edition manual*. San Antonio, TX: Psychological Corporation.

Beck, J. S., & Bieling, P. J. (2004). Cognitive therapy: Introduction to theory and practice. In M. J. Dewan, B. N. Steenbarger, R. P. Greenberg, & G. O. Gabbard (Eds.), *The art and science of brief psychotherapies: A practitioner's guide* (pp. 15–49). Washington, DC: American Psychiatric Press.

Brown, B. B. (1978). Social and psychological correlates of help seeking behavior among urban adults. *American Journal of Community Psychology, 6,* 425–439.

Budman, S. H., & Gurman, A. S. (1988). *Theory and practice of brief therapy*. New York: Guilford Press.

Cameron, C. L. (2006). Brief psychotherapy: A review. *American Journal of Psychotherapy, 60*(2), 147–152.

Corey, G. (2009). *Theory and practice of counseling and psychotherapy* (8th ed.). Belmont, CA: Brooks/Cole.

de Shazer, S., Dolan, S., Korman, Y., Tepper, T. S., McCollum, E. E., & Berg, I. K. (2005). *More than miracles: The state of the art of solution-focused therapy.* Binghamton, NY: Haworth Press.

Erickson, M. H. (1980). *Innovative hypnotherapy: Collected papers of Milton H. Erickson on hypnosis* (Vol. 4). E. L. Rossi (Ed.). New York: Irvington.

Goldfried, M. R. (2004). Integrating integratively oriented brief psychotherapy. *Journal of Psychotherapy Integration, 14,* 93–105.

Hartlaub, G. H., Martin, G. L., & Rhine, M. W. (1986). Recontact with the analyst following termination: A survey of seventy one cases. *Journal of the American Psychoanalytic Association, 34,* 895–910.

Macdonald, A. J. (2005). Brief therapy in adult psychiatry: Results from fifteen years of practice. *Journal of Family Therapy, 27,* 65–75.

Malan, D. (1979). *Individual therapy and the science of psychodynamics.* London: Routledge.

Mander, G. (2005). Suitability and context for brief therapy. *Psychodynamic Process, 11*(4), 417–428.

Manning, J., Beitman, B., & Dewan, M. J. (2004). Evaluating competence in brief psychotherapy. In M. J. Dewan, B. N. Steenbarger, R. P. Greenberg, & G. O. Gabbard (Eds.), *The art and science of brief psychotherapies: A practitioner's guide* (pp. 265–275). Washington, DC: American Psychiatric Press.

Patterson, V., Levene, H., & Breger, L. (1977). A one year follow-up study of two forms of brief psychotherapy. *American Journal of Psychotherapy, 31,* 76–82.

Rothwell, N. (2005). How brief is solution focused brief therapy? A comparative study. *Clinical Psychology and Psychotherapy, 12,* 402–405.

Shapiro, D. A., Barkham, M., Stiles, W. B., Hardy, G. E., Rees, A., Reynolds, S., et al. (2003). Time is of the essence: A selective review of the fall and rise of brief therapy research. *Psychology and Psychotherapy: Theory, Research and Practice, 76,* 211–235.

Stuart, S. (2004). Brief interpersonal psychotherapy. In M. J. Dewan, B. N. Steenbarger, R. P. Greenberg, & G. O. Gabbard (Eds.), *The art and science of brief psychotherapies: A practitioner's guide* (pp. 119–155). Washington, DC: American Psychiatric Press.

Tepper, T. S., Dolan, Y., McCollum, E. E., & Nelson, T. (2006). Steve de Shazer and the future of solution-focused therapy. *Journal of Marital and Family Therapy, 32*(2), 123–139.

Teyber, E. (2006). *Interpersonal processes in psychotherapy: A relational approach* (5th ed.). Pacific Grove, CA: Brooks/Cole.

Wettersten, K. B., Lichtenberg, J. W., & Mallinckrodt, B. (2005). Associations between working alliance and outcome in solution-focused brief therapy and brief interpersonal therapy. *Psychotherapy Research, 15*(1–2), 35–43.

White, J. R., & Freeman, A. S. (2000). *Cognitive-behavioral group therapy for specific problems and populations.* Washington, DC: American Psychological Association.

38

Motivational Interviewing

GRANT CORBETT

MOTIVATIONAL INTERVIEWING (MI) is a clinical style, a form of psychotherapy (W. R. Miller, personal communication, March 9, 2008), that is "a person-centered goal-oriented approach for facilitating change through exploring and resolving ambivalence" (Miller, 2006a, p. 138).

Historically, a client may have been labeled in denial or resistant if he or she expressed ambivalence. However, in MI, "feeling two ways" about an issue is considered normal and a common reason that people seek counseling. The developers, Drs. William R. Miller and Stephen Rollnick (2002), have described MI as helping shift an individual's "decisional balance" in favor of change. Decisions can be difficult when our options have both an up and a downside, leaving us feeling "two ways" about committing (you may know this as approach-avoidance).

Motivational interviewing facilitates motivation through a person-centered evoking and reinforcing of a counselee's desire, ability, reasons, need, and commitment to change (together referred to as *change talk*). Change talk is associated with improved outcomes, while arguments that clients verbalize for their current behavior (*status talk*) can reinforce a no-change position (Moyers & Martin, 2006; Moyers, Martin, Christopher, Houck, Tonigan et al., 2007). Motivational interviewing attempts to elicit the former and minimize the latter. This chapter will present an overview of the principles and skills of the counseling style.

EVIDENCE FOR EFFECTIVENESS

MOTIVATIONAL INTERVIEWING DEVELOPED in the alcohol treatment field, with numerous studies supporting its effectiveness. Later came evaluations in counseling contexts, such as motivating educational achievement (e.g., literacy acquisition), employment readiness, health promotion (e.g., fruit and vegetable consumption, physical activity), and marital communication. Other human service areas studied include child protection, criminal recidivism, and domestic-violence prevention.

Applications of MI in health and mental health are increasing. The former includes use and evaluation of the style in brain injury rehabilitation, cardiac care, chronic pain management, diabetes risk reduction and treatment, dietary change (e.g., eating disorders), drug-abuse treatment (including harm reduction and needle exchange), HIV/AIDS risk reduction, injury prevention and treatment, mammography screening, medical interviewing and treatment, medication adherence interventions (e.g., compliance in use of asthma controller inhalers), oral health care, osteoporosis prevention and treatment, speech/vocal therapy, and treatment retention.

Mental health studies have encompassed dual disorder management (i.e., substance use and mental illness), mental health treatment (e.g., for anxiety, bipolar disorder, depression, post-traumatic stress disorder [PTSD], and schizophrenia), problem gambling counseling, sexual behavior change (e.g., safer sex behaviors, and in interventions for sexual offenders, sex trade workers, and sexual addicts), tobacco use prevention and dependence treatment, and weight loss.

More than 180 randomized controlled trials (RCTs) have been completed (for a bibliography by area of application, see Rollnick, Miller, and Butler, 2008; or motivationalinterview.org).

Another level of evidence for MI can be found in systematic and meta-analytic reviews (Burke, Arkowitz, & Menchola, 2003; Burke, Dunn, Atkins, & Phelps, 2004; Dunn, Deroo, & Rivara, 2001; Hettema, Steele, & Miller, 2005; Knight, McGowan, Dickens, & Bundy, 2006; Rubak, Sandboek, Lauritzen, & Christensen, 2005). Particularly relevant to counseling is a paper by Rubak and colleagues (2005), who evaluated 72 RCTs that compared advice giving to MI. They found that in brief encounters of 15 minutes, 64% of the studies outperformed advice giving for a broad range of behavioral problems.

Thus, MI need not add additional time to sessions. Rather, MI may reduce length of sessions while improving outcomes, relative to advice giving.

PHILOSOPHY OF MOTIVATIONAL INTERVIEWING

MILLER INTRODUCED MI in a 1983 paper. He wrote the article during a sabbatical at the Hjellestad Clinic outside Bergen, Norway (W. R. Miller, personal communication, March, 2008; Moyers, 2004). During role-played interviews, questions from postgraduate psychologists led Miller to make explicit the approach he had "learned from my clients" (Miller, 1996, p. 835). This statement, that MI was learned from those with whom he worked, points to both the tradition and worldview of the approach.

To learn from those we counsel is to be client centered, the latter being rooted in the therapy of Carl Rogers and others before him (see chapter 36). Moyers (2004) describes this as an "emphasis on acceptance, egalitarianism and optimism regarding the client's ability to find the best solution for the problem under discussion" (pp. 291–292).

In MI, this "way of being"[1] with people is described as the "MI spirit," "consisting of collaboration, evocation and autonomy. . . . Without it, one can use MI methods, but it would not be MI" (Arkowitz & Miller, 2008, p. 4).

Specifically, studies show that the counselor's ability to convey this spirit is a predictor of using MI techniques and of increased client responsiveness during sessions (Moyers, Miller, & Hendrickson, 2005). Important as a starting point in learning MI is openness to this way of thinking about clients and consultation, at least a willing suspension of disbelief and active curiosity about the client's perspective.

PRINCIPLES OF MOTIVATIONAL INTERVIEWING

MILLER AND ROLLNICK (2002) proposed four guiding principles to help translate the MI spirit into practice. They are described here.

Express empathy. The use of empathy "is employed from the beginning and throughout the process of MI" (Miller & Rollnick, 2002, p. 37). Empathy may be misunderstood. Some think it is having had a common experience or being able to identify with the client. However, the latter is sympathy, which can result in a judgment (i.e., "It must be awful to feel that way"). Empathy is less about thinking than feeling what the person may be experiencing—in the moment.

Develop discrepancy. Motivational interviewing differs from Rogers's client-centered therapy by being intentionally goal-oriented (Miller

& Rollnick, 2002, p. 38). When the counselor ethically can move a client toward a target behavior (see discussion of ethics in the "Major Concerns for Motivational Interviewing" section), developing discrepancy is a primary means of resolving ambivalence in the direction of change. That is,

> to create and amplify, from the client's perspective, a discrepancy between presenting behavior and his or her broader goals and values . . . a discrepancy between the present state of affairs and how one wants it to be. (Miller & Rollnick, 2002, p. 38)

Roll with resistance. Given that ambivalence is normal, clients may find certain counselor behaviors or issues threatening. This may be observed as hesitancy or direct unwillingness to discuss a matter. The ability to roll with resistance is critical to avoid evoking and reinforcing status talk. Attempts to disagree, argue, or persuade the person to address a problem are likely to escalate defensiveness and counterarguments that are associated with lack of change. Motivational interviewing includes asking permission to give advice, to minimize the risk of resistance.

Support self-efficacy. Counseling outcomes are affected by hope and expectancy.[2] Thus, affirming a person's actions in the desired direction, and being optimistic, can help support self-efficacy. The techniques of MI follow from these four principles.

Techniques of Motivational Interviewing

As miller and Rollnick (2002) have emphasized,

> MI is a method of communication rather than a set of techniques. It is not a bag of tricks for getting people to do what they don't want to do. It is not something that one does *to* people. (p. 25)

However, MI does have techniques to elicit client speech from which change talk can be evoked and reinforced. The techniques consist of the microskills, used throughout, and the evoking and reinforcing of change talk and action steps.

The Microskills of MI

The microskills can be used in any counseling context. They are represented by the acronym OARS, which guide the practitioner to use the following.

Open-ended questions. An open-ended question differs from a closed-ended one (as the latter results in only a yes or no answer). The former should encourage the person to speak more about what he *or* she is thinking (rather than what we want to know).

Affirmations. As discussed, enhancing self-efficacy is an MI principle. This confidence can be increased by social reinforcement from the counselor. Note that an affirmation is not praise from a one-up position, which may be perceived as a judgment ("You are doing well; that's good"). An affirmation is an authentic valuing of the person's strengths, desires, and commitment ("I am pleased to hear that you are doing well").

Reflections. Reflection is about restating, or clarifying the meaning of, what the client communicates (verbally and nonverbally). It involves the following:

- Reflecting key content or the meaning behind what was expressed.
- Double-sided reflection. This is a form of summary that captures both sides of the ambivalence (e.g., "So you want to . . . and . . . you want to. . . . ").
- Amplified reflection. This overstates what the person says to create a discrepancy.
- Reflection with a twist, which involves initial agreement followed by a reframe.

Summaries. Summaries are a pulling together of several lines of thought expressed by a client. These have at least two purposes. First, when multiple issues have been presented, and you are unsure where to go next, a summary can help the person to identify what is most important. Second, summaries should collate change talk. This is a form of reinforcement and is a basis for evoking steps consistent with commitments.

THE TECHNIQUES FOR EVOKING AND REINFORCING CHANGE TALK

CHANGE TALK CONSISTS of preparatory language (DARN) and commitment language (C). Recently, activation (A) and taking steps (T) have been added. Here are examples of the content to be evoked and reinforced (with the first letters representing the foregoing):

- *Desire.* What they want, prefer, wish, and so forth.
- *Ability.* Words like able, can, could, possible.
- *Reasons.* "Why do it?" "What would be good about . . . ?"
- *Need.* Includes words such as important, have to, need to, matter, got to.

* *Commitment language.* "I need to," "I must," or "I am going to/ will/intend to do X when Y."
* *Activation.* "What are you ready and willing to do?"
* *Taking steps.* "What have you already done?"

There are several means to elicit change talk. The simplest way is to ask for it with open questions (e.g., What could you do to . . . [reference a stated desire])? Another is the use of rulers (also referred to as scaling questions). These can help you assess the importance of change and self-efficacy strength and evoke change talk.

* On a scale from 1 to 10, how important is it for you to . . . ? What would make importance (state a rating several points higher)?
* On a scale from 1 to 10, how confident are you that you could do . . . ? If your confidence were (state a rating several points higher), what would you be doing differently?

From the foregoing, MI evokes from the client the behaviors that they are willing to take, and the action steps to be taken.

MAJOR CONCERNS FOR MOTIVATIONAL INTERVIEWING

THERE HAVE BEEN no major critiques of the style. Published systematic and meta-analytic reviews suggest areas for additional research (Burke et al., 2003, 2004; Dunn et al., 2001; Hettema et al., 2005; Knight et al., 2006; Rubak et al., 2005). However, the following are challenges for MI.

The first is quality assurance. For example, some counselors say that they are already using the style. This may act as a barrier to learning the method and continuous improvement. For example, MI has advanced since publication of Miller and Rollnick's 2002 book. Thus, staff and trainers need to be updated on current research and practice. The name Motivational Interviewing is also appearing in workshop titles and books, yet the content does not cover MI as described in this chapter. Links to MI trainers and books can be found at motivational interview.org.

Second, MI has been entangled with the transtheoretical model (TTM; commonly referred to as the stages of change approach). This has caused confusion as to what the style is. Miller (2006b) clarifies as follows:

> Throughout its history, MI has often been associated and confused with the TTM in general, and in particular with its stages of change.

I'm clearly responsible in part for this, having included the TTM stages in many publications and presentations on MI. The two grew up together in the early 80s, and MI is a good example of an approach to help clients who are not yet "ready" for change. ICTAB-3 (Third International Conference on the Treatment of Addictive Behaviors in Scotland in 1984) was an early introduction of TTM to the addiction field and was also the first ICTAB at which MI was discussed. However, MI is explicitly not predicated on or derived from TTM. (p. 19)

Ethics in the use of MI is a final issue (Miller, 1994, 1995). As MI can guide a counselee toward a particular choice, the counselor needs to make principled decisions about evoking and reinforcing change talk.

CONCLUSION

MOTIVATIONAL INTERVIEWING IS a clinical style that is "a person-centered goal-oriented approach for facilitating change through exploring and resolving ambivalence" (Miller, 2006a, p. 138). Ambivalence is central to the philosophy and practice of MI. It is discrepancy, between a counselee's behaviors and how he or she wants to be, that is elicited and reinforced in the direction of change. Motivational interviewing has good evidence for effectiveness, and training in the style can potentially improve outcomes in a range of treatment contexts.

NOTES

1. "(MI) is fundamentally a way of being with and for people?—a facilitative approach to communication that evokes natural change" (Miller & Rollnick, 2002, p. 25).

2. Michael Lambert (1992) analyzed psychotherapy studies and concluded that four factors contribute to outcomes: (1) client and extra-therapeutic factors (said to account for 40% of change); (2) relationship factors (30%); (3) model/technique factors (15%); and (4) hope, and expectancy factors (15%).

REFERENCES

Arkowitz, H., & Miller, W. R. (2008). Learning, applying and extending motivational interviewing. In H. Arkowitz, H. A. Westra, W. R. Miller, & S. Rollnick (Eds.), *Motivational interviewing in the treatment of psychological problems* (pp. 1–25). New York: Guilford Press.

Burke, B. L., Arkowitz, H., & Menchola, M. (2003). The efficacy of motivational interviewing: A meta-analysis of controlled clinical trials. *Journal of Consulting and Clinical Psychology, 71*(5), 843–861.

Burke, B. L., Dunn, C. W., Atkins, D., & Phelps, J. S. (2004). The emerging evidence base for motivational interviewing: A meta-analytic and qualitative inquiry. *Journal of Cognitive Psychotherapy, 18*(4), 309–322.

Dunn, C., Deroo, L., & Rivara, F. P. (2001). The use of brief interventions adapted from motivational interviewing across behavioral domains: A systematic review. *Addiction, 96*(12), 1725–1742.

Hettema, J., Steele, J., & Miller, W. R. (2005). Motivational interviewing. *Annual Review of Clinical Psychology, 1,* 91–111. Retrieved March 2, 2008, from http://www.jennyhettema.com/annurev.clinpsy.1.pdf

Janis, I. L., and Mann, L. (1977). *Decision making: A psychological analysis of conflict, choice, and commitment.* New York: Free Press.

Knight, K. M., McGowan, L., Dickens, C., & Bundy, C. (2006). A systematic review of motivational interviewing in physical health care settings. *British Journal of Health Psychology, 11,* 319–332.

Lambert, M. J. (1992). Psychotherapy outcome research: Implications for integrative and eclectic therapists. In J. C. Norcross & M. R. Goldfried (Eds.), *Handbook of psychotherapy integration* (pp. 94–129). New York: Basic Books.

Miller, W. R. (1983). Motivational interviewing with problem drinkers. *Behavioural Psychotherapy, 11,* 147–172.

Miller, W. R. (1994). Motivational interviewing: III. On the ethics of motivational intervention. *Behavioural and Cognitive Psychotherapy, 22,* 111–123.

Miller, W. R. (1995). The ethics of motivational interviewing revisited. *Behavioural and Cognitive Psychotherapy, 23,* 345–348.

Miller, W. R. (1996). Motivational interviewing: Research, practice, and puzzles. *Addictive Behaviors, 21,* 835–842.

Miller, W. R. (2006a). Motivational factors in addictive behaviors. In W. R. Miller & K. M. Carroll (Eds.), *Rethinking substance abuse: What the science shows and what we should do about it* (pp. 134–150). New York: Guilford Press.

Miller, W. R. (2006b). State of the art and science of motivational interviewing. *MINT Bulletin, 13*(1), 16–20. Retrieved March 2, 2008, from http://motivationalinterview.org/mint/MINT13.1.pdf

Miller, W. R., & Moyers, T. B. (2006). The eight stages in learning motivational interviewing. *Journal of Teaching in the Addictions, 5*(1), 3–17.

Miller, W. R., & Rollnick, S. (2002). *Motivational interviewing: Preparing people for change* (2nd ed.). New York: Guilford Press.

Moyers, T. B. (2004). History and happenstance: How motivational interviewing got its start. *Journal of Cognitive Psychotherapy, 18*(4), 291–298.

Moyers, T. B., & Martin, T. (2006). Therapist influence on client language during motivational interviewing sessions. *Journal of Substance Abuse Treatment, 30*(3), 245–251.

Moyers, T. B., Martin, T., Christopher, P. J., Houck, J. M., Tonigan, J. S., & Amrhein, P. (2007). Client language as a mediator of motivational interviewing efficacy: Where is the evidence? *Alcoholism: Clinical and Experimental Research, 31*(10, Supple. S), 40S–47S.

Moyers, T. B., Miller, W. R., & Hendrickson, S. M. L. (2005). What makes motivational interviewing work? Therapist interpersonal skill as a predictor of client involvement within motivational interviewing sessions. *Journal of Consulting and Clinical Psychology, 73*(4), 590–598.

Rollnick, S., Miller, W. R, & Butler, C. C. (2008). *Motivational interviewing in health care.* New York: Guilford Press.

Rubak, S., Sandboek, A., Lauritzen, T., & Christensen, B. (2005). Motivational interviewing: A systematic review and meta-analysis. *British Journal of General Practice, 55,* 305–312. Retrieved March 2, 2008, from www .motivationalinterview.org/library/RubakMIreview.pdf

39

Gestalt Therapy

PHILIP BROWNELL

MANY COUNSELORS HAVE seen the training film of Fritz Perls working with "Gloria." This does not accurately depict gestalt therapy as it is practiced today. So, what is gestalt therapy? Gestalt has been described as an existential field theory and characterized as phenomenological behaviorism. A brief description of the practice of gestalt therapy is offered and presented below under its four primary theoretical constructs, but a more in-depth description following this same development can be found in *The Handbook for Theory, Research, and Practice in Gestalt Therapy* (Brownell, in press).

UNITY OF THEORY

THE UNITY OF gestalt therapy theory does not refer to one grand design originated by one comprehensive theorist. Rather, the endorsement of concomitant constructs and the assimilation of theoretical foundations fit into one comprehensive superstructure. The building materials may have been gathered from various places, but the building itself fits well together and has stood the tests of time as such.

Gary Yontef (1993) referred to this unity when he stated that each moment in gestalt therapy has two aspects that are always present—the dialogical relationship and awareness work that emerges through the use of a phenomenological method. One might add that these occur within a sphere of influence understood to gestalt therapists as "the field" and that the occasion is experiential and experimental, because it is ultimately undetermined. That is, in a therapeutic process (1) the therapist and the client are always in some form of meeting,

(2) they each have some degree of awareness around that, (3) for each there are various factors affecting how they experience what is going on, and (4) the entire interaction is alive and flowing through time in a fairly unpredictable fashion. It cannot be controlled, but it can be experienced and mined to the benefit of both client and therapist.

To practice gestalt therapy requires experiential training and supervision. The practitioner must entrust himself or herself to the process, feeling increasingly at home with the multifaceted events occurring in the "interpenetrating dimensions in which human living goes on: physical, affective, cognitive, interpersonal, social, economic, aesthetic, spiritual, and perhaps others" (Crocker, 1999, p. 338). Training in gestalt includes the theoretical support and grounding of the therapist as an important contribution to the work of the client.

Fused to all fibers of gestalt theory is gestalt therapy's theory of change. It is paradoxical, because it asserts that people change by "becoming more fully themselves not by making themselves become something or someone they are not" (Mackewn, 1997, p. 63). That is, one becomes what one is not by most fully being what one is. One achieves a future goal not by living in the fantasized eventuality but by living in the current experience that gave rise to the goal and likely includes this day's contribution to achieving it.

Finally, gestalt theory is unified in gestalt's holistic approach. Just as a person cannot be reduced to the mere sum of his or her parts, a whole person cannot be fully understood outside his or her situation, and that situation unfolds within a context. It is the relationship between one's foreground and one's background that gives significance to one's role in the situation, and that is experienced for each person from the first-person, subjective perspective—that Greek word from which Freud coined his term *ego*, which in Greek simply means *I*. The awareness of experiencing oneself in the situation, the awareness of being in connection with others in the situation, and the awareness that matters are affecting the situation, which is itself in flux, is an interconnected consideration—a unity. All aspects of gestalt therapy theory are always currently at play and cannot be dissected or eliminated for examination as if they had been operating in isolation.

PHENOMENOLOGICAL METHOD

THE PHENOMENOLOGICAL METHOD originated out of the thinking of Franz Brentano (Brentano, 1995; Jacquette, 2004) and Edmund Husserl (Husserl, 2001; Smith, 1995). From Brentano we inherited the construct of intentionality, and from Husserl we obtained our orientation to phenomenology.

An intentional object is that which has one's attention; thought is about something, feelings provide valence toward or away from something, and experience is of something. These are all aspects of intentionality. Brentano's act psychology not only influenced Husserl's development of phenomenological philosophy but also had a direct influence on the thinking of gestalt therapists (Yontef, 1993) who later recognized that contact, a central element in gestalt therapy, is the act (Crocker, 1999) of perceiver perceiving the perceived; it forms the awareness of self in one's environment and one reason for describing a person as an organism-environment being.

Husserl's considerations led him to conclude that a person's experience of the world is an intentional construct containing both directional and referential foci, and he believed the main task of phenomenology was to remove the layers of interpretation so that one might get close to the things themselves (Kirchner, 2000; Spinelli, 2005). He constructed what he called the phenomenological method in order to investigate experience in such a manner. It is this method, with its emphasis on increasing awareness of "what is," that has characterized gestalt therapy more than anything else among people superficially familiar with it. Indeed, the early experiential exercises comprising the first part of the seminal book *Gestalt Therapy* (Perls, Hefferline, & Goodman, 1951) were intentionally focused on increasing awareness.

The phenomenological method comprises three steps. This includes the rules of (1) *epoché,* (2) description, and (3) horizontalization (Spinelli, 2005). In the rule of epoché, one sets aside his or her initial biases and prejudices in order to suspend expectations and assumptions. In the rule of description, one occupies himself or herself with describing instead of explaining. In the rule of horizontalization, one treats each item of description as having equal value or significance. First one sets aside any initial theories with regard to what is presented in the meeting between therapist and client. Second, one describes immediate and concrete observations, abstaining from interpretations or explanations, especially those formed from the application of a clinical theory superimposed over the circumstances of experience. Third, one avoids any hierarchical assignment of importance such that the data of experience become prioritized and categorized as they are received. A gestalt therapist utilizing the phenomenological method might find himself or herself typically saying something like, "I notice a slight tension at the corners of your mouth when I say that, and I see you shifting on the couch and folding your arms across your chest . . . and now I see you rolling your eyes back." All this is not to say that the therapist never makes clinically relevant evaluations. Rather, when applying the phenomenological method, the therapist temporarily suspends the need for such interpretation or model building.

DIALOGICAL RELATIONSHIP

THE THERAPEUTIC RELATIONSHIP is perhaps one of the best-attested factors with regard to outcomes in psychotherapy. However, not all clinical perspectives approach it in the same way. Gestalt therapy is not hierarchical. Although there is a therapeutic contract and the therapist does serve the needs of the client, both client and therapist are people and they are human beings at the core of their meeting. Thus, each person is affected by the other. Overall, the gestalt therapist enters into a true relationship with the client, and the form of their contact has been characterized as dialogue (Jacobs, 1998; Melnick, Nevis, & Shub, 2005; Yontef, 1993). Therapeutic outcomes result as a product of the meeting between them, which occurs, as Martin Buber explained, with an alternating rhythm between what some call a more subjective encounter of person to person (I-Thou) and a more objective meeting of person to thing (I-It; Mackewn, 1997).

The intentionality in the I-It mode is to get business accomplished (even therapeutic business), and people are treated as means to that end. In extreme forms of this modality the accomplishment of tasks and the meeting of needs can be abusive to those objectified. However, it does not need to be, for the majority of our relating to one another is functionally goal oriented. Without it, we would not attend to our basic survival needs. In therapy, the therapist functions in this mode while gathering demographic information from the client, providing informed consent, and conducting a mental status exam.

The intentionality in relating from an I-Thou mode is to know another person and to be known by them. This comes in sparks of connection and interpersonal intimacy that feel exciting, may seem scary, and generate energy. They can be sustained briefly and are best thought of as dialogical moments. Therapists who operate within a persona of professionalism, what used to be called "professional distance," rarely experience dialogic moments and would likely be uncomfortable with them in a therapeutic relationship.

The contrast between these two modes is illustrated by the work of a gestalt therapist in a community mental health setting. One might easily relate to colleagues from the I-It mode while checking with the front desk for appointments, discussing issues during staff meeting or administrative supervision, checking with medical records, or conducting case management. There is also opportunity to experience the I-Thou mode while conducting therapy, engaging in clinical supervision, interacting with people in the community, or even while connecting with others personally during a number of the previous occasions (Brownell & Fleming, 2005).

To create the conditions under which a dialogic moment might occur, the therapist attends to his or her own presence, creates the space for the client to enter in and become present as well (called inclusion), and commits himself or herself to the dialogic process, surrendering to what takes place between them as opposed to attempting to control it. In presence, the therapist "shows up" as the whole and authentic person he or she is (Yontef, 1993) instead of assuming a role, false self, or persona. To practice inclusion is to accept however the client chooses to be present. It may be in a defensive and obnoxious stance or an overly sweet but superficially cooperative one. To practice inclusion is to support the presentation of the client, including his or her resistance, not as a gimmick but in full realization that that is how the client is present. Finally, the gestalt therapist is committed to the process, trusts in that process, and does not attempt to save himself or herself from it.

FIELD THEORETICAL STRATEGY

ALL THINGS HAVING affect for the client comprise the life space, or field, of the client. The field is a current consideration. That is, even though the field includes memory of the past and expectation of the future, it is only those aspects currently having affect. At the same time the field is a sphere of influence in which experience occurs. The dialogue between therapist and client occurs in a cocreated field as all-things-having-affect for the therapist meets all-things-having-affect for the client. In gestalt therapy, the field dynamics are central considerations, for even the phenomenological data for the individual client arises from that client as an organism-environment field (Parlett & Lee, 2005).

In field theory the *field* can be considered in two ways. There are ontological dimensions and there are phenomenological dimensions to one's field. The ontological dimensions are all those physical and environmental contexts in which we live and move. They are the office in which one works, the house in which one lives, the city and country of which one is a citizen, and so forth. The ontological field is the objective reality that supports our physical existence. The phenomenological dimensions are all mental and physical dynamics that contribute to a person's sense of self, one's subjective experience, but are not merely elements of the environmental context. This could be the memory of an uncle's inappropriate affection, one's color blindness, one's sense of the social matrix in operation at the office in which one works, and so forth.

It is the way in which gestalt therapists choose to work with field dynamics that makes what they do strategic. Some gestalt therapists choose to essentially observe and understand elements of the field having affect. Thus, they might detect that some aspect of the past is particularly relevant for the present. They might realize that something they do irritates the client. The gestalt therapist explores this possibility with the client, leading both to comprehend the *how* of the situation rather than just the *why* of it. Still other gestalt therapists might choose to introduce something into the field of the client, knowing that any change in the client's field will result in some kind of change in the client's experience. Thus, for a very depressed and isolated client, a therapist might arrange through family members for a home nurse to come and get the client up and out each day.

EXPERIMENTAL FREEDOM

GESTALT THERAPY IS considered an experiential therapeutic approach (Crocker, 1999). It is moving to action, away from mere talk therapy, that often has distinguished gestalt therapy from other counseling theories and therapeutic approaches. Through experiments, the therapist supports the client's direct experience of something new instead of merely talking about the possibility of something new. The entire therapeutic relationship could be considered experimental, because at one level it is the provision of corrective, relational experience for many clients. An experiment can be conceived of as a teaching method that creates an experience in which a client might learn something as part of his or her growth (Melnick et al. 2005). Experiments support the active self-exploration of the client. They make figures of interest more vibrant and they generate energy. They also intensify awareness and often, as in the case of the corrective experience mentioned in reference to the therapeutic relationship, they become healing in themselves. Thus, there is a corollary between nondirective play therapy in working with children and the experimental approach of gestalt therapists working with adults. Gestalt therapists working with children make this clear when they describe what they do in their work.

An experiment differs from an intervention in the usual sense of that word. A medical doctor listens to his or her patient and then prescribes medication. That prescription is an intervention, and the physician expects it to work in a customary fashion but with only minor differences, achieving the results for which it was prescribed. The gestalt therapist does not prescribe experiments thinking he or she knows what the direct result will be. To the contrary, no one really knows what the result will be, because an experiment is an intentional entry into novel experience for purposes of discovery. It can be supported and experienced, but it cannot be predicted or dispensed in doses designed to accomplish specific outcomes. That is why experiments have also been called *safe emergencies*. Often, the most vibrant experiments are not those that have become fixed in form, such as two-chair work or speaking subjectively as each part of one's dream. Rather, the most vibrant experiments emerge uniquely from the substance of the work taking place between client and therapist.

Finally, experiments can be negotiated between therapist and client, as when a therapist senses that an experiment might facilitate the process and asks if the client might be willing to try one. The client considers what is being proposed and decides if he or she wants to try it out to see what might happen. If they agree in such a negotiation, then they proceed. However, there are also unilateral experiments in which the therapist decides to influence the process with the client in a strategic fashion. Accordingly, the therapist might choose to self-disclose, remain purposefully silent, establish boundaries, give the client an introject, or intentionally assume the place the client usually sits in, leaving the therapist's chair empty. When the therapist conducts such a unilateral experiment it is still the safe emergency and takes place within the "container" of support provided for the client in the relationship between them.

UNITY OF PRACTICE

GESTALT THERAPY IS not like multimodal therapy, even though there are similarities. At first, it might seem that a gestalt therapist could choose to work according to one theoretical tenet or another. The therapist may choose to work this way and then at a choice point in the process to work that way (phenomenological method, dialogic relationship, field theoretical strategy, or experimental freedom). However, a person must realize that none of these tenets stands completely alone. Each is intertwined with the others. Elements of a dialogic relationship cannot cease from being experimental. Both the client and therapist are mutually growing in their knowledge and trust of one another. This all takes place within their relative fields as well as comprises a coconstructed field in their meeting, all of which results in the individual experiences of both therapist and client. Nonetheless, it is common for a therapist to be aware that at any given point in the process the emphasis is one thing or another. For instance, it is possible to form a matrix with gestalt's ways of working across the top, and the focal points of the work down the left side (Brownell & Fleming,

2005). Trainees in gestalt therapy training centers can track the process of work and discuss it by using such a matrix and following the turning points where a person working as therapist chose to do "this" here as opposed to "that" there.

RECOMMENDATIONS FOR FURTHER STUDY

FOR THOSE WHO wish to investigate gestalt therapy more, the reader can consult the sources in the reference section. It cannot be stated strongly enough that to practice gestalt therapy one must become trained, and that often means completing a 3- or 4-year, postgraduate level training program. The top gestalt therapy training organizations have Web sites, and there may exist such an organization close to where the reader lives.

In addition, regional and international associations of gestalt therapists provide support through associating, conferencing, and in many cases, they also help those desiring to learn more about gestalt therapy:

- The Association for the Advancement of Gestalt Therapy—an international community: www.aagt.org
- The European Association for Gestalt Therapy: www.eagt.org
- Gestalt Australia New Zealand: www.ganz.org.au

Furthermore, the reader will find online resources for study and discussion of gestalt therapy through the e-journal *Gestalt!* (www.g-gej .org), *Gestalt Review* (www.gestaltreview.com), the e-community known as Gstalt-L (www.g-gej.org/gstalt-l), and the gestalt forum at Behavior Online (www.behavior.net/forums/gestalt). At Gstalt-L and the gestalt forum it is possible to dialogue with seasoned gestalt therapists, organizational consultants, theorists, trainers, and growing trainees. These are vital opportunities to talk with those practicing gestalt therapy, taking the reader steps beyond merely reading this chapter.

REFERENCES

Brentano, F. (1995). *Psychology from an empirical standpoint*. New York: Routledge.

Brownell, P. (Ed.). (in press). *The handbook for theory, research, and practice in gestalt therapy*. Newcastle upon Tyne, UK: Cambridge Scholars Publishing.

Brownell, P., & Fleming, K. (2005). Gestalt therapy in community mental health. In A. Woldt & S. Toman (Eds.), *Gestalt therapy: History, theory, and practice* (pp. 257–277). Thousand Oaks, CA: Sage Publications.

Crocker, S. F. (1999). *A well-lived life: Essays in gestalt therapy*. Cambridge, MA: Gestalt Institute of Cleveland Press.

Husserl, E. (2001). *Logical investigations*. New York: Routledge.

Jacobs, L. (1998). Dialogue and paradox: In training with Lynne Jacobs, the "dialogue maven." *Gestalt!* 2(1). Retrieved April 6, 2007, from http://www.g-gej.org/2-1/jacobs.html

Jacquette, D. (2004). *The Cambridge companion to Brentano*. Cambridge, UK: Cambridge University Press.

Kirchner, M. (2000). Gestalt therapy theory: An overview. *Gestalt!* 4(3). Retrieved April 6, 2007, from http://www.g-gej.org/4-3/theoryoverview.html

Mackewn, J. (1997). *Developing gestalt counseling*. Thousand Oaks, CA: Sage Publications.

Melnick, J., Nevis, S. M., & Shub, N. (2005). Gestalt therapy methodology. In A. Woldt & S. Toman (Eds.), *Gestalt therapy: History, theory, and practice* (pp. 101–115). Thousand Oaks, CA: Sage Publications.

Parlett, M., & Lee, R. (2005). Contemporary gestalt therapy: Field theory. In A. Woldt & S. Toman (Eds.), *Gestalt therapy: History, theory, and practice* (pp. 41–63). Thousand Oaks, CA: Sage Publications.

Perls, F., Hefferline, R., & Goodman, P. (1951). *Gestalt therapy, excitement and growth in the human personality*. Guernsey, Channel Islands, UK: Souvenir Press/Guernsey Press.

Smith, B. (1995). *The Cambridge companion to Husserl*. Cambridge, UK: Cambridge University Press.

Spinelli, E. (2005). *The interpreted world: An introduction to phenomenological psychology* (2nd ed.). Thousand Oaks, CA: Sage Publications.

Yontef, G. (1993). *Awareness, dialogue, and process: Essays in gestalt therapy*. Highland, NY: Gestalt Journal Press.

Section F

Career Counseling, Human Growth and Development

40

Historical Perspectives in Career Development Theory

DAVID B. HERSHENSON

O F THE EIGHT core areas that the Council for Accreditation of Counseling and Related Educational Programs (2006) requires in all counselor education programs, two are concerned with development: (1) human growth and development, and (2) career development. One may ask why career development merits its own distinct category and is not just subsumed under human development. In all probability, the reasons for granting career development its unique identity are partially historical. Many in the field of counseling trace the start of modern professional counseling to Frank Parsons's opening of the Vocation Bureau of Boston in 1908 (e.g., Herr & Shahnasarian, 2001). Thus, a concern with career development provided the foundation for the field of counseling and so must remain distinctively enshrined in the identity of the profession. As an area of functioning, however, career has certain characteristics that differentiate it from other aspects of personal development. One's occupation gives structure to a large segment of most people's waking hours, is usually the principal source of sustenance, is frequently an index of social standing in the community, and is embedded in a broader social and economic context over which the individual has little control. Therefore, career development merits unique consideration for structural as well as for historic reasons.

HISTORICAL BACKGROUND

THE ROOTS OF our concern with human development (including career development) extend back to the Enlightenment of the 18th century, with its emphases on rational thinking, scientific method, and the rights of the individual. These principles are clearly reflected in Parsons's assertion that vocational choice involves the individual using "true reasoning" (Parsons, 1909, p. 5) to match his or her personal characteristics with the requirements and prospects of different occupations. Additionally, the concatenation of three 19th-century societal trends created a pressing need for a focus on career development: (1) the industrial revolution, with its upheaval of the traditional occupational opportunity structure; (2) urbanization, which resulted from the burgeoning need for factory labor at the same time as mechanized farming methods reduced the need for agricultural labor; and (3) immigration, which required large numbers of people to adapt to settings for which they were ill prepared (Herr, 2001). As the cumulative effects of these three trends crested in the United States around the turn of the 20th century, it is self-evident why the concern with career development, with its apotheosis in Parsons, arose when it did.

Parsons's (1909) dictum that occupational choice involved "three broad factors: (1) a clear understanding of . . . [one's] aptitudes, abilities, interests, ambitions, resources, [and] limitations . . . ; (2) a knowledge of the requirements . . . , advantages and disadvantages, compensation, opportunities, and prospects in different lines of work; (3) true reasoning on the relations of these two groups of facts" (p. 5) exclusively dominated the conception of career development for the first half of the 20th century. With the influx into the United States of large numbers of European psychologists and psychiatrists fleeing Nazi persecution in the period between the mid-1930s and mid-1940s, a new conception of developmental psychology arose to challenge, and then dominate, the assumption that behavior was controlled by rational processes. Reflecting this new emphasis on psychological development, between 1951 and 1966, a veritable tidal wave of new theories of career development appeared, based on the new paradigm that career development was a longitudinal, not purely rational developmental process (rather than a one-time, reasoned choice). Because this chapter takes a historical approach to the evolution of career development theories, the following review will cite the earliest publication of each theory in essentially its current form. More recent restatements of many of these theories may be found in Brown and Brooks (1996) or in Brown (2002), but the major constructs of each theory remain the same as presented here.

DEVELOPMENTAL/PERSONALITY THEORIES

THE FIRST RESEARCHERS to base their work on the new paradigm were Ginzberg, Ginsburg, Axelrad, and Herma (1951; respectively, an economist, a psychiatrist, a sociologist, and a psychologist). Based on their study of a group of male students from one prep school and one university in New York, they concluded that career development is a largely irreversible process of compromise that occurs between puberty and the end of adolescence. This process consists of three distinct phases: fantasy (to about age 11), tentative (ages 11–17 or 18; with sequential subphases of interests, capacity, values, and transition), and realistic (with sequential subphases of exploration, crystallization, and specification). Subsequently, Ginzberg (1972) revised the theory, concluding that the career development process did permit reversibility. Despite its methodological inadequacies, Ginzberg and colleagues (1951) was a groundbreaking study, in that it empirically demonstrated that career development is a longitudinal process. Once this beachhead was established, other theorists swarmed in to expand on the premise.

The most towering figure of this movement was Donald Super (1953, 1957), whose prolific and seminal writings on career development spanned more than 40 years. Super challenged Ginzberg and colleagues' (1951) conclusion that career choice is a compromise by adding that the choice process involved both synthesis and compromise. Super (1953) went even further in support of the new paradigm by declaring, "The process of vocational development is essentially that of developing and implementing a self-concept" (p. 190). This statement differed significantly from Parsons's view that occupational choice was a rationally determined one-time decision. In further adherence to the new developmental paradigm, Super (1957) went on to apply Charlotte Buehler's (1933) developmental life stages to mapping the process of career development. These five sequential stages were growth (ages 0–14), exploration (ages 15–24), establishment (ages 25–44), maintenance (ages 45–64), and decline (ages 65 and over). Interestingly, when Super reached the age of 65, he changed the name of the fifth stage from "decline" to "disengagement." In addition to proposing these life-span stages of career development, Super also proposed a life-space conception of occupation as one among a number of life roles (e.g., child, student, parent, worker, citizen, leisurite), each of which has greater or lesser salience at different times in one's life. Finally, Super (1957) suggested the notion of vocational (later changed to *career*) maturity as an index of how far along the career development process an individual had moved. Thus, while Super did not create a single, unified developmental theory, he did propose the most far-ranging set of concepts consistent with the new career development paradigm: occupation as implementation of the self concept, life-span career stages, life-space role salience, and career maturity.

In addition to Ginzberg and colleagues and Super, a number of part-theories consistent with this developmental paradigm were proposed. Several of these formulations focused on childhood experiences as the foundation for subsequent career development. Anne Roe (1956) proposed that in addition to genetic and cultural influences, people's career interests were determined by the nature of their relationship with their parents during childhood. Thus, children raised by parents who rejected or neglected them would tend to choose occupations that were not oriented toward people, such as technological and scientific fields, while children raised by parents who accepted them or were emotionally overinvolved with them would tend to choose occupations that were oriented toward people, such as sales, management, human services, and the arts. Bordin, Nachmann, and Segal (1963), basing their model on classical psychoanalytic theory, posited that an individual's level of psychosexual fixation determines his or her occupational choice. For example, those fixated at the oral stage would be attracted to occupations such as dentistry, while those fixated at the anal stage would favor occupations such as accounting. As one might expect, theories of this sort received little research support, because they failed to take into account the effects of the 10 to 15 years of intervening experience between early childhood and the age at which career choices are made.

More recently, Linda Gottfredson (1981, 1996) profited from these earlier attempts and instead focused on how children's career aspirations are circumscribed by considerations of gender typing and prestige of occupations. She posited that children tend to select an occupational goal that, most important, falls within that circumscribed zone and also permits them to implement their self-concept (a concept taken from Super). This choice generally involves a process of compromising on an alternative that is adequate, but not necessarily optimal. Gottfredson (1996) outlined four sequential stages of circumscription that occur between ages 3 and 14 (1. orientation to size and power, 2. orientation to sex roles, 3. orientation to social valuation, and 4. orientation to internal, unique self) and three types of compromise (anticipatory, experiential, and simulated). As her research has focused on children's current aspirations rather than their occupation chosen

415

*Historical
Perspectives
in Career
Development
Theory*

years later, her findings have been more supportive of her theory than was the case with Roe or Bordin and colleagues.

Finally, basing his work on Maslow's (1971) theory of needs structure, Liptak (2001) posited that career development must take into consideration both work and leisure roles, since needs that cannot be met in one domain may be met in the other.

MATCHING THEORIES

SEVERAL THEORIES HAVE sought to operationalize Parsons's (1909) idea that career choice involves matching the characteristics of the person with an occupation having compatible characteristics. While trying to stay within the new paradigm by casting his theory as a personality theory because it describes different types of persons, Holland (1966, 1973) was primarily concerned with the match (congruence) between these types and occupations that call for people of that type. The six types of persons and work environments he defined are realistic (focus on concrete, mechanical things); investigative (focus on intellectual or scientific problem solving); artistic (focus on imaginative, expressive activities); social (focus on teaching or helping people); enterprising (focus on controlling and managing); and conventional (focus on systematizing data). Since persons and occupations are rarely pure types, Holland used a three-type code (the three strongest type characteristics, in descending order) to characterize both persons and occupational environments. Holland found empirically that certain of the six types tend to cluster. Therefore, he arranged them around a hexagon in the order RIASEC, to show their degree of proximity. Thus, more people who are high on social are also high on artistic, but fewer people who are high on social are also high on realistic. Consistency is the extent to which people are high on adjacent types on the hexagon, and differentiation is the extent to which a person or environment is clearly high on some types and low on others. Undifferentiated persons have greater difficulty in choosing an occupation. Holland's system is widely used in good part because he developed a simple, well-researched instrument to determine one's type structure, the *Self-Directed Search* (Holland, 1985). Various guides are available that then allow one to locate occupations that are congruent with that pattern (e.g., Gottfredson & Holland, 1989). Considerable research supports the conclusion that people who are in congruent occupations are more satisfied with their choice of occupation.

The theory of work adjustment (TWA; Dawis & Lofquist, 1984; Lofquist & Dawis, 1969) also holds that correspondence between people and their work environment is necessary for a successful career.

Thus, the person's abilities must match the demands of the job for the worker to be judged as satisfactory, and the rewards offered by the job must match the worker's needs for the worker to feel satisfied. Research supports the theory's proposition that workers who are both satisfactory and satisfied will have longer tenure in their jobs.

COGNITIVE DECISION MAKING THEORIES

IN THE 1970S, a heightened interest in cognitive processing and in strategic decision making emerged across a range of academic disciplines (e.g., neurosciences, mathematics, psychology, economics, management). Consequently, a number of career theories were proposed to address Parsons's (1909, p. 5) third factor, "true reasoning." Even before that, however, Tiedeman and O'Hara (1963) proposed a pioneering theory of career decision making. Given the zeitgeist of the era in which they wrote, it is not surprising that they related their theory to Erikson's (1950) theory of psychosocial development. Tiedeman and O'Hara proposed a two-stage, longitudinal model of career decision making, which fits within the developmental paradigm. The first stage, Anticipation, included the four sequential phases of Exploration, Crystallization, Choice, and Clarification. The second stage, Implementation, included the three phases of Induction, Reformation, and Integration.

Following Bandura's (1977) publication of his social learning theory, several authors proposed career theories based on his principles. Krumboltz (1979) published his Social Learning Theory of Career Decision Making, which posited four types of factors that influence why people choose, remain in, or change their occupation. These factors were (1) genetic endowment and special abilities, (2) environmental conditions and events, (3) instrumental and associative learning experiences, and (4) task approach skills. Based on the interaction of these factors, people form beliefs about themselves and about the world of work, which they then act on in entering or preparing for an occupation.

The second theory that derived from Bandura's social learning theory was the Social Cognitive Career Theory (SCCT; Lent, Brown, & Hackett, 1994). This theory utilizes Bandura's (1986) constructs of self-efficacy, outcome expectations, and personal goals, which interact and affect career decision making. This theory has generated some strong supportive research that tracks the interaction of these elements in influencing career behaviors (Lent et al., 1994).

The wave of interest in cognitive science also led Peterson, Sampson, and Reardon (1991) to propose a Cognitive Information Processing theory, which essentially grafts a level of metacognitions (thinking about

417

*Historical
Perspectives
in Career
Development
Theory*

the decision-making process) onto Parson's three factors. Thus, one not only engages in Parsonian "true reasoning" but also examines the process by which he or she does so. This involves utilizing a five-stage cyclical process (CASVE) of (1) identifying a problem in one's career decision making (Communication), (2) interrelating the components of the problem (Analysis), (3) creating likely alternatives (Synthesis), (4) prioritizing alternatives (Valuing), and (5) forming means-end strategies (Execution).

Additionally, several part-theories were proposed that emphasized the role of a person's value system in arriving at career decisions. Katz (1966) viewed the career decision-making process as a series of sequential decisions that are largely based on one's value system. Brown and Crace (1996) asserted that high priority values are the most important determinants of career decisions and only choices that are consistent with the individual's values will produce satisfaction.

Finally, reflecting postmodern thinking, Young, Valach, and Collin (1996) posited that career development should be viewed as an action system that gains its personalized meaning through the interaction between the actor's purposive intent and the social context in which the act takes place.

ENVIRONMENTAL THEORIES

WHILE THE THEORIES of career choice and/or development that we have considered so far have focused on intrapsychic processes, sociologists and others have suggested theories of career development that attribute the process to external environmental factors. These theories include Status Attainment Theory (Blau & Duncan, 1967), which posits that one's level of occupational attainment is determined primarily by the social status of one's parents (which affects the level of education that one will achieve). At the time of its introduction, this theory proved a better predictor of career development than any of the intrapsychic theories.

A number of authors, including both sociologists (Miller & Form, 1951) and psychologists (Bandura, 1982; Cabral & Salomone, 1990; Mitchell, Levin, & Krumboltz, 1999), have posited that chance events, such as being in the right place at the right time, are major determinants of career development. As Super (1957) pointed out, part of the disagreement on the importance of chance events in determining careers results from a difference among scholars in the field as to definitions and conceptions of what constitutes chance. Another reason for career theorists to resist this concept is that it renders moot the theorists' attempts to define systematic processes of career development.

INTEGRATING THEORIES

HERSHENSON (2005) CONCLUDED that "there probably will never be a single, unified, comprehensive theory of career development..., because the career development process is too complex, too dependent on the idiosyncratic interaction of personal and environmental variables, and too contextually determined" (p. 150). Therefore, he proposed using a framework that consisted of six statuses within which constructs from diverse career theories can be organized. The notion of statuses (Helms, 1995) appears to best represent in vivo career development, because statuses avoid the necessarily sequential, one step at a time, implication of stages. Further, statuses allow for the simultaneous functioning of more than one process. The six career statuses, which were selected because they occur across demographic and cultural groups, are Imagining, iNforming, Choosing, Obtaining, Maintaining, and Exiting. These statuses form the acronym INCOME. For example, the Imagining status can bring together Ginzberg and colleagues' (1951) fantasy phase, Super's (1957) early Growth stage, Tiedeman and O'Hara's (1963) Exploration phase, the impact of early learning posited by the social learning theories (Krumboltz, 1979, and SCCT), the process of circumscription posited by Gottfredson (1981), and the impact of parental social status posited by Blau and Duncan (1967). In this way, constructs from a wide variety of career development theories can be brought together to inform a status that exists across diverse population groups.

REFERENCES

Bandura, A. (1977). *Social learning theory*. Englewood Cliffs, NJ: Prentice-Hall.

Bandura, A. (1982). The psychology of chance encounters and life paths. *American Psychologist, 37,* 747–755.

Bandura, A. (1986). *Social foundations of thought and action: A social-cognitive theory*. Englewood Cliffs, NJ: Prentice Hall.

Blau, P. M., & Duncan, O. D. (1967). *The American occupational structure*. New York: Wiley.

Bordin, E. S., Nachmann, B., & Segal, S. J. (1963). An articulated framework for vocational development. *Journal of Counseling Psychology, 10,* 107–116.

Brown, D. (Ed.). (2002). *Career choice and development* (4th ed.). San Francisco: Jossey-Bass.

Brown, D., & Brooks, L. (Eds.). (1996). *Career choice and development* (3rd ed.). San Francisco: Jossey-Bass.

Brown, D., & Crace, R. K. (1996). Values in life role choices and outcomes: A conceptual model. *The Career Development Quarterly, 44,* 211–223.

Buehler, C. (1933). *Der menschliche Lebenslauf als psychologisches Problem.* Leipzig: Hirzel.

Cabral, A. C., & Salomone, P. R. (1990). Chance and careers: Normative versus contextual development. *The Career Development Quarterly, 39,* 5–17.

Council for Accreditation of Counseling and Related Educational Programs. (2006). *2001 standards.* Retrieved September 14, 2007, from http://www.cacrep.org/2001Standards.html

Dawis, R. V., & Lofquist, L. H. (1984). *A psychological theory of work adjustment: An individual-differences model and its application.* Minneapolis: University of Minnesota Press. Erikson, E. H. (1950). *Childhood and society.* New York: W. W. Norton.

Erikson, E. H. (1950). *Childhood and society.* New York: Norton.

Ginzberg, E. (1972). Toward a theory of occupational choice: A restatement. *Vocational Guidance Quarterly, 20,* 169–176.

Ginzberg, E., Ginsburg, S. W., Axelrad, S., & Herma, J. L. (1951). *Occupational choice: An approach to a general theory.* New York: Columbia University Press.

Gottfredson, G. D., & Holland, J. L. (1989). *Dictionary of Holland occupational codes* (2nd ed.). Odessa, FL: Psychological Assessment Resources.

Gottfredson, L. S. (1981). Circumscription and compromise: A developmental theory of occupational aspirations. *Journal of Counseling Psychology, 28,* 545–579.

Gottfredson, L. S. (1996). A theory of circumscription and compromise. In D. Brown & L. Brooks (Eds.), *Career choice and development* (3rd ed., pp. 179–232). San Francisco: Jossey-Bass.

Helms, J. E. (1995). An update of Helm's White and people of color racial identity models. In J. G. Ponterotto, J. M. Casas, L. A. Suzuki, & C. M. Alexander (Eds.), *Handbook of multicultural counseling* (pp. 181–198). Thousand Oaks, CA: Sage Publications.

Herr, E. L. (2001). Career development and its practice: A historical perspective. *The Career Development Quarterly, 49,* 196–211.

Herr, E. L., & Shahnasarian, M. (2001). Selected milestones in the evolution of career development practices in the twentieth century. *The Career Development Quarterly, 49,* 225–232.

Hershenson, D. B. (2005). INCOME: A culturally inclusive and disability-sensitive framework for organizing career development concepts and interventions. *The Career Development Quarterly, 54,* 150–161.

Holland, J. L. (1966). *The psychology of vocational choice: A theory of personality types and model environments.* Waltham, MA: Blaisdell.

Holland, J. L. (1973). *Making vocational choices: A theory of careers.* Englewood Cliffs, NJ: Prentice-Hall.

Holland, J. L. (1985). *The Self-Directed Search professional manual.* Odessa, FL: Psychological Assessment Resources.

Katz, M. R. (1966). A model of guidance for career decision making. *Vocational Guidance Quarterly, 15,* 2–10.

Krumboltz, J. D. (1979). A social learning theory of career decision making. In A. M. Mitchell, G. B. Jones, & J. D. Krumboltz (Eds.), *Social learning and career decision making* (pp. 19–49). Cranston, RI: Carroll Press.

Lent, R. W., Brown, S. D., & Hackett, G. (1994). Toward a unifying social cognitive theory of career and academic interest, choice, and performance [Monograph]. *Journal of Vocational Behavior, 45,* 79–122.

Liptak, J. J. (2001). *Treatment planning in career counseling.* Belmont, CA: Wadsworth/Thompson Learning.

Lofquist, L. H., & Dawis, R. V. (1969). *Adjustment to work: A psychological view of man's problems in a work-oriented society.* East Norwalk, CT: Appleton-Century-Crofts.

Maslow, A. H. (1971). *The farther reaches of human nature.* New York: Penguin.

Miller, D. C., & Form, W. H. (1951). *Industrial sociology: An introduction to the sociology of work relations.* New York: Harper.

Mitchell, L. K., Levin, A. S., & Krumboltz, J. D. (1999). Planned happenstance: Constructing unexpected career opportunities. *Journal of Counseling and Development, 77,* 115–124.

Parsons, F. (1909). *Choosing a vocation.* Boston: Houghton Mifflin.

Peterson, G. W., Sampson, J. P., Jr., & Reardon, R. C. (1991). *Career development and services: A cognitive approach.* Pacific Grove, CA: Brooks/Cole.

Roe, A. (1956). *The psychology of occupations.* New York: Wiley.

Super, D. E. (1953). A theory of vocational development. *American Psychologist, 8,* 185–190.

Super, D. E. (1957). *The psychology of careers: An introduction to vocational development.* New York: Harper & Bros.

Tiedeman, D. V., & O'Hara, R. (1963). *Career development: Choice and adjustment.* New York: College Entrance Examination Board.

Young, R. A., Valach, L., & Collin, A. (Eds.). (1996). A contextual explanation of career. In D. Brown & L. Brooks (Eds.), *Career choice and development* (3rd ed., pp. 477–512). San Francisco: Jossey-Bass.

41

Occupational Choice and the Meaning of Work

ELLEN S. FABIAN

T HE MEANING THAT work has to an individual has been studied for decades, both in the sociological literature (e.g., Morse & Weiss, 1955) and the psychological and career literature (e.g., Crites, 1969; Gottfredson, 1996). Each of these perspectives has contributed to our understanding of the factors that influence how individuals find meaning and satisfaction in their work. More recently, career theorists have examined the extent to which job satisfaction is linked to life satisfaction and subjective well-being, suggesting the potential importance of career and work in providing meaning to an individual's life. The relationships between occupational choice, job satisfaction, and life satisfaction are important issues for counselors to consider no matter what specialty or setting they are in, as the problems or stress clients experience in one of these domains may affect the other and may overall decrease their sense of well-being. The purposes of this chapter are to (1) define job satisfaction; (2) examine the literature linking occupational choice to job satisfaction; and (3) describe the relationship between work satisfaction and well-being.

JOB SATISFACTION AND OCCUPATIONAL CHOICE

JOB SATISFACTION HAS been defined as "a pleasureable or positive emotional state resulting from the appraisal of one's job or job experiences" (Locke, 1976, p. 1300). The higher the degree of satisfaction with a job, the more likely an individual is to describe his or her work as meaningful (Arnold, Turner, Barling, Kelloway & McKee, 2007). Job satisfaction has been studied from different perspectives, including organizational or sociological perspectives and psychological or career perspectives. In the organizational literature, for example, job satisfaction is linked to work setting or environmental factors, such as task autonomy and variety, co-worker relationships, and organizational leadership and structure (Arnold et al., 2007), as well as more concrete factors such as wages and benefits (Piccolo & Colquitt, 2006). Not surprisingly, most studies have found that intrinsic job factors such as co-worker relationships and autonomy and diversity of job tasks—are more highly correlated with overall job satisfaction than extrinsic factors such as wages and benefits (Picollo & Colquitt, 2006). In fact one of the earliest studies demonstrating this finding arose from research conducted in the late 1920s by a Harvard business professor, Elton Mayo (Clark, 1999). In a series of industrial experiments, Mayo and his colleagues initially set out to explore how physical and environmental factors influenced worker productivity at the Hawthorne Plant in Cicero, Illinois. The findings of their seminal work were that worker productivity improved regardless of the experimental manipulation employed (Clark, 1999). This phenomenon, later coined the *Hawthorne effect*, influenced the development of organizational studies and industrial psychology in that it demonstrated the strength of intrinsic factors (in this case, workers' perception of management's interest in them) in influencing job performance and satisfaction. Over the succeeding decades, industrial psychologists and sociologists have provided strong evidence of the connections between workers' perceptions of intrinsic factors and their subsequent evaluations of the job (Franke & Kaul, 1978).

Factors contributing to job satisfaction have also been studied from the individualistic perspective that emerges from career counseling, rehabilitation counseling, counseling psychology, and related specialties. Career theories and theorists have often approached the issue of job satisfaction and the meaning of work from a person—environment interaction framework. This involves matching individual attributes, such as personality, skills, values, and needs, to environmental resources and supplies as a means of achieving job satisfaction (Tracey & Hopkins, 2001). Two of the best-known theories in this area include

Holland's theory of vocational choice (Holland, 1997) and Lofquist and Dawis's (1991) Theory of Work Adjustment (TWA). The next section of this chapter describes person-environment interaction theories that predict job satisfaction.

PERSON-ENVIRONMENT FIT MODELS OF OCCUPATIONAL CHOICE AND JOB SATISFACTION

TINSLEY (2000) REVIEWED the literature on person-environment fit models and their relationship to job satisfaction, concluding that these approaches "provide a valid and useful way of thinking about the interaction between the individual and the environment" (p. 150). Indeed, most counselors or psychologists working with clients around career choice issues approach it, at least in part, from a person-environment fit perspective. Many of the person-environment fit theories include a variety of career assessment techniques and tools that are intuitively valid and accessible to a variety of clients.

In general, person-environment fit models have supported the relationship between person-environment correspondence or congruence and a variety of outcomes, most notably job satisfaction (Tinsley, 2000). The best-known and well used of these theories is John Holland's theory of vocational choice (Holland, 1997). Holland's theory is based on measuring the fit or *congruence* between an individual's personality and the personality of the work environment. It proposes that people and occupational environments can be "characterized on the basis of the extent to which they resemble each of six 'pure types' and that a good match between person and environment will have a number of beneficial outcomes" (Arnold et al., 2007, p. 95). Holland's six types are hypothesized along a hexagonal dimension, with the placement along the hexagon indicating the degree of relationship among the six types. So, for example, the Artistic type in Holland's theory has the closest relationship to Social types, and the least relationship to Conventional ones (for more information on Holland's theory, see Holland, 1997). There are a number of assessment instruments available to measure an individual's Holland type, the most widely used being the Self-Directed Search (Holland, 1985). In Holland's theory, a match between the person and environment is referred to as congruence; it is hypothesized that higher indices of congruence result in greater job satisfaction and better job performance (Holland & Gottfredson, 1992). A great deal of subsequent research has attempted to measure the extent to which Holland's congruence predicts job satisfaction, with some equivocal findings, although the general consensus in the research literature is that the theory, and similar ones, are the most widely used and well supported in the field; in fact, a majority of career counselors rely on person-environment fit models in assisting clients with occupational choice.

Although there is some criticism regarding the static nature of Holland's congruence and similar constructs in other person-environment fit models, one related theory that may yield more complex and dynamic explanations for the relationship between person and environmental factors is the Theory of Work Adjustment (TWA; Lofquist & Dawis, 1969). This theory posits a dynamic relationship between the needs and values of the individual, and the demands and resources of the work environment. In this model, work adjustment is "viewed as a continuous process by which individual and environments seek to achieve and maintain a correspondence with each other" (Tinsley, 2000, p. 166). The degree to which this balance is achieved represents job satisfaction from the perspective of the employee, and job satisfactoriness from the perspective of the employer (for more information about the TWA, see Lofquist & Dawis, 1969, 1991). The TWA theory also incorporates a number of instruments assessing individual values and needs (Minnesota Importance Questionnaire; Rounds, Henley, Dawis, Lofquist, & Weiss, 1981), job satisfaction (Minnesota Satisfaction Questionnaire; Weiss, Dawis, England, & Lofquist, 1967), and reinforcers in the work environment (Minnesota Job Description Questionnaire; Borgen, Weiss, Tinsley, Dawis, & Lofquist, 1968). One of the hallmarks of the TWA model is the proposed reciprocal relationship between individual and environment, where each can cause change in the other. For example, employers can modify employee work schedules in order to accommodate workers with disabilities or those with child care and other responsibilities that require more flexibility. On the other hand, employees can voluntarily participate in health-promoting exercise and activities in order to reduce their absenteeism and increase their productivity.

There are many other person-environment interaction theories that generally support the conclusion that the better the match, the more satisfied the worker is and the better he or she performs (Tinsley, 2000). In addition, other types of career theories—such as developmental ones and social learning theories—have also explored the relationship between a variety of individual attributes and overall perceptions of the value and meaning of work (e.g., Jepsen & Sheu, 2003; Lent et al., 2005), as well as the relationship between positive work experiences and overall quality of life. The meaning of work and relationship to well-being are discussed in the next section.

THE MEANING OF WORK

CONTEMPORARY RESEARCH ON why people work emphasizes the linkages between work and all other domains of life—psychological and physical health, family, social participation, and subjective well-being. There is general consensus in psychological and sociological literature that work—whether it is paid or unpaid—is beneficial in that it positively affects mental health, provides structure and direction in people's lives, and may even improve psychological and physical illnesses (Arnold et al., 2007). The meaning that work has in an individual's life is important for counselors to consider, whether they are working with individuals who encounter significant challenges regarding work, such as people with disabilities, women who may experience role conflicts, or older people facing retirement. While all work is somewhat beneficial to most individuals (when compared to unemployment), it appears that it is positive or meaningful work that is most highly related to overall well-being (Westaby, Versenyi, & Hausmann, 2005), particularly in American society, where people are often defined by their work or their occupation.

It is also clear from decades of research that satisfaction with work is connected to satisfaction in other life domains. In this area, a number of studies have concluded that there is a modest, but significant, correlation between job satisfaction and life satisfaction, with positive life satisfaction spilling over into job satisfaction more commonly than the reverse (Judge & Watanabe, 1993). In other words, people who are happier in general are also happier in their jobs. However, the opposite effect can also occur—where negative work satisfaction can depress overall life satisfaction. This situation occurs most frequently when there is work and family conflict, a topic that has received a great deal of attention (Judge & Ilies, 2004) and one that is important for counselors to consider in career counseling.

WORK AND FAMILY

RESEARCH ON THE linkages between work and family—and the potential for conflict—has important implications for career counseling and counseling in general. The recent interest in this area has been stimulated by social trends, such as the increased number of women in the workforce, shifts in cultural values and expectations, and the movement away from gender-based roles both at work and in the family (Edwards & Rothbard, 2000). A consequence of these social trends has been more frequent role conflicts within families that can contribute to family distress and disintegration. These conflicts can include competing time demands, increases in psychological or physiological stress in one environment that can spill over into the other, and competing behavioral expectations between roles (Judge & Ilies, 2004). For example, women may function more independently in the workplace, yet be expected to perform more traditional dependent roles in the home. Whatever the source of the conflict, employers have begun to realize that they affect worker productivity and satisfaction and have developed organizational approaches to address them, such as onsite childcare facilities, telecommuting, flexible schedules, and liberal leave policies. In turn, counselors have been assisting clients and families to recognize the sources of family stress as a consequence of work and family linkages and encourage them to discover the value and meaning of work in order to sort through various role demands. A few career theorists, such as Nancy Schlossberg (Goodman, Schlossberg, & Anderson, 2006), can provide some guidance for counselors assisting adults and families in clarifying role expectations and managing crises and transitions.

WORK AND WELL-BEING

THE SAME SO-CALLED permeable boundary that exists between work and family (Judge & Ilies, 2004) also exists between work and well-being. Lent and Brown (2008) reiterate that "work is an important part of life for most adults, and the boundaries between work and other life domains are often permeable" (p. 12). They propose a bidirectional model that accounts for the spillover effects between job satisfaction and life satisfaction, suggesting that the strength of the linkages between the two is related to the individual's determination of the value or meaning attached to the worker role.

In terms of the contribution that work means to overall well-being or quality of life, a number of studies have examined this issue. Although the majority of them support the association between these two statuses (e.g., Judge & Watanabe, 1993; Heller, Judge, & Watson, 2002), there have been a few groups for whom employment may actually depress overall subjective well-being, for example, women (Starrin & Larsson, 1987); people with significant disabilities (Fabian, 1992); and individuals who derive little meaning or identity from their work (Hultman, Hemlin, & Hornquist, 2006). It appears that the relationship between work and well-being is a complex one (Lent & Brown, 2008), requiring counselors to carefully consider several issues, such as the intrinsic and extrinsic motivators to seek employment, whether the cost of going to work outweighs other life choices (like parenting), and cultural and social factors. The latter issue, in particular, has not been well studied in the literature.

IMPLICATIONS FOR COUNSELING INTERVENTIONS

THE LITERATURE ON occupational choice and the meaning of work clearly demonstrates the connection—in general, individuals who choose occupations based on skills, values, attributes, and personality are more likely to find satisfaction in their work. In turn, the satisfaction they receive from their work is more likely to influence their overall well-being or quality of life. These findings provide compelling support for counselors from a variety of disciplines to implement strategies that enable clients to engage in career exploration and decision making. They also implicitly suggest the role of counselors as advocates or consultants to employers as work environments—and the available supports—can also increase job satisfaction (Harris, Winskowski, & Engdahl, 2007). Recommendations for counselors are discussed below.

1. Empower individuals in the career choice process by helping them to understand the link between choice and satisfaction. This recommendation is no different than that found in most of the voluminous literature and textbooks on career development and counseling (e.g., Sharf, 2006). However, it is particularly incumbent on counselors to assist clients who may encounter the largest impediments to career choice—such as people with disabilities, people from socioeconomic disadvantaged barriers, or people of color—to understand the choice process, and to engage them in choice-promoting behaviors (such as hands-on exploration of different jobs, information interviews, internships and work experience trials). The link between articulation of vocational goals and various desirable outcomes—such as job satisfaction and job performance—has been established in the literature. Career choice resulting in articulation of concrete career goals empowers clients by making goal achievement viable.

2. Remain sensitive and aware of the so-called spillover effect between job satisfaction and life satisfaction, and help clients to sort out and address role conflicts between work and family. It is important for counselors to listen for underlying issues when clients present with career concerns or family concerns in terms of how these problems or stresses may overlap. Research has suggested a link between positive mood at work and mood at home (Judge & Ilies, 2004; Rothbard, 2001); the old adage about having a bad day at work and taking it out at home appears to have some truth. When clients can understand the link between the two, as well as the precipitating events or antecedents, they can develop coping

strategies to help contain the mood states (if negative) and address it in the appropriate environment. Of course, all of us have experienced the euphoria that comes from receiving a promotion, a good recommendation, or winning a contract on the job—generally these positive experiences have positive consequences in the home environment as well.

3. Counselors need to be aware of socioeconomic differences as they affect choice issues in career counseling. For example, there is some research suggesting that interest/job match is less important for working-class adults, particularly those for whom choice may have been constrained or circumvented as a result of life circumstances (Jepsen & Sheu, 2003). Adults reentering the workforce may also experience different kinds of financial pressures that depress career choice options. In these cases, the extrinsic factors in the work environment—for example, co-worker relations, employer sensitivity to family and accommodation issues—may be worth exploring in assisting these individuals to select jobs that will optimize their sense of well-being.

The nature of work and the nature of individual choice influence an individual's satisfaction with his or her job, and subjective well-being. In American society, work is an important aspect of people's lives and their identities. Research indicates that satisfaction in work potentially spills over into satisfaction in life; therefore, counselors' awareness of the way the occupational choice contributes to the meaning and importance of work is a critical component of counseling interventions.

REFERENCES

Arnold, K. A., Turner, N., Barling, J., Kelloway, E. K., & McKee, M. C. (2007). Transformational leadership and psychological well-being: The mediating role of meaningful work. *Journal of Occupational Health Psychology, 13*, 193–203.

Borgen, F. H., Weiss, D. J., Tinsley, H. E., Dawis, R. V., & Lofquist, L. H. (1968). *The measurement of occupational reinforcer patterns* (Minnesota Studies in Vocational Rehabilitation No. 25). Minneapolis: University of Minnesota Press.

Clark, D. A. (1999). *Hawthorne effect*. Retrieved February 15, 2008, from http://www.nwlink.com/~Donclark/hrd/history/hawthorne.html

Crites, J. O. (1969). *Vocational psychology*. New York: McGraw-Hill.

Edwards, J. R., & Rothbard, N. P. (2000). Mechanisms linking work and family: Clarifying the relationship between work and family constructs. *Academy of Management Review, 25*, 178–199.

Fabian, E. S. (1992). Supported employment and the quality of life: Does a job make a difference? *Rehabilitation Counseling Bulletin, 36,* 84–97.

Franke, R. H., & Kaul, J. D. (1978). The Hawthorne experiments: First statistical interpretation. *American Sociological Review, 43,* 623–643.

Goodman, J., Schlossberg, N. K., & Anderson, M. L. (2006). *Counseling adults in transition.* New York: Springer Publishing.

Gottfredson, L. (1996). Gottfredson's theory of circumscription and compromise. In D. Brown, L. Brooks et al. (Eds.), *Career choice and development* (3rd ed., pp. 179–232). San Francisco: Jossey-Bass.

Harris, J. I., Winskowski, A. M., & Engdahl, B. E. (2007). Types of workplace social support in the prediction of job satisfaction. *The Career Development Quarterly, 56,* 150–158.

Heller, D., Judge, T. A., & Watson, D. (2002). The confounding role of personality and trait affectivity in the relationship between job and life satisfaction. *Journal of Organizational Behavior, 23,* 815–835.

Holland, J. L. (1985). *The Self-Directed Search professional manual* (1985 ed.). Odessa, FL: Psychological Assessment Resources.

Holland, J. L. (1997). *Making vocational choices: A theory of vocational personalities and work environments* (3rd ed.). Odessa, FL: Psychological Assessment Resources.

Holland, J. L., & Gottfredson, G. D. (1992). Studies of the hexagonal model: An evaluation (or, the perils of stalking the perfect hexagon). *Journal of Vocational Behavior, 40,* 159–170.

Hultman, B., Hemlin, S., & Hornquist, J. L. (2006). Quality of life among unemployed and employed people in northern Sweden: Are there any differences? *Work, 26,* 47–56.

Jepsen, D. A., & Sheu, H. B. (2003). General job satisfaction from a developmental perspective: Exploring choice-job matches at two career stages. *The Career Development Quarterly, 52,* 162–179.

Judge, T. A., & Ilies, R. (2004). Affect and job satisfaction: A study of their relationship at work and at home. *Journal of Applied Psychology, 87,* 797–807.

Judge, T. A., & Watanabe, S. (1993). Another look at the job satisfaction-life satisfaction relationship. *Journal of Applied Psychology, 78,* 939–948.

Lent, R. W., & Brown, S. D. (2008). Social cognitive career theory and subjective well-being in the context of work. *Journal of Career Assessment, 16,* 6–21.

Lent, R. W., Singley, D., Sheu, H., Gainor, K. A., Breener, B. R., Trestiman, D., et al. (2005). Social cognitive predictors of domain and life satisfaction: Exploring the theoretical precursors of subjective well-being. *Journal of Counseling Psychology, 52,* 429–442.

Locke, E. A. (1976). The nature and causes of job satisfaction. In M. D. Dunnette (Ed.), *Handbook of industrial and organizational psychology* (pp. 1297–1349). Chicago: Rand McNally.

Lofquist, L. H., & Dawis, R. V. (1969). *Adjustment to work.* New York: Appleton-Century-Crofts.

Lofquist, L. H., & Dawis, R. V. (1991). *Essentials of person-environment-correspondence counseling*. Minneapolis: University of Minnesota Press.

Morse, N. C., & Weiss, R. W. (1955). The function and meaning of work and the job. *American Sociological Review, 20,* 191–198.

Piccolo, R. F., & Colquitt, J. A. (2006). Transformational leadership and job behaviors: The mediating role of core job characteristics. *Academy of Management Journal, 49,* 327–340.

Rothbard, N. P. (2001). Enriching or depleting? The dynamics of engagement in work and family roles. *Administrative Science Quarterly, 46,* 655–684.

Rounds, J. B., Henley, G. A., Dawis, R. V., Lofquist, L. H., & Weiss, D. J. (1981). *Manual for the Minnesota Importance Questionnaire: A measure of needs and values*. Minneapolis: University of Minnesota Press.

Sharf, R. S. (2006). *Applying career development theory to counseling* (4th ed.). Florence, KY: Brooks/Cole.

Starrin, B., & Larsson, G. (1987). Coping with unemployment—a contribution to the understanding of women's unemployment. *Social Science and Medicine, 25,* 163–171.

Tinsley, H. E. A. (2000). The congruence myth: An analysis of the efficacy of the person-environment fit model. *Journal of Vocational Behavior, 56,* 147–179.

Tracey, T. J. G., & Hopkins, N. (2001). Correspondence of interests and abilities with occupational choice. *Journal of Counseling Psychology, 48,* 178–189.

Weiss, D. J., Dawis, R. B., England, G. W., & Lofquist, L. H. (1967). *Manual for the Minnesota Satisfaction Questionnaire* (Minnesota Studies in Vocational Rehabilitation No. 22). Minneapolis: University of Minnesota Press.

Westaby, J. D., Versenyi, A., & Hausmann, R. C. (2005). Intentions to work during terminal illness: An exploratory study of antecedent conditions. *Journal of Applied Psychology, 90,* 1297–1305.

42

What Counselors Should Know About School-to-Work Transition

PAUL H. WEHMAN AND
JENNIFER TODD MCDONOUGH

EXPERTS IN THE fields of special education and rehabilitation recognize that the transition process must include the provision of quality services for all youth with disabilities as they prepare to leave school. In fact, the federal Office of Special Education and Rehabilitative Services (OSERS) has made school-to-work transition a national priority and regularly provides special discretionary funds to educational and community agencies that are establishing model transition programs. What does the transition process encompass? Why is transition important? What transition models are involved?

Perhaps one of the most significant reasons that transition from school to adulthood has emerged as a major area of interest for more than 25 years is because literally thousands of young people with disabilities are leaving special education with no jobs. Numerous post-21 outcome studies have repeatedly shown that people with mild as well as severe disabilities are unable to consistently gain good quality employment with decent pay and fringe benefits (Newman, 2001).

By most accounts more than 50% of young adults with disabilities are unemployed when they leave school, with figures much higher regarding those with severe disabilities. Many professionals have begun to question the validity of the secondary/special education curriculum and the efforts in providing effective teaching interventions for these students (Wehman & Kregel, 2004). Very serious concern has arisen that much of what happens in special education at the secondary level is not proving very useful or functional in the context of ultimately gaining employment and making successful transitions into adulthood (Wehman, 2006).

Transition for any student with a disability involves several key components, including (1) an appropriate school program; (2) formalized plans involving parents and the entire array of community agencies that are responsible for providing services; and (3) multiple, quality options for gainful employment and meaningful postschool education and community living (Dymond, Renzaglia, & Chun, 2008).

Although the goal of our educational system is to help students become productive members of society as adults, few schools have guided students with disabilities into meaningful employment opportunities appropriate for their abilities. Because most students with disabilities do not benefit from systematic transition from school to work, approximately 50% to 75% of all adults with disabilities are unemployed. Until recently, most parents of children with disabilities rarely considered the possibility of a career for their children after graduation.

The Individuals With Disability Education Improvement Act (IDEA, 2004) is specific about the responsibility of the local education agency for transition planning:

> The Individualized Education Program (IEP) for each student, beginning no later than age 16 (and at a younger age, if determined appropriate), must include a statement of transition services. . . . (sec. 602)
>
> (I) As used in this part, "transition services" means a coordinated set of activities for a child with a disability that:
>
>   (a) is designed to be within a results-oriented process, that is focused on improving the academic and functional achievement of the child with a disability to facilitate the child's movement from school to post-school activities, including post-secondary education, vocational education, integrated employment (including supported employment), continuing and adult education, adult services, independent living, or community participation;
>   (b) is based on the individual child's needs taking into account the child's strengths, preferences and interests; and,

(c) Include instruction, related services, community experiences, the development of employment and other post-school adult living objectives, and when appropriate, acquisition of daily living skills and functional vocational evaluation. (sec. 602)

A number of changes must occur in the way we help students secure meaningful, competitive employment. First, school programming needs to be revamped to include community-based job training. This involves teaching important skills directly at a site like a shopping mall or recreation center or job (Wehman & Kregel, 2004; Weiner & Zivolich, 2003). Second, parents and professionals must develop formal, written plans for transition similar to the IEP (Wehman & Wittig, in press). Third, schools and community agencies will have to work with businesses to develop a variety of meaningful employment options for citizens with disabilities (Wehman, Inge, Revell, & Brooke, 2007). In this chapter, we will address these issues.

TRANSITION PLANNING

TRANSITION FROM SCHOOL to work is a process that focuses on the movement of students with disabilities from school into the world of work (Wehman, 2006; Wehman & Wittig, in press). Facilitating a student's transition from a school program to the workplace requires movement through school instruction, planning for the transition process, and placement into meaningful community-integrated employment. Currently special education and vocational rehabilitation programs are required by legislation to cooperatively plan for the transition of students with disabilities into the work environment. A rehabilitation counselor's role in transition programs varies according to local needs and resources (Szymanski & Parker, 1996). In a few instances rehabilitation counselors are school-based and employed by a school district or cooperative of districts (Szymanski & Parker, 1996). However, most counselors are employed by state vocational rehabilitation agencies and often have limited time and resources to devote to the coordination of transition services. Whether a counselor is school-based or state agency–based, his or her activities may include career and psychosocial counseling, consultation with special education and vocational education teachers, and coordination with school, family, and community efforts in career planning and implementation. Additionally, job placement, coordination of job support service, referral to and coordination with adult services, and planning and coordination with postsecondary programs is also done regularly.

What are the key components that should be included in a transition planning process?

- Functional, community-referenced secondary educational curriculum
- Community-based service delivery
- Interagency planning and service delivery efforts
- Availability of an array of postsecondary options
- Availability of ongoing community-based support services
- Student, parent, and family involvement throughout the transition process.

INTERAGENCY PLANNING AND SERVICE DELIVERY EFFORTS

AN INTERAGENCY TRANSITION planning team should comprise professionals from various disciplines who provide direct educational services or who are targeted to provide adult services to transition-aged students and their families. The team's major responsibility is to develop, implement, and monitor the Transition IEP for the student (Wehman & Wittig, in press). The team should develop a plan that identifies the target adult outcomes in the areas of employment, community living, and recreation that the student and his or her family desire at the time of graduation (Wehman, 1995). The plan should identify the supports necessary to achieve and maintain these outcomes, the steps needed to achieve the desired outcomes, and who is responsible for each step.

The Transition IEP addresses goals in a number of postsecondary areas and goals that are not achieved while the student is in the secondary education program. This plan can serve to focus educational services on the development and practice of skills that will enhance opportunities for the students to achieve these goals upon completion of their secondary level program. Following are the key elements of a plan to consider:

- Does formal transition planning begin for students when they reach the age of 16?
- Are the appropriate school and adult service personnel involved?
- Has a transition planning meeting been held?
- Does the Transition IEP cover the appropriate target areas such as employment, postsecondary education, independent living services, financial and income needs, recreation and leisure needs, medical and therapeutic needs, social and recreational needs, transportation needs, and advocacy and legal needs?
- Does the plan reflect a true vision of the potential of the student or is it merely a plan that offers only what the service delivery system currently provides?

- Is the plan updated annually at a minimum?
- Are exit meetings held to finalize plans for the transition from school to employment?

POSTSECONDARY OPTIONS TO CONSIDER

EMPLOYMENT REPRESENTS A major element in the lives of people with or without disabilities. The type of work a person does, the amount of money he or she earns, and career advancement opportunities directly affect how individuals look at themselves (Wehman et.al., 2007). What is most important for individuals with disabilities is to develop multiple employment choices that reflect the array of job opportunities available to nondisabled workers in the same community. For example, the types of jobs and supports that need to be developed for those jobs are crucial to an effective transition plan for students with severe disabilities. Consider some of the following issues:

- Into what types of jobs are people being placed? Are these jobs reflective of the array of jobs available in the community? Are placements occurring only in entry-level positions?
- Do the jobs people are working provide a livable wage with benefits?
- Are people working in community-integrated jobs?
- Have the provision of training and ongoing support services been identified prior to placement?
- Once a placement has been initiated, has the fading process been implemented appropriately?
- Are all parties involved in the placement satisfied with the current outcome and level of support?
- Have appropriate arrangements been made for the transfer of case management activities to a long-term support agency (if one exists)?

CAREER/VOCATIONAL COUNSELING

CAREER AND JOB choices are difficult for everyone, but frequently students with disabilities have had little or no exposure to vocational options available within the community, thus making it very difficult to choose what type of job they want at graduation or as a career. The educational team, especially the rehabilitation counselor, should begin career/ vocational counseling with students by the time they reach 16 years of age. They should arrange to meet with the student, his or her family, and school personnel to discuss the array of employment opportunities available in the community. The counselor should act as a consultant to teachers and other school personnel involved in the development of the IEP to ensure that students are exposed to the variety of vocational opportunities available within the local economy. Concerted efforts on the part of all involved can provide the student with an experiential background that will enable him or her to make job/career choices as graduation nears.

CASE MANAGEMENT

TRADITIONALLY, REHABILITATION COUNSELORS working with a public agency have spent most of their time in case management rather than counseling responsibilities. However, these roles and responsibilities are changing as many rehabilitation counselors are now becoming licensed professional counselors. As a member of a transition planning team, the counselor may also assume a role of ensuring dissemination of accurate information to parents and educators. For example, here are some typical responsibilities of a case manager:

- Develop vendorship and purchase of service agreements
- Establish local agreements with key agencies
- Participate in local interagency transition planning
- Provide in-service training to school personnel and parents on the federal-state vocational rehabilitation criteria for eligibility and provision of services
- Attend individual transition planning meetings
- Serve as a member of the transition team throughout the secondary years
- Gather and interpret vocational assessment information
- Coordinate and monitor supported employment placement of postsecondary students
- Identify referral needs and ensure referrals are made to the appropriate agencies and/or services

Transition planning involves many different members of the educational team and the community as well as the choice of students and family members. This process is important as students plan for life after school.

THE SCHOOL'S ROLE IN IMPLEMENTING TRANSITION PLANNING

THE SERVICES AVAILABLE through the assistance of the vocational rehabilitation counselor and other adult services resources are most effective if the school program aggressively incorporates transition planning into middle school and secondary-level activities. This planning may include, for example, the family of a young adolescent with a disability signing up for service coordination assistance from local mental health/mental retardation (MH/MR) services programs as early in the student's school career as possible. The service coordinator is then invited to attend selective IEP meetings to assist with services such as living arrangements, respite services, and recreation.

There are a number of administrative procedures within the school necessary to implement effective transition planning. It is helpful first to designate the teacher who is responsible for the IEP as the transition service coordinator for a student. This teacher will then develop an Individualized Transition Plan (ITP) in cooperation with the MH/MR case manager, vocational rehabilitation (VR) counselor, and any other persons whom the student or family wishes to invite to transition-oriented IEP meetings. The written transition plan (ITP) can be filed with the active IEP and updated each time the IEP is reviewed. These procedures assist in establishing clear communication among all persons involved in long-range planning for a student. In instances where transition services are not being delivered and/or objectives are not being met in a timely manner, the IDEA legislation states that the school system is responsible for reconvening the transition committee. It is beneficial to indicate persons responsible for each objective and to set a timeline for carrying out specific strategies.

COMMUNITY-BASED INSTRUCTION WITH STUDENTS

MANY YOUTHS WITH disabilities and their families experience a sense of isolation from the community. A primary example of this isolation is the limited participation of youths with a disability in work and work-related activities. By encouraging and supporting middle school youth and high school students with disabilities to obtain ID cards, to develop and maintain résumés, and to seek out work opportunities, the school program can expand involvement in the community, knowledge of work requirements, and awareness of individual interests. These activities provide a firm base of information for the transition committees to use in helping the individual student to plan for postsecondary interests and services needs.

A formalized approach to expanding the community awareness and participation of a secondary-aged youth with a disability is the incorporation of community-based instruction and supported employment into the school activities (Wehman & Kregel, 2004). Community-based instruction is defined by Wehman (2006) as involving "teachers and other education personnel teaching educational objectives in natural environments, such as work sites, shopping malls, and restaurants" (p. 155). Training experiences in the community help students with a disability determine job preferences and develop a work history (Wehman & Walsh, 1999). The focus of community experiences can also move from training to actual employment as the student nears completion of secondary education.

RELATIONSHIP OF THE REHABILITATION ACT TO SCHOOL PROGRAMS AND YOUTH WITH DISABILITIES

THE REHABILITATION ACT Amendments of 1998 emphasize the provision of support and services through the rehabilitation system for high school students with disabilities exiting or preparing to exit school programs. The Rehabilitation Act Amendments contain a definition of transition services that matches what is contained in IDEA:

I. A coordinated set of activities for a student, designed within an outcome oriented process, that promotes movement from school to post school activities, including post secondary education, vocational training, integrated employment (including supported employment), continuing and adult education, adult services, independent living, or community participation.

II. The coordinated set of activities must be based upon the individual student's needs, taking into account the student's preferences and interests, and must include instruction, community experiences, the development of employment and other post school adult living objectives, and, if appropriate, acquisition of daily living skills and functional vocational evaluation. Transition services must promote or facilitate the achievement of the employment outcome identified in the student's individualized plan for employment (P.L. 105–202, sec. 361.55).

This definition is a balanced statement of how the transition process is embedded in the Rehabilitation Act Amendments. It is similar to, and coordinated with, IDEA's definition of what the school's transition responsibilities are. Why is this important to students? The reason is simple: parents and professionals alike can draw on the resources provided by this law to facilitate a student's transition from school to adulthood needs.

Part I of this definition focuses on services occurring after the individual exits the school program. These services reflect a representative sample of the wide array of postschool activities that might be used by individuals with a disability entering the adult community. At times these services are used in sequence, such as postsecondary education followed by employment. Services might also be used simultaneously, such as supported employment along with other adult services and community living supports.

Part II of the definition of transition services focuses on activities that may occur during the school program to support the preparation and planning for transition. This section emphasizes relating the school program to the community and the incorporation of postschool employment and daily living objectives into classroom activities and planning.

THE VOCATIONAL REHABILITATION COUNSELOR AND THE SCHOOL PROGRAM

T HE GOAL OF the cooperative relationship between the vocational rehabilitation program and the education system is to prevent any gap in services as youths with disabilities make the transition from school into their postsecondary activities. The number of persons with disabilities served at any one time by a VR counselor varies nationally. However, it is not unusual for an individual counselor to have responsibility for assisting 100 to 200 people at various stages of the VR process. Even those VR counselors who spend the majority of their time working with young people who have disabilities usually carry large caseloads. These counselors cannot possibly attend every IEP meeting for every student with a disability age 14 and older and still effectively respond to the multiple and diverse needs of the full range of persons for whom they coordinate services.

An example of how services would begin to be arranged for a student follows:

1. *Organizing the counselor role in transition efforts.* The manager of the local rehabilitation office participates on the county schools' transition advisory committee. Along with VR and school representatives, this committee includes a variety of adult services agencies involved in service coordination and funding, someone from the local community college, parents of students with disabilities, and employers.

2. *The counselor as information source and resource to the schools, youth with disabilities, and families.* The VR counselors make regular weekly itinerary visits to their individual schools and are available to consult generally with teachers, guidance staff, and others. The VR counselors participate in the practitioners committee that schedules transition meetings requiring involvement of external agencies and programs, identifies transition

barriers being experienced at the school level, and explores effective methods for the delivery of transition services.

3. *The counselor as resource at transition-oriented IEP meetings.* The VR counselor also participates on a more student-specific basis as individual school-based teams meet with youths who have disabilities and their families in transition-oriented IEP meetings. The counselor will explain generally about the vocational rehabilitation program, but the focus of this meeting is on the overall steps and resources needed for the youth to develop and reach his or her transition goals.

4. *What does the vocational rehabilitation counselor do?* The vocational rehabilitation counselor helps a client plan for and secure appropriate employment. This ideally should occur during the transition period from school to adulthood. Some students secure employment during their exiting school year, and the vocational rehabilitation counselor helps maintain contact and supports them in their work and community adjustment. Other students pursue postsecondary training/education in preparation for employment, and the counselor can potentially assist in planning and securing postsecondary activities leading to employment. Finally, some will seek employment directly on exiting their school program. They will need timely, well-planned job development and job placement assistance to bridge the gap between school and work.

Thus, the challenge for the VR counselor, the youth with a disability, and the school program is to design student-specific education, transition, and employment plans for a population whose individual interests and needs vary considerably. The vocational rehabilitation counselor can provide and/or coordinate a variety of services and supports, including job and career-oriented assessments, counseling, and guidance; sponsorship of postsecondary training; job development, analysis, placement, and restructuring; use of rehabilitation technology to assist, for example, in making job site accommodations; and identification and management of support services. The counselor must take leadership in individualizing the employment service plan and time the initiation and implementation of this plan to the student's school program and postsecondary interests.

CONCLUSION

IN ORDER FOR students with a disability to move effectively from school to work it is essential that the school and community resources are clear in their roles and responsibilities. The school must be focused on the students' in-school activities, involving both preparation and planning for living and working in the community. Objectives focused on working competitively and living in an independent, integrated fashion in the community should be emphasized in the student's educational program. Educators must be familiar with resources in the community that will be utilized as the student enters the adult community, and these resources should be brought into the school to assist in the planning of transition-oriented activities.

REFERENCES

Dymond, S. K., Renzaglia, A., & Chun, E. J. (2008). Inclusive high school service learning programs: Methods for and barriers to including students with disabilities. *Education and Training in Developmental Disabilities, 43*, 20–36.

Individuals With Disability Education Improvement Act of 2004. PL 108–446, 20 U.S.C. §§ 1400 *et seq*.

Newman, L. (2001). Montana/Wyoming careers through partnerships. *The Field Report 14*, 8–10.

Szymanski, E. M., & Parker, R. M. (Eds.). (1996). *Work and disability: Issues and strategies in career development and job placement*. Austin, TX: Pro-Ed.

Wehman, P. (1995). *Individual Transition Plans: A curriculum guide for teachers and counselors*. Austin, TX: Pro-Ed.

Wehman, P. (2006). *Life beyond the classroom: Transition strategies for young people with disabilities* (4th ed.). Baltimore: Paul H. Brookes.

Wehman, P., Inge, K. J., Revell, W. G., & Brooke, V. A. (2007). *Real work for real pay: Inclusive employment for people with disabilities*. Baltimore: Paul H. Brookes.

Wehman, P., & Kregel, J. (2004). *Functional curriculum for elementary, middle, and secondary age students with special needs* (2nd ed.). Austin, TX: Pro-Ed.

Wehman, P., & Walsh, P. N. (1999). Transition from school to adulthood: A look at the U.S. and Europe. In. P. Retish & S. Reiter (Eds.), *Persons with disabilities in society: An international perspective* (pp. 1–18). Mahwah, NJ: Lawrence Erlbaum Associates.

Wehman P., & Wittig, K. M. (in press). *Transition IEPs: A curriculum guide for teachers and transition practitioners* (3rd ed.). Austin, TX: Pro-Ed.

Weiner, J. S., & Zivolich, S. (2003). A longitudinal report for three employees in a training consultant model of natural support. *Journal of Vocational Rehabilitation, 18*, 199–202.

43

Career Counseling Across the Life Span

GLACIA ETHRIDGE, DAVID BURNHILL,
AND SHENGLI DONG

THE DEFINITION OF *career* encompasses one's vocational behavior across the life span (Brown, 2002). Thus, while we are using the phrase *life span,* it is rather unnecessary as the term career itself already includes this concept. Although the field of career counseling is developmental in both nature and definition, there are few theories that have specifically focused on this aspect of career counseling. Of these, Donald Supers's life work, spanning more than a half of the previous century, can be considered one of the first career theories based on developmental aspects of a person's career life (1990; Super, Savickas, & Super, 1996). Schlossberg's (1996) Adult Career Transition Model has also contributed significantly to current thinking in career development. However, theories such as Person-Environment (Parsons, 1909), Trait-Factor theories (Holland, 1985), and Social Cognitive Career Theory (SCCT; Lent, Brown, & Hackett, 1994), to name a few, while not being developmentally focused have contributed interventions that are highly efficacious. Thus it is not necessary that the theories that the career counselor draws on for interventions are derived from those that specifically call themselves developmental.

While it is not paramount for the theory on which the career counselor draws to be called developmental, it is vital that the underlying theoretical framework of any intervention be not only familiar to the counselor but also be proven to be efficacious. This chapter will focus on highlighting a few of those career development interventions that have been shown to be effective and how they can be appropriately utilized across a person's life span. As well, aspects of diversity offer their own unique challenges across the life span and are currently a priority topic in career development and will therefore be given a special emphasis in this chapter.

COUNSELING INTERVENTIONS FOR SCHOOL-AGED YOUTH AND ADOLESCENTS

BEFORE THE FORMAL entry into education, the child is introduced to the world of work through the medium of his or her parents, their peers, and even early childhood literature. Another important venture into the world of work at the preschool age is explored through the role modeling that takes place during play. These aspects of early career exploration continue into the school years, where young children are further exposed to the world of work; in fact, it is during these school years that the function of career counseling takes on a vital importance to the future career (and academic) development of the student by helping to guide and shape these ventures.

Lapan (2004) noted that in order to develop adaptive, resilient, and proactive approaches to both present and future career identities, youths must be aided in performing the following goals:

1. Develop a positive career-related self-efficacy expectation and attribution style (Albert & Luzzo, 1999; Lent, Brown, & Hackett, 1994, 2000)
2. Form vocational identities by utilizing self-directed career exploration and planning activities in order to establish effective educational and career goals with the ability to maintain these goals (Flum & Blustein, 2000)
3. Learn effective social and work readiness behaviors and skills (Bloch, 1996)
4. Strive for a greater understanding of self, the world of work, and the intersection of these two concepts (Parsons, 1909)
5. Be able to clarify personally valued vocational interests (Strong, 1927)
6. Have the ability to achieve academic success and to become self-regulated learners (Arbona, 2005; Lapan, Kardash, & Turner, 2002)

While the above list might not be exhaustive, it points to some of the goal areas of career development that have been derived from theoretical underpinnings. It therefore makes intuitive sense that both the goals of the career counselor and the interventions utilized should be directed toward these and similar key areas. Before utilizing intervention techniques it is crucial for the counselor to be aware of where the client is in terms of both his or her *life stage* and the *developmental tasks* that he or she is facing (Super et al., 1996). While this is particularly essential throughout the early school years (Herr, Cramer, & Niles, 2004), it remains just as important throughout the life span. For example, a 33-year-old adult may be ending his participation in playing indoor soccer (disengagement), yet at the same time may be initiating and seeking out other activities (exploration) and increasing his participation at work (Super et al., 1996).

Career guidance techniques in the elementary school setting might include curriculum infusion such as reading reference books and storytelling, group activities such as role playing, and finally, community involvement activities such as field trips and inviting local businesses to the school (Herr et al., 2004). In junior high and middle school the counselor must acknowledge the transitional nature of this period, where an emphasis is placed on helping students understand how present course selection can have future consequences. Interventions that aid in the timely, relevant, and accurate dissemination of career-related information is paramount at this stage. Using community resources, while key throughout all of the life span, is also vital at this stage (Herr et al., 2004; Lenz, 1984).

The major goals of career counseling for high school–age youth must involve specific planning of the next steps (Herr et al., 2004) either toward education, work, or both. This is also commonly referred to as *transition* counseling. Here, the counselor works to assist the student in clarifying life's various roles and in decision making. Techniques that can be employed in the high school setting and throughout the school years can involve individual and group counseling, structured classes and topical workshops, computer- and Internet-assisted programs and use of information systems, community career partnership programs, situational assessment, and last and least likely to be efficacious, self-directed career interventions (Lapan, 2004).

Some of the common links that can be found in regard to interventions utilized throughout the lower, middle, and high school and transition years tend to focus on the following: the dissemination of information, responding to individual characteristics of the students in a meaningful way, helping the student to explore the intersections of the world of self and the world of work, and helping the student to create and implement plans (Herr et al., 2004). It could also be argued that making changes on a systemic level, such as implementing a new career curriculum in the school, is another type of intervention that can be applied across all age groups.

COUNSELING INTERVENTION FOR MIDLIFE CAREER TRANSITION AND RETIREMENT TRANSITION

A DISTINCT TASK of midlife and older adults is characterized by the process of reevaluating an individual's career, determining a need for change, and preparing for the future (Erikson, 1963). Numerous personal, economic, technological, and sociocultural factors can create opportunities and challenges for midlife career transitions and retirement transitions. A mature adult may need to go through the following stages of career transitions: exploration, establishment, maintenance, and disengagement (Super, 1990) or "moving in," "moving through," "moving out," and "moving back again" (Schlossberg, Waters, & Goodman, 1995). The goals and tasks in each stage may differ. In addition, the goals and tasks can be further complicated by the nature of transitions: anticipated and unanticipated transitions (Schlossberg et al., 1995) and/or voluntary and involuntary transition (Isaacson & Brown, 1997).

In order to facilitate a positive transition in midlife and retirement, counselors should help clients to take the following actions (Gysbers, Heppner, & Johnston, 1998):

1. View themselves and their situations holistically in order to enable them to see the connections and relationships in their lives, families, and work
2. Understand and deal with complicated issues of psychological adjustment and career adjustment
3. Appreciate the diversity in the workplace
4. Develop support systems to buffer workplace and family stresses and strains
5. Recognize that grief and loss are natural reactions to change
6. Initiate positive changes by fully taking advantage of the resources and properly handling challenges

Counselors should take appropriate approaches to help clients solve specific problems during each stage of the career transition. According to Schlossberg and colleagues (1995), there are four major intervention stages that individuals encounter in transition for which they might seek help. In the *moving in* stage, counselors need to use practical ways to help newly employed individuals understand and navigate the joining up and adjustment process by utilizing various resources such as job clubs, employment services, support groups, and social and institutional networks (Schlossberg et al., 1995). The counselor should assist individuals to clarify their own unmet and unrealistic expectations and become aware of the significance of socializing processes and workplace diversity (Gysbers et al., 1998; Schlossberg et al., 1995). In addition, counselors need to empower individuals to establish positive self-efficacy by identifying and utilizing the resources in the following areas: situation, self, support, and strategies (Evan, Forney, & Guido-DiBrito, 1998; Schlossberg et al., 1995).

In the *moving through* stage, counselors need to assist individuals to properly deal with the sense of loneliness and feeling of incompetence that might accompany promotions (Schlossberg et al., 1995). Furthermore, counselors may help individuals recognize various factors that affect the career decision-making process, for example, multiple familial, socioeconomic, and occupational responsibilities and competing demands (Juntunen, Wegner, & Matthews, 2002). It is vital that counselors help individuals who feel caught in between redefine the notions of success and separate their failures and success at work from who they are as people (Schlossberg, 1996).

In the *moving out* stage, counselors should help individuals deal with feeling of grief and sense of loss that are common for people in this stage (Sterns & Subich, 2005). According to Schlossberg and colleagues (1995) and Schlossberg (2004), counselors should encourage individuals to establish and/or redefine their career and life goals, especially for those who intend to make a career change. For those individuals who are about to retire, counselors need to help individuals become aware of the multiple tasks and roles in preretirement and retirement transition (Glass & Flynn, 2000; Richardson, 1993). In addition, counselors should provide training and consultation related to pension benefits, health care, and life planning, which, in turn, may enhance individuals' physical, mental, and spiritual wellness (Fiske & Chiriboga, 1990; Stoltz-Loike, 1997; Tinsley & Bigler, 2002).

In the *trying to move in again* stage, counselors need to assist individuals to deal with the sense of frustration and anxiety by providing various emotional and informational supports (Schlossberg, 1996). Counselors need to involve individuals in exploring needs and potentials to learn new skills. It is essential that counselors assist individuals to develop new skills by providing training information and opportunities (Juntunen et al., 2002). In addition, counselors should empower individuals by helping them see the difference between long-term goals and short-term realities and striving for personal development and meaning (Schlossberg et al., 1995).

WORKING WITH DIVERSE POPULATIONS

IN WORKING WITH any of the population age groups that have been described throughout this chapter, career counselors must be cognizant of the culture that each client encompasses when considering any type of strategy or intervention. Women, persons of color, lesbians, gays, bisexuals, and transgendered in addition to people with disabilities, have often been marginalized, stigmatized, and socialized into stereotypical careers. In order to work effectively with any of these groups, career counselors should have some knowledge or understanding of strategies and techniques that are useful when working with people who may fall into more than one of these categories.

WOMEN

ACCORDING TO ISAACSON and Brown (1997), career counselors must be aware of the self-limiting stereotypes that restrict women's choices and be sensitive to the importance placed on families, be prepared to accept various lifestyles and explore the potential impact that may have in sustaining these lifestyles, and be cognizant of career options for women in nontraditional careers. Betz (2005) further contends that career counselors working with women should use the following strategies: "encourage high quality education; encourage women to take a lot of math, explore the client's outcomes expectations and barriers to her goal pursuits, with the idea of helping her to develop coping mechanisms, coping self-efficacy, and barrier-surmounting sources of social support" (pp. 268–269); and determine the role of culture and ethnicity as it relates to the woman's career choice. The role that the woman plays in her life must always be considered. Research has shown that women who are wives and mothers often play down their career aspirations due to familial obligations (Farmer, 1997).

PERSONS OF COLOR

IN WORKING WITH persons of color, career counselors need to be cognizant of their own stereotypes, prejudices, and misconceptions toward this population. Issacson and Brown (1997) suggest that before discussion of career options or interests of the clients, counseling should begin by identifying stressors (e.g., work-related, family, feelings of racial discrimination) as well as a discussion of how the client is coping with these stressors. The counselor is then encouraged to help the client identify supports that are available to help them cope with the stressors. It is essential at all times that counselors consider the client's culture in developing strategies and techniques.

In developing strategies and techniques, it is important that career counselors not negate the history of prejudice and discrimination that persons of color may have experienced. When working with diverse clients, career counselors must possess multicultural competence, including the awareness, knowledge, and skills required to assist diverse clients in any area (Sue, Arredondo, & McDavis, 1992). Multicultural competence is critical for career counselors, particularly because of the history of employment discrimination and stigma that people of color have experienced in the workplace (Alston & McCowan, 2001; Mpofu & Harley, 2006). This, in turn, can affect how the person may perceive himself or herself with respect to others. Career counselors should become familiar with racial identity development models, such as Cross's Black Identity Model and Kim's Asian Identity Model, to help facilitate the counseling process. When using identity development models, the career counselor must also consider the interaction between an individual's level of acculturation and identity development (Worthington, Flores, & Navarro, 2005).

LESBIAN, GAY, BISEXUAL, TRANSGENDERED

CAREER COUNSELORS NEED to be cognizant of sexual identity models, regardless of a person's developmental aspect. When working with lesbian, gay, bisexual, and transgendered (LGBT) individuals the counselor needs to consider the person's sexual identity, sexual orientation, and sexual identity management (Miller & Brown, 2005). Sexual identity issues and sexual orientation may have an effect on a person's vocational choice (Liddle, Luzzo, Hauenstein, & Schuck, 2004); therefore, these issues should be carefully considered when providing services to persons who are LGBT.

PEOPLE WITH DISABILITIES

CAREER COUNSELORS WORKING with individuals with disabilities must first and foremost be familiar with the American With Disabilities Act of 1990 (ADA; P.L. 101–336) as its underlying premise is to protect people with disabilities from employment discrimination. Once career counselors become familiar with the ADA, they also need to become cognizant of the personal characteristics of the individual; the interests, activities, and goals; gender; culture; the environment; the role of the family and other social supports; and the nature of the disability (i.e., specific impairments, severity of disability, time of onset, type of onset, visibility, stability, and pain; Patterson, DeLaGarza, & Schaller, 2005) for the individual with a disability. Hence, the career counseling process for clients with disabilities will involve addressing all of the aforementioned issues and may very well begin with an extensive psychological and/or vocational assessment(s), with consideration of not only the limitations but, more important, the assets of clients with disabilities in facilitating the career decision making process. In addition, knowledge of available state-of-the-art assistive technology or adaptive aids is critical regarding independence in the home and at work (de Jonge, Scherer, & Rodger, 2007). A final suggestion in working with persons with disabilities is to always use first-person language rather than using the disability to identify the person. For example, instead of the term *mentally ill persons,* it is more appropriate to use *persons who are mentally ill.*

CONCLUSION

It is imperative that career counselors understand that there is a sense of urgency and change in the job market that is inexorably tied into world economics and politics. This fluctuation in markets has been and will continue to impact not only the workplace, but also family structures, gender roles, and disability status. Due to the ever-changing nature of society and the workplace, career counselors and the field of career counseling need to continue efforts toward researching and developing solid knowledge bases regarding culturally appropriate interventions.

In addition, counselors need to be familiar with what stage clients are at in terms of both career and life development in order that they may help them to set appropriate goals and to utilize suitable counseling interventions. Career counselors who are working with clients from diverse cultural backgrounds should also understand the nature of transitions and other challenging and demanding roles faced by individuals during their career development. With this understanding, the counselor is able to apply different theories and strategies to provide the best possible services to individuals who are seeking career assistance.

RESOURCES

American Association for Retired Persons: http://www.aarp.org
Americans With Disabilities Act of 1990, 42 U.S.C. § 12101 *et seq.*
Medicare and Medicaid: http://www.hcfa.gov
National Wellness Institute: http://www.nationalwellness.org
Social Security: http://www.ssa.gov
Support group: http://fortyplus.org

REFERENCES

Albert, L. A., & Luzzo, D. A. (1999). The role of perceived barriers in career development: A social cognitive perspective. *Journal of Counseling and Development, 77,* 431–436.

Alston, R. J., & McCowan, C. J. (2001). African American women and disabilities: Rehabilitation issues and concerns. *Journal of Rehabilitation, 48,* 36–39.

Arbona, C. (2005). Promoting the career development and academic achievement of at-risk youth: College access programs. In S. D. Brown & R. W. Lent (Eds.), *Career development and counseling: Putting theory and research to work* (pp. 525–550). Hoboken, NJ: Wiley.

Betz, N. E. (2005). Women's career development. In S. D. Brown & R. W. Lent (Eds.), *Career development and counseling: Putting theory and research to work* (pp. 253–277). Hoboken, NJ: Wiley.

Bloch, D. T. (1996). Career development and workforce preparation: Educational policy versus school practice. *Career Development Quarterly, 45,* 20–40.

Brown, D. (2002). *Career choice and development* (4th ed.). San Francisco: Jossey-Bass.

de Jonge, D., Scherer, M., & Rodger, S. (2007). *Assistive technology in the workplace.* Amsterdam: Elsevier-Mosby.

Erikson, E. H. (1963). *Childhood and society* (2nd ed.). New York: W. W. Norton.

Evan, N., Fomey, D., & Guido-DiBrito, F. (1998). *Student development in college: Theory, research, and practice.* San Francisco: Jossey-Bass.

Farmer, H. S. (1997). What inhibits achievement and career motivation in women? *Counseling Psychologist, 6,* 12–14.

Fiske, M., & Chiriboga, D. A. (1990). *Change and continuity in adult life.* San Francisco: Jossey-Bass.

Flum, H., & Blustein, D. L. (2000). Reinvigorating the study of vocational exploration: A framework for research. *Journal of Vocational Behavior, 56,* 380–404.

Glass, J. C., & Flynn, D. K. (2000). Retirement needs and preparation of rural middle-aged persons. *Educational Gerontology, 26,* 109–134.

Gysbers, N. C., Heppner, M. J., & Johnston, J. A. (1998). *Career counseling: Process, issues and techniques.* Boston: Allyn & Bacon.

Herr, E. L., Cramer, S. H., & Niles, S. G. (2004). *Career guidance and counseling through the lifespan: Systematic approaches.* Boston: Allyn & Bacon.

Holland, J. L. (1985). *Manual for the Vocational Preference Inventory.* Odessa, FL: Psychological Assessment Resources.

Isaacson, L. E., & Brown, D. (1997). *Career information, career counseling, and career development* (6th ed.). Boston: Allyn & Bacon.

Juntunen, C. L., Wegner, K. E., & Matthews, L. G. (2002). Promoting positive career change in midlife. In C. Juntunen & D. Arkinson (Eds.), *Counseling across the lifespan: Prevention and treatment* (pp. 329–347). Thousand Oaks, CA: Sage Publications.

Lapan, R. T. (2004). *Career development across the K-16 years: Bridging the present to satisfying and successful futures.* Alexandria, VA: American Counseling Association.

Lapan, R. T., Kardash, C. A. M., & Turner, S. L. (2002). Empowering students to become self-regulated learners. *Professional School Counseling, 5,* 257–265.

Lent, R. W., Brown, S. D., & Hackett, G. (1994). Toward a unified social cognitive theory of career/academic interest, choice, and performance. *Journal of Vocational Behavior, 45,* 79–122.

Lent, R. W., Brown, S. D., & Hackett, G. (2000). Contextual supports and barriers to career choice: A social cognitive analysis. *Journal of Counseling Psychology, 47,* 36–49.

Lenz, J. G. (1984). Using community resources. In H. D. Burk & R. C. Reardon (Eds.), *Career development interventions* (pp. 191–211). Springfield, IL: Charles C. Thomas.

Liddle, B. J., Luzzo, D. A., Hauenstein, A. L., & Schuck, K. (2004). Construction and validation of the lesbian, gay, bisexual, and transgendered climate. *Journal of Career Assessment, 12,* 33–50.

Miller, M. J., & Brown, S. D. (2005). Counseling for career choice: Implications for improving interventions and working with diverse populations. In S. D. Brown & R. W. Lent (Eds.), *Career development and counseling: Putting theory and research to work* (pp. 441–465). Hoboken, NJ: Wiley.

Mpofu, E., & Harley, D. (2006). Racial and disability identity: Implications for the career counseling of African American with disabilities. *Rehabilitation Counseling Bulletin, 50,* 14–23.

Parsons, F. (1909). *On choosing a vocation.* Boston: Houghton Mifflin.

Patterson, J. B., DeLaGarza, D., & Schaller, J. (2005). Rehabilitation counseling practice: Considerations and interventions. In R. M. Parker, E. M. Szymanski, & J. B. Patterson (Eds.), *Rehabilitation counseling basics and beyond* (4th ed., pp. 155–186). Austin, TX: Pro-Ed.

Richardson, V. E. (1993). *Retirement counseling: A handbook for gerontology practitioners.* New York: Springer Publishing.

Schlossberg, N. K. (1996). A model of worklife transitions. In R. Feller & G. R. Walz (Eds.), *Career transitions in turbulent times: Exploring work, learning and careers* (pp. 93–104). Greensboro, NC: Eric Clearinghouse on Counseling and Student Services.

Schlossberg, N. K. (2004). *Retire smart retire happy: Finding your true path in life.* Washington, DC: American Psychological Association.

Schlossberg, N. K., Waters, E. B., & Goodman J. (1995). *Counseling adults in transition: Linking practice with theory.* New York: Springer Publishing.

Sterns, H. L., & Subich, L. M. (2005). Counseling for retirement. In S. D. Brown & R. W. Lent (Eds.), *Career development and counseling: Putting theory and research to work* (pp. 253–277). Hoboken, NJ: Wiley.

Stoltz-Loike, M. (1997). Creating personal and spiritual balance: Another dimension in career development. In D. P. Bloch & L. J. Richmond (Eds.),

Connections between spirit and work in career development (pp. 139–162). Palo Alto, CA: Consulting Psychologists Press.

Strong, E. K., Jr. (1927). *Vocational interest blank*. Palo Alto, CA: Stanford University Press.

Sue, D. W., Arredondo, P., & McDavis, R. J. (1992). Multicultural counseling competencies and standards: A call to the profession. *Journal of Counseling and Development, 70,* 477–486.

Super, D. E. (1990). A life-span, life space approach to career development. In D. Brown & L. Brooks (Eds.), *Career choice and development: Applying contemporary theories to practice* (pp. 197–261). San Francisco: Jossey-Bass.

Super, D. E., Savickas, M. L., & Super, C. M. (1996). The life-span, life-space approach to careers. In D. Brown, L. Brooks et al. (Eds.), *Career choice and development* (2nd ed., pp. 121–178). San Francisco: Jossey-Bass.

Tinsley, D. J., & Bigler, M. (2002). Facilitating transitions in retirement. In C. L. Juntunen & D. R. Atkinson (Eds.), *Counseling across the lifespan: Prevention and treatment*. Thousand Oaks, CA: Sage Publications.

Worthington, R. L., Flores, L. Y., & Navarro, R. L. (2005). Career development in context: Research with people of color. In S. D. Brown & R. W. Lent (Eds.), *Career development and counseling* (pp. 225–252). Hoboken, NJ: John Wiley & Sons, Inc.

44

Work, Careers, and Disability

Kim L. MacDonald-Wilson

I N THE UNITED STATES, work is one of the major life domains in which adults function. One of the first questions we ask when we meet someone is "What do you do?" Answering this question by stating "I am a ____" suggests that work is a major component of our identity. Satisfaction in work is also linked to well-being and satisfaction with other life domains (see chapter 41; Lent & Brown, 2008). There are an estimated 49.7 million (approximately 19.3 %) people in the United States who have a disability, and a significant proportion (12%) consists of people of working age (16–64) who experience limitations in working due to their disability (Waldrop & Stern, 2003). Approximately one in four people will develop a disability in their lifetimes (Waldrop & Stern, 2003), and for many of them, work will be affected. Given the prevalence of disability and prominence of work in our lives, counselors will likely face issues related to work for people with disabilities in their practice, even when it does not appear to be the primary issue bringing someone to counseling. This chapter will address work in the context of disability and provide a choose-get-keep framework for examining vocational development and work issues in counseling. Implications for counseling will be discussed.

NATURE OF WORK

I N MANY CULTURES, work is a central aspect of human life. The meaning of work to an individual is a complex interaction between workplaces, individuals, and society (Szymanski, Parker, Ryan, Merz,

Trevino-Espinoza, & Johnston-Rodriquez, 2003). The nature of work in the United States is changing, with layoffs and organizational restructuring, rapid changes in the labor market and economy, and increasing emphasis on use of technology in the workplace (Burke & Nelson, 1998; Storey, 2000). Access to the labor market is affected by one's education, gender, race and ethnicity, disability, and social culture of the workplace (Szymanski et al., 2003). Understanding the context of work and the role of the environment of work is important in choosing and planning interventions in counseling with people with disabilities.

NATURE OF DISABILITY AND WORK

M ANY HELPING PROFESSIONALS focus on the medical condition or diagnosis as defining disability. However, providing a medical diagnosis and description of symptoms is often not sufficient in determining the presence of disability, assessing functioning, or implementing rehabilitation services to improve functioning. A health condition interacts with environmental and personal factors to affect functioning (World Health Organization, 2001). The presence of a health condition or symptoms is not the sole cause of disability but may contribute to limitations in functioning, and not all health conditions lead to disability. A functional limitation is the inability to perform a physical, mental, or emotional action or a set of actions because of a physical or mental impairment (Brodwin, Parker, & DeLaGarza, 2003). Many individuals may be able to work in spite of having a medical condition or experiencing symptoms. It also follows that treating the symptoms may not necessarily improve functioning. What is essential is to understand how functioning is affected, particularly in work settings. Whether someone experiences disability in work depends in part on the impact of the health condition on functioning over time, the skills and expertise required by the position, the skills and expertise of the employee, supports available in the workplace, and the match or mismatch of the environmental demands with the employee's current abilities.

Although a discussion of the various types of limitations are beyond the scope of this chapter (see Brodwin et al., 2003; MacDonald-Wilson, Rogers, & Massaro, 2003, for additional detail), two examples may illustrate the distinctions between a medical and a functional understanding of disability. An individual with a physical condition such as rheumatoid arthritis (medical diagnosis) may have joint pain, stiffness, and swelling of the joints (symptoms). She may have difficulty climbing stairs (mobility limitation), lifting 10 pounds or more (lifting limitation), and typing (handling and fingering limitations). A person diagnosed with major depression and generalized anxiety disorder (medical diagnosis) may have depressed mood, feelings of anxiety and nervous energy (symptoms). He may have difficulty greeting customers (interpersonal limitation), prioritizing multiple tasks (cognitive limitation), and maintaining physical stamina throughout an 8-hour workday (physical limitation). In addition, other factors such as the labor market, gender, race and ethnicity, and culture may also play a role in the labor market participation of people with disabilities (Szymanski et al., 2003). Understanding how the health condition affects the individual's functioning in particular roles or environments is essential in determining how best to intervene when the work role is affected.

LEGISLATION RELATED TO WORK AND DISABILITY

THE LEGISLATIVE ENVIRONMENT also affects work and disability. There are a number of laws that directly relate to work and disability. For a more thorough review of such legislation, readers are referred to Bruyere and Brown (2003). One of the most important pieces of legislation is the Americans With Disabilities Act (ADA). The ADA defines a person with a disability in one of three ways:

1. The person has a physical or mental impairment that substantially limits one or more major life activities.
2. The person has a record of such an impairment.
3. The person is regarded as having such an impairment (Americans With Disabilities Act [ADA], 1990).

Counselors must be prepared to discuss the functional limitations that the individual experiences that may be attributed to a physical or mental impairment related to the first part of the definition of disability. The ADA also requires that employers provide reasonable accommodations to a qualified individual with a disability (Americans With Disabilities Act [ADA], 1990). An individual is qualified if he or she can perform the essential functions, or major duties, of the job with or without reasonable accommodation. This means that employers must make modifications to the work environment, the way that the job gets done, or in policies and procedures as long as it does not cause undue hardship, or create significant cost or disruption of business operations. Employers may not discriminate against a qualified individual with a disability if the person can do the job with or without reasonable accommodations. Counselors may be asked to provide employers with documentation related to the disability and need for reasonable accommodations. Examples of accommodations include but are not limited to the following:

1. Modifying the worksite (i.e., ramps, partitions, lighting)
2. Providing or modifying equipment or devices (i.e., software, teletypewriter [TTY] machines)
3. Job restructuring (i.e., exchanging minor duties)
4. Work schedule modifications (i.e., breaks, change in hours or days worked)
5. Providing qualified interpreters or readers
6. Reassignment to a vacant job (ADA, 1990; Job Accommodation Network [JAN], n.d.).

There are numerous benefits to accommodations to both the employee and the employer. An accommodation may provide the means to access the job or provide the support needed for the employee to function at maximum effectiveness. Employers also report that most accommodations are low cost, effective, and provide both direct and indirect benefits not only to the employee concerned but also to other employees and the company as a whole (JAN, n.d.). A number of resources are available on the requirements and provisions of the ADA. There are 10 regional Disability and Business Technical Assistance Centers (DBTACs) on the ADA that provide free technical assistance and information on all aspects of the ADA, including on Title I on Employment. These can be reached by calling 1-800-949-4232 to be connected with the closest regional ADA center or go to http://www.adata.org/. In addition, the Job Accommodation Network (JAN) is a free consulting service on worksite accommodations and technical assistance on the ADA and other disability-related legislation. It can be reached by calling 1-800-526-7234 (v), 1-877-781-9403 (TTY), or connecting to http://www.jan.wvu.edu/.

THE CHOOSE-GET-KEEP FRAMEWORK

ONE SIMPLE WAY of understanding the activities related to work for people with disabilities is to use the choose-get-keep framework (Anthony, Howell, & Danley, 1984; Danley & Anthony, 1987), an application of a psychiatric rehabilitation approach to vocational rehabilitation, later used to describe approaches to career planning (Danley, Hutchinson, & Restrepo-Toro, 1998; Unger, Danley, Kohn, & Hutchinson, 1987), supported employment (Danley, Sciarappa, & MacDonald-Wilson, 1992; MacDonald-Wilson, Mancuso, Danley, & Anthony, 1989), and supported education (Sullivan, Nicolellis, Danley, & MacDonald-Wilson, 1993). Choosing, getting, and keeping a job, career, and/or worker role is a process that the counselor facilitates and a set of tasks that the client does that can be used in any discipline, program model, or with any type of client. It is a simple framework that can be used by a counselor to organize counseling activities, and to orient the client to the process.

Vocational development may be affected by disability in a number of ways. Disability that occurs from birth, or in childhood or adolescence, may delay development of vocational identity (Hershenson & Liesener, 2003). Individuals may be involved in managing their health conditions, catching up with academic work, or may be denied opportunities to participate in typical vocational development tasks of similar-age peers, such as summer jobs, internships, or volunteer experiences. Individuals who are in the process of developing a vocational identity or career trajectory, and then acquire a disability later in life, may need to develop awareness of new strengths and limitations, revise their career goals, or explore accommodations and other supports that may facilitate return to work in the current job or with a new employer (see chapter 43). People who acquire a disability once a career is established may need assistance in choosing whether to work, exploring a new occupation or a new employer, or understanding work strengths and limitations. Depending on the nature and severity of disability and phase of vocational development, it may be necessary to provide assistance in finding a job, negotiating accommodations for the existing job, or exploring new career options.

One way to conceptualize this process is to identify the phase of vocational development and vocational role of focus by examining the primary vocational questions the person is facing and behavioral indicators of success in that role. Understanding where the person is in terms of vocational development may suggest the types of interventions needed to choose, get, or keep a vocational role. The counselor may then provide those interventions or coordinate with other service providers so that vocational needs are met (see Table 44.1).

CHOOSE

THE PROCESS OF developing a vocational identity is grounded in developmental career theories (Super, 1990; Super, Savickas, & Super, 1996). Super proposed life span stages of career development, and suggested that *vocational maturity* (later called *career maturity*) was an index of where a person was in the career development process (see chapter 40; Super, 1957). The notion of vocational identity can be an important one for counselors working with individuals on work- or career-related issues.

For most people with disabilities or other developmental challenges, these career issues become prominent in adolescence and early adulthood and may be revisited in later phases of adulthood, particularly if

TABLE 44.1   Vocational Identity (Career Maturity) Sample Questions, Behavioral Indicators, Service Needs

Vocational Roles	Phases of Vocational Development		
	Choosing	**Getting**	**Keeping**
Worker	Can I/Do I want to work?	How can I obtain work?	How can I continue working?
	Can evaluate compatibility of worker activities with personal interests, needs, and qualifications	*Can complete a general job application* *Can accurately describe general worker strengths and deficits*	*Can demonstrate work-related dependability, sociability, and adaptability*
	Motivational Interviewing **Job Tryouts** **World of Work Awareness**	**Work Readiness** **Work Adjustment**	**Transitional Employment** **Work Hardening**
Colleague/ Occupation Member	Can I/Do I want to work as a ___?	How can I become a ___?	How can I continue working as a ___?
	Can evaluate compatibility of occupational tasks with personal interests, needs, and qualifications	*Can demonstrate proficiency in technical skills associated with the occupation*	*Can learn new technical skills associated with changes in the occupation*
	Career Counseling	**Technical Training** **Higher Education** **Supported Education**	**In-service Training** **Education and Training** **Coping Skills**
Employee	Can I/Do I want to work as a ___ at ___?	How can I obtain employment as a ___ at ___?	How can I continue working as a ___ at ___?
	Can evaluate compatibility of places of employment with personal interests, needs, and qualifications	*Can locate specific employers* *Can contact specific employers* *Can present self positively in person and in writing*	*Can apply general worker and technical skills as required by specific employers*
	Career Counseling **Supported Employment**	**Job Search Skills** **Job Development/ SE Employment** **Search Firms**	**On-the-job Skills Training** **Supported Employment** **Accommodations** **Employer Services**

From "A Psychiatric Rehabilitation Approach to Vocational Rehabilitation," by K. S. Danley, E. S. Rogers, and D. B. Nevas, 1989, in *Psychiatric rehabilitation programs: Putting theory into practice* (pp. 81–131), edited by M. D. Farkas and W. A. Anthony. Copyright 1989 by K. S. Danley, E. S. Rogers, and D. B. Nevas. Adapted with permission.

the vocational development process is interrupted by disability. Some people with disabilities that first occur in childhood or adolescence may be delayed in undertaking early vocational development tasks because of focusing energies on illness or disability issues, while other people who experience disability later in life (and later in the vocational development process) may need to revisit their vocational decisions, understand the impact of disability on their work functioning and abilities, and redefine their vocational identities (chapters 40 and 43; Danley, Rogers, & Nevas, 1989; Hershenson & Liesener, 2003). Counselors can explore whether the individual is trying to answer the questions related to whether he or she wants to and feels able to work in any job, work in a particular occupation, or work in a particular job and setting. Depending on the vocational identity questions the individual is focusing on, the counselor may use or refer an individual for services, including motivational interviewing regarding readiness for making a change in work, career counseling, supported employment, or other interventions designed to answer the questions.

GET

PEOPLE WITH DISABILITIES may have a range of experiences and skills in obtaining work. For individuals whose disabilities affect interpersonal or cognitive functioning, professional support or placement services may be needed to develop job search skills or provide direct placement into employment (Hagner, 2003; Ryan, 2000). For others with experience and skills obtaining employment, referral to newly consolidated employment and training service centers such as One Stop Career Centers established under the Workforce Investment Act of 1998 (P. L. 105–220) may be useful. Counselors may focus on assisting the individual in identifying strengths, presenting self positively to employers, or addressing gaps in work history or need for accommodations in the hiring process. Individuals with significant disabilities may benefit from customized employment, where employment specialists work with employers to develop jobs that specifically match the skills and interests of the job seeker (Luecking, Fabian, & Tilson, 2004). Counselors may also refer individuals to supported employment services, where job coaches or employment specialists provide on-the-job training or other supports and other services to maintain people with the most severe disabilities in competitive employment (Cook et al., 2005; Wehman, Revell, Kregel, Kreutzer, Callahan, & Banks, 1990).

KEEP

SUSTAINING EMPLOYMENT OR a career requires a unique set of opportunities, skills, and supports for people with disabilities. Individuals who have been away from the world of work for a long period of time due to disability may first need to answer the question, "How can I continue to work?" The counselor may want to examine the demands of the job, the current skills and abilities of the worker, and nature of existing supports in determining the possibility of success in sustaining employment. These individuals may need assistance with *basic worker skills* needed for most jobs—dependability, sociability, and adaptability (Danley et al., 1992). Trial work periods, volunteer experiences, or work hardening may be useful strategies to develop or recover basic abilities to continue working. For people with the option of returning to the previous job, negotiating with the employer directly or its disability management office or an employee assistance program for a graduated return-to-work schedule may facilitate return to work. For individuals who are beginning a new career or returning to a modified job, the counselor may assess the person's ability to learn new skills through in-service training or training available on the job or other interventions to assist the person in demonstrating the *technical skills* needed for a particular occupation. Counselors may also help the individual develop coping skills to adapt to changes in the job or identify needed accommodations. Finally, exploration of both basic worker skills and technical skills needed in specific jobs in a particular employment setting are necessary to facilitate success in keeping a particular job.

In the keeping phase, job accommodations and other supports are an important component of success and satisfaction. Interventions leading to success at work should focus on not only the individual and his or her skills but also on accommodations and other supports that can lead to success. Examples of accommodations include raising the height of a workstation for an employee using a wheelchair, installing screen reader software for an employee with a visual disability, or negotiating later work hours for an employee whose psychotropic medications cause morning drowsiness. People with physical or sensory limitations may require physical environment modifications or equipment, while people with cognitive or emotional limitations may use interpersonal or cognitive accommodations such as changes in supervision, schedules, and breaks, or organizational software or personal devices (Butterfield & Ramseur, 2004; Cleveland, Barnes-Farrell, & Ratz, 1997; Hantula & Reilly, 1996; MacDonald-Wilson, Rogers, Massaro, Lyass, & Crean, 2002).

CONCLUSION

SUCCEEDING IN ONE'S work life and career is an important goal for many people. The experience of disability may disrupt vocational development and affect functioning in various work roles.

Counselors must consider the nature of work, specific strengths and limitations in functioning due to disability, and other factors such as culture, gender, race, supports, and the work environment in addressing work issues for people with disabilities. Understanding the unique situation of the individual in the choose-get-keep phases of vocational development and the primary vocational role of focus (worker, occupation member, employee) can provide direction regarding individual-focused and work environment–focused interventions that can facilitate achievement of the vocational goal.

REFERENCES

Americans With Disabilities Act of 1990, 42 U.S.C. §12101 *et seq*.

Anthony, W. A., Howell, J., & Danley, K. S. (1984). Vocational rehabilitation of the psychiatrically disabled. In M. Mirabi (Ed.), *The chronically mentally ill: Research and services* (pp. 215–237). Jamaica, NY: Spectrum Publications.

Brodwin, M., Parker, R. M., & DeLaGarza, D. (2003). Disability and accommodation. In E. M. Szymanski & R. M. Parker (Eds.), *Work and disability: Issues and strategies in career development and job placement* (pp. 201–246). Austin, TX: Pro-Ed.

Bruyere, S. M., & Brown, J. A. (2003). Legislation affecting employment for persons with disabilities. In E. M. Szymanski & R. M. Parker (Eds.), *Work and disability: Issues and strategies in career development and job placement* (pp. 27–52). Austin, TX: Pro-Ed.

Burke, R. J., & Nelson, D. (1998). Mergers and acquisitions, downsizing, and privatization: A North American perspective. In M. K. Gowing, J. D. Kraft, & J. C. Quick (Eds.), *The new organizational reality: Downsizing, restructuring, and revitalization* (pp. 21–54). Washington, DC: American Psychological Association.

Butterfield, T. M., & Ramseur, J. H. (2004). Research and case study findings in the area of workplace accommodations including provisions for assistive technology: A literature review. *Technology and Disability, 16*(4), 201–210.

Cleveland, J. N., Barnes-Farrell, J. L., & Ratz, J. M. (1997). Accommodation in the workplace. *Human Resource Management Review, 7*(7), 77–107.

Cook, J. A., Lehman, A. F., Drake, R., McFarlane, W. R., Gold, P. B., Leff, H. S., et al. (2005). Integrating psychiatric and vocational services: A multisite, randomized, controlled trial of supported employment. *American Journal of Psychiatry, 162*, 1948–1956.

Danley, K. S., & Anthony, W. A. (1987). The choose-get-keep model: Serving severely psychiatrically disabled people. *American Rehabilitation, 13*(4), 6–9, 27–29.

Danley, K., Hutchinson, D., & Restrepo-Toro, M. (1998). *Career planning curriculum for people with psychiatric disabilities*. Boston: Center for Psychiatric Rehabilitation, Boston University.

Danley, K., Rogers, E. S., & Nevas, D. (1989). A psychiatric rehabilitation approach to vocational rehabilitation. In M. D. Farkas & W. A. Anthony (Eds.), *Psychiatric rehabilitation: Putting concepts into practice* (pp. 81–131). Baltimore, MD: Johns Hopkins University Press.

Danley, K. S., Sciarappa, K., & MacDonald-Wilson, K. L. (1992). Choose-get-keep: A psychiatric rehabilitation approach to supported employment. In R. P. Liberman (Ed.), *Effective psychiatric rehabilitation* (New Directions in Mental Health Services, Vol. 53, pp. 87–96). San Francisco: Jossey-Bass.

Hagner, D. (2003). Job development and job search assistance. In E. M. Szymanski & R. M. Parker (Eds.), *Work and disability: Issues and strategies in career development and job placement* (pp. 343–373). Austin, TX: Pro-Ed.

Hantula, D. A., & Reilly, N. A. (1996). Reasonable accommodation for employees with mental disabilities: A mandate for effective supervision? *Behavioral Sciences and the Law, 14*(1), 107–120.

Hershenson, D. B., & Liesener, J. J. (2003). Career counseling with diverse populations: Models, interventions, and applications. In E. M. Szymanski & R. M. Parker (Eds.), *Work and disability: Issues and strategies in career development and job placement* (pp. 281–316). Austin, TX: Pro-Ed.

Job Accommodation Network (n.d.). Workplace accommodations: Low cost, high impact. *JAN's Accommodation Fact Sheet series*. Retrieved March 2, 2008, from http://www.jan.wvu.edu/media/LowCostHighImpact.pdf

Lent, R. W., & Brown, S. D. (2008). Social cognitive career theory and subjective wellbeing in the context of work. *Journal of Career Assessment, 16*, 6–21.

Luecking, R. G., Fabian, E. S., & Tilson, G. P. (2004). *Working relationships: Creating career opportunities for job seekers with disabilities through employer partnerships*. Baltimore: Paul H. Brookes.

MacDonald-Wilson, K. L., Mancuso, L. L., Danley, K. S., & Anthony, W. A. (1989). Supported employment for people with psychiatric disability. *Journal of Applied Rehabilitation Counseling, 20*(3), 50–57.

MacDonald-Wilson, K. L., Rogers, E. S., & Massaro, J. M. (2003). Identifying relationships between functional limitations, job accommodations, and demographic characteristics of persons with psychiatric disabilities. *Journal of Vocational Rehabilitation, 18*, 15–24.

MacDonald-Wilson, K. L., Rogers, E. S., Massaro, J. M., Lyass, A., & Crean, T. (2002). An investigation of reasonable workplace accommodations for people with psychiatric disabilities: Quantitative findings from a multisite study. *Community Mental Health Journal, 38*(1), 35–50.

Ryan, D. (2000). *Job search handbook for people with disabilities*. Indianapolis, IN: JIST.

Storey, J. A. (2000). "Fracture lines" in the career environment. In A. Collin & R. A. Young (Eds.), *The future of career* (pp. 21–36). Cambridge, UK: Cambridge University Press.

Sullivan, A. P., Nicolellis, D., Danley, K. S., & MacDonald-Wilson, K. (1993). Choose-get-keep: A psychiatric rehabilitation approach to supported education. *Psychosocial Rehabilitation Journal, 17*(1), 55–68.

Super, D. E. (1957). *The psychology of careers.* New York: Harper & Row.

Super, D. E. (1990). The life-span, life-space approach to career development. In D. Brown & L. Brooks (Eds.), *Career choice and development: Applying contemporary theories to practice* (pp. 197–261). San Francisco: Jossey-Bass.

Super, D. E., Savickas, M. L., & Super, C. M. (1996). The life-span, life-space approach to careers. In D. Brown, L. Brooks, et al. (Eds.), *Career choice and development* (2nd ed., pp. 121–178). San Francisco: Jossey-Bass.

Szymanski, E. M., Parker, R. M., Ryan, C., Merz, M. A., Trevino-Espinoza, B., & Johnston-Rodriquez, S. (2003). Work and disability: Basic constructs. In E. M. Szymanski & R. M. Parker (Eds.), *Work and disability: Issues and strategies in career development and job placement* (pp. 1–25). Austin, TX: Pro-Ed.

Unger, K. V., Danley, K. S., Kohn, L., & Hutchinson, D. (1987). Rehabilitation through education: A university-based continuing education program for young adults with psychiatric disabilities on a university campus. *Psychosocial Rehabilitation Journal, 10*(3), 35–49.

Waldrop, J., & Stern, S. M. (2003). Disability status 2000. *Census 2000 Brief, March 2003.* Washington, DC: U.S. Census Bureau, Economics and Statistics Administration, U.S. Department of Commerce. Retrieved March 1, 2008, from http://www.census.gov/prod/2003pubs/c2kbr-17.pdf

Wehman, P., Revell, W. G., Kregel, J., Kreutzer, J., Callahan, M., & Banks, P. D. (1990). Supported employment: An alternative model for vocational rehabilitation for persons with severe neurologic, psychiatric, or physical disability. In J. Kregel, P. Wehman, & M. S. Shafer (Eds.), *Supported employment for persons with severe disabilities: From research to practice* (Vol. 3, pp. 101–114). Richmond: Rehabilitation Center on Supported Employment, Virginia Commonwealth University.

Workforce Investment Act of 1998, P. L. 105–220, 29 U.S.C. §701 *et seq.*

World Health Organization. (2001). *The International Classification of Functioning, Disability and Health.* Geneva, Switzerland: Author.

45

Career Development Theories

BRIAN HUTCHISON AND SPENCER G. NILES

A CAREER IS defined as the course of events constituting a life (Super, 1976), including the total constellation of roles played over the course of a lifetime (Niles & Harris-Bowlsbey, 2005). Given the ever-changing social world we live in, both life events and roles evolve over time. Career development theory describes the lifelong process of shaping one's career, both psychologically and behaviorally, within the context of a society (Herr, Cramer, & Niles, 2004).

Existing theories vary in focus and scope in an effort to describe the complex process of career development. Savickas (2002) recognizes two types of career development theories, those that emphasize (1) individual differences (i.e., the way that people choose or find the environment that is the best occupational fit), and (2) individual development (i.e., how people display their career behavior over time). Herr and Cramer (1996) suggest that "existing career theories should be seen as complementary ways of knowing, not competing, and fully-developed alternative explanations of the same behavioral set or population." This chapter discusses career development theories in four different categories: (1) person-environment fit, (2) developmental, (3) social learning, and (4) postmodern career development theories.

PERSON-ENVIRONMENT FIT THEORIES

Holland's theory of person-environment interactions organizes a massive amount of information about job titles and the personality type that best fits each occupational type (Weinrach, 1984). This theory is based on four basic assumptions:

1. In our culture, most persons can be categorized as one of six types: realistic, investigative, artistic, social, enterprising, or conventional.
2. There are six kinds of environments: realistic, investigative, artistic, social, enterprising, and conventional.
3. People search for environments that will let them exercise their skills and abilities, express their attitudes and values, and take on agreeable problems and roles.
4. A person's behavior is determined by an interaction between personality and the characteristics of the environment (Holland, 1973, pp. 2–4).

The foundation of Holland's theory is the six corresponding categories used to describe both personality and environmental types. Below are brief descriptions of the six personality types identified by Holland (1973, pp. 14–18; 1994, pp. 2–3):

1. *Realistic.* Prefers ordered and systematic settings where they may manipulate tools, objects, and/or animals.
2. *Investigative.* Prefers to observe physical, biological, and/or cultural phenomena through symbolic, systemic, and creative investigation techniques.
3. *Artistic.* Prefers to create art forms or products through the manipulation of physical, verbal, or human materials in an ambiguous and free environment.
4. *Social.* Prefers to utilize human relations competencies to inform, train, develop, cure, or enlighten others.
5. *Enterprising.* Prefers to utilize skills of persuasion, interpersonal interaction, and leadership to manipulate others in pursuit of organizational or economic goals.
6. *Conventional.* Prefers to utilize clerical, computational, and business system competencies in an explicit, ordered, and systematic environment.

The foundation of Holland's model is the concept of *congruence,* or the degree of fit between an individual's personality type and work environment. This degree of fit is determined by identifying a person's Holland code, which is arrived at by identifying the person's three most prominent personality types. Holland's (1985) assessment instrument entitled the Self-Directed Search (SDS) is a typical measure used by counselors to identify a person's Holland code. Each person's Holland code is most often communicated by the first letter of the relevant types (i.e., SEA = Social, Enterprising, Artistic). A person with high congruence with his or her work environment would have a match between his or her personality (SEA) and work environment (also SEA) (Holland, 1973).

Two other concepts are important when applying Holland's theory. *Differentiation* describes the relative *strength* of the types constituting the person's Holland code. For example, if a person (or environment) resembles all six Holland codes equally, then this person (or environment) would be described as undifferentiated. Conversely, a person who has a great deal in common with the *social personality* type has relatively less in common with the remaining types contained in his or her Holland code. Accordingly, this individual would be considered differentiated.

Finally, consistency in regard to Holland types refers to the degree of *relatedness* among a person or his or her environment. To illustrate consistency, Holland uses a hexagonal model placing the Realistic, Investigative, Artistic, Social, Enterprising, and Conventional types located around the hexagon in that order to portray the relatedness among these types. Those located closer to each other on the hexagon have more in common with each other than those located farther apart. Low levels of differentiation and consistency can lead to difficulty in making career decisions and maintaining career achievement and satisfaction (Holland, 1973).

DEVELOPMENTAL THEORIES

THE LEADING DEVELOPMENTAL career theory is Donald Super's *life span, life space* theory (Super, Savickas, & Super, 1996). Super's theory drew on a variety of disciplines such as psychology and sociology and developed what he called a "differential-developmental-social-phenomenological career theory" (Super, 1969). Super (1990) lays the foundation of his work by proposing 14 assumptions on which the life span, life space, and self-concept theory is built. These assumptions made in his model suggest that (1) people are different based on their unique individual traits, and (2) these differences make them qualified for a number of different occupations. Occupations must be flexible enough in their characteristic requirements to allow a range of differing personality types to fit that particular occupation so that the job requirements can be fulfilled. Arising from personal preferences and situational experiences, people develop a *self-concept* or "picture of the self in some role, situation, or position, performing some set of functions, or in some web of relationships" (Super, 1963, p. 18). This changes with time and experience, although it becomes more stable as one matures. The *life span* then describes a series of developmental tasks that persons typically encounter as they attempt to implement their self-concepts. These stages include the following:

1. *Growth (ages 4–13).* Early development of an initial sense of self and the world of work.
2. *Exploration (ages 14–24).* Crystallizing and specifying one's future occupational preferences using knowledge of self and the world of work.
3. *Establishment (ages 25–45).* Stabilizing, consolidating, and advancing one's career preference.
4. *Maintenance (ages 45–65).* Holding, updating, and innovating within one's occupational environment.
5. *Disengagement (ages 65 and beyond).* Planning for retirement living, including lifestyle and postwork activities.

Over the course of life, one's self-concept and career pattern are influenced by one's parents' socioeconomic status, education, ability levels, and career maturity or degree of success in coping with career development demands. The degree of satisfaction the person obtains from work is related to the degree with which he or she is able to implement his or her self-concept in the context of his or her abilities, needs, values, interests, personality traits, and continually evolving self-concepts. In addition to implementing their self-concept in the world of work, people are also participating in the same process in other life roles. *Life space* acknowledges the degree of importance attached to nine different roles people typically play in their life span. These roles include son or daughter, student, leisurite, citizen, worker, spouse (or partner), homemaker, parent, and pensioner. According to Super (1980) a person's career comprises the total constellation of all nine life roles engaged in over the course of a lifetime.

The development of occupational aspirations through childhood and adolescence is presented from a sociological and developmental perspective by Gottfredson's (2002) theory of circumscription, compromise, and self-creation. This theory describes the way that youth modify their career aspirations based on their perceptions of gender, social prestige, and personal interest appropriateness. This modification of aspirations takes place throughout the life span, resulting in a person's "zone of acceptable occupational alternatives" or "social space" (Gottfredson, 2002, p. 91) from which they choose a career based on their perceived fit in society.

Circumscription describes the process of eliminating socially unacceptable occupations from one's aspirations based on gender and prestige. According to Gottfredson (1996) this process occurs through four stages of development:

1. *Orientation to size and power.* Between the ages of 3 and 5 children classify themselves as little and adults as big with the understanding that "big people" or adults work.
2. *Orientation to sex roles.* Between the ages of 6 and 8 children think dichotomously (i.e., good-bad, right-wrong) at the same time they become aware of gender roles. This leads to the development of tolerable sex-role boundaries as they identify certain jobs as either boy- or girl-appropriate.
3. *Orientation to social valuation.* Between the ages of 9 and 13 the person becomes aware of social class and occupational prestige leading him or her to develop a tolerable zone of occupations based upon two factors: (1) the lower level of occupations he or she is willing to consider based on ability level and the social reference group, and (2) the upper level of effort he or she is willing to exert in pursuing occupational aspirations.
4. *Orientation to the internal, unique self.* After 14 years of age adolescents become more self-aware and are able to determine which occupations are congruent with their unique self. This stage represents the shift from circumscribing or eliminating potential occupations to identifying those that are most acceptable from the zone of occupational aspirations that exists as a result of their circumscription process. It is from this zone that compromise is employed to narrow the range of occupations to pursue based on perceived external barriers to success (i.e., accessibility to entry into that occupation).

SOCIAL LEARNING THEORIES

BASED ON BANDURA'S (1986) social learning theory, the learning theory of career counseling (LTCC) acknowledges the role that a person's unique learning experiences play in career development as well as innate, developmental processes (Mitchell & Krumboltz, 1996). According to Mitchell and Krumboltz there are four factors that are identified as being influential in career decision making:

1. *Genetic endowment and special abilities.* Innate factors such as sex, race, and physical appearance interact with environmental events, leading to the rise of special abilities such as intelligence, athletic ability, and other special talents.

2. *Environmental conditions and events.* Cultural, economic, social, political, and natural forces create or eliminate opportunities in one's career path. Factors such as unemployment laws, natural disasters, family traditions, geographic location, and technological development all create the milieu in which a person develops his or her career identity.

3. *Instrumental and associative learning experiences.* Instrumental learning involves antecedents (the factors described above), behaviors (overt, cognitive, and emotional responses), and consequences (immediate and longer-term effects of one's behaviors as well as resulting self-talk). Associative learning occurs when a positive or negative stimulus interacts with a person's neutral stance toward the learning experience such as when a chance encounter affects one's career decision.

4. *Task approach skills.* Task approach skills have a reciprocal relationship in one's career development in that they both affect career decision outcomes and are often outcomes themselves. These skills include the consideration of one's genetic characteristics, special abilities, environmental factors, and learning experiences as well as characteristics such as work habits, cognitive process, problem-solving skills, and emotional responses.

These four factors influence people's beliefs about themselves and the world. These beliefs influence their occupational preferences and lead them to prefer occupations with tasks similar to those that they have been successful at, and where they have been valued by others. Additionally, persons who receive positive words from friends and family members have an increased image about themselves and the world.

Social cognitive career theory (SCCT) builds upon Bandura's social cognitive theory and Krumboltz's theory of career counseling or LTCC (Mitchell & Krumboltz, 1996). Lent and Brown (1996) suggest that this is achieved by being "more concerned with specific cognitive mediators through which learning experiences guide career behavior; with the manner in which variables such as interests, abilities, and values interrelate; and with the specific paths by which person and contextual factors influence career outcomes" (p. 377).

SCCT uses Bandura's (1986) triadic reciprocal model to outline the complex relationship between self-efficacy beliefs, outcome expectations, and personal goals in the career decision-making process. Self-efficacy beliefs, or beliefs about our ability to play a specific role in a specific domain, are shaped both positively and negatively by outcomes achieved within four domains: (1) personal performance accomplishments, (2) vicarious learning, (3) social persuasion, and (4) physiological states and reactions (Bandura, 1986). Outcome expectations are behavior-specific belief expectations that are developed in the context of extrinsic reinforcement (i.e., tangible rewards), self-directed consequences (i.e., pride of accomplishment), or outcomes resulting from the activity itself. Finally, personal goals influence one's determination to persist with behaviors over longer periods of time to achieve a specific outcome. The interaction of these three factors informs our beliefs about our ability to play a central role in our own career decision-making process.

POSTMODERN THEORIES

POSTMODERN CAREER DEVELOPMENT theories emphasize a person's subjective career development experience or his or her understanding of his or her career development journey as it takes place. Embracing a constructivist scientific perspective, these theories assume that there is no fixed truth for which one searches, as each of us constructs our own career. As such, these theories value multiculturalism as well as personal advocacy and agency in pursuit of an individual's career vision (Niles & Harris-Bowlsbey, 2005).

The narrative approach to career development emphasizes an understanding of the person's career plot with the person as the main character. This is played out in the story of his or her life or within the context of a specific career development task. The narrative provides organization for the context of the plot by giving it stages such as the beginning, middle, or end. The power of this theory comes from the temporal organization of one's career development providing context for understanding and perspective for intervention (Cochran, 1997).

The life chapters exercise is one tool a counselor might use to help a client organize his or her career journey to date. In this exercise, the client is encouraged to write the career plot of his or her life by choosing a title for a personal book, identifying and titling chapters that have occurred while identifying lessons learned from each, and then identifying and titling chapters that have yet to be written. This powerful exercise allows a client to construct the antecedents, current circumstances, and future goals of his or her career plot while providing a context for determining the steps needed to make the unwritten chapters the future reality. This process speaks to the heart of constructivist ideology, allowing a person to restore positive chapters and reverse negative ones through the writing of his or her future (Niles & Harris-Bowlsbey, 2005).

Contextual theories allow for the provision of contextual factors into the career development meaning-making process for individuals (Young, Valach, & Colling, 1996). Young and colleagues have identified four assumptions made by contextual career theories:

1. Acts are viewed as purposive and as being directed toward specific goals.
2. Acts are embedded in their context.
3. Change has a prominent role in career development. Because events take shape as people engage in practical action with a particular purpose, analysis and interpretation are always practical. Researchers look at action for a particular purpose.
4. Contextualism rejects a theory of truth based on the correspondence between mental representations and objective reality (p. 480).

Contextual theory views career development as dynamic, allowing for individuals to achieve meaning through their own actions within their social environment. In other words, people construct their careers through their actions (Young & Collin, 1992), allowing them to make sense of their lives (Young et al., 1996). These actions are taken in the context of the career construction process and take three forms: (1) manifest behaviors (i.e., explicit career-related actions), (2) internal processes (i.e., thoughts and feelings toward the action being manifested), and (3) social meaning (i.e., the meaning of the action to self and others). These goal-directed actions provide a framework for explaining a person's career development (Young, Valach, & Collin, 2002).

CONCLUSION

COLLECTIVELY, CAREER DEVELOPMENT theories provide rich explanations relative to how careers develop across the life span. The complex mix of intraindividual and extraindividual variables shaping career development presents an incredible challenge to career theorists. To fully appreciate the career development literature, one must understand multiple theories as each theory offers an important perspective. Integrating theoretical orientations related to individual difference and individual development provides the fullest explanation for those seeking to understand the career development process. Such integration also links career development to human development, which represents an important next step in the evolution of career development theories.

REFERENCES

Bandura, A. (1986). *Social foundations of thought and action: A social-cognitive theory*. Upper Saddle River, NJ: Prentice-Hall.

Cochran, L. (1997). *Career counseling: A narrative approach*. Thousand Oaks, CA: Sage Publications.

Gottfredson, L. S. (1996). A theory of circumscription and compromise. In D. Brown, L. Brooks, et al. (Eds.), *Career choice and development* (3rd ed., pp. 179–281). San Francisco: Jossey-Bass.

Gottfredson, L. S. (2002). Gottfredson's theory of circumscription, compromise, and self-creation. In D. Brown, et al. (Eds.), *Career choice and development* (4th ed., pp. 85–148). San Francisco: Jossey-Bass.

Herr, E. L., & Cramer, S. H. (1996). *Career guidance and counseling through the lifespan* (5th ed.). New York: HarperCollins.

Herr, E. L., Cramer, S. H., & Niles, S. G. (2004). *Career guidance and counseling through the lifespan: Systematic approaches* (6th ed.). Boston: Allyn & Bacon.

Holland, J. L. (1973). *Making vocational choices: A theory of careers*. Upper Saddle River, NJ: Prentice-Hall.

Holland, J. L. (1985). *Making vocational choices: A theory of vocational personalities and work environments* (2nd ed.). Upper Saddle River, NJ: Prentice-Hall.

Holland, J. L. (1994). Separate but unequal is better. In M. L. Savickas & W. B. Walsh (Eds.), *Convergence in career development theories: Implications for science and practice* (pp. 45–51). Palo Alto, CA: CPP Books.

Lent, R. W., & Brown, S. D. (1996). Social cognitive approach to career development: An overview. *The Career Development Quarterly, 44*, 310–321.

Mitchell, L. K., & Krumboltz, J. D. (1996). Krumboltz's learning theory of career choice counseling. In D. Brown, L. Brooks, & Associates (Eds.), *Career choice and development* (3rd ed., pp. 179–281). San Francisco: Jossey-Bass.

Niles, S. G., & Harris-Bowlsbey, J. (2005). *Career development interventions in the 21st century* (2nd ed.). Upper Saddle River, NJ: Pearson/Prentice-Hall.

Savickas, M. L. (2002). Career construction: A developmental theory of vocational behavior. In D. Brown & Associates (Eds.), *Career choice and development* (4th ed., pp. 149–205). San Francisco: Jossey-Bass.

Super, D. E. (1963). Self-concepts in vocational development. In D. E. Super, R. Starishevsky, N. Matlin, & J. P. Jordan, (Eds.), *Career development: Self-concept theory* (pp. 17–32). New York: College Entrance Examination Board.

Super, D. E. (1969). Vocational development theory: Persons, positions, processes. *The Counseling Psychologist, 1*, 2–9.

Super, D. E. (1976). *Career education and the meaning of work*. Washington, DC: Office of Education.

Super, D. E. (1980). A life-span, life-space approach to career development. *Journal of Vocational Behavior, 16*, 282–298.

Super, D. E. (1990). A life-span, life-space approach to career development. In D. Brown, L. Brooks, et al. (Eds.), *Career choice and development: Applying contemporary theories to practice* (2nd ed., pp. 197–261). San Francisco: Jossey-Bass.

Super, D. E., Savickas, M. L., & Super, C. (1996). A life-span, life-space approach to career development. In D. Brown, L. Brooks, et al. (Eds.), *Career choice and development* (3rd ed., pp. 121–128). San Francisco: Jossey-Bass.

Weinrach, G. (1984). Determinants of vocational choice: Holland's theory. In D. Brown, L. Brooks, et al. (Eds.), *Career choice and development: Applying contemporary theories to practice* (3rd ed., pp. 61–93). San Francisco: Jossey-Bass.

Young, R. A., & Collin, A. (Eds.). (1992). *Interpreting career: Hermeneutical studies of lives in context.* Westport, CT: Praeger.

Young, R. A., Valach, L., & Collin, A. (1996). A contextual explanation of career. In D. Brown, L. Brooks, et al. (Eds.), *Career choice and development* (3rd ed., pp. 477–508). San Francisco: Jossey-Bass.

Young, R. A., Valach, L., & Collin, A. (2002). A contextualist explanation of career. In D. Brown, L. Brooks, et al. (Eds.), *Career choice and development* (4th ed., pp. 206–254). San Francisco: Jossey-Bass.

46

Key Concepts and Techniques for an Aging Workforce

SUSANNE M. BRUYÈRE, DEBRA A. HARLEY,
CHARLENE M. KAMPFE,
AND JOHN S. WADSWORTH

OLDER WORKERS ARE one of the fastest-growing subsets of the American workforce. The U.S. Bureau of Labor Statistics predicts that between 2002 and 2012, the number of workers 55 years and older will grow by 50%. The aging population is likely to result in increasing numbers of people with disabilities in the workforce, who may have difficulty staying employed. The U.S. Census Bureau (2004) estimates that the 45–54- and 55–64-year-old population in the United States will grow by nearly 44.2 million (17%) and 35 million (39%) in the next 10 years. By the year 2010, this group will account for nearly half (44%) of the working-age population (20–64), and the number of people with disabilities between the ages of 50 and 65 will almost double (Weathers, 2006).

Effective counseling practices must increasingly include attention to preparing both individuals and their workplaces for the impact of the aging process. Proactive education about ways to maximize the productivity of an aging workforce, effective case management, and workplace accommodations can significantly contribute to maximizing aging-worker retention.

Older persons frequently experience dehumanizing situations or attitudes. They are often devalued by society, discriminated against with regard to employment, discouraged from making their own decisions about a variety of aspects of their lives, and forced to make residential relocations into institutions that may not encourage or allow independence of thought or action. The professional counselor's philosophy is antithetical to these practices.

Employment is a key aspect of the current social effort to promote financial independence, emotional health, and physical wellness among the growing population of older individuals. Both the need for economic support and the personal and social benefits of work may be important for persons of all ages. Some baby boomers are not waiting until retirement age to stop working; more than 4 million already have left the workforce due to retirement or disability. However, many older workers will need to work longer for the income it brings.

THEORETICAL AND CLINICAL CONSIDERATIONS

T HE AGING PROCESS is unique to every individual. Professional counselors have many opportunities to provide interventions that improve the quality of life for older persons. However, theoretical and philosophical models used in counseling older individuals are overwhelmingly grounded in the medical model, which emphasizes the identification and treatment of pathological physical changes that are associated with growing older. The medical model identifies a diagnosis, prescribes a protocol for intervention, and predicts a prognosis. As a dominant paradigm, this model asserts that the body is a physical mechanism that can be studied quantitatively through measurement of physiological function and can be treated as well at a strictly physical level. In many ways, the medical model disregards psychological concepts, emotional reactions, and subjective data. In addition, the medical model looks within the individual for a diagnosis of the problem, placing the physician above the person, and ignores the environment. This emphasis may lead counselors to anchor assessment results on biases against older adults. Ultimately, the medical model is too rigid, restrictive, and disempowering, because it adheres to the notion that aging itself is a type of impairment that with appropriate treatment can be either cured or altered.

A better understanding of aging is more closely aligned with the developmental model (Erikson, 1959). Erickson described human life in terms of stages—sequential developmental occurrences in which individuals experience developmental crises (e.g., change in employment status, loss, grief). He pointed out that old age is a time when people struggle to find meaning in the life they have lived, a sense of ego integrity, and satisfaction with a life well spent. The stage of life designated as *old age* involves numerous transitions (e.g., retirement, loss of autonomy, impaired health). The advantage for older people of the developmental model is its focus on wellness, planning for successful adaptations, and empowerment to realize the developmental goal and reach their full potential.

Developmental frameworks for counseling intervention have been reported to be successful in addressing a wide variety of concerns that impact older persons. Sexuality for older persons may be addressed through holistic and developmental frameworks that stress the potential for lifelong capacity to enjoy intimacy and sensual enjoyment. Career development may be presented as a lifelong, dynamic process that requires individuals to engage throughout their lifetime in the ongoing assessment, analysis, and synthesis of information about the world of work and self.

Persons who are aging successfully have a more integrative experience that includes acceptance of the past, resolution of conflicts, and reconciliation of reality with the ideal self than persons who utilize escape and obsessive reminiscence of the past. Life reviews may allow clients to integrate life experiences and create new meaning to promote the resolution of conflicts and reconciliation with others in preparation for life transitions and the termination of life. Life planning may assist older persons in clarifying transferable vocational or leisure skills, planning for age-related change, and goal setting.

Personal control is vital in maintaining mental health and life satisfaction. The ability to make decisions, self-regulate behavior, and control the environment is positively associated with psychological well-being. Paid work is recognized as an important source of well-being for older men and women because work provides a sense of independence and competence outside of immediate family networks. Counseling interventions that encourage personal control rather than focus on diagnosis and pathology may be more effective in promoting the well-being of older persons.

The aging population requires multiple services from various service professionals (e.g., counselors, health care providers, employment human resource departments). To better facilitate positive outcomes for aging populations, interagency collaboration offers an opportunity for enhanced employment outcomes. Casework is the common denominator, which cuts across various service professionals, and is relevant to deconstructing disincentives for either maintaining or returning to work. (See Harley, Donnell, & Rainey, 2003, for strategies and implications for functional integration collaboration for crossing professional borders.)

Counseling aids older adults in coping and meeting their needs in changing situations. However, fewer older adults than younger ones use mental health services and other related counseling services. Older individuals may associate counseling treatment with institutionalization or believe it is reserved for extremely disturbed individuals. They may also attribute emotional difficulties to the normal process of growing older, and they may believe that the inability to cope with difficulties is a sign of failure to age successfully.

Assessment may involve special considerations for older consumers. People with no recent experiences in standardized testing may find some assessments threatening and may require additional explanation to clarify what the test measures, its relevancy to the questions at hand, and the benefits of the actual results. Testing instruments must be chosen to be appropriate. Norms are not available on some instruments for age cohorts beyond 60 or 65 (e.g., Holland's Self-Directed Search; Holland, 1994). Even instruments that include older persons in the norm groups often only go to age 89 or 90 and thus would not necessarily be applicable to 100-year-olds (e.g., Wechsler Adult Intelligence Scales–Revised III [WAIS III]; Wechsler, 1997). Furthermore, the age range for older persons (e.g., 60–100 years) is great; there are very different functional levels, needs, and appropriate assessments within the 60–100 age groups. Test administrators need to assume responsibility for recognizing deficiencies of the instruments, and for selecting other appropriate instruments, if available.

Endurance must be a consideration in scheduling tests. People with sensory impairments, reduced energy levels, or disabling physical or mental conditions may benefit from accommodations during testing. Reflex speed typically decreases and sensory loss increases with age, so power tests may be more meaningful than speed tests. Abbreviated screening instruments may also be useful—shortened instruments to assess depression have been found to be as effective as longer ones, and a four-test short-form of the WAIS III has been found as effective as the full form in determining intellectual functioning in persons over age 65. Situational assessments or job trials may be more relevant to older persons than paper-and-pencil testing. Behavioral assessment is an important adjunct.

Tests of functional level can be an important source of information in vocational assessments and can further assist in career planning with older adults who wish to return to work. Specific instruments have been developed to determine functional status of older persons. For example, the Instrumental Activities of Daily Living (IADLs) scale (Nourhashemi et al., 2001) has been effectively used with women age 75 and older to assess independent living functioning and to successfully predict risk factors of frailty in older women who, at the time of the assessment, were healthy and living at home.

OPPORTUNITIES FOR OLDER WORKERS

IN A SOCIETY where careers and their role in society are a primary defining feature, the aging population, in a stage of development that does not focus on employment, is displaced. However, the increased need to remain in the workforce longer is presenting the aging population with numerous barriers.

People who are older are more likely than younger people to be adapting to the effects of sensory loss; to see themselves as being closer to death; to have a loss of role models for social demands they encounter; to experience significant loss of cohort groups, long-term friendships, and family members; to experience role changes, role reversals, and alterations in role expectations; to perceive changes in social support; and to experience changes in perception of time. Counselors can assist with adjustment to these circumstances.

As people age, chronic conditions are more prevalent. These conditions often do not prevent people from working or impair their daily living skills. Lifestyle, coping abilities, activity accommodations, medical care, external supports, physical and social environments, therapeutic regimens, and rehabilitation may mediate the severity of functional limitations and subsequent development of disabilities.

Premorbid personality is an important component in adaptation to disability. The effects of endurance, resilience, energy level, and stress are important in rehabilitation planning for persons of all ages and even more important when chronic, multiple, and severe conditions are combined with effects of aging.

Older workers are most at risk of disability or additional disability related to changes in sensory acuity. Approximately 14% of all individuals in the general population experience a hearing impairment by age 54. Visual impairments are also common, affecting approximately 15% of women and 12% of men over 65 (Hoyer & Roodin, 2003). Sensory impairments are a particularly significant source of functional limitation, regardless of chronological age, and these conditions often lead to a diminished ability to participate in everyday life. Employers are less familiar with accommodations for these types of impairments than for other disabilities and make them less frequently than they do other accommodations. This lack of experience lessens the likelihood that employers are prepared to deal with these disabilities. This barrier to continued productivity may affect older workers disproportionately.

People who are older experience the full range of disability, including mental illness and substance abuse. Approximately 15% to 20% of persons over age 65 have serious symptoms as a result of psychiatric disorders. Such symptoms may result from long-existing conditions such as personality disorders, from more recent situations such as severe depression related to medications, or may result from a combination of these. People who are older are more likely than people from other age groups to experience primary depression, that is, depression resulting from physical causes or drug side effects.

Substance abuse in older individuals can be a continuation of a past addiction, a new coping strategy, an abuse of prescription medication, or a condition associated with anxiety, depression, or cognitive disorders. It may resemble conditions that are associated with aging such as chronic pain, fatigue, or depression. Once identified, however, those who have this disorder may benefit from treatment.

Information regarding various social norms imposed on older individuals within different cultures, including ethnic and racial minority groups (e.g., roles, status, issues of respect), is needed. For example, older people from ethnic and racial minorities or Appalachian populations may rely heavily on informal networks and indigenous influence for intervention.

NEEDED PROACTIVE EMPLOYER RESPONSE

A MAJOR ISSUE for aging workers and their employers is the work environment, and whether it might be unfriendly and perhaps even discriminatory toward older workers. A significant factor influencing the decision to retain or eject older workers is no doubt the culture of the workplace itself. Age-based stereotyping perpetuates discriminatory practices and discourages elderly workers from remaining in or returning to the workplace.

Keeping the senior worker not only preserves valuable institutional knowledge and memory but also creates beneficial diversity in the workplace. Incentives and workplace supports will be needed to encourage employers to retain older workers and to encourage older workers to remain in the workforce. Employers must create workplace policies and practices and effective intergenerational inclusion initiatives that support worker retention.

Research suggests that employers discriminate against older workers in the job application process. In addition, the stereotypes that younger workers have of their older peers can greatly influence workplace dynamics. Traditional stereotypes of older workers (e.g., being inflexible, sicker, unwilling to learn new technology) continue to persist at many levels. Such stereotypes have clearly had an influence on older workers' (particularly men's) labor force participation in the past. Workers who experience age discrimination are more likely to leave their current employment setting and less likely to remain employed.

This may include adopting new management styles and work setting protocols that focus on an age-diverse workforce. Human resource policies and practices should reflect alternatives that will respond to the older workers' desire for flexible working hours, part-time positions, and the ability to choose what part of the work day they work. Flexible workplace, telecommuting options, and flex-time agreements can help fill this need.

Benefit plans may also create disincentives for retaining older workers. Many plans can send mixed messages to older workers; some create incentives to retire while others encourage continued labor force activity. Some employers are creating health care and retirement policies that offer incentives to older workers to stay engaged in the workforce, such as phased retirement, "in demand" workforce for specialized consulting, senior staff mentors for new workers, casual/part-time workers' programs, discounts on pharmaceuticals, specialized health screenings, long-term care insurance, preretirement planning, and prorated benefits for employees on flexible work schedules.

COUNSELOR PRACTICE, TRAINING, AND RESEARCH IMPLICATIONS

THE GROWING OLDER population, with its increased levels of disability and its desire and need to work, creates the opportunity for counselors to provide services to people who are older. To be able to confront myths and stereotypes, counselors will need to have knowledge of the intellectual, social, and emotional well-being of older adults. Counselor educators can prepare counselors-in-training for this task by including aging issues in the counselor education curriculum.

Personal experiences with various groups of people and social learning experiences shape one's viewpoint toward a group. Counselors-in-training may have had prior exposure to negative stereotypes about persons with disabilities; or been repeatedly exposed to negative stereotypes about aging (ageism); or have a prejudice against older persons (gerontophobia), or a fear of aging or of associating with older persons; and other attitudinal barriers or misconceptions. Both personal and societal attitudes toward the aging process and older populations are appropriate to explore in psychosocial coursework. Inclusion of material on multicultural aspects of human relationships is intended to increase trainees' multicultural awareness, knowledge, and skills through developing an understanding of one's personal values, attitudes, motivations, and behaviors.

Retraining, adaptive devices, physical therapy, and occupational therapies can assist workers injured on the job, regardless of their ages. However, counselors should be aware that age-related changes in stamina and healing may require that older employees who do receive on-the-job injuries may need to be afforded additional time and extended therapy to fully restore optimal functioning.

Infusion of information regarding this population into existing counselor accreditation–approved curricula is vital if the counseling profession is to become a resource for the development of strategies to maintain the economic independence of citizens who are older. Such courses can also expose counselors-in-training to the issues and attitudes that impact the employment of older workers, particularly those with disabilities.

Research is needed on the issues of aging workers, such as training needs, career transition issues, and retirement planning. Research is also needed on which accommodations, workplace modifications, and changes to policies and practices positively impact the retention and continued productivity of an aging workforce. Counselor practitioners are in a unique position to contribute to needed research design conceptualization, metrics, and analyses, to test the multiplicity of interventions we will be exploring in the coming years to keep our aging workforce healthy and intellectually engaged in the employment environment. Counselors are experientially qualified to provide the needed services to keep this population productive and more fully engaged in their communities and continuing employment.

RESOURCES

National Organizations/Associations

Adult Development and Aging, Division 20 of the American Psychological Association: http://www.apa.org/about/division/div20.html
American Association of Geriatric Psychiatry: http://www.aagpgpa.org/
American Association of Retired Persons (AARP): http://www.aagpgpa.org/
Association for Adult Development and Aging, A Division of the American Counseling Association: http://www.aadaweb.org/
The American Geriatrics Society: http://www.americangeriatrics.org

Council for Accreditation of Counseling Related Educational Programs (CACREP) Gerontological Counseling Standards: www.cacrep.org/2001standards .html

JOURNALS, SPECIFIC RELATED ARTICLES

American Psychological Association. *Psychology and aging.* Retrieved July 11, 2008, from http://www.apa.org/journals/pag/

Bruyère, S. M. (2006). Disability management: Key concepts and techniques for an aging workforce. *International Journal of Disability Management, 1,* 149–158.

Kampfe, C. M., Harley, D. B., Wadsworth, J. S., & Smith, S. M. (2007). Methods and materials for infusing aging issues into the rehabilitation curriculum. *Rehabilitation Education, 21,* 107–116.

Kampfe, C. M., Wadsworth, J. S., Smith, S. M., & Harley, D. A. (2005). The infusion of aging issues in the rehabilitation curriculum: A review of the literature. *Rehabilitation Education, 19,* 225–233.

REFERENCES

Erikson, E. H. (1959). *Identity and the life cycle: Psychological issues.* New York: International Universities Press.

Harley, D. A., Donnell, C., & Rainey, J. (2003). Interagency collaboration: Reinforcing professional bridges to serve aging populations with multiple service needs. *Journal of Rehabilitation, 69,* 32–37.

Holland, J. L. (1994). *Self-Directed Search.* Odessa, FL: Psychological Assessment Resources, Inc.

Hoyer, W. J., & Roodin, P. A. (2003). *Adult development and aging* (5th ed.). Boston: McGraw-Hill.

Nourhashemi, F., Andrieu, S., Gillette-Guyonnet, S., Vellas, B., Albarede, L., & Grandjean, H. (2001). Instrumental activities of daily living as a potential marker of frailty: A study of 7364 community-dwelling elderly women (the EPIDOS study). *The Journals of Gerontology, 56A,* M448–453.

U.S. Census Bureau. (2004). *U.S. Census Bureau population projections.* Retrieved October 7, 2007, from http://www.census.gov/ipc/www/usinterimproj/

Weathers, R. R. (2006). *Disability prevalence rates for an aging workforce.* Ithaca, NY: Cornell University, Rehabilitation Research and Training Center on Employment Policy.

Wechsler, D. (1997). *WAIS-III administration and scoring manual.* San Antonio, TX: The Psychological Corporation.

Section G

Assessment and Diagnosis

47

What Counselors Should Know About Personality Assessments

MARY LOUISE CASHEL

EFFORTS TO UNDERSTAND personality have a long history within the field of counseling and psychology. Cloninger (2008) defines personality as the underlying causes of individual behavior and experience within a person. Over the years, the practice of administering personality tests has become a significant role for many professional counselors. This chapter summarizes key information that can be found in many professional references and graduate texts (e.g., Beutler & Groth-Marnat, 2003; Lanyon & Goodstein, 1997; Todd & Bohart, 2005; Wiggins, 2003).

Personality assessments may be conducted for a variety of reasons. They can be used for the following purposes or to address related referral questions:

- To diagnose psychopathology or personality dysfunction
- To inform personnel selection or individual vocational development
- To predict future behavior (risk assessment)
- To identify malingering or other response styles
- To facilitate treatment planning, therapy, or supportive counseling.

Personality assessments are best conducted as a part of an overall psychological assessment. Todd and Bohart (1999) offered a concise definition of psychological assessment: "The process of collecting information in a systematic, objective, empirical way about an individual's intellectual functioning, behavior, or personality, so that predictions and decisions about them can be made" (p. 54). Personality functioning cannot be validly assessed in isolation of cognitive, intellectual, or social functioning. Each domain contributes to the functioning of the individual as a whole and informs the others.

The assessment process comprises multiple steps that include (1) clarifying the nature of the referral question; (2) selecting appropriate tests; (3) test administration; (4) test scoring and interpretation; (5) integrating test findings; and (6) compiling the psychological report. The second step, selection of measures, will ultimately determine the information the clinician obtains and conclusions he or she makes with respect to the referral question.

OVERVIEW OF PERSONALITY ASSESSMENT MEASURES

THERE ARE MANY measures the clinician can choose to assess personality functioning. These can be categorized based on their theoretical underpinnings, administration procedures, and response characteristics. A common categorization still found in many texts distinguishes *projective* from *objective* tests. The projective tests were derived from psychoanalytic theory and largely involve analysis of unconscious processes. These are measures individuals are asked to respond to in which there are ambiguous test stimuli with no readily apparent meaning. The assumption is that the person will interpret the material based on his or her own unconscious feelings, needs, desires, attitudes, motives, and other core aspects of personality. That is, the individual will "project" features of himself or herself and how he or she sees the world into the ambiguous stimuli.

PROJECTIVE TESTS

THERE ARE GENERALLY four types of projective tests: (1) association techniques (e.g., Rorschach Inkblot Test), for which examinees are asked to reflect upon a series of inkblots; (2) completion techniques (e.g., Sentence Completion Test), for which the examinee is asked to complete a sentence based on a general sentence stem or incomplete phrase; (3) choice or ordering techniques, such as adjective checklists or card sorts with which the examinee may be asked to describe himself or herself, other individuals, or situations; and (4) expressive/constructive techniques, which include storytelling tasks (e.g., Thematic Apperception Test [TAT]) and drawing tasks (e.g., the House-Tree-Person). Although a variety of scoring systems have been developed for interpretation of these measures, they still encompass a fair degree of subjectivity on the part of the examiner. They are very popular among many practicing clinicians, but the degree to which they demonstrate strong psychometric properties remains controversial among academicians and researchers.

OBJECTIVE TESTS

THE OBJECTIVE TESTS generally comprise self-report and multiscale measures such as the Minnesota Multiphasic Personality Inventory (MMPI/MMPI-2), the California Personality Inventory (CPI), and the Millon Clinical Multiaxial Inventory (MCMI/MCMI-III). They were referred to as objective measures primarily due to their scoring format, which utilizes a key, is uniform, and meets the highest standard of reliability; in fact, the administration and scoring of many of the objectives tests are completed on a computer. Interpretation of these measures is also more straightforward and primarily involves analysis of the score combinations. For many of these measures computer-generated interpretive programs are also available. However, clinicians are still called upon to use their professional judgment in integrating test findings with other information such as background information, behavioral observations, collateral information if available, and the results of other test findings. Most texts now refer to these tests more directly as self-report instruments or personality inventories.

Personality inventories can be defined as psychological measures that comprise a number of items concerning personal characteristics, thoughts, feelings, and behaviors. These tests are carefully constructed and standardized to assess a broad range of variables for comparison of groups or individuals within a normative group (Aiken, 1999). They can be further categorized based on the procedures used for test construction and their theoretical underpinnings. Rationally or theoretically derived measures were developed based on a specific conception of personality. Items are typically selected using professional judgment in adherence to a specific theory. These include measures such as the Myers-Briggs and MCMI-III, which assess features of personality as they relate to job preferences and personality disorders, respectively. Multivariate and factor analytic approaches have also been used in the scale development of personality inventories. In this process a large potential item pool is first generated by a panel of experts based on their professional judgment or common sense. Statistical procedures are then used to assess the degree to which the items interrelate to one another with consistency sufficient to form a scale to measure specific personality constructs. Such measures include the Neo-Personality Inventory (NEO-PI) and 16PF, which assess many characteristics of so-called normal personality functioning. Empirical or criterion-keyed strategies were used in the development of the MMPI/MMPI-2. Namely, individuals constituting known diagnostic groups completed a preliminary measure composed of items generated based largely on professional judgment. The items best discriminating among the groups were selected for each respective scale. The MMPI/MMPI-2 contains many scales relevant to personality and psychopathology, assessing constructs such as anxiety, depression, psychosis, and social functioning. Finally, some measures were developed using a combination of these approaches, such as the Personality Assessment Inventory, which is similar to the MMPI/MMPI-2, and was derived from a rational/theoretical and construct validational or factor analytic framework.

STRENGTHS AND LIMITATIONS OF PERSONALITY AND PROJECTIVE TESTS

AS WITH ANY tool, personality tests have their strengths and limitations. The advantages of projective measures include their freedom of response format and the depth of information they can potentially provide with respect to the examinee's personality functioning. Many practitioners assert that projective tests produce a more global and meaningful picture of the individual. Projective measures also have more limited face validity (i.e., what is being measured is less obvious to the examinee). Thus, it is generally more difficult for the examinee to intentionally manipulate his or her test results for projective measures. Alternatively, the scoring procedures for projective measures are usually more complex and time-consuming. The subjectivity that remains in most scoring systems reduces their reliability (i.e., consistency of measurement). Many of the constructs assessed are also difficult to evaluate by alternative methods, which makes establishing validity (i.e., accuracy of measurement) for these tools equally challenging.

Personality inventories have the advantages of ease and speed of administration. In most cases, the examiner simply reads the directions aloud and then allows the examinee to work independently at his or her individual pace. As noted above, the scoring procedures are straightforward and lend themselves well to research efforts to evaluate concurrent and predictive validity of the test measure. However, such measures have a fixed response format (i.e., true/false or a Likert scale) and do not generally allow the examinee to elaborate on or clarify responses to individual items. There is also an underlying assumption that the examinee is aware of and accurately perceives his or her psychological processes. Because most of the items are reasonably face valid in nature, personality inventories can be highly vulnerable to response sets. Response sets are characterized by intentional efforts on the part of the examinee to present himself or herself in a particular fashion (e.g., social desirability, malingering) or to answer items in a particular manner (e.g., endorsing all items as true or all items as false). Some clinicians may also argue that personality inventories are more limited in their ability to predict complex behaviors.

SELECTING APPROPRIATE TESTS

DECISIONS REGARDING WHICH measures to select for an assessment are typically made based on the nature of the referral question, characteristics of the client (e.g., cognitive functioning and reading skills), time constraints, and the theoretical preferences of the examiner. Having said this, research on test usage over the years demonstrates remarkable consistency among the measures most frequently used by practicing professionals. National surveys conducted in the 1960s suggested that the Rorschach, Thematic Apperception Test, and MMPI were among those most frequently included in psychological assessment batteries (Lubin, Wallis, & Paine, 1971; Sundberg, 1961).

The results of subsequent surveys conducted during the 1980s, and more recently, yielded very similar findings. Most recently, Camara, Nathan, and Puente (2000) analyzed survey data of psychological test usage among clinical psychologists and neuropsychologists who were all members of the American Psychological Association. Table 47.1 lists the personality measures that were reported most frequently by the clinical psychologists.

TABLE 47.1 Personality Measures Reported Most Frequently by Clinical Psychologists

Test	% of Sample
Minnesota Multiphasic Personality Inventory (MMPI) I and II	86
Rorschach Inkblot Test	77
Thematic Apperception Test	66
House-Tree-Person (H-T-P) Projective Technique	37
Millon Clinical Multiaxial Inventory (MCMI)	33
Human Figures Drawing Test	30
Sentence Completion Test	25

INTERPRETIVE CONSIDERATIONS

T HE INTERPRETATION OF personality test results is dependent upon a variety of considerations. First and foremost, there must be good evidence that the tests selected demonstrate reliability and validity for members of the socio-demographic group to which the examinee or client belongs. Normative data from which any scores are derived should include members of that group. Specific forms of reliability include internal consistency, test-retest, and interrater reliability if ratings are involved. Specific forms of validity include construct validity, concurrent validity, predictive and discriminant validity. If such information is limited, examiners should clearly make note of this limitation and be very cautious in drawing any conclusions.

In addition to considering the psychometric properties of the measures, examiners need to consider other individual, situational, or contextual factors that may affect the validity of test findings. As noted above, clients may be referred for personality assessments for a variety of reasons and may come either voluntarily or subject to the authority of an outside agency or court. The degree to which the client willingly participates in the evaluation should be observed and documented, in addition to the quality of rapport established with the examiner. Well-composed reports virtually always include a section on behavioral observations in which these issues are discussed.

Closely related to this is the issue of response style discussed earlier. Most personality inventories include scales specifically designed to assess the degree to which the examinee appears to have responded in an open and direct manner, without trying to intentionally manipulate the test results. When personality inventories are administered, the results section should first make comment on scores on these scales. Some of the projective measures (i.e., the Rorschach and TAT) also have suggested strategies for addressing these issues.

It is also useful to consider situational factors that could potentially impact test results. It is the responsibility of the examiner to sort out *state* versus *trait* responses, such as emotions, behaviors, and thought processing, that might reflect temporary or situational factors versus those that are more characteristic of the individual across different settings and time. For example, an individual who recently experienced a traumatic event such as a natural disaster, a house fire, or who just finalized an embittered divorce may produce very different results on some personality measures than that person might during otherwise normal circumstances.

Sociocultural factors should also be closely considered. For most personality measures, more limited information on reliability and validity is generally available for ethnic minorities. This is an especially important issue for clients for whom acculturation to the United States is an issue. Many experts suggest that explicit measures of acculturation should be included and interpreted in psychological assessment batteries for these individuals (Dana, 2000; Ponterotto, Gretchen, & Chauhan, 2000).

ETHICAL ISSUES

THERE ARE SPECIFIC professional standards to which practitioners must adhere when engaged in the practice of conducting or interpreting psychological assessments. These are delineated in the codes of ethics published by the American Psychological Association (APA, 2002), the American Counseling Association (ACA, 2003, 2005), and in the Standards for Educational and Psychological Testing (American Educational Research Association, American Psychological Association, and National Council on Measurement in Education, 1999). In addition to the interpretive issues discussed in the preceding section, professionals must be aware of test user qualifications and obligations regarding test selection, scoring, dissemination of findings, and special issues related to cultural sensitivity.

Counselors and psychologists may only administer and interpret measures and procedures for which they have appropriate training and competence. This requires specific training and supervision in the administration, scoring, and interpretation of each measure used, in addition to more general training in the basic principles of testing, measurement, and statistics for the social sciences. Test users cannot base assessment decisions on obsolete or outdated tests. This can pose a challenge at times to those in private practice or in agencies with limited budgets, as the cost of measures increase and updated versions are published more frequently.

Test users must adhere to standardized assessment procedures and document when assessments are not administered under standard conditions. Counselors and psychologists also retain the responsibility of ensuring the accuracy of their test scoring and interpretations, even when computerized programs are used to assist with this process. It may be tempting for many test users to simply "cut and paste" the findings provided by computer-generated reports into the results of their evaluations. Most professionals strongly discourage this practice because it can render the compilation of results essentially invalid. Thus, test users are called upon to consider the individual, sociocultural, and other contextual factors in drawing conclusions.

It is the responsibility of test users to explain the results of the findings to the client or examinee in language that is clear, comprehensible, and appropriate for his or her level of cognitive or intellectual functioning. Most assessment texts emphasize the need for test users to also carefully consider for whom the psychological report is written and refrain from incorporating unnecessary jargon that may impede clear communication of the findings. Related to this, all mental health professionals should be aware that clients have the right to request the results of their test findings, including the raw testing data (such as raw and scaled scores). In some cases, professionals may choose not to release the test data if it is believed that to do so would result in substantial harm to the client, misuse of the data, or would compromise the security of the test materials. Even in these cases, however, the release of such confidential information is subject to legal regulations. Counselors and psychologists, on the other hand, cannot release assessment results, or any other information subject to the Health Insurance Portability and Accountability Act (HIPAA) regulations, to any individual or agency without the informed, written consent of the examinee or client. The general exception to this is situations in which there is a court order.

Finally, for those that provide assessment services to ethnic, linguistic, and culturally diverse groups, there are additional standards summarized in the APA *Guidelines for Providers of Psychological Services to Ethnic, Linguistic, and Culturally Diverse Populations* (1990). Test users must educate themselves with respect to research and practice issues related to the populations they serve and be respectful of cultural beliefs, values, family, and community structures.

REFERENCES

Aiken, L. R. (1999). *Personality assessment methods and practices* (3rd ed.). Kirkland, WA: Hogrefe & Huber.

American Counseling Association. (2003). *Standards for qualifications of test users*. Alexandria, VA: Author.

American Counseling Association. (2005). *ACA code of ethics*. Alexandria, VA: Author.

American Educational Research Association, American Psychological Association, and National Council on Measurement in Education. (1999). *Standards for educational and psychological testing*. Washington, DC: American Educational Research Association.

American Psychological Association. (1990). *Guidelines for providers of psychological services to ethnic, linguistic, and culturally diverse populations*. Washington, DC: Author.

American Psychological Association. (2002). Ethical principles of psychologists and code of conduct. *American Psychologist, 57*, 1060–1073.

Beutler, L. E., & Groth-Marnat, G. (Eds.). (2003). *Integrative assessment of adult personality*. New York: Guilford Press.

Camara, W. J., Nathan, J. S., & Puente, A. E. (2000). Psychological test usage: Implications in professional psychology. *Professional Psychology: Research and Practice, 31*(2), 141–154.

Cloninger, S. (2008). *Theories of personality* (5th ed.). Saddle River, NJ: Pearson/Prentice-Hall.

Dana, R. H. (Ed.). (2000). *Handbook of cross-cultural and multicultural personality assessment*. Mahwah, NJ: Erlbaum.

Lanyon, R. I., & Goodstein, L. D. (1997). *Personality assessment* (3rd ed.). New York: Wiley.

Lubin, B., Wallis, R., & Paine, C. (1971). Patterns of psychological test usage in the United States: 1935–1969. *Professional Psychology: Research and Practice, 2,* 70–74.

Ponterotto, J. G., Gretchen, D., & Chauhan, R. V. (2000). Cultural identity and multicultural assessment: Quantitative and qualitative tools for the clinician. In L. Suzuki, J. G. Ponterotto, & P. Meller (Eds.), *The handbook of multicultural assessment* (2nd ed., pp. 67–99). San Francisco: Jossey-Bass.

Sundberg, N. D. (1961). The practice of psychological testing in clinical services in the United States. *American Psychologist, 16,* 79–83.

Todd, J., & Bohart, A. C. (Eds.). (1999). *Foundations of clinical and counseling psychology* (3rd ed.). New York: Addison-Wesley Education Publishers.

Todd, J., & Bohart, A. C. (Eds.). (2005). *Foundations of clinical and counseling psychology* (4th ed.). Long Grove, IL: Waveland Press.

Wiggins, J. S. (2003). *Paradigms of personality assessment*. New York: Guilford Press.

48

Understanding the Use of Aptitude Tests in Counseling

SUZANNE M. DUGGER

WHETHER YOU ARE a school counselor assisting students with developing their postsecondary educational and career plans, a college counselor helping students select a major and explore career and graduate school options, a rehabilitation counselor helping clients achieve greater levels of independence and productivity, or a community counselor addressing your clients' educational and/or career direction, you have undoubtedly found a need for objective information regarding your clients' skills and aptitudes. Students may be able to tell you whether they are stronger in math or writing, and clients may be able to tell you that they are more artistically than mechanically inclined, but you are left wondering how strong or weak their skills actually are in math, writing, art, or mechanics. Exactly what do they mean by being "bad at math" or "good at writing"? And do they have a firm foundation upon which to judge themselves as good or bad in these skill areas?

Counselors who have worked with clients on issues related to educational and career planning soon discover that self-report often doesn't suffice as a reliable indicator of skills and aptitudes. For a variety of reasons, clients may underestimate or overestimate their relative strengths and weaknesses. Low self-esteem, for example, may result in a person underestimating his or her skills and aptitudes. Culturally appropriate modesty may contribute to a person underreporting or downplaying skill level. Some personality disorders, in contrast, may lead to an inflated sense of skill/aptitude. Moreover, aside from such individual tendencies to underestimate or overestimate one's own aptitudes, a lack of broad exposure to the full range of aptitudes represented in a national sample makes it nearly impossible for even the most unbiased person to accurately assess his or her aptitude without the benefit of an objective measure.

The purpose of this chapter is to acquaint the professional counselor with the area of aptitude testing. It will provide information regarding the purpose of aptitude tests, three primary types of aptitude tests, and the most commonly used aptitude tests. Additionally, the chapter will address criticisms of aptitude testing along with guidelines for appropriate use of aptitude tests. Finally, the chapter will close with a discussion about the appropriate use of accommodations for clients with disabilities.

PURPOSE OF APTITUDE TESTS

APTITUDE TESTS ARE norm-referenced, standardized tests that are designed to measure a person's "ability to acquire a specific type of skill or knowledge" (Hood & Johnson, 2007, p. 71). They measure "a person's present performance on selected tasks to provide information that can be used to estimate how the person will perform at some time in the future or in a somewhat different situation" (Thorndike, 2005, p. 238). Generally speaking, counselors use aptitude tests when providing career or educationally related counseling. In each instance, the counselor would use the tests as one indicator of the client's potential to succeed in a given area.

To understand the concept of aptitude, it is important to distinguish this concept from *intelligence* and *achievement*. Binet, one of the developers of the Stanford-Binet Intelligence Test, defined intelligence as "a general ability to judge, to comprehend, and to reason well" (Hood & Johnson, 2007, p. 95). This is but one definition, however, and researchers in the field have long struggled to find a universally agreed-upon definition of intelligence. Some purport that the phrase *general mental ability* might best describe the majority of intelligence tests in existence (Aiken & Groth-Marnat, 2006, p. 114). Rather than focusing on a specific area in which a person has aptitude, intelligence tests purport to measure overall general ability. Intelligence, therefore, is a more global concept, and aptitude is, by definition, focused on specific areas of ability (Erford, 2007). Achievement tests, on the other hand, "attempt to measure what has already been learned or knowledge or skills that have

TABLE 48.1 Distinguishing Characteristics of Intelligence, Aptitude, and Achievement Tests

	Time Orientation	Scope	Construct Measured
Intelligence tests	Future	General	Overall ability to learn, comprehend, or reason
Aptitude tests	Future	Specific	Ability to learn specific knowledge or skills
Achievement tests	Past	Specific	Knowledge already learned or skills already acquired

been attained" (Hood & Johnson, 2007, p. 81). In contrast to intelligence and aptitude, both of which are forward-looking and address ability to learn in the future, the concept of achievement focuses on *past* learning or skill acquisition. Table 48.1 summarizes the distinguishing characteristics of these three related and often-confused concepts.

TYPES AND EXAMPLES OF APTITUDE TESTS

THE THREE PRIMARY types of aptitude tests are (1) scholastic aptitude tests; (2) vocational aptitude tests; and (3) measures of special abilities. Scholastic aptitude tests are designed to objectively assess a person's ability to be successful in future academic pursuits. Vocational aptitude tests, usually in the form of multi-aptitude test batteries, are intended to assess a person's aptitude to successfully learn knowledge and/or skills associated with various types of jobs. Measures of special abilities may be academically or vocationally oriented and are designed to focus more narrowly on a very specific aptitude.

Scholastic aptitude tests. A common reason for using scholastic aptitude tests is to predict a student's ability to succeed in higher levels of education. Given this, these tests are most often used at times of transition. Examples of this include scholastic aptitude tests given just before the transition from high school to college and scholastic aptitude tests administered prior to applying to graduate school. Table 48.2 identifies some of the most commonly used scholastic aptitude tests. For each of these tests, the most up-to-date information is available online, and many test publishers have sites specifically for counselors or educators who will be involved with the administration, interpretation, or use of test results.

Vocational aptitude tests. Given that vocational aptitude tests are intended to assess a person's aptitude to successfully learn knowledge and/or skills associated with various types of jobs, they are most commonly administered during the career exploration stage. Such tests are

TABLE 48.2 Commonly Administered Scholastic Aptitude Tests

Acronym	Test Name	Purpose	Web Site
PSAT/NMSQT	Preliminary Scholastic Assessment Test/ National Merit Scholarship Qualifying Test	Practice test for SAT Qualifying exam for the National Merit Scholarship	www.collegeboard.com/ prof/counselors/tests/ psat/news.html
ACT	American College Testing Assessment	College admissions	www.act.org/path/ secondary/
SAT	Scholastic Assessment Test	College admissions	www.collegeboard.com/ prof/counselors/
MAT	Miller Analogies Test	Graduate school admissions	www.milleranalogies.com
GRE	Graduate Record Examination	Graduate school admissions	www.ets.org/gre

frequently used in educational settings such as high schools to assist students in the career decision-making and educational planning process. They are also widely used within rehabilitation counseling settings in which clients with disabilities seek increased levels of independence and productivity. Key to this endeavor is the identification of vocational skills and career options. Whether used within educational or rehabilitation settings, the most widely used vocational aptitude tests tend to measure a broad array of aptitudes so as to identify relative strengths. Table 48.3 identifies several of the most commonly administered vocational multi-aptitude test batteries.

Measures of special abilities. In contrast with scholastic and vocational aptitude tests, which are designed to assess an individual's overall ability to acquire knowledge or skills in the academic and career arenas, respectively, a final type of aptitude test is even more specifically focused. Known as "measures of special abilities," these aptitude tests are narrowly focused on specific skills. Table 48.4 identifies several categories within which measures of special abilities may be organized. More detailed information about tests within these categories is offered by Drummond and Jones (2006) and by Erford and McNinch (2007).

CRITICISMS OF APTITUDE TESTS

LIKE ANY STANDARDIZED tests, aptitude tests have both advantages and disadvantages and their fair share of proponents and opponents. Clearly, no aptitude test can precisely and inarguably

TABLE 48.3 Commonly Administered Multi-Aptitude Test Batteries

Acronym	Test Name	Aptitudes Measured
DAT	Differential Aptitude Tests	*Subtests* Verbal Reasoning Numerical Ability Abstract Reasoning Clerical Speed and Accuracy Mechanical Reasoning Space Relations Spelling Language Usage
ASVAB	Armed Services Vocational Aptitude Battery	*Composite Scores* Verbal Skills Math Skills Science and Technical Skills *Subtests* General Science Arithmetic Reasoning Word Knowledge Paragraph Comprehension Mathematics Knowledge Electronics Information Auto and Shop Information Mechanical Comprehension
O*NET/GATB	O*NET Ability Profiler (replaced the General Aptitude Test Battery)	*Score Categories* Verbal Abilities Arithmetic Reasoning Computation Spatial Ability Form Perception Clerical Perception Motor Coordination Finger Dexterity Manual Dexterity

measure an individual's ability to acquire whatever skill or knowledge base focused upon by the test. To administer them with such an intention or to interpret their results in this manner is to practice assessment in counseling poorly and unethically. They are best utilized as but one assessment tool in a counselor's repertoire.

To understand the appropriate use of aptitude tests, it is useful to explore several common criticisms directed toward them. One criticism is that they measure but one factor related to future success in acquiring skill or knowledge: already achieved knowledge or skill. This is indeed true, but it need not be a reason to abandon the use of aptitude tests. Virtually all aptitude tests measure, to some extent, knowledge or

TABLE 48.4 Categories of Aptitude Tests for Measuring Special Abilities

Category	Example
Clerical aptitude	Hays Aptitude Test Battery–Revised
Computer aptitude	Computer Programmer Aptitude Battery
Creativity	Torrance Tests of Creative Thinking
Mechanical aptitude	Bennett Mechanical Comprehension Test–Third Edition
Musical aptitude	Musical Aptitude Profile–Fourth Edition
Psychomotor ability	Complete Minnesota Manual Dexterity Test
Sensory-perceptual skills	Developmental Test of Visual-Motor Integration

skills that have already been acquired by the test taker. With scholastic aptitude tests, for instance, a student's ability to succeed in future academic endeavors depends in part upon the degree to which he or she has already acquired academic knowledge and skills. As a hypothetical example, if there were an aptitude test to predict future ability to perform long division mathematics, it would surely include some assessment of the student's ability to add and subtract as these mathematical functions are necessary for long division.

Erford and McNinch's contention that "performance on tests measuring aptitudes is influenced not by previously learned content or instruction in an academic domain, but rather by previous, less formalized learning experiences" (2007, p. 357) represents an ideal. In reality, one will find that success on aptitude tests relies in part on formal educational achievement as well as on informal learning experiences (Lyman, 1998). A major difference, of course, is the purpose of the aptitude test. As discussed earlier in this chapter, aptitude tests differ from achievement tests in purpose. Whereas achievement tests are focused on measuring *past* learning, aptitude tests seek to predict *future* learning or skill acquisition. Savvy counselors will therefore understand that past acquisition of knowledge and skills may be relevant to future acquisition of knowledge and skills. In the event that there are academic or skill deficits, of course, remediation of these deficits may be useful in promoting greater success in the future.

A second criticism of aptitude tests addresses their goal of predicting future ability to learn or acquire skills. This criticism questions the value of aptitude tests in making these predictions and looks at the correlation between the aptitude test scores and future performance measures. Again using scholastic aptitude tests as an example, this criticism finds fault with aptitude tests because there is not a perfect relationship (a correlation of 1.00) between the aptitude test score and college grades. As articulated by Gregory (2007), "in 685 studies, the combined SAT Verbal and Math scores correlated .42, on average, with college first-year grade point average" (p. 254).

Even without specific correlation coefficients for criterion-related or predictive validity, however, seasoned counselors know that the ability to acquire a specific type of knowledge or skill does not necessarily equate to the future acquisition of such knowledge or skill. Employees with the aptitude to succeed on the job may or may not excel in actual job performance. Students with the ability to perform well in college may choose other postsecondary options. Those who do attend college may choose not to fully utilize their abilities and instead invest time and energy in other activities. Factors such as effort, motivation, and study habits also correlate with actual performance. There is wisdom, therefore, in using aptitude tests as but one predictor of future performance. Another predictor might include past performance. Indeed, "the College Board reports that the combination of SAT and high school grade point average correlated a robust .61 with freshman grades" (Gregory, 2007, p. 254). In other words, it is advisable to use more than one measure to estimate a person's future success in acquiring knowledge or skills. In seeking to predict college success, for example, it is clear that using both high school GPA and the SAT aptitude test score offers more predictive validity than when only relying on the SAT scores. When using aptitude tests appropriately, therefore, counselors must take great care not to use a single test result as the sole predictor of future performance. Again, aptitude tests are but one assessment tool in a counselor's repertoire.

A third common concern about aptitude tests is related to cultural bias. Critics point to data that show between-group differences across race. For example, "most minority students score lower than most white students on most maximum-performance tests" (Lyman, 1998, p. 45). As a result of such between-group differences, critics voice a concern about aptitude tests (and other maximum-performance tests) being culturally biased. "Critics who hypothesize that tests are biased against minorities assert that the test scores underestimate the ability of minority members" (Gregory, 2007, p. 276). In his thorough review of empirical studies focused on test bias in the predictive validity of aptitude tests, however, Gregory found that "extensive reviews of the empirical studies provide overwhelming evidence disconfirming the bias hypothesis" (p. 276). In summarizing these findings, Gregory reported that, although there may indeed be between-group differences with regard to aptitude test scores, there are also between-group differences in college grades. In synthesizing a myriad of empirical studies, he found that the aptitude tests appear to predict future performance equally well for racial minorities and Whites and that there is actually some evidence to suggest that some aptitude tests overestimate the future performance of racial minorities. Gregory suggested that between-group differences in performance on aptitude tests do not appear to be due to test bias but instead appear more likely to reflect social, genetic, and/or environmental differences across groups. Sound use of aptitude tests with racial minorities requires confirmation that the examinees are appropriately represented in the norming sample, that the possible need to use racially specific regression lines is explored, and that interpretation of test scores includes discussion of other factors that may influence future performance (Gregory, 2007).

GUIDELINES FOR ETHICAL USE OF APTITUDE TESTS

ANY COUNSELOR INVOLVED in the selection, administration, scoring, or interpretation of aptitude tests should become familiar with professional standards related to the use of standardized tests. Several sets of standards have been developed, and counselors should become familiar with each of them. Upon review of these standards, counselors will find that these various sets of standards complement one another, with each of them having a slightly different focus. Table 48.5 identifies several pertinent sets of standards.

Key to the ethical and appropriate use of aptitude tests is the appropriate administration and interpretation of the test. As described in the various sets of standards identified in Table 48.5, appropriate administration of aptitude tests requires strict adherence to the standardized administration instructions specified in the test manual. Indeed, meaningful inferences during the interpretation process depend upon

TABLE 48.5   Standards Addressing the Appropriate Use of Standardized Tests

Standards	Publisher	Year
Code of Fair Testing Practices in Education	Joint Committee on Testing Practices (JCTP)	2002
Responsibilities of Users of Standardized Tests–Third Edition	Association for Assessment in Counseling (AAC)	2003
Standards for Educational and Psychological Testing	American Educational Research Association (AERA), American Psychological Association (APA), and National Council on Measurement in Education (NCME)	1999
Standards for Multicultural Assessment	Association for Assessment in Counseling (AAC)	2003
Standards for Qualifications of Test Users	American Counseling Association	2003

proper administration. In most cases, an aptitude test should be administered in precisely the same manner to each examinee. An exception to this uniformity of administration procedures may be made when using aptitude tests with clients who have disabilities.

APTITUDE TESTING FOR CLIENTS WITH DISABILITIES

THE STANDARD TESTING procedures outlined in a test manual are often inappropriate for use in administering an aptitude test to a person with a disability. If a person with a visual impairment were to take a paper-and-pencil scholastic aptitude test under standardized administration procedures, for instance, he or she would be unable to see or read the print. Instead of reflecting scholastic aptitude, a low score on the test administered in this manner would instead reflect the examinee's visual impairment. Most test publishers therefore allow for testing accommodations when administering an aptitude test to a person with a disability in order to ensure that the test measures, as much as possible, the construct focused upon by the test rather than being unduly influenced by the person's disability.

Some of the disabilities that may render a person eligible for accommodations include visual impairments, hearing impairments, physical disabilities, medical conditions, and learning disabilities (College Board, 2007). The type of accommodation allowed for any given test is determined by the test publisher. In general, accommodations may be related to the way in which a test is presented, how a person may respond to or answer test questions, the length of time and number of breaks allowed during testing, the use of adaptive technologies, and the nature of the testing environment. In order to receive accommodations, the examinee must usually provide professional documentation of the disability or qualifying condition, and the test publisher then determines what accommodations to allow.

Just as it is important to extend accommodations for clients with disabilities in order to ensure that the test measures, as much as possible, the construct focused upon by the test, it is also essential to then interpret the test scores in the context of the accommodations. For example, if a person with attention deficit/hyperactivity disorder (AD/HD) is provided with a secluded room and extra time when taking an aptitude test, this needs to be noted in the reporting and interpreting of test results. This might be noted in a statement such as, "When taking the ASVAB in a secluded room and being allowed double time, John Doe performed at the 80th percentile in arithmetic reasoning."

CONCLUSION

ALTHOUGH APTITUDE TESTS have sometimes been the subject of criticisms, the use of standardized tests to predict future
performance is likely to continue on a widespread basis (Lyman, 1998).
To ensure that these tests are used appropriately with all clients, including those with disabilities and those of minority culture, it is essential
that counselors familiarize themselves with and adhere to professional
standards related to testing. As described in this chapter, counselors
who adhere to these professional guidelines will be best able to use
aptitude tests to assist clients with planning for their educational and
career futures.

REFERENCES

Aiken, L. R., & Groth-Marnat, G. (2006). *Psychological testing and assessment*
(12th ed.). Boston: Allyn & Bacon.

American Educational Research Association, American Psychological Asso-
ciation, and National Council on Measurement in Education. (1999).
Standards for educational and psychological testing. Washington, DC:
American Educational Research Association.

Association for Assessment in Counseling. (2003a). *Responsibilities of users of
standardized tests–third edition (RUST–3)*. Alexandria, VA: Author.

Association for Assessment in Counseling. (2003b). *Standards for multicultural
assessment*. Alexandria, VA: Author.

College Board. (2007). *Disability guidelines*. Retrieved December 9, 2007, from
http://professionals.collegeboard.com/guidance/tests/disabilities

Drummond, R. J., & Jones, K. D. (2006). *Assessment procedures for counselors
and helping professionals* (6th ed.). Upper Saddle River, NJ: Pearson
Merrill/Prentice-Hall.

Erford, B. T. (Ed.). (2007). *Assessment for counselors*. Boston: Lahaska Press.

Erford, B. T., & McNinch, K. (2007). Assessment of other aptitudes. In B. T. Erford
(Ed.), *Assessment for counselors* (pp. 357–384). Boston: Lahaska Press.

Gregory, R. J. (2007). *Psychological testing: History, principles, and applications*
(5th ed.). Boston: Allyn & Bacon.

Hood, A. B., & Johnson, R. W. (2007). *Assessment in counseling: A guide to the use
of psychological assessment procedures* (4th ed.). Alexandria, VA: American
Counseling Association.

Joint Committee on Testing Practices. (2002). *Code of fair testing practices in
education*. Washington, DC: Author.

Lyman, H. B. (1998). *Test scores and what they mean* (6th ed.). Boston: Allyn &
Bacon.

Thorndike, R. M. (2005). *Measurement and evaluation in psychology and education*
(7th ed.). Upper Saddle River, NJ: Pearson Education.

49

Understanding How to Use the *DSM–IV–TR*

EVA MILLER

THE *DIAGNOSTIC AND Statistical Manual of Mental Disorders (DSM–I)* (American Psychiatric Association [APA], 1952) was originally designed to collect statistical information about mental illness in the United States, namely World War II servicemen and veterans. Since then, the manual has undergone numerous revisions, with the latest being the *Diagnostic and Statistical Manual of Mental Disorders (DSM–IV–TR*; APA, 2000). The *DSM–IV–TR* is currently the most widely used manual for diagnosing mental disorders in the United States and is referred to by psychiatrists and other physicians as well as psychologists, social workers, nurses, rehabilitation therapists, counselors, and other health and mental health professionals who work with diverse client populations in both inpatient and outpatient settings. The primary uses of the manual are to (1) provide information about the course and prevalence related to the various disorders, (2) provide a means for common communication regarding clients' problems/concerns, (3) provide third-party reimbursement for mental health services, and (4) facilitate researchers' investigation of underlying causes and mechanisms of particular diagnostic conditions. The *DSM–IV–TR* is also widely used as an educational tool.

CRITICISMS OF THE *DSM*

ALTHOUGH RECOGNIZED AS being a profound assessment taxonomy in the mental health profession, the *DSM–IV–TR* and its preceding editions have been criticized about the validity of various diagnoses (e.g., atypical depression), the criteria required for diagnoses (e.g., the number of continuous weeks of depression required for a diagnosis of major depression), and for being cumbersome and not tied closely enough to clinical decision making (Westin, Hein, Morrison, Patterson, & Campbell, 2002).

Other criticisms include failing to consider the effects of labeling a person's behavior as being pathological or abnormal, failing to take into consideration personal values on the part of the professional who is making the diagnosis, subscribing to the medical model that assumes underlying neurological and medical disorders without taking into account a person's wider social context, and inadequate consideration of the developmental history and multicultural implications that can affect accurate diagnosis (Eriksen & Kress, 2006). For example, the *DSM–III* (APA, 1980) included the diagnosis of *ego-dystonic homosexuality*, which we know today can lead to harassment that may be internalized and potentially lead to depression, anxiety, guilt, self-hatred as well as substance abuse, prostitution, and even suicide (Ivey & Ivey, 1998). In addition, because most mental health settings require a *DSM* diagnosis for third-party insurance reimbursement, overdiagnosis, underdiagnosis, and misdiagnosis may lead to serious moral, ethical, and legal repercussions. Since Medicaid does not provide reimbursement for counseling services for individuals diagnosed with mental retardation, some clinicians will include a reimbursable coexisting diagnosis such as attention-deficit/hyperactivity disorder (AD/HD) despite knowing the symptoms of AD/HD are often seen in persons with mental retardation and there may be no need for two separate diagnoses. It is also noteworthy that if two mental health disorders overlap in symptomology, typically, the most severe diagnosis is the only one reported.

WHY MAKE A PSYCHIATRIC DIAGNOSIS?

FAUMAN (2002) OFFERS a number of excellent tips on the importance of making diagnoses using the *DSM–IV–TR* (APA, 2000). First, he points out that the use of diagnostic codes is fundamental to communicating a large amount of information about an individual's mental health. In essence, a diagnosis is a shorthand notion for a syndrome or cluster of clinical signs and symptoms that commonly occur together.

A second important function of diagnosis is that accurately diagnosing a client requires looking at the entire sequale of the person's condition versus simply focusing on only one or two of the major symptoms the client is reporting. For example, a person presenting with psychotic symptoms might be viewed as a good candidate for an antipsychotic medication; however, psychotic symptoms are not only associated with mental illnesses such as schizophrenia, but may also be present in major depressive disorders, dementia, bipolar disorders, and psychotic disorders due to a general medical condition. At a superficial level, these illnesses may look alike, but each has a different etiology and prognosis and each may warrant different treatment. The treatment for schizophrenia and major depressive disorder may not only require different psychotropic medications, but counseling and psychotherapy must also be tailored to the unique needs of the individual. For example, it would most likely be appropriate to use a cognitive behavior approach to treat depression whereas a person experiencing schizophrenia would be likely to benefit from an approach such as assertiveness training and socialization skills.

DSM–IV–TR AXES

A MULTIAXIAL ASSESSMENT involves an evaluation of each of the five axes specified in the *DSM–IV–TR*. Each axis refers to a different domain of information that is designed to help clinicians and counselors predict outcomes and develop treatment plans (Fauman, 2002).

AXIS I: CLINICAL DISORDERS AND OTHER CONDITIONS THAT MAY BE A FOCUS OF CLINICAL ATTENTION

AXIS I IS for reporting all the disorders or conditions (e.g., major depressive disorder, schizophrenia, and adjustment disorders) in the Classification except for *mental retardation* and *personality disorders* (which are coded on Axis II). Also reported on Axis I are *other conditions that may be a focus of clinical attention,* including *medication-induced movement disorders* (e.g., *neuroleptic-induced Parkinsonism*), *relational problems* such as *parent-child relational problem* and *partner relational problem,* and *problems related to abuse or neglect* (e.g., *physical abuse of child*).

When an individual presents with more than one Axis I disorder, all of these disorders should be reported on Axis I, with the principal diagnosis or the reason for the visit being indicated first. If no Axis I disorder is present, this should be coded as *V71.09 No diagnosis.* If an Axis I diagnosis is deferred pending the need to gather additional information to make a firm diagnosis, this should be coded as *799.9 Diagnosis deferred.*

AXIS II: PERSONALITY DISORDERS AND MENTAL RETARDATION

AXIS II INCLUDES all *personality disorders* and *mental retardation. Borderline intellectual functioning* (i.e., IQ in the 71–84 range) is the only other condition coded on Axis II. If a person has more than one Axis II diagnosis, both should be recorded. If a person has both an Axis I and an Axis II disorder, the principal diagnosis or the reason for the visit should be reported on the corresponding axis. For example, if the principal diagnosis is for major depressive disorder, which is coded on Axis I, this would be indicated as follows: *major depressive disorder (principal diagnosis).* If no Axis II disorder is present, this should be coded as *V71.09 No diagnosis.* If an Axis II diagnosis is deferred pending the need to gather additional information to make a firm diagnosis, this should be coded as *799.9 Diagnosis deferred.*

AXIS III: GENERAL MEDICAL CONDITIONS

AXIS III IS designed for reporting current general medical conditions such as diabetes, HIV/AIDS, and cancer that could be potentially relevant to understanding and managing an individual's mental disorder(s). These various conditions coincide with the *International Classification of Diseases,* Ninth Revision, Clinical Modification ([*ICD–9–CM*], from APA, 2000), which is the official coding system of the *DSM–IV–TR.* Most *DSM–IV–TR* Axis I and Axis II disorders have a numerical *ICD–9–CM* code that appears preceding the name of the mental disorder and accompanies the criteria set for the disorder. For example, mild mental retardation is coded as 317. Axis III is designed to facilitate the reporting of conditions classified outside the "Mental Disorders" chapter of the ICD–9–CM. Specifically, there is a section in the *DSM–IV–TR* that provides codes for medical conditions and medication-induced disorders that are coded on Axis III.

AXIS IV: PSYCHOSOCIAL AND ENVIRONMENTAL PROBLEMS

AXIS IV IS used to report psychosocial and environmental issues that may affect diagnosis, treatment, and prognosis of mental disorders identified on Axes I and II (APA, 2000). If an individual has multiple psychosocial or environmental problems, the clinician should note as many as he or she judges to be relevant and, generally, only those that have been present during the year preceding the evaluation. An example where a clinician may choose to report a problem that has persisted for more than a year and is still contributing to the mental disorder or has become the focus of treatment is a rape experience leading to post-traumatic stress disorder. Examples of environmental and psychosocial problems reported on Axis IV are problems with primary support groups (e.g., death of a family member, divorce, and sibling discord); educational and occupational problems; housing and economic problems; and problems with access to health care services such as inadequate health care services and a lack of transportation to health care facilities.

AXIS V: GLOBAL ASSESSMENT OF FUNCTIONING

AVIS V IS used to report an individual's overall level of functioning. The information on Axis V is helpful for treatment planning as well as for predicting outcomes. The *DSM–IV–TR* includes a Global Assessment of Functioning Scale (GAF) (APA, 2000, p. 34) that can be used for reporting overall client functioning. It should be noted, however, that impairments in functioning "do not include impairment in functioning due to physical or environmental limitations" (APA, 2000, p. 32). For example, a person with a visual or hearing impairment would not be given a lower GAF score based solely on the disability.

The GAF scale is divided into 10 ranges of functioning from 1–100 with two components; (1) symptom severity, and (2) level of functioning. "The GAF rating is within a particular decile if either the symptom severity or the level of functioning falls within the range" (APA, 2000, p. 32). If there is discordance noted between symptom severity and level of functioning, the final GAF should reflect the worse of the two. In most instances, ratings on the GAF scale should reflect the current time period; however, some clinicians prefer to include GAF scores that reflect both the current score as well as other relevant information such as highest level of functioning in the past year or level of functioning at the time of discharge (e.g., discharge from a mental health facility). Reporting a GAF score can be a fairly subjective process and scores often vary among clinicians; however, the *DSM–IV–TR* (APA, 2000) provides a method for determining an individual's GAF rating on page 33.

DSM–IV–TR CLASSIFICATION

THE FOLLOWING IS a listing of the 17 classifications found in the *DSM–IV–TR* (APA, 2000):

- Disorders Usually First Diagnosed in Infancy, Childhood, or Adolescence
- Delirium, Dementia, and Amnestic and Other Cognitive Disorders
- Mental Disorders Due to a General Medical Condition Not Elsewhere Classified
- Substance-Related Disorders
- Schizophrenia and Other Psychotic Disorders
- Mood Disorders
- Anxiety Disorders
- Somatoform Disorders
- Factitious Disorders
- Dissociative Disorders
- Sexual and Gender Identity Disorders
- Eating Disorders
- Sleep Disorders
- Impulse-Control Disorders Not Elsewhere Classified
- Adjustment Disorders
- Personality Disorders
- Other Conditions That May Be a Focus of Clinical Attention

Each of the preceding classifications of disorders includes subcategories of the corresponding disorders. For example, "Mood Disorders" include major depressive disorders and bipolar disorders, and "Anxiety Disorders" include disorders such as posttraumatic stress disorder and obsessive-compulsive disorder. In addition, each classification includes (1) diagnostic criteria associated with the disorder (e.g., type and duration of symptoms); (2) specific cultural, age-related, and gender features associated with the disorder; (3) the typical course of the disorder such as how long it takes the disorder to develop and how long it takes before symptoms remit (if they ever do remit); and (4) differential diagnosis, which describes other disorders that often mimic a particular disorder (e.g., differentiating between depression and bipolar disorder) (*DSM–IV–TR*, APA, 2000).

CRITERIA FOR DIFFERENTIAL DIAGNOSIS

The *DSM–IV–TR* (APA, 2000) identifies three criteria that should be considered in every diagnosis. These three criteria are to ensure that:

1. The disorder is not due to the direct effects of a substance (e.g., drug abuse);

2. The disorder is not due to the direct effects of a general medical condition (e.g., hypothyroidism); and
3. The disorder causes clinically significant distress or impairment in social, occupational, or other important areas of functioning.

The first and second criteria may be easier to detect as a clinician can refer individuals for drug testing and/or medical examinations and tests. The third criteria is relatively subjective in that it is often difficult to ascertain whether problems are clinically significant or if they are more closely related to things such as so-called normal developmental phases; cultural differences; or situational circumstances such as family discord, sexism, financial or occupational difficulties, malingering, or certain defense mechanisms an individual has developed to cope with a difficult situation. Therefore, a thorough initial diagnostic assessment that includes a complete social, family, work, medical, developmental, psychiatric, and substance abuse history is paramount. A complete understanding of how to conduct a comprehensive mental status exam and behavioral observations is also key to accurate diagnosis. Taking the time to talk with individuals about how they perceive their problems and how they may have coped with similar situations is also critical in diagnostic formulation.

CASE SAMPLE

MARIA FLORES IS a 42-year-old Hispanic female who was diagnosed with Human Immunodeficiency Virus (HIV) nine years ago. Despite undergoing protease inhibitor and antimicrobial treatment, Maria's condition has progressively worsened over the years. Her appetite is poor, and she has lost a considerable amount of weight. She is also easily fatigued, forgetful, has poor concentration and has difficulty with problem solving, such as being unable to arrange to have her two children, ages 17 and 15, picked up from school while her car is being repaired. Maria's affect is generally apathetic, and she has withdrawn from all social circles, including weekly gatherings with her parents and siblings. She has also stopped seeing the majority of her friends and spends most of her waking time watching TV. Her children have taken over most of the household chores, and her mother and sisters frequently drop off food they have prepared for Maria and her family. Maria's husband works as a mechanic and is seldom home. He and Maria rarely speak as Maria blames him for infecting her with HIV. Maria is also embarrassed to talk with her family and priest about the problems she and her husband are experiencing because she feels ashamed of her situation and believes her concerns should be kept within the family. Her husband refuses to discuss the situation with her and provides her with minimal emotional support. Instead, he spends most of his spare time with his friends. He has never admitted that he too is infected with HIV, but his condition is not nearly as severe as Maria's.

Maria frequently blames her husband and children for stealing her possessions by sneaking into her bedroom when she is asleep (all of which is unfounded). She also believes her best friend who died in an automobile accident 12 years ago talks to her and tells her to kill her husband for what he has done to her. Additional symptoms Maria experiences are hand tremors, rapid, repetitive movements, and she frequently loses her balance and falls. Maria's family worries about leaving her alone during the day and has begun to wonder if she might be better off living with her mother or in a long-term care facility. Maria is adamantly opposed to either of these considerations and refuses to discuss them. Her mood has become increasingly dysphoric, and she frequently contemplates suicide. She has never attempted suicide but has been severely depressed for the past few years.

RECOMMENDATIONS

1. Maria should be referred for a psychotropic medication review to address her depressive symptoms.
2. Maria's counselor should obtain written consent from Maria to have access to her medical records to gain a better understanding of Maria's prognosis.
3. Maria would most likely benefit from individual counseling to address her depression and adjustment to having HIV. The counseling should include:

    a. A person-centered approach that includes empathic listening, a nonjudgmental, supportive attitude, and reflection of her thoughts and feelings pertaining to her disability;

TABLE 49.1 *DSM-IV-TR* Diagnoses

Axis I	294.10	Dementia due to HIV disease
	296.34	Major depressive disorder, recurrent, severe, with psychotic features
Axis II	V71.09	No diagnosis
Axis III	042	HIV infection (symptomatic)
Axis IV		Problems with primary support group (marital discord and alienated from family and friends)
Axis V	GAF=40	(current)

b. A cognitive behavior approach that uses techniques such as Socratic questioning (e.g., "What do you have to lose by trying?"), helping Maria develop alternative views of her problems and new ways of behaving, challenging Maria's automatic and dysfunctional ways of thinking, asking Maria to provide reasons for her intense self-critical behavior, and helping Maria prioritize her goals;

c. An existential approach that focuses on increased awareness of death as a basic human condition and helping Maria explore her feelings relating to death;

d. The feasibility of Maria's desire to remain at home and long-term placement planning as her condition worsens; and,

e. Discussion surrounding a living will and end-of-life issues.

4. Maria should also be referred for family therapy to address her issues with her husband, her role as a mother, and to address the issues she has with her parents, siblings, and friends. Family therapy should be scheduled *after* Maria has begun to accept the reality that she is not at fault for her current condition and how she may benefit from reaching out to others who love and care about her.

5. Maria may also benefit from attending a support group for women with HIV.

CONCLUSION

DESPITE CRITICISMS THAT have arisen over the years, the *DSM* has continued to be a useful manual for providing valuable information about the course and prevalence of mental disorders and has provided a means for common communication regarding individuals' mental health problems. The *DSM–IV–TR* has also served as a valuable educational tool and has facilitated many researchers' investigations of underlying causes and mechanisms of particular diagnostic conditions. The publication date of the *DSM–V* is still unknown; however, as with previous editions, there will be many revisions designed to continue to improve the utility of this manual, which is heavily utilized by health and mental health professionals across the United States.

REFERENCES PERTAINING TO THE *DSM*

Frances, A., & Ross, R. (2001). *DSM–IV–TR case studies: A clinical guide to differential diagnosis.* Washington, DC: American Psychiatric Publishing.

Barlow, D. H. (2007). *Clinical handbook of psychological disorders: A step-by-step treatment manual* (4th ed.). New York: Springer Publishing.

REFERENCES

American Psychiatric Association. (1952). *Diagnostic and statistical manual of mental disorders*. Washington, DC: Author.

American Psychiatric Association. (1980). *Diagnostic and statistical manual of mental disorders* (3rd ed.). Washington, DC: Author.

American Psychiatric Association. (2000). *Diagnostic and statistical manual of mental disorders* (4th ed., text revision). Washington, DC: Author.

Eriksen, K., & Kress, V. E. (2006). The *DSM* and the professional counseling identity: Bridging the gap. *Journal of Mental Health Counseling, 28*(3), 202–217.

Fauman, M. A. (2002). *Study guide to DSM–IV–TR*. Washington, DC: American Psychiatric Publishing.

Ivey, A. E., & Ivey, M. B. (1998). Reframing *DSM–IV*: Positive strategies from developmental counseling and therapy. *Journal of Counseling and Development, 76,* 334–350.

Westin, D., Hein, A. K., Morrison, K., Patterson, M., & Campbell, L. (2002). Simplifying diagnosis using a prototype-matching approach: Implications for the next edition of the *DSM*. In L. E. Beutler & M. L. Malik (Eds.), *Rethinking the DSM: A psychological perspective* (pp. 221–250). Washington, DC: American Psychological Association.

50

Understanding Mental and Physical Functional Capacity Evaluations

IRMO MARINI

ERHAPS ONE OF the most interesting skills one can learn in working with persons with disabilities is to assess what their mental and physical residual capabilities are in order to transfer these abilities into work skills. This chapter will explore and discuss samples of a mental and physical functional capacity evaluation, then illustrate how each of these types of assessments may be used in establishing an appropriate work setting for clients with disabilities.

Mental and physical functional capacity evaluations tend to be most often used in Social Security court hearings in an effort to determine whether an individual is capable of working at any job commensurate with his or her skills and abilities. The primary difference between both types of evaluations is that mental functional capacity evaluations (MFCE) assess an individual's cognitive and emotional capacity, whereas a physical functional capacity evaluation (PFCE) focuses exclusively on an individual's physical capabilities. Each assessment is explored separately.

MENTAL FUNCTIONAL CAPACITY EVALUATION

THE MFCE CAN only be completed by a clinical or school psychologist with appropriate training in measurement and interpretation of psychometric tests including personality, intelligence, achievement, and aptitudes among other areas of assessment. It comprises essentially four sections; the first deals with an individual's *ability to understand, remember, and carry out instructions.* The second part assesses an individual's ability to *maintain sustained concentration and persistence.* The third area deals with *social interactions,* while the last area focuses on *adaptation to work changes.* The psychologist is asked to rate the individual on a five-point scale: (1) none—referring to the individual having no limitations; (2) slight—having some mild limitations but generally able to function well; (3) moderate—having moderate limitations but still capable of functioning satisfactorily; (4) marked—seriously limited in functioning but ability to work is not precluded; and (5) extreme—major limitation with no useful function. Although there are a few format variations available, areas covered in the assessment generally include understanding and remembering, sustained concentration and persistence, social interaction, and adaptation (see Table 50.1 for a full assessment).

The extreme ends of an MFCE assessment are easy to analyze; however, the *moderate* and *marked* areas depend on how many and which activities are checked or deemed problematic functionally. For example, if an individual had only one moderately checked limitation such as "ability to carry out detailed instructions," there would still prove to be many jobs available to perform in the unskilled labor market. If, however, the individual is assessed with moderate limitations in "understanding and remembering short, simple instructions" in addition to moderate limitations in "keeping up a normal work pace and responding appropriately to work pressures," this arguably may be enough to render an individual unemployable.

The MFCE is typically utilized in Social Security disability determination proceedings, but may also be used in guardianship hearings as well. Generally, persons assessed with this evaluation are those with psychiatric disabilities such as major depression, schizophrenia, or a personality disorder. Persons with intellectual disabilities such as mental retardation or head injury can also be evaluated with this assessment in the areas of work or living independently with or without supervision.

Persons with psychiatric disabilities, if assessed as having the capacity to work, are often recommended for jobs that do not involve much contact with the public, performing work involving simple and routine tasks that are deemed nonstressful (Fischler & Booth, 1999). Depending

TABLE 50.1 Mental Functional Capacity Evaluation

Name of Individual　　　　　　　*Social Security Number*

Please assist us in determining this individual's ability to do work-related activities on a sustained basis. "Sustained basis" means the ability to perform work-related activities 8 hours a day for 5 days a week, or an equivalent work schedule. Please give us your professional opinion of what the individual can still do despite his/her impairment(s). The opinion should be based on your findings with respect to medical history, clinical and laboratory findings, diagnosis, prescribed treatment and response, and prognosis.

For each activity shown below:

(1) Respond to the questions about the individual's ability to perform the activity. When doing so, use the following definitions for the rating terms:

- None — Absent or minimal limitations. If limitations are present, they are transient and/or expectable reactions to psychological stresses.
- Slight — There is some mild limitation in this area, but the individual can generally function well.
- Moderate — There is moderate limitation in this area, but the individual is still able to function satisfactorily.
- Marked — There is serious limitation in this area. The ability to function is severely limited but not precluded.
- Extreme — There is major limitation in this area. There is no useful ability to function in this area.

(2) Identify the factors (e.g., the particular medical signs, laboratory findings, or other factors described above) that support your assessment

	Slightly Limited	Moderately Limited	Markedly Limited	No Limitation	No Evidence
A. UNDERSTANDING AND MEMORY					
1. The ability to remember locations & worklike procedures	1.___	2.___	3.___	4.___	5.___
2. The ability to understand & remember very short & simple instructions	1.___	2.___	3.___	4.___	5.___
3. The ability to understand & remember detailed instructions	1.___	2.___	3.___	4.___	5.___

(continued)

TABLE 50.1 *(Continued)*

	Slightly Limited	Moderately Limited	Markedly Limited	No Limitation	No Evidence
B. SUSTAINED CONCENTRATION AND PERSISTENCE					
4. The ability to carry out very short & simple instructions	1.___	2.___	3.___	4.___	5.___
5. The ability to carry out detailed instructions	1.___	2.___	3.___	4.___	5.___
6. The ability to maintain attention & concentration for extended periods	1.___	2.___	3.___	4.___	5.___
7. The ability to perform activities within a schedule, maintain regular attendance, & be punctual within customary tolerances	1.___	2.___	3.___	4.___	5.___
8. The ability to sustain an ordinary routine without special supervision	1.___	2.___	3.___	4.___	5.___
9. The ability to work in coordination with or proximity to others without being distracted by them	1.___	2.___	3.___	4.___	5.___
10. The ability to make simple work-related decisions	1.___	2.___	3.___	4.___	5.___
11. The ability to complete a normal workday & workweek without interruptions from psychologically based symptoms and perform at a consistent pace without an unreasonable number & length of rest periods	1.___	2.___	3.___	4.___	5.___

C. SOCIAL INTERACTION

12. The ability to interact appropriately with the general public.
1. ___ 2. ___ 3. ___ 4. ___ 5. ___

13. The ability to ask simple questions or request assistance
1. ___ 2. ___ 3. ___ 4. ___ 5. ___

14. The ability to accept instructions and respond appropriately to criticism from supervisors
1. ___ 2. ___ 3. ___ 4. ___ 5. ___

15. The ability to get along with coworkers or peers without distracting them or exhibiting behavioral extremes
1. ___ 2. ___ 3. ___ 4. ___ 5. ___

16. The ability to maintain socially appropriate behavior and to adhere to basic standards of neatness and cleanliness.
1. ___ 2. ___ 3. ___ 4. ___ 5. ___

D. ADAPTATION

17. The ability to respond appropriately to changes in the work setting
1. ___ 2. ___ 3. ___ 4. ___ 5. ___

18. The ability to be aware of normal hazards & take appropriate precautions
1. ___ 2. ___ 3. ___ 4. ___ 5. ___

19. The ability to travel in unfamiliar places or use public transportation
1. ___ 2. ___ 3. ___ 4. ___ 5. ___

20. The ability to set realistic goals or make plans independently of others
1. ___ 2. ___ 3. ___ 4. ___ 5. ___

on level of education and past work experience, persons with psychiatric and intellectual disabilities are often recommended for work that is generally unskilled or semiskilled. Research has consistently shown that for persons with psychiatric disabilities, difficulties most often occur due to emotional problems not generally deriving from their job, but rather in the home setting (Fischler & Booth, 1999). In addition, persons with psychiatric disabilities longitudinally typically experience periodic episodes of decompensation, hospitalization, stabilization, and potential return to work if their disability is well managed, or chronic unemployment with low education if the disability is not well controlled.

Overall, the MFCE if used by skilled professionals can provide adequate work transition information regarding not only what an individual's intellectual and emotional capacity may be, but also indirectly provide ideas for the types of jobs for which this population may best be suited. The psychologist in consultation with the rehabilitation counselor, and client when feasible, should be able to agree on some viable options for employment.

PHYSICAL FUNCTIONAL CAPACITY EVALUATION

T HE PFCE IS totally different from the MFCE in that it focuses primarily on physical capacities only. The PFCE has several format variations; however, all assess essentially the same content criteria, and all are based on the Worker Trait Profile (WTP) found in the *Dictionary of Occupational Titles* (1991), a U.S. Department of Labor publication. The WTP lists seven criteria that essentially define in detail how jobs are performed. The seven criteria include the following:

1. *Strength*. Strength is defined as the amount of lifting an individual must be able to perform on the job. This includes *sedentary* (primarily seated jobs lifting a maximum of 10 pounds), *light* (lifting a maximum of 20 pounds occasionally, lift/carry 10 pounds frequently), *medium* (lifting a maximum of 50 pounds occasionally, lift/carry 10–25 pounds frequently), *heavy* (lifting a maximum of 100 pounds occasionally, lift/carry up to 50 pounds frequently), *very heavy* (lifting more than 100 pounds occasionally, and lift/carry 50–75 pounds frequently). Although not directly addressed, strength also considers to what degree a job may involve sitting, standing, and walking in an 8-hour workday.
2. *Physical demands*. Strength, defined above, is classified under physical demands but dealt with separately here. These include

525

*Understanding
Mental and
Physical Functiona
Capacity
Evaluations*

exertional and nonexertional commands, noting whether these tasks are performed *occasionally* (up to one-third of an 8-hour workday), *frequently* (2½ hours to 6 hours in an 8-hour work day), *constantly* (6 or more hours in an 8-hour workday), or *none* (meaning the task is not generally performed on the job). The categories include climbing, balancing, stooping, kneeling, crouching, crawling, reaching, handling, fingering, feeling, talking, hearing, taste/smell, near acuity, far acuity, depth perception, accommodation (eyes), color vision, and field of vision.

3. *Environmental conditions.* This section involves working under 14 different environmental conditions and once again rated as working under these conditions occasionally, frequently, constantly, or not at all. Environmental factors include exposure to weather, extreme cold, extreme heat, wet/humidity, noise intensity, vibration, atmospheric conditions (fumes, noxious odors), proximity to moving mechanical parts, exposure to electric shock, working in high exposed places, exposure to radiant energy, working with explosives, exposure to toxic chemicals, and other hazards.

4. *Specific vocational preparation* (SVP). This involves training obtained in a school, work setting, military, or other educational institution. By skill level, jobs are either classified as unskilled, semiskilled, or skilled work. A scale of vocational preparation ranges from 1–9, with one being unskilled work involving short demonstration only such as cleaning, a rating of four being indicative of semiskilled work such as a receptionist, and a rating of nine indicating skilled work such as a medical doctor.

5. *General educational development* (GED). Unlike SVP, general educational development refers to formalized academic education and is classified in three areas: reasoning, math, and language. Each of these three areas is graded in level of difficulty from 1–6, with the low score of one representing the simplest of skills required for the job, and six representing the highest level of educational attainment needed to perform the job.

6. *Aptitudes.* There are nine aptitudes rated on a scale from 1–5. A score of one pertains to the job requiring a high-level aptitude that the top 10% of the population can perform; a score of three is indicative of aptitude held by the middle third of the population; and a score of five recognizes that the aptitude requires the performance ability of the lowest 10% of the population. The eleven aptitudes include general intelligence; verbal ability; numerical ability; spatial ability; form perception; clerical perception; motor coordination; finger dexterity; manual dexterity; eyes/hand/foot coordination, and color discrimination. For example,

in considering the job of a neurosurgeon involving finger dexterity, this job would be classified as requiring finger dexterity of one, whereas the job of janitor would require a finger dexterity aptitude of four because fine-finger dexterity is not needed to perform the job.

7. *Temperaments.* This category relates to personal traits required by an individual to perform particular jobs, but without a rating scale, it only acknowledges whether certain traits are required for the job. These situations include working alone, directing others, expressing feelings, influencing others, making judgments, dealing with people, performing repetitive work, performing under stress, performing under precise work tolerances, working under specific instructions, and performing a variety of duties.

Although the full WTP includes these seven areas, an actual PFCE generally focuses on strength requirements, physical demands, and specific vocational preparation since its utility in the vast majority of cases is to assess persons with musculoskeletal injuries often involving low-back disc herniation with secondary complaints of chronic pain. This type of assessment is generally completed by a physical therapist or a physician in relation to what an individual's physical limitations may be, resulting in what types of work activities (if any) an individual can safely perform without fear of reinjury. A rudimentary example would be a construction worker who frequently performs heavy lifting but sustains an L4–L5 herniated disc and after therapy and/or surgery is limited in performing no more than light lifting/carrying. In this case, where the worker was once able to lift/carry up to 100 pounds, postinjury his available labor market should only consist of seeking out jobs that are either sedentary or light (lift/carry up to 20 pounds maximum) in nature.

The PFCE can be an effective tool for the rehabilitation counselor in establishing job options for a client postinjury that are, according to the evaluating medical professional, safe to engage in without fears of reinjury. Again, involving the client where feasible in the process becomes important in providing career counseling; however, generally, this is not the case in forensic matters. A sample PFCE can be found in Table 50.2.

REFERENCES

Dictionary of occupational titles (4th ed.). (1991). Indianapolis, IN: JIST.

Fischler, G., & Booth, N. (1999). *Vocational impact of psychiatric disorders: A guide for rehabilitation professionals.* Gaithersburg, MD: Aspen.

TABLE 50.2 Physical Functional Capacity Evaluation

PATIENT: **FACILITY:**

U.S. Department of Labor Definitions:

SEDENTARY WORK:	lift 10 # maximum and occasionally carry small objects
LIGHT WORK:	lift 20 # maximum; frequently lift/carry up to 10 #
MEDIUM WORK:	lift 50 # maximum; frequently lift/carry up to 25 #
HEAVY WORK:	lift 100 # maximum; frequently lift/carry up to 50 #

_____ It is my opinion that patient can now return to work without restrictions.

_____ Based on patient's demonstrated performance in our evaluation, the following limitations exist relevant to work activity:

1. **LIFT:**

	No Restriction	Occasionally (1%–33%)	Frequently (34%–66%)	Constantly (67%–100%)
a. up to 10 #	_____	_____	_____	_____
b. 11–20	_____	_____	_____	_____
c. 21–30	_____	_____	_____	_____
d. 31–50	_____	_____	_____	_____
e. 51–100	_____	_____	_____	_____

2. **CARRY:**

	No Restriction	Occasionally (1%–33%)	Frequently (34%–66%)	Constantly (67%–100%)
a. up to 10 #	_____	_____	_____	_____
b. 11–20	_____	_____	_____	_____
c. 21–30	_____	_____	_____	_____
d. 31–50	_____	_____	_____	_____
e. 51–100	_____	_____	_____	_____

3. **CAN THE PERSON PERFORM THE FOLLOWING TASKS:**

	No Restriction	Occasionally (1%–33%)	Frequently (34%–66%)	Constantly (67%–100%)
Pull–Seated	_____	_____	_____	_____
Pull–Standing	_____	_____	_____	_____
Bend	_____	_____	_____	_____
Squat	_____	_____	_____	_____
Crawl	_____	_____	_____	_____
Climb	_____	_____	_____	_____

4. **ASSUMING AN 8-HOUR WORKDAY WITH TWO FIFTEEN- (15) MINUTE BREAKS AND HALF-HOUR MEAL BREAK, I WOULD EXPECT THIS PERSON TO BE ABLE TO:**
   - Sit for _____ hours at a time, up to _____ hours over an 8–hour workday
   - Stand for _____ hours at a time, up to _____ hours over an 8–hour workday
   - Alternately stand/sit for_____ hours over an 8–hour workday
   - Walking for _____hours over an 8 –hour workday

5. **CAN THE PERSON USE HANDS FOR REPETITIVE ACTIONS SUCH AS:**

	Simple Grasping	Firm Grasp	Fine Manipulating
Right	Yes___No___	Yes___No___	Yes___No___
Left	Yes___No___	Yes___No___	Yes___No___

Estimated grip strength: Right_____ Left_____

(Continued)

TABLE 50.2 *(Continued)*

6. CAN THE PERSON USE FEET FOR REPETITIVE MOVEMENTS AS IN OPERATING FOOT CONTROLS?

Right	Left	Both
Yes____ No____	Yes____ No____	Yes____ No____

7. ANY RESTRICTIONS OF ACTIVITIES INVOLVED?

	None	Mild	Moderate	Total
Unprotected heights	____	____	____	____
Being around moving machinery	____	____	____	____
Exposed to marked changes in temperature and humidity	____	____	____	____
Drive automotive equipment	____	____	____	____
Exposure to dust, fumes, gas	____	____	____	____

8. CAN THE PERSON NOW RETURN TO PREVIOUS JOB?

9. COMMENTS: _____

_____

_____

_____

SIGNATURE:_____ **DATE:** _____

_____

51

The International Classification of Functioning, Disability, and Health (ICF): Applications for Professional Counseling

DAVID B. PETERSON

T HE INTERNATIONAL CLASSIFICATION of Functioning, Disability, and Health (ICF; WHO, 2001) is a classification system recently published by the World Health Organization (WHO). The ICF classifies "human functioning and disability" (p. 21), providing a new way for professional counselors to talk about health and human functioning. The ICF complements the use of diagnostic information with universal classifications of function, using a culturally sensitive, integrative, and interactive model of health and functioning that takes into account social and environmental aspects of health and disability (Üstün, Chaterji, Bickenbach, Kastanjsek, & Schneider, 2003).

Initially drafted as the *International Classification of Impairments, Disabilities, and Handicaps (ICIDH)* by the WHO (1980), the *ICF* was intended to complement its sister classification system, the *International Statistical Classification of Diseases and Related Health Problems (ICD;* WHO, 1992), currently in its tenth revision. The *ICD* was first formalized in 1893 as the Bertillon Classification or the International List of Causes of Death. The *ICD* provides an etiological classification of health conditions (e.g., diseases, disorders, injuries) related to mortality (death) and morbidity (illness), while the *ICF* provides a functional complement to the diagnosis-based *ICD*. Used together, they provide a comprehensive classification of human health and functioning.

WHY IS THE *ICF* IMPORTANT TO PROFESSIONAL COUNSELING?

THE *ICF* WAS endorsed for international use by the 54th World Health Assembly in 2001, and was subsequently accepted by 191 countries as the international standard to classify health and health-related states (Bruyère & Peterson, 2005). Those professionals working in health-related professions from nations represented in the World Health Assembly, including professional counselors, have been charged by WHO to become familiar with the *ICF*, use it where appropriate, and to become a part of its ongoing development.

DATA ON FUNCTIONING ENHANCES DIAGNOSTIC INFORMATION

DIAGNOSTIC INFORMATION ALONE, without functional data, may not adequately reflect an individual's health condition. Disease or impairment may manifest differently across individuals; similar functioning does not imply similar health conditions. Diagnoses alone do not sufficiently predict length of hospitalization (McCrone & Phelan, 1994) or treatment outcomes (Rabinowitz, Modai, & Inbar-Saban, 1994), levels of necessary care (Burns, 1991), types of service needs (National Advisory Mental Health Council, 1993), work performance (Gatchel, Polatin, Mayer, & Garcy, 1994), receipt of disability benefits (Bassett, Chase, Folstein, & Regier, 1998; Massel, Liberman, Mintz, & Jacobs, 1990; Segal & Choi, 1991), or integration into society (Ormel, Oldehinkel, Brilman, & vanden Brink, 1993).

531

*The International
Classification
of Functioning,
Disability, and
Health (ICF)*

DISABILITY IS UBIQUITOUS AND INCREASING

THE USE OF the *ICF* is important for a number of reasons, not the least of which is the prevalence of people with disabilities throughout the world. People with disabilities constitute one of the largest minority groups in the United States. Approximately 49.7 million people in the United States live with some type of chronic health condition or disability (U.S. Census Bureau, 2003). Of this number, 12.4 million (almost 25%) live with a physical, mental, or emotional condition causing difficulty in learning, remembering, or concentrating, and 21.3 million of those aged 16 to 64 live with a condition that affects the ability to work. Persons between the ages of 16 and 64 are less likely to be employed if disabled, and 8.7 million people with disabilities experience low socio-economic status (U.S. Census Bureau, 2003).

Within the next 15 years, it is estimated that chronic, disabling conditions and mental disorders will account for 78% of the global disease burden in developing countries (WHO, 2002, p. 13). Disability is quite common throughout the world, and related functional limitations and social implications are often important points of clinical focus and intervention for mental health professionals, including professional counselors.

MANAGED CARE AND MEDICAL INFORMATION MANAGEMENT

THE MANAGED CARE industry has caused health professionals to be more outcome-focused in their reports to third-party payers, rather than reporting only traditional diagnostic information (Tarvydas, Peterson, & Michaelson, 2005). The *ICF* provides a system to document functional outcomes that complement the diagnostic information in other health classification efforts (Peterson & Elliot, in press). Further, the *ICF* can also assist in managing the ever-increasing amount of medical information in health care today. Chute (2005) suggested that, while measures and classifications of functioning are the overall metric of organic well-being, the evolving knowledge base of medical information has outgrown our ability to consume it effectively. He suggested that systems like the *ICF* can help us to develop shared semantics, vocabularies, and terminologies, in a way that helps us to use medical knowledge effectively in treating people in health care settings.

UTILITY OF THE *ICF*

THE *ICF* CAN help stimulate significant developments in theory, research, policy, and practice applications (Bruyère & Peterson, 2005), the results of which can be used to help identify, mitigate, or remove societal hindrances to the full participation of people with disabilities in mainstream society. The *ICF* can be used to identify those who are disadvantaged by their experience of disability, compare their life experiences with those who are not disabled, and identify disparities in life experiences so that inequalities can be observed, measured, and ultimately remedied (Leonardi, Bickenbach, Üstün, Kostanjsek, & Chatterji, 2006).

OVERVIEW OF THE *ICF*

Several literature reviews have discussed and critiqued the *ICF* (see volume 25 of *Disability and Rehabilitation*, 2003; volume 50 of *Rehabilitation Psychology*, 2005; and volume 19 of *Rehabilitation Education*, 2005). While the *ICF* will be described briefly here, it is critical to note that such a brief overview is not an adequate substitute for reviewing the *ICF* in its entirety, studying the related literature, and attending training provided by those who are expert in its use (Peterson, 2005; Reed et al., 2005).

Models of Disability: *ICF's* Conceptual Framework

The medical model of disability guided early efforts to describe causes of mortality and morbidity, and has been relatively effective for detection and treatment of acute health problems (Peterson & Elliot, in press). The Medical Model emphasizes the diagnosis and treatment of disease, disorder, or injury; health problems are diagnosed and specialized services are prescribed to resolve the so-called problem (Kaplan, 2002).

In contrast, the Social Model of disability considers the role of environmental facilitators and barriers in health and functioning (Hurst, 2003; Smart, 2005). Within this paradigm, disability is not just a personal attribute, but a complex social construct reflecting the interaction between the individual and environment. Favored by advocates for the civil rights of persons with disability, this model suggests that any problem related to disability is not just due to the person with the disability, but rather is also influenced by societal attitudes and barriers in the environment (Olkin, 1999; Olkin & Pledger, 2003; Pledger, 2003; Ueda & Okawa, 2003).

More recent models of disability acknowledge the central role of social factors in understanding the causes and consequences of disability, supporting a more integrative, biopsychosocial model of disability, integrating useful aspects of both the medical and social models

533

*The International
Classification
of Functioning,
Disability, and
Health (ICF)*

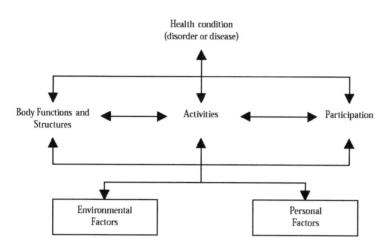

FIGURE 51.1   Interactions between the components of *ICF*.
From *The International Classification of Functioning, Disability, and Health* (p. 18),
by the World Health Organization, 2001, Geneva, Switzerland: Author. Copyright 2001 by
the World Health Organization. Reprinted with permission.

(Simeonsson, et al., 2003; Ueda & Okawa, 2003). The biospsychosocial
model of disability considers the interaction between disease/impair-
ment, disability, psychosocial stressors, and personal and environmental factors that account for various states of health and functioning.

The *ICF* is based on an integration of the medical and social models
of disability and addresses biological, individual, and societal perspectives on health, consistent with the biopsychosocial approach. The *ICF*
conceptual framework is depicted in Figure 51.1. The *ICF*'s interactive
conceptual framework illustrates how facilitators and barriers in the
environment are key factors in understanding disability and how advocacy occurs through social change (Hurst, 2003). The *ICF* permits separate
ratings along dimensions of body structure, function, and impairment
at the organ level, activity (versus activity limitation) and participation
(versus participation restriction) at the person level, and environmental
facilitators or barriers at the societal level.

ICF TERMINOLOGY

UNIVERSE OF WELL-BEING AND FUNCTIONING

THE *ICF* FOCUSES on health and well-being by referring to components of health that are typically a focus of health care professionals
(e.g., seeing, hearing, speaking, remembering, learning, walking), and to
components (health-related components of well-being) that are not typically a focus of health care systems (e.g., labor, education, employment,

social interactions, and transportation). Thus, the *ICF* was not designed to classify disability exclusively; it also classifies health and health-related states that make up a universe of well-being. Functioning then, according to the *ICF*, includes body functions, activities (and related limitations), and participation in society (and related restrictions).

IMPAIRMENT

THE *ICF* DEFINITIONS have a noticeably positive, health-oriented focus. *Impairments* are no longer defined as "problems," but as "a loss or abnormality in body structure or physiological function (including mental functions)." Impairments do not necessarily imply the presence of a disorder or disease but "represent a deviation from certain generally accepted population standards" of functioning, determined by "those qualified to judge physical and mental functioning according to these standards" (WHO, 2001, p. 12). The etiology of a particular dysfunction is not the focus of the *ICF*, but rather is the focus of its sister classification, the *ICD–10* (WHO, 1992).

DISABILITY

THE *ICF* CONCEPTUALIZES *disability* as an overarching term that refers to any impairments, activity limitations, or participation restrictions, or "the outcome or result of a complex relationship between an individual's health condition and personal factors, and of the external factors that represent the circumstances in which the individual lives" (WHO, 2001, p. 17). Within the *ICF*, disability is operationalized through "activity limitations" (p. 213). The antiquated term *handicap* is replaced by "participation restriction." Stated another way, "impairments are interactions affecting the body; activity limitations are interactions affecting [an] individual's actions or behavior; participation restrictions are interactions affecting [a] person's experience of life" (Leonardi et al., 2006, p. 1220; brackets are the author's).

THE *ICF* STRUCTURE

THE *ICF* IS made up of two parts, each with two components. The first part of the *ICF* describes the individual via *Functioning and Disability*; the second part addresses *Contextual Factors*. All components are further divided into chapters that contain categories of function within a given domain of health and health-related states. The units of classification are qualified with numeric codes that specify the magnitude or extent of disability or function in a given category or, within the case of environment, the extent to which a factor in the environment is a facilitator or a barrier.

535

*The International
Classification
of Functioning,
Disability, and
Health (ICF)*

The full version of the *ICF* provides four levels of classificatory precision, while the short version provides two levels of classification. In addition to an alphabetical index that organizes the hardcopy version of the *ICF*, there is an electronic version of the *ICF* that is searchable through the *ICF* browser (http://www.who.int/classifications/ICF/en/) or CD–ROM.

THE INDIVIDUAL

WITHIN THE FIRST part of the *ICF, Functioning and Disability,* there are two components. The *Body* component consists of two parallel classifications, *Body Functions* and *Body Structures.* The second component, *Activities and Participation,* covers domains of functioning from both an individual and societal perspective. The two components of functioning within the first part of the *ICF* can be expressed either as nonproblematic functioning or as disabilities (i.e., impairment, activity limitation, or participation restriction), and are operationalized through four separate but related constructs. *Body Functions and Structures* are interpreted through *changes in physiological systems* or *anatomical structures,* and *Activities and Participation* are interpreted through *capacity* and *performance.*

THE CONTEXT

THE SECOND PART of the ICF classification describes *Contextual Factors* through two components, *Environmental Factors* and *Personal Factors. Environmental Factors* are factors in the physical, social, or attitudinal world ranging from the immediate to more general environment. Environmental factors are qualified as either facilitating or hindering functioning. The second component of *Contextual Factors* is *Personal Factors,* which comprises personal attributes such as race, age, fitness, religion, lifestyle, habits, upbringing, coping styles, social background, education, profession, past and current experience, overall behavior pattern and character style, and individual psychological assets.

APPLYING THE *ICF*

BODY FUNCTIONS, STRUCTURES, ACTIVITIES AND PARTICIPATION

THE *BODY FUNCTIONS* component contains eight chapters that address "physiological functions of body systems (including psychological functions)" (WHO, 2001, p. 12). The *Body Structures* component contains eight chapters that parallel the *Body Functions* component and deal with "anatomical parts of the body such as organs, limbs, and their components" (p. 12). The *Activities and Participation* component contains nine chapters, with *Activities* addressing "the execution of a task or action by an individual" and *Participation* addressing "involvement in a life situation" (p. 14). In all instances, the *Body Functions and Structures* component is intended to be used with the *Activities and Participation* component. *Activity* is defined as the execution of a task or action by an individual such as sitting, copying, calculating, or driving. *Participation* is involvement in a life situation.

THE CONTEXT

THE *ENVIRONMENTAL FACTORS* component contains five chapters focusing on "the physical, social, and attitudinal environment in which people live and conduct their lives" (p. 171), organized from the immediate to more general environment. The Personal Factors component is not currently classified, but encourages consideration of personal circumstances such as socioeconomic status, race, gender, religion, or culture that may restrict full participation in society for reasons not related to health.

For each chapter, alphanumeric codes are used to indicate chapters (e.g., *b* for Body Functions, *s* for Body Structures, *d* for Activities and Participation, and *e* for Environmental Factors) and specific categories within each chapter. For example, the classification associated with the psychological function of emotion is found in the first chapter of *Body Functions* (its code begins with *b*) under the *Specific mental function* section, called *Emotional functions,* or alphanumeric code b152.

QUALIFIERS

THE *ICF* CODES have qualifiers to indicate a magnitude or level of health for a given code. For example, the *Body Function* component qualifies impairment with a Likert-type scale (ranging from "mild" to "complete" impairment) (WHO, 2001, p. 47). The domains of the *Activities and Participation* component are operationalized through the use of the qualifiers *Capacity* and *Performance*. *Capacity* "describes an individual's ability to execute a task or an action," or more specifically, "the highest probable level of functioning that a person may reach in a given domain at a given moment" (p. 15). One must apply the *Capacity* qualifier in the context of a "uniform" or "standard" environment; a heuristic for *Capacity* could be *what a person can do*. The *Performance* qualifier describes "what a person does in his or her

TABLE 51.1   Overview of the *ICF*

Two parts: (A dynamic interaction)	Part 1: Functioning and Disability		Part 2: Contextual Factors	
Each part has two components:	**Body Functions and Structures**	**Activities and Participation**	**Environmental Factors**	**Personal Factors**
Domains (Contain the categories or units of classification of the *ICF*)	1. Body Functions (including Psychological Functioning) 2. Body Structures	Life areas (tasks, actions)	External influences on functioning and disability	Internal influences on functioning and disability
Constructs (Defined through use of qualifiers that modify the extent or magnitude of function or disability)	Change in body function (physiological) Change in body structure (anatomical)	Capacity: Executing tasks in a standard environment ("can do") Performance: Executing tasks in the current environment ("does do")	Facilitating or hindering impact of features of the physical, social, and attitudinal world	Impact of attributes of the person
Positive aspect	Functioning Functional and structural integrity Activities Participation		Facilitators	*Not classified in the ICF*
Negative aspect	Disability Impairment Activity limitation Participation restriction		Barriers/ hindrances	

Note. Units of classification are situations, not people. From *The International Classification of Functioning, Disability, and Health* (p. 18), by the World Health Organization, 2001, Geneva, Switzerland: Author. Copyright 2001 by the World Health Organization. Adapted with permission.

current environment" (p. 15); a heuristic for *Performance* could be *what a person does do*. The *Performance* and *Capacity* qualifiers are rated on the same 0 to 4 scale as the first qualifier of *Body Functions and Structures,* substituting the term *difficulty* for *impairment.* An integrative overview of the *ICF* is illustrated in Table 51.1.

IMPLICATIONS FOR PROFESSIONAL COUNSELING

THE *ICF* HAS numerous implications for professional counseling. Disability should no longer be equated with diagnoses alone. Disability is not restricted to the services of any single health profession or medical specialty. Any health condition can have disabling features that can be understood (and rated) along the components in the *ICF* framework. The *ICF* provides an organizing scheme for understanding factors that can impose limitations and complicate or facilitate function and adjustment (Peterson & Elliot, in press).

Due to the international prevalence of disabilities, counselor education programs should systematically address disability issues within their didactic and clinical training. The *ICF*'s conceptual framework can inform curriculum development efforts. The *ICF* can also provide a framework to help counselors in training conceptualize functioning, disability, and health.

PROFESSIONALS' USE OF THE *ICF*

A VARIETY OF health professionals have applied the *ICF* to their respective paradigms of practice, including rehabilitation counseling (Bruyère, 2005; Peterson & Mpofu, in press), rehabilitation psychology (DiCowden, 2005; Peterson, 2005), nursing (Coenen, 2005), occupational therapy (Velozo, 2005), physical therapy (Mayo & McGill, 2005), and speech language pathology (Threats & Worrall, 2004). The emerging literature on the *ICF* suggests that the *ICF* will increasingly receive more attention from health professionals. The *ICF* has influenced many health care entities internationally, and is now in use in several countries including the United States, Australia, Canada, and the Netherlands (Bickenbach, 2003; Holloway, 2004; Madden, Choi, & Sykes, 2003). Work on the World Health Survey, built upon the *ICF* conceptual framework, has been implemented in 74 countries (Üstün et al., 2003).

Professional counselors can contribute to the ongoing development of the *ICF* by becoming familiar with the *ICF* itself, reviewing the related literature cited here, and attending training on its ethical use. One unique way in which counselors may contribute to the *ICF*'s ongoing development is to establish and refine concepts related to gender, race, age, fitness, religion, lifestyle, habits, coping styles, and individual psychological assets that may eventually be subsumed in the Personal Factors component, which is not yet classified.

CLINICAL IMPLEMENTATION

TO FACILITATE CLINICAL implementation of the *ICF* in the United States, the American Psychological Association and WHO are developing

The Procedural Manual and Guide for the Standardized Application of the ICF: A Manual for Health Professionals (Reed et al., 2005). Once the *Procedural Manual* is published, the guide can be used for training to promote consistent coding. Studies will be needed to evaluate the clarity and utility of the manual to clinical practice, and to validate the application of the *ICF* given the new implementation guidelines.

ETHICAL USE OF THE *ICF*

THE *ICF* IS designed as a system that requires the active participation of a consumer of health care services in a collaborative and informational process, and is not something that is done *to* a consumer (see Peterson & Threats, 2005). Eleven ethical provisions were established in the sixth Annex of the *ICF* (WHO, 2001, pp. 244–245) to reduce the risk of disrespectful or harmful use of the *ICF*. The 11 ethical provisions address three critical areas: (1) respect and confidentiality, (2) clinical use of the *ICF*, and (3) social use of *ICF* information.

CONCLUSION

THE USE OF the *ICF* in service delivery will simultaneously impact both academic and research discourse on disability. Coordinators of the WHO revision efforts for the *ICIDH* (WHO, 1980) included people with disabilities and disability advocates in the revision process, which led to important changes in the content and structure of the *ICF* (WHO, 2001); similar efforts will be ongoing as the *ICF* is revised over time.

Professional counselors need to know about the *ICF* and its importance as a new health classification tool. Most important, they need to participate in related research to positively impact the *ICF*'s ongoing development. Future research and implementation efforts with the *ICF* promise to (1) revolutionize the way stakeholders in health care delivery systems think about and classify health, (2) improve the quality of health care for individuals across the world, (3) generate innovative outcome-based research, and (4) influence culturally sensitive global health policy (Peterson & Rosenthal, 2005; Stucki, Ewert, & Cieza, 2003).

REFERENCES

Bassett, S. S., Chase, G. A., Folstein, M. F., & Regier, D. A. (1998). Disability and psychiatric disorders in an urban community: Measurement, prevalence and outcomes. *Psychological Medicine, 28,* 509–517.

Bickenbach, J. E. (2003). Functional status and health information in Canada: Proposals and prospects. *Health Care Financing Review, 24*(3), 89–102.

Bruyère, S. M. (2005). Using the *International Classification of Functioning, Disability, and Health (ICF)* to promote employment and community integration in rehabilitation. *Rehabilitation Education, 19*, 105–118.

Bruyère, S. M., & Peterson, D. B. (2005). Introduction to the special section on the *International Classification of Functioning, Disability, and Health (ICF)*: Implications for rehabilitation psychology. *Rehabilitation Psychology, 50*, 103–104.

Burns, C. (1991). Parallels between research and diagnosis: The reliability and validity issues of clinical practice. *The Nurse Practitioner, 16*, 42, 45, 49–50.

Chute, C. G. (2005, June). *The spectrum of clinical data representation: A context for functional status*. Symposium conducted at the meeting of the World Health Organization's North American Collaborating Center, Mayo Clinic, and Rochester, MN.

Coenen, A. (2005, June). *Mapping ICF to the International Classification for Nursing Practice (ICNP)*. Symposium conducted at the meeting of the World Health Organization's North American Collaborating Center, Mayo Clinic, Rochester, MN.

DiCowden, M. A. (2005, June). *The impact of ICF coding in practice*. Symposium conducted at the meeting of the World Health Organization's North American Collaborating Center, Mayo Clinic, Rochester, MN.

Gatchel, R. J., Polatin, P. B., Mayer, T. G., & Garcy, P. D. (1994). Psychopathology and the rehabilitation of patients with chronic low back pain disability. *Archives of Physical Medicine and Rehabilitation, 75*, 666–670.

Holloway, J. D. (2004, January). A new way of looking at health status. *Monitor on Psychology, 35*, 32.

Hurst, R. (2003). The international disability rights movement and the *ICF*. *Disability and Rehabilitation, 25*, 572–576.

Kaplan, R. M. (2002). Quality of life: An outcomes perspective. *Archives of Physical Medicine and Rehabilitation, 83*(Suppl. 2), S44–S50.

Leonardi, M., Bickenbach, J., Üstün, T. B., Kostanjsek, N., & Chatterji, S. (2006). Comment: The definition of disability: What is in a name? *The Lancet, 368*(9543), 1219–1221.

Madden, R., Choi, C., & Sykes, C. (2003). The *ICF* as a framework for national data: The introduction of the *ICF* into Australian data dictionaries. *Disability and Rehabilitation, 25*, 676–682.

Massel, H. K., Liberman, R. P., Mintz, J., & Jacobs, H. E. (1990). Evaluating the capacity to work of the mentally ill. *Psychiatry: Journal for the Study of Interpersonal Processes, 53*, 31–43.

Mayo, N. E., & McGill, J. (2005, June). *Standardizing clinical assessments to the ICF*. Symposium conducted at the meeting of the World Health Organization's North American Collaborating Center, Mayo Clinic, Rochester, MN.

McCrone, P., & Phelan, M. (1994). Diagnosis and length of psychiatric inpatient stay. *Psychological Medicine, 24*, 1025–1030.

541

*The International
Classification
of Functioning,
Disability, and
Health (ICF)*

National Advisory Mental Health Council. (1993). Health care reform for Americans with severe mental illness: Report of the National Advisory Mental Health Council. *American Journal of Psychiatry, 150*, 1447–1465.

Olkin, R. (1999). *What psychotherapists should know about disability*. New York: Guilford Press.

Olkin, R., & Pledger, C. (2003). Can disability studies and psychology join hands? *American Psychologist, 58*, 296–304.

Ormel, J., Oldehinkel, T., Brilman, E., & vanden Brink, W. (1993). Outcome of depression and anxiety in primary care: A three wave 3½ year study of psychopathology and disability. *Archives of General Psychiatry, 50*, 759–766.

Peterson, D. B. (2005). *International Classification of Functioning, Disability, and Health (ICF):* An introduction for rehabilitation psychologists. *Rehabilitation Psychology, 50*, 105–112.

Peterson, D. B., & Elliot, T. R. (2008). Advances in conceptualizing and studying disability. In R. Lent & S. Brown (Eds.), *Handbook of counseling psychology* (4th ed., pp. 212–230). Hoboken, NJ: Wiley.

Peterson, D. B., & Mpofu, E. (in press). Concepts and models in disability, functioning, and health. In T. Oakland & E. Mpofu (Eds.), *Assessment in rehabilitation and health*. New York: Springer Publishing.

Peterson, D. B., & Rosenthal, D. R. (2005). *The International Classification of Functioning, Disability, and Health (ICF)* as an allegory for history and systems in rehabilitation education. *Rehabilitation Education, 19*, 75–80.

Peterson, D. B., & Threats, T. T. (2005). Ethical and clinical implications of the *International Classification of Functioning, Disability, and Health (ICF)* in rehabilitation education. *Rehabilitation Education, 19*, 129–138.

Pledger, C. (2003). Discourse on disability and rehabilitation issues: Opportunities for psychology. *American Psychologist, 58*, 279–284.

Rabinowitz, J., Modai, I., & Inbar-Saban, N. (1994). Understanding who improves after psychiatric hospitalization. *Acta Psychiatrica Scandidavica, 89*, 152–158.

Reed, G. M., Lux, J. B., Bufka, L. F., Trask, C., Peterson, D. B., Stark, S., et al. (2005). Operationalizing the *International Classification of Functioning, Disability, and Health (ICF)* in clinical settings. *Rehabilitation Psychology, 50*, 122–131.

Segal, S. P., & Choi, N. G. (1991). Factors affecting SSI support for sheltered care residents with serious mental illness. *Hospital and Community Psychiatry, 42*, 1132–1137.

Simeonsson, R. J., Leonardi, M., Lollar, D., Bjorck-Akesson, E., Hollenweger, J., & Martinuzzi, A. (2003). Applying the *International Classification of Functioning, Disability, and Health (ICF)* to measure childhood disability. *Disability and Rehabilitation, 25*, 602–610.

Smart, J. (2005). The promise of the *International Classification of Functioning, Disability, and Health (ICF)*. *Rehabilitation Education, 19*, 191–199.

Stucki, G., Ewert, T., & Cieza, A. (2003). Value and application of the *ICF* in rehabilitation medicine. *Disability and Rehabilitation, 25,* 628–634.

Tarvydas, V. M., Peterson, D. B., & Michaelson, S. D. (2005). Ethical issues in case management. In F. Chan, M. Leahy, & J. Saunders (Eds.), *Case management for rehabilitation health professionals* (2nd ed., pp. 144–175). Osage Beach, MO: Aspen Professional Services.

Threats, T., & Worrall, L. (2004). Classifying communication disability using the *ICF. Advances in Speech-Language Pathology, 6*(1), 53–62.

U.S. Census Bureau. (2003, March). *Disability status: 2000.* Washington, DC: U.S. Department of Commerce, Economics and Statistics Administration.

Ueda, S., & Okawa, Y. (2003). The subjective dimension of functioning and disability: What is it and what is it for? *Disability and Rehabilitation, 25,* 596–601.

Üstün, T. B., Chaterji, S., Bickenbach, J., Kastanjsek, N., & Schneider, M. (2003). *The International Classification of Functioning, Disability, and Health:* A new tool for understanding disability and health. *Disability and Rehabilitation, 25,* 565–571.

Velozo, C. A. (2005, June). *Tutorial: Developing measures based on the ICF.* Symposium conducted at the meeting of the World Health Organization's North American Collaborating Center, Mayo Clinic, Rochester, MN.

World Health Organization. (1980). *ICIDH: International Classification of Impairments, Disabilities, and Handicaps. A manual of classification relating to the consequences of disease.* Geneva, Switzerland: Author.

World Health Organization. (1992). *International Statistical Classification of Diseases and Related Health Problems* (10th revision) *(ICD–10).* Geneva, Switzerland: Author.

World Health Organization. (2001). *ICF: International Classification of Functioning, Disability, and Health.* Geneva, Switzerland: Author.

World Health Organization. (2002). *Innovative care for chronic conditions: Building blocks for action.* Geneva, Switzerland: Author.

52

What Counselors Should Know About Vocational Assessment and Evaluation

STEVEN R. SLIGAR AND STEPHEN W. THOMAS

WHAT IS A VOCATIONAL EVALUATION?

VOCATIONAL EVALUATION (VE) or assessment is an employment outcome service that can provide added value to the counseling process. The definition adopted by the Vocational Evaluation and Work Adjustment Association (VEWAA) and found in the VEWAA Glossary (Dowd, 1993) is:

> A comprehensive process that systematically uses work, either real or simulated, as the focal point for assessment and vocational exploration, the purpose of which is to assist individuals with vocational development. Vocational evaluation incorporates medical, psychological, social, vocational, educational, cultural, and economic data into the process to attain the goals of evaluation.

The key points in VE are that it is planned, uses work as the lens for assessment, and incorporates data from other professions into the analysis of the consumer's employability skills. The benefit of using VE is twofold: It is efficient and effective. Consumers are able to identify a career and potential obstacles to achieve success in a short amount of time. The trial and error method of career selection is reduced because decisions are based on information that matches the interests, aptitudes, and skills of the consumer with the requirements of the job. Counselors are able to manage resources and plan more effectively as well as have a benchmark to use to measure progress.

Vocational evaluation operates under four paradigms as identified by the Thirtieth Institute on Rehabilitation Issues (2003). The first is empowerment, which at its root provides the consumer with information to enable the career decision making process. The consumer learns about personal strengths or areas for improvement, crystallizes interests, and makes plans as a result of the VE process. Along the way, the consumer is a partner in charting the course of evaluation, selecting evaluation tools, and formulating the results.

The second is a paradigm that identifies the importance of culture. There are three interrelated factors: the consumer's culture, the culture of the evaluator, and the culture of the tool used in the process. The evaluator makes adjustments in the selection, administration, interpretation, scoring, and reporting of the results based on these three factors.

The third paradigm incorporates universal design and assistive technology to ensure that equal opportunity is provided for all consumers. Universal design (UD) is used to improve efficiency in the operation of machines and tools and avenues for learning in the mainstream. Assistive technology (AT) is an application that ensures access for persons with disabilities. The uses of UD or AT are threefold: as a means to access the VE service, as the reason for referral to VE, or as a recommendation resulting from a VE.

The fourth paradigm recognizes the importance of individualization. The consumer has the right to a VE that is customized, that utilizes a variety of tools, and is of sufficient length to gather information to make decisions. One of the critical issues is the length of time for the VE. Consumers and counselors may want an evaluation that is comprehensive in scope, and yet, prefer that the whole process be conducted in a few hours. The time necessary for a vocational evaluation is posited on a continuum of service ranging from short 1–4 hour screenings or transferable skills assessments to 8 hours of career and interest testing to several days or weeks to conduct an on-the-job evaluation in the community.

545

*What Counselors
Should Know
About Vocational
Assessment and
Evaluation*

WHAT ARE THE TOOLS OF
THE PROFESSION?

THOMAS (1997) DESCRIBED three types of tools used by vocational evaluators: instruments, techniques, and strategies. Instruments are psychometric in nature and consist of various standardized tests such as interest, aptitude, intelligence, achievement, and others to obtain scores to compare the performance of the consumer with a norm group. Another type of instrument is a work sample, which may be purchased commercially or developed by an evaluation program. Typically, different instruments are used during VE. The results are usually compared against the requirements of a specific job or family of jobs or the entrance requirements for a training program to determine feasibility for placement or to identify gaps for remediation.

The second tool involves techniques in which the consumer is placed in a work-related situation and the resulting performance is measured against the criteria of the job. For example, if the consumer wants to work in a meat processing plant, then a tour may be arranged to experience the conditions, and if those are acceptable, then a short work experience is arranged to evaluate physical capacities and the consumer's skills to accept the workplace culture. This same technique may be applied to jobs ranging from computer programmer to civil engineer to hotel housekeeper. The evaluator uses behavioral observations, supervisor ratings, and knowledge of the job to determine the appropriateness of fit.

The third tool involves the use of strategies to determine the consumer's learning style and what type of work or learning modifications or accommodations are in order. Examples include modification of instructions (such as supplementing verbal instructions with a diagram for a person who has a learning disability), use of assistive technology (e.g., a screen reading program with speech emulation for a person who is blind), or application of learning style preferences to learn a job task (helping a visual learner to color code key words as a memory aid). Another aspect involves the identification of natural supports in the environment (a dirty window is a cue for a person with mental retardation that it is time to clean the window). When modifications or accommodations are identified, then the consumer and the counselor know how to plan for success in school or on the job.

WHAT IS THE VALUE OF VOCATIONAL
EVALUATION?

A VE IS DESCRIBED as a "professional discipline that most people, including people with disabilities, will want to use to help identify and achieve career goals" (Thirtieth IRI, 2003, p. 7). Counselors have found that an evaluation can answer differing levels of questions ranging from the specific (What is the consumer's keyboarding skills and interest?) to broader questions about the consumer's employability within a career field. A summary of research on the value of VE is offered in the Thirtieth Institute on Rehabilitation Issues (2003):

1. There are higher success rates when evaluation recommendations are followed as opposed to when they are not followed;
2. The more closely VE recommendations are followed, the higher the placement success rate; and
3. When a more comprehensive and individually tailored VE was administered, successful prediction was maximized. (p. 8)

Consumers who are transitioning from school to work, living with a disability, or experiencing difficulties with choosing, getting, or keeping a job are all able to benefit from VE.

REASONS FOR REFERRAL FOR A VE

ONE OF THE critical elements of a VE is the referral question(s). Counselors set the initial scope and length of the process with the reasons for referral. Johnson (2002) describes five different options for a VE based on the questions to be answered. These are presented below in order of complexity.

An itemized evaluation poses very specific questions that may require one to two tests and can be completed in a relatively short time (1–4 hours). Example questions: *What is the consumer's ability to use a numeric key pad? What are the consumer's math and reading achievement scores?*

A focused evaluation is conducted to determine feasibility for employment within a specific career goal or field. This may require some testing, use of a work sample(s) or situational assessment, and require several (4–10) hours to complete. Questions are similar to: *Can the consumer learn and perform the duties of a Certified Nurse's Aide? Does the consumer demonstrate the skills, temperaments, and behaviors of a customer service representative?*

An exploratory evaluation is useful for persons who are not sure of a career direction or, as the result of a disability, may need to change careers. A variety of tools, including education about different careers and a transferable skills analysis, is used to provide information so the consumer is able to make a decision as to which career holds the best potential for success. Time required for completion varies (6–24 hours) and may be spread over several days to allow time for the consumer to

547

*What Counselors
Should Know
About Vocational
Assessment and
Evaluation*

visit a job or educational site or to learn about various careers. Questions are broader in scope: *What are the consumer's general aptitudes, learning style, achievement levels, and interests? What career areas are matches with the consumer's work history given the etiology of the disability?*

A community-based assessment is beneficial for consumers who learn best from a real life and applied situation. This holistic process encompasses not only a hands-on job experience at an actual job site but also examines critically related skills such as mobility, social skills, and family or community supports. Time required for completion varies (6–40 hours) and may be spread over several days to allow for thorough exposure to the site and to determine typical behaviors associated with preparing for and returning from the site and actual on-the-job behaviors. Questions tend to be sociological in nature: *What work behaviors does the consumer exhibit on the job? What natural supports exist on the job and in the community that will help the consumer to get and keep a job?*

A comprehensive vocational evaluation is useful when none of the previous queries for information apply or have been useful. This is a very broad-based and holistic process that uses a combination of tools to answer questions related to employability (readiness to look for a job) and placeability (readiness for a specific job in the community) (Power, 2006). Career planning is an important element of this process, which varies in time (16–40 hours) and may be spread over several days to permit administration of several tests, intensive interviews, market analysis, job tryout, or other tools as may be needed. Questions are holistic in nature: *Considering the consumer's history of substance abuse, what are some viable employment options? The consumer's traumatic brain injury precludes a return to previous employment: What are some feasible career options and appropriate accommodations?*

HOW TO PREPARE A CONSUMER FOR A VE

THERE ARE SEVERAL factors to consider. First, with the consumer, determine the reason for the evaluation: how both of you plan to use the results. If the VE is to determine placeability, then the results will be used to find a job in the community. If the issue is support for a training program, then the results will help to determine the appropriateness of the program and what accommodations may be in order. Explain that a vocational evaluator may use one or a variety of tools to answer a specific question or to develop a profile compared with the requirements of a job, career, or education/training program. Regardless of the reason, the results will help to develop a plan for employment or career development. Some consumers may have anxiety about entering a testing situation: This needs to be managed with an emphasis on utilization of results and not on test scores. The Vocational Evaluation and Career Assessment Professionals (VECAP) Web site (vecap.org) has three videos about vocational evaluation, two from consumers and one from a parent, that explain about VE. Lastly, be sure the consumer knows where and when to go, whom to see (evaluator's name), what to wear, whether to bring a lunch, and understands the value of VE in the consumer's career development.

WHAT TO EXPECT FROM A VE REPORT

M OST VE REPORTS are completed within 5 days after the consumer completes the service. Formats vary, though reader-friendly versions will use headings for ease of location of information; jargon is used only when necessary; recommendations are actionable; and the referral questions are answered. A recent trend in empowerment-based evaluation is the use of portfolios as the process of the evaluation, and when the portfolio is completed, it also serves as the report.

WHO PROVIDES VE?

T HE PROFESSIONAL CREDENTIAL is Certified Vocational Evaluation Specialist (CVE) (see ccwaves.org). There are practicing vocational evaluators who have bachelor's degrees in rehabilitation or human services with several years of experience. Most vocational evaluators have a master's degree in VE, rehabilitation, or a closely related field.

CONCLUSION

V OCATIONAL EVALUATION OR career assessment is an employment outcome service that can add significant value to the counseling process. The field of VE is based on the premises of empowering the consumer with information to make a career choice; understanding and accepting the different cultures present in an evaluation; the importance and application of universal design and assistive technology; and the value of the consumer as demonstrated by individualized services. The evaluator uses a variety of tools, instruments (tests or work samples), techniques (situational assessment), and strategies (modifications and accommodations of the tasks). The value of VE lies in its efficiency and effectiveness as shown

549

*What Counselors
Should Know
About Vocational
Assessment and
Evaluation*

when recommendations are used in planning and placement. Referral questions are critical in determining the scope of the evaluation and helping to ensure that the experience is useful and meaningful. It is important that the counselor help prepare the consumer for the VE to leverage maximum benefit from the time spent with the evaluator. A report will be prepared by a qualified vocational evaluator, who usually has the designation of CVE.

REFERENCES

Dowd, L. (Ed.). (1993). *VEWAA glossary of terminology for vocational assessment, evaluation and work adjustment*. Menomonie: University of Wisconsin–Stout, Materials Development Center.

Johnson, C. (2002, February). *Career assessment services update*. Annapolis: Maryland State Department of Education, Division of Rehabilitation Services.

Power, P. W. (2006). *A guide to vocational assessment* (4th ed.). Boston: Pro-Ed.

Thirtieth Institute on Rehabilitation Issues. (2003). *A new paradigm for vocational evaluation: Empowering the VR consumer through vocational information*. Hot Springs, AR: University of Arkansas Rehabilitation Continuing Education Center.

Thomas, S. (1997). *Vocational evaluation: Philosophy and practice*. Greenville, NC: East Carolina University.

Section H

Counseling Couples, Families, and Groups

53

Family Assessment

SIMONE F. LAMBERT

OFTENTIMES WHEN WORKING with an individual client, counselors become frustrated and wish they could hear the other side of the story. With family counseling, however, additional perspectives and realities are available to be explored in that very moment. These multiple data points offer more depth in understanding the larger context for the challenges faced by an individual and his or her family. When families enter counseling, counselors enter a complex and rich world of invaluable information.

Family members often have different definitions of what is the problem or who has the problem. So the counselor must first discover the underlying issue that has caused this family to seek treatment. Understanding a family's presenting issue is paramount to accurate diagnosis and effective treatment.

Counselors develop these case conceptualizations through informal and formal assessments of the family. Gladding (2007) describes four different aspects of family life to assess: "pressures on the family, family history, family structure, and family process" (p. 415). More specific areas for assessment regarding structure and process include family members' perceptions of family roles, problem solving, boundaries, communication, and behaviors within the family (Pelsma, 2003). Assessment of these various family characteristics provides counselors with a glimpse into how the family is functioning overall and what are the problem areas for the family. Gladding notes assessment is an ongoing process, as the nature of these issues changes over time.

Fortunately, there are numerous assessments of family functioning to be used for clinical purposes with an individual, entire family, or a subsystem of a family. Instruments that are individually focused are completed by one person who responds to the questions with self in mind. Examples of instruments used in family counseling that are individually focused include the Myers-Briggs Type Indicator (MBTI) and the Minnesota Multiphasic Personality Inventory (MMPI). When individual test results of personality type are compared and contrasted for two or more family members, results can indicate areas of compatibility or potential conflict (Hood & Johnson, 2002). Other instruments focus on collecting data from two or more people about the family's presenting issue or one person's perception about the family's presenting issue, including relational issues. This chapter will focus on primarily assessing subsystems of the family or the family as a whole through informal and formal assessment tools.

Informal assessments of families naturally occur with each family seen in counseling. Counselors should be aware that assessment of a family begins at the point of the initial contact with the family. For instance, much information about the family is gleaned from which family member placed the original call and which family member advocated that the call be placed to schedule an appointment. Such information speaks to who may be the "identified client" or the reason for coming to counseling and who are the most motivated to seek treatment. Information given on the phone during an intake can help counselors to form a preliminary conceptualization of the family (Pelsma, 2003). Further data can be gathered informally by observing a family in the waiting room. During session, counselors can assess family dynamics through direct observation (Gladding, 2007). Family dynamics such as closeness and communication can be assessed by noting where family members sit in relation to each other and how they respond verbally and nonverbally to one another. Another example of informal observation of family dynamics, particularly family roles, is noting who the spokesperson for the family in session is compared to which family member initially set up the counseling appointment. These illustrations highlight how family assessment begins from the very first client contact and continues throughout treatment, regardless of whether a formal assessment instrument is completed.

Family techniques can also serve as informal family assessments. Data can be collected through family play therapy, family sculpting, and genograms. For instance, family play therapy offers an insight into parent–child interactions, as well as sibling interactions. This is an alternative means of collecting information from children who may not be old enough to complete a formal family assessment tool or not articulate to describe their perception of the family problem. For clients who respond better to creative approaches rather than formal testing or traditional talk therapy, family sculpting can be utilized. In this approach, information about family dynamics and functioning are demonstrated through sculpting or posing the family to visually represent an interaction among family members. This provides a powerful image of the presenting issue. Visual illustrations can also be constructed on paper. Genograms provide a pictorial written representation of family history and offer means of organizing a wide variety of information about the family, including health issues, addictions, marriages, events, and stressors (Pelsma, 2003). Genograms not only examine family constellation but also interpersonal relationships (Hood & Johnson, 2002). There are many creative tools to use as assessments in family counseling. Selection of these informal assessment approaches depends largely on the counselor's theoretical orientation and the client's presenting concern. Counselors should be intentional in selecting a technique to gather information in order to best address the specific treatment goals for their particular families in counseling.

Counselors may find that an objective, in-depth understanding of how the family is functioning is beneficial when developing a case conceptualization or treatment plan. Many formal assessment instruments are available and cover a wide variety of family-related issues (Gladding, 2007). There are many instruments that focus exclusively on marriage and couples, such as the Marital Satisfaction Inventory, Revised (MSI-R), Dyadic Adjustment Scale, or the Spouse Observation Checklist. Other instruments focus specifically on subsystems with parents and children or on overall family dynamics. There are numerous instruments for family counselors to select. The following is a description of frequently used instruments by counselors working with families; however, this is by no means an exhaustive list of assessment tools available.

Family-of-Origin Scale (FOS; Hovestadt, Anderson, Piercy, Cochran, & Fine, 1985)

- Purpose: perceived health in family of origin
- Scales: Autonomy and Intimacy
- Scoring: 40 questions with scores ranging from 40 to 200 (higher scores indicate better family health)
- See original source.

Personal Authority in the Family System Questionnaire (PAFS; Bray, Williamson, & Malone, 1984)

- Purpose: self-report on current interaction/relationships of three generations
- Scales: Dependence/Independence, Intergenerational Triangles, Intergenerational Intimidation, Personal Authority, and Intergenerational Fusion/Individuation

- Scoring: 132 items on 5-point Likert scale
- See original source.

Family Adaptability and Cohesion Evaluation Scale IV (FACES IV; Olson, Gorall, & Tiesel, 2007)

- Purpose: examines family structure, utilizing the circumplex model of family functioning
- Scales: Balanced Cohesion, Balanced Flexibility, Disengaged, Enmeshed, Rigid, and Chaotic
- Scoring: 42 items (can be scored with 20 additional items on Family Communication and Family Satisfaction scales, which come with the FACES IV package)
- Time: 15 minutes
- Ages: 12 to adult
- Cost: $95/FACES IV package (then unlimited duplication for purchaser)
- Publisher: Life Innovations, Inc.
- Web site: http://www.facesiv.com

Family Environment Scale (FES; Moos & Moos, 1994)

- Purpose: to examine family members' perceptions of their social environment (real, ideal, and expected)
- Scales: Relationship (Cohesion, Expressiveness, Conflict), Personal Growth (Independence, Achievement Orientation, Intellectual-Cultural Orientation, Active-Recreational Orientation, Moral-Religious Emphasis), and System Maintenance (Organization, Control)
- Scoring: 90 items (scoring key used with answer sheet; profile sheet available to interpret scores)
- Time: 15–20 minutes
- Reading level: sixth grade; translations available
- Cost: $30/25 booklets; $40/third edition manual; $15/25 answer sheets; $10/scoring key (bulk prices available)
- Publisher: Mind Garden, Inc.
- Web site: http://www.mindgarden.com/products/fescs.htm

Children's Version of the Family Environment Scale (CVFES; Pino, Simons, & Slawinowski, 1984)

- Purpose and scales same as FES, but 30-item Pictorial version for ages 5–11
- Scoring: 30 items (scoring key used with answer sheet; profile sheet available to interpret scores)
- Cost: $94.75/kit
- Publisher: Slosson Educational Publications, Inc.
- Web site: http://www.slosson.com/onlinecatalog

Family Assessment Device (FAD; Epstein, Baldwin, & Bishop, 1983)

- Purpose: assess family functioning
- Scales: problem solving, communication, roles, affective responsiveness (sharing of affection), affective involvement (emotional sensitivity), behavior control, and general functioning (boundaries)
- Scoring: 53 items rated using a 4-point Likert scale
- Time: 20 minutes
- See original source.

Parent-Child Relationship Inventory (PCRI; Gerard, 1994)

- Purpose: to understand how parents view their children and parenting itself
- Scales: Parental Support, Satisfaction With Parenting, Involvement, Communication, Limit Setting, Autonomy, and Role Orientation
- Scoring: AutoScore and computerized versions
- Time: 15 minutes
- Ages: parents ages 18–54 (for children ages 3–15)
- Cost: $99/kit (25 AutoScore answer sheets and manual)
- Publisher: Western Psychological Services
- Web site: http://www.wpspublish.com

Parent-Adolescent Communication scale (PAC; Barnes & Olson, 1982)

- Purpose: measures perceptions of communication among family members
- Scales: open and problem family communication
- Scoring: 20 items on each form (i.e., mother-child and father-child) and each item is rated on a 5-point Likert-type scale ranging from 1 (strongly disagree) to 5 (strongly agree)
- Reading level: fifth grade
- Cost: $30
- Publisher: Life Innovations, Inc.
- Web site: http://www.prepare-enrich.com/pdf/fip_order_form pdf

Stress Index for Parents of Adolescents (SIPA; Sheras, Abidin, & Konold, 1998)

- Purpose: detect stressful sectors of parent-adolescent interactions, including life circumstances
- Scales: Adolescent Domain (Moodiness/Emotional Labiality, Social Isolation/Withdrawal, Delinquency/Antisocial, and Failure

to Achieve or Persevere) and Parent Domain (Life Restrictions, Relationship With Spouse/Partner, Social Alienation, and Incompetence/Guilt)

   ❧ Scoring: 10 minutes to score 112 items (Likert and yes–no questions); responses recorded automatically on attached scoring sheet

   ❧ Time: 20 minutes (10 minutes to score)

   ❧ Ages: parents of adolescents ages 11–19

   ❧ Cost: $125/kit (manual, 25 reusable item booklets, and 25 hand-scorable answer sheet/profile forms)

   ❧ Publisher: Psychological Assessment Resources, Inc.

   ❧ Web site: http://www.parinc.com

Parenting Stress Index (PSI; Abidin, PAR Staff, & Noriel, 1995).

   ❧ Purpose: detect stressful sectors of parent-child interactions, related to dysfunctional parenting

   ❧ Scales: Child Domain (Adaptability, Acceptability, Demandingness, Mood, Hyperactivity and Distractibility, Reinforces Parent), Parent Domain (Depression, Attachment, Restrictions of Role, Sense of Competence, Social Isolation, Relationship With Spouse, and Parental Health), Life Stress, and Total Score

   ❧ Scoring: 120 items hand-scorable (36-item short form also available)

   ❧ Time: 20–30 minutes

   ❧ Ages: parents of 1-month- to 12-year-old children

   ❧ Cost: $125/kit (manual, 25 reusable item booklets, and 25 hand-scorable answer sheet/profile forms)

   ❧ Publisher: Psychological Assessment Resources, Inc.

   ❧ Web site: http://www.parinc.com

A word of caution for counselors to keep in mind is who completed the assessment instrument (i.e., parent, child, and spouse) and who was assessed (self-report or rating of someone else). Because the client is the family and each family member has a different perspective or reality of the situation, counselors need to be aware that the results from an assessment are a piece of the puzzle and not a definitive answer. Thus, if it is possible to have multiple family members complete assessments, more information can be utilized to further define the presenting concern and clarify the goals for treatment.

In selecting informal and formal assessments, counselors need to receive appropriate training for administering an instrument or applying a counseling technique to gather information. For instance, coursework or professional development should be obtained before attempting family play therapy or family sculpting. When first trying one of these approaches, supervision should be obtained to ensure accurate implementation and interpretation of results. The same holds true for formal assessments, which typically require a certain level of training to administer and analyze results. Test manuals and publisher catalogs often have the required training level necessary in regard to each instrument.

Counselors need to consider other responsibilities that come with administering assessments. When interpreting assessment data, the original sample in which the instrument was normed needs to be examined to determine whether the current family's demographics are represented among the initial sample. The validity and reliability for instruments need to be examined to ensure the test will effectively assess the family. Finally, counselors need to share the results in an appropriate and ethical manner with the family and any other third-party stakeholder as indicated by the family. For instance, some agencies may use family assessments to make critical decisions about family treatment and even child custody. This scenario emphasizes the need to take special care in the administering, scoring, and interpreting assessments and storing collected data.

Given all of the necessary provisions described above, assessments are still worth the effort. There are many benefits to collecting information from families that go beyond case conceptualization. By conducting family assessments at multiple points in time, effectiveness of treatment can be demonstrated to the family, the agency, and managed care. Assessments can document changes in performance to be used with managed care companies (Gladding, 2007). Testing can establish a need for further services in the community (i.e., additional sessions approved by health insurance or a referral to more intensive services) or in the schools (e.g., Individualized Education Plans). Thus, assessment results can indicate whether a client or family is suitable for a specific intervention, program, or facility. Concrete data also assists in procuring the necessary funding and resources to ensure that these services can be offered to the family.

While the hope is families improve with our services, sometimes there is not forward progress. In such a case, assessments can articulate the need for a different counseling approach with the family when improvement is not measured. Alternatively, assessments can offer a clear indication of success. Data can help to define when the counseling goal is met and assist clients in recognizing the progress they have made in treatment. Either way, family assessment data facilitates the provision of effective services for clients.

Families may seek counseling to work on a variety of presenting issues such as improving communication, reducing aggression/conflict, or increasing parenting effectiveness. The use of family assessments enables counselors to obtain a clear picture of how the family is functioning in a certain domain and to compare that with their desired level of functioning. Informal and formal assessments can be used throughout treatment to enlighten the counselor and family about the progress accomplished and areas for further improvement. Family assessments offer counselors the means to ensure clients obtain appropriate treatment.

Collecting family information was described as possible through a number of different assessment strategies. Select informal techniques and formal assessment instruments were discussed in this chapter. The benefits and precautions, including ethical implications, associated with testing families were described.

REFERENCES

Abidin, R. R. (1995). *Parenting Stress Index: Professional manual* (3rd ed.). Lutz, FL: Psychological Assessment Resources.

Barnes, H., & Olson, D. H. (1982). *Parent-Adolescent Communication*. Minneapolis, MN: Life Innovations.

Bray, J. H., Williamson, D. S., & Malone, P. E. (1984). Personal authority in the family system: Development of a questionnaire to measure personal authority in intergenerational family processes. *Journal of Marital and Family Therapy, 10,* 167–178.

Epstein, N. B., Baldwin, L. M., & Bishop, D. S. (1983). The McMaster Family Assessment Device. *Journal of Marital and Family Therapy, 9,* 171–180.

Gerard, A. B. (1994). *The Parent-Child Relationship Inventory: Manual.* Los Angeles: Western Psychological Services.

Gladding, S. T. (2007). Research and assessment in family therapy. In S. T. Gladding (Ed.), *Family therapy: History, theory, and practice* (4th ed., pp. 389–415). Upper Saddle River, NJ: Pearson.

Hood, A. B., & Johnson, R. W. (2002). Assessment of interpersonal relationships. In A. B. Hood & R. W. Johnson (Ed.), *Assessment of counseling* (3rd ed., pp. 273–284). Alexandria, VA: American Counseling Association.

Hovestadt, A. J., Anderson, W. T., Piercy, F. P., Cochran, S. W., & Fine, M. (1985). A family-of-origin scale. *Journal of Marital and Family Therapy, 11,* 287–297.

Moos, R. H., & Moos, B. S. (1994). *The Family Environment Scale manual.* Palo Alto, CA: Consulting Psychologists Press.

Olson, D. H., Gorall, D. M., & Tiesel, J. W. (2007). *FACES IV manual.* Minneapolis, MN: Life Innovations.

Pelsma, D. (2003). Assessing family issues related to the presenting problem. In D. M. Kaplan & Associates (Eds.), *Family counseling for all counselors* (pp. 87–119). Greensboro, NC: CAPS Publications.

Pino, C. J., Simons, N., & Slawinowski, M. J. (1984). *Children's Version of the Family Environment Scale.* Aurora, NY: Slosson Educational Publications.

Sheras, P. L., Abidin, R. R., & Konold, T. R. (1998). *Stress Index for Parents of Adolescents: Professional manual.* Odessa, FL: Psychological Assessment Resources.

54

Guidelines in Counseling Families

SIMONE F. LAMBERT

FAMILY COUNSELING OFFERS a valuable alternative or addition to addressing individual client concerns. By working with family members, counselors gain a broader context from accessing multiple perspectives about the presenting issue. Case conceptualization can occur in a shorter amount of time. In the age of managed care, producing rapid results is both desired and necessitated by third-party reimbursement requirements, and family counseling fits well with this paradigm. Family counseling tends to be short-term and solution-focused, where specific, attainable treatment goals are set for a definite end-point (American Association for Marriage and Family Therapy [AAMFT], 2002). Families may benefit more from intervals of brief problem-focused counseling, as opposed to long-term continuous counseling (Woody, 2004). Family counseling should then be tailored to resolve a particular issue in a limited timeframe.

Families seek services for assistance with a wide variety of concerns. Many therapeutic issues can be suitably addressed in family counseling, including mental health issues such as mood, anxiety, dissociative, and psychiatric disorders, as well as physical concerns such as chronic illness (Kaplan & Associates, 2003). Substance-related and process addictions (i.e., gambling addiction, sex addiction, etc.) are treated successfully with family counseling as a component of the treatment plan (Juhnke & Hagedorn, 2006). "Research indicates that marriage and family counseling is more effective than standard and/or individual

treatment for many mental health problems such as: adult schizophrenia, adult alcoholism and drug abuse, children's conduct disorders, adolescent drug abuse, anorexia in young adult women, childhood autism,
chronic physical illness in adults and children, and marital distress and
conflict" (AAMFT, 2002). Family counseling offers relief for many diverse presenting issues.

Contemporary family counselors assist with child concerns at home
or school, marital challenges (such as infidelity, separation, or divorce),
child–parent relational problems, family communication difficulties, conflicts in blended/remarried families, loss of a family member,
childhood trauma, and family violence. In addition, family counselors
can facilitate with developmental issues, life events, and transitions,
including starting a new marriage or adding children through birth,
remarriage, or adoption, parenting young children or adolescents, and
launching children to college or the workplace. World events also shape
family counseling, especially when working with military families and
refugee families. Today's families are struggling with many concerns
that can be addressed through family counseling.

In order to fully conceptualize the presenting issue, counselors con-
textualize the problem in part based on the family type. For example,
families typically are identified as nuclear, extended, single-parent, or
divorced/blended/remarried. Other categories that describe families
today include aging family, multigenerational family, grandparent-
headed family, dual-career family, child-free family, gay/lesbian family,
or military family. As noted previously, counselors do assist families in
transitioning through life cycles, which often leads to a change in family type. Families are not static; thus, family types will change over time
for an individual.

SYSTEMS PERSPECTIVE

SYSTEMS PERSPECTIVE REPRESENTS a shift from individual
to system dynamics, or how individuals within a system relate to
and influence one another. When change occurs, there is a ripple effect that impacts the entire system (family). The hope is that the system
then changes to support and sustain new behaviors of the individual or
family. Systems approaches can be utilized with an individual in counseling, since this perspective suggests that the change of one individual
affects the whole system.

Family Systems describes communication as a regulatory process,
whereby family members' verbal and nonverbal communications bi-
directionally influence the system. Furthermore, families attempt to

regulate themselves and maintain balance, referred to as homeostasis, to keep life management in check (Kaplan & Associates, 2003). When families get out of balance, it is often because the family roles become reversed, such as a parent taking the child's role or vice versa. Sometimes this is attributable to a life event or transition that the family has endured, such as a parent suffering with a chronic illness or becoming a single parent.

Boundaries help differentiate roles and functions of family members and need to be appropriately set for families to effectively function. If boundaries are too close between family members, then they are enmeshed; and if they are too distant, family members are disengaged (Kaplan & Associates, 2003). Thus, the goal is for families to be interdependent and to rely on one another in a healthy manner. Kaplan states, "Three problem-solving skills that promote healthy homeostasis in families are *the art of compromise, developing healthy family rules* and *becoming comfortable with change*" (p. 24).

Healthy families often have the following attributes:

* Sense of belonging to family system (cohesiveness/commitment)
* Accountability, give and take, and appreciation
* Effective communication, including quality and frequency (Kaplan & Associates, 2003)
* Sense of separateness and individuality (Individuation)
* Emotional barriers protect individual members (Boundaries)
* Religious/Spiritual orientation
* Ability to surpass crisis
* Desire to spend time together
* Encouragement of one another
* Clear roles
* Adaptability

Alternatively, dysfunctional families can be described as:

* Closed communication/Rigid patterns
* Poor self-esteem of parent(s)
* Expected to think, feel, and act the same
* Parents control via fear, punishment, guilt, or dominance
* Anxiety and tension when one person is pulled by other two (Triangular Relationships)
* Intergenerational coalitions or triangulation of two family members teaming up against another
* Disengaged or enmeshed
* Rigid or chaotic
* Subsystems out of hierarchy

Similar to individual counseling, the family counseling process can be divided into different phases of treatment: Case Conceptualization (ongoing), Initial Sessions, Middle Phase, Termination, and Follow-up. In order for this family counseling to be successful, counselors must build rapport with and engage all family members. This can be accomplished by demonstrating empathy, respect, and positive regard. With more people in the room, there are more verbal and nonverbal interactions to attend to between family members. Thus, family counselors must address both the process (how something is being communicated) and content (what is being communicated). Family therapists provide structure to sessions and redirect when the family goes off course. Throughout treatment, family counselors employ these central strategies and other specific techniques based on their theoretical perspective.

APPROACHES

WHILE IN THE past therapists attempted to be theoretical purists, the focus today is to integrate theoretical approaches and techniques to customize treatment for each family (Woody, 2004). Rather than being a theoretical purist, many counselors intentionally select theoretical interventions that go beyond one theoretical perspective. By integrating theoretical approaches, counselors can tailor counseling to best meet the needs of individual clients (Juhnke & Hagedorn, 2006).

Many of the theories that are applied to individual counseling can be applied to family counseling as well (i.e., cognitive behavior, gestalt, psychodynamic, etc.). There are other theoretical approaches that are specifically designed for family interventions (i.e., strategic, structural, Bowenian, solution-focused, etc.). The following is a list of theoretical approaches commonly used in family counseling, along with simplified descriptions and sample techniques from each approach.

TRADITIONAL THEORIES

Human Validation Process Model

- Goal: promote growth, self-esteem, and positive communication/interaction styles
- Techniques: sculpting and role playing

Experiential/Symbolic Family Counseling

- Goal: enable spontaneity, independence, and creativity
- Techniques: co-counseling, confrontation, and self-disclosure

Structural Family Counseling

- Goal: restructure family organization and establish boundaries
- Techniques: joining and accommodating

Strategic Family Counseling

- Goal: eliminate problem and change dysfunctional patterns
- Techniques: reframing, directives, and paradox

Social Constructionism

- Goal: deconstruct then co-construct new story
- Techniques: externalizing and reauthoring

Multigenerational Family Counseling

- Goal: differentiate self within system and understand family of origin
- Technique: genograms

CONTEMPORARY THEORIES

Behavioral Family Counseling

- Goal: promote change through consequences; learn, unlearn, or modify behavior
- Technique: contracting

Cognitive Behavior Family Counseling

- Goal: modify thoughts to change behaviors and interactions; teach communication and problem-solving skills
- Techniques: contingency contracting, modeling, role playing, thought stopping

Solution-Focused Family Counseling

- Goal: collaborate with the client to develop solutions
- Techniques: The Miracle Question (hypothetical solutions), Scaling Question (small changes), Coping Question (How has it been done before?), Exception Question (noting patterns and exceptions)

Narrative Family Counseling

- Goal: help families understand how they construct their realities and author their own stories
- Techniques: externalizing problem, using questions (exceptions and significance), letters, certificates, and celebrations

Family Play Counseling

* Goal: parents and young children have opportunity to be creative in their problem-solving strategies, become closer, and gain understanding
* Techniques: family play genogram, sand counseling, family puppet interviews, art counseling, and storytelling

Filial Counseling

* Goal: teach parents skills of structuring, empathic listening, imaginary play, and limit setting
* Technique: accompanies child-centered play counseling

Theraplay

* Goal: increase attachment, self-esteem, trust, and positive interactions with parents through playful approach; improve parenting skills
* Techniques: two therapists (one for parents and one for child)

SPECIAL POPULATIONS

WHEN WORKING WITH families, treatment needs to be tailored based on the specific circumstances presented by each family. Thus, the theoretical approaches described above need to be adjusted for the presenting issue and the family type. The following is a list of special populations, including the goal and techniques for each within family counseling.

Single-Parent Families

* Context: due to divorce, death, abandonment, unwed pregnancy, adoption, extended assignments
* Goal: focus on improving confidence, competence, efficiency, clear and functional boundaries and structures, and decision-making skills
* Techniques: communication methods, social support groups, bibliotherapy

Remarried Families

* Goal: focus on resolving loss and adapting to new people and situations
* Techniques: offer educational materials, help families form new traditions and rituals

‹ Approaches: structural, strategic, Bowen, and experiential family theories

Culturally Diverse Families

‹ Context: family acculturation level
‹ Goal: commitment to address internalized or externalized problem in counseling
‹ Techniques: identify past attempts at solutions; celebrate heritage and accomplishments

Family Addictions Counseling

‹ Context: substance abuse and other process addictions including sex, Internet, gambling, and eating
‹ Goal: relapse prevention, through improving environment, intrapersonal and interpersonal relations
‹ Techniques/Approaches: structural-strategic, Bowen, behavioral, Adlerian, multifamily, and community resources (support groups)

Domestic Violence

‹ Context: physical, sexual, psychological, and economic—power differential
‹ Goal: eliminate domestic violence
‹ Techniques/Approaches: conjoint family, intimate justice theory, and cognitive behavior therapies
‹ Resource: National Domestic Violence Hotline 1-800-799-SAFE (7233)

Child Abuse

‹ Context: physical, sexual, and psychological abuse, neglect, and abandonment
‹ Goal: eliminate child abuse
‹ Techniques/Approaches: Bowen and behavioral family therapies
‹ Resource: Childhelp National Child Abuse Hotline 1-800-4-A-CHILD

Families and Chronic Illness

‹ Context: emotions experienced upon diagnosis, including loss, grief, fear, acceptance, resignation, avoidance, denial, anger, and frustration

- ⟐ Goal: awareness of how a severe or chronic illness may affect all family members
- ⟐ Techniques: foster acceptance of illness; help families learn to live with illness

ETHICAL DECISION MAKING

WHEN CONDUCTING FAMILY counseling, ethical concerns often arise. Typical ethical dilemmas surround informed consent for all family members, multiple relationships, confidentiality, and legal issues (i.e., custody). When these or other concerns arise, counselors should consult ethical codes of profession (i.e., ACA, IAMFC, and/or AAMFT), seek supervision, and obtain case consultation. Counselors also need to be informed on best practices, current techniques, and strategies for family interventions by reviewing current literature and attending professional development workshops (Woody, 2004). Counselors should become trained in utilizing family counseling approaches prior to implementing them in session and should seek supervision as they begin to gain experience conducting family counseling.

CONCLUSION

THIS CHAPTER FOCUSED on presenting the benefits and approaches in utilizing family counseling. Special populations were addressed to tailor counseling based on the needs of specific families. Ethical considerations were outlined for family counselors.

RESOURCES

Blume, T. W. (2006). *Becoming a family counselor: A bridge to family therapy theory and practice*. Hoboken, NJ: Wiley.

Gil, E. (2003). Family play therapy: "The bear with short nails." In C. E. Schaefer (Ed.), *Foundations of play therapy* (pp. 192–218). Hoboken, NJ: Wiley.

Gladding, S. T. (2007). *Family therapy: History, theory, and practice* (4th ed.). Upper Saddle River, NJ: Pearson Education.

The International Association of Marriage and Family Counselors, a division of the American Counselors Association: www.iamfc.com

Lund, L. K., Zimmerman, T. S., & Haddock, S. A. (2002). The theory, structure, and techniques for the inclusion of children in family therapy: A literature review. *Journal of Marital and Family Therapy, 28*, 445–454.

Nichols, M. P., & Schwartz, R. C. (2005). *The essentials of family therapy* (2nd ed.). Boston: Pearson.

REFERENCES

American Association for Marriage and Family Therapy. (2002). *Frequently asked questions on marriage and family therapists.* Retrieved June 8, 2002, from http://www.aamft.org/faqs/index_nm.asp#what

Juhnke, G. A., & Hagedorn, W. B. (2006). *Counseling addicted families.* New York: Routledge.

Kaplan, D. M., & Associates. (2003). *Family counseling for all counselors.* Greensboro, NC: CAPS Publications.

Woody, R. H. (2004). Modern family interventions. *The American Journal of Family Therapy, 32,* 353–357.

55

Effective Counseling With Couples

NANCY NEWPORT

It is not a lack of love, but a lack of friendship that makes unhappy marriages.

—*Friedrich Nietzsche*

COUPLE THERAPY HAS entered a new era. It is only in the last few years that we have been given a clinical road map to effective work with relationships. Research now has demonstrated the causes of marital distress and satisfaction (Gottman, 1999), which include identifying and interrupting problematic patterns of interaction. John Gottman studied couples over a period of years to determine what factors cause couples to divorce and what happy relationships look like. Teaching couples the successful strategies he observed in happy marriages (cultivating friendship, kindness, and compassion) leads to greater marital satisfaction. Positive psychology (Seligman, 2006) research correlates the impact of positive and negative relationships on health and well-being and the role of optimism and a focus on strengths and resources in dealing with adversity. Richard Schwartz (1995) is broadening the "parts model" described by Virginia Satir (1978) that we all have parts or aspects of self. Our parts have a positive intention for us even in the face of problem behavior and sometimes these parts run the show, creating some of the havoc we experience in our relationships. Susan Johnson (2004) with emotionally focused therapy focuses on the emotional component of relationships and the recurring distressing emotional patterns that cause disconnection. Her research helps us take couples to a deeper level of healing personally and in relationships, particularly around attachment issues. Others have contributed to our understanding of how our current relationships tend to replicate or be triggered by relationships we had with our family of origin and how to identify those patterns that cause us pain and therefore become more conscious about interrupting these patterns with our mate. In addition, a 40-year longitudinal study conducted by the American Psychological Association (Hubble, Duncan, & Miller, 1996) concluded that the most significant factor in the success of any counseling was the relationship built between therapist and client. Building and sustaining a strong working alliance was deemed crucial to the outcome of the therapy. Couple therapy is now backed by a great deal of empirical evidence on how to help couples move through a repair of a relationship to a greater stability and satisfaction.

In this chapter, the latest of the science of couple therapy is combined with the art of therapy in a competency-based approach that considers individuals in the context of their family, culture, gender, values, and strengths. Competency-based therapy (Bertolino & O'Hanlon, 2002), which draws in part from the work of Milton H. Erickson, is one such approach known for its respect, optimism, hopefulness, collaboration, and strength-based focus. Sophisticated language patterns are utilized to create a change-friendly therapeutic environment that encourages hope and new possibilities while sustaining a strong working relationship.

ROLE OF THE THERAPIST

THE THERAPIST ACTS as a collaborator with the couple, and the therapy experience is a co-creation between the couple and the therapist. The clients have expertise on themselves. The therapist has expertise on change. Together, the collaboration unfolds in the direction of more conscious choices for each partner to improve the love relationship and their bond to one another. Clients teach you about themselves as they share their thoughts, emotions, and the behavioral patterns that compose their story, their view of the world and of their relationship. As the therapist learns the couple's story, it is appropriate for the therapist to share back or paraphrase his or her understanding of their story in order to stay on track and accurately perceive the couple's situation. The therapist's role is to be a guide and remain both an open-hearted and open-minded presence with each partner. As the clinician working with a couple or any member of the family, the therapist influences and is influenced by the family. This influence should be used mindfully, intentionally, and therapeutically.

THERAPEUTIC ALLIANCE

IT IS ESSENTIAL to establish a therapeutic alliance with both partners and to sustain that alliance throughout the therapy process.

Key Ingredients for Creating a Therapeutic Alliance

1. A nonjudging stance
2. A respectful collaborative demeanor
3. An optimistic and hopeful manner that says change is possible and sustainable
4. A nonpathologizing, normalizing approach with couples' concerns and challenges
5. Acknowledgment and validation throughout each session.

Acknowledging the concerns and perspectives of each person and validating his or her right to feel the way he or she does is a crucial aspect of joining and maintaining your connection to the couple. Acknowledgment and validation "tills the soil" by preparing couples to be ready and receptive to later planting the seeds of change. This technique not only creates a climate where clients feel heard and understood, but also serves as a powerful way of modeling for the couple (Bertolino & O'Hanlon, 2002), while continuing to acknowledge and validate a couple's concerns throughout the entire counseling journey. When this does not occur, therapists risk outpacing their clients and creating a disconnect that in turn can make a couple feel outpaced and judged as though they are doing therapy incorrectly. Therapists can sometimes make the mistake of becoming more invested in the couple making changes the couple is either not ready or willing to make. As a result, many couples drop out of therapy at this point, feeling not heard and supported. Therapists can lose sight of what the couple wants to change and get caught up in their own ideas of what the couple should be changing. Rarely do couples come to counseling requesting an "extreme makeover," and frequently only seek therapy to resolve a specific issue. When a couple feels successful at resolving a particular problem in therapy and is given the appropriate credit for the behavioral and attitudinal shifts they make, they are more likely to return for additional couples counseling about other, perhaps more serious, concerns in the future.

FOCUS ON CURRENT PROBLEMATIC INTERACTIONAL PATTERNS

THE PRIMARY FOCUS of therapy is on present-day external issues and internal responses that play out in interactional patterns between partners. If any family-of-origin patterns are addressed, it is in the context of how these patterns may perpetuate in the here and now. The problematic sequences of interaction are identified by the therapist and interruptions to those problem patterns are co-created, moving the partnership toward relationship repair and recovery. Gottman (1999) identified four particularly toxic interactional patterns that he calls the "Four Horsemen of the Apocalypse" (p. 27). Left unchecked, these behaviors are significant predicators of eventual divorce.

1. *Criticism*—"You never" or "You always"—attacks on the person rather than the behavior, focus on what's wrong rather than what may be going well.
2. *Contempt*—"I've got you figured out and it's not good." Sarcasm, eye rolling, hostility, and disgust.
3. *Defensiveness*—avoiding responsibility, defending his or her innocence, not listening, cross complaining.
4. *Stone walling*—withdrawing, acting unaffected, disconnecting.

Unhappy couples tend to be more negative with each other. Gottman (1999) found that couples who are very critical of one another are more brittle and defensive and more likely to focus on what is wrong at any given time rather than on what is right. Power struggles are frequent, and there is a tendency to rather be right (or at least prove his or her mate to be wrong) than to seek harmony and happiness. It is a healthy move to begin to reverse the amount of complaints and criticisms, and increase the amount of positive comments. A ratio of five positive comments to one criticism begins to put a greater investment into their collective emotional bank account and begins to reverse the negative momentum. Gottman (1999) actually found that happy couples tend to have a 20 to 1 ratio of positive to negative comments.

FIRST SESSION

MOST RELATIONSHIPS HAVE times of challenge with communication, problem resolution, connection, and intimacy issues. Couples tend to seek outside assistance with their relationship only after they have exhausted their own best efforts to resolve their differences. They come because they are in pain. The distress they are experiencing has fully grabbed their attention. It is vital to the success of the therapy that the counselor focus on what is currently troubling them early in the first session rather than taking an extensive history about their families of origin. The first session should be structured in such a way that the counselor gathers the following information on each partner: how they met, how they chose each other, what that felt like. Evoking good feelings about each other from their shared past will, for many, soften their position once they begin to describe why they have come to therapy. The counselor should express great interest in their positive history, asking open-ended questions in order to elicit additional positive history. The next step is to briefly inquire about demographic background regarding age, children, career, and length of marriage, spending only a few minutes before asking them to explain what has brought them to therapy. They will likely describe problematic patterns in their relationship and be generally unaware that they are describing problematic patterns as opposed to personal partner flaws. The therapist must listen carefully to each partner as the person expresses the interactional patterns that make him or her feel disconnected from the other person. The therapist needs to convey that he or she (1) honors and respects their individual perspectives, (2) that it is to be expected that they will each have their own way of perceiving things, (3) will not look for who is right or where the "truth" lies, and (4) will encourage them not to focus in that direction either.

This intervention done early in the first session tends to circumvent the arguing that could potentially transpire otherwise. Arguing does not help the therapeutic process move forward. As the therapist remains potent (e.g., firm, directive if necessary, yet very warm and kind) with the couple, they will see that they can both be safe in the room with the therapist. Again, acknowledge and validate their respective points of view by listening, asking clarification questions, and paraphrasing back to each partner what his or her specific concerns are about. The therapist must make sure the couple feels heard and understood. Once the couple verifies they have been understood, the next key question becomes how they want their relationship to be different. It's typical for many couples to first describe what they *don't* want, and in fact, a person often comes to therapy with a whole laundry list of what's wrong with his or her partner. While it is essential to acknowledge what they do not want, it is more fruitful to shift as soon as possible (while concomitantly maintaining the alliance created) to what their situation will look like when they are getting along well again. At the same time, the therapist cannot assume that a couple will necessarily want to stay together, therefore it becomes important to ask each of them if they love one another and want to stay in the relationship. The counselor may need to spend time alone with each partner if he or she thinks there is information or feelings one or both partners are not comfortable expressing in the presence of the other.

Therapists should also help couples formulate their complaints about areas of disconnection by teaching them how to express their discontent in a mature, constructive manner with a follow-up request for change (Gottman, 1999). How they deliver their messages plays an essential role in how their partner hears them. Partners should be encouraged to be specific regarding what behaviors they would like their partner to be doing in place of the perceived problem behavior. Talking in concrete language rather than vague terms tends to help clarify what each of them wants from the other. Finally, therapists need to assist each partner to increase his or her own willingness to be influenced and coached by the other.

By the end of the first session, the therapist has ideally begun to:

- Create a strong working alliance with each partner
- Develop an understanding of the interactional patterns causing distress in the relationship
- Plant seeds of hope for things to be different
- Create a climate in which both partners feel understood and validated
- Introduce couples to the concept of each of them having his or her own unique perspective (which will, over time, tend to circumvent future arguing over who is right/wrong about the past issues)
- Guide couples toward more effective communication together.

Before the second session, create a treatment plan for the couple that will best assist them in interrupting the problematic patterns and creating more healthy success patterns together. New therapists should check with supervisors or colleagues if they need assistance to identify the presenting distressing patterns. It takes repeated practice to gain proficiency in pattern identification and creating strategies to change those patterns.

Throughout the course of treatment, co-create with the couple task assignments that allow the couple to continue the counseling momentum during the times between appointments. John Gottman's books (1999, 2001) include many connection-oriented exercises for couples. Acknowledgment and validation must continue to be part of the therapist's communication style throughout the course of treatment.

INTERNAL AND EXTERNAL RESOURCES

PEOPLE COME TO therapy with strengths, skills, and abilities, as well as community resources. These may not be so obvious to them or they may have just misplaced them during the stress of the problem situation. As the couple's change agent, therapists should continually be on the alert for observed strengths they see in the partners and the partnership, and these strengths should be highlighted for the couple regarding what is healthy and strong in their relationship. Internal resources that couples can be made aware of by the therapist may include apparent love for each other; the ability to be loving, kind, generous; good decision-making skills; good common sense; a good sense of humor; an ability to be cool under pressure; and, any other talent or observed skills that could be utilized to help the couple move forward. Seeing the couple as resourceful and capable of making changes helps them see themselves that way also. Help them to reconnect to external sources of support such as family, friends, spiritual centers, groups, meetings, books, or seminars that could enhance their efforts at strengthening their relationship.

MOVING FROM ILLUSION TO ILLUMINATION: THE JOURNEY OF ROMANTIC LOVE

MANY COUPLES INITIALLY come to therapy in hopes of getting their partner to be like the person was when they first met. The belief that their mate really has "changed," and has become someone different from the person he or she was when they first met and fell in love with, is an illusion. People don't change so much as they reveal their true selves over time. This unfolding is expedited by situational stressors and pressures of the life lived together. One of nature's powerful ways of engaging individuals in the infatuation/attraction stage of a relationship is the release of neurotransmitters such as norepinephrine, phenylethylamine (PEA), and dopamine, which cloud judgment. It's a temporary love potion that lasts only a few months to a few years, and is physiologically not a state that can be indefinitely sustained (Love & Robinson, 1995). Since the majority of couples do not understand the biology behind attraction, it appears to them that their partner has changed in some less than desirable way because the partner no longer gets the same "high" he or she used to feel in his or her mate's presence. The romantic view couples once had of their partner's quirks begins to fade over time. For example, the lovely carefree way a partner has of living in the moment becomes an annoying habit of always being late. As couples move deeper into a relationship and the romantic high dissipates, individuals begin to see their partner's personality traits more clearly. In terms of longevity of a relationship, it is the friendship, the abiding connection to each other, that ultimately will sustain the relationship. Staying in love, sustaining love, depends on the friendship, the entwined roots, attending to the living, growing organism that is love. Couples will teach the therapist over time how deeply they want or are able to remain committed to that love possibility.

Ultimately, a counselor's greatest contribution to couples is to help them become more connected to each other, to treat each other at least as well as they would treat anyone else, to cultivate and grow their friendship, to deepen their interest in the other, and to build and sustain rituals and routines that strengthen their bond. As the architects of the family, couples set the tone for the health and safety of the entire family system.

EMOTIONAL LOVE LANGUAGE

IN THE COURTING stage, couples show their love in countless ways, verbalize their love expressively, and touch each other with passion, affection, and tenderness. After a while, most individuals unknowingly begin to narrow down their expression of love to the love language with which they most identify. Individuals unconsciously begin expressing the love language that is most like their own.

In reality, there are at least several love languages (Chapman, 1995), and it is generally unlikely that both partners share the same one. Love languages are based on the primary representational systems in which people relate to the world: visually, auditorally, and kinesthetically.

- *Visual* refers to the way things look—being taken places, presentation of things, gifts, preparing meals, meaningful looks, spending quality time, being there, acts of service.
- *Auditory* is how things sound—tempo, tone of voice, words of appreciation, affirmation.
- *Kinesthetic* is how things feel—physical touch, such as holding hands, or kissing in public could be a specific type of touch.

In order to discover the love language of each partner, explore with each of them a time when they felt deeply loved by their partner, and give them each time to access a specific memory and the feeling that goes with it. Once this memory has been accessed, the counselor can explore the following questions: "In order for you to feel those deep feelings of love, is it absolutely necessary that your partner show you that he or she loves you (1) by taking you places, buying you things, and looking at you in certain ways; or (2) talking to you, telling you things you like to hear; or (3) touching you, hugging you, or kissing you?" Therapists need to give each partner a moment between each question to fully consider each option.

A process of elimination should be employed to assist the couple in figuring out their primary strategy. It is important to note that human beings require all three modes of expressing love, but one or a combination of two is absolutely essential in order to feel deeply loved. And that's *the* one that is our primary love strategy. Once therapists discover each partner's primary love language, couples can then be coached on how to best meet their partner's needs and how to trigger their partner's love strategy deliberately.

PERSONAL JOURNEY OF THE THERAPIST

THE RELATIONSHIPS THAT therapists have in their own lives can ultimately affect the way they interact with clients about client issues. Therapists must be aware of their own bias in relationships, how they themselves are treating and are being treated by their partners, and how their own values and beliefs can impact counseling couples. The more personal growth and self-awareness therapists have and continue to develop, the more likely they will be fully present to their clients. Therapists cannot give what they do not have, and they cannot teach that which they have not learned.

CONCLUSION

AS A GLOBAL family, humans have not yet figured out how to get along together. The wars and strife we experience on an international level play out in our homes and in our hearts. Most couples have children and these children are directly impacted by how their parents get along. In the United States, more than half of all marriages end in divorce. Over the course of one's career, counselors will likely see couples in all different stages of union (dating, engaged, married, coupled/partnered, divorcing, divorced, remarried, blended). Our highest goal with couples is not whether they choose to stay together, but rather helping them learn to treat each other and themselves with love and compassion, and to live that love with their children. Virginia Satir (1978) frequently spoke of the direct connection between bringing healing to a family and the impact that creates for the greater community. Every couple a therapist assists in improving their capacity and their willingness to treat each other more lovingly is movement toward world harmony.

REFERENCES

Bertolino, B., & O'Hanlon, B. (2002). *Collaborative, competency-based counseling and therapy*. Boston: Allyn & Bacon.

Chapman, G. (1995). *The five love languages: How to express heartfelt commitment to your mate*. Chicago: Northfield Publishing.

Gottman, J. M. (1999). *The seven principles for making marriage work*. New York: Three Rivers Press.

Gottman, J. M. (2001). *The relationship cure—a five-step guide to strengthening your marriage, family and friendships*. New York: Three Rivers Press.

Hubble, M. A., Duncan, B. L., & Miller, S. D. (Eds.). (1996). *The heart and soul of change: What works in therapy*. Washington, DC: American Psychological Association.

Johnson, S. M. (2004). *The practice of emotionally focused couple therapy: Creating connection* (2nd ed.). NewYork: Brunner-Routledge.

Love, P., & Robinson, J. (1995). *Hot monogamy: Essential steps to more passionate intimate lovemaking*. New York: Plume.

Satir, V. (1978). *Your many faces*. Berkeley, CA: Celestial Arts.

Schwartz, R. C. (1995). *Internal family systems therapy*. New York: Guilford Press.

Seligman, M. (2006). *Learned optimism*. New York: Vintage.

56

A Guide to Having a Healthy Family

Samuel T. Gladding

S TUDIES REVEAL THAT healthy and functional families exist in virtually all cultures. They stay well and work efficiently because they are able to: (1) adapt to change, (2) set appropriate boundaries, (3) develop relationships through open communication, (4) promote responsibility, and (5) express confidence in themselves and their children (Cutler & Radford, 1999). In addition, they are optimistic about their future.

Health and well-being in these families is an interactive process associated with positive relationships and outcomes. In families, being healthy and well involves ethical accountability, such as promoting good relationships and balancing the give-and-take among members (Boszormenyi-Nagy & Ulrich, 1981). In regard to health and wellness, one cannot assume that healthy individuals necessarily come from continuously healthy and well-functioning families. In fact, highly resilient individuals who successfully overcome adversities do well in life (Walsh, 1995). However, being in a healthy family environment is an advantage for learning to build and maintain productive relationships.

Healthy, well-functioning families have a number of characteristics in common. For example, families that are most successful, happy, and strong are balanced. They seem to know what issues to address and how to problem solve these issues. Furthermore, they do not operate from either an extreme cognitive or emotional framework. They exert the right amount of energy in dealing with matters in the present, and they make realistic plans. Overall, in families with a sense of well-being, multiple forces and factors interact in complex but positive ways.

THE MARITAL UNIT

T HE MOST VITAL factor underlying a well-functioning family is the strength of the marital unit (Beavers, 1985). A healthy marriage is complex and multidimensional. It is intimate, flexible, and synergistic (Olson & Olson, 2000). In such relationships, partners adapt to each other and promote individual growth. Most successful marriages formed healthy relationships with their partner prior to becoming married. Couples who get along tend to work at keeping the marriage exciting and open and bringing those qualities to the family. They are able to be in touch with and express a wide array of emotions, communicate clearly, and are equalitarian and mutually supportive. Stabb (2005) suggests that "individuals who are successful in their intimate partnerships are willing to make sacrifices and report satisfaction about sacrificing itself" (p. 440).

CHARACTERISTICS OF HEALTHY FAMILIES

M ANY OF THE characteristics that distinguish healthy couples from dysfunctional ones also separate well-functioning families from those that function less well (McCoy, 1996). According to research (Krysan, Moore, & Zill, 1990; Stinnett & DeFrain, 1985), healthy and well-functioning families include the following characteristics:

* A commitment to the family and its individuals
* An appreciation for each other
* A willingness to spend time together
* Effective communication patterns
* A high degree of religious/spiritual orientation
* An ability to deal with crisis in a positive manner
* Encouragement of individuals
* Clear roles

Each of these characteristics will be addressed here.

COMMITMENT

AT THE CORE of healthy and well-functioning families is the idea of commitment. In strong families, members are devoted not only to the welfare of the family but also to the growth of each of the members. A commitment to the family is the basis for family members giving their time and energy to family-related activities.

Commitment involves staying loyal to the family and its members through both good and adverse life events. It is based on both emotion and intention. Couples and individuals who have not thought through their commitment to one another, or who are ambivalent about how committed they feel toward each other, have difficulty staying in a marriage and working together. The consequence of a lack of commitment can often result in infidelity (Pittman, 1990).

APPRECIATION

THE COMMITMENT THAT family members have toward one another is strengthened when they verbally or physically express their appreciation. In healthy and well-functioning families, "the marital partners tend to build the self-esteem of their mates by mutual love, respect, [and] compliments" (Thomas, 1992, p. 64). Other family members do likewise with each other. They avoid fights that take the form of personal attacks or violence.

WILLINGNESS TO SPEND TIME TOGETHER

HEALTHY FAMILIES SPEND both quantitative and qualitative time together. "The time they spend together needs to be good time; no one enjoys hours of bickering, arguing, pouting, or bullying. Time also needs to be sufficient; quality interaction isn't likely to develop in a few minutes together" (Stinnett & DeFrain, 1985, pp. 83–84).

Events that encompass both qualitative and quantitative time abound. They include family picnics, overnight campouts, vacations, and special nights out that involve entertainment, such as a play, ball game, or concert. They also encompass rituals and traditions such as celebrating birthdays and anniversaries, family interactions at mealtimes, and observing rites of passage together, such as graduations, weddings, and funerals. The idea behind spending time together is sharing thoughts, feelings, and identities. In the process, family members come to think of themselves as a cohesive unit instead of just a random group of individuals.

EFFECTIVE COMMUNICATION PATTERNS

COMMUNICATION IS CONCERNED with the delivery and reception of verbal and nonverbal information between family members. It includes skills in exchanging patterns of information within the family system (Brock & Barnard, 2008). When families are healthy and well-functioning, members attend to the messages from one another and pick up on subtle as well as obvious points. Within these families there is support, understanding, and empathy. There is no competition for "air time" or silence. Messages are sent and received in a sensitive and caring manner.

In the best of circumstances, there is frequent communication within families that includes seeking opportunities for sharing with each other. The messages between family members are clear and congruent. In addition, healthy families deal with a wide range of topics and are open to talking rather than remaining silent. When there is conflict these families seek to work out their differences through discussion. Family members seek to problem solve and are more likely than not to communicate in a positive tone.

Religious/Spiritual Orientation

A religious/spiritual orientation to life is a characteristic of "the vast majority of the world's families" (Prest & Keller, 1993, p. 137). Involvement in the religious/spiritual dimension of life also correlates with an overall sense of marital and family health and well-being. Spiritual beliefs and practices help families cope and be resilient, as well as find meaning and moral principles by which to live (Walsh & Pryce, 2003). According to research, religion and spirituality have traditionally played an important part in the lives of some groups more than others. For example, collective faith has been the cornerstone by which African Americans were supported and sustained from the "oppression of slavery" to the "civil rights movement" (Hampson, Beavers, & Hulgus, 1990, p. 308).

Regardless of the cultural group, individual family members in most families are frequently involved in life matters that can best be described as religious/spiritual (Campbell & Moyers, 1988). In addition, members of families often deal as a group with religious/spiritual questions during certain events such as deaths, births, and marriages. Couples who share a common faith or orientation toward religious matters and who are intrinsically motivated in their religious/spiritual orientation report more satisfaction in their relationships than those who are divided on these issues.

Ability to Deal With Crises in a Positive Manner

A number of different types of crises affect families over their lifespan. The most common type of crisis is an expected event that is predictable and actually occurs, for example, leaving one's family of origin to make a life for oneself, finding employment, or getting married. In these situations the general nature of the event is known but the specifics are always unique; hence, the crisis. Families that function well in these times use such coping strategies as negotiating, seeking advice from those who are more experienced, rehearsing, using humor, and expressing emotions to deal with such transitions (Goodman, Schlossberg, & Anderson, 2007).

There are also nonevents that are passive in the sense that they do not happen as envisioned or expected. Examples of a nonevent might be the failure of a couple to have children or to reach their financial goals in life. In such circumstances, families are thrown into a crisis that may or may not be recognized by others. Healthy families deal with these situations by openly expressing their emotions and supporting one another.

ENCOURAGEMENT OF INDIVIDUALS

BECAUSE FAMILIES WORK as systems, they are only as strong as their weakest members. Therefore, it behooves families to encourage the development of talents and abilities within their individual members. Such a process is generally done systemically in healthy families and is carried out over the family life cycle (Carter & McGoldrick, 1999).

Encouragement is especially important at certain times in the life cycle. Among the most crucial times encouragement is needed are with:

- School-aged children as they engage in the educational process
- Adolescents as they cope with physical changes and are influenced by their peer groups
- Young adults as they move from their parents' houses into their own psychological and physical spaces filled with dreams and possibilities. (Lambie & Daniels-Mohring, 1993)

CLEAR ROLES

ROLES ARE PRESCRIBED and repetitive behaviors involving a set of reciprocal activities with other family members. Roles in healthy and well-functioning families are clear, appropriate, suitably allocated, mutually agreed on, integrated, and enacted (Minuchin, 1974). Some roles are necessary, such as the provision of material resources. Others are unique and/or unnecessary, such as the acquiring of coins for a coin collection.

The exact roles within families are determined by such factors as age, culture, and tradition. Healthy families strive to make roles as interchangeable and flexible as possible.

CONCLUSION

THERE IS NO one factor alone that separates healthy and well-functioning families from others. Instead, there are combinations of qualities that combine to help families function in an optimal way. The marital unit is the basis for healthy functioning. If it is strong, then the couple along with the family should operate well. In addition, eight other factors have been identified as crucial in the health and well-being of families. These factors range from commitment, which is probably the most important, to appreciation, communication, encouragement, and clear roles. If a family is lacking in one or more of these qualities, it will not do as well as those families possessing all of these qualities.

As can be seen, health in a family is based on positive qualities and not on those that are negative or absent. Thus, while it may be helpful to give a critical evaluation of another family member from time to time, such a process on a regular basis may well lead to anger, feelings of rejection, or avoidance.

Therefore, accentuating and building on strengths and factors within a family's control appears to be the best way to create and maintain health. Fortunately, it is a process most family members can learn and do.

REFERENCES

Beavers, W. R. (1985). *Successful marriage*. New York: W. W. Norton.

Boszormenyi-Nagy, I., & Ulrich, D. N. (1981). Contextual family therapy. In A. S. Gurman & D. P. Kniskern (Eds.), *Handbook of family therapy* (pp. 159–186). New York: Brunner/Mazel.

Brock, G. W., & Barnard, C. P. (2008). *Procedures in marriage and family therapy* (4th ed.). Boston: Allyn & Bacon.

Campbell, J., & Moyers, B. (1988). *The power of myth*. New York: Doubleday.

Carter, B., & McGoldrick, M. (1999). *The expanded family life cycle* (3rd ed.). Boston: Allyn & Bacon.

Cutler, H. A., & Radford, A. (1999). Adult children of alcoholics: Adjustment to a college environment. *The Family Journal: Counseling and Therapy for Couples and Families, 7,* 148–153.

Goodman, J. E., Schlossberg, N. K., & Anderson, M. L. (2007). *Counseling adults in transition: Linking practice with theory*. New York: Springer Publishing.

Hampson, R. B., Beavers, W. R., & Hulgus, Y. (1990). Cross-ethnic family differences: Interactional assessment of white, black, and Mexican-American families. *Journal of Marital and Family Therapy, 16*, 307–319.

Krysan, M., Moore, K. A., & Zill, N. (1990). *Identifying successful families: An overview of constructs and selected measures*. Washington, DC: Child Trends.

Lambie, R., & Daniels-Mohring, D. (1993). *Family systems within educational contexts*. Denver, CO: Love.

McCoy, C. W. (1996). Reexamining models of healthy families. *Contemporary Family Therapy, 18*, 243–256.

Minuchin, S. (1974). *Families and family therapy*. Cambridge, MA: Harvard University Press.

Olson, D. H., & Olson, A. (2000). *Empowering couples: Building on your strengths*. Minneapolis: Life Innovations.

Pittman, F. (1990). *Private lies: Infidelity and betrayal of intimacy*. New York: W. W. Norton.

Prest, L. A., & Keller, J. F. (1993). Spirituality and family therapy: Spiritual beliefs, myths, and metaphors. *Journal of Marital and Family Therapy, 19*, 137–148.

Stabb, S. D. (2005). What the research tells us. In M. Harway (Ed.), *Handbook of couples therapy* (pp. 431–456). New York: Wiley.

Stinnett, N., & DeFrain, J. (1985). *Secrets of strong families*. Boston: Little, Brown.

Thomas, M. B. (1992). *An introduction to marital and family therapy: Counseling toward healthier family systems across the life span*. Upper Saddle River, NJ: Merrill/Prentice-Hall.

Walsh, F. (1995). From family damage to family challenge. In R. H. Mikesell, D. D. Lusterman, & S. H. McDaniel (Eds.), *Integrating family therapy* (pp. 587–606). Washington, DC: American Psychological Association.

Walsh, F., & Pryce, J. (2003). The spiritual dimension of family life. In F. Walsh (Ed.), *Normal family processes: Growing diversity and complexity* (3rd ed., pp. 337–372). New York: Guilford Press.

57

Theory and Practice of Counseling Families

JESSICA E. LAMBERT AND ROBERT A. WILLIAMS

THIS CHAPTER PROVIDES practitioners with a basic outline of considerations and techniques for conducting family therapy. This modality is not *individual therapy with a witness,* wherein the therapist is central and interacting with one family member at a time. Instead, family therapy is an interactive, active, and provocative experience for both clinician and family members.

Several schools of family therapy (e.g., structural, strategic, intergenerational) have evolved since the inception of family treatment in the 1950s, and a number of manual-based family treatments are available to clinicians (Henggeler, Schoenwald, Borduin, Rowland, & Cunningham, 1998; Liddle et al., 2001; Sexton & Alexander, 2005; Szapocznik & Williams, 2000). Although these approaches vary somewhat in how problems are conceptualized and treated, there are common elements in both the theoretical underpinnings and the intervention strategies. In the following chapter we first outline reasons for and against using a family modality, followed by basic principles underlying family therapy. Next we discuss how to get started in family therapy and highlight core intervention strategies that are common across most contemporary approaches.

REASONS FOR AND AGAINST FAMILY THERAPY

FAMILY THERAPY IS the appropriate choice of treatment for a number of presenting problems, including conflict among family members (Gottman, Driver, & Tabares, 2002); difficulties associated with divorce (Lebow & Rekart, 2006); remarriage of parents (Bray, 2001, 2005); adjustment to illness or death of a family member (McDaniel, Hepworth, & Doherty, 1992); and psychological (e.g., depression, anxiety; Diamond, Siqueland & Diamond, 2003) and behavioral problems (e.g., substance abuse, delinquency; Henggeler et al., 1998; Liddle, 2002; Sexton & Alexander, 2005; Szapocznik, Hervis, & Schwartz, 2003) of children and adolescents. Moreover, family therapy is appropriate for multiple ethnicities, gay and straight couples, persons with disabilities, and a range of diverse groups (Goldenberg & Goldenberg, 2001).

There are certain situations when family therapy may be inappropriate, or when other interventions (e.g., pharmacotherapy, individual therapy) are recommended before or in conjunction with family treatment. These include situations where psychopathology in one family member significantly interferes with the process of therapy; the risks of family therapy outweigh the advantages (e.g., risk of violence in the home); the family, as a whole, denies having problems; or when cultural or religious traditions are preferred over therapy (Glick, Clarkin, & Kessler, 1987).

BASIC PRINCIPLES

A DISTINGUISHING FEATURE of family therapy is the assumption that many presenting issues are associated with (though not necessarily caused by) difficulties in family functioning and, therefore, can often be most effectively addressed by working with or considering the family as a whole. Key underlying principles are outlined below.

SYSTEMS PERSPECTIVE

ACROSS MODELS, SYSTEMS theories assume that the family is a social system composed of interdependent individuals who can be best understood in relation to one another (P. Minuchin, 1985; S. Minuchin, 1974). Behavior within the family system is seen as reciprocally influenced; meaning, each member influences the family and the family influences each member (P. Minuchin, 1985). As such, a change in one member will generally produce a change in the system (Szapocznik & Kurtines, 1989). Therefore, family therapists carefully select treatment targets that will have a ripple effect on other family interactions.

STABILITY AND CHANGE

STABILITY AND CHANGE are inherent in family systems (P. Minuchin, 1985). All families strive to maintain stability, but problem families will sacrifice the well-being of individual family members to ensure stability. Change is the process of challenging interactions that maintain stability.

PATTERNS OF INTERACTION

OVER TIME, FAMILIES develop stable, repeating patterns of interaction, or ways of behaving toward one another, that help to negotiate the daily tasks of life, accomplish individual and collective goals, and meet the physical and emotional needs of the members (S. Minuchin, 1974). Interactions are governed by rules that are often unstated. These rules delineate acceptable and unacceptable behavior (e.g., "Don't express anger") and help to define family roles, or what is expected of each member (Minuchin & Fishman, 1981). Patterns of interaction have powerful implications for family functioning and for the functioning of each individual; thus changing maladaptive interactions is generally the focus of treatment (S. Minuchin, 1974).

FAMILY STORIES

CLINICIANS ARE WELL trained to look for the message within messages communicated to them in individual therapy. In family therapy, there is often a single family story (e.g., "We all agree that we just are not getting along"). Also, there are individual stories that build upon the family story ("My parents will not give me freedom"; "Our daughter is being distant and argumentative"). Family therapists must examine the message within these messages. In the parenthetical examples, one could hypothesize that the family is not getting along because they are having conflicts about what is the appropriate way to allow the daughter to move into womanhood. Madanes and Haley (1977) argue that there are two parts to a message: the content (what is said), and process (how it is said and the meaning of what was said). The therapist's job is to tentatively highlight what seems to be the underlying meaning of the content.

FAMILY FUNCTIONING

FAMILIES ARE IN a continuous process of change as they adjust to everyday life challenges and evolve through various developmental stages (e.g., birth of a child) (Minuchin & Fishman, 1981; Goldenberg & Goldenberg, 2001). A healthy family is able to negotiate life transitions and adapt stress such that the health and well-being of its individual members is supported. Although specific behaviors will vary by culture, in general, adaptive family functioning involves family roles that are developmentally appropriate (e.g., parent[s] in leadership and caregiver role); clear boundaries between the members (not enmeshed or disengaged); effective communication; and flexible, effective problem-solving and conflict-resolution strategies (Glick et al., 1987).

PROBLEMS AND SYMPTOMS

THE INFLUENCE OF intrapsychic, biological, and historical factors on the development of problems and symptoms is acknowledged by family therapists (Goldenberg & Goldenberg, 2007); however, the focus is generally directed toward recognizing and changing the ongoing processes or interactions that contribute to or maintain problems (Constantine, 1986). Presenting problems and symptoms may (1) result from mishandled solutions to everyday stresses and developmental transitions (Fisch, Weakland, & Segal, 1982; Waltzawick, Weakland, & Fisch, 1974); (2) be rooted in maladaptive patterns of interaction (S. Minuchin, 1974); (3) serve a function for the family system (Haley, 1963; Satir, 1967); or (4) relate to dysfunctional relational patterns passed down through generations in a family (Bowen, 1978).

THERAPEUTIC PARADOX

CLINICIANS ARE OFTEN baffled about why families ask for help, but "resist," especially when everyone agrees that there is a problem. This is sometimes referred to as a therapeutic paradox. Families enter into therapy with the intention to change, but resist change as a result of the need to keep the family stable. This relates to a definition of an unhealthy family, which is one that attempts to keep the family stable while sacrificing the well-being of an individual member.

GETTING STARTED

THE INITIAL PHASE of treatment involves several steps that may take more than one session, depending on the complexity of the problem and the willingness of members to participate in treatment (Glick et al., 1987; Minuchin, Nichols, & Lee, 2007). These include (1) forming a therapeutic alliance, (2) assessing the presenting problem and the interactions that maintain the problem, (3) reframing the problem, and (4) setting goals and establishing a therapeutic contract.

Therapeutic Alliance

As in individual therapy, establishing a strong therapeutic alliance is essential; however, the presence of multiple clients who are in conflict with one another or disagree over the need for treatment complicates this process (Friedlander, Escudero, & Heatherington, 2006). Therapists can form and maintain an alliance by (1) establishing rapport with each family member, (2) attending to and validating each person's experience, (3) making an effort to engage all family members in the process of therapy, and (4) helping members to develop and work toward mutually agreed upon, meaningful treatment goals (Diamond, Liddle, Hogue, & Dakof, 1999; Friedlander et al., 2006). The overarching aim is to join with the family, as a temporary member, and guide them in the process of change (Minuchin & Fishman, 1981; Szapocznik et al., 2003).

Assessment

The objective of the initial assessment is to gather sufficient information to begin formulating a case conceptualization and treatment plan. This involves assessing the nature of the problem that brought the family into treatment and assessing the patterns of interaction that maintain the problem. Information is obtained by eliciting *content* about the presenting issue and by observing the family's *process* of interacting with one another. Regarding specific content, the following questions are answered (Glick et al., 1987; Taibbi, 2007):

- What is the problem that brought the family into treatment (from each person's perspective)?
- What brings them into treatment now? Was there a recent crisis?
- What have they tried to solve the problem (what has worked, what has not)?
- What are each member's goals and expectations for therapy?

The following domains of functioning are assessed, based on the content information provided by the family and by observing the family's interaction processes (Glick et al., 1987):

- Family Roles
  - What roles do members play in the family? Are these adaptive?
  - Who is being blamed for the problem? Who is the identified patient?
  - Are family members siding with one another?

- Boundaries

  - What is the degree of emotional closeness among family members? Do they appear overly involved with one another (i.e., enmeshed) or distant (i.e., disengaged)?

- Communication

  - Is communication clear and direct? Do family members listen to one another?
  - Do family members express a range of feelings, or predominantly one?

- Problem-Solving, Conflict Resolution Skills

  - How effective and flexible are the family's problem-solving and conflict resolution skills?

Observing how family members respond to one another, both verbally and nonverbally, provides a wealth of assessment data that may not be evident in the self-report of members. However, family interaction patterns are complex, and problematic interactions may not be clear initially. To further assess these dynamics, the therapist can ask family members to discuss the problem among themselves during the first session (Haley, 1976). It is essential that therapists monitor the interaction closely. It is fine to allow some dysfunctional behavior to occur for the sake of assessment; however, allowing the dysfunctional behavior to continue too long is counterproductive, and verbal attacks or abusive behavior should be interrupted right away (Glick et al., 1987; Robbins, Turner, Alexander, & Perez, 2003; Taibbi, 2007). Notably, the assessment process is ongoing throughout treatment as the therapist continues to observe family interaction patterns and responses to interventions (Pinsof, 1995).

REFRAMING THE PROBLEM

FAMILIES OFTEN PRESENT to treatment when one member is symptomatic (e.g., daughter is depressed; son is using drugs) and typically view this individual, referred to as the identified patient, as the source of the family's difficulties (Minuchin & Fishman, 1981). As such, the task of the therapist is help family members gain awareness of the relational context of problems and to reframe the problem in a way that shifts blame away from any one member. Reframing the problem in the initial session instills hope by giving new meaning to the situation and opening the possibility for change (Sexton & Alexander, 2005). Reframes should have some degree of truth to them. For example, families that are in conflict, but show up for therapy are praised for their effort and investment in improving the family. Family members that are silent can be told that the therapist wants to honor his or her desire to be independent. When family conflict erupts, the therapist can label the experience as "passion" and as "everyone having a very strong interest in getting his or her opinion out there."

SETTING GOALS AND CONTRACTING FOR FUTURE SESSIONS

THE NEXT STEP is to collaborate with family members in establishing goals for treatment and contracting for future sessions. When conceptualizing goals, the therapist considers the issues as directly presented by the family, as well as the problematic interactions he or she has observed. It is recommended that therapists help families to articulate goals that are manageable, concrete, and specific (Hanna, 2006). Ideally, goals will be meaningful and beneficial to each of the members. Establishing a contract involves outlining the prospective course of therapy; that is, who will attend sessions, at what frequency, and the expected duration of treatment.

SUBSEQUENT SESSIONS: CORE INTERVENTIONS

SPECIFIC INTERVENTIONS IMPLEMENTED during the course of family therapy will vary according to the presenting problem, goals for treatment, and the theoretical orientation of the therapist. In general, interventions are aimed at changing the family's interaction patterns and challenging their joint family story (Minuchin & Fishman, 1981). This may involve reframing what is said, interrupting maladaptive interactions, providing the opportunity to practice more adaptive ways of interacting in session, teaching family members more effective communication and problem-solving skills, and helping family members to develop healthy boundaries (Glick et al., 1987; Hanna, 2006). Core techniques are described below.

FOCUSING

THERAPISTS MAY INITIALLY be overwhelmed by the vast amount of information that is presented by families, as well as the complexity of family interaction patterns (Minuchin & Fishman, 1981). To develop a meaningful focus for treatment, Hanna (2006) suggests that therapists look for recurring themes in the content and process, avoid shifting too quickly from topic to topic, and ask clients for permission to focus on a specific area. We recommend that therapists target one or two patterns that can have a ripple effect on other family interaction patterns. However, it is important that therapists not become so narrowly focused that they miss relevant information (Minuchin & Fishman, 1981).

BLOCKING DYSFUNCTIONAL PATTERNS

ONE OF THE most difficult challenges is interrupting family members who seem to have very important stories to tell. When should you interrupt? Why should you interrupt? Families enter therapy doing more of the same dysfunctional patterns, thus it is the therapist's ethical responsibility to disrupt these patterns. Blocking is interrupting. It is also *creating space* for other family members (Williams, 2005). Therapists can respectfully interrupt patterns by asking listeners *how they are feeling now, or what they are thinking now, or what would they like to say at this moment in response to all that they heard.*

ENACTMENTS: FACILITATING DIRECT COMMUNICATION

EXPERIENCE BEFORE EXPLANATION is a critical aspect of effective family therapy (Taibbi, 2007). An enactment is an in-session experience that (1) requires interactions between family members, (2) allows the therapist to observe how family members typically behave toward one another, (3) affords the opportunity to assess the affective and behavioral consequences of the interactions, and (4) sets the stage for changing problematic interactions. Enactments are effective not only in altering maladaptive patterned behaviors, but also in providing family members with a relational experience that may "effect deeper attitudinal, attributional and attachment shifts" (Butler & Gardner, 2003, p. 312). A typical example involves asking the family to discuss a problem in session, while the therapist facilitates (to varying degrees) communication between the members. The enactment can be followed by a discussion of the process to help members develop insight into problematic family dynamics and to clarify specific strategies for more effective interactions (Nichols & Fellenberg, 2000).

Butler and Gardner (2003) identified five different levels of enactments. In *Shielded enactments,* the therapist is highly centralized such that all communication goes through her. The therapist clarifies content, based on her understanding of what was said, and models effective communication. This is best used with highly volatile, abusive, and verbally aggressive situations. However, Taibbi (2007) warns clinicians to be careful to not overcontrol the session by excessively using shielded enactments. Often therapists overuse this stage of enactment to protect themselves from a disorganized and out-of-control session. *Buffered enactments* also have a highly centralized therapist. However, the therapist actively attempts to reframe and relabel statements made by family members. This stage is best used when caring and closeness in the family are moderate to strong, but family members' ability to express this care is problematic. *Face-to-Face, Talk-Turn enactments* have therapists that act as coaches. Communication is direct between family members, but the therapist gives family members specific instructions on what to say and how to say it. In *Episode enactments* the therapist is more of a facilitator, only moderately centralized in interactions. Communication between family members is direct, and is allowed to last longer because the communication is relatively successful. However, the therapist steps in on occasion to clarify, coach, reframe, and facilitate stronger communication. *Autonomous relationship enactment* is the most desired stage such that the therapist is highly decentralized and communication between family members is direct; that is, the therapist allows natural conversations to occur, intervening only when help is needed.

Enactments can be very effective with African Americans, White Americans, Latinos, and highly acculturated Asians, Asian Americans, and Pacific Islanders. However, in traditional Asian and Pacific Islander cultures, parents may view the directness of the interaction between parents and children to be a challenge to the parents' authority and status in the family. Therefore, a more centralized therapist role may be preferable when working with traditional Asian and Pacific Islander parents.

HIGHLIGHTING

MINUCHIN AND FISHMAN (1981) recommend that the therapist highlight important aspects of what a family member said in order to provide some focus for the session. In some instances, family members will talk a lot, offering a great deal of content. For example, they will tell the details of an argument with respect to who said what to whom. The therapist's task is to listen for and name the underlying emotional message. Was someone feeling hurt, sad, angry, exasperated, alienated, betrayed, and so forth? The therapist might say, "That sounds painful. I wonder if your mother can respond to the pain that you feel."

DIRECTIVES/HOMEWORK

DIRECTIVES OR HOMEWORK are opportunities for family members to try successful interactions at home, away from therapy. Directives must be interaction-focused, collaborative, clear, simple, and doable

(Haley, 1976). Ideally, the therapist will have had an in-session enactment that was a good start toward improved family interaction. Based on this relative success, the therapist may ask the family to try this interaction at home. If agreed, then the therapist works with the family to identify exactly what their individual roles will be in this directive. One example is a short 5- to 10-minute family meeting in which everyone simply makes a compliment of all family members present, without saying "but." Another example is that family members will say something positive to others without highlighting it. In the next session, the therapist asks family members if they noticed others' efforts. It is recommended that therapists always follow up on directives by asking how the family organized itself to do the directive or to explore why the directive did not work. In either case, the therapist needs to be curious about how the family handled the directive.

CONCLUSION

THIS CHAPTER PROVIDED a basic overview of considerations and techniques for conducting family therapy. The interventions presented here are by no means exhaustive. Family therapists have articulated a multitude of techniques to address specific clinical issues like engaging reluctant clients (Liddle, 2002), resolving conflict between family members (Hanna, 2006), and negotiating impasses in treatment (Taibbi, 2007). A recommended reading list is provided. Family therapy is a challenging endeavor that requires tremendous creativity and flexibility on the part of the clinician. The more sessions that clinicians conduct, the more effective they will be. However, we also encourage clinicians to be comfortable with making mistakes and being imperfect in the conduct of family therapy.

ADDITIONAL RECOMMENDED READING

Boyd-Franklin, N. (2003). *Black families in therapy: Understanding the African American experience* (2nd ed.). New York: Guilford Press.

Everett, C. A., & Everett, S. V. (1999). *Family therapy for ADHD*. New York: Guilford Press.

Gil, E. (1994). *Play in family therapy*. New York: Guilford Press.

Kilpatrick, A. C., & Holland, T. P. (2006). *Working with families: An integrative model based on need* (4th ed.). Needham Heights, MA: Allyn & Bacon.

Lee, E. (2000). *Working with Asian Americans*. New York: Guilford Press.

McGoldrick, M., Giordano, J., & Garci-Preto, N. (2005). *Ethnicity and family therapy* (3rd ed.). New York: Guilford Press.

Napier, A. Y., & Whitaker, C. (1978). *The family crucible: The intense experience of family therapy*. New York: Harper.

REFERENCES

Bowen, M. (1978). *Family therapy in clinical practice.* New York: Aronson.

Bray, J. H. (2001). Therapy with stepfamilies: A developmental systems approach. In D. D. Lusterman, S. H. McDaniel, & C. Philpot (Eds.), *Integrating family therapy: A casebook* (pp. 127–140). Washington, DC: American Psychological Association.

Bray, J. H. (2005). Family therapy with stepfamilies. In J. Lebow (Ed.), *Handbook of clinical family therapy* (pp. 497–515). New York: Wiley.

Butler, M. H., & Gardner, B. C. (2003). Adapting enactments to couple reactivity: Five developmental stages. *Journal of Marital and Family Therapy, 29,* 311–327.

Constantine, L. L. (1986). *Family paradigms: The practice of theory in family therapy.* New York: Guilford Press.

Diamond, G. M., Liddle, H. A., Hogue, A., & Dakof, G. A. (1999). Alliance building interventions with adolescents in family therapy: A process study. *Psychotherapy, 36,* 355–368.

Diamond, G. S., Siqueland, L., & Diamond, G. M. (2003). Attachment-based family therapy for depressed adolescents: Programmatic treatment development. *Clinical Child and Family Psychology Review 6,* 107–127.

Fisch, R., Weakland, J., & Segal, L. (1982). *The tactics of change: Doing therapy briefly.* San Francisco: Jossey-Bass.

Friedlander, M. L., Escudero, V., & Heatherington, L. (2006). *Therapeutic alliances with couples and families: An empirically informed guide to practice.* Washington, DC: American Psychological Association.

Glick, I. D., Clarkin, J. F., & Kessler, D. R. (1987). *Marital and family therapy* (3rd ed.). Orlando, FL: Grune & Stratton.

Goldenberg, H., & Goldenberg, I. (2001). *Counseling today's families* (4th ed.). Pacific Grove, CA: Wadsworth.

Goldenberg, H., & Goldenberg, I. (2007). *Family therapy: An overview* (7th ed.). Belmont, CA: Wadsworth.

Gottman, J. M., Driver, J., & Tabares, A. (2002). Building the sound marital house: An empirically derived couple therapy. In A. S. Gurman & N. S. Jacobson (Eds.), *Clinical handbook of couple therapy* (3rd ed., pp. 373–399). New York: Guilford Press.

Haley, J. (1963). *Techniques of family therapy.* New York: Basic Books.

Haley, J. (1976). *Problem-solving therapy.* San Francisco: Jossey-Bass.

Hanna, S. M. (2006). *The practice of family therapy: Key elements across models.* Belmont, CA: Thompson.

Henggeler, S. W., Schoenwald, S. K., Borduin, C. M., Rowland, M. D., & Cunningham, P. B. (1998). *Multisystemic treatment of antisocial behavior in children and adolescents.* New York: Guilford Press.

Lebow, J., & Rekart, K. N. (2006). Integrative family therapy for high conflict divorce with disputes over child custody and visitation. *Family Process, 46,* 79–91.

Liddle, H. A. (2002). *Multidimensional family therapy treatment (MDFT) for adolescent cannabis users.* Rockville, MD: Substance Abuse and Mental Health Services Administration.

Liddle, H. A., Dakof, G. A., Parker, K., Diamond, G. S., Barrett, K., & Tejeda, M. (2001). Multidimensional family therapy for adolescent drug abuse: Results of a randomized clinical trial. *American Journal of Drug and Alcohol Abuse, 27,* 651–688.

Madanes, C., & Haley, J. (1977). Dimensions of family therapy. *Journal of Nervous and Mental Disease, 165,* 88–98.

McDaniel, S. H., Hepworth, J., & Doherty, W. J. (1992). *Medical family therapy: A biopsychosocial approach to families with health problems.* New York: Basic Books.

Minuchin, P. (1985). Families and individual development: Provocations from the field of family therapy. *Child Development, 52,* 289–302.

Minuchin, S. (1974). *Families and family therapy.* Cambridge, MA: Harvard University Press.

Minuchin, S., & Fishman, H. C. (1981). *Family therapy techniques.* Cambridge, MA: Harvard University Press.

Minuchin, S., Nichols, M. P., & Lee, W. (2007). *Assessing families and couples: From symptom to system.* Boston: Pearson.

Nichols, M. P., & Fellenberg, S. (2000). The effective use of enactments in family therapy: A discovery-oriented process study. *Journal of Marital and Family Therapy, 26,* 143–142.

Pinsof, W. B. (1995). *Integrative problem-centered therapy.* New York: Basic Books.

Robbins, M. S., Turner, C. W., Alexander, J. F., & Perez, G. A. (2003). Alliance and dropout in family therapy for adolescents with behavior problems: Individual and systemic effects. *Journal of Family Psychology, 17,* 534–544.

Satir, V. (1967). *Conjoint family therapy: A guide to theory and technique.* Palo Alto, CA: Science and Behavior Books.

Sexton, T. L., & Alexander, J. F. (2005). Functional family therapy: A mature clinical model for working with at-risk adolescents and their families. In T. L. Sexton, G. R. Weeks, & M. S. Robbins (Eds.), *Handbook of family therapy: The science and practice of working with families and couples* (pp. 323–348). New York: Brunner-Routledge.

Szapocznik, J., Hervis, O. E., & Schwartz, S. (2003). *Brief strategic family therapy for adolescent drug abuse* (NIH Publication No. 03-4751). NIDA Therapy Manuals for Drug Addiction. Rockville, MD: National Institute on Drug Abuse.

Szapocznik, J., & Kurtines, W. M. (1989). *Breakthroughs in family therapy with drug-abusing and problem youth.* New York: Springer Publishing.

Szapocznik, J., & Williams, R. A. (2000). Brief strategic family therapy: Twenty-five years of interplay among theory, research, and practice in adolescent and behavior problems and drug abuse. *Clinical Child and Family Psychology Review, 3,* 117–134.

Taibbi, R. (2007). *Doing family therapy: Craft and creativity in clinical practice* (2nd ed.). New York: Guilford Press.

Waltzawick, P., Weakland, J. H., & Fisch, R. (1974). *Change: Principles of problem formulation and problem resolution.* New York: W. W. Norton.

Williams, R. A. (2005). A short course in family therapy: Translating research into practice. *The Family Journal: Counseling and Therapy for Couples and Families, 13,* 188–194.

58

Working With Individuals in Groups

ED JACOBS AND
CHRIS J. SCHIMMEL

O NE OF THE most difficult group leadership skills to master is the ability to work with an individual while keeping the other members engaged and involved (Jacobs, Masson, & Harvill, 2009). When leading any kind of growth, support, counseling, or therapy group, members will often bring up a concern that needs immediate and concentrated attention. Examples of this include a relationship break-up, dealing with their guilt, dealing with their medical diagnosis, or coping with their parent's drinking. It is essential for a leader to be able to concentrate on one member while simultaneously involving the rest of the group.

In this chapter, we focus on the specific skills and techniques required for working with individuals in a group setting. Our approach to group leading is an active, theory-driven, multisensory approach where the leader is actively involved in directing the personal work with an individual. Following are three examples of groups where there is a need for the leader to focus on one member:

Example 1: Fourth Session of an Alcohol Recovery Group

Leader: How was your Thanksgiving?

Don: Mine was good—we went to my grandparents and lots of family was there.

Jasmine: Mine was okay. My dad is in Iraq and it was not the same with him there.

Troy: (Voice shaking, on the verge of tears) Mine was terrible. My girlfriend broke up with me Wednesday night and I was all alone since I'd planned to be with her. I was hoping we'd get back together but she's dating this other guy now. I feel like I'm going insane.

Example 2: Second Session of a Therapy Group

Leader: Today, we're going to talk about guilt. On a 1–10 scale, how much does guilt play a role in your life—"10" being dominates your life and "1" is guilt is not an issue?

Members comment, giving various responses from "3"–"6"

Hector: (In a real depressed voice) Mine is a "10." For two years I've felt nothing but guilt. I had a car wreck two years ago where I severely injured a mother and two young children. It's awful. I can't get this out of my mind.

Example 3: Children of Divorce Group for 7th and 8th Graders

Leader: Does anyone have something they would like to talk about?

Felicia: (Crying) I do. My mom said we're going to have to move to Texas where her family lives. I have only been to Texas twice and I don't like my grandma and that's who we're going to live with. I've lived here all my life. All my friends are here! Mom says we're leaving at Christmas time and that's only two weeks from now.

There is no doubt that one member in each example needs help from the group and ideally the leader would focus on these people for 15–20 minutes. There are many different ways for the leader to proceed. Some intervention strategies are much more helpful than others. Many leaders who are not trained in working with individuals in a group will ask the member informational questions and then basically conduct individual counseling while the other members watch. This most often is not the best approach, especially if the leader is not a dynamic, creative counselor. Members get bored. We outline in this chapter how to avoid this most common mistake.

Unskilled leaders may also tend to handle this is by throwing the discussion open to members and the members begin to rescue, give advice, tell stories, or go off on tangents. This is not as helpful as what a skilled leader would do. In the remainder of this chapter we offer ideas and examples of how to effectively work with individuals while in groups.

CORE BELIEFS

1. People don't mind being led when they are led well (Jacobs et al., 2009). An active, intentional leadership model is the best approach in most growth, support, counseling, and therapy groups.
2. It is beneficial and advantageous to focus on individual members if the topic is a general one like relationships, parents, and self-worth. If the leader takes a member deeper into herself, other members will go deep within themselves especially if the leader involves the other members in the counseling.
3. Do not conduct individual counseling while the other members simply watch unless you are a highly skilled, exceptionally creative, and engaging counselor that provides an interesting exchange for the other members to watch and learn from. Even if your skills are exceptional in that regard, it is often best to involve the other members in some way.
4. It is therapeutic when members help members. Get input from the members. Often something that one member says to another is helpful to the working member and can provide the different perspective that the working member needs.
5. Do not do what the members can do. Give members the chance to ask questions and make comments. One common mistake is the leader asks all the questions when the questions being asked could easily be asked by the members.
6. Always monitor what is being said and remember to stay focused on the working member even though at times you may go to other members.

WAYS TO WORK WITH INDIVIDUALS

THERE ARE A number of techniques that group leaders who choose to focus on one member can use that will keep the other members involved. The key is to go to the members often but not have this detract from the member who is working on an issue. Too often leaders throw the discussion open to the group and members get off track and the working member is left hanging. In the initial moments of working with an individual and throughout the entire process, the effective leader thinks of ways to involve the other members. We briefly outline a number of valuable intervention strategies.

1. *Have the members ask questions* in order to gather more information. Instead of the leader asking, have the members ask. The leader can always tweak the questions if they seem off the mark.

2. *Have the members comment.* "Do any of you have a comment or reaction to what Hector has been saying?" Again, an effective leader monitors closely the reactions and comments so that they do not prohibit the work of or offend the member on which attention is being focused.

3. *Have the members share similar experiences* or ways they can relate. "Do you have similar experiences or can you relate to what is being said?"

4. *Have members vote.* Having members vote can be a simple and powerful way of engaging the members. Let's say Hector from the earlier example is talking about what a terrible person he is for causing the accident. The leader could use a voting technique.

   a. "How many of you think Hector was in a terrible accident?" All hands would go up.
   b. "How many of you think Hector is a bad person?" No hands would go up.

   The leader then asks members why they believe Hector isn't a bad person and he receives comments from members who historically seem to have good things to say. This way Hector would hear more rational comments rather than the irrational comments he's telling himself. (Note: This would be theory-driven in that the leader would be thinking rational emotive behavior therapy (REBT) and how Hector needs to tell himself something different. This is discussed later.)

5. *Have the working member do an intensive round.* Using rounds (where the working member voices something to every other member) is a powerful way to involve the members (Jacobs et al., 2009).

EXAMPLE 1

JANE HAS BEEN talking for 5 or so minutes about a relationship she's in and has told numerous stories that indicate the relationship is truly a harmful one—there is cheating, yelling, drinking, controlling, and so forth. She also has told painful stories about this relationship in previous sessions. The leader wants to help the member understand her private logic that is causing her to stay.

Leader:	Jane, I want you to look at each member one at a time and members, I want you to ask Jane why she stays with him. Start with Joe.
Joe:	(Looking at Jane) Why do you stay?
Jane:	(With obviously not much thought or insight) I don't know.
Leader:	(In a kind, supportive tone) Jane, I think you do know. Look at Cindy.
Cindy:	(Looking at Jane) Why do you stay in that?
Jane:	(Meekly) I stay because I love him.
Tom:	(Looking at Jane) Why do you put up with all that?
Jane:	(Starting to tear up) I stay because I am afraid.
Carol:	(Looking at Jane) Why do you stay? What are you afraid of?
Jane:	(Crying) I don't think anyone would want me. He says I'm trash.

Example 2

In a self-esteem group, a member (Cindy) has expressed feeling less than others because she's adopted. She's been on this theme for several minutes and the leader wants to get her to challenge her thinking. The leader decides to use a round. By doing this, the leader is not only trying to help the member but also hopes this helps other members to understand that no one is worth more than someone else.

Leader (to Cindy):	I want you to sit in front of each member and say to each person, "I'm less than you because I'm adopted." Each of you I want you to say, "No you're not—we're all equal. No one is better than anyone else."
Cindy:	(Moves and sits in front of Bobbi) I'm less than you because I'm adopted.
Bobbi:	No you're not. We're all equal. What else am I supposed to say?
Leader:	No one is better than anyone else.
Bobbi:	We're all equal. No one is better than anyone else.
Leader:	Move to the next person.
Cindy:	(To Tony) I'm less than you because I'm adopted.

Tony: Hey, you at least have parents that care about you. My parents are . . .

Leader: Tony, for now, just say "No you're not—we're all equal. No one is better than anyone else."

Tony: Oh, yeah. "No you're not—we're all equal. No one is better than anyone else."

Leader: Move to the next person. Really think about what is being said.

6. *Have members give feedback and comments.* After a member has worked on his issue for a while, the leader can involve the members by asking them to give the working member feedback. This is one of the most valuable aspects of group because it is good for the working member to hear other points of view, and it gives the leader as well as the members a chance to hear what others are thinking (Gladding, 2007). When doing this, the leader is alert to make sure what is being said has the potential to be helpful. Also, the leader makes sure the group does not veer off to another person or topic.

Example 1

Leader: (After Cindy has worked for several minutes): Any thoughts or comments for Cindy?

Bobbi: Cindy, it sure seems to me that you are miserable. You rated your life a 3. I think it would go up to a 6 if you got out of the bad relationship you are in. Maybe I'm wrong.

Leader: Anyone else have thoughts for Cindy?

Example 2

Leader: Given what Felicia has been saying, what would you like to share or say to her?

Fred: Felicia, it doesn't sound like there's any way you are going to get to stay here. Why don't we focus on the positives or possibilities?

Leader: That's a good idea.

Vicki: When I had to move 3 years ago I hated it and thought I'd never make friends. At first it was hard but now I have lots of friends. I e-mailed a lot and talked on the phone to my old friends and that helped. I also went back to my old home a couple of times during the first few months. Now this is home to me.

James: My parents don't let me do e-mail except on the weekends. Do any of you . . .

Leader: (Interrupting to redirect the group back onto Felicia) I want to stay focused on Felicia. Anyone else have something that may be helpful?

7. *Have members talk about the member.* The leader can use the *overhearing technique,* which is to have the members talk about the working member. This gives members a chance to try to express their support, frustrations, ideas, caring, and so forth for the working member. By doing it this way, many members get to share after hearing the working member work on his problem for a while. Also, the working member just listens and does not immediately react.

EXAMPLE 1

Leader: I want all of you to look at me and tell me what you are thinking or feeling about Troy's situation now that we've got a fairly good picture of what is going on. Troy, I want you to listen and see if anyone says anything that is helpful.

8. *Have members role play scenes that the working member is describing.* Often this is valuable for members playing the parts as well as the working member. Members can play out a work, family, relationship, or friend scene. The leader serves as the director and makes sure people play accurate roles.
9. *Teach the members a theory and then help them to apply it to the working member's issue.* We advocate that members be taught a theory such as REBT, transactional analysis (TA), Adlerian, or choice theory and then when a problem comes up, the leader can encourage members to use the theory (Jacobs et al., 2009). Gladding (2007) suggests that multiple theoretical models provide the richest experience for group members. Theory-driven group counseling is always more effective than when no theory is utilized (Corey, 2008).

EXAMPLE 1

Leader: Thinking back on what we covered last week about "thoughts cause feelings" and the ABC model, what do you think Hector is telling himself that is causing him more guilt? What could he tell himself? If you want, we can use the flipchart.

Karen: He's got to quit saying he's an awful person.

Leader: True enough. What does he need to tell himself?

EXAMPLE 2

Leader:	(Using TA) Which ego state do you think Ted is coming from—the Parent, the Adult, or the Child?
Fran:	He's coming from the Hurt Child. Sounds like his dad is coming from the Parent.
Leader:	Would others agree? (All members nod yes.) The key is for Ted to come from his Adult. This is true for many of you in here who said you still had major issues with one or both parents. We're going to focus on how to stay in the Adult when someone is coming from his Critical Parent. Ted, let's look further at your situation.

10. *Put working member on hold.* One skill that is useful is to periodically put the working member on "hold" to give him time to think and also to give the leader a chance to hear from others. With this technique, the leader would ask members to comment on what has been triggered for them.

EXAMPLE 1

Leader:	Cindy, let's do this. Take a couple of minutes and think about what all you've said and what we've said. While you are doing that, I'd like to hear from others. I saw many of you deep in thought. What has Cindy's work triggered for you?
Gloria:	I realize I'm a lot like Cindy. I don't look at all the bad stuff in my relationship. I'll work on my stuff when she's finished.
Bobbi:	I was thinking about how I don't think I deserve a good man, given all the crap from my past. I can say to Cindy it doesn't matter, but I'm not there yet with myself.
Leader:	We'll work on each of these concerns either today or at the next meeting. Cindy, where would you like us to pick up? What are you thinking about?

11. *Use creative props to keep everyone's attention.* One way to engage the other members when working with an individual is to use creative props (Jacobs, 1992). By using multisensory techniques when working with an individual, members stay focused and can usually relate to the prop being used. We'll give a few examples below:

EXAMPLE 1

Leader: Mary (who is crying), would you like to learn how to deal with your dad's comments when he's drunk?

Mary: (Weakly) Yes, it hurts so bad.

Leader: You need to use a shield (holds up a piece of Plexiglas). Actually, most of you need a shield since you live in a home where there's drug and alcohol abuse. When your dad comes at you, you need to block the comments with the shield. In a second I'm going to poke you on the arm while saying the mean things. (Leader does this.) Now I'm going to say the same things but I want you to use the shield. (Mary blocks the leader's pokes.)

Mary, which feels better?

Mary: Using the shield. Am I supposed to carry a shield?

Leader: No, it's symbolic of what you need to do. Let me say some more.

EXAMPLE 2

Leader: Carol, you say you can't control your anger (Leader is shaking a Coke bottle filled with Coke. Members are all watching.) Here, turn this toward yourself and open it.

Carol: (Jumps back) Heck no, I'm not opening that!

Leader: Good, you are exercising control. Would you like to learn how to do that with anger? It's like the Coke is your anger getting all shook up.

Bob: That's me. I get myself all shook up.

Jerry: Me too. How do I get control?

Leader: Let's work with Carol on her anger. I think this will be helpful to many of you.

One common mistake that leaders make is that they miss or fail to pick up on pockets of energy that are created when focusing on one member. Leaders can avoid this mistake and encourage more productive work among all group members when they effectively use their eyes. Leaders should train their group members that they will often use their eyes to scan the group for cues that they too are involved and engaged in the group. By using your eyes effectively, you can pick up on the energy of a person who may have something to add; you can help all members feel listened to and heard; you can gauge how members are reacting to what is being said; and you can connect members to each other by using your eyes to get them to look at each other. The idea is to try to keep your eyes moving so that you are constantly aware of the energy in the group (Jacobs et al., 2009).

CONCLUSION

OFTENTIMES DURING GROUP counseling, it becomes necessary to focus the work on one individual. However, involving all group members in the process is essential for productive group work. The process of including all group members takes great skill, much thought, and a lot of practice on the part of any group leader. If not well thought out and done purposefully, groups can become boring, ineffective, and difficult to lead. We hope this brief chapter gave you an overview of many skills and techniques that can be used to not only make group counseling more effective for all members, but also make groups interesting and stimulating for you, the leader.

REFERENCES

Corey, G. (2008). *The theory and practice of group counseling* (7th ed.). Pacific Grove, CA: Brooks/Cole.

Gladding, S. T. (2007). *Group work: A counseling specialty* (5th ed.). New York: Merrill.

Jacobs, E. (1992). *Creative counseling techniques: An illustrated guide*. Odessa, FL: Psychological Assessment Resources.

Jacobs, E. E., Masson, R. L., & Harvill, R. L. (2009). *Group counseling: Strategies and skills* (6th ed.). Pacific Grove, CA: Brooks/Cole.

59

Involuntary Members in a Group

Chris J. Schimmel, Ed Jacobs, and Jennifer R. Adams

MANY COUNSELORS WILL find themselves leading involuntary groups—groups with members who don't want to be there. These kinds of groups may include DUI (driving under the influence), short-term inpatient groups where members have had psychotic breaks or tried to commit suicide, long-term inpatient groups such as drug and alcohol treatment centers or adolescent treatment centers, and school groups where students are in trouble for their behavior, truancy, or failing. Anger management groups are usually involuntary as well. In each of these groups, many if not all of the members are involuntary and this certainly creates challenges for any group leader (Corey, 2008).

A good leader of involuntary groups needs to be dynamic, energetic, and engaging (Jacobs, Masson, & Harvill, 2009). She needs to be patient, flexible, and thick-skinned; that is, she needs to be prepared for negative reactions, and not take them personally. She needs to be able to cut off members when they are being negative or when they get off track. Also, the leader of a group consisting of nonvoluntary members needs to have numerous techniques for drawing out those members (Gladding, 2007).

In this chapter, we cover two kinds of situations where the leader has to deal with involuntary members; all members not wanting to be in the group, and one or more members not wanting to be there. In groups where the entire group does not want to be there, the leader must recognize that he or she has two purposes: (1) to try to cover the subject, such as anger, drinking and driving, and (2) to try to get the members to become voluntary; that is, to get the members to invest in the group experience instead of resisting learning from the experience. It is important for the leader to keep in mind that she cannot accomplish much if the members have a negative or bad attitude so the primary purpose of the first and second session is to "hook" them. When a leader attempts to hook group members, she is doing things to get them interested in what is being said; engaging them, and convincing them to understand that there is some value in what is being said and what others are saying. This approach often results in a group that began with involuntary members, then transformed into one that members can enjoy and look forward to participating.

COMMON MISTAKES

LEADERS FACED WITH involuntary members make a number of mistakes in the beginning that make leading the group much more difficult than it should be. Listed below are common mistakes that leaders make with involuntary members.

1. *Allow for a negative tone in the beginning.* Many leaders make the mistake of letting members express their negative feelings in the beginning in such a way that a negative tone is set. One member will say something and the others join in like a chorus. Often leaders make the mistake of asking members at the beginning what they expect or want and that opens the floodgates for all kinds of negative comments. The key is to try to set a positive tone and especially make sure that you don't let members begin in such a way that a negative tone is established.

2. *Put too much in the hands of the members.* In an involuntary group, the leader should not put responsibility for the group in the hands of the members. Said another way, the leader should plan the sessions and be very active. The leader needs to plan the group because members in an involuntary group will usually not have much that is positive to say during the first couple of sessions. Leaders who use a more facilitating leadership style often end up having to work very hard to get any kind of meaningful interaction to occur.

3. *Focus on content instead of process.* During the first couple of sessions, leaders of involuntary groups often mistakenly focus too much on the content (drinking, anger, poor grades) instead

of understanding that two purposes exist. The main purpose of any involuntary group is to get some, if not all, members to want to come to the group. In other words, there should be a strong emphasis on making the group interesting and engaging, so that the negativity starts to lessen. Members will not learn if they feel negative about coming to group.

4. *Engage in power struggles or come from a superior, one-up position.* Because these groups can be intimidating, beginning leaders often get in arguments or put the members down, which, in turn, sets up dynamics that are usually difficult to overcome. The key is for the leader to be very tuned in to the negative feelings of the members and to work hard to change those feelings. The leader should avoid putting members down for their negative feelings or behavior.

5. *Not informing court-mandated members that you are required to document their level of participation to probation officers or case managers.* It is important to let members know that they can choose not to participate but you, as the leader, have to verify their level of participation (Jacobs & Spadaro, 2003). When they know that a report is going to be turned in, this usually helps to get the members to participate more.

KEY STRATEGIES AND SKILLS FOR INVOLUNTARY GROUPS

USE SO-CALLED OUT *of the box techniques.* One of the best things that a leader can do with an involuntary group is to do something out of the ordinary (Jacobs, 1992). For example, in a mandatory group for teenagers who were caught using drugs at school, one leader started with:

> Leader: I know you don't want to be here so we're going to use the first ten minutes to bitch. I want you to get all your trash talking done with and put it in this trash can (puts a large trash can in the center of the group). You have ten minutes to bitch and then we're going to get down to business. All of you can talk at once and say all the negative things you are feeling about having to be here.

After 10 minutes, she dramatically put a lid on the trash can, removed the can, and firmly said, "Let's begin. I'm going to tell you how this can be valuable. I want you to fill out this short sentence-completion form." Although starting with negative energy is generally a mistake, the uniqueness of this situation did much to reduce the negative feelings about being in the group.

Another out of the box type strategy is to do something dramatic such as have someone dressed like a policeman come into the room right before the beginning of the group and fake an arrest or some other dramatic scene. This can be a good technique if the unique strategy is related to the purpose and stimulates members to talk about the desired topic.

Using bold, vivid movie or television scenes is another way to start an involuntary group. If the clip is a good one, members tend to forget that they have all these negative feelings about being in the group. The key is to find something that is engaging and relevant to the purpose of the group.

Use written exercises. One of the best ways to engage the members is to give them a brief writing task, such as to make a list or to complete some incomplete sentences. Members will usually make a list or finish some sentences if the list or sentences are interesting. When members are asked to read what they wrote, most will pay attention because they are curious to hear what others said, and if other members had a similar answer to their answers. For sentence completions, there only needs to be two to five sentences, such as:

1. The thing I dislike about school is _____.
2. One thing I'd change about school is _____.
3. I get angry when _____.
4. When I get angry, I _____.

Using lists can also be effective. For example, having members list five things that they think make them angry or list three things they like and three things they do not like about school can open up productive work.

Use creative techniques. One of the best ways to engage involuntary members is to use something that is creative. For anger groups, the leader could bring different lengths of thick string (e.g., 1/2 inch to 12 inches). The leader could then ask the members to pick the string that represents the length of their anger fuse. Usually most negative members will talk about their fuses.

For alcohol groups, using a large (3-foot-tall plastic bottle) beer bottle gets members' attention and the leader can show many ways where alcohol is a big problem. Members can relate to the size. The leader can swing the bottle, knocking things around or put the bottle between her and a member and show how alcohol prevents closeness. These demonstrations show the problems that come from having a drinking problem.

Use rounds. Rounds are exercises where you ask each member to say something such as a word or phrase or a number on a 1–10 scale (Jacobs et al., 2009). The value of rounds with involuntary members is that the leader is asking members to briefly say something as opposed to divulging a lot; however, even if members still initially want to maintain their silence, the leader should not perceive this as a problem. Most members will say something, and from this, the leader can have a better sense as to whether certain members will begin to become more engaged in sharing. For example:

Leader: In a word or phrase, when you think of school, what comes to mind? Or

Leader: I want each of you to say how you see yourself in regard to alcohol by selecting one of the following: "I have a serious problem with alcohol," "I may have a problem," or "I don't have a problem."

Use movement exercises. Since one major problem with involuntary members is getting them energized, the use of movement exercises can be very helpful in getting members engaged. By movement exercises, we mean any activity where the members have to move. It could mean moving along a continuum such as:

not angry at all ──────────→ very angry
math is easy──────────────→ math is very hard

The leader would have members stand in the center of the room lined up behind each other and then on the count of three, members move either right or left depending on how they felt about the issue being presented. Another movement activity involves having the members stand and show how they feel about the group using their arms and positioning themselves like a sculpture. For example:

Leader: I want you all to stand in a circle and in a minute I'm going to ask you to sculpt how you feel about the group. That is, if you hate the group and feel closed off, you could turn away from the circle with your arms folded; if you have some interest, you may put one foot forward and stand sort of open; if you don't like it, you can put your hands over your ears. Sculpt how you feel. Do you understand what I mean? (All nod.) Okay, on the count of three, sculpt how you feel.

These are just two examples of movement exercises. There are many more and certainly you can make up your own. Movement activities have a better chance of engaging involuntary members than almost any other kind of exercise (Jacobs et al., 2009).

Use inner circle, outer circle. As the involuntary group develops and the leader feels that some of the members are interested in talking, one technique that can be utilized is to have an inner circle and outer circle. The leader can say something like "For those of you wanting to discuss this topic, scoot your chairs to the middle and those of you who don't can sit quietly out of the circle." This serves a couple of purposes; mainly, members who want to gain from the group have the opportunity to do so, and resistant members don't have a chance to disrupt the flow of the group. Many times when this technique is employed, members on the outside circle pay attention and may even ask to speak and join the group. Even if they don't join, resistant members usually pay attention and gain value from the group by now wanting to learn from the experience.

DEALING WITH ONE OR TWO INVOLUNTARY MEMBERS

GROUPS IN TREATMENT centers and crisis care centers often have some members who want to be in the group and some who don't. In these groups, it is important for the leader to pay close attention to each person's level of interest or investment in the group process. If the leader does not do this, he may be "sucked in" by the involuntary member and may spend much of the group's time trying to get the member invested. Often leaders make the mistake of focusing on the negative, involuntary member when the member is not ready or wanting to share and this causes the involuntary member to have more hostility about having to be in the group. A skilled leader focuses on those members wanting to gain from the experience, while at the same time, assessing if the involuntary member seems ready to engage in the group (Corey, 2008).

ASSESSING READINESS

1. *Pay attention to the speech pattern, voice, and body language.* Skilled leaders can usually tell from how members speak (if they speak) if they seem open to the group process. If the leader does not pay attention or scan members for nonverbal gestures, she may call on or focus on a member who has real negative energy, which in turn affects the group process. By paying careful attention to speech patterns and body language, the leader can focus on those who seem to have energy for the group.

2. *Use dyads to find out how a member is feeling about the group.* Another technique that can be used to draw out members is for the leader to put them into *dyads* (groups of two) to talk about some topic relevant to the group. The leader then pairs herself with the involuntary, negative member(s) and asks them how they are feeling about the group and how they would like to participate, if at all. By using dyads, the leader can talk with, encourage, and possibly confront the member(s) somewhat privately, yet not involve the entire group. This way the group does not experience the hostile and negative reactions that can pollute the otherwise positive energy.

3. *Have member sit outside the group.* If one member is very negative, the leader may ask that specific member to sit outside the group. The member on the outside may listen, but is not allowed to interject negative comments. The outside member is permitted to sit, read, or draw. At any time the outside member can request to be part of the group if it is agreed that his participation will not be negative. A leader would do this as a last resort and do it in a way that it is not meant to be a punishment. This technique is meant to allow the group to be productive for the engaged members.

4. *Ask members to leave if this is an option.* It is important to understand that not all people benefit from groups, especially those who are mandated to attend. Skilled leaders who make sure their groups are engaging and relevant can frequently get members interested in a mandatory group, but there will be times when a member refuses to buy into the group process. Ideally the leader has the option to ask the member to leave, but, many times, agency policy dictates that the person has to attend the group.

5. *Purposefully use rounds, written or movement exercises.* These kinds of exercises may elicit some response from the involuntary member because he can participate without having to say very much. Leaders will sometimes use these exercises and then ask the resistant member about his responses in a sensitive way so as to not put the member on the spot or cause him to feel pressured to speak.

6. *Have members ask questions of other members.* The leader can conduct an exercise that has members ask other members questions. This strategy removes the leader from putting resistant members on the spot, and instead may be less anxiety-provoking for them by allowing other members to ask the questions.

7. *Do certain feedback exercises so the person has to be involved.* There are a number of feedback exercises that may get the involuntary member interested or more involved.

One simple exercise involves having members answer questions like "Who do you trust most in the group?" and "Who do you trust least?" or "Who do you feel most comfortable with?" and "Who do you feel least comfortable with?" By having members do this, the involuntary member is involved unless she leaves the room. She may not say anything but she will be listening to whether her name is called. The leader can then ask her how she feels about what was said.

Another feedback activity that may work is to have everyone write a word or a phrase on 3 x 5 cards for each member of the group and then give each member their feedback cards to read. Most of the time, the resistant member will read them and sometimes may react. Caution should be used with this technique in that the leader should only do this when she thinks there may be a chance that the member will open up or will react in a way that may start the process of his becoming involved in the group.

CONCLUSION

WORKING WITH INVOLUNTARY members is a tremendous challenge for group leaders. The key is to use activities that are interesting and engaging and often out of the box. Keep in mind that the primary purpose of the first couple of sessions of an involuntary group is to get some or all of the members to believe that the group experience can be helpful to them. Always look for members who seem to have some positive energy and work with them initially rather than focusing on resistant members.

REFERENCES

Corey, G. (2008). *The theory and practice of group counseling* (7th ed.). Pacific Grove, CA: Brooks/Cole.

Gladding, S. T. (2007). *Group work: A counseling specialty* (5th ed.). New York: Merrill.

Jacobs, E. (1992). *Creative counseling techniques: An illustrated guide*. Odessa, FL: Psychological Assessment Resources.

Jacobs, E. E., Masson, R. L., & Harvill, R. L. (2009). *Group counseling: Strategies and skills* (6th ed.). Pacific Grove, CA: Brooks/Cole.

Jacobs, E., & Spadaro, N. (2003). *Leading groups in corrections: Skills and techniques*. Lanham, MD: American Correctional Association.

60

Challenging Childhood Behaviors

JEANNIE A. GOLDEN

DEFINITION OF CHALLENGING CHILDHOOD BEHAVIORS

PROFESSIONAL COUNSELORS WORKING with children have many challenges that pose significant difficulties in behavioral and mental health treatment. Challenging behaviors in children include those behaviors that cause injury to self and others, cause property damage, that interfere with the acquisition of skills, or those that result in isolation (Doss & Reichle, 1989; McDougal, Nastasi, & Chafouleas, 2005; Reichle, 1996). Prevalence rates for challenging behaviors have increased significantly in recent years, to 14%–20% in children who are either typical or at-risk to 13%–30% in children who have developmental disabilities (Brandenburg, Friedman, & Silver, 1990; Reichle, 1996). These behaviors, which can be exhibited as early as the preschool years, tend to worsen over time (Kazdin, 1993). This is especially relevant for boys who are likely to follow a trajectory that will lead to problems with aggression into adulthood (Reid & Patterson, 1991). However, there is empirical evidence to support that behavior therapy and behavioral parent training (BPT) are the most effective ways of reducing challenging behaviors in school-aged children (Dumas, 1989; Garrett, 1985; Kazdin, 1987; McMahon & Wells, 1989; Serketich & Dumas, 1996). Thus, professional counselors are in an excellent position to impact challenging behaviors by providing BPT.

THE INITIAL MEETING

WHEN CHILDREN ARE brought to a counselor's office with challenging behaviors, there are several issues to consider from the start:

1. Counselors must gain the trust of parents so they will be honest with the counselor about their attempts to manage the child's behavior.
2. There are ethical concerns that some parents may possibly reveal information to the counselor about parenting practices that may lead the counselor to suspect child abuse.
3. Oftentimes, parents bring children in for therapy and view the problem as residing within the child. Thus, the parents may expect the counselor to "fix" their child, not recognizing their own need to change the way in which they interact and communicate with their child.
4. There may be a difference between how parents describe their parenting techniques and how they actually interact with and parent their children.
5. It is also more helpful to observe the children's behavior in multiple natural settings rather than to have the parent or teacher describe the behaviors.
6. Functional behavior assessment (FBA), which involves observing problem behavior and the antecedents of that behavior, is an invaluable tool for gathering information concerning reducing challenging behavior (Scott, Morris, & McNeil, 1996). However, acquiring naturalistic views of children's behavior and conducting FBAs may be very difficult and time-consuming. There are several ideas suggested in this chapter that will assist in the process.

BUILDING TRUST AND CONSIDERING ETHICAL DILEMMAS

BUILDING A TRUSTING relationship with parents can decrease the risks of ethical dilemmas within the counselor–parent relationship. This can be done by clearly stating the limits to confidentiality and describing treatment philosophies and strategies. Counselors can provide statements to parents about suspected child abuse reporting laws and discuss those laws before beginning parent interviews. It is also required by counselor licensure laws that counselors disclose their philosophy of working with parents and children. For example, the counselor may want to state: "It has been my experience that some children are more difficult to parent than others and that for those difficult children, there are some parenting techniques that have been found to be more effective than others. However, identifying the best techniques for a particular child depends on careful observation of that child in the settings where the problem behaviors occur." In making such a statement, you have openly expressed your philosophy and approach so there are no hidden agendas or surprises.

The professional counselor should provide parents the opportunity to express their thoughts, feelings, and concerns regarding the reason they brought their child in for therapy. Edelbrock, Crnic, and Bohnert (1999) demonstrated that accommodating the agenda of parents, among other modifications, improved the reliability of the Diagnostic Interview Schedule for Children (DISC) with 24 parents who brought their children into a university psychology clinic. Building trust and facilitating cooperation is also accomplished by counselors modeling for the parents that they can positively influence their child's behavior in the initial session. Providing parents with strategies that are simple and effective can help immediately to change their child's behaviors.

One of the best ways to present parenting strategies is to reframe rather than criticize their parenting style. It is also important to recognize, reflect, and comment on the child's and parent's strengths. An example of reframing from my own private practice is depicted in the following scenario:

> I had a divorced mom who had two sons, one who was having severe behavior problems including noncompliance, tantrums, fighting at school and not completing schoolwork and homework, bringing that son in for therapy. I found that it was difficult to be successful with this young boy without the cooperation of his dad and had invited him in to participate in his son's therapy many times. When he finally (after repeated invitations) came into my office, he was angry about his son being in therapy and told me that he was the one who could help his son, not me or any therapist. Rather than becoming defensive and pointing out how long it took for him to participate, I simply agreed with him that he was the most important person in his son's life and thanked him for coming in to therapy and showing commitment to his son. This response disarmed him and enabled him to be more cooperative in the therapy session.

Another way is to empathize with the child's and parent's feelings without getting defensive. Another example using empathy is described as follows:

> A mom who was frustrated with her teenage daughter began yelling at me that I wasn't helping her and that her daughter's behavior was getting worse. Again, I did not get defensive and simply starting empathizing with how difficult it must be to feel that she was losing the daughter she had who had been so loving and close and assured her that adolescence is not the final chapter of her daughter's life. This gave her the support and reassurance that she needed and that was a turning point in therapy in which she started to implement suggestions that I had been giving her for some time.

OBTAINING A TRUE PICTURE OF THE BEHAVIORS OF CHILDREN'S PARENTS AND TEACHERS

THERE ARE SEVERAL ways of obtaining a "true" picture of the child's behavior and the parents' and teachers' responses.

1. Find undergraduate or graduate students from local colleges or universities who are interested in receiving volunteer experience and/or college credit by assisting you in therapy. With written parent consent, they could make home and school visits to observe the child's behavior at critical times (i.e., at mealtime, bedtime, in certain classes, on the bus). These assistants could also gather information for functional behavioral assessments, could deliver behavior rating scales to teachers, as well as provide teachers and parents with assistance in record keeping in those settings (to be discussed later).

2. As the counselor, you may find it helpful to visit the child's school yourself to observe the child in the classroom and meet with the teacher. If this approach is taken, meet with the parents separately from their child, especially during the initial interview session. Once you have established some connection with the child, then the child will be more familiar with you during your classroom observations. This should provide you with a true picture of the child's behavior in this environment. Also, the counselor must secure written permission from the parent or guardian to contact school personnel or any other professionals who have information to better serve the child. If the child's problem behavior is occurring mostly at home, you could have the parents videotape or audiotape the interaction that occurs between them and their child. If the parents are unwilling or unable to do this, the next best alternative would be to have them bring the relevant props

(i.e., homework, hairbrush, sample meal) and have them role play in your office the behaviors observed at home. Private practice offices can be equipped with a children's room that has couches, chairs, desks, toys, kitchen supplies, writing materials, and other age-appropriate things that can effectively re-create home scenarios during role playing.

When conducting the initial interviews with the parents, keep in mind that specific information regarding the child's behaviors is important but often difficult to obtain from parents and teachers. Other observers may describe some children as aggressive, manipulative, unmotivated, inattentive, noncompliant, hyperactive, impulsive, or disrespectful. These terms are meant to facilitate communication among people by summing up a lot of behaviors in a single word. However, these descriptors are vague, subjective, opinionated, and vary by meaning and definition. For example, one person might view a child as *unmotivated* because the child does not complete his or her work. Other observers may view the child as unmotivated because the child consistently performs below his or her tested potential or because the child falls asleep in class. A child may fall asleep in class because the parents allow him or her to watch TV all night. It may be a fact that the child falls asleep in class; however, the teacher perceives the student as unmotivated. A counselor can assist the parent or teacher in changing the behavior of falling asleep in class, but cannot assist them in making a child motivated for school work.

Therefore, in the initial interview, it is essential for the counselor to evaluate the specific behaviors causing problems for the child. When the parent uses a vague term to describe the child's problem behaviors, the counselor can say something such as, "What does he do or say when he is being 'disrespectful'?" "Give me a play by play of the last time you can remember when he was 'disrespectful'." "What happened first?" "Tell me what happened next." "Then what happened next?"

It is also helpful to ask questions such as who, what, when, and where. It is recommended that *why* questions not be asked. This may prompt the teacher or parent to give an opinion about the child. Thus, you may not be getting the facts you need. Questions such as: *When does he usually yell, scream, and curse?, Who is there when this happens?, What is happening or what has been said just before this occurs?* and *What do people usually do or say in response?* can be very helpful in obtaining a more precise, detailed description of the behavior. There are a variety of tools for conducting a good behavioral interview. (See Table 60.1 for a format that I developed in my private practice for interviewing parents and teachers who have children that exhibit problematic or challenging behaviors.)

TABLE 60.1 Behavioral Assessment Interview

Behavioral Assessment Interview
Dr. Jeannie Golden
East Carolina University

Description of Individual	Background of Problem	Past Interventions	Perceived Needs
Typical "Bad" Day	Typical "Good" Day	Weekday Schedule and Expectations	Weekend Schedule and Expectations
Appropriate Behaviors to Exhibit		Task-Oriented	Behaviors to Reinforce
Behaviors to Extinguish (Minor)	Behaviors to Time Out (Major)	Short-Term Reinforcers (Social, Edible, Token, Back-Up)	
Long-Range Reinforcers (Material, Activity, Status)		Delivery of Reinforcers (Time/Place/ Schedule, Person Responsible)	
Available Consequences (Immediate-Extinguish, Loss of Tokens, Time Out, Delayed Loss of Privileges, Retribution, Lower Status)		Delivery of Consequences (Time/Place/Schedule)	
Method of Recording Behavior (Time/Place/Schedule, From Person Responsible)		Levels of Behavior (Baseline Level, Entry Criterion Level, Entry/Intermediate/Goal Criterion Level)	

CONDUCTING A FUNCTIONAL BEHAVIORAL ASSESSMENT (FBA)

THE BEST WAY to determine what causes and maintains problem behaviors is to identify the environmental antecedents and consequences. Assuming that you have identified one of the methods for gathering information in the child's home or school environment that has been outlined in the last section, you may want to use that opportunity to conduct a Functional Behavioral Assessment (FBA; Carr, 1994). Basically, an FBA is a means of finding the function or purpose of problem behavior by determining the antecedents of the behaviors (i.e., what happens right before) and the consequences of the behaviors (i.e., what happens right after). By identifying patterns of antecedent or consequences, clinicians can often identify what precipitates or causes as well as what reinforces or maintains problem behavior in children with emotional and behavioral disorders (Heckaman, Conroy, Fox, & Chait, 2000; Lane, Umbreit, & Beebe-Frankenberger, 1999). There is evidence that interventions based on information about specific antecedents and consequences can be very successful (Ervin, Kern, Clarke, Dunlap, & Friman, 2000).

When you ask informants such as parents and teachers why children exhibit problem behaviors, you will get their opinion of what causes such behaviors. For example, they may state "He gets angry when he doesn't get his way," or "He does it to get what he wants from his mother." These statements may or may not be true. Another possibility is that informants will give you a description of the child's behavior such as: "He does it because he's mean spirited like his dad," or "He does it because he has ODD [oppositional defiant disorder]." The latter I consider as the least helpful because the behaviors were used or inferred to make the diagnosis. Thus, it is circular reasoning to use the diagnosis as the explanation for the behavior. Refer to Golden (2007) for a complete description of how to conduct an FBA.

TEACHING PARENTS NEW WAYS OF INTERACTING WITH THEIR CHILDREN

ONCE THE FBA has been completed and the possible causes of the problem behavior have been identified, then the real challenge is teaching others how to deal with the child's negative behaviors. The counselor should begin by discussing the child's behaviors with the parents and teachers on how to facilitate more appropriate prosocial behaviors that can replace the child's problem behaviors. It is essential to teach parents and teachers how to reinforce those prosocial replacement behaviors. This is referred to in the literature as BPT, which has shown success in improving the behavior of children with externalizing behavior disorders (Kazdin, 1990, 1993, 1997; Weisz, Donenberg et al., 1995).

How a behavior plan is implemented depends a lot on the motivational and educational level of the parents. There may be other factors interfering with the parent's ability to focus on the behavior of their children, such as marital conflict, alcoholism, depression, or other mental health conditions. If this is the case these should be dealt with first through appropriate referrals (Reid & Patterson, 1991).

One important component of BPT is the existence of a handbook or manual in which specific instructions are provided, describing techniques that parents are to use. This will provide quality control as well as written material to use when the clinician/trainer is not available as a resource. The following is a list of excellent research-based approaches to parent training:

1. *Gerald Patterson's (1976) Living With Children*
2. *Forehand and McMahon (1981) Helping the Noncompliant Child*
3. *Carolyn Webster–Stratton and M. Jamila Reid (2007) Incredible Years and Teacher's Training Series*

4. *Russell Barkley's (1997) Defiant Children (New York: Guilford Press)*
5. *Glenn Latham's (1994) The Power of Positive Parenting: A Wonderful Way to Raise Children*

GOALS FOR PARENTS REGARDING CHILDREN'S BEHAVIORS AT HOME

THERE ARE SEVERAL goals for parents regarding behaviors at home:

A. Changes in the interactions of parents with their children:

1. Verbally reinforce the appropriate behaviors of children. It is important for parents to notice appropriate behaviors and reinforce them enthusiastically with the appropriate emotional intensity. Most children with challenging behaviors can reliably count on parents responding with negative emotional intensity when they exhibit inappropriate behavior. It is the typical response of most parents to problematic behavior and it reinforces (strengthens) the likelihood of problematic behaviors. It is the job of the counselor to turn this around by getting the parents to respond instead with positive emotional intensity to the child's appropriate behavior.

2. Ignore or react in a neutral manner when children exhibit "nuisance" behaviors or minor inappropriate behaviors such as fingers in mouth, whining, poor table manners, and so forth. It is always a good idea to choose your battles wisely with children. There are two important reasons for this. First, reacting to every little behavior can cause unnecessary friction between parents and children. Second, reacting to children's misbehavior in a negative emotional manner can reinforce misbehavior.

3. Refrain from making threats and becoming emotionally upset when children exhibit unacceptable behaviors (i.e. cursing, fighting, stealing). Serious behaviors should be followed with serious consequences (i.e., time out, fines, loss of privileges) delivered in a calm, matter-of-fact manner. Consider the highway patrolman. When issuing a ticket he does not yell, hit, or get emotionally excited. He delivers the ticket along with the comment "Have a nice day." If he were to yell and scream and give you no ticket you would probably laugh. The ticket is the consequence that serves to punish your behavior, not how the highway patrolman talks to you.

B. Ways that parents can provide more structure for their children:

1. Establish and state a few very specific, positively stated behavioral expectations (rules) to follow (weekly, monthly) in particular contexts.
2. Decide on short-term (daily) and long-term (weekly, monthly) rewards for children to earn for following rules.
3. Make a chart to post behavioral expectations (rules) and to monitor whether they were completed (followed).

(See Table 60.2 for additional ideas for helping parents to provide structure for their children.)

TABLE 60.2   What Children Need to Be Well Behaved and Happy

1.	**Children need structure and discipline:**	- Rules that are clear, direct, and simple. - Rewards for following rules. - Consequences for not following rules.
2.	**Words and physical punishment should not be used for discipline:**	- Don't remind, plead, nag, beg, reason, or explain to get compliance from children. - Don't criticize, scold, yell, scream, use derogatory labels, or express negative emotions to punish children for noncompliance. - Don't use physical punishment for noncompliance or misbehavior.
3.	**Words should be used to reward compliance and to build self-esteem:**	- Use clear, direct, and simple commands to encourage compliance. - Allow time for the child to comply (without repeating or explaining the command). - Reward compliance with praise. - Use complimentary phrases and express positive emotions to build self-esteem in children.
4.	**Consequences should be used to punish noncompliance or misbehavior and teach responsibility:**	- Withholding rewards, loss of privileges, ignoring, and time out are appropriate consequences. - Let children know ahead of time what the consequences are for noncompliance or misbehavior. - When children do not comply or misbehave, simply state that they have chosen the consequence through misbehavior (or say nothing at all) and provide the consequence in a calm, matter-of-fact manner.

(continued)

TABLE 60.2 *(Continued)*

5. **In learning complex skills (studying, completing homework, doing chores) or developing new habits (using table manners, going to bed, getting ready for school), children usually need more structure, clearly stated criteria and consequences, chances to show gradual improvement, and frequent rewards:**	- More structure, that is, lists, charts, assignment sheets, daily progress notes. - Clear criterion and consequences, that is, you must be up, dressed, eaten, teeth brushed, book bag full by 7:30 A.M. to watch morning cartoons. - A chance to show gradual improvement, that is, if you complete one chore on your list twice in one week without being asked, you get $1.00 bonus in your allowance. - Frequent rewards, that is, each day you bring home a good news note, you will get to stay up and watch TV one half-hour later that night.

IMPROVING CHILDREN'S BEHAVIORS AND PERFORMANCE AT SCHOOL

CLINICIANS CAN ALSO assist parents in improving their children's behaviors and performance at school. Collecting information or developing a monitoring form, from parent/teacher interviews and direct observation can assist with the child's academic performance and conduct. Often, teachers and parents make the mistake of focusing on academic grades rather than behaviors. Poor grades are more likely to improve when behaviors that lead to good grades (i.e., completing class work, writing down homework assignments and tests, bringing home books and notes, completing and handing in homework) are rewarded rather than when rewarding the upcoming good grades themselves. (See Table 60.3 for a sample school monitoring form.)

The child must be reinforced based on the information the teacher has provided on the form as well as for filling out the form and getting a signature. This is usually best accomplished by making the child's total access to money, and the specific amount of the allowance, dependent upon getting the form filled out with the signatures. With younger children, it is helpful to go over the form with the child and parents in the room at the same time and instruct, prompt, and reinforce the parents as to how to praise and reinforce the child. With older children, it is better to coach the parents ahead of time to praise and pay their children for all the behaviors they have done well, as reported and documented by the teacher. It is also important to refrain from criticizing or nagging the children about poor performance. It is interesting to observe

TABLE 60.3   Daily Report for School

Daily Report for School

Date _____   Day _____
Subject _____   Teacher _____

The following should be repeated for each of the child's classes:

	Points Available (A = 30/B = 20)	Points Earned
Assignment returned (grade) _____	_____	_____
Assignment handed in (yes/no) _____	____ 10 ____	_____
Class work completed (yes/no) _____	____ 25 ____	_____
Behavior appropriate (yes/no) _____	____ 25 ____	_____
New homework assignment _____	____ 10 ____	_____
Date of upcoming test _____	____ 10 ____	_____
	Teacher's Initials _____	

the looks of surprise and relief on the faces of the children when their parents emphasize and pay attention to their positive behaviors.

CONCLUSION

IN SUMMARY, THERE are many ways that counselors can impact the challenging behaviors of the children they see in treatment. Much of this impact will be indirect and involve changing negative behaviors of others in the child's environment. The more people that are involved (i.e., parents, teachers, grandparents, siblings) that are able to change the ways they respond to the child, the better chances they will have in improving the child's behaviors. After all, the clinician only sees the child weekly at best. The important people are those in their daily lives.

REFERENCES

Barkley, R. A. (1997). *Defiant children: A clinician's manual for assessment and parent training* (2nd ed.). New York: Guilford Press.

Brandenburg, N.A., Friedman, R. M., & Silver, S. E. (1990). The epidemiology of childhood psychiatric disorders: Prevalence findings from recent studies. *Journal of the American Academy of Child and Adolescent Psychiatry, 29*(1), 76–83.

Carr, E. (1994). Emerging themes in functional analysis of problem behavior. *Journal of Applied Behavior Analysis, 27,* 393–400.

Doss, S., & Reichle, J. (1989). Establishing communicative alternatives to the emission of socially motivated excess behavior: A review. *Journal of the Association for Persons With Severe Handicaps, 14*(2), 101–112.

Dumas, J. E. (1989). Treating antisocial behavior in children: Child and family approaches. *Clinical Psychology Review, 9,* 197–222.

Edelbrock, C., Crnic, K., & Bohnert, A. (1999). Interviewing as communication: An alternative way of administering the Diagnostic Interview Schedule for Children. *Journal of Abnormal Child Psychology, 27*(6), 447–453.

Ervin, R. A., Kern, L., Clarke, S., DuPaul, G. J., Dunlap, G., & Friman, P. C. (2000). Evaluating functional assessment-based intervention strategies for students with ADHD and comorbid disorders within the natural classroom context. *Behavioral Disorders, 25,* 344–358.

Forehand, R. L., & McMahon, R. J. (1981). *Helping the noncompliant child: A clinician's guide to parent training.* New York: Guilford Press.

Garrett, K. R. (1985). Elbow room in a functional analysis: Freedom and dignity regained. *Behaviorism, 13*(1), 21–36.

Golden, J. (2007). A new perspective on child and adolescent behavioral disorders, *Directions in Mental Health Counseling, 17,* 97–109.

Heckaman, K., Conroy, M., Fox, J., & Chait, A. (2000). Functional assessment-based intervention research on students with or at risk for emotional and behavioral disorders in school settings. *Behavioral Disorders, 25,* 196–210.

Kazdin, A. E. (1987). Treatment of antisocial behavior in children: Current status and future directions. *Psychological Bulletin, 102*(2), 187–203.

Kazdin, A. E. (1990). Premature termination from treatment among children referred for antisocial behavior. *Journal of Child Psychology and Psychiatry, 31,* 415–425.

Kazdin, A. E. (1993). Changes in behavioral problems and prosocial functioning in child treatment. *Journal of Child and Family Studies, 2,* 5–22.

Kazdin, A. E. (1997). Parent management training: Evidence, outcomes and issues. *Journal of the American Academy of Child and Adolescent Psychiatry, 36,* 1349–1356.

Lane, K., Umbreit, J., & Beebe-Frankenberger, M. (1999). Functional assessment research on students with or at risk for EBD. *Journal of Positive Behavior Interventions, 1,* 101–111.

Latham, G. (1994). *The power of positive parenting: A wonderful way to raise children.* Logan, UT: P & T Ink.

McDougal, J. L., Nastasi, B. K., & Chafouleas, S. M. (2005). Bringing research into practice to intervene with young behaviorally challenging students in public school settings: Evaluation of the behavior consultation team (BCT) project. *Psychology in the Schools, 42*(5), 537–551.

McMahon, R. J., & Wells, K. C. (1989). Conduct disorders. In E. J. Mash & R. A. Barkley (Eds.), *Treatment of childhood disorders* (pp. 73–132). New York: Guilford Press.

Patterson, G. R. (1976). *Living with children: New methods for parents and teachers* (revised ed.). Champaign, IL: Research Press.

Rayfield, A. R., Monaco, L., & Eyberg, S. M. (1999). Parent-child interaction therapy: Review and clinical strategies. In S. Russ and T. Ollendick (Eds.), *Handbook of psychotherapies for children and adolescents* (pp. 327–343). New York: Plenum.

Reichle, B. (1996). From is to ought and the kitchen sink: On the justice of distributions in close relationships. In L. Montada & J. Melvin (Eds.), *Current societal concerns about justice* (pp. 103–135). New York: Plenum Press.

Reid, J. B., & Patterson, G. R. (1991). Early prevention and intervention with conduct problems: A social interactional model for the integration of research and practice. In G. Stoner, M. R. Shinn, & H. M. Walker (Eds.), *Interventions for achievement and behavior problems* (pp. 715–739). Silver Spring, MD: National Association of School Psychologists.

Scotti, J. R., Morris, T. L., & McNeil, C. B. (1996). *DSM–IV* and disorders of childhood and adolescence: Can structural criteria be functional? *Journal of Consulting and Clinical Psychology, 64*(6), 1177–1191.

Serketich, W. J., & Dumas, J. E. (1996). The effectiveness of behavioral parent training to modify antisocial behavior in children: A meta-analysis. *Behavior Therapy, 27,* 171–186.

Webster-Stratton, C., & Reid, M. J. (2007). Incredible years and teachers training series: A head start partnership to promote social competence and prevent conduct problems. In P. Tolin, J. Szapocznik, & S. Sambrano (Eds.), *Preventing youth substance abuse* (pp. 67–88). Washington, DC: American Psychological Association.

Weisz, J. R., Donenberg, G. R., Han, S. S., & Weiss, B. (1995). Bridging the gap between laboratory and clinic in child and adolescent psychotherapy. *Journal of Consulting and Clinical Psychology, 63,* 688–701.

Section I

Counseling Specific Populations

61

Counseling Individuals With Disabilities

COUNSELORS SEEK TO understand their clients, and then based on that understanding, establish a therapeutic alliance and, in cooperation with the client, develop treatment goals. Greater numbers of persons with physical, cognitive, emotional, and psychiatric disabilities will seek counseling services due to the following factors: (1) the growing number of people with all types of disabilities; (2) more complete integration of people with disabilities (PWDs) into the broader culture; (3) growing awareness that anyone can acquire a disability; and (4) rising Disability Rights movement, which is advocating for civil rights and a higher standard of living for PWDs (Smart & Smart, 2006). In order to meet minimum standards of practice, counselors of all theoretical orientations, specializations, and professional settings will be required to become proficient in disability issues. According to the U.S. Bureau of the Census, 18% of the population of the United States experiences a disability (U.S. Bureau of the Census, 2006).

Despite the fact that disability is a natural part of human existence for everyone, counselors may not be prepared to work with PWDs and often hold restrictive beliefs and false stereotypes of PWDs, thus unintentionally reinforcing the status quo found in the larger culture. Like everyone else, PWDs have multiple identities, roles, functions, environments, and assets, and therefore, PWDs will require the services of counselors in all specialty areas: aging and adult development; gay, lesbian, bisexual, and transsexual issues; multicultural concerns; community mental health, school counseling; college and university counseling, group counseling; marriage and family counseling; career counseling; and spiritual, ethical, and religious values.

However, counselors (with the exception of rehabilitation counselors) typically are not trained in disability issues, or may have received training that is based on the biomedical model of disability, which considers disability to be a pathological attribute located solely within the individual. Counselors may avoid dealing with disability issues, or they have restrictive ideas about the roles of PWDs, and therefore counselors may not expand the range of roles and behaviors available to their clients with disabilities. Many of our assumptions about the disability experience and the individuals who have disabilities, although based on ostensible kindness and good intentions, are inaccurate and may impede the counseling process. Inaccurate assumptions will lead to faulty case conceptualizations and problem formulation.

Although the biomedical model will never be abandoned, it is being challenged and questioned further, as other models shape the self-identity of PWDs and more accurately reflect the daily lives of PWDs (Smart, 2001). These newer models conceptualize disability as an interaction among the individual and the environment, both physical and social. Disability is no longer thought to be a private misfortune, but rather a societal concern.

The following suggestions are offered in order to give counselors a clearer understanding of their clients with disabilities:

1. Counselors should engage in an ongoing examination of clients' feelings about the experience of disability and the resulting interaction of the counselor's own identity with that of the client. The disability of the client may arouse feelings of existential questioning, anxiety, and defensiveness in the counselor, much of it the result of the biomedical model that views disability as a tragic inferiority. In subtle ways, the disability of the client may be stress-inducing to the counselor. Many people without disabilities (PWODs) "harbor unspoken anxieties about the possibility of disablement, to us or to someone close to us" (Longmore, 2003, p. 132). If counselors are able to accept their own vulnerability to disability, "it will be less likely that they will experience a negative, emotional response to a client with a disability. Countertransference, and other emotional reactions to the disability of the client may prevent the counselor from fully understanding the client and therefore negatively affect the counseling relationship" (Smart & Smart, 2006, p. 37).

2. Counselors should recognize that most individuals with disabilities do not accept the basic tenets of the biomedical model. Often, PWDs view their disability as a valued part of their identity, are proud of their mastery of the disability, see positive aspects and experiences in the disability, and would choose not to eliminate the disability if they were given a choice. Indeed, many individuals with disabilities do not reject their disability, but they refuse the inferiority, pathology, and deviance aspects of the disability *role*. They understand that there is nothing in their disability that warrants prejudice and discrimination. In contrast, many individuals without disabilities, including counselors, may believe that the acquisition of a disability automatically results in a social devaluation.

3. Counselors should guard against sympathy and lowered expectations. Frequently, PWDs are praised for minor accomplishments and widely held standards are lowered or simply waived. Sympathy and lowered expectations are stigmatizing and prejudicial and results in withholding honest feedback from the client, reduces the range of opportunities open to the individual, fosters dependence and passivity, and communicates to clients with disabilities that they are not perceived to be capable. Praise for minor accomplishments can be insulting because it questions the individual's credibility and competence. Further, it is not much of a compliment when PWODs are surprised when an individual with a disability succeeds.

4. Counselors should understand the power of *spread*. Essentially, spread is the process of ascribing greater limitations to the disability and, at the same time, discounting and underrating the strengths and abilities of the individual with a disability. Shouting to a person who is blind is an example of spread. This overgeneralization of the effects of the disability, taken to the extreme, can lead to the false conceptualization of the individual with a disability as "a twisted body, twisted soul." In other words, because of the disability, the individual is bitter, angry, idealizes normality, and is resentful of PWODs.

5. Counselors should understand that being an individual with a disability is a normative role, imposed by those in power, people *without* disabilities. These rules include making others comfortable with their disability; complying with all treatment; always being cheerful, never expressing anger or other seemingly negative emotions, keeping their aspirations and needs at a modest level, and always being grateful for accommodations and services. Most important, however, is the socially imposed criteria of "appearing normal." Ranging from minor inconvenience and irritation

to painful and useless treatments, to further disablement and even death, these rules are not always benign and PWDs justifiably resent them. Frequently, PWDs will sacrifice functioning for the appearance of normality, such as not wearing hearing aids or wearing uncomfortable and unfunctional prostheses in public. These social expectations can be exhausting burdens for PWDs. If the individual chooses not to comply with these externally imposed rules, he or she may be considered to have "a chip on her or his shoulder" or to have not accepted the disability. There are times when PWDs capitulate to these rules in order to receive services and benefits. Each PWD, therefore, must negotiate a balance between autonomy and society's expectations. The counselor should understand that the individual with the disability is the expert on his or her disability and its management.

6. In an effort to give meaning to a wide array of information about the disability, the counselor may make generalizations and categorizations based on the client's medical diagnosis. Counselors may not always feel competent and comfortable with many disability issues. Nonetheless, clients are not their medical diagnosis. In addition, not all of the failings and difficulties of the individual are due to the disability. For many clients, the disability is not the "presenting problem."

7. Counselors should recognize that the disability is an important aspect of the individual's identity, but the disability does not comprise the individual's entire identity, nor is it often the most important part of the individual's identity. Like most people, individuals with disabilities consider their family roles and their professional/work functions as the most important aspects of their identity. Therefore, counselors should obtain a deep and complete understanding of the client, including the varied identities, functions, and environments of the client. The disability, and its demands, is not the motivator of every decision of the client. In addition, disability identity also constantly changes and develops, as all identities do.

8. Counselors should be willing to listen to the PWD's experience of prejudice and discrimination. Prejudice and discrimination against PWDs is often not seen or acknowledged. Nonetheless, managing and responding to prejudice and discrimination are daily tasks for PWDs. Two disability scholars explained: "Unkind words against homosexuals, African-Americans, Hispanics, and other minorities at least prompt rebuke from people who, though not members of these stigmatized groups, still recognize the prejudice. But prejudice against individuals with disabilities commonly goes undetected by a general public too unaware of its own feelings to recognize

what has been said or written as prejudicial" (Fleischer & Zames, 2001, p. xv). Davis (1997) considers the prejudice and discrimination against PWDs to be greater than any other group, including racial and ethnic minorities: "People with disabilities have been isolated, incarcerated, observed, written about, operated on, instructed, implanted, regulated, treated, institutionalized, and controlled to a great degree probably unequal to that experienced by any other minority group" (p. 1). Clients with disabilities may wish to discuss their experiences with paternalism, being a forced representative, being objectified, infantilized, sexualized, and marginalized. At times, PWDs are made to feel that they are burdens or drains on the economy or unwanted mistakes. On the other hand, counselors should avoid ascribing all of the client's difficulties to prejudice and discrimination.

9. Counselors should understand the importance of a group identity for their clients with disabilities. As a group, people with disabilities want cultural and social authority over their identity rather than being defined from the outside. In the past, the medical professions and the popular media acted as cultural translators of the disability experience. Indeed, many PWDs feel that they have been exploited and misrepresented by the media. While the disability of every individual is a unique experience, there are common experiences and shared values among people with disabilities. A group identity for PWDs will result in political gains. Individuals with disabilities want full civil rights and equal opportunities while maintaining their identity as individuals with disabilities. Access to health care, employment, accessible environments, provision of assistive technology, and enforcement of civil rights are important issues for PWDs. Many individuals with disabilities consider their experiences to be valuable and important parts of human life and because of this, PWDs want their history and viewpoints integrated into the broader American culture. Not every client with a disability will be a political activist, but PWDs understand that collective gains will result in a better quality of life for everyone with a disability.

10. Counselors should understand the way in which the popular media depicts disability often results in assaults upon the self-esteem of the PWD. From super crips to Disney fairytales to charity telethons to slasher movies, PWDs view the misrepresentation and demeaning sensationalization and exaggeration of disability as another form of unquestioned and unchallenged prejudice and discrimination. In contrast, most PWODs do not recognize many of these false stereotypes. Indeed, the modern media depicts disability in much the same way as Charles Dickens did in the mid-19th century.

The media often reinforces such myths as disability is a punishment for some wrongdoing, PWDs are continuously embittered by their disability, and the PWD is helpless, dependent, and passive. The popular media simply reinforces the power structure between PWODs and PWDs. Indeed, often there is a wise, strong PWOD who assists the PWD in accepting his or her disability. Frequently, audiences are led to believe that the individual is his or her disability when PWDs are shown as having no family life, no job, and no social life. People with disabilities (actually the false representation of PWDs) are big moneymakers for the media.

11. Counselors should understand "disability exhaustion." Disability exhaustion is often the result of dealing with layers and layers of bureaucracy and negotiating a system that is often contradictory. One mother of a child with a disability described: "The system can be overwhelming. The system consumes manpower—her dad, me, maybe grandma. We need to make sure that the services are adequate—that all the documentation and paperwork is up to date. That her wheelchairs, braces, crutches are up to date. Sometimes we are assessed, to see if she is still disabled." Another woman with a disability reported: "What percentage of my time is spent maintaining my relationship with the funding agencies who keep me alive? It goes up in a crisis period. It's 25% of my time" (National Public Radio, 1998). Another individual with a disability stated: "Sometimes the warrior in me gets tired" (Putnam et al., 2003). Disability exhaustion can occur when environments are not accessible and accommodations are not in place. Inaccessible environments send a clear message to individuals with disabilities: They are not wanted.

12. Counselors should understand the impact of institutionalized "enforced idleness." According to national polls, most PWDs express a desire to work. However, a combination of public perceptions and laws and policies with built-in financial disincentives prevents many PWDs from working. Eric Weihenmayer (2001), the man who was blind and climbed Mt. Everest, could not get a dishwasher's job in Cambridge, Massachusetts. He wrote: "Too big, too small, too fast, too hot, like a twisted version of the three bears—the story repeated itself again and again. I had thought that somehow, that with my force of will, with my ingenuity, with my tenacity, I could eventually win people over and get what I wanted out of life. I hadn't realized that there were doors that would remain locked in front of me. I wanted so badly to break through, to take a battering ram to them, to bash them into a million splinters, but the doors were locked too securely and their surfaces were impenetrable. I never got a dishwasher's job in Cambridge, but I did choke down

an important lesson, that people's perceptions of our limitations are more damaging than those limitations themselves, and it was the hardest lesson that I ever had to swallow" (pp. 127–128).

13. Counselors should empower their clients. Barnes, Mercer, & Shakespeare (1999) stated, "their [PWDs] lives are saturated with unequal encounters with professionals" (p. 82). In many of these experiences with professionals, PWDs have not been allowed input into their treatment, were not permitted to ask questions, and were not given direct answers to their questions. Additionally, many of these professionals were gatekeepers to obtaining resources and benefits and, because of this, PWDs submitted to this paternalism. Counselors can empower clients with disabilities by listening and supporting them and not assuming that they know what is best for the client. The client can be empowered to become active and engaged in the counseling process by setting appropriate goals. Finally, counselors should guard against the idea that the life of a PWD is not worthy of investment (when compared to the live of a PWOD) (McCarthy, 2003).

14. Counselors should understand the meaning of *chronic*. Most PWDs are happy, have family roles, and many work. Zola (1991) explained: "Our daily living is not filled with dramatic accomplishments but with mundane ones. And most of all, our physical disabilities are not temporary ones to be overcome once-and-for-all, but ones we must face again and again for the rest of our lives. That is what chronic means" (p. 161).

The general public likes to hear stories of *super crips* or *overcomers*, individuals with disabilities who have accomplished great goals. To think that most PWDs (or most PWODs) can achieve these accomplishments by simply working harder or trying harder is "wish fulfillment by people without disabilities" (Linton, 1998, p. 18). The media loves super crips probably because these individuals decrease our fear of acquiring a disability. Nonetheless, the public's fascination with superachieving, exceptional PWDs does not reflect the reality of daily life of most PWDs.

Counselors are in a unique position to understand the relationships between personal characteristics of a client, his or her developmental stage of life, and the context and environment in which the client lives. In order to provide ethical and effective services to clients with disabilities, counselors will need to seek out further training on the experience of disability. Certainly, information about each client's identity and feelings about his or her disability must come from that individual, but obtaining a broad knowledge of the disability experience is essential. Interagency collaboration will become more important as counselors assist clients with disabilities. Health care systems, vocational rehabilitation, and Social Security agencies can work with counselors in order to provide comprehensive services for clients with disabilities. While assisting clients on a one-to-one basis can make a contribution to the larger society, counselors should also intervene at institutional and political levels, advocating for changes in systems and politics. Professional counseling organizations can also provide support and advocacy for individuals with disabilities. Individual counselors and the counseling profession are faced with the task of questioning our assumptions about disability and the individuals who experience them.

REFERENCES

Barnes, C., Mercer, G., & Shakespeare, T. (1999). *Exploring disability: A sociological introduction*. Cambridge, UK: Polity.

Davis, L. J. (Ed.). (1997). *The disability studies reader*. New York: Routledge.

Fleischer, D. Z., & Zames, F. (2001). *The disability rights movement: From charity to confrontation*. Philadelphia: Temple University Press.

Linton, S. (1998). *Claiming disability: Knowledge and identity*. New York: New York University Press.

Longmore, P. K. (2003). *Why I burned my book and other essays on disability*. Philadelphia: Temple University Press.

McCarthy, H. (2003). The disability rights movement: Experiences and perspectives of selected leaders in the disability community. *Rehabilitation Counseling Bulletin, 46,* 209–223.

National Public Radio. (May, 1998). *Disability History Project. What's Work Got to Do With It?* Retrieved July 11, 2008, from http://iris.npr.org/programs/disability/ba_shows.dir/work.dir/

Putnam, M., Greenen, S., Powers, L., Saxton, M., Finney, S., & Dautel, P. (2003). Health and wellness: People with disabilities discuss barriers and facilitators to well-being. *Journal of Rehabilitation, 69,* 37–45.

Smart, J. F. (2001). *Disability, society, and the individual*. Austin, TX: Pro-Ed.

Smart, J. F., & Smart, D. W. (2006). Models of disability: Implications for the counseling profession. *Journal of Counseling and Development, 84,* 29–40.

U.S. Bureau of the Census. (2006, July 26). *Facts for Americans: Americans with disabilities*. Retrieved July 11, 2008, from http://www.census.gov/prod/www/stastistical-abstract.html

Weihenmayer, E. (2001). *Touch the top of the world: A blind man's journey to climb farther than the eye can see*. New York: Dutton.

Zola, I. K. (1991). Communication barriers between "the able-bodied" and "the handicapped." In P. M. Ferguson, D. L. Ferguson, & S. J. Taylor (Eds.), *Interpreting disability: A qualitative reader* (pp. 157–164). New York: Columbia Teachers College Press.

62

Psychiatric Disability: A Biopsychosocial Challenge

GREGORY G. GARSKE

PROFESSIONAL COUNSELORS REPRESENTING a variety of specialties provide mental health services to individuals with psychiatric disabilities. According to the National Institute of Mental Health revised figures for 2006, approximately 26.2% of Americans ages 18 and older experience a diagnosable mental disorder in a given year. When applied to the U.S. Census, this figure translates to 57.7 million people. While mental disorders are widespread in the population, about 6% experience a serious mental illness (SMI). Mental disorders are now considered to be the leading cause of disability in the United States and Canada for ages 15–44; see http://www.nimh.nih.gov/publicat/numbers.cfm for the details. Although some gains have been made in service provision for persons with SMI, the increasing number of individuals with severe and lifelong psychiatric disabilities continues to challenge the counseling profession.

Under the Americans With Disabilities Act of 1990, the term *disability* includes (1) mental impairment that substantially limits one or more of the major life activities of an individual; (2) a record of such an impairment; or (3) being regarded as having such an impairment. The term *mental illness* generally includes a broad range of mental and emotional disorders. The term *psychiatric disability* is used when the mental illness significantly interferes with the performance of major life activities such as learning, thinking, communicating, and sleeping, among others (Anthony, Cohen, Farkas, & Gagne, 2002). In order to have a psychiatric disability, a person must first have a psychiatric diagnosis. Primarily these diagnoses include schizophrenia, affective disorders, and anxiety disorders. It is estimated that 2.2 million adults have schizophrenia, 18.8 million American adults have depressive disorders, and another 19.1 million adults have anxiety disorders.

BIOPSYCHOSOCIAL FACTORS

FROM A BIOPSYCHOSOCIAL perspective, the biological component relates to relationships among normal biology, disease processes, and genetic influences. The psychological component addresses those factors that include thoughts, feelings, perceptions, motivation, and reaction to illness. The sociological part examines cultural, environmental, and familial influences. Understanding how clients function at all levels can help provide a more complete clinical picture.

Severe psychiatric illnesses are persistent mental or emotional disorders that significantly interfere with a person's ability to carry out such primary aspects of daily life as self-care, household management, interpersonal relationships, and school or work (Garske, 2002). Due to the complexity of severe psychiatric disorders, the whole person and his or her relation to his or her environment must be considered. Most mental illnesses are "complex" in pathophysiology. That is, their causes and mechanism should be analyzed from several perspectives, running the gamut from genes to environment (Andreasen, 2001). As an example, schizophrenia may be considered from a bio-psycho-social perspective. Due to the chemical imbalances, medication management may be required to handle some of the biological concerns. At the same time, individuals with schizophrenia may experience accompanying personal and interpersonal issues. Similar to physical disability, it is possible to conceptualize psychosocial aspects of psychiatric disability as the internal and external factors that, when combined, create individualized responses not attributable to the disabling condition alone. These internal (intrapersonal) and external (interpersonal) and environmental factors are those psychological and social factors that play a primary role in adjustment to disability.

BIOLOGICAL CONSIDERATIONS

IN ORDER TO work effectively with people with mental disorders, counselors and other therapists need to obtain an understanding of how the brain works and sometimes malfunctions. According to the American Counseling Association (ACA), the practice of professional counseling is the application of mental health, psychological, or human development principles, through cognitive, affective, behavioral, or systemic intervention strategies that address wellness, personal growth, or career development, as well as pathology (http://www.counseling.org). Andreasen and Black (2006) indicated that the normal healthy brain is a complex, miraculous, and ingeniously created organ. Individuals have a unique brain with particular capacities that can be enhanced through learning and productive work or wasted through intellectual inactivity and unhealthy living habits. This same brain can also become "broken" in many ways that lead to disorders known as mental illnesses. Although a standard social definition of mental illness may not exist, it can be understood as a severe and persistent biologically based mental disorder that may interfere with social functioning. Primary aspects of daily life, such as self-care, interpersonal relationships, and work or schooling, can be disrupted and necessitate occasional hospital or crisis care (Walsh, 2000).

The workings of the brain are indeed complex. Andreasen and Black (2006) explained that the brain expands its communicating and thinking power by multiplying connectivity through an average of 1,000–10,000 synapses per cell. It was further noted that the synopses are "plastic" in that they remodel themselves continuously in response to changes in their environment and the inputs they receive. The disturbances in thought, emotion, and behavior we observe are ultimately due to aberrations in the brain. Understanding those aberrations and methods to correcting them is the ultimate challenge.

In order to gain a working knowledge of psychiatric disorders, counselors must receive specific training in regard to client interviewing, diagnosis and assessment, and the manifestations of the specific disorders. Another biological aspect related to the treatment of persons with psychiatric disabilities relates to pharmacologic treatment. The treatment of mental illness underwent a dramatic shift with the introduction of psychotropic drugs. Before the introduction of these medications, individuals with severe mental illness were institutionalized for decades. In the second half of the 20th century, state mental health institutions were radically depopulated, resulting in a greater number of individuals with severe psychiatric disability in the community. While counselors may not prescribe psychotropic drugs, many of their clients may be medicated. Current and future clinicians should remain educated about the ever-changing psychotropic medications used to treat mental disorders. The *Handbook of Clinical Psychopharmacology* by Preston, O'Neil, and Talaga (2005) is a widely used resource for counselors. Counselors need to understand the effects of these medications as well as the related side effects. For example, side effects of traditional antipsychotic medications may include dystonic reactions, akathisia, and Parkinsonism. The dystonic reactions involve acute muscular spasms that occur mainly in the head or neck. Akathisia is an inner restlessness manifested as an inability to sit still. The Parkinsonism side effect involves rigidity of joints, tremors, and a slowing of movements (Bond & Meyer, 1999).

PSYCHOSOCIAL CONSIDERATIONS

THE ECOLOGICAL POINT of view was popularized by Kurt Lewin (1935) with his famous equation B = f(P,E), which states that behavior is a function of both the person and the environment. In similar fashion, mental health practitioners are reminded that in order to change behavior, it is necessary to alter the perception and the abilities of individuals, as well as the characteristics of their environment (Teed & Scileppi, 2007). Psychosocial aspects of any disability are important factors in the treatment and rehabilitation of the individual. Yet, the concept continues to be nebulous in nature. Like adjustment to physical disability, adjustment to psychiatric disability can be a very complicated and individualized process based on the combination of psychological, social, and disability-related components.

Counselors need to remain mindful of the individuality of the coping process. According to Lazarus and Folkman (1984), psychological stress is a particular relationship between the person and the environment that persons with disability perceive as taxing or exceeding their resources and endangering their well-being. It was further explained that coping is the process through which the demands of the person in relation to the environment may be perceived as highly emotionally stressful to the individual with the disability.

A variety of psychological factors may affect an individual's management of psychiatric disability. To begin with, a person's personality can affect the way in which he or she interacts with the environment. The manner in which people think, feel, and perceive may characterize and determine how they deal with their surroundings. It is vital to remember that no two individuals' psychological makeup is the same. Consequently, their methods of adjustment to their mental health matters will vary.

Sociological factors can also impact a person's coping success with psychiatric disabilities. Sociological aspects of a disability involve reactions of other individuals, the environment, and society toward the person with a psychiatric disability. Society often holds a negative view of people with psychiatric disabilities. These negative attitudes lead to stigma and labeling of the person as having a "spoiled identity." Issues of dysfunction, disability, and disadvantage are more often more difficult to deal with than the actual impairments. An inability to perform valued tasks and roles and the resultant loss of self-esteem are significant barriers to recovery.

PSYCHIATRIC REHABILITATION APPROACH

WHILE THE *DIAGNOSTIC* and *Statistical Manual of Mental Disorders* (DSM–IV–TR; American Psychiatric Association [APA], 2000) does not support a specific theoretical orientation, counselors are required to tailor therapeutic efforts to the needs of the client and their environment. Obviously, services are essential for meeting the basic human needs of people who are severely mentally ill, be they in the areas of securing food, clothing, housing, financial assistance, or even social, vocational, educational, and recreational opportunities. Mental health service providers need to focus on the integration of psychosocial treatments into the service systems that respond to the needs of individuals with psychiatric disabilities. Hogarty (2002) noted that beyond medication, service systems certainly are necessary, but it appears that psychosocial treatments might ultimately constitute the sufficient program components required for a successful recovery and maintenance of function.

Psychiatric rehabilitation efforts focus on persons who have experienced psychiatric disabilities rather than on individuals who are simply dissatisfied, unhappy, or socially disadvantaged. Persons with psychiatric disability have diagnosed mental illnesses that limit their capacity to perform certain tasks and functions and their ability to perform certain roles.

Definitions of rehabilitation essentially converge around the idea that the client should achieve the best life adjustment in his or her environment. It appears that health and rehabilitation professionals have little difficulty in understanding this concept in relation to physical disability, yet many practitioners do not understand what is involved in the principles and practices of psychiatric rehabilitation. While there are obvious differences between the two treatment approaches, the psychiatric rehabilitation approach is based on a rehabilitation model, the same model of impairment-disability-handicap that underlies the field of physical rehabilitation. Psychiatric rehabilitation typically involves helping individuals gain or improve the skills and obtain the resources and support they require to attain their goals. The mission of psychiatric rehabilitation as defined by Anthony et al. (2002) is to help persons with long-term psychiatric disabilities to increase their functioning so that they are successful and satisfied in the environments of their choice, with the least amount of ongoing professional intervention. According to Pratt, Gill, Barrett, & Roberts (1999), psychiatric rehabilitation has three generally accepted goals. Psychiatric rehabilitation services are designed to help persons with severe mental illness to achieve (1) recovery, (2) maximum community integration, and (3) the highest possible quality of life.

Psychiatric rehabilitation practice is guided by the basic philosophy of rehabilitation in that people with disabilities require skills and environmental supports to fulfill the role demands of their living, learning, social, and working environments. Pratt et al. (1999) recommended 12 guiding principles for psychiatric rehabilitation. These were identified as: (1) individualization of all services; (2) maximum client involvement, preference, choice; (3) normalized and community-based services; (4) strength focus; (5) situational assessment; (6) treatment and rehabilitation integration through a holistic approach; (7) ongoing, accessible, coordinated services; (8) vocational focus; (9) skills training; (10) environmental modification and supports; (11) partnership with the family; and (12) evaluative, assessment, outcome-oriented focus. It was emphasized that these principles are important tools for providing day-to-day guidance in clinical situations and for systematizing the practice of psychiatric rehabilitation.

PSYCHIATRIC REHABILITATION PRACTICES

TRADITIONALLY, MEDICATION AND psychotherapy were the two major treatment approaches, with little attention given to preventing or reducing functional limitations or handicaps to social performance. Community treatment of the person who is severely psychiatrically impaired should focus on the teaching of those coping skills necessary to live as independently as possible in his or her community. People with SMI experience numerous limitations in everyday functioning, some of which include (1) difficulties with interpersonal situations, including the most basic ones (greeting a friend on the street, paying for a purchase in a store); (2) problems coping with stress (including minor hassles, such as finding an item in a store); and (3) difficulty concentrating, and lack of energy or initiative. Whether persons with SMI have never learned social skills or have lost them, most of these individuals have marked skill deficits in social skills and interpersonal situations. It is the presence or absence of such skills, rather than symptoms, that is the determining factor related to rehabilitation outcome. Psychosocial programs must encompass the development of learning or relearning of skills and competencies required for successful interpersonal and social functioning as well as those needed for specific vocational pursuits. Psychosocial programs may provide training in activities of daily living, such as cooking, shopping, housekeeping, and budgeting. Whatever diagnostic category these individuals may fit into, or whatever specific mental symptom they manifest, they are all characterized by a relative inability to master age-appropriate tasks. Therefore, the individual's functional impairment may result in the inability to live independently and to sustain gainful employment and the neglect of personal hygiene and health needs. Consequently, the individuals may experience a breakdown in social support systems, and, in extreme cases, even an inability to provide for basic nutrition and emergent medical problems. According to Anthony et al. (2002), the preferred method of increasing a client's skills or abilities is a skills-training approach. In such an approach, the intent of the rehabilitation diagnosis, as opposed to the traditional psychiatric diagnosis, is to identify those specific client skill deficits that are preventing the person from functioning more effectively in his or her living, learning, and/or work community.

The primary strategies emphasized in state-of-the-art rehabilitation efforts with people who have severe mental illness include the strengthening of client skills and competencies and strengthening environmental supports (Anthony et al., 2002). The use of traditional approaches, such as medications, hospitalization, and dynamic psychotherapy have limited effectiveness when applied to the socialization and work aspects of individuals with SMI. Psychiatric rehabilitation practice should be guided by the basic philosophy of rehabilitation; that is, persons with disabilities require skills and environmental supports to fulfill the role demands of various living, learning, and working environments. Highly endorsed client skill strengthening approaches involve social and independent living skills training, symptom management, and job finding programs. Environmental support strengthening approaches identified as critical include family behavior management and the use of peer groups in the transition to community living. Finally, supported employment was cited as a critical service component, which places equal emphasis on both the strengthening of client skills and competencies and environmental supports.

An emphasis on community-based treatment has resulted in a major shift in treatment methods for individuals with SMI. Although improvements have been made, much remains to be accomplished in the 21st century. Part of the solution rests in the need for qualified counselors who subscribe to the humane principles and practices of psychiatric rehabilitation.

REFERENCES

American Psychiatric Association. (2000). *Diagnostic and statistical manual of mental disorders* (4th ed., text revision). Washington, DC: Author.

Andreasen, N. C. (2001). *Brave new brain: Conquering mental illness in the era of the genome*. New York: Oxford University Press.

Andreasen, N. C., & Black, D. W. (2006). *Introductory textbook of psychiatry*. Washington, DC: American Psychiatric Publishing.

Anthony, W., Cohen, M., Farkas, M., & Gagne, C. (2002). *Psychiatric rehabilitation*. Boston: Center for Psychiatric Rehabilitation.

Bond, G. R., & Meyer, P. S. (1999). The role of medications in the employment of people with schizophrenia. *Journal of Rehabilitation, 65*(4), 9–16.

Garske, G. G. (2002). Psychiatric rehabilitation in America: A work in progress. *The Rehabilitation Professional, 10,* 153–58.

Hogarty, G. E. (2002). *Personal therapy for schizophrenia and related disorders: A guide to individualized treatment*. New York: Guilford Press.

Lazarus, R. S., & Folkman, S. (1984). *Stress appraisal, and coping*. New York: Springer.

Lewin, K. (1935). *A dynamic theory of personality*. New York: McGraw-Hill.

Pratt, C. W., Gill, K. J., Barrett, N. M., & Roberts, M. M. (1999). *Psychiatric rehabilitation*. San Diego: Academic Press.

Preston, J. D., O'Neal, J. H., & Talaga, M. C. (2005). *Handbook of clinical psychomaracology for therapists*. Oakland, CA: New Harbinger Publications.

Teed, E. L., & Scileppi, J. A. (2007). *The community mental health system: A navigational guide for providers*. Boston: Allyn & Bacon.

Walsh, J. (2000). Clinical case management with persons having mental illness: A relationship-based perspective. Belmont, CA: Brooks/Cole.

63

Counseling Criminal Justice Clients

DAVID J. SIMOURD

C OUNSELING CRIMINAL JUSTICE clients can be both
fascinating and clinically rewarding. The fascinating aspect of
this work relates to the intriguing nature that crime plays in
society. It is human nature to be curious about nonordinary events
such as criminal behavior. This basic curiosity has become almost an
obsession based on how much attention crime assumes in the popular media and entertainment industry. The entertainment industry,
unencumbered by the requirement to provide even the slimmest of
facts, provides a rich and constant diet of crime through television
series and movies. In reality, the portrayal of crime in these medi-
ums tends to be overdramatized, overplayed, and quite often simply
inaccurate. The line between fact (what is actually true) and fantasy
(what people believe is true) related to crime and criminal behavior
has become quite blurred. The intent of this chapter is to offer a brief
overview of central issues for counselors who may be interested in
providing therapeutic service to criminal justice clients. The chapter will cover four main areas: (1) an overview of clients served, (2) a
description of relevant "best practices" in working with criminal justice clients, (3) a presentation of therapeutic targets, and (4) suggestions for clinical practice.

MYTH OF CRIMINAL BEHAVIOR

THE GENERAL PUBLIC (which includes counselors) often overestimates the frequency of crime and the number of people involved in crime. The general myth often sensationalized by the media and entertainment industry portrayals is that crime is rampant and that a considerable proportion of the population is involved in criminal conduct. In actuality, crime statistics reported by the Federal Bureau of Investigation (FBI) show, for example, that for the year 2006, there were 473.5 violent crimes per 100,000 people and 3,334.5 property crimes per 100,000 people in the United States. Combining these two rates into a total crime rate and dividing by the population results in a 3.8% crime prevalence rate. This would indicate that in general terms, 4% of the U.S. population committed an offence in 2006. This rate is remarkably stable across time and is very comparable to other countries of similar demographic and economic background. Whether a 4% crime rate is good, bad, or indifferent depends on your point of view.

CRIMINAL JUSTICE CLIENTS

THE TERM FORENSIC is Latin, meaning "before the courts" and essentially relates to issues of jurisprudence (i.e., conviction/ acquittal and sentencing). There is a strong history of psychiatry (forensic psychiatrist) and psychology (forensic psychologist) in this area, which may have led to a layperson conceptualization of the term *forensic* as related to the converged notions of crime and mental illness. However, the term *forensic* has expanded in recent years to imply specialization in a range of fields from science (e.g., anthropology: forensic anthropologist) to commerce (e.g., accounting: forensic accountant). Parenthetically, the first "forensic accountant" may well have been the bookkeeper whose testimony helped convict the notorious 1930s gangster Al Capone of tax evasion. The expanded and generic use of the term *forensic* has created some confusion on who specifically clients are and what therapeutic issues should be addressed.

The predominant clinical activity within a truly forensic jurisprudence context relates to the determination of mental competencies. That is, was the accused of "sound mind" when he or she committed the criminal act and does he or she understand the court process? Assessment of the accused's mental competencies is of central concern in this context rather than any counseling per se. The courts are particularly interested in knowing whether the accused has a mental health impairment that could explain and/or mitigate his or her criminal actions. As it turns out, very few accused persons before the courts have significant mental health issues or compromised mental competencies. Research has found that less than 7% of offenders are diagnosed with schizophrenia. Personality disorders, on the other hand, are much more common among criminal justice clients with between 50% to 100% of clients receiving a formal diagnosis (antisocial personality disorder and substance abuse disorders are the most common). The general picture that emerges is that criminal justice clients are more likely to be "bad" rather than "mad."

Given that criminal justice clients are more likely to have life management difficulties rather than psychiatric disturbance suggests that counselors can play a significant role in therapeutically modifying client characteristics. Criminal justice clients spend proportionally less time involved with court proceedings than they do with postcourt agencies such as correctional facilities, probation/parole, and other community support agencies. In other words, less time "before the courts" and more time within the criminal justice system. Considering the fact that far greater therapeutic activities with offenders occur beyond the courtroom, the term *criminal justice clients* may be more reflective of the clients served. This would include all clients who are involved with the criminal justice system, be it during their time in custody following sentencing or in the community.

Now that a general understanding of the extent of the potential criminal behavior is established, the typical setting for counseling criminal justice clients is explored. Counseling noncriminal justice clients often occurs in a professional office in some type of setting. For criminal justice clients, there are two main settings: in custody or out of custody. In-custody settings are typically locked facilities such as jails or prisons. In these settings, security of the institution has precedence over all other activities and there is strict adherence to "inmate movement," times when clients may move from their locked locations (i.e., single cells or dormitory). Custody settings typically are not endowed with professional office arrangements, and as such, there are often limits on available space. Counseling criminal justice clients who are incarcerated requires flexibility in both time (when and for how long clinical sessions can last) and setting (i.e., office type). The situation of having to interview a client while locked in a jail cell with the client or standing outside the cell and discussing personal matters through the bars of a cell is certainly not unheard of, but fortunately is a rare occurrence. Counseling criminal justice clients who are out of custody is much easier from a setting perspective because there are virtually no time or setting considerations; at least, none that are different from working with noncriminal justice clients.

CORRECTIONAL BEST PRACTICES

CONSIDERABLE ADVANCES HAVE occurred in recent years in assessment and treatment technology in what is commonly referred to as "correctional best practices." This extensive knowledge base has led to greater insights into the effective delivery of offender rehabilitation services and provides distinct road maps to successful therapeutic outcomes with offenders. More important are the clients themselves. While the background circumstances surrounding the actions of criminal justice clients can be remarkably similar, there is a uniqueness in the manner in which they lead their lives and ultimately find themselves in conflict with the law. In this way, each client is different, requiring different therapeutic approaches and different clinical goals and expectations.

These clinical advances, however, were only achieved because of direct challenges to offender rehabilitation that have subsequently been dismissed due to strong empirical evidence. The most influential comment is attributed to Robert Martinson (1974, p. 25), who after reviewing the extant offender treatment literature stated: "with few and isolated exceptions, the rehabilitation efforts that have been reported so far have had no appreciable effect on recidivism" (p. 25). The rhetoric of the phrase "nothing works" has persisted in criminal justice for more than 30 years.

The problem with the Martinson literature was that it was based on the traditional narrative research review process. In this approach, studies are selected and reviewed according to subjective criteria, which is vulnerable to considerable discretion and bias on the part of the reviewer. The scientific world changed dramatically in 1981 when Glass, McGraw, and Smith introduced a more objective and quantitative approach to literature review called *meta-analysis*. The first meta-analyses in corrections sought to respond to the "nothing works" issue by examining the degree to which treatment produced positive outcomes through reductions on reoffending. In the Andrews, Zinger, and colleagues (1990) study, effect sizes (which were based on recidivism rates) were compared between those offenders receiving treatment and those offenders not receiving treatment. The overall results indicated that treatment produced, on average, a 10% reduction in recidivism, which is a positive outcome. However, more detailed analysis found the following results:

Custody without treatment:	7% *increase* in recidivism
Insight-oriented therapy:	5% *increase* in recidivism
Unstructured skill-based therapy:	14% *reduction* in recidivism
Structured skill-based therapy:	30% *reduction* in recidivism

The general pattern of these results has been replicated in subsequent meta-analysis over the years. The take-home message for counselors from this empirical evidence is that correctional treatment "works" in reducing recidivism and that skill-based services of a cognitive behavioral type such as restructuring produce the best results. Insight-orientated treatment approaches actually have been shown to increase recidivism.

It is one thing to know that therapeutic activities with criminal justice clients produce a positive outcome (primarily measured by way of reduced reoffending), it is quite another to work directly with clients to effect change. Research has convincingly shown that clinical improvement among criminal justice clients is maximized when clinicians attend to the three principles of the Risk/Need/Responsivity (Andrews, Bonta, & Hoge, 1990) model of offender rehabilitation. These three principles are:

> *Risk principle:* Match intensity of service with risk level of cases (high-risk cases should receive intensive service whereas low-risk cases should receive minimal, if any, service).
> *Need principle:* Target criminogenic factors (those directly related to criminality).
> *Responsivity principle:* (1) General responsivity (employ cognitive behavioral, skill-based strategies). (2) Specific responsivity (match treatment strategies to the unique learning styles, personalities, and motivations of the client).

A brief elaboration of these principles is offered. The essence of the Risk Principle is that clinical services can be delivered in various so-called dosages, and the dosage should be paired with the problem level of the client. A common example of this concept in everyday practice is that of headache pain and dosage of medication in which the dosage of medication is linked to the severity of pain.

Applying the Risk Principle in clinical practice with criminal justice clients suggests that clinical services should be titrated to the degree of presenting problem, with the presenting problem among criminal justice clients defined as low versus high risk to reoffend. One of the clearest demonstrations of the risk principle among criminal justice clients is a study by Bonta, Wallace-Capretta, & Rooney (2000). In a posthoc study, these authors examined the risk level of clients (as determined by scores on a standardized assessment measure of criminal risk potential) and the level of clinical service (defined by the number of rehabilitation programs completed). There were four main comparisons: (1) low risk—low service, (2) low risk—high service, (3) high risk—low service, and (4) high risk—high service. The recidivism rates for the four combinations were as follows: low risk—low service

(15% reoffending), low risk—intensive service (32% reoffending), high risk—low service (56% reoffending), high risk—intensive service (32% reoffending). What is apparent is that low-risk clients who received clinical service beyond their required risk level had greater reoffending (32% instead of 15%) and that high-risk clients who had insufficient clinical service reoffended at a higher rate than expected (56% instead of 32%). The key, therefore, is to properly match the level of service to the risk level of the client.

Criminal justice clients often have multiple life management difficulties, some related to their criminality and some not. The key in working with criminal justice clients is to focus clinical attention on the factors most responsible for their antisocial behavior. These factors are routinely referred to as need areas and relate specifically to the Need Principle. There is a distinction between two types of need areas: criminogenic and noncriminogenic. Criminogenic need areas are those issues that are directly linked to the client's criminal behavior. As will become clearer later during the discussion of criminal risk factors, criminal attitudes and criminal friends are two examples of risk factors that are strongly linked to criminal behavior. Noncriminogenic risk factors, on the other hand, are those issues that are only weakly related to the client's criminal behavior. Low self-esteem is an excellent example of a noncriminogenic risk factor as research shows that this is virtually unrelated to criminal behavior. Counselors are encouraged to focus on the criminogenic need areas of clients and largely ignore the noncriminogenic areas.

The last of the three main clinical principles is the Responsivity Principle. The general theme of this concept is that clinical services are maximally effective when they are tailored as best as possible to client characteristics. There are two separate types of responsivity considerations, those that relate generally to criminal justice clients and those related specifically to each client. General Responsivity relates generically to all criminal justice clients. Research and clinical practice in all human service activities indicates that cognitive behavioral techniques produce optimum therapeutic approaches. Specific Responsivity relates to the unique personal, situational, and environmental characteristics of each client that makes him or her more amenable to clinical service. For example, clients vary on their degree of shyness. A person who is very shy would be expected to improve better in individual clinical sessions rather than group-oriented sessions, because he or she is likely to experience excessive anxiety in group settings. For clients to achieve their greatest clinical potential, they must receive services that are sensitive to these dimensions.

How do the risk/need/responsivity concepts apply in clinical practice for a typical criminal justice client? In the typical scenario, you are referred a client who has been convicted of a property-based crime for "counseling." An assessment of the client's criminal risk potential and specific need areas is completed, which reveals that he or she is at moderate risk to reoffend with problems in the area of employment, criminal thinking, criminal peers, and poor self-esteem. Further information reveals that the client is not overly intelligent and is weakly motivated to change his or her lifestyle. Attending to the risk principle, you schedule the client for reasonably frequent sessions, such as biweekly. Cognizant of the need principle, clinical activities are focused first on altering his or her criminal attitudes, then on altering his or her peer group such that he or she associates less with antisocial peers and more with prosocial peers. Clinical work is concluded with the client by addressing deficits in his or her employment eligibility. Virtually no clinical attention is directed to issues of self-esteem for two reasons. First, this is a noncriminogenic issue and second, because the client's views of himself or herself are likely to improve naturally as the client shows improvements in other aspects of his or her life. Finally, in attending to the responsivity principle, sessions in relatively short bursts that are interesting to the client are conducted (to sustain his or her attention and motivation) and use of abstract concepts is kept to a bare minimum (to address the low-intelligence issue).

THERAPEUTIC TARGETS

GOAL SETTING IS a constant theme in counseling contexts. Without goals, counselors and clients can easily lose sight of the germane clinical issues and what ultimately is to be achieved. Although personal well-being is often the therapeutic goal when working with noncriminal justice clients, generally speaking, personal well-being is not a clinical goal when working with criminal justice clients; however, it is often an indirect outcome of positive change. The primary clinical goal among criminal justice clients is reduced reoffending. The clinical challenge is to assist clients in modifying the factors and/or circumstances that gave rise to their criminal conduct such that it does not repeat itself. Resistance to clinical activities is quite common as clients do not generally enjoy, and in some cases genuinely fear, altering some of their comfortable behaviors such as abusing substances, associating with irresponsible peers, and having a free-spirited and unstable lifestyle. However, their well-being will certainly improve if they engage in less criminality, which results in less victimization and less contact with the criminal justice system.

One way to assist criminal justice clients in achieving improved clinical outcomes is to address the deficits in their lifestyle that are linked to their criminal risk potential. Criminal justice clients typically have multiple deficit areas of varying degrees of impairment. Determining which issue to address in what sequence of clinical contact can be a daunting task. One way to address this issue is to focus clinical attention on the factors related to clients' criminal risk potential (recalling that the predominant goal in working with criminal justice clients is to reduce their likelihood of reoffending). The research evidence from meta-analysis literature reviews on the predictors of criminal behavior can be helpful guides in this regard. Extensive research on the dominant risk factors for criminal behavior exists for different types of offenders, including adult male offenders (Gendreau, Little, & Goggin, 1996), juvenile male offenders (Cottle, Lee, & Heilbrun, 2001), juvenile female offenders (Simourd & Andrews, 1994), adult sex offenders (Hanson & Bussiere, 1998), and diagnosed psychiatric offenders (Bonta, Law, & Hanson, 1998).

Perusal of the meta-analytic literature reviews by Andrews, Bonta, and Wormith (2006) describe the "central eight" as the most relevant risk/need factors to consider when delivering clinical services to criminal justice clients. In order of importance, these factors and the way to improve them include:

1. *History of antisocial behavior* (early and continuing involvement in antisocial acts)—develop alternative behavior to high-risk situations,
2. *Antisocial personality* (adventurous, pleasure seeking, weak self-control)—develop problem-solving skills and general self-management,
3. *Antisocial cognition* (attitudes, values, beliefs supportive of crime)—reduce procriminal thinking and enhance prosocial thinking,
4. *Antisocial associates* (close association with criminal others and relative isolation from prosocial others)—reduce association with negative peers,
5. *Family/marital* (poor family and/or marital support and poor monitoring of behavior)—reduce conflict and enhance positive relationships,
6. *School/work* (low levels of performance and satisfaction in school or work)—enhance performance and rewards,
7. *Leisure/recreation* (low levels of involvement and satisfaction in anticriminal pursuits)—enhance involvement and rewards,
8. *Substance abuse* (abuse of alcohol or drugs)—reduce substance abuse and enhance alternatives to drug abuse.

As can be seen by this rank ordering of risk factors, greater clinical attention should be dedicated to the personal characteristics of clients such as those related to his or her thinking and immediate social relations. Modest clinical attention should be directed at the client's social achievement such as family relations and work situation, while less clinical attention should be devoted to issues of the client's free time and use of substances.

SUGGESTIONS FOR CLINICAL PRACTICE

THE META-ANALYTIC research and notions of the "central eight" risk/need factors inform clinicians as to the more potent criminal risk factors, which by extension indicates that they represent relevant therapeutic change targets. However, the degree to which any one factor is present quite often varies from client to client. The challenge to counselors is to customize a treatment plan for each client that addresses the relevant risk factors, but does so within the context of the risk/need/responsivity principles. Achieving this balance offers clients the greatest opportunity to improve their lives and reduce criminality. To accomplish this, counselors must accurately determine the relevant risk factors by way of assessment measures and be flexible in the delivery of clinical services. For example, the client profile noted above indicated that employment, criminal attitudes, and criminally oriented friends were the client's main problem areas. The research on risk factors indicates that criminal attitudes and friends are among the top risk factors whereas employment is a mid-range risk factor. It may be, however, the client has severe difficulty with employment and a minor problem with attitudes and peers. In this instance, it would be clinically appropriate to dedicate more attention to employment issues because it is a more serious issue with respect to criminal potential (which is consistent with the risk principle) than the other two issues, even though the research ranks it a lower criminal risk factor. These types of situations are quite common when working with criminal justice clients.

Is there such a thing as a typical criminal justice client? The simple answer is no—just like there is no typical client with an anxiety disorder, a mood disorder, or phobia. Criminal justice clients are unique in their own ways either by the type of offence they commit, the reasons why they committed their offence, and their responsiveness to altering their lifestyles. There are, however, common themes that occur among criminal justice clients. The general portrait of the criminal justice client is a person who commits a property-based crime who has a history of engaging in deviant behavior, has a positive belief system toward crime, has friends who are involved in crime to some degree, has family relationship and work problems, is involved in some fashion with illicit substances, and is modestly motivated to alter his or her lifestyle. Counselors can influence successful clinical outcomes with criminal justice clients by (1) determining the most relevant risk factors of the client, those linked to his or her criminality, and focusing clinical attention on those factors; (2) delivering the appropriate number of clinical sessions; and (3) counseling the client in a way that he or she can understand them the best. In many ways, this approach is similar to working with noncriminal justice clients.

In summary, working with criminal justice clients is both fascinating and clinically rewarding work. Although the crime rate is relatively low across many countries and jurisdictions, the sheer number of citizens in conflict with the law suggests that there is a sizeable criminal justice client group that may require therapeutic services. Counselors can be maximally effective in their clinical work if they provide skill-based services that address relevant criminogenic risk of their clients and do so in a manner that they can learn the best.

REFERENCES

Andrews, D. A., Bonta, J., & Hoge, R. D. (1990). Classification for effective rehabilitation: Rediscovering psychology. *Criminal Justice and Behavior, 17*, 19–52.

Andrews, D. A., Bonta, J., & Wormith, S. J. (2006). The recent past and near future of risk/need assessment. *Crime and Delinquency, 52*, 7–27.

Andrews, D. A., Zinger, I., Hoge, R. D., Bonta, J., Gendreau, P., & Cullen, F. T. (1990). Does correctional treatment work? A psychologically informed meta-analysis. *Criminology, 28*, 369–404.

Bonta, J., Law, M., & Hanson, K. (1998). The prediction of criminal and violent recidivism among mentally disordered offenders: A meta-analysis. *Psychological Bulletin, 123*, 123–142.

Bonta, J., Wallace-Capretta, S., & Rooney, J. (2000). A quasi-experimental evaluation of an intensive rehabilitation supervision program. *Criminal Justice and Behavior, 27*, 312–329.

Cottle, C. C., Lee, R. J., & Heilbrun, K. (2001). The prediction of criminal recidivism in juveniles: A meta-analysis. *Criminal Justice and Behavior, 28*, 367–394.

Gendreau, P., Little, T., & Goggin, C. (1996). A meta-analysis of the predictors of adult offender recidivism: What works. *Criminology, 34*, 575–607.

Glass, G. V., McGraw, B., & Smith, M. S. (1981). *Meta-analysis in social research.* Beverly Hills, CA: Sage Publications.

Hanson, R. K., & Bussiere, M. T. (1998). Predicting relapse: A meta-analysis of sexual offender recidivism studies. *Journal of Consulting and Clinical Psychology, 66*, 348–362.

Martinson, R. (1974). What works?—Questions and answers about prison reform. *The Public Interest, 10*, 22–54.

Simourd, L. A., & Andrews, D. A. (1994). Correlates of delinquency: A look at gender differences. *Forum on Corrections Research, 6*, 26–31.

64

Sexual Abuse Treatment

NOREEN M. GRAF

THE TERMS *SEXUAL* abuse and *sexual assault* are frequently used interchangeably in the literature to indicate sexual acts with a person who does not, or cannot, give consent. When these acts are also accompanied by physical force or harm, death threats, incapacitating substances, or kidnapping, the term *aggravated sexual abuse* is applied. The U.S federal criminal code distinguishes between "sexual contact" and "sexual acts." *Sexual contact* involves intentional touching of genitals, breasts, buttocks, anus, inner thigh, or groin without penetration. *Sexual acts* include penile penetration of the vagina or anus, contact between the mouth and genitals or anus, penetration of the vagina or anus with an object, or directly touching the genitals of a person under age 16 (U.S.C., Title 18, Chapter 109A, § 2241–2233, 2006).

PREVALENCE, TYPE, AND RISK

SEXUAL ABUSE IS commonplace, but the actual prevalence of sexual abuse is difficult to determine because there is no central agency responsible for the gathering and assimilation of this data. Abuse can be reported to a number of agencies that do not share information such as government and legal entities, medical facilities, mental health services, or faith-based organizations. Conversely, the abuse may not be reported at all due to the sensitivity of the topic and the perceived and actual undesirable outcomes that may result from reporting a crime.

Estimates of prevalence vary considerably depending upon the population sampled, the sampling method, and whether the definition includes noncontact sexual acts. In a meta-analysis of studies, Rind, Tromovitch, and Bauserman (1998) concluded that the sexual abuse of males ranges from 3% to 37% (M = 17%) and the sexual abuse of females ranges from 8% to 71% (M = 28%).

Despite appalling statistics, disclosure and reporting of abuse is uncommon. In a review of studies of adults who were sexually abused as children, London, Bruck, Ceci, and Shuman (2005) noted that the large majority of children who are sexually abused do not disclose the abuse as children, and only 10% to 18% of sexual abuse is ever reported. In part, this may be due to the fact that perpetrators of sexual abuse are most frequently a family member or a close family friend. In a national study that included 8,000 women, 60% of rapes against women occurred when the victims were below the age of 18 and 80% of the victims knew their perpetrators. However, only 16% of the rapes were reported (Kilpatrick, Edmunds, & Seymour, 1992).

Studies to determine factors that make children more susceptible to sexual abuse have determined that, aside from age and gender, other risk factors are associated with childhood sexual abuse and include coming from a low-income household, living in a single-parent household (Sobsey & Doe, 1991), and having a disability (Glover-Graf & Reed, 2006).

COMMON SYMPTOMS

To understand the needs of this population, it is essential to understand the numerous potential effects of sexual abuse. Unresolved sexual abuse may result in somatic reactions (Schachter, Stalker, & Teram, 2001), negative thoughts and beliefs about the self, negative emotions, destructive behaviors, and interpersonal problems. Negative feelings include chronic anger, fear, shame, and guilt. A low self-esteem and perceived powerlessness, self-blame, and worthlessness are strongly related to interpersonal problems and destructive behavior problems. Negative or destructive behavior may include eating disorders, sleep disorders, anxiety attacks, self-injury, sexual promiscuity, and substance abuse (Blume, 1990; Courtois, 1988; Sanderson, 2006). Interpersonal problems may involve isolation from others, a lack of personal boundaries, lack of trust in others, and an inability to sustain relationships (Briere, 1992).

LONG-TERM EFFECTS

T HE LONG-TERM EFFECTS of sexual abuse have been noted as revictimization (Messman-Moore & Long, 2000), posttraumatic stress disorder (PTSD) and other dissociative disorders, somatoform disorders, emotional dysregulation, depression, anxiety, sexual dysfunction, learning difficulties, behavior problems, and neuroses (Gauthier, Stollak, Meese, & Arnoff, 1996; Kendall-Tackett, Williams, & Finkelhor, 1993). Depression is a typical response to sexual abuse and major depressive disorder (MDD) may also emerge as a long-term result of abuse. Victims experience feelings of helplessness and hopelessness, suicide ideation and/or attempts, and difficulty with sleeping, eating, concentrating, and daily functioning. About a third of rape victims experience MDD in their lifetime (Kilpatrick et al., 1992).

Another potential long-term effect of sexual abuse is PTSD, which involves the development of particular symptoms following a traumatic event, including persistent reexperiencing of the event; intrusive thoughts; nightmares; avoidance of situations, feelings, and thoughts related to the assault; and hyperarousal. Most women who have been raped experience these symptoms after their assault and may initially be diagnosed with acute stress disorder, an earlier form of PTSD. About a third of victims will go on to develop PTSD in their lifetimes (Tjaden & Thoennes, 2000).

Other long-term effects are suggested by studies related to illegal behaviors. Childhood abuses are estimated to increase delinquency and criminality by 40% (Widom, 1992). A number of studies have noted that between 76% and 90% of prostitutes were victims of childhood sexual abuse (Weisburg, 1985). Revictimization has also been noted among survivors of sexual abuse because adults who have previous histories of sexual abuse may repeatedly enter abusive relationships. Russell (1999) found a strong correlation between childhood incest and later adult sexual abuse and spousal abuse. Additionally, Vanderbilt (1992) noted that 40% of sexual perpetrators were also childhood abuse victims.

TREATMENT APPROACHES

B EFORE TREATMENT CAN be initiated, a comprehensive assessment must be performed, including a detailed history of the sexual abuse, the frequency of abuse, relationship to perpetrators, trauma characteristics, response to the trauma, current coping capacity, support system access, and current symptoms. Substance abuse assessment, depression, and PTSD screens should be applied as indicated.

Clients may enter treatment at a number of stages following the sexual abuse. It is important to initially assess the client's state of crisis. Crisis is defined as "a perception or experiencing of an event or situation as an intolerable difficulty that exceeds the person's current resources and coping resources" (James & Gilliland, 2001, p. 3). Clients may experience crisis immediately following a traumatic event or may come to reexperience a crisis stage during a number of different life events (e.g., initiation of dating, marriages, divorces, birth of a child), or they may also enter crises at later stages due to unresolved issues and/or inadequate coping skills. When clients enter therapy in a crisis state, therapists should follow a crisis theory model that focuses upon alleviating immediate distress. This may be followed up with longer-term therapy.

Treatment approaches for sexual abuse include psychotherapy to deal with the emotional issues related to the abuse; cognitive behavior therapies to change negative emotions, thoughts, and behaviors associated with the abuse and to develop positive coping strategies; group therapy to provide the benefits of group sharing and learning; eye-movement desensitization and reprocessing (EMDR) to deal with reconnection and reprocessing of traumatic memories; prolonged exposure (PE) to desensitize victims to the effects of the abuse; and expressive therapies including art therapy, music therapy, and phototherapy to express the feelings and impact of the abuse. Medication is sometimes used in combination with therapy to assist in symptom tolerance, including sleep, antidepressant, and antianxiety medications, particularly if the victim suffers from depression, sleep disorders, panic disorders, or anxiety disorders.

Psychodynamic psychotherapy is a form of therapy that focuses around uncovering, exploring, and processing unconscious thoughts and feelings through talk therapy. If defense mechanisms such as denial are keeping clients from connecting with their feelings, anxiety and maladaptive behaviors may result. Psychotherapy is often used in combination with other therapies as described below.

Cognitive behavior therapies (CBT) are considered the most effective in treatment for sexual abuse. However, this may be combined with psychodynamic therapy, particularly if the client has childhood abuse issues and/or is unaware of, or disconnected from, feelings associated with the trauma. Trauma-focused CBT typically involves behavioral relaxation training paired with gradual exposure to the distressing traumatic events. Continual pairing of the events with relaxation is intended to subdue the impact of the memories of the event. New cognitively focused information related to the current meaning of the event, beliefs about the self, the world, and the individual's future are also introduced. Faulty thinking related to the victim's behavior at the time of the trauma and the victim's responsibility for the event is also challenged on a cognitive level (Deblinger & Heflin, 1996). Cognitive processing therapy (CPT) is a cognitive therapy that is specifically designed to treat rape victims with depression and PTSD through the use of exposure through writing and reading detailed accounts of their rape experience (Resnick & Schnicke, 1993). Stress Innoculation Training (SIT) is another form of CBT that was developed to deal with anxiety following rape. Treatment components include education, coping-skills training, relaxation and breathing techniques, thought-stopping, positive self-talk, assertiveness training, and role playing.

Prolonged exposure (PE) therapy involves the prolonged and repeated exposure to the trauma-related objects and situations that evoke anxiety. During PE, therapists will instruct the individual to repeatedly recount the abuse in detail. Clients may also tape-record these sessions and continue to listen to their accountings until the anxiety associated with recalling the event is substantially diminished. Later treatment involves exposure to anxiety-producing triggers such as dark places or dating. Both SIT and PE have been shown to be effective in treatment of PTSD related to sexual assault (Foa et al., 1999).

Eye-movement desensitization and reprocessing (EMDR) uses elements from psychodynamic therapy, cognitive behavior therapy, and exposure therapy. The therapy involves an eight-phase process of exposure to trauma using tactile, auditory, and visual stimulation to activate both the left and right hemispheres of the brain in order to process the traumatic event both cognitively and emotively (Shapiro, 2002). This therapy has been shown to reduce trauma-related symptoms with greater efficiency than exposure therapy or CBT (Korn & Leeds, 2002).

Group therapy in combination with individual therapy is frequently considered the most appropriate treatment for victims of sexual abuse. Groups may vary in length and be long-term or time-limited and deal with a number of relevant issues. Group therapy is often an important part of the healing process for women who are victims of sexual assault. Therapy may help reduce isolation and encourage supportive relationships. Friendships may also develop that are built upon trust and mutual concern. For many women, the group may also serve as "family" where they are able to work through family problems and rehearse for future family-of-origin encounters without fear. Self-esteem may also be improved because members view their contributions to the group as meaningful and helpful to others. Reality testing is also a benefit of group treatment because members of the group are able to share their beliefs about responsibility and blame for abuse as well as their feelings about the events. Members will often blame themselves for the abuse but will rarely believe that other group members were responsible for the abuse they experienced. Group members can also practice new behaviors and social skills (Faller, 1993).

Expressive therapy is a form of therapy that uses the arts as a means of expressing and exploring feelings. Art, music, drama, dance, play, and writing have been used for the treatment of both adults and children to develop therapeutic relationships, break down defenses, facilitate communication, and for cathartic release (Bow, 1993). Glover-Graf (2007) suggested the use of photography therapy as a communication tool for better understanding and exploring sexual abuse.

COUNSELING FOCUS

T HE MAIN GOALS of treatment for sexual abuse are to process and overcome the negative effects of abuse, including the physical, cognitive, emotional, interpersonal, and behavioral consequences of abuse. Treatment can also result in personal growth and transcendence in which the victims develop a greater personal strength and awareness. Depending upon the victim's needs and desires, treatment can last from months to years.

PHYSICAL COUNSELING ISSUES

IMMEDIATE PHYSICAL CONCERNS following a sexual assault include sustained injuries, sexually transmitted diseases, and pregnancy. The National Violence Against Women's Study estimates that about 5% of adult females who are raped become pregnant. Fifty percent of these pregnancies are voluntarily terminated, 11% are spontaneously aborted, and 39% elect to give birth with 6% of these births resulting in adoptions. Women making decisions about keeping or terminating pregnancy may require considerable counseling regarding options available as well as dealing with the psychological impact of an undesired pregnancy resulting from rape (Tjaden & Thoennes, 2000).

The Centers for Disease Control estimates the risk of contracting sexually transmitted diseases (STDs), including gonorrhea, Chlamydia, and syphilis to range from less than 1% to 17%. The risk of contacting HIV from rape is estimated at less than 1%. While these risks are generally low, anxiety about contracting STDs is prevalent for some time because some STDs take up to a year to rule out. Additionally, some studies have shown higher rates of chronic physical complaints among victims of abuse, including lower back pain, gynecological problems, gastrointestinal disorders, pelvic pain, and headaches (Schachter et al., 2001). However, for some victims, even touching of the body can be experienced as painful. Body contact or even clothing that restricts movement may be intolerable.

COGNITIVE COUNSELING ISSUES

THOUGHTS AND BELIEFS about the nature of abuse trauma and about the self may need to be addressed in counseling because feelings and behaviors may be affected by thinking. Victims may believe they are responsible for the abuse due to failure to defend themselves, or their choices in persons to date and places to visit. Victims may also internalize messages from society regarding their behavior or clothing as contributing to the perpetrator's assault. Adults who experience sexual abuse as a child may think they were responsible and blame themselves for the seduction of the adult, for failure to defend themselves from the abuse, for any positive physical or emotional pleasure they may have had in relation to the sexual experiences, for failure to report the abuse, for the negative consequences of reporting the abuse (impact on the family and punitive consequences to the perpetrator), or for the subsequent abuse of other persons due to failure to report. The invasiveness of sexual abuse and the feelings of guilt can also have a strong impact upon self-esteem. The victims may see themselves as damaged, dirty, and powerless (Briere, 1992).

EMOTIONAL COUNSELING ISSUES

EMOTIONAL CONSEQUENCES OF abuse often involve feelings of depression, anger, anxiety, fear, numbing, guilt, and shame. Guilt is often triggered by a sense of responsibility for the occurrence of the sexual abuse. Therapy also addresses the anxiety and fear that may result from the sexual abuse experience itself. While physical violence or rendering the victim unable to defend herself through chemicals or restraint may not always be present, threats of violence or harm to the victim or other loved persons or pets may be equally damaging to the psyche. In children where coercion is most often used, this may be coupled with verbal threats to the stability and unity of the family, or threats of physical harm. Victims may develop phobic reactions to a specific person, or groups of persons (e.g., adult males), or to environmental triggers (e.g., dark rooms), or even specific behaviors elicited by others. These fears can lead to avoidance of: public places, social contact with others, intimate and trusting relationships, and engagement in activities (Blume, 1990; Briere, 1992; Courtois, 1988).

Anger and rage may also be experienced by the survivor of sexual abuse and may be experienced directly or may be displaced onto others since it may not be possible to express the anger directly to the known or unknown assailant. In longer-term abuse or childhood abuse, anger expressed at the time of the abuse may have led to greater violence at the time of abuse, leading to the belief that it is unsafe to express anger and to anger suppression. This inability to feel and express anger may persist, or anger may become a pervasive emotion and victims may constantly feel inner hostility and rage. Counseling for anger may include assisting the client to experience the anger and directing it at the cause so that the victim may move toward resolution (Blume, 1990).

BEHAVIOR COUNSELING ISSUES

A NUMBER OF behavioral consequences may also require therapy. Physical boundaries are frequently a problem for survivors, particularly those who were abused as children. A sense of appropriate physical distance and appropriate touching is often unclear to victims, sometimes leading to sexual avoidance or highly sexualized behaviors. Adults may isolate themselves from all sexual contact, or may exhibit promiscuous sexual behaviors, potentially adding to the cycle of revictimization. Those who avoid all sexual contact or associations with sexuality seek to avoid the feelings they associate with sexual acts. They may dress in ways to make themselves appear unattractive to others, may not attend to personal hygiene, or manipulate the size of their body through excessive or diminished eating to make themselves unapproachable or invisible. Those who act out sexually appear to have internalized a belief that they have been reduced to a sexual purpose and behave accordingly, sometimes dressing in revealing and suggestive clothing, using sexualized behaviors, and sometimes turning to prostitution. Other behavior problems have been noted such as self-abusive acts, including suicide attempts, substance abuse, eating disorders, and self-harm. Some of the most common forms of self-injury occur among clients with a history of sexual abuse. These include self-mutilation through cutting and burning (including "branding" with heated objects), picking at skin or wounds, hair-pulling, self-hitting with objects, and multiple piercing or tattooing. While these behaviors may appear to be self-punitive, their intent may be directed toward feeling and demonstrating self-control over one's own body in an attempt to reclaim the self. Counseling focus should therefore not merely be aimed at behavior extinction, but at establishing a deep sense of self-ownership and control. Self-abuse issues may require separate specialized treatment, depending on the severity of the behavior (Blume, 1990; Briere, 1992; Courtois, 1988).

INTERPERSONAL COUNSELING ISSUES

AT THE ROOT of interpersonal problems are issues of power and control, the feeling that one has little or no control over what happens to him or her, and the fear that someone, even someone trusted, will harm him or her. Therefore, counseling must address the difficulty and reluctance to trust others that can lead to the avoidance of establishing close and intimate relationships. Treatment issues generally include a strong emphasis upon building trust. If the victim was abused in childhood and/or by a known adult, the ability to trust others may be severely impacted. In intrafamilial sexual abuse, lack of trust may be pervasive because those charged with protection violated the child's personal boundaries. In addition, the nonoffending parent failed to protect the child. When other trusted adults or adults who hold a position of authority are perpetrators, this too causes the child to have difficulty placing trust in others, potentially leading to a lifelong pattern of relationship problems due to the lack of ability to form trusting bonds (Russell, 1999). A number of additional issues may require therapeutic interventions if the sexual abuse was intrafamilial, including addressing the mother–victim relationship and the perpetrator–victim relationship.

Finally, it is important to consider that elimination of negative consequences and restoration to the previous sense of self and previous level of functioning are important goals; however, as with any type of trauma, there is opportunity for growth and transcendence to higher levels of functioning, and greater clarity of life's purpose and meaning.

REFERENCES

Blume, E. S. (1990). *Secret survivors: Uncovering incest and its aftereffects in women.* New York: Wiley.

Bow, J. N. (1993). Overcoming resistance. In C. Schaefer (Ed.), *The therapeutic powers of play* (pp. 17–39). Northvale, NJ: Jason Aronson.

Briere, J. N. (1992). *Child abuse trauma: Theory and treatment of the lasting effects.* Newbury Park, CA: Sage Publications.

Courtois, C. A. (1988). *Healing the incest wound.* New York: W. W. Norton.

Deblinger, E., & Heflin, A. H. (1996). *Cognitive behavioral interventions for treating sexually abused children.* Thousand Oaks, CA: Sage Publications.

Faller, K. C. (1993). *Child sexual abuse: Intervention and treatment issues.* Retrieved September 1, 2007, from http://www.childwelfare.gov/pubs/usermanuals/sexabuse/sexabuse.pdf

Foa, F. B., Dancu, C. V., Hembree, E. A., Jaycox, L. H., Meadows, E. A., & Street, G. P. (1999). A comparison of exposure therapy, stress inoculation training, and their combination for reducing posttraumatic stress disorder in female assault victims. *Journal of Consulting and Clinical Psychology, 59,* 715–723.

Gauthier, L., Stollak, G., Meese, L., & Arnoff, J. (1996). Recall of childhood neglect and physical abuse as differential predictors of current psychological functioning. *Child Abuse and Neglect, 20,* 549–559.

Glover-Graf, N. M. (2007). Therapeutic photography for sexual abuse survivors. In S. L. Brooke (Ed.), *The use of the creative therapies with sexual abuse survivors* (pp. 86–101). Springfield, IL: Charles C. Thomas.

Glover-Graf, N. M., & Reed, B. J. (2006). Abuse against women with disabilities. *Rehabilitation Education, 20,* 43–56.

James, R. K., & Gilliland, B. E. (2001). *Crisis intervention strategies* (4th ed.). Belmont, CA: Wadsworth.

Kendall-Tackett, K. A., Williams, L. M., & Finkelhor, D. (1993). Impact of sexual abuse on children: A review and synthesis of empirical studies. *Psychological Bulletin, 113,* 164–180.

Kilpatrick, D. G., Edmunds, C. N., & Seymour, A. K. (1992). *Rape in America: A report to the nation.* Arlington, VA: National Victim Center and Charleston, SC, Medical University of South Carolina.

Korn, D. L., & Leeds, A. M. (2002). Preliminary evidence of efficacy for EMDR resource development and installation in the stabilization phase of treatment of complex posttraumatic stress disorder. *Journal of Clinical Psychology, 58,* 1465–1487.

London, K., Bruck, M., Ceci, S. J., & Shuman, D. W. (2005). Disclosure of child sexual abuse: What does the research tell us about the ways that children tell? *Psychology, Public Policy, and Law, 11,* 194–226.

Messman-Moore, T. L., & Long, P. J. (2000). Child sexual abuse and revictimization in the form of adult sexual abuse, adult abuse, and adult psychological maltreatment. *Journal of Interpersonal Violence, 15,* 489–502.

Resnick, P. A., & Schnicke, M. K. (1993). *Cognitive processing therapy for rape victims: A treatment manual.* Newbury Park, CA: Sage Publications.

Rind, B., Tromovitch, P., & Bauserman, R. (1998). A meta-analytic examination of assumed properties of child sexual abuse using college samples. *Psychological Bulletin, 124,* 22–53.

Russell, D. E. H. (1999). *The secret trauma: Incest in the lives of girls and women* (2nd ed.). New York: Basic Books.

Sanderson, C. (2006). *Counseling adult survivors of child sexual abuse* (3rd ed.). London: Jessica Kingsley.

Schachter, C., Stalker, C., & Teram, E. (2001). *Handbook on sensitive practice for health professionals: Lessons from women survivors of childhood sexual abuse.* Ottawa, Canada: National Clearinghouse on Family Violence.

Shapiro, F. (2002). EMDR 12 years after its introduction: A review of past, present, and future directions. *Journal of Clinical Psychology, 58,* 1–22.

Sobsey, D., & Doe, T. (1991). Patterns of sexual abuse and assault. *Sexuality and Disability, 9*(3), 243–259.

Tjaden, P., & Thoennes, N. (2000). *Full report of the prevalence, incidence, and consequences of intimate partner violence against women: Findings from the National Violence Against Women Survey.* Report for Grant 93-IJ-CX-0012. Washington, DC: National Institute of Justice.

United States Code. (2006). Title 18, Part One, Chapter 109A—Sexual Abuse.

Vanderbilt, H. (1992, February). Incest: A chilling report. *Lear's,* 49–64.

Weisburg, D. K. (1985). *Children of the night: A study of adolescent prostitution.* Lexington, MA: Lexington Books.

Widom, C. S. (1992). *The cycle of violence.* Washington, DC: National Institute of Justice, U.S. Department of Justice.

65

Disaster Mental Health Response and Stress Debriefing

MARK A. STEBNICKI

W E ARE IN the midst of a paradigm shift in the counseling and allied helping professions when it comes to dealing with extraordinary stressful and traumatic events that have taken place in the United States. Catastrophic events have accelerated world-wide within the last seven years. In America, the horrific terrorist attacks of Tuesday, September 11, 2001, and Hurricane Katrina that took place on August 29, 2005, left emotional, physical, spiritual, and environmental scars upon our minds, bodies, and spirits. The desolation left in the aftermath has created a sort of historical trauma among Westerners that seems to have prompted a consciousness shift within the counseling field and other helping professions. Fires, floods, drought, school shootings, and other critical incidents require our complete and full attention to survivors, families, and communities of such events. For many, Planet Earth does not appear to be a safe place to live because of the multitude of critical events. Despite that most Americans may be far from the epicenter of such critical incidents, many are affected at some level of consciousness. As a consequence, some of us may be experiencing the emotional, social, physical, spiritual, and occupational exhaustion that is associated with empathy fatigue. Thus, we need to cultivate and train new generations of counselors that are skilled and competent at providing disaster mental health response and stress debriefing counseling services.

While medical professionals, police, and rescue workers all prepare for the physical rescue in the multitude of disaster scenarios, counselors and other mental health professionals are called to provide the mental health rescue. Today, many counselors and other human service professionals are required to have training in the various models of crisis intervention (see resources section). These include, but are not limited to American Red Cross (ARC) Disaster Mental Health response, Acute Traumatic Stress Management (ATSM), Critical Incident Stress Debriefing (CISD), Critical Incident Stress Management (CISM), and National Organization for Victims' Assistance (NOVA) Group Crisis response model. There are many other crisis response models where teams of first responders are formed such as Homeland Security, Environmental Protection Agency, computer and Internet security specialists, the commercial airline industry, public schools and higher education, private corporations, faith-based and charity organizations, and others to serve in a specific settings or in groups.

Indeed, there are multiple opportunities for professional counselors to prepare, plan, and intervene in a variety of critical incidents. The consequence of such extraordinary stressful and traumatic events affects a wide range of the population who require specialists to work with children and adolescents, college students, middle-aged and older adults, and others who have been victimized. New clients and consumers of mental health, rehabilitation, and allied health services seem to be emerging who are secondary survivors of traumatic events. These include, but are not limited to, spouses, children, and family members that have a loved one serving in Iraq and Afghanistan; soldiers who have come home with traumatic physical injuries and chronic and persistent mental health conditions; and a new population of survivors of sexual abuse perpetrated by online predators and some members of the clergy.

This chapter offers (1) a practical approach for facilitating disaster mental health and stress debriefing groups using a combination of crisis response models; (2) specific guidelines for structuring such interventions and responding to individuals and groups; and (3) resources to assist in personal and professional growth in the specialty area of disaster mental health response. Additionally, three case scenarios are provided at the end of the chapter for the purpose of practicing the skills of disaster mental health and stress debriefing interventions.

DISASTER MENTAL HEALTH RESPONSE AND STRESS DEBRIEFING

THERE ARE A variety of models and strategies that disaster mental health professionals utilize during a crisis event. Certain models are preferred because of the type of setting (e.g., schools, hospitals, government agencies); however, there is no one model superior to the others that can comprehensively address the survivor's mental and emotional needs in all situations. Accordingly, it is important to evaluate the efficacy of the intervention and its use for a particular critical incident. One of the most important elements common to all settings is the rapport and connection that a competent crisis counselor can establish with the survivor. The quality of the working relationship is paramount in facilitating and reinforcing coping and resiliency skills as well as supports and resources for the survivor of critical incidents. The ability to intently listen, attend to, and empathically respond can therapeutically empower survivors with the necessary and sufficient conditions for coping within the first few hours, days, and weeks after a critical event.

Accordingly, the primary purpose of a disaster mental health intervention is to facilitate brief interventions in a highly dynamic and supportive environment that focus on (1) identifying the person's behavioral, affective, somatic, interpersonal, cognitive, and spiritual capacities that increase the individual's safety and security needs; (2) creating an empathic environment and opportunity for the individual to talk about the trauma experience for the purpose of psychological first aid; and (3) reducing acute stress and offering an environment that can cultivate the seeds of hope to restore balance and normalcy by building resiliency. Most practitioners and researchers agree that disaster mental health response should not serve in place of longer-term therapeutic interventions. Thus, the skilled practitioner understands that creating a supportive, safe, empathetic, and compassionate environment is the first therapeutic step in the survivor's overall mental health, wellness, and healing.

PREINTERVENTION STRUCTURE

INITIALLY, THE PREINTERVENTION and planning stage is critical in assessing, coordinating, and communicating with others on the disaster team concerning the trauma survivors' psychological, spiritual, and medical/physical level of functioning. The nature and timing of the traumatic event (e.g., 24 hours, 48 hours, 5 days postdisaster) will determine the mental health interventions that will be required. The mental health professional should first select individuals and/or groups that may be closest to the epicenter of the critical event or those that are most at-risk psychologically. Other groups may be formed by those individuals and groups that are secondary survivors or further from the epicenter.

Begin by establishing a rapport with the individual or group members in a private area if possible. Once the group or individual session is formed then the disaster mental health professional should (1) make sure to introduce himself or herself and others on the disaster response team and begin to establish a rapport with the survivor, (2) explain the purpose and intention of the stress debriefing or intervention, (3) ask for permission to talk with the survivor, (4) discuss issues of confidentiality, (5) provide a professional statement of disclosure and emphasize the counselor's role as mental health specialist, (6) encourage personal disclosure with the survivor but only at the level the person feels most comfortable when discussing the traumatic experience, and (7) focus on interventions and educate the individual or group, and reinforce that the counselor is there for emotional/psychological support with the intention of empowering them with resources that will help build short-term coping and resiliency skills.

COMPASSION AND EMPATHY: ESTABLISHING SAFETY AND SECURITY

THE COUNSELOR/MENTAL HEALTH specialist should provide opportunities for individuals to receive positive human contact (compassionate communication and appropriate physical touch) and to reaffirm their needs for physical and psychological safety and security. Use the skills of listening, attending, and empathic responding to validate the survivor's experience. Mental health professionals must be aware of the behavioral, affective, somatic, interpersonal, cognitive, and spiritual responses to acute and posttraumatic stress (see Table 65.1). Most of all, they must create an environment that reinforces the survivors' safety and security needs, as well as provide hope for the future.

During this first phase of intervention, individuals and groups are extremely concerned with how they will cope with the losses, suffering, grief, and catastrophic critical incident. There is a tendency to feel an overwhelming sense of hopelessness, discouragement, mental, physical, and spiritual exhaustion. Thus, it is critical to use statements that encourage and reflect their positive traits of internal locus of control and things in their lives that they can and cannot control. Reinforce the individual or group's coping and resiliency skills from past events of adversity.

VENTILATION, VALIDATION, AND EMPATHY

ENCOURAGE INDIVIDUALS TO talk and tell their story about the stressful and traumatic event. Allow and give permission to the individual or group participants in a stress debriefing or crisis response to ventilate. The professional counselor can use this as therapeutic leverage to validate the participant's feelings/emotions about the critical event. Reassure the person that his or her sadness and grief are very normal responses to a nonordinary or traumatic event. Assure the

TABLE 65.1   Children and Adolescents' Response to Acute Stress and Trauma

Physical	Cognitive	Emotional	Behavioral
Fatigue	Tendency to blame others	Anxiety	Changes in normal activities
Insomnia		Severe panic (rare)	
Muscle tremors	Confusion	Grief	Change in speech
Twitches	Poor attention	Denial	Withdrawal from others
Difficulty or rapid breathing	Inability to make decisions	Survivor guilt/ self- blame	Emotional outbursts
Bowel and bladder problems	Heightened or lowered alertness	Emotional numbness	Change in communication
Elevated BP	Poor concentration	Uncertainty	Suspiciousness
Rapid heartbeat	Forgetfulness	Loss of emotional control	Inability to rest
Chest pain	Trouble identifying known objects or people	Fear of loss/of going crazy	Substance abuse
Headaches			Intensified startle reflex
Visual difficulties	Increased or decreased awareness of surrounding	Depression	
Nausea/vomiting		Lack of capacity for enjoyment	Antisocial acts
Thirst			Pacing
Loss of appetite	Poor problem solving	Apprehension	Erratic movements
Dizziness		Intense anger	Decreased personal hygiene
Excessive sweating	Loss of a sense of time, place, or person	Irritability	Diminished sexual drive
Chills		Agitation	
Weakness		Helplessness	Appetite disturbance
Fainting	Disturbed thinking	Mistrust	
	Nightmares	Feelings of worthlessness	Prolonged silences
	Inescapable images		Accident prone–ness
	Flashbacks	Apathy/boredom	
	Suicidal ideas		
	Disbelief		
	Change in values		
	Search for meaning		

person that he or she will not always feel this sense of overwhelming grief. The person may never forget the traumatic event; however, with time, the intensity of emotion will ease or diminish.

The professional crisis responder will want to reinforce that being open and honest with one's feelings and emotions is healthy for one's overall well-being. Disclosure of feelings, emotions, or the individual's story concerning the traumatic event is very individualized. The ethical and competent disaster mental health practitioner knows that he or she should never force emotions or shame individuals for not disclosing, especially early on in the grieving and healing process (e.g., 24–48 hours posttrauma). Many trauma survivors require a period of silence as a coping response before talking to someone that may initially be a stranger or an acquaintance. Overall, it is essential that the trauma specialist emphasize to the survivor that he or she should only disclose at the level he or she is most comfortable with at this time.

The disaster mental health or stress debriefing team should reemphasize that the focus of the session or group will allow the survivor to cultivate his or her coping and resiliency skills. When the survivor is ready, reinforce that it is healthy to "talk about it, and by putting our heads together, we may be able to see how we can get our lives back to normal or back to balance again." Facilitators may use the following questions:

- Where were you when this incident happened?
- Try and remember back to this event. What were some of the things that you saw, heard, felt, smelled, and experienced?
- What other memories stood out for you?
- Since the time of this incident, how have you been affected? Can you describe how this event has significantly impacted your life right now?
- How did your family and friends react to this incident?

The crisis responder should use the skills of attending, listening, empathic reflection, paraphrasing, clarifying, and summarizing to facilitate individual or group interventions. Educate the survivors on the mental, physical, cognitive, spiritual, and other things they may experience during this particular time of their lives. Despite the fact that many persons who have been through extraordinary stressful and traumatic events may feel like they are victims, reinforce the idea that they are actually *survivors* of the traumatic event. Clarify for the participants that they may doubt their mental and physical abilities, cognitive skills, judgment, and capacity for coping and resiliency, but "it won't always feel this way."

PREDICTION, PREPARATION, AND MAKING MEANING OF THE EVENT

ENCOURAGE THE PERSON to try and think about how he or she can get back to normal again and how to reconnect with his or her life (e.g., job, school, friends, family, regular routines). As a professional mental health crisis responder, you may feel the need to provide all the answers. However, your most effective strategies are those that (1) educate the person about psychosocial reaction to trauma, loss, and grief; and (2) facilitate meaning of the critical event and brainstorm ideas for healing, support, and building capacity for coping and resiliency. Facilitators may ask the following questions:

- What have you discovered about yourself in this experience?
- What keeps you going through this painful time right now?
- Have you made any sense of this painful experience?
- After all that you have been through, what do you expect to face in the next few days, weeks, months?
- What are some things that help you to continue on after all that you've been through?
- How do you think that your family, friends, or community will continue to be affected?
- What other concerns do you have about your future?
- What are some things (coping strategies) that you can do (today) to help you prepare for getting back to normal again at (school, work, home, and parenting)?
- Are there any specific things that you could share with others that might help them through this event, to help them cope right now?
- If I came in contact with you a few weeks or months from now, what might I notice that would be different about you? What would you be feeling or thinking?

In critical incident or crisis response, the individual's sense of self, safety, and security is a significant stressor in his or her life. The critical event may have taken away the person's sense of meaning and hope for having a so-called normal life ever again. However, the professional and competent crisis counselor is compelled to help the survivor begin a path of healing and facilitate strategies that allow the person to heal at his or her own pace. Thus, it is important for the professional counselor or crisis responder to recognize that finding meaning in an extraordinary stressful or traumatic event occurs at different levels of consciousness for the survivor. With time, some of the physical, emotional, and psychological trauma begins to scar over as the survivor attempts to integrate the traumatic experience into his or her existential or perhaps spiritual worldview. Accordingly, the professional must make a holistic assessment of the individual and then facilitate appropriate interventions at the survivor's level of understanding and perception toward the critical incident.

CORE MESSAGES AND FACILITATIVE RESPONSES OF WHAT TO COMMUNICATE TO CHILDREN, ADOLESCENTS, AND ADULTS

THE SEASONED DISASTER mental health or trauma specialist knows how to communicate words of comfort and compassion that are culturally sensitive. Although the professional cannot prepare to intervene in every environmental setting or disaster scenario, it is essential that the counselor gather information prior to convening a stress debriefing session or group. For example, it is important to anticipate any cultural differences (e.g., racial/ethnic identity, gender, rural versus urban settings, physical disability) so that interventions can be facilitated in a culturally responsive manner. It is beyond the scope of this chapter to provide a comprehensive list of guidelines for multiple populations and settings. However, the list of resources provided at the end of this chapter should provide professional counselors additional information for increasing their knowledge and skills in disaster mental health response. The following section offers some guidelines and facilitative responses that may be helpful with different groups and individuals.

Children and Adolescents

- Assure the child/adolescent that feeling frightened, sad, or confused is very normal given all that the child has been through and that it's healthy to express emotions. It will help them get better similar to when they are feeling sick or injured (i.e., flu, colds, healing a broken bone).
- Explain to the child/adolescent that part of what he or she is feeling emotionally and physically will actually help him or her feel better and more balanced in his or her life. Say to the child, "You are not a weak person. Most kids and even adults feel the same way you do after an experience like yours." It especially helps heal emotions when kids verbalize their feelings.
- Reinforce that it is important for them to accept help and support for a while until they feel better and less sad. We are not totally independent in our lives. Everyone needs some help from others at some point in his or her life.
- Reassure the child/adolescent that right now, it may take a lot of effort and focus to do his or her normal daily routine (i.e., school, homework, sports, other activities). Allow each person time to transition back to his or her normal routines. The more the child practices doing his or her routine, the easier it will become.

- Explain to the child/adolescent that he or she does not have to share his or her thoughts and feelings with everyone, but it's OK to share them with you, or someone he or she trusts.
- Say to the child/adolescent: "You have been through something very few others have and it's normal to feel sad. Crying over something sad and terrible is not the same as acting like a baby."
- Say to the child/adolescent: "People's hearts can hurt the same way a broken bone does. Hurting is just part of healing, and broken hearts do heal, just like broken bones."

Facilitative Responses for Adults

- I'm sorry this has happened to you. I can't imagine what you are going through right now.
- I'm glad you're safe right now; let's think of some ways that you can feel even more safe.
- It is hard to forget or stop the pain because this is something too painful to forget.
- What you are feeling right now is very normal. What you have been through is very abnormal.
- Feeling sad only means that you are a human being.
- Your feelings may change from day to day. You may have many different feelings all at the same time. It may feel confusing to you at times because of all that you have been through.
- You may never completely forget or be able to erase what happened. As time goes on, you will feel less frightened or sad, and things will begin to feel normal again.
- You will feel happy again. If you get upset again, that's OK. This is just your heart telling you how much you miss him or her right now. It's OK to remember.

SUICIDE RISK AND LETHALITY

TRADITIONAL MODELS FOR assessing the potential risk of suicide focus primarily on the lethality of the individual and the intended level of threat to complete an act of suicide. Despite the statistical significance of a plethora of epidemiological research that has identified at-risk populations, the fact remains that persons who have sustained some level of loss, extraordinary stressful or trauma event, are in the highest risk category for lethality and completing an act of suicide. Thus, the professional crisis responder should never rely on statistics to determine a person's level of lethality during a time of chaos and tragedy.

A natural response of the trauma survivor early on is to feel a sense of physical, cognitive, and emotional numbness. This is an extremely difficult period of time for the individual and his or her loved ones. The person is typically feeling very disorganized and out of touch with his or her mind, body, and spirit. Crisis interventions must center on the person's level of coping skills and capacity for resiliency, as opposed to assessing characteristics of acute stress or the person's sense of hopelessness, powerlessness, and level of lethality.

In the context of establishing contact with the person, a foundational beginning point is that the person is a *survivor* of a critical incident rather than a *victim*. Accordingly, interventions addressing the person's level of lethality should begin with the facilitation of compassion, connection, and using resiliency as therapeutic leverage. If the individual can view himself or herself as a *survivor* of a traumatic event, then this should provide an opportunity to refocus the crisis intervention on potential support systems and resources.

The BASICS Model of Crisis Response

The Behavioral, Affect, Somatic, Interpersonal, Cognitive, and Spiritual (BASICS) model is based on Slaideu's (1990) application of Lazarus's (1981) multimodal assessment and has recently been presented by Echterling, Presbury, and Edson-McKee (2005, p. 13) as an assessment of lethality and suicide ideation. The strength of the BASICS model, as delineated below, is that it offers prompts for a multimodal assessment of the survivor's resiliency traits and coping skills. The acronym (BASICS) was developed to guide the crisis counselor through critical areas of survivor evaluation and is defined in the following holistic areas: Behavioral (what people do); Affective (how people feel); Somatic (how people respond physically); Interpersonal (how people relate to others); Cognitive (how people think); Spiritual (what people believe and value). This protocol may be helpful for disaster mental health professionals to integrate assessment items with empathic responses to evaluate the survivor's suicide ideation as well as developing the survivor's residuals.

Behavioral. Note the person's appearance and nonverbal communication that might indicate a suicide risk. Is the person only hinting at the possibility of hurting self or others, or is he or she openly verbalizing suicide intention? If the person openly states: *"I'm thinking of killing myself . . ."* respond empathically to the person's pain: *"It takes a lot of courage to talk about this—I can't imagine how this must feel to you. . . . Tell me more specifically what you mean by this."* If preparations are being made by the person (gathering of the implements), ask directly: *"Are you planning to do anything right now to carry out your plan?"* If previous attempts have been made by the individual, this places the person in a high-risk category. State: *"You said that you've tried to kill yourself in the past. . . . I'm very concerned about your safety and would like to ask you some questions about this issue. . . ."* If the person has chosen life, then this is an opportunity to begin assessing the individual's coping resources. You might state: *"What did you tell yourself when you talked yourself out of hurting yourself?"* Or, *"How were you able to get through that terrible event without trying to kill yourself?"*

Affective. Evaluate the individual's level/intensity of feelings of fear, rage, depression, or mood disorder that would place him or her in a high-risk category. You could state: *"I can't imagine what you are going through right now. . . . Other people that have been through what you have been through have feelings like yours (hopeless, depression, and thoughts of suicide) . . . sometimes these feelings pass. . . . I'm concerned about you. . . . What are you feeling right now?"* You could use a scaling technique: *"On a scale of 1 to 10 with 1 being no hope whatsoever and 10 feeling very hopeful . . . where are you right now? What might be different in your life right now if you felt more hopeful?"*

Somatic. If someone has been injured and you sense he or she is in a high-risk category, you might state: *"I'm sorry this has happened to you, you've shared that you are struggling now. . . . I've had this question running through my mind, are you thinking about hurting yourself?"* Or in a less direct way: *"Now that you're dealing with this injury that threatens your life, how are you finding the will or the strength to continue on?"*

Interpersonal. The fewer supports there are in the person's life, the higher risk the person will be for suicide. Assess the support from family, friends, and/or social group by asking: *"Who are the important people in your life? . . . How can they be more involved in your situation right now?"*

Cognitive. An occasional, vague, nondescriptive, and fleeting moment of suicide ideation is not uncommon during the time of a crisis. It is important to check the individual's thoughts about this if you feel the lethality is high. You might say directly: *"I'm sensing that you really want to end it all now."* Or, *"You suggested that you might want to end it all right now—do you have a plan or idea how you would do this?"* This is an opportunity to explore coping resources and the person's internal emotional and psychological strengths. Try to tap this energy source and state: *"It sounds like you've maybe got some ideas about an alternative possibility. . . . Tell me more about this."*

Spiritual. A particular troubling sign of high risk is when someone is expressing the belief system that he or she no longer matters to anyone, or life has no meaning. Someone who is feeling a profound sense of spiritual alienation may see suicide as his or her only choice. You might state: *"After all that's just happened to you it sounds like you're wondering if there's any point to your life right now. . . . What would need to happen for you to begin feeling better about going on with your life?"*

CONCLUSION

DISASTER MENTAL HEALTH and trauma counseling is a challenging field. There is a noticeable change in the types of individuals and groups being served by professional counselors. Thus, there is an enormous need for qualified and competent mental health professionals who can provide disaster mental health relief and stress debriefing groups in a wide range of critical incidents. Client stories that have such themes as physical or sexual abuse, psychological trauma, or loss, pain, and suffering can adversely affect the mind, body, and spirit of the professional counselor. Many professionals who work this close to the epicenter are naturally predisposed to an empathy fatigue experience. Thus, it is essential that counselor self-care approaches be initiated for working at such intense levels of service.

SCENARIO 1: CRITICAL INCIDENT: SCHOOL BUS CRASH SCENARIO

TWO NIGHTS AGO, three busloads of your middle school 7th–8th graders were returning home from a daylong field trip. As the three buses were driving back at night in a strong rainstorm, the bus in the middle slid off into a ditch, crashed, and was turned on its side. Apparently, there was a car that the bus driver was trying to avoid. Currently, we do not have much information beyond this; an investigation is pending.

The bus that crashed had about 35 riders. Two of the students, Marcus and Joy, sustained some broken bones and a moderate brain injury. They are both listed in critical condition at Dare County Hospital. Marcus has a reputation of being somewhat "obnoxious and irritating" to others. He is an average student with poor interpersonal skills and does not handle problem solving well. Marcus spends time living between his grandparents' and mother's house and is not involved in any extracurricular school activities. Joy is an academically talented student, plays on the girls softball team, and belongs to a number of school clubs. The remaining children were treated and released with only minor injuries of cuts and bruises. The bus driver also went to the hospital and is listed in stable condition.

Roles

Teacher. You have Marcus and Joy in your class as well as many of the other adolescents that were injured. You have contact with these students on a daily basis. You were riding in the bus that was following behind the bus that crashed. You didn't actually see the crash, but you heard the students on your bus scream and then you passed by the bus that was lying off in the ditch.

Girls softball coach. Joy is one of the star softball players on your team and you have coached her for the last two seasons. Three of the other adolescents who sustained minor injuries are also on the team. However, you've got the Regional Tournament coming up, and you really need Joy.

School nurse. You really don't have much contact with Joy, but you see Marcus several times a month because he always seems to have frequent injuries during gym class. You were on the field trip and riding on the bus in front of the one that crashed. No one on your bus saw or heard anything until a few minutes later when your bus driver heard the emergency call over the radio.

School counselor. You see Marcus regularly to coordinate outside social services for him and his mother. Although he is not one of your favorite students, he does follow through on things.

Mental health case worker. You don't know Joy or any of the other youth that were injured. You see Marcus twice per month for family intervention services. You do have infrequent contact with some of the kids who were riding in the other two buses.

School principal. You have frequent contact with Marcus because of his behavior problems. You've got a soft spot in your heart for Marcus because you can relate with his family situation, which reminds you of your own as you were growing up between two homes while in school.

SCENARIO 2: CRITICAL INCIDENT: TOXIC CHEMICAL SPILL SCENARIO

ONE AUGUST AFTERNOON in a rural community in your state (population about 20,000 residents), a train carrying tanker cars of chemicals derailed in the center of town. Before emergency disaster personnel knew what was contained in the tanker cars, many people within a mile or so of the accident become ill with flulike symptoms from the toxic fumes. Officials of this small rural town had to wait about 2 hours before federal officials could identify exactly what chemicals were being transported by this train. The local hospital emergency department was in chaos because of the overwhelming number of local residents being transported there for emergency medical treatment of some unknown toxin. Fortunately, there were no related deaths, only some lingering upper respiratory effects from the exposure to the chemicals.

At the time of the accident, a local daycare facility was swimming at the local public pool close to the downtown area. In all the confusion and chaos during the train derailment, one particular 4-year-old child who could not swim was left unattended for a very brief period of time (less than 1 minute). Sadly, little Leslie drowned. You have been called in to provide mental health disaster relief to this rural community 4 days after this toxic spill. Discuss and role play the following:

1. Discuss the characteristics of such a critical incident (e.g., transportation disaster, sociocultural aspects, existing county/town infrastructure, time of day or month of event, duration or intensity of this transportation event, effects of media coverage).
2. Discuss the types of losses that individuals in this rural community have sustained.
3. Anticipate and discuss some of the familiar feelings/emotions, thoughts, or stories that you would expect to encounter after such an incident.
4. Who might be the persons most affected (emotionally, behaviorally, physically, cognitively, and spiritually) by this critical incident (e.g., populations such as elderly or disabled, children, family members, friends, firefighters, police, paramedics, rescue personnel, other surrounding support systems, daycare facility workers)?
5. What coping mechanisms and resiliency factors would you want to assess/evaluate and facilitate with this community?

Role Play Scenario
{Discuss how you might set up or arrange your crisis intervention. Role play one on one with partner, each taking different roles; if time allows, role play Group Crisis.}

* Town mayor
* Emergency service personnel (firefighters, paramedics, police)
* Parent with child in daycare setting
* Lifeguard on duty at time of drowning
* Director of daycare facility and daycare teachers
* Parent of "Little Leslie"
* Director of parks, pools, and recreation
* Create your own role.

SCENARIO 3: CRITICAL INCIDENT: TORNADO SCENARIO

ONE NIGHT IN March 1999, there were about 30 tornados that ripped through the central part of the state of Arkansas. One particular rural town (population about 5,000) was almost entirely destroyed and about the only thing left standing was the local school. You are called to the school gymnasium within 48 hours of this critical incident to do a stress debriefing with many of the towns' folk. Discuss and role play the following:

1. Discuss the characteristics of such a critical incident (e.g., natural disaster, sociocultural aspects, existing county/town infrastructure, time of day or month of event, duration or intensity of this weather event, effects of media coverage).
2. Discuss the types of losses that individuals in this small rural community have sustained.
3. Anticipate and discuss some of the familiar feelings/emotions, thoughts, or stories that you would expect to encounter after such an incident.
4. Who might be the persons most affected (emotionally, behaviorally, physically, cognitively, and spiritually) by this critical incident (e.g., populations such as elderly or disabled, family members, friends, firefighters, police, paramedics, rescue personnel, other surrounding support systems)?
5. What coping mechanisms and resiliency factors would you want to assess/evaluate and facilitate with the townspeople?

Role Play Scenario

{Discuss how you might set up or arrange your crisis intervention. Role play one on one with partner, each taking different roles; if time allows, role play Group Crisis.}

- Town mayor
- Emergency service personnel (firefighters, paramedics, police)
- Parent of school-aged children
- School principal
- Schoolteacher
- Older person with roots in community for 100-plus years
- Create your own role.

DISASTER MENTAL HEALTH RESOURCES

WEB SITES

American Academy of Child and Adolescent Psychiatry (AACAP): www.aacap.org

The American Academy of Experts in Traumatic Stress (AAETS): www.aaets.org

American Counseling Association (ACA): www.counseling.org

American Psychiatric Association (APA): www.psych.org

American Psychological Association (APA): www.apa.org

American Red Cross (ARC): www.redcross.org

Centers for Disease Control and Prevention (CDCP): www.cdc.gov

National Association of School Psychologists (NASP): www.nasponline.org

National Association of Social Workers (NASW): www.naswdc.org

National Institute on Mental Health (NIMH): www.nimh.nih.gov

National Mental Health Association (NMHA): www.nmha.org

Substance Abuse Mental Health Services Administration (SAMHSA): www.samhsa.gov

BOOKS AND ARTICLES

Bass, D. D., & Yep, R. (2002). *Terrorism, trauma, and tragedies: A counselor's guide to preparing and responding.* Alexandria, VA: American Counseling Association Foundation.

Davis, M., Robbins Eshelman, E., & McKay, M. (1995). *The relaxation and stress reduction workbook* (4th ed.). Oakland, CA: New Harbinger Publications.

Johnson, K. (2000). *School crisis management: A hands-on guide to training crisis response teams.* Alameda, CA: Hunter House.

Lerner, M. D. (2006). *It's OK not to be OK . . . right now: How to live through a traumatic experience.* New York: Mark Lerner Associates.

Mitchell, J. T., & Everly, G. S. (1996). *Critical incident stress debriefing: An operations manual for the prevention of traumatic stress among emergency service and disaster workers* (2nd ed.). Ellicott City, MD: Chevron Publishing.

Stebnicki, M. A. (2001). The psychological impact on survivors of extraordinary stressful and traumatic events: Principles and practices in critical incident response for rehabilitation counselors. *New Directions in Rehabilitation, 12*(6), 57–72.

Stebnicki, M. A. (2008) *Empathy fatigue: Healing the mind, body, and spirit of professional counselors.* New York: Springer.

REFERENCES

Echterling, L. G., Presbury, J. H., & Edson-McKee, J. (2005). *Crisis intervention: Promoting resilience and resolution in troubled times.* Columbus, OH: Pearson, Merrill/Prentice-Hall.

Lazarus, A. A. (1981). *The practice of multimodal therapy.* New York: McGraw-Hill.

Slaideu, K. A. (1990). *Crisis intervention: A handbook for practice and research* (2nd ed.). Boston: Allyn & Bacon.

66

Substance Abuse Assessment

Lloyd R. Goodwin, Jr.

SUBSTANCE ABUSE IS the nation's number one health problem, straining the health care system and contributing to the ill health and death of millions of Americans every year. According to the Schneider Institute for Health Policy report (2001):

> There are more deaths, illnesses and disabilities from substance abuse than from any other preventable health condition. Of the more than two million deaths each year in the United States, approximately one in four is attributable to alcohol, tobacco and illicit drug use, with tobacco causing about 430,700 deaths, followed by more than 100,000 for alcohol and nearly 16,000 for illicit drugs. (p. 6)

PREVALENCE OF PSYCHOACTIVE SUBSTANCE USE

PSYCHOACTIVE SUBSTANCE USE disorders (SUDs) wreak havoc on American society. Families are destroyed, jobs lost, and relationships ruined. Chronic substance abuse often results in a decline in both physical and mental health status in users who then require care from medical and mental health professionals in hospitals, rehabilitation programs, and specialized substance abuse treatment facilities. In spite of the many potential consequences, America remains a nation of psychoactive substance users.

In 2005, according to the national survey by the Substance Abuse and Mental Health Services Administration (SAMHSA, 2006), an estimated 19.7 million Americans (8.1% of the population) aged 12 or older were current illicit drug users, and had used an illicit drug the month prior to the survey interview. The illicit drugs most frequently used were marijuana (14.6 million or 6.0% of the population), prescription-type psychotherapeutic drugs used nonmedically (6.4 million; 2.6%), cocaine (2.4 million; 1.0%), hallucinogens (1.1 million; 0.4%), and methamphetamine (257,000; 0.2%). However, the incidence of illicit drug use pales in comparison to the use of legal psychoactive substances. An estimated 80% of Americans regularly use mild stimulants in the form of caffeine, with an average intake of 200 to 250 mg per day (Patton & Beer, 2001). There are 126 million people (51.8% of Americans) who currently drink alcoholic beverages and 71.5 million people (29.4%) who are current users of tobacco products (SAMHSA, 1999).

Psychoactive Substance Abuse

Most users of psychoactive substances do not abuse or become dependent on the substances they use. However, a small percentage of psychoactive substance users do become abusers. Also, not all substances have the same addiction potential. Some substances such as nicotine and crack cocaine have higher addiction potential than other substances such as marijuana.

Prevalence of SUDs. Analysis of the 2005 National Survey on Drug Use and Health (SAMHSA, 2006) indicated that an estimated 22.2 million (9.1%) of the population aged 12 or older were classified with SUDs in the past year based on criteria specified in the *Diagnostic and Statistical Manual of Mental Disorders,* 4th edition (American Psychiatric Association [APA], 1994). Of the 22.2 million classified with a SUD, 3.6 million were dependent on or abused illicit drugs but not alcohol, and 15.4 million were dependent on or abused alcohol but not illicit drugs. The illicit drugs with the highest levels of past-year dependence or abuse were marijuana (4.1 million), followed by cocaine (1.5 million), and pain relievers (1.5 million). It is estimated that the ratio of problem drinkers (i.e., alcohol abusers) to those severely dependent on alcohol is about 4:1 (Institute of Medicine, 1990).

Lifetime risk of acquiring a SUD. Nearly 25% of adults will have a SUD (either substance abuse or dependence) in their lifetime. Alcohol dependence occurs in 14% of Americans, including 20% of men and 8% of women (Kessler et al., 1994). The prevalence of SUDs rises through the teen years, peaks between ages 18 and 20, and then declines gradually over the next 40 years (Office of Applied Studies, 2002).

It is often assumed that most people who drink to excess are probably alcoholics. However, a recent survey of 4,761 New Mexico adults found that while 16.5% drank alcohol in excess of national guidelines, only 1.8% met the criteria for alcohol dependence. This study suggests that most excessive drinkers are binge drinkers and not alcohol dependent (Woerle, Roeber, & Landen, 2007).

CO-OCCURRING PROBLEMS

INDIVIDUALS WITH SUDs have high rates of additional health and social problems that increase the difficulty of treatment. Such co-occurring problems as mental health disorders; HIV, hepatitis C, sexually transmitted diseases, and other infectious diseases; crime victims; illegal activity; involvement in the criminal justice system; family dysfunction; homelessness; and vocational problems often complicate substance abuse treatment. As Dennis and Scott (2007) point out, individuals who abuse multiple substances or have other co-occurring problems are more likely to experience difficulties with treatment and medication adherence including shorter stays, administrative discharges, compromised functional status, difficult community adjustment, reduced quality of life, and worse outcomes. Integrated care is recommended when individuals have SUDs combined with co-occurring problems.

IMPACT OF SUDS ON SOCIETY AND COUNSELING

THE ECONOMIC COST of substance abuse to the U.S. economy each year is estimated at more than $414 billion (Schneider Institute for Health Policy, 2001). In 2002, the estimated economic cost of illicit drug abuse alone was more than $180 million (Robert Wood Johnson Foundation, 2006). The annual cost of alcohol use disorders (AUDs) exceeds $185 billion (National Institute on Alcohol Abuse and Alcoholism [NIAAA], 2000), and approximately 100,000 individuals die each year from alcohol-related disease or injury (McGinnis & Foege, 1999). The estimated cost of health care resulting from AUDs in the United States is estimated at more than $26 billion per year (U.S. Department of Health and Human Services [DHHS], 2000). Health care expenses for substance abuse problems absorbed 25% of Medicare costs and 20% of Medicaid costs in 1995, according to the Robert Wood Johnson Foundation (American Hospital Association, 2001). Individuals with alcohol-related medical illnesses have more frequent hospitalizations and longer hospital stays than individuals without alcoholism (Walker, Howard, Lambert, & Suchinsky, 1994).

Many treated and untreated people with SUDs receive services from counselors working in schools, rehabilitation, criminal justice, employee assistance programs, and other mental health settings. It is a fact that SUDs often complicate or prevent effective counseling services and related mental health treatment for individuals with co-occurring physical and mental disorders, sabotaging the best counseling, treatment, and rehabilitation plans.

ASSESSMENT OF SUBSTANCE USE DISORDERS (SUDS)

A COMPREHENSIVE SUBSTANCE abuse assessment will focus on the whole person and not just the presenting SUD. Substance abuse affects the whole person, including the biological, psychological, social, and spiritual aspects of the individual. Substance abuse also affects the systems that individuals interact with such as families, schools, work, and human service agencies. This holistic biopsychosocialspiritual model of addiction is necessary to formulate comprehensive and effective assessment and treatment plans. Substance abuse assessments may include screening, comprehensive assessment, or diagnosis of SUDs.

SUBSTANCE ABUSE SCREENING

FAMILIARITY WITH SOME simple substance abuse screening procedures and tools can be helpful for counselors treating individuals with substance abuse issues. A number of free, brief, and sensitive substance abuse screening instruments in the public domain are available that can be incorporated into routine client assessment by mental health professionals. Once counselors identify individuals with possible SUDs, they can conduct a more comprehensive assessment or refer these clients to a qualified substance abuse professional for assessment and treatment.

COMPREHENSIVE SUBSTANCE ABUSE ASSESSMENT

COMPREHENSIVE ASSESSMENT AND treatment planning are essential to successful substance abuse rehabilitation and require the same holistic perspective as other mental and physical health problems (Goodwin, 1986). Substance abuse assessment and treatment occur concurrently with individuals with SUDs. As Washton and Zweben (2006) point out, "An assessment is not intended to proceed in linear fashion, follow the same template for all patients, or obtain information at the expense of developing rapport, trust, and a working therapeutic relationship with the patient" (p. 123). Establishing a safe and therapeutic climate is a priority so that clients can lower defenses and openly and honestly share information about their substance use and consequences without fear of rejection or judgment.

FUNCTION OF SUBSTANCE ABUSE ASSESSMENT

A SUBSTANCE USE assessment serves five major functions: (1) to facilitate the development of rapport and a therapeutic alliance with the client; (2) to determine the nature and extent of the client's substance use, consequences, and triggers that initiate use; (3) to gain a holistic view of the client including physical, psychosocial, spiritual aspects, including any environmental or human service systems the client is involved with; (4) to assess the client's readiness and motivation to change; and (5) to provide feedback to the client about counseling and treatment needs and establish a basis for developing a rehabilitation plan in conjunction with the client.

SUBSTANCE ABUSE ASSESSMENT DOMAINS

A COMPREHENSIVE ASSESSMENT includes domains related to substance use and related issues, including history of psychoactive substance use and abuse; consequences of substance use; history of presenting problems; family-of-origin, marital, and family history; current living arrangement; physical health status, including infectious diseases and medication use; psychological functioning, including mental status, cognitions (e.g., cognitive style of thinking, beliefs, injunctions), cognitive impairment, and coexisting mental disorders; history of trauma, abuse, and violence; treatment history of mental health and SUDs; social relationships, including support network; cultural issues, strengths, and identities; language and speech issues; developmental issues; educational status; vocational status; legal history and current status; spirituality views, issues, and available supports; problem areas; strengths and assets, including coping skills; physical, sensory, or mobility limitations; relapse history and potential; motivational level for treatment and current stage of change; and diagnostic impressions.

SUBSTANCE ABUSE ASSESSMENT INSTRUMENTS

NO MATTER HOW comprehensive, no assessment instrument can replace the clinical interview in accurately determining the presence and extent of SUDs. However, assessment instruments can be helpful in verifying, supporting, or clarifying the diagnosis of SUDs.

Substance abuse screening instruments. Commonly used substance abuse screening instruments include the Alcohol Use Disorders Identification Test (AUDIT; Babor, De La Fuente, & Saunders, 1989), CAGE questionnaire (Mayfield, McLeod, & Hall, 1974), Drug Abuse Screening Test (DAST; Skinner, 1982), Michigan Alcohol Screening Test (MAST; Selzer, 1971); Short MAST (Selzer, Vinokur, & Van Rooijen, 1974); Simple Screening Instrument for Substance Abuse (SSI-SA; Center for Substance Abuse Treatment, 1994), and Substance Abuse Subtle Screening Inventory (SASSI; Miller, 2000). All of these screening instruments, except for the commercially produced SASSI, are in the public domain and are available at no cost from the National Clearinghouse on Alcohol and Drug Information, or they can be downloaded from the Web sites listed at the end of this chapter. Although the SASSI is one of the most widely used assessment instruments, according to a recent review of research on substance abuse screening instruments by Feldstein and Miller (2007), there is little advantage, if any, of the SASSI when compared to other instruments in screening for SUDs. These researchers found no independent empirical evidence that the SASSI is more sensitive or accurate in detecting SUDs, or less susceptible to falsification in screening for SUDs through its indirect (subtle) scales than simpler direct scales.

Comprehensive substance abuse instruments. The Addiction Severity Index—5th Edition (ASI; McLellan, Luborsky, Woody, & O'Brien, 1980; McLellan et al., 1992; Treatment Research Institute, 2007) and the Comprehensive Drinker Profile (CDP; Miller & Marlatt, n.d.) are substance abuse assessment instruments in the public domain that provide a more comprehensive assessment of individuals with SUDs than the screening instruments mentioned in the previous section. The ASI (Treatment Research Institute, 2007) is designed to be administered as a semistructured interview to individuals who present with SUDs. This instrument gathers information about seven areas of a patient's life: medical, employment/support, drug and alcohol use, legal, family history, family/social relationships, and psychiatric problems. Using a 10-point scale ranging from 0 to 9, the interviewer rates the severity of an individual's problems in each of the seven areas, based on historical and current information. Composite scores are based only on current information and are indicators of the present status of the patient. Thus the ASI is useful for evaluating treatment outcomes, since successive composite scores can be used to summarize change in patient status. English, Spanish, and Native American versions of the ASI, including the administration and scoring manual, can be downloaded at no cost from the Treatment Research Institute Web site at http://www.tresearch.org. The CDP is another assessment instrument that provides a comprehensive history and current status of an individual's alcohol use and abuse and is helpful for treatment planning. The CDP can be downloaded at no cost at the Center on Alcoholism, Substance Abuse, and Addictions (CASAA) Web site at http://casaa.unm.edu/inst/CDP.pdf.

Cognitive behavioral assessment instruments. Helpful instruments to assess cognitive behavioral factors, including beliefs about psychoactive substance use, include the Alcohol Effects Questionnaire (SAMHSA, 1999) and the Alcohol Expectancy Questionnaire—III (Adult) (SAMHSA, 1999), which examine possible psychological effects and beliefs about alcohol use; the Inventory of Drinking Situations (Annis, 1982a), which helps clients identify situations associated with drinking; the Situational Confidence Questionnaire (Annis, 1982b; SAMHSA, 1999) and the Brief Situational Confidence Questionnaire (SAMHSA, 1999), which help clients identify the degree of their confidence in their ability to handle the situations associated with drinking; the Cognitive Appraisal Questionnaire (Annis, 1982c), which helps clients identify cognitive factors that might interfere with their self-efficacy; and the Cognitive Self-Assessment Inventory (Goodwin, 2002a), which helps clients identify cognitions (thoughts, beliefs, injunctions, and cognitive styles of thinking) that may be associated with emotional distress, or "buttons" (Goodwin, 2002b) that can lead to substance use.

Stages of change, treatment readiness, and expectations. The Stages of Change Readiness and Treatment Eagerness (SOCRATES; Miller & Tonigan, 1996), the Readiness to Change Questionnaire (Treatment Version) (RCQ-TV; SAMHSA, 1999), and the University of Rhode Island Change Assessment (URICA; SAMHSA, 1999) instruments can help clinicians identify clients' motivation to change substance abuse behavior and can assist in treatment planning. The Alcohol (and Illegal Drugs) Decisional Balance Scale and the Alcohol and Drug Consequences Questionnaire (ADCQ) can assist clinicians in assessing the pros and cons of drinking and other drug use for clients (SAMHSA, 1999). The What I Want From Treatment questionnaire by Miller and Brown (1999) can be useful in determining what clients expect, want, and need from substance abuse treatment.

Most of the commonly used substance use assessment instruments are readily available at no cost from government publications (e.g., Center for Substance Abuse Treatment, 1994, 1995, 2005) and can be ordered from the National Clearinghouse for Alcohol and Drug Information (www.ncadi.samhsa.gov/) or downloaded online at no cost from Web sites such as PROJECT CORK (http://www.projectcork.org/clinical_tools/index.html) and the Center on Alcoholism, Substance Abuse, and Addictions (http://casaa.unm.edu/inst.html).

Diagnosis of SUDs. The criteria in the *Diagnostic and Statistical Manual–Fourth Edition–Text Revision* (*DSM–IV–TR*; APA, 2000) are used to help assess and diagnose SUDs, including substance abuse and dependence. According to Maxmen and Ward (1995), intoxication and withdrawal are the most prevalent substance-related disorders.

ONLINE SUBSTANCE ABUSE RESOURCES

INFORMATION ON PSYCHOACTIVE SUBSTANCES AND TREATMENT OF SUBSTANCE USE DISORDERS (SUDs)

Addiction Technology Transfer Centers: http://www.nattc.org
Center for Substance Abuse Prevention: http://csap.samhsa.gov
Center for Substance Abuse Treatment: http://csat.samhsa.gov
National Clearinghouse on Alcohol and Drug Information: http://ncadi.samhsa.gov
National Institute on Alcoholism and Alcohol Abuse: http://www.niaaa.nih.gov
National Institute on Drug Abuse: http://www.nida.nih.gov
Substance Abuse and Mental Health Services Administration: http://www.samhsa.gov

DOWNLOADABLE SUBSTANCE ABUSE ASSESSMENT RESOURCES

Center on Alcoholism, Substance Abuse, and Addictions (associated with the University of New Mexico): http://casaa.unm.edu/inst.html
Join Together (associated with Boston University) provides an online screening tool for alcohol use disorders (AUDs) at http://www.alcoholscreening.org/index.asp
PROJECT CORK (associated with Dartmouth Medical School): http://www.projectcork.org/clinical_tools/index.html
Treatment Research Institute (TRI): http://www.tresearch.org; TRI was founded by A. Thomas McLellan, Ph.D., one of the developers of the Addiction Severity Index, Jack Durell, M.D., and a small team of colleagues from the University of Pennsylvania.

REFERENCES

American Hospital Association. (2001). Substance abuse takes a big bite of health care spending. *AHA News, 37*(17), 9.
American Psychiatric Association. (2000). *Diagnostic and statistical manual of mental disorders* (4th ed., text revision). Washington, DC: Author.

Annis, H. M. (1982a). *Inventory of Drinking Situations*. Toronto: Addiction Research Foundation of Ontario.

Annis, H. M. (1982b). *Situational Confidence Questionnaire*. Toronto: Addiction Research Foundation of Ontario.

Annis, H. M. (1982c). *Cognitive Appraisal Questionnaire*. Toronto: Addiction Research Foundation of Ontario.

Babor, T. F., De La Fuente, J. R., & Saunders, J. (1989). *AUDIT: Alcohol Use Disorders Identification Test: Guidelines for use in primary health care*. Geneva, Switzerland: World Health Organization.

Center for Substance Abuse Treatment. (1994). *Screening and assessment for alcohol and other drug abuse among adults in the criminal justice system*. Treatment Improvement Protocol (TIP) #7 (DHHS Publication No. SMA 94–2076). Rockville, MD: Substance Abuse and Mental Health Services Administration.

Center for Substance Abuse Treatment. (1995). *Simple screening instruments for outreach for alcohol and other drug abuse and infectious diseases*. Treatment Improvement Protocol (TIP) #11 (DHHS Publication No. SMA 94–2094). Rockville, MD: Substance Abuse and Mental Health Services Administration.

Center for Substance Abuse Treatment. (2005). *Substance abuse treatment for persons with co-occurring disorders*. Treatment Improvement Protocol (TIP) #42 (DHHS Publication No. SMA 05–3992). Rockville, MD: Substance Abuse and Mental Health Services Administration.

Dennis, M., & Scott, C. K. (2007). Managing addiction as a chronic condition. *Addiction Science and Clinical Practice, 4*(1), 45–55.

Feldstein, S. W., & Miller, W. R. (2007). Does subtle screening for substance abuse work? A review of the Substance Abuse Subtle Screening Inventory (SASSI). *Addiction, 102*, 41–50.

Goodwin, L. R., Jr. (1986). A holistic perspective for the provision of rehabilitation counseling services. *Journal of Applied Rehabilitation Counseling, 17*(2), 29–36.

Goodwin, L. R., Jr. (2002a). *Cognitive Self-Assessment Inventory*. Victoria, BC, Canada: Trafford.

Goodwin, L. R., Jr. (2002b). *The button therapy book: How to work on your buttons and the button-pushers in your life*. Victoria, BC, Canada: Trafford.

Institute of Medicine. (1990). *Broadening the base of treatment for alcohol problems*. Washington, DC: National Academy Press.

Kessler, R. C., McGonagle, K. A., Zhao, S., Nelson, C. B., Hughes, M., Eshleman, S., et al. (1994). Lifetime and 12-month prevalence of *DSM–III–R* psychiatric disorders in the United States: Results from the National Comorbidity Survey. *Archives of General Psychiatry, 51*(1), 8–19.

Maxmen, J. S., & Ward, N. G. (1995). *Essential psychopathology and its treatment* (2nd ed.). New York: W. W. Norton.

Mayfield, D., McLeod, G., & Hall, P. (1974). The CAGE questionnaire: Validation of a new alcoholism screening instrument. *American Journal of Psychiatry, 131*, 1121–1123.

McGinnis, J., & Foege, W. (1999). Mortality and morbidity attributable to use of addictive substances in the United States [Abstract]. *Proceedings of the Association of American Physicians, 111,* 109–118.

McLellan, A. T., Kushner, H., Metzger, D., Peters, R., Smith, I., Grissom, G., et al. (1992). The fifth edition of the Addiction Severity Index. *Journal of Substance Abuse Treatment, 9*(3), 199–213.

McLellan, A. T., Luborsky, L., Woody, G. E., & O'Brien, C. P. (1980). An improved diagnostic instrument for substance abuse patients: The Addiction Severity Index. *Journal of Nervous and Mental Disorders, 168,* 26–33.

Miller, G. A. (2000). *Adult SASSI-3 manual.* Springville, IN: SASSI Institute.

Miller, W. R., & Brown, J. M. (1999). *Enhancing motivation for change in substance abuse treatment.* In Substance Abuse and Mental Health Services Administration (SAMHSA), Treatment Improvement Protocol (TIP) Series 35. Center for Substance Abuse Treatment (DHHS Publication No. SMA 99–3354). Rockville, MD: Substance Abuse and Mental Health Services Administration.

Miller, W. R., & Marlatt, G. A. (n.d.). Center on Alcoholism, Substance Abuse, and Addictions (CASAA; undated). *Comprehensive Drinker Profile.* Retrieved February 26, 2007, from http://casaa.unm.edu/inst/CDP.pdf

Miller, W. R., & Tonigan, J. S. (1996). Assessing drinkers' motivations for change: The Stages of Change Readiness and Treatment Eagerness Scale (SOCRATES). *Psychology of Addictive Behaviors, 10*(2), 981–989.

National Institute on Alcohol Abuse and Alcoholism. (2000). *Updating estimates of the economic costs of alcohol abuse in the United States: Estimates, update methods, and data.* Report prepared by the Lewin Group for the NIAAA. Rockville, MD: National Institutes of Health, U.S. Department of Health and Human Services.

Office of Applied Studies. (2002). *Results from the 2001 National Household Survey on Drug Abuse: Vol. 1. Summary of national findings* (DHHS Publication No. SMA 02–3758). Rockville, MD: Substance Abuse and Mental Health Services Administration.

Patton, C., & Beer, D. (2001). Caffeine: The forgotten variable. *International Journal of Psychiatry in Clinical Practice, 5,* 231–236.

Robert Wood Johnson Foundation. (2006, August). *Economic benefits of treating substance abuse outweigh costs.* Research Highlight Number 7. Retrieved March 3, 2007, from http://www.rwjf.org/files/research/Research%20 Highlight%207%200605.pdf

Schneider Institute for Health Policy. (2001). *Substance abuse: The nation's number one health problem.* Prepared by the Schneider Institute for Health Policy, Brandeis University for the Robert Wood Johnson Foundation, Princeton, NJ. Retrieved March 2, 2007, from http://www.rwjf.org/files/ publications/other/SubstanceAbuseChartbook.pdf

Selzer, M. L. (1971). The Michigan Alcohol Screening Test: The quest for a new diagnostic instrument. *American Journal of Psychiatry, 127,* 1653–1658.

Selzer, M. L., Vinokur A., & Van Rooijen, L. A. (1974). Self-administered Short Michigan Alcohol Screening Test (SMAST). *Journal of Studies on Alcohol, 15,* 276–280.

Skinner, H. A. (1982). Drug Abuse Screening Test. *Addictive Behavior, 7,* 363–371.

Substance Abuse and Mental Health Services Administration. (1999). *Enhancing motivation for change in substance abuse treatment.* Treatment Improvement Protocol (TIP) Series 35. Center for Substance Abuse Treatment (DHHS Publication No. SMA 99–3354). Rockville, MD: Author.

Substance Abuse and Mental Health Services Administration. (2006). *Results from the 2005 National Survey on Drug Use and Health: National findings.* Office of Applied Studies. (NSDUH Series H-30, DHHS Publication No. SMA 06-4194). Rockville, MD: Author.

Treatment Research Institute. (2007). *Addiction Severity Index* (5th ed.). Retrieved February 25, 2007, from http://www.tresearch.org/resources/instruments.htm#top

U.S. Department of Health and Human Services. (2000). *Tenth special report to Congress on alcohol and health.* Bethesda, MD: Author. Retrieved January 23, 2007, from pubs.niaaa.nih.gov/publications/10report/intro.pdf

Walker, R. D., Howard, M. O., Lambert, M. D., & Suchinsky, R. (1994). Psychiatric and medical comorbidities of veterans with substance use disorders. *Hospital Community Psychiatry, 45,* 232–237.

Washton, A. M., & Zweben, J. E. (2006). *Treating alcohol and drug problems in psychotherapy practice: Doing what works.* New York: Guilford Press.

Woerle, S., Roeber, J., & Landen, M. G. (2007). The prevalence of alcohol dependence among excessive drinkers in New Mexico. *Alcoholism: Clinical and Experimental Research, 31*(2), 293–298.

67

Treatment for Substance Use Disorders

Lloyd R. Goodwin, Jr.

I N 2005, APPROXIMATELY 3.9 million persons aged 12 or older received some kind of treatment for problems related to the use of alcohol or illicit drugs (Substance Abuse and Mental Health Services Administration [SAMHSA], 2006). Substance abuse treatment programs and clinical counseling approaches are designed to treat a variety of substance use disorders (SUD)s. Treatment approaches may include a combination of medical (e.g., pharmacotherapy) and psychosocial approaches. Therapeutic programs for individuals with SUDs include hospital-based inpatient programs, mutual-help groups (e.g., Alcoholics Anonymous and Narcotics Anonymous); detoxification programs; partial hospitalization; intensive outpatient programs; therapeutic communities; halfway houses; pharmacotherapy-based interventions such as methadone programs for opioid addicts, naltrexone for alcoholics, and nicotine replacement therapies for tobacco addicts; employee assistance programs; prison-based programs and community-based criminal justice programs such as drug courts; boot camps; school-based programs; and specialty programs for particular populations such as adolescents, women (e.g., perinatal programs for pregnant addicts and halfway houses that accommodate children of single parents), and culturally diverse groups such as African Americans, Hispanic Americans, Asian Americans, and Native American Indians.

CLIENT-TREATMENT MATCHING

FOLLOWING A COMPREHENSIVE substance abuse assessment the substance abuse counselor determines the type of substance abuse treatment program that best meets the individual's clinical needs. In many communities, the type of treatment modality that individuals are referred to may be determined more by the availability of treatment resources and the financial status of individuals, instead of ideal client-treatment matching criteria.

The American Society of Addiction Medicine's (ASAM) five levels of care. The patient placement criteria developed by the ASAM (1996) are widely used in substance abuse treatment programs. The ASAM criteria have five levels of care: Level 0.5—Early Intervention; Level I—Outpatient Services; Level II—Intensive Outpatient/Partial Hospitalization Services; Level III—Residential Inpatient Services; Level IV—Medically Managed Intensive Inpatient Services.

ASAM criteria for determining levels of care. The ASAM uses criteria along six different dimensions to determine the most appropriate level of care. These dimensions are: (1) acute intoxication, (2) withdrawal potential, (3) biomedical conditions and complications, (4) emotional or behavioral conditions and complications, (5) treatment acceptance or resistance, and relapse potential, and (6) recovery environment. After conducting a substance abuse assessment, a substance abuse counselor matches the client to the appropriate level of care and type of treatment. "In general, the least restrictive environment for treatment should be used unless the severity of the substance use disorder and related medical, psychiatric, and social problems is such that structured or medically monitored treatment is needed" (Daley & Marlatt, 2006, p. 39).

PRINCIPLES OF EFFECTIVE TREATMENT

THIRTEEN PRINCIPLES OF effective treatment for SUDs have been described by a panel of substance abuse experts (National Institute on Drug Abuse [NIDA], 1999): (1) No single treatment is appropriate for all individuals. Matching treatment settings, interventions, and services to each individual's needs and problems is needed; (2) Treatment needs to be readily available; (3) Effective treatment attends to multiple needs of the individual, not just his or her drug use; (4) An individual's treatment and services plan must be assessed continually and modified as necessary to ensure that the plan meets the person's changing needs; (5) Remaining in treatment for an adequate period of time is critical for treatment effectiveness; (6) Counseling (individual and/or group) and other behavioral therapies are critical components of effective treatment for addiction; (7) Medications are an important element of treatment for many patients, especially when combined with counseling and other behavioral therapies; (8) Addicted or drug-abusing individuals with coexisting mental disorders should have both disorders treated in an integrated way; (9) Detoxification is only the first stage of addiction treatment and by itself does little to change long-term drug use; (10) Treatment does not need to be voluntary to be effective; (11) Possible drug use during treatment must be monitored continuously; (12) Treatment programs should provide assessment for HIV/AIDS, hepatitis B and C, tuberculosis, and other infectious diseases as well as counseling to help patients modify or change behaviors that place themselves or others at risk; (13) Recovery from drug addiction can be a long-term process and frequently requires multiple episodes of treatment.

GOALS OF EFFECTIVE TREATMENT

TREATMENT GOALS FOR individuals with SUDs include motivation toward abstinence, moderation of use, or drug substitution (e.g., methadone for heroin). Supporting goals include (1) creating a healthy lifestyle that includes drugless alternatives to satisfy the same motivations to use psychoactive substances; (2) developing support systems that may include a mutual-help group such as Alcoholics Anonymous; (3) enhancing social skills, including assertion and refusal skills; (4) practicing stress management and relaxation techniques; (5) attaining stable and supportive family relationships; (6) enhancing vocational and educational functioning and career goals; (7) attaining a stable housing arrangement and financial security; (8) enhancing physical health status; (9) improving mental health status by better managing psychological and emotional issues such as shame, guilt, depression, and anxiety; (10) learning how to recognize and express feelings and increase self-esteem, self-efficacy, and more effective problem-solving and decision-making skills; (11) developing healthy leisure, recreational, and social activities; (12) resolving or avoiding legal problems; and (13) addressing relevant spiritual issues and practicing centering and transcendental practices such as meditation or prayer.

SUBSTANCE ABUSE COUNSELING

COUNSELORS APPLY A variety of counseling theories and approaches to substance abuse problems. Lewis, Dana, and Blevins (2002) provide some general guidelines for substance abuse counseling. These include: (1) Use a respectful and positive approach with all clients; (2) View substance abuse problems on a continuum from nonproblematic to problematic use rather than as an either/or situation; (3) Provide treatment that is individualized, both in goals and in methods; (4) Provide multidimensional treatment that focuses on the social and environmental aspects of long-term recovery; (5) Remain open to new methods and goals as research findings become available; and (6) Use a multicultural perspective to meet the needs of diverse client populations.

Stages of change. Prochaska, Norcross, and DiClemente (1994) have described six stages of change that people go through in changing harmful behaviors, including SUDs. These stages are (1) the *precontemplation stage* when individuals do not recognize that a problem exists; (2) the *contemplation stage* when individuals believe that a problem might exist and give some consideration to the possibility of changing their behaviors though they are not quite ready and are ambivalent about changing; (3) the *preparation stage* when individuals decide to change and make plans to do so; they know change is best, but they're not sure how to begin; (4) the *action stage* when individuals take active steps toward change, such as entering treatment; and (5) the *maintenance stage,* which involves activities to maintain the change such as implementing a relapse prevention plan.

Motivational interviewing (MI) and motivational enhancement therapy (MET). These therapies, MI (Miller & Rollnick, 1991, 2002) and MET (Miller, Zweben, DiClemente, & Rychtarik, 1995), are often used by substance abuse professionals in conjunction with the stages of change model described by Prochaska et al. (1994). Both MI and MET are nonauthoritative approaches to help people free up their own motivations and resources. These approaches shift the focus away from denial and toward increasing motivation to change. Both MI and MET help counselors identify individuals' stage of change, resolve ambivalence about change, strengthen commitment for change, and increase motivation to move through the stages of change toward successful recovery and rehabilitation.

Other substance abuse counseling strategies. Many of the individual, group, and family counseling theories and techniques used to treat other mental health problems are also used to treat individuals with SUDs. Group work, including group therapy, theme groups, and psychoeducational groups, are the counseling modalities most often used in substance abuse treatment programs. Commonly used counseling strategies include stress management and relaxation skill training; skills training in such areas as assertiveness, refusal, problem solving, decision making, social and behavioral self-control, and drugless alternatives; relapse prevention planning, including identification of substance use cues and triggers such as certain people, places, and emotional states, and a plan for action when the desire to use psychoactive substances occurs; behavioral counseling, including contingency contracting and management and cue extinction procedures; and cognitive behavioral strategies that teach individuals how their thoughts (e.g., "stinking thinking"), beliefs, and injunctions may hinder their recovery. Use of a global psychological self-help method such as the six-step Button Therapy method (Goodwin, 1981, 2002) for identifying and removing potentially self-defeating cognitions and coping with stressors (i.e., "Button-Pushers") is especially helpful when individuals become emotionally distressed. It is also useful to help individuals select appropriate support networks that may include mutual-help groups such as Alcoholics Anonymous (McCrady, Horvath, & Delaney, 2003; Sias & Goodwin, 2007).

SUBSTANCE ABUSE COUNSELOR INFLUENCE ON TREATMENT OUTCOME

ALTHOUGH THE MILLER, Wilbourne, and Hettema (2003) review focused on substance abuse treatment methods, there were also some interesting findings on substance abuse therapist variables. Therapists' rates of successful treatment outcome varied from 25% to 100%, and therapist empathy was found to be a key factor in successful treatment.

Counselor empathy. Several studies found that the more empathy expressed by the therapist during treatment, the less likely his or her clients were to drink following treatment (Miller & Baca, 1983; Miller, Benefield, & Tonigan, 1993; Valle, 1981). In one study, therapist empathy accounted for two-thirds of the variance in client outcomes at 6 months, one-half at 12 months, and one-quarter at 24 months. By far the strongest predictor of clients' treatment outcomes was the therapist to whom they were assigned, even though all therapists were using the same treatment method (Miller & Baca, 1983, cited in Miller et al., 2003).

As Miller et al. (2003) point out, "It is clear that client outcomes are influenced not only by what we do in treatment but also by how we do it. . . . Therapist empathy is one of the better-specified determinants of effective treatment" (p. 39). Accurate empathy involves the ability to actively listen and reflect an accurate understanding of the client's experience. Miller et al. (2003) further suggest that, "[therapist empathy] has little or nothing to do with identification, with having had a similar experience oneself. Rather, empathy is skillful active listening. Its opposite, perhaps, is a 'listen-to-me' authoritarian approach" (p. 39).

Confrontation. The use of confrontation is often associated with substance abuse counseling. In one study (Miller et al., 1993) cited by Miller et al. (2003), the researchers "were able to predict half of the variance in clients' drinking outcomes at 12-month follow-up from one therapist behavior during treatment: The more the therapist confronted, the more the client drank" (p. 39). In the Miller et al. (1993) study, "therapist 'confronting' responses consisted of challenging, disagreeing, head-on disputes, incredulity, emphasizing negative client characteristics, and sarcasm. . . . In general, client resistance behaviors were strongly correlated with therapist confrontational responses. Positive, self-motivational client responses, on the other hand, were related to therapist listening and restructuring" (p. 458). As Miller et al. (1993) pointed out, "In every study in which therapist characteristics have been systematically evaluated and effects were found, more favorable outcomes have been associated with a therapeutic style approximating what Rogers termed *accurate empathy*" (p. 455).

Shaming and punishing. Miller and Carroll (2006) indicate that, "No scientific evidence supports belittling, shaming, and castigating addicted people; taking away their children and social benefits; and incarcerating them for extended periods" (p. 263). These strategies will often have a paradoxical effect and drive the person to increased substance abuse.

Therapist tone of voice. Another therapist variable affecting treatment retention and outcome is tone of voice. One study found that the more anger in the counselor's tone of voice, the less likely clients were to stay in treatment or to change their drinking (Milmoe, Rosenthal, Blane, Chafetz, & Wolf, 1967).

Hope and faith. Hope and faith appear to influence treatment outcomes as well. A therapist's expectation that a client will change or not can be a powerful self-fulfilling prophecy (Leake & King, 1977). Similarly, the client's own level of hope or optimism about change (i.e., self-efficacy), as well as the therapist's belief in the efficacy of the treatment, can enhance outcomes (Miller et al., 2003).

EVIDENCE-BASED TREATMENTS

THE SUBSTANTIAL RESEARCH on treatment approaches for alcohol use disorders has been summarized by Miller et al. (2003). Their review of 381 controlled trials of 99 different treatment modalities, involving 75,000 clients, concluded that, "First, there is clearly reason for optimism in the treatment of alcohol use disorders. This review reveals 18 treatment methods with a positive balance of evidence" (p. 40). However, in a narrative review of the treatment outcome research, the authors noted that,

> [A]lthough the scientific literature points to a list of treatment approaches with reasonable evidence of positive benefit, this list overlaps little with those components often employed in U.S. alcoholism treatment programs. . . . The negative correlation between scientific evidence and treatment-as-usual remains striking, and could hardly be larger if one intentionally constructed treatment programs from those approaches with the least evidence of efficacy. (p. 41)

Thus, most of the currently available evidence-based treatment approaches with demonstrated efficacy are infrequently used in substance abuse treatment programs.

Cost effectiveness of substance abuse treatment. Substance abuse treatment more than pays for itself in terms of costs to society. The California Drug and Alcohol Treatment Assessment (CALDATA) study of treatment outcomes over a 3- to 5-year period following treatment, conducted by the State of California and duplicated by several other states, found that there was continual abstinence in approximately 50% of individuals treated, crime was abated in 74% of those treated, and the state enjoyed savings of $7 for every $1 spent on treatment (Ettner et al., 2005; Inaba & Cohen, 2004; Robert Wood Johnson Foundation, 2006a). Economic studies across settings, populations, methods, and time periods have consistently found positive net economic benefits of substance abuse treatment. The primary economic benefits come from reduced crime, including incarceration and victimization costs, and posttreatment reduction in health care costs (Belenko, Patapis, & French, 2005; Robert Wood Johnson Foundation, 2006b). In addition, the most effective treatment models are not necessarily the costliest ones. One earlier study found that a more expensive treatment was not likely to produce more effective results (Holder, Longabaugh, Miller, & Rubonis, 1991). More than three-quarters of the people accessing addiction treatment receive some kind of public assistance (SAMHSA, 2006).

TREATMENT OUTCOMES

INABA AND COHEN (2004) point out that, "Several studies have confirmed that treatment for people with SUDs result[s] in long-term abstinence along with tremendous health, social, and spiritual benefits to patients" (p. 384). According to Dr. Alan I. Leshner, former director of the National Institute on Drug Abuse (cited in Inaba & Cohen, 2004):

> Treatment is effective. Scientifically based drug addiction treatments typically reduce drug abuse by 40% to 60%. These rates are not ideal, of course, but they are comparable to compliance rates seen with treatment for other chronic diseases, such as asthma, hypertension, and diabetes. Moreover, treatment markedly reduces undesirable consequences of drug abuse and addiction, such as unemployment, criminal activity, and HIV/AIDS or other infectious diseases, whether or not patients achieve complete abstinence. (p. 379)

Benefits to society include social, financial, and quality-of-life gains, including reductions in criminal activity, health care expenditures, dependence on public assistance, and increases in employment earnings (Carr et al., 2008).

PATHWAYS OF ADDICTION AND RECOVERY

THE PATH OF many individuals with SUDs is marked by cycles of recovery, relapse, repeated treatments, often spanning many years before ending in stable recovery, other disabilities, or death (Anglin, Hser, & Grella, 1997; Hser, 1997; Scott, Foss, & Dennis, 2005; Simpson, Joe, & Broome, 2002; White, 1996). Between 58% and 60% of people who meet the criteria for a SUD at some time in their lives eventually achieve sustained recovery (Dawson, 1996; Dennis & Scott, 2007; Kessler, 1994; Robins & Regier, 1991).

Natural recovery. Many, if not most, individuals with substance abuse problems manage to recover on their own without the assistance of professional treatment or mutual-help groups (Burman, 1997; Humphreys, Moos, & Finney, 1995; Sobell, Ellingstad, & Sobell, 2000; Toneatto, Sobell, Sobell, & Rubel, 1999; Watson & Sher, 1998). In one review of the literature, "Estimates of the prevalence of nontreatment recoveries ranged from 87.5% to 53.7% depending on the definition of prior alcohol problems employed" (Cunningham, 1999a, p. 463). Between 80% and 90% of individuals quit smoking tobacco, one of the most addictive substances, on their own without treatment (Fiore et al., 1990; Orleans et al., 1991).

Professional substance abuse treatment. The majority of all prior substance abusers have never come in contact with any drug treatment services (Cunningham, 1999a, 1999b). Estimates of the ratio of untreated to treated individuals with alcohol problems in the general population range from 3:1 to 13:1 (Roizen, 1977). Although a significant proportion of individuals recover from alcohol problems without treatment, such recoveries appear less common among individuals with more severe SUDs, particularly when addiction is accompanied by mental disorders (Cunningham, 1999a; Scott et al., 2005). A subset of individuals with SUDs suffer from a more chronic version whereby they cycle through periods of relapse, treatment reentry, recovery, and incarceration, often lasting several years (Anglin et al., 1997; Scott et al., 2005). Compared with individuals with alcohol-related problems who do not obtain timely help, those who enter either Alcoholics Anonymous or treatment relatively soon after initiating help-seeking improve more quickly and achieve higher long-term remission rates (Moos & Moos, 2005; Timko, Moos, Finney, & Lesar, 2000).

Substance abuse counseling interventions. In addition to mutual-help groups such as Alcoholics Anonymous and Narcotics Anonymous (Gossop, Stewart, & Marsden, 2007; Scott et al., 2005; Sias & Goodwin, 2007), several counseling approaches have shown promise in reducing SUDs, including group therapy, marital and family therapy, cognitive behavior therapy, motivational interviewing and enhancement therapy, brief interventions, social skills training, relaxation training, systematic desensitization, problem solving, relapse prevention, and integrative models (French et al., 2008; Miller et al., 2003; Winters, Stinchfield, Latimer, & Lee, 2007). In one study (French et al., 2008), skills-focused psychoeducational group therapy was the least expensive and most cost-effective intervention when compared to functional family therapy, individual cognitive behavior therapy, and integrative treatment combining joint individual and family therapy for adolescents with a substance use disorder. Substance abuse services and treatment outcomes are affected by factors in the external political and economic environment of a facility, by internal program-level variables, and by client characteristics (Ghose, 2008).

Chronic nature of SUDs. Sixty-two percent of individuals in publicly funded substance abuse treatment in 2002 met the diagnostic criteria for dependence, 16% met the criteria for abuse, and 22% met the criteria for other substance-related problems such as acute intoxication and mental health problems aggravated by substance use. Sixty-four percent were reentering treatment: 23% for the second time, 22% for the third or fourth time, and 19% for the fifth or more time (Office of Applied Studies, 2005). Approximately half of the clients entering public or private substance abuse treatment are doing so for the first time. Clients entering substance abuse treatment for the first time tend to be younger, more educated, more steadily employed, and they tend to have less serious drug use and criminal involvement, and fewer family and mental health problems than clients with a prior treatment history (Anglin et al., 1997; Cacciola, Dugosh, Foltz, Leahy, & Stevens, 2005). On average, people reach sustained recovery only after three to four episodes of different kinds of treatment over a number of years (Anglin et al., 1997; Dennis, Scott, Funk, & Foss, 2005; Grella & Joshi, 1999; Hser, 1997; Hser, Grella, Chou, & Anglin, 1998; Scott, Dennis, & Foss, 2005). The estimated median time from first use to at least 1 drug-free year was 27 years, and the median time from first treatment episode to last use was 9 years in one study (Dennis et al., 2005). In sum, most individuals with SUDs require multiple treatment episodes over several years to reach stable recovery (Dennis & Scott, 2007). Psychoactive SUDs need to be viewed like other chronic relapsing disorders such as arthritis, asthma, cystic fibrosis, diabetes, heart disease, hypertension, and obesity in that they typically require long-term versus acute treatment. Scott and Dennis (2003) developed a Recovery Management Checkup model to provide ongoing monitoring for relapse and reducing the time from relapse to treatment reentry. Substance use disorders are typically chronic disorders where multiple substance use, comorbid mental disorders, and multiple treatment admissions over many years is the norm (Dennis et al., 2005).

TREATMENT DEMAND

IN 2005, 23.2 million (9.5% of the population aged 12 or older) persons needed treatment for a SUD. However, only 2.3 million (9.9%) of those in need of treatment received treatment at a specialty facility. Thus, 20.9 million persons (8.6% of the population aged 12 or older) needed treatment for a SUD but did not receive treatment at a substance abuse facility (SAMHSA, 2006). There are many reasons why individuals with SUDs don't enter treatment. One reason is the lack of treatment resources to accommodate the treatment need. Another reason is the placement of treatment-seeking individuals with SUDs on a waiting list.

> Substance users who wait for treatment services are less likely to enter treatment and often continue to use drugs, placing them at heightened risk for health complications such as overdose and exposure to infectious diseases such as hepatitis and HIV. . . . The likelihood of treatment-seeking substance abusers actually entering treatment after assessment is often less than 50%. . . . In part, this is related to substance abusers' limited tolerance for treatment wait time, with longer waits associated with higher rates of pretreatment attrition . . . longer wait time for an assessment is influenced by being court referred, less belief in having a substance abuse problem, and less desire for change. A shorter wait to actually enter treatment is predicted by having a case manager, being more ready for treatment, and having less severe employment and alcohol problems. (Carr et al., 2008, p. 193)

FAMILY ISSUES

S UBSTANCE ABUSE CAN be viewed as a family illness. It is estimated that a person addicted to psychoactive substances affects at least four to six other people, especially family members. Hook (2008) estimates that substance abuse affects approximately 45%–68% of the U.S. population. It is estimated that, in the United States, 25% of children under the age of 18 are living with a parent in need of treatment of a SUD (Kinney, 2003). Psychoactive substance use also affects future generations through women taking substances during pregnancy, the genetic transmission by substance abusing parents, and family psychosocial effects, including modeling of parental and sibling substance abuse.

Psychoactive substances and pregnancy. Approximately 5.5% of U.S. women giving birth used illicit drugs and 18.8% drank alcohol sometime during their pregnancy (National Institute on Drug Abuse, 1994). Most psychoactive substances can have a deleterious effect on the developing fetus. Probably the best-known harmful effect of psychoactive substances on the developing fetus is that of *fetal alcohol syndrome (FAS)* and the less severe *fetal alcohol effects.* According to Kinney (2003), FAS is the most preventable cause of mental retardation and developmental disabilities in the United States.

Genetic predisposition. There is an increased incidence of substance abuse in children of substance abusers versus children of nonsubstance abusing parents. Heredity can influence SUDs, behavioral addictions, and some mental disorders. Studies of twins along with other human and animal studies estimate the influence of genetics on substance abuse at between 40%–60% (Bierut et al., 1998; Blum, Cull, Braverman, & Comings, 1996; Eisen et al., 1998; Kendler, Aggen, Tambs, & Reichborn-Kjennerud, 2006; Lynskey et al., 2006; Schuckit, 1986, 2000).

Family system, homeostasis, and coping styles. Viewing the family as a system is a common perspective in mental health disciplines. Central to family systems theory is the belief that changes in any part (i.e., any family member) of the system affect all of the others. The other family members, in response, make changes to maintain the balance within the family system. Substance abuse by a family member affects the homeostatic balance of the entire family system. Families tend to strive for homeostatic balance when confronted with the disrupting stressor of a substance abusing family member. Families utilize numerous coping strategies to adapt to the stress within a family system. Sharon Wegscheider (1981), a student of Virginia Satir, gave titles of the *family hero, scapegoat, lost child,* and *mascot* to family roles played by children in the alcoholic family. Claudia Black (1981), another early pioneer in the promotion of treatment for children of alcoholics, defined their role behavior in two categories: (1) the misbehaving and obviously troubled children, and (2) the mature, stable, overachieving, behaving children. She termed the roles of young children of alcoholics as the *responsible ones, adjusters,* and *placaters*. These roles identified by Wegscheider and Black were adaptations of the family dysfunctional communication patterns identified earlier by Satir (Bandler, Grender, & Satir, 1976; Satir, 1988) of *placater, blamer, computer (super reasonable),* and *distracter*. Children often blame themselves for the pain in the family and try to fix it by rigidly playing out their role in the system, often at the expense of their own mental health. In times of stress, these roles tend to become rigid in an attempt to cope and survive. These childhood coping styles can last into adulthood and affect relationships and work in both negative and positive ways, depending on how these patterns are channeled.

Three basic approaches family members adopt in living with an alcoholic include (1) keeping out of the way of the drinker and managing one's own life; (2) caregiving, counseling, and controlling; and (3) resigning and maintaining a façade. The approach most commonly chosen differs by gender and between spouse and children. The spouse is often involved with caregiving, counseling, and controlling. Children are more likely to keep out of the way of the drinker and manage their own lives. Women more than men are more likely to selectively keep out of the drinker's way while also engaged in caregiving while men are more likely to adopt resignation. The husband is more likely to leave an alcoholic wife than vice versa, and the female alcohol-dependent member is much more likely to be divorced than is her male counterpart (Kinney, 2003).

Although substance abuse can be viewed as a symptom of a dysfunctional family system, it is difficult to determine if the substance abuse caused the family system dysfunction or is the result of a dysfunctional family system (Lawson & Lawson, 1983).

Enabling. For a variety of reasons family members may unwittingly adopt certain behaviors that allow the substance abuse to continue. Enabling occurs whenever the actions of family members, or others, protect the substance abusing family member from the consequences of substance abuse. While trying to cope with the embarrassment, shame, and financial consequences of living with a substance abusing family member, family members may make excuses and cover up the consequences of substance abuse. As Kinney (2003) points out, "Ironically, while sparing the alcohol-dependent person from experiencing the consequences and thus the associated pain, the family members absorb the pain themselves" (p. 203).

Codependency. Family and friends of individuals caught up in substance abuse are usually affected to some degree. It is difficult to watch a loved one travel down a self-destructive path. Codependency refers to the phenomenon of being affected by the substance abuser to the point that one becomes hopeful and happy when the substance abuser takes a break from his or her substance abuse and responsibly performs his or her life functions, and becomes discouraged and distressed when the substance abuse behavior returns. In codependency, happiness or distress is dependent upon the status of the substance abuser at any given time. In its more extreme form the codependent may attempt to meet the substance abuser's needs to the exclusion of his or her own needs. The codependent individual may become hypervigilant and live in a chronically distressed state waiting for the substance abuser to fall off the wagon or to call from the police station asking to be bailed out. It is no wonder that many family members and friends eventually cut loose the substance abuser from their lives for their own welfare and survival.

Boundaries and family rules. Families with a substance abusing member often have many boundary issues and family rules. As Lawson and Lawson (1983) point out:

> Disengaged or rigid boundaries are frequently seen in alcoholic families with the result of isolation of family members from each other and isolation of the family from the community. The disengagement of family members is perpetuated by family rules such as: it is not safe to comment on alcoholism or drug addiction, it is not wise to confront the alcoholic or addict, and it is essential to the survival of the family to protect the alcoholic or addict so things don't get worse. . . . Researchers have reported that young adults and adolescents with drug problems often describe their families as chaotic and disengaged. (p. 182)

Family therapy. Studies indicate that including the spouse or other family members in substance abuse treatment improves treatment outcome. Family therapy appears to be effective, and in some cases, better than individual therapy (Friedman, Tomko, & Utada, 1991; Joanning, Quinn, Thomas, & Mullen, 1992; Liddle, Dakog, Diamond, Barrett, & Tejeda, 2001; Liddle & Diamond, 1991; O'Farrell & Fals-Stewart, 2003; O'Farrell, Murphy, Alter, & Fals-Stewart, 2008; Piercy & Frankel, 1989; Quinn, Kuehl, Thomas, & Joanning, 1988; Rowe & Liddle, 2003; Stanton & Shadish, 1997; Szapocznik, Kurtines, Foot, Perez-Vidal, & Hervis, 1986).

SUBSTANCE ABUSE COUNSELING SPECIALISTS

MANY MENTAL HEALTH disciplines, including counseling, psychology, and psychiatry, have found it necessary to develop a specialty area of practice in substance abuse counseling along with specialty certifications. Also, substance abuse counseling is evolving as a separate profession with its own unique body of knowledge, specialized preparation needs and competencies, certifications and licensure, and accreditation standards. The substance abuse field is at a crossroad with two evolving trends that attract substance abuse professionals. One trend is the development of substance abuse counseling as a separate profession with its own independent accreditation and licensure mechanisms. The other trend is the development of substance abuse counseling as a specialization, including specialty certification, within other, more established mental health professions (Goodwin, 2006).

The substance abuse field has an extensive body of knowledge as well as specialty assessment, counseling, and treatment strategies. Mental health professionals are advised to attain specialty preservice or continuing education preparation in order to work effectively with individuals with SUDs and their families. There are many institutions of higher education that offer substance abuse courses, including online distance education courses that are available to practitioners in the field. In addition, there are many continuing education workshops in the substance abuse area (Goodwin, 2006). Individuals with SUDs have unique issues and problems that are often life-changing and sometimes life-threatening and deserve qualified mental health professionals knowledgeable in the substance abuse field to serve them. Because substance use and abuse is found in every mental health, school, and health care setting, all professional counselors should attain enough education to recognize the signs and symptoms of SUDs, provide substance abuse screenings, and know when to refer to more qualified substance abuse professionals for more comprehensive assessment and treatment.

In summary, SUDs are best viewed as chronic, relapsing biopsychosocialspiritual disorders that are treatable with successful outcomes. Substance use disorders are analogous to other chronic relapsing disorders such as asthma, hypertension, and diabetes in that slips and relapses often occur following acute treatments. Healing or management of the illness often requires continued monitoring and successive acute care treatments when the illness flares up. With continued care, successive treatments, and continual monitoring, individuals with SUDs can increase the interval between abusive episodes until the individual achieves either full abstinence or more responsible substance use, and a more stable life-fulfilling recovery. Successful long-term recovery requires the adoption of a healthy lifestyle and continued mindfulness that SUDs are chronic, relapsing disorders that can rear their ugly heads if one becomes negligent in maintaining life-enhancing attitudes, beliefs, and behaviors. Eventually, the majority of individuals can be expected to recover from SUDs with abstinence or reductions in substance use, along with improved health, social, vocational, and spiritual functioning. With patience, persistence, tolerance, empathy, and compassion, counselors can help individuals and their families successfully recover from this devastating and potentially life-threatening disorder.

ONLINE SUBSTANCE ABUSE RESOURCES

INFORMATION ON PSYCHOACTIVE SUBSTANCES AND TREATMENT OF SUBSTANCE USE DISORDERS (SUDs)

Addiction Technology Transfer Centers: http://www.nattc.org

Center for Substance Abuse Prevention: http://csap.samhsa.gov

Center for Substance Abuse Treatment: http://csat.samhsa.gov

National Clearinghouse on Alcohol and Drug Information: http://ncadi.samhsa.gov

National Institute on Alcoholism and Alcohol Abuse: http://www.niaaa.nih.gov

National Institute on Drug Abuse: http://www.nida.nih.gov

Substance Abuse and Mental Health Services Administration: http://www.samhsa.gov

DOWNLOADABLE SUBSTANCE ABUSE ASSESSMENT RESOURCES

Center on Alcoholism, Substance Abuse, and Addictions (associated with the University of New Mexico): http://casaa.unm.edu/inst.html

Join Together (associated with Boston University) provides an online screening tool for alcohol use disorders (AUDs) at http://www.alcoholscreening.org/index.asp

PROJECT CORK (associated with Dartmouth Medical School): http://www.projectcork.org/clinical_tools/index.html

Treatment Research Institute (TRI): http://www.tresearch.org; TRI was founded by A. Thomas McLellan, Ph.D., one of the developers of the Addiction Severity Index, Jack Durell, M.D., and a small team of colleagues from the University of Pennsylvania.

REFERENCES

American Society of Addiction Medicine. (1996). *Patient placement criteria for the treatment of substance-related disorders* (2nd ed.). Chevy Chase, MD: American Society of Addiction Medicine.

Anglin, M. D., Hser, Y. I., & Grella, C. E. (1997). Drug addiction and treatment careers among clients in the Drug Abuse Treatment Outcome Study (DATOS). *Psychology of Addiction Behaviors, 11*(4), 308–323.

Bandler, R., Grender, J., & Satir, V. (1976). *Changing with families.* Palo Alto, CA: Science and Behavior Books.

Belenko, S., Patapis, N., & French, M. T. (2005). *Economic benefits of drug treatment: A critical review of the evidence for policy makers.* Treatment Research Institute at the University of Pennsylvania. Retrieved February 26, 2007, from http://www.tresearch.org/resources/specials/2005FebEconomicBenefits.pdf

Bierut, L. J., Dinwiddie, S. H., Begleiter, H., Crowe, R., Hesselbrock, V., Nurnberger, J. I., Jr., et al. (1998). Familial transmission of substance dependence: Alcohol, marijuana, cocaine, and habitual smoking: A report from the collaborative study on the genetics of alcoholism. *Archives of General Psychiatry, 55*(11), 982–988.

Black, C. (1981). *It will never happen to me.* Denver, CO: M.A.C. Publishers.

Blum, K., Cull, J. G., Braverman, E. R., & Comings, D. E. (1996). Reward deficiency syndrome. *American Scientist, 84,* 132–145.

Burman, S. (1997). The challenge of sobriety: Natural recovery without treatment and self-help groups. *Journal of Substance Abuse, 9,* 41–61.

Cacciola, J. S., Dugosh, K., Foltz, C., Leahy, P., & Stevens, R. (2005). Treatment outcomes: First time versus treatment-experienced clients. *Journal of Substance Abuse Treatment, 28,* S13–S22.

Carr, J. A. C., Xu, J., Redko, C., Lane, D. T., Rapp, R. C., Gioris, J., et al. (2008). Individual and system influences on waiting time for substance abuse treatment. *Journal of Substance Abuse Treatment, 34,* 192–201.

Cunningham, J. A. (1999a). Resolving alcohol-related problems with and without treatment: The effects of different problem criteria. *Journal of Studies on Alcohol, 60*(4), 463–466.

Cunningham, J. A. (1999b). Untreated remissions from drug use: The predominant pathway. *Addictive Behaviors, 24*(2), 267–270.

Daley, D. C., & Marlatt, G. A. (2006). *Overcoming your alcohol or drug problem: Effective recovery strategies. Therapist guide* (2nd ed.). New York: Oxford University Press.

Dawson, D. (1996). Gender differences in the risk of alcohol dependence: United States, 1992. *Addiction, 91*(12), 1831–1842.

Dennis, M., & Scott, C. K. (2007). Managing addiction as a chronic condition. *Addiction Science and Clinical Practice, 4*(1), 45–55.

Dennis, M. L., Scott, C. K., Funk, R., & Foss, M. A. (2005). The duration and correlates of addiction and treatment careers. *Journal of Substance Abuse Treatment, 28*(Suppl. 1), S51–S62.

Eisen, S. A., Lin, N., Lyons, M. J., Scherrer, J. F., Griffith, K., True, W. R., et al. (1998). Familial influences on gambling behavior: An analysis of 3,359 twin pairs. *Addiction, 93*(9), 1375–1384.

Ettner, S. L., Huang, D., Evans, E., Ash, D. R., Handy, M., Jourabchi, M., et al. (2005). Benefit-cost in the California Treatment Outcome Project: Does substance abuse treatment "pay for itself"? *Health Services Research, 41*(1), 192–213. DOI: 10.1111/j.1475–6773.2005.00466.x. Retrieved July 11, 2008, from http://www.blackwell-synergy.com/action/doSearch

Fiore, M. C., Novotny, T. E., Pierce, G. A., Giovino, G. A., Hatziandreu, E. J., Newcomb, P. A., et al. (1990). Methods used to quit smoking in the United States. Do cessation programs help? *Journal of the American Medical Association, 263*(20), 2760–2765.

French, M. T., Zavala, S. K., McCollister, K. E., Waldron, H. B., Turner, C. W., & Ozechowski, T. J. (2008). Cost-effectiveness analysis of four interventions for adolescents with a substance use disorder. *Journal of Substance Abuse Treatment, 34,* 272–281.

Friedman, A. S., Tomko, I. A., & Utada, A. (1991). Client and family characteristics that predict better family therapy outcome for adolescent drug abusers. *Family Dynamics of Addiction Quarterly, 1*(1), 77–93.

Ghose, T. (2008). Organizational and individual level correlates of posttreatment substance use: A multilevel analysis. *Journal of Substance Abuse Treatment, 34*(2), 249–262.

Goodwin, L. R., Jr. (1981). Psychological self-help: A five-step model. *Journal of Humanistic Psychology, 21*(1), 13–27.

Goodwin, L. R., Jr. (2002). *The button therapy book: How to work on your buttons and the button-pushers in your life.* Victoria, BC, Canada: Trafford.

Goodwin, L. R., Jr. (2006). A comprehensive substance abuse counselor education program: From specialty certificate to PhD. *Journal of Teaching in the Addictions, 5*(2), 59–80.

Gossop, M., Stewart, D., & Marsden, J. (2007). Attendance at Narcotics Anonymous and Alcoholics Anonymous meetings, frequency of attendance and substance use outcomes after residential treatment for drug dependence: A 5-year follow-up study. *Addiction, 103,* 119–125.

Grella, C. E., & Joshi, V. (1999). Gender differences in drug treatment careers among clients in the National Drug Abuse Treatment Outcome Study. *American Journal of Drug and Alcohol Abuse, 25*(3), 385–406.

Holder, H., Longabaugh, R., Miller, W. R., & Rubonis, A. V. (1991). The cost effectiveness of treatment for alcoholism: A first approximation. *Journal of Studies on Alcohol, 52*(6), 517–541.

Hook, M. K. (2008). Addiction and families. In D. Capuzzi and M. D. Stauffer (Eds.), *Foundations of addictions counseling* (pp. 325–352). Boston: Pearson/ Allyn & Bacon.

Hser, Y. I. (1997). Drug treatment careers: A conceptual framework and existing research findings. *Journal of Substance Abuse Treatment, 14*(6), 543–558.

Hser, Y. I., Grella, C., Chou, C. P., & Anglin, M. D. (1998). Relationships between drug treatment careers and outcomes: Findings from the National Drug Abuse Treatment Outcome Study. *Evaluation Review, 22*(4), 496–519.

Humphreys, K., Moos, R. H., & Finney, J. W. (1995). Two pathways out of drinking problems without professional treatment. *Addictive Behaviors, 20,* 427–441.

Inaba, D. S., & Cohen, W. E. (2004). *Uppers, downers, all arounders* (5th ed.). Ashland, OR: CNS Publications.

Joanning, H., Quinn, W., Thomas, F., & Mullen, R. (1992). Treating adolescent drug abuse: A comparison of family systems therapy, group therapy, and family drug education. *Journal of Marital and Family Therapy, 18*(4), 345–356.

Kendler, K. S., Aggen, S. H., Tambs, K., & Reichborn-Kjennerud, T. (2006). Illicit psychoactive substance use, abuse and dependence in a population-based sample of Norwegian twins. *Psychological Medicine, 36*(7), 955–962.

Kessler, R. C. (1994). The National Comorbidity Survey of the United States. *International Review of Psychiatry, 6,* 365–376.

Kinney, J. (2003). *Loosening the grip: A handbook of alcohol information* (7th ed.). Boston: McGraw-Hill.

Lawson, A., & Lawson, G. (1983). *Alcoholism and the family: A guide to treatment and prevention.* Austin, TX: ProEd.

Leake, G. J., & King, A. S. (1977). Effect of counselor expectations on alcoholic recovery. *Alcohol Health and Research World, 11*(3), 16–22.

Lewis, J. A., Dana, R. Q., & Blevins, G. A. (2002). *Substance abuse counseling* (3rd ed.). Pacific Grove, CA: Brooks/Cole.

Liddle, H. A., Dakog, G. A., Diamond, G. S., Barrett, K., & Tejeda, M. (2001). Multidimensional family therapy for adolescent substance abuse: Results of a randomized clinical trial. *American Journal of Drug and Alcohol Abuse, 27,* 651–687.

Liddle, H. A., & Diamond, G. S. (1991). Adolescent substance abusers in family therapy: The critical initial phase of treatment. *Family Dynamics of Addiction Quarterly, 1*(1), 55–68.

Lynskey, M. T., Agrawal, A., Bucholz, K. K., Nelson, E. C., Madden, P. A. F., Todorov, A. A., et al. (2006). Subtypes of illicit drug users: A latent class analysis of data from an Australian twin sample. *Twin Research and Human Genetics, 9*(4), 523–530.

McCrady, B. S., Horvath, T., & Delaney, S. I. (2003). Self-help groups. In R. H. Hester & W. R. Miller (Eds.), *Handbook of alcoholism treatment approaches: Effective alternatives* (3rd ed., pp. 165–187). Boston: Allyn & Bacon.

Miller, W. R., & Baca, L. M. (1983). Two-year follow-up of bibliotherapy and therapist-directed controlled drinking training for problem drinkers. *Behavior Therapy, 14,* 441–448.

Miller, W. R., Benefield, R. G., & Tonigan, J. S. (1993). Enhancing motivation for change in problem drinking: A controlled comparison of two therapist styles. *Journal of Consulting and Clinical Psychology, 61,* 455–461.

Miller, W. R., & Carroll, K. M. (2006). *Rethinking substance abuse: What science shows, and what we should do about it.* New York: Guilford Press.

Miller, W. R., & Rollnick, S. (1991). *Motivational interviewing: Preparing people to change addictive behavior.* New York: Guilford Press.

Miller, W. R., & Rollnick, S. (2002). *Motivational interviewing: Preparing people to change addictive behavior* (2nd ed.). New York: Guilford Press.

Miller, W. R., Wilbourne, P. L., & Hettema, J. E. (2003). What works? A summary of alcohol treatment outcome research. In R. H. Hester & W. R. Miller (Eds.), *Handbook of alcoholism treatment approaches: Effective alternatives* (3rd ed., pp. 13–63). Boston: Allyn & Bacon.

Miller, W. R., Zweben, A., DiClemente, C. C., & Rychtarik, R. G. (1995). *Motivational enhancement therapy manual: A clinical research guide for therapists treating individuals with alcohol abuse and dependence.* Project MATCH Monograph Series Vol. 2. Rockville, MD: National Institute on Alcohol Abuse and Alcoholism.

Milmoe, S., Rosenthal, R., Blane, H. T., Chafetz, M. E., & Wolf, I. (1967). The doctor's voice: Postdictor of successful referral of alcoholic patients. *Journal of Abnormal Psychology, 72,* 78–84.

Moos, R. H., & Moos, B. S. (2005). Sixteen-year changes and stable remission among treated and untreated individuals with alcohol use disorders. *Drug and Alcohol Dependence, 80,* 337–347.

National Institute on Drug Abuse. (1994). *National pregnancy and health survey* [Press release]. Rockville, MD: National Clearinghouse for Alcohol and Drug Information.

National Institute on Drug Abuse. (1999). *Principles of drug addiction treatment: A research based guide.* NIH Publication No. 00–4180. Bethesda, MD: National Institutes of Health.

O'Farrell, T. J., & Fals-Stewart, W. (2003). Alcohol abuse. *Journal of Marital and Family Therapy, 29*(1), 121–146.

O'Farrell, T. J., Murphy, M., Alter, J., & Fals-Stewart, W. (2008). Brief family treatment intervention to promote continuing care among alcohol-dependent patients in inpatient detoxification: A randomized pilot study. *Journal of Substance Abuse Treatment, 34,* 363–369.

Office of Applied Studies. (2005). *Treatment episode data set (TEDS): 2002. Discharges from substance abuse treatment services* (DHHS Publication No. SMA 04–3967). Rockville, MD: Substance Abuse and Mental Health Services Administration.

Orleans, C. T., Schoenbach, V. J., Wagner, E. H., Quade, D., Salmon, M. A., Pearson, D. C., et al. (1991). Self-help quit-smoking interventions: Effects of self-help materials, social support instructions, and telephone counseling. *Journal of Clinical and Consulting Psychology, 59,* 439–448.

Piercy, F. F., & Frankel, B. R. (1989). The evolution of an integrative family therapy for substance-abusing adolescents: Toward the mutual enhancement of research and practice. *Journal of Family Psychology, 3*(1), 5–25.

Prochaska, J. O., Norcross, J. C., & DiClemente, C. C. (1994). *Changing for good: The revolutionary program that explains the six stages of change and teaches you how to free yourself from bad habits.* New York: William Morrow.

Quinn, W. H., Kuehl, B. P., Thomas, F. N., & Joanning, H. (1988). Families of adolescent drug abusers: Systemic interventions to attain drug-free behavior. *American Journal of Drug and Alcohol Abuse, 14*(1), 65–87.

Robert Wood Johnson Foundation. (2006a, August). *Economic benefits of treating substance abuse outweigh costs*. Research Highlight Number 7. Retrieved March 3, 2007, from http://www.rwjf.org/files/research/Research%20Highlight%207%200605.pdf

Robert Wood Johnson Foundation. (2006b, August). *Treatment of chemical dependency may reduce medical utilization and costs*. Research Highlight Number 6. Retrieved March 3, 2007, from http://www.rwjf.org/files/research/Research%20Highlight%206%200605.pdf

Robins, L. N., & Regier, D. A. (1991). *Psychiatric disorders in America*. New York: Macmillan.

Roizen, R. (1977). *Barriers to alcoholism treatment*. Berkeley, CA: Alcohol Research Group.

Rowe, C. L., & Liddle, H. A. (2003). Substance abuse. *Journal of Marital and Family Therapy, 29*(1), 97–120.

Satir, V. (1988). *The new peoplemaking*. Palo Alto, CA: Science and Behavior Books.

Schuckit, M. A. (1986). Genetic and clinical implications of alcoholism and affective disorder. *American Journal of Psychiatry, 143*(2), 140–147.

Schuckit, M. A. (2000). Genetics of the risk for alcoholism. *American Journal of Addiction, 9*(2), 103–112.

Scott, C. K., & Dennis, M. L. (2003). *Recovery management checkup (RMC) protocol for people with chronic substance use disorders*. Blomington, IL: Chestnut Health Systems. Available from the author at cscott@cheastnut.org

Scott, C. K., Foss, M. A., & Dennis, M. L. (2005). Pathways in the relapse-treatment-recovery cycle over 3 years. *Journal of Substance Abuse Treatment, 28*(Suppl.), 563–572.

Sias, S. M., & Goodwin, L. R., Jr. (2007). Students' reactions to attending 12-step meetings: Implications for counselor education. *Journal of Addictions and Offender Counseling, 27*, 113–126.

Simpson, D. D., Joe, G. W., & Broome, K. M. (2002). A national 5-year follow-up of treatment outcomes for cocaine dependence. *Archives of General Psychiatry, 59*(6), 538–544.

Sobell, L. C., Ellingstad, T. P., & Sobell, M. B. (2000). Natural recovery from alcohol and drug problems: Methodological review of the research with suggestions for future directions. *Addiction, 95*, 749–764.

Stanton, M. D., & Shadish, W. R. (1997). Outcome, attrition, and family-couple treatment for drug abuse: A meta-analysis and review of the controlled, comparative studies. *Psychological Bulletin, 122*, 170–191.

Substance Abuse and Mental Health Services Administration. (2006). *Results from the 2005 National Survey on Drug Use and Health: National findings.*

Office of Applied Studies (NSDUH Series H-30, DHHS Publication No. SMA 06-4194). Rockville, MD: Author.

Szapocznik, J., Kurtines, W. M., Foot, F., Perez-Vidal, A., & Hervis, O. (1986). Conjoint versus one-person family therapy: Further evidence for the effectiveness of conducting family therapy through one person with drug-abusing adolescents. *Journal of Consulting and Clinical Psychology, 54*(3), 395–397.

Timko, C., Moos, R., Finney, J. W., & Lesar, M. D. (2000). Long-term outcomes of alcohol-use disorders: Comparing untreated individuals with those in Alcoholics Anonymous and formal treatment. *Journal of Studies on Alcohol, 61*, 529–540.

Toneatto, T., Sobell, L. C., Sobell, M. B., & Rubel, E. (1999). Natural recovery from cocaine dependence. *Psychology of Addictive Behaviors, 13*, 259–268.

Valle, S. K. (1981). Interpersonal functioning of alcoholism counselors and treatment outcome. *Journal of Studies on Alcohol, 42*, 783–790.

Watson, A. L., & Sher, K. J. (1998). Resolution of alcohol problems without treatment: Methodological issues and future directions of natural recovery research. *Clinical Psychology: Science and Practice, 5*, 1–18.

Wegscheider, S. (1981). *Another chance: Hope and help for the alcoholic family*. Palo Alto, CA: Science and Behavior Books.

White, W. L. (1996). *Pathways from the culture of addiction to the culture of recovery: A travel guide for addiction professionals* (2nd ed.). Center City, MN: Hazelden.

Winters, K. C., Stinchfield, R., Latimer, R. R., & Lee, S. (2007). Long-term outcome of substance-dependent youth following 12-step program. *Journal of Substance Abuse Treatment, 33*(1), 61–69.

68

Counseling the Terminally Ill and Their Families

KRISS A. KEVORKIAN

Death is nothing more than a migration of the soul from this place to another.

—Plato

BEFORE ANY DISCUSSION regarding counseling the terminally ill can be explored, it is important to differentiate the meaning between grief, bereavement, and mourning. *Grief* is the reaction or response to loss. *Bereavement* refers to the state of being deprived of something, often a loss through death; and *mourning* is the process of coping with grief and loss. The following chapter explores various issues concerning providing counseling services to clients with terminal illness and their families, providing guidelines in counseling clients with terminal illness, working with terminally ill children, bereavement counseling strategies, and caregivers support.

COMMUNICATING WITH THE TERMINALLY ILL AND THEIR FAMILIES

COUNSELING PEOPLE FACING death, and their families as they observe the decline of their loved one, requires compassion, empathy, and a conscious understanding of living and dying. Dass

(2000) noted three frequently recurring questions surrounding death: (1) "How do you deal with the processes of dying? (2) What happens to me at the moment of death? (3) What will happen to me after I die?" (p. 150). In order to counsel the dying and their loved ones, it is important to understand how you, the counselor, respond to these questions and your comfort in doing so.

Necessary skills for counselors working with the dying are *listening, supporting,* and *guiding.* People want to share their stories of life, both the good and the bad. Some want to learn from the process of dying and want to help teach others about it as well. As counselors, a great deal of trust is bestowed upon us to help guide and support those in grief. The most important skill we can offer is listening.

> Malini Mundle, MA, a counseling psychologist in New Delhi, India, shares, [The patients] are not the done unto's but the doers, actively participating as best they can to make the last stage meaningful and through their narratives and discourse giving their lives value. They gratefully acknowledge the support to get this work done. Counselors will find that stepping out of the box is the best gift they can give themselves when they are with these living individuals whose present journey is coming to an end. (M. Mundle, personal communication, December 7, 2007)

The terminally ill client has been through a series of losses, sometimes a long one, a roller coaster of recurring hope and despair, and increasing debilitation with ongoing pain. At some point, curative treatment is no longer an option. If the person is lucky, the attendant physician is compassionate and knows how to give bad news. If that isn't the case, in addition to acting as counselor, it is fitting and important to also act as an advocate. Assess how both patient and family are coping and what their needs might be. If the terminally ill person is not being properly cared for in regard to physical health and well-being, not being included in details of care, or not being communicated to with dignity and respect, the patient and family may be hurt and angry, and these factors can impede the family's grieving process. In such instances, counselors should consider offering to facilitate a family meeting with the physician in order to bridge a communication gap between the patient, family, and physician. If the physician is unwilling to participate, educate and empower the family to speak with another physician to get the answers they need.

In our death-denying culture, it is often extremely difficult to hear that one has an illness. The crucial component for counseling the dying is honest communication. Families often want to protect their loved one from the diagnosis of being terminally ill; however, the person is likely to know that he or she is dying. Facilitating honest communication between the terminally ill person and the family is important to help ensure that the person is not isolated from them, which can occur when families are overly protective.

Some Guidelines When Communicating With the Terminally Ill

1. Let the individual set the tone. Light conversation can often lead the way toward deeper, more meaningful conversations; however, the client has to find a comfort level first. Test the waters and then move at the pace set by the client.
2. Most ill people want an opportunity to share how they are feeling, and family might not be open to those discussions. Facilitate communication, to help everyone hear how each person is feeling. This is beneficial twice: at the time of the initial sharing and also when the family has lost their loved one, since they had the opportunity to share what they wanted and needed to share.
3. Listen and reflect. And where possible, teach the family to do so as well. This can be difficult for some, especially when an ill person remains silent either by choice or by inability. Some people benefit more from being silent than from speaking. In either case, educate the family that they can still share with their loved one by communicating through words, music, or touch, if acceptable to the ill one. Encourage family members to hold hands with their loved one or stroke the person's hair. Teach them how to perform a hand or foot massage (or have available a health worker who can teach them). While some family members might not feel comfortable, others may at least try. Actively engaging in this way can release the anxiety that some people have in sitting alone with a person who does not speak and may be dying.
4. Remain within your scope of practice. Counselors need to be aware of their role and scope of expertise for ethical reasons. Although counselors are frequently asked medical or spiritual/religious questions by the family or ill loved one, counselors are reminded to limit their responses relative to their expertise in the matter. Although some counselors may be trained to deal with spiritual or medical questions, they should be prepared to refer when necessary to medical personnel or religious leaders as warranted.
5. Be willing to be silently present. Communication is nonverbal as well as verbal. Stay still and focused. If you are fidgeting and looking at your watch, you will create a very uncomfortable situation for your client and greatly limit the level of trust that might have developed. Many people are uncomfortable being around people who are sick, and people who are ill become adept at sensing this, so your body language matters. Spiritual leaders speak of *being*

present with people, conscious of the person, sharing the moment of just *being,* when immense energy and sharing can take place.

6. Always allow hope. As dying people have shared, *one never truly knows what tomorrow may bring.* As such, counselors should not diminish client or family hope for cure or view such behavior as denial where the impending death must be accepted as a reality; however, counselors need to balance the hope of the family while at the same time supporting the family to prepare for the inevitable.

7. Encourage and support a life review, if one is in progress. A life review helps bring about closure to a dying person, whether it is happening consciously or unconsciously. There are many books that can help families ask questions of their dying loved one to prompt a life review that also have a place to record responses (see Resources). These discussions can also be tape-recorded or video-taped in order to keep them for others. The dying person might have specific stories to share with children who are too young to completely understand.

Common questions asked to prompt a life review include:

- What was your childhood like? Where and with whom?
- What activities did you participate in?
- What sort of work were you involved in?
- Who was your first love and what was that like?

Questions young people might ask of elders might include, What was the world like when you were my age? What type of music did you listen to?

8. Ask if the dying person would like to hear music, and if so, what kind, either to help stir memories or for comfort. Music can be extremely effective in calming the fear and chaos that can accompany the dying process.

9. Be tolerant when a person carries on conversations that seem to be occurring in real time but with no one physically present. A dying person might be speaking with a loved one who has passed on and is perceived as now being there to help. For some family members, this can be frightening. Educate them about this phenomenon and encourage their tolerance, especially since this is an experience that can occur for the person who is dying as well as for a bereaved person.

10. Avoid using the words *I understand* or *I can imagine.* Grief is an individual process. Just as we live differently, we grieve differently, and we will die differently. Always remember to *leave your agenda and beliefs at the door.*

While the terminally ill person experiences losses in health and activities of daily living, the family is experiencing *anticipatory mourning*, the expectation of losses that are not quite yet reality. For example, if the patriarch of the family is dying, the family may become aware of all the roles he has played: father, bookkeeper, cook, driver. The family can then begin to expect losses to come as the father declines and dies. The family unit may change; roles may become reversed if a child begins providing care to the parent. Caregiving issues discussed later may surface, and lack of proper coping skills might affect how the family is managing with the impending loss.

COUNSELING TERMINALLY ILL CHILDREN

Honest communication is particularly important when working with terminally ill children and their families. Communicating honestly with dying children gives them the respect that they deserve and allows them to discuss issues not often discussed with family, particularly grief. It is best for adults to be quiet and listen. More often than not, children are kept out of the loop regarding issues of their own health care; here is another situation when advocacy is called for because children should be allowed to participate in their care if they choose.

Be rigorously authentic with young clients; they will know if you are not and this can jeopardize their trust. Ask what the child enjoyed doing prior to being diagnosed, did he or she enjoy sports, and if so, which ones? What kind of music does he or she enjoy? Remember that as counselors, we meet the client where he or she is at the time. Does the child want to discuss his or her illness/grief with you? What does the child believe happens at the time of death and after death? Few people who are dying really have an opportunity to share how they are feeling about the diagnosis and everything else they're dealing with as the dying process progresses. The same is true for children. Listen and support the child, and remind him or her that you are also there to help the family through this process as well. The child might want to make sure that family members will be supported after the death.

COUNSELING THE BEREAVED

After the death of the terminally ill person, family members may continue to need emotional support and counseling. Others might prefer to participate in a support group or do both. Some people may need time to adjust to the loss and may choose to get counseling at a later time. In any case, educating a person about the grieving process is truly validating.

Grief can manifest itself in many ways, including behavioral, physical, and spiritual. Feelings can include sadness, anger, guilt, anxiety, fatigue, and shock. Physical sensations can include tightness in the throat or chest, dry mouth, lack of energy, and shortness of breath. Cognitive responses may include disbelief, confusion, and sometimes a sense of the presence of the deceased. Behavioral issues may include disruptions in sleep or appetite, crying, dreaming of the deceased, loss of interest, and social withdrawal. Social manifestations may include problems functioning in an organization or family and difficulties with interpersonal relationships. Spiritual issues may include searching for meaning, or anger or hostility toward a religious leader or God.

Worden (1982, 1991, 2002) describes four tasks of mourning:

- Accepting the reality of the loss
- Experiencing the pain or emotional aspects of the loss
- Adjusting to an environment in which the deceased is missing
- Relocating the dead person within one's life and finding ways to memorialize the person.

These tasks are not linear in any way, but a means to assist the bereaved in healing. A person might be managing well with one task but having difficulty with others.

Keep in mind that children who are grieving will understand what's happening and what you are saying at whatever developmental level they have reached. A thorough developmental assessment is important to understand how much they are able to comprehend. A useful technique to understanding just how much a child understands is to ask the family members to explain the situation and then *ask* the child what he or she heard. This allows one to clearly identify if information is being properly presented and received. It is also a good tool to use with adults who are having difficulty hearing what is being said. Children should be asked if they want to visit a loved one in the hospital or to attend the funeral. Adults are often in so much grief themselves that the children and their emotional needs can be overlooked.

Neimeyer (2000) in a man-on-the-street survey asked people how long they thought grief lasted. The responses ranged from 48 hours to 2 weeks. The truth is that grief lasts a lifetime. Since grief is not a part of our school curriculum, we learn how to grieve from those we see around us. For most people, the greatest concern is whether they are grieving the *right* way. Teach your clients that the grieving process is unique to each person but that there are healthy and unhealthy coping skills. Validate their concerns and provide support.

It is a lifelong process, not a quick fix. People do not *recover* from grief; *recover* means to bring back to normal position or condition (Merriam-Webster, 2007). One adjusts to the loss of a loved one, one doesn't recover from it; one learns to view the loss differently as one grows and matures.

CAREGIVER SUPPORT

WHEN FAMILY MEMBERS or loved ones act as primary caregivers for a dying person, issues of fear, guilt, and resentment can often hinder the mental well-being of both the terminally ill person and the caregiver.

Encourage and advocate caregiver support. Recommend that hospice families hire caregivers, if financially feasible, to avoid the issues that can develop as the terminally ill person declines and their needs increase. When a parent is dying, it's best if the children can remain the children and not take on the role-reversal issues that come with caring for a parent. If finances are not available to hire caregivers, encourage and assist family members to seek out the help they need that often may be found in places of worship, senior centers, volunteer programs, and hospice services, which include some levels of respite care.

Many family caregivers find that they truly are the best equipped to manage the care of their loved ones, once taught by nurses and mental health professionals regarding how to care for their loved one. It is often difficult for family caregivers to take breaks and take some time for themselves. If this is the case, time should be spent with the caregiver providing emotional support and suggesting healing therapies, such as Reiki (a Japanese technique for stress reduction and healing) or guided imagery (a relaxation technique to help reduce stress and promote well-being), to relieve the stress, frustration, and worry that come with caregiving. Counselors should also look for signs of caregiver resentment, anger, or frustration toward other family members for not pitching in to help.

The following is a list of strategies to emphasize for caregivers:

- Take care of yourself first and foremost!
- If you need support, ask for it.
- Utilize caregiver support networks and online resources to connect you to others who might be in similar situations who can help.
- Eat well, exercise, and get enough sleep.
- Talk with counselors or a spiritual leader who can help you with the many emotional issues that arise when caring for another.

As our population ages, more and more people are going to find themselves acting as caregivers either professionally or as family members. This growing phenomena as Americans age will require supportive counseling for bereavement and dependency issues.

CONCLUSION

THE SKILLS REQUIRED for those working with this population are honest and open communication, great listening skills, compassion, empathy, and genuine interest in the well-being of others, both living and dying.

Strategies to keep in mind when working with the dying and the bereaved are:

- Understand how you view dying and death.
- Leave your own beliefs and agenda at the door.
- Listen to clients and their families.
- Remember communications skills listed in the chapter.
- Always allow hope.
- Help others listen to children as they would to adults.
- Encourage caregiver support.

Information about education and training in grief counseling is available from the Association for Death Education and Counseling at www.adec.org.

SUGGESTED READING

Balk, D. E., Wogrin, C., Thornton, G., & Meagher, D. K. (Eds.). (2007). *Handbook of thanatology: The essential body of knowledge for the study of death, dying and bereavement*. Northbrook, IL: ADEC.

Blackman, S. (1997). *Graceful exits: How great beings die*. Boston: Shambala.

Callanan, M., & Kelley, P. (1993). *Final gifts*. New York: Bantam.

Corr, C. A., Nabe, C. M., & Corr, D. M. (2007). *Death and dying, life and living* (5th ed.). Belmont, CA: Wadsworth/Thomson.

DeSpelder, L. A., & Strickland, A. L. (2005). *The last dance: Encountering death and dying* (7th ed.). New York: McGraw-Hill.

Doka, K. J. (1993). *Living with life-threatening illness: A guide for patients, their families and caregivers*. New York: Lexington.

Elison, J., & McGonigle, C. (2003). *Liberating losses: When death brings relief*. Cambridge, MA: Perseus.

LaGrand, L. (1997). *After death communication: Final farewells*. St. Paul, MN: Llewellyn.

RESOURCES

Advance Health Care Directives: http://www.finalchoices.calhealth.org/advance_health_care_directives.htm

Dougy Center for Grieving Children and Families: http://www.dougy.org

Hospice Foundation of America: http://www.hospicefoundation.org

Metta Institute offers an End-of-Life Care Practitioner Program: http://www.mettainstitute.org/EOLprogram.html

Palliative Care Network directory gives palliative care professionals access to colleagues worldwide to provide educational support: http://www.palliativecarenetwork.com/default.htm

REFERENCES

Dass, R. (2000). *Still here: Embracing aging, changing, and dying.* New York: Riverhead.

Merriam-Webster. (2007). *Dictionary.* Retrieved December 10, 2007, from http://www.merriam-webster.com/dictionary/recover

Neimeyer, R. A. (2000). *Lessons of loss: A guide to coping.* Memphis, TN: University of Memphis.

Worden, J. W. (1982). *Grief counseling and grief therapy: A handbook for the mental health practitioner.* New York: Springer.

Worden, J. W. (1991). *Grief counseling and grief therapy: A handbook for the mental health practitioner* (2nd ed.). New York: Springer.

Worden, J. W. (2002). *Grief counseling and grief therapy: A handbook for the mental health practitioner* (3rd ed.). New York: Springer.

69

Assistive Technology and Persons With Disabilities

MARCIA J. SCHERER

A **SSISTIVE TECHNOLOGIES OR** *devices* are tools for enhancing the independent functioning of people who have physical limitations or disabilities. An assistive technology device (ATD), as initially defined in the Technology-Related Assistance of Individuals With Disabilities Act of 1988 (P.L. 100–407), is any item, piece of equipment, or product system, whether acquired commercially off the shelf, modified or customized, that is used to increase, maintain, or improve functional capabilities of individuals with disabilities. This definition of ATDs has been used in each piece of legislation related to persons with disabilities passed since 1988, and it is a common definition used in the field. Assistive technologies or devices are really just what the term implies—they assist individuals in getting around, doing personal and household tasks, participating in meetings at their places of work, and so on. Examples of ATDs are listed in Table 69.1.

Assistive technology devices range from low-tech aids such as built-up handles on eating utensils to high-tech, computerized systems to help persons with disabilities live independently and enter the workforce. Over time, increased use of these devices has impacted community practices. For example, independent mobility by battery-powered wheelchair required accessible buildings and modified transportation systems.

TABLE 69.1 Examples of Assistive Technology Devices: ABLEDATA Product Categories From www.abledata.com

Walking
  Major Categories: Canes, Crutches, Standing, Walkers

Wheeled Mobility
  Major Categories: Wheelchairs (Manual, Sport, and Powered), Wheelchair Alternatives (Scooters), Wheelchair Accessories, Carts, Transporters, Stretchers

Seating
  Major Categories: Seating Systems, Cushions, Therapeutic Seats

Transportation
  Major Categories: Mass Transit Vehicles and Facilities, Vehicles, Vehicle Accessories

Personal Care: Products to aid in activities of daily living
  Major Categories: Bathing, Carrying, Child Care, Clothing, Dispenser Aids, Dressing, Drinking, Feeding, Grooming/Hygiene, Handle Padding, Health Care, Holding, Reaching, Smoking, Toileting, Transfer

Computers: Products for using desktop and laptop computers and other kinds of information technology
  Major Categories: Software and Hardware, Computer Accessories

Controls: Products that provide the ability to start, stop, or adjust electric or electronic devices
  Major Categories: Environmental Controls, Switches

Blind and Low Vision: Products for people with visual disabilities
  Major Categories: Computers, Information Storage, Kitchen Aids, Labeling, Magnification, Office Equipment, Orientation and Mobility, Reading, Recreation, Sensors, Telephones, Typing, Writing (Braille)

Communication: Products to help people with disabilities related to speech, writing, and other methods of communication
  Major Categories: Alternative and Augmentative Communication, Headwands, Mouthsticks, Signal Systems, Telephones, Typing, Writing

Deaf and Hard of Hearing: Products for people with hearing disabilities
  Major Categories: Amplification, Driving, Hearing Aids, Recreational Electronics, Signal Switches, Speech Training, Telephones, Timers

Deaf Blind: Products for people who are both deaf and blind

Orthotics: Braces and other products to support or supplement joints or limbs
  Major Categories: Head and Neck, Lower Extremity, Torso, Upper Extremity

Prosthetics: Products for amputees
  Major Categories: Lower Extremity, Upper Extremity

Recreation: Products to assist with leisure and athletic activities
  Major Categories: Crafts, Electronics, Gardening, Music, Photography, Sewing, Sports, Toys

Safety and Security: Products to protect health and home
  Major Categories: Alarm and Security Systems, Child Proof Devices, Electric Cords, Lights, Locks

Architectural Elements: Products that make the built environment more accessible
  Major Categories: Indoors, Outdoors, Vertical Lift, Houses, Lighting, Signs

TABLE 69.1 *(Continued)*

Education: Products to provide access to educational materials and instruction in school and in other learning environments
  Major Categories: Classroom, Instructional Materials

Workplace: Products to aid people with disabilities at work
  Major Categories: Agricultural Equipment, Office Equipment, Tools, Vocational Assessment, Vocational Training, Work Stations

Home Management: Products to assist in cooking, cleaning, other household activities as well as adapted furniture and appliances
  Major Categories: Food Preparation, Housekeeping

There is currently no category for cognitive support technologies.

MATCHING PERSON AND TECHNOLOGY

THE DESIRE FOR—and reactions to—assistive technology devices are highly individual. Ultimately, the goal of rehabilitation and counseling professionals is to match an individual with an ATD that will enhance the person's capabilities and quality of life. Regardless of the type of device, an individual will either use it or not use it, to varying degrees. Nonuse can consist of device discard, or avoidance of use altogether (e.g., a person will not show up for an evaluation or fitting or will not purchase it). Use can be full-time and done willingly, or partial and done inappropriately or reluctantly. Partial use most frequently occurs when users:

1. experience fatigue or discomfort when using the device,
2. have other options than the device, or
3. use a device in one setting but not another.

THE DESIRABILITY OF A MODEL FOR MATCHING PERSON AND TECHNOLOGY

THE FACTORS THAT influence the use or nonuse of more optional assistive technology devices (not essential to the user) can be viewed as follows:

1. The characteristics of the *Milieu* or setting(s) where the device is to be used.
2. The pertinent features of the individual's *Personality,* priorities, and preferences.
3. The salient characteristics of the assistive *Technology* device itself.

Matching people with the most appropriate ATD involves the consideration of many factors and influences within the above three domains. The Matching Person and Technology (MPT) model (Scherer, 2005) was first developed in 1989 to organize these influences and is shown in Figure 69.1.

Considering these factors provides both a broad and an in-depth profile of where persons may be at a particular point in time with their devices. For example, a person may look like a partial or reluctant device user as far as the *milieu factors,* but appear to be an optimal user according to the characteristics listed for *personality* and *technology*. Thus, the *milieu* in which the device will be used may need some modification so the person can derive maximal satisfaction and functional gain from the device. While the characteristics and resources of the person will ultimately determine the consumer's choice of one product over a competing one, all of these influences interact with and determine one another. That is why the outermost circle reflects an ongoing, iterative, dynamic process of user–product evaluation, selection, accommodation (or adjustment), and use.

Device use is interactive; changes in one set of factors will have an effect on the others. For example, optimal use of one ATD may likely lead to enthusiasm for trying another device, improved self-confidence, and expanded social and community participation. It is often the case that a person will use one device well but have qualms about using

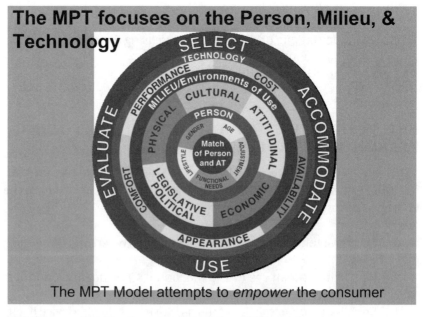

FIGURE 69.1 Matching Person and Technology (MPT) model.

a second device at the same time. Sometimes, the introduction of a new device can make the use of an existing one more complicated or cumbersome.

ASSESSING THE MATCH OF PERSON AND TECHNOLOGY

Documenting a person's goal achievement before and after the device is used can:

1. help provide the rationale for funding a device or training for that device,
2. demonstrate an individual's improvement in performance and participations over time, and
3. help organize information typifying the needs of an organization's consumers.

To achieve this, an assessment process emerged from the Matching Person and Technology model that consists of checklist-type instruments to record consumer goals and preferences, views of the benefits to be gained from a device, and changes in self-perceived outcome achievement over time. The instruments are listed in Table 69.2.

DESCRIPTION OF THE ASSISTIVE TECHNOLOGY DEVICE PREDISPOSITION ASSESSMENT

WE WILL FOCUS on the Assistive Technology Device Predisposition Assessment (ATD PA), which was developed by studying differences between ATD users and nonusers. It inquires into individuals' subjective satisfaction with current functioning in many areas and where the most improvement is desired. The consumer version has two forms: The Person Form consists of three sections.

- Section A: subjective ratings of cognitive/sensory, mobility/lower extremity, and upper extremity capabilities (9 items),
- Section B: subjective well-being (12 items),
- Section C: personal and psychosocial resources (33 items).

The Device Form consists of 12 items inquiring into the consumer's views of and expectations for using a particular device (12 items). Companion professional forms exist so that comparisons of professional and consumer views can be made.

TABLE 69.2   The Matching Person and Technology Assessments

The MPT assessments take a personal approach to assessing the potential technology need, choosing the most appropriate technology given the user's needs and goals, the technology features, and environmental support.

Features

- Provides a general technology screening and evaluation as well as specific technology matching.
- Instruments are applicable across individuals, types of technology, and environments of use.
- Based on underlying MPT model with multiple research studies testing the model with different populations and technology use situations.
- Specific instruments can be completed in approximately 15 minutes; a more comprehensive battery in approximately 45 minutes.

Step One: *Initial Worksheet for the Matching Person and Technology (MPT) Model* identifies initial goals and potential interventions supportive of goal achievement.

Step Two: *History of Support Use* notes supports used in the past, satisfaction with those supports, and those which are desired and needed but not yet available to the consumer.

Step Three: *Specific Technology Matching:* The consumer completes his or her version of the appropriate form depending on the type of technology under consideration. Companion professional forms exist to evaluate shared perspectives:

General: *Survey of Technology Use*
Assistive: *Assistive Technology Device Predisposition Assessment*
Educational: *Educational Technology Device Predisposition Assessment*
Workplace: *Workplace Technology Device Predisposition Assessment*
Healthcare: *Healthcare Technology Device Predisposition Assessment*

Step Four: The consumer and professional discuss factors that may indicate problems with optimal use of the technology.

Step Five: After problem areas have been noted, the professional and consumer work to identify specific intervention strategies and devise an action plan to address the problems.

Step Six: A follow-up assessment is conducted to determine any adjustments or accommodations needed to the technology and to inquire into goal achievement and whether the consumer has changed priorities. For assistive technologies, specific follow-up forms have been developed that can be used to correlate initial and follow-up information and assess AT outcomes. For the other types of technologies being matched with a consumer (general, educational, workplace) administering the same forms pre- and post-technology will provide an idea of changes in the consumer perspectives of that device or product.

Source: Institute for Matching Person & Technology, Inc. Reprinted with permission.

EVIDENCE FOR THE USEFULNESS OF THE ASSISTIVE TECHNOLOGY DEVICE PREDISPOSITION ASSESSMENT

DATA SHOW THAT the ATD PA is highly reliable and predictive when results are compared from the time of device selection to subsequent follow-up (Scherer & Sax, in press; Scherer, Sax, Vanbeirvliet, Cushman, & Scherer, 2005). In a recent study, 139 individuals were followed over time in order to understand their continued or discontinued use of mobility devices (canes, walkers, wheelchairs, and crutches). Participants were enrolled in a rehabilitation outcomes study (Jette, Keysor, Coster, Ni, & Haley, 2005) and had diagnoses of hip fracture, stroke, or complex medical conditions. All completed the ATD PA at baseline and 6 months follow-up.

Respondents were divided into three groups according to their ATD PA Device Form total scores: weak, moderate, strong predisposition at baseline, and match at 6-month follow-up. Discriminant function analyses showed that the 45 Section B and Section C items strongly differentiated the three groups at both baseline and follow-up (overall Wilks's Lambda was significant at the $p = .01$ level or better). The percent correctly predicted into weak, moderate, strong match at follow-up was 98.7%, which indicates strong accurate prediction. General Linear Model (GLM) multivariate analyses showed that the ATD PA baseline data strongly discriminated the participants into continued, discontinued, or substituted use of the initial ATD at 6 months follow-up ($F = 2.07$, $df = 16$ and 194, $p = .01$) (Graves, Scherer, & Sax, 2006). The subscale scores separately differentiated the groups as follows:

A. Cognitive/sensory ($F = 4.20$, $df = 2$ and 104, $p = .01$); Mobility ($F = 6.50$, $df = 2$ and 104, $p = .002$); Upper extremity ($F = 4.78$, $df = 2$ and 104, $p = .01$);

B. Subjective well-being ($F = 9.07$, $df = 2$ and 104, $p = .001$);

C. Social support ($F = 3.06$, $df = 2$ and 104, $p = .05$); engagement in therapy ($F = 4.76$, $df = 2$ and 104, $p = .01$); resistance to change ($F = 6.45$, $df = 2$ and 104, $p = .002$).

In another study (Furhmann, 2007), 43 adults with spinal cord injury completed the ATD PA and were categorized into three groups according to time since injury. Those injured 1–3 years ago rated themselves as having the highest well-being and activity levels. Patients injured less than 1 year ago rated themselves having the lowest well-being. Depending on the time since injury, discriminant analyses showed that the three groups had statistically significant different perceptions of well-being and activity level ($p = .00$) and could be grouped accurately

100% of the time. In addition, the three groups showed different SCI educational needs (p = .00; 100% accurate classification).

EMPOWERING PERSONS WITH DISABILITIES

THE MPT REPRESENTS an evolution from a philosophy that emphasized the desirability of persons with disabilities striving to be like nondisabled persons to a philosophy of empowerment, that is, persons with disabilities have the right to be self-determining and to make their own choices about their lives and to achieve the quality of life each believes is personally best (Scherer, 2005). Persons with disabilities want as much emphasis placed on their community participation as on their physical capabilities, creating as much need to change and accommodate the environment as equip the person.

Thanks in part to ATDs, more individuals with disabilities can now lead more independent lives, live in their communities, attend regular schools, and seek professional careers. Concomitantly, we are hearing the plea to move away from the *medical model* of rehabilitation (with an emphasis on individual limitations) to a *social model* (with an emphasis on inclusion and participation and support for this through universal design, legislation, and societal attitudes of acceptance). Each of these models, however, has something to offer the consumer selecting ATDs. While there is not a pure *medical* or *social* model, and each houses a range of adherents who are more or less inclined toward consumer inclusion (that is, extreme perspectives in each is exclusionary of individual preferences), the *individual choice and empowerment* perspective recognizes the value of, and need for, the inclusionary supporters in each. This blended approach is depicted in Figure 69.2.

For the *individual choice and empowerment* perspective to succeed, a complex mix of characteristics needs to be considered that includes the person's personal characteristics, expectations, prior experiences and opportunities, and psychosocial environment. It also depends on aspects of the disability and the type and amount of rehabilitation and "empowering resources," opportunities, and choices available.

The individual empowerment model believes that *both* environmental modification and "equipping the individual" are necessary. This more comprehensive perspective sees the environment as presenting barriers and challenges, but also as stimulating and offering opportunities for accomplishment. Thus, ATDs must pass the acid test of fostering autonomy and participation and contributing to a positive identity, enhanced self-esteem, and improved quality of life *as defined by that particular person*. Empowering individuals means looking beyond environmental accommodations and individual functional

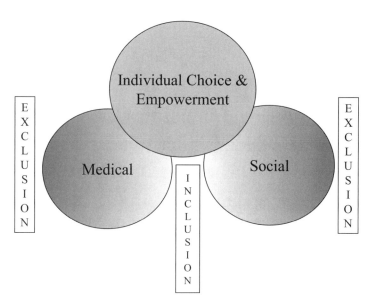

FIGURE 69.2   The medical and social models have a range of perspectives. The extremes in each exclude individual choice.

capabilities to the achievement of a higher quality of life and participation in all desired roles and activities. Assistive technology devices can be important enablers, and a poor match of person and technology (or no technology provision at all) can be considered a barrier, yet other supports and services are just as important. Figures 69.3 and 69.4 depict the need for the consideration of comprehensive, interacting, elements impacting the consumer and, focusing on the match with ATD in particular, the need to work from an empowering model such as the MPT.

Counseling services need to be an integral part of rehabilitation programs. Unlike most other professionals, counselors are very adept at working with subjective, multidimensional, interactive and individualized factors. Individuals want and need opportunities to discuss feelings, attitudes, preferences, goals and priorities, and counselors are highly skilled listeners. The identification of goals needs to be a first step, and then the provision of the ATDs, supports, and resources to achieve them. In this way, rehabilitation interventions are best accepted and adopted by the consumer. Counseling needs to be given a further priority because it will ultimately save many dollars and pay for itself in helping persons who are depressed, who abuse substances, who need to develop new coping strategies and new relationships, and who need to come to terms with barriers to their own functioning, sense of connection and belonging, and motivation. Counseling specialists,

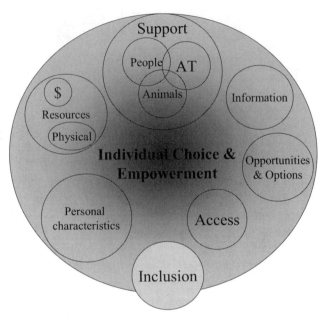

FIGURE 69.3 Being informed and being heard: identifying, then communicating, preferences and priorities.

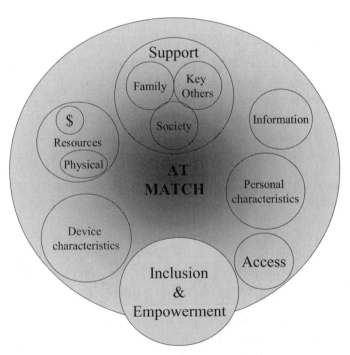

FIGURE 69.4 A good match of person and technology requires comprehensive considerations.

trained to have an interactive, comprehensive, and interdisciplinary approach to problem intervention: "look at the whole picture: pride, motivation, confidence, coping, one's outlook on life—all those elusive things" (Scherer, 2005, pp. 193–194).

RECOMMENDED WEB SITE RESOURCES

ABLEDATA. This site is a national database of information on thousands of products that are available for people with disabilities: http://www.abledata.com

Alliance for Technology Access. A national network of community-based resource organizations to provide information and support to increase the access and use of assistive technology: http://www.ataccess.org

DisabilityInfo.gov. The site organizes information and issues concerning disabilities into nine categories, listed as color-coded tabs at the top of every page. Simply select the tab of your desired category, and links related to that topic will appear on the left: http://www.disabilityInfo.gov

Job Accommodation Network. An international toll-free consulting service that provides information about job accommodations and the employability of people with disabilities: http://janweb.icdi.wvu.edu

RESNA's Technical Assistance Project Library. Summarizes key legislation and provides links to resources such as an AT bibliography: http://www.resna.org/taproject/library

RECOMMENDED BOOKS

de Jonge, D., Scherer, M., & Rodger, S. (2007). *Assistive technology in the workplace.* St. Louis, MO: Mosby.

Scherer, M. J. (2004). *Connecting to learn: Educational and assistive technology for people with disabilities.* Washington, DC: American Psychological Association.

Scherer, M. J. (Ed.). (2002). *Assistive technology: Matching device and consumer for successful rehabilitation.* Washington, DC: American Psychological Association.

REFERENCES

Fuhrmann, T. (2007). *Assessing the concerns of SCI patients in order to improve treatment.* Basic Science and Clinical Research: 2007 Student Research Poster Session, University of Rochester Medical Center, Rochester, NY.

Graves, D., Scherer, M. J., & Sax, C. (2006). Dimensional structure of the Assistive Technology Device Predisposition Assessment. *Archives of Physical Medicine and Rehabilitation, 87*(10), E23.

Jette, A. M., Keysor, J., Coster, W., Ni., P., & Haley, S. (2005). Beyond function: Predicting participation in a rehabilitation cohort. *Archives of Physical Medicine and Rehabilitation, 86*(11), 2087–2094.

Scherer, M. J. (2005). *Living in the state of stuck: How assistive technology impacts the lives of people with disabilities* (4th ed.). Cambridge, MA: Brookline Books.

Scherer, M. J., & Sax, C. (in press). Measures of assistive technology predisposition and use. In E. Mpofu & T. Oakland (Eds.), *Assessment in Rehabilitation and Health*. Boston: Allyn & Bacon.

Scherer, M. J., Sax, C., Vanbeirvliet, A., Cushman, L. A., & Scherer, J. V. (2005). Predictors of assistive technology use: The importance of personal and psychosocial factors. *Disability and Rehabilitation, 27*(21), 1321–1331.

70

Counseling Issues in College Students

PERRY C. FRANCIS

C OLLEGE IS A time of great change for many students of all ages. The traditional student, defined as the 18- to 24-year-old, will generally develop a keener sense of identity as he or she moves out from under the influence of parents and into a college residence hall or other living arrangement. He or she will be faced with the many daily decisions, from the mundane to the monumental, that were, at one time, made by or with his or her parents (VonSteen, 2000). The nontraditional student will have different pressures. This student is an adult learner (25 years of age and older) who returns to school while trying to balance family, employment, finances, and finals. In many cases this student has been making his or her own decisions for some time and is returning to school to improve his or her lot in life or earn a professional degree and move into a new career or expand a current career (Benshoff & Bundy, 2000). Each brings to the consultation room his or her own unique needs and characteristics that affect the counseling relationship, assessment of issues, and use of interventions that ultimately lead to the successful completion of counseling. Awareness of these unique issues and characteristics will help the counselor provide appropriate services to the college client.

THE TRADITIONAL STUDENT

Y OUNG ADULTS (18–24 years of age) go through many developmental changes as they traverse the time between graduation from high school to their establishment in an occupation. For many, this time is spent in furthering their education in an assortment of educational institutions from community and technical colleges to 4-year universities with doctoral degree granting status. This population of young adults has a number of characteristics that sets them apart from their peers who are not furthering their formal education in college settings. These students attend college for two major reasons. The first is to obtain employment that will lead to financial success and comfort. The second reason, which is related to the first, is to obtain careers that will allow them to balance their professional lives with family and helping others. These students equate being well off financially with being able to raise a family and care for themselves and others. They are not solely focused on themselves and making money. Instead, many see helping others as a very important value (Pryor, Hurtado, Saenz, Santos, & Kron, 2007).

More students are also working while in college. This means learning to balance work schedules with class schedules and other academic responsibilities. This is reflected in the fact that most freshman report receiving some aid from family and friends and using savings set aside for the purpose of obtaining a college education (Pryor et al., 2006).

Their suicide rate is substantially less than the same age group who are not in school (Schwartz, 2006). Although their suicide rate is less, when a suicide occurs, it is often given more attention than their peers who complete a suicide and are not in school (Franke, 2004; Gose, 2000). While their suicide rate is lower, more and more traditional students are arriving on college campuses with prescriptions for psychotropic medications, a perceived greater level of psychological problems, larger amounts of stress, and greater expectations to succeed from family (Gallagher, 2006; Lippincott, 2007). Those students who are coming to campus with formally diagnosed severe and/or persistent mental illnesses are not going to the counseling center on campus at any greater rate than the rest of the student body. While the negative perception of obtaining counseling services has diminished for the traditional college-aged population, those students with a severe or persistent mental illness continue to struggle with the desire to be accepted by their peers and therefore hide their diagnosis from friends and professors on campus (Megivern, 2001).

The source of the stress for many college students is varied and can present difficulty for treatment (Lago, 2002). They include coping with alcohol and other drugs use and abuse, unwanted sexual experiences (both prior to attending college and while in college), unwanted pregnancies, sexually transmitted diseases, and eating disorders (VonSteen, 2000). The unintended consequences to these problems include academic difficulties, relationship problems with peers inside and outside of residence halls, and, in some cases, dropping out of college.

Of particular note is the use and abuse of alcohol. For many, the idea of binge drinking is part of the developmental process of the college experience. A newfound freedom is explored as the student, away from home for the first time, tests the limits of his or her freedom by participating with peers in alcohol-fueled gatherings. While the rates of use and associated problems seem to have decreased, the amount of alcohol consumed and the prevalence of alcohol-related problems significantly increased, with more reported deaths and incidence (Sullivan & Wodarski, 2004).

This group of students is also incredibly technologically savvy. They are inundated with multiple ways to communicate, research, and relate to each other without ever meeting face to face. The average undergraduate uses technology as a means of communication approximately 5½ hours per day. This includes written and verbal notes, with instant and text messaging for short notes and cell phone conversations for the more personal conversations (Diamanduros, Jenkins, & Downs, 2007). Many students may have classes that include online components where the whole class meets infrequently and other classes where the students do not meet at all. While this provides greater flexibility for students, it can bring with it other unintended consequences. The student who struggles with social skills can find himself or herself increasingly isolated, having only virtual relationships with people via the World Wide Web, thus missing opportunities to develop personally and professionally. In our increasingly diverse college environment and world, being able to learn how to relate to many different people on a personal and professional level is part of the unofficial curriculum of a college education (VonSteen, 2000).

THE NONTRADITIONAL STUDENT

THE ADULT STUDENT is generally 25 years of age or older and is attending college to start, continue, or complete a degree program that was delayed due to family, finances, or other circumstances or is pursuing additional education to maintain or further himself or herself in an occupation or to change occupations. Other reasons for beginning or returning to school include planned or unplanned transitions in one's life, including a change in marital status or unemployment, or a desire for contact with others who share similar goals. They have been labeled as *adult learners, reentry students,* or *returning students.* In most cases they not only carry the responsibilities of school (full- or part-time), they also have the additional responsibility of family, employment, and other adult issues that are not shared by their traditional student counterparts. These added responsibilities also contribute to their being geographically anchored to one location and limiting their choice of colleges to ones within driving distance or that are accessible through online means (Benshoff & Bundy, 2000; Gary, 2007).

Adult learners who have never had a college experience or whose experience is in the distant past may bring to the classroom significant levels of doubt or anxiety that affect their ability to succeed in the academic setting. Often they have to become proficient in the use of newer technologies in the classrooms and libraries that were not available to them when they left high school. This creates an additional amount of material to be learned in the life of a student whose time is already stretched by job and family (Carney-Crompton & Tan, 2002). In many cases the services offered by the college (e.g., financial aid, counseling services, tutoring) are tailored to the traditional student who may be on campus full-time while the nontraditional student comes to campus only for class and oftentimes in the evening. Seeking student services can become a frustration when all the student service offices are closed when the nontraditional student is on campus.

While nontraditional students have different hurdles to negotiate to attend college when compared to their traditional peers, they bring with them qualities that often support their education. They view education as an investment whose payoff may be more immediate not only to themselves, but to their families. This brings a greater sense of commitment, purpose, and motivation to the classroom. Their learning is supported by a real-life experience that may be missing in traditional college students. They seek more practical, hands-on learning, which can be immediately connected to their lives, jobs, and careers (Klein, 1990). This is complemented by better time management and study skills, which leads to less stress and a more positive college experience (Benshoff & Bundy, 2000).

DIAGNOSTIC ISSUES

THE PROFESSIONAL COUNSELOR who works with the college population is faced with unique diagnostic issues when conceptualizing the client. The traditional-aged college student is traversing many transitions and developmental stages that bring about stresses and strains that can affect the general mental health of the student. It is also during this time that many clinical mental health disorders begin to manifest themselves (Lippincott, 2007). The professional counselor is aware of and uses both a developmental understanding as well as a clinical understanding of the student who presents himself or herself for counseling services. To favor one mode of understanding over another may lead to under- or overdiagnosing of the student and the application of poor treatment planning and implementation. VonSteen (2000) uses the example of a female freshman who presents with body image concerns and homesickness after coming to college and gaining weight. From a purely developmental perspective, the client may be struggling with her newfound independence and autonomy while gaining weight as a result of the environmental change in moving from the family home and diet to a residence hall and institutionally prepared food. Counseling would center on normalizing the weight gain while offering the client nutritional and exercise information. In addition, the counselor may address adjustment to college and responsibility and autonomy issues. The counselor, whose sole focus is from a clinical perspective, may link the client's behavior to disordered eating patterns and poor body image and self-esteem. The counselor may seek a referral for psychotropic medications and further evaluation for a mental illness. While each approach has its own merit, to provide treatment based solely upon one or the other is to miss the possible developmental and environmental influences associated with this age group or to inadequately address the short- and long-term consequences of an untreated eating disorder. As seen in this example, the counselor does not conceptualize the client from one perspective but rather uses both approaches in a continuum, taking into account all variables.

DEVELOPMENTAL ISSUES

THE MAJOR DEVELOPMENTAL issues that traditional-aged college students face center on separation and individuation from their family of origin (Lapsely & Edgerton, 2002). It often requires that the students renegotiate their relationships with their families as they move toward more autonomy and independence. This can be complicated by the fact that, in most cases, families are paying the bills for college and still seek to have some influence on the life and behavior of the students. This sets up a conflict between the students and their families as the student begins to make decisions or act out or experiment with new behaviors in ways that are developmentally appropriate but challenging to the family's values and morals.

College is also a time of experimentation as students seek to find out what the boundaries are for themselves and others. The problems that occur when this process does not develop smoothly center around relationship difficulties, issues of self-esteem, academic and career concerns, stress and psychosomatic symptoms, as well as the use and abuse of alcohol and other drugs (Bishop, Gallagher, & Cohen, 2000). The severity of each is dependent on the coping ability and style of the students as well as the foundation from which students launch.

Nontraditional students have their own developmental and environmental issues that, when placed under stress, can cause problems that bring them into counseling. In many cases nontraditional students have to renegotiate family roles and tasks as they take on the additional responsibility of their academic programs. When family support is lacking or roles in the family do not evolve to accommodate the additional money, time, and responsibility that are required when someone returns to school, relationship problems occur that impact the nontraditional student's ability to be successful (Gary, 2007).

CLINICAL ISSUES

THERE IS A growing perception among college counseling center directors that more students are coming to college with more severe psychological problems (Gallagher, 2006; Kadison & DiGeronimo, 2005). Research in this area is difficult at best due to several factors, including the different diagnostic systems each center employs, the different populations at each campus, and the type, amount, and depth of counseling and intervention provided by the counseling center (Bishop et al., 2000). At the same time, with advances in psychotropic medication, earlier and more sophisticated diagnosis, and intervention at the advent of mental illness in children, and disability accommodations provided for students with mental illnesses, the population of students with severe or persistent mental illnesses is rising on our college campuses (Collins & Mowbray, 2005). Additionally, the age of onset for many major mental illnesses is late adolescence and early adulthood, or the traditional age of most college students. This requires the counselor working with this population to be trained in the prevention and treatment of developing mental illness (Kadison & DiGeronimo, 2005).

The major mental illnesses that are presented by these students while on campus include, but are not limited to, schizophrenia and other psychotic disorders, bipolar disorders, major depression, personality disorders (with borderline personality features being especially prominent) (Kadison & DiGeronimo, 2005; Lippincott, 2007). Because of the combination of developmental boundary testing, and individuation and autonomy issues, borderline behaviors are especially prominent in this population (Lippincott, 2007).

ASSESSMENT

GIVEN THE WIDE range of mental health issues that can be presented by both the traditional and nontraditional college student, it is incumbent upon the counselor to use a detailed assessment interview that includes not only a history of the presenting problem, but a developmental history of the client and, if necessary, a family mental health history as well. In this way, as the picture of the problem or issue becomes clearer, the counselor can then focus his or her attention toward a more developmental or clinical assessment and intervention.

It is important for the counselor to take note of the living arrangements of the students he or she is assessing. In large, residential colleges and universities students live in high-density housing. While many colleges are moving to less dense housing situations, students are still living on top of one another and this situation can lead to increased conflicts and stress, especially for students who are unaccustomed to such arrangements. Additionally, sleep and eating patterns are occasionally disrupted and bring about conflicts that must then be negotiated between roommates.

If more formal assessments are needed, inventories, checklists, and assessments may be employed that are focused on the traditional and nontraditional college-aged population, if appropriate (e.g. College Adjustment Scale, Inventory of Common Problems, Symptom Check List-90, Revised, Millon College Counseling Inventory, Millon Clinical Multiaxial Inventory-III, MMPI-II, etc.). Many of these tests can provide both a developmental and clinical assessment that, combined with a detailed initial interview, will give the counselor a comprehensive picture of the student's issues and problems (Bishop et al., 2000; Lippincott, 2007).

STUDENT DEVELOPMENT THEORY

THE COUNSELING PROFESSION uses a developmental framework in the conceptualization of clients (Neukrug, 2007). College presents students with many new and unique situations that go beyond normal developmental theory. College student development theory can aid the counselor in understanding, in more detail, the developmental stages of their college-aged clients. This helps in client conceptualization and the tailoring of interventions for successful counseling (Evans, Forney, & Guido-DiBrito, 1998).

Student development theories can be categorized into two broad categories: (1) psychosocial and identity development, and (2) cognitive–structural development. Each theory category presents a different approach to how students develop in the college environment. Psychosocial/identity theories focus on how students define themselves, their relationships, and the direction they want to take their lives based on that information. The students move through their development based upon interaction of their internal biological clocks and psychological challenges as they interact with their environment. This mix of internal change, social norms and pressures, coping skills, the resolution of developmental tasks, and the college environment help to form the student's identity. The work of Chickering (1969) and Josselson (1987) are examples of this category applied to college students.

Cognitive–structural theories see change taking place as a result of assimilation and accommodation. This integrating of new information and modifying existing or creating new cognitive structures is strongly fostered in the college environment where new experiences and knowledge (both formal and informal) are daily occurrences. In college, not only is cognitive and intellectual development fostered, so is ethical and moral development. The work of Perry (1970) exemplifies not only the intellectual development of the average college student, but the moral and ethical development as well.

CONCLUSION

COLLEGE IS A time of great excitement, growth, and change for all students. The vast majority make it through their college years having lived up to the emotional and intellectual challenges that college presents and have fond memories of their experiences. It is also a time of great developmental challenges and the onset of many psychiatric illnesses (Kadison & DiGeronimo, 2005; Kitzrow, 2003). While the vast majority of students never see the inside of the college counseling center or meet with a counselor off campus, their mental health needs are growing and professional counselors will need to be prepared to work with this population in order to help them successfully navigate the rigors and joys of the college experience.

REFERENCES

Benshoff, J. M., & Bundy, A. P. (2000). Nontraditional college students. In D. C. Davis & K. M. Humphrey (Eds.), *College counseling: Issues and strategies for a new millennium* (pp. 133–151). Alexandria, VA: American Counseling Association.

Bishop, J. B., Gallagher, R. P., & Cohen, D. (2000). College students' problems: status, trends, and research. In D. C. Davis & K. M. Humphrey (Eds.), *College counseling: Issues and strategies for a new millennium* (pp. 89–110). Alexandria, VA: American Counseling Association.

Carney-Crompton, S., & Tan, J. (2002). Support systems, psychological functioning, and academic performance of nontraditional female students. *Adult Education Quarterly, 52*(2), 140–154.

Chickering, A. W. (1969). *Education and identity.* San Francisco: Jossey-Bass.

Collins, M. E., & Mowbray, C. T. (2005). Higher education and psychiatric disabilities: National Survey of Campus Disability Services. *American Journal of Orthopsychiatry, 75*(2), 304–315.

Diamanduros, T., Jenkins, S. J., & Downs, E. (2007). Analysis of technology ownership and selective use among undergraduates. *College Student Journal, 41*(1), 970–977.

Evans, N. J., Forney, D. S., & Guido-DiBrito, F. (1998). *Student development in college.* San Francisco: Jossey-Bass.

Franke, A. H. (2004, June 25). When students kill themselves, college may get the blame. *The Chronicle of Higher Education, 50,* B18–B19.

Gallagher, R. P. (2006). *National survey of counseling center directors.* Alexandria, VA: International Association of Counseling Services.

Gary, J. M. (2007). Counseling adult learners: Individual interventions, group interventions, and campus resources. In J. A. Lippincott & R. B. Lippincott (Eds.), *Special populations in college counseling* (pp. 99–113). Alexandria, VA: American Counseling Association.

Gose, B. (2000, February 25). Elite colleges struggle to prevent student suicides. *The Chronicle of Higher Education, 46,* A54–A55.

Josselson, R. (1987). *Finding herself: Pathways to identity development in women.* San Francisco: Jossey-Bass.

Kadison, R., & DiGeronimo, T. F. (2005). *College of the overwhelmed: The campus mental health crisis and what to do about it.* San Francisco: Jossey-Bass.

Kitzrow, M. A. (2003). The mental health needs of today's college students: Challenges and recommendations. *NASPA Journal, 41*(1), 165–179.

Klein, J. D. (1990). An analysis of the motivational characteristics of college reentry students. *College Student Journal, 24*(3), 281–286.

Lago, C. (2002). The university and the wider community. In N. Stanley & J. Manthorpe (Eds.), *Students' mental health needs* (pp. 145–167). London: Jessica Kinglsey.

Lapsely, D. K., & Edgerton, J. (2002). Separation-individuation, adult attachment style, and college adjustment. *Journal of Counseling and Development, 80*(4), 484–492.

Lippincott, J. A. (2007). When psychopathology challenges education: Counseling students with severe psychiatric disorders. In J. A. Lippincott & R. B. Lippincott (Eds.), *Special populations in college counseling: A handbook for mental health professionals.* Alexandria, VA: American Counseling Association.

Megivern, D. M. (2001). Educational functioning and college integration of students with mental illness: Examining the roles of psychiatric symptomatology and mental health service use. *Dissertation Abstracts International Section A: Humanities and Social Sciences Vol. 62* (10-A) (April 2002): 3574.

Neukrug, E. (2007). *World of the counselor: An introduction to the counseling profession* (Vol. 3). Pacific Grove, CA: Brooks/Cole.

Perry, W. G. (1970). *Forms of intellectual and ethical development in the college years: A scheme.* Troy, MO: Holt, Rinehart & Winston.

Pryor, J. H., Hurtado, S., Saenz, V. B., Korn, J. S., Santos, J. L., & Kron, W. S. (2006). *The American freshman.* Los Angeles: University of California, Higher Education Research Institute.

Pryor, J. H., Hurtado, S., Saenz, V. B., Santos, J. L., & Kron, W. S. (2007). *The American freshman: Forty-year trends, 1966–2006.* Los Angeles: University of California, Higher Education Research Institute.

Schwartz, A. J. (2006). College student suicide in the United States: 1990–1991 through 2003–2004. *Journal of American College Health, 54*(6), 341–352.

Sullivan, M., & Wodarski, J. (2004). Rating college students' substance abuse: A systematic literature review. *Brief Treatment and Crisis Intervention, 4*(1), 71–91.

VonSteen, P. G. (2000). Traditional-age college students. In D. C. Davis & K. M. Humphrey (Eds.), *College counseling: Issues and strategies for a new millennium* (pp. 111–131). Alexandria, VA: American Counseling Association.

71

School Violence: Prevalence, Impact, Assessment, and Treatment

JoLynn V. Carney

VIOLENCE AMONG YOUTH is a real concern that many people, organizations, and communities work diligently to combat (Jimerson & Furlong, 2006; McCann, 2002). Youth violence takes on many forms from destruction of property to interpersonal assaults. In fact, we can think of violence on a continuum from least damaging (put downs) to most lethal (murder and suicide). Early intervention can occur when counselors are knowledgeable about youth violence facts such as prevalence, various types, impact, and treatment options. This chapter specifically focuses on violence in the nations' schools by providing (1) an overview of youth violence, including risk/protective factors, (2) assessment items for preventing violence, and (3) suggestions of intervention/prevention strategies for reducing youth violence and its impact.

PREVALENCE AND TYPES

NATIONAL ESTIMATES INDICATE that youth compared to adults are twice as likely to be victims of serious crimes and three times as likely to be victims of simple assaults. Approximately 40%

of violent crimes committed by adolescents against adolescents take place in or around schools (Fitzpatrick, 1999). This is no surprise since up to 53 million youth spend a majority of their time in and around their schools. The distribution of serious violent crime varies among schools based on size and location (urban versus rural). The main questions to answer are: "How big of a current problem is school violence and how does it impact students?" Reflecting back on past school problems places this question in context and is quite revealing since studies showed the most common discipline issues in the 1940s were talking, chewing gum, and making noise, while by the 1990s school problems included weapon carrying/use (murder and suicide), assaults, gangs, and drug/alcohol abuse.

A recent survey of school students found that more than one-third reported being in a fight at school during the academic year with 4% of students requiring medical attention for their injuries. Seventeen percent of students indicated that they had carried a weapon to school within the last 30 days (Centers for Disease Control and Prevention [CDC], 2004). National data indicate that 71% of public schools experienced at least one violent incident and 12% of students reported experiencing victimization at school (Miller, 2003).

The use of the term *school violence* first began in the 1990s and is defined as a multidimensional construct involving aggression and criminal acts in schools. The term *targeted school violence* was coined by the U.S. Secret Service and the U.S. Department of Education to describe a subset of school-associated violent deaths in which the perpetrator(s) preselect the school, students, administrators, and/or faculty as targets (Reddy Randazzo et al., 2006).

Types of school violence range from nonfatal to fatal incidents aimed at property, other individuals, or self (e.g., vandalism, trespassing, insults, chronic bullying, assaults, rape, robbery, homicide, and suicide). The most commonly reported type of school violence is chronic bullying, which occurs daily in schools and has negative consequences for millions of students. There is widespread agreement (e.g., students/parents, educators, mental health professionals, medical professionals, and community/political leaders) that youth violence has a significant impact on perpetrators, targets, and witnesses. Increasing counselors' awareness for risk factors of potentially violent behavior is important to assist them in intervening effectively.

SOCIAL-ECOLOGICAL RISK FACTORS

RISK FACTORS ARE not contained just in individuals or environments. Counselors must look to the broader contextual characteristics of personal traits/dispositions interacting with characteristics of the situation and social setting in order to fully understand risk factors for violence potential. Beginning with the environmental context, risk factors for violence based within the *school* system include *larger* school size, *older* students, and the presence of *drugs* and *gang* activity. *Timing* is also a significant risk factor with violent deaths at school more likely to occur during transition periods such as start/end of the day or at lunch. Additionally, homicides are more likely to occur at the beginning of new semester versus another other time during the academic year (DeVoe et al., 2004). This timing also parallels highest risk of student suicide. *Location* within the school can also be seen as increasing risk of violence. Several key zones are entrances, hallways/stairs, cafeterias, and restrooms. Schools are a part of the larger community and several *neighborhood* risk factors contribute to violence levels (e.g., socioeconomic status, transient nature of the population, and community involvement).

Socialization within family and peer groups plays a major role in development and continuation of violence potential (U.S. Department of Health and Human Services, 2001). Family factors are powerful predictors for aggressive behavior in children. *Conflictual families* that expose youth to interfamily violence, drug abuse, inconsistent/harsh discipline, violent problem-resolution strategies, and/or little to no involvement/supervision create poor prosocial learning environments that foster a climate of acceptance for antisocial beliefs/attitudes and behaviors.

Peer social networks are definitely influential by supporting behaviors that the group considers normative. Associations with delinquent peer groups, and/or involvement in gangs, can reinforce negative norms that might lead to violent behaviors. Isolation from any peer group can also increase violence potential. Being rejected by peers creates a host of issues that in some cases can culminate in the marginalized youth(s) acting aggressively and taking hostile actions in retaliation for their treatment.

Specific *individual issues* and *behaviors* can also be additional contributors to violent actions. *Mental health disorders* are seen as being at the core of maladaptive aggression in youth. Comorbid with violent behaviors include disorders such as attention deficit (ADD, AD/HD), anxiety, depression, oppositional defiant disorder (ODD), conduct disorder, and substance abuse. Many of these disorders are also comorbid with each other and can create a complex symptomology pattern. For example, early onset of AD/HD has been shown to predict earlier onset of conduct disorder and violent offending. Diagnosis of conduct disorder and depression puts youth at three times the suicide risk as depression alone. Approximately 2.2 million students in the year 2005 experienced at least one major depressive episode. The students who had a major depressive episode were more than twice as likely to have used drugs as those who had not experienced a major depressive episode. The availability and prevalence of drugs at school creates a significant risk factor for at least 9.5 million students in the United States (Office of Applied Studies, Substance Abuse and Mental Health Services Administration, 2005).

Violent youth often display *poor control* and have low capacity for cognitive/emotional *empathy* or respect for others. They tend to have limited anger management and coping skills, low frustration tolerance, high/narcissistic self-images, focus on perceived injustices, and blame others, or in cases of suicidal youth, blame themselves and have low/insecure self-images. These traits can make a lethal combination. For example, an inability to control behaviors manifests itself through impulsive decisions/actions, while the lack of empathy for potential targets does not dampen their immediate reaction to attack. Table 71.1 provides a succinct list of risk and protected factors compiled for this chapter from several sources: U.S. Department of Education and the U.S. Department of Health and Human Services.

INITIAL ITEMS FOR ASSESSING VIOLENCE POTENTIAL

ASSESSING VIOLENCE POTENTIAL is to *prevent*, not predict, violence. The optimal goal is to identify both perpetrator(s) and target(s) *prior to* any violent incident. A caution on threats of violence is prudent here. Threats should be taken seriously, but not be a necessary condition to initiate a violence potential assessment as threats are not the most reliable indicator of risk.

A few structured assessment tools do exist for counselors to use. One such measure is the Structured Assessment of Violence Risk in Youth (SAVRY) that has 24-risk factor items (e.g., history, social/contextual, and individual) as well as an additional 6-protective factor items (Borum, Bartel, & Forth, 2002). Counselors do not necessarily need published assessment measures, but can investigate youth violence potential through a series of initial *triage* questions that assess individual, family, peer/school dynamics. Assessment areas to be answered should focus on the following:

Individual

- Previous history violent behavior and exposure to violence/abuse
- History of substance abuse and its relationship to impulse control and judgments/insight
- Adequacy of coping skills (cognitive/emotional development), potential triggers (loss, including loss of status, failure, bullying),

TABLE 71.1 Social-Ecological Risk and Protective Factors

Risk Factors

School

- Larger school size
- Older students
- Presence of drug/gang activity
- Timing (start/end of day)
- Location (restrooms, hallways)
- Lack of involvement in school activities
- Poor academic performance/school failure
- Low commitment to school

Family

- Exposure to volence and family conflict
- Parental drug abuse/criminality
- Harsh, lax, or inconsistent discipline
- Lack of parent/caregiver involvement
- Low emotional attachment to parent/caregiver
- Poor family functioning
- Poor monitory/superivsion of children
- Low parental education/income

Individual Issues and Behaviors

- History of early aggression
- Mental health issues
- Substance use/abuse
- Social cognitive or information-processing deficits

Neighborhood

- Diminished economic opportunity
- Econimically disadvantaged residents
- High levels of transiency
- Low community participation
- Socially disorganized neighborhoods

Peer

- Delinquent peer group
- Involvement in gangs
- Social rejection by peers

- Poor behavioral control
- Low intellectual level
- Antisocial beliefs/attitudes

Protective Factors

School/Peer

- Commitment to school
- Involvement in social activities

Individual Issues and Behaviors

- Mental health intervention
- Positive relationship with at least one caring adult
- Positive social orientation
- Intolerant attitude toward deviance
- High intelligence

Family

- Warm, nurturing parenting style
- Clear limit setting/respect for autonomy

and reactions to perceived challenges (violence is *the* answer, hopelessness, suicidal ideation)
- Identified or identifiable mental health diagnosis
- Capacity to carry out the violence (intention/motivation, plan, and weapons) relative to capacity for cognitive/emotional empathy and respect for others

Family

- Relationships among family members (connected/distant), parenting style (harsh, inconsistent) and parental supervision (friends, TV/movies, video games, Internet sites)
- Family violence and drug abuse patterns and acceptance of pathological behaviors
- Available weapons in the home

School/Peers

- Peer relationships and culture, including use of drugs/alcohol
- School culture on violence (intolerance/tolerance of disrespectful behavior)
- School culture on discipline (equitable/arbitrary)
- Students connectedness/attachment to the school

Answers to these areas of assessment provide information for evaluating *threat level* (transient/low, serious substantive/medium, or very serious substantive/high) and *type* (direct, indirect, veiled or conditional). The following examples demonstrate threat/type differences.

A *transient* threat (indirect, veiled, and vague) was made soon after a shouting and pushing incident between two girls in the hallway. One female student told friends, "I'm going to get her someday."

A *serious substantive* threat (more direct and plausible) occurred between two male students who had been antagonizing each other. One student wrote a note that said, "Meet me tonight at the park so I can take care of you once and for all."

A *very serious substantive* threat (direct and poses imminent danger) was reported when a male student who was being chronically peer-abused told another student that he was bringing his uncle's gun to school tomorrow to "pay them back and end it for me too."

Prevention assessment focuses on individual issues (behaviors and personality) and situational characteristics (family/peer/school dynamics). Data that have been gathered from multiple sources, including past records, school personnel/students, parents/caregivers, and others with pertinent information, ultimately provide information on the "what, when, where, and to whom" aspects of violence potential.

An in-depth intake interview and decisions about treatment options are the next steps in reducing the threat of violence.

INTERVENTION ISSUES AND OPTIONS

FIGURE 71.1 PROVIDES a specific image of youth violence with a primary intervention message to intervene with youth as early as possible to reduce the amount/level of violence perpetrated by youth and to minimize the impact of violence on targets. Intervening in lower-level violence interrupts the build-up of violence. For instance, research has shown that prior to rape, many youth were first in trouble for harassment and robbery. Likewise, investigations have found that prior to murder and/or suicide students have experienced chronic bullying. Early intervention is also important for those who witness violence. Exposure to increasingly violent behaviors can traumatize or desensitize bystanders, either of which decrease the potential that witnesses will lend support to victims.

Violent youth often report a belief that use of violence helps them gain a desired outcome, including enhanced self-esteem and social image. This belief seems to be a learned cognition based on previous exposure to violence and its outcomes. Many violent youth are themselves either victims or witnesses to violence. Research studies have shown the individuals who are bullies and are also victimized typically are at high risk for experiencing internalizing symptomology (e.g., depression, anxiety).

Being the target of violence can take a tremendous toll on an individual. Victimization leaves targets feeling shame, embarrassment, and

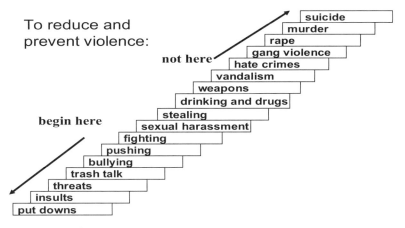

FIGURE 71.1 Violence continuum.

fear of continued and/or escalated violence against them. The overall impact of violence on victims as well as witnesses includes (1) mental health issues such as lowered self-esteem, depression, posttraumatic stress disorder [PTSD], suicidal ideation/completions, and/or homicidal ideation/completion, and (2) academic problems such as failing grades, daily fear-based reluctance to attend school, and truancy.

Treatment options range from individual and/or family focused to schoolwide prevention focused. Counseling individuals affected by violence can be accomplished through a variety of therapeutic orientations with *cognitive behavior therapy* addressing both thoughts and behaviors. The focus of therapy involves increasing productive function (e.g., anger management, relaxation techniques, and alternative problem-solving skills) and decreasing unproductive thinking and behaviors (e.g., violence is *the* answer to problems). *Psychotropic medications* may also be used as an adjunct to counseling, but side effects must be closely monitored because in some cases aggression toward self and others may actually increase.

Family therapy is a vitally important treatment modality. *Parent training* (PT) teaches parents/caregivers positive parenting skills such as the use of reinforcement to increase wanted behaviors and to decrease disruptive behaviors. *Behavioral family therapy* (BFT) is another recommended treatment for violent youth and their families. Addressing maladaptive family patterns has been shown to be successful by improving functioning for youth and families. For a complete discussion of BFT see Juhnke and Guill Liles (2000).

Schoolwide prevention programs are a viable vehicle for reducing school violence by creating a school climate that is intolerant of violence. Blueprints for Violence Prevention identifies 12 programs that have been effective in reducing adolescent violent behavior and substance abuse. A few examples of these diverse programs include Olweus Bullying Prevention Program, Life Skills Training, Functional Family Therapy, Multisystemic Therapy, and Project Towards No Drug Abuse. Information on each of these programs can be found online at http://www.colorado.edu/cspv/blueprints/model/overview.html

CONCLUSION

ASSESSING AND TREATING potentially violent youth, targets, and witnesses are important to prevent violence. Counselors should gather information from multiple sources on multiple issues as no one personality profile for a violent youth or targets exists. Focusing on behaviors and placing those behaviors in a social-ecological context provides the clearest understanding of potential risk and directs treatment options and modalities. Behavioral, personality, familial, social, and school dynamics are key components that provide counselors with vital information necessary to effectively identify and treat potentially violent youth, targets, and witnesses.

An emerging research area that can add another dimension to understanding focuses on biobehavioral components associated with youth violence. This research gathers typical self-report and observational data, but also collects biomarkers (e.g., stress hormone cortisol and/or testosterone) from participants The emergence of minimally intrusive techniques for collecting biological data from saliva samples is increasingly giving researchers the ability to compare student self-reported trauma reaction to school violence with actual biological responses as measured through cortisol levels present in their saliva (Hazler, Carney, & Granger, 2006). My interest in furthering the counseling research on youth violence incorporates the use of biomarkers to enhance our understanding, and quite possibly, more closely tailor our intervention/prevention efforts in the future.

REFERENCES

Borum, R., Bartel, P. A., & Forth, A. (2002). *SAVRY: Structured assessment of violence risk in youth*. Lutz, FL: Psychological Assessment Resources.

Centers for Disease Control and Prevention. (2004). Youth risk behavior surveillance–United States. *Morbidity and Mortality Weekly Report, 53*(SS02), 1–96.

DeVoe, J. F., Peter, K., Kaufman, P., Miller, A., Noonan, M., Snyder, T. D., et al. (2004). *Indicators of school crime and safety: 2004* (NCES 2005–002/NCJ 205290). U.S. Departments of Education and Justice. Washington, DC: Government Printing Office.

Fitzpatrick, K. M. (1999). Violent victimization among America's school children. *Journal of Interpersonal Violence, 14*, 1055–1069.

Hazler, R. J., Carney, J. V., & Granger, D. A. (2006). Integrating biological measures into the study of bullying. *Journal of Counseling and Development, 84*, 298–307.

Jimerson, S. R., & Furlong, M. J. (2006). *Handbook of school violence and school safety*. Mahwah, NJ: Erlbaum.

Juhnke, G. A., & Guill Liles, R. (2000). Treating adolescents presenting with comorbid violence and addictive behaviors: A behavioral family therapy model. In S. S. Sandhu & C. Blalock Aspy (Eds.), *Violence in American schools: A practical guide for counselors* (pp. 319–334). Alexandria, VA: American Counseling Association.

McCann, J. T. (2002). *Threats in schools: A practical guide for managing violence*. New York: Haworth.

Miller, A. M. (2003). *Violence in U.S. public schools: 2000 school survey on crime and safety* (NCES 2004–314) Revised. U.S. Department of Education, National

Center for Education Statistics. Washington, DC: Government Printing Office.

Office of Applied Studies, Substance Abuse and Mental Health Services Administration. (2005). *Results from the 2004 National Survey on Drug Use and Health: National findings* (DHHS Publication No. SMA 05–4062, NSDUH Series H-28). Rockville, MD: Author.

Reddy Randazzo, M., Vossekuil, B., Fein, R., Borum, R., Modzeleski, W., & Pollack, W. (2006). Threat assessment in schools: Empirical support and comparisons with other approaches. In S. R. Jimerson & M. J. L. Furlong (Eds.), *Handbook of school violence and school safety* (pp. 147–156). Mahwah, NJ: Erlbaum.

U.S. Department of Health and Human Services. (2001). *Youth violence: A report of the Surgeon General.* Retrieved June 15, 2007, from http://www.sur geongeneral.gov/library/youthviolence

72

Services for PTSD and Poly-Trauma Service Members and Veterans

Debra A. Harley

V ETERANS RETURNING FROM Iraq face very specific psychosocial adjustment and transition issues. One assumption of service members who were involved in combat zones is that they are impacted by their experiences. Some have growth-promoting and maturing experiences. Others acquire the traumatizing effects of combat that can be both devastating and transformative in potentially damaging ways, which can be manifested across the lifespan (Litz & Orsillo, 2004). Many service members returning from war experience a high rate of posttraumatic stress disorder (PTSD), alcohol and drug addictions, and various other psychological stressors. Mental health conditions that typically follow traumatic events include PTSD, depression, alcohol and substance abuse disorders, panic disorder, phobias, and transient psychotic reactions (Keane, 2006). In fact, mental health experts predict because of the intensity of warfare and intimacy with the enemy in Afghanistan and Iraq, 15% or more of service members returning from these conflicts will develop PTSD (Hoge et al., 2004). Given that the U.S. military is involved in the Iraqi war, information presented in this chapter will focus on data and resources for this particular conflict.

This chapter addresses the essential features of PTSD and other poly-trauma disorders and transitional needs of service members and veterans. Although poly-trauma is a diagnosis that encompasses a variety of conditions, diseases, and injuries (Christy & Company, 2007), the focus in this chapter is on psychological trauma. Information is presented on (1) a model of the etiology of PTSD and psychological poly-trauma, (2) components of quality assessment, including cultural and gender dimensions of assessment, and (3) treatment issues.

In a study of soldiers returning home from Iraq and Afghanistan who were seeking treatment for PTSD and other mental health conditions, Kellicker (2004) found that there was a strong correlation between being shot at, handling dead bodies, knowing someone who was killed, or killing the enemy and the subsequent development of PTSD. Of those who met the criteria for a mental disorder, only 38% to 45% expressed an interest in receiving help, and only 23% to 45% reported receiving help within a year after returning home. In fact, the participants who screened positive for a mental disorder were least likely to seek treatment because of the fear of being stigmatized, jeopardizing their careers, or other barriers to their personal and professional life.

Other data indicated that for troops and service members returning from Iraq, 26% reported mental disorders (Government Accountability Office, 2004). One in six soldiers met the screening criteria for major depression, generalized anxiety disorder, or PTSD. More than one in four has come home with health problems that require medical or mental health treatment (Department of Defense, 2004). Almost 1,700 service members returning from the war in 2007 said they harbored thoughts of hurting themselves or that they would be better off dead, nearly 20,000 reported nightmares or unwanted war recollections, and more than 3,700 said they had concerns that they might hurt or lose control around family, friends, or significant others (Army Center for Health Promotion and Preventive Medicine, 2007).

Both veterans and active duty service personnel may encounter frightening experiences (e.g., military-related harassment such as sexual, racial, ethnic trauma, loss related to family members missing or deceased), which can exacerbate traumatic stress response. These types of stress reactions often lead veterans to increase their medical utilization. Because far fewer veterans experiencing traumatic stress reactions seek mental health services, health care professionals, as opposed to mental health care professionals, are the primary providers of services for those with PTSD (National Center for Posttraumatic Stress Disorder [NCPSD], 2007). The NCPSD reported that the relationship between trauma exposure and increased health care utilization appears to be mediated by the diagnosis of PTSD.

The psychological, social, and emotional toll of war can be immediate, acute, and chronic. Litz and Orsillo (2004) described the characteristics of adaptation to the stressors of war as follows. *The immediate interval* "refers to psychological reactions and functional impairment that occur in the war-zone during battle or while exposed to other severe stressors during war" (p. 21). War-zone stressors can include being fired upon, having a low morale, increased physical demands, as well as the behavioral and emotional effects of circulating norepinephrine, epinephrine, and cortisol. The *acute adaptation interval* includes "the period from the point at which the soldier is objectively safe and free from exposure to severe stressors to approximately one month after return to the U.S., which corresponds to the one-month interval during which acute stress disorder (ASD) may be diagnosed according to *DSM–IV*" (p. 23). The *chronic phase* of adjustment "is the burden of war manifested across the life-span" (p. 23). Psychosocial adaptation to war, over time, is not linear and continuous, and ASD is not a necessary precondition for chronic impairment.

MODEL OF ETIOLOGY OF PTSD AND PSYCHOLOGICAL POLY-TRAUMA

THE CAUSES OF PTSD and poly-trauma are numerous and vary depending upon individual characteristics. Posttraumatic stress disorder includes behavioral changes that are generated by emotional distress, biochemical pathways, and neurological symptoms (Currey, 2007). Diathesis-stress models identify the following characteristics and causes of combat-related PTSD and poly-trauma: (1) individual characteristics constitute diatheses, (2) diatheses can be genetic, psychological, physiological, or contextual, (3) life and death exposures vary in frequency, intensity, and severity, (4) recovery environment varies considerably, and (5) responses to the exposures are a function of the individual's diatheses, the events, and the recovery environment (Keane, 2006).

In a meta-analysis of risk factors for PTSD and poly-trauma, Brewin, Andrews, and Valentine (2000) found the following characteristics as contributing factors: (1) severity of the traumatic event, (2) absence of social support postevent, (3) additional life stressors, (4) adverse childhood events, (5) low socioeconomic status, intelligence, and education, (6) prior traumatic exposure, and (7) gender. Keane presented a model of the etiology of PTSD and poly-trauma. According to Keane, PTSD and poly-trauma emerge from either *generalized psychological* or *generalized biological vulnerability,* which leads to experience of trauma. Next, the individual experiences a *true alarm* or alternative intense basic emotion, such as anger or distress, followed by a *learned alarm* or strong mixed emotions. The subsequent step is *anxious apprehension* (focused on reexperienced emotions), then *avoidance* or numbing of emotional response, which is eventually moderated by social support and ability to cope, which leads to PTSD and poly-trauma.

Often, service members and veterans must deal with transitions, a turning point that has significant disruption on established patterns of personal and social identity (Moos, 1990). Schlossberg (1981) developed a model for analyzing human adaptation to transition. The model represents a framework in which positive, negative, ordinary, and dramatic transitions can be analyzed, and possible interventions formulated. Given that people react and adapt differently to transitions, Schlossberg's model attempts to understand and help adults as they face nonpredictable transitions of life (Schlossberg, Waters, & Goodman, 1995).

COMPONENTS OF QUALITY ASSESSMENT

THE DEPARTMENT OF Defense uses two approaches to identify service members at risk for PTSD: the combat stress control program and the postdeployment health assessment questionnaire. The combat stress control program identifies service members at risk for PTSD by training all service members to identify the early onset of combat stress, which if left untreated, could lead to PTSD. The postdeployment health assessment questionnaire is used to screen service members for physical ailments and mental health issues commonly associated with deployments, including PTSD (General Accountability Office, 2004). Assessment of PTSD and poly-trauma requires multi-method and interdisciplinary approaches. These include clinical diagnostic interviews, structured clinical interview for *DSM–IV*, psychological testing, and neurobiological testing (reactivity measures) (Keane & Barlow, 2002); and various PTSD and poly-trauma scales (Screen for Posttraumatic Stress Symptoms [SPTSS] and Clinician Administered PTSD Scale [CAPS], Weathers, Keane, & Davidson, 2001). The specific areas for assessment include psychological symptoms (e.g., CAPS, which is available at http://www.ncptsd.org/publications/assessment/ncinstruments.html.

The Posttraumatic Checklist-Civilian (PCL-C) is recommended rather than the PCL-Military because it is important to assess the veteran's responses to military and nonmilitary traumatic events when determining treatment needs (Carlson, 2002). Other assessments that are recommended include trauma inventories such as Trauma History Screen (TSC; Carlson, 2004) and the Traumatic-Related Dissociation Scale (TRDS; Carlson & Waedel, 2000). The Development Risk and Resilience Inventory (DRRI) is also an important and useful assessment tool (King, King, & Vogt, 2003). There are also assessments to measure the veteran's functioning and quality of life (QOL), including SF-36 from veterans Medical Outcome Study (MOS) the World Health Organization's (WHO) disability tools, and assessments to distinguish the person's disability QOL from their level of functioning; as well as various personality assessments (e.g., Minnesota Multiphasic Personality Inventory–2) (Keane, 2006).

Other relevant areas of assessment include (1) neuropsychological (i.e., cognition, memory, attention, information processing, neuroimaging) (Keane, 2006), (2) depression (Beck Depression Inventory–Short Form [BDI-SF]; Beck & Steer, 2000), (3) traumatic grief (i.e., Screen for Complicated Grief [SCG]), alcohol abuse (i.e., Alcohol Use Disorders Identification Test [AUDIT]; Goldman, Brown, & Christian, 2000), (4) anger (i.e., State-Trait Anger Expression Inventory [STAX-I]; Spielberger, 1988), (5) guilt and shame (Kubany et al., 1995). Women who may be exposed to a number of traumatic stressors not assessed by other combat measures can benefit from other specific assessments of military stressors (i.e., Life Stressors Checklist; Wolfe & Kimerling, 1997). Each of these domains can be adequately addressed both during an interview or more intensive assessment.

CULTURAL ASPECTS OF ASSESSMENT

TWO ADDITIONAL AREAS of assessment are the significance of cultural data (Haley, 2002) and gender issues (Vogt, 2007) for the care of veterans and service members. The counseling, rehabilitation, and medical literature on cultural diversity has examined the inequality in service and care between non-White and White individuals (Smedley, Stith, & Nelson, 2003; Smith, 2004; Wilson, Harley, & Alston, 2001; Wilson, Turner, Lui, Harley, & Alston, 2002). Many racial minority groups tend to seek services during crisis periods and may abruptly discontinue treatment when the crisis is over (Castillo, n.d.; Dixon & Vaz, 2005). For veterans and service members of minority groups, assessment must also consider the effects of co-occurring situations (subject to racist remarks) and historical events (e.g., racial discrimination, oppression, dehumanizing treatment) on behavior and adjustment. For example, Americans of Arab descent may experience conflict between their American identity and identity related to their heritage (Litz & Orsillo, 2004). The psychological risk for minority groups through the persistent presence of racism needs to be assessed in the context of PTSD and poly-trauma.

When assessing minority groups, consideration should be given to the following: (1) the individual level of acculturation, (2) avoidance of generalization and viewing themes on a continuum, (3) awareness of language differences and fluency (especially among Latinos), (4) the definition of family (extends beyond the nuclear family), and (5) definitions of tolerable behavior (Castillo, n.d.). When assessing clients it is important to gather information on contexts that may be relevant from the client's perspective. Smith (2004) suggested that practical guidelines for contextual multicultural assessment for psychological functioning reflect the numerous complexities of the individual and the importance of context, including (1) the interactions of identity, particularly those listed in the ADDRESSING (Hays, 2001) and RESPECTFUL frameworks (D'Andrea & Daniels, 2001), (2) macro-level factors, (3) strengths and opportunities as well as difficulties and limitations, (4) recognition of when trauma has occurred, (5) physiology, physical illness, and related genetic predispositions that impact mental functioning, (6) identity and wellness factors most salient for a particular individual, (7) prevalence and incidence data, (8) overlap of psychological symptoms, (9) selection of instruments that are most appropriate to hypotheses generated about the individual, interpretion of the results in light of other evidence, and then making decisions about severity of symptoms and diagnosis, and (10) recognition of interventionist bias (positive and negative).

WOMEN IN THE MILITARY

THE ASSESSMENT OF women requires attention to the impact of sexual or gender harassment. Women in the military are at high risk for exposure to traumatic events, especially during times of war, and are more than twice more likely to develop PTSD than men (10% versus 4%) (Vogt, 2007). Women in the military may experience unwanted sexual touching or verbal conduct of a sexual nature from other unit members, commanding officers, or civilians in the war zone, which creates a hostile work environment. In addition, harassment may be played out as deliberate sabotage, gossip and rumors, and indirect threats. In civilian and military life these types of experiences are devastating for victims and create stress, powerlessness, and rage (Litz & Orsillo, 2004). Women are likely to develop PTSD if they (1) have a past mental health problem (e.g., depression or anxiety), (2) experienced a very severe or life-threatening trauma, (3) were sexually assaulted, (4) were injured during the event, (5) had a severe reaction at the time of the event, (6) experienced other stressful events afterward, and (7) do not have good social support (King & King, 2007; Vogt, 2007). In addition, women may take longer to recover from PTSD. Given the current situation in Iraq with approximately 15% of all military personnel being women, a growing number of women are now being exposed to combat (Vogt, 2007).

Overall, a comprehensive assessment is a precursor for effective treatment. Important variables to assess when working with veterans of the Iraq war include (1) work functioning, (2) interpersonal functioning, (3) recreational and self-care, (4) physical functioning, (5) psychological symptoms, (6) past distress and coping, (7) previous traumatic events, and (8) deployment-related experiences. Dr. Richard Selig, program manager and coordinator of the Trauma and Transition Resource Program for the VA's Eastern Kansas Health Care System, indicated that assessing and interfacing with veterans and service members should occur "in the context of systems—the structure of a person's life and interactions at familial, community, and organizational levels" (Currey, 2007, p. 16). The key point is that assessment of each of these domains can be useful as a starting point for assessing PTSD and/or poly-trauma and more generally to establish a sense of the potential risk and resiliency factors that may impact on the veteran's current and future functioning (Litz & Orsillo, 2004).

TREATMENT ISSUES

TREATMENT OF VETERANS and service members diagnosed with PTSD and/or poly-trauma is individualized and specific to their circumstances. Nevertheless, some strategies are useful and applicable across veterans to prevent problems such as family breakdown, social withdrawal, and isolation, employment issues, and substance abuse (Ruzek et al., 2004). Each of these areas can pose problems for veterans upon return to civilian life. The possibility exists that a multidisciplinary team (i.e., mental health/psychiatric, vocational rehabilitation, medical, social work) can minimize negative and/or long-term consequences in these areas. It is important to note that veterans with concurrent PTSD and TBI (traumatic brain injury) are increasingly common, compounding care and long-term alternatives (Currey, 2007).

The key to aiding veterans and service members in adjustment to postdeployment environments is seamless transitions (Currey, 2007). Three critical areas to address in treatment include (1) general considerations in care (i.e., connect veterans with each other, offer practical help with specific problems, attend to broad needs of the person), (2) methods of care (i.e., education about posttraumatic stress reactions, training in coping skills, exposure therapy, cognitive restructuring, family counseling), and (3) pharmacotherapy (i.e., pharmacologic treatment of acute stress reaction [ASR], ASD, and PTSD) (Ruzek et al., 2004).

The Department of Veterans Affairs (VA) and Department of Defense (DoD) developed clinical practical guidelines for the management of posttraumatic stress (VA/DoD, 2004). The goal of the guidelines was to create an algorithm to aid field personnel and health care workers in identifying, assessing, and/or training service members and veterans who have survived traumatic events. The guidelines offer a decision tree for prevention, assessment, and treatment with full annotation across a broad range of posttraumatic disorders.

CONCLUSION

GIVEN THE PROTRACTED extent of the war in Iraq, the number of service members returning with PTSD and poly-trauma is expected to continue at an alarming rate. It is in the postdeployment environment that service providers will need to understand how to provide care through an integrated systems approach for service members and veterans with PTSD and poly-trauma. Readjustment issues are expected of this population, and if they persist, the service members should seek help from a mental health professional. Acute behavioral changes, erratic, unexpected, or out-of-character behavior signal a need for intervention (Currey, 2007). Understanding PTSD and poly-trauma is a complex process that involves a variety of conditions and circumstances. In fact, the most effective treatment approach is a comprehensive one, consisting of a life care plan through a team of professionals.

REFERENCES

Army Center for Health Promotion and Preventive Medicine. (2007). *USACHPPM health information operations weekly update*. Retrieved July 5, 2007, from http://chppm-www.apgea.army.mil/

Beck, A. T., & Steer, R. A. (2000). Beck Depression Inventory. In Task Force for the Handbook of Psychiatric Measures (Ed.), *Handbook of psychiatric measures* (pp. 519–522). Washington, DC: American Psychiatric Association.

Brewin, C. R., Andrews, B., & Valentine, J. D. (2000). Meta-analysis of risk factors for posttraumatic stress disorders in trauma-exposed adults. *Journal of Consulting Clinical Psychology, 68*, 748–766.

Carlson, E. B. (2002, November). *Challenges to assessing traumatic stress histories in complex trauma survivors*. Paper presented at the Annual Meeting of the International Society of Traumatic Stress Studies, Baltimore, MD.

Carlson, E. B. (2004). Appendix D. Assessment of Iraq war veterans: Selecting assessment instruments and interpreting results. *The Iraq war guide* (2nd ed.). Retrieved June 26, 2007, from http://www.ncptsd.va.gov

Carlson, E. B., & Waedel, L. (2000, November). *Preliminary psychometric properties of the Trauma Related Dissociation Scale*. Paper presented at the Annual Meeting of the International Society for Traumatic Stress Studies, San Antonio, TX.

Castillo, D. T. (n.d.). *Cultural dimensions in the assessment and treatment of Hispanic veterans with PTSD*. Retrieved June 26, 2007, from http://www.ncptsd.va.gov/ptsd101/dodules/casrillo_cultural.html

Christy & Company. (2007). *Poly-trauma: Aftermath of the Iraq war: An overview of the injuries and disease suffered by U.S. soldiers*. Retrieved August 14, 2007, from http://www.associatedcontent.com

Currey, R. (2007). PTSD in today's war veterans: The road to recovery. *Social Work Today, 7,* 13–16.

D'Andrea, M., & Daniels, J. (2001). Respectful counseling: An integrative multidimensional model for counselors. In D. Pope-Davis & H. Coleman (Eds.), *The intersection of race, class, and gender in multicultural counseling* (pp. 417–466). Thousand Oaks, CA: Sage Publications.

Department of Defense. (2004). *Posttraumatic stress disorder: VA/DoD. clinical practice guidelines*. Retrieved July 5, 2007, from www.oqp.med.va.gov/cpg/PTSD/PTSD_Base.htm

Dixon, C. G., & Vaz, K. (2005). Perceptions of African Americans regarding mental health counseling. In D. A. Harley & J. M. Dillard (Eds.), *Contemporary mental health issues among African Americans* (pp. 163–174). Alexandria, VA: American Counseling Association.

Goldman, M., Brown, S., & Christian, B. (2000). Alcohol Expectancy Questionnaire (AEQ). In Task Force for the Handbook of Psychiatric Measures (Ed.), *Handbook of psychiatric measures* (pp. 476–477). Washington, DC: American Psychiatric Association.

Government Accountability Office. (2004, September). *VA and defense health care—More information needed to determine if VA can meet an increase in demand for post-traumatic stress disorder services* (DHHS Publication No. GAO–04–1069). Washington, DC: Author.

Haley, J. A. (2002). The importance of cultural assessment. *Spinal Cord Injury Nurses, 19,* 177–180.

Hays, P. (2001). *Addressing cultural complexities in practice: A framework for clinicians and counselors*. Washington, DC: American Psychological Association.

Hoge, C. W., Castro, C. A., Messer, S. C., McGurk, D., Cotting, D. I., & Koffman, R. L. (2004). Combat duty in Iraq and Afghanistan, mental problems, and barriers to care. *New England Journal of Medicine, 351,* 13–22.

Keane, T. M. (2006). *Issues in the assessment of PTSD*. Retrieved July 5, 2007, from www.ncptsd.va.gov/

Keane, T. M., & Barlow, D. H. (2002). Posttraumatic stress disorder. In D. H. Barlow (Ed.), *Anxieties and its disorders* (pp. 418–453). New York: Guilford Press.

Kellicker, P. G. (2004). *Less than half of soldiers with mental health problems seek treatment*. Retrieved June 26, 2007, from http://www.iraqwarveterans.org/readjustment_development.htm

King, D. W., King, L. A., & Vogt, D. S. (2003). *Manual for the Development Risk and Resilience Inventory (DRRI): A collection of measures for studying development-related experiences in military veterans*. Boston: National Center for PTSD.

King, L. A., & King, D. W. (2007, May 22). *Traumatic stress in female veterans.* Retrieved August 14, 2007, from http://www.ncptsd.va.gov

Kubany, E. S., Abueg, F. R., Owens, J. A., Brennan, J. A., Kaplan, A. S., & Watson, S. B. (1995). Initial examination of a multidimensional model of trauma-related guilt: Applications to combat veterans and battered women. *Journal of Psychopathology and Behavioral Assessment, 17,* 353–376.

Litz, B., & Orsillo, S. M. (2004). The returning veteran of the Iraq war: Background issues and assessment guidelines. *The Iraq war clinician guide* (2nd ed.). Retrieved June 26, 2007, from http://www.ncptsd.va.gov

Moos, R. H. (1990). *Coping with life crisis: An integrated approach.* New York: Plenum Press.

National Center for Posttraumatic Stress Disorder. (2007, May 22). *PTSD in Iraq war veterans: Implications for primary care.* Retrieved June 26, 2007, from http://www.ncptsd.va.gov

Ruzek, J. I., Curran, E., Friedmann, M. J., Gusman, F. D., Southwick, S. M., Swales, P., et al. (2004). Treatment of the returning Iraq war veteran. *The Iraq war clinician guide* (2nd ed.). Retrieved June 26, 2007, from http://www.ncptsd.va.gov

Schlossberg, N. K. (1981). A model for analyzing human adaptation to transition. *The Counseling Psychologists, 9,* 2–18.

Schlossberg, N. K., Waters, E. B., & Goodman, J. (1995). *Counseling adults in transition: Linking practice with theory.* New York: Springer.

Smedley, B. D., Stith, A. Y., & Nelson, A. R. (2003). *Unequal treatment: Confronting racial and ethnic disparities in health care.* Washington, DC: The National Academies Press.

Smith, T. B. (2004). *Practicing multiculturalism: Affirming diversity in counseling and psychology.* Boston: Pearson.

Spielberger, C. D. (1988). *Manual for the State-Trait Expression Inventory: STAXI.* Odessa, FL: Psychological Assessment Resources.

Veterans Affairs and Department of Defense. (2004). *VA/DoD clinical practice guideline for the management of post-traumatic stress: Version 1.0* (V101(93) P–1633). Washington, DC: Office of Performance and Quality.

Vogt, D. (2007, July 13). *Women, trauma and PTSD.* Retrieved August 14, 2007, from http://www.ncptsd.va.gov

Weathers, F. W., Keane, T. M., & Davidson, J. R. T. (2001). Clinician-Administered PTSD Scale: A review of the first ten years of research. *Depression and Anxiety, 156,* 132–156.

Wilson, K. B., Harley, D. A., & Alston, R. J. (2001). Race as a correlate of vocational rehabilitation acceptance: Revisited. *Journal of Rehabilitation, 67,* 35–41.

Wilson, K. B., Turner, T., Lui, J., Harley, D. A., & Alston, R. J. (2002). Perceived vocational rehabilitation service efficacy by race: Results of a national customer survey. *Journal of Applied Rehabilitation Counseling, 33,* 26–34.

Wolfe, J., & Kimerling, R. (1997). Gender issues in the assessment of PTSD. In J. Wilson & T. M. Keane (Eds.), *Assessing psychological trauma and PTSD* (pp. 192–238). New York: Guilford Press.

73

Counseling Older Adults: Practical Implications

Eva Miller and Chuck Reid

ADULTS AGE 65 and over represent the fastest-growing segment of people in the United States, composing approximately 12.4% (37 million) of the total population and this number is projected to increase by 20% by 2030 (U.S. Census Bureau, 2000). As such, counselors will increasingly be faced with meeting the demands of older persons and their families. According to Myers and Harper (2004), an estimated one-third of older adults have mental health problems for which intervention is needed, including depression, anxiety, substance abuse, and dementia; however, these estimates fail to incorporate normative developmental issues such as transition to retirement, grandparenthood, health- and disability-related issues, sensory deficits, and economic hardship. Moreover, only a small proportion of older adults (approximately 6% to 8%) are actually seen in community mental health clinics and outpatient mental health settings, and an even smaller percentage is seen by private counseling practitioners (Myers & Harper, 2004). The purpose of this chapter is to discuss the major mental health disorders experienced by older adults, to identify the most effective counseling approaches and psychotropic medications used to address the mental health needs of older adults, and to provide an overview of best practice counseling and treatment interventions used to address the mental health needs of older adults.

DEPRESSION

DEPRESSION HAS BEEN noted to be the most significant and widespread mental health disorder of later life, affecting as many as 15% of older persons at any given time (Smyer & Qualls, 1999) and 50% of older adults residing in nursing homes (Serby & Yu, 2003). Suicide is the 18th leading cause of death among older adults, with rates being highest among older men (Surgeon General, 2008). Although depression and related mood disorders often go undiagnosed and undertreated in older adults, research has generally shown these individuals benefit from both counseling and psychotropic medication for treatment of depression and comorbid disorders such as anxiety, substance abuse, and dementia (Lewis & Trizinski, 2006; Zalaquett & Stens, 2006).

In an overview of the literature regarding major depression and dysthymia (a low-grade, chronic form of depression), Zalaquett and Stens (2006) examined the effectiveness of four commonly used individual therapies for treating older adult depression: (1) cognitive behavior therapy (CBT), (2) interpersonal therapy (IPT), (3) brief dynamic therapy (BDT), and (4) reminiscence therapy (RT) and life review (LR) therapy. Some of the most effective CBT techniques included initial assessment of clients' cognitive and sensory impairments; assessing their knowledge, attitudes, and misconceptions about the counseling process; and tailoring counseling based on their needs. For example, it was found that some older adults who had difficulties in assuming active participation in counseling due to cognitive impairments benefited from tape-recorded sessions, the establishment of moderate treatment goals, and extended treatment for those with lifelong problems.

Interpersonal therapy (IPT) is indicated for older persons who need to change their behavior in current personal relationships. Therapy begins with establishing rapport, educating clients about how treatment works, and assuming an active role by focusing on pragmatic solutions (Zalaquett & Stens, 2006). Some of the most common issues addressed with older adults using this form of therapy have been dependency, chronic health problems, and significant losses that often lead to depression. Older adults who have limited opportunities to engage in new interpersonal relationships (e.g., those residing in nursing homes) may be encouraged to tolerate problematic relationships and find acceptable alternatives such as changing roommates and sitting next to compatible residents during mealtimes.

Brief dynamic therapy (BDT) is indicated for older clients who are experiencing adjustment disorders, traumatic stress disorders, and grief-related issues (Kennedy & Tanenbaum, 2000). This type of therapy is time-limited (approximately 15 sessions) and includes exploration of unconscious processes as they relate to lifetime developmental issues. An essential adaptation of BDT for working with older adults includes helping clients regain a positive self-perception and self-mastery while preventing the development of dependency. This approach has also been shown to be especially efficacious for treating major depression among older adults.

Reminiscence therapy (RT) and life review (LR) therapy are based on Erickson's (1950) theory of psychosocial development and are used to assist older adults struggling to find meaning in their lives and those dealing with stressful situations such as the realization of their own mortality. Techniques include homework assignments that involve finding mementos, photographs, journals, and other memorabilia from one's life to share with the counselor in an effort to resolve past issues and increase tolerance for dealing with present conflict. Older adults participating in RT and LR therapy often experience a wide array of emotions, including rage, resentment, and distrust (Kennedy & Tanenbaum, 2000). These types of responses require counselors to demonstrate a commitment to listen and understand what clients are experiencing while reviewing issues of their past and dealing with current issues such as life-threatening illnesses, losses, and relocation form their homes.

Active treatment with psychotropic medications can also improve symptoms of depression in older persons. Selective serotonin reuptake inhibitors (SSRIs) such as Lexapro, Effexor, Zoloft, Remeron, and Celexa are some of the most commonly used medications to treat depressive symptoms. Cymbalta is also therapeutic for treating depression, especially if the person has comorbid chronic pain associated with diseases such as osteoporosis and rheumatoid arthritis. The most common side effects found with SSRIs are gastrointestinal upset (e.g., nausea and vomiting), increased anxiety, restlessness or akathisia, insomnia, headaches, and sexual dysfunction. It should be noted that these symptoms usually remit within 1 month (with the exception of sexual dysfunction), which is typically the amount of time it takes for the medication to reach therapeutic effectiveness.

ANXIETY DISORDERS

ACCORDING TO KRAUS, Kunik, & Stanley (2007), a substantial number of older adults experience anxiety, with an estimated 10% meeting the *Diagnostic and Statistical Manual of Mental Disorders, Fourth Edition, Text Revision* (*DSM–IV–TR;* American Psychiatric Association [APA], 2000) diagnostic criteria for anxiety disorders. The prevalence of anxiety is even higher for older adults with coexisting medical and other mental health disorders. Cognitive behavior therapy is often indicated for older adults who are experiencing anxiety and entails identifying and challenging maladaptive ways of thinking (Kraus et al.). This approach also involves educating clients about anxiety and teaching them self-monitoring techniques to increase awareness of their symptoms and having them track their progress during therapy. Counselors can develop brief checklists to assist clients in tracking their symptoms. Other techniques used to treat anxiety among older adults include problem solving; increasing behaviors that are likely to bring them pleasure such as going out with friends, watching a movie, or volunteering at a charitable organization; and spending time with family members. Reminding clients to focus on one goal at a time may also alleviate stress and the feeling of being overwhelmed.

Others (e.g., Steffens, 2007) emphasize the importance of spirituality when working with older persons experiencing anxiety and other mental health problems. According to Steffens, counselors are often conflicted about how much to push religious and spiritual issues with their older clients; therefore, he suggests that a good clinical rule of thumb is that if faith has been one of the areas impacted by physical and/or mental illness, the person should be encouraged to reconnect with spiritual and religious activity. Supportive therapy has also been indicated for working with older individuals with anxiety. This approach entails providing direction and guidance, focusing on external circumstances related to the person's difficulties, encouraging adaptive functioning, and problem solving. For many older adults, this approach is nonthreatening in that it involves empathic reflection of concerns they are currently facing, including declining physical abilities, medical problems, housing concerns, and economic constraints.

Ativan, BuSpar, Xanax, Restoril, and Klonopin are some of the most commonly prescribed benzodiazepines for treating anxiety among adults of all ages. Common side effects include sedation; psychomotor impairment; anterograde amnesia such as decreased recall and confusion; and paradoxical reactions such as excitement, agitation, and confusion. Older persons are especially susceptible to these adverse effects. Physical dependence and withdrawal is also seen with the use of benzodiazepines, which occurs after 2 to 3 months of chronic use. Symptoms include nervousness, anxiety, insomnia, tremor, and seizures. Therefore, it is suggested that these agents be used in acute situations and not long-term, due to the potential for abuse. For maintenance use, it has been suggested that SSRIs may be the best choice of treatment (Lowinson, Riuz, Millman, & Langrod, 2005).

DEMENTIA

T HE MOST COMMON cause of dementia in later life is Alzheimer's disease (AD), which affects an estimated 4.5 million Americans (National Institute on Aging, 2007). The disease usually begins after age 60, and risk increases with age. Approximately 5% of men and women ages 65 to 74 have AD, and nearly half of those age 85 and older may have the disease. Alzheimer's disease involves the parts of the brain that control thought, memory, and language. Common symptoms include asking the same questions repeatedly; becoming lost in familiar places; being unable to follow directions; becoming disoriented; personality changes; and neglecting personal safety, hygiene, and nutrition. People with dementia also lose their abilities at different rates. On average, people with AD live from 8 to 10 years after they are diagnosed, although the disease can last for as many as 20 years (National Institute on Aging, 2007).

Vascular dementia (VD) constitutes the second leading form of dementia and results from a series of small strokes or changes in the brain's blood supply, which often results in the death of brain tissue (National Institute on Aging, 2007). The location in the brain where the stroke occurs determines the seriousness of the problem and the symptoms that arise. Symptoms that have a sudden onset may be a sign of VD. People with VD are likely to show signs of improvement or remain stable for long periods of time, then quickly develop new symptoms if additional strokes occur.

Reality orientation therapy (ROT) is commonly used for working with persons with dementia and is used primarily in long-term care settings (Myers & Harper, 2004). Informal ROT (24-hours method) is a continual process that requires staff to convey to clients constant repetition of information such as date, day of the week, time of day, and current location through the use of verbal cues and environmental aides (e.g., showing them a calendar or holiday decorations displayed in the facility). Class ROT involves a more formal didactic group therapy in which clients, depending on their level of confusion, meet from 30 to 60 minutes per day (Metitieri et al., 2001). Counselors may also choose to use this approach on a one-to-one basis with clients who show advanced signs of confusion.

Validation therapy (VT), which is widely used in counseling older persons with dementia, focuses on the emotional and psychological consequences of short-term memory loss. Like ROT, VT can be used in one-to-one conversations or for group work. The premise of VT involves accepting disoriented older persons who live in their past and helping them "sum up" their lifetime (Morton & Bleathman, 1991).

The assumption of VD is that the behavior and speech of disoriented persons has an underlying meaning and that they return to the past in an attempt to resolve unfinished conflicts by expressing previously hidden feelings (Morton & Bleathman, 1991). Counselors, in turn, validate what the client is saying rather than correcting factual errors so that meaningful conversation can take place on the issues that are important to the person with dementia. Group therapy involves choosing relevant topics that have universal meanings such as anger, separation, and loss and assisting clients in verbalizing their unresolved feelings about these topics.

Counseling approaches such as behavior therapy and reminiscence therapy are also widely used for counseling persons with dementia. For example, people with late-stage dementia often benefit from a behavioral approach that focuses on functional abilities such as hygiene and grooming, appropriate verbalizations (e.g., verbal praise for speaking calmly when frustrated versus yelling at others), and physically aggressive behavior. A combination of all the aforementioned techniques may be indicated for persons with dementia, depending on their disposition/temperament, current situation, and degree of cognitive impairment.

Although counseling approaches have been known to be beneficial for persons with dementia, researchers have not found a specific cause or cure for AD and, therefore, treatment is often limited to pharmacological interventions such as Aricept, Cognex, Namenda, and the Exelon patch, which are designed to slow the progression of the disease. Common side effects of these medications are diarrhea, dizziness, drowsiness, fatigue, nausea, and vomiting.

DELIRIUM AND PSYCHOSIS

ACCORDING TO THE *DSM–IV–TR* (APA, 2000) delirium is seen in approximately 10%–15% of older persons who are hospitalized and up to 60% of nursing home residents age 75 and older. Symptoms of delirium include a disturbance of consciousness (i.e., reduced clarity of the environment) with reduced concentration and attention. Additional symptoms include changes in cognition such as memory problems, disorientation, dysarthria or slurred speech, visual hallucinations, disorganized or delusional thought processes, and sleep disturbance. The onset of delirium is acute and usually remits within hours to days; however, if left untreated, symptoms may progress to coma, seizures, and death (APA, 2000). Delirium is often confused with dementia and counselors are encouraged to consult the *DSM–IV–TR* and other mental health professionals if they are having difficulty formulating an accurate diagnosis.

Psychosis (e.g., hallucinations and delusions) is also commonly seen in older adults. There are many causes of psychosis; however, Vitamin B-12 and thiamine deficiencies, anesthesia, hypoglycemia, thyroid abnormalities, urinary tract and respiratory infections, overstimulation, anticonvulsants, neuroleptics, steroids, and antihypertensives can cause psychotic symptoms in older adults. Antipsychotic medications are frequently prescribed for older persons with psychosis and severe agitation, which is frequently seen in individuals with delirium and dementia. Some of the most commonly prescribed medications are classified as atypical antipsychotics and include Risperdal, Geodon, Seroquel, and Zyprexa. Side effects of these medications include sedation, weight gain, orthostatic hypotension/dizziness, and akathisia/restlessness.

SUBSTANCE MISUSE AND ABUSE

SPECIFIC ISSUES FOR older adults are the misuse of over-the-counter (OTC) and prescription drugs (Reid & Kampfe, 2000), excessive alcohol use (Reid & Kampfe, 2000; Stevens-Smith & Smith, 1959) and, with the aging of the baby boomer population, the use and abuse of cocaine and other illicit drugs. This population has been known to experiment with illicit drugs and, as they age, the boomers may become one of the higher risk groups for substance abuse (Kausch, 2002). The following provides an overview of some of the most commonly recognized issues in these areas.

OVER-THE-COUNTER DRUGS

THE MISUSE OF over-the-counter (OTC) and prescription drugs in the older population is not clearly established as many older persons may not be aware they are misusing these drugs. However, older adults represent the largest consumers of OTC and prescription drugs in the United States, with an estimated 12% taking 10 prescription drugs and 23% taking at least five prescription drugs (Shepler, Grogan, & Steinmetz-Pater, 2006). Medication noncompliance for this age group is reported to range from 25% to 59% (Russell, Conn, & Jantarakupt, 2006).

Many age-related medical conditions such as insomnia, arthritis, constipation, and gastric maladies can be treated with OTC medications but are often inappropriately used. Physical, social, and economic factors such as impaired mobility, sensory deficits, limited finances, and limited access to physicians all reinforce the practice of excessive OTC medication use in older adults. Failure to take into account the physical changes of aging, cognitive impairment, and the perception that OTC medications are not harmful may contribute to patterns of dependence and abuse (Russell et al., 2006). The physiological changes caused by aging also affect the pharmacokinetics of chemicals ingested, including reduced activity of major metabolic pathways, altered absorption due to diminished gastrointestinal blood flow, and slowed renal excretion of drugs. These changes increase active drug concentrations and increase the possibility for toxicity among the geriatric population (Shepler et al., 2006).

PRESCRIPTION DRUGS

OVER-THE-COUNTER AND PRESCRIPTION drugs are often used in combination by older persons as are prescription and psychotropic medications (Shepler et al., 2006). Many of the physiological factors are similar to the overuse of OTC drugs. Misuse of medications may go undetected because the symptoms of misuse may also be symptoms of physical conditions associated with older age. Examples include tremors, unsteadiness, constipation, depression, malnutrition, memory loss, drowsiness, fatigue, falling, and anxiety (Crome & Crome, 2005). These symptoms can be perceived by medical professionals as conditions unrelated to drug use. Drug misuse can manifest itself in a number of ways, including excessive use, medication sharing, inconsistent use, underuse, and the taking of numerous drugs without medical supervision (Crome & Crome, 2005). Polypharmaceutical practice among older persons may result in adverse effects and adverse drug interactions. For example, they may be more susceptible to falls, confusion, anorexia, fatigue, and urinary retention (Shepler et al., 2006).

ALCOHOL AND ILLICIT DRUGS

EXCESSIVE DRUG AND alcohol use is a potential issue for older adults and these issues are becoming more prevalent as the baby boomer generation matures (Kausch, 2002; Reid & Kampfe, 2000). Older persons are at risk for alcohol and drug abuse for a number of reasons, including social, medical, and emotional difficulties. In addition to loss of body functions, older adults may have issues with families, friends, income, occupations, independent living, and autonomy. Grief, decreased mobility, reduced social support, increased time on their hands, and disempowerment may also lead to drug and alcohol abuse (Myers, 1990).

Some older adults use alcohol as a means of coping with stress and other life issues such as loneliness, depression, and boredom. Symptoms of alcohol-related stress coping can take a number of forms such as falling or sustaining other injuries. Psychological issues of alcohol-related stress coping include sexual dysfunction, sleep problems, depression, and anxiety. Alcohol use in the older population may also result in de-creased social and family support (Hunter & Gillen, 2006).

Alcohol can induce cognitive changes and dementia, both of which accelerate the aging process (Atkinson & Kofoed, 1982). Decreased tes-tosterone production due to alcohol use can lead to impotence, which is often mistaken for the effects of aging. Alcohol-induced chronic gastritis can lead to iron-deficiency anemia. Liver toxicity is another well-known complication of alcohol abuse, which may be mistaken as a product of old age. Additionally, vitamin and nutritional deficiencies due to excessive drinking are often mistakenly attributed to old age (Lowinson et al., 2005).

The precise number of older people who use or who have used il-licit drugs is difficult to ascertain, but it is indicated that these num-bers will increase as will the number of older people with drug-induced maladies (Kausch, 2002; Lowinson et al., 2005). Areas of concern for older adults are shortened lifespans due to drug use and drug-related HIV/AIDS infection and other sexually transmitted diseases, vascular sclerosis, and dental problems. Neurological problems due to drug use is indicated in cases of stroke, mood changes, and seizures. Cocaine and amphetamines use can cause intracranial hemorrhage.

Counselors can do a number of things to assist older people in deal-ing with drug and alcohol abuse, including identifying risk factors for each person, assisting individuals in finding new meaning in life and dealing with losses, and attempting to understand the role of drugs in their coping repertoire and replacing these with appropriate coping skills (Hunter & Gillen, 2006). Counselors can also assist older persons in developing social supports and promoting opportunities for social interaction. Examples include involving family members in the person's life, encouraging hobbies, and identifying social support networks.

Counselors should also educate themselves about the signs of exces-sive alcohol and substance abuse, noting that some medical conditions may have similar symptoms to drug or alcohol abuse. Becoming familiar with the signs of drug and alcohol abuse and watching for a deteriora-tion in level of functioning is also indicated. Finally, providing informa-tion to older persons about illicit drugs and medications so they become more aware of the potential harm they may be inflicting upon them-selves is also highly recommended for this segment of the population.

BEST PRACTICES

THE FOLLOWING COUNSELING and treatment interventions are designed to provide counselors with a handy reference guide for working with older adults.

- Older adults are often uncomfortable with the counseling process and may require longer time for rapport-building as well as an overview of what counseling entails.
- Older persons have a propensity to self-disclose somatic complaints instead of psychosocial concerns and may benefit from *specific* questions pertaining to their mental health and related issues.
- Be aware of sensory deficits and accommodate accordingly (e.g., do not be afraid to inquire as to whether the person can adequately hear you).
- Do not be afraid to touch older persons (e.g., hold their hand, hug them) as this is often the only form of physical contact they receive outside of personal care.
- Complete routine mental status examinations due to fluctuating cognitive symptoms.
- Be well familiarized with *all* medications your client is taking (not just psychotropic medications) as drug interactions are common—consult with pharmacology personnel.
- Use a multidisciplinary team approach as older persons receive numerous services that can impact counseling (e.g., family members; social workers; physicians and nurses; occupational, physical, and speech therapists; dietary staff; activity directors; and financial and benefits coordinators.
- *Advocate* for your clients and teach them assertiveness skills as they are often unfamiliar with available services or may be too passive to address their own needs.

REFERENCES

American Psychiatric Association. (2000). *Diagnostic and statistical manual of mental disorders* (4th ed., text revision). Washington, DC: Author.

Atkinson, R. M., & Kofoed, L. L. (1982). Alcohol and drug abuse in old age: A clinical perspective. *Substance and Alcohol Actions/Misuse, 3,* 353–368.

Crome, I., & Crome, P. (2005). At your age what does it matter? Myths and realities about older people who use substances. *Drugs: Education, Prevention and Policy, 12*(5), 343–347.

Erickson, E. H. (1950). *Childhood and society.* New York: W. W. Norton.

Hunter, I. R., & Gillen, M. C. (2006). Alcohol as a response to stress in older adults: A counseling perspective. *Life span, 5*(2), 114–126.

Kausch, O. (2002). Cocaine abuse in the elderly. *Journal of Nervous and Mental Diseases, 190*(8), 562–564.

Kennedy, G. J., & Tanenbaum, S. (2000). Psychotherapy with older adults. *American Journal of Psychotherapy, 54,* 386–407.

Kraus, C. A., Kunik, M. E., & Stanley, M. A. (2007). Use of cognitive behavioral therapy in late-life psychiatric disorders. *Geriatrics, 62*(6), 21–26.

Lewis, M. M., & Trizinski, A. L. (2006). Counseling older adults with dementia who are dealing with death: Innovative interventions for practitioners. *Death Studies, 30,* 777–787.

Lowinson, J. H., Riuz, P., Millman, R. B., & Langrod, J. G. (2005). *Substance abuse: A comprehensive textbook* (4th ed.). New York: Williams & Wilkins.

Metitieri, T., Zanetti, O., Geroldi, C., Frisoni, G. B., De Leo, D., Dello Buono, M., et al. (2001). Reality orientation therapy to delay outcomes of progression in patients with dementia: A retrospective study. *Clinical Rehabilitation, 15,* 471–478.

Morton, I., & Bleathman, C. (1991). The effectiveness of validation therapy in dementia-A pilot study. *International Journal of Geriatric Psychiatry, 6,* 327–330.

Myers, J. E. (1990). *Empowerment for life.* Ann Arbor, MI: ERIC Counseling and Personal Services Clearinghouse.

Myers, J. E., & Harper, M. C. (2004). Evidence-based effective practices with older adults. *Journal of Counseling and Development, 84,* 207–218.

National Institute on Aging. (2007). Alzheimer's information: General information. Retrieved March 4, 2008, from http://www.nia.nih.gov/Alzheimers/AlzheimersInformation/GeneralInfo/#howmany

Reid, C. R., & Kampfe, C. M. (2000). Multicultural issues. In A. Sales (Ed.), *Substance abuse counseling* (pp. 215–246). Greensboro, NC: ERIC.

Russell, C. L., Conn, V. S., & Jantarakupt, P. (2006). Older adult medication compliance: Integrated review of randomized controlled trials. *American Journal of Health Behavior, 30*(6), 636–650.

Serby, M., & Yu, M. (2003). Overview: Depression in the elderly. *The Mount Sinai Journal of Medicine, 70,* 69–74.

Shepler, S. A., Grogan, T. A., & Steinmetz-Pater, K. (2006). Keep your older patients out of medication trouble. *Nursing, 36*(9), 44–47.

Smyer, M. A., & Qualls, S. H. (1999). *Aging and mental health.* Malden, MA: Blackwell.

Steffens, D. C. (2007). Spiritual considerations in suicide and depression among the elderly. *Southern Medical Journal, 100*(7), 748–749.

Stevens-Smith, P., & Smith, R. L. (1959). *Substance abuse counseling: Theory and practice.* Columbus, OH: Merril.

Surgeon General. (2008). Mental health: A report by the Surgeon General: Older adults and mental health. Retrieved July 16, 2008, from http://www.surgeongeneral.gov/library/mentalhealth/chapter5/sec3.html

U.S. Census Bureau. (2000). The 65 years and over population: 2000. Retrieved January 25, 2008, from http://www.census.gov/population/www/cen2000/briefs.html

Zalaquett, C. P., & Stens, A. N. (2006). Psychosocial treatments for major depression and dysthymia in older adults: A review of the research literature. *Journal of Counseling and Development, 84,* 192–201.

Section J

Contemporary Issues in Counseling

74

Positive Psychology

CHRISTOPHER PETERSON AND NANSOOK PARK

POSITIVE PSYCHOLOGY IS the scientific study of what goes right in life, from birth to death (Peterson, 2006). It is the study of optimal experience, people being their best and doing their best. Positive psychology is a newly christened approach within psychology that takes seriously as a subject matter those things that make life most worth living. Everyone's life has peaks and valleys, and positive psychology does not deny the low points. Its signature premise is more nuanced: What is good about life is as genuine as what is bad and therefore deserves equal attention from mental health practitioners. Positive psychology assumes that life entails more than avoiding or undoing problems and that explanations of the good life must do more than reverse accounts of problems.

BACKGROUND

POSITIVE PSYCHOLOGY HAS a very long past but only a very short history. The field was named in 1998 as one of the initiatives of Martin Seligman in his role as president of the American Psychological Association (Seligman & Csikszentmihalyi, 2000). A trigger for positive psychology was Seligman's realization that psychology since World War II had focused much of its efforts on human problems and how to remedy them.

The yield of this focus on pathology has been considerable, but there has been a cost. Much of scientific psychology has neglected the study of what can go right with people and often has little to say about the psychological good life. More subtly, the underlying assumptions of psychology have shifted to embrace a disease model of human nature. People are seen as flawed and fragile, casualties of cruel environments or bad genetics. This worldview has even crept into the common culture, where many people have become self-identified victims.

Positive psychology challenges the assumptions of the disease model. It calls for as much focus on strength as on weakness, as much interest in building the best things in life as in repairing the worst, and as much attention to fulfilling the lives of healthy people as to healing the wounds of the distressed. Psychologists interested in promoting human potential need to start with different assumptions and to pose different questions from their peers who assume only a disease model.

The most basic assumption that positive psychology urges is that human goodness and excellence are as authentic as disease, disorder, and distress. Positive psychologists argue that these topics are not secondary, derivative, or otherwise suspect. The good news is that these generalizations about business-as-usual psychology are simply that—generalizations. There are many good examples of psychological research, past and present, that can be claimed as positive psychology (Snyder & Lopez, in press).

The very long past of positive psychology stretches at least to the Athenian philosophers in the West and to Confucius and Lao-Tsu in the East. In the writings of these great thinkers can be found the same questions posed by contemporary positive psychologists. What is the good life? Is virtue its own reward? What does it mean to be happy? Is it possible to pursue happiness directly, or is fulfillment a byproduct of other pursuits? What roles are played by other people and society as a whole?

Within psychology, the premises of positive psychology were laid out long before 1998. Setting the immediate stage for positive psychology as it currently exists were humanistic psychology as popularized by Carl Rogers and Abraham Maslow; utopian visions of education like those of Alexander Sutherland Neill; primary prevention programs based on notions of wellness as pioneered by George Albee and Emory Cowen; work by Albert Bandura and others on human agency and efficacy; studies of giftedness; conceptions of intelligence as multiple; and studies of the quality of life among medical and psychiatric patients that went beyond an exclusive focus on their symptoms and diseases. And the field of counseling psychology itself has contributed a great deal to the positive perspective (Lopez et al., 2006).

Today's positive psychologists do not claim to have invented notions of happiness and well-being, to have proposed their first theoretical accounts, or even to have ushered in their scientific study. Rather, the contribution of contemporary positive psychology has been to provide an umbrella term for what had been isolated lines of theory and research and to make the self-conscious argument that what makes life worth living deserves its own field of inquiry within psychology, at least until all of psychology embraces the study of what is good along with the study of what is problematic.

The framework of positive psychology provides a comprehensive scheme for describing and understanding the good life (Seligman, 2002). The field can be divided into three related topics:

- Positive subjective experiences (happiness, pleasure, gratification, fulfillment, flow)
- Positive individual traits (strengths of character, talents, interests, values)
- Positive institutions (families, schools, businesses, communities, societies)

A theory is implied here: Positive institutions facilitate the development and display of positive traits, which in turn facilitate positive subjective experiences.

The word *facilitate* avoids strict causal language. It is possible for people to be happy or content even in the absence of good character, and people can have good character even when living outside the realm of positive institutions. But matters are simpler when institutions, traits, and experiences are in alignment. Doing well in life probably represents a coming together of all three domains.

When positive psychology was first described, its stated goal was not to move people from –5 to 0—the presumed goal of business-as-usual psychology—but rather from +2 to +5 (Seligman, 2002). This assertion is useful in highlighting what is novel about positive psychology but does not do justice to this new field and what it might help people to achieve. Even if it is conceded that positive psychology has little to say about severe mental illness (a point that itself could be argued), positive psychology certainly speaks clearly to the typical person with circumscribed problems who seeks out counseling. Whatever the presenting complaints, such people also bring assets and strengths that can be used to resolve their problems. Indeed, when asked how they can tell that treatment has been effective, even individuals with *DSM* diagnoses describe their own view of "remission" in positive psychology language, spontaneously mentioning that they would be more optimistic and that they would function well (Zimmerman et al., 2006).

The relevance of positive psychology to counseling psychology is thus obvious and multifold. First, positive psychology provides a way to conceive the goals of treatment that go beyond the vision inherent in a disease model. Second, positive psychology provides the counselor strategies of assessment that ascertain domains of strength and competence and progress within these domains. Third, positive psychology also makes available a variety of specific techniques and exercises to be used in the context of a therapy that can make the life of a client more fulfilling. Finally, positive psychology can be used to frame the counselor's entire model of intervention.

The skeptic might object that "good" counselors have long made use of the positive perspective in their work with clients (cf. Saleebey, 1992). So what is new here? The value of positive psychology to counseling is that it makes the positive stance explicit and systematic. It also provides some concrete resources for counselors to use in their work.

TREATMENT GOALS

POSITIVE PSYCHOLOGY CAN be criticized for being value-laden, a charge that applies to all approaches to helping professions. The offsetting virtue is that the values inherent in positive psychology are clearly stated. The real question is whether these values are idiosyncratic or culture-bound. At a certain level of abstraction, the vision of psychological well-being that emerges from positive psychology seems ubiquitous if not universal. So, positive psychology assumes that people are doing well when they experience more positive feelings than negative feelings, are satisfied with their lives as they have been lived, have identified what they do well and use these talents and strengths on an ongoing basis, are highly engaged in what they do, are contributing members of a social community, and have a sense of meaning and purpose in their lives. Health and safety, of course, provide an important context for psychological well-being. It is difficult to imagine a cultural group in which these are not valued. Respect for human diversity need not entail extreme cultural relativism. In any event, the positive psychology vision of optimal functioning provides ultimate goals for treatment that can be discussed with a client.

ASSESSMENT STRATEGIES

ASSESSMENT HAS LONG been a staple of psychology, and much of it has been tilted—understandably—toward identifying weaknesses, deficiencies, and problems. The positive psychology perspective is that business-as-usual assessment should be expanded (not replaced) to include attention to areas of strength and competence. Positive psychology also implies that *DSM* Axis V (global assessment of functioning) should be taken as seriously by diagnosticians as the other axes.

More specifically, positive psychologists have developed an impressive set of measurement instruments that allow someone doing assessment to break through the zero point of deficiency measures. For example, the "best" one can score on typical measures of depression is zero, but this lumps together people who are blasé with those who are filled with zest and joy. The distinction seems well worth making, and the self-report surveys and interviews developed by positive psychologists allow it.

Space does not permit a detailed presentation of positive psychology measures, but Table 74.1 provides representative examples. Fuller descriptions of these and other measures can be found in Lopez and Snyder (2003), Peterson and Seligman (2004), and Ong and van Dulmen (2006). Many of the popular positive self-report surveys are available online at no cost at www.authentichappiness.org. Upon completion of a survey, individual feedback is provided, which means that clients can be directed to this Web site and asked to keep a record of their scores.

Most of the existing positive psychology measures were developed for research purposes, which means they are most valid when aggre-

TABLE 74.1 Positive Psychology Measures

Positive affect
  e.g., Positive and Negative Affect Schedule (PANAS), Profile of Mood States (POMS)

Happiness
  e.g., Authentic Happiness Inventory (AHI)
  e.g., Orientations to Happiness Scale [measures endorsement of pleasure, engagement, meaning]

Life Satisfaction
  e.g., Satisfaction with Life Scale
  e.g., Marital Satisfaction
  e.g., Work Satisfaction
  e.g., Leisure Satisfaction

Positive traits
  e.g., Values in Action Inventory of Strengths (VIA) [measures positive traits]
  e.g., Ryff and Singer's Psychological Well-Being Scales
  e.g., Search Institute's Developmental Assets [for youth]

Values
  e.g., Values Inventories of Rokeach, Schwartz, Scott, and others

Interests
  e.g., Strong-Campbell Vocational Interest Blank (SVIB)

Abilities
  e.g., multiple intelligences

Social Support and Attachment
  e.g., The Multidimensional Scale of Perceived Social Support
  e.g.., Adult Attachment Style Questionnaire

gated to yield conclusions about groups of people. They, of course, can be used ipsatively, to describe the psychological characteristics of an individual, but the cautious use of these descriptions is a point of discussion and departure in counseling. None is a strong diagnostic test, and none should be treated as if it were. Such prudence is appropriate for all psychological assessment, but it is worth emphasizing in the special case of positive psychology measures. The last thing that a client needs to believe about herself is that she is not kind or loving simply because an online test says so.

SPECIFIC TECHNIQUES

POSITIVE PSYCHOLOGISTS HAVE provided ample demonstrations of brief interventions that at least in the short term boost happiness, satisfaction, and fulfillment. In some cases, there is good evidence for their sustained effectiveness and their ability to alleviate depression (Seligman, Steen, Park, & Peterson, 2005). See Table 74.2 for some examples. Fuller descriptions of these and other interven-

TABLE 74.2 Positive Psychology Techniques and Interventions

Exercises to increase positive feelings
   e.g., performing acts of kindness
   e.g., savoring
   e.g., writing a gratitude letter

Exercises to decrease negative feelings
   e.g., turning one's head to see the positive

Exercises to increase life satisfaction
   e.g., counting one's blessings

Exercises to develop talents and strengths
   e.g., using talents and/or signature strengths of character in novel ways

Exercises to increase engagement
   e.g., finding a challenging hobby

Exercises to increase social connectedness
   e.g., being a good teammate
   e.g., active-constructive responding

Exercises to increase meaning and purpose
   e.g., performing secret good deeds
   e.g., writing one's own legacy
   e.g., working for a valued institution

Exercises to increase health and safety
   e.g., worrying about the right things

tions can be found in Linley and Joseph (2004), Peterson and Seligman (2004), and Peterson (2006).

Some caveats are in order if these techniques are used in the context of counseling. First, they are not therapies per se but simply exercises to be deployed as part of an overall treatment plan. The counselor must ascertain a client's readiness to change in the particular ways requested in the exercise. Second, none of these techniques is akin to a crash diet or an antibiotic. To the degree that they have lasting effects, it is because clients integrate them into their regular behavioral routines. Counting blessings for a week will likely make a person happier for that week, but only if the person becomes habitually grateful will there be a more enduring effect. Third, these exercises are typically presented as one-size-fits-all, but there is no reason to think that they are equally useful for all clients. Nothing is known about the match of an exercise with a client's particular presenting problems or with a client's age, gender, social class, or ethnicity. Fourth, all interventions run the risk of unintended harm, and while positive psychologists would like to believe that their techniques avoid iatrogenic effects, this assertion cannot be made with thorough confidence.

TOWARD POSITIVE TREATMENT

POSITIVE PSYCHOLOGY IS a perspective, and no single theory underlies this perspective. What positive psychology has instead are numerous micro-theories, and it is not clear that any of these have the power or scope to frame an entire therapy. As positive psychologists begin to propose full-blown approaches to psychotherapy consistent with the premises of positive psychology, they turn to existing therapies for the overall model of treatment. For example, the quality of life therapy described by Frisch (2006) is an instance of cognitive therapy. The positive psychotherapy sketched by Seligman, Rashid, and Parks (2006) draws heavily on the cognitive behavior approach. Joseph and Linley (2006) based their positive therapy on humanistic psychology. Other plausible frameworks might be interpersonal therapy or conjoint family therapy.

It is difficult to predict the future of psychological treatment from a positive perspective, but perhaps it will someday be seen as an instance of eclectic or integrative psychotherapy. Regardless, counselors using a positive approach can learn much from the decades of lessons that emerged from business-as-usual therapists who focused on the problems of their clients. Does positive treatment work? One cannot rely on testimonials from individual clients. What about its efficiency? Are benefits of positive treatment evident only in comparison to "no treatment," or does the positive approach represent value added to existing treatments? How robust are any effects, and how long do they last? Is positive treatment more effective in increasing strengths than in decreasing problems?

The major drawback of the popularity of positive psychology is precisely that it is popular, and the perspective has attracted many adherents enamored of the positive but not necessarily of the science of psychology that sets positive psychology apart from the positive thinking approach associated with Émile Coué, Norman Vincent Peale, and contemporary self-help gurus. Attaining the good life is difficult but not impossible, and a prudent application of ideas from positive psychology can help people live better.

REFERENCES

Frisch, M. B. (2006). *Quality of life therapy*. New York: Wiley.

Joseph, S., & Linley, P. A. (2006). *Positive therapy: A meta-theory for positive psychological practice*. East Sussex, UK: Routledge.

Linley, P. A., & Joseph, S. (Eds.). (2004). *Positive psychology in practice*. New York: Wiley.

Lopez, S. J., Magyar-Moe, J. L., Petersen, S. E., Ryder, J. A., Krieshok, T. S., O'Byrne, K. K., et al. (2006). Counseling psychology's focus on positive aspects of human functioning. *The Counseling Psychologist, 34,* 205–227.

Lopez, S. J., & Snyder, C. R. (Eds.). (2003). *Positive psychological assessment: A handbook of models and measures*. Washington, DC: American Psychological Association.

Ong, A. D., & van Dulmen, M. (Eds.). (2006). *Handbook of methods in positive psychology*. New York: Oxford University Press.

Peterson, C. (2006). *A primer in positive psychology*. New York: Oxford University Press.

Peterson, C., & Seligman, M. E. P. (2004). *Character strengths and virtues: A classification and handbook*. Washington, DC: American Psychological Association/New York: Oxford University Press.

Saleebey, D. (Ed.). (1992). *The strengths perspective in social work practice*. New York: Longman.

Seligman, M. E. P. (2002). *Authentic happiness*. New York: Free Press.

Seligman, M. E. P., & Csikszentmihalyi, M. (2000). Positive psychology: An introduction. *American Psychologist, 55,* 5–14.

Seligman, M. E. P., Rashid, T., & Parks, A. C. (2006). Positive psychotherapy. *American Psychologist, 61,* 774–788.

Seligman, M. E. P., Steen, T. A., Park, N., & Peterson, C. (2005). Positive psychology progress: Empirical validation of interventions. *American Psychologist, 60,* 410–421.

Snyder, C. R., & Lopez, S. (Eds.). (in press). *Handbook of positive psychology* (2nd ed.). New York: Oxford University Press.

Zimmerman, M., McGlinchey, J. B., Posternak, M. A., Friedman, M., Attiullah, N., & Boerescu, D. (2006). How should remission from depression be defined? The depressed patient's perspective. *American Journal of Psychiatry, 163,* 148–150.

75

Empathy Fatigue in the Counseling Profession

MARK A. STEBNICKI

I N TRADITIONAL NATIVE American philosophy, it is told that each time you heal someone you give away a piece of yourself. The journey to become a medicine man or woman requires an understanding that the healer at some point in time will become wounded and requires healing (Tafoya & Kouris, 2003). As in Native American culture, many counseling professionals in the West also encounter a wounded healer type of experience. I refer to this phenomenon as empathy fatigue. It results from a state of psychological, emotional, mental, physical, spiritual, and occupational exhaustion that occurs as the counselors' own wounds are continually revisited by their clients' life stories of chronic illness, disability, trauma, grief, and loss (Stebnicki, 1999, 2000, 2001, 2007, 2008).

Similar observations and measurements of counselor impairment and fatigue syndromes have been noted in the nursing, psychology, counseling, and mental health literature. For example, compassion fatigue, first introduced in the nursing literature by Joinson (1992) and then expanded by Figley (1995), Stamm (1995), and others in psychology, suggests that therapists who deal with survivors of extraordinarily stressful and traumatic events are more prone to compassion fatigue or a secondary traumatic stress (STS) type of reaction as a result of feeling compassion and empathy toward others' pain and suffering. McCann and Perlman (1989) refer to this experience as "vicarious traumatization" where the therapist becomes deeply emotionally affected by the client's traumatic stories. Consequently, the professional counselor experiences a special type of burnout (Maslach, 1982, 2003) where there is an organizational-environmental impact on the person who feels emotionally and physically exhausted, depleted, and has reached the point of depersonalization with their professional colleagues.

Many counselors spend a tremendous amount of time and energy acting in compassionate and empathic ways searching for the meaning of their client's mind, body, and spirit that has been lost to trauma, incest, addictions, and other stressors that prompt questions concerning the meaning of their lives. As a consequence, professional counselors become affected by the same persistent or transient physical, emotional, and psychological symptoms as their clients. Thus, empathy fatigue is a type of counselor impairment that affects the whole self: mind, body, and spirit. Identifying counselor impairment or fatigue syndromes requires the use of self-care practices to maintain competent and ethical practice in the counseling profession. This chapter provides a description of the empathy fatigue experience from a mind, body, and spiritual growth perspective. The chapter that follows offers a functional risk factor assessment as well as self-care resources for professional counselors who experience counselor impairments and professional fatigue syndromes such as empathy fatigue.

WHAT IS EMPATHY FATIGUE AND HOW IS IT SIMILAR TO OTHER COUNSELOR IMPAIRMENTS?

EMPATHY FATIGUE, AS opposed to other fatigue syndromes and counselor impairments (e.g., compassion fatigue, burnout, vicarious traumatization), is experienced by professional counselors who primarily use person-centered and empathy-focused interactions to build rapport with their clients so they can achieve a therapeutic working relationship. Throughout the history of the helping professions the most fundamental approach to helping others has been rooted in compassion and empathy. Empathy has been discussed in the counseling and psychology literature as a skill that can be both developed and learned if facilitated properly in therapeutic interactions (Barone et al., 2005). In fact, empathy has a rich history of being at the core of most humanistic theoretical orientations within counselor education and training programs. Accordingly, possessing the skills of empathy is a prerequisite for becoming a competent helper and is a person-centered approach that practitioners can facilitate to increase interpersonal effectiveness and enhance client outcomes (Corey & Corey, 2003; Egan, 1998; Ivey & Ivey, 1999; Truax & Carkhuff, 1967). The richness of using the skills of basic and advanced level empathy can build a strong client-counselor relationship. If facilitated competently by the therapist, empathy can (1) help increase client self-awareness, (2) be a motivation for personal growth and change, and (3) cultivate new ways of thinking, feeling, and acting to achieve optimal levels of mind, body, and spiritual wellness.

Carl Rogers (1980) talked passionately about empathy and empathic listening as a "way of being" with a client. However, there is an emotional and physical cost to entering the private perceptual world of the client because the counselor may be a "sponge" for their client's emotional and physical pain. The conscious and unconscious absorption of the client's emotional, physical, spiritual, and existential issues is a natural artifact of helping others at intense levels of service. This is because many counselors are in so-called high touch professions and are at the epicenter of their client's life stories. Many client stories contain themes of extraordinary stressful and traumatic events, pain and suffering, and result in client transference and negative countertransference of toxic energy during the session. Accordingly, there is a shadow side to facilitating empathic approaches with clients during counseling interactions. If the experience of empathy fatigue is not recognized by self and others then it can potentially lead to a deterioration of the counselor's resiliency or coping abilities.

Rogers (1980) appeared to have an understanding of counselor fatigue syndromes. He observed a significant need for therapists to rebalance their minds, bodies, and spirits after spending countless hours in psychotherapy sessions. As I have observed, counselors who work with routine professional practice issues may experience empathy fatigue also. This may include professionals who work with clients who have experienced loss of a loved one (i.e., grief, divorce, extramarital affairs), substance abuse (i.e., family, legal, career issues), career development issues (i.e., company downsizing, work-related job stress, career transitions), chronic health conditions (i.e., cancer, HIV/AIDS), and generalized anxiety, depression, and other general stress conditions.

This author hypothesizes that empathy fatigue may be different from other types of counselor impairment and fatigue syndromes. This is primarily because empathy fatigue (1) is viewed as a counselor impairment that can occur early on in one's career due to an interaction of variables that include, but are not limited to, personality traits, general coping resources, age and developmental related factors, opportunities to build resiliency, organizational and other environmental supports, and the interrelationship between the person's mind, body, and spiritual development; (2) many times goes unrecognized by the individual and the professional counseling setting or environment because of its subtle characteristics; (3) may be experienced as both an acute and cumulative type of emotional, physical, and spiritual stressor that does not follow a predictable linear path to total burnout or fatigue; and (4) is a highly individualized experience for most individuals, because the counselor's perception toward the client's story and life events differs depending upon the issues presented during session.

In view of this hypothesis, professional counselors who experience empathy fatigue appear to have a diminished capacity to listen and respond empathically to their client's stories that contain various themes of acute and cumulative psychosocial stress, not necessarily stories of acute and posttraumatic stress. Consequently, the professional counselor acquires feelings of grief, loss, detachment, anxiety, depression, and a type of professional burnout, in which he or she feels like his or her therapeutic interactions with others have very little meaning and purpose in the client's overall life.

A NEW LOOK AT COUNSELOR IMPAIRMENT AND FATIGUE SYNDROMES

HEALING THE MINDS, bodies, and spirits of professional counselors should be a collective responsibility among professional counseling associations, as well as counselor educators, clinical supervisors, and the counselor's work setting. One of the most troubling aspects of counselor impairment and fatigue syndromes is that counselor educators, supervisors, and professional counseling associations have been slow to prepare counselor trainees/supervisees for cultivating self-care approaches. We do a good job of preparing competent and ethical practitioners for diagnosing and treating a variety of mental health conditions and addressing other counseling related issues; however, the role and function of professional counselors have expanded significantly in the last 10 years. Today, many counselors provide mental health and disaster relief services to those involved in a multitude of extraordinary stressful and traumatic events (e.g., hurricanes, fires, floods, school shootings, workplace violence). Consequently, providing the mental health rescue to those at the epicenter of critical incidents profoundly affects the mind, body, and spirit of professional counselors.

Maintaining personal and professional wellness in one's career goes beyond acquiring continuing educational credits at conferences and workshops. Rather, some counselors will require a transformative personal experience to continue in their chosen profession. There appears to be some promise for addressing issues in counselor impairment and fatigue syndromes that have drawn the interest of some state and national professional counseling associations. For example, the American Counseling Association's (ACA) Taskforce on Counselor Wellness and Impairment (ACA, 2003) has recognized the importance of self-care approaches to increase counselor wellness. The ACA Web site (www. counseling.org) provides a variety of stress and compassion fatigue self-reporting instruments for the identification and prevention of counselor impairment and fatigue syndromes. It also offers resources for building capacity for occupational and career wellness.

It is essential to maintain well-qualified, competent, and ethical professionals to serve those who are challenged by significant life issues. Other professional organizations such as the American Medical Association (AMA), American Psychological Association (APA), and American Nurses Association (ANA) are also interested in decreasing professional impairment and fatigue syndromes. These professional associations have focused organizational efforts by optimizing the individual's professional growth and development in cultivating programs of self-awareness and self-care. Overall, counselor impairment and fatigue syndromes have a significant negative impact on the counselor's mental, physical, and spiritual functioning. If ignored or left unrecognized, some counselors may be practicing unethically, as they may be exhibiting characteristics of counselor impairment (e.g., substance abuse or other mental health issues).

THE EXPERIENCE OF EMPATHY FATIGUE FROM A MIND, BODY, AND SPIRITUAL PERSPECTIVE

CARL JUNG APPEARED to have an understanding of counselor fatigue syndromes as he observed the need for therapists to rebalance their mind, body, and spirit after spending countless hours in psychotherapy sessions with their clients. Jung was inspired by the belief that humans are spiritual beings, not just biological, instinctual, or behavioral organisms. He explored manifestations of the soul and the process of transforming the mind, body, and spirit into a greater awareness of the self to increase one's purpose in life. In Jung's view, regaining psychic equilibrium, soul-searching, and self-discovery appear to be paramount in maintaining one's therapeutic practice.

Client stories that have such themes as addictions, physical or sexual abuse, and psychological trauma can adversely affect the mind, body, and spirit of the counselor. Remembering emotions related to such painful or traumatic events and re-creating an internal "emotional scrapbook" can be extremely painful and difficult for clients as well as counselors. This is especially relevant for new professional counselors who have not had the opportunity to cultivate self-care strategies for professional wellness.

New studies on the mind–body connection report that the shared emotions and physiological arousal experienced between client and therapist can contribute to our knowledge of how empathic connections are developed during counseling sessions. For example, Marci, Ham, Moran, and Orr (2007) looked at 20 client–therapist pairs, with the client being treated for mood and anxiety disorders. The researchers specifically focused on the therapeutic relationships that were formed during psychotherapy sessions. They then took measures of the physiological reactions of both client and therapist and the client's perceived level of empathy as expressed by the therapist. They found that when high positive emotions and empathy were experienced by the client and therapist, then similar physiological responses were experienced as measured by electrical skin conductance recordings, heart rate, voice dynamics, and body movement.

It appears that a much stronger working alliance or social–emotional attachment is formed in therapy than once perceived. Because an empathetic connection forms between client and therapist, there appears to be a potential for some degree of emotional and physical exhaustion experienced by intense, cumulative, and regular therapeutic interactions.

Emotions and the Brain: The Neuroscience of Empathy Fatigue

In the study of emotions and the brain, it is hypothesized that there are discrete, basic, and universal emotions that persons react to on a mind, body, and spiritual dimension (Bar-On & Parker, 2000; Mayne & Bonanno, 2001). Despite that many individuals express universal emotions (e.g., anger, love, happiness, sadness) with varying levels of experience and intensity, Mayne and Ramsey (2001) indicate that this only constitutes a measure of personal experience and a self-report of emotional expression. From a purely dynamic physiological state, emotions involve different body systems and are measured much differently by neuroscientists than experimental psychologists. This is important to understand because our individual perception of critical events will determine how our parasympathetic and sympathetic nervous system is activated during times of an actual or anticipated stressful event. After prolonged periods of physiological stress such as seen by professionals who work with the traumatized, it is evident that chronic activation of the stress response has both a physiological and emotional cost. Consequently, professionals who work at such intense levels of service may experience anxiety and depressive disorders and may account for some aspects of the emotional and physical fatigue experienced by those who report counselor fatigue syndromes such as empathy fatigue.

Kabat-Zinn (1990; see Berger, 2006) indicates that empathy fatigue can be scientifically measured in the brain because there are specific neurological pathways to empathetic responses. The complexities of studying how emotions affect our mind, body, and spirit require studying such problems from a multidisciplinary perspective that includes the fields of psychology, neurology, immunology, and biology. The discipline of psychoneuroimmunolgy (PNI) has provided a model by which researchers can study emotions and the brain. The task of PNI researchers is a difficult one because as Sapolsky (1998) suggests, our emotions, particularly the stress response, have their own unique physiological arousal patterns of magnitude, frequency, and intensity. This is so, in part, because people differ in how they turn on their stress mechanism and other emotional responses in the brain. As Sapolsky (1998) notes, if we are constantly trying to mobilize energy, we never have the opportunity to store it, so we can use this source of energy for calm and relaxed states of consciousness. Accordingly, there is a physical and emotional cost to persistent sympathetic arousal because of the heavy secretion of glucocorticoids released in the body that are markers for depression and anxiety disorders.

Brothers (1989) points to the amygdale-cortical pathway in the brain as part of the key neural circuitry that underlies the emotions associated with the empathy response. The amygdale appears to be the specific structure of the brain that orchestrates the most intense electrical activation when reading, interpreting, or trying to understand the emotions of others. Over time, the counselor's inability to express a healthy and facilitative emotional response (such as empathy) based on the client's expression of such feelings as stress, grief, or trauma appears to have a bio-psycho-social-spiritual cost to the counselor. In other words, the chronic and cumulative activation of the emotional brain and habitual repression of emotions can compromise our immune system, which increases our resistance to infections, chronic illness, and diseases (Pert, Dreher, & Ruff, 2005; Sapolsky, 1998; Weil, 1995).

Despite that we have no control over our autonomic nervous system, we do have some degree of control over our voluntary nervous system such as observed during a biofeedback session. Thus, becoming attuned to things we do have control over in life is central to the care we can provide for ourselves and our clients.

EMPATHY FATIGUE AS THE WOUNDED SPIRIT

CLEARLY, THE SEARCH for personal meaning in one's chronic illness, disability, or traumatic experience is an existential and spiritual pursuit (Stebnicki, 2006). In many cultures, the most significant and meaningful questions relate to where we came from before birth and where we will transcend at the time of our death (Pedersen, 2000). The wounded healer searches for existential meaning in the significance of his or her chosen occupation as a professional helper. Such questions as *How could life and death, joy and suffering, love, self-acceptance, and healing exist all within the same day in the lives of my clients?* are disorienting and call on a divine source to acquire a deeper level of understanding.

Professionals who have experienced a wounded spirit should be open to questioning their own spiritual health so they can cope with their client's existential and spiritual experience of loss, grief, trauma, or extraordinary stressful life events. Professional counselors should not feel obligated to provide all the answers to knowing everything that God, our higher power, spirit guides, or the universe has to teach us. For some professionals, this ambiguity and parallel experience of spiritual confusion may reach beyond the range of ordinary human experiences. Thus, the counselor would likely benefit from the assistance of a spiritual or religious helper who can facilitate an understanding of such existential and/or spiritual questions.

Some authors (Pargament & Zinnbauer, 2000; Shafranske & Malony, 1996) have suggested that counselors have an ethical obligation to explore the spiritual aspects of their client's life because it is consistent with facilitating counseling approaches within a holistic-wellness and multicultural framework. Spiritual connectedness is a cultural attribute and can be a form of social support that empowers individuals with chronic illnesses and disabilities to cope with their environment (Harley, Stebnicki, & Rollins, 2000). Spirituality plays a prominent role in the lives of individuals from many different cultural and ethnic backgrounds. Thus, to work effectively with the client's spiritual identity and worldview, it has been suggested throughout the literature that counselor educators and supervisors need to intentionally prompt their supervisee to inquire about the client's spiritual health (Bishop, Avila-Juarbe, & Thumme, 2003; Cashwell & Young, 2004; Polanski, 2003; Stebnicki, 2006).

The fact that many counselors cannot ethically share their client's stories with anyone outside of the therapeutic environment or supervision session creates a kind of shroud of secrecy that many counselors take home with them. Consequently, the compassionate and empathic helper may go home at the end of the day and perhaps withdraw into a privileged communication frame of consciousness.

Multiple client stories of extraordinary stressful and traumatic events, as well as exposure to clients with chronic illness and life-threatening disabilities, many times place the professional helper at risk for feeling helpless and hopeless. So the question becomes who pays attention to, and takes care of, the wounded healer. Nouwen (1972) speaks to this type of counselor fatigue experience from his concept of the *wounded healer*. He suggests that paradoxically we withdraw into ourselves, thus creating a sacred space for no other person to enter. Miller (2003) suggests that from the wounded healer framework, as the counselor brings a compassionate spirit to the counseling relationship, the client's expectations of the counselor is that he or she does not have any psychological, emotional, or spiritual vulnerabilities. Thus, the counselor is seen as a role model for emotional and spiritual well-ness by the client who feels wounded. However, the counselor may not be dealing openly and honestly with the client if he or she has difficulties sharing or disclosing his or her own wounded soul alongside of the client (Miller & Baldwin, 1987).

Facilitating empathic approaches in the counseling relationship requires that we help our clients unfold the layers of their stress, grief, loss, or traumatic experiences by searching through their emotional scrapbooks. The search for personal meaning and purpose of our client's pain and suffering may contribute to our own spiritual fatigue experience. If counselors are mindful of this experience, and view this as an opportunity for nurturing personal growth and development, then they may create opportunities for resiliency so they can replenish their wounded spirits.

CONCLUSION

THE EXPERIENCE OF empathy fatigue is both similar and different from other types of counselor impairment or professional fatigue syndromes. Thus, it is hypothesized that the cumulative effects of multiple client sessions throughout the week may lead to a deterioration of the counselor's resiliency or coping abilities. Professional counselors who interact with clients who experience daily hassles and stressful life events may be at the same risk level as those professionals who assist those who are traumatized.

As the professional counselor engages in therapeutic interactions, this may predispose the counselor to experience an empathy fatigue reaction that ranges on a continuum of low, moderate, and high. However, there are multiple risk factors that should be considered and are identified in the Empathy Fatigue Risk-Factor Functional Assessment (Stebnicki, 2000) that will be discussed in Chapter 76.

Consequently, the cumulative effects of multiple client stories can result in the depletion of the professional counselor's empathic energies, resulting in empathy fatigue. Developing a clearer understanding of the risk factors associated with empathy fatigue is pivotal in developing self-care strategies for the professional counselor.

REFERENCES

American Counseling Association. (2003). *ACA Taskforce on Counselor Wellness and Impairment*. Retrieved March 3, 2006, from http://www.counseling.org/wellness_taskforce/index.htm

Bar-On, R., & Parker, J. D. (2000). *The handbook of emotional intelligence: Theory, development, assessment, and application at home, school, and in the workplace*. San Francisco: Jossey-Bass.

Barone, D. F., Hutchings, P. S., Kimmel, H. J., Traub, H. L., Cooper, J. T., & Marshal, C. M. (2005). Increasing empathetic accuracy through practice and feedback in a clinical interviewing course. *Journal of Social and Clinical Psychology, 24*(2), 156–171.

Berger, R. M. (2006). Prayer: It does a body good. *Sojourners Magazine, 35*(2), 17.

Bishop, D. R., Avila-Juarbe, E., & Thumme, B. (2003). Recognizing spirituality as an important factor in counselor supervision. *Counseling and Values, 48*(1), 34–46.

Brothers, L. (1989). A biological perspective on empathy. *American Journal of Psychiatry, 146*(1), 1–16.

Cashwell, C. S., & Young, J. S. (2004). Spirituality in counselor training: A content analysis of syllabi from introductory spirituality courses. *Counseling and Values, 48*(2), 96–109.

Corey, M. S., & Corey, G. (2003). *Becoming a helper* (4th ed.). Pacific Grove, CA: Wadsworth Group/Brooks/Cole.

Egan, G. (1998). *The skilled helper: A problem-management approach to helping* (6th ed.). Pacific Grove, CA: Brooks/Cole.

Figley, C. R. (1995). *Compassion fatigue: Coping with secondary traumatic stress disorder in those who treat the traumatized*. Bristol, PA: Brunner/Mazel.

Harley, D. A., Stebnicki, M. A., & Rollins, C. W. (2000). Applying empowerment evaluation as a tool for self-improvement and community development with culturally diverse populations. *Journal of Community Development Society, 31*(2), 348–364.

Ivey, A. E., & Ivey, M. B. (1999). *Intentional intervention and counseling: Facilitating client development in a multicultural society*. Pacific Grove, CA: Brooks/Cole.

Joinson, C. (1992). Coping with compassion fatigue. *Nursing, 22*(4), 116–122.

Kabat-Zinn, J. (1990). *Full catastrophe living: Using the wisdom of your body and mind to face stress, pain, and illness*. New York: Dell.

Marci, C., Ham, J., Moran, E., & Orr, S. (2007). Physiologic correlates of perceived therapist empathy and social-emotional process during psychotherapy. *Journal of Nervous and Mental Disorders, 195*, 103–111.

Maslach, C. (1982). *The burnout: The cost of caring*. Englewood Cliffs, NJ: Prentice-Hall.

Maslach, C. (2003). *Burnout: The cost of caring*. Cambridge, MA: Malor Books.

Mayne, T. J., & Bonanno, G. A. (2001). *Emotions: Current issues and future directions*. New York: Guilford Press.

Mayne, T. J., & Ramsey, J. (2001). The structure of emotion: A nonlinear dynamic systems approach. In T. J. Mayne and G. A. Bonanno (Eds.), *Emotions: Current issues and future directions* (pp. 1–37). New York: Guilford Press.

McCann, L. & Perlman, L. A. (1989). Vicarious traumatization: A framework for understanding the psychological effects of working with victims. *Journal of Traumatic Stress, 3*(1), 131–149.

Miller, G. (2003). *Incorporating spirituality in counseling and psychotherapy: Theory and technique*. Hoboken, NJ: Wiley.

Miller, G. D., & Baldwin, D. C. (1987). Implications of the wounded-healer paradigm for the use of the self in therapy. In M. Baldwin & V. Satir (Eds.), *The use of self in therapy* (pp. 130–151). New York: Haworth Press.

Nouwen, H. J. M. (1972). *The wounded healer*. New York: An Image Book/Doubleday.

Pargament, K. L., & Zinnbauer, B. J. (2000). Working with the sacred: Four approaches to religious and spiritual issues in counseling. *Journal of Counseling and Development, 78*, 162–171.

Pedersen, P. (2000). *A handbook for developing multicultural awareness* (3rd ed.). Alexandria, VA: American Counseling Association.

Pert, C. B., Dreher, H. E., & Ruff, M. R. (2005). The psychosomatic network: Foundations of mind-body medicine. In M. Schlitz, T. Amorok, & M. Micozzi (Eds.), *Consciousness and healing: Integral approaches to mind-body medicine* (pp. 61–78). St. Louis, MO: Elsevier, Churchill, & Livingstone.

Polanski, P. J. (2003). Spirituality and supervision. *Counseling and Values, 47*(2), 131–141.

Rogers, C. R. (1980). *A way of being*. Boston: Houghton Mifflin.

Sapolsky, R. M. (1998). *Why zebras don't get ulcers: An updated guide to stress, stress-related diseases, and coping*. New York: W. H. Freeman.

Shafranske, E. P., & Malony, H. N. (1996). Religion and the clinical practice of psychology: The case for inclusion. In E. P. Shafranske (Ed.), *Religion and the clinical practice of psychology*. Washington, DC: American Psychological Association.

Stamm, B. H. (1995). *Compassion fatigue: Coping with secondary traumatic stress disorder in those who treat the traumatized*. New York: Brunner-Routledge.

Stebnicki, M. A. (1999, April). *Grief reactions among rehabilitation professionals: Dealing effectively with empathy fatigue.* Presentation made at the NRCA/ ARCA Alliance Annual Training Conference, Dallas, TX.

Stebnicki, M. A. (2000). Stress and grief reactions among rehabilitation professionals: Dealing effectively with empathy fatigue. *Journal of Rehabilitation, 6*(1), 23–29.

Stebnicki, M. A. (2001). Psychosocial response to extraordinary stressful and traumatic life events: Principles and practices for rehabilitation counselors. *New Directions in Rehabilitation, 12*(6), 57–71.

Stebnicki, M. A. (2006). Integrating spirituality in rehabilitation counselor supervision. *Rehabilitation Education, 20*(2), 137–159.

Stebnicki, M. A. (2007). Empathy fatigue: Healing the mind, body, and spirit of professional counselors. *Journal of Psychiatric Rehabilitation, 10*(4), 317–338.

Stebnicki, M. A. (2008). *Empathy fatigue: Healing the mind, body, and spirit of professional counselors.* New York: Springer.

TaFoya, T., & Kouris, N. (2003). Dancing the circle: Native American concepts of healing. In S. G. Mijares (Ed.), *Modern psychology and ancient wisdom: Psychological healing practices from the world's religious traditions* (pp. 125–146). New York: Haworth Integrative Healing Press.

Truax, C. B., & Carkhuff, R. R. (1967). *Towards effective counseling and psychotherapy.* Chicago: Aldine.

Weil, A. (1995). *Spontaneous healing.* New York: Ballantine.

76

Empathy Fatigue: Assessing Risk Factors and Cultivating Self-Care

MARK A. STEBNICKI

EMPATHY FATIGUE RESULTS from a state of mental, emotional, social, physical, spiritual, and occupational exhaustion that occurs as the counselor's own wounds are continually revisited by his or her clients' life stories of chronic illness, disability, trauma, grief, loss, and extraordinary stressful events (Stebnicki, 2008). It is of paramount importance that counselor educators, supervisors, and concerned others recognize this negative shift within the professional counselor's mind, body, and spirit that may signal an empathy fatigue experience. This chapter offers (1) areas to consider in a risk factor assessment of empathy fatigue, (2) a recently developed tool (Global Assessment of Empathy Fatigue [GAEF]) that may be used for screening and identifying professionals that may be experiencing this unique counselor fatigue syndrome, and (3) resources for self-care of empathy fatigue.

There is a plethora of valid, reliable, and even home-grown self-report instruments in the counseling and psychology literature that relate to one's mental health and well-being. Each has its own focus as it relates to one's personal, emotional, physical, and spiritual wellness. Most of the assessments that relate to counselor impairment and fatigue syndromes are subjective measures of the professional's experience of acute and secondary traumatic stress (i.e., compassion fatigue) or cumulative stress (i.e., burnout). A content analysis of these self-report items generally includes a subjective rating of one's mental, emotional, and physical exhaustion or fatigue. Self-care assessment and screening instruments rarely if ever address the level of one's spiritual fatigue such as theorized in the GAEF listed at the end of this chapter.

Generally, the core elements or content in self-care assessments as it relates to counselor impairments typically evaluate one's (1) self-awareness (awareness of significant factors that hinder personal growth and development as a counselor), (2) self-regulation (a conscious and unconscious process of decreasing physical, emotional, cognitive, and behavioral impulses for the intent of maintaining balance in the mind, body and spirit), and (3) achieving balance (using holistic or wellness strategies for the purpose of reconnecting to the self in relation to one's internal and external environment) (Baker, 2003). Currently, there are no self-care assessments that measure the experience of empathy fatigue as it relates to one's mind, body, and spiritual development. This author offers the GAEF as a global measure of functioning with the experience of empathy fatigue. Further development of an empathy fatigue measure is underway at the time of this writing and will be presented in future publications.

THE FATIGUE EXPERIENCE

LONGEVITY FOR MAINTAINING competent and ethical practice can be quite a challenge for professional counselors who work in intense person-centered environments. Many counselors, especially those just entering the profession, *feel fatigued* and may have a sense that there is something physiologically wrong with them. They may also attribute their sense of fatigue to specific emotional, behavioral, and cognitive characteristics as it relates to their general feeling of wellness. However, some researchers report *fatigue* primarily as a physiological experience with less emphasis on the psychological or emotional component. Yet, mental or emotional fatigue can be equally debilitating and reflects an important variable in measuring correlates of empathy fatigue. Accordingly, mental or emotional fatigue can reduce the individual's psychological capacity and competence for the mental and emotional aspects of his or her job, thereby decreasing his or her capacity for expressing empathy.

Measuring the construct of empathy fatigue requires both qualitative and quantitative measures and requires using various raters in the professional counselor's environment (e.g., clinical supervisor, clients, colleagues). It requires viewing this special type of fatigue syndrome from a biopsychosocial and spiritual dimension to gain a wider perspective of the person's experience. The importance of measuring the degree and level of empathy fatigue is to develop a screening or functional assessment tool to determine the professional's risk factors that may lead to counselor impairment and fatigue. Ultimately, the true focus of developing a screening or assessment tool for empathy fatigue is for professional counselors to begin cultivating self-care practices.

There are multiple variables that coexist on the empathy fatigue continuum that theoretically range from low, moderate, to high. Qualitative measures of the person's experience of empathy fatigue can be assessed in several areas that include, but are not limited to (1) the counselor's developmental level of competence and functioning, (2) whether the precipitating event of fatigue has triggered an acute response, (3) the cumulative nature of a particular stressor as it relates to the individual, (4) the counselor's previous coping abilities, or adaptive-maladaptive behaviors, and (5) the counselor's previous exposure to critical incidents. To begin the self-assessment process, consider asking the following questions as it relates to your experience of empathy fatigue:

- How do I experience the intensity of my client's interpersonal issues of extraordinary stress, loss, grief, life transition/adjustment, and mental health functioning?
- What things have I discovered about myself in regard to working with clients who have life adjustment issues, daily hassles, or stress?
- Which life areas of my own have I been challenged with as I hear my client's life stories?
- What are some specific coping skills or approaches that I have used, or can use in the future to keep me balanced in my mind, body, and spirit?
- What are some things I learned about my coping abilities and resiliency traits for working in my chosen profession?
- What specific resources have helped me get through adversity in my past?
- What sense, purpose, or meaning have I found as a result of my empathy fatigue experience?
- What advice could I give to my colleagues about dealing with empathy fatigue?

Measuring the empathy fatigue experience requires openness to the idea that impaired professionals experience much more than a negative shift in their physical, emotional, psychological, cognitive, and spiritual well-being. Rather, the professional may be at risk for substance abuse and other mental health conditions that could impair his or her perceptions and ability to work competently and ethically with clients.

EMPATHY FATIGUE DOMAINS FOR CONSIDERATION

STEBNICKI (2000) OFFERS a functional risk-factor assessment for empathy fatigue that may assist professional counselors, counselor educators, and supervisors to identify and recognize risk factors. The items in this particular functional assessment were developed from a meta-analysis of similar counselor impairments and fatigue conditions as noted in the literature (e.g., burnout, compassion fatigue, secondary traumatic stress, depression, substance abuse, other mental health conditions). In the current development of an empathy fatigue measure, consideration will be given to content items that address the spiritual dimension. There is a constellation of areas to consider within the experience of empathy fatigue that includes, but is not limited to, the professional's:

1. *Current and Preexisting Personality Traits and States:* type A personality traits, unrealistic or high expectations by the person, need for recognition, pattern of cynicism.
2. *History of Emotional or Psychiatric Problems:* underlying mental health issues or behaviors that may interfere with the counselor's competency, direct or indirect exposure to critical incidents, lethality issues or harm to self and others.
3. *Maladaptive Coping Behaviors:* patterns of alcohol or substance abuse, increased use of tobacco, caffeine, food.
4. *Age and Experience-Related Factors:* younger professionals new to counseling versus older professionals' coping abilities, experience in working with different types of clients/consumers, experience in crisis response.
5. *Organizational and System Dynamics at the Counselor's Place of Work:* organization or system is insensitive to or unappreciative of emotional needs of counselor, organization or system's openness to trying new approaches.
6. *Specific Job Duties of Counselor in Which the Counselor Is Employed:* direct service versus supervisory, caseload size, work overly demanding, time-consuming.

7. *Unique Sociocultural Attributes:* values, beliefs, cultural identity that may be different from that of the organization/employer.
8. *Response to Handling Past Critical and Other Stressful Life Events:* level of exposure to trauma or secondary traumatic stress (STS) and counselor's ability to cope, identification of any counselor isolation, detachment, or dissociative issues.
9. *Level of Support and Resources:* individual, group, or family support, ability to seek out assistance.
10. *Spirituality:* counselor questioning the meaning and purpose of life, occupation, spiritual and/or religious beliefs, anger toward God or religious affiliation, any spiritual emergencies.

Generally, there are multiple risk factors in empathy fatigue that complicate one's competence and ethics, personal and professional relationships, and hinder one's capacity for personal coping and resiliency. Thus, consideration must be given to assessing empathy fatigue from a holistic perspective. Developing domains before scale items are essential in the scale development process. Other analysis and statistical procedures will also assist the researcher in the design process. The following domains are suggested by which to measure the construct of empathy fatigue:

- *Individual Traits:* Current and preexisting personality traits, any history of emotional or psychiatric problems, maladaptive coping behaviors.
- *Family:* Level of support and resources, family history of poor coping abilities, lack of clear expectations and rules for occupation or career.
- *Sociocultural:* Worldview, personal cultural identity, choice of occupation, family and extended family members, coping resources, age, gender, race, ethnicity, disability.
- *Developmental Level:* Experience level of counselor: practicum, internship, postgraduate, or expert.
- *Occupational Setting:* Organizational and system dynamics, setting where professional is employed, specific job duties, responsibilities, and position within the organization.
- *Physical Attributes:* Medical–physical status, chronic illness, disability, health status, nutritional intakes, and lifestyle factors related to health.
- *Cognitive Behavioral:* Dysfunctional thought patterns, ability to motivate oneself, flexibility in problem-solving tasks.
- *Religious–Spiritual:* Connection to higher power, God, spirit helpers, patterns of religious practices in terms of rituals, ceremonies.

GLOBAL ASSESSMENT OF FUNCTIONING IN THE THEORETICAL MEASUREMENT OF EMPATHY FATIGUE

THE GLOBAL ASSESSMENT of Empathy Fatigue (GAEF) rating scale is a theoretical measure of the holistic experience of empathy fatigue (see Table 76.1). The GAEF is categorized according to five different levels of functioning. Level V indicates the highest level and Level I the lowest level of the hypothetical construct of empathy fatigue. It is hypothesized that professional helpers may experience and project this felt-sense of empathy fatigue in seven distinct content areas that are contained within each of the five levels: (1) cognitively, (2) behaviorally, (3) spiritually, (4) process/counseling skills, (5) emotionally, (6) physically, and (7) occupationally. Table 76.1 delineates each of these areas that may be observed by self and others in the professional helper's environment. The theoretical constructs involved in measuring this type of counselor impairment are currently being researched. As the GAEF is in its theoretical stage of development, the construct of empathy fatigue is differentiated theoretically from other counselor impairment and fatigue syndromes. There is no empirical evidence as of yet to report, however.

The intent and purpose of the GAEF in its early stage of development is to provide a means of viewing the overall level of functioning as the professional helper experiences empathy fatigue. The content contained within each of the five levels of functioning is based on a comprehensive review of the counselor impairment and fatigue literature in counseling, psychology, mental health, as well as biopsychosocial research in the fields of nursing and medicine (see Stebnicki, 2008). The GAEF rating scale was also guided by the present author's clinical experiences.

Counselor impairments appear to involve a constellation of states, traits, behaviors, and other factors that encompass the person's experience of working with clients that have a diversity of issues ranging from daily hassles, life adjustment issues, to extraordinary stressful and traumatic events. It is difficult to determine universal traits or states of counselor impairment because each professional experiences and perceives his or her clients' general levels of stress differently. It is much like the difficulties in studying stressful life events. Overall, it is hypothesized that there are both conscious and unconscious factors that relate to the professional counselor's experience of stress and fatigue. Further, the frequency, intensity, level of intrusion, and avoidance of critical issues are considered to be both acute and cumulative in nature. Thus, some counselors may perceive more relevance of certain characteristics within each of the content areas in the GAEF than

TABLE 76.1 Global Assessment of Empathy Fatigue Rating Scale (GAEF)

	Level V	Level IV	Level III	Level II	Level I
Cognitive	❖ Diminished concentration ❖ Preoccupied ❖ Disorganized thoughts ❖ Detachment from client	❖ Diminished concentration ❖ Preoccupied ❖ Slightly disorganized thoughts ❖ Detachment ❖ Possible irrational thinking	❖ Exhibit some diminished concentration ❖ Somewhat preoccupied ❖ Thought organization loose ❖ Fair focus on therapeutic process ❖ Quiet attending of counselor to internal thoughts and feelings ❖ Having an "off day"	❖ Slight problems in concentration ❖ Occasionally preoccupied ❖ Need to continually refocus ❖ Good focus on therapeutic process ❖ Some response to internal thoughts and feelings ❖ Thoughts of hopefulness	❖ Slight problems in concentration and thought organization ❖ More preoccupied than usual ❖ Responding to internal thoughts and feelings more than usual, but therapeutic process good
Behavioral	❖ Impatience ❖ Irritability ❖ Aggression	❖ Impatient ❖ Irritable ❖ Competitive	❖ Exhibit signs of restlessness or impatience ❖ Slightly inattentive eye contact ❖ Slightly strained vocal tone and pace of speech	❖ Physical signs of being restless or impatient, but controls behavior ❖ Eye contact good ❖ Occasionally strained vocal quality and pace of speech	❖ Exhibit physical signs of restlessness or impatience, but controls behavior ❖ Eye contact good ❖ Vocal quality and pace of speech good, but sometimes strained

(continued)

TABLE 76.1 *(Continued)*

	Level V	Level IV	Level III	Level II	Level I
	⬩ Cynical with client ⬩ Hypervigilance ⬩ Poor eye contact ⬩ Strained, erratic, slow, or fast-paced speech	⬩ Very cautious ⬩ Eye contact fair ⬩ Somewhat strained, erratic, slow, or fast-paced speech ⬩ Somewhat cynical with clients			
Spiritual	⬩ Detached from spiritual support ⬩ Lack meaning and purpose in faith or spiritual beliefs ⬩ Communication of these deficits	⬩ Lack some meaning and purpose with regard to faith or spiritual beliefs ⬩ Some detachment of spiritual support ⬩ Communication of lack of meaning and purpose spiritually	⬩ Confusion regarding meaning and purpose with regard to faith or spiritual beliefs ⬩ Separation from spiritual support	⬩ Sense of awareness of refocusing on meaning and purpose with regard to faith or spiritual beliefs ⬩ Attempts to remain connected spiritually ⬩ Makes attempts to become reconnected to spiritual support	⬩ Sense of connectedness to faith restored after self-reassurance ⬩ Attempts to become reconnected to spiritual support
Process Skills	⬩ Lack of rapport with client ⬩ Strained working alliance	⬩ Rapport difficult to establish ⬩ No working alliance	⬩ Longer time to establish rapport ⬩ Working alliance achieved more slowly	⬩ Working alliance takes longer to achieve but remains stable ⬩ Empathic response more genuine, deeper, more frequent	⬩ Rapport takes slightly longer to establish ⬩ Working alliance takes somewhat longer to achieve, but work with client remains intact and stable

❖ Nonexistent attending and listening	❖ Poor attending and listening	❖ Listening and attending to clients fair to good	❖ Session goes beyond data gathering	❖ Attending and listening is appropriate
❖ No genuine empathetic responses	❖ Gather information in session vs. processing client story	❖ Empathetic responses more genuine	❖ Nonverbal incongruencies in session	❖ Integration of client content, experience, and affect better
❖ Resistant	❖ Superficial empathic responses	❖ Session involves gathering basic information	❖ Avoids dealing with countertransference	❖ Few missed therapeutic opportunities
❖ Apprehensive	❖ Some degree of countertransference	❖ Some missed opportunities in therapeutic interactions	❖ Uses some open-ended questioning, solution-focused probes, or brainstorming techniques	❖ Empathic responses somewhat deeper
❖ Hypersensitive	❖ Little use of open-ended questioning	❖ Responses have only basic empathy	❖ Rapport takes longer to establish, but eventually is good	❖ Somewhat hesitant to explore new areas of client support and resources
❖ High degree of counter-transference	❖ Little use of solution-focused probes	❖ Somewhat resistant or apprehensive	❖ Working alliance takes longer to achieve	❖ Some nonverbal incongruencies
❖ Lack of open-ended questioning	❖ Little use of brainstorming techniques with clients	❖ Little nonverbal interest during session	❖ Ongoing therapeutic work with client remains intact and stable	❖ Increased interest in understanding countertransference
❖ Lack of solution-focused probes	❖ Somewhat resistant or apprehensive during session	❖ Some degree of countertransference	❖ Attending and listening is good	❖ Open-ended questioning, solution-focused probes, and brainstorming techniques used
❖ Diminished use of brainstorming techniques	❖ Show little nonverbal interest during testing	❖ Little use of open-ended questioning		
❖ Basic information gathering sessions vs. processing client story		❖ Little use of solution-focused probes		
❖ Misses opportunities to integrate client content, experience, and affect		❖ Little use of brainstorming techniques		

(continued)

TABLE 76.1 *(Continued)*

	Level V	Level IV	Level III	Level II	Level I
Emotional	• Diminished affective state • Moodiness • Sadness • Tearfulness • Negative • Pessimistic • Clear high and low emotions • Depleted • Exhausted	• Somewhat diminished affective state • Moodiness • Slight mood swings • Moderate level of sadness • Emotionally fatigued • Exhausted • Negative • Pessimistic	• Affective state fair • Slight moodiness • Dysthymic • Appears emotionally tired • Negative • Pessimistic	• Affective state good • Sense of dysthymic mood • Slightly emotionally tired • Feeling negative or pessimistic	• Affective state could be better • Sense of a slightly "down" mood • Somewhat emotionally tired • Slightly negative • Pessimistic, but initiates self-correction
Physical	• Shallow breathing • Sweating • Fatigue • Discomfort while sitting	• Shallow breathing • Slight sweating • Fatigue • Facial grimacing	• Exhibit tiredness • Sighs of frustration with breath • Facial grimacing • Lack of appetite	• Exhibits slight tiredness but takes steps to avoid fatigue • Occasional signs of frustration • Uses internal dialogue to relax • Some discomfort while sitting	• Slight tiredness • Takes steps to avoid fatigue • Occasional sighs of frustration • Uses internal dialogue to relax

	(Severe)	(Moderate-Severe)	(Moderate)	(Mild-Moderate)	(Mild)
	❖ Dizziness ❖ Nausea ❖ Disturbance in visual acuity ❖ Facial grimace of pain ❖ Muscle tremors or twitches ❖ Severe headache	❖ Feelings of wooziness ❖ Lack of appetite due to upset stomach ❖ Occasional muscle tremors or twitches ❖ Moderate degree of headache ❖ Disturbance in visual acuity	❖ Occasional muscle twitches ❖ Slight sense of headache ❖ Dry eyes	❖ Appetite and eating habits somewhat irregular ❖ Muscles slightly tense ❖ Needs constant reminder to rebalance physical wellness	❖ Appetite and eating habits somewhat irregular ❖ Muscles feel slightly tense ❖ Constant reminder to rebalance wellness
Occupational	❖ Missing at least one day of work per week ❖ Cancelling sessions ❖ Not showing up for sessions ❖ Avoids meetings ❖ Avoids colleague at work ❖ Leaves work early every day ❖ Sick or cynical sense of humor ❖ Poor coping skills ❖ Shows little resiliency ❖ Difficulty separating professional and personal life	❖ Missing 2–3 days of work per month ❖ Rescheduling client appointments ❖ Avoids meetings ❖ Avoids colleagues at work ❖ Leaves work early on average ❖ Consistently cuts sessions short ❖ Exhibits cynical sense of humor ❖ Difficulties separating professional and personal life ❖ Struggling ❖ Exhibiting decreased coping abilities and resiliency	❖ Missing 1–2 days of work per month ❖ Some avoidance of starting session on time ❖ Hope for client "no shows" ❖ Cuts session shorter than usual ❖ Makes excuses to try and leave meetings and work early ❖ Superficial contact with colleagues at work ❖ Exhibits inappropriate sense of humor ❖ Some difficulties separating professional and personal life ❖ Some difficulties with coping abilities and resiliency	❖ May feel the need to take off 1–2 days of work per month ❖ Has thoughts of client "no shows" ❖ Occasionally makes excuses for leaving meetings early ❖ Minimal contact with colleges at work ❖ Has difficulties transitioning to social self ❖ Some difficulties separating professional and personal life ❖ Better coping abilities and resiliencies	❖ May feel the need to take off 1–2 days of work per month ❖ Thoughts of client "no shows" ❖ Conducts sessions on time and for usual duration ❖ Will make excuses for leaving meetings early ❖ Contact with colleagues less than usual ❖ Exhibits usual sense of humor ❖ Difficulties transitioning to social self ❖ Some difficulties separating professional and personal life ❖ Better coping skills and resiliency

other areas. The theoretical continuum ranging from Level V (most impaired) to Level I (least impaired), it is hoped, can provide an anchor or benchmark for the optimal level of functioning for professional helpers within each of the content domains.

USE OF DIFFERENT RATERS

THE GAEF SHOULD be used to rate the professional helper's current level of functioning. Because individual behaviors, states, and traits are often dependent upon the environment in which they are observed, observations should be documented based on multiple raters as listed below. A time sampling method should be used because the individual may differ in his or her experience of empathy fatigue with regard to events that take place at different times throughout the day (e.g., morning, afternoons, evenings, weekends, before client sessions, after client sessions, every other day). Persons considering rating themselves and/or others using the GAEF should be open to, and understand, the limitations and bias that are found in other subjective ratings of experiences such as mood, affect, personality, stress, attitude, motivation, level of satisfaction, and job burnout, as well as measures of spiritual well-being.

- *Self-Ratings by the Professional:* The individual himself or herself may use the GAEF as a self-report measure.
- *Ratings by the Professional's Colleagues:* The professional may request the involvement of his or her clinical supervisor, peer mentor, or another professionals to rate his or her observations independently on the GAEF measure.
- *Ratings by Clients/Consumers:* Ratings may be carried out according to a well-designed scheme within the work environment that uses interrater agreement by the therapist's client/consumer and/or a triad of raters (i.e., client, therapist, and independent observer).
- *Ratings by Independent Observers Outside the Work Environment:* The therapist may request ratings by close professional colleagues.
- *Ratings by Another Objective Individual:* The professional may request ratings by others (i.e., personal therapists) who are closely committed to the professional's personal goals of self-care and personal growth.

As the rater(s) view the GAEF rating scale as shown in Table 76.1, they should rate the level of empathy fatigue experienced primarily within the last 2 weeks. Although the professional helper may not relate with all characteristics within each level, the therapist should choose the attributes that he or she identifies with more so than not. Also, the rater(s) may consider using the GAEF Levels (V, IV, III, II, & I) for each of the seven content areas and deriving a rating (i.e., Level V in Cognitive Behavioral; Level III in Spiritual, Physical).

CULTIVATING COUNSELOR RESILIENCY

A CONSISTENT FINDING IN resiliency psychology research suggests that persons' attitudes and beliefs play a key role in the degree of resiliency that is exhibited or expressed. Resilient professionals almost always appear to posses a higher degree of internal locus of control, are inwardly directed, self-motivated, and thrive despite adverse conditions. Anecdotal evidence from professional helpers who have bounced back from adversity in their lives such as substance addiction, divorce, loss of a loved one, career transition, or traumatic stress have chosen to live in an optimal state of mental and physical well-being. They have incorporated the following principles, some of which are universal, in cultivating a resilient mind, body, and spirit:

Making a Choice. Professional helpers make a thinking, feeling, and behavioral choice on a daily basis when they must deal with client adversity. At the end of the day, counselors can choose to vent with their colleagues (and be a good listener for others) and not take home all their client's stories of adversity. If they take on this stress (consciously or unconsciously) this may already be added to their own wounded soul. Thus, the alternative would be to choose more healthy thoughts and emotions. The act of choosing a healthier outlook basically is a choice to take responsibility for one's own thoughts and emotions. There will always be a professional responsibility of helping another person in a compassionate and empathic way. However, resilient professionals know how to manage client adversity throughout their work, home, social, and interpersonal lives. Thus, not moving forward into one's own program of personal wellness would be self-defeating. The alternative would inevitably be bleak by constantly ruminating over the client's adversity at the end of the day. Thus, making a choice to change one's stream of thoughts and emotions about a client's adversity can be very empowering for some therapists. Negative and destructive thought patterns must be replaced with a plan of personal self-care and wellness. This must be reinforced and supported by colleagues and others in the counselor's environment to be successful. Accordingly, professional counselors need to create opportunities to help cultivate personal wellness and self-care approaches.

Positive Thinking. The power of positive thinking is about believing in yourself, having faith in your abilities, and having a high level of confidence that you can effect a positive outcome with your clients. As counselors struggle with their own as well as their client's issues, it is easier for therapists to see the barriers and obstacles to living from a positive frame of reference. The counselor may have many negative recurring thoughts about the client's life in general. However, this can turn into a self-fulfilling prophecy. Professional counselors need to practice positive redirection in their thinking so that it can become a routine and intentional way of living.

Taking Self-Responsibility. Shifting blame to others does not provide an opportunity for the therapist to develop resiliency behaviors (e.g., "My clients drive me crazy sometimes by really pushing my buttons; if they think that they have problems, they should have seen the client from my previous session"). Metaphorically, "when you point a finger at someone else, there are four fingers pointing back at you." Taking responsibility is a challenge for many counselors despite that we advocate the same with our clients. Many professionals were never taught how to do this. For example, some clients may be in denial of their son or daughter's substance abuse behaviors and may be enabling the adolescent. The consequences of the adolescent's bad choices may be hindered by the therapist who has taken on all the emotional responsibility, or perhaps identifying with the adolescent's parent. Taking self-responsibility is learned behavior that can generalize to other areas of the therapist's life. We all need to learn how to model self-responsibility and give up some control to the client. Allowing our clients to take safe risks and fail can be very therapeutic at times. It can build resiliency and promote healthy choices. Meanwhile, we may learn how our clients can live without our assistance. Overall, we should be internally responsible for our own thoughts, emotions, and actions and learn how to build resiliency traits.

Self-Motivation. Resilient individuals find their own unique style of internal motivation with school, work, home, socially, emotionally, and in other ways. Persons who have bounced back and pulled through adverse critical incidents demonstrate to others that they know how to achieve optimal and realistic control in their lives. These types of professional helpers tend to have an increased level of emotional, physical, and spiritual well-being. They are persistent with the tasks they take on and have an innate sense for knowing how to achieve their life goals. Many professionals have had the opportunity to observe healthy role models in their environment. They were fortunate to have a colleague, clinical supervisor, life coach, teacher, religious or spiritual leader, or others who have cared about them to help them overcome the more difficult challenges in their lives.

CHOOSING HEALTHY EMOTIONS

THE INTENTIONAL AND conscious use of empathy during client–counselor sessions appears to be integral to the helper's ability to establish a therapeutic relationship with the client so that they may achieve an optimal working alliance. However, there is a cost to having to be empathically available to clients all week that has cumulative effects on the mind, body, and spirit of professional counselors. To achieve an optimal level of self-care we should recognize that it is essential to approach our profession in an emotionally healthy, responsible, and effective way. The following five elements are offered as a way to build counselor resiliency:

1. Realize that your experiences, thoughts, and feelings are all interconnected, which can affect you physically, emotionally, cognitively, and spiritually. Unhealthy thoughts and emotions may hinder your spiritual growth. Likewise, life without an existential or spiritual meaning can hinder growth and development of your thoughts and emotions. As we have learned from the collective wisdom of various indigenous groups of people and belief systems throughout the centuries, achieving a balance between the mind, body, and spirit will offer us harmony.

2. All thoughts, feelings, and emotions occur naturally during therapeutic interactions. It is important to be aware of how you express your thoughts and feelings to others and how these unfold in your own life. How you perceive various thoughts, feelings, and client issues may determine how you integrate such material into your mind, body, and spirit. The wealth of your being depends on an honest and direct relationship of your mind, body, and spiritual self.

3. It is okay to have negative, hurtful, or painful thoughts or feelings toward self and others. We should not place a value or judgment on positive or negative emotions; they are all just emotions. Rather, this is a natural cue from your mind, body, and spirit that signals you need to communicate your thoughts, emotions, or experiences to someone you trust to help resolve specific life issues.

4. Verbalizing thoughts and feelings to a trusted colleague, supervisor, friend, or another professional helper will improve your mood and perceptions toward yourself and others. This does not mean that you are a burned-out, impaired, or fatigued professional. Rather, the expression or request for assistance should signal to others that you care about the state of your personal and professional growth and that you value self-care activities. All therapists need help from others throughout their careers.

5. It may take multiple attempts to try and get in touch with your thoughts and feelings and express these appropriately. As time goes on, it will become easier.

The professional helper's search for meaning, purpose, and how to deal with adversity in life is an ongoing life task. The alternative to ignoring some of the basic resiliency principles is that we may miss the opportunity for resolving conflict, obtain good closure to specific life tasks, learn how to deal with the inter- and intrapersonal demands of stressors, and most of all, learn the art of how to be a tough-minded optimist. We can model healthy choices, exercising the power of positive thinking, take responsibility for things that we can control, and motivate ourselves for success. These are the essential self-care strategies for building counselor resiliency.

RESOURCES

American Counseling Association's (ACA) Taskforce on Counselor Wellness and Impairment: http://www.counseling.org/wellness_taskforce/tf_re sources.htm. The ACA is the largest professional counseling association in North America. This is a very comprehensive source for counselor self-care. There are multiple assessment and screening tools for professional counselors that include wellness, professional quality of life, traumatic stress, and a variety of other assessments.

Gift From Within: http://www.giftfromwithin.org. Gift is an international not-for-profit organization for survivors of traumatic stress. This particular organization is dedicated to PTSD survivors and advocates multiple supports from family, friends, and peers. Educational materials, list of retreats, workshops, and online support are offered.

Green Cross Foundation and Green Cross Academy of Traumatology: http://www.greencross.org. Green Cross is a professional organization of traumatologists founded by Dr. Charles Figley and colleagues who have developed the foundational research and educational materials related to compassion fatigue.

Mark Lerner Associates, Inc.: http://www.marklernerassociates.com. Dr. Lerner is a clinical psychologist and traumatic stress consultant with an international reputation in organizations and individuals that have experienced extraordinary stressful and traumatic events in their lives. Dr. Lerner offers consultations, workshops, and educational and training materials for individuals and organizations to thrive and survive after traumatic events.

RECOMMENDED BOOKS

Brennan, B. A. (1987). *Hands of light: A guide to healing through the human energy field*. New York: Bantam Books.

Davis, M., Robbins Eshelman, E., & McKay, M. (1995). *The relaxation and stress reduction workbook* (4th ed.). Oakland, CA: New Harbinger.

Fanning, P. (1994). *Taking control of your life*. Oakland, CA: New Harbinger.

Figley, C. R. (2002). *Treating compassion fatigue*. New York: Brunner-Routledge.

Fox, M., & Sheldrake, R. (1996). *The physics of angels: Exploring the realm where science and spirit meets*. San Francisco: HarperSanFrancisco.

Goodwin, L. R. (2002). *The button therapy book: A practical psychological self-help book and holistic cognitive counseling manual for mental health professionals*. Victoria, BC, Canada: Trafford.

Hauck, R. (1994). *Angels: The mysterious messengers*. New York: Ballantine.

Ingerman, S. (1991). *Soul retrieval: Mending the fragmented self*. San Francisco: HarperSanFrancisco.

Kabat-Zinn, J. (1990). *Full catastrophe living: Using the wisdom of your body and mind to face stress, pain, and illness*. New York: Dell.

Kabat-Zinn, J. (1994). *Wherever you go there you are: Mindfulness meditation in everyday life*. New York: Hyperion.

LeShun, L. (1974). *A self-discovery guide of how to meditate*. Boston: Bantam.

Maslach, C. (2003). *Burnout: The cost of caring*. Cambridge, MA: Malor Books.

McKay, M., Davis, M., & Fanning, P. (1997). *Thoughts and feelings: Taking control of your moods and your life*. Oakland, CA: New Harbinger.

Mehl-Madrona, L. (1997). *Coyote medicine: Lessons from Native American healing*. New York: Fireside/Simon & Schuster.

Merton, T. (1961). *New seeds of contemplation*. New York: New Directions.

Mitchell, K. K. (1994). *Reiki: A torch in daylight*. St. Charles, IL: Mind Rivers Publications.

Monaghan, P., & Diereck, E. G. (1999). *Meditation: The complete guide*. Navato, CA: New World Library.

Moodly, R., & West, W. (2005). *Integrating traditional healing practices into counseling and psychotherapy*. Thousand Oaks, CA: Sage Publications.

Myers, J. E., & Sweeney, T. J. (2005). *Counseling for wellness: Theory, research, and practice*. Alexandria, VA: American Counseling Association.

Schaper, D., & Camp, C. A. (2004). *Labyrinths from the outside in: Walking to spiritual insight—A beginner's guide*. Woodstock, VT: Skylight Paths.

Seaward, B. L. (1997). *Stand like mountain flow like water*. Deerfield Beach, FL: Health Communications.

Seaward, B. L. (2006). *Essentials of managing stress*. Sudbury, MA: Jones and Bartlett.

Weiss, L. (2004). *Therapist's guide to self-care*. New York: Brunner-Routledge.

REFERENCES

Baker, E. K. (2003). *Caring for ourselves: A therapist's guide to personal and professional well-being*. Washington, DC: American Psychological Association.

Stebnicki, M. A. (2000). Stress and grief reactions among rehabilitation professionals: Dealing effectively with empathy fatigue. *Journal of Rehabilitation, 6*(1), 23–29.

Stebnicki, M. A. (2008). *Empathy fatigue: Healing the mind, body, and spirit of professional counselors*. New York: Springer.

77

Counselor Burnout

TED F. RIGGAR

BURNOUT IS A biopsychosocial concept defined as comprising a number of distinct work-related symptoms: emotional and mental exhaustion, physical depletion, decreased sense of professional efficacy, negative self-evaluation, depersonalization, cynicism, apathy, and indifference. The burnout syndrome involves a wide range of causes, consequences, and coping strategies, and is often cited as a reason why counselors do not perform more effectively. It is clear that considerable money, time, and effort are lost each year in human services because of personnel who can no longer function or cope successfully in their jobs. More than just the financial loss is the emotional and psychological pain suffered by the professionals.

Virtually all burnout studies find the same relevant factors as causal, varying only by occupation, current societal factors, and type of organizational structure and processes. Recently, Kleiman (2007) noted common causal factors such as the nature of one's work, interpersonal relationships, and organizational practices. Ivancevich and Duening (2006) suggest that burnout is the index of the disparity between what people are and what they have to do. For them, burnout "represents an erosion in values, dignity, spirit and will" (p. 75).

FACTORS RELATED TO BURNOUT: CAUSES AND SOURCES

RIGGAR (1985) EXAMINED more than 1,000 published articles on burnout and compiled an annotated bibliography of the most thorough and significant characteristics. The categorical taxonomy was based on (1) causes and sources, (2) signs and symptoms, and (3) coping strategies. Table 77.1 highlights major characteristics of burnout within each of these three categories.

ORGANIZATIONAL STRATEGIES IN BURNOUT

To AID HUMAN service administrators, managers, and supervisors to organize appropriate interventions, each of the organizational strategies is examined in some detail. The first issue to deal with is personnel. Personnel are often caught in a quality–quantity dilemma. This problem refers to trying to achieve job performance requirements while functioning in a competent and acceptable manner. The individual attempts to fulfill personal, professional, and social activities while directing his or her efforts toward some standard of productivity set forth by the organization for which he or she works. Vague and ambiguous productivity goals and standards unduly complicate the process for the individual. Too often the specific demands to be met are not known. Job expectations can be achieved only by clear-cut performance standards and carefully delineated job goals. This will be the only way that the counselor will know what is to be achieved within the organization for which he or she works.

The complexity of work, particularly the repetitiveness and difficulty with discrete job tasks, is related to the self-directed nature of the counselor's work ethic. The ability to use initiative, intelligence, experience, and independent judgment is crucial in a human service work setting. Repetitive tasks of the counselor (i.e., documentation, report writing) can make little use of one's intellectual capacity, which can lead to negative reactions to the organization and job itself. The organizational environment also must provide counselors with challenge and opportunity for accomplishing important self-rewarding job tasks. Organizations that allow counselors some degree of job autonomy, self-direction, and job independence will certainly decrease and prevent the risk of organizational burnout.

Professional Training of Personnel

Training professional personnel is a constant activity in most human service settings. It is possible to prevent, reduce, or even cure burnout through training activities. Personal growth and development that includes seminars, workshops, courses, and continuing education have proven effective in helping counselors perform as competent and ethical counselors. Regardless of job classification, the training of all organizational personnel can lessen job anxiety

TABLE 77.1   Burnout

Personal Causes	Organizational Causes	Environmental Causes
Loss/separation	Disequilibrium	Tedium
Communications	Clients/patient politics	Rewards
Type A behavior	Tedium/tension	Society/economy
Pollyanna Principle	Communication	Conflicts
Personal standards	Feedback	Physical factors
Conflict/crises	Management	Living
Relationships	Supervision	
Fear	Changes	
	Involvement	
	Rewards	
	Role	
	Decisions	
	Time	
	Status	

Signs and Symptoms

Physical:	*Emotional/Mental:*	*Organizational:*
Substance abuse	Mental illness	Job dissatisfaction
Susceptibility to illness	Depression	Unprofessionalism
Pain/tension	Rigidity	Involvement
Cardiopulmonary	Marital conflict	Administration
Sleep problems	Family conflict	Turnover
Fatigue	Loss of coping	Attitudes toward
Isolation	Cynicism	clients/patients
Physiological changes	Passivity	Absenteeism/tardiness
	Aggression	Decreased productivity
	Self-esteem	Personnel activity

Coping Strategies

Personal:	*Organizational*:
Biofeedback	Job definition
Planning	Involvement
Support systems	Tasks
Relaxation	Training
Meditation	Management/supervision
Exercise/nutrition	Sharing/communication
Leisure time	Performance standards
Personal	Expectations
Psychological	Conflict resolution
	Rest

and stress. Employees who feel that the organization is concerned for their overall well-being have an increased attitude and positive feeling toward self and others in their work environment. Strategies that have been effective in reducing organizational burnout include improving employee job skills, orientation sessions, regular in-service activities, and allowing the time and money to attend classes and courses.

Thus, reciprocal caring results in an increase in positive feelings and attitudes about one's job and the overall organizational environment.

The relationship between burnout and job expectations has specific origins. These factors involve change and motivation. Personal expectations are unduly affected by potentially threatening changes in the organization's structure or job requirements. Generally, resistance to and inability to cope with changes occurs due to potential threatened loss. Loss of job, control, or status is most frequently noted. Basically, personnel have the expectation that greater efforts result in improved performance, which leads to increased rewards.

For human service administrators, burnout is often associated with how their superiors and subordinates view supervisory job responsibilities. For example, new managers tend to continue in their practitioner role, while perhaps not performing the expected supervisory functions. Continuation of practitioner responsibilities and activities can lead to burnout of all parties. However, this can be easily remedied by clear-cut job definitions and descriptions. Often a certain organizational hierarchy exists that ranks personnel by seniority, age, competence, pay, and so forth. Supervisors who ignore these attributes and receive preferential treatment or privileges outside of the recognized system risk alienating other subordinates. To assure consistency and avoid frustration and anxiety leading to burnout, it is necessary to clearly and formally define both the job and its roles.

Organizational Conflict

Conflict in any counseling agency, human service organization, or rehabilitation treatment facility is inevitable because a hemostatic organization is one that does not change. Thus, conflict resolution must be structured by whatever organizational methods are used to resolve employee conflicts and the process must be established and known to all before they are called into play.

It is likely that managers and supervisors either cause or do not prevent the majority of burnout as evidenced in the human services. This is especially the case if conflict resolution policies are absent from the organization. Generally, administrative failures in this area center on a certain lack of understanding of supervision duties or have an unwillingness to delegate such responsibilities. Supervisors must be receptive to subordinate's ideas, by listening and assessing the practicality of such approaches. Thus, supervisors must be willing to let go of tasks so that the subordinates can learn new ways of approaching work. Organizational burnout may also be caused through poor supervision, which restricts intellectual flexibility.

While an organizational support system, through the formal administrative hierarchy, is critical, it is also necessary for subordinate and supervisor to establish appropriate communication at the person-to-person level. Especially in the clarification of organizational issues and goals, the subordinate must be able to share the perceptions of his or her supervisor who likely has a broader view. Judgment, consideration, openness, and a high degree of mutual respect and understanding of others' viewpoints and problems are required by human service supervisors. Allowing personnel to vent their frustrations and anxieties may also help avoid employee and organizational burnout.

THE PSYCHOLOGICAL, EMOTIONAL, AND PHYSICAL FATIGUE IN BURNOUT

COUNSELOR FATIGUE, EITHER mental or physical, may lead to burnout through long-term cumulative effects. Counselor burnout may often be cured by complete removal from the work environment. Seeking a new, less stressful position, or modifying the organizational environment, should reduce counselor burnout, but at a slower rate than complete withdrawal of all work activity. However, this approach should only be used when coping strategies and preventative approaches have failed.

As an affective reaction to work and the organization as a whole, personal involvement combines both motivation and willingness to work. Personal involvement in this sense denotes the relationship between a person's job performance and self-esteem. The degree of interaction, compliance, motivation, and cooperation the counselor maintains or engages in pursuant to specific job tasks is dependent upon how the job assignment, job performance itself, enhances or decreases the counselor's self-esteem.

Over the last 30 years, a myriad of variables on burnout in human service organizations have been delineated. The first known significant fact is that burnout is an entirely negative experience. Unlike stress, which is necessary to build healthy emotional muscles and to prepare counselors for handling crisis and emergency situations, burnout has no positive attributes. Secondly, burnout is always an individual internal psychological experience for the person involved. While jobs may be the same and sociocultural variables constant, the ever-changing individual perceives burnout on an individual level. Because burnout is an individual experience, group burnout does not exist. Although an organization may have high rates of absenteeism, tardiness, and turnover, the results for each individual are widely variable.

For over three decades the most common measure of the burnout syndrome has been the Maslach Burnout Inventory (MBI; Maslach, Jackson, & Leiter, 1996). Ongoing revision of the MBI reflects occupational and societal changes due to new variables being identified (Barnett, Brennan, & Gareis, 1999).

ORGANIZATIONAL WORK LIFE AND BURNOUT

MASLACH AND LEITER (1997) have provided six areas in organizational work life wherein job mismatches or lack of harmony may instigate burnout. These include (1) employee workload, (2) control over job, (3) organizational rewards, (4) sense of community, (5) sense of fairness, and (6) matching of personal and organizational values. Personal experiences concomitant to burnout include (1) energy, (2) involvement, (3) effectiveness, (4) physical symptoms, and (5) commitment.

Although burnout has often been cited as a reason for poor performance of personnel, few human service administrators, managers, or supervisors have developed and implemented organizational administrative approaches to deal with the problem of burnout. Failure to develop appropriate management-based programs may be due, in part, to factors surrounding the investigation of the syndrome or the dissemination of information concerning the problem. Burnout appears to be a significant personnel problem most neglected by human service administrators. The personal consequence of burnout is the same whether it is due to (1) the lack of knowledge or understanding of the complex research findings, (2) lack of prevention activities by organizational administrators and supervisors (Riggar, Garner, & Hafer, 1984), or (3) limited management awareness of the manifestations (i.e., causes/sources, signs/symptoms) of the burnout syndrome.

CONCLUSION

MASLACH (2003) NOTES that "effective interventions have yet to be developed and evaluated" (p. 189) for burnout prevention at all levels of the organization. It is evident from the literature that the top four reasons counseling professionals left their jobs were (1) little advancement potential, (2) little job satisfaction, (3) stress burnout, and (4) personality differences with management/supervision. Clearly, these variables are closely associated to job burnout that encompasses a holistic set of variables. As Layne, Hohenshil, and Singh (2004) point out "that it is the occupation stress inherent in the job functions of counselors, and not individual coping resources or demographic variables, that accounts for the turnover intentions of counselors" (p. 19). It is clear that preventing, reducing, and eliminating burnout begins with effective management intentions that are realistic, genuine, and in tune with the organization and employee's job-related stressors (Maslach & Leiter, 1997).

REFERENCES

Barnett, R. C., Brennan, R. T., & Gareis, K. C. (1999). *Journal of Applied Biobehavioral Research, 4*(2), 65–78.

Ivancevich, J. M., & Duening, T. N. (2006). *Management: Skills, application, practice, and development.* Cincinnati, OH: Atomic Dog Publishing.

Kleiman, L. S. (2007). *Human resource management.* Cincinnati, OH: Atomic Dog Publishing.

Layne, C. M., Hohenshil, T. H., & Singh, K. (2004). The relationship of occupational stress, psychological strain, and coping resources to the turnover intentions of rehabilitation counselors. *Rehabilitation Counseling Bulletin, 48,* 19–30.

Maslach, C. (2003). Job burnout: New directions in research and intervention. *Current Directions in Psychological Science, 12*(5), 189–192.

Maslach, C., Jackson, S. E., & Leiter, M. P. (1996). *The Maslach Burnout Inventory* (3rd ed.). Palo Alto, CA: Consulting Psychologists Press.

Maslach, C., & Leiter, M. P. (1997). *The truth about burnout.* San Francisco: Jossey-Bass.

Riggar, T. F. (1985). *Stress burnout: An annotated bibliography.* Carbondale: Southern Illinois University Press.

Riggar, T. F., Garner, W. E., & Hafer, M. (1984). Rehabilitation personnel burnout: Organizational cures. *Journal of Rehabilitation Administration, 8*(3), 94–104.

78

Religion and Spirituality in Counseling

PERRY C. FRANCIS

ELIGION EXERTS A major influence in the lives of many people in our culture. When asked in a recent Gallup poll: "How important would you say religion is in your own life—very important, fairly important, or not very important?", 27% responded with fairly important and 57% responded with very important (Gallup, 2007). A separate but related issue, spirituality, also influences the lives of many people (Zinnbauer et al., 1997), guiding their decisions, choices, and how they view the world. Taken together, religion and spirituality have been a part of our world since time began, defining cultural boundaries, influencing the arts, affecting the direction of health care, causing and ending wars, and generally impacting the development of humanity (Zinnbauer & Pargament, 2005).

Religious and/or spiritual clients bring their beliefs and values into the consultation room as a part of their identity and culture. Increasingly, these clients, who once were avoiding the consultation room out of fear the counselor may see their faith as a symptom of pathology, are now venturing in and seeking services from both secular and faith-based mental health professionals, expecting their beliefs and values to be accepted and respected (Belare, Young, & Elder, 2005). Additionally, they view the discussion of religious and/or spiritual concerns as part of the counseling process and are expecting their counselor to be capable of including that discussion as part of the therapy (Rose, Westefeld, & Ansley, 2001). As noted by Rose et al.:

> One client noted that talking to clergy "isn't always an option." Religious or spiritual persons struggling with issues such as abortion, sexual orientation, or extramarital affairs might be more comfortable discussing the religious and spiritual implications of these problems with a counselor. (p. 68)

The mental health profession has recognized this shift as evidenced by a call for and an increase in published research (Worthington, Kurusu, McCullough, & Sandage, 1996), professional books targeted to the subject of spirituality and religion within counseling and psychology (Cashwell & Young, 2005; Frame, 2003; Richards & Bergin, 1997; Shafranske, 1996), an increased emphasis on including this subject as part of training counselors, especially as part of a multicultural framework and competencies (Hage, Hopson, Siegal, Payton, & DeFanti, 2006; Young, Cashwell, Wiggins-Frame, & Belare, 2002), and the recognition that psychopathology and mental illness are not correlated with religiousness and/or spirituality (Genia, 2000). Additionally, there is increased debate in the literature on how to address, use, and intervene using religious and spiritual techniques and the ethical implications related to those professional and practice issues (Helminiak, 2001; Watts, 2001).

Mental health professionals will work with clients who are going to bring their religious and spiritual concerns into the consultation room. This will require those professionals to have an increased knowledge of and sensitivity to those concerns as they impact the session and the relationship between the client and the counselor. These religious and spiritual beliefs and behaviors are used by clients to provide ritual, support, and meaning in both good and bad times and can be accessed by the counselor to offer help and healing in the consultation room.

RELIGION AND SPIRITUALITY: A MULTIDIMENSIONAL CONCEPT

To begin developing a knowledge base about religion and spirituality that is helpful for the working counselor, it is important to define each term. As those definitions are developed, it will become apparent each is a multidimensional concept. While they are separate terms, in practice they intersect each other in both the abstract and concrete applications of a person's life. It is also worthwhile to note that while the profession struggles to define each term for the sake of research and practice (C. R. Hall, Dixon, & Mauzey, 2004; W. R. Miller & Thoresen, 2003), clients have developed their own definitions that may or may not be similar with the counselor's understanding of each. It is the wise clinician who seeks to understand not only how the profession may define and operationalize these concepts, but also how the client understands and lives out these concepts.

RELIGION AND RELIGIOUSNESS

RELIGION CAN BE seen primarily as a social construct that helps provide boundaries to the belief systems it represents. In this way it serves as a way to define and differentiate between the different orthodoxies of the world's faith systems (C. R. Hall et al., 2004; Hill et al., 2000). It implies that adherents are to follow a set of beliefs in thought and action that can be understood as being religious or religiousness. This might include participation in the public and private rituals of that religion. It might also be implied that a person who cognitively and behaviorally follows the beliefs and rituals of his or her religion is a spiritual person, especially if the person integrates his or her beliefs into his or her meaning of life. At the same time, another person may be seen as only religious and not spiritual if he or she is going through the motions for social or business reasons and never really integrating the belief system into his or her understanding of life (Frame, 2003). It is essential for the counselor to be able to understand the difference when working with a religious client.

It is important to note that religion and religiousness do not necessarily represent a rigid or fixed set of ideas or theology. Instead, they may be a reflection of the dynamic growth and development of the human spirit as an individual seeks to understand the world and his or her place within it (Pargament, 1999).

SPIRITUALITY

SPIRITUALITY IS OFTEN understood as how a person lives out his or her religion in the world. This definition narrowly ties spirituality to religion when, in fact, it is much broader. While religion and spirituality are closely connected, spirituality differs in that a spiritual person does not have to be tied to a religion (Hill & Pargament, 2003; W. R. Miller & Thoresen, 2003). More broadly understood, spirituality can be seen as a person's search for his or her ultimate meaning and place in the world. That search may include a relationship that is developed with a transcendent or divine power beyond oneself that may be considered sacred. This sacred relationship may include an altruistic side that seeks the best in self and others and creates an appreciation for the values of one's culture and morals (Wiggins-Frame, 2005).

DEVELOPING A MULTICULTURAL VIEW OF RELIGION AND SPIRITUALITY

A S THE COUNSELOR begins to develop the therapeutic relationship with the client, it is important to create a safe environment so the client feels comfortable in bringing to the session those important issues that are in need of exploration and remediation. This requires the counselor to develop an open ecumenical and multicultural stance. The counselor must go beyond an awareness of his or her own cultural background and develop an understanding and appreciation of the client's religious and spiritual tradition (or lack of one) and how that impacts his or her development and worldview (Bergin, Payne, & Richards, 1996). From there the counselor can consciously determine how his or her own religious/spiritual development influences his or her work with clients from different religious/spiritual backgrounds. This openness is communicated to the client and contributes to a therapeutic environment of mutual understanding and respect in which the client and counselor can learn from each other about the views they bring to the consultation room.

This open ecumenical/multicultural stance is not based upon a nondenominational approach that does not consider religious denominations, but one that has an appreciation for what each religious denomination brings to the culture of the client and his or her individual development (Hagedorn, 2005). It also allows the counselor, when appropriate, to take advantage of the denominational leaders and community as a source of consultation, education, and social support. Additionally, the counselor should ensure that any techniques or interventions that are employed are sensitive to the denomination's traditions and beliefs (Richards & O'Grady, 2005).

In that light, the counselor should begin developing a worldview of religion and spirituality. As our globe becomes increasingly smaller and travel and relocation more ubiquitous, there is an increase in the number of different religions that are present in our culture. With those religions comes a set of values and behaviors that may conflict with the counselor's values. This can interfere with the therapeutic alliance if not addressed at the appropriate time. It would also be a therapeutic error to assume that an intervention based upon one client's religion can be used with another client who comes from a different religious belief system. When those values and behaviors are in too much conflict with those of the counselor, additional education and/or supervision for the counselor or a referral for the client may be in order (Richards & O'Grady, 2005).

Another ecumenical and multicultural consideration is the appropriate use of religious and spiritual language. Those clients who present as highly or rigidly religious may resist engaging the counselor in discussions concerning religious practices or behaviors unless traditional religious language is used. On the other hand, clients who identify as highly spiritual but do not identify with any religious practices or who have an aversion to religion may also resist any discussions without the use of spiritual language and symbols (Worthington & Sandage, 2001). Assessing the client's needs in this area is a sign of respect that helps to build trust between the client and counselor.

RELIGIOUS, SPIRITUAL, AND MORAL DEVELOPMENT

THE PROFESSION OF counseling is deeply rooted in the concept of human growth and development. It is used to develop theory, design interventions, and guide therapy. The growth of faith, spirituality, and morality or values is also a developmental process that is defined by theory (Worthington, 1989). While faith development theory is not as well developed when compared to other developmental theories, it can help the counselor build a therapeutic relationship, conceptualize the client's issues, and tailor interventions that are more effective. Additionally, a faith development theory can also be helpful in assessing the level of religious or spiritual maturity of the client, which also helps in the conceptualization and assessment of the client's problem. As with use of any developmental theory and assessment, the cultural context of the client needs to be considered for its effect on development (G. Miller, 2005). A client's level of faith development must also be seen through the lens of his or her social, cognitive, and emotional development. Religion and/or spirituality are often used in times of normative and nonnormative life transitions. Clients may use their faith adaptively or defensively to help them through those transitions and an accurate understanding of both their social/cognitive/emotional development and faith development is critical in the accurate conceptualization of the client (Worthington, 1989).

This coincides with Fowler's (1981) developmental view that the power of childhood images and memories of faith do not diminish over time but are involved in a person's ongoing development. These memories help in the development of a worldview that is used to construct meaning, structure facts and cognitions and their relationships with one another, and to provide a framework for interpersonal relationships (Lownsdale, 1997). As Maslow pointed out (as cited in Lownsdale, 1997, p. 50):

> The human needs a framework of values, a philosophy of life, a religion or religion-surrogate to live by and understand by, in about the same sense that he needs sunlight, calcium, or love. . . . What a man needs but doesn't have, he seeks for unceasingly.

There are several faith and moral development theories and it is important to note that not all theories are solely faith-based, although their concepts intersect on the development of morals and values. Many involve the development of "life structures" (Levinson, 1978), moral development (Gilligan, 1993; Kohlberg, 1969), or Jungian individualism (C. S. Hall & Norbdy, 1973). For those clients who may not identify with or are hostile to formal religions but who see themselves as spiritual, moral, or persons with values, these theories can be helpful tools for conceptualization and intervention. Other models of development focus on the growth and maturity of faith from childhood to adulthood (Allport, 1950; Fowler, 1981) or the development of faith and concepts of god in childhood alone (Coles, 1990). Each, used with other developmental theories, is helpful in working with religious and spiritual issues in counseling.

RELIGION, SPIRITUALITY, AND ASSESSMENT

WHEN MAKING AN assessment of a client who presents as strongly religious or spiritual, it is recommended that consideration of those issues be a part of the determination of diagnosis, if one is used, and the etiology of the presenting problem. As the counselor includes those variables, he or she should consider the (1) religious status of the client, (2) level of religious maturation and how the client reached that level, and (3) if the client is at any transition points in his or her development (Worthington, 1989).

If it is determined that the client's religious or spiritual issues are having an impact on the creation, maintenance, or resolution of his or her problems, a more comprehensive assessment of that interaction needs to be undertaken. Worthington (1989, pp. 589–592) identified eight issues that need to be considered when conducting such an assessment:

1. How formal should the assessment be? Given the strength and depth of the religious or spiritual issues and how intertwined they are with the presenting problems, the counselor will need to

determine if a formal or informal assessment is necessary as well as the use of any formal inventories or instruments.

2. To what degree is the content of the person's faith to be assessed versus the process of *faithing*? The client's *what* and *how* of his or her faith will need to be assessed by the counselor. This cannot be done without understanding that a person's faith is held in the context of his or her culture and life events.

3. How is religion involved in the life of the client? The counselor will need to determine how the client's religion or spirituality plays a part in his or her daily life and functioning. Is it used as a defense mechanism, part of normal coping, life enhancing or detracting from the client's normal functioning? This requires the counselor to have an understanding of human growth and development and faith development.

4. How mature is the client in his or her religious life as well as in his or her cognitive, moral, and socioemotional lives? Related to the previous item, the counselor will need to assess if the client's developmental areas are (1) interrelated, (2) differentially developed, and (3) underdeveloped.

5. To what degree, if any, is the client's religion related to the diagnosis? It is important for the counselor to understand if the behaviors associated with a client's religion or spirituality are within a normal range or part of the psychological disorder. This requires the counselor to be educated about the beliefs and practices of a client's religious expression.

6. To what degree is the client's religion involved in the etiology of the problem? Using a developmental perspective, the counselor assesses the origins of the problems and the coping mechanisms of the client. With the religious or spiritual client, the counselor also seeks to assess the extent to which religion or spirituality influences the creation, maintenance, or improvement of the presenting issues.

7. Who is the client? As with most counseling, when religious or spiritual issues are involved in counseling, the goals of the client may include more than the individual. The client is part of a larger system of people and organizations that now include a religious organization that impacts the goals and direction of the client.

8. Is the counselor competent to deal with the client's personal issues and the religious implications for the client? Clients with religious or spiritual issues will come with many different faith perspectives. It is important for the counselor to determine if he or she is competent to deal with these issues as part of the counseling process. It is not enough to simply say you disagree with a client's religious belief or values system to refer her or him to another therapist (Hermann & Herlihy, 2006). Issues of competency

or countertransference will need to be present before the counselor can refer the client to another professional.

There are many different assessments and inventories that can be used with clients who present with religious or spiritual issues (Fitchett, 1993; T. W. Hall, Tisdale, & Brokaw, 1994). Like all instruments, it is incumbent upon the counselor to become familiar with the instrument's appropriate usage and its relationship to the needs of the client and counselor.

INTERVENTIONS

THE USE OF specific interventions with religious or spiritual clients can take on many forms. Before the counselor uses any intervention she or he needs to first be aware that many religious clients fear being asked to participate in exercises or interventions that are contrary to their belief system or being misunderstood by the counselor who would pathologize the client due to his or her religious beliefs (Worthington, 1989). Demonstrating respect for a client's faith system is required before the use of any intervention.

There are two models for integrating secular and religious techniques into a counseling session, implicit and explicit integration (Tan, 1996). Implicit integration refers to a more "covert" (p. 368) approach that does not directly or systematically use religious practices (e.g., prayer or reading of sacred text) as interventions. While religious issues may not be brought up directly, they will be dealt with respect for the values and beliefs of the client. Clients who want to deal with issues of religion more directly may need the counselor to adopt a more explicit approach.

An explicit approach deals more directly and systemically with the spiritual and religious issues in the session. Uses of religious resources are more common and overt. The spirituality of both the counselor and the client are considered part of the foundation for effective therapy. Clients from more orthodox belief systems seem to prefer this method of counseling. Caution needs to be practiced to ensure that the counselor is not proselytizing or imposing his or her own practices and values upon the client with the use of specific interventions (Tan, 1996).

CONCLUSION

CLIENTS ARE INCREASINGLY bringing their beliefs, values, and faith systems into the consultation room. In many cases, these religious and spiritual beliefs are used as coping mechanisms and support in times of trouble and discomfort. These beliefs and value are part of what makes up the cultural picture of the client and can be used by the skillful and sensitive counselor to help the client navigate the counseling process toward healing and wholeness.

REFERENCES

Allport, G. W. (1950). *The individual and his religion*. London: Macmillan.

Belare, C., Young, J. S., & Elder, A. (2005). Inclusion of religious behaviors and attitudes in counseling: Expectations of conservative Christians. *Counseling and Values, 49*(2), 82–94.

Bergin, A. E., Payne, I. R., & Richards, P. S. (1996). Values in psychotherapy. In E. P. Shafranske (Ed.), *Religion and the clinical practice of psychology* (pp. 297–326). Washington, DC: American Psychological Association.

Cashwell, C. S., & Young, J. S. (Eds.). (2005). *Integrating spirituality and religion into counseling: A guide to competent practice*. Alexandria, VA: American Counseling Association.

Coles, R. (1990). *The spiritual life of children*. Boston: Houghton Mifflin.

Fitchett, G. (1993). Spiritual assessment in pastoral care: A guide to selected resources. *Journal of Pastoral Care Publication Monograph, 4*.

Fowler, J. W. (1981). *Stages of faith: The psychology of human development and the quest for meaning*. San Francisco: HarperCollins.

Frame, M. W. (2003). *Integrating religion and spirituality into counseling: A comprehensive approach*. Pacific Grove, CA: Thomson Brooks/Cole.

Gallup, G. (2007). *Poll topics a to z: Religion*. Retrieved April 18, 2007, from http://www.galluppoll.com/content/default.aspx?ci=1690

Genia, V. (2000). Religious issues in secularly based psychotherapy. *Counseling and Values, 44*(3), 213–221.

Gilligan, C. (1993). *In a different voice: Psychological theory and women's development*. Cambridge, MA: Harvard University Press.

Hage, S. M., Hopson, A., Siegal, M., Payton, G., & DeFanti, E. (2006). Multicultural training in spirituality: An interdisciplinary review. *Counseling and Values, 50*(3), 217–234.

Hagedorn, W. B. (2005). Counselor self-awareness and self-exploration of religious and spiritual beliefs: Know thyself. In C. S. Cashwell & J. S. Young (Eds.), *Integrating spirituality and religion into counseling: A guide to competent practice* (pp. 63–84). Alexandria, VA: American Counseling Association.

Hall, C. R., Dixon, W. A., & Mauzey, E. D. (2004). Spirituality and religion: Implications for counselors. *Journal of Counseling and Development, 82,* 504–507.

Hall, C. S., & Norbdy, V. J. (1973). *A primer of Jungian psychology*. New York: Mentor.

Hall, T. W., Tisdale, T. C., & Brokaw, F. (1994). Assessment of religious dimensions in Christian clients: A review of selected instruments for research and clinical use. *Journal of Psychology and Theology, 22*(4), 395–421.

Helminiak, D. A. (2001). Treating spiritual issues in secular psychotherapy. *Counseling and Values, 45*(3), 163–189.

Hermann, M. A., & Herlihy, B. R. (2006). Legal and ethical implications of refusing to counsel homosexual clients. *Journal of Counseling and Development, 84*(4), 414–418.

Hill, P. C., & Pargament, K. I. (2003). Advances in the conceptualization and measurement of religion and spirituality: Implications for physical and mental health research. *American Psychologist, 58*(1), 64–74.

Hill, P. C., Pargament, K. I., Hood, R. W., Jr., McCullouch, M. E., Swyers, J. P., Larson, D. B., et al. (2000). Conceptualizing religion and spirituality: Points of commonality, points of departure. *Journal for the Theory of Social Behavior, 30*(1), 51–77.

Kohlberg, L. (1969). The development of children's orientations toward a moral order. I. Sequence in the development of moral thought. *Vita Humana, 6*, 11–33.

Levinson, D. J. (1978). *The seasons of a man's life.* New York: Ballantine.

Lownsdale, S. (1997). Faith development across the life span: Fowler's integrative work. *Journal of Psychology and Theology, 28*(1), 49–63.

Miller, G. (2005). Religious/spiritual life span development. In C. S. Cashwell & J. S. Young (Eds.), *Integrating spirituality and religion into counseling: A guide to competent practice* (pp. 105–122). Alexandria, VA: American Counseling Association.

Miller, W. R., & Thoresen, C. E. (2003). Spirituality, religion, and health. *American Psychologist, 58*(1), 24–35.

Pargament, K. I. (1999). The psychology of religion and spirituality? Yes and no. *The International Journal for the Psychology of Religion, 9*(1), 3–16.

Richards, P. S., & Bergin, A. E. (1997). *A spiritual strategy for counseling and psychotherapy.* Washington, DC: American Psychological Association.

Richards, P. S., & O'Grady, K. A. (2005). Working with the religiously committed client. In G. P. Koocher, J. C. Norcross, & S. S. Hill (Eds.), *Psychologists' Desk Reference* (2nd ed., pp. 338–341). New York: Oxford University Press.

Rose, E. M., Westefeld, J. S., & Ansley, T. M. (2001). Spiritual issues in counseling: Clients' beliefs and preferences. *Journal of Counseling Psychology, 48*(1), 61–71.

Shafranske, E. P. (Ed.). (1996). *Religion and the clinical practice of psychology.* Washington, DC: American Psychological Association.

Tan, S. Y. (1996). Religion in clinical practice: Implicit and explicit integration. In E. P. Shafranske (Ed.), *Religion and the clinical practice of psychology* (pp. 365–387). Washington, DC: American Psychological Association.

Watts, R. E. (2001). Addressing spiritual issues in secular counseling and psychotherapy: Reponse to Helminiak's (2001) views. *Counseling and Values, 45*(3), 207–217.

Wiggins-Frame, M. (2005). Spirituality and religion: Similarities and difference. In C. S. Cashwell & J. S. Young (Eds.), *Integrating spirituality and religion into counseling: A guide to competent practice* (pp. 11–29). Alexandria, VA: American Counseling Association.

Worthington, E. L., Jr. (1989). Religious faith across the life span: Implications for counseling and research. *Counseling Psychologist, 17*(4), 555–612.

Worthington, E. L., Jr., Kurusu, T. A., McCullough, M. E., & Sandage, S. J. (1996). Empirical research on religion and psychotherapeutic processes and outcomes: A 10-year review and research prospectus. *Psychological Bulletin, 119*(3), 448–487.

Worthington, E. L., Jr., & Sandage, S. J. (2001). Religion and spirituality. *Psychotherapy, 38*(4), 473–478.

Young, J. S., Cashwell, C. S., Wiggins-Frame, M., & Belare, C. (2002). Spiritual and religious competencies: A national survey of CACREP-accredited programs. *Counseling and Values, 47*(1), 22–33.

Zinnbauer, B. J., & Pargament, K. I. (2005). Religiousness and spirituality. In R. F. Paloutzian & C. L. Park (Eds.), *Handbook of the psychology of religion and spirituality* (pp. 21–42). New York: Guilford Press.

Zinnbauer, B. J., Pargament, K. I., Cole, B. C., Rye, M. S., Butter, E. M., Belavich, T. G., et al. (1997). Religion and spirituality: Unfuzzying the fuzzy. *Journal for the Scientific Study of Religion, 36*(4), 549–564.

79

Counseling Persons With Chronic Pain

CARRIE WINTEROWD AND WENDY SIMS

PAIN AND ITS ORIGINS

PAIN IS AN "unpleasant sensory and emotional experience associated with actual or potential tissue damage or described in terms of such damage" (Merskey & Bogduk, 1994, p. 209). Pain can be malignant (cancer-related) or benign (non–cancer-related). It can also be acute or chronic in nature (Winterowd, Beck, & Gruener, 2003). The majority of clients seeking counseling services (either self- or other-referred) tend to have benign chronic pain.

Acute pain has duration lasting seconds to months and is typically the result of an identifiable origin, including tissue damage from an infection, injury, inflammation, or surgery. The majority of acute pain experiences are nociceptive in nature, meaning that sensory receptors (nociceptors) located on select peripheral nerve endings detect noxious stimuli and send pain messages to the brain via the spinal cord (Nicholson, 2003). Acute pain can function to protect and warn the individual of imminent or actual tissue damage (Woolf & Mannion, 1999). Acute pain can be relieved with treatment, medication, and healing of tissue.

Chronic pain is pain that persists beyond the time one would expect normal healing to occur (Merskey & Bogduk, 1994). The origin of chronic pain can be associated with an identifiable injury or disease;

however, the origin of chronic pain is sometimes unidentifiable, making management of chronic pain symptoms challenging. Unrelenting suffering and distress often accompany the complex nature of chronic pain. Chronic pain typically arises from nociceptive pain, neuropathic pain, or a combination of both (otherwise known as mixed pain). Neuropathic pain stems from a lesion or malfunction often in the peripheral nervous system, the dorsal root ganglion, or the central nervous system (Woolf & Mannion, 1999).

Pain has also been defined as idiopathic or unspecified pain, which is undiagnosed pain. Psychogenic pain is pain that has been diagnosed as being psychological in nature. It should be noted that psychological factors can influence the experience of pain in all clients who have chronic pain.

PREVALENCE OF CHRONIC PAIN

HEALTH CARE PROVIDERS are encountering increasing numbers of patients seeking relief from chronic pain. Approximately 10% to 30% of people in the United States live with the burden of enduring symptoms of intractable malignant or nonmalignant chronic pain (Turk & Nash, 1993). Chronic pain ratings among veterans range as high as 50% (Clark, 2002).

The prevalence of chronic pain continues to increase despite major advances in research, technology, and management practices (Turk & Burwinkle, 2005). Chronic pain is reported to be debilitating, expensive, and one of the top reasons for health care visits and work absences (World Health Organization, 2001). It has been estimated that annual spending on specialized treatment for pain exceeds $1.5 billion (Turk, 2001).

TYPES OF PAIN

ONE OF EVERY eight adult Americans will likely experience back pain in his or her lifetime, which is one of the most common reasons people seek treatment in emergency rooms and are absent from work (Dillard, 2002). Site-specific pain is reported more often than widespread pain (Hardt, Jacboson, Goldberg, Nickel, & Buchwald, 2008), the most common locations being in the lower extremities (including hips, legs, knees, feet, ankles) and back (Hardt et al., 2008; Portenoy, Ugarte, Fuller, & Haas, 2004). Women report significantly more headache pain than men (Hardt et al., 2008).

DEMOGRAPHIC CHARACTERISTICS

CLIENTS WITH CHRONIC pain tend to be women (Hardt et al., 2008; Portenoy et al., 2004) from lower socioeconomic status backgrounds who have fewer years of education (Portenoy et al., 2004). Reports of chronic pain are highest among those aged 50–59 and lowest for those age 70 and above, with the exception of headache pain, which is highest among those aged 30–59 (Hardt et al., 2008).

Racial differences in the experience of chronic pain have been noted in the literature. Researchers found Hispanics/Mexican Americans report less pain chronic pain than Whites and African Americans (Hardt et al., 2008) and are less likely to visit a doctor for pain (Portenoy et al., 2004). African Americans report more chronic pain and/or more physical impairment than Whites (Cano, Mayo, & Ventimiglia, 2006) and are more likely to have used prescription medication than Hispanics or Whites (Portenoy et al., 2004). There is some evidence that socioeconomic status (i.e., educational level and income) mediates the relationship between race and pain (Cano et al., 2006; Portenoy et al., 2004).

COMMON EXPERIENCES AND CHARACTERISTICS

PEOPLE SUFFERING FROM chronic pain experience a number of psychological and psychosocial problems, including depression, anxiety, anger, grief, changes in eating and sleeping patterns, decreases in mobility, activity level, daily functioning, work performance, and social interactions (Breen, 2002), and unfavorable health perceptions (Gureje, Von Korff, Simon, & Gater, 1998). Chronic pain is especially draining and damaging to a person's mental well-being as its complexity spans physical sensations, mental and psychological exhaustion, social disruptions, and financial burdens of accumulating medical costs, and loss of work (Tumlin, 2001).

TYPICAL COGNITIONS/EMOTIONS/ BEHAVIORS

THERE IS A large amount of empirical support for the relationship between negative, unrealistic, and catastrophic thinking and having chronic pain (Severeijns, Vlaeyen, Van Den Hout, & Weber, 2001). How clients think about their pain has a significant impact on how they perceive pain sensations, how they feel emotionally, and what they do when they are in pain. Most people who have chronic pain have beliefs about their pain (i.e., "The pain is uncontrollable"), themselves (i.e., "I am inadequate/dysfunctional"), and their bodies (i.e., "My body has betrayed me") as well as their relationships with others (i.e., "People don't care about me or my pain"), and about their future (i.e., "This pain will make my life miserable"; Winterowd et al., 2003).

When clients think negatively about themselves and their chronic pain condition, they are more likely to feel a variety of distressing emotions, for example, feeling depressed, anxious, angry, and/or guilty, which can result in increased muscle tension and a hyperaroused state, activating more pain messages, thus increasing the pain experience. Thinking negatively about chronic pain can also reinforce self-defeating behaviors, such as inactivity and social isolation (Winterowd et al., 2003).

CHRONIC PAIN TREATMENTS

CLIENTS WHO HAVE chronic pain are often involved in concurrent pain treatments in addition to counseling services. They are often under the medical care of one or more physicians (i.e., primary care physicians, pain specialists) who diagnose and treat their pain (Winterowd et al., 2003). Pharmacological treatments of chronic pain can include nonsteroidal inflammatory drugs (NSAIDS), antidepressants, antiepileptics, capsaicin cream, and opioid analgesics (Marcus, 2000). Steroid injections may be recommended for unremitting pain as a next course of action.

In addition to medical treatments, persons with chronic pain often undergo rehabilitation therapies. Physical therapists use low impact exercise, stretches, cold or heat treatments, and application of transcutaneous electrical nerve stimulation (TENS) units to recondition and strengthen muscles and joints. Occupational therapists instruct pain patients on proper body posture and movements as well as monitor daily activity levels. Recreational therapists focus on helping the patient maintain enjoyment of leisure activities. Massage therapy is also considered a treatment for chronic pain conditions as a benefit of relaxing muscle groups and improving circulation (Winterowd et al., 2003).

Clients who are overweight are at risk for increased pain due to additional strain and tension on joints and muscles. Overweight or obese persons can seek treatment from a dietician or nutritionist for help with achieving a healthy diet or for help reaching an optimal weight before being considered for surgical treatment (Winterowd et al., 2003).

After less invasive treatments are considered, some clients may become candidates for surgical procedures to repair tissue or neurological damage. Orthopedic surgeons treat muscle tissue damage or pathology whereas neurosurgeons treat nerve damage or pathology. Some common invasive procedures include diskectomies, laminectomies, joint replacements, and spinal fusions. Implantable devices such as spinal cord stimulation and intrathecal drug therapy for pain management also require invasive procedures.

Counseling is often recommended for clients with chronic pain to cope more effectively with the pain and its consequences. Clients are often reluctant to see a counselor or psychotherapist because they fear that seeking such services implies that their pain is psychogenic in nature and thus not real. However, counselors and psychotherapists can help clients understand that counseling services are an integral part of chronic pain management programs in teaching them how to cope better (or manage) with their pain and their moods, and to enhance their functioning in various life roles.

EMPIRICAL SUPPORT FOR COUNSELING APPROACHES

COGNITIVE BEHAVIOR THERAPIES (including adaptations of Donald Meichenbaum's, Aaron Beck's, and Albert Ellis's approaches) and behavioral therapies are more effective in helping clients cope with their chronic pain and its consequences compared to other treatments and control groups (i.e., not being in therapy at all; Hoffman, Papas, Chatkoff, & Kerns, 2007; Morley, Eccleston, & Williams, 1999; van Tulder et al., 2000). There is also recent evidence for utilization of Acceptance and Commitment Therapy, one particular cognitive behavioral approach, in the treatment of persons with chronic pain (Dahl & Lundgren, 2006).

Multidisciplinary pain treatment programs that incorporate cognitive behavior therapy and behavioral therapy approaches are significantly more successful than programs that use only one treatment or programs with no other treatments (Flor, Fydrich, & Turk, 1992). The cognitive behavioral approach to counseling has a positive effect when combined with active treatments such as medications, physical therapy, and medical treatments for chronic pain clients in treating pain, thoughts about pain, and pain behavior problems (Morley et al., 1999). Researchers found that multidisciplinary pain management programs consisting of therapeutic dialogue, physical activity, and education have the potential to improve coping strategies and health-related quality of life for clients with chronic pain (Dysvik, Vinsnes, & Eikeland, 2004).

Mind–body interventions, particularly mindfulness meditation, have been used effectively, as part of stress management and/or relaxation programs, to help people cope with chronic pain (Morone & Greco, 2007), as well as enhance physical and psychological functioning (McCraken, Gauntlett-Gilbert, & Vowles, 2007).

Given the findings mentioned above, the majority of chronic pain management programs tend to incorporate cognitive and/or behavioral approaches to counseling, including some mindfulness-based practices, such as mindfulness meditation.

Overall Goals of Counseling

Individual and/or group counseling approaches can be used with chronic pain clients. Couples and/or family counseling may also be recommended. Some of the main goals in working with clients with chronic pain from a cognitive behavioral/mindful approach (whether it be individual and/or group counseling) are to (1) help clients understand their pain (via pain monitoring, e.g., keeping a pain diary) as well as learning strategies to cope with their pain and their lives; (2) learning relaxation, mindfulness meditation (including "experiencing" without judgment, being in the moment), as well as distraction techniques; (3) thinking more realistically about their pain and experiences (including identifying, evaluating, and modifying negative, unrealistic thoughts and beliefs about their pain and their feelings about their pain using automatic thought records and core belief worksheets as well as imagery work; see Winterowd et al., 2003); (4) managing their activity levels given their pain; (5) learning how to be more assertive with others about their experience and become more active in their treatment, rehabilitation, and recovery; and (6) learning problem-solving skills (Gatchel, 2005; Winterowd et al., 2003). Although it is rare for clients to become pain free, cognitive behavioral/mindfulness-oriented counseling approaches teach clients how cope with their chronic pain (including a radical acceptance of pain, without judgment) and to enhance their functioning in various life roles (Winterowd et al., 2003).

Key Elements of a Counseling Program

Assessment Interview. Counselors should conduct an intake interview prior to the start of counseling to include (1) a thorough assessment of the client's pain, including his or her descriptions of the pain, where it is located, its duration, intensity, frequency, any particular fluctuations in pain as well as what makes pain better or worse; (2) the client's emotions, thoughts, and behaviors when in pain; (3) efforts to cope with chronic pain (including activity levels, communication styles, and spiritual/religious beliefs); (4) potential physical limitations related to the pain as well as the other conse-quences of having chronic pain (e.g., role limitations, financial and/or legal difficulties); (5) other psychosocial stressors that affect pain (e.g., personality, relationship issues, environment); and (6) medical/health care history, including how the pain condition developed, types of treatments received for pain, including pain medications prescribed, as well as other relevant information, including family history, social history (friends, dating, partnerships, children), educational and work history, substance use history, and any significant events or traumas (Winterowd et al., 2003).

If clients have not been evaluated by a physician or specialist, appropriate referrals should be made to ensure an interdisciplinary team approach to chronic pain management. Other health care professionals such as physicians, nurses, physical and/or occupational therapists, and nutritionists should be consulted with and included in chronic pain management counseling goals/plans.

COURSE OF CHRONIC PAIN COUNSELING SESSIONS

T HE COURSE OF counseling from a cognitive behavioral/mindful perspective (usually 12 sessions in duration) typically starts with a focus on pain management, and then moves to other concerns or issues (Winterowd et al., 2003). Building a good relationship with clients is the first step in the change process. Many clients are seeking not only support but also direction in managing their pain and their moods. Therefore, counselors may need to be more active and directive in the counseling process than they might with other clients. The focus on this counseling approach is to help clients change the way they think about themselves and their pain (to be more realistic and hopeful) and to learn new coping strategies to address their pain and their lives, including relaxation, mindfulness meditation, assertiveness training, and problem-solving skills.

BEHAVIORAL INTERVENTIONS

CLIENTS WITH CHRONIC pain typically want some quick solutions in the early phase of counseling so that they can experience some pain relief as soon as possible. The primary behavioral interventions used in helping clients manage pain include pain monitoring (e.g., identifying and tracking pain and its intensity over time and across situations), activity scheduling and monitoring (e.g., tracking activity levels, adding more enjoyable activities to daily life, and modifying activities based on pain levels), relaxation training (e.g., deep breathing, guided imagery, and progressive muscle relaxation), and distraction techniques. See Winterowd et al. (2003) for more information.

Mindfulness-based interventions can also be incorporated at this point, including mindfulness-based meditation (i.e., body scan meditation, eating and/or walking meditations) practices (e.g., see Segal, Williams, & Teasdale, 2002). During these practices, clients are taught to focus in on their breathing and learn to breathe into different parts of their body with the goal of experiencing the symptoms of the body (i.e., chronic pain, emotions, and thoughts) without judgment. Through this here-and-now experience of *being*, clients learn to develop a different relationship with their thoughts, feelings, and chronic pain.

Cognitive Interventions

WHEN PEOPLE DEVELOP negative thoughts and beliefs about their pain, they often think of their pain and its consequences in terms of losses, threats, and disappointments (Winterowd et al., 2003). It is important for clients to learn how to identify, evaluate, and modify their negative self-talk, imagery, (i.e., automatic thoughts) and core beliefs related to their pain and distress. In addition to the mindfulness practices mentioned earlier, clients learn to develop a different relationship with their thoughts and beliefs by viewing themselves as observers or investigators of their thoughts, images, and assumptions to catch/notice them, identify possible errors in thinking (e.g., all-or-nothing thinking, personalization, shoulds/musts, overgeneralizing), and putting these thoughts to the test to see if they are helpful and/or accurate (via thought records, behavioral experiments, and core belief worksheets; see Winterowd et al., 2003 for more information). The underlying motivations for thinking negatively and the consequences for doing so can also be clarified. As clients go through the process of evaluating their negative thoughts and beliefs about their pain, they begin to realize the unrealistic or unhelpful nature of their thoughts and consider the possibility of changing them.

As part of the change process, counselors and clients can role play how to "talk back" to their negative, unrealistic thoughts about their pain. For example, the client could play the role of the negative thoughts about their pain and the counselor could play the role of the "realistic" thoughts. The roles can then be switched to build clients' assertiveness skills in generating their own realistic responses, so that when the negative thoughts pop into their minds outside of session, they are better able to respond to them in more helpful and realistic ways (Winterowd et al., 2003).

Clients with chronic pain can have very vivid, catastrophic images of the pain itself, images of being in pain, images of how people will react to them or relate to them given their pain, and images of the future with pain (Winterowd et al., 2003). To help address negative images related to pain and suffering, clients can learn how to take control of these images by using distraction strategies (i.e., turning down or stopping images) or by changing the image in some way (i.e., directing the images, coping in the image; see Winterowd et al., 2003 for more information).

PROBLEM-SOLVING STRATEGIES

WHEN CLIENTS' NEGATIVE thoughts and beliefs about their pain and life events are indeed accurate, problem-solving strategies can help them cope by deciding what they want to do about the problem. There are several steps to this process, including identifying the problem, breaking down the problem into smaller steps, developing a list of possible solutions, taking one step toward a solution, and evaluating the results of the solution (Beck, 1995; Winterowd et al., 2003).

ASSERTIVENESS TRAINING

CHRONIC PAIN CLIENTS can experience a number of stressors related to their medical care, including the demands of treatment, following these treatment plans, managing their relationships with physicians and staff, and dealing with unrelieved pain despite medical and pharmacological intervention (Winterowd et al., 2003), which can result in a lot of anger and frustration toward oneself and others, including health care providers (Okifuji, Turk, & Curran, 1999), friends, family, employers, and coworkers. These clients need to learn how to communicate directly with a variety of people about their experience of pain, their emotions and thoughts, and their wants and needs. Clients learn to (1) listen to what other people are saying first; (2) keep an open mind when communicating with others; (3) share their own thoughts and feelings in a nonblaming way; (4) get to the main messages or key points when communicating; and (5) be concrete and specific when offering feedback to others (Winterowd et al., 2003).

For more detailed information about counseling clients who have chronic pain, see *Cognitive Therapy With Chronic Pain Patients* (Winterowd et al., 2003).

REFERENCES

Beck, J. S. (1995). *Cognitive therapy: Basics and beyond*. New York: Guilford Press.
Breen, J. (2002). Transitions in the concept of chronic pain. *Advances in Nursing Science, 24,* 48–59.

Cano, A., Mayo, A., & Ventimiglia, M. (2006). Coping, pain severity, interference, and disability: The potential mediating and moderating roles of race and education. *The Journal of Pain, 7,* 459–468.

Clark, J. D. (2002). Chronic pain prevalence and analgesic prescribing in a general medical population. *Journal of Pain and Symptom Management, 23,* 131–137.

Dahl, J., & Lundgren, T. (2006). Acceptance and commitment therapy (ACT) in the treatment of chronic pain. In R. Baer (Ed.), *Mindfulness-based treatment approaches: Clinician's guide to evidence base and applications* (pp. 285–306). San Diego, CA: Elsevier Academic Press.

Dillard, J. (2002). *The chronic pain solution.* New York: Bantam Books.

Dysvik, E., Vinsnes, A. G., & Eikeland, O. (2004). The effectiveness of a multidisciplinary pain management programme managing chronic pain. *International Journal of Nursing Practice, 10,* 224–234.

Flor, H., Fydrich, T., & Turk, D. (1992). Efficacy of multidisciplinary pain treatment centers: A meta-analytic review. *Pain, 49,* 221–230.

Gatchel, R. J. (2005). *Clinical essentials of pain management.* Washington, DC: American Psychological Association.

Gureje, O., Von Korff, M., Simon, G. E., & Gater, R. (1998). Persistent pain and well-being: A World Health Organization study in primary care. *Journal of the American Medical Association, 280,* 147–151.

Hardt, J., Jacobson, C., Goldberg, J., Nickel, R., & Buchwald, D. (2008). Prevalence of chronic pain in a representative sample in the United States. *Pain Medicine,* doi:10.1111/j.1526–4637.2008.00425.x.

Hoffman, B. M., Papas, R. K., Chatkoff, D. K., & Kerns, R. D. (2007). Meta-analysis of psychological interventions for chronic low back pain. *Health Psychology, 26,* 1–9.

Marcus, D. A. (2000). Treatment of nonmalignant chronic pain. *American Family Physician, 61,* 1331–1338.

McCracken, L. M., Gauntlett-Gilbert, J., & Vowles, K. E. (2007). The role of mindfulness in a contextual cognitive-behavioral analysis of chronic pain-related suffering and disability. *Pain, 131,* 63–69.

Merskey, H., & Bogduk, N. (Eds.). (1994). *Classification of chronic pain: Description of chronic pain syndromes and definition of pain terms.* Seattle: IASP Press.

Morley, S., Eccleston, C., & Williams, A. (1999). Systematic review and meta-analysis of randomized controlled trials of cognitive behaviour therapy and behaviour therapy for chronic pain in adults, excluding headache. *Pain, 80,* 1–13.

Morone, N. E., & Greco, C. M. (2007). Mind-body interventions for chronic pain in older adults: A structured review. *Pain Medicine, 8,* 359–375.

Nicholson, B. (2003). Responsible prescribing of opioids for the treatment of chronic pain. *Drugs, 63,* 17–32.

Okifuji, A., Turk, D. C., & Curran, S. L. (1999). Attachment and pain: Investigations of anger targets and intensity. *Journal of Psychosomatic Research, 47,* 1–12.

Portenoy, R. K., Ugarte, C., Fuller, I., & Haas, G. (2004). Population-based survey of pain in the United States: Differences among White, African American, and Hispanic subjects. *The Journal of Pain, 5,* 317–328.

Segal, Z. V., Williams, J. M. G., & Teasdale, J. D. (2002). *Mindfulness-based cognitive therapy for depression: A new approach to preventing relapse.* New York: Guilford Press.

Severeijns, R., Vlaeyen, J. W. S, Van Den Hout, M. A., & Weber, W. E. J. (2001). Pain catastrophizing predicts pain intensity, disability, and psychological distress independent of the level of physical impairment. *Clinical Journal of Pain, 17,* 165–172.

Tumlin, T. R. (2001). Treating chronic-pain patients in psychotherapy. *Journal of Clinical Psychology, 57*(11), 1277–1288.

Turk, D. C. (2001). Treatment of chronic pain: Clinical outcomes, cost-effectiveness, and cost benefits. *Drug Benefit Trends, 13*(9), 36–38.

Turk, D. C., & Burwinkle, T. M., (2005). Clinical outcomes, cost-effectiveness, and the role of psychology in treatments for chronic pain sufferers. *Professional Psychology: Research and Practice, 36,* 219–226.

Turk, D. C., & Nash, J. M. (1993). Chronic pain: New ways to cope. In D. Goleman & J. Gurin (Eds.), *Mind body medicine: How to use your mind for better health* (pp. 111–130). Yonkers, NY: Consumer Reports Books.

van Tulder, M., Ostelo, R., Vlaeyen, J., Linton, S., Morley, S., & Assendelft, W. (2000). Behavioral treatment for chronic low back pain. *Spine, 26,* 270–281.

Winterowd, C., Beck, A., & Gruener, D. (2003). *Cognitive therapy with chronic pain patients.* New York: Springer.

Woolf, C. J., & Mannion, R. J. (1999). Neuropathic pain: Aetiology, symptoms, mechanisms, and management. *The Lancet, 353,* 1959–1964.

World Health Organization. (2001). *The world health report: 2001: Mental health: New understanding, new hope.* Retrieved January 28, 2004, from http://www.who.int/whr2001/2001/

80

Psychiatric Medicines: What Every Counselor Should Know

NORMAN L. KELTNER AND JOAN S. GRANT

THIS BRIEF CHAPTER can serve as no more than an introduction to psychiatric (or psychotropic) drugs. For more extensive coverage on the topic, readers are referred to *Psychotropic Drugs* (4th ed., 2005) by Norman L. Keltner and David Folks. The value of a chapter concerning psychiatric medications is easily defended. Many individuals (e.g., patients, clients, consumers) who use counseling services take these medications, particularly for conditions such as depression and anxiety where these medications are prescribed extensively.

This chapter addresses the more prevalent major drug classifications, including antipsychotics, antidepressants, antimanic, and antianxiety drugs. Subclasses will be identified when appropriate such as the selective serotonin reuptake inhibitors (SSRIs) subclass of antidepressants. Some representative drugs for a specific subclass will also be discussed; for example, the specific drug fluoxetine (Prozac) will be addressed from the SSRI subclass. In addition, brand names will be used in cases where a drug is commonly known by that name. Table 80.1 includes a list of drugs with both generic and brand names identified.

TABLE 80.1 Generic and Brand Names of Frequently Prescribed
Psychotropic Drugs

Antipsychotic	Antidepressant	Antimanic	Antianxiety
Traditional Drugs	*SSRIs*	*Older Drug*	*Benzodiazepines*
Chlorpromazine (Thorazine)	Citalopram (Celexa)	Lithium (Eskalith,	Alprazolam (Xanax) Clonazepam
Fluphenazine (Prolixin)	Escitalopram (Lexapro) Fluoxetine (Prozac)	Lithane, Lithobid, etc.)	(Klonopin) Diazepam (Valium)
Haloperidol (Haldol)	Fluvoxamine (Luvox)	*Anticonvulsants*	Lorazepam (Ativan)
Thioridazine (Mellaril)	Paroxetine (Paxil) Sertraline (Zoloft)	Carbamazepine (Tegretol)	*SSRIs*
SGAs	*TCAs*	Divalproex (Depakote)	See antidepressant column
Clozapine (Clozaril)	Amitriptyline (Elavil)	Lamotrigene	
Olanzapine (Zyprexa)	Clomipramine (Anafranil)	(Lamictal) Oxcarbazepine	
Risperidone (Risperdal)	Desipramine (Norpramin)	(Trileptal) Valproic acid	
Quetiapine (Seroquel)	Imipramine (Tofranil) Nortriptyline	(Depakene)	
Ziprasidone (Geodon)	(Pamelor)	*SGAs* See anti-	
Aripiprazole[a] (Abilify)	*Novel Antidepressants* Bupropion	psychotic column	
	(Wellbutrin)		
	Duloxetine (Cymbalta)		
	Mirtazapine (Remeron)		
	Venlafaxine (Effexor)		

[a] Sometimes aripiprazole is referred to as a third-generation antipsychotic. SGAs = Second-Generation Antipsychotics; SSRIs = Selective Serotonin Reuptake Inhibitors; TCAs = Tricyclic Antidepressants.

A discussion of pharmacokinetics and pharmacodynamics is limited but is introduced in the review of antianxiety drugs to illustrate treatment strategies. Finally, a brief but meaningful review of the side effects of these medications is addressed.

ANTIPSYCHOTICS

Older drugs (1950–1990): Thorazine, Mellaril, Haldol, Prolixin
Newer drugs (1990–present): Clozaril, Risperidone, Zyprexa, Seroquel, Geodon, Abilify

As were the antidepressant, antimanic, and antianxiety drugs, antipsychotics were stumbled upon while looking for something else. They

---

BOX 80.1   Basic Review of Receptors

Most drugs work by affecting what are called receptors. Receptors are protein molecules typically embedded in the surface membrane of a cell. When receptors are stimulated or blocked by a drug, a cell behaves differently than before the drug was given. In the case of mental health problems, the cells are nerve cells (or neurons) in the brain. Almost all of the drugs we will discuss modify receptor function and, in turn, modify neuron responses. In some mental disorders neurons need to work faster or better (think of depression) and in other mental disorders neurons need to slow down (think of mania).

---

were "invented" around 1950 in France, found their way into American state hospitals about 1954 or so, and were fine-tuned and then totally overhauled. That is, the first antipsychotic, chlorpromazine (Thorazine), was "discovered" while searching for a better antihistamine. It was studied in a state hospital and made an immediate hit. Consumers improved. How did it work? It worked by blocking a certain dopamine receptor in a certain part of the brain (see the discussion of receptors in Box 80.1). This drug was fine-tuned and tweaked and eventually many, many other drugs were developed. This tweaking continued until about 1990. At that time antipsychotic drugs were overhauled. The atypical or second-generation antipsychotics (SGAs) were born.

Why was an overhaul necessary? The old 1950–1990 drugs (referred to as traditional antipsychotics) caused a lot of side effects in order to get at that "certain receptor in that certain part of the brain." For example, in order to stop hallucinations effectively, consumers often developed Parkinsonism-type side effects, experienced slowed thinking, and acquired feminine features (caused by an elevation of prolactin). The search began for a drug that could effectively reduce psychotic thinking while not causing these major side problems. There also are a group of symptoms in schizophrenia that these older drugs did not address, the negative symptoms, but which SGAs do address.

Positive Symptoms	**Negative Symptoms**
Hallucinations	Apathy, Anergia (lack of energy)
Delusions	Avolition (lack of motivation)
Disorganized thinking	Anhedonia, Cognitive problems

NEUROCHEMICAL THEORY OF SCHIZOPHRENIA

THE NEUROCHEMICAL THEORY of schizophrenia simply states there is too much dopamine in a specific area of the brain. While this explanation is simple and probably inadequate, the fact remains that all antipsychotic drugs block dopamine receptors, thus attacking this problem directly. Unfortunately, while there probably is too much dopamine in a specific part of the brain, the traditional drugs did not block dopamine just in that specific area. Hence, the side effect issues previously noted.

ATYPICAL OR SECOND-GENERATION ANTIPSYCHOTIC DRUGS

THE FIRST ATYPICAL antipsychotic or SGA was Clozaril. Since then, in order of market availability, Risperidone, Zyprexa, Seroquel, Geodon, and Abilify have been added. Now when one considers that schizophrenia is a lifetime disorder and that drug treatment will last a lifetime as well, cost of medication became a significant issue. The older drugs are inexpensive (about $20/month or less) while the newer drugs are expensive (about $300 to $700/month). When calculated for a lifetime, the difference in cost is substantial.

So, what do the SGAs have to offer for this financially crippling difference (maybe more than $300,000 over a lifetime just in drug costs for a single drug)? The answer is three things. The SGAs (1) cause fewer Parkinsonian side effects (properly called extrapyramidal side effects [EPSEs]); (2) actually cause an improvement in cognition and the so-called negative symptoms of schizophrenia; and (3) do not cause an elevation of prolactin and thus feminizing characteristics (impotence, decreased libido, enlarged breasts, etc.). Box 80.2 provides critical information about several very important concepts when working with consumers treated with antipsychotics.

Important Facts/Points

1. The traditional antipsychotics are good antipsychotics, especially concerning positive symptoms; are inexpensive; but cause EPSEs, feminizing features, and a few other side effects.
2. The SGAs are good antipsychotics for both positive and negative symptoms, are very expensive, and cause fewer side effects.
3. The SGAs are not without problems, however. There is a growing concern that these drugs cause weight gain, Type 2 diabetes, and some alter the heartbeat (Geodon may be the worst offender). See Box 80.2 to review key issues.

**BOX 80.2   Important Concepts for Consumers Taking
Antipsychotics**

Extrapyramidal Side Effects (EPSEs): These are movement disorders and come in a variety of forms, for example, dystonia, dyskinesia, akathisia. They are more likely to occur with the older drugs but can occur with the SGAs too. Basically, these drugs cause a reaction in the brain similar to what is going on in Parkinson's disease. By blocking dopamine, a neurochemical imbalance is created. Parkinson's disease is caused by a deficiency of dopamine. By blocking dopamine receptors, the body "thinks" there is a deficiency of dopamine.

Hyperprolactinemia: This is an elevation in prolactin which the older, traditional drugs are more likely to cause. Symptoms include enlarged breasts, lactation, impotence, and so forth. Obviously, such symptoms would be troublesome and embarrassing, particularly for a young man.

Type 2 Diabetes and Weight Gain: This is caused by the newer drugs. Simply put, many people become obese on the SGAs and also develop insulin resistance (which decreases the amount of glucose entering cells, thus causing high blood sugars). This is the reason many people prescribed SGAs also require an oral hypoglycemic such as metformin (Glucophage).

Agranulocytosis: This is a severe drop in white blood cells that can expose the body to a severe and even fatal infection. Only one of these drugs typically causes agranulocytosis, Clozaril. Because of this fear, consumers taking Clozaril must have weekly or biweekly blood samples drawn for testing.

ANTIDEPRESSANTS

Older drugs: Elavil, Pamelor
Newer drugs: Prozac, Paxil, Zoloft, Celexa, Lexapro, Effexor,
    Wellbutrin

The antidepressants were "discovered" in the early to mid-1950s. These drugs help reduce and sometimes eliminate depression. Although discussing the monoamine oxidase inhibitors (MAOIs) cannot be fully addressed here, one cannot pick up a bottle of cough syrup at the drugstore without noting a prohibition against taking the cough medicine if prescribed MAOIs. Why? These drugs (i.e., MAOIs) can have serious and sometimes fatal interactions with other drugs and even certain foods. They are rarely prescribed because people can get into trouble very easily with these agents. Therefore, the implication for a counselor is that your consumers know the potential side effects of these drugs, that they are not to take over-the-counter medications or prescription drugs unless approved by their primary physician, and they know potential food interaction with MAOIs.

Neurotransmitter Theory of Depression

Depression, from a biochemical perspective, is thought related to a deficiency in serotonin and/or norepinephrine. Most of us are familiar with the serotonin theory because we have seen television advertising depicting Zoloft blocking little serotonin molecules from reentering the neuron, thus building up the amount of serotonin to interact with another neuron. The norepinephrine view, sometimes referred to as the catecholamine hypothesis, is just as convincing though less familiar. All antidepressants work by manipulating these neurotransmitters.

How Antidepressants Work

All of the antidepressants, except the MAOIs mentioned above, work by blocking serotonin, norepinephrine, and sometimes dopamine (e.g., Wellbutrin) from reentering the nerve cell it was released from (this process is known as reuptake). The SSRIs do this just for serotonin, hence the modifier *selective*. The older drugs called tricyclic antidepressants (TCAs) block the reuptake of both serotonin and norepinephrine. As noted, Wellbutrin prevents dopamine from being absorbed back into the neuron it was released from (called a presynaptic neuron), while Effexor and Cymbalta increase both serotonin and norepinephrine based on dosage, that is, at lower dosages mostly serotonin is increased but at higher dosages, norepinephrine increases as well. Again, antidepressants increase serotonin and/or norepinephrine and at least one of these drugs increases dopamine.

SSRIs, TCAs, and Other Antidepressants

Major side effects of the SSRIs are sexual dysfunction (see Box 80.3) and gastrointestinal upset. Since dopamine is "good for sex," it is not surprising that the dopamine-enhancing antidepressant, Wellbutrin, is often added to an SSRI in order to treat the sexual dysfunction caused by the SSRI. Other ways of addressing SSRI-induced sexual dysfunction include lowering the dosage, changing to a non-SSRI, or even waiting to see if the problem goes away.

The TCAs are good antidepressants, as good as the SSRIs and much less expensive, but they are not prescribed as often because they cause

BOX 80.3   Psychiatric Drugs and Sexual Function

It is important to keep in mind one simple but powerful idea: dopamine enhances sex and serotonin inhibits sex. As dopamine levels climb (think cocaine, methamphetamine, or even a drug for Parkinson's disease), sexual behaviors increase. Conversely, when dopamine levels go down, the opposite occurs. When serotonin levels go up, sex is inhibited. Tragically perhaps, the two most common psychiatric drug classes are antipsychotics (which block dopamine) and antidepressants (which often increase serotonin). Sexual behavior can be divided into three phases: libido (desire), arousal (erection/lubrication), and orgasm. The drug management of psychosis and depression unfortunately attacks all three phases; however, what we see most often is dysfunction in the last phase, orgasm. In other words, many men can perform sexually but cannot complete the sex act. In a phrase, dopamine good, serotonin bad!

a couple of important side effects. For instance, it is not uncommon for people taking one of these medications to have a drop in blood pressure, difficulty urinating, or constipation. The most serious problem associated with TCAs are reports of heart attacks caused by these drugs interfering with the way the heart beats.

Effexor, Cymbalta, and Wellbutrin are each unique drugs. Moreover, they appear to be safe and effective. Space does not allow for their discussion.

Important Facts/Points

1. SSRIs are the most common drugs prescribed for depression.
2. SSRIs are associated with sexual dysfunction and this causes major problems for many consumers.
3. TCAs are effective antidepressants but cause blood pressure problems and have been implicated in a few deaths related to heart attacks.
4. Effexor, Cymbalta, and Wellbutrin appear to be good antidepressants. Wellbutrin is often added to an SSRI to improve the SSRI-induced sexual dysfunction.

ANTIMANIC DRUGS

Older drug: Lithium
Newer drugs: Anticonvulsants, Atypical Antipsychotics or Second-Generation Antipsychotics (SGAs)

Lithium, a naturally occurring element in the same column as potassium and sodium on the Periodic Table, is still considered the gold standard for treating bipolar disorder. Lithium is a good drug but the difference in dose between what will help a patient and what might harm a patient is very small (this is referred to as a narrow therapeutic range).

Because of this fact, lithium blood levels are drawn routinely. For some consumers it might be every day while for others it might be every 6 months. What the prescriber is looking for is a blood level of lithium at least 0.6 mEq/L but not greater than 1.0 mEq/L (this is the narrow therapeutic range noted above). Levels that extend past 1.5 are considered toxic. At levels around 3.0 to 4.0 consumers become very disoriented and can die. Therefore, lithium is an effective drug but it must be consistently monitored.

The anticonvulsants, particularly divalproex (or valproic acid), are first-line (or preferred) drugs for bipolar disorder too. Why an anticonvulsant? Well, just remember how talkative and how fast thoughts fly in bipolar consumers you have treated. Someone has likened these rapid mental maneuverings to a seizure—an emotional seizure! If so, an anticonvulsant makes perfect sense.

Divalproex (Depakote) or valproic acid (Depakene) are basically the same drug. We use the generic terms in this case because the generic forms are most often prescribed (i.e., cheaper). This is an excellent drug but it too requires close watch of its blood level (50–125 mcg/ml). At blood levels higher than 125, toxicity may occur. Divalproex works by slowing nerve cell firing. It does this in three different ways but to describe those actions is beyond the scope of this chapter. Nonetheless, the neurons that are firing way too fast are slowed down and the patient is then better able to receive your counseling.

Finally, several SGAs are approved for bipolar disorder. Since psychotic symptoms and mental disorganization are common features of bipolar disorder, it makes sense that antipsychotic drugs would have a role to play in the stabilization and maintenance of bipolar disorder.

Important Facts/Points

1. Lithium blood levels must be monitored.
2. Divalproex blood levels must be monitored.
3. Compliance, or the taking of medications as prescribed, is an ongoing battle. The reason is twofold:

   a. There is a sense of exhilaration to be derived from the manic high.
   b. Consumers often feel that they do not need medication or at least do not take it any longer.

ANTIANXIETY DRUGS

Older drugs: Benzodiazepines such as Valium, Ativan, Xanax
Newer drugs: SSRIs

People have been attempting to subdue their feelings of anxiety with some sort of chemical for thousands of years. Alcohol is a classic example of a chemical that was used and is still used by people to feel less anxious.

BENZODIAZEPINES

THE MOST FAMILIAR antianxiety agents are the benzodiazepines. This class of drugs includes Valium, Ativan, and Xanax, among others. These drugs are very good at making people feel less anxious. They do so by slowing down neuronal firing. In anxiety, neurons are firing too fast in certain parts of the brain. By taking a Valium or similar drug, those neurons slow down. This happens because Valium makes the neuron take in "extra" chloride (which has a negative charge), thus making it more difficult for the neuron to fire. If a person takes enough Valium, he or she will feel relaxed and maybe go to sleep. Indeed, Ativan is often prescribed to people who struggle to sleep.

The downside of these wonderful drugs is that they make people feel so relaxed that they want to take more and more in order to sustain that "peaceful, easy feeling." Unfortunately, this quest can lead to addiction and these drugs are addicting. In fact, though you cannot die from an overdose on a benzodiazepine alone (i.e., not mixed with other drugs), people can die (and have) from cold-turkey withdrawal. To be clear, however, many people have died from overdosing on benzodiazepines when combined with other central nervous system depressants, such as alcohol.

SSRIs

THE BEST DRUGS for anxiety are the SSRIs. While SSRIs do not work rapidly, over time these agents are effective anxiolytics. We have not discussed pharmacokinetics nor pharmacodynamics. Admittedly, these can be boring topics but a brief mention here is in order.

Pharmacokinetics is the study of what the body does to a drug. There are four major pharmacokinetic processes: absorption (getting the drug from the stomach to the blood), distribution (getting the drug from the bloodstream to the brain in the case of psychotropic drugs), metabolism (breaking the drug down to an inactive form), and excretion (getting the drug out of the body). As any one of these processes is affected, the drug's effects can be affected.

Pharmacodynamics is the study of what the drug does to the body. In the case of SSRIs, this is a slow process of several weeks, about how long it takes for them to have a clinical effect. What we tell consumers is this: Benzodiapines are like aspirins. They have an immediate effect but when they wear off, the headache comes back. The SSRIs do not have an immediate effect but they hold promise of actually changing the way neurons behave and thus actually "curing" the anxiety. However, when people are miserable they are not interested in a long-term approach, so we typically suggest treating anxiety with a combination of benzodiazepines and SSRIs, then tapering the benzodiazepines once the SSRIs start achieving their pharmacodynamic manipulation of neurons.

CONCLUSION

THESE FEW PAGES have provided a brief overview of psychiatric medicines. Antipsychotic drugs are used primarily to treat schizophrenia. The most commonly used antispsychotic agents prescribed are the SGAs. These drugs potentially combat both positive and negative symptoms with a decreased risk of causing extrapyramidal side effects (EPSEs) and elevated prolactin (e.g., impotence, etc.). On the other hand, weight gain and Type 2 diabetes are major concerns.

Antidepressants are commonly prescribed drugs for depression and for anxiety. These drugs are frequently prescribed by general practitioners and by psychiatric professionals. The SSRIs do not cause the blood pressure and heart-altering problems caused by the older antidepressants, but they do cause significant sexual dysfunction and gastrointestinal upset. These drugs are also first-line agents in the treatment of anxiety.

Antimanic agents include the natural element lithium and an array of anticonvulsants. Though lithium is still considered the gold standard, divalproex is more commonly prescribed today due to a better side effect profile. Other anticonvulsants such as Tegretol and Lamictal are also prescribed for bipolar disorder but were not reviewed in this text. Finally, SGAs such as Zyprexa, Seroquel, and Abilify are prescribed for bipolar disorder and have proven effective after careful study.

Anxiety remains a significant problem in our society and is most often treated with benzodiazepines and SSRIs. The benzodiazepines have an immediate effect but no lasting effect; SSRIs are almost the opposite. They do not have an immediate effect but if taken consistently over time, they will gradually alleviate anxiety in most consumers.

RECOMMENDED READING

Keltner, N. L. (2005). Genomic influences on schizophrenia-related neurotransmitter systems. *Journal of Nursing Scholarship, 37*(4), 322–328.

Keltner, N. L. (2006). Metabolic syndrome: Schizophrenia and atypical neurotransmitter systems. *Perspectives in Psychiatric Care, 42*(3), 204–207.

Keltner, N. L., & Folks, D. G. (2005). *Psychotropic Drugs* (4th ed.). St. Louis, MO: Elsevier, Churchill, & Livingstone.

Keltner, N. L., & Kelly, J. (2003).The ABCs of psychopharmacology. *Perspectives in Psychiatric Care, 39*(3), 123–126.

Keltner, N. L., Schwecke, L. H, & Bostrom, C. (2007). *Psychiatric Nursing.* St. Louis, MO: Elsevier, Churchill, & Livingstone.

81

Testifying Issues and Strategies as an Expert Witness

IRMO MARINI

THE SPECIALIZATION OF forensic expert testimony in mental health has traditionally been precluded for counselors and dominated primarily by psychologists and psychiatrists. The American Board of Forensic Psychology, established in 1978, restricts its membership to those with PhDs in psychology from an American Psychological Association accredited program. With more than several hundred thousand licensed professional counselors in the United States, the National Board of Forensic Evaluators was originated in 2000 to meet the growing need for forensic mental health evaluators. Certified individuals are typically contracted to assess, report, and provide expert testimony in cases such as sexual abuse, personal injury, substance abuse, domestic violence, child custody, malingering, competency, delinquency, and divorce. Eligibility requires a state license to practice mental health counseling, marriage and family counseling, or social work, plus 3 years postlicensed experience (see www.theHoffmanInstitute.com for details). Individuals are allowed to take deficiency courses if they have not graduated from one of the three eligible programs; therefore, a licensed professional counselor (LPC) can take additional coursework to be eligible for the training and certification exam.

This chapter focuses on the applicable laws related to providing expert testimony and their impact on how counselors must prepare and present their findings in court. Legal definitions and differences in deposing or discovery testimony versus trial testimony are outlined. A third area of coverage addresses the procedures a forensic counselor needs to be aware of before, during, and after having testified. Knowing the order and relevant issues involved at each procedural step becomes important regarding testimony preparation. A practical look at the specific skills counselors should have in order to effectively work in the forensic field is discussed next as well as specific strategies in preparing for and testifying in a courtroom.

LAWS AFFECTING THE TESTIMONY OF COUNSELORS AS EXPERTS

PRIOR TO 1993, expert witnesses were allowed to give opinions based solely on their education, training, and experience without definitively having to qualify their conclusions, even if their opinions were not a generally accepted practice or supported by research in their field. As such, it was not uncommon to find experts with wildly diverging views testifying on behalf of the plaintiff or defense regarding the same case.

The admissibility of such testimony came to an end in 1993, however, in the *Daubert v. Merrill Dow Pharmaceuticals* decision where an expert witness's testimony was disqualified. This decision redefined for the federal court system who could be qualified as an expert (Field, 2000). The Daubert decision noted that expert testimony must be founded on a methodology that was empirically supported and applied to the facts of the issue (Weed, 1998). In addition, any theory or technique used had to be generally accepted by the profession and subjected to peer review and publication. Currently, 26 states have adopted Daubert as the standard while the others refer to a 1923 case, *Frye v. United States*, that earlier clarified who could be considered an expert. The Daubert decision applies to the Federal Rules of Evidence 702 in federal cases (Gunn & Gunn, 1998).

In 1999, in another court decision, *Kumho Tire Co. v. Carmichael*, admissibility of expert testimony surfaced again (Blackwell, 1992). It addressed witness qualifications, admissibility of opinions that included what methods were used to render conclusions, the reliability and validity of those methods, whether the methods were commonly relied upon by other experts, and whether the expert's conclusions had been subjected to peer review and/or published. If most of the criteria are not met, the expert could be disqualified from testifying (Countiss & Deutsch, 2002).

TESTIMONY IN LITIGATION

SINCE THIS IS a new field and counselors are just now becoming certified in it, they may be employed in a variety of ways. In the areas requiring such services discussed earlier, counselors will be asked to assess, report, and testify to specific issues such as child custody, substance abuse, malingering, and so on. Following the interview and work-up of a case, the expert is often called to give a *deposition* prior to a potential court appearance. There are two types of depositions. In the *evidentiary* deposition, the expert procedurally provides testimony in the same manner he or she would in court; however, the setting is generally not a courtroom but rather a conference room. The testimony is sometimes videotaped and is always transcribed by a court reporter, and it is typically videotaped if the expert will not be able to testify live in court. In this instance, the expert will want to discuss with the retaining attorney in advance as to whether any visual or multimedia aids such as PowerPoint should be used in the deposition to visually illustrate major opinions.

The other type of deposition is called a *discovery*. In this type of deposition, the opposing attorney conducts the majority of questioning in order to learn more about the expert's qualifications, what and how conclusions were made, and to observe how credible the witness may appear in court. Although the questions are generally asked by the opposing attorney without a judge or jury present, court procedures still apply. The attorney who retained the expert's services will also be present and typically will only ask follow-up questions if clarification of the expert's earlier testimony needs to occur, and will otherwise only object to the opposing attorney's questions if deemed irrelevant or inappropriate.

In both types of depositions, the expert is typically subpoenaed weeks prior to the deposition and is required to bring certain materials to the deposition, which are generally marked as exhibits (Elliott, 1998). These materials usually include the expert's resume or vitae, a copy of his or her report, and any drafts, all notes taken, audio- or videotapes pertaining to the case, testing or assessment materials and results, a listing of all previous depositions and court testimony cases, and any published books or studies relied upon in forming opinions. Postdeposition, it is also advised that counselors meet with the retaining attorney for feedback and to review any apparent areas of weakness uncovered during the deposition so these may be addressed prior to trial (Blackwell, 1992).

COURTROOM PROCEDURES

K NOWLEDGE OF COURTROOM procedures and the order with which testimony is presented becomes particularly important for the expert in preparing to render his or her opinions. Before the trial date, the expert and retaining attorney should engage in a pretrial conference regarding how the expert's findings can best be conveyed to the jury. This discussion typically involves issues such as how the expert's findings will be solicited, use of multimedia aids, and specific areas the expert should be prepared to address (Blackwell, 1992).

DIRECT EXAMINATION

DIRECT EXAMINATION IS conducted by the retaining attorney and should present no surprises to the expert that have not been previously discussed. Prior to the court's delving into the counselor's opinions of the case, however, he or she must first be rendered as "qualified" to testify as an expert (Gunn & Gunn, 1998). As such, the retaining attorney will begin by asking the expert a number of personal background questions that may include:

1. Name, job title, and affiliation,
2. Education, degrees, certifications, and/or licenses,
3. Professional work experience, particularly those acquired skills related to why the witness should be considered an expert,
4. Professional affiliations, publications, and presentations related to the field of specialization,
5. Any awards or honors that connote peer recognition for excellence in the field.

Once the retaining attorney is satisfied his or her witness has adequately conveyed the extent of his or her qualifications, the attorney will move to qualify the witness as an expert to the judge. If there is some doubt, the opposing counsel has the right to *voir dire* or further question the witness's qualifications before a decision is made as to whether the expert is indeed qualified. If for some reason the witness is deemed not to be an expert, he or she is excused from testifying.

Once qualified, direct examination continues again with the retaining attorney laying the foundation for how the expert came to his or her conclusions. In this stage of testimony, the retaining attorney will generally proceed with the following order of questioning:

1. When were you contacted about this case and what were you asked to do?

2. What materials did you review in this case?
3. How do you typically perform assessments in cases such as this?
4. What kind of information did you gather in this case and who did you consult or interview for this information?
5. Did you perform any testing or other analysis regarding the client?
6. Could you explain to the jury what those tests assess and your overall findings?
7. Would you explain to the jury what your overall conclusions are?

It is further important to note that in the legal arena, an expert's opinions must simply have a "probability" of occurring (having a 51% or greater chance of occurring) and not be absolute (Gunn & Gunn, 1998). Experienced counselors generally listen closely to opposing counsel's questions during cross-examination where counsel can attempt to solicit contradicting opinions from the expert by asking about the "possibility" of a situation. For example, the expert under direct examination may opine that an alleged malingerer with a low-back injury collecting workers' compensation and caught on videotape reshingling his roof is indeed malingering and therefore not totally disabled from a vocational standpoint. Under cross-examination from the opposing plaintiff counsel, however, a question may be, "Isn't it possible that my client was simply having one good day but the vast majority of time he is in extreme pain and unable to work?" In this instance, opposing counsel is attempting to have the expert contradict himself or herself by saying "yes," after he or she has just opined otherwise (the individual is malingering).

It is important for the expert to explain to the jury that although it is "possible" (less than a 51% probability) the plaintiff had one good day, based on the medical work restrictions as well as the plaintiff's testimony about not being able to lift anything over 10 pounds, climb, stoop, or bend, malingering would be a more probable likelihood. It is also useful for counselors to define for the jury the difference between probability and possibility, and the fact that probability has a much greater likelihood of occurring, while possibility is considered as speculation.

Cross-Examination

DURING THIS STAGE of testimony, opposing counsel has the opportunity to question the expert's qualifications, methodology, and findings. If opposing counsel has not previously voir dired the expert during direct examination, questions regarding qualifications will be limited but perhaps specific to questioning the extensiveness of experience or training the expert has with the case in question. Although it may not be enough to exclude testimony, lack of experience with the specific disability in question can undermine an expert's credibility.

Regarding the cross-examination approach, opposing counsel typically asks many similar questions to those asked during deposition, especially those that counsel believed were poorly answered. Opposing counsel may attempt to "impeach" the expert's testimony if it is inconsistent with what was stated during deposition or direct examination, again with the intent of undermining credibility for the jury. No matter which side you as the expert are testifying for, it becomes critical to remain *objective and consistent* with your methodology and testimony. If you had given contradictory testimony in other cases, opposing counsel will access and use this information against you to damage credibility.

If the expert has excellent qualifications, opposing counsel will instead focus on discrediting the expert's report itself. Counsel will question the expert's methodology, conclusions, and assumptions or inferences made (Blackwell, 1992). Other than these general guidelines in the strategies opposing counsel may employ, typical areas of questioning will/can include the following:

1. How much do you charge per hour and how much have you charged in this case? (designed to illustrate the expert's monetary incentives).
2. How many plaintiff cases have you been retained and how many defense cases? (designed to show you are biased toward one side or another).
3. Be alert for questions that begin with "Wouldn't you agree with me that . . ." This type of question is designed to get the expert to discuss the "possibility" rather than probability of something occurring and is generally set up to draw out an inconsistent opinion from the expert.

Blackwell (1992) also notes the three basic rules experts should adhere to during cross-examination, including telling the truth, listening to the question before answering, and looking directly at the attorney questioning you.

RE-DIRECT EXAMINATION AND RE–CROSS-EXAMINATION

FOLLOWING CROSS-EXAMINATION, THE retaining attorney has the opportunity to ask additional questions of the vocational expert. Generally, this occurs only when opposing counsel has effectively damaged the expert's credibility in terms of qualifications, methodology, and/or concluding opinions or to further clarify earlier testimony. In re–cross-examination, opposing counsel may again focus on areas of weakness regarding certainty of opinions. Blackwell (1992) indicates how opposing counsel may ask a question that does not require the expert to answer, but is designed to be argumentative of a previously answered question with the intent of making the expert's response sound implausible or biased.

POSTTRIAL CONFERENCE

REGARDLESS THE OUTCOME of the trial, counselors can benefit by obtaining feedback from the retaining attorney regarding how the expert's testimony was perceived in terms of strengths and weaknesses. Attorney feedback regarding testimony delivery, demeanor, perceived trustworthiness, and credibility can help the counselor enhance his or her skills.

TESTIFYING STRATEGIES FOR THE VOCATIONAL EXPERT

PRIOR TO THIS point, we have discussed key legal rulings for testifying experts, courtroom procedures, types of questioning, and strategy of questioning tactics used by plaintiff and defense attorneys. Finally, we explore specific strategies for counselors to remember when called to testify in court:

1. The expert witness is there to educate the jury and provide his or her objective findings in layperson language without advocating for or against the client.
2. The most credible expert witnesses remain calm and nonemotional while testifying. You should not appear smug, sarcastic, argumentative, or defensive. Again, your duty is to educate the jury in a similar manner you might otherwise educate students in a classroom.
3. You are not expected to know all the answers, and it is recommended to say "I don't know" rather than to guess an answer and be challenged for it later.
4. Experts must remember to testify only to matters related to their area of expertise, and not testify beyond the boundaries of their education, training, or experience.
5. Listen to the question carefully before answering. This not only gives you a moment to formulate your answer but also allows the

retaining attorney to object to inappropriate questioning and can interrupt the cross-examiner's rhythm (Blackwell, 1992).

6. If the cross-examiner is badgering you or being argumentative about a response, let the judge know you have answered the question as best you can (Blackwell, 1992).

7. Split your eye contact time between the attorney asking questions and the jury in explaining your opinions. If multimedia is being used for illustration, present the information as if the jury was a classroom of students by directly addressing them while drawing their attention to relevant areas of the screen.

8. If uncertain as to how to answer a question, it is appropriate to ask the judge about responding. Similarly, you may ask the judge if you can qualify an answer if a yes/no response were required but further explanation is warranted because your response will otherwise be mischaracterized or misconstrued.

9. Experts are often advised to only answer the question and not to volunteer any further information. This recommendation does not apply to instances where further clarification of a point is necessary to make sure the jury understands.

10. Image and behavior play an important role in an expert's credibility and trustworthiness. Males should wear a dark suit with a conservative tie, women either a business dress or suit with low heels. The old adage, "Never let them see you sweat" is also relevant in testifying. If you become confused or flustered from fielding tough questions, you must maintain your composure and convey a confident demeanor. When leaving the stand, a slight nod to the jury may be appropriate, again, trying not to look dejected or triumphant.

Other dynamics in testifying, or presenting to audiences in general, relate to the concepts of the primacy and recency affect. These concepts are based on the understanding that people are most attentive at the beginning and ending of a speech or address. Some jurors often lose interest or even fall asleep during the middle parts of testimony, therefore, it becomes important to plan out the best way to explain the expert's findings.

CONCLUSION

THE GROWING NEED for forensic mental health evaluators plays a significant role in scientifically and methodologically providing the court with valuable knowledge in helping to render more informed decisions. Regardless who retains the expert, testimony must be objective, consistently applied to all cases, and follow the same generally accepted protocol in the expert's field. Experts need to be familiar with the laws concerning admissible evidence for experts as well as courtroom procedures.

There are numerous strategies counselors can benefit from in the delivery of their testimony, including physical appearance/dress, demeanor, visual aids, language, and style of explaining one's findings. The most credible and trustworthy expert is one who is confident and can remain calm under duress, stay objective, and educate the jury using nontechnical terms.

REFERENCES

Blackwell, T. L. (1992). *The vocational expert primer*. Athens, GA: Elliott & Fitzpatrick.

Countiss, R. N., & Deutsch, P. M. (2002). The life care planner, the judge and Mr. Daubert. *Journal of Life Care Planning, 11*(1), 35–47.

Elliott, T. C. (1998). A plaintiff's attorney's perspective on life care plans. In R. O. Weed (Ed.), *Life care planning and case management handbook* (pp. 371–380). Boca Raton, FL: CRC Press.

Field, T. (2000). *A resource for the rehabilitation consultant on the Daubert and Kumho rulings*. Athens, GA: Elliott & Fitzpatrick.

Gunn, L. D., & Gunn, T. R. (1998). A defense attorney's perspective on life care plans. In R. O. Weed (Ed.), *Life care planning and case management handbook* (pp. 381–398). Boca Raton, FL: CRC Press.

Weed, R. O. (1998). *Life care planning and case management handbook*. Boca Raton, FL: CRC Press.

Appendix A

NOEL A. YSASI, MARK A. STEBNICKI,
AND IRMO MARINI

PROFESSIONAL COUNSELING ASSOCIATIONS AND ORGANIZATIONS

THE FOLLOWING IS a list and description of the various associations and organizations that identify with the counseling profession. Professional counseling associations and organizations have grown significantly within the last 30 years at the state, national, and international level. A comprehensive directory of all known associations and organizations is not the intent of this resource. Rather, Appendix A offers a brief description and Web site address of the various nationally known professional counseling associations and their related divisions within the multitude of counseling specialties in North America. Please note that there is a plethora of other organizations whose membership comprises primarily consumers of counseling services. These peer-related and consumer organizations are not listed because of the enormity of this base of consumer and self-help organizations.

AMERICAN COUNSELING ASSOCIATION

THE AMERICAN COUNSELING Association (ACA) is a not-for-profit, professional counseling organization that serves nearly 45,000 members. Founded in 1952, ACA is the largest counseling association both nationally and internationally. This organization represents professional counselors in a diversity of practice settings. The ACA states that its mission "is to enhance the quality of life in society by promoting the development of professional counselors, advancing the counseling profession, and using the profession and practice of counseling to promote respect for human dignity and diversity."

The ACA also has been instrumental in setting professional and ethical standards for the counseling profession, and it has been instrumental in the counselor accreditation and licensure process. It also represents the interests of the professional counselors before Congress and federal agencies, and strives to promote recognition of professional counselors to the public and the media.

The following is a brief description and list of Web site addresses for each of ACA's 19 counseling divisions. The home page for ACA is http://www.counseling.org.

Association for Assessment in Counseling and Education (AACE) http://www.theaaceonline.com

Originally, the Association for Measurement and Evaluation in Guidance, AACE was chartered in 1965. The purpose of AACE is to promote the effective use of assessments in the counseling profession. It publishes a quarterly journal, *Measurement and Evaluation in Counseling and Development,* in which reviews and evaluations of new, revised, or upcoming assessment instruments are provided. A subscription to the division newsletter (*NewsNotes*) offers nationwide and international news, legislative updates, and articles of concern to diagnosticians as well as updates of upcoming events.

Association for Adult Development and Aging (AADA) http://www.aadaweb.org/index.html

Chartered in 1986, AADA serves as the central organization dedicated to professional development and advocacy related to adult development and aging issues. This association promotes counseling concerns across the life span. Overall, AADA cultivates partnerships with other professional counseling associations and organizations to help improve the standards for care of adults as well as older adults.

Association for Creativity in Counseling (ACC) http://www.aca-acc.org

The Association for Creativity in Counseling (ACC) is a forum for counselors, counselor educators, creative arts therapists, and counselors in training to explore unique and diverse approaches to counseling. Its goal is to promote greater awareness, advocacy, and understanding of diverse and creative approaches to counseling. The *Journal of Creativity in Mental Health,* the official journal of the ACC, is an interdisciplinary journal for educators and practitioners that examines the benefits and practical applications of using creativity to help deepen self-awareness and build healthy relationships. This refereed journal explores how creative, diverse, and relational therapeutic approaches can be used by therapist and client to cultivate self-discovery, personal growth, and positive relations with family and others.

American College Counseling Association (ACCA) http://www.col legecounseling.org

This association is one of the newest divisions of the American Counseling Association. Chartered in 1991, the focus of ACCA is to foster student development in colleges, universities, and community colleges. It works in collaboration with other organizations related to higher education, and provides the necessary leadership and advocacy for counselors. The ACCA publishes the *Journal of College Counseling (JCC)* twice a year that focuses on research, professional issues, and innovative practices in counseling.

Association for Counselors and Educators in Government (ACEG) http://www.dantes.doded.mil/dantes_web/organizations/ aceg/index.htm

Originally the Military Educators and Counselors Association, ACEG was chartered in 1984. Dedicated to counseling clients and their families in local, state, and federal government or in military-related agencies, ACEG extends itself to all branches of the military and the family members of active or retired personnel, and to civilian employees of government agencies such as the Department of Defense. It aims in developing administrators, counselors, and educators in the government setting while promoting only the highest standards of professionalism for these professionals.

Association for Counselor Education and Supervision (ACES) http:// www.acesonline.net/index.asp

Originally the National Association of Guidance and Counselor Trainers, ACES was the founding association of ACA in 1952. The ACES emphasize the need for quality education and supervision of counselors for all work settings. Its mission is to improve the practice of professional counseling by endorsing effective counselor education and supervision. The quarterly journal, *Counselor Education and Supervision,* publishes manuscripts that deal with research, theory development, and program applications that relate to counselor education and supervision.

Association for Lesbian, Gay, Bisexual and Transgender Issues in Counseling (ALGBTIC) http://www.algbtic.org/index.htm

ALGBTIC acknowledges individuals from diverse sociocultural backgrounds that represent differences in race, ethnicity, class, gender, sexual orientation, age, and belief systems in order to endorse a greater awareness and understanding of gay, lesbian, bisexual, and transgender issues. The ALGBTIC provides an avenue for counselors to find community, common ground, support, and resources. This organization educates counselors to the unique needs of client identity development and a nonthreatening counseling environment by aiding in the reduction of stereotypical thinking and homoprejudice. The quarterly *Journal of LGBT Issues in Counseling* was introduced in 2006. This journal addresses counseling issues that relate to the development of gay, lesbian, bisexual, and transgender individuals.

Association for Multicultural Counseling and Development (AMCD) http://www.amcdaca.org/amcd/default.cfm

Originally the Association of Non-White Concerns in Personnel and Guidance, the Association for Multicultural Counseling and Development (AMCD) was chartered in 1972. This organization seeks to develop programs focused on improving ethnic and racial empathy and understanding. Further, AMCD strives to improve cultural, ethnic, and racial empathy and understanding by promoting programs to advance and sustain personal growth opportunities for members from diverse cultural backgrounds. It fosters the philosophy that enhancing an understanding of cultural diversity is an influential source for changing attitudinal barriers.

American Mental Health Counselors Association (AMHCA) http:// www.amhca.org

Chartered in 1978, AMHCA represents mental health counselors, advocating for client access to quality services within the health care industry. It also advocates for the profession of mental health counseling through state licensing boards, advocacy, education, and professional counselor development. The AMHCA publishes the quarterly *Journal of Mental Health Counseling,* which features articles addressing all aspects of practice, theory, research, and professionalism that relate to mental health counseling.

American Rehabilitation Counseling Association (ARCA) http://www.ar caweb.org

The ARCA is an association of rehabilitation counseling practitioners, educators, and students who are concerned with advocating the development and quality of life for persons with chronic illnesses and disabilities throughout the life span. It promotes excellence in rehabilitation counseling practice, research, consultation, and professional development. It is interested in eliminating environmental and attitudinal barriers through public education, legislation, and promoting the rights of persons with disabilities. It publishes a quarterly journal, *Rehabilitation Counseling Bulletin (RCB)*, which incorporates empirical research and clinical practice implications for rehabilitation counselors.

American School Counselor Association (ASCA) http://www.school counselor.org

Since 1953 ASCA has endorsed school counseling professionals and has focused on activities that shape the personal, educational, and career development of students. Its members also work with parents, educators, and community members to provide a positive learning environment. The ASCA advocates that school counseling professionals work with parents and educators to develop a constructive learning environment for students. Its journal, *Professional School Counseling*, is published six times a year and addresses practice, theory, and research issues that assist school counseling professionals to stay on top of the latest issues.

Association for Spiritual, Ethical, and Religious Values in Counseling (ASERVIC) http://www.aservic.org

Originally the National Catholic Guidance Conference, ASERVIC was chartered in 1974. It is devoted to professionals who believe that spiritual, ethical, religious, and other human values are essential to the full development of the person and to the discipline of counseling. The ASERVIC publishes the quarterly journal, *Counseling and Values*. The journal accepts theoretical, philosophical, or empirical manuscripts that deal with the ethical, religious, and spiritual values that correlate with counseling. The journal also publishes free intellectual inquiry into spiritual, ethical, religious, and personal/social values related to the counseling profession.

Association for Specialists in Group Work (ASGW) http://www.asgw.org

Chartered in 1973, ASGW provides professional leadership in the field of group work and establishes standards for ethical and competent practice of group work. It was established to encourage excellence in group work training, practice, and research at both the national and international levels. It publishes the quarterly *Journal for Specialists in Group Work*. Issues in this journal relate to practitioners, counselor educators and supervisors, and researchers interested in group work.

Counseling Association for Humanistic Education and Development (C-AHEAD) http://www.c-ahead.com

The C-AHEAD was a founding association of ACA chartered in 1952 and provides a forum for the exchange of information related to humanistically oriented counseling practices. It promotes individual change that reflects the growing body of knowledge about humanistic principles as applied to human development and potential. It promotes the development of the physical, mental, emotional, and the spiritual aspects of the person. It publishes the *Journal of Humanistic Education and Development* on a quarterly basis. Articles published in the journal cover a wide range of topics related to the mission and purpose of C-AHEAD.

Counselors for Social Justice (CSJ) http://counselorsforsocialjustice.com

This is a community of counselors, counselor educators, graduate students, and school and community leaders. Its membership seeks equity and advocates an end to oppression and injustice affecting clients, students, counselors, families, communities, schools, workplaces, governments, and other social and institutional systems. The *Journal for Social Action in Counseling and Psychology* is available twice a year electronically and its intent is to encourage systemic and social change through activism.

International Association of Addictions and Offender Counselors (IAAOC) http://www.iaaoc.org

Originally the Public Offender Counselor Association, IAAOC was chartered in 1972. The IAAOC advocates the development of effective counseling and rehabilitation programs for people with substance abuse problems, other addictions, adults, and juvenile public offenders. Members consist of professional counselors and others interested in the addictions or forensic criminal justice fields. The *Journal of*

Addictions and Offender Counseling is published twice a year and promotes research in areas of addictions, offender counseling, and other topics related to its mission and goals of the association.

International Association of Marriage and Family Counselors (IAMFC) http://www.iamfc.com

Chartered in 1989, IAMFC members promote the development of healthy family systems through prevention, education, and therapy. The membership is devoted to help increase the competent and ethical practice working with couples and families. It offers a journal, the *Family Journal,* and a newsletter available three timers per year, the *Family Digest.* The journal and newsletter focus on current research and practice issues and other activities related to the organization's mission.

National Career Development Association (NCDA) http://ncda.org

Originally the National Vocational Guidance Association, NCDA was one of the founding associations of ACA chartered in 1952. The mission of NCDA is to promote career development for all people across the life span through public information, member services, conferences, and publications. It publishes a quarterly journal for its members, *Career Development Quarterly.* The journal offers its membership articles related to theory, research, practice, and other issues related to NCDA's mission.

National Employment Counseling Association (NECA) http://geo cities.com/employmentcounseling/

NECA, originally the National Employment Counselors Association, was chartered in 1966. The commitment of NECA is to offer professional leadership to professional counselors who work in employment and/or career development settings. It offers its members a quarterly, the *Journal of Employment Counseling.* This journal publishes articles related to the theory, research, and practice of professionals working in career counseling and other community, state, and federal employment agencies.

OTHER ASSOCIATIONS AND ORGANIZATIONS THAT IDENTIFY WITH PROFESSIONAL COUNSELING

American Psychological Association (APA) http://www.apa.org

Based in Washington, DC, APA's Web site states that it is a scientific and professional organization that represents the profession of psychology in the United States. With 148,000 members, APA is the largest association of psychologists worldwide. There are 53 professional divisions within this organization. To view each of these divisions, go to http://www.apa.org/about/division.html for a complete list.

Canadian Association of Rehabilitation Professionals, Inc. (CARP) http://www.carpnational.org/whoarewe.html

Established in the early 1970s, CARP is a national nonprofit association that represents rehabilitation counseling professionals who provide a continuum of rehabilitation services. Its members are primarily in eastern Canada, regions within New Brunswick, Nova Scotia, Newfoundland, Labrador, and Prince Edward Island. Its philosophy suggests that rehabilitation counseling professionals partner with persons with disabilities and their families to provide services such as assessment, counseling for disability adjustment, career and vocational counseling, case management, coordination of disability services, job placement services, as well as other services needed to improve the quality of life and functioning of persons with chronic illnesses and disabilities. The CARP has interest in increasing the competence and professionalism of rehabilitation counselors and publishes an interdisciplinary code of ethics, the *Canadian Code of Ethics for Rehabilitation Professionals*. To ensure that rehabilitation professionals meet certain standards of competence and ethical behavior, CARP has a registry for the designation of such professionals, the Registered Rehabilitation Professional (RRP).

National Rehabilitation Counseling Association (NRCA) http://nrca-net.org

Based in Manassas, VA, NRCA became independent in 2005 from its former umbrella organization, the National Rehabilitation Association (NRA). It was chartered in 1958 and represents rehabilitation counselors who work in a variety of employment settings that include, but are not limited to, private rehabilitation insurance and case management companies, state-federal system of vocational rehabilitation, rehabilitation counselor education, community-based rehabilitation facilities, and other general rehabilitation counseling settings. The NRCA publishes the *Journal of Applied Rehabilitation Counseling (JARC)* on a quarterly basis. Articles in this peer-reviewed journal include topics on rehabilitation counselor theory, research, education, and practice.

Professional Association of Rehabilitation Counselors (PARC) http://
parc1.homestead.com/title.html

The PARC is a national association of counselors who primarily possess a graduate degree in rehabilitation, substance abuse, and clinical
counseling. Its membership practices in a variety of work settings and
possesses occupational titles such as mental health, substance abuse,
clinical, and rehabilitation counselor. It has specialty divisions for
substance abuse counselors, clinical mental health counselors, rehabilitation counselor educators, and general rehabilitation counseling.
It was founded by Dr. Lloyd Goodwin, Professor and Director of the
Substance Abuse and Clinical Counseling Program at East Carolina
University (ECU). The majority of its membership lives and works in
North Carolina and are alumni of ECU's rehabilitation counseling and
substance abuse and clinical counseling programs.

Appendix B

SELF-STUDY EXAM FOR *PCDR*

Note: The co-editors of the PCDR *requested that each contributor/author submit four multiple-choice questions based on the chapter they wrote. A total of 323 multiple-choice questions were developed for this self-study exam. The questions are separated into each counseling domain or content area. They are based on the core content and knowledge areas of the CACREP and CORE accredited standards for counselor training programs. The self-study examination for the PCDR is independent of any accreditation, credentialing, or counselor licensure entity or organization. The intention of the self-study examination is to assist preprofessional counselors in the general preparation of their counselor licensure and/or certification exam. It is recognized that there is a variety of specialty areas within the counseling field. Thus, this exam may not include all content items related to the counselor's specialty area and academic training. The answers to the self-study exam can be found in Appendix C.*

The Identity of Professional Counselors

1. Although professional growth of the supervisee and the supervisory relationship are important elements within the clinical

---

Note of thanks: The authors of the *PCDR* would like to thank Kit Roberson for the initial formatting of the 323 questions contained in the self-study examination.

supervision process, according to Bernard and Goodyear, which statement below suggests an even stronger obligation from the supervisor-supervisee perspective?

   a. Client welfare and protection is of paramount importance and supersedes the personal and professional needs of the supervisee.

   b. Supervisee skill development and trying out new counseling techniques on clients should have the strongest commitment in the supervisor-supervisee relationship.

   c. Education and consultation has a stronger obligation in the supervisory working alliance.

   d. Personal growth by the supervisee has the strongest obligation because without this element, the new professional counselor could have personal issues that may contaminate the client-counselor or even supervisory relationship.

2. Clinical supervision encompasses a variety of techniques, approaches, and formats. Thus, deciding on which clinical supervision format is appropriate for each supervisee:

   a. depends solely on the supervisee's work setting.

   b. basically depends upon the overall needs of the supervisee.

   c. should only be done after an assessment of the supervisory working alliance.

   d. really depends on the availability and willingness of the supervisor to supervise.

3. Which statement most accurately depicts developmental models (DM) of supervision?

   a. DM of supervision is the most widely researched of the supervision models and examines the supervisee's personal and professional growth and cognitive development as a counselor.

   b. DM of supervision looks at how the supervisory roles of counselor, consultant, and teacher affect the supervisory working alliance and relationship.

   c. DM of supervision investigates the intercorrelations between the supervisee's clients, work setting, and the therapeutic approaches facilitated in therapy.

   d. DM of supervision measures the supervisee's level of empathy facilitated during therapeutic interactions and then interposes other strategies and techniques as the supervisee develops professionally.

4. Which statement best reflects some of the technological advances currently being utilized in clinical supervision?

   a. Because of video conferencing capabilities, supervisees never have to receive face-to-face supervision.

   b. In most settings, e-mail supervision is adequate for supervisee growth and development as a counselor.

   c. The most affordable and technologically efficient approach to supervision is telephone conferencing along with weekly case notes submitted via e-mail.

   d. The manner in which technology is used to enhance the supervision process depends on the needs of the supervisee, the work setting, availability of technology, and other related factors.

5. Which statement about credentialing is most accurate as it relates to the counseling profession?

   a. Certification in a counseling specialty is required by most state statutes prior to being licensed to practice in the field of counseling.

   b. Licensure to practice in the counseling profession is regulated by state law and is required for reimbursement of services by third-party and private payers.

   c. Certification is a process that almost all counselor educational programs must acquire in order to identify themselves as a counselor education and training program.

   d. Certification to practice in the counseling profession is based on state counseling statutes and has the benefit of legally being able to receive reimbursement from third-party payers for services rendered.

6. Which statement best characterizes the American Counseling Association (ACA)?

   a. ACA is an accreditation body that accredits professional counselors as well as counselor training programs.

   b. ACA is a national counselor licensing board that oversees regulatory boards for all professional counselors.

   c. ACA is considered a professional counseling association that advocates and promotes the competent and ethical practice of the counseling profession.

   d. ACA is national organization that regulates third-party reimbursement rates for professional counselors.

7. The National Credentials Registry (NCR) was established for the purpose of:

   a. issuing a professional counseling certification for all professional counselors.
   b. assisting licensed professional counselors with the process of portability of their counseling license across the different state licensing boards.
   c. issuing a license to all professional counselors so they may practice across different states.
   d. attracting more counselors to the counseling field.

8. One of the primary purposes of the licensed professional counselor's professional disclosure statement is to:

   a. inform the client/consumer of the counselor's educational background, professional experiences, and describe the counselor's scope of practice.
   b. assist the licensed counselor with third-party reimbursement for services.
   c. satisfy the requirements of counselor accreditation entities that govern the practice of counseling across different states.
   d. try and limit the potential conflicts of interest between the client and counselor and to monitor fees for reimbursement from third-party payers.

9. Counseling, as a profession, evolved from which of the following?

   a. was mandated in federal law and regulations.
   b. development and maturation of specialty areas of practice.
   c. outgrowth of clinical psychology.
   d. began as a large group of general counselors, followed by specialization.

10. What was the first professional association to comprehensively represent counselors?

   a. National Counseling Association.
   b. American Psychological Association.
   c. American Personnel and Guidance Association.
   d. National Career Guidance Association.

11. Which was the first state to achieve state counselor licensure in 1975?

   a. Virginia.
   b. Texas.
   c. California.
   d. Vermont.

12. Certification began in this country with which of the following groups?

    a. rehabilitation counselors.
    b. mental health counselors.
    c. teachers and school counselors.
    d. addictions counselors.

13. Guidance and consultation involves assisting clients with:

    a. psychological change.
    b. life choices and decisions.
    c. identifying values.
    d. b and c.

14. Rehabilitation counselors work with which population?

    a. older adults.
    b. persons with disabilities and chronic illness.
    c. persons with substance abuse issues.
    d. all of the above.

15. A core set of knowledge areas for counselors has been identified by which of the below professional entities?

    a. CACREP.
    b. CORE.
    c. NBCC.
    d. a and b.

16. Which of the following is most accurate in regard to the current state of counselor licensure?

    a. Licensure laws are standard across all 50 states.
    b. Once a counselor is licensed, the license can be easily transferred to any other state.
    c. Licensure laws vary considerably across states in title and practice domains.
    d. Social workers and psychologists can sit for counseling licensing exams.

Professional, Ethical, and Practice Management Issues in Counseling

17. Successful private practice counselors are able to:

    a. challenge their belief system in order to see themselves as businesspersons.
    b. be at the right place at the right time.

c. charge fees above what is usual and customary.

d. not take insurance or deal with managed health care.

18. A marketing plan should target:

    a. other counselors already in private practice.

    b. both clients and referrals sources.

    c. the medical community.

    d. those clients that are in your niche market.

19. *Cross-Pollination* refers to:

    a. an approach to public speaking.

    b. how to be an entrepreneur in the business world.

    c. practice expansion based on networking with others who work with the client.

    d. developing multiple income streams.

20. The prospect of private practice for counselors will continue to be:

    a. a viable career path.

    b. an elusive goal.

    c. a part-time endeavor.

    d. only for doctorate-level counselors.

21. The current *ACA Code of Ethics* requires counselors to break confidentiality when there is:

    a. clear and imminent danger.

    b. serious and foreseeable harm.

    c. insufficient contact.

    d. possible danger.

22. The concept of dual relationships has been replaced with the concept of:

    a. multiple relationships.

    b. comingled relationships.

    c. conjoint relationships.

    d. beneficial versus harmful relationships.

23. If a counselor uses a technique that is neither grounded in theory nor has an empirical or scientific foundation, the counselor must:

    a. never use it again.

    b. read at least one journal article about the technique.

    c. label the technique as unproven or developing.

    d. consult on the appropriate use of the technique with a trusted peer.

24. When conducting distance counseling through the Internet, a counselor must:

    a. use a video camera whenever possible.
    b. verify client identification.
    c. allow for electronic scheduling via the Internet.
    d. ensure that the client has a printed copy of the informed consent document.

25. This type of insurance offers the most freedom of choice for the client:

    a. Point of Service Plan (POS).
    b. Indemnity Insurance.
    c. Health Maintenance Organization (HMO).
    d. Preferred Provider Organization (PPO).

26. The "back door" method of accessing managed care panels:

    a. allows you to be an ad hoc or one-time provider of service for a plan.
    b. makes you only an associate for that plan.
    c. requires much documentation.
    d. has the plan send you clients.

27. The National Provider Identifier is:

    a. a standard unique identifier for health care providers.
    b. a Web-based program to help find the right provider.
    c. necessary to be licensed.
    d. mandated by the federal government.

28. Electronic billing:

    a. can be very difficult.
    b. is currently mandated.
    c. can only be done by third-party billers.
    d. is facilitated by billing software.

29. The three key players in the world of electronic billing are:

    a. payers, providers, and clearinghouses.
    b. providers, software vendors, and clearinghouses.
    c. software vendors, providers, and billing services.
    d. software vendors, clearinghouses, and payers.

30. The two types of self-service electronic billing solutions are:

    a. all-service and partial-service billing.
    b. Web-based and computer-based.

c. broadband and dial-up.

d. direct-connect and regular connect.

31. The four key ingredients of an effective practice Web site are:

a. keyword-rich text, balanced design, simple navigation, and clear call-to-action.

b. balanced design, meta description, several domain names, and clear call-to-action.

c. balanced design, complex navigation, educational text, and clear call-to-action.

d. balanced design, simple navigation, educational text, and clear call-to-action.

32. The only two direct ways of increasing Web site visibility are:

a. SEO and PPC.

b. submitting online articles and SEO.

c. PPC and keyword-rich text.

d. SEO and meta keywords.

33. Which statement best depicts the intent of the professional disclosure statement (PDS)?

a. The PDS discloses to clients the nature and boundary of the counseling relationship, provides important information regarding the counselor's background, and the services the counselor is competent to offer.

b. The PDS is a written statement basically indicating that the client has been fully informed of his or her rights and responsibilities, the services that the counselor is competent to offer, and provides a signed document suggesting that the client has been fully informed.

c. The PDS acts as a contract that the client and counselor sign suggesting that the counselor will honor his or her commitment to providing appropriate therapeutic services to the client.

d. The PDS is a legally binding agreement in almost all jurisdictions that delineates the nature and boundaries of the counseling relationship and the limits to client-counselor confidentiality.

34. Which of the following items are required to be addressed in the professional disclosure statement?

a. an explanation of possible dual relationships within the client-counselor session.

b. third-party billing and reimbursement information.

c. the notification process for the counselor's retirement or death.

d. all of the above are required.

35. The primary goal of state licensing boards, national certification entities, and accreditation agencies is to:

   a. ensure that professional counselors have the appropriate training.

   b. monitor and protect the welfare of clients/consumers of counseling services.

   c. serve as an advocate for issues related to professional counselor licensure laws.

   d. receive consumer complaints and administer appropriate consequences to counselors.

36. Which statement most accurately depicts the professional counselors' obligation to understand state law and codes of ethics?

   a. Counselors should have a healthy respect for and advanced knowledge of state statutes because both the law and codes of ethics could help or hurt them in times of a consumer/client complaint.

   b. Counselors should always abide by state statutes first before they consider counselor codes of ethics when it comes to an ethical dilemma.

   c. Counselors are not expected to have advanced knowledge of state laws, but should have an understanding of specific statutes that relate to the counseling profession and try to keep a healthy balance to avoid ethical conflicts.

   d. Counselors should always adhere to counselor codes of ethics first before they consider state statutes that govern the counseling profession.

37. In *Tarasoff v. Regents of the University of California* the federal courts:

   a. ruled that professional counselors have the ability to commit their clients involuntarily to a state mental health institution.

   b. decided that professional counselors are generally immune from lawsuits when providing mental health treatment to their clients.

   c. found that state counselor licensure laws supersede those of federally mandated statutes.

   d. have defined the counselor's duty to protect individuals who may be in danger due to threats made by a client through a documented record of such an event.

38. Which of the following *are not* typically offered as guidance in ethical decision-making models?

   a. Counselors are almost always offered precise suggestions and advice on dealing with a variety of specific ethical dilemmas.
   b. Counselors typically have a model for determining if there a conflict between two ethical principles such as autonomy or beneficence.
   c. Counselors are provided with guidance on formulating a general plan of action.
   d. Counselors are offered ways to problem solve through issues of whether an ethical dilemma exists at all.

Case Management and Consultation Issues

39. Intake interviews:

   a. are typically open-ended discussions in which clients are encouraged to talk about whatever they want.
   b. are part of the counseling assessment process.
   c. gather information in a systematic way.
   d. are more concerned with gathering information than with building rapport.

40. The format of an intake interview:

   a. should remain consistent despite the context in which the counselor is working.
   b. is influenced by the organization in which the counseling takes place, funding requirements, and the severity of the client's presenting concerns.
   c. leave little room for empathic connection.
   d. has no common elements that are typical of all counseling intake interviews.

41. Informed consent:

   a. means letting clients know how much services will cost.
   b. is not relevant when working with minors.
   c. is an ethical imperative.
   d. outlines the information about the counselor and the counseling process necessary for clients to make an informed decision about whether to engage in the intake process.

42. A Mental Status exam:

   a. is a totally separate part of the intake interview.
   b. varies in formality depending on where and to whom it is administered.

c. assesses current functioning.

d. can only be done by a physician.

43. Which of the following is *not* commonly included in a referral?

    a. background information, such as demographics and presenting symptoms.

    b. specific referral questions or specific services being purchased.

    c. documentation (e.g., test and medical exam results, educational records) held by the agency.

    d. timelines, specific dates, or guidelines as to when important events will be completed.

44. Which of the following is false?

    a. To be most efficient and effective, the counselor should largely manage the referral process without input from the client.

    b. The success of the referral will depend, in large part, on the knowledge of the professional counselor.

    c. As a resource broker, the professional counselor has a secondary client—the potential service provider.

    d. A resource broker is a professional who helps the client to use vendors who can provide services necessary to meet the client's goals.

45. Which of the following is *not* identified as an area in which service providers may be evaluated?

    a. outcome.

    b. cost.

    c. responsiveness to client needs.

    d. responsiveness to organization needs.

46. Which of these did Moxley (1989) identify as important knowledge areas for resource brokers?

    a. availability, appropriateness, acceptability, and accessibility of community resources.

    b. whether eligibility requirements are need-based, diagnosis-based, or means-tested.

    c. quality of service, identified through past experience, evaluation studies, and accrediting bodies.

    d. all of the above.

47. Treatment plans:

    a. are a tool that primarily helps the counselor stay on track.

    b. are essential for clients seeking third-party reimbursement.

c. require little input from the client.

d. are an important part of the counseling process and benefit clients, counselors, and the field of psychotherapy.

48. Treatment plans:

a. have a standard format regardless of setting.

b. should be tied to diagnostic concerns rather than clients' primary issues.

c. should reflect clients' primary concerns and diagnostic considerations.

d. should always be action-oriented.

49. Bill is in the precontemplative stage of change. His treatment plan will likely be most effective if:

a. the focus is on identifying small changes that Bill can initiate.

b. the focus is on validating his feelings and exploring his reluctance to change.

c. the focus is on referring Bill to a support group that will encourage desired changes.

d. the focus is on identifying resources to facilitate change.

50. Culturally competent counselors:

a. understand that regardless of culture, clients need the counselor to identify important steps in the treatment.

b. view treatment planning as most appropriate for clients from the majority culture.

c. always refer minority clients to resources that are culturally similar to the client's.

d. take the client's level of acculturation, preferred coping styles, and ideas about what promotes health into account when developing treatment plans.

51. Sue and Sue (2003) cite statistics indicating that minority clients working with a White counselor typically do not return for a second session approximately _____ of the time:

a. 10%.

b. 25%.

c. 50%.

d. 75%.

52. Prochaska and DiClemente (1983) describe six stages of change individuals may make. Which of the following is not one of those stages?

a. psychosocial stage.

b. maintenance stage.

c. precontemplation stage.
d. action stage.

53. Perhaps the most important strategy for counselors to practice during the first session is to:

a. make sure the client signs the informed consent statement.
b. not answer the phone when with the client.
c. develop a rapport with a warm, caring, and empathic attitude.
d. make sure to set up the next appointment before the client leaves.

54. To increase the likelihood clients will return for a second session, counselors should:

a. give clients an appointment card showing a "no show" fee policy.
b. give the client some relevant homework assignment.
c. give the client an affirmation card to read daily.
d. all of the above.

55. According to the empirical evidence, one of the three key predictors of client acceptability of homework activities is *not:*

a. the link between treatment goals and the content of the activity.
b. perceived ability to complete the activity.
c. whether the homework was selected from a predetermined schedule.
d. the difficulty level of the activity.

56. Specific homework assignments may involve which of the following?

a. information gathering.
b. the application of learned skills.
c. more experientially oriented activities.
d. all of the above.

57. As a guideline, when willingness/readiness/confidence ratings are less than ____ should the therapist renegotiate the homework activity:

a. 90%.
b. 70%.
c. 50%.
d. 30%.

58. When reviewing homework, which of the following is *not* recommended as facilitative of client engagement with homework activities?

    a. discussing the quantity and quality of completed homework activities.
    b. reviewing practical obstacles to activities.
    c. expressing disappointment with the client for not completing the activity.
    d. asking about the client's beliefs about the costs and benefits of the activity.

59. A public or private agency within a geographic area that provides a service for our clients, ourselves, or our organization and may or may not charge a fee is a definition for:

    a. client service.
    b. referral source.
    c. community resource.
    d. community outreach.

60. Which agency sets quality standards for organizations that credential various professionals?

    a. National Commission for Certifying Agencies (NCCA).
    b. National Association of Competence Assurance (NOCA).
    c. Certification of Licensure Boards Commission (CLBC).
    d. Commission on Accreditation of Rehabilitation Facilities (CARF).

61. If a counselor was interested in finding a community resource that would assist persons with disabilities, a good place to begin the search would be the Department of:

    a. Justice.
    b. Disability.
    c. Social Services.
    d. Health and Human Services.

62. Which of the following benefit systems are legislated by the state and are not dependent upon policyholder selection of services?

    a. Social Security.
    b. auto insurance.
    c. long-term disability.
    d. Workers Compensation.

Multicultural Counseling Issues

63. One of the most successful U.S.-facilitated sterilization programs involved:

    a. African American females.
    b. Puerto Rican females.
    c. Mexican females.
    d. Asian females.

64. Racial tensions between African Americans and White Americans have occurred largely because of:

    a. the involuntary sterilization of African American females.
    b. the large number of unfairly incarcerated African American males.
    c. what appears to be periodic blatant acts of prejudice and discrimination by Whites.
    d. the involuntary sterilization of African American males.

65. The immigration of Asians to America came to an abrupt halt as a result of the:

    a. 1848 Chinese Exclusion Act.
    b. 1882 Chinese Exclusion Act.
    c. Executive Order 9066 signed by President Roosevelt.
    d. 1896 Land Treaty Act.

66. In working with American Indians, counselors need to be able to:

    a. be aware of their intense anger and resentment toward White people.
    b. acknowledge the psychosocial impact of oppression inflicted on its peoples.
    c. treat and understand these clients as they would any White client.
    d. realize that past transgressions toward American Indians are largely forgotten today.

67. Approximately what percentage of Native American Indians live on what is referred to as reservation or Indian lands?

    a. 33%.
    b. 50%.
    c. 75%.
    d. 15%.

68. The 2005 U.S. Census found that:

    a. Native American Indians are three times as likely to live in poverty as Whites in the U.S. population.

b. Native American Indians are generally not considered to live in poverty because of economically sound tribal governments.

c. Native American Indians are twice as likely to live in poverty as other minorities in the U.S. population.

d. Native American Indians are twice as likely to live in poverty as Whites in the U.S. population.

69. "Status and Trends in the Education of American Indians and Alaska Natives" (2005) reports:

a. only 30% of the total Native population have high school degrees or less.

b. almost 60% of the total Native population have high school degrees or less.

c. Natives between the ages of 18 and 24 are more likely to be enrolled in a college or university than their White, Asian, and Black peers.

d. approximately 24% of the total Native population has completed at least a bachelor's degree.

70. The following is true about Native American Indians:

a. Native American Indian culture emphasizes youthfulness.

b. Native American Indians maintain a government-to-government relationship with the United States.

c. Native youth are not allowed to participate in tribal ceremonies and rituals.

d. Native American Indians do not perceive themselves as living in more than one culture.

71. Which of the following is *true* regarding the health of African Americans?

a. African Americans are underrepresented among AIDS cases.

b. African Americans and Whites are about equally covered when it comes to health insurance.

c. African Americans males experience fewer health issues than Whites.

d. The average life span of African Americans is up to seven years shorter than that of White Americans.

72. Which of the following is *not true* regarding African Americans?

a. African American families are becoming more matriarchal.

b. African American males and females value assertiveness and although the home may be headed by women, men are often around providing support.

    c. African American incarceration rates are similar to those of other groups.

    d. African American men have the lowest graduation rate of any group from NCAA Division I institutions.

73. What has been found to be related to the stages of racial identity in African Americans?

    a. their preference for counselor ethnicity.

    b. African Americans at the preencounter stage preferred a White counselor.

    c. Although the stage of identity is a factor, most prefer a counselor who showed "cultural sensitivity."

    d. all of the above.

74. What has been found regarding African American youth?

    a. Unemployment rates among this population are low.

    b. Homicide is the top cause of death.

    c. Most do not feel that race is a factor in terms of how people are judged.

    d. Their suicide rate is lower than that of White youth.

75. Acculturative stress refers to:

    a. the stress of having a culture.

    b. the process of adopting American cultural patterns.

    c. difficulties that arise in navigating mainstream culture.

    d. the stress of discarding one's culture of origin.

76. Filial piety is an important concept in:

    a. understanding how Asian Americans may feel about parents and elders.

    b. assessing the degree of empathy that Asians may feel.

    c. generating a sense of sympathy for those less fortunate.

    d. learning how Asians may worship at shrines.

77. Acupuncture is:

    a. a barbaric torture practice using needles.

    b. an alternative medicine approach based on Chinese theory about balancing yin and yang forces.

    c. used by Asian Americans to heal illness.

    d. a therapy practice that originated in Japan.

78. A gestalt therapy approach with an Asian American client may be:

    a. highly indicated due to the well-known emotional repression.

    b. used sensitively if there is a strong therapeutic alliance and the client is highly acculturated.

c. forbidden because Asian clients may terminate counseling abruptly.

d. ineffective because Asian clients want to be told what to do.

79. Research regarding the need for mental health services among Hispanics/Latinos has increased in the past decades due primarily to all of the following reasons except:

a. issues associated with immigration.
b. level of acculturation.
c. increased prevalence of mental illness in their native country.
d. discrimination.

80. Why is it important for a mental health professional to know about the role of stereotypes among Hispanics/Latinos (H/L)?

a. H/Ls may develop a pathology due to a fixation of wanting to overcome them and live just like their Anglo American counterparts.
b. Stereotypes are a clear indication of a mental health disorder and it would be important to address these early in the first session.
c. Stereotypes influence and affect their socialization through gender role expectations as well as family relations, family functioning, and overall family system. These have been shown to have an impact in the development of psychopathology.
d. Stereotypical behaviors among H/Ls, such as with attachment styles, religious practices, and patriarchal beliefs, are considered a deviation from the norm and need to be remedied to facilitate the client's integration within an American community.

81. Research suggests that among Hispanic/Latinos, there appears to be a consensus about what they would like to get out of the counseling experience. For example:

a. they prefer when the counselor gives advices, asks questions, and focuses on current problems, especially family issues.
b. H/Ls fare better when the counseling professional speaks very little and the session is not structured.
c. H/Ls prefer to have their loved ones present from the beginning as they feel that their problems are due to the family, spouse, and/or children.
d. they would like to be able to limit counseling to one session and receive medication for their physical illnesses since they do not believe in mental illness.

82. Some suggestions for approaching/treating Hispanic/Latinos in psychotherapy include all of these except to:

    a. engage the client by describing his or her role within the family and community. Even though psychotherapy has an individualistic approach, with H/Ls, the family unit is probably considered more important than the single unit.
    b. clarify the significance and meaning of psychotherapy. Address any misperceptions and ask the client what he or she expects to get out of psychotherapy.
    c. address the client initially with a level of formality and respect, especially if the clinician is bilingual.
    d. address negative internal dialogue and irrational beliefs as soon as possible, especially if they are about family. It is unfair that the client be burdened with wanting to be an ideal family member, who is to fix all the family problems.

83. Which statement best characterizes Middle Eastern Americans' identity?

    a. Many Middle Eastern Americans have various social and political identities and affiliations with Palestinians, Jordanians, Egyptians, Lebanese, Iraqis, Syrians, and Yemenis, which also refer to their country of origin.
    b. Middle Eastern Americans have a variety of religious identities that includes, but is not limited to, Greek Orthodox, Antiochian Orthodox, Protestant, Sunni Muslims, and Shiite Muslims.
    c. The majority of Middle Eastern Americans are Christians, although Islam is the predominant religion practiced throughout the Middle Eastern world.
    d. All of the above characterize Middle Eastern Americans.

84. Which statement most accurately depicts the Middle Eastern American family?

    a. Development of an individual identity separate from that of the family or the community is typically not valued or encouraged.
    b. Individual identity separate from that of the family is respected but only among first-generation Middle Eastern American families.
    c. Arranged marriages are practiced among most Middle Eastern Americans but generally among Orthodox Sunni Muslims.
    d. Extended families are usually not accepted among Middle Eastern Americans.

85. Middle Eastern Americans' acculturation experiences:

 a. are generally no different from that of Hispanic Americans.
 b. are generally positive because most Middle Easterners have great wealth that makes transition to the United States much easier than other groups of lower socioeconomic status.
 c. are really based on country of origin, length of time spent in the United States, and the reasons for emigration.
 d. are typically positive socially for most Middle Easterners.

86. Many Middle Easterners generally are skeptics when it comes to mental health services in America because:

 a. mental illness is a difficult concept to grasp among Middle Eastern Americans.
 b. there is a general fear of being stereotyped as *crazy*.
 c. few Middle Easterners have been exposed to Western mental health services.
 d. all of the above.

87. The largest of the European groups that have settled in the United States are:

 a. persons that are from German ancestry.
 b. the Irish.
 c. Eastern Europeans primarily who are Polish.
 d. persons that are from Italian heritage.

88. Work as a predominant value of the European American cultural identity tends to be strongest among which of the following European American groups?

 a. French.
 b. British and Germans.
 c. Italians.
 d. Irish.

89. The expression of feelings tends to be most difficult in which European cultures?

 a. British.
 b. Irish.
 c. Germans.
 d. All of the above groups are found to have difficulty with self-disclosure of feelings.

90. Which statement best reflects Southern and Eastern European family values?

    a. There is a rugged individualism among Southern and Eastern European women, and men in the family respect and honor such family values.
    b. Southern and Eastern European men are typically married and have extramarital affairs that are acknowledged and tend to be tolerated by the spouse.
    c. Moving out of the house, going away to college, or marrying outside the culture could each be viewed by the family as an act of betrayal and might become a presenting problem in counseling.
    d. The appropriate expression of feelings is an important part of family communication.

91. Single-identity models are often used to describe a progressive sequential process of individual:

    a. nonacceptance to acceptance of one's cultural identity.
    b. experiences of traditional cultural values.
    c. self-esteem and self-concept.
    d. integration of the self with societal group norms.

92. The emergence of multiculturalism within the field of psychology has helped bring attention to and emphasized the importance of:

    a. psychological assessment with people of color.
    b. sociocultural factors that affect psychological well-being and development.
    c. experiences of family dynamics in social settings.
    d. majority cultural social group membership dynamics.

93. LGB people of color may often experience the coming-out process as:

    a. similar to White LGB individuals.
    b. different due to cultural factors and experiences of *isms.*
    c. different due to their nonmembership with the dominant culture.
    d. the same given that both groups identify as LGB.

94. When working with LGB people of color, mental health professionals should:

    a. be familiar with the coming-out process.
    b. focus on helping the client move through the stages of the coming-out process.

    c. help the client focus on ways in which to integrate his or her multiple social identities.

    d. help the client become aware that being out publicly will help him or her feel a part of the LGB community.

95. Availability of mental health services in rural communities is most affected by:

    a. lack of insurance.

    b. low population densities.

    c. the downsizing of rural mental health centers due to the Rural Health Services Reintegration Act of 1988.

    d. low salaries paid to mental health providers.

96. Dual relationships in rural settings result in:

    a. the potential exclusion of many people who are in need from receiving services.

    b. the necessity of close supervision.

    c. violations of ACA ethical guidelines.

    d. problems only when there is a sexual relationship.

97. Barriers to acceptability discussed in the chapter on rural mental health include all the following but:

    a. self-reliance in managing problems.

    b. stigma.

    c. cross-cultural differences.

    d. enmeshed family structures.

98. Counseling in rural settings can result in:

    a. burnout.

    b. cultural enrichment.

    c. isolation.

    d. all the above.

99. Deaf culture includes:

    a. a historical understanding of the Deaf community.

    b. common theatrical and artistic expressions.

    c. social groups.

    d. all of the above.

100. Which are myths about Deaf people?

    a. Deaf people have greater vision than other people.

    b. Deaf people tend to socialize with other deaf people.

    c. Deaf parents always have deaf children.

    d. a and c.

101. What environmental condition(s) should a counselor be cognizant of when working with a client who is Deaf or hard of hearing in regard to fostering efficient communication?

    a. water temperature in the restroom.
    b. glare from windows.
    c. air temperature.
    d. number of exits.

102. Important considerations for working with persons who are Deaf include:

    a. if they use sign language.
    b. if they speech read.
    c. if they require an interpreter.
    d. all of the above.

Counseling Theories and Techniques

103. Freud labeled the process by which clients pushed disturbing early memories into their subconscious:

    a. transference.
    b. regression.
    c. repression.
    d. penis envy.

104. Which of the following is not considered one of Freud's unconscious defense mechanisms?

    a. projection.
    b. rationalization.
    c. denial.
    d. fixation.

105. Kohut inspired the self psychology movement that emphasized:

    a. cognitive reframing.
    b. empathy.
    c. token economy.
    d. behavioral analysis.

106. The relational movement of psychoanalysis emphasizes:

    a. not knowing and courting surprises rather than interpretation.
    b. taking responsibility for one's actions.
    c. reliving traumatic childhood memories.
    d. interpreting a client's subconscious thoughts.

107. Cognitive behavior therapy represents the work of:

    a. Albert Ellis.
    b. Aaron T. Beck.
    c. Sigmund Freud.
    d. a broad range of theorists and clinicians.

108. Cognitive behavior therapy developed from:

    a. the low frustration tolerance of individuals who wanted to feel better quickly.
    b. a combination of behavioral and psychodynamic approaches.
    c. the requirements of managed care.
    d. none of the above.

109. A basic premise of cognitive behavior therapy is that:

    a. thoughts cause feelings and behaviors.
    b. feelings cause thoughts and behaviors.
    c. feelings and thoughts have no connection.
    d. there is an interaction between thoughts, feelings, and behavior.

110. Cognitive behavior therapy emphasizes interventions that are:

    a. vague and amorphous.
    b. clear, targeted, and explicit.
    c. designed to cause the client maximum discomfort.
    d. all of the above.

111. The founder and primary developer of reality therapy was:

    a. Robert Wubbolding.
    b. Carl Rogers.
    c. William Glasser.
    d. Aaron Beck.

112. Which of the following is not one of the five basic needs assumed by reality therapy?

    a. power.
    b. fun.
    c. freedom.
    d. expression.

113. The first stage of helping clients in reality therapy is:

    a. evaluation of their current behaviors.
    b. goal establishment.
    c. confronting current behaviors.
    d. creating a "do plan."

114. Reality therapy is unique in that it:

    a. has a strong focus on client/counselor relationship.
    b. emphasizes homework assignments.
    c. has a goal-setting stage.
    d. does not view psychiatric diagnosis or symptoms as useful in therapy.

115. What is the core aim of E-H therapy?

    a. happiness.
    b. expressiveness.
    c. transformation.
    d. freedom.

116. The key to the cultivation of freedom in E-H therapy is:

    a. analysis.
    b. Socratic dialogue.
    c. presence.
    d. philosophical clarification.

117. The main difference between E-H therapy and other therapies, such as cognitive behaviorism and psychoanalysis, is:

    a. the experiential level of contact.
    b. the stress on philosophy.
    c. the stress on optimism.
    d. therapist disclosure.

118. E-H therapy is best characterized by:

    a. positive regard.
    b. confrontation.
    c. problem solving.
    d. attunement to the ambiguities of life.

119. In REBT, a belief is considered irrational when:

    a. it is illogical.
    b. it is logical but premised improperly.
    c. it causes emotional dysfunction.
    d. all of the above.

120. One assumption in REBT is that:

    a. one's past dictates personality.
    b. activating events cause emotional disturbance.
    c. we can minimize disturbances with insight.
    d. early childhood beliefs are instilled by adolescence.

121. In REBT, the main disturbance-causing idea contains a demand on:

    a. the self.
    b. others.
    c. the world.
    d. all of the above.

122. The role of coping statements in REBT is:

    a. providing the answers to the disputed ideas.
    b. meant to make you feel better.
    c. rewards.
    d. helpful releasers of rage.

123. Which method was developed by Teodoro Ayllon and Nathan Azrin to help remotivate long-term inpatients who had become institutionalized?

    a. systematic desensitization.
    b. the exposure principle.
    c. the token economy.
    d. cognitive therapy.

124. Which method did H. G. Jones use to help the anxious dancer perform in public again?

    a. graded reeducation.
    b. acceptance and commitment therapy.
    c. assertiveness training.
    d. hypnosis.

125. The dream reorganization method has been applied to which clinical problem or disorder:

    a. head-banging.
    b. sleep-walking.
    c. specific phobias.
    d. recurrent traumatic nightmares.

126. Which pair correctly links a particular problem area with a treatment intervention that has been found to be helpful in that application?

    a. performance anxiety; the token economy.
    b. depression; behavioral activation.
    c. traumatic nightmares; positive reinforcement.
    d. bizarre behavior; biofeedback.

127. Which of the following statements is *incorrect?*

    a. Feminist therapy was developed to address the sexism within clinical practice.

b. Contemporary feminist therapy includes men as clients.
c. Feminist counselors utilize standardized techniques.
d. Various feminist therapies exist.

128. Which of the following statements is *incorrect* regarding the tenet of empowerment?

a. It solely focuses on the effect of women's work in their families.
b. It allows clients to address their feelings of anger.
c. It allows clients to perceive opportunities to change the responses from the wider society.
d. It allows for the understanding of the interplay between the external environment and the inner realities of clients.

129. Which of the following is *not* a tenet of multiracial feminism?

a. interlocking inequalities.
b. understandings of diverse women.
c. importance of a feminist identity.
d. intersectional nature of hierarchies.

130. Rather than using the term *pathology,* why might feminist counselors prefer to use the phrase *problems in living or coping strategies?*

a. The concerns of clients are not inextricably connected to social and political factors that influence their personal choices.
b. It is understood that behaviors and mental processes are congruent with living in an oppressive society.
c. Economic factors rarely influence the lives of clients.
d. It is important for clients to adapt to a dysfunctional environment.

131. Which one of the following is *not* a key concept in disability-affirmative therapy?

a. disability culture and community.
b. models of disability.
c. integrating disability into the case formulation.
d. body image enhancement.

132. The socioeconomic background of clients with disabilities should be explored, because:

a. such clients are more likely to have grown up in families living below the poverty line.
b. such clients are more likely to have a parent with a disability.

c. adults with disabilities are more likely to be married.

d. children with disabilities are more likely to attend separate schools.

133. Disability-affirmative therapy encourages:

a. clients to embrace the social model of disability.
b. clients to embrace the medical model of disability.
c. counselors to embrace the social model of disability.
d. counselors to embrace the medical model of disability.

134. Important issues that are *less* likely to emerge with clients with disabilities, compared to nondisabled clients, include:

a. pain and fatigue.
b. marital issues.
c. medical traumas.
d. sexual abuse.

135. Disabilities vary along several important dimensions. Generally these include:

a. age of onset, degree of uncertainty, and degree of visibility.
b. age of onset, degree of pain, and proximity to the face.
c. degree of pain, degree of uncertainty, and proximity to the face.
d. degree of pain, degree of fatigue, and effects on mobility.

136. Adler used the term *individual psychology* in order to:

a. emphasize the indivisible nature of our personalities.
b. lesson the idea of the essential unity of the individual.
c. promote reductionism in psychology.
d. none of the above are correct.

137. Adlerians believe that all behavior is:

a. creative.
b. goal-directed.
c. change-directed.
d. punishment-avoidant.

138. Adler believed that all people have three basic life tasks. These include work, friendship, and:

a. communication.
b. love-intimacy.
c. superiority.
d. self-actualization.

139. The task of Adlerian psychotherapy is one of:

a. encouraging the development of social interest.
b. promoting the development of a more effective lifestyle.

c. redirecting and refocusing behavior goals.

d. all of the above.

140. Overall, most brief therapists seem to agree that the following number of sessions is sufficient for stimulating positive, enduring changes in clients with mental illness:

a. Less than 10 sessions.

b. 10 to 15 sessions.

c. 12 to 25 sessions.

d. 25 to 50 sessions.

141. Budman and Gurman (1988) utilize the interpersonal-developmental-existential (I-D-E) perspective in exploring with clients:

a. trust issues.

b. why the client has chosen this point in time to come for counseling.

c. financial concerns.

d. when clients first notice they have a problem.

142. Which of the following is *not* one of the most salient issues in conducting brief therapy?

a. giving homework exercises after the first session.

b. involving significant others as the situation calls.

c. directly confronting clients about their reluctance to change.

d. making use of other therapeutic groups such as Alcoholics Anonymous.

143. When considering terminating therapy, brief therapists generally acknowledge that:

a. clients are essentially cured.

b. it is natural for clients to return to counseling if future crises occur.

c. clients will generally have ongoing problems over the remainder of their lives.

d. if it wasn't for insurance limits, most clients could benefit from more therapy sessions.

144. Motivational interviewing is a:

a. directive style based on empathic advice giving.

b. person-centered, goal-oriented approach to resolving ambivalence.

c. means for breaking through denial and resistance.

d. none of the above.

145. Evidence for the effectiveness of motivational interviewing is:

    a. insufficient at this time.
    b. awaiting meta-analysis reviews.
    c. based on more than 180 randomized controlled trials.
    d. limited to the alcohol treatment field.

146. Motivational interviewing is based on:

    a. the transtheoretical model (commonly called the stages of change approach).
    b. learning from clients.
    c. psychotherapeutic theories.
    d. none of the above.

147. The principles of motivational interviewing do not include:

    a. expressing empathy.
    b. developing discrepancy.
    c. confronting resistance.
    d. supporting self-efficacy.

148. The phenomenological method consists of three steps:

    a. the rule of epoché, the rule of description, and the rule of horizontalization.
    b. the rule of experiment, the rule of containment, and the rule of confrontation.
    c. the short step (also called "the hop"), the medium step (simply known as "the step"), and the long step (also called "the jump").
    d. observing, bracketing, and describing.

149. To create the conditions in which a dialogic moment might occur, the therapist:

    a. practices presence, inclusion, and commitment to dialogue.
    b. makes that a treatment goal and presses the client to become more authentic.
    c. does nothing because gestalt therapy is a paradoxical approach.
    d. abandons professionalism and tells the client all about his or her personal life.

150. Why are experiments also called "safe emergencies"?

    a. because that is a cute, humanistic buzzword.
    b. because they lead to a novel experience that is unde-termined.

c. because they are interventions designed to achieve predict-able results.

d. to emphasize that they are always without risk.

151. What does it take to become a gestalt therapist?

   a. reading the seminal book, *Gestalt Therapy,* by Perls, Hefferline, and Goodman.
   b. taking a class on experiential therapies in an accredited graduate program.
   c. graduating from a recognized postgraduate-level gestalt therapy training institute or center.
   d. attending an international conference for gestalt therapy produced by the Association for the Advancement of Gestalt Therapy—An International Community (AAGT–AIC).

Career Counseling, Human Growth and Development

152. Frank Parsons posited that vocational choice involves all of the following except:

   a. self-knowledge.
   b. knowledge about occupations.
   c. knowledge about social structure.
   d. using true reasoning.

153. Donald Super's contributions to career development theory included all of the following except:

   a. a life-span model of career stages.
   b. the triadic reciprocal model.
   c. a life-space model of salient roles.
   d. the concept of career maturity.

154. Social cognitive career theory employs all of the following constructs except:

   a. outcome expectations.
   b. personal goals.
   c. self-efficacy.
   d. task approach skills.

155. In the INCOME framework, N stands for:

   a. iNforming.
   b. kNowing.
   c. iNtuiting.
   d. iNvesting.

156. In terms of the meaning of work, the "Hawthorne" effect showed that:

    a. workers did not care what management did.
    b. workers responded to work environment changes no matter what the circumstances.
    c. workers responded only to positive changes in the environment.
    d. workers did not respond at all.

157. One theory that explains how workers and work environments influence each other in a dynamic fashion is:

    a. career counseling theory.
    b. the theory of well-being.
    c. Super's developmental theory.
    d. the Theory of Work Adjustment.

158. Research regarding work and qualify of life has generally shown that:

    a. being employed generally positively influences quality-of-life satisfaction.
    b. there is no relationship between work and life satisfaction.
    c. these are independent domains of functioning.
    d. studies on subjective well-being have yet to be conducted.

159. An example of an intrinsic motivating factor for work would be:

    a. salary.
    b. benefits.
    c. variety of job tasks.
    d. availability of transportation.

160. According to the Individuals With Disability Education Improvement Act of 2004, transition services should focus on:

    a. postsecondary education and vocational education.
    b. integrated employment and adult services.
    c. independent living and community participation.
    d. all of the above.

161. An interagency transition planning team's major responsibility is to:

    a. create an IEP suitable to the student's educational needs.
    b. create an IEP suitable to the student's vocational needs.
    c. develop, implement, and monitor the transition IEP for the student.
    d. ensure that the school prepares the student to be independent in the community.

162. The rehabilitation counselor should work with the educational team to:

    a. act as a consultant in the development of IEPs and ensuring that students are exposed to a variety of vocational opportunities.
    b. begin looking at vocational opportunities for students aged 14 and older.
    c. ensure that the student has acquired the necessary skills to live independently in the community upon graduation from school.
    d. provide in-depth career and vocational counseling for students when they turn 16.

163. During the transition process, the student should be afforded opportunities to include:

    a. job development, assessment, and job site training.
    b. community experiences, employment, and functional daily living skills.
    c. only activities that relate to increasing the academic capacity of the student.
    d. only activities that relate to vocational options following exit of the school.

164. In working with diverse populations, career counselors should possess the following:

    a. knowledge, skills, and awareness.
    b. patience, understanding, determination.
    c. knowledge pertaining to all diverse populations.
    d. many years of professional experience working with diverse populations.

165. The following are all common links in regard to interventions that can be utilized throughout the lower, middle, and high school years except:

    a. dissemination of information.
    b. responding in a meaningful way to individual characteristics.
    c. computerized assessment techniques.
    d. helping the student to create and implement plans.

166. Schlossberg's Integrative Model of the transition process included all of the following except:

    a. moving in.
    b. moving out.

    c. maintenance.
    d. moving through.

167. The coping resources involve all of the following except:

    a. situation.
    b. sharing.
    c. support.
    d. self.

168. A disability is primarily a function of:

    a. a medical diagnosis and symptoms that are acute and severe.
    b. a physical or mental impairment that requires intensive medical treatment.
    c. an interaction of a health condition, environmental and personal factors that affect functioning.
    d. limitations in functioning that can be attributed to race or ethnicity, gender, and cultural factors.

169. Having difficulty concentrating on a conversation due to hearing voices for someone diagnosed with schizophrenia is an example of:

    a. a functional limitation.
    b. a psychiatric diagnosis.
    c. a symptom of a psychiatric condition.
    d. a medical impairment.

170. A file clerk who is Deaf spends most of his workday filing medical records. He asks to trade duties filling in answering phones for the receptionist on her lunch break with another clerical worker who occasionally sorts incoming mail. This is an example of:

    a. an undue hardship.
    b. a medical impairment.
    c. an unqualified employee.
    d. a reasonable accommodation.

171. A 43-year-old female plumber that you see in counseling was in a serious car accident and experienced a spinal cord injury that left her paralyzed from the waist down. She is unable to return to her job as a plumber and is feeling depressed because she has no idea what kind of work she can do. Based on assessing her phase of vocational development and vocational role, what type of vocational intervention would you recommend?

    a. job search skills training.
    b. career counseling.

c. in-service training.
d. work adjustment training.

172. Which statement best describes Holland's theories of person-environment fit?

a. Holland organizes information on job titles and personality types and hypothesizes that there are six different personality types that would fit within specific occupations and would be a good job match.
b. Holland suggests that interactions between the person and his or her environment may not predict the best job matches; rather, it would be the individual's expressed interests that are most important.
c. Although Holland theorizes about personality types often, he suggests that specific developmental aspects of the person's life are what predict the range of job matches for the individual.
d. Holland suggests that one's self-concept that was developed in early childhood is the best predictor of good job matches.

173. In social cognitive career theory (SCCT), self-efficacy beliefs play a specific role that both positively and negatively affects our career decision-making process but are based on:

a. personal performance and accomplishments.
b. vicarious learning opportunities.
c. physiological states and reactions.
d. all of the above.

174. Which career development theory(s) would best value multiculturalism?

a. person-environment fit.
b. social learning theories.
c. postmodern theories.
d. developmental theories.

175. The following is an effective approach for working with older persons:

a. using a developmental counseling model.
b. conducting life reviews.
c. administering a life planning protocol.
d. all of the above.

176. The following is a key consideration in assessment with older adults:

a. administration may require additional explanation to clarify what the test measures.

b. relevant norms may not be available.

c. endurance may be an issue in scheduling tests.

d. all of the above.

177. A key consideration for an older worker in staying successfully attached to the workplace is:

a. effective intergenerational inclusion initiatives.

b. proximity to place of residence.

c. accommodation for visual and hearing impairments.

d. a and c.

178. A critical component of a counseling curriculum that addresses knowledge development about the aging population is:

a. personal experiences with older persons.

b. exposure to the medical model.

c. functional integration collaboration for crossing professional borders.

d. a and c.

179. The Rorschach Inkblot Test can be categorized in which form of projective test?

a. completion techniques.

b. expressive/constructive techniques.

c. choice or ordering techniques.

d. association techniques.

180. The MMPI was developed using which approach to test development?

a. rational or theoretical.

b. multivariate or factor analytic.

c. empirical or criterion-keyed.

d. a combination of each of these methods.

181. The advantages of projective tests include all of the following except:

a. freedom-of-response format.

b. limited face validity.

c. complexity of scoring procedures.

d. reliability and validity.

182. The advantages of objectives tests include all of the following except:

a. freedom-of-response format.

b. limited face validity.

c. complexity of scoring procedures.
d. reliability and validity.

183. The personality test administered the most frequently over the last 40 years is the:

   a. Rorschach Inkblot Test.
   b. MCMI.
   c. House-Tree-Person.
   d. MMPI.

Assessment and Diagnosis

184. Aptitude tests are generally used in:

   a. academic counseling.
   b. career counseling.
   c. personal counseling.
   d. a and b.

185. Achievement is to aptitude as:

   a. past is to future.
   b. past is to present.
   c. present is to past.
   d. present is to future.

186. The Miller Analogies Test (MAT) is an aptitude test used for:

   a. qualifying exam for the National Merit Scholarship.
   b. college admissions.
   c. graduate school admissions.
   d. career placement.

187. The Differential Aptitude Test (DAT) is a:

   a. Scholastic Aptitude Test.
   b. Vocational Aptitude Test.
   c. measure of special abilities.
   d. none of the above.

188. Mental retardation is reported on:

   a. Axis I.
   b. Axis II.
   c. Axis III.
   d. Axis IV.

189. If an individual has more than one *DSM–IV–TR* diagnosis on the same axis, the one that should be listed first is the:

   a. principal diagnosis.
   b. one that is the least severe.

c. reason for the visit.

d. a and c.

190. If there is discordance noted between symptom severity and level of functioning, the final GAF score should reflect the:

a. average of the two.

b. worse of the two.

c. best of the two.

d. none of the above.

191. Which of the following is *not* one of the three criteria that should be considered in every *DSM* diagnosis?

a. The disorder is not due to the direct effects of a substance.

b. The disorder is not due to the direct effects of a general medical condition.

c. The disorder causes clinically significant distress among others closely involved with the person.

d. The disorder causes clinically significant distress or impairment in social, occupational, or other important areas of functioning.

192. *Mental functional capacity evaluations* can generally only be completed by:

a. rehabilitation and counselor educators.

b. clinical and school psychologists.

c. marriage and family therapists.

d. clinical social workers.

193. Which of the following categories is not considered a level of functioning using the *mental functional capacity evaluation?*

a. no difficulty functioning.

b. profound difficulty functioning.

c. moderate difficulty functioning.

d. marked difficulty functioning.

194. A *physical functional capacity evaluation* is generally used to assess an individual's:

a. ability to live independently in the home.

b. ability to socialize in the community.

c. physical capacity to perform specific work duties.

d. physical capacity to perform activities of daily living.

195. Which of the following is not one of the *worker trait profile* categories utilized in a physical functional capacity evaluation?

a. specific vocational preparation.

b. strength demands.

c. physical demands.
d. psychological demands.

196. The *International Classification of Functioning (ICF)* is a classification system for defining:

a. human functioning and disability.
b. multicultural differences in counseling.
c. family differences in functioning.
d. specific anatomy of various diseases.

197. The *ICF* is useful for documenting:

a. functional outcomes for insurance companies.
b. functional outcomes for clients.
c. cross-classification information for the *DSM–IV*.
d. cross-classification information with CPT codes.

198. The *ICF* most closely espouses the philosophy of:

a. the medical model paradigm.
b. the social model of disability.
c. the moral model of disability.
d. none of the above.

199. The classification of *contextual factors* found in the *ICF* contains two subclassifications; they are:

a. body functions and mental functions.
b. physical and mental capacity functions.
c. environmental factors and personal factors.
d. clinical and procedural factors.

200. One determining factor that differentiates vocational evaluation from psychometric testing is the use of:

a. vocational interest inventories.
b. real or simulated work.
c. other specialists' reports for background information.
d. industrial norms.

201. The three tools of the vocational evaluator are:

a. instruments, techniques, and strategies.
b. instruments, techniques, and situational assessment.
c. techniques, strategies, and work samples.
d. strategies, accommodations, and psychometric tests.

202. Which of the following is a poor referral question?

a. What is the consumer's rate of manipulation for the bobbin tender job?

b. What are the supports necessary for the consumer to work at the Acme Supply House as a cleaner?

c. Preinjury, the consumer was a teacher's aide; is this still a viable job, and if so, what accommodations may be needed?

d. Can you please conduct a vocational evaluation of the consumer?

203. Which of the following is not a consideration in the preparation of the consumer for a vocational evaluation?

a. the consumer understands the reason for the evaluation.
b. the names of the tests that may be administered.
c. the location of the VE office.
d. whether to bring a lunch.

Counseling Couples, Families, and Groups

204. According to Gladding (2007), there are four important areas to assess when working with families. Which of the following was *not* one of those four?

a. family history.
b. individual personalities.
c. pressures on the family.
d. family structure.

205. Informal assessments begin _____:

a. at the initial contact.
b. at the first session.
c. when an instrument is completed.
d. none of the above.

206. To assess a family's overall functioning, use of the _____ would be an appropriate instrument:

a. Parent-Child Relational Inventory (PCRI).
b. Parent-Adolescent Communication scale (PAC).
c. Family Environment Scale (FES).
d. Myers-Briggs Type Indicator (MBTI).

207. A disadvantage to collecting data through family assessments is _____:

a. developing a clear case conceptualization and diagnosis.
b. selecting appropriate interventions.
c. procuring resources and funding for services.
d. none.

208. Family counseling has been shown to be effective with which of the following presenting issues?

    a. schizophrenia.
    b. substance abuse.
    c. anorexia.
    d. all of the above.

209. In structural family counseling, the goal is to _____:

    a. help families understand how they construct realities and author their own stories.
    b. differentiate self within system and understand family of origin.
    c. restructure family organization and establish boundaries.
    d. eliminate problem and change dysfunctional patterns.

210. Special populations in family counseling work include:

    a. single-parent families.
    b. remarried families.
    c. families struggling with an addiction.
    d. all of the above.

211. _____ is an ethical concern for family counselors:

    a. ensuring confidentiality for all family members.
    b. obtaining informed consent only from person completing paperwork.
    c. seeking supervision only when in graduate coursework.
    d. all of the above.

212. Acknowledgment and validation are:

    a. essential ongoing communication strategies to effectively join and keep pace with each person in the relationship.
    b. important only early in treatment.
    c. useful to convince clients to make changes they need to make.
    d. strategies to plant seeds of change.

213. Clients feel outpaced and judged:

    a. when the therapist gets too invested in the outcome.
    b. when the therapist stops acknowledging and validating.
    c. when the therapist sides with one person in the relationship.
    d. all of the above.

214. Problematic pattern interruptions need to be:

    a. co-created by therapist and couple.
    b. explored based solely on family of origin history.

c. discouraged as not helpful.

d. left to the couple to decide.

215. As the couple's counselor it is not the counselor's role to:

a. collaborate with the couple.

b. be of influence with the couple intentionally.

c. interpret the couple's motives.

d. identify and highlight client resources.

216. Which items depict a healthy and well-functioning family?

a. Healthy families must function on both a cognitive and emotional level of communication for interactions to be at an optimal level of functioning.

b. One family member with leadership qualities must be chosen by the other members to help resolve conflicts.

c. A healthy, well-balanced family has members that are happy, successful, and can work together to problem solve conflicts.

d. Families that have a strong father or mother role model function oftentimes better than those families in which both partners share role modeling.

217. Which statement is most accurate about the marital unit overall?

a. The most successful marriages are those that formed healthy relationships prior to becoming married.

b. The most successful marriages are those that have good financial support that is distributed across all family members.

c. Marriages that do not function well are those in which either partner has to make sacrifices for the other or for the good of the family.

d. Marriages that do not thrive are those in which either partner has a chronic illness or disability.

218. At the core of healthy and well-functioning families is:

a. the freedom to allow everyone to do their own thing and to live as they choose.

b. the commitment and appreciation of each member.

c. the amount of time that the family can spend together.

d. actions that mean well, but do not necessarily have to be verbally communicated.

219. From a family systems perspective, problems and symptoms may be:

a. a result of mishandled solutions to everyday stresses.

b. serving a function for the family system.

   c. rooted in maladaptive patterns of interaction.

   d. all of the above.

220. In family therapy, an enactment is an intervention that:

   a. requires interaction among family members.

   b. requires the therapist to facilitate communication between members.

   c. involves no interaction between family members.

   d. a and b.

221. Across family systems theories behavior is:

   a. regarded as linear (i.e., one behavior causes another).

   b. seen as reciprocally influenced.

   c. not as important as unconscious processes.

   d. none of the above.

222. When assessing a family it is important that the therapist consider:

   a. the content information articulated by the family members.

   b. the family interaction processes that are observed.

   c. a and b.

   d. none of the above.

223. One way to engage members in the session when the leader is working with one individual is to:

   a. threaten to have them thrown out of the group for not paying attention.

   b. use a creative prop in the work with the individual.

   c. allow other members to leave the room while the leader works with one individual.

   d. let the other members completely take over the individual counseling.

224. The authors mention counseling theories as an essential part of the group counseling process, especially when counseling one individual in front of the entire group. Which of the following theories can be used effectively for this purpose?

   a. rational emotive behavior therapy.

   b. transactional analysis.

   c. choice theory.

   d. all of the above.

225. At times when focusing on one member of the group, it may become necessary to "put the working member on hold" because:

   a. the group will get tired of listening to the same member ramble on.

b. you really only want to focus on one member for a few minutes.

c. putting that member "on hold" will allow the person time to think and get input from others.

d. the group will need a break and it is better to take a break when only one member has been working.

226. One technique that can be used when working with an individual in front of the group is the "overhearing" technique. That is, the working individual member sits quietly while the other members talk about him or her. Advantages to this technique are:

a. this allows the working member to take a break and listen to reactions from the entire group.

b. it helps the member realize that people will talk behind his or her back.

c. it allows the other group members to express their support, encouragement, or frustrations with the individual's progress.

d. a and c.

227. The authors of the group therapy chapter discuss using techniques that they consider "out of the box." One reason to use more unorthodox techniques is to:

a. create an environment of high energy that will engage and interest the members.

b. fill time so you don't have to hear members complain about being in the group.

c. ensure that members will leave the group and tell their friends about the out-of-the-ordinary things you did.

d. attempt to get the involuntary members to feel so uncomfortable that they ask to leave the group.

228. The advantages of using writing techniques to draw out involuntary members include the following:

a. writing techniques allow members to feel more comfortable if they can read what they write.

b. even the most negative member may have interest in hearing what other members write.

c. they allow leaders to gauge the reading/writing levels of clients.

d. a and b.

229. In groups where all members are deemed involuntary, the leader has what purpose?

a. to change the agency policy so that no groups are structured this way.

b. to attempt to get the members to be more voluntary.
c. to cover the subject matter of the group.
d. b and c.

230. Benefits of using the "inner circle–outer circle" technique with involuntary groups are that it:

a. allows members who want to benefit from the group the opportunity to do that.
b. prevents resistant members from disrupting the flow of the group.
c. may encourage the resistant members who choose to sit outside the group to actually pay closer attention to what is being said.
d. all of the above.

231. Determining the reasons for children's challenging behaviors is best accomplished by:

a. finding the correct diagnosis.
b. identifying the antecedents and consequences of children's behaviors.
c. administering standardized tests.
d. having parents and teachers fill out checklists regarding children's behaviors.

232. In order to assist parents with their children's challenging behaviors it is important to:

a. test the children and make the correct diagnosis.
b. observe the children and make the correct diagnosis.
c. test the children and get their parents to be specific about their behaviors.
d. observe the children and get their parents to be specific about their behaviors.

233. In order to gain the trust and participation of parents it is best to be:

a. upfront and honest with parents as well as being empathetic and avoiding defensiveness.
b. careful not to disagree with their parenting techniques as well as being empathetic and avoiding defensiveness.
c. upfront and honest with parents as well as confrontational about their parenting techniques.
d. careful not to disagree with their parenting techniques and to avoid being totally honest about what you think.

234. A therapist working with parents of children with challenging behaviors:

    a. may need to deal with marital conflict, alcoholism, or depression.
    b. may need to refer parents for help with marital conflict, alcoholism, or depression.
    c. should always follow the agenda that the parents have brought to the therapy session.
    d. should always follow his or her own agenda, that is, to help these parents with their children.

235. Effective interventions for children with challenging behavior problems:

    a. should be selected on the basis of the appropriate diagnosis.
    b. should be selected based on the skills and preferences of the therapist.
    c. should be based on the function of the challenging behavior and the identification of an appropriate replacement behavior.
    d. should be based on the expressed desires of the children and their parents.

236. Goals for parents when interacting with their children who have challenging behaviors include:

    a. providing lots of exciting praise and positive reinforcement for appropriate behavior.
    b. providing strong admonishment and lengthy lectures for minor or nuisance behaviors.
    c. providing immediate and punishing consequences with a strong display of anger for more serious behaviors.
    d. all of the above.

Counseling Specific Populations

237. More recent conceptualizations of disability emphasize that:

    a. disability is a private concern.
    b. disability is a societal concern.
    c. disability is not the concern of most counseling specialties because the main identity of people with disabilities (PWDs) is their disability.
    d. the number of individuals with disabilities continues to decline.

238. Lowered expectations of PWDs:

    a. are prejudicial and stigmatizing.
    b. allow the PWD to accept the limitations of the disability.
    c. protect the PWD from negative and harmful feedback.
    d. assist counselors in understanding that widely held standards of accountability are not appropriate for most PWDs.

239. The disability of the client may arouse anxiety in the counselor due to:

    a. the fact that PWDs can be exhausting burdens for counselors.
    b. most often, PWDs resent PWODs and therefore a therapeutic alliance will be difficult to form.
    c. all clients with disabilities should be referred to rehabilitation counselors because the disability is the main identity of these clients.
    d. many counselors lack the training and preparation in disability issues.

240. The biomedical model of disability is being questioned and challenged because:

    a. PWDs refuse the disability role of pathology, inferiority, and deviance.
    b. prejudice and discrimination against PWDs are widely recognized.
    c. PWDs want their collective history and experiences incorporated into the wider culture.
    d. almost one-fifth of the American population reports some type of disability.

241. The primary strategies emphasized in state-of-the-art rehabilitation efforts with people who have severe mental illness include _____:

    a. hospitalization.
    b. strengthening of client skills.
    c. medication only.
    d. psychotherapy only.

242. Mental health practitioners are reminded that in order to change behavior, it is necessary to alter both the perception and the abilities of individuals, as well as their _____:

    a. environments.
    b. medications.

c. health insurance.
d. treatment methods.

243. In order to have a psychiatric disability, a person must first have a _____:

    a. predisposing condition.
    b. prescription for psychotropic drugs.
    c. psychiatric diagnosis.
    d. family history of mental illness.

244. Psychiatric rehabilitation services are designed to help persons with severe mental illness to achieve all of the following except _____:

    a. recovery.
    b. maximum community integration.
    c. the highest quality of life.
    d. reliance on others.

245. Which of the following organizations and models provide opportunities for training in disaster mental health and crisis response?

    a. American Red Cross.
    b. Acute Traumatic Stress Management.
    c. National Organization for Victims Assistance.
    d. all of the above.

246. Skilled practitioners in disaster mental health response:

    a. should first do a behavioral before a psychological assessment on the individual.
    b. can facilitate both short- and long-term crisis interventions.
    c. must facilitate individual crisis response before any group interventions.
    d. should establish a safe environment with the individual, using a holistic assessment approach, and facilitate short-term brief interventions.

247. What are some common characteristics within the preintervention structure of disaster mental health response?

    a. Use a high level of empathy, open-ended questions about the critical incident, and plan for future support and resources.
    b. Establish a client rapport, discuss confidentiality, coordinating, and communicating with other members of the disaster response team.

    c. Communicate assurance with the survivor that everything will be alright and with time the person will not remember the critical event.

    d. Provide handouts detailing the psychological, emotional, physiological, and cognitive response to critical incidents trying to normalize the event.

248. Which of the following is *not* an appropriate facilitative response to children during disaster mental health interventions?

    a. "You may be feeling sad now, but this will all be over with soon and you'll have very little memory of this event."

    b. "You may be feeling sad, frightened, or confused now, this is normal, it's healthy to talk about your feelings because it will help you get better."

    c. "If you work hard now at school, your life will get back to normal soon."

    d. "You should share your thoughts and feelings with everyone you come in contact with about this event, because this will help you feel more normal again."

249. Studies on the Risk Principle of case classification have shown:

    a. low-risk clients who receive excessive intervention have negative outcomes.

    b. high-risk clients who receive inferior intervention have negative outcomes.

    c. high- and low-risk clients who receive proper intervention have the best outcomes.

    d. all of the above.

250. A clinician has a so-called slow learner type client in an anger management group and makes extensive use of concrete problem-solving examples. This is an example of:

    a. the clinician being insensitive to the client's abilities.

    b. attending to client needs.

    c. the responsivity principle of case management.

    d. ignoring risk factors.

251. Reviews of the correctional treatment literature show:

    a. treatment has no effect on offenders.

    b. criminal sanctions (e.g., prison) reduces reoffending.

    c. treatment reduces reoffending by approximately 10%.

    d. insight-oriented offender programs work particularly well.

252. Which of the following pairs of criminogenic needs are from the "Central Eight"?

a. self-esteem and substance abuse.
b. criminal attitudes and criminal companions.
c. IQ and educational achievement.
d. socially disadvantaged neighborhood and employment.

253. Which of the following is frequently considered the most appropriate form of treatment for survivors of sexual abuse?

a. EMDR.
b. expressive therapy.
c. group therapy.
d. cognitive behavior therapy.

254. The percent of sexual abuse that is ever reported is:

a. 5% to 10%.
b. 10% to 18%.
c. 20% to 29%.
d. 50% to 58%.

255. Factors associated with childhood sexual abuse include all of the following except:

a. living in a low-income household.
b. having a disability.
c. living in a single-parent household.
d. living in a household with more than three children.

256. Hyperarousal, a potential effect of sexual abuse, is a symptom of:

a. PTSD.
b. depression.
c. sexual dysfunction.
d. regressive behaviors.

257. Which statement is most accurate when it comes to choosing a model or strategies to facilitate disaster mental health response?

a. It is important to evaluate the efficacy of each model for each particular critical incident because there are no superior models that can comprehensively address all disaster response scenarios.
b. Regardless of the model or strategy chosen, the quality or chemistry of the working relationship is of paramount

importance in facilitating coping and resiliency skills, as well as supports and resources for the survivor of critical incidents.

c. Facilitating the skills of intense attending, listening, and empathic responding can therapeutically empower survivors with the necessary and sufficient conditions for coping with a traumatic incident.

d. All of the above are accurate.

258. Which of the following most accurately depicts the strength of the BASICS model of crisis response?

a. The BASICS model assists the crisis counselor in normalizing client emotions and building resiliency and coping skills early on.

b. The BASICS model offers crisis counselors a tool to measure the behavioral attributes or intensity and impact that a particular traumatic event has had in the survivor's life.

c. The BASICS model offers crisis counselors a multimodal assessment for evaluating the survivor's lethality and coping skills as it relates to critical areas of the health of one's mind, body, and spirit.

d. The BASICS model trains beginning-level crisis counselors on the fundamentals of crisis counseling and the basic techniques and strategies.

259. Which statement characterizes the Prediction, Preparation, and Meaning stage and the goals used to facilitate disaster mental health response?

a. The crisis counselor discusses openly with the survivor the confidential nature of the relationship and prepares the survivor for finding meaning of the critical incident.

b. The crisis counselor facilitates strategies that include empathic attending, listening, and responding.

c. The crisis counselor uses informal diagnostic assessment tools to predict coping skills of the survivor and prepare the person with resources that will assist him or her for coping.

d. The crisis counselor educates the survivor on the psychosocial reaction to loss and grief and facilitates meaning of the critical event by brainstorming and facilitating interventions to build coping and resiliency skills.

260. Which core message or facilitative response would *not* be appropriate to use when working with a child or adolescent who has recently survived a critical incident?

a. Explain to the child/adolescent that talking about the incident will actually help him or her feel better emotionally and physically.

b. Reinforce that it is important for him or her to accept help and support for a while until he or she feels better and much less sad.

c. Reassure the child/adolescent that right now, it may take a lot of effort and focus to do his or her normal daily routine (i.e., school, homework, sports, other activities).

d. Let the child/adolescent know that with time he or she will totally forget about the incident and the child/adolescent should focus more on his or her future.

261. Which of the following statement best characterizes substance abuse assessment?

a. Substance abuse assessment should be a comprehensive and holistic process that is individualized with an emphasis on establishing a working relationship that is direct and honest with the client.

b. Substance abuse assessment is a process whereby the counselor administers a mix of standardized and multi-modal assessments that reveals the client's true addictive behaviors.

c. Substance abuse assessment should be a holistic process with the primary focus on assessing the individual's environment that is most problematic for him or her.

d. Substance abuse assessment should begin with significant others because the client typically will not disclose the most accurate information regarding his or her substance abuse or addictive behaviors.

262. One of the primary functions of substance abuse assessment is to:

a. have the client openly disclose what he or she is feeling, thinking, and experiencing.

b. assess the client's motivation for change.

c. gain an understanding of the client's emotional and psychological functioning.

d. determine if the client can go 30 days without the use of an addictive substance.

263. Which statement is most accurate as it relates to the Substance Abuse Subtle Screening Inventory (SASSI)?

a. The SASSI is an appropriate assessment instrument to use over most other assessments except with non-English-speaking clients.

b. In private practice settings the Addiction Severity Index (ASI) is a more user-friendly instrument than the SASSI to administer and reveals better information on the client's strengths and weaknesses.

c. Researchers suggest that since the SASSI is most widely used, this instrument has better reliability and validity data than any other SUD assessment instrument.

d. Researchers found no independent empirical evidence that the SASSI is more sensitive or accurate in detecting SUDs than any other instruments.

264. Which of these therapist variables was found by research to be a key factor related to successful treatment outcome?

a. therapist empathy.
b. confrontation.
c. shame and punishing.
d. therapist tone of voice.

265. Which of these is *not* included in the stages of change model by Prochaska, Norcross, and DiClemente (1992)?

a. precontemplation.
b. contemplation.
c. maintenance.
d. commitment.

266. The stages of change model by Prochaska, Norcross, and DiClemente is often used in conjunction with what therapy(s):

a. motivational interviewing.
b. gestalt therapy.
c. solution-focused therapy.
d. behavioral counseling.

267. A good comprehensive assessment instrument for individuals with a substance use disorder is:

a. AUDIT.
b. CAGE.
c. SASSI.
d. ASI.

268. What is grief?

a. an emotion felt when a loved one has died.
b. the reaction to loss.
c. synonymous with bereavement.
d. what some people feel only when a loved one dies.

269. Define anticipatory mourning:

    a. the grief a person feels watching a loved one die.
    b. the expectation of losses that have not yet become a reality.
    c. describes how the terminally ill person is feeling about how his or her life is ending.
    d. how we anticipate we will feel when a loved one dies.

270. How do children grieve?

    a. just like adults.
    b. in their own unique ways.
    c. they don't grieve because they cannot understand what grief is.
    d. they cry and act out, but believe their loved one will return.

271. For many individuals grief may last:

    a. a lifetime.
    b. 2 weeks.
    c. until one recovers from it.
    d. 48 hours.

272. Assistive technology (AT) was first defined in the:

    a. 1988 Tech Act.
    b. 1990 American With Disabilities Act.
    c. 1990 Individual With Disabilities Education Act.
    d. 1998 Assistive Technology Act.

273. Mobility assistive technologies refer to devices such as:

    a. wheelchairs, walkers, and canes.
    b. grooming and eating devices.
    c. accessible transportation.
    d. ramps and lifts.

274. What does RESNA stand for?

    a. Residential and Environmental Services National Association.
    b. Rehabilitation Engineering and Assistive Technology Society of North America.
    c. Research in Educational Services National Association.
    d. Re-engineering Systems National Association.

275. In the MPT model, *milieu* refers to:

    a. the system of AT service delivery in France.
    b. the system of AT service delivery in Quebec.

c. the built and attitudinal environments of AT use.
d. the need to reduce complexity.

276. The traditional college student (18–24 years of age) is perceived as coming to campus with _____ level of psychological problems, stress, and expectations to succeed by family than previous generations:

a. a lesser.
b. a greater.
c. a moderate.
d. the same.

277. An issue that must be taken into account when providing counseling and diagnostic services on a college campus is _____:

a. knowing the difference between normal developmental issues and the clinical presented by the college student.
b. knowing that most issues presented are of a developmental nature.
c. understanding that most students will, in time, work through their issue with some minor interventions.
d. having a clear clinical diagnosis to begin treatment planning.

278. The suicide rate among traditional college students is _____ as the same age group (18–24 years of age) of adults who are not attending college:

a. substantially more.
b. about the same.
c. slightly more.
d. substantially less.

279. The nontraditional college student is generally _____ proficient in the use of the newer technologies than what the traditional college student has mastered while growing up:

a. less.
b. more .
c. equally.
d. substantially less.

280. Comorbid disorders associated with youth violence include all except:

a. substance abuse.
b. bipolar disorder.

    c. ADHD disorder.

    d. conduct disorder.

281. Risk factors for potential violence include all except:

    a. high social capital.

    b. history of violent behaviors.

    c. witnessing violence.

    d. inconsistent discipline at home and school.

282. Witnessing violence can lead to:

    a. trauma reactions.

    b. desensitization.

    c. mental health issues.

    d. all of the above.

283. The most common type of school violence is:

    a. school shooting.

    b. physical assaults.

    c. bullying.

    d. vandalism.

284. The psychological, social, and emotional toll of war can be immediate, acute, and chronic. The period in which a soldier is objectively safe and free from exposure to severe stressors to approximately 1 month after return to civilian life is known as the _____ interval:

    a. immediate.

    b. acute.

    c. chronic.

    d. trauma.

285. Risk factors for posttraumatic stress disorder (PTSD) and poly-trauma include which of the following characteristics?

    a. low socioeconomic status, intelligence, and education.

    b. gender, adverse childhood events, and absence of social support postevent.

    c. severity of the traumatic event, prior traumatic exposure, and additional life stressors.

    d. all of the above.

286. Assessment of PTSD and poly-trauma requires which of the following?

    a. medical and military approaches.

    b. physical and combat stress control program.

  c. multimethod and interdisciplinary approaches.
  d. creative and longitudinal approaches.

287. Women are more likely to develop PTSD if ____:

  a. their mother had PTSD.
  b. they have a support network composed of only women.
  c. they were officers at the low organizational level.
  d. they had a severe reaction at the time of the event.

288. The major difference between dementia of the Alzheimer's type (DAT) and delirium is:

  a. DAT is a reversible disease.
  b. delirium is a reversible condition.
  c. delirium entails a gradual onset.
  d. the cause of DAT is well known.

289. The type of counseling that involves having older persons produce mementos, photographs, and other memorabilia to share with the counselor is:

  a. brief dynamic therapy.
  b. reminiscence or life review therapy.
  c. cognitive behavior therapy.
  d. interpersonal therapy.

290. Some of the most commonly prescribed psychotropic medications for depression among older persons are:

  a. Ativan and Xanax.
  b. Geodon and Seroquel.
  c. Effexor and Celexa.
  d. Namenda and Aricept.

291. The average older adult takes an average of _____ prescription medications:

  a. 2–3.
  b. 6–7.
  c. 5–10.
  d. 15–18.

Contemporary Issues in Counseling

292. Positive psychology is:

  a. the modern version of the power of positive thinking.
  b. the science of hedonism.
  c. the scientific study of what makes life most worth living.
  d. what psychology has always done.

293. Positive psychology:

   a. assumes that human strengths are as genuine as human problems.
   b. believes that people are responsible for their problems.
   c. ignores human problems.
   d. reinterprets human problems as good experiences.

294. Which of these is *not* a major topic of concern to positive psychology?

   a. subjective experiences.
   b. individual traits.
   c. institutions.
   d. all of these are major topics of concern.

295. Which theory is most widely used by positive psychology practitioners?

   a. behavioral.
   b. cognitive behavior.
   c. humanistic.
   d. none of the above.

296. Which statement best describes the Global Assessment of Empathy Fatigue (GAEF) scale?

   a. The GAEF is a theoretical measure of the holistic experience of empathy fatigue.
   b. The GAEF is a valid and reliable instrument used as a screening tool for empathy fatigue.
   c. The GAEF is a valid risk factor functional assessment scale used to predict the prevalence and incidence of empathy fatigue.
   d. The GAEF is a biopsychosocial measure of empathy fatigue.

297. Which statement best depicts the professional concerns with counselor impairment syndromes?

   a. Counselor impairment syndromes are primarily a cluster of personality traits.
   b. Counselor impairments are primarily independent personality states.
   c. It is hypothesized that counselor impairments have multidimensional characteristics so it is difficult to predict who may be more or less at-risk for this experience.
   d. It is hypothesized that younger, less experienced professionals are the individuals most affected by counselor impairments.

298. The measurement of counselor impairment and fatigue syndromes is complicated because:

    a. it depends on who is observing such a subjective phenomenon.
    b. subjective rating, self-report instruments may not be the best means of capturing the essence of such phenomenon.
    c. researchers believe that counselor fatigue is not a well-defined construct.
    d. all of the above pose difficulties in measuring counselor impairments.

299. Which statement best characterizes counselor resiliency?

    a. Possessing a positive frame of reference when engaged in client issues is all important when determining the level or degree of counselor resiliency.
    b. The most resilient counselors are those that have had an extraordinary stressful or traumatic event occur in their past; without this it is not possible to build resiliency traits.
    c. Attitudes and beliefs about specific mental health conditions and issues play a key role in determining how resilient the counselor may be in response to specific client issues.
    d. Choosing healthy emotions by the counselor is all that is needed when confronted with strong negative client emotions during session.

300. Which statement best describes the theoretical construct of empathy fatigue (EF)?

    a. EF results from a combination of cumulative emotional stress, job burnout, counselor resiliency traits, and negative forms of countertransference.
    b. EF results from a state of psychological, emotional, mental, physical, spiritual, and occupational exhaustion that occurs as the counselors' own wounds are continually revisited by their clients' life stories of chronic illness, disability, trauma, grief, and loss.
    c. EF results from counselors who have poor coping skills when it comes to dealing with clients who have issues of acute traumatic stress.
    d. EF basically has the same effects as vicarious traumatization.

301. Which general statement is most accurate when describing the similarities and differences in empathy fatigue and other counselor impairments?

    a. Empathy fatigue is experienced by professional counselors who primarily use person-centered and empathy-focused interactions to build rapport with their clients for the purpose of building a therapeutic working alliance with clients.

b. There is a clear association between the trait of empathy and job burnout; those who possess higher levels of empathy become fatigued and burned-out at much higher rates than those that do not possess such traits.

c. Those professionals that engage in primarily case management duties tend to suffer from job burnout as opposed to empathy fatigue because empathy is not really needed for these types of occupations.

d. Empathy fatigue is more readily apparent than compassion fatigue or job burnout, because the latter is rarely exhibited in the work setting.

302. Which statement most parsimoniously depicts the recent research regarding the mind-body connection as it relates to counselor impairment and fatigue syndromes?

a. When high positive emotions and empathy are experienced between client and therapist, then similar physiological responses are experienced as measured by electrical skin conductance recordings, heart rate, voice dynamics, and body movement.

b. Because empathetic connections are formed between client and therapist and can be measured both physiologically and psychologically, there appears to be potential for some degree of emotional and physical exhaustion by counselors who engage in therapeutic interactions with clients who disclose themes of an intense nature.

c. Although one's perception of critical events differs in terms of parasympathetic and sympathetic nervous system activation, it is the frequency, intensity, and cumulative nature of physiological stress and emotional arousal that creates counselor fatigue.

d. All of the above are accurate.

303. Self-care approaches for preprofessional and professional counselors are essential for competent and ethical practice within the profession of counseling because:

a. clients may perceive their therapist to be an unskilled professional otherwise.

b. continuing educational credits are required for counselor licensure.

c. continual self-awareness and personal growth are essential for maintaining one's personal and professional wellness, especially in working with persons who have intense needs.

d. counselor impairment and fatigue syndromes are readily apparent among self and others, so self-care approaches must be taken as a prevention approach.

304. Burnout is:

a. a factor in employment that can be prevented, cured, or eliminated.
b. a psychobiosocial concept.
c. a leading cause of job loss in the United States.
d. an employment function caused by emotional exhaustion.

305. Burnout is:

a. an entirely personal, individual, and negative experience.
b. useful to allow the "weeding out" of less productive counselors.
c. harmful when it becomes a majority or group syndrome.
d. a form of stress that can be inoculated for via training.

306. Human service administrators usually:

a. plan preventative programs, usually involving training, to alleviate symptoms of burnout.
b. understand the parameters of personnel burnout because it is the budgetary item related to absenteeism, tardiness, and turnover.
c. use the wealth of burnout research to develop continuing and consistent programs to deal with burnout.
d. ignore burnout until it leads to poor work productivity or disruptions due to lack of trained personnel.

307. Preventing, reducing, and eliminating burnout initially involves:

a. management involvement.
b. counselors training.
c. qualified supervisors.
d. clients who understand the stresses of the counseling profession.

308. _____ can be seen primarily as a social construct that helps provide boundaries to the belief system it represents:

a. religiosity.
b. spirituality.
c. religion.
d. religious-centered psychotherapy.

309. _____, broadly understood, can be seen as a person's search for his or her ultimate meaning and place in the world:

a. religiosity.
b. spirituality.

c. religion.
d. psychotherapy.

310. When assessing the religious or spiritual development of a client, the counselor should adopt a _____ approach that respects the traditions, language, and cultural understanding that contributes to the client's development:

a. denominational.
b. nondenominational.
c. neutral.
d. therapeutic.

311. Tan (1996) suggests there are two models for integrating secular and religious techniques into a counseling session. _____ integration refers to a more "covert" approach that does not directly or systemically use religious practices. While religious issues may not be brought up, they will be dealt with respectfully:

a. explicit.
b. nondirect.
c. implicit.
d. direct.

312. Which of the following is *not* a characteristic of chronic pain?

a. The origin of chronic pain might be unidentifiable.
b. The prevalence of chronic pain is decreasing given new medical technologies.
c. Chronic pain lasts longer than the normal expected healing time.
d. Persons with chronic pain commonly experience negative effects on their mental well-being.

313. Negative cognitions or beliefs about pain can lead to _____:

a. self-defeating behaviors, negative emotions, and increased pain messages.
b. noncompliance with pain treatments.
c. improved social relationships with others.
d. increased physical and social activities.

314. Clients with chronic pain usually seek concurrent pain management treatments. How can counseling benefit the client with chronic pain?

a. Clients can learn that their pain is probably psychogenic.
b. Clients can incorporate coping skills, relaxation techniques, and education for managing pain, mood, and psychosocial changes.

c. Clients can get recommendations for the best noninvasive and invasive medical procedures to treat their pain.

d. Clients can be reassured that they will be pain-free at the completion of treatment.

315. Cognitive behavior therapies are empirically supported as efficacious in counseling persons with chronic pain alone or as part of a multidisciplinary approach. What cognitive techniques can be useful when counseling clients with chronic pain?

a. monitoring pain and activity levels and practicing relaxation.

b. identifying and evaluating possible solutions for the pain condition.

c. communicating directly their pain experiences with physicians, counselors, family, friends, and coworkers.

d. examining and modifying negative thinking, unrealistic beliefs, and assumptions related to pain and distress.

316. Extrapyramidal side effects (EPSEs) caused by antipsychotic drugs are related to Parkinson's disease because both are related to:

a. a decrease in dopamine activity.

b. an increase in dopamine activity.

c. decreased serotonin activity.

d. decreased norepinephrine activity.

317. Which of the following SSRI side effects would be a special concern for Mr. Johnson, a 35-year-old depressed lawyer?

a. dry mouth.

b. anorgasmia.

c. constipation.

d. miosis (i.e., constricted pupils).

318. Mr. Smith is taking lithium and he tells you the lab just mailed him his lithium level report. His level was 1.0 mEq.L. Your reaction should be to:

a. tell Mr. Smith to contact his physician immediately.

b. thank Mr. Smith for sharing his lab results and assure him his levels are fine.

c. contact the physician and ask for guidance in this situation.

d. ask Mr. Smith to hold a dose or two so that his system can self-regulate.

319. Benzodiazepines given alone can usually cause all but one of the following:

a. dependence.

b. withdrawal.

c. death from overdose.
d. abuse problems.

320. Counselors providing testimony in evidentiary depositions generally do so if:

a. they are testifying about malingering.
b. they are unable to appear live in court.
c. they are testifying about their qualifications.
d. they live out of state.

321. One of the main goals of the expert when testifying is to:

a. display his or her conviction and dedication in the case.
b. show the jury how knowledgeable he or she is in forensic matters.
c. educate the jury in an objective manner.
d. advocate for the side that retained his or her services.

322. When an attorney intends to *voir dire* an expert witness, this action pertains to:

a. asking the expert how he arrived at his conclusions.
b. asking the expert to define what methods she used in developing her report.
c. asking the expert more specific questions regarding his qualifications.
d. asking the expert what she charges for cases and how much she charged in this case.

323. Which one of the following is *not* a recommended strategy for counselors to use while testifying:

a. remaining calm and confident while testifying.
b. asking the judge whether you can explain your answer when relevant.
c. saying "I object" to questions you feel are inappropriately asked by opposing counsel.
d. saying "I don't know" to questions where you are uncertain of the answer.

Appendix C

ANSWER KEY FOR SELF-STUDY EXAM FOR *PCDR*

The Identity of Professional Counselors

1. a
2. b
3. a
4. d
5. b
6. c
7. b
8. a
9. b
10. c
11. a
12. c
13. d
14. d
15. d
16. c

Professional, Ethical, and Practice Management Issues in Counseling

17. a
18. b

19. c
20. a
21. b
22. d
23. c
24. b
25. b
26. a
27. a
28. d
29. d
30. b
31. d
32. a
33. a
34. d
35. b
36. c
37. d
38. a

Case Management and Consultation Issues

39. c
40. a
41. d
42. c
43. c
44. a
45. b
46. d
47. d
48. c
49. b
50. d
51. c
52. a
53. c
54. d
55. c
56. d
57. b
58. c
59. c

60. b
61. d
62. d

Multicultural Counseling Issues

63. b
64. c
65. b
66. b
67. a
68. d
69. b
70. b
71. d
72. c
73. c
74. b
75. c
76. a
77. b
78. b
79. c
80. c
81. a
82. d
83. d
84. a
85. c
86. d
87. a
88. b
89. d
90. c
91. a
92. b
93. c
94. c
95. b
96. a
97. a
98. d
99. d

100. d
101. b
102. d

Counseling Theories and Techniques

103. c
104. d
105. b
106. a
107. d
108. b
109. d
110. b
111. c
112. d
113. b
114. d
115. d
116. c
117. a
118. d
119. d
120. c
121. d
122. a
123. c
124. a
125. d
126. b
127. d
128. a
129. b
130. b
131. d
132. a
133. c
134. b
135. a
136. a
137. c
138. b
139. d

140. c
141. b
142. c
143. b
144. b
145. c
146. b
147. c
148. a
149. a
150. b
151. c

Career Counseling, Human Growth and Development

152. c
153. b
154. d
155. a
156. b
157. d
158. a
159. c
160. d
161. c
162. a
163. b
164. a
165. c
166. c
167. b
168. c
169. a
170. d
171. b
172. a
173. d
174. c
175. d
176. d
177. d
178. d

179. d
180. d
181. d
182. c
183. d

Assessment and Diagnosis

184. d
185. a
186. c
187. b
188. b
189. d
190. b
191. c
192. b
193. b
194. c
195. d
196. a
197. a
198. a
199. c
200. b
201. a
202. d
203. b

Counseling Couples, Families, and Groups

204. b
205. a
206. c
207. d
208. d
209. c
210. d
211. a
212. a
213. d
214. c
215. b
216. c
217. a

218. b
219. d
220. d
221. b
222. c
223. b
224. d
225. c
226. d
227. a
228. d
229. d
230. d
231. b
232. d
233. a
234. b
235. c
236. a

Counseling Specific Populations

237. b
238. a
239. d
240. a
241. b
242. a
243. a
244. a
245. d
246. d
247. b
248. b
249. d
250. c
251. c
252. b
253. c
254. b
255. d
256. a
257. d
258. c

259. d
260. d
261. a
262. b
263. d
264. a
265. d
266. a
267. d
268. b
269. b
270. b
271. a
272. a
273. a
274. b
275. c
276. b
277. a
278. d
279. a
280. b
281. a
282. d
283. c
284. b
285. d
286. c
287. d
288. b
289. b
290. c
291. c

Contemporary Issues in Counseling

292. c
293. a
294. d
295. d
296. a
297. c
298. d
299. c

300. b
301. a
302. d
303. c
304. b
305. a
306. d
307. c
308. c
309. b
310. a
311. c
312. b
313. a
314. b
315. d
316. a
317. b
318. b
319. c
320. b
321. c
322. c
323. c

Index

For Reference

Not to be taken from the library